SECOND EDITION

Invitation to the Life Span
CANADIAN EDITION

Kathleen Stassen Berger

Bronx Community College
City University of New York

Susan S. Chuang

University of Guelph

WORTH PUBLISHERS
A MACMILLAN HIGHER EDUCATION COMPANY

In loving memory of my lovely and darling mother who inspired me every day.
Susan S. Chuang

Publisher: Kevin Feyen
Associate Publisher: Jessica Bayne
Developmental Editor: Edward O'Connor
Project Editors: Janice Dyer; Debbie Smith, First Folio Resource Group Inc.
Copy Editor: Arleane Ralph
Executive Marketing Manager: Katherine Nurre
Media Editor: Lauren Samuelson
Senior Project Editor: Vivien Weiss
Art Director and Cover Designer: Barbara Reingold
Interior Designer: Lyndall Culbertson
Photo Researchers: Donna Ranieri, Deborah Anderson, Maria DeCambra
Illustrations: Todd Buck Illustrations, MPS Limited, TSI Graphics, Inc.
Production Manager: Barbara Seixas
Composition: Tom Dart, First Folio Resource Group Inc.
Printing and Binding: RR Donnelley
Cover Art: Sandra Dionisi

ISBN-13: 978-1-4641-4198-0
ISBN-10: 1-4641-4198-3

Printed in the United States of America

First printing

Worth Publishers
41 Madison Avenue
New York, NY 10010
www.worthpublishers.com

Credit is given to the following sources for permission to use the photos indicated:

Author Photos

Worth Publishers: p. iii (left)
Malcolm Taylor, p. iii (right)

Part Openers

David M. Phillips / Science Source, pp. xxii–1
Scott Hancock / Jupiter Images, pp. iv, 90–91
Craig Pershouse / Getty Images, p. 172
Olaf Krüger / imagebrok / age fotostock, pp. iv, 246–247
Grove Pashley / Corbis, pp. v, 324
commerceandculturestock / Getty Images, p. 392
Alamy, pp. v, 490

Chapter Openers

© Erin Moroney LaBelle / The Image Works, p. 2
Jade Brookbank / Getty, pp. vi, 48
Andrew Chuang, pp. vii 92
Nabi Lukic / Getty Images, p. 136
KidStock / Blend Images / Corbis, pp. vii, 174
Daniel Boag / Getty Images, p. 210
Floresco Productions / Corbis, pp. viii, 248
Gary John Norman / Getty Images, p. 290
KidStock / Blend Images / Corbis, pp. viii, 332
Patrick Sheandell O'Carroll / PhotoAlto / Corbis, pp. ix, 358
Westend61 / Getty Images, pp. ix, 394
Patrice Coppee / Getty Images, pp. ix, 426
Yellow Dog Productions Inc. / Getty Images, p. 460
punchstock, pp. x, 492
Ryan McVay / Getty Images, pp. xi, 528
Buddhika Weerasinghe / Reuters / Corbis, pp. xi, 564

Brief Contents

About the Authors

KATHLEEN STASSEN BERGER received her undergraduate education at Stanford University and Radcliffe College, earned an M.A.T. from Harvard University, and an MS and PhD from Yeshiva University. Her broad experience as an educator includes directing a preschool, serving as chair of philosophy at the United Nations International School, teaching child and adolescent development to graduate students at Fordham University and undergraduates at Montclair State University in New Jersey and at Quinnipiac University in Connecticut, as well as teaching social psychology to inmates at Sing Sing Prison.

Throughout most of her professional career, Berger has taught at Bronx Community College of the City University of New York, first as an adjunct and for the past two decades as a full professor. She has taught introduction to psychology, child and adolescent development, adulthood and aging, social psychology, abnormal psychology, and human motivation. Her students—who come from many ethnic, economic, and educational backgrounds and who have a wide range of ages and interests—consistently honour her with the highest teaching evaluations.

Berger is also the author of *The Developing Person Through the Life Span* and *The Developing Person Through Childhood and Adolescence.* Her developmental texts are currently being used at more than 900 schools worldwide and are available in Spanish, French, Italian, and Portuguese, as well as English. Her research interests include adolescent identity, multi-generational families, immigration, and bullying, and she has published many articles on developmental topics in the *Wiley Encyclopedia of Psychology* and in publications of the American Association for Higher Education and the National Education Association for Higher Education. She continues teaching and learning every semester and in every edition of her books.

SUSAN S. CHUANG received her undergraduate degree in criminology and sociology at the University of Toronto. At the University of Rochester, in New York, she earned an MS in elementary education, and an MS and PhD in human development. She also received post-doctoral training at the National Institutes of Health, in Maryland.

Chuang's lines of research include parenting, fathering, parent–child relationships, child and adolescent development, and school readiness in various sociocultural contexts (e.g., North American, Asian, and Latino countries). She also focuses on settlement and immigration issues.

Chuang collaborates with various local and national organizations and leads community-based projects across Canada. She conducts workshops on various topics, including parenting, parent–child relationships, youth development, and studying tips and strategies. Audiences range from youth to young adults to parents of all ages.

Chuang is the co-editor of books such as *On New Shores: Understanding Immigrant Fathers in North America* and *Immigrant Children: Change, Adaptation, and Cultural Transformation,* and of special journal issues that focus on families and immigration, including *Sex Roles* (2009) and the *Journal of Family Psychology* (2009). She is currently the editor of Springer Science+Business Media's series Advances in Immigrant Family Research. The first book in the series is *Gender Roles in Immigrant Families.* In addition, Chuang organizes the On New Shores international conferences, which focus on immigrant families. They feature leading scholars from various disciplines as well as community and governmental agencies and other non-academic delegates.

Contents

Preface

In our daily lives, we experience many different situations, whether they are with our families and friends, peers from school, or the communities in which we live. We also witness others' experiences, in person, on television, and in social media. During and after these events, we may try to figure out why a particular situation occurred, what impact it will have on those involved, and what will happen in the future.

As we try to make sense of our world, we create *theories* to better understand our circumstances and those of others. We take into consideration the characteristics of individuals—gender, personality traits, age, and ethnicity, to name a few. We then include external factors that we deem relevant to a situation, such as a person's family background, past life events, and the neighbourhood or country in which the person grew up. In spite of the myriad individual and contextual factors, we realize that there are commonalities among diverse people as well.

Family Pride Grandpa Charilaos is proud of his tavern in northern Greece (central Macedonia), but he is even more proud of his talented grandchildren, including Maria Soni (shown here). Note her expert fingering. Her father and mother also play instruments—is that nature or nurture?

We hope that this textbook will provide you with greater clarity on how we live, answer some questions you may have, and hopefully have you asking more! This textbook is just the beginning, an *invitation* to understand the complexities of your life, your family and friends' lives, and the lives of all the other billions of humans alive now or who have lived.

Education occurs in hundreds of ways. Writing this book is one of our contributions; studying it is one of yours. We strove to make this text both challenging and accessible to every student. You deserve a book that respects your intellect and experiences, without making development seem dull or obscure.

Overall, we believe that a better world is possible because today's students—you—will become tomorrow's leaders. We hope that the knowledge you gain from reading this book will help you and your loved ones develop with more joy and fulfillment, and that you will share with others the insights that you gain into humanity—from one generation to the next.

To learn more about the specifics of this text, including the material that is new to the Canadian edition, read on. Or simply turn to Chapter 1 and begin your study.

New to this Canadian Edition

One thing you'll notice from the first page of this book is that this is a truly *Canadian* textbook. This book has been thoroughly revised so that it speaks to our students—not only through Canadian examples and Canadian statistics, but by highlighting current research done by Canadians. The lives of Canadians are clearly at the centre of the textbook. There is a deliberate focus on Aboriginal children and families, French-Canadians and bilingualism, and issues of immigration (Susan's area of specialty). Here are some of the specifically Canadian highlights for each chapter:

CHAPTER 1: THE SCIENCE OF HUMAN DEVELOPMENT
- Sudden infant death syndrome (SIDS) in Canada, p. 6
- The effect of Canadians' socioeconomic status on their development, pp. 11–12
- The multicultural context in Canada, pp. 14–16

ZHIYU WENG

Sensory Exuberance Human animals are unusual in that all the senses function at birth, but motor skills develop slowly. This Ontario boy loves to grab the rings, or even bend over to taste and bite them, even though he cannot yet sit up unsupported.

Danger Ahead This boy thinks like the teenager he is. He ignores the risks.

ZAYAN 1904 / GETTY IMAGES

Education in Process These students, checking the Internet on the steps in San Miguel de Allende in Mexico, illustrate why some scholars claim that college and university students learn more from each other than from their professors.

JEREMY WOODHOUSE / AGE FOTOSTOCK

Ongoing Features

While this book has been thoroughly updated and Canadianized, many characteristics of the first edition were acclaimed and have therefore been retained in this new edition.

Writing That Communicates the Excitement and Challenge of the Field

An overview of the science of human development should be lively, just as real people are. Each sentence conveys tone as well as content. Chapter-opening vignettes bring student readers into the immediacy of development. Examples and explanations abound, helping students make the connections among theory, research, and their own experiences.

Up-to-Date Coverage

Our mentors welcomed curiosity, creativity, and skepticism; as a result, we are both eager to read and analyze thousands of articles and books on everything from autism to zygosity. The recent explosion of research in neuroscience and genetics has challenged both of us, once again, first to understand and then to explain many complex findings and speculative leaps. Our students continue to ask questions and share their experiences, always providing new perspectives and concerns.

The best of the new concepts are integrated into the text, including hundreds of new references on topics such as the genetics of delinquency, infant nutrition, bipolar and autism spectrum disorders, high-stakes testing, drug use and drug addiction, the importance of attachment, brain development throughout childhood and into the last years of our lives, and neurocognitive disorders.

RESEARCH ON THE BRAIN

Every major section of the book includes a section on the brain, often enhanced with charts and photos to help students understand its inner workings. The following list highlights some of this material:

- The implication of low serotonin levels in SIDS, p. 6
- The role of neurotransmitters and growth factors such as GDNF in depression, p. 19
- PET scans of brains of a depressed and a non-depressed person, p. 20
- Effect of the short allele of 5-HTTLPR on stress reactions, p. 23
- Prenatal growth of the brain, pp. 60–62; illustrated, p. 62
- Teratogenic effects on brain development, pp. 73–74; 78–79
- Brain development in the first two years, pp. 95–101
- Measurements of brain function applied to evaluate Piaget's sensorimotor intelligence, pp. 120–121
- Epigenetic effects on brain development, pp. 123–124
- Brain developments that support social emotions, pp. 141–142
- The effect of stress on brain development, pp. 143–144
- Synchrony and brain maturation, p. 148

HENRIK WEIS / CULTURA / CORBIS

Idyllic Two 8-year-olds, each with a 6-year-old sister, are day-dreaming or exploring in a very old tree beside a lake in Denmark—what could be better?

BRITA KASHOLM-TENGVE / GETTY IMAGES

Bonded That fathers enjoy their sons is not surprising, but notice the infant's hand reaching for Dad's face. At this age, infants show their trust in adults by grabbing and reaching. Synchrony and attachment are mutual.

- Attachment and brain development, p. 152
- The effect of lead exposure on brain development, p. 180
- Brain development in early childhood (prefrontal cortex, myelination, lateralization, the limbic system), pp. 184–189; illustrated, pp. 185–186
- The effects of physical exercise on the brain, p. 253
- Collaboration of cortical regions in selective attention, pp. 261–262
- Unusual brain patterns in children with bipolar disorder and ADHD, pp. 279–280
- Use of brain scans to identify neurological problems that make reading difficult, p. 280
- Brain abnormality as a possible factor in bullying, p. 315
- The role of the pituitary gland in hormone production, pp. 328–329
- Adolescent brain development; heightened arousal of reward areas of the brain, pp. 337–339
- Proportion of grey matter from childhood through adolescence, p. 338
- Benefits of adolescent brain development, pp. 354–355
- The impact of sexual abuse on the brain, pp. 374–375
- Neurological factors as predictors of delinquency in adolescence, p. 382
- The impact of alcohol on the adolescent brain, p. 386
- Brain development and postformal thought, p. 402
- The aging brain: Neurological changes in adulthood, p. 432
- Fluid intelligence and overall brain health, p. 446
- Complications in calculating adult IQ due to brain changes, p. 447
- Brain changes due to experience and expertise, p. 455
- Brain function and personality, p. 466
- The aging brain: Neurological changes in late adulthood, pp. 504–506
- Brain-shrinkage interference with multi-tasking in late adulthood, pp. 505–506
- Skills practice and improvement of brain function in late adulthood, p. 509
- Specific genes associated with Alzheimer's disease (AD); scans of progress of AD, pp. 514–515
- Correlation between vascular neurocognitive disorder and the ApoE4 allele, p. 515
- Repeated concussions as a precursor of neurocognitive disorder, p. 516
- Expression of creativity and its impact on brain health, p. 521–522
- Brain activity in response to disappointment: Differences between old, emotionally healthy individuals; old, depressed individuals; and young individuals, p. 533
- Brain death as determining factor in declaring a person legally dead, pp. 576–577

An Interdisciplinary Approach

Cognizant of the interdisciplinary nature of human development, we reflect research in biology, sociology, education, anthropology, political science, and more—as well as psychology. Genetics and social contexts are noted throughout. The variations and hazards of infant day care and preschool education are described; the implications of various family structures throughout the life span are explored; the pivotal role of school and the workplace is noted; and so on.

Coverage of Diversity

Cross-cultural, international, multi-ethnic, sexual orientation, wealth, age, gender—all these words and ideas are vital to appreciating how children develop. Research uncovers surprising similarities and notable differences: We have much in common, yet each human being is unique. From the discussion of social contexts in Chapter 1 to the coverage of cultural differences in mourning in the Epilogue, each chapter highlights possibilities and variations. New is the inclusion of genetic susceptibility, another source of variation.

New research on family structures, immigrants, bilingualism, emerging adults, and ethnic differences in health are among the many topics that illustrate human diversity. Respect for human differences is evident throughout. You will note that examples and research findings from many parts of the world are included, not as add-on highlights, but as integral parts of the description of each age.

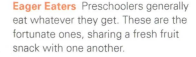

Happy Grandfathers No matter where they are, grandparents and grandchildren often enjoy each other partly because conflict is less likely, as grandparents are usually not as strict as parents are. Indeed, Sam Levinson quipped, "The reason grandparents and grandchild get along so well is that they have a common enemy."

Student Support

This book was designed for today's students. Each chapter begins with a brief real-life vignette to help students connect to the chapter content. Key terms appear in boldface type in the text; they are defined in the margins and again in a glossary at the end of the book. The outline on the first page of every chapter and the system of major and minor subheads facilitate the survey-question-read-write-review (SQ3R) approach. Chapters end with a brief summary, a list of key terms, and key questions for review. Then application exercises suggest ways to apply concepts to everyday life.

Each major section of a chapter closes with "Key Points," allowing students to pause and reflect on what they have just read. Active learning is also stressed in "Observation Quizzes" that inspire readers to look more closely at photographs, tables, and graphs, as well as in "Especially for …" questions in the margins. Each "Especially for …" question is addressed to a specific population—such as parents, nurses, educators, psychologists, or social workers—who are asked to apply what they've just read. Furthermore, we chose each photograph and wrote each caption with the expectation that students will learn from it. (This Preface offers a selection of the photographs that appear in the book.)

Critical thinking is encouraged throughout—not just in the Opposing Perspectives boxes. Every chapter challenges myths, research designs, and cultural assumptions. A series of features called "A View from Science" apply the research that shapes theory, practice, and application.

Eager Eaters Preschoolers generally eat whatever they get. These are the fortunate ones, sharing a fresh fruit snack with one another.

LEARNING OBJECTIVES

Much of what students learn from this course is a matter of attitude, approach, and perspective—all hard to quantify. In addition, there are specific learning objectives, which supplement the key terms that should also be learned. New to this edition, two sets of objectives are listed for each chapter. Each question asked at the beginning of each chapter ("What Will You Know?") correlates with a major heading in the chapter and focuses on general ideas that students might remember and apply throughout their lives.

At the end of each chapter are more specific learning objectives ("What Have You Learned?") that also connect to each major heading within the chapter but ask more specific questions about the chapter content. Suggestions and grading rubrics for these questions are available in the test bank that goes along with the book.

OPPOSING PERSPECTIVES

New to this edition are boxed features on controversial and exciting topics in development—from prenatal sex selection to the right to die. These high-interest sections are introduced in every chapter and provide students with enough information on both sides of an issue that they can practise assessing arguments, looking at the evidence, and coming up with their own conclusions. A complete list of these new features is included in the table of contents.

Supplements

As instructors, we know that supplements can make or break a class. Students are now media savvy and instructors use tools that did not exist when they were in university or college. Many supplements are available for both students and professors.

In particular, we both know how important good quality assessment materials are to students who use them to study—and to instructors who use them to see how well students are doing in class. We personally revised and approved every question in the Test Bank and Learning Curve quiz bank—adding more challenging and analytical questions to meet students' and instructors' needs, and double- and triple-checking the accuracy of each question.

LaunchPad

A comprehensive web resource for teaching and learning development, LaunchPad combines rich media resources and an easy-to-use platform. For students, it is the ultimate online study guide, with videos, an e-Book, and the LearningCurve adaptive quizzing system. For instructors, LaunchPad is a full course space where they can post class documents, easily assign and grade quizzes, and assess and record students' progress. LaunchPad can be previewed at www.worthpublishers.com/launchpad/bergerchuang1e. You'll find the following in our LaunchPad:

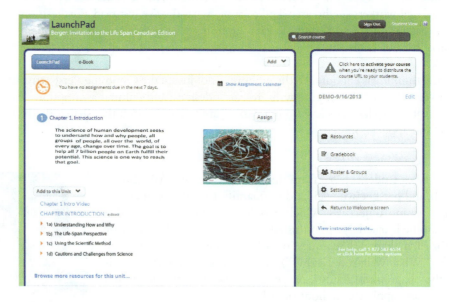

LEARNINGCURVE QUIZZING SYSTEM

The LearningCurve quizzing system is designed based on the latest findings from learning and memory research. It combines adaptive question selection, immediate and valuable feedback, and a game-like interface to engage students in a learning experience that is unique to them. Each LearningCurve quiz is fully integrated with other resources in LaunchPad through the Personalized Study Plan, so students will be able to review material with Worth's extensive library of videos and activities. And state-of-the-art question analysis reports allow instructors to track the progress of individual students as well as their class as a whole. A team of dedicated instructors—including Lisa Hager, Spring Hill College; Jessica Herrick, Mesa State College; Sara Lapsley, Simon Fraser University; Rosemary McCullough, Ave Maria University; Wendy Morrison, Montana State University; Emily Newton, University of California, Davis; Curtis Visca, Saddleback College; and Devon Werble, East Los Angeles Community College—have worked closely to develop more than 5000 quizzing questions specifically for this book. In addition, we reviewed every question to make sure that it was accurate and that it corresponded to the content of this new Canadian book.

Human Development Videos

In collaboration with dozens of instructors and researchers, Worth has developed an extensive archive of video clips. This collection covers the full range of the course, from classic experiments (like the Strange Situation and Piaget's conservation tasks) to investigations of children's play, adolescent risk taking, and the effects of Alzheimer's disease. Instructors can assign these videos to students through LaunchPad or choose one of 50 popular video activities, which combine videos with short-answer and multiple-choice questions. For presentation purposes, our videos are available in a variety of formats to suit your needs, including download and flash drive.

Instructor's Resources

Now fully integrated with LaunchPad, this collection of resources, written by Richard O. Straub (University of Michigan, Dearborn), has been hailed as the richest collection of instructor's resources in developmental psychology. The resources include learning objectives, springboard topics for discussion and debate, handouts for student projects, course planning suggestions, ideas for term projects, and a guide to audiovisual and online materials.

Interactive Presentation Slides

A new extraordinary series of "next-generation" interactive presentation lectures give instructors a dynamic yet easy-to-use new way to engage students during classroom presentations of core developmental psychology topics. Each lecture provides opportunities for discussion and interaction and enlivens the psychology classroom with an unprecedented number of embedded video clips and animations from Worth's library of videos. In addition to these animated presentations, Worth offers a set of pre-built slide sets with all chapter art and illustrations. These slides can be used as is or can be customized to fit individual needs.

Test Bank and Computerized Test Bank

The test bank, prepared by Jessica Herrick (Colorado Mesa University), Victoria Van Wie (Lone Star College), and Susan Chuang, includes at least 100 multiple-choice and 70 fill-in, true-false, and essay questions for each chapter. Good test questions are critical to every course, and we have gone through each and every one of these test questions with care. We have added more challenging questions, and questions are keyed to the textbook by topic, page number, and level of difficulty.

The Diploma computerized test bank, available on a dual-platform CD-ROM for Windows and Macintosh, guides instructors step by step through the process of creating a test. It also allows them to quickly add an unlimited number of questions; edit, scramble, or re-sequence items; format a test; and include pictures, equations, and media links. The accompanying gradebook enables instructors to record students' grades throughout the course and includes the capacity to sort student records, view detailed analyses of test items, curve tests, generate reports, and add weights to grades.

The CD-ROM is also the access point for Diploma Online Testing, which allows instructors to create and administer secure exams over a network or over the Internet. In addition, Diploma has the ability to restrict tests to specific computers or time blocks. Blackboard-formatted versions of each item in the Test Bank are available on the CD-ROM.

Thanks

We would like to thank the academic reviewers who have read this book in every edition and who have provided suggestions, criticisms, references, and encouragement. They have all made this a better book. We want to mention especially those who have reviewed this Canadian edition:

Sherry Beaumont, University of Northern British Columbia

Debashis Dutta, Renison University College and Conestoga College

Frank Elgar, McGill University

Wendy Ellis, King's University College

Lana-Lee Hardacre, Conestoga College

Antonia Henderson, Langara College

Jacqueline Kampman, Thompson Rivers University

Cheryl Kier, Athabasca University

Laura Loewen, Okanagan College

Michael MacDonald, Oakland University

Michael Mueller, University of Guelph

Nancy Ogden, Mount Royal University

Rick Owens, George Brown College

Carol Prechotko, Cambrian College of Applied Arts and Technology

Kim Roberts, Wilfrid Laurier University

William Roberts, Thompson Rivers University

Scott Ronis, University of New Brunswick

Nicholas Rule, University of Toronto

Sandra Wiebe, University of Alberta

We would also like to thank those dedicated and thoughtful instructors who met with us to discuss the challenges and rewards of teaching life span development.

Melanie Doyle, Dawson College

Susan Finch, Dawson College

Michael Mueller, University of Ontario Institute of Technology

Kim Roberts, Wilfrid Laurier University

Emily Schryer, University of Waterloo

Jan Schumacher, Georgian College

Saima Sheikh, Humber College

A Note from Susan

I would like to first thank my wonderful parents who were my constant supports, always encouraging me to do my best, and my family and friends who provided great photos for the textbook. Many thanks to Jessica Bayne for reaching out to me to Canadianize this textbook. Her leadership, patience, and understanding throughout this process have made this a great learning experience. I am very grateful to my friend and colleague, Robert Moreno (Syracuse University, New York), for providing insightful comments on all of the chapters. Many thanks to the editorial, production, and photo research people at First Folio Resource Group Inc. for their attention to detail and always being positive and encouraging throughout this process, especially Debbie Smith, Tom Dart, Janice Dyer, and Maria DeCambra. I would also like to thank Ed O'Connor, my developmental editor, and the rest of the staff at Worth Publishers who helped make this book a reality, including Christine Burak, Julia Jevmenova, Tracey Kuehn, Rosemary McCullough, Katherine Nurre, Catherine Michaelsen, Lauren Samuelson, Barbara Seixas, and Vicki Tomaselli. Finally, at the University of Guelph, I would particularly like to thank all my students, including Jessica Furtado, Jenny Glozman, Kevin De Leon, Andrea Patterson, and Diana Truong, for their tireless efforts on the textbook, test bank, and LearningCurve.

Susan S. Chuang
February 2014

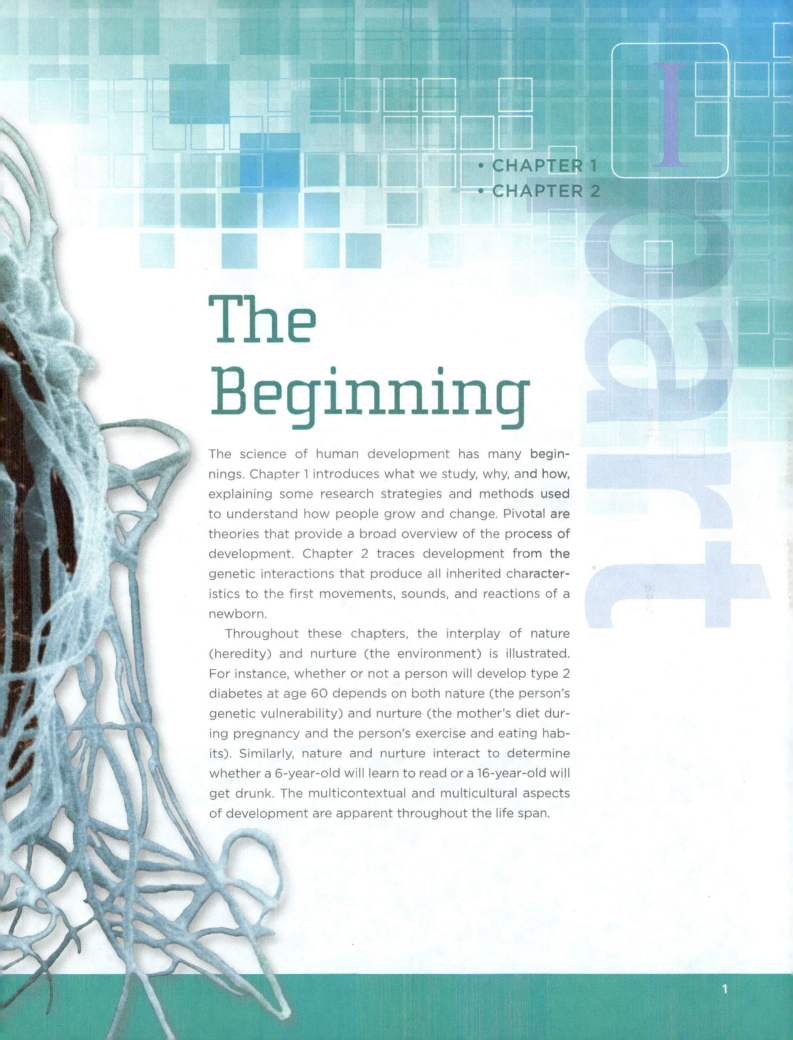

The Beginning

The science of human development has many beginnings. Chapter 1 introduces what we study, why, and how, explaining some research strategies and methods used to understand how people grow and change. Pivotal are theories that provide a broad overview of the process of development. Chapter 2 traces development from the genetic interactions that produce all inherited characteristics to the first movements, sounds, and reactions of a newborn.

Throughout these chapters, the interplay of nature (heredity) and nurture (the environment) is illustrated. For instance, whether or not a person will develop type 2 diabetes at age 60 depends on both nature (the person's genetic vulnerability) and nurture (the mother's diet during pregnancy and the person's exercise and eating habits). Similarly, nature and nurture interact to determine whether a 6-year-old will learn to read or a 16-year-old will get drunk. The multicontextual and multicultural aspects of development are apparent throughout the life span.

CHAPTER OUTLINE

THE SCIENCE OF HUMAN
Development

WHAT WILL YOU KNOW?

■ What are the complexities of studying all kinds of people?

■ Why are theories considered so important in science?

■ What special methods do developmentalists use to study change over time?

■ Why do scientific conclusions need to be interpreted with caution?

I am holding my daughter's bent right leg in place with all my strength. A nurse holds her left leg while Bethany pulls on a sheet tied to a metal structure over her bed. The midwife commands, "Push ... push ... push." Finally, a head is visible, small and wet, but perfect. In a moment, body and limbs emerge, all 4139 grams of Caleb, perfect as well. Apgar is 9, and every number on the monitor is good. Bethany, smiling, begins to nurse. Decades of learning, studying, teaching, praying, and mothering have led me to this miracle at 6:11 A.M., my first-born with her first-born. Celestial music is ringing in my ears. The ringing grows louder. Suddenly I am on the floor, looking up at six medical professionals: I have fainted.

"I am fine," I insist, getting back on the couch where I spent the night. They still stare at me.

"You need to go to triage."

"No, I am fine. Sorry I fainted."

"Hospital policy."

"No. I belong here."

"We must send you to triage, in a wheelchair."

What should I say to make them ignore me and focus on Caleb?

Another nurse wisely adds, "You can refuse treatment."

Of course. I remember now; the law requires patient consent.

So I am wheeled down the hall, wait for the elevator, go to Admitting, explain that I was with my labouring daughter all night with no food or sleep. I fainted, but I am fine. I refuse treatment.

The admitting nurse takes my blood pressure—normal—and checks with her supervisor.

"I refuse treatment," I repeat, standing up to walk back.

"OK. Wait. Sit down. Someone must wheel you back. Hospital policy."

Both Blissful Kathleen's grandson, Caleb, rests after an arduous journey, as Kathleen rejoices after crying and fainting.

I acquiesce. My immediate priority is my daughter and grandson, not policy change. I am back before the placenta is delivered.

I am thankful, but puzzled. Bethany chose me for her birth partner because of my knowledge, experience, and steadiness. I can interpret numbers, jargon, monitors, body language, medical competence, hospital cleanliness, hall noises, and more. I do not panic, and I know that Bethany is strong, healthy, and conscientious. I was grateful but not surprised that Caleb was perfect. I told the triage nurse that I had not slept or eaten all night—true, but I have gone without sleep and food before, never fainting. What happened this time? ●

—Kathleen Berger

THIS INCIDENT IS A FITTING INTRODUCTION FOR CHAPTER 1, which begins to explain what we know, what we don't know, and how we learn about human development. Emotions mix with intellect, family bonds with professional competence, contexts with cultures, personal experiences with academic knowledge. Much is known and yet new questions arise, surprises occur. I learned more about physiology, relationships, and cognition because I fainted. I also thought more about my own aging (one reason I fainted) as well as about the effects of genetics and of prenatal care (part of the reason Caleb and Bethany were fine). This chapter, and those that follow, will help you learn as well.

Understanding How and Why

The **science of human development** *seeks to understand how and why people—all groups of people, all over the world, of every age—change over time.* The goal is to help all 7 billion people on Earth fulfill their potential. This science is one way to reach that goal.

Developmentalists recognize that growth over the life span is *multidirectional, multicontextual, multicultural, multidisciplinary,* and *plastic,* five terms that will be explained soon. First we need to emphasize that developmental study is a *science.* It depends on theories, data, analysis, critical thinking, and sound methodology, just like every other science. All scientists ask questions and seek answers to figure out the "how and why."

Science is especially necessary when the topic is human development: Lives depend on the answers. People disagree vehemently about what pregnant women should eat, whether babies should be left to cry, when children should be punished, under which circumstances adults should marry, or divorce, or retire, or die. Opinions are subjective, arising from emotions and culture. Scientists seek to progress from opinion to truth, from subjective to objective, from wishes to evidence.

The Scientific Method

As you may realize, facts may be twisted, and applications sometimes spring from assumptions, not from data. To avoid unexamined opinions and to rein in personal biases, researchers follow five steps of the **scientific method** (see Figure 1.1):

1. *Begin with curiosity.* On the basis of theory, prior research, or a personal observation, pose a question.

2. *Develop a hypothesis.* Shape the question into a **hypothesis,** a specific prediction that can be tested.

3. *Test the hypothesis.* Design and conduct research to gather **empirical evidence** (data).

---

science of human development
The science that seeks to understand how and why people of all ages and circumstances change or remain the same over time.

scientific method
A way to answer questions that requires empirical research and data-based conclusions.

hypothesis
A specific prediction that can be tested.

empirical evidence
Evidence based on data from scientific observation or experiments; not theoretical.

4. *Draw conclusions.* Use the evidence to support or refute the hypothesis.

5. *Report the results.* Share the data, conclusions, and alternative explanations.

As you see, developmental scientists begin with curiosity and then seek the facts, drawing conclusions after careful research. **Replication**—repeating the procedures and methods of a study with different participants—is often a sixth and crucial step (Jasny et al., 2011). Are the findings from this replication study similar to the original study? Scientists study the reported procedures and results of other scientists. They read publications, attend conferences, send emails, and sometimes move from one nation to another to collaborate. Conclusions are revised, refined, and confirmed after replication.

The implications of those conclusions spread beyond science, involving religion, politics, and ethics. One of the most famous scientists of all time said, "Science without religion is lame; religion without science is blind" (Einstein, 1954/1994, p. 49). Some of the politics and ethics of scientific research are discussed at the end of this chapter. Every chapter of this book, and every "Opposing Perspectives" feature, describes the interaction of empirical data with moral values.

The Nature–Nurture Controversy

A good example of the need for science concerns a great puzzle of development, the *nature–nurture debate*. **Nature** refers to the influence of the genes that people inherit. **Nurture** refers to environmental influences, beginning with the health and diet of the embryo's mother and continuing a lifetime, including family, school, community, and society.

The nature–nurture debate has many other names, among them *heredity–environment* and *maturation–learning*. Under whatever name, the basic question is: *How much of any characteristic, behaviour, or emotion is the result of genes and how much is the result of specific experiences?* Some people are predisposed to believe that most traits are inborn, that children are innately good or bad, naturally innocent or evil. Other people stress nurture, crediting or blaming parents, or circumstances, or drugs, or food (as in "You are what you eat").

Developmentalists have learned that neither belief by itself is accurate. The question is "how much," not "which," because both genes and the environment affect every characteristic: Nature always affects nurture, and then nurture affects nature. Some scientists think that even "how much" is misleading, as it implies that nature and nurture each contribute a fixed amount when actually their dynamic interaction is crucial (Gottlieb, 2007; Meaney, 2010; Spencer et al., 2009). I fainted at Caleb's birth because of the interaction of at least seven factors (low blood sugar, lack of sleep, physical exertion, gender, age, relief, joy), all influenced by both nature and nurture, all combining to land me on the floor.

Scientific Method

1. Curiosity

2. Hypothesis

3. Test

4. Conclusion

5. Report

And Replicate

FANCY COLLECTION / SUPERSTOCK

PHOTODISC

YURI ARCURS / ALAMY

MOODBOARD / SUPERSTOCK

MASTERFILE (ROYALTY-FREE DIV.)

FIGURE 1.1 Process, Not Proof Built into the scientific method—in questions, hypotheses, tests, and replications—is a passion for possibilities, especially unexpected ones.

replication
The repetition of a study, using different participants.

nature
A general term for the traits, capacities, and limitations that each individual inherits genetically from his or her parents at the moment of conception.

nurture
A general term for all the environmental influences that affect development after an individual is conceived.

A VIEW FROM SCIENCE

Sudden Infant Death*

Coverage of every topic in this book is based on research that follows the scientific method. Here we present one topic, **sudden infant death syndrome (SIDS),** to illustrate. Every year until the mid-1990s, tens of thousands of 2- to 6-month-old infants died of SIDS (called *crib death* in North America, *cot death* in England, nameless but nonetheless tragic in many developing nations). Tiny babies smile at their caregivers, wave at rattles that their small fingers cannot yet grasp, go to sleep, but never wake up. For many years, as parents mourned, scientists asked why (*step 1*) and tested hypotheses (the cat? the quilt? unpasteurized honey? homicide? spoiled milk?) to no avail: Sudden infant death was a mystery.

Then a scientist named Susan Beal studied every SIDS death in South Australia, seeking factors that might be causes. She learned that some circumstances did not matter (such as birth order) and others increased the risk (such as maternal smoking and lambskin blankets).

A breakthrough came when Beal noticed an ethnic variation: Australian babies of Chinese descent died far less often of SIDS than did Australian babies of European descent. Genetic?

Sleeping Safely Sudden infant death syndrome occurred too often in many nations before 1990, but not in Mongolia (shown here) or other Asian countries. The reason, as scientists hypothesized and later confirmed, is that Asian parents put their children "back to sleep."

SEAN SPRAGUE / THE IMAGE WORKS

OBSERVATION QUIZ

Back-sleeping babies sometimes squirm, making the blankets covering them come loose—another risk factor for SIDS. What detail makes that unlikely here? (see answer, page 8) ➡

Most experts thought so. But Beal's scientific observation led her to note that Chinese babies slept on their backs, contrary to the Australian (as well as European and North American) custom of stomach-sleeping. She developed a new hypothesis (*step 2*): Sleeping position matters.

To test her hypothesis (*step 3*), Beal convinced a large group of non-Chinese parents to put their newborns to sleep on their backs. Almost none of the infants died suddenly. After several years of data, she drew a surprising conclusion (*step 4*): Back-sleeping protected against SIDS. Her published reports (*step 5*) (Beal, 1988) caught the attention of doctors in the Netherlands, where pediatricians for some time had been telling parents that babies should sleep on their stomachs. Two Dutch scientists (Engelberts & de Jong, 1990) recommended back-sleeping; thousands of parents took heed. SIDS was reduced in Holland by 40 percent in one year—a stunning replication (*step 6*).

In Canada in 1993, the federal government and several public health organizations began recommending that parents place their babies on their backs to sleep. SIDS rates had been falling since the late 1980s, but after the government launched a formal "Back to Sleep" campaign in 1999, the rate of SIDS in Canada fell by 50 percent over the next five years. Researchers believe this significant reduction can be directly linked to the increase in the number of babies who were put to sleep on their backs, as well as to lower smoking rates among pregnant women.

Stomach-sleeping is a proven, replicated risk, but it is not the only one: SIDS still occurs. Beyond sleeping position, and factors such as cigarette smoke in the household and low birth weight, other risks include a brain-stem abnormality that produces too little serotonin (a neurotransmitter), soft blankets or pillows, and bed-sharing (when infants sleep in their parents' beds) (Duncan et al., 2010; Ostfeld et al., 2010). In Canada, there is currently a higher incidence of SIDS among infants born prematurely and with low birth weight or those born to low-income or Aboriginal parents (Public Health Agency of Canada, 2011a). As with almost every development, a combination of nature and nurture produces the outcome.

---

*Each chapter includes a feature entitled A View From Science that is intended to help readers to understand the scientific process as well as to learn details of a topic of interest. For both reasons, don't skip over these features.

sudden infant death syndrome (SIDS) The term used to describe an infant's unexpected death; when a seemingly healthy baby, usually between 2 and 6 months old, suddenly stops breathing and dies unexpectedly while asleep.

The Life-Span Perspective

The **life-span perspective** (Fingerman et al., 2011; Lerner, 2010) takes into account all phases of life, not just the first two decades, which were once the sole focus of developmental study. By including the entire life (see Table 1.1), this perspective leads to a new understanding of human development as multidirectional, multicontextual, multicultural, multidisciplinary, and plastic (Baltes et al., 2006; Staudinger & Lindenberger, 2003). Ages are only a rough guide to "change over time."

life-span perspective An approach to the study of human development that takes into account all phases of life, not just childhood or adulthood.

Development Is Multidirectional

The traditional idea—that all development advances until about age 18, steadies, and then declines—has been refuted by life-span research. Multiple changes, in every direction, characterize the life span. If any particular human trait were to be charted over time, it would be apparent that some traits appear and disappear, with increases, decreases, and zigzags (see Figure 1.2).

Sometimes *discontinuity* is evident: Change can occur rapidly and dramatically, as when caterpillars become butterflies. Sometimes *continuity* is found: Growth can be gradual, as when redwoods grow taller over hundreds of years. Some characteristics do not seem to change at all: A zygote is XY or XX, male or

TABLE 1.1 Age Ranges for Different Stages of Development

Infancy	0 to 2 years
Early childhood	2 to 6 years
Middle childhood	6 to 11 years
Adolescence	11 to 18 years
Emerging Adulthood	18 to 25 years
Adulthood	25 to 65 years
Late adulthood	65 years and older

As you will learn, developmentalists are reluctant to specify chronological ages for any period of development, since time is only one of many variables that affect each person. However, age is a crucial variable, and development can be segmented into periods of study. Approximate ages for each period are given here.

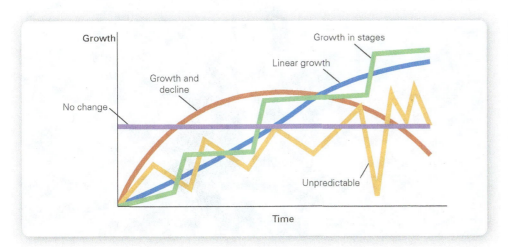

FIGURE 1.2 Patterns of Developmental Growth Many patterns of developmental growth have been discovered by research. Although linear (or near-linear) progress seems most common, scientists now find that almost no aspect of human change follows the linear pattern exactly.

critical period
A time when a particular type of
developmental growth (in body
or behaviour) must happen if it
is ever going to happen.

sensitive period
A time when a certain type of development is most likely to happen or
happens most easily, although it may
still happen later with more difficulty.
For example, early childhood is considered a sensitive period for language
learning.

female, and that chromosomal sex remains throughout the life span. Of course, the significance of that biological fact changes over time.

There is simple growth, radical transformation, improvement, and decline as well as stability, stages, and continuity—day to day, year to year, and generation to generation. Not only does the direction of change vary over the life span, but each characteristic follows a distinct pattern: Losses in some specific skills and abilities occur at the same time as gains in others. For example, when babies begin talking, they lose some ability to distinguish sounds from other languages; when adults retire, they may become more creative.

The speed and timing of impairments or improvements vary as well. Some changes are sudden and profound because of a **critical period,** either a time when something *must* occur to ensure normal development or the only time when an abnormality might occur. For example, the human embryo grows arms and legs, hands and feet, fingers and toes, each over a critical period between 28 and 54 days after conception. After that it is too late: Unlike some insects, humans never grow replacement limbs.

Tragically, between 1957 and 1961, thousands of newly pregnant women in 30 nations took *thalidomide,* an anti-nausea drug. This change in nurture (via the mother's bloodstream) disrupted nature (the embryo's genetic program). If an expectant mother ingested thalidomide during the 26 days of that critical period, her newborn's limbs were malformed or absent (Moore & Persaud, 2007). Specifics (for example, whether arms and legs, or just arms, or only hands were missing) depended on exactly when she swallowed the pill. Surprisingly, if an expectant woman took thalidomide before day 28 or after day 54, no harm occurred.

Life has very few such critical periods. Often, however, a particular development occurs more easily—but not exclusively—at a certain time. Such a time is called a **sensitive period.** An example is language. If children do not start speaking their first language between ages 1 and 3, they might do so later (hence, the first years are not critical), but their grammar is usually impaired (hence, these years are sensitive). Similarly, childhood is a sensitive period for learning to pronounce a second or third language with a native accent.

As is often the case with development, sweeping generalizations (like those in the preceding sentence) do not apply in every case. Accent-free speech *usually* must be learned before puberty, but some teenagers or adults with exceptional nature and nurture (naturally adept at hearing and then immersed in a new language) master a second language flawlessly (Birdsong, 2006; Muñoz & Singleton, 2011).

Life-Span Plan This 25-year-old, Diana Truong, is currently in the Master of Teaching program at the Ontario Institute for Studies in Education (OISE). Worldwide, emerging adulthood is a period of exploration and change. Over the next several years, Diana may decide to teach older students rather than younger students, stay in school to get her PhD, or change fields completely.

DIANA TRUONG

Development Is Multicontextual

The second insight from the life-span perspective is that development is multi-contextual. It takes place within many contexts, including physical surroundings (climate, noise, population density, etc.) and family configurations (married couple, single parent, same-sex couple, extended family, and more). Developmentalists who study the life span take dozens of contexts into account, as explained throughout this book. Examining these contexts provides researchers a better understanding of what may be universal or developmental, relevant and similar for all individuals, or dependent on cultural context.

ECOLOGICAL SYSTEMS The Russian-American psychologist Urie Bronfenbrenner (1917–2005) stressed contexts by recommending that developmentalists take an **ecological-systems approach** (see Figure 1.3) (Bronfenbrenner & Morris, 2006). Ecology is the branch of biology that deals with the relation of living things to their environment and to each other; Bronfenbrenner believed that each person is affected by many social contexts and interpersonal relations. Before he died, he renamed his approach the *bioecological theory* to stress the important role that biology plays in development, recognizing that systems within the body (such as the sexual reproductive system and the cardiovascular system) affect all the external systems.

Bronfenbrenner developed his theory of ecological systems by stressing that all relationships the individual person has with other people and with various social contexts are interconnected. He started with the most immediate, direct relationships

Cat, Duck, or Dog? Nine-year-old Sun Minyl is listening to his teacher attentively before circling the correct animal and writing "cat" in his workbook. This activity is not difficult at his age, but Sun Minyl has an extra challenge: he is learning in English, not in his first language, Chinese, at a school near Shanghai.

ecological-systems approach
The view that in the study of human development, the person should be considered in all the contexts and interactions that constitute a life. (Later renamed *bioecological theory*.)

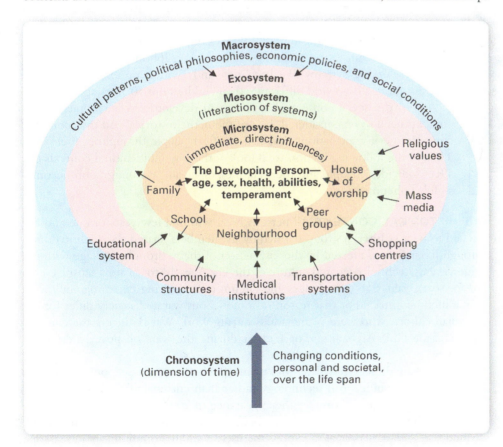

FIGURE 1.3 The Ecological Model Each person is affected by interactions among overlapping systems, which provide the context of development. *Microsystems*—family, peer groups, classroom, neighbourhood, house of worship—intimately shape human development. Surrounding and supporting the microsystems are the *exosystems*—external networks, such as local educational, medical, employment, and communications systems—that influence the microsystems. Influencing both of these systems is the *macrosystem,* which includes cultural patterns, political philosophies, economic policies, and social conditions. *Mesosystems* refer to interactions among systems, as when parents and teachers coordinate to educate a child. Bronfenbrenner eventually added a fifth system, the *chronosystem,* to emphasize the importance of historical time.

the child has with his or her immediate family and then worked outward to other environments that might affect the child indirectly.

The ecological-systems approach recognizes various systems that surround individuals and have lasting effects on them. Most obvious are *microsystems*, which are those basic, personal relationships each of us has with family, friends, and peers. Also important are *exosystems*—relationships between individual people and local institutions such as church and school—and *macrosystems*, which consist of the broader social setting and include such influences as government policies, economic trends, and cultural values.

Because he appreciated the dynamic interaction among all the systems, Bronfenbrenner included a fourth system, the *mesosystem*, consisting of the connections among all the other systems. One example of a mesosystem is the interface between employment (exosystem) and family life (microsystem). These connections include not only the direct impact of family leave, retirement, and shift work, but also indirect macrosystem influences from the economy that affect unemployment rates, minimum wage standards, and hiring practices—each of which may affect the family microsystem as well as each individual in the family, always influenced by the overall culture.

For instance, if one person in a dual-earner couple becomes unemployed, he or she usually does more household cooking and cleaning, but specifics depend on whether the unemployed person is a man (3 additional hours per week) or a woman (6 additional hours) (Gough & Killewald, 2011). Gender differences are also affected by national norms: Women in Italy do much more domestic work than men, but this is less true in Sweden (Cooke & Baxter, 2010). It is obvious now, but not when Bronfenbrenner first wrote, that mesosystems provide crucial connections between the various contexts that affect each person.

Throughout his life, Bronfenbrenner also stressed the role of historical conditions on human development, and therefore he included a fifth system, the *chronosystem* (literally "time system"). For example, children growing up with advanced communication technologies such as cellphones, the Internet, and social networking systems like Facebook and Twitter are experiencing and learning about their world differently than children did 50 years ago.

As you can see, a contextual approach to development is complex; many contexts need to be considered. Two of them, the historical and the economic contexts, merit explanation now, as they affect people throughout their lives. Then in the following section we'll look at the way multicultural contexts can affect individual people and their families, especially as immigration becomes a global phenomenon.

Twenty-First-Century Manners
If this boy removed his elbows from the table but kept texting, what would you say about his manners? What would your parents say? Your grandparents?

"Hey! Elbows off the table."

WILLIAM HAEFELI / THE NEW YORKER COLLECTION WWW.CARTOONBANK.COM

cohort
A group defined by the shared age of its members, who, because they were born at about the same time, move through life together, experiencing the same historical events and cultural shifts.

THE HISTORICAL CONTEXT All persons born within a few years of one another are said to be a **cohort,** a group defined by its members' shared age. Cohorts travel through life together, affected by the interaction of their chronological age with the values, events, technologies, and culture of the era. Ages 18 to 25 are a sensitive period for social values, so experiences and circumstances during emerging adulthood have a lifetime impact. For that reason, attitudes about war and society differ for the Canadian cohorts who were young adults during World War II, during the conflicts in Korea, the Gulf, Afghanistan, or Iraq, or during the wars on poverty, drugs, or terrorism.

As Canadian thinker Marshall McLuhan (1911–1980) pointed out, sometimes advances in communications technology rather than current political issues constitute a historical context. Consider the appearance in 2004 of the social networking service Facebook. Founder Mark Zuckerberg's mission was to make the world more "connected," allowing people to express themselves and to communicate in real time

with their family members and friends, all the while making new friends. Thanks to the World Wide Web, Facebook quickly became a global phenomenon. By 2013, there were more than 945 million monthly users, more than 80 percent of whom were outside North America (Facebook Newsroom, 2013).

Think of the many ways Facebook may have affected the development of the cohort popularly known as Generation Z, or the Internet Generation: people born roughly between 1990 and 2001. For example, to what extent will this cohort's notions of privacy and friendship differ from those of their parents and grandparents? These are questions that developmentalists might pose as the basis for research studies. Researchers in Australia who surveyed Internet users there found that Facebook and other online social networks can allow people to develop relationships they would be reluctant to pursue in person. This in turn increases their psychological well-being and strengthens their ties with neighbours and friends (Bargh & McKenna, 2004). These online sites can also decrease the challenges of social interactions and encourage more self-disclosure (Bargh, McKenna, & Fitzsimons, 2002; Tidwell & Walther, 2002).

THE SOCIOECONOMIC CONTEXT Another influential context of development is a person's **socioeconomic status (SES)**. Sometimes SES is called *social class* (as in *middle class* or *working class*). SES reflects not just income but other aspects, including level of education and occupational status.

Consider two Canadian families. In both, the family composition includes an infant, an unemployed mother, and a father who earns $15 000 a year. The SES of family 1 would be low if the father were a high school dropout who washes dishes for a living and lives in an urban slum. The SES of family 2 would be higher than that of family 1 if the father were a graduate student who works as a teaching assistant, and his family lived in graduate housing on campus. So, the father's level of education and social status (a graduate student obviously has a greater *potential* income than a dishwasher) are taken into consideration when determining the family's SES.

As this example shows, annual income alone does not determine poverty. Rates of inflation also have to be considered, as when the cost of food or gas or other necessities goes up. In Canada, the federal government has no official definition of poverty, low income, or income adequacy. Statistics Canada uses household income to determine whether a family is "living in straitened circumstances." If a family spends a greater proportion of its income (at least 20 percent more than the average Canadian family) on basic necessities such as food, clothing, and shelter, then it falls beneath what the agency calls a "low income cut-off," or LICO rate (Campaign 2000, 2011).

Statistics Canada calculates both a before-tax and after-tax LICO rate. It is the after-tax LICO that most non-governmental agencies and media outlets in Canada

Same Situation, Far Apart: Times are Changing Seniors in the twenty-first century live decades longer than did earlier cohorts, affording them opportunities that were previously unavailable. In 1950 in Peru, average life expectancy was 45. Now in Lima, newlyweds Carmen Mercado, age 64, and Jorge de la Cruz, age 74 *(left)*, can expect a decade of wedded bliss. While Carmen and Jorge were courting, Hazel Soares *(right)* was studying, which culminated in her graduation from Mills College in Oakland, California, at age 94.

socioeconomic status (SES)
A person's position in society as determined by income, wealth, occupation, education, and place of residence. (Sometimes called *social class*.)

use to identify poverty rates in the country. In 2009, the after-tax LICO for one parent with one child under the age of 18 in a large urban centre was $22 420. Nationwide, about 9.5 percent of Canadians fell below this rate, which meant that about 3.2 million people, including 639 000 children, were living in poverty.

Who is at greatest risk of living in poverty in Canada? Female-headed households, Aboriginal peoples, immigrant families, and families that include children with disabilities all have higher-than-average rates of poverty (D. I. Hay, 2009). In 2009, more than half (52 percent) of single mothers with children under the age of 6 were living in poverty. Among First Nations, one in every four children was growing up poor. The extent to which families are vulnerable to poverty also depends on the region in which they live. Comparing child poverty rates among provinces in 2009, Manitoba and British Columbia had the highest rates at 16.8 and 16.4 percent respectively, and Prince Edward Island the lowest rate, at 9 percent (Campaign 2000, 2011).

A question for developmentalists is: At what age does low SES do the most damage? In infancy, a family's low SES may mean less nutritional foods that could stunt the developing brain. In adolescence, low SES could mean a neighbourhood where guns and drugs are readily available. In adulthood, job and marriage prospects are reduced for those with low SES. In late adulthood, accumulated stress over the decades, including the stress of poverty, overwhelms the body's reserves, causing disease and death (Hoffmann, 2008).

According to Statistics Canada's 2009 after-tax LICO rate, seniors had a lower incidence of poverty (5.2 percent) than any other age group, but the fact remains that those seniors who are poor may suffer more. This highlights the role of ideology: SES is a powerful lifelong influence, but the data does not dictate which age group most needs financial relief, nor the problems of the near-poor, who do not qualify for certain social assistance programs.

FIGURE 1.4 The Rich Live Longer As you see, there is a difference in life expectancy between the rich and poor, with those in the highest tax bracket (Q5) living the longest.

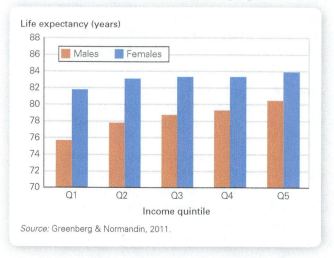

Life expectancy (years)

Source: Greenberg & Normandin, 2011.

Also important is how nations differ in their response to SES and whether those responses change over time. For example, in Canada, as in the United States, there is a gap in life expectancy between the rich and poor, as evident from Figure 1.4.

What to do about age, economic, national, and historical differences is a political rather than a developmental question. Voters choose leaders who decide policies that affect people of various ages and incomes. At best, developmentalists provide data, not prescriptions.

Development Is Multicultural

In order to study "all kinds of people, everywhere, at every age," as developmental science must do, it is essential that people of many cultures be included. For social scientists, **culture** is "the system of shared beliefs, conventions, norms, behaviours, expectations and symbolic representations that persist over time and prescribe social rules of conduct" (Bornstein et al., 2011, p. 30).

Thus, culture is far more than food, clothes, or rituals; it is a set of ideas that people share. This makes culture a powerful **social construction,** a concept constructed, or made, by a society. Social constructions affect how people think and behave, what they value, ignore, and punish. Because culture is so basic to thinking and emotions,

culture
A system of shared beliefs, norms, behaviours, and expectations that persist over time and prescribe social behaviour and assumptions.

social construction
An idea that is based on shared perceptions, not on objective reality. Many age-related terms, such as childhood, adolescence, yuppie, and senior citizen, are social constructions.

KUTTIG-RF-KIDS / ALAMY

Family Pride Grandpa Charilaos is proud of his tavern in northern Greece (central Macedonia), but he is even more proud of his talented grandchildren, including Maria Soni (shown here). Note her expert fingering. Her mother and father also play instruments. Is that nature or nature?

people are usually unaware of their cultural values. Just as fish do not realize that they are surrounded by water, people often do not realize that their assumptions about life and death arise from their own culture.

Sometimes people use the word *culture* to refer to large groups of other people, as in "Asian culture" or "Latino culture." That invites stereotyping and prejudice, since such large groups include people of many cultures. For instance, people from Korea and Japan are aware of notable cultural differences between themselves, as are people from Mexico and Guatemala. Furthermore, individuals within those cultures sometimes rebel against expected beliefs, conventions, norms, and behaviours.

Culture influences everything we say, do, or think, but the term "culture" needs to be carefully used. Ideally, pride in one's national heritage adds to personal happiness, but sometimes cultural pride is destructive of both the individual and the community (Morrison et al., 2011; Reeskens & Wright, 2011).

DEFICIT, OR JUST DIFFERENCE? Humans tend to believe that they, their nation, and their cultures are a little better than others. This way of thinking has benefits. Generally, people who like themselves are happier, prouder, and more willing to help others. However, that belief becomes destructive if it reduces respect and appreciation for others. Developmentalists recognize the **difference-equals-deficit error,** the assumption that people unlike us (different) are inferior (deficit). Think back to high school and the various cliques and groups of people there. Did some groups of students think that they were better than the rest?

The difference-equals-deficit error is one reason a multicultural approach is necessary. Various ways of thinking or acting are not necessarily wrong or right, better or worse. The scientific method, which requires empirical data, is needed for accurate assessments.

Sometimes a difference may be connected to an asset (Marschark & Spencer, 2003). For example, cultures that discourage dissent also foster harmony. The opposite is also true—cultures that encourage conflict also value independence. Whatever your personal judgment on this, the opposite opinion has some merit. A multicultural understanding requires recognition that some differences signify strengths, not weaknesses.

A multicultural perspective helps researchers realize that whether a difference is an asset or not depends partly on the cultural context. Is the toddler who has a large

difference-equals-deficit error
The mistaken belief that a deviation from some norm is necessarily inferior to behaviour or characteristics that meet the standard.

ARNELL MANALANG / ALAMY

Feet Between Feet This child is completely enclosed by his mother's body as she reads to him, unlike the side-by-side position typical among European-Canadians. What cultural values does each position teach?

vocabulary better than the one who knows few words? Is the mother who reads to her child every day better than the mother who does not? Yes to both questions in middle-class United States culture. A European-American criticism of Mexican-Americans is that parents rarely read to their children. But this criticism may reflect the difference-equals-deficit error; cross-cultural research finds that many Mexican-American families use other ways to foster language, such as storytelling (Hammer et al., 2011).

Another important reason to have a multicultural perspective is to be more sensitive to our biases and how we socially construct our knowledge. For example, for a long time, many researchers concluded that Chinese societies promote interdependence whereas Western countries such as Canada and the United States promote independence. However, researchers such as Chao (1994, 1995) and Chuang (2006) have found that Chinese-American and Chinese-Canadian mothers do support their young children's independence, even though how they define independence may vary. Chinese-American mothers define independence as self-reliance, the ability to do things without the parents' assistance; American parents define it as self-expression (Chao, 1994). As for Chinese-Canadian mothers, they define independence both as self-reliance and as an expression of self (Chuang, 2006). For all these reasons, it is important for researchers to understand how people are defining, interpreting, and making meaning of their development and their world around them.

THE MULTICULTURAL CONTEXT IN CANADA The Canadian identity is rooted in multiculturalism and the diversity it encourages. Historically, this diversity has had two major manifestations—among the "three founding peoples" at the time of Confederation, and among the waves of immigrants who arrived after the country's immigration policies were liberalized in the 1960s.

The three founding peoples consist of the Aboriginal peoples, the French, and the English. As the Constitution Act acknowledges, the Aboriginal peoples themselves are subdivided as First Nations, Inuit, and Métis. Among the various First Nations peoples across the country, there is also much diversity of languages and cultures.

For various reasons, the English gradually came to be the "dominant" culture in Canada as a whole, and both the Aboriginal peoples and the French have struggled to maintain their distinct identities in the face of this dominance.

For the French, language has always been key to their sense of identity. The right to use French in the courts and Parliament was enshrined in the British North America Act, 1867 and the Constitution Act, 1982, and over the years various federal and provincial/territorial laws have further defined and strengthened these rights. Canada is officially a bilingual nation, and the Official Languages Act states that all federal services must be available in both English and French. It's also important to remember that the French presence is not limited to Quebec; there are significant francophone communities in New Brunswick (the only officially bilingual province in Canada), Ontario, Manitoba, Saskatchewan, and Alberta.

One question we'll pursue throughout this text is: What are the developmental implications of living in a bilingual country? What effects might this have on patterns of language acquisition, on education in general, and on a person's world view? Could it be that Canadians are a little more cosmopolitan, a little more open to other opinions than their American neighbours, because of the presence of the French and official bilingualism?

Another question we'll consider is: To what extent have cultural conflicts between Aboriginal peoples and the rest of Canadian society had developmental impacts on Aboriginal persons of all ages? Perhaps the most dramatic example of these conflicts is the residential school system of the twentieth century, when Aboriginal children were taken from their parents and home communities and sent away to schools run by Christian churches. In these schools, young people were forbidden to speak their own language, to participate in their own cultural practices, and for the most part to communicate with their own family members.

The negative consequences of these schools were so obvious and grave that the entire system was eventually dismantled and the Canadian government issued a formal apology to all Aboriginal peoples in 2008, calling the residential school system "a sad chapter in our history." Developmentally speaking, are there lessons to be learned, not just from the residential schools legacy, but from traditional Aboriginal teachings on child rearing and education?

To a large extent, residential schools were an attempt by the government to *assimilate* Aboriginal peoples into the dominant culture of the time to, in the chilling words of one government official, "kill the Indian in the child." As the government began to abandon this policy in the 1960s, Aboriginal peoples also acquired, for the first time in Canadian history, the rights of full citizenship. At the same time, Canada began to liberalize its immigration laws, which had always favoured white Europeans and discouraged immigration from Asia, Africa, and South America.

Slowly and sometimes grudgingly, Canadian society began to welcome, even to celebrate, diversity. Part of what makes this cultural diversity possible is what John Berry, emeritus professor at Queen's University in Kingston, calls **acculturation.** This is the process of cultural and psychological changes that individuals face as they come into contact with a new culture (Berry et al., 1989). Specifically, it involves all the adjustments immigrants have to make to adapt to their new surroundings while still maintaining their own cultural practices and beliefs.

In Canada, the acculturation process has been made easier than in some other countries because of certain government policies and programs that are rooted in the country's history. As noted above, before the 1960s, Canada's ethnoprofile was largely European, white, and, except in Quebec, English speaking. Then in 1962 and 1967, largely for economic reasons, the federal government reformed the Immigration Act to remove all existing racial barriers. The result was a major transformation in the number of immigrants coming to Canada from countries in the developing world, a transformation that over the years has completely changed the ethnic profile of Canadian immigration (see Figure 1.5).

To accommodate this change in its immigrant population, the Canadian government under Pierre Trudeau adopted an official policy of multiculturalism in 1971. In 1988, this policy became law through the adoption of the Canadian Multiculturalism Act, whose stated objective is to "recognize and promote the understanding that multiculturalism reflects the cultural and racial diversity of Canadian society and acknowledges

acculturation
The process of cultural and psychological change that occurs when individuals come into contact with a new culture.

FIGURE 1.5 A Changing Society
The liberalization of Canadian immigration laws in the 1960s had obvious and long-term impacts on the ethnic composition of Canadian society. In terms of the regional origin of immigrants, which region had the greatest decline over the 45-year period illustrated here? Which had the greatest increase? How might these changes affect human development in this country?

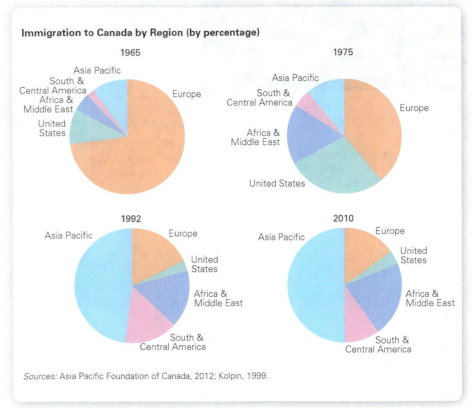

Immigration to Canada by Region (by percentage)

Sources: Asia Pacific Foundation of Canada, 2012; Kolpin, 1999.

the freedom of all members of Canadian society to preserve, enhance and share their cultural heritage" (Minister of Justice, 1988).

To strengthen the country's commitment to immigrant Canadians, the federal and provincial/territorial governments now provide funds to support numerous services and programs specifically targeted to newcomers. By 2011, there were close to 1000 immigrant serving agencies (ISAs)—largely community-based, not-for-profit organizations—across Canada. Numerous community organizations also provide free services and programs for local immigrant families. From a developmental point of view, these types of social support systems help mitigate some of the negative experiences that are often associated with the acculturation process, such as poverty, depression, and family conflicts.

Mentoring Children Lev Vygotsky lived from 1896 to 1934, when war, starvation, and revolution led to the deaths of millions. Throughout this political turmoil, Vygotsky focused on the role of parents in their children's learning. Here he is shown with his daughter Gita, who later worked with some of her father's students to publish his manuscripts.

LEARNING WITHIN A CULTURE Russian cognitive developmentalist Lev Vygotsky (1896–1934) was a leader in describing the interaction between culture and education (Wertsch & Tulviste, 2005). He noticed that adults from the many Russian cultures (Asians and Europeans, of many religions) taught their children whatever beliefs and habits they might need as adults.

Vygotsky (discussed in more detail in Chapter 5) believed that *guided participation* is a universal process used by mentors to teach cultural knowledge, skills, and habits. Guided participation can occur via school instruction but more often happens informally, through "mutual involvement in several widespread cultural practices with great importance for learning: narratives, routines, and play" (Rogoff, 2003, p. 285). One example is book reading, as just explained.

Inspired by Vygotsky, Barbara Rogoff studied cultural transmission in Guatemalan, Mexican, Chinese, and American families. Adults always guide children, but clashes occur if parents and teachers are of different cultures. In one such misunderstanding, a teacher praised a student to his mother:

> **Teacher:** Your son is talking well in class. He is speaking up a lot.
> **Mother:** I am sorry.
>
> *[Rogoff, 2003, p. 311]*

ETHNIC AND RACIAL GROUPS It is easy to confuse culture, ethnicity, and race, because these terms sometimes overlap (see Figure 1.6). People of an **ethnic group** share certain attributes, almost always including ancestral heritage and usually national origin, religion, and language (Whitfield & McClearn, 2005). As you can

ethnic group
People whose ancestors were born in the same region and who often share a language, culture, and religion.

FIGURE 1.6 Overlap—But How Much? Ethnicity, culture, and race are three distinct concepts, but they often—though not always—overlap. Which set of circles do you think is more accurate?

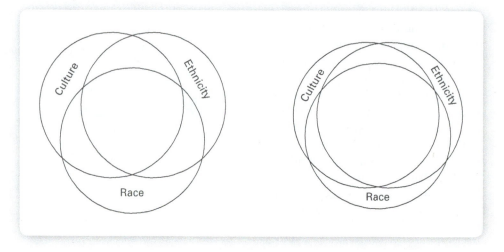

OPPOSING PERSPECTIVES

Using the Word *Race**

The term **race** has been used to categorize people on the basis of physical differences, particularly outward appearance. Historically, most North Americans believed that race was real, an inborn biological characteristic. Races were categorized by colour: white, black, red, and yellow (Coon, 1962).

It is obvious now, but was not a few decades ago, that no one's skin is really white (like this page) or black (like these letters) or red or yellow. Social scientists are now convinced that race is a social construction, and that colour terms exaggerate minor differences.

Genetic analysis confirms that the concept of *race* is based on a falsehood. Although most genes are identical in every human, those genetic differences that distinguish one person from another are poorly indexed by appearance (Race, Ethnicity, and Genetics Working Group of the American Society of Human Genetics, 2005). Skin colour is particularly misleading, since dark-skinned people with African ancestors have particularly "high levels of genetic population diversity" (Tishkoff et al., 2009, p. 1035), and since dark-skinned people whose ancestors were not African share neither culture nor ethnicity with Africans.

Race is more than a flawed concept; it is a destructive one. It was used to justify racism, expressed in myriad laws and customs, with slavery, lynching, and segregation directly connected to the idea that race was real. Racism continues in less obvious ways (some highlighted later in this book), undercutting the goal of our science of human development—to help all of us fulfill our potential.

Since race is a social construction that continues to lead to racism, some social scientists believe that the term should be abandoned. Ethnic and cultural differences may be significant for development, but racial differences are not. This realization is embedded in the way the United States census reports differences. Race categories began decades ago

*Every page of this text includes information that requires critical thinking and evaluation. In addition, once in each chapter you will find a feature entitled Opposing Perspectives in which an issue is highlighted that has compelling opposite perspectives.

and the original *white* and *black* terms remain. However, Hispanics, first counted separately in 1980, "may be of any race."

A study of census categories used by 141 nations found that only 15 percent use the word *race,* and that almost all of them were once slave-holding nations. The United States is the only nation that separates the racial category from the ethnic one (Morning, 2008), another indication that *race* may be a word of another era. The Canadian census form asks three questions to determine ethnicity: one relating to ancestry, one referring to Aboriginal affiliation, and a third asking about ethnic origin. Although the word *race* does not appear on the census form, the third question still contains categories for *White* and *Black*.

Cognitively, labels encourage stereotyping, and labelling people by race leads to the notion that superficial differences in appearance are significant (Kelly et al., 2010). To avoid racism, one possibility is to avoid using the word *race,* thereby becoming colour-blind.

But there is a powerful, opposite perspective. In a nation with a history of racial discrimination, reversing that history may require recognizing race, allowing those who have been harmed to be proud of their identity. The fact that race is a social construction, not a biological distinction, does not make it meaningless. Particularly in adolescence, people who are proud of their racial identity are likely to achieve academically, resist drug addiction, and feel better about themselves (Crosnoe & Johnson, 2011).

Furthermore, documenting ongoing racism requires data to show that many medical, educational, and economic conditions—from low birth weight to college and university graduation, from family income to health insurance—reflect disparities along racial lines. To overcome such disparities, race must first be recognized.

As you see, strong arguments support both sides of this issue. In this book, we refer to ethnicity more often than to race, but we use race or colour when the original data are reported that way.

see from this definition, ethnic groups often share a culture, but this is not necessary. Some people of a particular ethnicity differ culturally (consider people of Irish descent in Ireland, Australia, and Canada), and some cultures include people of several ethnic groups (consider British culture).

Ethnicity is a social construction, affected by the social context, not a direct outcome of biology. That makes it nurture, not nature. For example, African-born people who live in Canada typically consider themselves African, but African-born people living on that continent identify with a more specific ethnic group.

race

A group of people regarded as distinct from other groups on the basis of appearance, typically skin colour. Social scientists think race is a misleading concept, as biological differences are not signified by outward appearance.

Similar identity becomes strengthened and more specific (Sicilian, not just Italian; South Korean, not just East-Asian) when others of the same ethnic group are nearby and when members of other groups emphasize differences. Race is also a social construction—and a misleading one. There are good reasons to abandon the term, and good reasons to keep it, as the following section explains.

Development Is Multidisciplinary

Scientists often specialize, studying one phenomenon in one species at one age. Such specialization provides a deeper understanding of the rhythms of vocalization among 3-month-old infants, for example, or of the effects of alcohol on adolescent mice, or of widows' relationships with their grown children. (The results of these studies inform later sections of this book.)

However, human development requires insights and information from many scientists, past and present, in many disciplines. Our understanding of every topic benefits from multidisciplinary research; scientists hesitate to apply conclusions about human life until they are substantiated by several disciplines.

GENETICS AND EPIGENETICS The need for multidisciplinary research became particularly apparent with the onset of genetic analysis. The final decades of the twentieth century witnessed dozens of genetic discoveries, leading to a momentous accomplishment at the turn of the century: The Human Genome Project mapped all the genes that make up a person. To the surprise of many, it is now apparent that every trait—psychological as well as physical—is influenced by genes (see Chapter 2).

At first, it seemed that genes might determine everything, that humans became whatever their genes destined them to be—heroes, killers, or ordinary people. However, research from many disciplines quickly revealed the limitations of genetic research. Yes, genes affect every aspect of behaviour. But even identical twins, with identical genes, differ biologically, psychologically, and socially (Poulsen et al., 2007).

epigenetic
Referring to the effects of environmental forces on the expression of an individual's, or a species', genetic inheritance.

The realization that genes alone do not determine development soon led to the further realization that all important human characteristics are **epigenetic.** The prefix *epi-* means "with," "around," "before," "after," "beyond," or "near." The word *epigenetic,* therefore, refers to the environmental factors that surround the genes, affecting genetic expression.

Some "epi" influences occur in the first hours of life as biochemical elements silence certain genes, in a process called *methylation.* The degree of methylation for people changes over the life span, affecting genes (Kendler et al., 2011). In addition, other epigenetic influences occur, including some that impede development (e.g., injury, temperature extremes, drug abuse, and crowding) and some that facilitate it (e.g., nourishing food, loving care, and active play). Research far beyond the discipline of genetics, or even the broader discipline of biology, is needed to discover all the epigenetic effects.

The inevitable epigenetic interaction between genes and the environment (nature and nurture) is illustrated in Figure 1.7. That simple diagram, with arrows going up and down over time, has been redrawn and reprinted dozens of times to emphasize that genes interact with environmental conditions again and again in each person's life (Gottlieb, 2010).

Epigenetic research is especially important in treating diseases that impair the brain and devastate human development. As one group of researchers explains, "Clearly, the brain contains an epigenetic 'hotspot' with a unique potential to not only better understand its most complex functions, but also to treat its most vicious diseases" (Gräff et al., 2011, p. 603). Genes are always important; some are expressed, affecting development, and some are never noticed, from generation to generation,

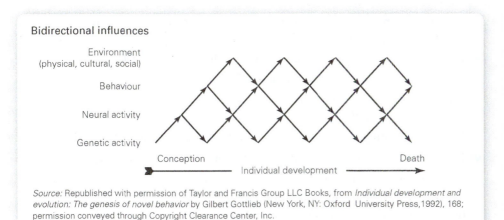

Source: Republished with permission of Taylor and Francis Group LLC Books, from *Individual development and evolution: The genesis of novel behavior* by Gilbert Gottlieb (New York, NY: Oxford University Press, 1992), 168; permission conveyed through Copyright Clearance Center, Inc.

FIGURE 1.7 An Epigenetic Model of Development Notice that there are as many arrows going down as going up, at all levels. Although development begins with genes at conception, it requires that all four factors interact.

unless circumstances change. The reasons are epigenetic; factors beyond the genes are crucial (Issa, 2011; Skipper, 2011).

MULTIDISCIPLINARY RESEARCH ON DEPRESSION Consider the importance of many disciplines in understanding depression, which results in 65 million lost years of productive life per year around the world (P. Y. Collins et al., 2011). There is no doubt that depression is partly genetic and neurological—certain brain chemicals make people sad and uninterested in life. There is also no doubt that depression is developmental: Depression increases and decreases throughout the life span (Kapornai & Vetró, 2008; Kendler et al., 2011).

For instance, the incidence of clinical depression suddenly rises in early adolescence, particularly among girls. Throughout life, whether or not a person becomes depressed is affected by chemicals in the brain—not only by neurotransmitters such as dopamine and serotonin, but also by growth factors such as GDNF (glial cell line-derived neurotrophic factor), the product of one gene that makes neurons grow or stagnate (Uchida et al., 2011).

Child-rearing practices have an impact as well. Typically, depressed mothers smile and talk to their infants less than other mothers, and then the infants become less active and verbal. A researcher who studies mother–infant interaction told non-depressed mothers with their 3-month-olds to do the following for only three minutes:

> To speak in a monotone, to keep their faces flat and expressionless, to slouch back in their chair, to minimize touch, and to imagine that they felt tired and blue. The infants … reacted strongly, … cycling among states of wariness, disengagement, and distress with brief bids to their mother to resume her normal affective state. Importantly, the infants continued to be distressed and disengaged … after the mothers resumed normal interactive behavior.
>
> *[Tronick, 2007, p. 306]*

Thus, even three minutes of mock-depressive behaviour makes infants act depressed. If a mother is actually depressed, her baby will be, too.

Many genetic, biochemical, and neurological factors distinguish adults with depression from other adults (Kanner, 2012; Poldrack et al., 2008). However, their moods and behaviours are powerfully affected by experience and cognition (Huberty, 2012; van Praag et al., 2004). Again, nature is affected by nurture. A person with depressing relationships and experiences is likely to develop the brain patterns characteristic of depression, as well as vice versa. Overall, at least 12 factors are linked to depression:

● Low serotonin in the brain, as a result of an allele of the gene for serotonin transport *(neuroscience)*

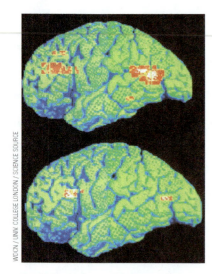

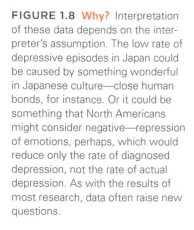

Red Means Stop The red areas on the top PET scan show abnormally low metabolic activity and blood flow in a depressed person's brain, in contrast to the normal brain shown in the bottom scan.

- Childhood caregiver depression, especially postpartum depression with exclusive mother-care *(psychopathology)*
- Low exposure to daylight, as in winter in higher latitudes *(biology)*
- Malnutrition, particularly low hemoglobin *(nutrition)*
- Lack of close friends, especially when a person enters a new culture, school, or neighbourhood *(anthropology)*
- Diseases, including Parkinson's and AIDS, and drugs to treat diseases *(medicine)*
- Disruptive event, such as a breakup with a romantic partner *(sociology)*
- Death of mother before age 10 *(psychology)*
- Absence of father during childhood—especially because of divorce, less so because of death or migration *(family studies)*
- Family history of eating disorders (not necessarily of the depressed person) *(genetics)*
- Poverty, especially in a nation where some people are very wealthy *(economics)*
- Low cognitive skills, including illiteracy and lack of exposure to other ideas *(education)*.

As you see, each of these factors arises from research in a different discipline (italicized). Of course, disciplines overlap. Lack of close confidants, for instance, is noted by anthropologists, but also by sociologists and psychologists. Furthermore, culture, climate, and politics all have an effect, although the particulars are debatable. For example, consider the national differences in Figure 1.8. There are at least six explanations for the disparity in the incidence of depression between one nation and another—some genetic, some cultural, and some a combination of the two.

A multidisciplinary approach is crucial in alleviating every impairment, including depression. Currently in North America, a combination of cognitive therapy, family therapy, and antidepressant medication is often more effective than any one of these three alone. International research finds that depression is relatively high in some populations in some places (e.g., among half the women in Pakistan) and low in others (e.g., among about 3 percent of the non-smoking men in Denmark), again for a combination of reasons (Flensborg-Madsen et al., 2011; Husain et al., 2011; von dem Knesebeck et al., 2011).

As already noted in our discussion of nature and nurture, of SIDS, and of the story of watching Caleb's birth, no single factor determines any outcome. In fact, some people who experience one, and only one, of the factors above never experience depression. It is a combination that makes a person depressed. As you will now learn, for genetic and other reasons, some people are severely affected by circumstances that

FIGURE 1.8 Why? Interpretation of these data depends on the interpreter's assumption. The low rate of depressive episodes in Japan could be caused by something wonderful in Japanese culture—close human bonds, for instance. Or it could be something that North Americans might consider negative—repression of emotions, perhaps, which would reduce only the rate of diagnosed depression, not the rate of actual depression. As with the results of most research, data often raise new questions.

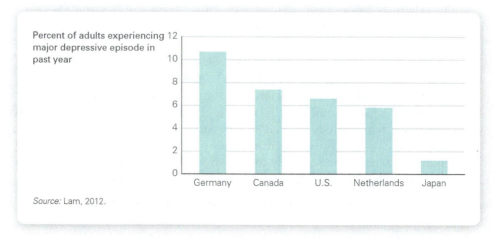

Percent of adults experiencing major depressive episode in past year

Source: Lam, 2012.

do not bother others. The multidisciplinary approach to the life span adds a measure of caution to every scientist: No one is able to predict with certainty the future developmental path for anyone.

Development Is Plastic

The term *plasticity* denotes two complementary aspects of development: Human traits can be moulded (as plastic can be) and yet people maintain a certain durability of identity (as plastic does). The concept of plasticity in development provides both hope and realism—hope because change is possible, and realism because development builds on what has come before.

DYNAMIC SYSTEMS The concept of plasticity is basic to the contemporary understanding of human development. This is evident in one of the newest approaches to understanding human growth, an approach called **dynamic systems.** The idea is that human development is an ongoing, ever-changing interaction between the body and mind and between the individual and every aspect of the environment, including all the systems described in the ecological approach. The dynamic-systems approach began in disciplines that focus on changes in the natural world.

> Seasons change in ordered measure, clouds assemble and disperse, trees grow to a certain shape and size, snowflakes form and melt, minute plants and animals pass through elaborate life cycles that are invisible to us, and social groups come together and disband.
>
> *[Thelen & Smith, 2006, p. 271]*

Note the key word *dynamic:* Physical and emotional influences, time, and each person and every aspect of the environment are always interacting, always in flux, always in motion. This approach builds on many aspects of the life-span perspective already described, including that development is multidirectional, multicontextual, multicultural, and multidisciplinary. With any developmental topic, stage, or problem, the dynamic-systems perspective urges us to consider all the interrelated aspects, every social and cultural factor, over days and years.

AN EXAMPLE OF INTERACTING SYSTEMS My sister-in-law contracted rubella (called German measles) early in her third pregnancy, a fact not recognized until David was born, blind and dying. Heart surgery two days after birth saved his life, but surgery at 6 months to remove a cataract destroyed that eye. Malformations of his thumbs, ankles, teeth, feet, spine, and brain became evident. David did not walk or talk or even chew for years. Some people wondered why his parents did not place him in an institution. Yet dire early predictions—from me as well as many others—have proven false. David is a productive adult, and happy. When I questioned him about his life he said, "I try to stay in a positive mood" (David Stassen, personal communication, 2011).

Remember, plasticity cannot erase a person's genes, childhood, or permanent damage. David's disabilities are always with him (he still lives with his parents). But his childhood experiences gave him lifelong strengths. His family loved and nurtured him (consulting the Kentucky School for the Blind when he was a few months old, enrolling him in four preschools and then in public kindergarten at age 6). By age 10, David had skipped a year of school and was a fifth grader, reading at the eleventh-grade level. He learned a second and a third language. In young adulthood, after one failing semester (requiring family assistance again), he earned several As and graduated from college.

David now works as a translator of German texts, which he enjoys because, he says, "I like providing a service to scholars, giving them access to something they

dynamic-systems approach
A view of human development as an ongoing, ever-changing interaction between a person's physical and emotional being and between the person and every aspect of his or her environment, including the family and society.

Kathleen's STORY

GREG STASSEN

Kathleen's Nephews Michael, Bill, and David (left to right) are adults now, with quite different personalities, abilities, offspring (4, 2, and none), and contexts (in Massachusetts, Pennsylvania, and California). Yet despite distinct genes, prenatal life, and childhood influences, they shared the influence of Glen and Dot, Kathleen's brother and sister-in-law—evident here in their similar, friendly smiles.

differential sensitivity
The idea that some people are more vulnerable than others are to certain experiences, usually because of genetic differences.

would otherwise not have" (David Stassen, personal communication, 2007). As his aunt, I have seen him repeatedly defy predictions. All five of the characteristics of the life-span perspective are evident in David's life, as summarized in Table 1.2.

DIFFERENTIAL SENSITIVITY As just noted, plasticity emphasizes that people can and do change, that predictions are not always accurate. This is sometimes frustrating to scientists, who seek to prevent problems by learning what is particularly risky or helpful for healthy development.

Three insights have improved predictions. Two of them you already know: (1) nature and nurture always interact, and (2) certain periods of life are sensitive periods, more affected by particular events than others. This was apparent for David: his inherited characteristics affected his ability to learn and his early childhood education (a sensitive period for language learning) has helped him throughout his life.

The third factor to aid prediction and thus target intervention is a more recent discovery, **differential sensitivity.** The idea is that some people are more vulnerable than others to particular experiences.

Can you remember something you heard in childhood that still affects you, such as a criticism that stung or a compliment that motivated you? Now think of what that same comment meant to the person who uttered it, or what it might have meant to another child. A particular comment stayed with you, but for most people, the same words would be forgotten. That is differential sensitivity.

Generally, many scientists have found many genes, or circumstances, that work both ways—they predispose people to being either unusually successful or pathological (Belsky et al., 2012; Kéri, 2009). This idea is captured in the folk saying "Genius is close to madness": The same circumstance (brilliance) can become a gift for an entire society or a burden for the affected individual, or it can have little effect.

TABLE 1.2 **Five Characteristics of Development**

Characteristic	Application in David's Story
Multidirectional. Change occurs in every direction, not always in a straight line. Gains and losses, predictable growth, and unexpected transformations are evident.	David's development seemed static (or even regressive, as when early surgery destroyed one eye) but then accelerated each time he entered a new school or college.
Multidisciplinary. Numerous academic fields—especially psychology, biology, education, and sociology, but also neuroscience, economics, religion, anthropology, history, medicine, genetics, and many more—contribute insights.	Two disciplines were particularly critical: medicine (David would have died without advances in surgery on newborns) and education (special educators guided him and his parents many times).
Multicontextual. Human lives are embedded in many contexts, including historical conditions, economic constraints, and family patterns.	The high SES of David's family made it possible for him to receive daily medical and educational care. His two older brothers protected him.
Multicultural. Many cultures—not just between nations but also within them—affect how people develop.	Appalachia, where David and his family lived, has a particular culture, including acceptance of people with disabilities and willingness to help families in need. Those aspects of that culture benefited David and his family.
Plasticity. Every individual, and every trait within each individual, can be altered at any point in the life span. Change is ongoing, although neither random nor easy.	David's measured IQ increased from about 40 (severely mentally retarded) to about 130 (far above average), and his physical disabilities became less crippling as he matured. Nonetheless, because of a virus contracted before he was born, the course of his life changed forever.

Here is one example that began with African-American 11-year-old boys in rural Georgia (Brody et al., 2009). Early puberty is a sensitive period, when young adolescents seek to rebel against parents, preachers, and teachers, and when the allure of alcohol, marijuana, and sexual intercourse is strong. Yet if a boy can resist those hazards until he is more mature, his future is much brighter. A team of researchers hoped they could protect these Georgia boys from future harm, and they sought scientific evidence to prove or disprove their hypothesis.

Accordingly, they randomly divided parents and sons into two groups: (1) a group that had no intervention, and (2) a group that attended seven seminars designed to increase racial pride, family support, honest communication, and compliance with parents' rules. These features are in keeping with replicated research that finds that pride and parental involvement protect against early sex and drug use.

The first follow-up, five years later, was disappointing. The intervention seemed to have had almost no effect. Both groups of boys drank, smoked, or had sex at similar rates. However, remember that scientists constantly keep up with the work of other scientists, reading published research from many disciplines. By the first follow-up, research on genetics and differential sensitivity had begun appearing in the academic literature, so the Georgia researchers decided to assess (via a saliva test) whether each boy had the short or long version of a particular gene (called 5-HTTLPR).

That small genetic difference turned out to be critical: Those with the long version developed just as well whether they were in the intervention group or not. However, teenagers with the short version who attended the seminars were less likely to have early sex or to use drugs than those who had the short gene but not the family training (see Figure 1.9). The sensitivity provided by nature (the small difference in the code for 5-HTTLPR) allowed the special nurture (the seminars) to have an impact.

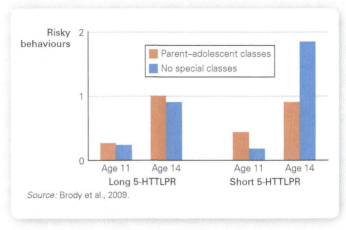

Source: Brody et al., 2009.

FIGURE 1.9 **Differential Sensitivity** The risk score for these boys was a simple 0 to 3, with 1 point for each of the following: drank alcohol, smoked marijuana, had sex. As shown, most had done none of these at age 11, and, by age 14, most had done one (usually drunk beer). However, some of those at genetic risk had done all three, and many had done two. For them, and only them, the seven-session intervention made a difference.

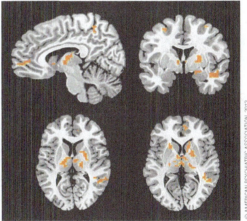

© AMERICAN PSYCHIATRIC ASSOCIATION, 2012

Many Brain Regions More than a dozen brain areas are more reactive to stress when a person has only the short allele of 5-HTTLPR. That is shown in these brain scans from a study of healthy college women who were paid to undergo an experiment involving 12 episodes without shocks, 13 with moderate shocks, and 13 with stronger (painful but not extreme) shocks. Uncertainty increased stress: The women did not know exactly when or how strong the shocks would be. People with only the short version of 5-HTTLPR were much more anxious overall, with more areas of their brains activated (shown here in red), compared with those who had the long version.

KEY ᵱoints

- Development is multidirectional, with gains and losses evident at every stage and in every domain.

- Development is multicontextual, with the ecological context from the immediate family to the broad social environment affecting every person. Cohort and socioeconomic status have powerful impacts.

- Cultural influences are sometimes unrecognized until another culture is understood. Social constructions, including ethnicity and race, are tangled with cultural values, making culture not only crucial but complex.

- Many academic disciplines provide insight on how people grow and change over time, as the interaction of all the developmental contexts and domains cannot be fully grasped by any one discipline.

- Each person's development is plastic, with the basic substance of each individual life mouldable by contexts and events, sometimes in differential ways, making every person unlike any other person.

Theories of Human Development

As you read earlier in this chapter, the scientific method begins with observations, questions, and theories (step 1). These lead to specific hypotheses that can be tested (step 2). A *theory* is a comprehensive and organized explanation of many phenomena; a *hypothesis* is more limited and may be proven false. Theories are generalities; hypotheses are specific. Data are collected through research (step 3), conclusions are drawn (step 4), and the results are reported (step 5) and replicated.

Although developmental scientists are intrigued by all their observations, theories are crucial to start the scientific process. Theories sharpen their perceptions and organize the thousands of behaviours they observe every day. Every **developmental theory** is a systematic statement of principles and generalizations, providing a framework for understanding how and why people change over the life span. We need theories to "help us describe and explain developmental changes by organizing and giving meaning to facts and by guiding future research" (P. H. Miller, 2011, p. 25). Theories connect facts with patterns, weaving the details of life into a meaningful whole.

You will encounter dozens of theories throughout this text, each one useful in organizing data and developing hypotheses. Six major theories that apply to the entire life span are introduced here; more details about each of them appear later in this text.

developmental theory
A group of ideas, assumptions, and generalizations that interpret and illuminate the thousands of observations that have been made about human growth. A developmental theory provides a framework for explaining the patterns and problems of development.

Psychoanalytic Theory

Inner drives and motives are the foundation of **psychoanalytic theory.** These basic underlying forces are thought to influence every aspect of thinking and behaviour, from the smallest details of daily life to the crucial choices of a lifetime (Dijksterhuis & Nordgren, 2006). Psychoanalytic theory is often treated as a *stage theory* because it sees each child going through distinct and sequential levels or stages. Each stage in a child's development builds upon the last and prepares for the next. For example, in developing math skills, children need to learn what numbers are before they can add. Once they can add, the next step is subtraction, then multiplication, and then division. Skipping or failing to master one stage will lead to problems in the next. Many psychoanalytic theorists believe that human development proceeds in just such a fashion, in clearly defined and complementary stages.

psychoanalytic theory
A theory of human development that holds that irrational, unconscious drives and motives, often originating in childhood, underlie human behaviour.

FREUD'S STAGES Psychoanalytic theory originated with Sigmund Freud (1856–1939), an Austrian physician who treated patients suffering from mental illness. He listened to their dreams and fantasies and constructed an elaborate, multi-faceted theory.

According to Freud, development in the first six years occurs in three stages, each characterized by sexual pleasure centred on a particular part of the body. Infants experience the *oral stage,* so named because the erotic body part is the mouth, followed by the *anal stage* in early childhood, with the focus on the anus. In the preschool years (the *phallic stage*), the penis becomes a source of pride and fear for boys and a reason for sadness and envy for girls.

In middle childhood comes *latency,* a quiet period that ends when one enters the *genital stage* at puberty. Freud was the most famous theorist who thought that development stopped after puberty and that the genital stage continued throughout adulthood (see Table 1.3).

Freud maintained that at each stage, sensual satisfaction (from stimulation of the mouth, anus, or genitals) is linked to developmental needs, challenges, and conflicts. How people experience and

Freud at Work In addition to being the world's first psychoanalyst, Sigmund Freud was a prolific writer. His many papers and case histories, primarily descriptions of his patients' bizarre symptoms and unconscious sexual urges, helped make the psychoanalytic perspective a dominant force for much of the twentieth century.

AKG / SCIENCE SOURCE

TABLE 1.3 Comparing Stages: Freud and Erikson

Approximate Age	Freud (Psychosexual)	Erikson (Psychosocial)
Birth to 1 year	*Oral Stage* The lips, tongue, and gums are the focus of pleasurable sensations in the baby's body, and sucking and feeding are the most stimulating activities.	*Trust vs. Mistrust* Babies either trust that others will care for their basic needs, including nourishment, warmth, cleanliness, and physical contact, *or* develop mistrust about the care of others.
1–3 years	*Anal Stage* The anus is the focus of pleasurable sensations in the baby's body, and toilet training is the most important activity.	*Autonomy vs. Shame and Doubt* Children either become self-sufficient in many activities, including toileting, feeding, walking, exploring, and talking, *or* doubt their own abilities.
3–6 years	*Phallic Stage* The phallus, or penis, is the most important body part, and pleasure is derived from genital stimulation. Boys are proud of their penises; girls wonder why they don't have one.	*Initiative vs. Guilt* Children either want to undertake many adult-like activities *or* internalize the limits and prohibitions set by parents. They feel either adventurous *or* guilty.
6–11 years	*Latency* Not really a stage, latency is an interlude during which sexual needs are quiet and children put psychic energy into conventional activities like schoolwork and sports.	*Industry vs. Inferiority* Children busily learn to be competent and productive in mastering new skills *or* feel inferior, unable to do anything as well as they wish they could.
Adolescence	*Genital Stage* The genitals are the focus of pleasurable sensations, and the young person seeks sexual stimulation and sexual satisfaction in heterosexual relationships.	*Identity vs. Role Confusion* Adolescents try to figure out "Who am I?" They establish sexual, political, and vocational identities *or* are confused about what roles to play.
Adulthood	Freud believed that the genital stage lasts throughout adulthood. He also said that the goal of a healthy life is "to love and to work."	*Intimacy vs. Isolation* Young adults seek companionship and love *or* become isolated from others because they fear rejection and disappointment. *Generativity vs. Stagnation* Middle-aged adults contribute to the next generation through meaningful work, creative activities, and raising a family, *or* they stagnate. *Integrity vs. Despair* Older adults try to make sense out of their lives, either seeing life as a meaningful whole *or* despairing at goals never reached.

resolve these conflicts—especially those related to weaning (oral), toilet training (anal), male roles (phallic), and sexual pleasure (genital)—determines their personality patterns, because "the early stages provide the foundation for adult behavior" (Salkind, 2004, p. 125). For example, Freud believed that the gratification of needs helped children develop a sense of independence.

ERIKSON'S STAGES Many of Freud's followers became famous theorists themselves. The most notable in human development was Erik Erikson (1902–1994), who described eight developmental stages, extending Freud's five-stage theory to old age. Perhaps this extension was influenced by his own adult life, when he made several dramatic moves. He was a wandering artist in Italy, a teacher in Austria, and a Harvard professor in the United States.

Spiked Hair and Piercings This adolescent thinks that she is a nonconformist; her spiked red hair and multiple tattoos and piercings are certainly unlike those of her mother or grandmother. But she is similar to adolescents everywhere—seeking to establish their own distinct identity.

TED STRESHINSKY / TIME LIFE PICTURES / GETTY IMAGES

A Legendary Couple In his first 30 years, Erikson frequently changed nations, schools, and professions. Then he met Joan. In their first five decades of marriage, they raised a family and wrote several books. If he had published his theory at age 73 (when this photograph was taken) instead of in his 40s, would he still have described his life as a series of crises?

learning theory
A theory of human development that describes the laws and processes by which observable behaviour is learned.

behaviourism
A learning theory based on the idea that behaviours can be trained and changed in response to stimuli in the environment.

Erikson named two polarities at each stage (which is why the word *versus* is used in each), but he recognized that many outcomes between these opposites are possible (Erikson, 1963). For most people, development at each stage leads to neither extreme. For instance, the generativity-versus-stagnation stage of adulthood rarely involves a person who is totally stagnant—no children, no work, no creativity. Instead, most adults are somewhat stagnant and somewhat generative.

Like Freud, Erikson believed that adults' problems echo their childhood conflicts. For example, an adult who cannot form a secure, close relationship with someone else (intimacy versus isolation) may not have resolved the crisis of infancy (trust versus mistrust). However, Erikson's stages differ significantly from Freud's in that, first, Erikson's theory was a life-span theory with a specific crisis at each stage of life, from infancy to old age. Second, Erikson emphasized the importance of family and culture, not sexual urges. He called his theory *epigenetic*, partly to stress that the social environment strongly influences genes and biological impulses.

Before psychoanalytic theory, most scientists ignored the first years of life. Both Freud and Erikson noted that psychological conflicts—especially in childhood within families—affect people throughout their lives, an insight that developmentalists now accept.

Learning Theory

From the beginning, psychoanalytic theory was criticized by scientists who said it was difficult to measure internal motives and drives, especially those stemming from the unconscious mind. Out of this criticism came **learning theory,** which focuses on overt behaviours that can be directly observed. Learning theory argues that behaviour is influenced by the social environment and by how people are rewarded or punished when they act in certain ways. Two important learning theories are behaviourism and social learning theory.

BEHAVIOURISM **Behaviourism** arose in direct opposition to the psychoanalytic emphasis on unconscious, hidden urges (differences are described in Table 1.4). Early in the twentieth century, John B. Watson (1878–1958) argued that scientists should examine only what they could observe and measure. According to Watson, if psychologists focus on behaviour, they will realize that anything can be learned. Watson wrote:

> Give me a dozen healthy infants, well-formed, and my own specified world to bring them up in and I'll guarantee to take any one at random and train him to become any type of specialist I might select—doctor, lawyer, artist, merchant chief, and yes, even beggar-man and thief, regardless of his talents, penchants, tendencies, abilities, vocations, and race.
>
> *[Watson, 1924/1998, p. 82]*

Many other psychologists, especially in the United States, agreed. They found that the unconscious motives and drives that Freud described were difficult (or impossible) to verify via the scientific method (Uttal, 2000). For instance, researchers found that, contrary to Freud's view, parents' approach to toilet training did not determine a child's later personality. Thus, behavioural psychologists believed that what children learn, especially in regard to social behaviour, is acquired from their environment.

For every individual at every age, from newborn to centenarian, behaviourists have identified laws to describe how environmental responses shape what people do. All behaviour, from reading a book to robbing a bank, follows these laws. Every action is learned, step by step. As the saying goes, "monkey see, monkey do."

ARCHIVES OF THE HISTORY OF AMERICAN PSYCHOLOGY, THE UNIVERSITY OF AKRON

An Early Behaviourist John Watson was an early proponent of learning theory. His ideas are still influential and controversial today.

TABLE 1.4 Psychoanalytic Theory vs. Behaviourism

Area of Disagreement	Psychoanalytic Theory	Behaviourism
The unconscious	Emphasizes unconscious wishes and urges, unknown to the person but powerful all the same	Holds that the unconscious not only is unknowable but also may be a destructive fiction that keeps people from changing
Observable behaviour	Holds that observable behaviour is a symptom, not the cause—the tip of an iceberg, with the bulk of the problem submerged	Looks only at observable behaviour—what a person does rather than what a person thinks, feels, or imagines
Importance of childhood	Stresses that early childhood, including infancy, is critical; even if a person does not remember what happened, the early legacy lingers throughout life	Holds that current conditioning is crucial; early habits and patterns can be unlearned, even reversed, if appropriate reinforcements and punishments are used
Scientific status	Holds that most aspects of human development are beyond the reach of scientific experiment; uses ancient myths, the words of disturbed adults, dreams, play, and poetry as raw material	Is proud to be a science, dependent on verifiable data and carefully controlled experiments; discards ideas that sound good but are not proven

CONDITIONING The specific laws of learning apply to **conditioning,** the processes by which responses become linked to particular stimuli. There are two types of conditioning: classical and operant.

More than a century ago, Ivan Pavlov (1849–1936), a Russian scientist who won a Nobel Prize for his work on animal digestion, noticed that his experimental dogs drooled not only when they saw and smelled food but also when they heard the footsteps of the attendants who brought the food. This observation led Pavlov to perform experiments in which he conditioned dogs to salivate when they heard a specific sound.

SOVFOTO

Pavlov began by ringing a bell just before presenting food to the dogs. After a number of repetitions of the ringing-then-food sequence, the dogs began salivating at the sound, even when no food was present. This simple experiment demonstrated **classical conditioning** (sometimes called *respondent conditioning*), a process in which, over time, a person or animal learns to associate a neutral stimulus (the sound) with a meaningful stimulus (the food) to elicit a response (salivation).

The most influential North American behaviourist was B. F. Skinner (1904–1990). He agreed with Watson that psychology should focus on the scientific study of behaviour, and that classical conditioning explains some behaviour. However, Skinner stressed another type of conditioning, **operant conditioning** (sometimes called *instrumental conditioning*). In operant conditioning, animals perform some action and then a response occurs. If the response is useful or pleasurable, the animal is likely to repeat the action. If the response is painful, the animal is not likely to repeat the action. In both cases, the animal has learned. Pleasant consequences are sometimes called *rewards,* and unpleasant consequences are sometimes called *punishments.* Behaviourists hesitate to use those words, however, because what people commonly think of as a punishment can actually be a reward, and vice versa. For example, parents punish their children by withholding dessert, by giving them a time out, by not letting them play, by speaking harshly to them, and so on. But if a particular

conditioning
According to behaviourism, the processes by which responses become linked to particular stimuli and learning takes place. The word "conditioning" is used to emphasize the importance of repeated practice, as when an athlete conditions his or her body to perform well by training for a long time.

A Contemporary of Freud
Ivan Pavlov was a physiologist who received the Nobel Prize in 1904 for his research on digestive processes. It was this line of study that led to his discovery of classical conditioning.

classical conditioning
A learning process in which a meaningful stimulus (such as the smell of food to a hungry animal) gradually comes to be connected with a neutral stimulus (such as a particular sound) that had no special meaning before the learning process began. (Also called *respondent conditioning.*)

operant conditioning
A learning process in which a particular action is followed either by something desired (which makes the person or animal more likely to repeat the action) or by something unwanted (which makes the action less likely to be repeated). (Also called *instrumental conditioning.*)

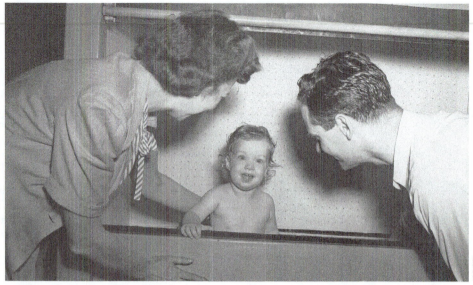

Rats, Pigeons, and People
B. F. Skinner is best known for his experiments with rats and pigeons, but he also applied his knowledge to human problems. For his daughter (shown here), he designed a glass-enclosed crib in which temperature, humidity, and perceptual stimulation could be controlled to make her time in the crib enjoyable and educational.

reinforcement
A technique for conditioning a particular behaviour in which that behaviour is followed by something desired, such as food for a hungry animal or a welcoming smile for a lonely person.

Susan's STORY

social learning theory
An extension of behaviourism that emphasizes that other people influence each person's behaviour. The theory's basic principle is that even without specific reinforcement, every individual learns many things through observation and imitation of other people.

Still Social Even in his 80s, Albert Bandura is on the faculty at Stanford University, where he is continuing his research on the effects of modelling on behaviour, feelings, and thought patterns.

child dislikes the dessert, being deprived of it is actually a reward, not a punishment. Another child might not mind a time out, especially if he or she craves quiet time. For that child, the intended punishment (a time out) is actually a reward (quiet).

Any consequence that follows a behaviour and makes the person (or animal) likely to repeat that behaviour is called a positive **reinforcement,** not a reward. Once a behaviour has been conditioned, humans and other creatures will repeat it even if reinforcement occurs only occasionally. Similarly, an unpleasant response makes a creature less likely to repeat a certain action.

This insight has practical application. Early responses are crucial for development because children learn habits that endure. For example, when I was a child, my father would come home, announce his arrival, and hope to be greeted by his four children, to no avail. So at one point, he started yelling out, "Chocolate bars!" whenever he arrived home, and we all came running to pull the treats from his pockets. After a while, the chocolate bars stopped, but by then we had developed the habit of giving our father a warm welcome at the end of the day. In this way, my father reinforced family solidarity.

The science of human development has benefitted from behaviourism. The theory's emphasis on the origins and consequences of observed behaviour led to the realization that many actions that seem to be genetic, or to result from deeply rooted emotional problems, are actually learned. And if something is learned, it can be unlearned. No longer are "the events of infancy and early childhood … the foundation for adult personality and psychopathology," as psychoanalysts believed (Cairns & Cairns, 2006, p. 117). People *can* change; plasticity continues throughout one's life.

SOCIAL LEARNING THEORY A major extension of behaviourism is **social learning theory,** which was first described by Albert Bandura (b. 1925), who was born and raised in Alberta. He is currently a professor emeritus at Stanford University. Social learning theory notes that, because humans are social beings, they learn from observing others, even without personally receiving any reinforcement.

This form of learning theory is often called *modelling* because people learn by observing role models. For example, researchers have found that children who witness domestic violence are influenced by it. As the multicontextual approach would predict, what they learn varies. In a family in which the father often hits the mother, one son might identify with the abuser and another with the victim. Later in adulthood, because of their past social learning, one man might slap his wife and spank his children, while his brother might be fearful and apologetic at home. They learned opposite lessons. Differential sensitivity may also be evident: a third sibling may not be affected in adulthood by past memories of domestic violence.

Cognitive Theory

In a third type of theory, each person's ideas and beliefs are of central importance. According to **cognitive theory,** thoughts and expectations profoundly affect actions. Cognitive theory has dominated psychology since about 1980 and has branched into many versions, each adding insights about human development. The word *cognitive* refers not just to thinking but also to attitudes, beliefs, and assumptions.

The most famous cognitive theorist was a Swiss scientist, Jean Piaget (1896–1980). Unlike other scientists of the early twentieth century, Piaget realized that babies are themselves like "little scientists." They are curious and thoughtful, creating their own interpretations about their world. Piaget began by observing his own three infants; later he studied thousands of older children (Inhelder & Piaget, 1958).

From this work, Piaget developed the central theme of cognitive theory: How people think (not just what they know) changes with time and experience, and human thinking influences human actions. Piaget maintained that cognitive development occurs in four major age-related periods, or stages: *sensorimotor, preoperational, concrete operational,* and *formal operational* (see Table 1.5).

Intellectual advancement occurs throughout one's life because humans seek *cognitive equilibrium*—that is, a state of mental balance. An easy way to achieve this balance is to interpret new experiences through the lens of pre-existing ideas. For example, infants discover that new objects can be grasped in the same way as familiar objects; older adults speak fondly of the good old days as embodying values that should endure.

Sometimes, however, a new experience is jarring and incomprehensible. The resulting experience is one of *cognitive disequilibrium,* an imbalance that initially creates confusion. As Figure 1.10 illustrates, disequilibrium leads to cognitive growth because it forces people to adapt their old concepts. Piaget describes two types of adaptation:

- *Assimilation,* in which new experiences are interpreted to fit into, or assimilate with, old ideas
- *Accommodation,* in which old ideas are restructured to include, or accommodate, new experiences.

Listen and Learn Jean Piaget called himself a "genetic epistemologist"—one who studies how children gain knowledge about the world as they grow up. He learned about children by listening carefully to them as they spoke—especially to their incorrect explanations, which no one had paid much attention to before.

cognitive theory
A theory of human development that focuses on changes in how people think over time. According to this theory, our thoughts shape our attitudes, beliefs, and behaviours.

TABLE 1.5 Piaget's Periods of Cognitive Development

Age Range	Name of Period	Characteristics of the Period	Major Gains During the Period
Birth to 2 years	Sensorimotor	Infants use senses and motor abilities to understand the world. Learning is active; there is no conceptual or reflective thought.	Infants learn that an object still exists when it is out of sight (object permanence) and begin to think through mental actions.
2–6 years	Preoperational	Children think magically and poetically, using language to understand the world. Thinking is egocentric, causing children to perceive the world from their own perspective.	The imagination flourishes, and language becomes a significant means of self-expression and of influence from others.
6–11 years	Concrete operational	Children understand and apply logical operations, or principles, to interpret experiences objectively and rationally. Their thinking is limited to what they can personally see, hear, touch, and experience.	By applying logical abilities, children learn to understand concepts of conservation, number, classification, and many other scientific ideas.
12 years through adulthood	Formal operational	Adolescents and adults think about abstractions and hypothetical concepts and reason analytically, not just emotionally. They can be logical about things they have never experienced.	Ethics, politics, and social and moral issues become fascinating as adolescents and adults take a broader and more theoretical approach to experience.

FIGURE 1.10 **Challenge Me** Most of us, most of the time, prefer the comfort of our conventional conclusions. According to Piaget, however, when new ideas disturb our thinking, we have an opportunity to expand our cognition with a broader and deeper understanding.

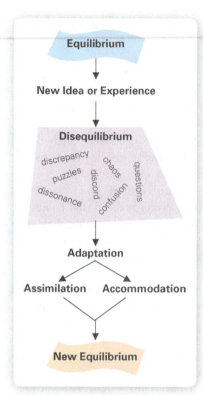

Equilibrium

↓

New Idea or Experience

↓

Disequilibrium

discrepancy chaos
puzzles discord questions
dissonance confusion

↓

Adaptation

↙   ↘

Assimilation   **Accommodation**

↓

New Equilibrium

Like Father, Like Son It's not difficult to figure out where this boy got the idea to show off his biceps!

OBSERVATION QUIZ
Behind the posturing, what indicates that this boy models himself after his parent? (see answer, page 32) →

family systems theory
A theory of human behaviour that focuses on the family as a unit or functioning system, with each member having a role to play and rules to respect.

Accommodation requires more mental energy than assimilation, but it is sometimes necessary because new ideas and experiences may not fit into existing cognitive structures. Accommodation produces significant intellectual growth. For example, think of cognitive structures as filing cabinets. A child has a family cat that is black and white. Learning that this animal is called a "cat," the child creates a "cat folder." When the child meets a brown cat, she has no trouble learning that in spite of its difference in colour, it is also a "cat" and can be filed away into the "cat folder." This new information becomes *assimilated* (added) in the "cat folder." Now, when the child meets a dog, she may at first think that it's a cat, since it also has four legs and a long tail. However, her parents tell her that this new animal is actually a dog! She now needs to make a "dog folder" to *accommodate* this new information.

Another influential cognitive theory, called *information processing*, differs from Piaget's theory. Information-processing theory (which is discussed in Chapter 3) describes the steps of cognition with details, not stages, and with attention to perceptual and neurological processes. Many researchers (in addition to those influenced by information-processing theory) now think that some of Piaget's conclusions were mistaken. However, every developmentalist appreciates Piaget's basic insight: Thoughts can influence emotions and actions.

Systems Theory

Many useful twenty-first-century developmental theories describe systems that involve the interaction of various forces and people. The word *systems* captures the idea that a change in one part of a person, family, or society affects every aspect of development because each part is connected to all the other parts (Spencer et al., 2006).

Human development depends on systems. Consider examples from the three domains of development. Some systems are physiological, such as the immune system, which includes many kinds of immune cells. Some systems are cognitive, such as language, with sounds, words, and grammar all working together to produce communication. And some are social, such as the members of a family, workers in a factory, or citizens of a town. Minor dysfunctions can be overcome, but a major dysfunction can bring the whole system to a dead stop.

We have already considered one important systems theory earlier in this chapter, Urie Bronfenbrenner's ecological-systems approach. Here we will examine another and more recent way of understanding human development called family systems theory.

FAMILY SYSTEMS THEORY As Bronfenbrenner focused on various microsystems to help explain development, **family systems theory** focuses on the family as a unit or functioning system with its own set of rules that keep it operating over time. Systems theory is useful in understanding the complex interactions among family members, including the way they make decisions, set and achieve certain goals, and create rules

How to Think About Flowers A person's stage of cognitive growth influences how he or she thinks about everything, including flowers. (a) At the preoperational stage, flowers fit into the egocentric scheme. Claire, a young girl from British Columbia, wants to touch, smell, and pick the flowers, not realizing how others might perceive such actions. (b) At the adult's formal operational stage, flowers can be part of a larger, logical scheme—either to earn money or to cultivate beauty. Thinking is an active process from the beginning of life until the end.

to regulate behaviours. Much of family systems theory developed from the work and writings of the renowned therapist Salvador Minuchin (b. 1921) in the 1970s.

According to Minuchin (1974), it is impossible to understand how families operate without considering the concept of *wholeness*. Each family member makes up a part of the whole, and each member is connected with every other member. This *interdependence* of family members means that what affects one has an effect on every other member and on the family as a whole.

Think of a time in your own family history when something significant happened. Perhaps your grandfather died, your mother got a promotion that meant moving to another city, or your parents divorced. Whether for good or bad, the whole family has to react in such a situation, and every reaction results in some kind of change. Whenever this happens, the family system makes an effort to stabilize itself, to return to a state of balance or what theorists call *homeostasis*.

The way family members influence each other in a back-and-forth fashion is called *reciprocal interaction and feedback*. When one member behaves in a certain way, this calls forth a reaction (or reciprocal interaction) from another. However, this interplay of cause and effect does not end there. *Feedback* also occurs, a type of reaction that sparks yet another response and keeps the exchange going. For example, a baby may smile at her mother, causing the mother to smile back and move closer. At this, the baby provides feedback by laughing, and the mother starts tickling the baby to make her laugh again.

Over time, *patterns* emerge in every family whereby behaviours become regulated, allowing each member to anticipate other members' actions. Three factors are responsible for regulating behaviours: rules, roles, and communication styles.

Parents or guardians usually decide what the *rules* will be, providing a common understanding for acceptable and unacceptable behaviours. Rules can either be explicit, as when parents tell teens exactly what their curfew is, or implicit, as when it is simply understood that children will enhance their career prospects by going to university or college.

Each person assumes a specific *role* in the family (as mother, father, son, or daughter), and with a role comes a set of expected behaviours and responsibilities. For instance, a 15-year-old son's role might involve being a good student, keeping a clean room, and doing some of the household chores.

Communication styles are important in determining the quality of family relationships. There are three types of communication styles: verbal, nonverbal, and contextual. Verbal communications consist of the words spoken out loud among family members. These words are usually accompanied by some type of nonverbal communication such as bodily gestures and facial expressions. Both verbal and nonverbal communications are delivered within a specific context that usually enhances the message in some way. For example, when parents force a child to say "sorry," this is a very different context from when a child spontaneously and willingly offers an apology (Beevar & Beevar, 1998).

As families develop their own unique sets of patterns, they also create certain *boundaries* that are useful in setting limits for acceptable behaviours. Boundaries can either strengthen or weaken the health of a family system. Families that are *open systems* have boundaries that are flexible, and they are willing to exchange information and interactions with other families and individual people. In contrast, *closed systems* set inflexible boundaries and are unwilling to accept outside information and interactions. For example, many families refuse to discuss mental health issues or to seek therapy for a family member until the illness has escalated to a dangerous level.

Humanism

humanism
A theory that stresses the potential of all human beings for good and the belief that all people have the same basic needs, regardless of culture, gender, or background.

Many scientists are convinced that there is something hopeful, unifying, and noble in the human spirit, something ignored by psychoanalytic theory and behaviourism. The limits of those two major theories were especially apparent to Abraham Maslow (1908–1970), one of the founders of **humanism.** Maslow believed that all people—no matter what their culture, gender, or background—have the same basic needs and drives. He arranged these needs in a hierarchy (see Figure 1.11):

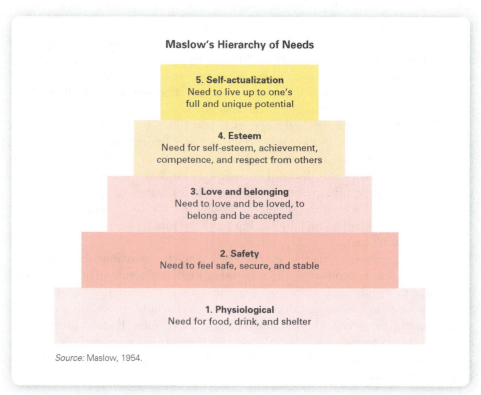

Maslow's Hierarchy of Needs

5. Self-actualization
Need to live up to one's full and unique potential

4. Esteem
Need for self-esteem, achievement, competence, and respect from others

3. Love and belonging
Need to love and be loved, to belong and be accepted

2. Safety
Need to feel safe, secure, and stable

1. Physiological
Need for food, drink, and shelter

Source: Maslow, 1954.

FIGURE 1.11 Moving Up, Not Looking Back Maslow's hierarchy is like a ladder: Once a person stands firmly on a higher rung, the lower rungs are no longer needed. Thus, someone who has arrived at step 4 might devalue safety (step 2) and be willing to risk personal safety to gain respect.

1. *Physiological:* needing food, water, warmth, and air
2. *Safety:* feeling protected from injury and death
3. *Love and belonging:* having loving friends, family, and a community
4. *Esteem:* being respected by the wider community as well as by oneself
5. *Self-actualization:* becoming truly oneself, fulfilling one's unique potential.

At self-actualization, when basic needs have been met, people can be fully themselves—creative, spiritual, curious, appreciative of nature, and able to respect everyone else. The person has "peak experiences" when life is so intensely joyful that time stops and self-seeking disappears.

Maslow contended that everyone must satisfy each lower level before moving higher. A starving man, for instance, may risk his life to secure food (level 1 precedes level 2), or an unloved woman might not care about self-respect because she needs affection (level 3 precedes level 4). People may be destructive and inhumane, not self-actualizing, because of unmet lower needs.

Although humanism does not postulate stages, a developmental application of this theory is that satisfying childhood needs is crucial for later self-acceptance. Thus, when babies cry in hunger, that basic need should be met. People may become thieves or even killers, unable to reach their potential, if they were unsafe or unloved as children.

This theory is prominent among medical professionals because they realize that pain can be physical (the first two levels) or social (the next two) (Majercsik, 2005; Zalenski & Raspa, 2006). Even the very sick need love and belonging (family should be with them) and esteem (the dying need respect).

Evolutionary Theory

Charles Darwin's basic ideas about evolution were first published 150 years ago (Darwin, 1859), but serious research on human development inspired by evolutionary theory is quite recent (Gangestad & Simpson, 2007, p. 2).

According to this theory, nature works to ensure that each species does two things: survive and reproduce. Consequently, many human impulses, needs, and behaviours evolved to help humans survive and thrive over 100 000 years (Konner, 2010). Evolutionary theory has intriguing explanations for many phenomena in human development, including women's nausea in pregnancy, 1-year-olds' attachment to their parents, puberty in young adolescents, emerging adults' sexual preferences, parents' investment in their children, and the increase in neurocognitive disorder, cancer, and other diseases in late adulthood.

To understand human development, this theory contends, humans need to recognize what was adaptive thousands of years ago. For example, it is irrational that many people are terrified of snakes (which cause 1 death in a billion), but virtually no one fears automobiles (which cause about 1 death in 5000). Evolutionary theory suggests that the fear instinct evolved to protect life when snakes killed many people, which was true until quite recent history. Our fears have not caught up to modern life.

Some of the best human qualities, such as cooperation, spirituality, and self-sacrifice, may have also originated thousands of years ago when groups of people survived because they took care of one another. Childhood itself, particularly the long period when children depend on others while their brains grow, can be explained via evolution (Konner, 2010). So can the fact that, unlike chimpanzees, human mothers prefer fathers to be involved in their children's lives, and they accept assistance from other relatives and even strangers. Shared child care allows women to have children every two years or so, unlike chimpanzees who wait at least four years between births (Hrdy, 2009).

KEY Points

- Developmental theories provide a crucial framework, enabling people to understand and study life.
- Psychoanalytic theory posits stages of development. Freud emphasized unconscious urges; Erikson stressed eight stages of psychosocial development, from infancy through old age.
- Learning theory focuses on the fact that people's behaviours are influenced by their social environment. Two learning theories are behaviourism and social learning theory. Behaviourism contends that people have learned most of what they do either through association or reinforcement. Social learning theory states that individuals can learn by observation and modelling.
- Cognitive theory stresses that the way people think affects their behaviour. Piaget's stages are one example.
- Systems theory emphasizes that human development takes place within the context of some type of system, a complex set of relationships in which each part is related to and affected by every other part. Family systems theory focuses on the interrelationships of family members and how one individual affects the others.
- Humanism recognizes universal human needs that must be met for people to reach the highest level, self-actualization, thereby becoming the best they can be.
- Evolutionary theory explains emotions and actions on the basis of their contribution to survival and reproduction in past millennia.

scientific observation
A method of testing a hypothesis by unobtrusively watching and recording participants' behaviour in a systematic and objective manner—in a natural setting, in a laboratory, or in searches of archival data.

Can They See Her? No. This scientist is observing three boys who are deaf through a window that is a mirror on the other side. Her observations will help them learn to communicate.

Using the Scientific Method

There are hundreds of ways to design scientific studies and analyze their results, and researchers continually try to make sure that their data are valid and convincing. Often statistical measures help scientists discover relationships between various aspects of the data. (Some statistical perspectives are presented in Table 1.6.) Every research design, method, and statistical measure has strengths as well as weaknesses. Now we describe three basic types of research designs—observation, the experiment, and the survey—and then three ways developmentalists study change over time.

Observation

Scientific observation requires researchers to record behaviour systematically and objectively. Observations often occur in a naturalistic setting (such as a home, school, or public park), where people behave as they usually do and ideally where the observer can be ignored or go unnoticed. Scientific observation can also occur in a laboratory, where scientists record human reactions in various situations, often with wall-mounted video cameras and the scientist in another room.

Observation is crucial in developing hypotheses, as Beal did when she wanted to understand what caused sudden infant death syndrome. However, observation provides issues to explore, not proof. For SIDS, observed differences

TABLE 1.6 Statistical Measures Often Used to Analyze Research Results

Measure	Use
Effect size	Indicates how much one variable affects another. Effect size ranges from 0 to 1: An effect size of 0.2 is called small, 0.5 moderate, and 0.8 large.
Significance	Indicates whether the results might have occurred by chance. A finding that chance would produce the results only 5 times in 100 is significant at the 0.05 level. A finding that chance would produce the results once in 100 times is significant at 0.01; once in 1000 times is significant at 0.001.
Cost benefit analysis	Calculates how much a particular independent variable costs versus how much it saves. This is particularly useful for analyzing public spending. For instance, one cost-benefit analysis showed that every dollar that the Ontario provincial government has invested in full-day kindergarten yields $2.42 in benefits (The Centre for Spatial Economics, 2010).
Odds ratio	Indicates how a particular variable compares to a standard, set at 1. For example, one study found that the odds ratio of Canadian university students finding employment related to their field of study is 5.267 for those in health sciences, 2.018 for those in education, and 1.951 for those in mathematics/computer/information sciences (Boudarbat & Chernoff, 2009).
Factor analysis	Hundreds of variables could affect any given behaviour. In addition, many variables (such as family income and parental education) may overlap. To take this into account, analysis reveals variables that can be clustered together to form a factor, which is a composite of many variables. For example, SES might become one factor, child personality another.
Meta-analysis	A "study of studies." Researchers use statistical tools to synthesize the results of previous, separate studies. Then they analyze the accumulated results, using criteria that weight each study fairly. This approach improves data analysis by combining the results of studies that were too small, or too narrow, to lead to solid conclusions.

Sources: Alasuutari et al., 2008; Duncan & Magnuson, 2007; Hubbard & Lindsay, 2008.

Who Participates? For all these measures, the characteristics of the people who participate in the study (formerly called subjects, now called participants) are important, as is the number of people who are studied.

between Chinese and Australian infants included prenatal care, maternal diet, parental age, breastfeeding, facial features, baby blanket fabrics, and more. Beal's hypothesis that the crucial difference was sleeping position needed an experiment.

The Experiment

The **experiment** is the usual research method used to establish what causes what. In the social sciences, experimenters typically impose a particular treatment on a group of volunteer participants (formerly referred to as *subjects*) or expose them to a specific condition and then note whether their behaviour changes.

In technical terms, the experimenters manipulate an **independent variable,** which is the imposed treatment or special condition (also called the *experimental variable;* a *variable* is anything that can vary). They note whether this independent variable affects whatever they are studying, called the **dependent variable** (which *depends* on the independent variable).

Thus, the independent variable is the new, special treatment; any change in the dependent variable is the result. In Beal's research, convincing some European-Australian parents to put their infants to sleep on their backs (the independent variable) was crucial to connect cause (sleeping position) and effect (survival).

The purpose of an experiment is to find out whether an independent variable affects the dependent variable. In a typical experiment (as diagrammed in Figure 1.12), two groups of participants are studied. One group is called the *experimental group,* which gets a particular treatment (the independent variable). The other group is the *comparison group* (also called the *control group*), which does not. When the

experiment
A research method in which the researcher tries to determine the cause-and-effect relationship between two variables by manipulating one (the independent variable) and then observing and recording the ensuing changes in the other (the dependent variable).

independent variable
In an experiment, the variable that is introduced to see what effect it has on the dependent variable. (Also called *experimental variable.*)

dependent variable
In an experiment, the variable that may change as a result of whatever new condition or situation the experimenter adds. In other words, the dependent variable depends on the independent variable.

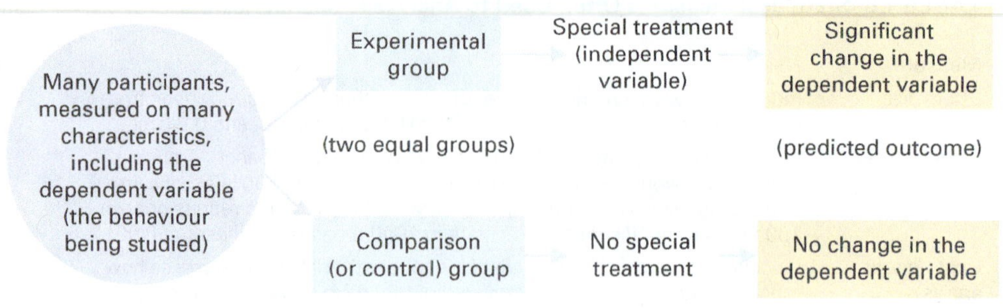

FIGURE 1.12 How to Conduct an Experiment The basic sequence diagrammed here applies to all experiments. Many additional features, especially the statistical measures listed in Table 1.6 and various ways of reducing experimenter bias, affect whether publication occurs. (Scientific journals reject reports of experiments that were not rigorous in method and analysis.)

Procedure:

1. Divide participants into two groups that are matched on important characteristics, especially the behaviour that is the dependent variable on which this study is focused.

2. Give special treatment, or intervention (the independent variable), to one group (the experimental group).

3. Compare the groups on the dependent variable. If they now differ, the cause of the difference was probably the independent variable.

4. Publish the results.

scores, or results, of the experimental group and control group are significantly different, based on statistical analysis, then we know that the particular treatment was effective, for better or worse.

Another example of an experiment in this chapter was the study involving 11-year-old African-American boys and their parents. As you remember, half of them (the experimental group) attended special seminars, while the other half (the comparison group) did not. Having that comparison was crucial in showing that the seminars made a difference for the boys with the short version of the 5-HTTLPR gene.

◆ **ESPECIALLY FOR Nurses** In the field of medicine, why are experiments conducted to test new drugs and treatments? (see response, page 38) →

The Survey

A third research method is the **survey.** Information is collected from a large number of people by interview, questionnaire, or some other means. This is a quick, direct way to obtain data.

survey
A research method in which information is collected from a large number of people by interviews, written questionnaires, or some other means.

Unfortunately, although surveys may be quick and direct, they are not necessarily accurate. When pollsters try to predict elections, they survey thousands of potential voters. They hope that the people they survey will vote as they say they will, that undecided people will follow the trends, and that people who refuse to tell their opinion, or who are not included, will be similar to those surveyed. None of this is certain. Some people lie, some change their minds, some (especially those who don't have phones or who never talk to strangers) are never counted.

Also, survey answers are influenced by the wording and the sequence of the questions. For example, class evaluations of professors and the courses they teach are used at many universities and colleges. One could imagine that if students found a certain professor charismatic and funny, the positive ratings for that professor would be higher if students were asked "Was the professor able to engage with the students?" instead of "Was the professor well organized?" Course ratings might also be higher if the questions about the professor came first, followed by those about the course content and structure, since the students' good feelings for the professor would carry over to the course itself.

Another factor that affects survey results is that respondents present themselves as they would like to be perceived. For example, a survey done for CBC News in

2011 asked Canadians if they believed they were overweight. About 44 percent said they were overweight, 7 percent admitted to being obese, and 43 percent stated that they were at a healthy weight. According to Dr. Arya Sharma, obesity management professor at the University of Alberta, two-thirds of Canadians are overweight and 24 percent are clinically obese (CBC News, 2011a)!

To understand responses in more depth, another method can be used—the **case study,** which is an in-depth study of one person. Case studies usually require personal interviews, background information, test or questionnaire results, and more. Although in some ways case studies seem more accurate than more superficial measures, in other ways they are not: The assumptions and interpretations of the researcher are more likely to bias the results than would a survey that has been validated on hundreds of participants.

Even if accurate, the case study applies only to one person, who may be quite unlike other people. For instance, the report on David is a case study, but David is unique: Other embryos exposed to rubella may have quite different lives than David's.

case study
An in-depth study of one person, usually requiring personal interviews to collect background information and various follow-up discussions, tests, questionnaires, and so on.

Studying Development over the Life Span

In addition to conducting observations, experiments, and surveys, developmentalists must measure how people *change or remain the same over time,* as our definition of the science of human development stressed. Remember that systems are dynamic, ever-changing. To capture that dynamism, developmental researchers use one of three basic research designs: cross-sectional, longitudinal, or cross-sequential (see Figure 1.13 on page 40).

CROSS-SECTIONAL RESEARCH The quickest and least expensive way to study development over time is with **cross-sectional research,** in which groups of people of one age are compared with people of another age. For instance, in Canada in 2012, an estimated 92 percent of men aged 25 to 44 were in the labour force, but only 69 percent of those aged 55 to 64 were (Statistics Canada, 2012b). It seems that one-quarter of all men stop working between ages 45 and 55.

Cross-sectional design seems simple. However it is difficult to ensure that the various groups being compared are similar in every way except age. In this example, the younger men, on average, may have had more education than the older ones. Thus, what seems to be the result of age might actually have to do with schooling: Perhaps education, not age, accounted for the higher employment rates of the younger adults. Or perhaps age discrimination was the problem. The older adults may have wanted jobs but been unable to get them.

cross-sectional research
A research design that compares groups of people who differ in age but are similar in other important characteristics.

Compare Groups These diverse groups seem ideal for cross-sectional research. The younger ones *(left)* have their hands all over each other and express open-mouth joy—but with age, even smiling classmates, like these high school friends *(right),* are more restrained. However, with cross-sectional research, it is not certain whether such contrasts are the direct result of chronological age or the result of other variables—perhaps income, cohort, or culture.

Five Stages of Life These photos show Susan in infancy (age 7 months), middle childhood (age 9 years), adolescence (age 12), emerging adulthood (age 23), and adulthood (age 30). Continuity (her smile) and discontinuity (her hair) are both evident in longitudinal research.

JAMES CHUANG

longitudinal research
A research design in which the same individuals are followed over time and their development is repeatedly assessed.

✦ **ESPECIALLY FOR Future Researchers** What is the best method for collecting data? (see response, page 41) →

RESPONSE FOR Nurses (from page 36) Experiments are the only way to determine cause-and-effect relationships. If we want to be sure that a new drug or treatment is safe and effective, an experiment must be conducted to establish that the drug or treatment improves health. ●

LONGITUDINAL RESEARCH To help discover whether age itself rather than cohort or economic differences causes a developmental change, scientists undertake **longitudinal research.** This requires collecting data repeatedly on the same individuals as they age. Longitudinal research is particularly useful in tracing development over many years (Elder & Shanahan, 2006).

For example, in 1994 two agencies of the Canadian government began collaborating on the National Longitudinal Survey of Children and Youth (NLSCY). About 25 000 children were questioned every two years until they reached adulthood. The objective of the NLSCY was to gather information about the critical factors affecting child development in Canada, and then to use this information for policy analysis and program development.

The data collected by the NLSCY has also been very useful for developmental researchers in Canadian universities. As an example, with the wealth of information gathered over time, one group of researchers was able to explore the effects of maternal depression on emotional disorders in adolescents (Naicker et al., 2012). Based on survey responses of more than 900 children, their findings revealed that adolescents who were initially exposed to their mothers' depression between the ages of 2 and 5 were twice as likely to experience some form of emotional disorder than children who were not exposed to maternal depression at this age. However, those exposed to maternal depression in the first postpartum year or after the age of 5 were not significantly affected. This discovery allowed the research team to conclude that there is a sensitive period for initial exposure to maternal depression that may negatively affect children's mental health many years later.

It is important to note, however, that longitudinal research has several drawbacks. Over time, participants may withdraw, move to an unknown address, or die. These losses can skew the final results if those who disappear are unlike those who stay, as they usually are. Another problem is that participants become increasingly aware of the questions or the goals of the study and that awareness may cause them to change in ways that differ from most other people.

Probably the biggest problem comes from the historical context. Science, popular culture, and politics alter life experiences, and those changes limit the current relevance of data collected on people born decades ago. Results from longitudinal studies of people born in 1900, as they made their way through childhood, adulthood,

and old age, may not be relevant to people born in 2000. Regarding male employment, voluntary retirement before age 60 has been less common over the past decade not because people have changed but because the exosystem has.

Furthermore, longitudinal research requires years of data. For example, alarm about possible future harm caused by ingesting *phthalates* (chemicals used in manufacturing) in plastic baby bottles and infant toys leads many parents to use glass baby bottles. But perhaps the risk of occasional shattered glass causes more harm than the chemicals in plastic, or perhaps the mother's use of cosmetics, which puts phthalates in breast milk, is a much greater source of the chemicals than any bottles (Wittassek et al., 2011). Could breastfeeding harm infants? The benefits of breast milk probably outweigh the dangers, but we want answers now, not in decades.

CROSS-SEQUENTIAL RESEARCH Scientists have discovered a third strategy, combining cross-sectional and longitudinal research. This combination is called **cross-sequential research** (also referred to as *cohort-sequential* or *time-sequential research*). With this design, researchers study several groups of people of different ages (a cross-sectional approach) and follow them over the years (a longitudinal approach).

A cross-sequential design lets researchers compare findings for a group of, say, 18-year-olds with findings for the same individuals at age 10, as well as with findings for groups who were 18 a decade or two earlier and with findings for groups who are currently 10 years old (see Figure 1.13). Cross-sequential research is the most complicated, in recruitment and analysis, but it lets scientists disentangle age from history.

One well-known cross-sequential study (the Seattle Longitudinal Study) found that some intellectual abilities (vocabulary) increase even after age 60, whereas others (speed) start to decline at age 30 (Schaie, 2005). This confirms the multidirectional nature of development. This study also discovered that declines in math ability are more closely related to education than to age, a finding that neither cross-sectional nor longitudinal research alone could reveal.

Some more recent cross-sequential research focuses on the mental health of children. Cross-sequential studies find that many factors are influential throughout childhood, but that some harm schoolchildren more than babies. Father absence or unemployment is one of them (Sanson et al., 2011).

cross-sequential research
A hybrid research design in which researchers first study several groups of people of different ages (a cross-sectional approach) and then follow those groups over the years (a longitudinal approach). (Also called *cohort-sequential research* or *time-sequential research*.)

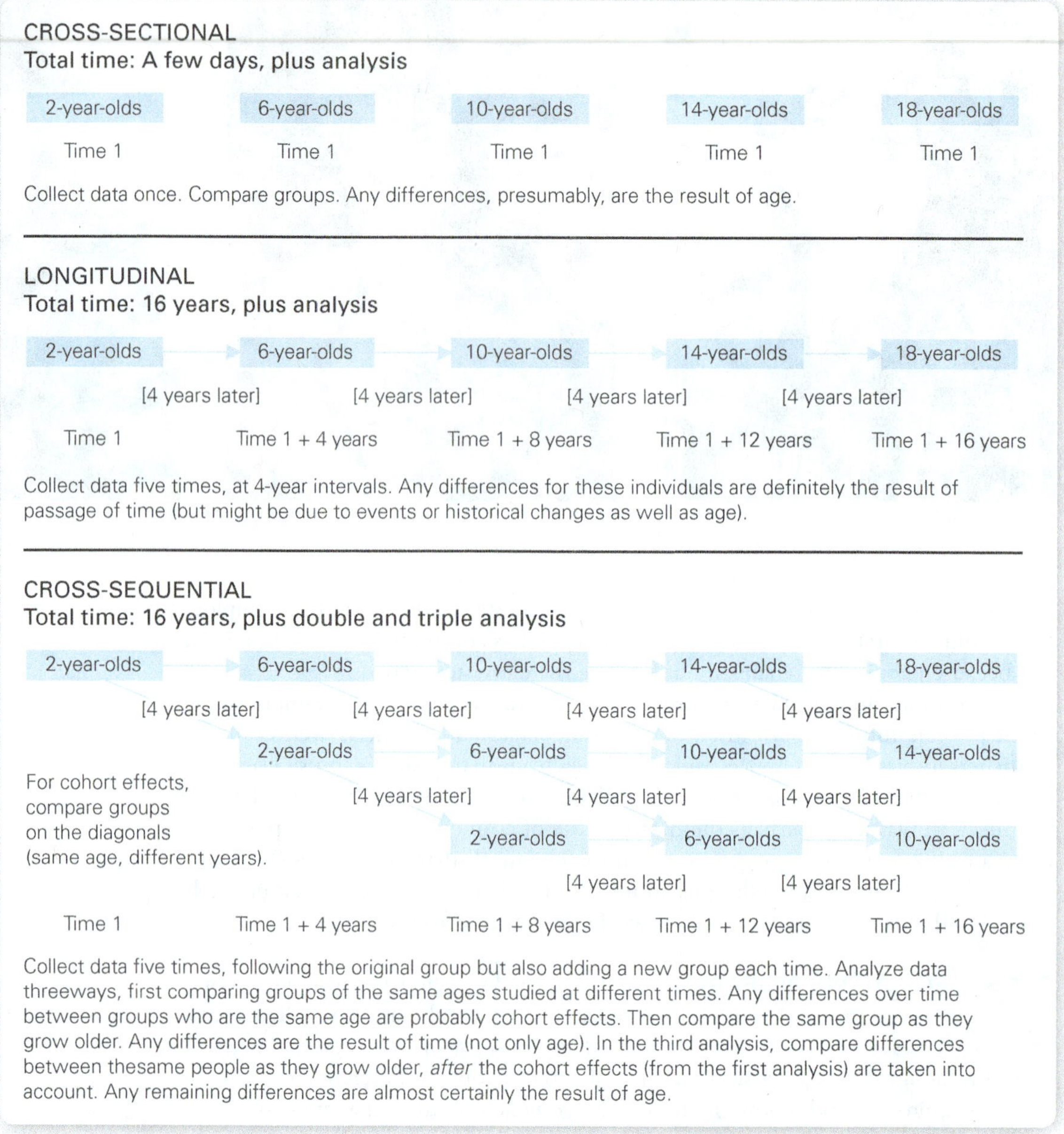

CROSS-SECTIONAL
Total time: A few days, plus analysis

2-year-olds	6-year-olds	10-year-olds	14-year-olds	18-year-olds
Time 1	Time 1	Time 1	Time 1	Time 1

Collect data once. Compare groups. Any differences, presumably, are the result of age.

LONGITUDINAL
Total time: 16 years, plus analysis

2-year-olds	→ 6-year-olds	→ 10-year-olds	→ 14-year-olds	→ 18-year-olds
[4 years later]	[4 years later]	[4 years later]	[4 years later]	
Time 1	Time 1 + 4 years	Time 1 + 8 years	Time 1 + 12 years	Time 1 + 16 years

Collect data five times, at 4-year intervals. Any differences for these individuals are definitely the result of passage of time (but might be due to events or historical changes as well as age).

CROSS-SEQUENTIAL
Total time: 16 years, plus double and triple analysis

2-year-olds	6-year-olds	10-year-olds	14-year-olds	18-year-olds
[4 years later]	[4 years later]	[4 years later]	[4 years later]	
	2-year-olds	6-year-olds	10-year-olds	14-year-olds
	[4 years later]	[4 years later]	[4 years later]	
		2-year-olds	6-year-olds	10-year-olds
		[4 years later]	[4 years later]	
Time 1	Time 1 + 4 years	Time 1 + 8 years	Time 1 + 12 years	Time 1 + 16 years

For cohort effects, compare groups on the diagonals (same age, different years).

Collect data five times, following the original group but also adding a new group each time. Analyze data threeways, first comparing groups of the same ages studied at different times. Any differences over time between groups who are the same age are probably cohort effects. Then compare the same group as they grow older. Any differences are the result of time (not only age). In the third analysis, compare differences between thesame people as they grow older, *after* the cohort effects (from the first analysis) are taken into account. Any remaining differences are almost certainly the result of age.

FIGURE 1.13 Which Approach Is Best? Cross-sequential research is the most time-consuming and complex, but it yields the best information. One reason that hundreds of scientists conduct research on the same topics, replicating one another's work, is to gain some advantages of cross-sequential research without waiting for decades.

KEY Points

- Scientists use many methods because none is perfect.
- Careful and systematic observation can discover phenomena that were unnoticed before.
- Experiments uncover what causes what; specifically, how the independent variable affects the dependent variable.
- Surveys are quick, and case studies are detailed, but both are vulnerable to bias.
- To study change over time, cross-sectional, longitudinal, and cross-sequential designs are used, each with advantages and disadvantages.

Cautions and Challenges from Science

There is no doubt that the scientific method illuminates and illustrates human development as nothing else does. Facts, hypotheses, and possibilities have all emerged that would not be known without science—and people of all ages are healthier, happier, and more capable than people of previous generations as a result.

For example, infectious diseases in children, illiteracy in adults, depression in late adulthood, and racism and sexism at every age are much less prevalent today than a century ago. Science deserves credit for all these advances. Even violent death is less likely, with scientific discoveries and education likely reasons (Pinker, 2011).

Developmental scientists have also discovered unexpected sources of harm. Video games, cigarettes, television, shift work, and asbestos are all less benign than people first thought.

Although the benefits of science are many, so are the pitfalls. We now discuss three potential hazards: misinterpreting correlation, depending too heavily on numbers, and ignoring ethics.

RESPONSE FOR Future Researchers (from page 38) There is no best method for collecting data. The method used depends on many factors, such as the age of participants (e.g., infants can't complete questionnaires), the question being researched, and the time frame. ●

Correlation and Causation

Probably the most common mistake in interpreting research is the confusion of correlation with causation. A **correlation** exists between two variables if one variable is more (or less) likely to occur when the other does. Thus, there is a relationship or link between one variable and the other. A correlation is *positive* if both variables tend to increase together or decrease together, *negative* if one variable tends to increase while the other decreases, and *zero* if no connection is evident.

To illustrate: From birth to age 9, there is a positive correlation between age and height (children grow taller as they grow older), a negative correlation between age and amount of sleep (children sleep less as they grow older), and zero correlation between age and number of toes (children do not have more or fewer toes as they grow older). (Now try taking the quiz on correlation in Table 1.7.)

correlation
A number that indicates the degree of relationship between two variables, expressed in terms of the likelihood that one variable will (or will not) occur when the other variable does (or does not). A correlation indicates only that two variables are related, not that one variable causes the other to occur.

TABLE 1.7 Quiz on Correlation

Two Variables	Positive, Negative, or Zero Correlation?	Why? (Third Variable)
1. Ice cream sales and murder rate	_____	_____
2. Learning to read and number of baby teeth	_____	_____
3. Child gender and sex of parent	_____	_____

For each of these three pairs of variables, indicate whether the correlation between them is positive, negative, or non-existent. Then try to think of a third variable that would determine the direction of the correlation. The correct answers are printed upside down below.

Expressed in numerical terms, correlations vary from +1.0 (the most positive) to −1.0 (the most negative). Correlations are almost never that extreme; a correlation of +0.3 or −0.3 is noteworthy; a correlation of +0.8 or −0.8 is astonishing.

Many correlations are unexpected. For instance, first-born children are more likely to develop asthma than are later-born children, teenage girls have higher rates of mental health problems than do teenage boys, and newborns born to immigrants weigh more than do newborns of non-immigrants. (All these correlations are discussed later.) At this point, the important caution to remember is *correlation is not causation*. Just because two variables are correlated, that does not mean that one causes the other; it only proves that they are connected somehow. Many mistaken and even dangerous conclusions are drawn because people misunderstand correlation.

Quiz Answers:
1. Positive; third variable: heat
2. Negative; third variable: age
3. Zero; each child must have a parent of each sex; no third variable

Quantity and Quality

A second caution concerns how heavily scientists should rely on data produced by **quantitative research** (from the word *quantity*). Quantitative research data can be categorized, ranked, or numbered and thus can be easily translated across cultures and for diverse populations. One example of quantitative research is the use of children's school achievement scores to measure the effectiveness of education.

Since quantities can be easily summarized, compared, charted, and replicated, many scientists prefer quantitative research. Statistics require numbers. Quantitative data are easier to replicate and less open to bias, although researchers who choose this method have some implicit beliefs about evidence and verification (Creswell, 2009).

When data are presented in categories and numbers, some nuances and individual distinctions are lost. Many developmental researchers thus turn to **qualitative research** (from *quality*)—asking open-ended questions, reporting answers in narrative (not numerical) form. Qualitative researchers are "interested in understanding how people interpret their experiences, how they construct their world" (Merriam, 2009, p. 5). Qualitative research reflects cultural and contextual diversity, but it is also more vulnerable to bias and harder to replicate.

Developmentalists use both quantitative and qualitative methods (Creswell, 2009). Sometimes they translate qualitative research into quantifiable data; sometimes they use qualitative studies to suggest hypotheses for quantitative research.

One caution applies especially to qualitative research: Scientists must not leap to conclusions on the basis of one small study. In the same way, personal experiences may suggest topics and hypotheses, but the particulars of our lives are no substitute for empirical research on hundreds of other people. Another caution applies to quantitative research: The accuracy of the conclusions depends on exactly how the numbers were defined and collected—a truth that is obvious when you realize that a score of A (80–100 percent) in one class is easier to get than a B (70–79 percent) in another.

quantitative research
Research that provides data that can be expressed with numbers, such as ranks or scales.

qualitative research
Research that considers qualities instead of quantities. Descriptions of particular conditions and participants' expressed ideas are often part of qualitative studies.

◆ **ESPECIALLY FOR People Who Have Applied to College, University, or Graduate School** Is the admissions process based on quality or quantity? (see response, page 44) →

A Bite Worse Than Its Bark A crucial question for all scientists is whether their research is ethical and will help solve human problems.

off the mark.com by Mark Parisi

... AND I FIGURE BY GENETICALLY COMBINING TREES AND PITBULLS, THE RAIN FORESTS MIGHT HAVE A FIGHTING CHANCE...

Ethics

The most important caution for all scientists, especially for those studying humans, is to uphold ethical standards in their research. Each academic discipline and professional society involved in the study of human development has a *code of ethics* (a set of moral principles) and specific practices within a scientific culture to protect the integrity of research and research participants.

Ethical standards and codes are increasingly stringent. In Canada, most educational and medical institutions have a *Research Ethics Board* (REB), a group that permits only research that follows certain guidelines. Although REBs often slow down scientific study, some research conducted before they were established was clearly unethical, especially when the participants were children, members of minority groups, prisoners, or animals (Blum, 2002; Washington, 2006).

PROTECTION OF RESEARCH PARTICIPANTS Researchers must ensure that participation is voluntary, confidential, and harmless. In Western nations, this entails the *informed consent* of the participants—that is, the participants must understand and agree to the research procedures and know any risks involved.

If children are involved, consent must be obtained from the parents as well as the children, and the children must be allowed to end their participation at any time. In some other nations, ethical standards require consent of the village elders and heads of families, in addition to that of the research participants themselves (Doumbo, 2005).

Historically, shocking examples of unethical practices—from not treating syphilis to neglecting babies—include some "studies carried out by respected psychologists and published in the finest journals of the day. We've come a long way since then, baby. And babies are grateful." (Stephen L. Black, personal communication, 2005).

Protection of participants may conflict with the goals of science. The Canadian Psychological Association suggests ways to resolve this conflict. Its four guiding principles are

1. *respect for the dignity of persons,* which includes such factors as non-discrimination, informed consent, and confidentiality

2. *responsible caring,* which involves competence and the intention to maximize benefits while minimizing harm

3. *integrity in relationships,* which emphasizes an objective approach to research and the complete avoidance of any conflict of interest

4. *responsibility to society,* which involves the general development of knowledge that will benefit society as a whole.

Note that all four of these principles should be followed, if possible, but they are ranked in order of importance: Respect for individuals is most important (Canadian Psychological Association, 2010).

IMPLICATIONS OF RESEARCH RESULTS Once a study has been completed, additional issues arise. Scientists are obligated to promote "accuracy, honesty, and the obvious prohibitions of fraud or misrepresentation" (Canadian Psychological Association, 2000).

Deliberate falsification is rare. When it does occur, it leads to ostracism from the scientific community, dismissal from a teaching or research position, and, sometimes, criminal prosecution. Another obvious breach of ethics is to "cook" the data, or distort one's findings, in order to make a particular conclusion seem to be the only reasonable one. This is not as rare as it should be. Tenure, promotion, and funding all encourage scientists to publish, and publishers to seek, remarkable findings. Researchers recognize the "file-drawer" problem—studies that do not demonstrate significant findings are relegated to personal files rather than publication, creating a bias in the scientific literature in favour of those studies that do demonstrate statistically significant results. This is problematic since it may be important to know that findings were not significant. Awareness of this danger is leading to increased calls for replication (Carpenter, 2012).

Insidious dangers include unintentionally slanting the conclusions and withholding publication of a result, especially when there is "ferocious … pressure from commercial funders to ignore good scientific practice" (Bateson, 2005, p. 645). Similarly, non-profit research groups and academic institutions pressure scientists to produce publishable results.

Ethical standards cannot be taken for granted. As stressed at the beginning of this chapter, researchers, like all other humans, have strong opinions, which they expect research to confirm. Therefore, they might try (sometimes without even realizing it) to achieve the results they want. One team explains:

> Our job as scientists is to discover truths about the world. We generate hypotheses, collect data, and examine whether or not the data are consistent with those

✦ **ESPECIALLY FOR** Future Researchers and Science Writers Do any ethical guidelines apply when an author writes about the experiences of family members, friends, or research participants? (see response, page 44) →

hypotheses … [but we] often lose sight of this goal, yielding to pressure to do whatever is justifiable to compile a set of studies we can publish. This is not driven by a willingness to deceive but by the self-serving interpretation of ambiguity.

[Simmons et al., 2011, pp. 1359 & 1365]

RESPONSE FOR People Who Have Applied to College, University, or Graduate School (from page 42) Most institutions of higher education emphasize quantitative data—GPA or LSAT, GRE, GMAT, and MCAT scores, for example. Decide for yourself whether this is fairer than a more qualitative approach. ●

Obviously, collaboration, replication, and transparency are essential ethical safeguards for all scientists.

What Should We Study?

Finally, the most important ethical concern for developmentalists is to study issues that will help "all kinds of people, everywhere, of every age" live satisfying and productive lives. Consider these questions, for instance:

- Do we know enough about prenatal drug abuse to protect every fetus?
- Do we know enough about poverty to enable everyone to be healthy?
- Do we know enough about same-sex relationships, or polygamy, or single parenthood, or divorce, to make sure all people develop well no matter what their family structure?
- Do we know enough about dying to enable everyone to die with dignity?

RESPONSE FOR Future Researchers and Science Writers (from page 43) Yes. Anyone you write about must give consent and be fully informed about your intentions. They can be identified by name only if they give permission. For example, family members gave permission before anecdotes about them were included in this text. David, for example, read the first draft of his story (see pages 21–22) and is proud to have his experiences used to teach others. ●

The answer to all these questions is a resounding *NO*. The reasons are many, but a major one is that these topics are controversial. Some researchers avoid them, fearing unwelcome and uninformed publicity (Kempner et al., 2005). Few funders are eager to support scientific studies of drug abuse, poverty, non-standard families, or death, partly because people have strong opinions on these issues that may conflict with scientific findings and conclusions. Religion, politics, and ethics shape scientific research, sometimes stopping investigation before it begins. Yet developmentalists must study whatever benefits the human family.

The next cohort of developmental scientists will build on what is known, mindful of what needs to be explored. Remember that the goal is to help all 7 billion people on Earth fulfill their potential. Much more needs to be learned. This book is only a beginning.

KEY Points

- Correlation is not causation. Two variables may be related, not necessarily because one causes the other, but perhaps because a third variable affects both.
- Quantitative research is easier to analyze and compare, but qualitative study captures more nuances.
- Research ethics require that the participants be respected; they must give informed consent, and confidentiality must be assured.
- Scientists need to study and report data on many issues that are crucial for the optimal development of all people.

SUMMARY

Understanding How and Why

1. The study of human development is a science that seeks to understand how people change or remain the same over time. As a science, it begins with questions and hypotheses and then gathers empirical data, drawing conclusions that are shared (usually published) with other scientists, who replicate the study to confirm, modify, or refute the conclusions.

2. Nature and nurture always interact. Each human characteristic is affected by both genes (nature) and environment (nurture) and by their interaction. Epigenetically, the environment affects genes.

The Life-Span Perspective

3. Development is multidirectional, multicontextual, and multicultural. That means that gains and losses are apparent throughout life, that an ecological approach that considers the immediate contexts (family, school) as well as broader contexts (historical conditions, economic status) is essential, and that each culture embraces values and assumptions about human life.

4. Culture, ethnicity, and race are social constructions, concepts created by society. Culture includes beliefs and patterns; ethnicity refers to ancestral heritage. The social construction of "race" has been misused, so some social scientists want to abandon it whereas others want to use it to combat racism.

5. Development also needs to be understood using the methods and viewpoints of many disciplines. For example, to understand the cause of psychological depression, at least a dozen factors from a dozen disciplines are helpful.

6. Development is plastic, which means that although inborn traits and childhood experiences affect later development, patterns and possibilities can change throughout life.

Theories of Development

7. Psychoanalytic theory, as originated by Freud, emphasizes that human actions and thoughts originate from unconscious impulses and childhood conflicts. Erikson went beyond Freud: He described eight stages of psychosocial development, each reflecting the age, culture, and context of the individual.

8. Learning theory focuses on how overt behaviours are influenced by the social environment. One learning theory, behaviourism, stresses that people of all ages develop according to the associations and reinforcements that accompany their actions. Another learning theory, social learning theory, acknowledges that humans are social beings whose behaviours are shaped by observing the behaviours of others.

9. Cognitive theory emphasizes that thought processes affect all human behaviours and assumptions. Piaget described how these change with age; information-processing theory stresses the step-by-step advances in cognition.

10. Systems theory focuses on the idea that a change in one part of a system—be it a body, a family, or a society—affects every other part of the system and the system as a whole.

11. Humanism stresses that all humans have basic needs that must be met for people to reach their full potential, becoming self-actualized.

12. Evolutionary theory traces the inborn impulses that arise from past millennia of human life, and that enable humans to survive and reproduce successfully. This perspective explains some irrational fears as well as some noble human traits.

Using the Scientific Method

13. Several specific research designs help scientists understand human development. Scientific observation, the experiment, and the survey each provide insights and discoveries that were not apparent before the research. Each also has liabilities, so before a scientific community will accept a conclusion several methods are typically used.

14. An additional challenge for developmentalists is to study change over time. Two traditional research designs are often used: cross-sectional research (comparing people of different ages) and longitudinal research (studying the same people over time). A third method, cross-sequential research (combining the two other methods), is more complicated, but also provides more reliable conclusions.

Cautions and Challenges from Science

15. A correlation shows that two variables are related. However, it does not prove that one variable *causes* the other. The relationship of variables may be opposite to the one expected, or it may be the result of a third variable.

16. Quantitative research provides data that is numerical, and thus is often used to compare children in different contexts and cultures. By contrast, qualitative research captures the nuance of individual lives. Both are needed.

17. Ethical behaviour is crucial in all the sciences. Not only must participants be protected and data be kept confidential (primary concerns of Research Ethics Boards), but results must be fairly reported, honestly interpreted, and replicated. Scientists must be mindful of the implications of their research.

18. Appropriate application of scientific research depends partly on the training and integrity of the scientists. The most important ethical question is whether scientists are designing, conducting, analyzing, publishing, and applying the research that is most critically needed to help the entire human family develop well.

acculturation (p. 15)
behaviourism (p. 26)
case study (p. 37)
classical conditioning (p. 27)
cognitive theory (p. 29)
cohort (p. 10)
conditioning (p. 27)
correlation (p. 41)
critical period (p. 8)
cross-sectional research (p. 37)
cross-sequential research (p. 39)
culture (p. 12)

dependent variable (p. 35)
developmental theory (p. 24)
difference-equals-deficit error (p. 13)
differential sensitivity (p. 22)
dynamic-systems approach (p. 21)
ecological-systems approach (p. 9)
empirical evidence (p. 4)
epigenetic (p. 18)
ethnic group (p. 16)
experiment (p. 35)
family systems theory (p. 30)

humanism (p. 32)
hypothesis (p. 4)
independent variable (p. 35)
learning theory (p. 26)
life-span perspective (p. 7)
longitudinal research (p. 38)
nature (p. 5)
nurture (p. 5)
operant conditioning (p. 27)
psychoanalytic theory (p. 24)
qualitative research (p. 42)
quantitative research (p. 42)
race (p. 17)
reinforcement (p. 28)

replication (p. 5)
science of human development (p. 4)
scientific method (p. 4)
scientific observation (p. 34)
sensitive period (p. 8)
social construction (p. 12)
social learning theory (p. 28)
socioeconomic status (SES) (p. 11)
sudden infant death syndrome (SIDS) (p. 6)
survey (p. 36)

WHAT HAVE YOU LEARNED?

1. What are the five steps of the scientific method?

2. What basic question is at the heart of the nature–nurture controversy?

3. Give an example of discontinuity and of continuity as it relates to your development.

4. What does it mean to say that development is multicontextual?

5. How does the exosystem affect your life today?

6. What are some cohort differences between you and your parents?

7. What factors comprise a person's socioeconomic status?

8. Give an example of a social construction. Why is it a construction, not a fact?

9. Explain the concept of guided participation, as described by Vygotsky.

10. What is the difference between race and ethnicity?

11. How do both specialization and multidisciplinary research add to our understanding of a topic?

12. What is the difference between "genetics" and "epigenetics"?

13. In what two ways is human development plastic?

14. What is implied about human development when it is described as dynamic?

15. Give an example that explains the concept of "differential sensitivity."

16. What main idea underlies Freud's psychoanalytic theory?

17. What is the main difference between Erikson's theory of human development and Freud's?

18. How can behaviourism be seen as a reaction to psychoanalytic theory?

19. How do classical and operant conditioning differ?

20. Why is social learning also called modelling?

21. What is the basic idea of cognitive theory?

22. According to Maslow, what is the five-step hierarchy of people's basic needs and drives?

23. How does the theory of evolution help explain human development?

24. Explain the following concept: "Observation provides issues to explore, not proof."

25. Why do experimenters use a control (or comparison) group as well as an experimental group?

26. What are the strengths and weaknesses of the survey method?

27. Why would a scientist conduct a cross-sectional study?

28. What are some advantages and disadvantages of longitudinal research?

29. Explain the following statement: Cross-sequential research combines cross-sectional and longitudinal research.

30. Why does correlation not prove causation?

31. Why do some researchers prefer quantitative research while others prefer qualitative research?

32. Why is it important for academic disciplines and professional societies to follow codes of ethics?

33. What is one additional question about development that should be answered?

APPLICATIONS

1. It is said that culture is pervasive but that people are unaware of it. List 30 things you did today that you might have done differently in another culture.

2. How would your life be different if your parents were much higher or lower in SES than they are? What if you had been born in another cohort?

3. Design an experiment to answer a question you have about human development. Specify the question and the hypothesis and then describe the experiment, including the sample size and the variables.

>>ONLINE CONNECTIONS

To accompany your textbook, you have access to a number of online resources, including LearningCurve, which is an adaptive quizzing program; critical thinking questions; and case studies. For access to any of these links, go to www.worthpublishers.com/launchpad/bergerchuang1e. In addition to these resources, you'll find links to video clips, personalized study advice, and an e-Book. Among the videos and activities available online is the following:

■ *What's Wrong with This Study?* This activity allows you to review some of the pitfalls in various research designs.

CHAPTER OUTLINE

FROM CONCEPTION
to Birth

WHAT WILL YOU KNOW?

- How do genes affect each individual?
- What birth practices are best for mother, father, and newborn?
- How can serious birth disorders be avoided?
- Is alcoholism genetic or cultural?

In graduate school, I had a friend named Don, whose wife, Donna, had a difficult pregnancy. She couldn't keep her food down and did not gain much weight over her nine-month term. All Don could do was be supportive and try to make the pregnancy go as well as possible.

On the day Donna went into labour, the birth process was prolonged; the baby did not seem ready to come out. The doctors advised Donna to walk around, so that is what she did. Arm in arm with Don, she walked up and down the hallways—for hours.

At one point, Donna needed to use the washroom, and since she was so close to giving birth, Don and the nurse followed close behind. As Donna sat on the toilet, Don started to cry.

"What's wrong?" asked Donna, alarmed. "Why are you crying?"

"Nothing! I'm just so happy I'll be a father soon."

It turned out to be sooner than he thought, since the baby chose that moment to arrive—feet first! As the two feet came out, the doctor and nurses acted quickly to make sure that the rest of the delivery was safe.

As you will see later in this chapter, coming out feet first, also known as a breech birth, is not the preferred way for a baby to arrive. Baby Delaney gave everyone quite a scare, but in the end she turned out to be a healthy and very happy child. ●

—Susan Chuang

Here is happy and healthy Delaney *(right)* with her sister, Deagan, enjoying the fall weather.

THE PASSAGE FROM CONCEPTION TO BIRTH IS A complex process, one that is often fraught with difficulties and surprises. As you will learn in this chapter, in spite of everything that can go wrong, most babies are born healthy and develop normally. Ensuring that this happens is not just the mother's responsibility but that of all the important people who surround her. These include the father, the extended family members, the mother's circle of friends, and the team of medical professionals, to name just a few.

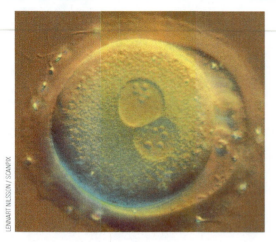

LENNART NILSSON / SCANPIX

The Moment of Conception This ovum is about to become a zygote. It has been penetrated by a single sperm, whose nucleus now lies next to the nucleus of the ovum. Soon, the two nuclei will fuse, bringing together about 20 000 genes to guide development.

zygote
The single cell that is formed from the fusing of two gametes, a sperm and an ovum.

DNA (deoxyribonucleic acid)
The molecule that contains the chemical instructions for cells to manufacture various proteins.

chromosome
One of the 46 molecules of DNA (in 23 pairs) that each cell of the human body contains and that, together, contain all the genes. Other species have more or fewer chromosomes.

gene
A small section of a chromosome; the basic unit for the transmission of heredity. A gene consists of a string of chemicals that provide instructions for the cell to manufacture certain proteins.

gamete
A reproductive cell; that is, a sperm or an ovum that can produce a new individual if it combines with a gamete from the other sex to form a zygote.

The Beginning of Life

Every person starts life as a single cell, called a **zygote.** Each zygote is distinct from every other human cell ever created, yet that cell contains genes that have been passed down for thousands of years. The first hours of development are a compelling example of both the universal and the unique characteristics of each human being.

Genes and Chromosomes

First we will focus on the universal. All living things are composed of cells that promote growth and sustain life according to instructions in their molecules of **DNA (deoxyribonucleic acid)** (see Figure 2.1). Each molecule of DNA is called a **chromosome.** Chromosomes contain units of instructions called **genes,** with each gene located on a particular chromosome.

Additional DNA and RNA (another molecule) surround each gene. In a process called *methylation,* this material enhances, transcribes, connects, empowers, silences, and alters genes (Shapiro, 2009). This non-genetic material used to be called *junk*— no longer. Thousands of scientists seek to discover what these molecules do, but no one now thinks they are junk (Wright & Bruford, 2011). Methylation continues throughout life, and can alter a gene's expression even after the person is born. This is part of epigenetics, explained in Chapter 1.

With one important exception, every cell in each person normally has copies of that person's 46 chromosomes, arranged in 23 pairs. That one exception is the reproductive cell, called a **gamete.** Each gamete—*sperm* in a man and *ovum* in a woman—has only 23 chromosomes, one from each of a person's 23 pairs of chromosomes.

Generally, at conception, the genes on each chromosome of the sperm match with the genes on the same chromosome of the ovum. For instance, the eye-colour gene from the father on chromosome 15 matches with an eye-colour gene from the mother on the zygote's other chromosome 15.

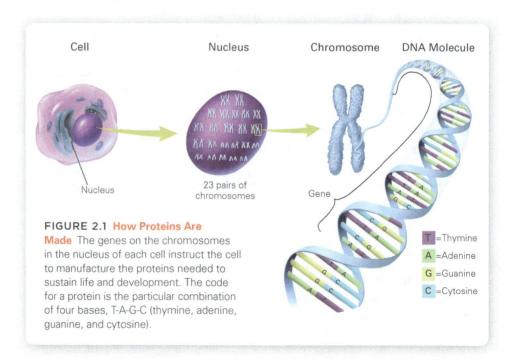

Cell Nucleus Chromosome DNA Molecule

Nucleus

23 pairs of chromosomes

Gene

T = Thymine
A = Adenine
G = Guanine
C = Cytosine

FIGURE 2.1 How Proteins Are Made The genes on the chromosomes in the nucleus of each cell instruct the cell to manufacture the proteins needed to sustain life and development. The code for a protein is the particular combination of four bases, T-A-G-C (thymine, adenine, guanine, and cytosine).

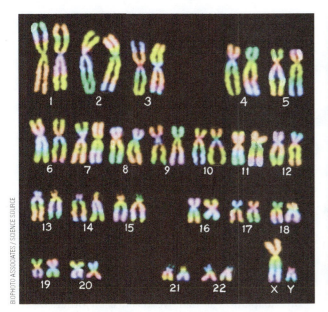
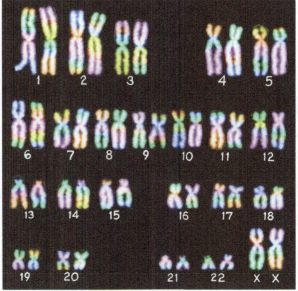

Uncertain Sex Every now and then, a baby is born with "ambiguous genitals," meaning that the child's sex is not abundantly clear. When this happens, a quick analysis of the chromosomes is needed, to make sure there are exactly 46 and to see whether the 23rd pair is XY or XX. The karyotypes shown here indicate a typical baby boy *(left)* and girl *(right)*.

Variations Among People

Now let's focus on the unique part of life. Since each gamete has only one of each person's pair of chromosomes, each person can produce 223 different gametes, more than 8 million versions of their chromosomes (actually 8 388 608). When a sperm and an ovum combine, they create a new cell in which one of those 8 million possible gametes from the father interacts with one of the 8 million possible gametes from the mother. In theory, your parents could have given you an astronomical number of siblings, each unique.

More variations occur because the DNA code contains 3 billion pairs of chemicals organized in triplets (sets of three pairs), each of which specifies production of one of 20 possible amino acids. Those amino acids combine to produce proteins, and those proteins combine to produce a person. Small variations or repetitions (called *copy number* variations) in the base pairs or triplets could make a notable difference in the proteins, and thus, eventually, in the person.

And that is what happens. Some triplets on some genes have transpositions, deletions, or repetitions not found in other versions of the same gene. Each of these variations is called an **allele** of that gene. Genes that have various alleles are called *polymorphic* (literally, "many forms") and each variation is a *single-nucleotide polymorphism* (abbreviated SNP).

Most alleles cause only minor differences (such as the shape of an eyebrow); some seem to have no effect; some are notable, even devastating. Alleles make one person unlike another. One difference in a triplet could make a person tall, or artistically talented, or red-haired (see Figure 2.2).

Every zygote inherits many alleles from its sperm or ovum, and that means that many gene pairs do not exactly match in every triplet. In addition, mutations that are not in either parent occur as the gametes form. That makes each person a little bit unusual. As one expert said, "What's cool is that we are a mosaic of pieces of genomes. None of us is truly normal" (Eichler, quoted in J. Cohen, 2007a, p. 1315).

allele
Any of the possible forms in which a gene for a particular trait can occur.

Phenotype		Allele 1	Allele 2	Allele 3
	Long	×	—	—
	Short	—	—	—
	Curly	×	—	×
	Wiry	—	×	—

FIGURE 2.2 One Species, A Billion Variations Dogs immediately recognize other dogs, even from a distance, despite dramatic differences in size, shape, colouring (of tongues and eyes as well as coats), and, as shown here, in hair. Minor code variations become marked for differences—long or short, curly or straight, wiry or limp.

genotype
An organism's entire genetic inheritance, or genetic potential.

phenotype
The observable characteristics of a person, including appearance, personality, intelligence, and all other traits.

genome
The full set of genes that are the instructions to make an individual member of a certain species.

Each individual's collection of genes is called his or her **genotype.** It was once thought that the genotype led directly to facial characteristics, body formation, intelligence, personality, and so on, but this is much too simplistic.

Because of the numerous epigenetic effects, as well as the interactions among the genes themselves, the **phenotype,** which is a person's actual appearance and behaviour, reflects much more than the genotype. The genotype is the beginning of diversity; the phenotype is the actual manifestation of it.

Genetic diversity not only distinguishes each person (you can immediately spot a close friend in a crowd) but also allows adaptation. We are the only species that thrives on every continent, from the poles to the equator. One of the best parts of our adaptation is that we teach each other. If we suddenly found ourselves in a climate we had never experienced, we would quickly learn how to dress, where to sleep, and what to eat from the other people who already had adapted to that place.

Thanks to our genetic diversity, even devastating diseases have not killed us all. For example, a few people have alleles that defend them from HIV, which causes AIDS (Aouizerat et al., 2011). Similarly, genotype differences allowed some of our ancestors to survive tuberculosis, malaria, the Black Death, and other scourges.

More on Shared and Divergent Genes

The entire packet of instructions to make a living organism is the **genome.** There is a genome for every species, from *Homo sapiens* to the smallest insect, and even for every kind of plant. A worldwide effort to map all the human genes led to the *Human Genome Project,* which was virtually completed in 2003 and continues to reveal surprises to this day.

The first surprise was that any two men or women, of any ethnicity, share 99.5 percent of their genetic codes. Similarly, codes for humans and chimpanzees are 98 percent the same (although chimp genes are on 48, not 46, chromosomes). The genomes for humans and every other mammal are at least 90 percent the same. All these shared genes allow scientists to learn about human genetics from other creatures, especially mice, by transposing, deactivating, enhancing, and duplicating their genes.

The more scientists experiment, the more they are amazed. Until 2001, scientists thought humans had about 100 000 genes, but that turned out to be a gross overestimate. The Human Genome Project found only about 20 000–23 000 genes. Genomes from other creatures led to more surprises: Dogs and mice have more genes than humans, and mice have several times more. The precise count is still unknown, partly because of another surprise: It is not always clear where one gene ends and another begins (Pennisi, 2007).

A more recent international project, called the HapMap, aims to spot all the variations in the human genome. HapMap has found 11 million differences among the 3 billion chemical pairs in humans (Hinds et al., 2005). Some genes are exactly identical for every person, but some have dozens of alleles—mostly rare, but not always. Humans are all alike, all one species, yet because of those 11 million differences, each of us is unique.

Applications of HapMap research are problematic. Much remains to be understood about the connection between alleles in the genotype and actual characteristics of the phenotype. The sheer number of variations is daunting. Scientists know that "genomics is not destiny. Indeed, if genomic sequence 'determines' anything behaviourally, it determines diversity" (Landis & Insel, 2008, p. 821).

THE 23RD PAIR The difference between one person and another, and one species and another, begins with the genes, but is much more epigenetic than genetic. The material surrounding a gene can halt, or expand, the instructions from that gene. Hormones, or proteins, or other factors that shape the phenotype begin with a gene but do not end with that. Consider sex differences: They originate from one gene (SRY) on one chromosome, as the following explains.

In 22 of the 23 pairs of human chromosomes that each person inherits, the chromosomes of each pair are closely matched. They are called *autosomes*, and they could be inherited by a male or female.

The 23rd pair of chromosomes is a special case. In females, it is composed of two large X-shaped chromosomes. Accordingly, it is designated **XX.** In males, the 23rd pair has one large X-shaped chromosome with many genes and one quite small chromosome, with only a few genes, which is Y-shaped. That 23rd pair is called **XY.**

Because a female's 23rd pair is XX, every ovum that her body creates contains either one X or the other—but always an X. Because a male's 23rd pair is XY, when his body splits his 46 chromosomes to make gametes, half of his sperm carry an X chromosome and half carry a Y.

The Y chromosome has the SRY gene that directs the developing fetus to make male organs. Thus, the sex of the developing organism depends on which sperm penetrates the ovum—either an X sperm, which creates a girl (XX), or a Y sperm, which creates a boy (XY) (see Figure 2.3). That SRY gene also directs hormone production that affects the brain, skeleton, body fat, muscles, and much more from the moment of conception to the last breath in old age.

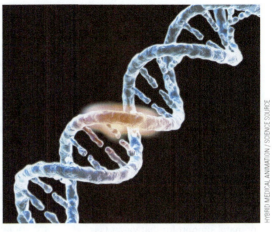

Twelve of 3 Billion Pairs This is a computer illustration of a small segment of one gene, with several triplets. Even a small difference in one gene, such as a few extra triplets, can cause major changes in a person's phenotype.

XX
A 23rd chromosome pair that consists of two X-shaped chromosomes, one each from the mother and the father. XX zygotes become females.

XY
A 23rd chromosome pair that consists of an X-shaped chromosome from the mother and a Y-shaped chromosome from the father. XY zygotes become males.

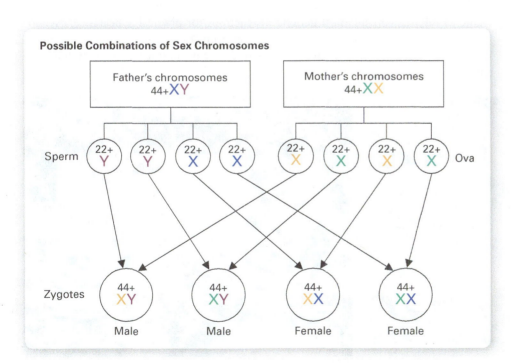

Possible Combinations of Sex Chromosomes

Father's chromosomes
44+XY

Mother's chromosomes
44+XX

Sperm: 22+Y 22+Y 22+X 22+X   22+X 22+X 22+X 22+X :Ova

Zygotes: 44+XY (Male) 44+XY (Male) 44+XX (Female) 44+XX (Female)

FIGURE 2.3 Determining a Zygote's Sex Any given couple can produce four possible combinations of sex chromosomes; two lead to female children and two, to male. In terms of the future person's sex, it does not matter which of the mother's Xs the zygote inherited. All that matters is whether the father's Y sperm or X sperm fertilized the ovum. However, for X-linked conditions (conditions linked to genes on the X chromosome), it matters a great deal because typically one, but not both, of the mother's Xs carries the trait.

At conception, there are about 120 males for every 100 females, perhaps because Y sperm swim faster and reach the ovum first (remember, they carry fewer genes so they are lighter than the X sperm). However, male embryos are more vulnerable than female ones (because of fewer genes, again?) so they are less likely to survive prenatally. At birth, the boy:girl ratio is about 105:100. When conditions are stressful (as in a famine), male embryos suffer more. For example, in many African nations (including South Africa, the Congo, Ghana, Nigeria, Kenya, and Ethiopia), the ratio at birth is 102 males per 100 females. In China and India, the ratio is currently higher—more than 110 boys to 100 girls—for reasons that are explained in the feature on the opposite page.

But first note that all the male/female differences—from the toy trucks given to 1-day-old boys to the survival rates of older women—begin with that one gene and influence every part of the body and every aspect of the culture. In turn, how infants are socialized in their culture affects the expression of that gene.

Obviously the impact of that SRY gene is much more than the quantitative fact that it is only one of about 20 000 genes, and only 0.005 percent of the genotype. The SRY gene, via epigenetic factors, affects thousands of other genetic and environmental influences that make for more sex differences than might be expected from 0.005 percent of the genome. Likewise, many other genes are similarly enhanced, promoted, and guided by other genetic material and a myriad of cultural forces.

TWINS There is one major exception to genetic diversity. Although every zygote is genetically unique, not every newborn is.

About once in every 250 human conceptions, the zygote not only duplicates but splits apart completely, creating two, or four, or even eight separate zygotes, each genetically identical to that first single cell. If each separate cell implants and grows, multiple births occur. One separation results in **monozygotic twins,** from one *(mono)* zygote (also called *identical twins*). Two or three separations create monozygotic quadruplets or octuplets. (An incomplete split creates *conjoined twins,* formerly called Siamese twins.)

Because monozygotic multiples originate from the same zygote, they have the same genotype, with identical genetic instructions for physical appearance, psychological traits, vulnerability to diseases, and everything else. However, because nurture always affects nature, even before birth, identical twins do not have exactly the same phenotype.

✦ **ESPECIALLY FOR Biologists** Many people believe that the differences between the sexes are primarily socio-cultural, not biological. Is there any prenatal support for that view? (see response, page 57) ➔

monozygotic twins
Twins who originate from one zygote that splits apart very early in development. (Also called *identical twins.*)

OBSERVATION QUIZ
Can you tell which pair of twins shown below is monozygotic? (see answer, page 58) ➔

Same Birthday, Same (or Different?) Genes Twins who are of different sexes are dizygotic, sharing only half of their genes. Many same-sex twins are dizygotic as well. One of these twin pairs is dizygotic; the other is monozygotic.

OPPOSING PERSPECTIVES

Choosing a Boy

Historically most couples believed that whether a newborn was male or female was up to chance, or God, or fate. If nurture had any role, people thought it occurred via the mother, particularly her diet, prayers, or sleeping position. Although boys were often preferred, most parents accepted whatever came.

For many couples, "whatever came" was more than accepted: Healthy newborns were welcomed. I (Kathleen) have four daughters and no sons. I am convinced this is for the best, and I bristle when anyone implies otherwise. Among my reasons: my children did not suffer from boy/girl rivalry; same-sex siblings more easily share the same room, the same chores, and the same clothes; my husband and I are better parents for girls than boys. (Probably I would have created a different list of reasons if I had had a boy.)

But some human history is appalling. Female infanticide was accepted in almost every nation. It was so common in the Arab world that Mohammed explicitly forbade it. Wife-blaming was evident in every nation and era: One reason Henry VIII conspired to have his second wife, Anne Boleyn, beheaded was because she did not bear a boy.

Now humans know better than to blame mothers. But knowing more about conception has allowed couples to select sex before birth by (1) inactivating X or Y sperm before conception, (2) undergoing in vitro fertilization and then inserting only male or female embryos, or (3) aborting XX or XY fetuses. Should that be legal?

In China, the government implemented a one-child policy (officially the "family planning policy") in 1979 in reaction to the country's overpopulation. Certain groups were exempted from this policy, including families in rural areas, ethnic minorities, and parents without any siblings themselves.

On the positive side, this policy cut the birth rate in half and lifted millions of families out of poverty. But it also led to more abortions when amniocentesis revealed a female fetus, and to more newborn girls being available for adoption because their parents wanted to try for a boy. The sex ratio escalated from 107 male newborns for every 100 girls in 1979 to 121 male newborns for every 100 girls in 2005. This meant there was an overall excess of 1.1 million men, and for the population under the age of 20, there were 32 million more males than females (Zhu & Hesketh, 2009).

National governments have come to recognize the problems created by an imbalance of males and females. Consequently, many nations have changed, or are considering changing, public policy. For example, in China and India, prenatal sex determination is now illegal. Unfortunately, prenatal sex selection still occurs (Greenhalgh, 2008). The most recent Chinese census reports 118 male newborns for every 100 girls (Hvistendahl, 2011). Many other Asian nations also have more young boys than girls.

The changes in public policy seem logical, but now consider the opposite view. Most North Americans approve of personal choice, including in sexual matters. For example, if a couple wants four or more children even though that means a greater financial burden on other people in society, they are not stopped—no one-child or two-child policy interferes.

Similarly, most fertility doctors in North America believe that sex selection is a reproductive right (Puri & Nachtigall, 2010). As one fertility doctor said, "Reproductive choice, as far as I'm concerned, is a very personal issue. If it's not going to hurt anyone, we go ahead and give them what they want" (Steinberg, quoted in Grady, 2007).

Freedom of individual choice—not just in the sex of a baby but also in sexual activity, sexual partner, contraception, prenatal care, and abortion—often clashes with social values, expressed by governments, religious groups, and many people. Balancing personal freedom and community needs has never been easy; now that sex selection is possible, yet another dilemma arises. Viewed from the outside, two opposing perspectives can both seem valid.

AP PHOTO / MANISH SWARUP

My Strength, My Daughter That's the slogan these girls in New Delhi are shouting at a demonstration against abortion of female fetuses in India. The current sex ratio of children in India suggests that this practice still occurs.

Usually, monozygotic twins develop their own identities while enjoying twinship. They might both have inherited athletic ability, for instance, but one chooses basketball and the other, soccer. One monozygotic twin writes:

> Twins put into high relief *the* central challenge for all of us: self-definition. How do we each plant our stake in the ground, decide how sensitive, callous, ambitious, cautious, or conciliatory we want to be every day? … Twins come with a built-in constant comparison, but defining oneself against one's twin is just an amped-up version of every person's lifelong challenge: to individuate, to create a distinctive persona in the world.
>
> [Pogrebin, 2009, p. 9]

Dizygotic twins, also called *fraternal twins,* occur about twice as often as monozygotic twins. They began life as two zygotes created by two ova fertilized by two sperm. (Usually, the ovaries release only one ovum per month, but sometimes two or more ova are released.) Dizygotic twins, like any other siblings, have half their genes in common. Their phenotypes may differ in obvious ways (about half are male/female pairs) or they can look quite similar, again like other siblings.

The tendency to ovulate more than one ovum is influenced by genes, so if a woman has one set of twins, she is more likely to have another set (Painter et al., 2010). Her daughters also have a 50/50 chance of inheriting her twin-producing X. A son from that family is not particularly likely to have twins because he is not the one who ovulates, but his daughter is, because she has an X from his mother, and half the time it happens to be the multiple-ovulation X.

Genetic Interactions

No gene functions alone. Thus almost every trait is polygenic (affected by many genes) and multifactorial (influenced by many factors). Almost daily, researchers describe new complexities in polygenic and multifactorial interaction. It is apparent that "phenotypic variation … results from multiple interactions among numerous genetic and environmental factors" (Nadeau & Dudley, 2011, p. 1015). Here we describe a few of the complexities that occur at conception.

Some genes are **additive genes.** Their effects *add up* to make the phenotype. When genes interact additively, the phenotype reflects all the genes that are involved. Height, hair curliness, and skin colour, for instance, are influenced by additive genes. Indeed, height is probably influenced by 180 genes, each contributing a very small amount (Enserink, 2011).

Less common are *non-additive* genes, which do not contribute equal shares. In one non-additive form of heredity, alleles interact in a **dominant–recessive pattern,** in which one allele, the *dominant gene,* is far more influential than the other, the *recessive gene.* When someone inherits a recessive gene that is not expressed in the phenotype, that person is said to be a **carrier** of that gene: The recessive gene is *carried* on the genotype.

Most recessive genes are harmless. For example, blue eyes are determined by a recessive allele and brown eyes by a dominant one, which means that a child conceived by a blue-eyed person and a brown-eyed person will usually have brown eyes. "Usually" is accurate, because sometimes a brown-eyed person is a carrier of the blue-eye gene. In that case, in a blue-eye/brown-eye couple, every child will have at least one blue-eye gene (from the blue-eyed parent) and has a 50/50 chance of having another blue-eye gene (from the other parent) (see Figure 2.4).

It is also possible for both parents to be carriers, and then their children have one chance in four to inherit the recessive gene from both parents. The complexity of dominant–recessive inheritance is also evident in blood type.

dizygotic twins

Twins who are formed when two separate ova are fertilized by two separate sperm at roughly the same time. (Also called *fraternal twins.*)

additive gene

A gene that adds something to some aspect of the phenotype. Its contribution depends on additions from the other genes, which may come from either the same or the other parent.

dominant–recessive pattern

The interaction of a pair of alleles in such a way that the phenotype reveals the influence of one allele (the dominant gene) more than that of the other (the recessive gene).

carrier

A person whose genotype includes a gene that is not expressed in the phenotype. Such an unexpressed gene occurs in half the carrier's gametes and thus is passed on to half the carrier's children, who will most likely be carriers, too. Generally, the characteristic appears in the phenotype only when such a gene is inherited from both parents.

Like Mother, Like Daughter?

Shyness is inherited, but since this mother seems not to have the gene, her daughter must have inherited this trait from her father—unless nurture has taught the mother to be outgoing and the daughter to be shy.

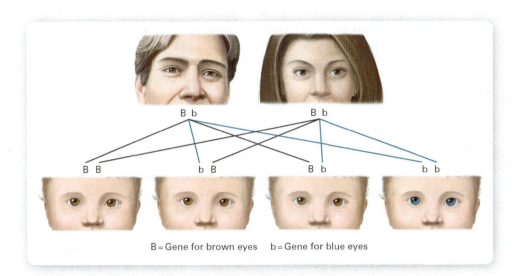

FIGURE 2.4 Recessive Genes
If two brown-eyed parents both carry the blue-eye gene, they have one chance in four of having a blue-eyed child. Other recessive genes include those for red hair, Rh-negative blood, and many genetic diseases.

B = Gene for brown eyes   b = Gene for blue eyes

It is quite possible for a child's blood type to be unlike either parent's, even though the interactions of their genotypes produced it.

A special case of the dominant–recessive pattern occurs with genes that are **X-linked** (located on the X chromosome). If an X-linked gene is recessive—as are the genes for most forms of colour-blindness, many allergies, several diseases (including hemophilia and Duchenne muscular dystrophy), and some learning disabilities—the fact that it is on the X chromosome is critical (see Table 2.1).

Since the Y chromosome is much smaller than the X chromosome, an X-linked recessive gene almost never has a dominant counterpart on the Y. Therefore, recessive traits carried on the X chromosome affect the phenotypes of sons more often than those of daughters because the daughters are protected by their other X chromosome, which usually will have the dominant gene. This explains why males with an X-linked disorder inherited it from their mothers, not their fathers. Thanks to

X-linked
A gene carried on the X chromosome. If a male inherits an X-linked recessive trait from his mother, he expresses that trait because the Y from his father has no counteracting gene. Females are more likely to be carriers of X-linked traits but are less likely to express them.

✦ **ESPECIALLY FOR Future Parents**
Suppose you wanted your daughters to be short and your sons to be tall. Could you achieve that? (see response, page 58) →

RESPONSE FOR Biologists (from page 54) Only one of the 48 human chromosomes determines sex, and the genitals develop last in the prenatal sequence. Sex differences are apparent before birth, but they are relatively minor. ●

TABLE 2.1 The 23rd Pair and X-Linked Colour Blindness

23rd Pair	Phenotype	Genotype	Next Generation
1. XX	Normal woman	Not a carrier	No colour blindness from mother
2. XY	Normal man	Normal X from mother	No colour blindness from father
3. XX	Normal woman	Carrier from father	Half her children will inherit her X. The girls with her X will be carriers; the boys with her X will be colour-blind.
4. XX	Normal woman	Carrier from mother	Half her children will inherit her X. The girls with her X will be carriers; the boys with her X will be colour-blind.
5. XY	Colour-blind man	Inherited from mother	All his daughters will have his X. None of his sons will have his X. All his children will have normal vision, unless their mother also had an X for colour blindness.
6. XX	Colour-blind woman (rare)	Inherited from both parents	Every child will have one X from her. Therefore, every son will be colour-blind. Daughters will be only carriers, unless they also inherit an X from the father, as their mother did.

ANSWER TO **OBSERVATION QUIZ**
(from page 54) The Chinese girls are the monozygotic twins. If you were not sure, look at their eyebrows, their nose, and the shapes of their faces, compared with the boys' head shapes and personality. ●

their mothers, and because of their own Y chromosome, 20 times more boys than girls are colour-blind (McIntyre, 2002).

Thousands of disabilities begin with genes and chromosomes, as described at the end of this chapter. First, however, we consider the more usual case: the development of a healthy embryo, fetus, and baby.

KEY ℘oints

- Each person's 46 chromosomes and 20 000 or so genes are inherited from his or her parents, with diversity and commonality part of the process.
- The 23rd pair of chromosomes produces a male (XY) or female (XX), with the father's gamete the determining factor.
- Monozygotic twins are genetically identical, and dizygotic twins share only half of their genes, like other siblings.
- Genes interact with each other in an additive or dominant–recessive manner, always affected by epigenetic factors.

From Zygote to Newborn

The most dramatic and extensive transformation of the entire life span occurs before birth. To make it easier to study, prenatal development is often divided into three main periods. The first two weeks are called the **germinal period;** the third through the eighth week is the **embryonic period;** the ninth week until birth is the **fetal period** (see Table 2.2 for alternative terms).

Germinal: The First 14 Days

Within hours after conception, the zygote begins *duplication* and *division*. First, the 23 pairs of chromosomes carrying all the genes duplicate, forming two complete sets of the genome. These two sets move toward opposite sides of the zygote, and the

germinal period
The first two weeks of prenatal development after conception, characterized by rapid cell division and the beginning of cell differentiation.

embryonic period
The stage of prenatal development from approximately the third through the eighth week after conception, during which the basic forms of all body structures, including internal organs, develop.

fetal period
The stage of prenatal development from the ninth week after conception until birth, during which the fetus grows in size and matures in functioning.

RESPONSE FOR Future Parents
(from page 57) Yes, but you wouldn't want to. You would have to choose one mate with whom to conceive your sons, and another for your daughters, and you would have to use sex-selection methods. Even so, it might not work, given all the genes of your genotype. More importantly, the effort would be unethical, unnatural, and possibly illegal. ●

TABLE 2.2 Timing and Terminology

Popular and professional books use various phrases to segment pregnancy. The following comments may help clarify the phrases used.

- *Beginning of pregnancy:* Pregnancy begins at conception, which is also the starting point of *gestational age*. However, the organism does not become an embryo until about two weeks later, and pregnancy does not affect the woman (and cannot be confirmed by blood or urine testing) until implantation. Paradoxically, many obstetricians date the onset of pregnancy from the date of the woman's last menstrual period (LMP), about 14 days *before* conception.

- *Length of pregnancy:* Full-term pregnancies last 266 days, or 38 weeks, or 9 months. If the LMP is used as the starting time, pregnancy lasts 40 weeks, sometimes referred to as 10 lunar months (a lunar month is 28 days long).

- *Trimesters:* Instead of *germinal period, embryonic period,* and *fetal period,* some writers divide pregnancy into three-month periods called *trimesters*. Months 1, 2, and 3 are called the *first trimester;* months 4, 5, and 6, the *second trimester;* and months 7, 8, and 9, the *third trimester.*

- *Due date:* Although doctors assign a specific due date (based on the woman's LMP), only 5 percent of babies are born on that exact date. Babies born between three weeks before and two weeks after that date are considered "full term" or "on time." Babies born earlier are called *preterm;* babies born later are called *post-term.* The words *preterm* and *post-term* are more accurate than *premature* and *post-mature.*

(a)

(b)

(c)

ALL ANATOMICAL TRAVELOGUE / SCIENCE SOURCE

First Stages of the Germinal Period The original zygote divides into *(a)* two cells, *(b)* four cells, and then *(c)* eight cells. Occasionally at this early stage, the cells separate completely, forming the beginning of monozygotic twins, quadruplets, or octuplets.

single cell splits neatly down the middle into two cells, each containing the original genetic code. These two cells duplicate and divide, becoming four, which themselves duplicate and divide, becoming eight, and so on. If the two-celled organism is artificially split apart and each of those two separated cells is allowed to develop (illegal for humans, successful with mice), that creates monozygotic twins. Every cell of both would have the same DNA.

Those first cells are **stem cells,** able to direct production of any other cell and thus to become a complete person. After about the eight-cell stage, duplication and division continue but a third process, *differentiation,* begins. Soon cells specialize, taking different forms and reproducing at various rates, depending on where they are located. They are no longer omnipotent stem cells (some cells in adults can also take on other functions, but they are not nearly as adaptable as early stem cells) (Slack, 2012). For instance, even though every cell carries the complete code, differentiation means that some cells become part of an eye, others part of a finger, still others part of the brain. As one expert explains, "We are sitting with parts of our body that could have been used for thinking" (Gottlieb, 1992/2002, p. 172).

About a week after conception, the multiplying cells (now numbering more than 100) separate into two distinct masses. The outer cells form a shell that will become the *placenta* (the organ that surrounds and protects the developing creature), and the inner cells form a nucleus that will become the embryo.

The first task of the outer cells is **implantation**—that is, to embed themselves in the nurturing lining of the uterus. This is far from automatic; about 50 percent of natural conceptions and an even larger percentage of in vitro conceptions never implant (see Table 2.3). Most new life ends before an embryo begins (Sadler, 2012).

stem cells
Cells from which any other specialized type of cell can form.

implantation
The process, beginning about 10 days after conception, in which the developing organism burrows into the tissue that lines the uterus, where it can be nourished and protected as it continues to develop.

embryo
The name for a developing human organism from about the third through the eighth week after conception.

Embryo: From the Third Through the Eighth Week

The start of the third week after conception initiates the *embryonic period,* during which the formless mass of cells becomes a distinct being—not yet recognizably human but worthy of a new name, **embryo.** (The word *embryo* is often used loosely, but each stage of development has a particular name; here, embryo refers to the developing human from day 14 to day 56.)

TABLE 2.3 Vulnerability During Prenatal Development

The Germinal Period
An estimated 60 percent of all zygotes do not grow or implant properly and thus do not survive the germinal period. Many of these organisms are abnormal; few women realize they were pregnant.

The Embryonic Period
About 20 percent of all embryos are aborted spontaneously, most often because of chromosomal abnormalities. This is usually called an early miscarriage.

The Fetal Period
About 5 percent of all fetuses are aborted spontaneously before viability at 22 weeks or are stillborn, defined as born dead after 22 weeks. This is much more common in developing nations.

Birth
Because of all these factors, only about 31 percent of all zygotes grow and survive to become living newborn babies. Age is crucial. One estimate is that less than 3 percent of all conceptions after age 40 result in live births.

Sources: Bentley & Mascie-Taylor, 2000; Corda et al., 2012; Laurino et al., 2005.

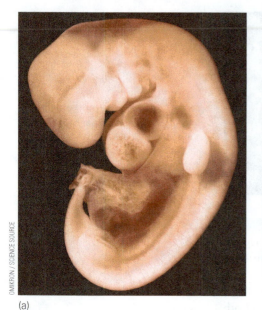

OMIKRON / SCIENCE SOURCE

(a)

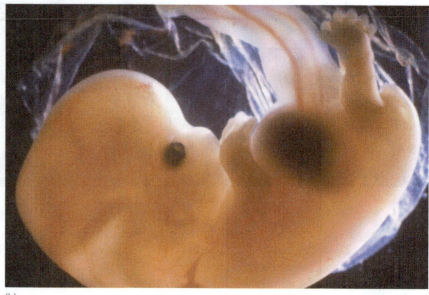

PETIT FORMAT / SCIENCE SOURCE

(b)

The Embryonic Period *(a)* At 4 weeks past conception, the embryo is only about 3 millimetres long, but already the head has taken shape. *(b)* By 7 weeks, the organism is about 2½ centimetres long. Eyes, nose, the digestive system, and even the first stage of finger and toe formation can be seen.

fetus
The name for a developing human organism from the start of the ninth week after conception until birth.

ultrasound
An image of a fetus (or an internal organ) produced by using high-frequency sound waves. (Also called *sonogram*.)

There's Your Baby For many parents, their first glimpse of their future child is an ultrasound image. This is Alice Morgan, 63 days before birth.

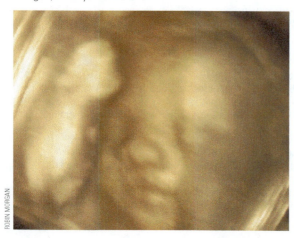

ROBIN MORGAN

At about day 14, a thin line (called the *primitive streak*) appears down the middle of the embryo, becoming the neural tube 22 days after conception and eventually developing into the central nervous system, brain, and spinal column (Sadler, 2012). The head appears in the fourth week, as eyes, ears, nose, and mouth start to form. Also in the fourth week, a minuscule blood vessel that will become the heart begins to pulsate.

By the fifth week, buds that will become arms and legs emerge. The upper arms and then forearms, palms, and webbed fingers grow. Legs, knees, feet, and webbed toes, in that order, are apparent a few days later, each having the beginning of a skeletal structure. Then, 52 and 54 days after conception, respectively, the fingers and toes separate (Sadler, 2012).

As you can see, prenatally, the head develops first, in a *cephalocaudal* (literally, "head-to-tail") pattern, and the extremities form last, in a *proximodistal* (literally, "near-to-far") pattern. This is true for all living creatures, part of universal genetic instructions.

At the end of the eighth week after conception (56 days), the embryo weighs just 1 gram and is about 2½ centimetres long. It has all the organs and body parts (except sex organs) of a human being, including elbows and knees. It moves frequently, about 150 times per hour, but such movement is random and imperceptible to the mother, who may not even realize that she is pregnant.

Fetus: From the Ninth Week Until Birth

The organism is called a **fetus** from the ninth week after conception until birth. The fetal period encompasses dramatic change, from a tiny, sexless creature smaller than the final joint of your thumb to a boy or girl about 51 centimetres long.

In the ninth week, sex organs develop, soon visible via **ultrasound** (also called *sonogram*). The male fetus experiences a rush of the hormone testosterone, affecting the brain (Morris et al., 2004; Neave, 2008).

By 3 months, the fetus weighs about 87 grams and is about 7.5 centimetres long. Of course, fetal growth rates do vary—some 3-month-old fetuses do not quite weigh 80 grams and others already weigh 100.

As prenatal growth continues, the cardiovascular, digestive, and excretory systems develop. The brain increases about six times in size from the fourth to the sixth month, developing many new neurons (*neurogenesis*) and synapses (*synaptogenesis*). Indeed, up to half a million brain cells per minute are created at peak growth during mid-pregnancy (Dowling, 2004).

This brain growth is critical because it enables regulation of all the body functions, including breathing (Johnson, 2010). That allows the fetus to reach the **age of viability,** when a preterm newborn might survive. Thanks to intensive medical care, the age of viability decreased dramatically in the twentieth century, but it now seems stuck at about 22 weeks (Pignotti, 2010) because even the most advanced technology cannot maintain life without some brain response.

According to an international report published in 2012, Canada has a preterm birth rate of almost 8 percent, while the U.S. rate is 12 percent, the worst among G8 countries (Howson et al., 2012). Canada's preterm birth rate has increased almost 25 percent from the early 1990s, when it stood at 6.5 percent (Canadian Institute for Health Information, 2009). Reasons for the increase include the greater number of older women who are having babies and the rise in rates of multiple pregnancies, often the result of taking fertility drugs. Other factors include increased rates of obesity, which can lead to high blood pressure and diabetes, and more cases of medically induced labour and Caesarean sections before pregnancies reach full term (Howson et al., 2012).

As the brain matures and the *axons,* or nerve fibres, connect, the organs of the body begin to work in harmony, fetal movement as well as heart rate quiet down during rest, and the heart beats faster during activity (which may be when the mother is trying to sleep).

Attaining the age of viability simply means that life outside the womb is *possible* (see Figure 2.5). Each day of the final three months improves the odds, not only of survival but also of life without disability (Iacovidou et al., 2010). A preterm infant born in the seventh month is a tiny creature requiring intensive care for each gram of nourishment and every shallow breath. The care and complications of preterm infants (especially conditions associated with low birth weight) are discussed at the end of this chapter. Usually, however, full-term infants are ready to thrive at home on the mother's milk—no expert help, oxygenated air, or special feeding required. The fetus typically gains at least 2.1 kilograms in the third trimester, increasing to about 3.4 kilograms at birth (see At About This Time).

By full term, human brain growth is so extensive that the *cortex* (the brain's advanced outer layers) forms several folds in order to fit into the skull (see Figure 2.6). Although some large

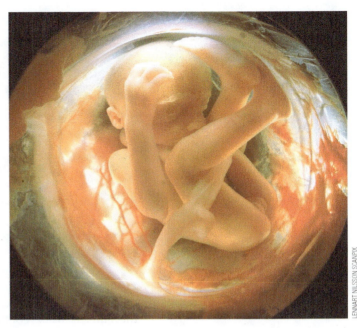

LENNART NILSSON SCANPIX

Viability This fetus is in mid-pregnancy, a few weeks shy of viability. As you can see, the body is completely formed. Unseen is the extent of brain and lung development, which will take at least another month to become sufficiently mature to allow for survival.

age of viability
The age (about 22 weeks after conception) at which a fetus may survive outside the mother's uterus if specialized medical care is available.

FIGURE 2.5 **Each Critical Day** Even with advanced medical care, survival of extremely preterm newborns is in doubt. These data come from a thousand births in Sweden, where prenatal care is free and easily obtained. As you can see, the age of viability (22 weeks) means only that an infant might survive, not that it will. By full term (not shown), the survival rate is almost 100 percent.

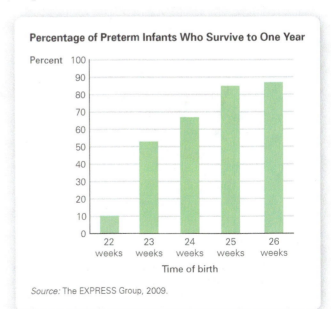

Percentage of Preterm Infants Who Survive to One Year

Source: The EXPRESS Group, 2009.

One of the Tiniest Rumaisa Rahman was born after 26 weeks and 6 days, weighing only 244 grams. Nevertheless, she has a good chance of living a full, normal life. Rumaisa gained 2270 grams in the hospital and then, six months after her birth, went home. Her twin sister, Hiba, who weighed 590 grams at birth, had gone home two months earlier. At their one-year birthday, the twins seemed normal, with Rumaisa weighing 6800 grams and Hiba 7711 grams (CBS News, 2005).

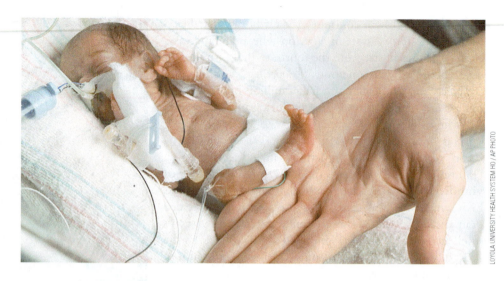

mammals (whales, for instance) have bigger brains than humans (although not bigger in relation to one's size), no other creature needs as many folds as humans do, because the human cortex contains much more material than the brains of non-humans. Those mammals that have bigger brains than humans also have far bigger bodies: Proportionally, human brains are largest.

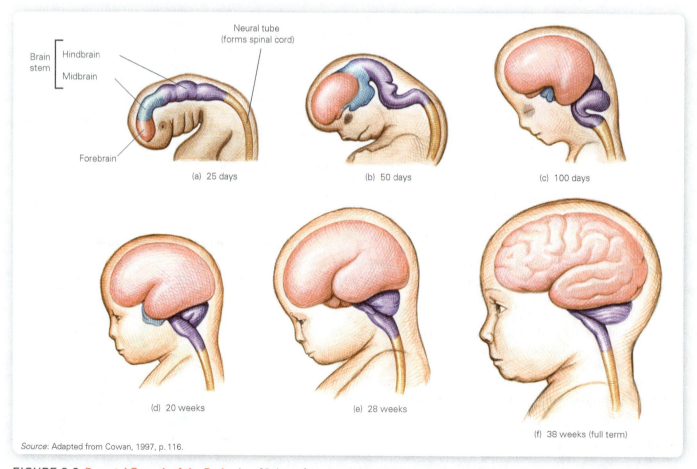

Source: Adapted from Cowan, 1997, p. 116.

FIGURE 2.6 Prenatal Growth of the Brain Just 25 days after conception (a), the central nervous system is already evident. The brain looks distinctly human by day 100 (c). By the 28th week of gestation (e), at the very time brain activity begins, the various sections of the brain are recognizable. When the fetus is full term (f), all the parts of the brain, including the cortex (the outer layers), are formed, folding over one another and becoming more convoluted, or wrinkled, as the number of brain cells increases.

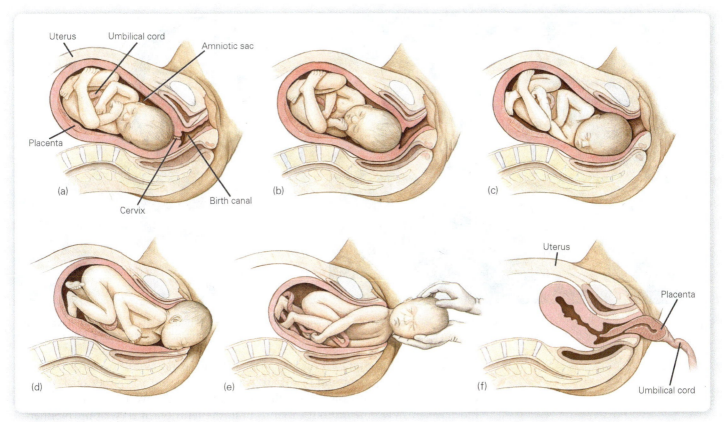

FIGURE 2.7 A Normal, Uncomplicated Birth (a) The baby's position as the birth process begins. (b) The first stage of labour: The cervix dilates to allow passage of the baby's head. (c) Transition: The baby's head moves into the "birth canal," the vagina. (d) The second stage of labour: The baby's head moves through the opening of the vagina ("crowns") and (e) emerges completely, followed by the rest of the body about a minute later. (f) The third stage of labour is the expulsion of the placenta. This usually occurs naturally, but it is crucial that the whole placenta be expelled, so birth attendants check carefully. In some cultures, the placenta is ceremonially buried, to commemorate the life-giving role it plays.

Finally, a Baby

About 38 weeks (266 days) after conception, the fetal brain signals the release of hormones, specifically *oxytocin*, which prepares the fetus for delivery and starts labour. The average baby is born after 12 hours of active labour for first births and 7 hours for subsequent births (Moore & Persaud, 2003), although labour may take twice or half as long. The definition of "active" labour varies, which is one reason some women believe they are in active labour for days and others say 10 minutes. (Figure 2.7 shows the stages of birth.)

Women's birthing positions also vary—sitting, squatting, lying down. Some women give birth while immersed in warm water, which helps the woman relax (the fetus continues to get oxygen via the umbilical cord). However, some physicians believe water births increase the rate of infection, and the underwater emergence of the head is difficult for the medical team to monitor (Tracy, 2009).

AT ABOUT THIS TIME
Average Prenatal Weights*

Period of Development	Weeks Past Conception	Average Weight	Notes
End of embryonic period	8	1 g	Most common time for spontaneous abortion (miscarriage).
End of first trimester	13	85 g	
At viability (50/50 chance of survival)	22–25	565–900 g	A birth weight less than 1000 g is extremely low birth weight (ELBW).
End of second trimester	26–28	900–1400 g	Less than 1500 g is very low birth weight (VLBW).
End of preterm period	35	2500 g	Less than 2500 g is low birth weight (LBW).
Full term	38	3400 g	Between 2500 and 4000 g is considered normal weight.

*Actual weights vary. For instance, normal full-term infants weigh between 2500 and 4000 grams; viable preterm newborns, especially twins or triplets, weigh less than shown here.

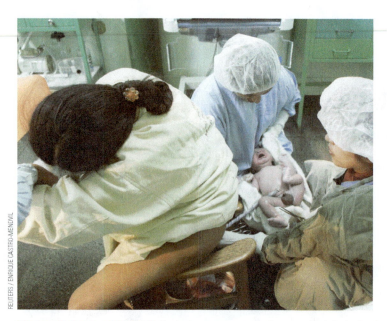

Choice, Culture, or Cohort? Both these women (in Peru on the left, in England on the right) chose methods of labour that are not typical in Canada, where birthing stools and birthing pools are uncommon. In both nations, most births occur in hospitals—a rare choice a century ago.

Preferences and opinions on birthing positions (as on almost every other aspect of prenatal development and birth) are partly cultural and partly personal. In general, physicians find it easier to see the head emerge if the woman lies on her back. However, many women find it easier to push the fetus out if they sit up. Neither of these generalities is true for every individual.

THE NEWBORN'S FIRST MINUTES Newborns usually breathe and cry on their own. Between spontaneous cries, the first breaths of air bring oxygen to the lungs and blood, and the infant's colour changes from bluish to pinkish. (Pinkish refers to blood colour, visible beneath the skin, and applies to newborns of all hues.) Eyes open wide; tiny fingers grab; even tinier toes stretch and retract. The full-term baby is instantly, zestfully, ready for life.

One assessment of newborn health is the **Apgar scale** (see Table 2.4), first developed by Dr. Virginia Apgar. When she earned her MD in 1933, Apgar wanted to work in a hospital but was told that only men did surgery. Consequently, she became an anesthesiologist. Apgar saw that "delivery room doctors focused on mothers and paid little attention to babies. Those who were small and struggling were often left to die" (Beck, 2009, p. D-1). To save those young lives, Apgar developed a simple rating scale of five vital signs—colour, heart rate, cry, muscle tone, and breathing—to alert doctors when a newborn was in crisis.

Apgar scale
A quick assessment of a newborn's body functioning. The baby's heart rate, respiratory effort, muscle tone, colour, and reflexes are given a score of 0, 1, or 2 twice—at one minute and five minutes after birth—and each time the total of all five scores is compared with the ideal score of 10 (which is rarely attained).

TABLE 2.4 Criteria and Scoring of the Apgar Scale

	Five Vital Signs				
Score	Colour	Heartbeat	Reflex Irritability	Muscle Tone	Respiratory Effort
0	Blue, pale	Absent	No response	Flaccid, limp	Absent
1	Body pink, extremities blue	Slow (below 100)	Grimace	Weak, inactive	Irregular, slow
2	Entirely pink	Rapid (over 100)	Coughing, sneezing, crying	Strong, active	Good; baby is crying

Source: Apgar, 1953.

Since 1950, birth attendants worldwide have used the Apgar (often using the name as an acronym: Appearance, Pulse, Grimace, Activity, and Respiration) at one minute and again at five minutes after birth, assigning each vital sign a score of 0, 1, or 2. If the five-minute Apgar is 7 or higher, all is well.

MEDICAL ASSISTANCE AT BIRTH The specifics of birth depend on the parents' preparation, the position and size of the fetus, and the customs of the culture. In developed nations, births almost always include sterile procedures, electronic monitoring, and drugs to dull pain or speed contractions. In addition, many aspects of birth depend on who delivers the baby—doctor, midwife, or the parents themselves.

Midwives are as skilled at delivering babies as physicians, but in most nations only medical doctors perform surgery, such as **Caesarean sections (C-sections)**, whereby the fetus is removed through incisions in the mother's abdomen. A new endeavour in Africa to teach midwives to perform Caesareans is projected to save a million lives per year.

Caesareans are usually safe for mother and baby and have many advantages for hospitals (easier to schedule, quicker, and more expensive than vaginal deliveries, which means that hospitals make more money on C-sections), but they also bring more complications after birth and reduce breastfeeding (Malloy, 2009). Given that, it is not surprising that Caesareans are controversial. The World Health Organization (WHO) suggests that they are medically indicated in 15 percent of births. In some nations there are far fewer than that; in others, many more (see Figure 2.8).

According to the Canadian Institute for Health Information (CIHI), there are no agreed-upon benchmarks for conducting C-sections on mothers in Canada (CIHI, 2010). From 2008 to 2009, the national rate of C-sections stood at 26 percent, well above the WHO-recommended rate of 15 percent, and there has been a 45 percent increase since 1998. Such figures inevitably raise questions about the appropriateness of the care mothers are receiving. Are Canadian doctors performing too many Caesareans? If so, is this putting mothers and/or infants at risk?

For reasons nobody quite understands, C-section rates vary widely by region across Canada. For instance, in Manitoba in 2008–2009, the rate was 11 points lower (14 percent) than the national rate. CIHI has calculated that if all the provinces' rates for primary C-sections, or C-sections for first-time mothers, were similar to Manitoba's, 16 200 fewer Caesareans would be performed across Canada. This would represent a potential annual savings of $36 million in acute care services (CIHI, 2010).

Examining the rates in other countries, China's rate of Caesareans increased from 5 percent in 1991 to 46 percent in 2008 (Guo et al., 2007; Juan, 2010). In the United States, the rate rose every year between 1996 and 2009 (from 21 percent to 34 percent, with notable state variations, from 22 percent in Utah to 39 percent in Florida) (Menacker & Hamilton, 2010).

Less studied is the *epidural,* an injection in a particular part of the spine of the labouring woman to alleviate pain. Epidurals are often used in hospital births, but they increase the rate of Caesarean sections and decrease the readiness of newborn infants to suck immediately after birth (Bell et al., 2010).

Caesarean section (C-section)
A surgical birth, in which incisions through the mother's abdomen and uterus allow the fetus to be removed quickly, instead of being delivered through the vagina.

FIGURE 2.8 Too Many Caesareans or Too Few? Rates of Caesarean deliveries vary widely from nation to nation. Aside from China, Latin America has the highest rates in the world (note that 40 percent of all births in Chile are by Caesarean), and sub-Saharan Africa has the lowest rates (the rate in Chad is less than half of 1 percent). The underlying issue is whether some women who should have Caesareans do not get them, while other women have unnecessary Caesareans.

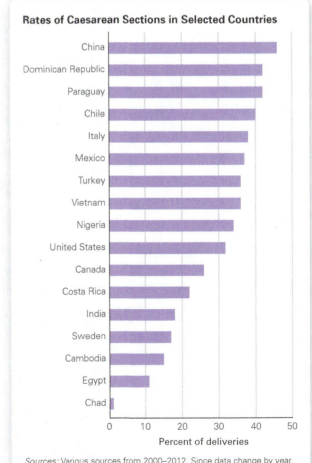

Rates of Caesarean Sections in Selected Countries

Sources: Various sources from 2000–2012. Since data change by year and sources provide different rates, this chart is approximate.

From Day One For various reasons, some countries have much higher rates of Caesarean deliveries than others. This new mother in Brazil, which has a high C-section rate, has safely delivered her baby and, with the encouragement of the hospital, is breastfeeding him from the very beginning.

Another medical intervention is *induced labour,* in which labour is started, speeded, or strengthened with a drug. The rate of induced labour in many developed nations has more than doubled since 1990, up to 20 to 25 percent. The reasons are sometimes medically warranted (such as when a woman develops eclampsia, which could kill the fetus) and sometimes not (Grivell et al., 2012). Induction increases the rate of complications, including the need for Caesareans.

ALTERNATIVES TO HOSPITAL TECHNOLOGY Questions of costs and benefits abound. For instance, C-section and epidural rates vary more by doctor, hospital, day of the week, and region than by medical circumstances. This is partly an economic issue; in the United States, the C-section rate increases when the birth is fully covered by insurance. But it also is true in Sweden, where obstetric care is paid for by the government (Schytt & Walderenström, 2010).

Most Canadian births now take place in hospital labour rooms with high-tech facilities and equipment nearby. In 2011, 98.4 percent of Canadian births were hospital births, while 1.6 percent were non-hospital births, for example, in *birthing centres* or at home (Statistics Canada, 2013j). Some home births were planned while others were unexpected because labour was too quick. The latter situation is hazardous if no one is nearby to rescue a newborn in distress (Tracy, 2009).

In some European nations, many births occur at home by plan (30 percent in the Netherlands). In Europe, home births have fewer complications than in hospitals—perhaps because pregnant women requesting home births are screened to disallow those at risk (such as an older woman having twins), or perhaps because the women are more relaxed at home. In the Netherlands, special ambulances called *flying storks* speed mothers and newborns to hospitals if needed. Dutch research finds home births better for mothers and no worse for infants than hospital births (de Jonge et al., 2009).

In most hospitals in the twentieth century, women giving birth laboured alone. Fathers and other family members were kept away and only doctors and nurses attended the birth. No longer. Almost everyone now agrees that other people should always be with a labouring woman. Relatives or friends are often present, midwives have often replaced doctors, and sometimes a **doula** provides practical as well as emotional support for the mother and other family members. Many studies have found that doulas benefit anyone giving birth, rich or poor, married or not (Vonderheid et al., 2011). For example, in one study 420 middle-class married women who arrived at a hospital in labour with their husbands were randomly assigned a doula or not. Those with doulas had fewer Caesareans (13 versus 25 percent) or epidurals (65 versus 76 percent) (McGrath & Kennell, 2008).

In Canada, women can also make use of a licensed midwife instead of an obstetrician. Besides assisting at a baby's birth, midwives provide various other services, including physical examinations and screening tests. They work in partnership with other health professionals. In 2009, midwives attended about 10 percent of all births in Ontario, and 20 percent of those births occurred at home (College of Midwives of Ontario, n.d.).

The New Family

The fact that mothers are now less lonely during labour stems in part from the recognition that people are social creatures, seeking support from their families and their societies. Birth marks the beginning of a new family; ideally, each family member—newborn, mother, and father—shares the experience.

THE NEWBORN Before birth, developing humans already contribute to their families via fetal movements and hormones that cause protective impulses in the mother early in pregnancy and nurturing impulses at the end (Konner, 2010). The appearance of the newborn (big hairless head, tiny feet, and so on) stirs the human heart, as is evident in adults' brain activity and heart rates when they see a baby.

Newborns are responsive social creatures, listening, staring, sucking, and cuddling. In the first day or two after birth, a professional might administer the **Brazelton Neonatal Behavioral Assessment Scale (NBAS),** which records 46 behaviours, including 20 reflexes. Parents watching the NBAS are amazed at their newborn's competence—and this fosters early parent–child connection (Hawthorne, 2009). Technically, a **reflex** is an involuntary response to a particular stimulus. Humans of every age reflexively seek to protect themselves (the eye blink is an example). The speed and strength of reflexes varies, even among newborns, who have three sets of protective reflexes:

- *Reflexes that maintain oxygen supply.* The *breathing reflex* begins even before the umbilical cord, with its supply of oxygen, is cut. Additional reflexes that maintain oxygen are reflexive *hiccups* and *sneezes,* as well as *thrashing* (moving the arms and legs about) to escape something that covers the face.

- *Reflexes that maintain constant body temperature.* When infants are cold, they *cry, shiver,* and *tuck their legs* close to their bodies. When they are hot, they try to *push away* blankets and then stay still.

- *Reflexes that manage feeding.* The *sucking reflex* causes newborns to suck anything that touches their lips—fingers, toes, blankets, and rattles, as well as natural and artificial nipples of various textures and shapes. The *rooting reflex* causes babies to turn their mouths toward anything that brushes against their cheeks—a reflexive search for a nipple—and start to suck. *Swallowing* is another reflex that aids feeding, as is *crying* when the stomach is empty and *spitting up* when full.

Each of these 13 reflexes (in italics) normally causes a caregiving reaction, as the new parents do what seems necessary to protect their newborn. Thus reflexes affect human interaction. In addition, newborn senses are also responsive to people: New

doula
A woman who helps with the birth process. Doulas are trained to offer support to new mothers, including massage and suggestions for breast-feeding positions.

Brazelton Neonatal Behavioral Assessment Scale (NBAS)
A test often administered to newborns that measures responsiveness and records 46 behaviours, including 20 reflexes.

reflex
An unlearned, involuntary action or movement in response to a stimulus. A reflex occurs without conscious thought.

Never Underestimate the Power of a Reflex
For developmentalists, newborn reflexes are mechanisms for survival, indicators of brain maturation, and vestiges of evolutionary history. For family members, they are mostly delightful and sometimes amazing. Both of these viewpoints are demonstrated by star performer Wyatt, who was born on March 1, 2013 in Brampton, Ontario. He is seen here sucking peacefully on his finger; grasping the finger of his big sister, Nicole; and stepping eagerly forward on legs too tiny to support his body.

babies listen more to voices than to traffic, for instance, and they stare at faces more than at machines. Typically, when a baby stares at a new parent, the parent talks and the baby listens.

couvade
Symptoms of pregnancy and birth experienced by fathers.

A Good Beginning The joy and bonding between this expectant couple and their unborn child is a wonderful sign. Their alliance is crucial for the healthy social and emotional development of their child.

NEW FATHERS From conception on, fathers' involvement in their children's lives is vitally important and has a strong impact on children's development. Fathers-to-be help mothers-to-be stay healthy, nourished, and drug-free. They are present at ultrasounds and they help with the labour and birth. Some fathers-to-be even have their own biological and psychological experiences with pregnancy and birth, in a condition known as **couvade.** For example, levels of stress hormones correlate between expectant fathers and mothers, probably because they reflect each others' emotions (Berg & Wynne-Edwards, 2002). Beyond that, many fathers experience weight gain and indigestion during pregnancy and pain during labour. Indeed, among some Latin American indigenous peoples, fathers go through the motions of labour when their wives do, to help ensure an easy birth.

After their children's birth, fathers are involved in the day-to-day care of their infants. This active involvement—a shift from the days when a father's main role was as breadwinner—can partially be explained by the less traditional division of roles and responsibilities of mothers and fathers, including the increased participation of women in the labour force, and by fathers' wanting to be closer to their children (Beaupré et al., 2010). In addition, some researchers suspect that a general cultural shift and changing attitudes toward parenting roles is partly responsible for the greater number of fathers who are primary caregivers to their children (Marshall, 2008).

In Canada, fathers' increased use of paid parental leave from work is evidence of their increased involvement in the care of their children. In 2000, only 3 percent of eligible Canadian fathers took this time off, but by 2006 the rate had increased to 20 percent. A large part of the increase was due to rule changes, especially in Quebec where the provincial government instituted a "daddy days" policy that allows for up to five weeks of paid paternal leave that cannot be transferred to the mother.

The move away from traditional parenting roles is evident among European-Canadians as well as among the country's immigrant communities. For example, one recent study found that Chinese-Canadian fathers are actively involved in rearing their young children, and their direct involvement ranges from playing with and caring for their infants and toddlers to cooperating with mothers on making decisions about child care (Chuang & Su, 2009).

NEW MOTHERS About half of all women experience physical problems after giving birth, such as incisions from a C-section, painfully sore nipples, or problems with urination (Danel et al., 2003). However, worse than any physical problems are psychological ones. When the birth hormones decrease, between 8 and 15 percent of women experience **postpartum depression,** a sense of inadequacy and sadness (called *baby blues* in the mild version and *postpartum psychosis* in the most severe form) (Perfetti et al., 2004). With postpartum depression, baby care (feeding, diapering, bathing) feels very burdensome.

Sometimes the first sign that something is amiss is that the mother is euphoric after birth. She cannot sleep, stop talking, or keep from worrying about the newborn. Some of this is normal, but family members and medical personnel need to be alert, as a crash might follow the high.

Maternal depression can have a long-term impact on the child, one of the many reasons why postpartum depression should be quickly recognized and treated. Fathers are usually the first responders; they may be instrumental in getting the help the mother and baby need (Cuijpers et al., 2008; Goodman & Gotlib, 2002). This is easier said than done. Fathers may become depressed as well; in such cases, other people need to step in.

From a developmental perspective, causes of postpartum depression (such as marital problems) sometimes predate pregnancy; others (such as financial stress) occur during pregnancy; others correlate with birth (especially if the mother is alone); and still others (health, feeding, or sleeping problems) are specific to the particular infant. Successful breastfeeding may mitigate maternal depression, in part by increasing levels of oxytocin, a bonding hormone. This is one of the many reasons a lactation counsellor (who helps with breastfeeding techniques) may be a crucial member of the new mother's support team.

BONDING The active involvement of both parents in pregnancy, birth, and newborn care helps establish the **parent–infant bond,** the strong, loving connection that forms as parents hold, examine, and feed their newborn. Factors that encourage parents (biological or adoptive) to nurture their newborns have lifelong benefits, proven with mice, monkeys, and humans (Champagne & Curley, 2010).

Early skin-to-skin contact, which was welcomed a few decades ago because it reduced the impersonal medicalization of hospital births, helps establish this bond. The importance of this contact has recently become apparent with **kangaroo care,** in which the newborn lies between the mother's breasts, skin-to-skin, listening to her heartbeat and feeling her body heat. Many studies find that kangaroo-care newborns sleep more deeply, gain weight more quickly, and spend more time alert than do infants with standard care (Ludington-Hoe, 2011).

Kangaroo care was first used with low-birth-weight newborns, but it also benefits healthy newborns. Fathers also can provide kangaroo care, benefitting babies

postpartum depression
The sadness and inadequacy felt by some new mothers in the days and weeks after giving birth.

A Teenage Mother This week-old baby, born in an economically disadvantaged village in Myanmar (Burma), has a better chance of survival than he might otherwise have had because his 18-year-old mother has bonded with him.

SHEHZAD NOORANI / AGE FOTOSTOCK

parent–infant bond
The strong, loving connection that forms as parents hold, examine, and feed their newborn.

kangaroo care
A child-care technique in which a new mother holds the baby between her breasts, like a kangaroo that carries her immature newborn in a pouch on her abdomen.

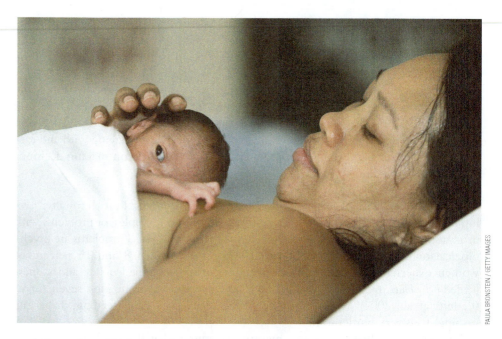

A Beneficial Beginning This new mother in a maternity ward in Manila is providing her baby with kangaroo care.

and themselves (Feeley et al., 2013). Months later, infants who are given kangaroo care tend to flourish, either because of improved infant adjustment to life outside the womb or because of increased parental sensitivity and effectiveness. Probably both. Oxytocin is released during kangaroo care, which is beneficial for everyone (Ludington-Hoe, 2011).

KEY Points

- The germinal period ends 2 weeks after conception with implantation. This period is followed by the development of the embryo, as the creature takes shapes.

- At 8 weeks after conception, fetal life begins, with 7 months of brain and body maturation, as well as life-saving weight gain, from about 85 grams at 3 months to about 3 kilograms at full term.

- Full-term birth is a natural event, assisted by drugs and other medical measures in developed countries.

- Human social interaction begins even before birth, as mothers, fathers, and babies respond to each other.

Problems and Solutions

The early days of prenatal life place the developing person on a path toward health and success—or not. Fortunately, resilience is apparent from the beginning; healthy newborns are the norm, not the exception.

From the moment of conception to the days and months after birth, many biological and psychological factors protect each new life. We now look at specific problems that may occur and how to prevent or minimize them. Always remember dynamic systems—every hazard is affected by dozens of factors. As one scientist stresses, "genes and their products almost never act alone, but in networks with other genes and proteins and in the context of the environment" (Chakravarti, 2011, p. 15).

Abnormal Genes and Chromosomes

Perhaps half of all zygotes have serious abnormalities of their chromosomes or genes. Most of them never grow or implant—an early example of the protection built into nature. However, some newborns with serious genetic problems survive and live close to a normal life—especially if protective factors are present (Nadeau & Dudley, 2011).

CHROMOSOMAL MISCOUNTS About once in every 200 births, an infant is born with 45, 47, or even 48 or 49 chromosomes instead of the usual 46. Each of these produces a recognizable *syndrome,* a cluster of distinct characteristics that occur together. The variable that most often correlates with an odd number of chromosomes is the age of the mother, presumably because her ova become increasingly fragile by midlife. The father's age is also relevant, again probably because his gametes become less robust with age (Brenner et al., 2009).

The most common extra-chromosome condition that results in a surviving child is **Down syndrome,** also called *trisomy-21* because the person has three (tri) copies of chromosome 21. No individual with Down syndrome is identical to another, but most have specific observable characteristics—a thick tongue, round face, slanted eyes, distinctive body proportions. Many also have hearing problems, heart abnormalities, muscle weakness, and short stature. They are usually slower to develop intellectually, especially in language, and they reach their maximum intellectual potential at about age 15 (Rondal, 2010). Some are severely intellectually disabled; others are of average or above-average intelligence. That extra chromosome affects the person throughout his or her life, but family context, educational efforts, and possibly medication can improve the person's prognosis (Kuehn, 2011).

Another common problem occurs at the 23rd pair of chromosomes. Not every person has two, and only two, sex chromosomes. About 1 in every 500 infants is born with only one sex chromosome (no Y) or with three or more (not just two) (Hamerton & Evans, 2005). Such children have many challenges, especially in sexual maturation and fertility. The specifics depend on the particular configuration as well as on other genetic factors (Mazzocco & Ross, 2007).

Down syndrome
A condition in which a person has 47 chromosomes instead of the usual 46, with three rather than two chromosomes at the 21st position. People with Down syndrome typically have distinctive characteristics, including atypical facial features (thick tongue, round face, slanted eyes), heart abnormalities, and language difficulties. (Also called *trisomy-21.*)

An Artist in the Making Daniel, seen here painting a brightly coloured picture on a big canvas has trisomy-21. He attends the only school in Chile where children with and without special needs share classrooms.

REUTERS / CLAUDIA DAUT

GENE DISORDERS Everyone is a carrier of genes or alleles that *could* produce serious diseases or disabilities in the next generation. Given that most disorders are polygenic and that the mapping of the human genome is recent, the exact impact of each allele is not yet known (Couzin-Frankel, 2011a). It is likely that common complex disorders arise from an accumulation of genetic defects in many genes (Chakravarti, 2011). Although most disorders result from many genes, single-gene disorders have been studied for decades. Our accumulated knowledge of them can help us understand more complex disorders.

Most of the 7000 *known* single-gene disorders are dominant and easy to identify as such: Half the offspring of parents with a dominant disorder will also have the disorder (in other words, it will be expressed in their phenotype) and half will escape the gene, and hence the disorder, completely.

If the condition is fatal in childhood, it will, of course, never be transmitted. Thus, all common dominant disorders either begin in adulthood (Huntington disease and early-onset Alzheimer disease, for instance) or have relatively mild symptoms.

One disorder once thought to be dominant is *Tourette syndrome,* which may make a person have uncontrollable tics and explosive verbal outbursts. But most people with Tourette syndrome have milder symptoms, such as an occasional twitch or a controllable impulse to speak inappropriately. Recent research finds a complex inheritance: probably multiple genes and epigenetic factors rather than a single dominant gene (Woods et al., 2007).

The number of recessive disorders is probably in the millions, most of them rare. For example, Canadian writer Ian Brown's son Walker was born with a genetic disorder so rare it occurs only once in every 300 000 births. The resulting syndrome creates very serious developmental difficulties. *The Boy in the Moon,* Brown's 2009 account of Walker's birth and development, gives a moving description of what it is like to live with (and to love) a child who is severely disabled:

> Tonight I wake up in the dark to a steady, motorized noise. Something wrong with the water heater. *Nnngah.* Pause. *Nnngah. Nnngah.*
>
> But it's not the water heater. It's my boy, Walker, grunting as he punches himself in the head, again and again.
>
> He has done this since before he was two. He was born with an impossibly rare genetic mutation, cardiofaciocutaneous syndrome, a technical name for a mash of symptoms. He is globally delayed and can't speak, so I never know what's wrong. No one does. There are just over a hundred people with CFC around the world. The disorder turns up randomly, a misfire that has no certain cause or roots; doctors call it an orphan syndrome because it seems to come from nowhere.
>
> [Brown, 2009]

Other recessive conditions are much more common, including cystic fibrosis, thalassemia, and sickle-cell anemia. About 1 in 12 North Americans is a carrier for one of them. The reason these three are common is that carriers are protected from lethal diseases. For example, carriers of the sickle-cell trait are unlikely to die of malaria, a deadly killer in central Africa. As a result, over the centuries, African carriers were more likely than non-carriers to survive. Similarly, the single cystic fibrosis gene is more common among people whose ancestors came from northern Europe because carriers of that gene may have been protected against cholera. Prenatal and even preconception tests can detect many disorders (see Table 2.5).

Teratogens

teratogen
Any agent or condition, including viruses, drugs, and chemicals, that can impair prenatal development, resulting in birth defects or complications.

Possible problems can occur after conception as well, because many toxic substances, illnesses, and experiences can harm a fetus. Every week scientists discover an unexpected **teratogen,** which is anything—drugs, viruses, pollutants, malnutrition,

TABLE 2.5 Methods of Prenatal and Preconception Testing*

Method	Description	Risks, Concerns, and Indications
Preconception blood tests	Test for nutrients (especially iron); for diseases (syphilis, HIV, herpes, hepatitis B); for carrier status (cystic fibrosis, sickle-cell anemia, Tay-Sachs disease, thalassemia, etc.).	Might require postponement of pregnancy for counselling, treatment.
Pre-implantation testing	After in vitro fertilization, one cell is removed from each zygote at the four- or eight-cell stage and analyzed.	Not entirely accurate; requires in vitro fertilization and rapid assessment, delaying implantation. Used when couples are at high risk of known, testable disorders.
Tests for pregnancy-associated plasma protein A (PAPPA) and human chorionic gonadotropin	Blood tests are usually done at about 11 weeks to indicate levels of these substances.	Low levels correlate with chromosomal miscounts and slow prenatal growth, but false-positive or false-negative results can occur.
Alpha-fetoprotein assay	Blood is tested for alpha-fetoprotein (AFP) level, often combined with other blood tests and repeat sonogram.	High AFP indicates neural-tube defects or multiple embryos; low AFP indicates Down syndrome. Normal levels change weekly; accurate conception dating required.
Sonogram (ultrasound)	High-frequency sound waves produce a "picture" of the fetus, often done several times, from 6 to 38 weeks. Detects many problems, anticipates complications.	Reveals head or body malformations, excess brain fluid, Down syndrome (via fetal neck measurement), and several diseases. Estimates fetal age and growth, reveals multiple fetuses and placental position. No known risks, unlike the X-rays that it has replaced.
Chorionic villus sampling (CVS)	A sample of the chorion (part of the placenta) obtained (via sonogram and syringe) at 10 weeks and analyzed. Cells of placenta are genetically identical to fetal cells, so CVS indicates genetic conditions.	Can cause spontaneous abortion (rare).
Amniocentesis	Some fluid inside the placenta is withdrawn (via sonogram and syringe) at 16 weeks; cells cultured and analyzed.	Can cause spontaneous abortion (rare). Detects abnormalities later in pregnancy than other tests but is very accurate.

*Many newer tests are experimental, soon to be offered to the general public. Therefore, this list is partial, to illustrate that many tests are used at various times during pregnancy to indicate possible problems.

stress, and more—that increases the risk of prenatal abnormalities. Many abnormalities can be avoided, many potential teratogens do no harm, and much damage can be remedied.

Some teratogens cause no physical defects but affect the brain, making a child hyperactive or antisocial, or resulting in the child having a learning disability. These are **behavioural teratogens.** About 20 percent of all children have difficulties that *could* be connected to behavioural teratogens, although the link is not straightforward: The cascade is murky, in part because the impact of the environment varies (Bell & Robinson, 2011).

One of my students described her little brother as follows:

> I was nine years old when my mother announced she was pregnant. I was the one who was most excited. … My mother was a heavy smoker, Colt 45 beer drinker. … I asked, "Why are you doing it?" She said, "I don't know."
>
> During this time I was in the fifth grade and we saw a film about birth defects. My biggest fear was that my mother was going to give birth to an infant with fetal alcohol syndrome (FAS). … My baby brother was born right on schedule. The doctors claimed a healthy newborn. … Once I heard healthy, I thought everything was going to be fine. I was wrong, then again I was just a child. … My baby brother never showed any interest in toys … he just cannot get the right words out of his mouth … he has no common sense. …

[J., personal communication]

behavioural teratogens
Agents and conditions that can harm the prenatal brain, impairing the future child's intellectual and emotional functioning.

Kathleen's STORY

My student wrote: "Why hurt those who cannot defend themselves?" J. blames her mother for drinking beer, although genes, postnatal experiences, and the lack of information and services that could have prevented harm (for instance, some drug rehab programs do not accept pregnant women) may have contributed to her brother's lack of "common sense." Just as every teratogen can be mitigated by other circumstances, every one can be made worse. An understanding of risk is crucial.

Risk Analysis

Risk analysis discerns which chances are worth taking and how risks are minimized. Let's pick an easy example: Crossing the street is a risk, yet it would be worse to avoid all street crossing. Knowing this, we cross carefully, looking both ways.

Although all teratogens increase the *risk* of harm, none *always* causes damage. The impact of teratogens depends on the interplay of many factors, both destructive and protective, an example of the dynamic-systems perspective.

FIGURE 2.9 Critical Periods in Human Development The most serious damage from teratogens (green bars) is likely to occur early in prenatal development. However, significant damage (purple bars) to many vital parts of the body can occur during the last months of pregnancy as well. Behavioural teratogens also affect the fetus throughout development.

Birth Defects from Teratogens: Time of Exposure and Effect on Major Organs

Source: Adapted from K. L. Moore & Persaud, 2003.

THE CRITICAL TIME One crucial factor in the effect of a teratogen is *timing*—the age of the developing embryo or fetus when it is exposed to the teratogen (Sadler, 2012). Some teratogens cause damage only during a *critical period* (see Chapter 1) (see Figure 2.9).

Obstetricians recommend that *before* pregnancy occurs, women should avoid drugs (especially alcohol), supplement a balanced diet with extra folic acid and iron, and update their immunizations. Indeed, preconception health is at least as important as health during pregnancy.

In recent years, Canadian women have been more active and aware of the importance of preconception health as a strategy to optimize a healthy birth. Through public awareness campaigns, discussions with health care providers, and preconception classes, expectant mothers and fathers have gained the knowledge, skills, motivation, opportunity, access, and supportive environments that make it easier to engage in healthy behaviours (McGreary, 2007). (See Figure 2.10 for examples of changes in prenatal health behaviours.)

The first days and weeks after conception (the germinal and embryonic periods) are critical for body formation, but the entire fetal period is a sensitive time for brain development. Further, preterm birth is a risk factor that is affected by nutrition and drugs throughout pregnancy.

Timing may be important even before conception. When pregnancy occurs soon after a previous pregnancy, risk increases, perhaps because a woman's body may need time to recover from birth. For example, second-born children are twice as likely to be autistic if they are born within a year of the first-born child than if they are born several years later (Cheslack-Postava et al., 2011). Mothers who are under age 16 or over age 40 have higher rates of genetic, prenatal, and birth complications.

The critical and sensitive period concepts are helpful in understanding **cerebral palsy** (difficulties with movement control resulting from brain damage), which was once thought to be caused solely by birth procedures (excessive medication, slow breech birth, or use of forceps to pull the fetal head through the birth canal). We now know that cerebral palsy results from genetic vulnerability, teratogens, and maternal infection (J. R. Mann et al., 2009), and not only insufficient oxygen to the fetal brain at birth.

cerebral palsy
A disorder that results from damage to the brain's motor centres. People with cerebral palsy have difficulty with muscle control, so their speech and/or body movements are impaired.

FIGURE 2.10 For the Sake of the Baby According to one study in Ontario, there were significant changes in prenatal health behaviours between 2002 and 2008. Specifically, when compared to their last pregnancy, women were more likely to consult their health care provider about improving their health, quit/cut down on their smoking, and/or begin taking folic acid. In fact, many of these behaviour changes began even before conception (Best Start Resource Centre, 2009).

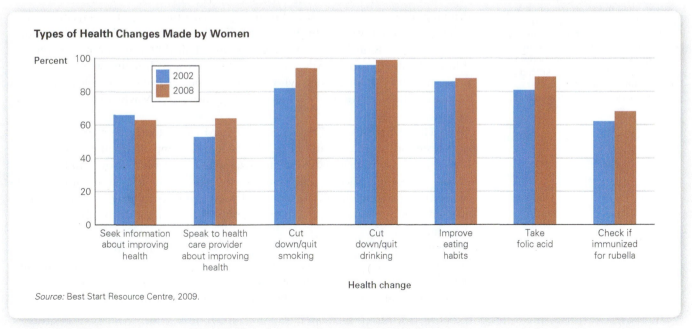

Types of Health Changes Made by Women

Source: Best Start Resource Centre, 2009.

anoxia
A lack of oxygen that, if prolonged, can cause brain damage or death.

A lack of oxygen is **anoxia,** which often occurs for a second or two during birth, indicated by a slower fetal heart rate. To prevent prolonged anoxia, the fetal heart rate is monitored during labour. Avoiding anoxia is also the reason that two of the five Apgar ratings indicate oxygen level. How long anoxia can continue without harming the brain depends on genes, birth weight, gestational age (preterm newborns are more vulnerable), drugs (either taken by the mother before birth or given during birth), and many other factors. Insufficient oxygen may begin long before birth. Thus, anoxia is part of a cascade that may cause cerebral palsy or other problems. Inadequate oxygen during pregnancy is a serious condition, which is why listening to the fetal heartbeat is part of every prenatal visit.

threshold effect
A situation in which a certain teratogen is relatively harmless in small doses but becomes harmful once exposure reaches a certain level (the threshold).

HOW MUCH IS TOO MUCH? A second factor affecting the harm from any teratogen is the dose and/or frequency of exposure. Some teratogens have a **threshold effect;** they are virtually harmless until exposure reaches a certain level, at which point they "cross the threshold" and become damaging. This threshold is not a fixed boundary: Dose, timing, frequency, and other teratogens affect when the threshold is crossed (O'Leary et al., 2010).

Thresholds are difficult to set because one teratogen may increase the harm from another. Consider alcohol. Early in pregnancy, an embryo exposed to heavy drinking can develop **fetal alcohol syndrome (FAS),** which distorts the facial features (especially the eyes, ears, and upper lip). Later in pregnancy, alcohol is a behavioural teratogen, the cause of *fetal alcohol effects (FAE),* leading to hyperactivity, poor concentration, impaired spatial reasoning, and slow learning (Niccols, 2007; Streissguth & Connor, 2001). Health Canada (2005) estimates that the Canada-wide rate for FAS is 1 to 3 per every 1000 live births; for FAE, the Canadian rate is 30 per 1000. These rates are much higher for some First Nations and Inuit communities. Together, FAS and FAE are the leading causes of preventable birth defects in Canada. However, some pregnant women drink alcohol with no evident harm to the fetus. FAS is more apparent when women are poorly nourished and cigarette smokers (Abel, 2009). If occasional drinking during pregnancy always caused FAS, almost everyone born in Europe before 1980 would be affected. As for FAE, hyperactivity and slow learning are so common that FAE cannot be blamed for every case.

fetal alcohol syndrome (FAS)
A cluster of birth defects, including abnormal facial characteristics, slow physical growth, and intellectual disabilities, that may occur in the child of a woman who drinks alcohol while pregnant.

Currently, Health Canada advises all Canadian women who are pregnant or even thinking of becoming pregnant to avoid taking any alcohol whatsoever: "STOP drinking alcohol now if you are planning to become pregnant" (Health Canada, 2005). By contrast, women in the United Kingdom receive conflicting advice about drinking an occasional glass of wine (Raymond et al., 2009), and French women are told to abstain, but many have not heard that message (Toutain, 2010). Total abstinence requires that all women who might become pregnant avoid a legal substance that most adults use routinely. Wise? Probably. Necessary? Maybe not.

✦ **ESPECIALLY FOR Judges and Juries** How much protection, if any, should the legal system provide for fetuses? Should alcoholic women who are pregnant be jailed to prevent them from drinking? What about people who enable them to drink, such as their partners, their parents, bar owners, bartenders? (see response, page 79) ➞

GENETIC VULNERABILITY Genes are a third factor that influences every aspect of conception, pregnancy, and birth. Consider what happens when a woman carrying dizygotic twins drinks alcohol, for example. The alcohol in the mother's blood stream reaches the placenta and then the embryos via the umbilical cord. Thus, the twins' blood alcohol levels are equal. However, one twin may be more severely affected than the other because their alleles for the enzyme that metabolizes alcohol may differ.

Genetic vulnerability is a particular example of differential susceptibility, as described in Chapter 1. Genetic protections or hazards are suspected for many birth defects (Sadler, 2012). A protective factor seems to be the X chromosome; male fetuses (only one X) are more vulnerable to teratogens than females (XX) (Lewis & Kestler, 2012).

Since fathers provide 23 chromosomes, they are as likely as mothers to provide genetic protection or vulnerability. Maternal genes have an additional role: They affect a mother's body and thus the environment of the womb. One maternal allele results in low levels of folic acid during pregnancy. Via the umbilical cord, this can produce *neural-tube defects*—either *spina bifida,* in which the tail of the spine is not enclosed properly (in healthy embryos, enclosure occurs at about week 7), or *anencephaly,* when part of the brain is missing.

Neural-tube defects are more common in certain ethnic groups (Irish, English, and Egyptian) than in others. For these groups, folic acid supplements before pregnancy are strongly recommended. Although the allele that causes low folic acid in women is rare among Asians and Africans, it is still beneficial for pregnant women of these backgrounds to take supplemental folic acid as it is not harmful.

In 1998, both Canada and the United States created laws that required folic acid to be added to packaged cereal products such as white flour, enriched pasta, and cornmeal. The aim of these measures is to protect every woman, even if she does not expect to become pregnant. A Canadian study found that the rate of neural-tube defects in Canada dropped by 46 percent since these laws were enacted, which means that as many as 170 fewer babies a year are growing up with conditions such as spina bifida (De Wals et al., 2007).

APPLYING THE RESEARCH Risk analysis cannot precisely predict the results of genetic vulnerability, teratogenic exposure, or birth complications in individual cases. However, much is known about what individuals and society can do to reduce the risks. Table 2.6 lists some teratogens and their possible effects, as well as preventive measures.

Remember that the outcomes vary. Many fetuses are exposed with no evident harm. The opposite occurs as well: About 20 percent of all serious defects occur for reasons unknown. Women are advised to maintain good nutrition and avoid teratogens, especially drugs and chemicals (pesticides, cleaning fluids, and many cosmetics contain teratogenic chemicals). Some medications are necessary (e.g., for women who have epilepsy, diabetes, severe depression) and should be continued, but caution should begin *before* pregnancy is confirmed.

Sadly, the cascade of teratogens is most likely to begin with women who are already vulnerable. For example, cigarette smokers are more often drinkers (as was J.'s mother); those whose jobs involve chemicals and pesticides are more often malnourished; low-SES women are more likely to give birth early, and they are less likely to get prenatal care and be admitted to modern hospitals (Ahmed & Jaakkola, 2007; A. S. Bryant et al., 2010; Hougaard & Hansen, 2007).

The benefits of early prenatal care are many: Women can be told which substances to avoid, they can learn what to eat and what to do, and they may be diagnosed and treated for some conditions (syphilis and HIV among them) that harm the fetus only if early treatment does not occur. As noted earlier, prenatal tests (of blood, urine, and fetal heart rate, as well as ultrasound) and even preconception tests can identify many disorders (see Table 2.5 on page 73). When complications (such as twins, gestational diabetes, infections) arise, early recognition increases the chance of a healthy birth.

One obvious effect of early prenatal care is that the risk of low birth weight is reduced. As you will now see, an underweight newborn is vulnerable in dozens of ways. Indeed, the United States' rate of infant death is higher than many other nations largely because of more underweight babies. In Canada, the rate of infant death is also higher than for many industrialized countries, but the reasons for this are complex, as you will see in the feature A View from Science: Why Are Infant Mortality Rates in Canada So High? (page 82).

TABLE 2.6 Teratogens: Effects of Exposure and Prevention of Damage*

Teratogens	Effects of Exposure on Fetus	Measures for Preventing Damage
Diseases		
Rubella (German measles)	In embryonic period, causes blindness and deafness; in first and second trimesters, causes brain damage.	Get immunized before becoming pregnant.
Toxoplasmosis	Brain damage, loss of vision, intellectual disabilities.	Avoid eating undercooked meat and handling cat feces, garden dirt during pregnancy.
Measles, chicken pox, influenza	May impair brain functioning.	Get immunized before getting pregnant; avoid infected people during pregnancy.
Syphilis	Baby is born with syphilis, which, untreated, leads to brain and bone damage and eventual death.	Early prenatal diagnosis and treatment with antibiotics.
AIDS	Baby may catch the virus. Without treatment, illness and death are likely during childhood.	Prenatal drugs and Caesarean birth make AIDS transmission rare.
Other sexually transmitted infections, including gonorrhea and chlamydia	Not usually harmful during pregnancy but may cause blindness and infections if transmitted during birth.	Early diagnosis and treatment; if necessary, Caesarean section, treatment of newborn.
Infections, including infections of urinary tract, gums, and teeth	May cause premature labour, which increases vulnerability to brain damage.	Get infection treated, preferably before becoming pregnant.
Pollutants		
Lead, mercury, PCBs (polychlorinated biphenyls); dioxin; and some pesticides, herbicides, and cleaning compounds	May cause spontaneous abortion, preterm labour, and brain damage.	Most common substances are harmless in small doses, but pregnant women should avoid regular and direct exposure, such as drinking well water, eating unwashed fruits or vegetables, using chemical compounds, and eating fish from polluted waters.
Radiation		
Massive or repeated exposure to radiation, as in medical X-rays	In the embryonic period, may cause abnormally small head (microcephaly) and intellectual disabilities; in the fetal period, suspected but not proven to cause brain damage. Exposure to background radiation, as from power plants, is usually too low to have an effect.	Get sonograms, not X-rays, during pregnancy; pregnant women who work directly with radiation need special protection or temporary assignment to another job.
Social and Behavioural Factors		
Very high stress	Early in pregnancy, may cause cleft lip or cleft palate, spontaneous abortion, or preterm labour.	Get adequate relaxation, rest, and sleep; reduce hours of employment; get help with housework and child care.
Malnutrition	When severe, may interfere with conception, implantation, normal fetal development, and full-term birth.	Eat a balanced diet (with adequate vitamins and minerals, including, especially, folic acid, iron, and vitamin A); achieve normal weight before getting pregnant, then gain 10–15 kg during pregnancy.
Excessive, exhausting exercise	Can affect fetal development when it interferes with pregnant woman's sleep, digestion, or nutrition.	Get regular, moderate exercise.
Medicinal Drugs		
Lithium	Can cause heart abnormalities.	Avoid all medicines, whether prescription or over-the-counter, during pregnancy unless they are approved by a medical professional who knows about the pregnancy and is aware of the most recent research.
Tetracycline	Can harm teeth.	
Retinoic acid	Can cause limb deformities.	
Streptomycin	Can cause deafness.	
ACE inhibitors	Can harm digestive organs.	
Phenobarbital	Can affect brain development.	
Thalidomide	Can stop ear and limb formation.	

TABLE 2.6 (Continued)

Teratogens	Effects of Exposure on Fetus	Measures for Preventing Damage
Psychoactive Drugs		
Caffeine	Normal use poses no problem.	Avoid excessive use: Drink no more than three cups a day of beverages containing caffeine (coffee, tea, cola drinks, hot chocolate).
Alcohol	May cause fetal alcohol syndrome (FAS) or fetal alcohol effects (FAE).	Stop or severely limit alcohol consumption during pregnancy; especially dangerous are three or more drinks a day or four or more drinks on one occasion.
Tobacco	Reduces birth weight, increases risk of malformations of limbs and urinary tract, and may affect the baby's lungs.	Stop smoking before becoming pregnant; if already pregnant, stop smoking immediately.
Marijuana	Heavy exposure may affect the central nervous system; when smoked, may hinder fetal growth.	Avoid or strictly limit marijuana consumption.
Heroin	Slows fetal growth and may cause premature labour; newborns with heroin in their bloodstream require medical treatment to prevent the pain and convulsions of withdrawal.	Get treated for heroin addiction before becoming pregnant; if already pregnant, gradual withdrawal on methadone is better than continued use of heroin.
Cocaine	May cause slow fetal growth, premature labour, and learning problems in the first years of life.	Stop using cocaine before pregnancy; babies of cocaine-using mothers may need special medical and educational attention in their first years of life.
Inhaled solvents (glue or aerosol)	May cause abnormally small head, crossed eyes, and other indications of brain damage.	Stop sniffing inhalants before becoming pregnant; be aware that serious damage can occur before a woman knows she is pregnant.

* The field of toxicology advances daily. Research on new substances begins with their effects on nonhuman species, which provides suggestive (though not conclusive) evidence. This table is a primer; it is no substitute for careful consultation with a professional who knows the recent research.

Sources: Gupta, 2011; Mann & Andrews, 2007; O'Rahilly & Müller, 2001; Reece & Hobbins, 2007; Sadler, 2012; Shepard & Lemire, 2004.

Low Birth Weight

Some newborns, especially preterm babies, are small and immature. With modern hospital care, tiny infants usually survive, but it would be better for everyone—mother, father, baby, and society—if all newborns were in the womb for at least 35 weeks and weighed more than 2500 grams.

Low birth weight (LBW) is defined by the World Health Organization as weight under 2500 grams. LBW babies are further grouped into **very low birth weight (VLBW),** under 1500 grams, and **extremely low birth weight (ELBW),** under 1000 grams.

Recently, some researchers have examined the issue of birth weight by taking ethnicity into consideration. One Canadian study noted that babies of immigrant mothers from regions of the world other than Europe and North America are often smaller than those of domestically born mothers. Some of these smaller babies run the risk of being classified LBW and subjected to unnecessary tests and hospitalizations when actually they are a normal weight for newborns from their world region. The researchers concluded that "birthweight curves [standards] need to be modified for newborns of immigrant mothers originating from non-European/Western nations" (Ray et al., 2012, p. 159).

low birth weight (LBW)
A body weight at birth of less than 2500 grams.

very low birth weight (VLBW)
A body weight at birth of less than 1500 grams.

extremely low birth weight (ELBW)
A body weight at birth of less than 1000 grams.

RESPONSE FOR Judges and Juries (from page 76) The law punishes women who jeopardize the health of their fetuses, but a developmental view would consider the micro-, exo-, and macrosystems. ●

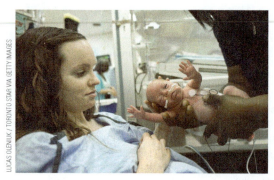

Doing Great Survival is uncertain for extremely low birth weight newborns, such as Owen (shown here) and his twin brother, Oliver. However, Owen and Oliver's chances are excellent, partly because they are receiving specialized care at the neonatal intensive care unit (NICU) at Mount Sinai Hospital in Toronto. Medical advances, such as those at Mount Sinai Hospital, have led to decreased mortality rates of at-risk babies.

preterm birth
A birth that occurs three or more weeks before the full 38 weeks of the typical pregnancy have elapsed—that is, at 35 or fewer weeks after conception.

small for gestational age (SGA)
Having a body weight at birth that is significantly lower than expected, given the time since conception. For example, a 2265-gram newborn is considered SGA if born on time but not SGA if born two months early. (Also called *small-for-dates*.)

MATERNAL BEHAVIOUR Fetal weight normally doubles in the last three months of a full term pregnancy, with 900 grams of that gain occurring in the final three weeks. Thus, a baby born **preterm** (three or more weeks early; no longer called *premature*) is usually LBW.

Preterm birth correlates with many of the teratogens already mentioned, an example of the cascade that leads to newborns with evident problems. The prenatal environment itself may cause early labour as well. Indeed, when the environment of the womb is harmful, as when multiple fetuses reduce nourishment to each individual fetus, hormones can precipitate labour.

Early birth is only one cause of low birth weight. Some fetuses gain weight slowly throughout pregnancy and are **small for gestational age (SGA)** (also called *small-for-dates*). For example, a full-term baby weighing only 2500 grams and a 30-week-old fetus weighing 1000 grams are both SGA. The former is one gram shy of LBW and the latter, if born, is ELBW *and* SGA. Maternal or fetal illness might cause SGA, but maternal drug use before and during pregnancy is the most common underlying cause. Every psychoactive drug slows fetal growth; tobacco is implicated in 25 percent of all LBW births worldwide.

Another common reason for slow fetal growth is maternal malnutrition. Women who begin pregnancy underweight, who eat poorly during pregnancy, or who gain less than 1.3 kilograms per month in the final six months are likely to have an underweight infant. Malnutrition (not age) is the primary reason teenagers often have small babies. Unfortunately, many of the risk factors just mentioned—underweight, undernutrition, underage, and smoking—tend to occur together.

FATHERS AND SIGNIFICANT OTHERS The causes just mentioned of low birth weight focus on the pregnant woman: If she takes drugs or is undernourished, her fetus suffers. Conversely, if she take cares to nourish herself, to not take drugs, and to avoid exhaustion, she can help protect the baby's prenatal health. However, the more we learn about birth problems, the more important fathers—and grandmothers, neighbours, and communities—are discovered to be. As an editorial in a journal for obstetricians explains: "Fathers' attitudes regarding the pregnancy, fathers' behaviours during the prenatal period, and the relationship between fathers and mothers … may indirectly influence risk for adverse birth outcomes" (Misra et al., 2010, p. 99).

Much Canadian research over the last two decades bears out the idea that fathers have strong impacts on the health and well-being of their newborn babies. For example, a team of researchers from Ottawa examined the links between paternal age and adverse birth outcomes (Chen et al., 2007). They found that, compared with fathers in their 20s or older than 40, teenage fathers were more likely to have children who experienced preterm birth, low birth weight, low Apgar scores, and neonatal mortality.

Although there are no clear reasons why teenage fathers might contribute to an increased rate of negative birth outcomes, the researchers speculated about several causes. First, biology itself might play a role, since younger men tend to have more immature sperm, which lead to "abnormal placentation," or difficulties in implanting properly in the nourishing environment of the placenta.

Second, socioeconomic factors may have an influence, since teenage fathers often come from economically disadvantaged families and have less education than older fathers. Parents from disadvantaged backgrounds are less likely to make use of prenatal care services, which leads to a greater risk of poor birth outcomes. Also the social dynamics between teenage parents may have negative consequences for newborns, since men of this age tend to be more prone to violence and have fewer financial resources to support their spouses than older men have.

Finally, lifestyle factors can play a role, because drinking, smoking, and the use of illegal drugs, which are all more common with teenage fathers, can lead to adverse birth outcomes (Chen et al., 2007).

CONSEQUENCES OF LOW BIRTH WEIGHT Early death is the most obvious hazard of low birth weight. But problems do not end with survival. When compared with newborns conceived at the same time but born later, very low-birth-weight infants are later to smile, hold a bottle, walk, and talk.

As months go by, cognitive, visual, and hearing impairments emerge. High-risk newborns are more likely to cry more, pay attention less, disobey, and experience language delays as they get older (Aarnoudse-Moens et al., 2009; Spinillo et al., 2009).

Longitudinal research studies find that, compared with the average child in middle childhood, formerly SGA children have smaller brain volume, and those who were preterm have lower IQs (van Soelen et al., 2010). Even in adulthood, risks persist: Adults who were LBW are more likely to have heart disease and diabetes.

However, remember that risk analysis gives odds, not certainties—and remember that many factors (including the genes and prenatal care already described and caregiving explained in the following chapters) affect each child. Although low birth weight is a risk to be avoided if possible, some tiny newborns, by age 4 years, are normal in brain development and in every other way (Claas et al., 2011; Spittle et al., 2009).

COMPARING NATIONS The low-birth-weight rate in Canada is about 6 percent. This rate is higher than that of some northern European nations, such as Sweden, which has an LBW rate of 4 percent, and lower than that of countries such as the United States, which has an LBW rate of about 8 percent. In several South Asian nations, including India, more than 20 percent of infants weigh less than 2500 grams (see Figure 2.11).

What factors other than being born preterm may affect the baby's birth weight? Historically, personal factors such as smoking, alcohol and drug use, poor nutrition before and during pregnancy, and high stress have put a mother at risk for a low birth weight baby. Key environmental factors have been poverty, single or teenage parenthood, and living with a violent partner.

Lending a Hand Fathers-to-be play an important role in expectant mothers' and babies' well-being. With the support of her partner, this mother-to-be is likely to eat well, avoid drugs, and rest when she is tired.

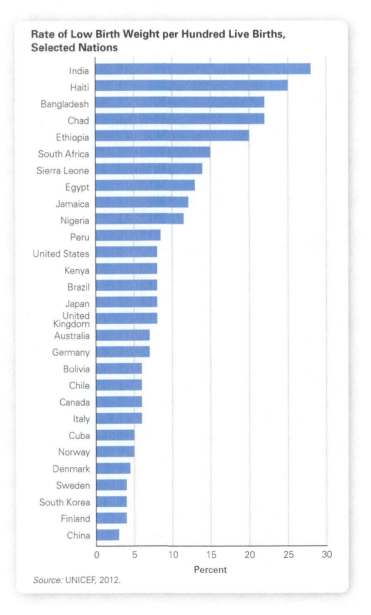

Rate of Low Birth Weight per Hundred Live Births, Selected Nations

Source: UNICEF, 2012.

FIGURE 2.11 **Getting Better** Some public health experts consider the rate of low birth weight to be indicative of national health, since both are affected by the same causes. If that is true, the world is getting healthier, since the LBW world average was 28 percent in 2009 but is now 16 percent. When all nations are included, 47 report LBW at 6 per 100 or lower, which suggests that many nations (including Canada and the United States) could improve.

However, according to a 2009 report from Vital Signs Canada (VSC), some factors that have historically contributed to low birth weight are declining across the country, including smoking among pregnant women and incidence of teenage pregnancy (VSC, 2009). Other factors, such as the increasing number of older women (aged 35–49) who are giving birth, the increased use of assisted reproductive technologies and Caesarean sections, and greater numbers of multiple births, all contributed to a 17 percent increase in low-birth-weight babies over the 10-year period from 1995–2004 (VSC, 2009).

As for the United States, the Department of Agriculture found an increase in *food insecurity* (measured by skipped meals, use of food stamps, and outright hunger) in the past decade. Food insecurity directly affects LBW, and it also increases chronic illness, which itself correlates with LBW (Seligman & Schillinger, 2010). In 2008, about 15 percent of U.S. households were considered food insecure, with rates higher among women in their prime reproductive years than among middle-aged women or men of any age. These rates increased with the economic recession of 2008–2010; if food insecurity is one explanation for LBW rates, rates of LBW will continue to increase.

Worldwide, far fewer low-birth-weight babies are born now than 20 years ago, and neonatal deaths have been reduced by one-third as a result (Rajaratnam et al., 2010). Some nations, China and Chile among them, have shown dramatic improvement. In 1970 about half of Chinese newborns were LBW; recent estimates put that number at 4 percent (UNICEF, 2012). By contrast, in other nations, notably in sub-Saharan Africa, the LBW rate is steady or rising because global warming, AIDS, food shortages, wars, and other problems affect pregnancy.

infant mortality rate
The rate, per 1000 live births, at which babies of less than one year of age die.

A VIEW FROM SCIENCE

Why Are Infant Mortality Rates So High in Canada?

The **infant mortality rate (IMR)** is defined as the number of deaths that occur before a child's first birthday per 1000 live births. Tracking this rate is important because it acts as an indicator of children's health and well-being in a particular society over time. It also provides a standard we can use to judge the effectiveness of a country's health system as a whole. As the Organisation of Economic Cooperation and Development (OECD) noted in a 2009 report, "the infant mortality rate … reflects the economic and social conditions for the health of mothers and newborns, as well as the effectiveness of health systems" (p. 246).

Given the importance of the IMR, the question becomes how well is Canada performing compared with other nations? Apparently rather poorly, according to the OECD report just mentioned. In ranking 17 industrialized nations, the OECD placed Canada second to last, with an IMR of 5.1, ahead of only the United States (see Figure 2.12). This result led the Conference Board of Canada to call Canada's IMR "shockingly high for a country at Canada's level of socio-economic development." André Lalonde, vice-president of the Society of Obstetricians and Gynaecologists of Canada, lamented, "We're losing our reputation. We have fallen way behind" (Priest, 2010).

Thanks to medical advances, between 1960 and 1980 Canada's IMR did drop significantly, from 27 deaths per 1000 live births to 10. After 1980, the rate continued to improve but not in as dramatic a fashion. After 2000, it stabilized to between 5.5 and 5.0 but stubbornly resisted all attempts to push it below the 5.0 mark. Nonetheless, since the 1960s, many other industrialized countries have improved at greater speed and have achieved lower rates. For example, Japan's 2009 IMR was 2.6, just about half that of Canada's.

To some extent, relatively high IMR in Canada may stem from the way "live birth" is defined across nations. For instance, Canadian officials define a live birth as a newborn that takes a breath or shows other signs of life (Statistics Canada, 2011a). In contrast, both France and the Netherlands define a live birth as a baby who meets the minimal weight of 2500 grams or 22 weeks gestation (EURO-PERISTAT et al., 2008). Plainly, a baby who meets the European standards has a better chance of surviving than one who was born before 22 weeks gestation or who weighed less than 2500 grams but still managed to draw a breath after delivery.

Other researchers have suggested that the higher Canadian rates are due in part to the prevalence of new technologies for delivering preterm or VLBW babies

(Milan, 2011). Thus, many more babies are given a greater chance of living who may have been stillborn in years past. Since they are so fragile, however, a number of them die in infancy. New fertility programs also lead to multiple births, and since these babies tend to be born preterm, they are at a higher risk of early death (Conference Board of Canada, 2012).

Researchers also recognize that there are important environmental or socioeconomic factors that contribute to Canada's high IMR. These include the growing gap between rich and poor and high rates of child poverty and teen pregnancies (Warick, 2010; Raphael, 2010). Another factor that can have an effect is isolation, as with remote villages in rural regions where quality health care can be difficult to access and where poor water quality and substandard housing are persistent concerns.

All of these environmental factors have particular relevance for Aboriginal peoples in Canada. According to most researchers, the IMR among First Nations is twice as high as that for the general population, while the rate for Inuit communities is three to four times higher (Smylie et al., 2010). Federal government initiatives to lower the IMR, especially in Aboriginal communities, include the Maternal Child Health Program, the Canada Prenatal Nutrition Program, Aboriginal Head Start, and Early Childhood Development programs (Native Women's Association of Canada, 2012).

Thanks in part to these and other initiatives, in 2009 Canada's IMR finally cracked the 5.0 barrier and registered at 4.9. However, by current measure, Canada's IMR is still significantly higher than that of most other industrialized countries.

FIGURE 2.12 Poor Grade for Canada In its report on infant mortality, the Conference Board of Canada assigned Canada a grade of "C" for its relatively high infant mortality rate compared with other industrialized countries. Twelve of the 17 listed countries had rates below 4, while Canada's was 5.1. What could be some reasons for such a wealthy country having a relatively high rate of infant mortality?

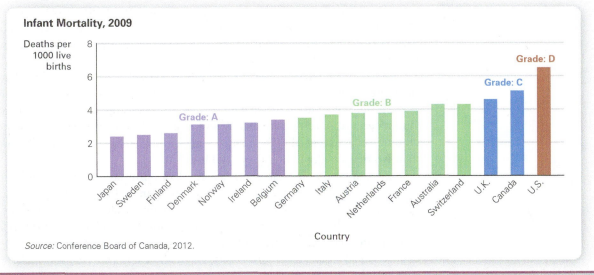

Infant Mortality, 2009

Source: Conference Board of Canada, 2012.

KEY Points

- Zygotes with abnormal chromosomes and genes are common: Most are spontaneously aborted early after conception. Survivors (e.g., those with Down syndrome) benefit from good care.

- Although hundreds of teratogens can harm the fetus, many future babies are protected by genes, timing (late), dose (small), and frequency (rare).

- Fathers, future grandparents, and cultures reduce risks, making sure expectant mothers are well fed, rested, and drug-free.

- Newborns born early and small for gestational age are at risk for many problems, at birth and throughout the life span.

- Infant mortality rates in Canada are considered high when compared with rates in other countries.

Nature and Nurture Connected

We close this chapter with a detailed look at two phenomena—alcoholism and near-sightedness—that illustrate the connections among genes, prenatal care, developmental age, and culture. The interaction is dynamic, not simple, but understanding it has many practical applications for parents, professionals, and everyone else.

Alcoholism

At various times, people have considered alcohol and drug abuse to be a moral weakness, a social scourge, or a personality defect. Attention has been on alcohol, in part because fermentation is natural and universal, present in every culture and era, and in part because alcoholism is a far more common addiction than any other.

In various times and places, alcoholics were locked up, doused with cold water, or burned at the stake. Alcohol has been declared illegal (as in Ontario from 1916 to 1927 and in Alberta from 1916 to 1924), deemed sinful (in Islam, Mormonism, and many other religions), and considered sacred (as in many Jewish and Catholic rituals). Science has now learned that the human reaction to alcohol is affected by dozens of alleles as well as by diverse cultural practices, so any universal prohibition or veneration will affect individuals in opposite ways. Differential sensitivity again!

As you might expect, alcoholism begins with genes that create an addictive pull that can be overpowering, extremely weak, or somewhere in between. To be specific, each person's biochemistry reacts to alcohol, causing sleep, nausea, aggression, joy, relaxation, forgetfulness, sexual urges, or tears.

How bodies metabolize alcohol allows some people to "hold their liquor" and therefore drink too much, whereas others (including many East Asians) sweat and become red-faced after just a few sips, an embarrassing response that may lead to abstinence. Candidate genes and alleles for alcoholism have been identified on every chromosome except the Y chromosome (ironic, since, internationally, more men than women are alcoholics) (Epps & Holt, 2011).

Inherited psychological traits affect alcoholism as much as biological ones (Macgregor et al., 2009). A quick temper, sensation seeking, or high anxiety encourage drinking. It is impossible to specify how much alcoholism is genetic or cultural because these influences are "inexorably intertwined" (Dick, 2011, p. 225); the relationship between nature and nurture varies by age and context (Young-Wolff et al., 2011). For example, some contexts (such as fraternity parties) make it hard to avoid alcohol; other contexts (a church social in a "dry" county) make it difficult to swallow anything stronger than lemonade. Age is also pivotal. Adolescents experience more pleasure, and less pain, from being drunk than people older or younger (Spear, 2011). Consequently, they get drunk more often—and have higher rates of car accidents, temper tantrums, and unprotected sex while drinking.

Biological sex (XX or XY) and gender (cultural) also affect the risk of alcoholism. For biological reasons (body size, fat composition, metabolism), women become drunk on less alcohol than men, but how much a woman drinks depends on her social context.

For example, in Japan, both sexes inherit the same genes for metabolizing alcohol, yet Japanese men—not women—drink more alcohol than their peers elsewhere. When Japanese women immigrate to the United States, their alcohol consumption is said to increase about fivefold (Higuchi et al., 1996; Makimoto, 1998). Their alcoholism increases as well. For all immigrants, alcohol consumption is related to the original culture, the stress of immigration, and norms of the country to which they immigrate—increasing or decreasing depending on specifics (Szaflarski et al., 2011)

As you have read, prenatal exposure to alcohol may seriously impair the fetus, but it also is more likely that a baby born to a drinking mother will become an alcoholic later on. Is that a genetic, prenatal, or childhood effect, or all three?

Nearsightedness

Age, genes, and culture affect vision as well. First consider age. Newborns focus only on things within 60 centimetres of their eyes; vision improves steadily until about age 10. At puberty, the eyeball changes shape, which increases nearsightedness (myopia); eyeball shape changes again in middle age, decreasing nearsightedness but increasing farsightedness (hyperopia).

Now consider genes. A study of British twins found that the gene that governs eye formation (Pax6) has many alleles that increase nearsightedness (Hammond et al., 2004). This research found *heritability* of almost 90 percent, which means that if one monozygotic twin was nearsighted, the other twin was almost always nearsighted, too.

However, **heritability** is a statistic that indicates only how much of the variation in a particular trait *within a particular population* in a particular context and era can be traced to genes. For example, the heritability of height is very high (about 95 percent) when children receive good medical care and ample nourishment, but it is low (about 20 percent) when children are malnourished. Thus, the 90 percent heritability of nearsightedness among the British children may not apply elsewhere.

Instead, visual problems may be caused by the environment. In some African nations, heritability of vision is close to zero: Severe vitamin A deficiency is the main reason some children see less well than others. Scientists are working to develop a strain of maize (the local staple) high in vitamin A. If they succeed, heritability will increase and overall vision will improve (Harjes et al., 2008).

heritability
A statistic that indicates what percentage of the variation in a particular trait within a particular population, in a particular context and era, can be traced to genes.

But what about children who are well nourished? Is their vision entirely inherited? Cross-cultural research suggests not. One report claims that "myopia is increasing at an 'epidemic' rate, particularly in East Asia" (Park & Congdon, 2004, p. 21). The first published research on this phenomenon appeared in 1992, when scholars noticed that, in army-mandated medical exams of all 17-year-old males in Singapore, 26 percent were nearsighted in 1980 but 43 percent were nearsighted in 1990 (Tay et al., 1992).

Further studies found nearsightedness increasing from 12 to 84 percent between ages 6 and 17 in Taiwan, with increases in myopia during middle childhood also in Singapore and Hong Kong (cited in Grosvenor, 2003). One author claims "very strong environmental impacts" on Asian children's vision (Morgan, 2003, p. 276). Why could that be? One clue

A First Pair of Glasses This girl from South Korea may require glasses because she spends a lot of time studying and less time playing outdoors.

is that, unlike earlier generations or children in other nations, since 1980 East Asian children have become amazingly proficient in math and science because they study intensely, in school and after school. As their developing eyes focus on the print in front of them, those with a genetic vulnerability to myopia may lose acuity for objects far away—which is exactly what nearsightedness means.

A study of Singaporean 10- to 12-year-olds found a correlation between nearsightedness (measured by optometric exams) and high achievement, especially in language (presumably reflecting more reading). Correlation is not causation, but statistics (odds ratio of 2.5, significance of 0.001) strongly suggest a link (Saw et al., 2007).

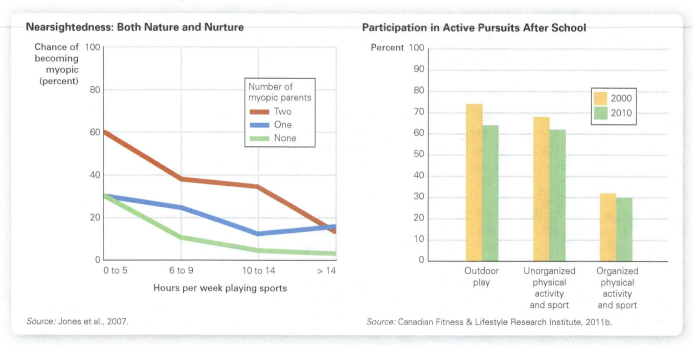

Nearsightedness: Both Nature and Nurture

Chance of becoming myopic (percent)

Number of myopic parents
— Two
— One
— None

Hours per week playing sports

Source: Jones et al., 2007.

Participation in Active Pursuits After School

Percent

2000
2010

Outdoor play | Unorganized physical activity and sport | Organized physical activity and sport

Source: Canadian Fitness & Lifestyle Research Institute, 2011b.

FIGURE 2.13 Go Out and Play!
If both your parents are nearsighted, chances are you will be, too—but not if you play sports at least six hours a week. The dramatic correlation between childhood myopia and playing sports does *not* prove causation: Some children who wear glasses choose to avoid sports. Nonetheless, parents and schools should encourage children to play outside every day. In 2010, only about 64 percent of all children did so, a 10 percent decline over the course of 10 years.

Ophthalmologists believe that the underlying cause is not time spent studying but inadequate time spent in daylight. An editorial in a leading U.S. journal for ophthalmologists explains:

> The probability of becoming myopic by the eighth grade is about 60% if a child has two myopic parents and does less than 5 hours per week of sports/outdoor activity. … [It is] about 20% if a two-myopic-parent child does 14 hours or more per week of sports/outdoor activity.

> *[Mutti & Zadnik, 2009, p. 77]*

Between the early 1970s and the early 2000s, nearsightedness in the U.S. population increased from 25 to 42 percent (Vitale et al., 2009). Urbanization, video games, homework, and fear of strangers have kept many contemporary North American children indoors doing close work much of the time, unlike earlier generations who played outside for hours each day. The correlation between nearsightedness and lack of outside play is striking (see Figure 2.13).

A vision scientist from Ohio State University says: "We're kind of a dim indoors people nowadays. … If you ask me, I would say modern society is missing the protect effect of being outdoors" [Mutti, quoted in Holden, 2010, p. 17].

However, correlation is not cause. To prove a causal link, a longitudinal experiment would require some children to stay indoors while others from the same families (to control for genes) play outside. Since that is hypothesized to harm those who stay inside, that research would be unethical (see Chapter 1) as well as impossible. Nonetheless, many applications arise from this apparent connection and from many other ideas from this chapter.

Practical Applications

Since genes affect every disorder, no one should be blamed or punished for inherited problems. However, knowing that genes do not act in isolation can lead to preventive measures, before, during, and after prenatal development.

For instance, if alcoholism is in their genes, women can avoid alcohol before, during, and after pregnancy. Further, parents can keep alcohol out of their home, hoping their children become cognitively and socially mature before drinking. (If alcohol is available at home, most children taste it before age 10.) Similarly, if nearsightedness runs in the family, parents can make sure that children play outdoors every day.

Of course, outdoor play and abstention from alcohol are recommended for every child, as are dozens of other behaviours, such as flossing the teeth, saying "please," getting enough sleep, eating vegetables, and writing thank-you notes. However, no parent can enforce every recommendation.

Awareness of genetic risks alerts parents to set priorities and act on them, and helps professionals advise pregnant women. Some recommendations should be routine (e.g., prenatal vitamins including folic acid) because it is impossible to know who is at risk. Others are tailored to the individual, such as weight gain for underweight women.

Care must be taken to keep pregnancy and birth from being an anxious time, filled with restrictions and fears about diet, diseases, drugs, and other possible dangers. Anxiety itself may reduce sleep, impair digestion, and raise blood pressure—all of which hinder development—and then may make birth complicated and postpartum depression likely.

Indeed, stress reduces the chances of conception, increases the chance of prenatal damage, and slows down the birth process. A conclusion from every page of this chapter is that risks are apparent in every moment of conception, pregnancy, and birth but those risks can be minimal if everyone, fathers as well as mothers, professionals as well as community members, does what is needed to ensure that newborns begin life eager and able to live 80 more healthy years.

KEY Points

- Nature and nurture always interact. Whether a particular genetic vulnerability becomes a lifelong problem depends a great deal on the environment.
- Alcoholism is affected by genes for metabolism and personality, but also by social context.
- Nearsightedness has increased in the past decades, particularly in East Asia but also in North America. Less time for outdoor play is the suspected reason.
- Knowing genetic risks helps parents avoid triggers for problems and hopefully reduces generalized anxiety, which itself can be a teratogen.

SUMMARY

The Beginning of Life

1. Genes are the foundation for all development. Human conception occurs when two gametes (an ovum and a sperm, each with 23 chromosomes) combine to form a zygote, 46 chromosomes in a single cell.

2. Every cell of every human being has a unique genetic code made up of about 20 000–23 000 genes, some in variations called *alleles*. The environment interacts with the genetic instructions for every trait.

3. The sex of an embryo depends on the sperm: A Y sperm creates an XY (male) embryo; an X sperm creates an XX (female) embryo. Twins occur if a zygote splits in two (monozygotic, or identical, twins) or if two ova are fertilized by two sperm (dizygotic, or fraternal, twins).

4. Genes interact in various ways; sometimes additively, with multiple genes contributing to a trait, and sometimes in a dominant–recessive pattern. While the genotype of each person is always determined by the combined genotypes of the parents, the phenotype (apparent characteristics) may be quite different from the genotype.

From Zygote to Newborn

5. The first two weeks of prenatal growth are called the germinal period. The cells differentiate, as the developing organism implants itself in the lining of the uterus.

6. The period from the third through the eighth week after conception is called the embryonic period. The heart begins to beat, and the eyes, ears, nose, and mouth form. By the eighth

week, the embryo has the basic organs and features of a human, with the exception of the sex organs.

7. The fetal period extends from the ninth week until birth. By the 12th week, all the organs and body structures have formed. The fetus attains viability at 22 weeks, when the brain is sufficiently mature to regulate basic body functions.

8. The average fetus gains approximately 2000 grams during the last three months of pregnancy. Maturation of brain, lungs, and heart ensures survival of virtually all full-term babies.

9. Medical intervention can speed contractions, dull pain, measure health via the Apgar scale, and save lives. However, some measures seem unnecessary. The goal is a balance, protecting the baby but also allowing parental involvement and control.

10. Many women feel unhappy, incompetent, or unwell after giving birth. Postpartum depression gradually disappears with appropriate help; fathers are particularly crucial to the well-being of mother and child, although they, too, are vulnerable to depression.

Problems and Solutions

11. Often a zygote has more or fewer than 46 chromosomes. Such zygotes usually do not develop; the main exceptions are those with three chromosomes at the 21st location

(Down syndrome, or trisomy-21) or an odd number of sex chromosomes.

12. Thousands of teratogens, especially drugs and alcohol, have the potential to harm the embryo or fetus. Actual harm occurs because of a cascade: Genes, critical periods, dose, and frequency all have an impact.

13. Birth complications, such as unusually long and stressful labour that includes anoxia (a lack of oxygen to the fetus), have many causes. Low birth weight (under or 2500 grams) may arise from multiple births, placental problems, maternal illness, genes, malnutrition, smoking, drinking, and drug use.

Nature and Nurture Connected

14. Alcoholism is partly genetic, but not completely. It is particularly crucial that children who are genetically vulnerable avoid early exposure to alcohol.

15. Nearsightedness is also partly genetic, but understanding heritability (the impact of genes within a population, not necessarily within an individual) helps show that the increase in nearsightedness is affected by the childhood environment.

16. Nature and nurture interact to cause virtually all human problems; understanding genes, prenatal development, birth, and childhood all increase the odds that a newborn will have a long and healthy life.

KEY TERMS

additive gene (p. 56)
age of viability (p. 61)
allele (p. 51)
anoxia (p. 76)
Apgar scale (p. 64)
behavioural teratogens (p. 73)
Brazelton Neonatal Behavioral Assessment Scale (NBAS) (p. 67)
carrier (p. 56)
cerebral palsy (p. 75)
Caesarean section (C-section) (p. 65)
chromosome (p. 50)
couvade (p. 68)

dizygotic twins (p. 56)
DNA (deoxyribonucleic acid) (p. 50)
dominant–recessive pattern (p. 56)
doula (p. 67)
Down syndrome (p. 71)
embryo (p. 59)
embryonic period (p. 58)
extremely low birth weight (ELBW) (p. 79)
fetal alcohol syndrome (FAS) (p. 76)
fetal period (p. 58)
fetus (p. 60)

gamete (p. 50)
gene (p. 50)
genome (p. 52)
genotype (p. 52)
germinal period (p. 58)
heritability (p. 85)
implantation (p. 59)
infant mortality rate (IMR) (p. 82)
kangaroo care (p. 69)
low birth weight (LBW) (p. 79)
monozygotic twins (p. 54)
parent–infant bond (p. 69)
phenotype (p. 52)

postpartum depression (p. 69)
preterm birth (p. 80)
reflex (p. 67)
small for gestational age (SGA) (p. 80)
stem cells (p. 59)
teratogen (p. 72)
threshold effect (p. 76)
ultrasound (p. 60)
very low birth weight (VLBW) (p. 79)
X-linked (p. 57)
XX (p. 53)
XY (p. 53)
zygote (p. 50)

WHAT HAVE YOU LEARNED?

1. What is the relationship among DNA, chromosomes, and genes?

2. Use the concept of gametes to explain why your parents could have given you millions of different siblings.

3. What surprises came from the Human Genome Project?

4. How is the sex of a zygote determined?

5. What are the differences among monozygotic twins, dizygotic twins, and other siblings?

6. When talking about genes, what is meant by a "dominant–recessive pattern"?

7. What are three major developments in the germinal period?

8. What body parts develop during the embryonic period?

9. What major milestone is reached about halfway through the fetal period?

10. What role does the hormone oxytocin play in birth?

11. What five vital signs does the Apgar scale measure?

12. What are some advantages and disadvantages of Caesarean sections?

13. In what ways do doulas support women before, during, and after labour?

14. What three sets of protective reflexes are typically seen in newborns? Give three examples of reflexes from each set.

15. How do fathers experience pregnancy?

16. What are the signs of postpartum depression?

17. What are the results of kangaroo care?

18. What are the consequences if an infant is born with trisomy-21?

19. Why are a few recessive traits (such as the sickle-cell trait) quite common?

20. What teratogens harm the developing baby, and what types of harm can they cause?

21. How does the timing of exposure to a teratogen affect the risk of harm to the fetus?

22. What are the potential consequences of drinking alcohol during pregnancy?

23. What factors increase or decrease the risk of spina bifida?

24. What are the benefits of prenatal care?

25. What are the differences among LBW, VLBW, and ELBW?

26. List at least four reasons why a baby might be born LBW.

27. What are some potential consequences of low birth weight?

28. In what ways do biology, psychology, and culture influence the risk of alcoholism?

29. In what ways do age, genes, and culture affect vision?

30. How might an awareness of genetic risks influence parents' behaviour before, during, and after pregnancy?

APPLICATIONS

1. Pick one of your traits, and explain the influences that both nature and nurture have on it. For example, if you have a short temper, explain its origins in your genetics, your culture, and your childhood experiences.

2. Draw a genetic chart of your biological relatives, going back as many generations as you can, listing all serious illnesses and causes of death. Include ancestors who died in infancy. Do you see any genetic susceptibility? If so, how can you overcome it?

3. Go to a nearby greeting-card store and analyze the cards about pregnancy and birth. Do you see any cultural attitudes (e.g., variations depending on the sex of the newborn or of the parent)? If possible, compare those cards with cards from a store that caters to another economic or cultural group.

4. Interview three mothers of varied backgrounds about their birth experiences. Make your interviews open-ended—let the mothers choose what to tell you, as long as they give at least a 10-minute description. Then compare and contrast the three accounts, noting especially any influences of culture, personality, circumstances, or cohort.

>> ONLINE CONNECTIONS

To accompany your textbook, you have access to a number of online resources, including LearningCurve, which is an adaptive quizzing program; critical thinking questions; and case studies. For access to any of these links, go to www.worthpublishers.com/launchpad/bergerchuang1e. In addition to these resources, you'll find links to video clips, personalized study advice, and an e-Book. Among the videos and activities available online are the following:

- *Brain Development.* A three-dimensional animation follows brain development from the formation of the neural tube until birth.

- *Periods of Prenatal Development.* A series of detailed animations show the stages of prenatal development from fertilization to birth.

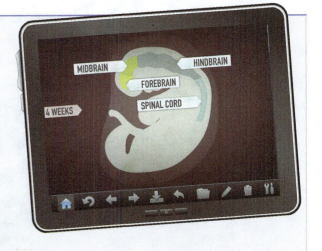

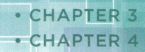
The First Two Years

Adults don't change much in a year or two. They might have longer, greyer, or thinner hair; they might gain or lose weight; they might learn something new. But if you saw friends you hadn't seen for two years, you'd recognize them immediately.

Imagine caring for a newborn 24 hours a day for a month and then leaving for two years. On your return, you might not recognize him or her. The baby would have quadrupled in weight, grown 30 centimetres taller, and sprouted a new head of hair. Behaviour and emotions change, too—less crying, but new laughter and fear—including fear of you.

A year or two is not much compared with the 80 or so years of the average life. However, in their first two years humans reach half their adult height, learn to talk in sentences, and express almost every emotion—not just joy and fear but also love, jealousy, and shame. The next two chapters describe these radical and awesome changes.

CHAPTER OUTLINE

THE FIRST TWO YEARS:
Body and Mind

3

WHAT WILL YOU KNOW?

- What part of an infant grows most in the first two years?
- How are newborn humans the opposite of newborn kittens?
- Does immunization protect or harm babies?
- If a baby doesn't look for an object that disappears, what does that mean?
- Why talk to babies who are too young to understand words?

Our first child, Bethany, was born when I was in graduate school. I studiously memorized developmental norms, including sitting at 6 months, and walking and talking at 12. But although Bethany had not yet taken her first step at 14 months, I was not worried. I told my husband that genes were more influential than anything we did. I had read that babies in Paris are among the latest walkers in the world, and my grandmother was French. My speculation was bolstered when our next two children, Rachel and Elissa, were also slow to walk.

Fourteen years after Bethany, Sarah was born. I could afford a full-time caregiver, Mrs. Todd. She thought Sarah was the most advanced baby she had ever known, except for her own daughter, Gillian. I told her that Berger children walk late.

"She'll be walking by a year," Mrs. Todd told me. "Gillian walked at 10 months."

"We'll see," I graciously replied, confident of my genetic explanation.

Mrs. Todd bounced my delighted baby on her lap, day after day, and spent hours giving her "walking practice." Sarah's first step was at 12 months, late for a Todd, early for a Berger, and a humbling lesson for me. ●

—*Kathleen Berger*

RUIZHI ZHANG

Developmental Changes Infants are very small, as seen by Isaiah, the son of Susan Chuang's colleague. At 5 months, he can fit in a pail! However, very soon he will have grown too big for the pail, and will be walking and talking. Children change dramatically in the first two years of life.

As a scientist, I know that a single case proves nothing. Sarah shares only half her genes with Bethany. My daughters are only one-eighth French, a fraction I had ignored when Sarah's sisters were infants.

Nonetheless, as you read about development, remember that caregiving enables babies to grow, move, and learn. Development is not as straightforward and automatic, nor as genetically determined, as it once seemed. It is multidirectional, multicontextual, multicultural, and plastic. Parents express their devotion in many ways, some massaging infant bodies every day, some talking in response to every noise. No wonder babies vary.

Growth in Infancy

In infancy, growth is so rapid and the consequences of neglect are so severe that gains are closely monitored. Medical checkups, including measurements of height, weight, and head circumference, occur often in developed nations because these measurements provide the first clues as to whether an infant is progressing as expected—or not.

Body Size

Weight gain is dramatic. Newborns lose a bit of weight in the first three days of life and then gain about 30 grams a day for several months. Birth weight typically doubles by 4 months and triples by a year. A typical 3175-gram newborn would be approximately 9525 grams at 12 months.

Physical growth in the second year is slower but still rapid. By 24 months, most children weigh almost 13 kilograms. They have added more than 30 centimetres in height—from about 51 centimetres at birth to about 86 centimetres at age 2 (see Figure 3.1). This means that 2-year-olds are half their adult height and about a fifth of their adult weight, four times heavier than they were at birth (see Figure 3.2).

Each of these numbers is a **norm,** which is an average, or standard, for a particular population. The "particular population" for the norms just cited is North American infants. Remember, however, that genetic diversity means that some perfectly healthy newborns are smaller or larger than these norms, as we discussed in Chapter 2.

norm
An average, or standard, measurement, calculated from the measurements of many individuals within a specific group or population.

FIGURE 3.1 Gender Differences
Boys and girls grow at almost the same rate throughout childhood. Compare this graph to the one on weight (Figure 3.2), and note that already by age 2, genetic growth patterns are disturbed by overfeeding and underfeeding.

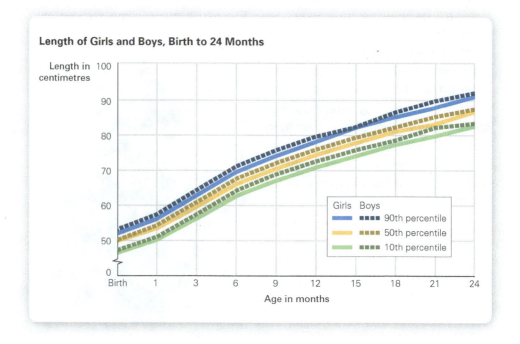

Length of Girls and Boys, Birth to 24 Months

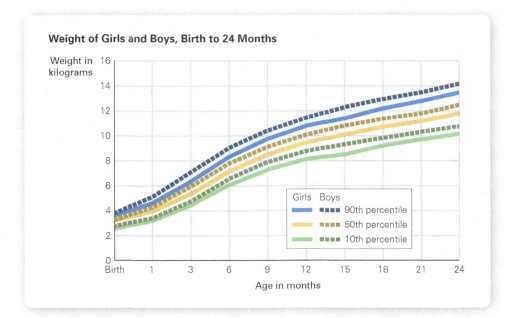

Weight of Girls and Boys, Birth to 24 Months

FIGURE 3.2 **Eat and Sleep** The rate of increasing weight in the first weeks of life makes it obvious why new babies need to be fed, day and night.

At each well-baby checkup (monthly at first), a doctor or nurse measures the baby's growth and compares it to that baby's previous numbers. A baby who always has been average (50th percentile) becomes worrisome if the percentile changes a lot, either up or down. Abnormal growth may signify a problem; that's why early checkups are vital.

Prenatal and postnatal brain growth (measured by head circumference) is crucial for later cognition (Gilles & Nelson, 2012). If teething or a stuffed nose slow weight gain, nature protects the brain, a phenomenon called **head-sparing.** From two weeks after conception to 2 years, the brain grows more rapidly than any other part of the body, from about 25 percent of adult weight at birth to almost 75 percent. Over the same two years, brain circumference increases from about 36 to 48 centimetres (see Figure 3.3).

FIGURE 3.3 **Growing Up** Two-year-olds have already reached half their adult height and three-fourths of their adult brain size.

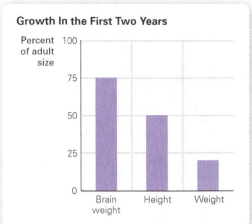

Growth In the First Two Years

Brain Development

The brain is essential throughout life; it is discussed in every chapter of this book. We begin now with the basics—neurons, axons, dendrites, neurotransmitters, synapses, and the cortex, especially the prefrontal cortex.

BRAIN BASICS Communication within the central nervous system (CNS)—the brain and spinal cord—begins with nerve cells, called **neurons.** At birth, the human brain has billions of neurons, most of them (about 70 percent) in the **cortex,** the brain's six outer layers. The cortex is crucial: Most thinking, feeling, and sensing occur in the cortex (Johnson, 2010). The final part of the brain to mature is the **prefrontal cortex,** the area for anticipation, planning, and impulse control. It is virtually inactive in the first months of infancy, and gradually becomes more efficient in childhood and adolescence (Wahlstrom et al., 2010).

Different areas of the brain have specialized functions. Some regions deep within the skull maintain breathing and heartbeat, some in the midbrain underlie emotions and impulses, and some in the cortex allow perception and cognition. For instance, there is a visual cortex, an auditory cortex, and an area dedicated to the sense of touch for each body part—including for each finger of a person or each whisker of a rat (Barnett et al., 2006).

head-sparing
A biological mechanism that protects the brain when malnutrition disrupts body growth. The brain is the last part of the body to be damaged by malnutrition.

neuron
One of billions of nerve cells in the central nervous system, especially in the brain.

cortex
The outer layers of the brain in humans and other mammals. Most thinking, feeling, and sensing involve the cortex.

prefrontal cortex
The area of the cortex at the very front of the brain that specializes in anticipation, planning, and impulse control.

axon
A fibre that extends from a neuron and transmits electrochemical impulses from that neuron to the dendrites of other neurons.

dendrite
A fibre that extends from a neuron and receives electrochemical impulses transmitted from other neurons via their axons.

synapse
The intersection between the axon of one neuron and the dendrites of other neurons.

neurotransmitter
A brain chemical that carries information from the axon of a sending neuron to the dendrites of a receiving neuron.

Within and between areas of the central nervous system, neurons are linked to other neurons by intricate networks of nerve fibres called **axons** and **dendrites** (see Figure 3.4). Each neuron has a single axon and numerous dendrites, which spread out like the branches of a tree. The axon of one neuron meets the dendrites of other neurons at intersections called **synapses,** tiny gaps that are critical communication links within the brain.

To be more specific, axons and dendrites do not touch at synapses. Instead, neurons communicate by sending electrochemical impulses (called **neurotransmitters**) through their axons to synapses, to be picked up by the dendrites of other neurons. The dendrites bring messages to the cell bodies of their neurons, which, in turn, convey the messages via their axons to the dendrites of other neurons.

EXPERIENCES AND PRUNING At birth, the brain contains at least 100 billion neurons, more than a person needs. However, the newborn's brain has far fewer dendrites and synapses than the person will eventually possess. During the first months and years, rapid growth and refinement in axons, dendrites, and synapses occur, especially in the cortex. Dendrite growth is the major reason that brain weight triples from birth to age 2 years (Johnson, 2010).

An estimated fivefold increase in dendrites in the cortex occurs in the 24 months after birth, with about 100 trillion synapses being present at age 2 years. According to one expert, 40 000 new synapses are formed every second in the infant's brain (Schore & McIntosh, 2011).

FIGURE 3.4 How Two Neurons Communicate The link between one neuron and another is shown in the simplified diagram at right. The infant brain actually contains billions of neurons, each with one axon and many dendrites. Every electrochemical message to or from the brain causes thousands of neurons to fire, each transmitting the message across the synapse to neighbouring neurons. The electron micrograph directly below shows neurons greatly magnified, with their tangled but highly organized and well-coordinated sets of dendrites and axons.

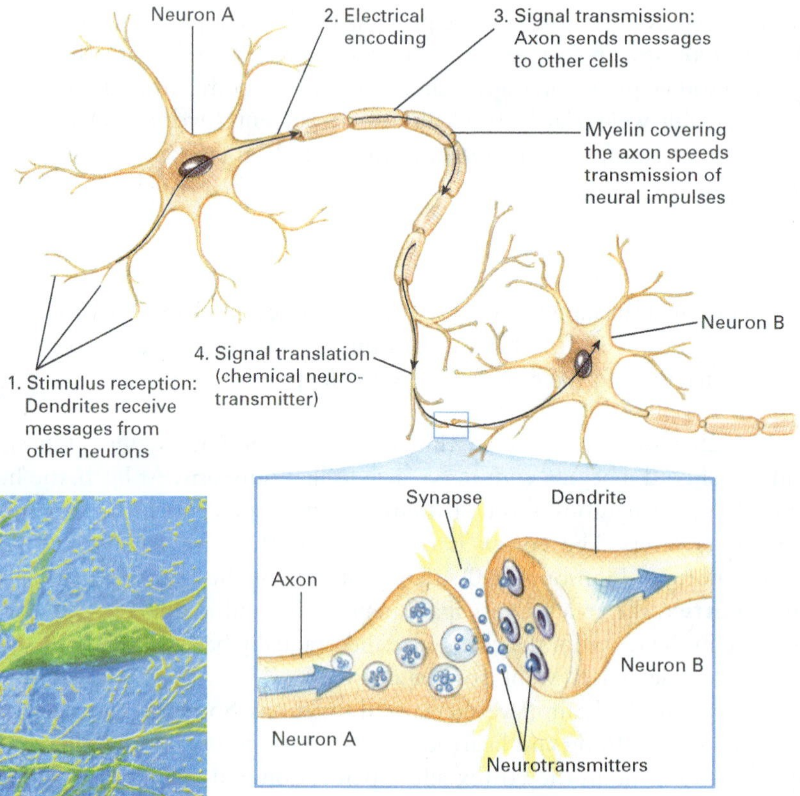

Neuron A

2. Electrical encoding

3. Signal transmission: Axon sends messages to other cells

Myelin covering the axon speeds transmission of neural impulses

Neuron B

1. Stimulus reception: Dendrites receive messages from other neurons

4. Signal translation (chemical neurotransmitter)

Synapse

Dendrite

Axon

Neuron B

Neuron A

Neurotransmitters

In the synapse, or intersection between an axon and many dendrites, neurotransmitters carry information from one neuron to another.

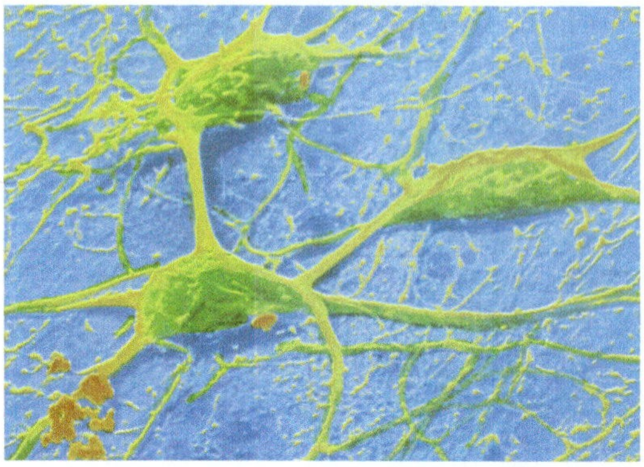

CNRI / SCIENCE SOURCE

This extensive postnatal brain growth is highly unusual for mammals. Why does it occur in humans? Although prenatal brain development is remarkable, it is limited by the simple fact that the human pelvis is relatively small and the head must be relatively small as well to make birth possible. Thus there is an acceleration of growth after birth. In fact, unlike other species, humans must nurture and protect their offspring for more than a decade as children's brains continue to develop (Konner, 2010).

Early dendrite growth is called **transient exuberance:** *exuberant* because it is so rapid and *transient* because some of it is temporary. The expansive growth of dendrites is followed by **pruning.** Just as a gardener might prune a rose bush by cutting away some growth to enable more, or lovelier, roses to bloom, unused brain connections atrophy and die (Stiles & Jernigan, 2010).

The specifics of brain structure and growth depend on genes and maturation but even more on experience (Stiles & Jernigan, 2010). Some dendrites wither away because they are never used—that is, no experiences have caused them to send a message to other neurons. Expansion and pruning of dendrites occur for every aspect of early experience, from noticing musical rhythms to understanding emotions (Scott et al., 2007). Strangely enough, this loss of dendrites increases brainpower. The space between neurons in the human brain, for instance—especially in regions for advanced, abstract thought—is far greater than the space in chimpanzee brains (Miller, 2010). The densely packed neurons of chimps make them less intelligent than people, probably because humans have more space for dendrite formation. This allows more synapses and thus more complex thinking.

Some children with intellectual disabilities have "a persistent failure of normal synapse pruning" (Irwin et al., 2002, p. 194). That makes thinking difficult. For example, one sign of autism is more rapid brain growth, suggesting too little pruning (Hazlett et al., 2011). Yet just as too little pruning creates problems, so does too much pruning. Brain sculpting is attuned to experience: The appropriate links in the brain need to be established, protected, and strengthened while inappropriate ones are eliminated. One group of scientists speculates that "lack of normative experiences may lead to overpruning of neurons and synapses, both of which may lead to reduction of brain activity" (Moulson et al., 2009, p. 1051). Another group suggests that infants who are often hungry, or hurt, or neglected develop brains that compensate—and cannot be reprogrammed even if circumstances change. The hungry baby

Same Boy, Much Changed All three photos show the same child, first at 3 months, then at 12 months, and finally at 24 months. Note the rapid growth in the first two years, especially apparent in head proportions and use of the legs.

transient exuberance
The great but temporary increase in the number of dendrites that develop in an infant's brain during the first two years of life.

pruning
When applied to brain development, the process by which unused connections in the brain atrophy and die.

becomes the obese adult, the neglected child rejects attention, and so on, always with the interaction of nature and nurture (van IJzendoorn et al., 2012).

William Greenough and his colleagues explored the plasticity of the brain and discovered that experiences influence how the brain develops and matures. They believed that there are two types of categorization schemes present in the brain, depending on the type of information that is to be stored. The first type of scheme is the *experience-expectant* information storage, which includes the environmental information that is common to all people (e.g., seeing contrast, borders, or patterns). The second type of scheme is called *experience-dependent*, which stores important and specific information, unique to the individual (e.g., sources of food). Thus, new synaptic connections are made in response to each person's experiences and what needs to be remembered (Greenough et al., 1987).

PLASTICITY OF THE BRAIN During the prenatal stage, the brain develops rapidly, as various parts take on their specialized functions. Some of this development is automatic, due to genetically predetermined pathways. However, the brain is also very vulnerable to environmental influences, and these influences can set the stage for major neurological patterns in the future (e.g., competence, health, and well-being) (Mustard, 2006). Thus, the brain is high in **plasticity,** meaning that it can be modified and changed by environmental circumstances. For example, infants raised in an environment with minimal sensory stimulation have been found to have a different brain structure and weight than infants who have been raised in enriched settings (Cicchetti, 2003; Couperus & Nelson, 2006).

One advantage of the brain's plasticity is the ability to compensate or take over the functions of certain areas that may have been damaged by disease or accident. However, as just noted, such plasticity also means the brain is highly vulnerable to impoverished or restricted environments, and this can lead to damage that is significant enough to have serious implications for future development.

Some researchers have found that language and literacy assessment can provide an indication of overall brain development in the early years. The sounds of the language that infants are exposed to have been found to influence how the auditory neurons function. For example, during the first 7 to 8 months, if infants are exposed to two languages (e.g., English and French), they are more likely to speak each language idiomatically, that is, with no discernible accent. Those who learn two languages during their early years have a larger left brain (Mustard, 2006), which may assist with language acquisition and fluency.

plasticity
The ability to be modified or changed.

Electric Excitement Milo's delight at his mother's facial expressions is visible, not just in his eyes and mouth, but also in the neurons of the outer layer of his cortex. Electrodes map his brain activation, region by region and moment by moment. Every month of life up to age 2 shows increased electrical excitement.

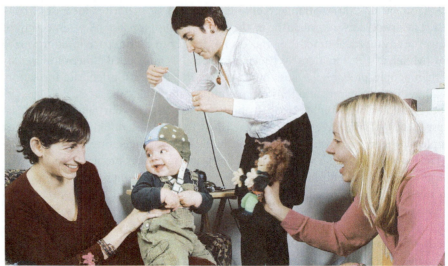

A VIEW FROM SCIENCE

Face Recognition

Unless you have prosopagnosia (face blindness, relatively rare), one part of your brain, the *fusiform face area*, is astonishingly adept at face recognition. This area is primed among newborns, although it has yet to reflect experience: Newborns stare at monkey faces as well as at human ones, and at pictures and toys with faces as well as at live faces.

Soon, experiences (such as seeing one's parents again and again) refine perception (de Heering et al., 2010). By 3 months, most babies smile more readily at familiar people and are more accurate at differentiating faces from their own species and their own ethnic group (called the *own-race effect*).

The own-race effect is the result of limited multi-ethnic experiences, not innate prejudice. Children of one ethnicity, adopted and raised exclusively among people of another ethnicity, recognize differences among people of their adopted group more readily than differences among people of their biological group.

The importance of early experience is further evidenced in two studies. In one, over the course of three months, 6-month-old infants were repeatedly (more than 30 times) shown a book of pictures of six monkey faces, each with a name written on the page (see photo).

For one-third of the babies, the parents read the names while showing the pictures; another one-third of the parents said only "monkey" as they turned each page; and the final one-third simply turned pages. At 9 months, all the infants viewed pictures of six *unfamiliar* monkeys. The infants who had repeatedly seen named monkeys were better at distinguishing one new monkey from another than the infants who saw the same picture book but did not hear each monkey's name (Scott & Monesson, 2010).

The second study was premised on the fact that many children and adults do not notice the individuality of newborns. Some even claim that "all babies look alike." However, the study found that 3-year-olds with younger siblings were much better at recognizing differences between photos of unfamiliar newborns than were 3-year-olds with no younger brothers or sisters (Cassia et al., 2009). This shows that experience matters, contributing to development of dendrites in the fusiform face area.

REPRINTED FROM *NEUROPSYCHOLOGIA*, 48, SCOTT, L. ET AL. EXPERIENCE-DEPENDENT NEURAL SPECIALIZATION DURING INFANCY, 1857–1861. COPYRIGHT 2010 WITH PERMISSION FROM ELSEVIER.

Dario   Boris   Anice   Iona   Flora   Louis

Distinguishing Between Faces If you heard that Dario was quite different from Louis or Boris, would you stare at unfamiliar monkey faces more closely in the future? For 6-month-olds, the answer is yes.

HARM AND PROTECTION Most infants develop well within their culture, and head-sparing usually ensures that baby brains are sufficiently nourished. For brain development, it does not matter whether a baby hears French or Farsi, or sees emotions dramatically or subtly (e.g., throwing oneself to the floor or merely pursing the lips). However, infant brains do not develop well without certain experiences that all humans need.

Because of brain plasticity and its consistent development, parents and others in the infants' social world play an important role in the baby's brain development. There are many simple and efficient ways of promoting healthy development. To begin with, parents need to provide a stimulating environment, which can include talking and singing to the baby, playing, massaging, and engaging in other sensory activities, all of which provide fodder for brain connections. Severe lack of stimulation (e.g., no

✦ **ESPECIALLY FOR Parents of Grown Children** Suppose you realize that you seldom talked to your children until they talked to you, and that you often put them in cribs and playpens. Did you limit their brain growth and their sensory capacity? (see response, page 101) →

shaken baby syndrome (SBS) A life-threatening injury that occurs when an infant is forcefully shaken back and forth, a motion that ruptures blood vessels in the brain and breaks neural connections.

talking at all) stunts the brain. As the saying goes, "use it or lose it." As one review of early brain development explains, "enrichment and deprivation studies provide powerful evidence of … widespread effects of experience on the complexity and function of the developing system" (Stiles & Jernigan, 2010, p. 345).

This does not mean that babies require spinning, buzzing, multi-textured, and multicoloured toys. In fact, such toys may be a waste of time and money since infants can be overstimulated by them; babies usually cry or go to sleep when that happens, to avoid bombardment. While there is no evidence that such overstimulation harms the infant brain, it is clear that babies are just as fascinated by simple objects and facial expressions as they are by complicated ones.

A simple application of what has been learned about the prefrontal cortex is that hundreds of objects, from the very simple to the quite elaborate, can capture an infant's attention. There is also a tragic implication: The brain is not yet under thoughtful control, since the prefrontal cortex is not well developed. Unless adults understand this, they might get angry if an infant keeps crying. Infants cry as a reflex to pain (usually digestive pain); they are too immature to *decide* to stop crying, as adults do.

If a frustrated caregiver reacts to crying by shaking the baby, it can cause a life-threatening condition called **shaken baby syndrome (SBS),** which occurs when infants are shaken back and forth sharply and quickly. Because the brain is still developing, shaking stops the crying because blood vessels in the brain rupture and fragile neural connections break. Pediatricians consider shaken baby syndrome an example of *abusive head trauma* (Christian et al., 2009). Death is the worst possible result; lifelong intellectual impairment is the more likely one.

According to one study of 364 injured children under the age of 5 years who were admitted to pediatric hospitals across Canada, 69 (19 percent) of the children died outright of their injuries. Of those who survived, 55 percent suffered long-term neurological damage and 65 percent had visual impairments. Only 22 percent of survivors showed no signs of continuing developmental impacts when they were released from hospital (King et al., 2003). The study also found that in cases where the abuser was identified, it was usually a parent, either the biological father (50 percent), the stepfather or partner (20 percent), or the biological mother (12 percent). Such statistics have encouraged researchers and government agencies to develop remedial programs that will raise parental awareness of the serious nature of SBS, and offer advice on ways to avoid the frustration that can lead parents to shake a baby who won't stop crying.

In 2004, the state of New York passed a law requiring mothers of newborns to watch a 15-minute video on SBS before leaving hospital. One of the project coordinators has credited this program with reducing the incidence of SBS in western New York by 50 percent (CBC, 2005). A temporary program in Vancouver that distributed information booklets and DVDs to mothers of newborns also showed promising results (Barr et al., 2009). All such efforts indicate the importance of education in lowering the rates of what Health Canada has called "a preventable tragedy" (Public Health Agency of Canada, 2012b).

The fact that infant brains respond to their circumstances suggests that waiting until evidence shows that a young child has been mistreated is waiting too long. In the first months of life, babies adjust to their world, becoming withdrawn and quiet if their caregivers are depressed or becoming loud and demanding if that is the only way they get fed. Such adjustments set patterns that are destructive later on. Thus, understanding development as dynamic and interactive means helping caregivers from the start, not waiting until destructive systems are established (Tronick & Beegly, 2011). The word "systems" is crucial here. Almost every baby experiences something stressful—a caregiver yelling, or a fall off the bed, or a painful stomach. Fortunately, **self-righting**—an inborn drive to remedy deficits—is built into the human system. Infants with few toys develop their brains by using whatever objects are available, and infants whose mothers are neglectful may develop close bonds with someone else who provides daily stimulation.

Human brains are designed to grow and adapt; plasticity is apparent from the beginning of life (Tomalski & Johnson, 2010). It is the patterns, not the moments, of neglect or maltreatment that harm the brain.

self-righting
The inborn drive to remedy a developmental deficit; literally, to return to sitting or standing upright after being tipped over. People of all ages have self-righting impulses, for emotional as well as physical imbalance.

Sleep

One consequence of brain maturation is the ability to sleep through the night. Newborns cannot do this. Normally they sleep 15–17 hours a day, in one- to three-hour segments. Hours of sleep decrease rapidly with maturity: The norm per day for the first 2 months is 14¼ hours; for the next 3 months, 13¼ hours; and for 6 to 17 months, 12¾ hours. Variation is particularly apparent in the early weeks. As reported by parents (who might exaggerate), one new baby in 20 sleeps nine hours or fewer per day, and one in 20 sleeps 19 hours or more (Sadeh et al., 2009).

Sleep specifics vary not only because of biology (age and genes), but also because of the social environment. With responsive parents, full-term newborns sleep more than low-birth-weight babies, who are hungry every two hours. Babies who are fed cow's milk and cereal sleep more soundly—easier for parents but not ideal for the baby. Social environment has a direct effect: If parents respond to pre-dawn cries with food and play, babies wake up early every morning (Sadeh et al., 2009).

Over the first months, the relative amount of time in various stages of sleep changes. Babies born preterm may always seem to be dozing. Full-term newborns dream a lot; about half their sleep is **REM (rapid eye movement) sleep,** with flickering eyes and rapid brain waves. That indicates dreaming. REM sleep declines over the early weeks, as does "transitional sleep," the dozing, half-awake stage. At 3 or 4 months, quiet sleep (also called *slow-wave sleep*) increases, as does time alert and wide awake.

Overall, 25 percent of parents of children under age 3 years report that their babies have sleeping problems, according to an Internet study of more than 5000 North Americans (Sadeh et al., 2009). Sleep problems are more troubling for parents than for infants. This does not render them insignificant; overtired parents may be less patient and responsive (Bayer et al., 2007). Patience is also needed to ensure the baby's sleep position is properly "back to sleep," to protect against sudden infant death syndrome (see Chapter 1).

One problem for parents is that advice about where infants should sleep varies, from contending that infants should sleep beside their parents—who must immediately respond to every cry (Nicholson & Parker, 2009)—to advising that infants need their own room, should be allowed to "cry it out" so they will not be spoiled, and can learn to soothe themselves. Both sets of advice make sense, as the following explains.

RESPONSE FOR Parents of Grown Children (from page 100) Probably not. Brain development is programmed to occur for all infants, requiring only the stimulation that virtually all families provide—warmth, reassuring touch, overheard conversation, facial expressions, movement. Extras such as baby talk, music, exercise, mobiles, and massage may be beneficial, but are not essential. ●

REM (rapid eye movement) sleep
A stage of sleep characterized by flickering eyes behind closed lids, dreaming, and rapid brain waves.

Protective Sleeping It matters little what infants sleep in—bassinet, cradle, crib, or Billum bag made from local plants in Papua, New Guinea, as shown here. In fact, this kind of bag is very useful since babies can easily be carried in it. It can also be used for carrying food, tools, and much else. What does matter is the infant's sleeping position—always on the back, like this healthy infant.

PETER SOLNESS / GETTY IMAGES

OPPOSING PERSPECTIVES

Where Should Babies Sleep?

Traditionally, most middle-class North American infants slept in cribs in their own rooms; it was feared that they would be traumatized by the parents' sexual interactions. By contrast, infants in Asia, Africa, and Latin America slept with their parents, a practice called **co-sleeping.** People in those cultures believed that parent–child separation at night was cruel.

Even today, at baby's bedtime, Asian and African mothers worry more about separation, whereas European and North American mothers worry more about lack of privacy. A study in 19 nations confirms that parents act on their fears: The extremes were 82 percent of babies in Vietnam sleeping with their parents compared to 6 percent of babies in New Zealand (Mindell et al., 2010) (see Figure 3.5).

At first, this may seem to be a matter of income: Families of low socioeconomic status (SES) are less likely to have an extra room. But even wealthy Japanese families often co-sleep, and many poor Western families find a separate space for their children to sleep. Co-sleeping is a matter of custom, not merely income (Kohyama et al., 2011).

The argument for co-sleeping is that it is easier to respond to infants in the middle of the night, especially if a baby is hungry or scared. When parents opt for co-sleeping, they are less exhausted since they can reach over to feed or comfort their baby. Breastfeeding, often done every hour or two at first, is easier with co-sleeping—one reason many high-SES North Americans now practise it.

Yet the argument against co-sleeping rests on a chilling statistic: Sudden infant death is more common when babies sleep beside their parents (Gettler & McKenna, 2010; Ruys et al., 2007). In fact, the Public Health Agency of Canada (2011a) strongly recommends that infants under 4 months be placed on their backs in their own crib, cradle, or bassinet. Young infants should not share an adult's bed, couch, or armchair at bedtime.

Furthermore, adult beds, unlike cribs, are often soft, with comforters, mattresses, and pillows that increase the risk of suffocation (Alm, 2007). A commercial solution is a "co-sleeper," which is a baby bed designed to be next to the parents' bed but not in it. That way, the dangers of *bed-sharing* are avoided. Privacy issues remain, however.

One reason for opposing views is that every adult is affected by his or her long-past babyhood and seeks to avoid the mistakes of his or her parents. This phenomenon is called *ghosts in the nursery* because the parents bring

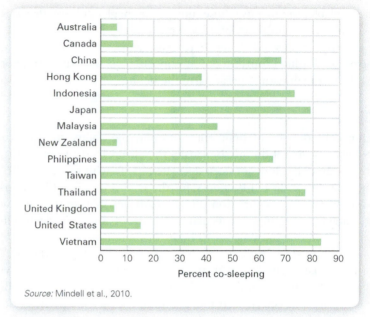

Source: Mindell et al., 2010.

FIGURE 3.5 **Awake at Night** Why the disparity between Asian and non-Asian rates of co-sleeping? It may be that Western parents use a variety of gadgets and objects—monitors, night lights, pacifiers, cuddle cloths, sound machines—to accomplish the same thing Asian parents do by having their infant next to them.

decades-old memories into the bedrooms of their children. Those ghosts can push for either co-sleeping or separate rooms.

One study found that, compared with Israeli adults who had slept near their parents as infants, those who had slept communally with other infants (as sometimes occurred on a kibbutz) often interpreted their own infants' nighttime cries as distress requiring comfort (Tikotzky et al., 2010). In other words, a ghost from the past is affecting current behaviour; when parents think their crying babies are frightened, lonely, and distressed, they want to respond quickly. Quick responses are more possible with co-sleeping. On the other hand, if parents' only private time and place is in their bedroom at night, the marriage may suffer if the baby sleeps there.

A developmental perspective begins with what we know: Infants learn from their earliest experiences. If babies become accustomed to bed-sharing, they will crawl into their parents' bed when they are long past infancy. Parents might lose sleep for years because they wanted more sleep when their babies were small.

Of course, that concern reflects a cultural norm as well. According to an ethnographic study, by the time Mexican Mayan children are 5 years old, they choose when, how

long, and with whom to sleep (Gaskins, 1999), a practice that bewilders many other North Americans.

Developmentalists hesitate to declare any particular pattern best (Tamis-LeMonda et al., 2008) because the issue is "tricky and complex" (Gettler & McKenna, 2010, p. 77). Sleeping alone may encourage independence and individuality—traits appreciated in some cultures, and not so much in others. Interestingly, one British study found that mothers and fathers who adjusted to sleeping with their infants felt this bonding experience was more rewarding than disruptive. They also found that it encouraged more involvement on the part of the father in nighttime caregiving (Ball et al., 2000).

Infant at Risk? Sleeping in the parents' bed is a risk factor for SIDS in North America, However, in Japan, 97 percent of infants sleep next to their parents, yet infant mortality is only 3 per 1000. What explains this difference in infant mortality?

✦ **ESPECIALLY FOR New Parents** You are aware of cultural differences in sleeping practices, which raises a very practical issue: Should your newborn sleep in bed with you? (see response, page 104) ➡

co-sleeping
A custom in which parents and their children (usually infants) sleep together in the same room.

KEY Points

- Weight and height increase markedly in the first two years; the norms are three times the baby's birth weight by age 1, and **30 centimetres taller** than birth height by age 2.
- Brain development is rapid during infancy, particularly development of the axons, dendrites, and synapses within the cortex.
- Since experience shapes the infant brain, the infant's environment plays an important role; pruning eliminates unused connections.
- Where and how much infants sleep is shaped by brain maturation and family practices.

Perceiving and Moving

People who don't know infants might think they are passive creatures at first, unable to do much. But that is far from the truth: Developmentalists have traced the immediate and rapid development of every skill.

The Senses

Every sense functions at birth. Newborns have open eyes, sensitive ears, and responsive noses, tongues, and skin. Indeed, very young babies seem to attend to everything without much judgment. For instance, in the first months of life, they smile at strangers and put almost anything in their mouths (Adolph & Berger, 2005).

Why are new infants not more cautious? Because sensation precedes perception, and perception leads to cognition. In order to learn, babies need to begin by responding to every sensation that might be significant.

sensation
The response of a sensory system (eyes, ears, skin, tongue, nose) when it detects a stimulus.

perception
The mental processing of sensory information when the brain interprets a sensation.

RESPONSE FOR New Parents (from page 103) From psychological and cultural perspectives, babies can sleep anywhere as long as the parents can hear them if they cry. The main consideration is safety: Infants should not sleep on a mattress that is too soft. Otherwise, each family should decide for itself. ●

Sensation occurs when a sensory system detects a stimulus, as when the inner ear reverberates with sound or the retina and pupil of the eye intercept light. Thus, sensations begin when an outer organ (eye, ear, nose, tongue, or skin) meets anything that can be seen, heard, smelled, tasted, or touched. Sensation at birth is affected by genetic selection over more than 100 000 years. Humans cannot hear what mice hear, or see what bats see, or smell what puppies smell; humans do not need those sensory abilities. However, survival requires people to respond to other people, and newborns innately do so (Konner, 2010; Lloyd-Fox et al., 2009).

Perception occurs when the brain notices and processes a sensation. This happens in the cortex, usually as the result of a message from one of the sensing organs, such as from the eye to the visual cortex. If a particular sensation occurs often, it connects with past experience, making a particular sight worth interpreting (M. E. Diamond, 2007).

Some sensations are beyond comprehension at first. A newborn has no idea that the letters on a page might have significance, that the mother's face should be distinguished from the father's, or that the smells of roses and garlic have different connotations. Perceptions require experience. Infants' brains are especially attuned to their own repeated social experiences, and that is how perception occurs. Thus, a newborn named Emily has no concept that *Emily* is her name. However she is born with crucial sensations, including the brain and auditory capacity to hear sounds in the usual speech range (not the high sounds that only dogs can hear) and an inborn preference for repeated patterns and human speech.

By about 4 months, when her auditory cortex is rapidly creating and pruning dendrites, the repeated word *Emily* is perceived as well as sensed, especially because that sound emanates from the people Emily has come to love (Saffran et al., 2006). By 6 months, Emily may open her eyes and turn her head when her name is called. It will take many more months before she says "Emmy" and still longer before she knows that *Emily* is indeed her name.

Thus, perception follows sensation, when senses are noticed by the brain. Then cognition follows perception, when people think about what they have perceived. (Later, cognition no longer requires sensation: People imagine, fantasize, and hypothesize.) The sequence from sensation to perception to cognition requires that an infant's sense organs function. No wonder the parts of the cortex dedicated to the senses develop rapidly: That is the prerequisite for human intellect. Now, some specifics.

TOUCH AND PAIN The sense of touch is acute in infants, with wrapping, rubbing, and cradling all soothing to many new babies. Some infants relax when held by their familiar caregiver, even when their eyes are closed. The ability to be comforted by touch is one of the important skills tested in the Brazelton Neonatal Behavioral Assessment Scale (NBAS, described in Chapter 2).

Although newborns respond to being securely held, soon they prefer specific, familiar touches. Caressing, swaddling, kissing, massaging, tickling, bouncing, and rocking are various means of soothing infants.

Pain is not one of the five senses, but it is often connected to touch. Some babies cry when being changed because sudden coldness on their skin is distressing. Some touches seem to be intrusive and produce crying.

Since the process of myelination, which speeds the transmission of nerve impulses between neurons, is not complete in infant brains, scientists have debated for years whether newborns experience pain to the same degree as adults. Now, the consensus seems to be that newborns do feel some kind of pain when undergoing procedures such as circumcision or setting a broken bone.

In a recent longitudinal study on infant pain response to heel pricking (routine after birth), Williams and her colleagues concluded that preterm infants do indeed experience pain right after birth and that their pain response increases as they get older (Williams et al., 2009). Many physiological measures, including stress hormones, erratic heartbeats, and rapid brain waves, are now studied to assess pain in preterm infants.

One tool designed to measure pain in both preterm and full-term infants is called the Neonatal Infant Pain Scale, which was developed at the Children's Hospital of Eastern Ontario (Lawrence et al., 1993). It uses five parameters to assess infant pain: facial expression, cry, breathing patterns, movement of arms and legs, and state of arousal.

HEARING AND SEEING The sense of hearing develops during the last trimester of pregnancy, which means that fetuses hear sounds in the womb. Since infants have experiences with their mothers' voice prenatally, they develop voice/sound preferences. Some studies have shown that human fetuses seem to recognize and respond more positively to the sound of their own mother's voice than to that of other women (Kisilevsky et al., 2003). They also often develop a preference for female voices to male voices, but do not seem to have a preference for their father's voice over other male voices (Brazelton, 1978; DeCasper & Fifer, 1980).

Researchers have also explored the hearing abilities of fetuses starting at 24 weeks after gestation. For example, DeCasper and Fifer (1980) had pregnant mothers read *The Cat in the Hat* twice a day 6.5 weeks before they were to give birth. After birth, those infants who had heard this story in the womb were more likely to suck on a pacifier faster (an indication that they recognized the story) each time their mothers read this story rather than another story.

For newborns, familiar, rhythmic sounds, such as a heartbeat, are soothing—one reason kangaroo care reduces newborn stress (see Chapter 2). Newborn hearing is routinely checked because the sense of hearing is normally quite acute: If a newborn seems deaf, early remediation may allow language to develop normally.

By 4 months of age, infants have developed perceptions of speech, as is evident in the Emily example. Babies expect the rhythms, segmentation, and cadence of the words they hear long before they understand meaning (Minagawa-Kawai et al., 2011).

Vision is the least mature sense at birth. Although the eyes open in mid-pregnancy and are sensitive to bright light (if the pregnant woman is at the beach in a bikini, for instance), the fetus has nothing much to see. Newborns are legally blind; they focus only on things 10 to 75 centimetres away (Bornstein et al., 2005).

Almost immediately, experience combines with maturation of the visual cortex to improve the ability to see shapes and then notice details, with vision improving so rapidly that researchers are hard-pressed to describe the day-by-day improvements (Dobson et al., 2009). By 2 months, infants not only stare at faces but also, after perception and then cognition occur, smile. (Smiling can occur earlier, but not because of perception.)

As perception builds, visual scanning improves. Thus, 3-month-olds look closely at the eyes and mouth, smiling more at smiling faces than at angry or expressionless ones. They pay attention to patterns, colours, and motion (Kellman & Arterberry, 2006).

✦ **ESPECIALLY FOR Nurses and Pediatricians** The parents of a 6-month-old have just been told that their child is deaf. They don't believe it because, as they tell you, the baby babbles as much as their other children did. What do you tell them? (see response, page 107) →

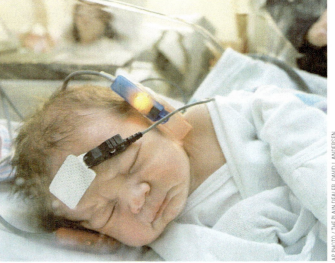

Before Leaving the Hospital Many hospitals require that newborns, such as 1-day-old Henry, have their hearing tested via vibrations of the inner ear in response to various tones. The computer interprets the data and signals any need for more tests—as is the case for about 1 baby in 100. Normal newborns hear quite well; Henry's hearing was fine.

AP PHOTO / THE PLAIN DEALER, DAVID I. ANDERSEN

Depth Perception This toddler is crawling on the experimental apparatus called a visual cliff. She stops at the edge of what she perceives as a drop-off.

binocular vision
The ability to focus the two eyes in a coordinated manner to see one image.

Learning About a Lime Like her peers, Jacqueline's curiosity leads to taste and then to a slow reaction, from puzzlement to tongue-out disgust. Her responses demonstrate that the sense of test is acute in infancy and that quick brain reactions are still to come.

Because **binocular vision** (coordinating both eyes to see one image) is impossible in the womb (nothing is far enough away to need two eyes), many newborns seem to use their two eyes independently, momentarily appearing wall-eyed or cross-eyed. Normally, visual experience leads to rapid development of focus and binocular vision; usually between 2 and 4 months, both eyes can focus on a single object (Wang & Candy, 2010). This helps in the development of depth perception, which has been demonstrated in 3-month-olds, although it was once thought to develop much later due to infants' reactions on an experimental apparatus called the visual cliff (see photo).

SMELLING AND TASTING Through the amniotic fluids, infants develop their senses of taste and smell while still in the womb. Schaal and colleagues (2000) found that women who consumed anise-flavoured products during pregnancy gave birth to babies who showed a marked preference for the smell of anise during the first few days after birth. Another group of researchers discovered that infants who were exposed to the flavour of carrot juice, either through amniotic fluid or breast milk, enjoyed eating carrot-flavoured cereal more than plain cereal once they started consuming solid food (Mennella et al., 2001).

Some herbs and plants contain natural substances that are medicinal. The foods of a particular culture may aid survival: Bitter foods provide some defence against malaria, spicy ones preserve food and thus work against food poisoning, and so on (Krebs, 2009). Thus, developing a taste for family food may be life-saving.

Adaptation also occurs for the sense of smell. When breastfeeding mothers used a chamomile balm to ease cracked nipples during the first days of their baby's lives, those babies preferred that smell almost two years later, compared with babies whose mothers used an odourless ointment (Delaunay El-Allam et al., 2010). Amazingly, 4-day-old infants can discriminate between the smell of their own mother's breast milk and that of another mother's milk (Porter & Reiser, 2005).

As babies learn to recognize each person's scent, they prefer to sleep next to their caregivers, and they nuzzle into their caregivers' chests—especially when the adults are shirtless. One way to help infants who are frightened of the bath (some love bathing, some hate it) is for the parent to get in the tub with the baby. The smells of the adult's body mix with the smell of soap, making the experience comforting.

Motor Skills

The most dramatic **motor skill** (any movement ability) is independent walking; this is one reason why Mrs. Todd was determined that Sarah would walk by the age of 1 year (see the beginning of this chapter). Walking and all other motor skills, from the newborn's head-lifting to toddler's stair-climbing, develop gradually over the first two years. The first evidence is in reflexes, already explained in Chapter 2.

Caregiving and experience matter. Reflexes become skills if they are practised and encouraged. As you saw in the chapter's beginning, the foundation for Sarah's walking was laid by Mrs. Todd's experience and caregiving when Sarah was only a few months old, long before her first step.

GROSS MOTOR SKILLS Deliberate actions that coordinate many parts of the body, producing large movements, are called **gross motor skills.** These emerge directly from reflexes and proceed in a cephalocaudal (head-down) and proximodistal (centre-out) direction. Infants first control their heads, lifting them up to look around. Then they control their upper bodies, their arms, and finally their legs and feet.

Sitting develops gradually, a matter of developing the muscles to steady the top half of the body. By 3 months, most babies can sit propped up in someone's lap. By 6 months, they can usually sit unsupported. Standing, and then walking, takes longer.

Crawling is another example of this head-down and centre-out direction of skill mastery. When placed on their stomachs, many newborns reflexively try to lift their heads and move their arms as if they were swimming. As they gain muscle strength, infants wiggle, attempting to move forward by pushing their arms, shoulders, and upper bodies against whatever surface they are lying on.

Usually by 5 months or so, they use their arms, and then legs, to inch forward (or backward) on their bellies. Exactly when this occurs depends partly on how much "tummy time" the infant has had, which is affected by culture (Zachry & Kitzmann, 2011).

Between 8 and 10 months after birth, most infants lift their midsections and crawl on "all fours," coordinating the movements of their hands and knees. Crawling depends on experience as well as maturation. Some normal babies never do it, especially if the floor is cold, hot, or rough, or if they have always lain on their backs (Pin et al., 2007). It is not true that babies *must* crawl to develop normally.

All babies figure out some way to move before they can walk (inching, bear-walking, scooting, creeping, or crawling), but many resist "tummy time" by rolling over and fussing (Adolph & Berger, 2005). Overweight babies master gross motor skills later than thinner ones: Practice is harder when the body is heavy (Slining et al., 2010).

The dynamic systems underlying motor skills have three interacting elements, each illustrated here with an example related to walking.

1. *Muscle strength.* Newborns with skinny legs and 3-month-olds buoyed by water make stepping movements, but 6-month-olds on dry land do not; their legs are too chubby for their underdeveloped muscles.

2. *Brain maturation.* The first leg movements—kicking (alternating legs at birth and then both legs together or one leg repeatedly at about 3 months)—occur without much thought. As the brain matures, deliberate leg action becomes possible.

3. *Practice.* Unbalanced, wide-legged, short strides become a steady, smooth gait.

motor skills
The learned abilities to move some part of the body, in actions ranging from a large leap to a flicker of the eyelid. (The word *motor* here refers to movement of muscles.)

gross motor skills
Physical abilities involving large body movements, such as walking and jumping. (The word *gross* here means "big.")

RESPONSE FOR Nurses and Pediatricians (from page 105) Urge the parents to begin learning sign language and investigate the possibility of cochlear implants. Babbling has a biological basis and begins at a specified time, in deaf as well as hearing babies. If their infant can hear, sign language does no harm. If the child is deaf, however, non-communication may be destructive. ●

Young Expert This infant is an adept crawler. Note the coordination between hands and knees, as well as the arm and leg strength needed to support the body in this early version of push-ups. This boy will probably be walking soon.

RICK GOMEZ / MASTERFILE

Bossa Nova Baby? This boy in Brazil demonstrates his joy at acquiring the gross motor skill of walking, which quickly becomes dancing whenever music plays.

fine motor skills
Physical abilities involving small body movements, especially of the hands and fingers, such as drawing and picking up a coin. (The word *fine* here means "small.")

pincer movement
The use of the thumb and forefinger to pick up objects.

The first item, *muscle strength*, may explain why newborns' innate stepping reflexes disappear. When newborns are held upright, they show well-coordinated walking movements—stepping. However, it is not until two months later that these stepping movements can be purposefully accomplished by the infant. Some researchers believe that stepping disappears because of the effects of gravity on muscle function (Thelen et al., 1982). As infants gain weight, they dramatically increase their leg mass, which alters the dynamics of their moving limbs. Thus, the strength of the leg muscle is not sufficient to lift the leg or to support the infant's full weight when in an upright position.

The last item in the list, *practice*, is powerfully affected by caregiving before the first independent step. Some adults spend hours helping infants walk (holding their hands, or the back of their shirts) or providing walkers (dangerous if not supervised).

Once toddlers can walk themselves, at around 1 year old, they practise obsessively, barefoot or not, at home or in stores, on sidewalks or streets, on lawns or in mud. They fall often, but that does not stop them; they average between 500 and 1500 walking steps per hour so that by the end of each day, they have taken 9000 walking steps and travelled the length of 29 football fields (Adolph et al., 2003).

FINE MOTOR SKILLS Small body movements are called **fine motor skills.** Finger movements are fine motor skills, enabling humans to write, draw, type, tie, and so on. Movements of the tongue, jaw, lips, and toes are fine movements, too.

Actually, mouth skills precede finger skills by many months (newborns can suck; chewing precedes drawing by a year or more). Every culture encourages finger dexterity, so children practise finger movements. However, mouth skills such as spitting or chewing are not praised.

Regarding hand skills, newborns have a strong reflexive grasp but lack control. During their first 2 months, babies excitedly stare and wave their arms at objects dangling within reach. By 3 months, they can usually touch such objects, but they cannot yet grab and hold on unless an object is placed in their hands, partly because their eye–hand coordination is limited.

By 4 months, infants sometimes grab, but their timing is off: They close their hands too early or too late. Finally, by 6 months, with a concentrated, deliberate stare, most babies can reach, grab, and hold almost any object that is of the right size. Some can even transfer an object from one hand to the other. Almost all can hold a bottle, shake a rattle, and yank a sister's braids. Once grabbing is possible, babies practise it enthusiastically: "From 6 to 9 months, reaching appears as a quite compulsive behaviour for small objects presented within arm's reach" (Atkinson & Braddick, 2003, p. 58).

Toward the end of the first year and throughout the second, finger skills improve, as babies master the **pincer movement** (using thumb and forefinger to pick up tiny objects) and self-feeding (first with hands, then fingers, then utensils) (Ho, 2010).

As with gross motor skills, fine motor skills are shaped by culture and opportunity. For example, infants given "sticky mittens" (with Velcro) that allow grabbing master hand skills sooner than usual. Their perception advances as well (Libertus & Needham, 2010; Soska et al., 2010).

In the second year, grabbing becomes more selective. Toddlers learn when *not* to pull at a sister's braids, or Mommy's earrings, or Daddy's glasses. However, as you will learn, the curiosity of the "little scientist" may overwhelm this inhibition.

Dynamic Sensory-Motor Systems

The entire package of sensations and motor skills furthers three goals:

1. social interaction
2. comfort
3. learning.

Physiologically, young human infants are, an unusual combination of motor immaturity (they cannot walk for many months), sensory acuteness, and curiosity (Konner, 2010). What a contrast to kittens, for instance, who are born deaf, with eyes sealed shut, and who stay beside their mother although they can walk.

Compare a kitten to a human newborn, listening and looking from day one, eager to practise every motor skill as soon as possible. An amusing example is rolling over. At about 3 months, infants can roll over from their stomach to the back, but not vice versa. Many a baby rolls over, fusses until someone puts him or her stomach down again, and then immediately rolls over again, only to fuss once more.

Sensory Exuberance Human animals are unusual in that all the senses function at birth, but motor skills develop slowly. This Ontario boy loves to grab the rings, or even bend over to taste and bite them, even though he cannot yet sit up unsupported.

The most important experiences are perceived with interacting senses and skills, in dynamic systems (see Chapter 1). Breast milk, for instance, is a mild sedative, so the newborn literally feels happier at mother's breast, connecting that pleasure with taste, touch, smell, and sight. But for all those joys to occur, the infant must actively suck at the nipple (an inborn motor skill, which becomes more efficient with practice).

Similarly, 6-month-olds coordinate their senses and skills, expecting lip movements to synchronize with speech, for instance (Lewkowicz, 2010), and making responsive noises themselves. For toddlers, crawling and walking are part of dynamic systems; they are used to explore, and thus sensations lead to perception and cognition.

Piaget named the first two years of cognitive development "sensorimotor" for good reason, as you will soon see. But first, there is one obvious prerequisite for all the growth already described—staying alive.

KEY Points

- All the senses function at birth, with hearing the most acute sense and vision the least developed.
- Every sense allows perception to develop and furthers social interaction, as caregivers are recognized by sight, touch, smell, and voice.
- Gross motor skills follow a genetic timetable for maturation; they are also affected by practice and experience.
- Fine motor skills also develop with time and experience, combining the senses as part of the dynamic systems.

Surviving in Good Health

Although precise worldwide statistics are unavailable, at least 10 billion children were born between 1950 and 2010. More than 2 billion of them died before age 5 years. Although 2 billion is far too many, twice as many would have died without recent public health measures. As best we know, in earlier centuries more than half of all newborns died in infancy.

TABLE 3.1 Deaths of Children Under Age 5 in Selected Countries, 2010

Country	Number of Deaths per 1000	Country	Number of Deaths per 1000
Iceland	2**	Russia	12*
Japan	3**	Mexico	17**
Singapore	3**	China	18**
Sweden	3**	Brazil	19**
Italy	4**	Vietnam	23**
Australia	5*	Iran	26**
Spain	5**	Philippines	29**
United Kingdom	5*	India	63**
Canada	6*	Nigeria	143*
New Zealand	6*	Afghanistan	149*
United States	8*	Sierra Leone	174*

*Reduced by at least one-third since 1990.
**Reduced by half or more since 1990.

Source: World Health Organization, 2012b.

Better Days Ahead

In the twenty-first century, 99.9 percent of newborns in developed nations who survive the first month (when the sickest and smallest may die) live to adulthood. Even in the poorest nations, where a few decades ago many children died before age 5 years, now about 80 percent live (see Table 3.1).

The world death rate in the first five years of life has dropped about 2 percent per year since 1990 (Rajaratnam et al., 2010). Most nations have improved markedly on this measure since 1990. Only when war destroys families and interferes with public health measures (as it has in Afghanistan) are nations not improving this statistic.

Public health measures (clean water, nourishing food, immunization) are the main reasons for the higher rate of survival. When women realize that a newborn is likely to survive to adulthood, they have fewer babies, and that advances the national economy. Infant survival and maternal education are the two main reasons the world's 2010 fertility rate is half what the rate was in 1950 (Bloom, 2011; Lutz & Samir, 2011).

If doctors and nurses were available in underserved areas, the current infant death rate would be cut in half—immediately by newborn survival and widespread immunization, and soon via measures to help the whole population, such as better food distribution, less violence, and clean water (Farahani et al., 2009). For example, every year in Africa 1 million people die of malaria, most of them undernourished children. Immediate drug treatment can save lives, but many victims live far from medical help, and some anti-malaria drugs are no longer effective (Kun et al., 2010).

One innovation has cut the malaria death rate in half: bed nets treated with insect repellant that drape over sleeping areas (Roberts, 2007) (see photo). Over the long term, however, systemic prevention means making mosquitos sterile—a promising research effort now entering clinical trials (James et al., 2011).

Immunization

Immunization primes the body's immune system to resist a particular disease. Immunization (also called *vaccination*) is said to have had "a greater impact on human mortality reduction and population growth than any other public health intervention besides clean water" (J. P. Baker, 2000, p. 199).

No immunization is yet available for malaria. Thousands of scientists are working to develop one, and some clinical trials seem promising (Vaughan & Kappe, 2012). However, immunization has been developed for measles, mumps, whooping cough, smallpox, pneumonia, polio, and rotavirus, which no longer kill hundreds of thousands of children each year.

It used to be that the only way to become immune to these diseases was to catch them, sicken, and recover. The immune system would then produce antibodies to prevent recurrence. Beginning with smallpox in the nineteenth century, doctors discovered that giving a vaccine—a small dose of the virus—to healthy people who have not had the disease stimulates the same antibodies.

SPECIFIC DISEASES Stunning successes in immunization include the following:

● Smallpox, the most lethal disease for children in the past, was eradicated worldwide as of 1971. Vaccination against smallpox is no longer needed.

immunization
A process that stimulates the body's immune system to defend against attack by a particular contagious disease. Immunization may be accomplished either naturally (by having the disease) or through vaccination (often by having an injection). (Also called *vaccination*.)

LOUISE GUBB / CORBIS

Well Protected Disease and early death are common in Africa, where this photo was taken, but neither is likely for 2-year-old Salem. He is protected not only by the nutrition and antibodies in his mother's milk, but also by the large blue net that surrounds them. Treated bed nets, like this one provided by the Carter Center and the Ethiopian Health Ministry, are often large enough for families to eat, read, and sleep in together, without fear of malaria-infected mosquitos.

- Polio, a crippling and sometimes fatal disease, is rare. Widespread vaccination, begun in 1955, eliminated polio in the Americas. Only 784 cases were reported anywhere in the world in 2003. In the same year, however, rumours halted immunization in northern Nigeria. Polio reappeared, sickening 1948 people in 2005, almost all in West Africa. Then public health workers and community leaders campaigned to increase immunization, and Nigeria's polio rate plummeted. Meanwhile, poverty and new conflicts in South Asia prevented immunization (De Cock, 2011; World Health Organization, 2012a). Worldwide, 223 cases were reported in 2012. In 2013, only three countries, Afghanistan, Nigeria, and Pakistan, had an epidemic of polio (World Health Organization, 2013a). Since 1988, there has been a 99 percent decrease in cases (See Figure 3.6).

- Measles (rubeola, not rubella) is disappearing, thanks to a vaccine developed in 1963. Prior to that time, about 300 000 children were affected by measles each year in Canada alone. About 300 of these children died each year and another 300 suffered permanent brain damage. After the introduction of the measles vaccine, the number of cases dropped dramatically to about 50 a year (Public Health Agency of Canada, 2014).

✦ **ESPECIALLY FOR Nurses and Pediatricians** A mother refuses to have her baby immunized because she wants to prevent side effects. She wants your signature for a religious exemption, which in some jurisdictions allows the mother to refuse vaccination because she says it is for religious reasons. What should you do? (see response, page 112) ➔

FIGURE 3.6 Not Yet Zero Many public health advocates hope polio will be the next infectious disease to be eliminated worldwide, as is the case in almost all of North America. The number of cases has fallen dramatically worldwide (a). However, there was a discouraging increase in polio rates from 2003 to 2005 (b).

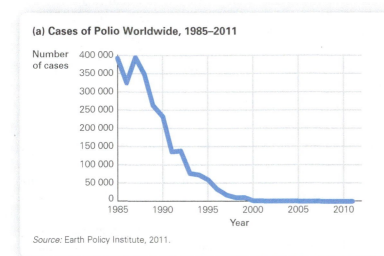

(a) Cases of Polio Worldwide, 1985–2011

Source: Earth Policy Institute, 2011.

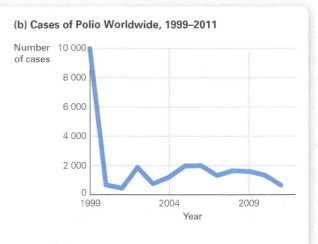

(b) Cases of Polio Worldwide, 1999–2011

- Canada began publicly funding a vaccination program for varicella (chicken pox) in 2004. Since then, hospitalization rates for varicella dropped from an average of 288 per year to 114 per year (Public Health Agency of Canada, 2012c).

Immunization protects children not only from temporary sickness, but also from complications, including deafness, blindness, sterility, and meningitis. Sometimes the damage from illness is not apparent until decades later. Childhood mumps, for instance, can cause sterility and doubles the risk of schizophrenia (Dalman et al., 2008).

Some people cannot be safely immunized, including the following:

- Embryos, who may be born blind, deaf, and brain-damaged if their pregnant mother contracts rubella (German measles)

- Newborns, who may die from a disease that is mild in older children

- People with impaired immune systems (HIV-positive, aged, or undergoing chemotherapy), who can become deathly ill.

Fortunately, each vaccination of a child stops transmission of the disease and thus protects others, a phenomenon called *herd immunity*. Although specifics vary by disease, usually if 90 percent of the people in a community (a herd) are immunized, the disease does not spread to those who are vulnerable. Without herd immunity, some community members die of a "childhood" disease.

PROBLEMS WITH IMMUNIZATION Some infants react to immunization by being irritable or even feverish for a day or so, to the distress of their parents. In addition, many parents are concerned about the potential for even more serious side effects. Whenever something seems to go amiss with vaccination, the media broadcasts it, which frightens parents. As a result, the rate of missed vaccinations has been rising over the past decade. This horrifies public health workers, who, taking a longitudinal and society-wide perspective, are convinced that the risks of the diseases are far greater than the risks from immunization. A hypothesis that the MMR (measles-mumps-rubella) vaccine causes autism has been repeatedly disproved (Mrozek-Budzyn et al., 2010; Shattuck, 2006). (More on autism in Chapter 7.)

True Dedication This young Buddhist monk lives in a remote region of Nepal, where, until recently, measles was a fatal disease. Fortunately, a UNICEF porter carried the vaccine over mountain trails for two days so that this boy—and his whole community—could be immunized.

Doctors agree that vaccines "are one of the most cost-effective, successful interventions in the history of public health" and lament that that success has made parents, physicians, and governments less vigilant (Hannan et al., 2009, p. S571). For example, lack of immunization is blamed for a spike in infant whooping cough cases across Canada in 2012.

Nutrition

Infant mortality worldwide has plummeted in recent years. Several reasons have already been mentioned: fewer sudden infant deaths (explained in Chapter 1), advances in prenatal and newborn care (explained in Chapter 2), and, as you just read, immunization. One more measure has made a huge difference: better nutrition.

BREAST IS BEST Ideally, nutrition starts with *colostrum,* a thick, high-calorie fluid secreted by the mother's breasts at birth. After about three days, the breasts begin to produce milk. Compared with formula based on cow's milk, human milk is sterile,

Same Situation, Far Apart: Breastfeeding Breastfeeding is universal. None of us would exist if our foremothers had not successfully breastfed their babies for millennia. Currently, breastfeeding is practised worldwide, such as shown here in Laos and Canada. It is no longer the only way to feed infants, and each culture has particular practices.

always at body temperature, and rich in iron, vitamins, and other newly discovered nutrients for brain and body (Drover et al., 2009).

Babies who are exclusively breastfed are less often sick. In infancy, breast milk provides antibodies against any disease to which the mother is immune and decreases allergies and asthma. Disease protection continues throughout life, because babies who are exclusively breastfed for 6 months are less likely to become obese (Huh et al., 2011) and thus less likely to develop diabetes and heart disease.

Breast milk is especially protective for preterm babies; if a preterm baby's mother cannot provide breast milk, physicians recommend milk from another woman (Schanler, 2011). (Once a woman has given birth, her breasts produce milk for decades if they continue to be stimulated.) In addition, the specific fats and sugars in breast milk make it more digestible and better for the brain than any substitute (Drover et al., 2009; Riordan, 2005). (See Table 3.2 for other benefits of breast milk.)

The composition of breast milk adjusts to the age of the baby, with milk for premature babies distinct from that for older infants. Quantity increases to meet the demand: Twins and even triplets can grow strong while being exclusively breastfed for months.

Not all mothers are able to breastfeed as some may have health conditions or take medication that could harm the infant. Formula feeding is preferable only in unusual or challenging cases, such as when the mother is HIV-positive or uses toxic or addictive drugs. Even then, however, breast milk may be advised. In some African nations, HIV-positive women are encouraged to breastfeed because their infants' risk of catching HIV from their mothers is lower than the risk of dying from infections, diarrhea, or malnutrition as a result of bottle-feeding (Cohen, 2007b; Kuhn et al., 2009).

Doctors worldwide recommend breastfeeding with no other foods—not even juice. Some pediatricians suggest adding foods (rice cereal and bananas) at 4 months; others want mothers to wait until 6 months (Fewtrell et al., 2011). For breast milk to meet the baby's nutritional needs, the mother must be well-fed and hydrated (especially important in hot climates) and should avoid alcohol, cigarettes, and other drugs.

Breastfeeding was once universal, but by the middle of the twentieth century many mothers thought formula feeding was more modern. Fortunately, that has changed again. In 2005, the Canadian Paediatric Society (CPS) began recommending that newborn infants be exclusively breastfed for the first 6 months (Boland, 2005). By 2009, 87 percent of Canadian mothers were breastfeeding their most recent baby for at least a short period of time. In the same year, just under 25 percent of mothers were following

✦ **ESPECIALLY FOR New Parents**
When should parents decide whether to feed their baby only by breast, only by bottle, or using some combination? When should they decide whether or not to let their baby use a pacifier? (see response, page 116) ➞

> ### TABLE 3.2 The Benefits of Breastfeeding
>
> **For the Baby**
>
> Balance of nutrition (fat, protein, etc.) adjusts to age of baby
>
> Breast milk has micronutrients not found in formula
>
> Less infant illness, including allergies, ear infections, stomach upsets
>
> Less childhood asthma
>
> Better childhood vision
>
> Less adult illness, including diabetes, cancer, heart disease
>
> Protection against many childhood diseases, since breast milk contains antibodies from the mother
>
> Stronger jaws, fewer cavities, advanced breathing reflexes (less SIDS)
>
> Higher IQ, less likely to drop out of school, more likely to attend college or university
>
> Later puberty, less teenage pregnancy
>
> Less likely to become obese or hypertensive by age 12
>
> **For the Mother**
>
> Easier bonding with baby
>
> Reduced risk of breast cancer and osteoporosis
>
> Natural contraception (with exclusive breastfeeding, for several months)
>
> Satisfaction of meeting infant's basic need
>
> No formula to prepare; no sterilization
>
> Easier travel with the baby
>
> **For the Family**
>
> Increased survival of other children (because of spacing of births)
>
> Increased family income (because formula can be expensive)
>
> Less stress on father, especially at night
>
> *Sources:* Beilin & Huang, 2008; Riordan & Wambach, 2009; Schanler, 2011; U.S. Department of Health and Human Services, 2011.

the CPS recommendation and exclusively breastfeeding their infants for at least six months (see Figure 3.7) (Statistics Canada, 2011b).

Although statistics for breastfeeding of Aboriginal children have some serious limitations, one earlier survey found that 73 percent of off-reserve Aboriginal children aged 3 months and younger were breastfed. Although this is lower than the national average, it still represents an upward trend (Turcotte & Zhao, 2004).

Worldwide, about half of all 2-year-olds are still nursing, usually at night. How long a mother breastfeeds is strongly affected by her experiences in the first week, when encouragement and practical help are most needed (DiGirolamo et al., 2005).

FIGURE 3.7 A Smart Choice
Midway through the twentieth century, educated women in North America were taught that formula was the smart, modern way to provide nutrition—but no longer. Today, more education for women correlates with more breast milk for babies. In 2009, 27 percent of Canadian women with a post-secondary degree or diploma breastfed exclusively for 6 months—no juice, no water, and no cereal. This was about 3 percentage points higher than the national average for that year.

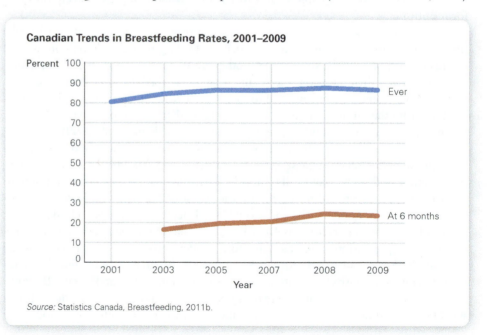

Canadian Trends in Breastfeeding Rates, 2001–2009

Source: Statistics Canada, Breastfeeding, 2011b.

Ideally, nurses visit new parents weekly at home; such visits (routine in some countries, rare in others) increase the likelihood that breastfeeding will continue.

MALNUTRITION **Protein-calorie malnutrition** occurs when a person does not consume sufficient food to sustain normal growth. That form of malnutrition occurs for roughly one-third of the world's children in developing nations: They suffer from **stunting,** being short for their age because chronic malnutrition prevented them from growing (World Bank, 2010). Stunting is most common in the poorest nations (see Figure 3.8).

Even worse is **wasting,** when children are severely underweight for their age and height (two or more standard deviations below average). Many nations, especially in East Asia, Latin America, and central Europe, have seen improvement in child nutrition in the past decades, with an accompanying decrease in wasting and stunting.

In some other nations, primarily in Africa, wasting has increased. And in several nations in South Asia, about half the children over age 5 years are stunted and half of them are also wasted, at least for a year (World Bank, 2010). In terms of development, the worst effect is that energy is reduced and normal curiosity is absent (Osorio, 2011).

One common way to measure a particular child's nutritional status is to compare weight and height with the detailed norms presented in Figures 3.1 and 3.2. For example, a sign of poor nutrition would be a long child who doesn't weigh a lot (underfeeding) or a short child who weighs a lot (overfeeding), as compared to the norms. Remember that some children may simply be genetically small, but all children should grow rapidly in the first two years.

Chronically malnourished infants and children suffer in three ways (World Bank, 2010):

1. Their brains may not develop normally. If malnutrition has continued long enough to affect height, it may also have affected the brain.

2. Malnourished children have no body reserves to protect them against common diseases. About half of all childhood deaths occur because malnutrition makes a childhood disease lethal.

3. Some diseases result directly from malnutrition, such as **marasmus** during the first year, when body tissues waste away, and **kwashiorkor** after age 1, when growth slows down, hair becomes thin, skin becomes splotchy, and the face, legs, and abdomen swell with fluid (edema).

protein-calorie malnutrition
A condition in which a person does not consume sufficient food of any kind. This deprivation can result in several illnesses, severe weight loss, and even death.

stunting
The failure of children to grow to a normal height for their age due to severe and chronic malnutrition.

wasting
The tendency for children to be severely underweight for their age as a result of malnutrition.

marasmus
A disease of severe protein-calorie malnutrition during early infancy, in which growth stops, body tissues waste away, and the infant eventually dies.

kwashiorkor
A disease of chronic malnutrition during childhood, in which a protein deficiency makes the child more vulnerable to other diseases, such as measles, diarrhea, and influenza.

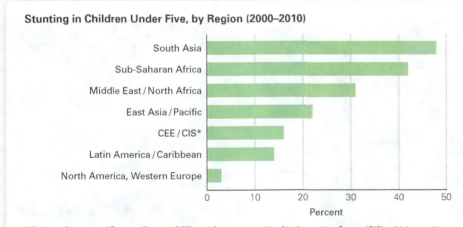

Stunting in Children Under Five, by Region (2000–2010)

South Asia
Sub-Saharan Africa
Middle East / North Africa
East Asia / Pacific
CEE / CIS*
Latin America / Caribbean
North America, Western Europe

0   10   20   30   40   50
Percent

*Refer to Central and Eastern Europe (CEE) and Commonwealth of Independent States (CIS), which together comprise the countries of central Europe as well as those that made up the former Soviet Union.

Source: UNICEF, 2012.

FIGURE 3.8 Genetic? The data show that basic nutrition is still unavailable to many children in the developing world. Some critics contend that Asian children are genetically small and therefore Western norms make it appear as if India and Africa have more stunted children than they really do. However, children of Asian and African descent born and nurtured in North America are as tall as those of European descent. Thus, malnutrition, not genes, accounts for most stunting worldwide.

Prevention, more than treatment, stops childhood malnutrition. In fact, some children hospitalized for marasmus or kwashiorkor die even after feeding, because their digestive systems are already failing. Prevention starts with prenatal nutrition and breastfeeding, with supplemental iron and vitamin A for mother and child.

A study of two poor African nations (Niger and Gambia) found several specific factors that reduced the likelihood of wasting and stunting: breastfeeding, both parents at home, water piped to the house, a tile (not dirt) floor, a toilet, electricity, immunization, a radio, and the mother's secondary education (Oyekale & Oyekale, 2009). Overall, "a mother's education is key in determining whether her children will survive their first five years of life" (United Nations, 2011, p. 26).

POVERTY AND NUTRITION Poverty has strong and well-documented negative impacts on nutrition and brain development in infants and young children. Its effects are not limited to nations in Africa and Asia; childhood poverty is a widespread and stubborn problem in Canada, too. This problem has grown worse over the past 20 years, despite the federal government's announced commitment in 1989 to eliminate poverty among children by the year 2000. In 2010, 979 000 or 14.5 percent of all Canadian children were living in poverty. Among Aboriginal peoples in Canada, the childhood poverty rate stands at a very troubling 25 percent (Campaign 2000, 2011).

Poor nutrition, often resulting from poverty, has been directly linked to lower scores on tests of vocabulary, reading comprehension, arithmetic, and general knowledge. Poor nutrition in infancy can also have negative impacts on a child's physical growth and motor skill development, and it can affect a child emotionally, resulting in a withdrawn or mistrustful personality (Brown & Pollitt, 1996).

Other risk factors for children in poverty include maternal drug abuse and depression. Specifically, substance abuse by a pregnant woman can stunt the growth of neurons in her baby's brain and lead to serious neurological disorders (Jones, 1997). Depressed mothers affect their infants' brain development because they are less likely to provide the stimulation babies need at critical points in their growth. This can result in children who are less active and have shorter attention spans (Belle, 1990).

Finally, children living in poverty are more likely to experience the chronic and elevated levels of stress that produce the hormone cortisol, which in large doses kills brain cells. This has negative impacts on memory and emotional development and on a child's ability to concentrate (Gunnar, 1998).

RESPONSE FOR New Parents (from page 113) Both decisions should be made within the first month. If parents wait until the infant is 4 months or older, they may discover that they are too late. It is difficult to introduce a bottle to a 4-month-old who has been exclusively breastfed or a pacifier to a baby who has already adapted the sucking reflex to a thumb. ●

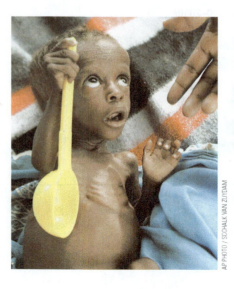 

Same Situation, Far Apart: Children Still Malnourished Infant malnutrition is common in nations at war, like Afghanistan (right), or with crop failure, like Niger (left). UNICEF relief programs reach only half the children in either nation. The children in these photographs are among the lucky ones who are being fed.

Infant Cognition

The rapid physical growth of the human infant, just described, is impressive, but intellectual growth during infancy is even more awesome. Concepts and sentences—non-existent in newborns—are evident by age 1 and consolidated by age 2. We begin with Jean Piaget, who many consider to be the most influential researcher of all time in the area of cognitive developmental psychology (Birney et al., 2005).

Sensorimotor Intelligence

Piaget called cognition in the first two years **sensorimotor intelligence** because infants learn through their senses and motor skills. He subdivided this period into six stages (see Table 3.3).

sensorimotor intelligence
Piaget's term for the way infants think—by using their senses and motor skills—during the first period of cognitive development.

STAGES ONE AND TWO: SIMPLE REFLEXES AND PRIMARY CIRCULAR REACTIONS For the first two stages, infants focus primarily on themselves. Stage one, called the *stage of simple reflexes,* includes the neonatal reflexes that infants use during their first month of life, the foundations of infant thought. During this stage, the newborn's motor reflexes evoke certain brain reactions.

Soon sensation leads to perception, which ushers in stage two, *first acquired adaptations* or *primary circular reactions* (also called the *stage of first habits*). This stage lasts from one month to four months. It is a primary circular reaction because this is when infants begin to put together two separate actions or sensations, such as looking and touching or listening and touching, to form a habit. For example, the infant places her thumb in her mouth, finds it soothing, and begins to suck. Over time, the two separate actions become one combined action, repeated over and over (circular).

Newborns reflexively suck anything that touches their lips. By about 1 month, they have adapted this reflex to bottles or breasts, pacifiers or fingers, each requiring specific types of tongue-pushing. This adaptation is a sign that infants have begun to interpret their perceptions; as they accommodate to pacifiers, they are thinking.

Time for Adaptation Sucking is a reflex at first, but adaptation begins as soon as an infant differentiates a pacifier from her mother's breast, or realizes that her hand has grown too big to fit into her mouth. This infant's expression of concentration suggests that she is about to make that adaptation and suck just her thumb from now on.

F/STOP / PUNCHSTOCK

TABLE 3.3 The Six Stages of Sensorimotor Intelligence

For an overview of the stages of sensorimotor thought, it helps to group the six stages into pairs. The first two stages involve the infant's responses to its own body.

Stage One (birth to 1 month)	*Simple reflexes:* sucking, grasping, staring, listening
Stage Two (1–4 months)	*Primary circular reactions (the first acquired adaptations):* accommodation and coordination of reflexes *Examples:* sucking a pacifier differently from a nipple; grabbing a bottle to suck it

The next two stages involve the infant's responses to objects and people.

Stage Three (4–8 months)	*Secondary Circular Reactions (making interesting sights last):* responding to people and objects *Example:* clapping hands when mother says "patty-cake"
Stage Four (8–12 months)	*Coordination of secondary circular reactions (new adaptation and anticipation):* becoming more deliberate and purposeful in responding to people and objects *Example:* putting mother's hands together in order to make her start playing patty-cake

The last two stages are the most creative, first with action and then with ideas.

Stage Five (12–18 months)	*Tertiary circular reactions (new means through active experimentation):* experimentation and creativity in the actions of the "little scientist" *Example:* putting a teddy bear in the toilet and flushing it
Stage Six (18–24 months)	*Mental representations (new means through mental combinations):* considering before doing, which provides the child with new ways of achieving a goal without resorting to trial-and-error experiments *Example:* before flushing, remembering that the toilet overflowed and mother was angry the last time, and hesitating

---

STAGES THREE AND FOUR: SECONDARY CIRCULAR REACTIONS AND COORDINATION OF SECONDARY CIRCULAR REACTIONS In stages three and four, reactions are no longer confined to the infant's body; they are an *interaction* between the baby and something else in the external world. During stage three (4 to 8 months), infants attempt to produce exciting experiences, *making interesting events last.* Infants will continue to repeat those actions over and over because of their consequences. For example, realizing that rattles make noise, they wave their arms and laugh whenever someone puts a rattle in their hand. The sight of something delightful—a favourite book, a smiling parent—can trigger active efforts for interaction.

Next comes stage four (8 months to 1 year), *coordination of secondary circular reactions* or *new adaptation and anticipation,* also called the *means to the end* because babies have goals that they try to reach. At this stage, infants begin to show *intentionality.* Often they ask for help (fussing, pointing, gesturing) to accomplish what they want. Thinking is more innovative because adaptation is more complex. For instance, instead of always smiling at Daddy, an infant might first assess Daddy's mood and then try to engage. Stage-three babies know how to continue an experience; stage-four babies initiate and anticipate.

That initiation is *goal-directed,* not random. For instance, babies who are breast-fed indicate that they are hungry, lifting up their mothers' shirts. They also inform caregivers when they do not want to eat, keeping their mouths firmly shut if they are full or if the food on the spoon is not what they want. If the caregivers have been using sign language, among the first signs learned before age 1 are "eat" and "all done."

OBJECT PERMANENCE Piaget thought that, at about 8 months, babies first understand **object permanence**—the concept that objects or people continue to exist when they are no longer in sight. As Piaget predicted, beginning at about 8 months, infants search for toys that have fallen from the crib, rolled under a couch, or disappeared under a blanket. Babies who are blind also acquire object permanence toward the end of their first year, reaching for an object that they hear nearby (Fazzi et al., 2011).

Piaget developed a basic experiment to measure object permanence: An adult shows an infant an interesting toy and then covers it with a lightweight cloth. The results are as follows:

- Infants younger than 8 months do not search for the object (by removing the cloth).
- At about 8 months, if infants are given the opportunity to search immediately (by removing the cloth), they do so; however, if they have to wait a few seconds before beginning to search, they forget that the object was there.
- By 2 years, children fully comprehend object permanence, progressing through several stages of ever-advanced cognition (Piaget, 1954).

Piaget believed that an infant's failure to search before 8 months of age was evidence that the baby had no concept of object permanence—that "out of sight" literally means "out of mind." However, researchers who track infants' eye movements and brain activity believe that Piaget was mistaken because even infants younger than 8 months do look longer at the correct spot (the cloth covering the toy). Indeed, some scientists believe that infants as young as 2 and 3 months of age can represent fully hidden objects (Cohen & Cashon, 2006). Other scientists are not convinced (Kagan, 2008), arguing that looking and reaching are two different and non-interchangeable tasks.

Piaget further tested this ability by conducting the following type of experiment. A research assistant (RA) shows an infant an attractive toy and places it under one of two cloths, cloth A. The infant looks, and reaches for the toy under cloth A. The RA places the toy under cloth A several more times, allowing the infant to reach for it each time. Then, the RA changes the hiding spot and places the toy under cloth B, right in front of the infant. Which cloth will the infant lift up? Cloth A. This is called **A-not-B error.**

STAGES FIVE AND SIX: TERTIARY CIRCULAR REACTIONS AND MENTAL REPRESENTATION
In their second year, infants start experimenting in thought and deed—or, rather, in the opposite sequence: deed and thought. They act first (stage five) and think later (stage six).

Stage five (12 to 18 months) is called *tertiary circular reactions* or *new means through active experimentation,* when goal-directed anticipation (stage four) becomes more expansive and creative. This is when infants become *intentional* and *purposive,* knowing what they are going to do before they actually do it. Toddlers delight in squeezing all the toothpaste out of the tube, taking apart an electronic device, or uncovering an anthill, activities they have never seen an adult do. Piaget referred to stage-five toddlers as **little scientists** who "experiment in order to see." Their devotion to discovery is familiar to every adult scientist—and to every parent.

Finally, in the sixth stage (ages 18 to 24 months), toddlers enter the stage of *new means through mental combinations.* Thankfully, stage-six infants use thought and memory, which deter the little scientists somewhat. Stage-six infants can even pretend. They can also think through a problem to discover a solution and then act upon it. For instance, a toddler sitting on the floor may want to play with his toy that is at the

object permanence
The realization that objects (including people) still exist even if they can no longer be seen, touched, or heard.

ARIEL SKELLEY / AGE FOTOSTOCK

Exploration at 15 Months Taste and smell are primary senses for adults when eating, but for Jonathan, and other 15-month-olds, the best way to investigate food is to squish it in his hands, observe any changes in colour and texture, and listen for any sounds.

A-not-B error
The tendency to reach for a hidden object where it was last found rather than in the new location where it was last hidden.

✦ **ESPECIALLY FOR Parents of Toddlers** One parent wants to put away all the breakable or dangerous objects because a toddler is now able to move around independently. The other parent says that the baby should learn not to touch certain things. Who is right? (see response, page 123) →

little scientist
The stage-five toddler (age 12 to 18 months) who experiments without anticipating the results, using trial and error in active and creative exploration.

deferred imitation
A sequence in which an infant first perceives something done by someone else and then performs the same action hours or even days later.

TOOGA PRODUCTIONS, INC. / GETTY IMAGES

Imitation This 14-month-old toddler demonstrates deferred imitation, copying her parents who she has seen using their tablet.

mirror neurons
Cells in an observer's brain that respond to an action performed by someone else in the same way they would if the observer had actually performed that action.

end of his blanket. The toddler realizes that if he pulls the blanket, the toy will come closer and closer until he can reach it.

Piaget also described **deferred imitation,** another stage-six intellectual accomplishment, when mental combinations allow children to copy behaviour they noticed hours or even days earlier (Piaget, 1945/1962). He wrote about his daughter, Jacqueline, who observed another child

> who got into a terrible temper. He screamed as he tried to get out of a playpen and pushed it backward, stamping his feet. Jacqueline stood watching him in amazement, never having witnessed such a scene before. The next day, she herself screamed in her playpen and tried to move it, stamping her foot lightly several times in succession.
>
> *[Piaget, 1945/1962, p. 63]*

PIAGET RE-EVALUATED As detailed by hundreds of developmentalists, many infants reach the stages of sensorimotor intelligence earlier than Piaget predicted (Oakes, 2011). Not only do 5-month-olds show surprise when objects seem to disappear (evidence of object permanence before 8 months, as described earlier), but some babies younger than 1 year also pretend and defer imitation (both stage-six abilities, according to Piaget).

A major limitation of Piaget's method for determining what infants could think is that it relied only on direct observation of behaviour, such as noticing whether or not a baby pulled away a cloth to search for a hidden object. Scientists now have many ways of measuring brain activity long before any observable evidence is apparent (see Table 3.4) (Johnson, 2010).

Some require millisecond video analysis, such as whether an infant stares at a disappearing object for 20 or 30 milliseconds. Before any conclusions are drawn, data from dozens of infants need to be analyzed statistically.

Other techniques involve brain scans. For example, in functional magnetic resonance imaging (fMRI), a burst of electrical activity measured by blood flow within the brain is recorded, indicating that neurons are firing. This leads researchers to conclude that a particular stimulus has been noticed and processed, even if the infant takes no action.

Brain scans are one way to investigate **mirror neurons,** an astonishing discovery that arose from careful research on monkeys—something not done in Piaget's day. About two decades ago, scientists were surprised to discover that a particular region of a macaque monkey's brain responded to actions the monkey had merely observed, as if it had actually performed those actions itself (Gallese et al., 1996).

For example, when one macaque saw another reach for a banana, the same brain areas were activated (lit up in brain scans) in both monkeys. Mirror neurons in the F5 area of the observing macaque's premotor cortex responded to what was observed. Using increasingly advanced technology, neuroscientists have now found mirror neurons in several parts of the human brain (Keysers & Gazzola, 2010).

Many scientists are particularly interested in the implications for infant cognition. Perhaps the avid watching and listening that babies do enable them to learn long before Piaget realized. Because of mirror neurons, their understanding of objects, language, or human intentions might be far more advanced than researchers have demonstrated (Diamond & Amso, 2008; Rossi et al., 2011; Virji-Babul et al., 2012).

Scientists are now convinced that infants have memories, goals, deferred imitation, and mental combinations well in advance of the timing that Piaget proposed for his stages (Bauer et al., 2010; Morasch & Bell, 2009). Piaget was correct to describe babies as eager learners. He simply underestimated how rapidly that learning occurs.

TABLE 3.4 Some Techniques Used by Neuroscientists to Understand Brain Function

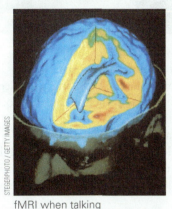

EEG, normal brain

Technique
EEG (electroencephalogram)

Use
Measures electrical activity in the top layers of the brain, where the cortex is.

Limitations
Especially in infancy, much brain activity of interest occurs below the cortex.

ERP when listening

Technique
ERP (event-related potential)

Use
Notes the amplitude and frequency of electrical activity (as shown by brain waves) in specific parts of the cortex in reaction to various stimuli.

Limitations
Reaction within the cortex signifies perception, but interpretation of the amplitude and timing of brain waves is not straightforward.

fMRI when talking

Technique
fMRI (functional magnetic resonance imaging)

Use
Measures changes in blood flow anywhere in the brain (not just the outer layers).

Limitations
Signifies brain activity, but infants are notoriously active, which can make fMRIs inaccurate.

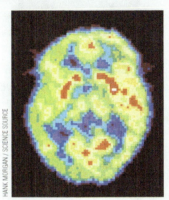

PET scan of sleep

Technique
PET (positron emission tomography)

Use
PET (like fMRI) reveals activity in various parts of the brain. Locations can be pinpointed with precision, but PET requires injection of radioactive dye to light up the active parts of the brain.

Limitations
Many parents and researchers hesitate to inject radioactive dye into an infant's brain unless a serious abnormality is suspected.

For both practical and ethical reasons, these techniques have not been used with large, representative samples of normal infants. One of the challenges of neuroscience is to develop methods that are harmless, easy to use, and comprehensive for the study of normal children. A more immediate challenge is to depict the data in ways that are easy to interpret and understand.

Information Processing

Piaget's four periods of cognition contrast with **information-processing theory,** a perspective originally modelled after computer functioning, including input, memory, programs, calculation, and output.

Information-processing research has found that many concepts and categories develop in very young brains. Even math concepts may begin as early as 3 months, advancing throughout the first year (Libertus & Brannon, 2009). For instance, 6-month-olds can detect the difference between a display of 8 dots and one of 16 dots, but not until 9 months of age can they distinguish between 8 and 12 dots (Lipton & Spelke, 2003).

· The information-processing perspective has uncovered many notable aspects of infant cognition. Babies are thought to be little scientists in the first year of life. As one scientist summarizes, "Rather than bumbling babies, they are individuals who … can learn surprisingly fast about the patterns of nature" (Keil, 2011, p. 1023).

The term *infant* (or *childhood*) *amnesia* refers to the belief that adults and older children can remember almost nothing that took place before the age of 2 years. Information processing has revealed otherwise. We now focus on one specific aspect of the information-processing perspective—memory.

information-processing theory
A perspective that compares human thinking processes, by analogy, to computer analysis of data, including sensory input, connections, stored memories, and output.

Goals and Cognition Much of infant intellectual development is about goal-directed behaviour. This Ottawa toddler has already learned that opening his mouth for his father will encourage his father to keep feeding him ice cream.

MEMORY Evidence for infant memory comes from innovative experiments in which 3-month-olds were taught to make a mobile move by kicking their legs (Rovee-Collier, 1987, 1990). The infants lay on their backs, in their own cribs, connected to a mobile by means of a ribbon tied to one foot.

Virtually all the infants began making some occasional kicks (as well as random arm movements and noises) and realized, after a while, that kicking made the mobile move. They then kicked more vigorously and frequently, sometimes laughing at their accomplishment. So far, this is no surprise—self-activated movement is highly reinforcing to infants, a part of dynamic perception.

When some infants had the mobile-and-ribbon apparatus reinstalled in their cribs *one week later,* most started to kick immediately. Their reaction indicated that they remembered their previous experience. But when other 3-month-old infants were retested *two weeks later,* they began with only random kicks. Apparently they had forgotten.

Then the lead researcher, Carolyn Rovee-Collier, developed another experiment. Two weeks after the initial training, the infants watched the mobile move but were *not* tied to it and were positioned so that they could *not* kick. This experience of

Selective Amnesia As we grow older, we forget about spitting up, nursing, crying, and almost everything else from our early years. However, strong emotions (love, fear, mistrust) may leave lifelong traces.

looking, but not kicking, was a **reminder session.** The next day, when they were again connected to the mobile and positioned so that they could move their legs, they kicked as they had learned to do two weeks earlier. Apparently, watching the mobile move on the previous day had revived their faded memory. The information about making the mobile move was stored in their brains, but they needed processing time to retrieve it. The reminder session provided that time.

Other research finds that repeated reminders are more powerful than single reminders, and that context is crucial, especially for infants younger than 9 months old: Being tested with the same mobile in the same room as the initial experience aids memory (Rovee-Collier & Cuevas, 2009).

Scientists now believe that an infant's memory begins to develop prenatally, when the baby is still in the womb. For example, one Canadian study used technologies such as ultrasound and image processing to measure a fetus's heart rate while listening to its mother and a female stranger reading passages in English and Mandarin. The fetuses showed an increase in heart rate when they heard their mother's voice and their native language, indicating they had developed memories of the voices and languages to which they were repeatedly exposed (Kisilevsky et al., 2009).

So, very young infants *can* remember, even if they cannot later put memories into words. Memories are particularly evident when

- experimental conditions are similar to those of real life
- motivation is high
- retrieval is strengthened by reminders and repetition.

THE ACTIVE BRAIN The crucial insight from information processing is that the brain is a very active organ, even in infancy, so that the particulars of experiences and memory are critically important in determining what a child knows or does not know. Soon generalization is possible. In another study, after 6-month-olds had had only two half-hour sessions with a novel puppet, a month later they remembered the experience—an amazing feat of memory for babies who could not talk or even stand up (Giles & Rovee-Collier, 2011).

reminder session
A perceptual experience that is intended to help a person recollect an idea, a thing, or an experience, without testing whether the person remembers it at the moment.

RESPONSE FOR Parents of Toddlers (from page 119) It is easier and safer to babyproof the house because toddlers, being little scientists, want to explore. However, both parents should encourage and guide the baby. A couple may choose to leave out a few untouchable items if that will prevent a major conflict between them. ●

MARINA RAITH / GETTY IMAGES

Active Learning The objects and people that these infants experience influence their brain development and memory.

Memory Aid Personal motivation and action are crucial to early memory, which is why Noel has no trouble remembering which shape covers the photograph of herself as a baby.

Other research finds that toddlers transfer learning from one object or experience to another. They learn from many people and events—from parents and strangers, from other babies and older siblings, from picture books and family photographs (Hayne & Simcock, 2009). The dendrites and neurons of the brain change to reflect early experiences and memories. Infants do not simply copy what they have seen, they think about it. For example, 15-month-old infants were shown an adult playing with a toy in a particular way. A day later, they were given another toy, one they had never seen. They tried to play with it as they remembered from the day before. This was especially true if, on the previous day, the toddler had also been allowed to play with the toy (Yang et al., 2010). Action strengthens memory.

Many studies show that infants remember not only specific events and objects, but also patterns and general goals (Keil, 2011). Some examples come from research, such as infants' memory of syllables and rhythms that they have heard, or their understanding of how objects move in relation to others; additional examples arise from close observations of babies at home, such as their understanding of what they expect from Mommy as compared to Daddy, or what details indicate bedtime. Every day of their young lives, infants are processing information and storing conclusions.

KEY Points

- Infants demonstrate cognitive advances throughout their first years.
- Piaget described cognition in the first two years as sensorimotor development, a period that has six stages, from reflexes to new exploration and deferred imitation.
- Piaget said that object permanence begins at 8 months, but more recent research finds that it starts earlier.
- Information-processing theory traces the step-by-step learning of infants. Each advance is seen as the accumulation of many small advances, not as a new stage.
- Very young infants can store memories, especially if they are given reminder sessions.

Language

No other species has anything approaching the neurons and networks that support the 6000 or so human languages. The human ability to communicate, even at age 2 years, far surpasses that of full-grown adults from every other species. This includes dolphins, ravens, and chimpanzees, all with much better communication mechanisms than was formerly believed.

Here we describe the specific steps in human language learning, "from burp to grammar" as one scholar put it (Saxton, 2010, p. 2). We then ask: How do babies do it?

AT ABOUT THIS TIME
The Development of Spoken Language in the First Two Years

Age*	Means of Communication
Newborn	Reflexive communication—cries, movements, facial expressions.
2 months	A range of meaningful noises—cooing, fussing, crying, laughing.
3–6 months	New sounds, including squeals, growls, croons, trills, vowel sounds.
6–10 months	Babbling, including both consonant and vowel sounds repeated in syllables.
10–12 months	Comprehension of simple words; speech-like intonations; specific vocalizations that have meaning to those who know the infant well. Babies who are deaf express their first signs; hearing babies also use specific gestures (e.g., pointing) to communicate.
12 months	First spoken words that are recognizably part of the native language.
13–18 months	Slow growth of vocabulary, up to about 50 words.
18 months	Naming explosion—three or more words learned per day. Much variation: Some toddlers do not yet speak.
21 months	First two-word sentence.
24 months	Multiword sentences. Half the toddler's utterances are two or more words long.

*The ages of accomplishment in this table reflect norms. Many healthy children with normal intelligence attain these steps in language development earlier or later than indicated here.

The Universal Sequence

The timing of language acquisition varies; the most advanced 10 percent of 2-year-olds speak more than 550 words, and the least advanced 10 percent speak fewer than 100 words—a fivefold difference (Merriman, 1999). But, although timing varies, the sequence is the same worldwide (see At About This Time). Even children who are deaf who become able to hear before age 3 (thanks to cochlear implants) follow the sequence (Ertmer et al., 2007).

LISTENING AND RESPONDING Infants who can hear begin learning language before birth, via brain connections. They prefer the language their mother speaks over an unheard language; newborns of bilingual mothers respond to both languages and differentiate between them (Byers-Heinlein et al., 2010).

Newborns look closely at facial expressions, apparently trying to connect words and expressions, to understand what is being communicated. By 6 months, infants can tell whether a person is speaking their native language or not, just by looking at the person's mouth movements (no sound) (Weikum et al., 2007). The ability to distinguish sounds and gestures in the language (or languages) of caregivers improves over the first year, while the ability to hear sounds never spoken in the native language deteriorates (Narayan et al., 2010).

Adults everywhere use higher pitch, simpler words, repetition, varied speeds, and exaggerated emotional tones when they speak to infants (Bryant & Barrett, 2007). This special language form is sometimes called *baby talk*, since it is talk directed to babies, and sometimes called *motherese* or *parentese*, since mothers and other caregivers—including fathers and siblings—universally speak it. In fact, all of these may be misleading terms; scientists prefer the more formal designation, **child-directed speech.**

child-directed speech
The high-pitched, simplified, and repetitive way adults speak to infants. (Also called *baby talk*, *motherese*, or *parentese*.)

Same Situation, Far Apart: Before Words The Polish babies learning sign language (*left*) and four-month-old Claire, from Victoria, British Columbia (*right*) are all doing what babies do: trying to understand communication long before they are able to talk.

No matter what term is used or who is speaking it, child-directed speech captures infant attention and thus fosters learning.

Sounds are preferred over content. Infants like alliteration, rhymes, repetition, rhythm, and varied pitch (Hayes & Slater, 2008; Schön et al., 2008). Think of your favourite lullaby (itself an euphonious word). All infants listen to whatever they can and appreciate the sounds they hear. Even music is culture-specific: 4- to 8-month-olds seem to like their own native music best (Soley & Hannon, 2010).

babbling

The extended repetition of certain syllables, such as *ba-ba-ba,* that begins when babies are between 6 and 9 months old.

BABBLING At first, babies mostly listen. By 6 months they start practising sounds, repeating certain syllables (*ma-ma-ma, da-da-da, ba-ba-ba*), a phenomenon referred to as **babbling.** Responses from other people encourage babbling (this is the age of "making interesting events last").

Toward the end of the first year, babbling begins to sound like the infant's native language; infants imitate what they hear in accents, cadence, consonants, and so on.

Who is Babbling? Probably both the 6-month-old and the 27-year-old. During every day of infancy, mothers and babies communicate with noises, movements, and expressions.

Gestures also become more specific, with all babies (deaf as well as hearing) expressing concepts with gestures sooner than with speech (Goldin-Meadow, 2006).

One early gesture is pointing, typical in human babies at 10 months. Pointing is an advanced social gesture that requires understanding another person's perspective. Most animals cannot interpret pointing; most 10-month-old humans can look toward the place another person is pointing at and can point themselves, even at the place where an object should be but no longer is (Liszkowski et al., 2009).

FIRST WORDS Finally, at about 1 year, the average hearing baby utters a few words, although some hearing babies do not begin to talk until about 18 months. Caregivers usually understand the first words before strangers do, which makes it hard for researchers to pinpoint exactly what a 12-month-old can say.

Spoken vocabulary increases gradually (perhaps one new word a week). However, 6- to 15-month-olds learn meanings rapidly; they understand about 10 times more words than they can say (Schafer, 2005; Snow, 2006). Initially, the first words are merely labels for familiar things (*mama* and *dada* are common), but each can convey many messages. Imagine meaningful sentences encapsulated in "Dada!" "Dada?" and "Dada." Each is a **holophrase,** a single word that expresses an entire thought.

Careful tracing of early language from the information-processing perspective finds periods when vocalization seems to slow down before a burst of new talking, as perception and action are interdependent (Pulvermüller & Fadiga, 2010). This means that sometimes, with a new perceptual understanding, it takes time for verbal output to reflect that neurological advance. This slowdown before a language spurt is not evident in every infant, but many seem temporarily quieter before a burst of new words (Parladé & Iverson, 2011).

Once vocabulary reaches about 50 *expressed* words (understood words are far more extensive), it builds rapidly, at a rate of 50 to 100 words per month, with 21-month-olds saying twice as many words as 18-month-olds (Adamson & Bakeman, 2006). This language spurt is called the **naming explosion** because many early words are nouns (Waxman & Lidz, 2006).

✦ **ESPECIALLY FOR Caregivers** A toddler calls two people "Mama." Is this a sign of confusion? (see response, page 129) ➞

holophrase
A single word that is used to express a complete, meaningful thought.

naming explosion
A sudden increase in an infant's vocabulary, especially in the number of nouns, that begins at about 18 months of age.

Show Me Where Pointing is one of the earliest forms of communication, emerging at about 10 months.

Cultural Differences

Early sequence and sounds of languages are universal, but there are many differences that soon emerge. For instance, about 30 languages of the world use a click sound as part of spoken words; infants there become adept at clicking. Similarly, the rolled "r," the enunciated "l" or "th," and the difference between "b" and "v" are mastered by infants in some languages but not others, depending on what they hear.

Although all new talkers say more nouns than any other parts of speech, the ratio of nouns to verbs varies from place to place. For example, by 18 months, English-speaking infants use relatively more nouns but fewer verbs than Chinese or Korean infants do. Why?

One explanation goes back to the language itself. Mandarin and Korean are "verb-friendly" in that verbs are placed at the beginning or end of sentences, which makes them easier to learn. In English, verbs occur in various positions within sentences, and their forms change in illogical ways (e.g., *go, gone, will go, went*). This irregularity makes English verbs harder to learn than nouns.

An alternative explanation considers the entire social context: Playing with a wide range of toys and learning about dozens of objects are crucial in North American culture, whereas East Asian cultures emphasize human interactions—specifically, how one person responds to another.

Accordingly, North American infants are expected to learn to name many objects, whereas Asian infants are expected to act on objects and respond to people. Thus, Chinese toddlers might learn the equivalent of *come, play, love, carry, run,* and so on before Canadian ones (Chan et al., 2009). This is the result of experience, not genes. A toddler of Chinese ancestry growing up in an English-speaking Canadian home has the learning patterns of other English-speaking toddlers.

A simpler explanation is that young children are sensitive to the sounds of words, with some sounds more salient than others. Verbs are learned more easily if they sound like the action (Imai et al., 2008), and such verbs may be more common in some languages than others.

In English, most verbs are not onomatopoeic, although perhaps *jump, kiss,* and *poop*—all learned relatively early on—are exceptions. The infant preference for sounds may be one reason why many English-speaking toddlers who have never been on a farm nonetheless know that a cow says "moo" and a duck says "quack."

grammar
All the methods—word order, verb forms, and so on—that languages use to communicate meaning, apart from the words themselves.

PUTTING WORDS TOGETHER **Grammar** includes all the methods that languages use to communicate meaning. Word order, prefixes, suffixes, intonation, verb forms, pronouns and negations, prepositions and articles—all of these are aspects of grammar, all varying by whatever language the infant hears (Saxton, 2010).

Grammar can be discerned in holophrases but becomes obvious between 18 and 24 months, when two-word combinations begin (Tomasello, 2011). For example, in English, "Baby cry" and "More juice" follow the proper word order. No child asks, "Juice more," and already by age 2 children know that "cry baby" has an entirely different meaning than "Baby cry." Soon the child combines three words, usually in subject–verb–object order in English (for example, "Mommy read book"), rather than any of the five other possible sequences of those words.

Young children can master two languages, not just one. The crucial variable is how much speech in both languages the child hears. Listening to two languages does not necessarily slow down the acquisition of grammar, but "development in each language proceeds separately and in a language specific manner" (Conboy & Thal, 2006, p. 727). In Canada, where English and French are the official languages, many infants acquire both. This is referred to as *bilingual first language acquisition* (BFLA).

Statistics Canada estimates that in 2006, almost 18 percent of the population was fluent in both French and English (Corbeil & Blaser, 2009).

A review by Fred Genesee of McGill University is one of several recent studies to explore whether BFLA in any way strains a child's language-learning ability or leads to delays in the language-acquisition process (Genesee, 2009). As Genesee (2008, 2009) points out, this type of research is important because of the number of people—including some parents, teachers, speech pathologists, and educational policy-makers—who fear that BFLA may have negative impacts on a child's ability to learn either language properly. In their research, Genesee and other scientists have debunked three common misconceptions:

1. *Children who are bilingual have greater difficulty in learning grammar than children who speak one language.* In fact, bilingual children have similar rates of language development as monolingual children, at least in their dominant language (Nicoladis & Genesee, 1996; Paradis & Genesee, 1996). (Note that for various reasons, most dual-language learners become more proficient in one language than the other [Genesee, 2009].)

2. *Children who are monolingual speak their first words sooner and learn words faster than children who are bilingual.* Again, research shows that monolingual and bilingual children produce their first words at about the same time. They also show similar rates in the growth of their vocabulary (Pearson et al., 1993; Pearson & Fernandez, 1994).

3. *Dual-language learners face more communication challenges than monolingual children.* Actually, bilingual children have about the same number of communication challenges as children who speak only one language. Interestingly bilingual children often become more skilled in interpersonal communications at an earlier age since they switch between languages depending on context and the preferences of the person they are speaking to (Vihman, 1998).

Indeed, some evidence suggests that children are statisticians: They implicitly track the number of words and phrases and learn those expressed most often. That is certainly the case when children are learning their mother tongue; it is probably true when learning a second language as well (Johnson & Tyler, 2010).

Bilingual toddlers soon realize differences between languages, adjusting tone, cadence, and vocabulary when speaking to a monolingual person. Most bilingual children have parents who are also bilingual; hence, these children mix languages because they know their parents will understand.

Note that mixing languages is a cultural adaptation, not a sign of mental deficiency. In fact, bilingual children and adults seem to have a cognitive advantage over monolingual people, as noted in Chapter 5.

How Do They Do It?

Worldwide, people who are not yet 2 years old already speak their native tongue. They continue to learn rapidly: Some teenagers compose lyrics or deliver orations that move thousands of their co-linguists. How is language learned so easily and so well? Answers come from three schools of thought, one emphasizing learning, one emphasizing culture, and the third stressing evolution.

THEORY ONE: INFANTS NEED TO BE TAUGHT The seeds of the first perspective were planted more than 50 years ago, when the dominant theory in North American psychology was behaviourism, or learning theory. The essential idea was

✦ **ESPECIALLY FOR Educators** An infant daycare centre has a new child whose parents speak a language other than the one the teachers speak. Should the teachers learn basic words in the new language, or should they expect the baby to learn their language? (see response, page 130) →

RESPONSE FOR Caregivers (from page 127) Not at all. Toddlers hear several people called "Mama" (their own mother, their grandmothers, their cousins' and friends' mothers) and experience mothering from several people, so it is not surprising if they use "Mama" too broadly. They will eventually narrow the label down to the one correct person. ●

that all learning is acquired, step by step, through association and reinforcement. Just as Pavlov's dogs learned to associate the sound of a tone with the presentation of food (see Chapter 1), behaviourists believe that infants associate objects with words they have heard often, especially if reinforcement occurs.

B. F. Skinner (1957) noticed that spontaneous babbling is usually reinforced. Typically, every time the baby says "ma-ma-ma-ma," a grinning mother appears, repeating the sound as well as lavishing the baby with attention, praise, and perhaps food. Skinner believed that most parents are excellent instructors, responding to their infants' gestures and sounds, thus reinforcing speech (Saxton, 2010).

The core ideas of this theory are:

- parents are expert teachers, although other caregivers help
- frequent repetition is instructive, especially when linked to daily life
- well-taught infants become well-spoken children.

RESPONSE FOR Educators (from page 129) Probably both. Infants love to communicate, and they seek every possible way to do so. Therefore, the teachers should try to understand the baby and the baby's parents, but they can also teach another language. ●

Behaviourists note that some 3-year-olds converse in elaborate sentences; others just barely put one simple word with another. Such variations correlate with the amount of language each child has heard. Parents of the most verbal children teach language throughout infancy—singing, explaining, listening, responding, and reading to their children every day, even before 1 year of age (Forget-Dubois et al., 2009) (see Figure 3.9).

THEORY TWO: CULTURE FOSTERS INFANT LANGUAGE The second theory arises from the sociocultural reason for language: communication. According to this perspective, infants communicate because humans are social beings, dependent on one another for survival and joy. Each culture has practices that further social interaction; talking is one of those practices.

It is the emotional messages of speech, not the words, that are the focus of early communication, according to this perspective. In one study, people who had never heard English (Shuar hunter–gatherers living in isolation near the Andes Mountains) listened to tapes of North American mothers talking to their babies. The Shuar successfully distinguished speech conveying comfort, approval, prohibition, and

FIGURE 3.9 Maternal Responsiveness and Infants' Language Acquisition Learning the first 50 words is a milestone in early language acquisition, as it predicts the arrival of the naming explosion and the multiword sentence a few weeks later. Researchers found that the 9-month-old infants of highly responsive mothers (top 10 percent) reached this milestone as early as 15 months. The infants of nonresponsive mothers (bottom 10 percent) lagged significantly behind.

OBSERVATION QUIZ
Why does the blue line end at 18 months? (see answer, page 132) →

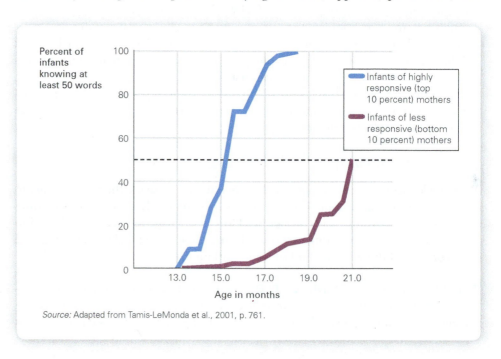

Source: Adapted from Tamis-LeMonda et al., 2001, p. 761.

attention, without knowing any of the words (Bryant & Barrett, 2007). Thus, the social content of speech is universal, which is why babies learn whatever their culture provides.

For example, many 1-year-olds enjoy watching television and videos, but the evidence implies that they learn from it only when adults are actively involved in teaching. In a controlled experiment, 1-year-olds learned vocabulary much better when someone directly taught them than when the same person taught on a video (Roseberry et al., 2009). This suggests personal, social language acquisition, not impersonal learning.

According to theory two, then, social impulses, not explicit teaching, lead infants to learn language "as part of the package of being a human social animal" (Hollich et al., 2000). Those same impulses are evident in all the ways infants learn. According to this theory, people differ from the great apes in that they depend on others within their community and thus learn whatever way their culture uses to communicate. Every infant (and no chimpanzee) masters words and grammar to join the social world in which he or she finds himself (Tomasello & Herrmann, 2010).

Cultures vary not only in the languages they speak, but also in how they communicate, some using gestures and touch more than words. A learning theorist might consider the quieter, less verbal child to be developmentally delayed, but this second perspective contends that the crucial aspect of language is social communication, and that the quieter child may simply be communicating in another way. Language is not necessarily spoken.

THEORY THREE: INFANTS TEACH THEMSELVES A third theory holds that language learning is innate; adults need not teach it, nor is it a by-product of social interaction. It arises from the universal human impulse to imitate. As already explained in the research on memory, infants and toddlers observe what they see and apply it—not slavishly, but according to their own concepts and intentions. This may be what they do with the language they hear as well (Saxton, 2010).

The seeds of this perspective were planted soon after Skinner proposed his theory of verbal learning. Noam Chomsky (1968, 1980) and his followers felt that language is too complex to be mastered merely through step-by-step conditioning. Although behaviourists focus on variations among children in vocabulary size, Chomsky focused on similarities in language acquisition—the universals, not the differences.

Noting that all young children master basic grammar at about the same age, Chomsky cited this *universal grammar* as evidence that humans are born with a mental structure that prepares them to seek some elements of human language—for example, the use of a raised tone at the end of an utterance to indicate a question. Chomsky labelled this hypothesized mental structure the **language acquisition device (LAD),** which enables children to derive the rules of grammar quickly and effectively from the speech they hear every day, regardless of whether their native language is English, Thai, or Urdu.

Other scholars agree with Chomsky that infants are innately ready to use their minds to understand and speak whatever language is offered. All babies are eager learners, and language may be considered one more aspect of neurological maturation (Wagner & Lakusta, 2009). This idea does not strip languages and cultures of their differences in sounds, grammar, and almost everything else, but the basic idea is that "language is a window on human nature, exposing deep and universal features of our thoughts and feelings" (Pinker, 2007, p. 148).

The various languages of the world are all logical, coherent, and systematic. Infants are primed to grasp the particular language they are exposed to, making caregiver speech "not a 'trigger' but a 'nutrient'" (Slobin, 2001, p. 438). There is no need for a

✦ **ESPECIALLY FOR Nurses and Pediatricians** Bob and Joan have been reading about language development in children. Because they are convinced that language is "hard-wired," they believe they don't need to talk to their 6-month-old son. How do you respond? (see response, page 132) ➡

language acquisition device (LAD) Chomsky's term for a hypothesized mental structure that enables humans to learn language, including the basic aspects of grammar, vocabulary, and intonation.

trigger, according to theory three, because the developing brain quickly and efficiently connects neurons and dendrites to support whichever language the infant hears.

Research supports this perspective as well. As you remember, newborns are primed to listen to speech (Vouloumanos & Werker, 2007), and all infants babble *ma-ma* and *da-da* sounds (not yet referring to mother or father). No reinforcement or teaching is required; all infants need is for dendrites to grow, mouth muscles to strengthen, neurons to connect, and speech to be heard.

ALL TRUE? Which of these three perspectives is correct? Perhaps all of them. In one monograph that included details and results of 12 experiments, the authors presented a *hybrid* (which literally means "a new creature, formed by combining other living things") of previous theories (Hollich et al., 2000).

Since infants learn language to do numerous things—indicate intention, call objects by name, put words together, talk to family members, sing to themselves, express their wishes, remember the past, and much more—some aspects of language learning may be best explained by one theory at one age and other aspects by another theory at another age. Although originally developed to explain acquisition of first words, mostly nouns, this **hybrid theory** also explains learning verbs: Perceptual, social, and linguistic abilities combine to make that learning possible (Golinkoff & Hirsh-Pasek, 2008).

After intensive study, another group of scientists also endorsed a hybrid theory, concluding that multiple attentional, social and linguistic cues contribute to early language (Tsao et al., 2004). It makes logical and practical sense for nature to provide several paths toward language learning and for various theorists to emphasize one or another of them (Sebastián-Gallés, 2007), and for some children to learn better one way, and others another way (Goodman et al., 2008).

Some scholars, inspired by evolutionary theory, think that language is the crucial trait that makes humans unlike any other species—that "language is entwined with human life" (Pinker, 2007, p. viii). If that is true, then there must be many paths to language learning, to ensure that every human learns.

Adults need to talk often to infants (theory one), encourage social connections (theory two), and appreciate the innate abilities of the child (theory three). As one expert concludes,

> in the current view, our best hope for unraveling some of the mysteries of language acquisition rests with approaches that incorporate multiple factors, that is, with approaches that incorporate not only some explicit linguistic model, but also the full range of biological, cultural, and psycholinguistic processes involved.
>
> *[Tomasello, 2006, pp. 292–293]*

The idea that every theory is correct in some way may seem uncritical, naïve, and idealistic. However, a similar conclusion was arrived at by scientists extending and interpreting research on language acquisition. They contend that language learning is neither the direct product of repeated input (behaviourism) nor the result of a specific human neurological capacity (LAD). Instead, different aspects of language may have evolved in different ways, and as a result a piecemeal and empirical approach is needed (Marcus & Rabagliati, 2009). In other words, a single theory that explains how babies learn language does not reflect the data: Humans accomplish this feat in many ways.

Infants are active learners not only of language (as just outlined) and of perceptions and motor skills (as explained in the first half of this chapter), but also of everything else in their experience. Active and interactive social and emotional understandings are described in the next chapter.

---

hybrid theory
A perspective that combines various aspects of different theories to explain how language, or any other developmental phenomenon, occurs.

RESPONSE FOR Nurses and Pediatricians (from page 131) While much of language development is indeed hard-wired, many experts assert that exposure to language is required. You don't need to convince Bob and Joan of this point, though—just convince them that their baby will be happier if they talk to him. ●

ANSWER TO **OBSERVATION QUIZ**
(from page 130) By 18 months, every one of the infants of highly responsive mothers (top 10 percent) knows 50 words. Not until 30 months do all the infants with quiet mothers reach the naming explosion. ●

KEY Points

- Infants pay close attention to the sounds and rhythms of speech, comprehending far more than they can say.
- Infants learn rapidly to communicate and to speak, starting with cries in the first weeks and progressing to words by 1 year and sentences before age 2.
- Culture affects the timing and types of words acquired.
- Some experts emphasize the importance of adult reinforcement of early speech; others suggest that language learning is innate; others believe it is a by-product of social impulses.
- A hybrid explanation suggests that language learning occurs in many ways, depending on the specific age, culture, and goals of the infant.

SUMMARY

Growth in Infancy

1. In the first two years of life, infants grow longer, gain weight, and increase in head circumference—all indicative of development. Birth weight doubles by 4 months, triples by 1 year, and quadruples by 2 years, when toddlers weigh about 12 to 14 kilograms. Similarly, length increases by more than 30 centimetres in the second year of life, making 2-year-olds half their adult height.

2. Brain size increases even more dramatically, from about 25 to 75 percent of adult weight in the first two years. Complexity increases as well, with cell growth, development of dendrites, and formation of synapses. Both growth and pruning aid cognition. Experience is vital for brain development.

3. Sleep gradually decreases over the first two years. As with all areas of development, variations in sleep patterns are normal, caused by both nature and nurture. Bed-sharing is the norm in many developing nations, and co-sleeping is increasingly common in developed ones.

Perceiving and Moving

4. At birth, the senses already respond to stimuli. Prenatal experience makes hearing the most mature sense. Vision is the least mature sense at birth, but it improves quickly. Infants use all their senses to strengthen their early social interactions.

5. Infants gradually improve their motor skills as they begin to grow and as brain maturation increases. Gross motor skills are soon evident, from rolling over to sitting up (at about 6 months), from standing to walking (at about 1 year), from climbing to running (before age 2).

6. Babies gradually develop the fine motor skills to grab, aim, and manipulate almost anything within reach. Experience, time, and motivation allow infants to advance in all their motor skills.

Surviving in Good Health

7. About 2 billion infant deaths have been prevented in the past half-century because of improved health care. One major innovation is immunization, which has eradicated smallpox and virtually eliminated polio and measles. More medical professionals are needed to prevent, diagnose, and treat the diseases that still cause many infant deaths in developing nations.

8. Breastfeeding is best for infants, partly because breast milk helps them resist disease and promotes growth of every kind. Most babies are breastfed at birth, but in North America only one-third are exclusively breastfed for three months, as doctors worldwide recommend.

9. Severe malnutrition stunts growth and can cause death, both directly through marasmus or kwashiorkor and indirectly through vulnerability if a child catches measles, an intestinal disorder, or some other illness.

Infant Cognition

10. Piaget realized that very young infants are active learners, seeking to understand their complex observations and experiences. Sensorimotor intelligence develops in six stages, beginning with reflexes and ending with mental combinations.

11. Infants gradually develop an understanding of objects. As shown in Piaget's classic experiment, infants understand object permanence and begin to search for hidden objects at about 8 months. Other research finds that Piaget underestimated infant cognition in the timing of object permanence and in many other ways.

12. Another approach to understanding infant cognition is information-processing theory, which looks at each step of the thinking process, from input to output. Each week, infants understand more about numbers, objects, patterns of speech, and so on.

13. Infant memory is fragile but not completely absent. Reminder sessions help trigger memories, and young brains learn motor sequences long before they can remember with words.

Language

14. Language learning may be the most impressive cognitive accomplishment of infants, distinguishing the human species from other animals. Eager attempts to communicate are apparent in the first weeks and months. Infants babble at about 6 to 9 months, understand words and gestures by 10 months, and speak their first words at about 1 year.

15. Vocabulary begins to build very slowly until the child knows approximately 50 words. Then the naming explosion begins. Toward the end of the second year, toddlers put words together, showing that they understand the rudiments of grammar.

16. Various theories explain how infants learn language as quickly as they do. The three main theories emphasize different aspects of early language learning: that infants must be taught, that their social impulses foster language learning, and that their brains are genetically attuned to language. Each theory seems true for some aspects of language acquisition.

KEY TERMS

A-not-B error (p. 119)
axon (p. 96)
babbling (p. 126)
binocular vision (p. 106)
child-directed speech (p. 125)
co-sleeping (p. 102)
cortex (p. 95)
deferred imitation (p. 120)
dendrite (p. 96)
fine motor skills (p. 108)
grammar (p. 128)
gross motor skills (p. 107)

head-sparing (p. 95)
holophrase (p. 127)
hybrid theory (p. 131)
immunization (p. 110)
information-processing theory (p. 121)
kwashiorkor (p. 115)
language acquisition device (LAD) (p. 131)
little scientist (p. 119)
marasmus (p. 115)
mirror neurons (p. 120)
motor skills (p. 107)

naming explosion (p. 127)
neuron (p. 95)
neurotransmitter (p. 96)
norm (p. 94)
object permanence (p. 119)
perception (p. 104)
pincer movement (p. 108)
plasticity (p. 98)
prefrontal cortex (p. 95)
protein-calorie malnutrition (p. 115)
pruning (p. 97)

REM (rapid eye movement) sleep (p. 101)
reminder session (p. 123)
self-righting (p. 101)
sensation (p. 104)
sensorimotor intelligence (p. 117)
shaken baby syndrome (SBS) (p. 100)
stunting (p. 115)
synapse (p. 96)
transient exuberance (p. 97)
wasting (p. 115)

WHAT HAVE YOU LEARNED?

1. In what ways do a baby's weight and length change in the first two years?

2. Describe the process of communication within the central nervous system.

3. Why is pruning an essential part of brain development?

4. What should caregivers remember about brain development when an infant cries?

5. How do a baby's sleep patterns change over the first 18 months?

6. What is the relationship among perception, sensation, and cognition?

7. How does an infant's vision change over the first three months?

8. Give examples to describe how an infant's gross motor skills develop over the first year.

9. Describe how a baby's hand skills develop over the first two years.

10. Why has there been a decrease in infant mortality rates? What other measures could lead to a further decrease?

11. What is the purpose of immunization?

12. In what ways does herd immunity save lives?

13. Why has the rate of immunization decreased over the past decade?

14. What are the reasons for and against breastfeeding until a child is at least 1 year old?

15. In what ways does malnutrition affect infants and children?

16. Why did Piaget call cognition in the first two years "sensorimotor intelligence"?

17. Describe the first two stages of sensorimotor intelligence.

18. In sensorimotor intelligence, what is the difference between stages three and four?

19. Why is the concept of object permanence important to an infant's development?

20. What does the active experimentation of the stage-five toddler suggest for parents?

21. Why did Piaget underestimate how rapidly early cognition occurs?

22. What conditions help 3-month-olds remember something?

23. What have researchers discovered about the way adults talk to babies?

24. How would a caregiver who subscribes to the behaviourist theory of language learning respond when an infant babbles?

25. What is typical of the rate and nature of the first words that infants speak?

26. What indicates that toddlers use some grammar?

27. According to behaviourism, how do adults teach infants to talk?

28. According to sociocultural theory, why do infants try to communicate?

29. What is Chomsky's theory about how young children learn language?

30. What does the hybrid model of language learning suggest to caregivers?

APPLICATIONS

1. Immunization regulations and practices vary, partly for social and political reasons. Ask at least two faculty or administrative staff members what immunizations students at your college must have and why. If you hear, "It's the law," ask why.

2. Observe three infants (whom you do not know) in public places such as a store, playground, or bus. Look closely at body size and motor skills, especially how much control each baby has over legs and hands. From that, estimate the age in months, then ask the caregiver how old the infant is.

3. Many educators recommend that parents read to babies even before the babies begin talking. How would advocates of each of the three hypotheses about language development respond to this advice?

4. Test an infant's ability to search for a hidden object. Ideally, the infant should be about 7 or 8 months old, and you should retest over a period of weeks. If the infant can immediately find the object, make the task harder by pausing between the hiding and the searching or by secretly moving the object from one hiding place to another. Describe this experiment in detail.

>>ONLINE CONNECTIONS

To accompany your textbook, you have access to a number of online resources, including LearningCurve, which is an adaptive quizzing program; critical thinking questions; and case studies. For access to any of these links, go to www.worthpublishers.com/launchpad/bergerchuang1e. In addition to these resources, you'll find links to video clips, personalized study advice, and an e-Book. Among the videos and activities available online are the following:

- *Language Development in Infancy.* How easy is it to understand a newborn's coos? Or a 6-month-old's babbling? But we can almost all make out the voice of a toddler singing "Twinkle, Twinkle." Video clips from a variety of real-life contexts bring to life the development of children's language.

- *Infant Reflexes.* Do you have trouble distinguishing the Moro from the Babinski? Video clips will help clarify what they look like in newborns.

CHAPTER OUTLINE

THE FIRST TWO YEARS:
Psychosocial Development

4

WHAT WILL YOU KNOW?

- How do smiles, tears, anger, and fear change from birth to age 2?
- Does a baby's temperament predict lifelong personality?
- What are the signs of a healthy parent–infant relationship?
- Do the six major theories and the hundreds of human cultures differ in their understanding of infant development and caregiving practices?

My 1-week-old grandson cried. Often. Again and again. Day and night. For a long time. He and his parents were living with me while they looked for an apartment. I was the dog-walker and dinner-cooker, not caregiver, so I didn't mind the crying for myself. But I did mind for my sleep-deprived daughter.

"Give him a pacifier," I told her.

"No, that causes 'nipple confusion,'" she said.

"I never heard of that. What have you been reading? Give him a pacifier."

My daughter knows that I value research and evidence, not hearsay or anecdote. She replied, "The American Academy of Pediatrics says no pacifiers for breastfed babies in the first month. Here it is on their website."

That quieted me, but soon I developed another worry—that my son-in-law would resent fatherhood. He spent many hours, day and night, carrying my grandson while my daughter slept.

"It seems to me that you do most of the baby-comforting," I told him.

"That's because Elissa does most of the breast-feeding," he answered with a smile.

I learned in those months. In the decades since my children were infants, pediatricians have new recommendations and fathers are more active partners. ●

—*Kathleen Berger*

THIS CHAPTER OPENS BY TRACING INFANTS' EMOTIONS AS their brains mature and their experiences accumulate, noting temperamental and cultural differences. This leads to an exploration of caregiver–infant interaction, particularly synchrony, attachment, and social referencing. For every aspect of caregiving, fathers as well as mothers are included.

Then we apply each of the six theories introduced in Chapter 1. After the theories are explained, we apply them to a controversial topic in infant psychosocial development: Who should provide daily care?

Many specifics vary depending on culture and cohort, but some universal psychosocial needs are apparent. With or without pacifiers or patient parents, most infants thrive, as long as their basic emotional needs are met.

AT ABOUT THIS TIME
Ages When Emotions Emerge

Birth	Crying; contentment
6 weeks	Social smile
3 months	Laughter; curiosity
4 months	Full, responsive smiles
4–8 months	Anger
6–9 months	Fear of social events (strangers, separation from caregiver)
12 months	Fear of unexpected sights and sounds
18 months	Self-awareness; pride; shame; embarrassment

Emotional Development

In the first two years, infants progress from reactive pain and pleasure to complex patterns of social awareness (see At About This Time) (Lewis, 2010). This is a period of high emotional responsiveness (Izard et al., 2002), expressed in speedy, uncensored reactions—crying, startling, laughing, raging—and, by toddlerhood, in complex responses, from self-satisfied grins to mournful pouts. As always, culture and experience influence the norms of development. This is especially true for emotional development after the first eight months.

Early Emotions

The earliest emotions, also called primary emotions, emerge within the first 6 months (Izard, 1978). At first, there is pleasure and pain. Newborns are happy and relaxed when fed and drifting off to sleep. They cry when they are hurt or hungry, tired or frightened (as by a loud noise or a sudden loss of support). Some infants have bouts of uncontrollable crying, called colic—probably the result of immature digestion. About 20 percent of babies cry excessively, defined as more than three hours a day, for more than three days a week, for more than three weeks (Kim, 2011).

SMILING AND LAUGHING Soon, additional emotions become recognizable (Lavelli & Fogel, 2005). Curiosity is evident as infants (and people of all ages) respond to objects and experiences that are new but not too novel. Happiness is expressed by the **social smile,** evoked by a human face at about 6 weeks. A social smile is a

social smile
A smile evoked by a human face, normally first evident in infants about 6 weeks after birth.

Smiles All Around Joy is universal when an infant smiles at her beaming grandparents. This particular scene takes place in Kazakhstan, in central Asia.

CHRISTOPHER HERWIG / GETTY IMAGES

developmental milestone as it indicates that the infant is intentionally communicating with others (e.g., inviting adults to interact with her, or responding to somebody else's smile). Preterm babies smile a few weeks later because the social smile is determined by cognition (development of the brain), which is less developed for preterm babies.

Infants worldwide express social joy, even laughter, between 2 and 4 months (Konner, 2007; Lewis, 2010). Among the Navajo, whoever brings forth that first laugh gives a feast to celebrate the baby's becoming a person (Rogoff, 2003). Laughter builds as curiosity does; a typical 6-month-old laughs loudly upon discovering new things, particularly social experiences that have the right balance between familiarity and surprise, such as Daddy making a funny face.

ANGER AND SADNESS The positive emotions of joy and contentment are soon joined by negative emotions, more frequent in infancy than later on (Izard, 2009). Anger is evident at 6 months, usually triggered by frustration, such as when infants are prevented from moving or grabbing.

To see how infants responded to frustration, researchers gently restrained children's arms from behind for 2 minutes or until 20 seconds of hard crying ensued (Mills-Koonce et al., 2011). Hard crying is a common reaction when infants are strapped in, caged in, closed in, or even just held in place when they want to explore.

In infancy, anger is a healthy response to frustration, unlike sadness, which also appears in the first months. Sadness indicates withdrawal and is accompanied by an increase in the body's production of **cortisol,** the primary stress hormone.

In a series of experiments, 4-month-olds were taught to pull a string to see a picture, which they enjoyed—not unlike the leg-kicking described in Chapter 3. Then the string was disconnected. Most babies reacted by angrily jerking the string. Some, however, quit trying and looked sad (Lewis & Ramsay, 2005); their cortisol levels increased. This suggests that anger relieves stress, but that some babies learn to repress their anger.

Since sadness produces physiological stress (e.g., cortisol), sorrow negatively impacts the infant. All social emotions, particularly sadness and fear, probably shape the brain (Fries & Pollak, 2007; Johnson, 2010). As you learned in Chapter 3, experience matters.

FEAR Fear in response to some person, thing, or situation (not just starting in surprise) is evident at about 6 to 9 months and soon becomes more frequent and obvious (Witherington et al., 2004). Two kinds of social fear are typical:

- **Separation anxiety**—clinging and crying when a familiar caregiver is about to leave
- **Stranger wariness**—especially when an unfamiliar person moves too close, too quickly.

Separation anxiety is normal at age 1 year, intensifies by age 2, and usually subsides after that. Fear of separation interferes with infant sleep. For example, if infants fall asleep next to familiar people, they may wake up terrified if they are alone (Sadeh et al., 2010). Some babies become accustomed to a transitional object, such as a teddy bear or blanket, that comforts them as they transition from sleeping in their parents' arms to sleeping alone.

Transitional objects are not pathological; they are the infant's way to cope with anxiety. However, if separation anxiety remains strong after age 3, it is considered an emotional disorder and is accompanied by physiological signs of distress (Kossowsky et al., 2012).

cortisol
The primary stress hormone; fluctuations in the body's cortisol level affect human emotion.

separation anxiety
An infant's distress when a familiar caregiver leaves, most obvious between 9 and 14 months.

stranger wariness
An infant's expression of concern—a quiet stare while clinging to a familiar person, or a look of fear—when a stranger appears.

Developmentally Correct Both Santa's smile and Olivia's grimace are age-appropriate reactions. Babies between the ages of 6 to 9 months often have a fear of strangers, as Olivia, 7 months, shows here.

REUTERS / SUZANNE PLUNKETT

Strangers—especially those who move or appear unlike familiar caregivers—merit stares, not smiles, at age 1. This is a good sign: Infant memory is active and engaged. Many 1-year-olds fear not only strangers but also anything unexpected, from the flush of the toilet to the pop of a jack-in-the-box, from closing elevator doors to the tail-wagging approach of a dog. With repeated experience and reassurance, older infants might enjoy flushing the toilet (again and again) or calling the dog (and crying if the dog does not come).

Every aspect of early emotional development interacts with cultural beliefs, expressed in parental actions. There seems to be more separation anxiety and stranger wariness in Japan than in Germany because Japanese infants have very few experiences with separation from the mother, whereas in Germany, infants are more likely to experience time apart from their mothers (Saarni et al., 2006).

Toddlers' Emotions

Emotions take on new strength during toddlerhood. This is evident in temper tantrums. Toddlers are famous for fury, when something angers them so much that they yell, scream, cry, and do something physical—throwing a chair, throwing a punch, or throwing themselves on the floor. Logic is beyond them; if adults respond with anger or teasing, that makes it worse. Soon sadness comes to the fore, and then comfort (not acquiescence or punishment) is helpful (Green et al., 2011).

Gradually, more complex emotions emerge as toddlers develop a sense of themselves in relation to others (social awareness) and of their own uniqueness as a person (self-awareness).

SOCIAL AWARENESS Temper can be seen as an expression of selfhood. So can these new and more complex emotions: pride, shame, empathy, jealousy, embarrassment, and disgust. These emotions require social awareness, which emerges from family interactions and is shaped by culture (Mesquita & Leu, 2007).

Pride is experienced when the toddler feels joy at doing something successfully (Stipek et al., 1992). For example, many North American parents encourage toddler pride (saying, "You did it yourself!"), but Asian families typically discourage pride. Instead, they cultivate modesty and shame. Shame happens when a child thinks he or she has failed to meet the standards and expectations set by family or culture. This emotion then makes the child want to hide or disappear (Lewis, 1992).

Embarrassment occurs when a toddler feels confused and awkward as the result of unwanted attention. For example, a little boy can feel embarrassed simply from being stared at or pointed at by strangers. The difference between embarrassment and shame that shame stems from a sense of failure, but embarrassment is a result of unwanted attention from others, such as when an older person points at a child and exclaims, "Isn't she adorable!"

The emotion of empathy allows a young child to actually share another person's feelings. It is not uncommon for a toddler to look sad in the presence of a playmate who is crying and to pat that other child on the back (Lewis, 2007). Jealousy, on the other hand, makes a child want what someone else has, whether that something is a toy or food or attention.

Disgust as a physical reaction to an unpleasant taste or smell is evident very early. Even infants younger than 6 months will immediately spit out food that tastes bad or smells unpleasant. Disgust at a more complex level is strongly influenced by other people and age. For example, 18-month-olds (but not younger infants) express disgust at touching a dead animal (Stevenson et al., 2010).

By age 2, most children display the entire spectrum of emotions, and they begin to regulate their reactions, with more fear or boldness depending on experience

✦ **ESPECIALLY FOR Nurses and Pediatricians** Parents come to you concerned that their 1-year-old hides her face and holds on to them tightly whenever a stranger appears. What do you tell them? (see response, page 142) ➜

(Saarni et al., 2006). For example, many toddlers hide behind their parents when a dog approaches. Depending on how their mother or father reacts to the dog, and their prior experience with pets, the toddler may peek out and perhaps pet the dog himself or herself.

SELF-AWARENESS In addition to social awareness, another foundation for emotional growth is **self-awareness,** the realization that one's body, mind, and activities are distinct from those of other people (Kopp, 2011). Closely following the new mobility that results from walking, an emerging sense of "me" and "mine" leads to a new consciousness of others at about age 1.

Very young infants have no sense of self—at least of self as most people define it (Harter, 2006). In fact, a prominent psychoanalyst, Margaret Mahler, theorized that for the first 4 months, infants see themselves as part of their mothers. At about 5 months, they begin to spend several months developing self-awareness (Mahler et al., 1975).

Some aspects of selfhood emerge before age 1, but

> more complex self-representations are reflected [in] … self-referential emotions. … By the end of the second year and increasingly in the third [ages 1 and 2] the simple joy of success becomes accompanied by looking and smiling to an adult and calling attention to the feat; the simple sadness of failure becomes accompanied either by avoidance of eye contact with the adult and turning away or by reparative activity and confession. …
>
> *[Thompson, 2006, p. 79]*

In a classic experiment known as the mirror/rouge test (Lewis & Brooks, 1978), 9- to 24-month-olds looked into a mirror after a dot of rouge had been surreptitiously put on their noses. If they reacted by touching their noses, that meant they knew the mirror showed their own faces. None of the babies younger than 12 months old showed that self-recognition, although they sometimes smiled and touched the dot on the "other" baby in the mirror. However, between 15 and 24 months, babies became self-aware, touching their noses with curiosity and puzzlement. Self-recognition usually emerges at about 18 months, along with two other advances: pretending and using first-person pronouns (*I, me, mine, myself, my*) (Lewis, 2010).

self-awareness
A person's realization that he or she is a distinct individual whose body, mind, and actions are separate from those of other people.

Who Is That? At 18 months, this boy is at the beginning of self-awareness, testing to see whether his mirror image will meet his finger.

KEY Points

- Newborns experience such basic emotions as distress and contentment, expressed by crying or looking relaxed.
- Older babies feel curiosity, joy, anger (when they are kept from something they want), and fear (when something unexpected occurs).
- Toddlers express many emotions that indicate awareness of themselves and others, such as empathy, jealousy, and embarrassment.
- Cultural expectations and parental actions influence emotions.

Brain and Emotions

As the brain develops rapidly, not only do infants' cognitive abilities increase (as you read in Chapter 3), but their emotional abilities increase as well (Johnson, 2010). When the infant's brain responds to various experiences in his or her environment, important connections (neural pathways) are formed.

RESPONSE FOR Nurses and Pediatricians (from page 140) Stranger wariness is normal up to about 14 months. This baby's behaviour sounds like secure attachment. ●

Links between expressed emotions and brain growth are complex and are difficult to assess and describe (Lewis, 2011). Compared to the emotions of adults, discrete emotions during early infancy are murky and unpredictable. For instance, an infant's cry can be triggered by pain, fear, tiredness, surprise, or excitement; laughter can quickly turn to tears. Furthermore, infant emotions may erupt, increase, or disappear for unknown reasons (Camras & Shutter, 2010).

Growth of the Brain

Many specific aspects of brain development support social emotions (Lloyd-Fox et al., 2009). For instance, the social smile and laughter appear as the cortex matures (Konner, 2010). The same is probably true for fear, self-awareness, and anger. The maturation of a particular part of the cortex (the anterior cingulate gyrus) is directly connected to emotional self-regulation, allowing a child to express or hide feelings (Posner et al., 2007).

Infants' early emotional experiences guide the way that they will deal with those feelings in the future. For example, when infants experience stress, if trusted adults help them deal with the stressful event, infants develop constructive ways of dealing with future negative events. However, if infants repeatedly experience high levels of stress with little or a lack of positive adult support, the pathways that allow them to experience fear, anger, and frustration strengthen. This has future implications, as these children may be less likely to explore their environment or try new experiences, which are important for continued development and growth (Onunaku, 2005).

Thus, parents can greatly affect the "wiring" of the infant's brain through the types of interactions they have with their infants. The unique ways that families interact is cultural; culture helps determine the infants' developmental characteristics. For example, when and how babies are fed and parents' response to infant cries and temper tantrums are influenced by the family's culture.

Cultural differences may become encoded in the infant brain, called "a cultural sponge" by one group of scientists (Ambady & Bharucha, 2009). It is difficult to measure how infant brains are influenced by their context, but one study of adults (Zhu et al., 2007), half born in the United States and half in China, found that in both groups, a particular area of the brain (the medial prefrontal cortex) was activated when the adults judged whether certain adjectives applied to them. However, only in the Chinese was that area also activated when they were asked whether those adjectives applied to their mothers.

Researchers consider this to be "neuro-imaging evidence that culture shapes the functional anatomy of self-representation" (Zhu et al., 2007, 1310). They speculate that brain activation occurs because the Chinese participants learned, as babies, that they are closely aligned with their mothers, whereas the Americans learned to be independent. (A related cultural difference is explored in the Opposing Perspectives discussion of proximal and distal parenting later in this chapter.)

Providing a Stimulating Environment William lies comfortably with his father, Charles, as his mother, Maricyl, tries to make William smile at their home in Mississauga, Ontario. Both parents have cerebral palsy, a physical disability, but like other parents, they are able to provide a stimulating and nurturing environment that infants need to develop.

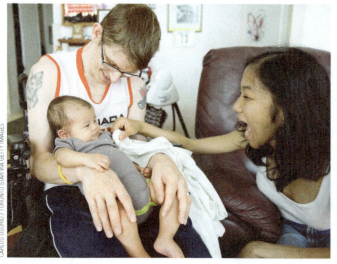

CARLOS OSORIO / TORONTO STAR VIA GETTY IMAGES

PARENTS' ROLE IN EARLY BRAIN DEVELOPMENT AND EMOTIONAL DEVELOPMENT Although parents' interactions are encompassed within culture, researchers disseminate some universal advice to parents and service providers to help them support their children's brain development in the early years. A research and advocacy organization, From Zero to Three, provides the following suggestions for healthy optimal brain development:

- Respond to the infant's initiated acts (e.g., smiles, cries, babbles).
- Praise the infant when a new skill/ability is mastered.
- Talk, sing, read, and play with the infant.
- Provide interesting things for the infant to touch, smell, and chew on.
- Encourage the infant to vocalize and babble.

[Zero to Three, n.d.]

MEMORY All emotional reactions, particularly those connected to self-awareness, depend partly on memory (Harter, 2006; Lewis, 2010). As already explained in Chapter 3, memory is fragile at first and gradually improves as dendrites and axons connect over the first year. No wonder toddlers are more quickly angered than younger babies when teased by an older sibling, and are more likely to resist entering the doctor's office. Unlike young infants, they have vivid memories of the previous time a sibling frustrated them or the doctor gave them a needle.

Memory for events and places is evident, but memory for people is even more powerful. Particular people (typically those the infant sees most often) arouse strong emotions. Even in the early weeks, faces are connected to sensations. For example, a breastfeeding mother's face is connected to sucking and relief of hunger. The tentative social smile at every face, which occurs naturally as the brain reaches six weeks of maturity, soon becomes a much quicker and fuller smile when an infant sees his or her parent. This occurs because the neurons that fire together become more closely and quickly connected to each other (via dendrites and neurotransmitters) with repeated experience.

Social preferences form in the early months and are connected with an individual's face, voice, touch, and smell. This is one reason adopted children are placed with their new parents in the first days of life whenever possible, unlike 100 years ago, when adoptions were delayed until after age 1. It also is a reason to respect an infant's reaction to a babysitter: If a 6-month-old screams and clings to the parent when the sitter arrives, perhaps another caregiver needs to be found. (Do not confuse this with separation anxiety at 12 months—a normal, expected reaction.)

STRESS Emotions are connected to brain activity and hormones, but the connections are complicated—affected by genes, past experiences, and additional hormones and neurotransmitters not yet understood (Lewis, 2011). One link is clear: Excessive stress (increasing cortisol) harms the developing brain (Adam et al., 2007). The hypothalamus (discussed further in Chapter 5), in particular, grows more slowly if an infant is often frightened.

Brain scans of children who were discovered to have been maltreated in infancy show abnormal responses to stress, anger, and other emotions, and even to photographs of frightened people (Gordis et al., 2008; Masten et al., 2008). This research has led many developmentalists to suspect that abnormal neurological responses are caused by early abuse.

Quebec researchers Michael Meaney and Gustavo Turecki at the Douglas Mental Health University Institute have explored how environment can modify genes, from genetics to epigenetics. Specifically, they studied a gene called NR3C1, which produces a protein that helps individuals decrease the concentration of stress hormones in the body. The researchers examined 36 brains post-mortem: 12 were victims of suicide who had experienced childhood abuse; 12 were victims of suicide but had not been subjected to abuse; and 12 were control brains. The results were written in the neurons: Those who were abused had epigenetic modifications that had altered their functioning of the NR3C1 gene. They found that the glands that secrete stress hormones were on constant alert, making these individuals more vulnerable to anxiety and depression, and even more suicidal (Douglas Institute, 2013). Conversely, the NR3C1 gene can be activated to decrease the quantity of stress hormones. But activating this gene needs an epigenetic switch—for humans, this includes a hug (or cuddling, a nurturing, soothing behaviour).

The likelihood that early caregiving affects the brain throughout life leads to obvious applications (Belsky & de Haan, 2011). Since infants learn emotional responses, caregivers need to be consistent and reassuring. This is not always easy—remember that some infants cry inconsolably in the early weeks. As one researcher noted:

> An infant's crying has two possible consequences: it may elicit tenderness and desire to soothe, or helplessness and rage. It can be a signal that encourages attachment or one that jeopardizes the early relationship by triggering depression and, in some cases, even neglect or abuse.
>
> *[Kim, 2011, p. 229]*

Sometimes parents are blamed, or blame themselves, when their infant keeps crying. This is not helpful: Parents who feel guilty or incompetent may become angry at their baby, which may lead to unresponsive parenting, an unhappy child, and a hostile parent. But a negative relationship between difficult infants and their parents is not inevitable. Most colicky babies have loving parents and, when the colic subsides, a warm, reciprocal relationship develops. Developmentalists refer to this kind of mutual relationship as goodness of fit—that is, an adjustment that allows for smooth infant–caregiver interaction.

Kathleen's STORY

Temperament

This chapter began by describing universals of infant emotions, and then explained that brain maturation undergirds those universals. You just read that parents should not blame themselves when a baby cries often and rarely sleeps. Who, then, is to blame? When my friend had a difficult infant, she laughingly said that she and her husband wanted to exchange her for another model. And my daughter with my crying grandson (in the opening of this chapter) was upset when I said my babies were all easy. She felt I was bragging or forgetful, not sympathetic.

GENES AND EMOTIONS Certainly not all babies are easygoing. Infant emotions are affected by alleles and prenatal events, and the uniqueness of each person means that some babies are difficult from the moment they are born. Developmentalists recognize the impact of genes and prenatal experiences. Some devote their lives to discovering alleles that affect specific emotions (Johnson & Fearon, 2011). For example, researchers have found that the 7-repeat allele of the DRD4 VNTR gene, when combined with the 5-HTTLPR genotype, results in 6-month-olds who are difficult—crying often, hard to distract, slow to laugh (Holmboe et al., 2011).

Temperament is defined as the "biologically based core of individual differences in style of approach and response to the environment that is stable across time and situations" (van den Akker et al., 2010, p. 485). "Biologically based" means that these traits originate with nature, not nurture. Confirmation that temperament arises from the inborn brain comes from an analysis of the tone, duration, and intensity of infant cries after the first inoculation, before much experience outside the womb. Cry variations at this every early stage were correlated with later temperament (Jong et al., 2010).

Temperament is not the same as personality, although temperamental inclinations may lead to personality differences. Generally, although personality traits (e.g., honesty and humility) are fairly stable over the course of one's life, they are learned or

✦ ESPECIALLY FOR Pediatricians and Nurses Parents come to you with their fussy 3-month-old. They say they have read that temperament is "fixed" before birth, and they are worried that their child will always be difficult. What do you tell them? (see response, page 146) ➜

temperament
Inborn differences between one person and another in emotions, activity, and self-regulation. It is measured by the person's typical responses to the environment.

acquired, and influenced by the individual's environment, whereas temperamental traits (e.g., shyness and aggression) are genetic.

Of course, heredity and experience always interact, as shown in Figure 4.1. Although temperament originates with genes, the expression of emotions over the life span is modified by experience—the result of child-rearing methods, culture, and learning (Rothbart & Bates, 2006). How this happens will be clearer with examples.

RESEARCH ON TEMPERAMENT In laboratory studies of temperament, infants are exposed to events that are frightening or attractive. Four-month-olds might see spinning mobiles or hear unusual sounds. Older babies might confront a noisy, moving robot or a clown who quickly moves close. At such experiences, some children laugh (and are classified as "easy"), some cry ("difficult"), and some are quiet ("slow to warm up").

These three categories (easy, difficult, slow to warm up) come from the New York Longitudinal Study (NYLS), which started in 1956 and continued for several decades, investigating infants' individual types of personality and temperament. The NYLS was the first large study to recognize that each newborn has distinct inborn traits (Thomas & Chess, 1977). Nine characteristics were identified, and infants were scored on a three-point scale (low, medium, high) for their level and extent of each one:

1. motor activity
2. rhythmicity or regularity of functions, such as eating, sleeping, wakefulness
3. response to new people or objects (accepts or withdraws from situation)
4. adaptability to changing environment
5. sensitivity to stimuli
6. energy level of responses
7. general mood or disposition (e.g., cheerful, crying, friendly, cranky)
8. distractibility
9. attention span and persistence in an activity.

Researchers believed that infants can be behaviourally profiled from the scores of these nine characteristics. According to the NYLS, by 3 months, infants manifest these nine traits that cluster into four categories (the three described above and "hard to classify"). The proportion of infants in each category was as follows:

- easy – 40 percent
- difficult – 10 percent
- slow to warm up – 15 percent
- hard to classify – 35 percent.

Easy children are generally positive in mood, have regular bodily functioning, are adaptable and have a positive approach to new situations, and have a low or medium intensity of response. For parents, these infants pose few problems in caring for and training them.

Difficult children, on the other hand, have irregular bodily functions, usually display intense reactions, tend to withdraw from new situations, are slow to adapt to changes in their environment, generally have negative moods, and are seen as crying a lot. Difficult children tend to be more trying for parents, requiring them to be more consistent in their interactions and training, and more tolerant of their children's behaviours.

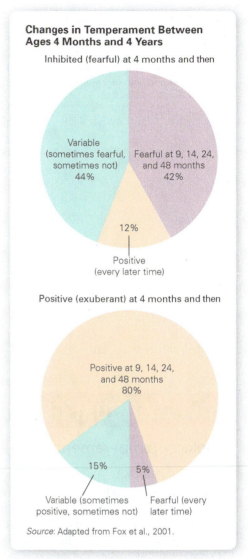

Changes in Temperament Between Ages 4 Months and 4 Years

Inhibited (fearful) at 4 months and then

- Variable (sometimes fearful, sometimes not) 44%
- Fearful at 9, 14, 24, and 48 months 42%
- Positive (every later time) 12%

Positive (exuberant) at 4 months and then

- Positive at 9, 14, 24, and 48 months 80%
- Variable (sometimes positive, sometimes not) 15%
- Fearful (every later time) 5%

Source: Adapted from Fox et al., 2001.

FIGURE 4.1 Do Babies' Temperaments Change?
Sometimes. Especially if they were fearful. Adults who are reassuring help children overcome an innate fearfulness. If fearful children do not change, it is not known whether it is because their parents are not sufficiently reassuring (nurture) or because they are temperamentally more fearful (nature).

RESPONSE FOR Pediatricians and Nurses (from page 144) It's too soon to tell. Temperament is not truly "fixed" but variable, especially in the first few months. Many "difficult" infants become happy, successful adolescents and adults. ●

Slow-to-warm-up children are fairly low in activity level, tend to withdraw, are slower to adapt to new situations, are somewhat negative in mood, and have a low intensity of reaction.

Later research confirms again and again that newborns differ temperamentally and that some are unusually difficult. However, although the NYLS began a rich research endeavour, the nine dimensions of the NYLS have not held up in later large studies (Caspi & Shiner, 2006; Zentner & Bates, 2008). Generally, only three (not nine) dimensions of temperament are clearly present in early childhood (Else-Quest et al., 2006; van den Akker et al., 2010). Although each study uses somewhat different terms, the following three dimensions of temperament are apparent:

1. effortful control – able to regulate attention and emotion, to self-soothe
2. negative mood – fearful, angry, unhappy
3. surgency – active, social, not shy, exuberant.

Research has also linked temperament to social skills and adjustment. For example, children who are negative, impulsive, and unregulated tended to have poorer peer relationships, and behaviourally inhibited children were more likely to be more anxious and depressed. However, these children with less than ideal temperaments are not doomed. Parents can influence children's temperament so that they can develop optimally by adjusting their demands and expectations with their children's temperament (goodness of fit).

A VIEW FROM SCIENCE

Linking Temperament and Parenting—A Canadian Perspective

As noted, thousands of scientists have studied infant temperament. In one study, a team of Canadian researchers from Quebec sought, among other things, to find whether there is a link between a specific environmental factor—harsh parenting—and aggressive behaviour in young children (Vitaro et al., 2006). This question is important because children who are overly aggressive will face greater difficulties in socializing with their peers. In turn, not having friends in school has a negative impact on children's academic motivation and performance.

Participants were from the Quebec Longitudinal Study of Child Development (Jetté & Des Groseilliers, 2000) and included 1516 families. In their study, the researchers focused on both reactive and proactive types of aggression. Children who display reactive aggression are usually responding to pre-existing conditions (whether perceived or real) such as provocation, frustration, or threats. The most frequent response is anger. Children who display proactive aggression often try to manipulate or dominate others for their own purposes.

Harsh parenting is often associated with parents who show little warmth toward their children but punish them freely. In this study, the researchers measured harsh parenting by rating parents' responses to a series of statements, such as: "When my baby cries, he/she gets on my nerves" and "I have shaken my baby when he/she was particularly fussy."

Both mothers and fathers were first surveyed when their children were 17 months old. Then, when each child was 6 years old, the mother and the child's teacher reported on the child's tendencies toward reactive and proactive aggression. The report included answers to such questions as: "In the past 12 months, how often would you say that [this] child reacted in an aggressive manner when teased or threatened?" (reactive aggression), or "… used physical force to dominate other children?" (proactive aggression).

With both types of aggression, the data were clear—harsh parenting of infants predicted aggressive behaviours in older children. The study thus established an explicit connection between nurture and the temperamental trait of aggression. (It is unclear whether parents who engaged in harsh parenting when their child was 17 months continued this line of behaviour throughout their child's lives, although this is most likely.)

The research also showed that children's negative emotionality at age 17 months predicted the level of reactive aggression at 6 years of age. Given such a link, the importance and advantages of early intervention and education strategies, such as those for the prevention of shaken baby syndrome (see Chapter 3), are obvious.

The Development of Social Bonds

As you have already seen in this chapter, the social context has a powerful impact on development. So does the infant's age, via brain maturation. Regarding emotional development, the baby's age determines specific social interactions that lead to growth—first synchrony, then attachment, then social referencing.

Synchrony

Early parent–child interactions are described as **synchrony,** a mutual exchange that requires split-second timing for parent and child to match each other ("the meeting of the minds"). Synchrony is a joy for both participants, and also is a powerful learning experience. In every episode, infants learn to read others' emotions and develop social skills, such as taking turns and watching expressions.

Synchrony is evident in the first three months, becoming more frequent and elaborate as the infant matures (Feldman, 2007). The adult–infant partnership usually begins with the adult imitating the infant (not vice versa); adults rarely smile at young infants until the infants smile at them, several weeks after birth. Then adults usually grin broadly and talk animatedly to their babies (Lavelli & Fogel, 2005).

In addition to careful timing, synchrony also involves rhythm and tone (Van Puyvelde et al., 2010). Metaphors for synchrony are often musical—a waltz, a jazz duet—to emphasize that each partner must be attuned to the other. This helps infants connect their internal state with external expressions understood within their culture. Synchrony is particularly apparent in Asian cultures, perhaps because of a focus on interpersonal sensitivity (Morelli & Rothbaum, 2007).

synchrony
A coordinated, rapid, and smooth exchange of responses between a caregiver and an infant.

Same Situation, Far Apart: Sweet Synchrony Differences in gender and nation (England and Cuba) are obvious but superficial. The essence of early parent–infant interaction in both situations is synchrony.

Synchrony is evident not only by direct observation, as when watching a caregiver play with an infant too young to talk, but also via computer calculation of the millisecond timing of smiles, arched eyebrows, and so on (Messinger et al., 2010). One study found that mothers who took longer to bathe, feed, and diaper their infants were also most responsive. Apparently, some parents combine caregiving with emotional play, which takes longer but also allows more synchrony.

still-face technique
An experimental practice in which an adult keeps his or her face unmoving and expressionless in face-to-face interaction with an infant.

NEGLECTED SYNCHRONY What if there is no synchrony? If no one plays with an infant, what will happen? Experiments using the **still-face technique** have addressed these questions (Tronick, 1989; Tronick & Weinberg, 1997). In still-face experiments, an infant faces an adult who responds normally while two video cameras simultaneously record their interpersonal reactions. Frame-by-frame analysis reveals that parents instinctively synchronize their responses to the infants' movements, with exaggerated tone and expression. Babies reciprocate with smiles and flailing limbs.

To be specific, long before they can reach out and grab, infants respond excitedly to caregiver attention by waving their arms. They are delighted if the adult moves closer so that a waving arm touches the face or, even better, a hand grabs hair. You read about this eagerness for interaction in Chapter 3, when infants try to "make interesting sights last" or when they babble in response to adult speech. Meanwhile, adults open their eyes wider, raise their eyebrows, smack their lips, and emit nonsensical sounds—all in response to tiny infant actions.

In the next phase of the experiment, on cue, the same adult does not move closer but instead erases all facial expression, staring quietly with a "still face" (a motionless face) for a minute or two. Sometimes by 2 months, and clearly by 6 months, infants are upset by still faces, especially from their parents (less so from strangers). Babies frown, fuss, drool, look away, kick, cry, or suck their fingers. By 5 months, they also vocalize, as if to say, "Pay attention to me" (Goldstein et al., 2009).

Many types of studies have reached the same conclusion: Synchrony is vital. Responsiveness aids psychosocial and biological development, evident in heart rate, weight gain, and brain maturation (Moore & Calkins, 2004; Newnham et al., 2009). Particularly in the first year, babies of depressed mothers suffer unless someone else is a sensitive partner (Bagner et al., 2010). In the following section, we examine the next stage in child–adult bonding: attachment.

Attachment

attachment
A bond that an infant forms with a caregiver; a tie that binds them together in space and endures over time.

Toward the end of the first year, face-to-face synchrony almost disappears. Once infants can move around, they are no longer content to respond to adult facial expressions and vocalizations. Another connection, called attachment, overtakes synchrony. **Attachment** is the lasting emotional bond that infants develop with a caregiver. Unlike temperament, which focused on the infant, attachment is based on relationships.

British psychoanalyst and researcher John Bowlby first developed a comprehensive theory to explain attachment (1969, 1973a, 1973b, 1988). His work was carried on and expanded upon by American-Canadian developmentalist Mary Ainsworth. Ainsworth received her PhD from the University of Toronto, worked with Bowlby in London, and then performed seminal studies on mother–infant relationships in Central Africa (Ainsworth, 1967). (We will look at Ainsworth's contribution to attachment theory research in detail later in this chapter.)

As is often the case, both Bowlby and Ainsworth grounded their work in that of other scientists, especially in the fields of psychoanalysis and ethology (the study of animals with the focus on behavioural patterns in natural environments). Bowlby was influenced by the work of psychoanalyst René Spitz (1946), who studied infants in a Colorado orphanage. Spitz tried to explain why, even though these children received adequate food and physical care, they failed to thrive. According to Freud, if basic needs are met, infants would bond with their mothers. Instead, the orphaned infants lost weight, grew passive, and showed no positive feelings for the nurse who fed them (Rutter, 2006). Spitz came to believe that the children suffered a kind of emotional deprivation from the loss of their mothers, and that this sense of loss had lasting negative impacts on their development.

Researcher Harry Harlow's work also had an important influence on the development of attachment theory. In Harlow's classic study (1958), rhesus monkeys were taken from their mothers shortly after birth and placed in a cage with two mechanical "mothers." One was made of wire and had a feeding bottle. The other was covered in soft terrycloth and had no bottle. Surprisingly, all the infant monkeys spent much more time clinging to the cloth mother than the wire one, only going to the wire mother to feed. From this and later experiments, Harlow concluded that an infant's love for its mother is based more on emotional needs than physical requirements such as hunger and thirst.

Bowlby used the term "maternal deprivation" to describe the emotional trauma suffered by infants who lose their mother or other beloved caregiver. He also believed that the evolutionary need for protection reinforced children's profound attachment to their maternal or principal caregiver. "The infant and young child," Bowlby stated in one of his early works, "should experience a warm, intimate, and continuous relationship with his mother (or permanent mother substitute) in which both find satisfaction and enjoyment" (1951, p. 179). Bowlby argued that not experiencing this fundamental relationship would have serious impacts on a child's mental health.

Although it is most evident at about age 1 year, attachment begins before birth and influences relationships throughout life (see At About This Time). Adults' attachment to their parents, formed decades earlier, affects their behaviour with their own children as well as their relationship with their partners (Grossmann et al., 2005; Kline, 2008; Simpson & Rholes, 2010; Sroufe et al., 2005).

In recent years, research on infant attachment has looked beyond Western parenting practices; in Canada, the caregiver-infant relationship within Aboriginal families has merited closer attention. Researchers Cindy Hardy and Sherry Bellamy from British Columbia (2013) have pointed out that the Western perspective of attachment theory is simplistic in comparison to how Aboriginal peoples view family life.

For many Aboriginal families in Canada (and elsewhere), the themes of holism, balance, and respect inform the way children are instructed in their views of health and sickness, and their relations to others (Adelson, 2007). The Medicine Wheel, for example, is one of the models that represents First Peoples' worldview of the interactions and balance among mind, emotions, spirit, and body (Mitchell & Maracle, 2005), and the interconnectedness with all person's relations, community, and the land (Vukic et al., 2011). So, researchers in this area need to pay attention to the history, ancestors, extended family, and community to which the caregiver and child are connected, as these connections influence parenting.

SIGNS OF ATTACHMENT Infants show their attachment through proximity-seeking (such as approaching and following their caregivers) and by maintaining contact (such as touching, snuggling, and holding). Proximity-seeking is evident when a baby cries if the mother wants privacy when she goes to the bathroom, or if a backward-facing car seat prevents the baby from seeing the parent. Some parents in the front passenger seat reach back to give a hand, which sometimes reassures the

AT ABOUT THIS TIME
Stages of Attachment

Birth to 6 weeks	*Preattachment*. Newborns signal, via crying and body movements, that they need others. When people respond positively, the newborn is comforted and learns to seek more interaction. Newborns are also primed by brain patterns to recognize familiar voices and faces.
6 weeks to 8 months	*Attachment in the making*. Infants respond preferentially to familiar people by smiling, laughing, babbling. Their caregivers' voices, touch, expressions, and gestures are comforting, often overriding the infant's impulse to cry. Trust develops.
8 months to 2 years	*Classic secure attachment*. Infants greet the primary caregiver, play happily when the caregiver is present, and show separation anxiety when the caregiver leaves. Both infant and caregiver seek to be close to each other (proximity) and frequently look at each other (contact). In many caregiver–infant pairs, physical touch (patting, holding, caressing) is frequent.
2 to 6 years	*Attachment as launching pad*. Young children seek their caregiver's praise and reassurance as their social world expands. Interactive conversations and games (hide-and-seek, object play, reading, pretending) are common. Children expect caregivers to comfort and entertain.
6 to 12 years	*Mutual attachment*. Children seek to make their caregivers proud by learning whatever adults want them to learn, and adults reciprocate. In concrete operational thought, specific accomplishments are valued by adults and children.
12 to 18 years	*New attachment figures*. Teenagers explore and make friendships on their own, using their working models of earlier attachments as a base. With more advanced, formal operational thinking, shared ideals and goals become more influential.
18 years on	*Attachment revisited*. Adults develop relationships with others, especially relationships with romantic partners and their own children, influenced by earlier attachment patterns. Past insecure attachments from childhood can be repaired rather than repeated, although this does not always happen.

Source: Adapted from Grobman, 2008.

baby. However, contact-maintaining need not be physical: visual or verbal connections are often sufficient.

Research on attachment has occurred in dozens of nations, with people of many ages. Attachment seems to be universal, but specific manifestations vary. For instance, Ugandan mothers never kiss their infants but often massage them, contrary to Western custom. Adults who are securely attached to each other might remain in contact via daily phone calls, emails, or texts, and keep in proximity by sitting in the same room as each reads quietly. Some scholars believe that attachment, not only of mother and infant but also of fathers, grandparents, and non-relatives, is the reason that *Homo sapiens* thrived whereas other species became extinct (Hrdy, 2009).

SECURE AND INSECURE ATTACHMENT As infants make sense of their social world, they develop an internal working model, a cognitive framework that is comprised of mental representations for interpreting their world, self, and others. So, how the situation will be evaluated, what is expected, and what infants will do are guided by the internal working model. Simply put, Bowlby (1969) believed that their first relationship (primary caregiver) will act as the prototype for future relationships.

Mary Ainsworth first developed a way of studying Bowlby's attachment theory by conducting experiments that identified different types of attachment that infants might have with their caregivers. Based on Ainsworth's work, attachment is now classified into four types, A, B, C, and D (see Table 4.1).

Infants with **secure attachment** (B) feel comfortable and confident because their parents are generally responsive and sensitive to their needs. "Responsive" and "sensitive" are terms that need to be distinguished because they describe two different types of behaviour. If a baby cries and a parent immediately goes over to the baby to see what the matter is, this is responsive behaviour. However, does the parent know why the baby is crying? Is the baby hungry? Does the baby's diaper need to be changed? Does the baby want to be held? That is when parents need to be sensitive to the needs of their infants (and later on, to those of their children). When parents are responsive and sensitive, infants learn that they can trust their parents to protect them and to ensure their well-being. The caregiver is also a *base for exploration*, providing assurance and enabling exploration. A toddler might, for example, scramble down from the caregiver's lap to play with an intriguing toy, but periodically look back and vocalize (contact-maintaining) or bring the toy to the caregiver for inspection (proximity-seeking).

By contrast, insecure attachment (A and C) is characterized by fear, anxiety, anger, or indifference in children whose parents are not consistently sensitive or responsive to their needs. Some insecure children play independently without maintaining contact; this is **insecure-avoidant attachment** (A). The opposite reaction is also insecure: some children are unwilling to leave the caregiver's lap, which is **insecure-resistant/ambivalent attachment** (C).

Ainsworth's original schema identified only A, B, and C types of attachment. Later researchers discovered a fourth category (D), **disorganized attachment.** Type D infants may shift from hitting to kissing their mothers, from staring blankly to crying hysterically, or from pinching themselves to freezing in place.

Among the general population (not among infants with special needs), almost two-thirds of infant attachments are secure (B). Their mothers' presence gives them courage to explore; her departure causes distress; her return elicits positive social contact (such as smiling or hugging) and then more playing. A balanced reaction, being concerned but not overwhelmed by comings and goings, indicates security. (Reference here to the mother is deliberate, as most early research was on mother–infant attachment; later research included fathers, siblings, and other caregivers.)

About one-third of infant attachments are insecure, either indifferent (A) or unduly anxious (C). About 5 to 10 percent of infants fit into none of these categories and are labelled disorganized (D). Disorganized infants have no evident strategy for social interaction (even an avoidant or resistant one, A or C). Sometimes they

secure attachment
A relationship in which an infant obtains both comfort and confidence from the presence of his or her caregiver.

insecure-avoidant attachment
A pattern of attachment in which an infant avoids connection with the caregiver, as when the infant seems not to care about the caregiver's presence, departure, or return.

insecure-resistant/ambivalent attachment
A pattern of attachment in which an infant's anxiety and uncertainty are evident, as when the infant becomes very upset at separation from the caregiver and both resists and seeks contact on reunion.

disorganized attachment
A type of attachment that is marked by an infant's inconsistent reactions to the caregiver's departure and return.

TABLE 4.1 **Patterns of Infant Attachment**

Type	Name of Pattern	In Playroom	Mother Leaves	Mother Returns	Toddlers in Category (%)
A	Insecure-avoidant	Child plays happily.	Child continues playing.	Child ignores her.	10–20
B	Secure	Child plays happily.	Child pauses, is not as happy.	Child welcomes her, returns to play.	50–70
C	Insecure-resistant/ambivalent	Child clings, is preoccupied with mother.	Child is unhappy, may stop playing.	Child is angry; may cry, hit mother, cling.	10–20
D	Disorganized	Child is cautious.	Child may stare or yell; looks scared, confused.	Child acts oddly— may scream, hit self, throw things.	5–10

become hostile and aggressive, difficult for anyone to relate to (Lyons-Ruth et al., 1999). Unlike the first three types, disorganized infants have elevated levels of cortisol in reaction to stress (Bernard & Dozier, 2010).

MEASURING ATTACHMENT Ainsworth (1973) developed a now-classic laboratory procedure called the **Strange Situation** to measure attachment. The procedure takes place in a location that is unfamiliar to the infant, which is likely to increase the infant's need for his or her parent. In a well-equipped playroom, an infant is observed for eight episodes, each lasting three minutes. First, the infant and his or her parent are together in the playroom. Then, the infant is exposed to separations from and reunions with the parent, as well as two interactions with a stranger, one with the parent in the room and one with the parent out of the room. During these episodes, observers rate the infant's behaviour according to

Strange Situation
A laboratory procedure for measuring attachment by evoking infants' reactions to the stress of various adults' comings and goings in an unfamiliar playroom.

- *Exploration of the toys.* A secure toddler plays happily.
- *Reaction to the caregiver's departure.* A secure toddler notices when the caregiver leaves and shows some sign of missing him or her.
- *Reaction to the caregiver's return.* A secure toddler welcomes the caregiver's reappearance, usually seeking contact, and then plays again.

In this procedure, the infant's behaviour in response to these situations indicates the quality or security of the child's attachment.

Attachment is not always measured via the Strange Situation. Instead, surveys and interviews are also used. Sometimes parents answer 90 questions about their children's characteristics, and sometimes adults are interviewed extensively (according to a detailed protocol) about their relationships with their own parents, again with various specific measurements (Fortuna & Roisman, 2008).

Research measuring attachment has revealed that some behaviours that might seem normal are, in fact, a sign of insecurity. For instance, an infant who clings to the caregiver and refuses to explore the toys in the new playroom might be type A. Likewise, adults who say their childhood was happy and their mother was a saint, especially if they provide few specific memories, might be insecure. And young children who are immediately friendly to strangers may never have formed a secure attachment (Tarullo et al., 2011). A new diagnostic category in DSM-5, reactive attachment disorder, recognizes that some children never form an attachment at all, even an insecure one.

Assessments of attachment, developed and validated for middle-class North Americans, may not be culturally appropriate elsewhere. Infants who seem dismissive or clingy may not always be insecure, as cultures differ. Everywhere, however, infants are attached to their parents, and everywhere secure attachment predicts academic success and emotional stability (Erdman & Ng, 2010; Molitor & Hsu, 2011; Rothbaum et al., 2011).

Insecure Attachment and Social Setting

At first, developmentalists expected secure attachment to "predict all the outcomes reasonably expected from a well-functioning personality" (R. A. Thompson & Raikes, 2003, p. 708). But this expectation turned out to be naive.

Securely attached infants are more likely to become secure toddlers, socially competent preschoolers, high-achieving schoolchildren, and capable parents (R. A. Thompson, 2006) (see Table 4.2). Attachment affects early brain development, one reason these later outcomes occur (Diamond & Fagundes, 2010). However, A, B, C, or D status may shift with family circumstances, such as divorce, abuse, or income loss.

Harsh contexts, especially the stresses of poverty, reduce the incidence of secure attachment (Seifer et al., 2004; van IJzendoorn & Bakermans-Kranenburg, 2010), and insecure attachment correlates with many later problems. However, correlation is not causation, and thus insecure attachment may not be the direct cause of those problems.

Many aspects of low SES make low school achievement, hostile children, and fearful adults more likely. The underlying premise—that responsive early parenting leads to secure attachment, which buffers stress and encourages exploration—seems valid, but attachment behaviours in the Strange Situation are only one indication of the quality of the parent–child relationship.

INSIGHTS FROM ROMANIA No scholar doubts that close human relationships should develop in the first year of life and that the lack of such relationships has dire consequences. Unfortunately, thousands of children born in Romania are proof. When Romanian dictator Nicolae Ceausescu outlawed birth control and abortions in the 1980s, illegal abortions became the leading cause of death for Romanian women aged 15 to 45 (Verona, 2003), and more than 100 000 children were abandoned to crowded, impersonal, state-run orphanages. The children experienced severe deprivation, including virtually no normal interaction, play, or conversation (Rutter et al., 2007).

In the two years after Ceausescu was ousted and executed in 1989, thousands of those children were adopted by North American, western European, and Australian families. Those who were adopted before 6 months of age fared best; synchrony was established via play and caregiving. Most of them developed normally.

For those adopted after 6 months, and especially after 12 months, early signs were encouraging: skinny infants gained weight and grew faster than other 1-year-olds, developing motor skills they had lacked (Park et al., 2011). However, the impact of early social deprivation soon became evident in their emotions and cognition. Many were overly friendly to strangers throughout childhood, a sign of insecure attachment (Tarullo et al., 2011). At age 11, they scored an average of only 85 on

---

TABLE 4.2 **Predictors of Attachment Type**

Secure attachment (type B) is more likely if:

- The parent is usually sensitive and responsive to the infant's needs.
- The infant–parent relationship is high in synchrony.
- The infant's temperament is "easy."
- The parents are not stressed about income, other children, or their marriage.
- The parents have a working model of secure attachment to their own parents.

Insecure attachment is more likely if:

- The parent mistreats the child. (Neglect increases type A; abuse increases types C and D.)
- The mother is mentally ill. (Paranoia increases type D; depression increases type C.)
- The parents are highly stressed about income, other children, or their marriage. (Parental stress increases types A and D.)
- The parents are intrusive and controlling. (Parental domination increases type A.)
- The parents are active alcoholics. (Alcoholic father increases type A; alcoholic mother increases type D.)
- The child's temperament is "difficult." (Difficult children tend to be type C.)
- The child's temperament is "slow to warm up." (This correlates with type A.)

Danger Ongoing Look closely and you can see danger. That bent crib bar could strangle an infant, and that chipped paint could contain lead. These three Romanian infants (photographed in 1990) escaped those dangers to be raised in loving adoptive homes. Unfortunately, the damage of social isolation (note the sheet around the crib) could not be completely overcome: some young adults who spent their first year in an institution like this still carry emotional scars.

the Wechsler Intelligence Scale for Children (WISC) IQ test, 15 points below normal (Rutter et al., 2010).

These children are now young adults, many with serious emotional or conduct problems. The cause is more social than biological. Even those who were relatively well nourished at adoption, or who caught up to normal growth, often became impulsive and angry teenagers. Apparently, the stresses of adolescence and emerging adulthood exacerbated the cognitive and social strains on these children and their families (Merz & McCall, 2011).

Romanian infants are no longer available for international adoption, but some are still abandoned. Research confirms that early emotional deprivation, not genes or nutrition, is their greatest problem. Romanian infants develop best in their own families, second best in foster families, and worst in institutions (Nelson et al., 2007). To the best of our knowledge, this applies to infants everywhere: Families usually care for their babies better than strangers do.

Fortunately, institutions have improved somewhat; more recent adoptees are not as impaired as those 1990 Romanian orphans (Merz & McCall, 2011). However, some infants in every nation are still deprived of healthy interactions, and the early months seem to be a sensitive period for emotional development. Children need parents, biological or not (McCall et al., 2011).

PREVENTING PROBLEMS All infants need love and stimulation; all seek synchrony and then attachment—secure if possible, insecure if not. Without some adult support, infants become disorganized, adrift, and emotionally troubled. Extreme early social deprivation is very difficult to overcome.

Since synchrony and attachment develop over the first year, and since more than one-third of all parents have difficulty establishing secure attachments, many developmentalists seek to discover what particularly impairs these parents and what can be done. We know that secure attachment is more difficult when parents were abused as children, when families are socially isolated, when mothers are young adolescents, or when infants are unusually difficult (Berlin et al., 2011).

If biological parents cannot care for their newborns, foster or adoptive parents need to be found quickly so synchrony and attachment can develop (McCall et al., 2011). Sometimes children are placed in kinship care, especially with their grandparents. In Canada, provincial governments have begun to emphasize using the least intrusive form of intervention when placing a child in foster care. This means they are now providing financial support for kinship care through their foster care systems. As a result, the number of children under 18 years in Canada who were living with grandparents instead of parents increased by 20 percent from 1991 to 2001. When grandparents serve as a child's primary caregivers, this is known as a "skipped generation household." By 2001, there were 56 700 Canadian grandparents in skipped generation households (Fuller-Thomson, 2005).

This trend is especially evident among First Nations, whose children, according to Indian and Northern Affairs Canada, are four to six times more likely than other Canadian children to come into the care of child welfare agencies (Fuller-Thomson, 2005). Since the early 1980s, the federal and provincial governments have been handing over responsibility for child welfare on reserves to First Nations' agencies. In developing protocols for placing at-risk infants into foster care, these agencies emphasize the need to keep the children within their home communities whenever possible, and preferably within the extended family. For this reason, grandparents are often the preferred caregivers when parents, for whatever reason, cannot perform this role themselves. Placing infants and young children with their grandparents not only avoids the disruption and trauma associated with handing them over to strangers, but also has the advantage of keeping the children in a culturally similar milieu where they will feel more at home and comfortable (Fuller Thomson, 2005).

If high-risk birth parents believe they can provide good care, early support may avoid later problems. Success has been reported when skilled professionals come to the home to nurture secure relationships between infant and caregiver (Lowell et al., 2011). In fact, if a professional helps parents in the first days after birth, perhaps by using the NBAS (mentioned in Chapter 2) to encourage bonding, problems need never start (e.g., Nugent et al., 2009).

Social Referencing

Social referencing refers to infants seeking emotional responses or information from other people. You may see this when you approach a toddler and she starts looking back and forth between her parent and you. She is looking for facial and body cues from her parent to see if she should be afraid. A parent's reassuring glance or cautionary words, a facial expression of alarm, pleasure, or dismay—those are social references.

After age 1, when infants can walk and are little scientists, their need to consult others becomes urgent. Social referencing is constant, as toddlers search for clues in gazes, faces, and body position, paying close attention to emotions and intentions. They focus especially on their familiar caregivers, but they also use relatives, other children, and even strangers to help them assess objects and events. They are remarkably selective: even at 16 months, they recognize which strangers are reliable references and which are not (Poulin-Dubois & Chow, 2009).

Social referencing has many practical applications. Consider mealtime. Caregivers the world over smack their lips, pretend to taste, and say "yum-yum," encouraging toddlers to eat their first beets, liver, or spinach. For their part, toddlers become astute at reading expressions, insisting on the foods that the adults *really* like. Through this process, some children may develop a taste for raw fish or curried goat or smelly cheese—foods that children in other cultures might refuse. Similarly, toddlers use social cues to understand the difference between real and pretend eating (Nishida & Lillard, 2007), as well as to understand which toys, emotions, and activities are encouraged or forbidden.

Fathers as Social Partners

Fathers enhance their children's social and emotional development in many ways (Lamb, 2010). Synchrony, attachment, and social referencing are all apparent with fathers, sometimes even more than with mothers. This was doubted until researchers found that some infants are securely attached to their fathers but not to their mothers (Bretherton, 2010). Further, fathers elicit more smiles and laughter from their infants than mothers do.

Close father–infant relationships can teach infants (especially boys) appropriate expressions of emotion (Boyce et al., 2006), particularly anger. The results may endure: Teenagers are less likely to lash out at friends and authorities if, as infants, they experienced a warm, responsive relationship with their father (Trautmann-Villalba et al., 2006). Close relationships with infants help men, too, by reducing the risk of depression (Borke et al., 2007; Bronte-Tinkew et al., 2007).

In some cultures and ethnic groups, fathers spend much less time with infants than mothers do (Parke & Buriel, 2006; Tudge, 2008). Culture and parental attitudes

social referencing
Seeking information about how to react to an unfamiliar or ambiguous object or event by observing someone else's expressions and reactions. That other person becomes a social reference.

Same Situation, Far Apart: Bonded That fathers enjoy their sons is not surprising, but notice the infants' hands—one clutching Dad's hair tightly and the other reaching for Dad's face. At this age, infants show their trust in adults by grabbing and reaching. Synchrony and attachment are mutual, in Ireland *(left)*, Kenya *(right)*, and everywhere.

are influential: Some women believe that child care is their special domain (Gaertner et al., 2007), while some fathers think it unmanly to dote on an infant. This is not equally true everywhere. For example, Denmark has high rates of father involvement. At birth, 97 percent of Danish fathers are present, and five months later, most Danish fathers say that every day they change diapers (83 percent), feed their infants (61 percent), and play with them (98 percent) (Munck, 2009).

Research on ethnic minority fathers in North America has increased in recent years, particularly on fathers in immigrant families (Chuang & Moreno, 2011; Chuang & Tamis-LeMonda, 2013). Earlier views of these fathers tended to reinforce stereotypes and generalizations. They often portrayed fathers as strict or distant. However, more recent studies have not substantiated such views.

To illustrate, studies on immigrant Chinese-Canadian and mainland Chinese families with 1-year-olds showed that Chinese fathers in both communities demonstrate a more egalitarian and child-centred framework in their parenting approach. When fathers were asked what their roles and responsibilities were in their families, both Chinese-Canadian and Chinese fathers stated that their roles are multi-dimensional: economic provider, caregiver, playmate, educator/trainer, and household chore performer (Chuang & Su, 2008). When mothers and fathers were asked to recount their daily activities over the last few days, they both recalled fathers spending time with their toddlers, including changing their diapers and feeding and playing with them. Fathers also did household chores (Chuang, 2013; Chuang & Su, 2008).

Less rigid sex roles seem to be developing among parents in many nations. One example of historical change is the number of married mothers with children under age 6 who are employed in Canada. The employment rate in 2009 for this population was 64.4 percent, as compared to 27.6 percent in 1976 (Statistics Canada, 2010a). Note the reference to "married" mothers: About half the mothers of infants in Canada are not married, and their employment rates are even higher. As detailed later in this chapter, often fathers—not necessarily married to the mothers—help care for infants when mothers are at the workplace.

One sex difference seems to endure: Mothers engage in more caregiving and comforting, and fathers in more high-intensity play (Kochanska et al., 2008). When asked to play with their baby, mothers typically caress, read, sing, or rely on traditional games such as peekaboo. Fathers are more exciting: They move their infant's limbs in imitation of walking, kicking, or climbing, or they swing the baby through the air, sideways, or even upside down. Mothers might say, "Don't drop him"; fathers and babies laugh with joy.

Since the 1970s, father–infant research has tried to answer three questions:

1. Can men provide the same care as women?

2. Is father–infant interaction different from mother–infant interaction?

3. How do fathers and mothers interact to provide infant care?

Many studies over the years have answered yes to the first two. On the third question, the answer depends on the family (Bretherton, 2010). Usually mothers are caregivers and fathers are playmates, but not always—each couple, given their circumstances (which might include being immigrant, low-income, or same-sex), finds their own way to complement each other to help their infant thrive (Lamb, 2010).

A constructive parental alliance is not guaranteed, whether or not the parents are legally wed. Sometimes neither parent is happy with their infant, with themselves, or with each other. One study reported that 7 percent of fathers of 1-year-olds were depressed, and they were four times as likely to spank as non-depressed fathers (40 percent versus 10 percent) (See Figure 4.2) (Davis et al, 2011).

Family members are affected by each other's moods: Paternal depression correlates with maternal depression, and with sad, angry, and disobedient toddlers. Cause and consequence are intertwined. When infants are depressed, or anxious, or hostile, the family triad (mother, father, baby) all need help.

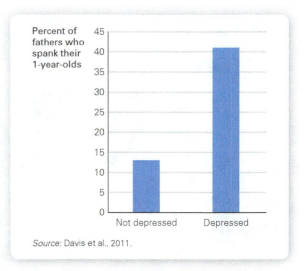

Source: Davis et al., 2011.

FIGURE 4.2 **The Effects of Depression** Toddlers are naturally curious and careless, often taxing the patience of parents. However, research shows that fathers who were depressed were more likely to spank their children. Both depression and spanking are affected by financial stress, marital conflict, and cultural norms.

KEY Points

- Caregivers and young infants engage in split-second interaction, evidence of synchrony.

- Attachment between people is universal, apparent in infancy with contact-maintaining and proximity-seeking as 1-year-olds play.

- Toddlers use other people as social references, to guide them in their exploration.

- Fathers are as capable as mothers in social partnerships with infants, although they may favour physical, creative play more than mothers do.

Theories of Infant Psychosocial Development

We now consider again the theories discussed in Chapter 1 in greater depth. As you will see, theories lead to insight and applications, preparing us for the final topic of this chapter, non-parental care of infants, with a special focus on infant daycare.

Psychoanalytic Theory

Psychoanalytic theory connects biosocial and psychosocial development. Sigmund Freud and Erik Erikson each described two distinct stages of early development. Freud (1935, 1940/1964) wrote about the *oral stage* and the *anal stage*. Erikson (1963) called his first stages *trust versus mistrust* and *autonomy versus shame and doubt*.

✦ **ESPECIALLY FOR Nursing Mothers** You have heard that if you wean your child too early, he or she will overeat or become an alcoholic. Is it true? (see response, page 159) ➞

All Together, Now Toddlers in an employees' daycare program at a flower farm in Colombia learn to use the potty on a schedule.

trust versus mistrust
Erikson's first crisis of psychosocial development. Infants learn basic trust, if the world is a secure place where their basic needs (for food, comfort, attention, and so on) are met.

autonomy versus shame and doubt
Erikson's second crisis of psychosocial development. Toddlers either succeed or fail in gaining a sense of self-rule over their actions and their bodies.

A Mother's Dilemma Infants are wonderfully curious, as this little boy demonstrates. Parents, however, must guide as well as encourage the drive toward autonomy. This mother makes sure her son does not crush or eat the flower.

FREUD: ORAL AND ANAL STAGES According to Freud (1935), the first year of life is the *oral stage,* so named because the mouth is the young infant's primary source of gratification. In the second year, with the *anal stage,* the infant's main pleasure comes from the anus—particularly from the sensual pleasure of bowel movements and, eventually, the psychological pleasure of controlling them.

Freud believed that the oral and anal stages are fraught with potential conflicts that have long-term consequences. If a mother frustrates her infant's urge to suck—weaning the infant too early, for example, or preventing the child from sucking a thumb or a pacifier—the child may become distressed and anxious, eventually becoming an adult with an oral fixation. Such a person is stuck (fixated) at the oral stage and therefore eats, drinks, chews, bites, or talks excessively, in quest of the mouth-related pleasure denied in infancy.

Similarly, if toilet training is overly strict or if it begins before the infant is mature enough, parent and infant may become locked in a conflict over the toddler's refusal, or inability, to comply. The child develops an anal personality and becomes an adult who seeks self-control, with an unusually strong need for regularity in all aspects of life.

ERIKSON: TRUST AND AUTONOMY According to Erikson, the first psychosocial crisis of life is **trust versus mistrust,** when infants learn whether the world can be trusted to satisfy basic needs. Babies feel secure when food and comfort are provided with "consistency, continuity, and sameness of experience" (Erikson, 1963, p. 247). If social interaction inspires trust, the child (later the adult) confidently explores the social world.

The second crisis is **autonomy versus shame and doubt,** beginning at about 18 months, when self-awareness emerges. Toddlers want autonomy (self-rule) over their own actions and bodies. Without it, they feel ashamed and doubtful. Like Freud, Erikson believed that problems in early infancy could influence one's personality later in life, creating adults who are suspicious and pessimistic (mistrusting) or easily shamed (lacking autonomy).

Erikson was aware of cultural variations. He knew that mistrust and shame could be destructive or not, depending on norms and expectations of each ethnic group and family. Some cultures encourage independence and autonomy; in others, "shame is a normative emotion that develops as parents use explicit shaming techniques" to encourage children's loyalty and harmony within their families (Mascolo et al., 2003, p. 402).

Learning Theory

According to learning theory, even very young children pick up behavioural cues from those around them. Behaviourism focuses on the way parents use positive and negative reinforcements as the means of shaping a child's behaviour. In contrast, social learning theory stresses the way that children learn to behave by observing and imitating their parents and other adults.

BEHAVIOURISM From the perspective of behaviourism, emotions and personality are shaped as parents reinforce or punish a child. Behaviourists believe that parents who respond joyously to every glimmer of a grin will have children with a sunny disposition. The opposite is also true:

Failure to bring up a happy child, a well-adjusted child—assuming bodily health—falls squarely upon the parents' shoulders. [By the time the child is 3] parents have already determined … [whether the child] is to grow into a happy person, wholesome and good-natured, whether he is to be a whining, complaining neurotic, an anger-driven, vindictive, over-bearing slave driver, or one whose every move in life is definitely controlled by fear.

[Watson, 1928, pp. 7, 45]

Hammering Bobo These images are stills from the film of Bandura's original study in which frustrated 4-year-olds imitated the behaviour they had observed an adult perform. The children used the same weapon as the adult, with the same intent—hitting the doll with a hammer, shooting it with a toy gun, or throwing a large ball at it.

SOCIAL LEARNING THEORY Later behaviourists recognized that infants' behaviour also has an element of **social learning,** through which infants learn from the people around them. Albert Bandura conducted a classic experiment (Bandura, 1977) in which young children were frustrated by being told they could not play with some attractive toys; they were then left alone with a mallet and a rubber toy clown (Bobo) after seeing an adult hit the toy. Both boys and girls pounded and kicked Bobo as the adult had done, indicating that they had learned from observation.

Since that experiment, developmentalists have demonstrated that social learning occurs throughout life (Morris et al., 2007; Nielsen, 2006). In many families, toddlers express emotions in various ways—from giggling to cursing—just as their parents or older siblings do. A boy might develop a hot temper if his father's outbursts seem to win his mother's respect; a girl might be coy or passive-aggressive if that is what she has seen. These examples are deliberately sexist: Social learning theories believe that gender roles, in particular, are learned.

Social learning theorists acknowledge inborn temperament but stress that children follow the role models they see. Shyness may be inborn, for instance, but parents who model social interaction, greeting their many friends warmly, will help a withdrawn child become more outgoing (Rubin et al., 2009). Often parents unwittingly encourage certain traits in their children by how they respond to their infants. This is evident in the effects of proximal versus distal parenting, as you will now learn.

social learning
The acquisition of behaviour patterns by observing the behaviour of others.

RESPONSE FOR Nursing Mothers
(from page 157) Freud thought so, but there is no experimental evidence that weaning, even when ill-timed, has such dire long-term effects. ●

Cognitive Theory

Cognitive theory holds that thoughts and values determine a person's perspective. Early experiences are important because beliefs, perceptions, and memories make them so, not because they are buried in the unconscious (psychoanalytic theory), or are the result of repeated reinforcement (behaviourism).

According to many cognitive theorists, early experiences help infants develop a set of assumptions that become a frame of reference for later in life. This set of assumptions is known as a **working model** (Johnson et al., 2010). It is a "model" because early relationships form a prototype, or blueprint, for later interactions; it is "working" because, although it is used, it is not necessarily fixed or final, but is modified as new information becomes available.

working model
In cognitive theory, a set of assumptions that the individual uses to organize perceptions and experiences. For example, a person might assume that other people are trustworthy and be surprised by an incident that suggests this working model of human behaviour was erroneous.

OPPOSING PERSPECTIVES

Proximal and Distal Parenting

Should a parent carry an infant most of the time, or will that spoil the baby? Should babies have a large number of toys, or will that make them too materialistic?

These questions refer to the distinction between **proximal parenting** (being physically close to a baby, often holding and touching) and **distal parenting** (keeping some distance—providing toys, feeding by putting finger food within reach, talking face-to-face instead of communicating by touch). Caregivers tend to behave in proximal or distal ways very early, when infants are only 2 months old (Kärtner et al., 2010).

The research finds notable cultural differences, not only with newborns but also with older children (Keller et al., 2010). For example, a longitudinal study comparing child-rearing methods of the Nso people of Cameroon with those of Greeks in Athens found marked differences in proximal and distal parenting (Keller et al., 2004). In that study, 78 mothers were videotaped as they played with their 3-month-olds. Coders (who did not know the study's hypothesis) counted frequency of proximal play (e.g., carrying, swinging, caressing, exercising the child's body) and distal play (e.g., face-to-face talking) (see Table 4.3). The Nso mothers were proximal, holding their babies all the time and almost never using toys or bottles. The Greek mothers were relatively distal, using objects almost half the time.

The researchers hypothesized that proximal parenting would result in toddlers who were less self-aware but more compliant—traits needed in an interdependent and cooperative society such as that of rural Cameroon. By contrast, distal parenting might produce children who were self-aware but less obedient, as needed when a culture values independence and self-reliance.

The predictions were accurate. At 18 months, these same infants were tested on self-awareness (via the mirror/rouge test) and obedience to their parents. The African toddlers (proximal) didn't recognize themselves in the mirror but were compliant; the opposite was true of the Greek toddlers (distal).

TABLE 4.3 Infants in Rural Cameroon and Urban Greece

	Cameroon	Athens, Greece
I. Infant–mother play at 3 months		
Percent of time held by mother	100%	31%
Percent of time playing with objects	3%	40%
II. Toddler behaviour at 18 months		
Self-recognition	3%	68%
Immediate compliance with request	72%	2%

Source: Adapted from Keller et al., 2004.

✦ **ESPECIALLY FOR Statisticians**
Note the sizes of the samples in Table 4.3 and in the description of the Costa Rica study on page 161: 78 mother–infant pairs in Cameroon and Greece and 12 pairs in Costa Rica. Are these samples large enough to draw conclusions? (see answer, page 162) →

Not Just a Snapshot Proximal and distal patterns are pervasive, affecting every moment of infant care. For example, in North America, babies often travel in strollers, while in other cultures they are strapped to their mothers' bodies.

Replicating their own work, the researchers studied a dozen mother–infant pairs in Costa Rica. In that country, caregiver–infant distance was midway between the Nso and the Greeks, as was later toddler behaviour (Keller et al., 2004).

The researchers then reanalyzed all their data, child by child. They found that, even apart from culture, proximal or distal play at 3 months was highly predictive: Greek mothers who, unlike most of their peers, were proximal parents had more obedient toddlers. Further research in several other nations confirmed the consequences of these two forms of parenting (Borke et al., 2007; Kärtner et al., 2011).

For every aspect of infant care, cultural attitudes have some impact, but for the proximal/distal response, culture is especially pivotal. Is independence valued over dependence, Is autonomy more important than compliance? Cultures differ in their answers. If a mother asks her toddler to put away some toys that he or she did not use (a test sometimes used to measure compliance), and the toddler puts them away without protest, is that wonderful or disturbing?

Answers may depend on whether rebellious independence or law-abiding morality is the quality most needed in a particular society. If you have an answer that you believe is best, you can figure out whether to pick up your baby (proximal) or give her a pacifier (distal) when she cries, whether to breastfeed her (proximal) until she is 2 years old or switch her to bottle-feeding as soon as possible (distal). Of course, many other factors influence whether or not a woman will breastfeed in Canada, but worldwide, those cultures that are proximal also tend to be those where breastfeeding continues for months and even years.

✦ **ESPECIALLY FOR Pediatricians** A mother complains that her child refuses to stay in the car seat, spits out disliked foods, and almost never does what she says. How should you respond? (see response, page 163) ➡

Ideally, infants develop a working model of the self as valued, loved, and competent and a working model of parents as emotionally available, loving, sensitive and supportive (Harter, 2006). However, reality does not always conform to this ideal. A 1-year-old girl might develop a model, based on her parents' inconsistent responses to her, that people are unpredictable. She will continue to apply that model to everyone: Her childhood friendships will be insecure and her adult relationships will be guarded.

To use Piaget's terminology, such a girl develops a cognitive schema to organize her perceptions. According to cognitive theory, an infant's early experiences are not themselves necessarily crucial, but the interpretation of those experiences is (Olson & Dweck, 2009). In this way, working models formed in childhood echo for a lifetime. A hopeful message from cognitive theory is that people can rethink and reorganize their thoughts, developing new models. Our mistrustful girl might marry a faithful and loving partner and gradually develop a better working model.

proximal parenting
Caregiving practices that involve being physically close to the baby, with frequent holding and touching.

distal parenting
Caregiving practices that involve remaining distant from the baby, providing toys, food, and face-to-face communication with minimal holding and touching.

Systems Theory

As you read in Chapter 1, family systems theory focuses on the family as a unit in which each member has a certain role and a number of responsibilities. Because Bowlby's primary agenda with attachment theory was to challenge his psychoanalytic colleagues' assumptions that children only love their mothers because they provide oral gratification, Bowlby overlooked fathers.

Michael Lamb (1976), a leading researcher in the field of fathering, conducted a series of experiments evaluating infants' attachment with mothers and fathers. Lamb found that infants' level of approach to and contact-seeking with mothers and fathers were similar, and infants tended to show more affiliative behaviours, such as smiling, vocalizing, and proffering toys, to fathers than to mothers. Thus, fathers make a unique contribution to their children's development.

Recently, researchers have focused especially on fathers and on the way their roles and responsibilities have changed over time. For example, fathers now share caregiving responsibilities with mothers instead of primarily being as the economic breadwinner in the family. One reason for this is that the mother's role has changed too, since many mothers are now contributing to the household income through their own careers (Chuang, 2009).

Stranger Danger Brad Graham and his 21-month-old son, Cameron, are spending time together at a farmer's market in Chatham, Ontario, on Halloween. Cameron is seeking comfort from his father after being scared by Frankenstein. No matter what parents say, children react according to their inborn temperament.

According to Statistics Canada (2010c), although fathers are assuming more caregiving duties than in the past, mothers still spend more time on average in this role than fathers. For example, in 2010, women with children 4 years and younger spent 6 hours 33 minutes per day as caregivers compared with fathers spending 3 hours 7 minutes.

Humanism

Remember that Maslow described a hierarchy of needs (physiological, safety/security, love/belonging, success/esteem, and self-actualization), with the lower levels being prerequisites for higher ones. Infants begin at the first level: Their emotions serve to ensure that physiological needs are met. That's why babies cry when they are hungry or hurt. Basic survival needs must be satisfied to enable the person to reach higher levels (Silton et al., 2011).

Humanism reminds us that caregivers also have needs, and their needs influence how they respond to infants. Self-actualized people are no longer needy for themselves, so they can nurture an infant well. But most young parents are at level 3 or 4, seeking love or respect. They may be troubled by "ghosts in the nursery" (first mentioned in Chapter 3 in the discussion of infant sleep). Their own babyhood experiences often include unmet needs, and that interferes with their ability to nurture.

For example, although all experts endorse breastfeeding as the best way to meet infants' physiological needs, many mothers stop breastfeeding after trying for a few days, and many fathers feel excluded if the mother spends most of her time and attention on nursing. This may puzzle the experts but not the humanist theorists, who realize that a parent's needs may clash with the infant's needs (Mulder & Johnson, 2010). For instance, one mother of a 1-year-old said:

RESPONSE FOR Statisticians (from page 160) Probably not. These studies are reported here because the results were dramatic (see Table 4.3) and because the two studies pointed in the same direction. Nevertheless, replication by other researchers is needed. ●

My son couldn't latch so I was pumping and my breasts were massive and I'm a pretty small woman with big breasts and they were enormous during pregnancy. It has always been a sore spot for me and I've never loved my breasts. And that has been hard for me in not feeling good about myself. And I stopped pumping in January and slowly they are going back and I'm beginning to feel some confidence again and that definitely helps. Because I felt overweight, your boobs are not your own and you are exhausted and your body is strange it's just really hard to want to share that with someone. They think you are beautiful, they love it and love you the way you are but it is not necessarily what you feel.

[quoted in Shapiro, 2011, p. 18]

This woman's need for self-respect was overwhelming, causing her to stop breast-feeding in order to feel some confidence about her shape. Her husband's love of her body, or her son's need for breastfeeding, did not help, because she was not at level 3 (love and belonging) and her "strange" body attacked her self-esteem (level 4).

Her personal needs may have been unmet since puberty (she says, "I've never loved my breasts"). She blames her husband for not understanding her feelings and her son who "couldn't latch." Since all babies learn to latch with time and help, her deciding that he couldn't do so suggests something amiss in synchrony and attachment—unmet baby needs because of unmet mother needs.

By contrast, some parents understand their baby's need for safety and security (level 2) even if they themselves are far beyond that stage. Kevin is an example.

> Kevin is a very active, outgoing person who loves to try new things. Today he takes his 11-month-old daughter, Tyra, to the park for the first time. Tyra is playing alone in the sandbox, when a group of toddlers joins her. At first, Tyra smiles and eagerly watches them play. But as the toddlers become more active and noisy, Tyra's smiles turn quickly to tears. She … reaches for Kevin, who picks her up and comforts her. But then Kevin goes a step further. After Tyra calms down, Kevin gently encourages her to play near the other children. He sits at her side, talking and playing with her. Soon Tyra is slowly creeping closer to the group of toddlers, curiously watching their moves.
>
> *[Lerner & Dombro, 2004, p. 42]*

Evolutionary Theory

Remember that evolutionary theory stresses two needs: survival and reproduction. Humans are extraordinarily good at those tasks. We have much bigger brains, proportionally, than any other creature, which allows us to use our genetic diversity to aid our own survival and that of our children, in every climate and continent.

It takes about 20 years of maturation before the human brain is fully functioning. A child must be nourished, protected, and taught by adults for much longer than offspring of any other species. Infant and parent emotional development help ensure such lengthy protection.

EMOTIONS FOR SURVIVAL Infant emotions are part of the evolutionary mandate. All the emotions described in the first part of this chapter—from the hunger cry to the temper tantrum—can be seen from this perspective (Konner, 2010).

For example, newborns are extraordinarily dependent, unable to walk or talk, or even sit up and feed themselves, for months after birth. They must attract adult devotion—and they do. That first smile, the sound of infant laughter, and their role in synchrony are all powerfully attractive to adults—especially to parents. Adults call their hairless, chinless, round-faced, small-limbed creatures "cute," "handsome," "beautiful," and "adorable," and willingly spend hours carrying, feeding, changing, and cleaning them.

If humans were only motivated by objective reward, caregiving would make no sense—but many adults think that parenting is worth every sacrifice. Children are costly, from birth on. Food (breast milk requires the mother to eat more), diapers, clothes, furniture (such as cribs and strollers), medication, toys, and child care (either hiring someone or unpaid labour from someone not employed) are just a start. Before a child becomes financially independent, many parents have paid for a bigger

RESPONSE FOR Pediatricians (from page 161) Consider the origins of the misbehaviour—it may be a combination of the child's inborn temperament and the mother's distal parenting. That could contribute to the child's being stubborn and independent. Acceptance is more warranted than anger. ●

house, education, vacations, and much more. These are just the financial costs; the emotional costs are greater.

None of this would occur without the parents making a major investment in each child—and that is exactly what human biology and culture foster. Hormones, specifically oxytocin, do much more than trigger birth and promote breastfeeding; they increase the impulse to bond with others, especially one's children. Both men and women have oxytocin in their blood and saliva, and this hormone continues to be produced as caregiving needs require (Feldman et al, 2011).

Evolutionary theory holds that, over human history, proximity-seeking and maintaining contact fostered species survival by keeping toddlers near their caregivers and keeping caregivers vigilant. Infants fuss at the still face, fear separation, and laugh when adults play with them, all to sustain parent–child interdependence. We inherited these emotional reactions from our great-great- … grandparents, who would have died without them. Bonding, and then synchrony, and then attachment, are greater and more durable for humans than for other animals. Toddlers attend to nuances of adult expressions (social referencing) to establish the relationships between self and others.

The dependence is mutual. It is almost impossible not to dote on a baby who grins at the sight of your face and pays attention when you frown. Thus it is part of human nature for babies to evoke caregiving, and for caregivers to attend to babies.

ALLOCARE Evolutionary social scientists note that if mothers were the exclusive caregivers of each child until children were adults, a given woman could bear only one or two offspring—not enough for the species to survive. The reason humans have more children, which is essential for species survival, is **allocare,** the care of children by people other than the biological parents (Hrdy, 2009).

Compared to many other species, human mothers are willing to let other people help with child care, and other people are eager to do so (Kachel et al., 2011). Throughout the centuries, the particular person to provide allocare has varied by culture and ecological conditions. Often fathers helped, but not always. Some men were far away, fighting, or hunting, or seeking work; some had several wives and children. In those situations, other women (daughters, grandmothers, sisters, friends) and sometimes other men provided allocare. In several cultures, infants were breastfed by several lactating women, especially in the beginning before the mother's milk became plentiful. All this can be explained by evolutionary theory. Of course, as you just read, other theories are plausible as well. Cultural variations in allocare are vast, and each theory can be used to justify certain variations.

Non-parental Care

It is estimated that about 134 million babies will be born each year from 2010 to 2021 (United Nations, 2011). Most newborns will be cared for primarily or exclusively by their mothers, with allocare increasing from ages 1 to 20. Some infants, even in the first months of life, are cared for by relatives, typically fathers in North America and grandmothers in most other nations (Leach,

allocare
Literally, "other-care"; the care of children by people other than the biological parents.

Same Situation, Far Apart: Caregiving Historically, grandmothers have often played an important role in caring for their grandchildren. Even today, grandmothers still provide extensive care, as shown by these two—in North America and China.

FABRICE TROMBERT PHOTOGRAPHY INC. / GETTY IMAGES

CHAU DOAN / LIGHTROCKET VIA GETTY IMAGES

2009). Worldwide, only about 15 percent of infants (birth to age 2 years) receive daily care from a non-relative who is paid and trained to provide it.

Many people believe that their own family's or culture's practices are best and that other patterns harm either the infant or the mother. This is another example of the difference-equals-deficit error.

Statistics on the precise incidence and consequences of various forms of infant care in each nation are difficult to find or interpret because it is difficult to keep statistics on the many different types of child care arrangements (Leach, 2009). Further, patterns of infant care are part of a complex web of child-rearing: it is difficult to connect any one particular pattern with one particular outcome.

INTERNATIONAL COMPARISONS Centre-based care is common in countries such as France, Israel, China, and Sweden, where it is heavily subsidized by governments. It is scarce in other regions, such as South Asia, Africa, and Latin America, where there is little government support for centre-based care. North America is in between these extremes, but variation from place to place is apparent.

Involvement of relatives in infant care also varies. Worldwide, fathers are increasingly involved in baby care. Some nations provide paid leave at birth for fathers as well as mothers. Several nations provide paid family leave that can be taken by either parent or shared between them. Some nations mandate that a job be held for a woman who takes an unpaid maternity leave. Most developing nations provide limited paid leave for mothers (India does not allow women to be employed in the first six weeks after birth) but not fathers (see Table 4.4).

Note that these are policies, not always practices. In many nations, parents have intense, unregulated employment and take off only a day or two for birth. Also note that underlying such policies are theories about what is best for infants. When nations mandate paid leave, the belief is that infants need parental care and that employers should encourage that to occur.

In Canada, 70 percent of infants are cared for exclusively by their mothers (no other relatives or babysitters) throughout their first year (Côté et al., 2008). This is in contrast to the United States, which is similar in ethnic diversity but has higher rates of maternal employment: 20 percent of American infants are cared for only by their mothers. These differences are affected by culture more than by universal psychosocial needs of babies and parents. In the United States, federal policy mandates that a job be held for a parent who takes unpaid leave of up to 12 weeks unless the company has fewer than 50 employees, and almost no company pays for paternal leave. As a result, most mothers return to work soon after giving birth.

One might hope that centuries of maternal, paternal, and allocare would provide clear conclusions about effective practices. Unfortunately, the evidence is mixed.

TYPES OF NON-MATERNAL CARE In the twenty-first century, most mothers prefer that their baby's father become the chief alternate caregiver. In Canada, many parents coordinate their work schedules so one or the other parent is always present, an arrangement that may help the infant and the budget but not the marriage, as parents have much less time together (Meteyer & Perry-Jenkins, 2010). Grandmothers are also often caregivers in the first year, less so as children become more mobile and social (Leach, 2009).

When parents turn to paid non-relatives, wealthier families may hire someone to come to the home. Many parents use **family daycare,** in which one caregiver looks

> **TABLE 4.4 Parental Leave Policies in Selected Nations**
>
> - Canada: 50 weeks of shared leave (either parent), at about three-fourths pay.
> - Sweden: 16 months, close to full pay, shared (e.g., both parents can take 8 months) but at least 2 months is reserved for the father.
> - Denmark: 52 weeks, shared, full pay; at least 2 weeks is reserved for the father and at least 18 weeks for the mother.
> - Bulgaria: 52 weeks, full pay; shared by mother, father, and grandmother.
> - Brazil: 5 days for the father and 120 days for the mother at full pay.
> - Kenya: 2 weeks for the father and 2 months for the mother at full pay.
> - Indonesia: 2 days for the father and 3 months for the mother at full pay.
> - Lebanon: 1 day for the father and 7 weeks for the mother at full pay.
> - Australia: 18 weeks for the father and 18 weeks for the mother at minimal wage.

family daycare
Child care that includes several children of various ages and usually occurs in the home of a woman who is paid to provide it.

Same Situation, Far Apart: Daycare Options Winnipeg, Manitoba *(top),* is on the opposite side of the world from Dhaka, Bangladesh *(bottom),* but daycare is needed in both places, as shown here.

OBSERVATION QUIZ

What cultural differences do you notice? (see answer, page 168) →

centre daycare

Child care that occurs in a place especially designed for the purpose, where several paid adults care for many children. Usually, the children are grouped by age, the daycare centre is licensed, and providers are trained and certified in child development.

after a small group of young children in her (almost never his) home. The quality of family daycare varies; infants and toddlers often get less attention than 3- and 4-year-olds (Kryzer et al., 2007).

Providing physical care and ensuring safety are only the beginning of quality caretaking, although those factors tend to be the focus when parents seek allocare. Evolutionary theory notes that survival of infants was far from guaranteed in earlier centuries. Ideally, each baby also experiences many hours each day of personalized social interaction.

Another option is **centre daycare,** in which licensed and specially educated adults care for several infants in a place especially designed for them. Most centres separate infants from older children, a good strategy from the humanist perspective, since it allows everyone's developmental needs to be met. In Canada in 2003, about 28 percent of children between the ages of 6 months and 5 years attended a daycare centre funded by the province or territory. In Quebec, thanks to generous provincial subsidies that started in 1997, the rate was much higher at 52 percent (Bushnik, 2006).

Ideally, an infant daycare centre has ample safe space, appropriate equipment, trained providers, and two adults for a group of five or fewer infants (de Schipper et al., 2006; NAEYC, 2012) (see Table 4.5). Such a setting advances both cognitive and social skills: Babies are intrigued by other babies, and they learn from them.

No matter what form of care is chosen, responsive, individualized care with stable caregivers seems best (Morrissey, 2009). Caregiver change is especially problematic for infants because it doesn't allow synchrony to develop. Each simple gesture or sound that a baby makes not only merits an encouraging response, but also requires interpretation by someone who knows that particular baby well. "Baba" could refer to a bottle, baby, blanket, banana, or some other item that does not even begin with the /b/ sound. This example emphasizes the importance of synchrony.

TABLE 4.5 High-Quality Daycare

High-quality daycare during infancy has five essential characteristics:

1. *Adequate attention to each infant.* A small group of infants (no more than five) needs two reliable, familiar, loving caregivers. Continuity of care is crucial.

2. *Encouragement of language and sensorimotor development.* Infants need language—songs, conversations, and positive talk—and easily manipulated toys.

3. *Attention to health and safety.* Cleanliness routines (e.g., handwashing), accident prevention (e.g., no small objects), and safe areas to explore are essential.

4. *Professional caregivers.* Caregivers should have experience and degrees/certificates in early childhood education. Turnover should be low, morale high, and enthusiasm evident.

5. *Warm and responsive caregivers.* Providers should engage the children in active play and guide them in problem solving. Quiet, obedient children may indicate unresponsive care.

THE EFFECTS OF INFANT DAYCARE The evidence is overwhelming that good preschool education (discussed in Chapter 5) benefits children, especially in cognition. However, as the National Institute of Child Health and Human Development (NICHD) states, when it comes to infants, disagreements about the merits of different forms of child care remain (NICHD Early Child Care Research Network, 2005). A major problem is that quality varies a great deal. Some caregivers with no training look after many infants, and the result is inadequate care.

Some babies seem far more affected than others by the quality of their care (Phillips et al., 2011; Pluess & Belsky, 2009). The main concern is that some infants with extensive non-maternal care will become more aggressive later on (Jacob, 2009). As one review explained: "This evidence now indicates that early non-parental care environments sometimes pose risks to young children and sometimes confer benefits" (Phillips et al., 2011). Differential sensitivity is evident: For genetic and familial reasons, the choice about how best to provide care for an infant varies from case to case.

Consider three examples. First, in England, one study found that infants who were not exclusively in their mothers' care were less advanced emotionally at age 5 years (Fergusson et al., 2008). Most of those infants were cared for by grandmothers, especially when the mothers were young and poor. As you know from your understanding of correlation, however, low SES itself is associated with several variables, in addition to non-maternal care, that might account for the delayed emotional development reported in this study. In this case, the relevant variables may include the grandmothers' low SES, the mothers' immaturity, and the households' financial stress. Any of those could be the reason for the 5-year-olds' emotional immaturity. Or their behaviour could be the direct result of non-maternal infant care; the data tells us correlation, not cause.

Second, a large study in Canada found that infant girls seem to develop equally well in various care arrangements. However, boys are more complex. Boys from high-income families with infant allocare fared less well than similar boys in exclusive maternal care: By age 4, they were slightly more assertive or aggressive and had more emotional problems (e.g., a teacher might note that such a boy "seems unhappy").

The opposite was true for boys from low-income families: On average, they benefitted from non-maternal care in infancy, again according to teacher reports. The researchers insist that no policy implications can be derived from this study, partly because care varied so much in quality, location, and provider (Côté et al., 2008). Research in the United States on low-income families also finds that centre care is beneficial for low-SES families (Peng & Robins, 2010).

The third study may be the most solid research, in that it is longitudinal and began with a large and diverse sample. The Early Child Care Research Network of the NICHD has followed the development of more than 1300 children from birth to age 11 years. Researchers found many cognitive benefits of early daycare, especially in language development. Attachment to mothers seemed as secure for babies in daycare as for babies with exclusive maternal care. Some babies in infant care were also securely attached to their caregivers, which is a good sign.

Like other, smaller studies, the NICHD research confirms that the mother–child relationship is pivotal. The NICHD study and the consensus of many researchers in North America is that parents are the most important influence on child development, and that infant daycare, even for 40 hours a week before age 1, has much less influence on child development than does the warmth of the mother–infant relationship (Phillips et al., 2011).

However, the NICHD study also found that infant daycare is detrimental when the mother is insensitive and the infant spends more than 20 hours a week in a poor-quality program (McCartney et al., 2010). In particular, boys with extensive

✦ ESPECIALLY FOR Daycare Providers A mother who brings her child to you for daycare says that she knows she is harming her baby, but economic necessity compels her to work. What do you say? (see response, page 169) ➝

non-maternal care became more quarrelsome as they matured, having more conflicts with their teachers than did the girls or other boys with a different mix of maternal traits and daycare experiences.

What can be concluded from these three studies? Nothing definitive. Each study is complex: International variations, uncertainty about quality and extent of care (both at home and elsewhere), and the fact that choices are not random (for instance, maternal employment and hence allocare are more likely in families with educated parents, but less likely if the couple are married and financially secure) make general conclusions elusive.

Family income, culture, religion, and education affect choice of care, and those same variables affect child development. The fact that boys are more affected than girls may indicate something about biological sex, or that difficult boys are more often placed in daycare, or that cultures encourage traits in boys that are discouraged in girls. Indeed, not every study finds that boys are more affected—again, there are many possible reasons to explain a lack of gender differences, just as there are many reasons to explain the presence of gender differences.

ANSWER TO **OBSERVATION QUIZ** (from page 166) The Bangladeshi children are dressed alike and they are all of the same ethnicity. The children from Winnipeg are dressed differently and are of different ethnicities. ●

MATERNAL EMPLOYMENT IN INFANCY Closely tied to the issue of infant day-care is the issue of maternal employment. Once it was assumed that mothers should stay home with their children, as recommended by psychoanalytic and behaviourist theory. That assumption has been challenged, partly by the idea that mothers have needs that merit attention (humanism), and by historical evidence that exclusive maternal care was far from typical over the centuries (evolutional theory).

A summary of the longitudinal outcomes of non-maternal infant care finds "externalizing behaviour is predicted from a constellation of variables in multiple contexts ... and no study has found that children of employed mothers develop serious emotional or other problems solely because their mothers are working outside the home" (McCartney et al., 2010, pp. 1, 16). Indeed, findings from the Quebec Longitudinal Study of Child Development research revealed that children generally benefit if their mothers are employed (Goldberg et al., 2008). The most likely reasons are that maternal income reduces parental depression and increases family wealth, making parent more likely to use formal child care, which all correlate with happier and more successful children (Geoffroy et al., 2012).

A time-use study found that mothers who worked full time outside the home spent almost as much time playing with their babies (14½ hours a week) as did mothers with no outside jobs (16 hours a week) (Huston & Aronson, 2005). To make more time for their babies, they spent half as much time on housework, less time with their husbands, and almost no time on leisure. The study concludes:

> There was no evidence that mothers' time at work interfered with the quality of their relationship with their infants, the quality of the home environment, or children's development. In fact, the results suggest the opposite. Mothers who spent more time at work provided slightly higher quality home environments.
>
> [Huston & Aronson, 2005, p. 479]

This is a comforting conclusion for employed mothers, but again other interpretations are possible. It may be that the women who were able to find worthwhile work were more capable of providing a quality home environment than the women who were unemployed. Further, the fact that employed mothers had less time with their husbands or less personal time for leisure may not bode well for the child's future.

Marriage relationships benefit from shared activities, so couples who rarely enjoy each other's company are likely to be less dedicated to each other. This may be particularly a problem for the men, because men who are devoted to their wives are more likely to be active and involved fathers. Father involvement correlates with child happiness and success. The opposite is also true.

As you see, every study reflects many variables, just as every theory has a different perspective on infant care. Given that, and given divergent cultural assumptions, it is not surprising that researchers find mixed evidence on infant care and caregivers. Many factors are relevant: infant sex and temperament, family income and education, and especially the quality of care at home and elsewhere.

Thus, as with many topics in child development, questions remain. What is definite is that each infant needs personal responsiveness from at least one person—ideally from both mother and father, but another relative or a non-relative can suffice. Someone should be a partner in the synchrony duet, a base for secure attachment, and a social reference who encourages exploration. If the baby has that, infant emotions and experiences—cries and laughter, fears and joys—will ensure that development goes well.

RESPONSE FOR Daycare Providers (from page 167): Reassure the mother that you will keep her baby safe and will help develop the baby's mind and social skills by fostering synchrony and attachment. Also tell her that her interactions with her baby will continue to be strong, which is most important for her baby's psychosocial development. ●

KEY Points

- All theories recognize that infant care is crucial: Psychosocial development depends on it.

- Psychoanalytic theory stresses early caregiving routines, with Freud and Erikson differing in specifics.

- Behaviourists emphasize early learning, and cognitive theories emphasize early thinking. In both cases, lifelong patterns are said to begin in infancy.

- Social learning focuses on how infants learn behaviours from their social environment, such as using role models.

- Family systems theory stresses the importance of all family members, such as fathers who also play an important role in their children's lives.

- Humanists recognize that everyone—adults as well as infants—have basic needs they seek to fulfill.

- According to evolutionary theory, inborn impulses provide the interdependence that humans need for survival.

- Infant daycare and maternal employment are now common in North America, but worldwide they remain controversial.

SUMMARY

Emotional Development

1. Two emotions, contentment and distress, appear as soon as an infant is born. Smiles and laughter are evident in the early months. Anger emerges with restriction and frustration, between 4 and 8 months of age, and becomes stronger by age 1.

2. Reflexive fear is apparent in very young infants. Fear of something specific, including fear of strangers and of separation, appears toward the end of the first year.

3. In the second year, social awareness produces more selective fear, anger, and joy. As infants become increasingly self-aware, emotions emerge that encourage an interface between the self and others—specifically, pride, shame, empathy, jealousy, embarrassment, and disgust. Self-recognition (on the mirror/ rouge test) emerges at about 18 months.

Brain and Emotion

4. Stress impedes early brain and emotional development. Some infants are particularly vulnerable to the effects of early mistreatment.

5. Temperament is a set of genetic traits whose expression is influenced by the context. Inborn temperament is linked to later personality, although plasticity is also evident.

The Development of Social Bonds

6. Sometimes by 2 months, and clearly by 6 months, infants become more responsive and social, and synchrony begins. Infants are disturbed by a still face because they expect and need social interaction.

7. Attachment, measured by the baby's reaction to the caregiver's presence, departure, and return in the Strange Situation, is crucial. There are four types of attachment: insecure-avoidant or indifferent (A); secure (B); insecure-resistant/ambivalent or overly dependent (C); and disorganized (D). Secure attachment provides encouragement for infant exploration. Some children never form an attachment at all, even an insecure one.

8. As they play, toddlers engage in social referencing, looking to other people's facial expressions and body language to detect what is safe, frightening, or fun.

9. Infants frequently use fathers as partners in synchrony, attachment, and social referencing, developing emotions and exploring their world within the context of paternal caregiving.

Theories of Infant Psychosocial Development

10. According to all major theories, caregiver behaviour is especially influential in the first two years. Freud stressed the mother's impact on oral and anal pleasure; Erikson emphasized trust and autonomy.

11. Behaviourists focus on learning; parents teach their babies many things, including when to be fearful or joyful. Cognitive theory holds that infants develop working models based on their experiences.

12. Humanism notes that some adults are stuck in their own unfinished development, and this impairs their ability to give infants the loving responses that they need.

13. Evolutionary theorists recognize that both infants and caregivers have impulses and emotions, developed over the centuries, that foster survival of each new member of the human species.

14. The impact of non-maternal care depends on many factors; it varies from one nation to another and probably from one child to another. Although each theory focuses on a different aspect of this controversy, all agree that quality of care (responsive, individualized) is crucial, no matter who provides that care.

KEY TERMS

allocare (p. 164)
attachment (p. 149)
autonomy versus shame and doubt (p. 158)
centre daycare (p. 166)
cortisol (p. 139)

disorganized attachment (p. 151)
distal parenting (p. 160)
family daycare (p. 165)
insecure-avoidant attachment (p. 151)
insecure-resistant/ambivalent attachment (p. 151)

proximal parenting (p. 160)
secure attachment (p. 151)
self-awareness (p. 141)
separation anxiety (p. 139)
social learning (p. 159)
social referencing (p. 155)
social smile (p. 138)

still-face technique (p. 148)
Strange Situation (p. 152)
stranger wariness (p. 139)
synchrony (p. 147)
temperament (p. 144)
trust versus mistrust (p. 158)
working model (p. 159)

WHAT HAVE YOU LEARNED?

1. What are the first emotions to appear in infants?

2. What experiences trigger anger and sadness in infants?

3. What do 1-year-olds fear?

4. How do emotions differ between the first and second year of life?

5. How do family interactions and culture shape toddler's emotions?

6. What is known and unknown about the impact of brain maturation on emotions?

7. How are memory and emotion connected?

8. How does stress affect early brain development?

9. Why are temperamental traits more apparent in some people than others?

10. How might synchrony affect early emotional development?

11. Give examples of how infants and caregivers demonstrate proximity-seeking and contact-maintaining behaviours.

12. Describe the four types of attachment. How might each affect later life?

13. How do negative circumstances (e.g., divorce, abuse, low SES) affect attachment?

14. What can be done to improve the parent–child bond?

15. How is social referencing important in infancy?

16. How does father involvement affect infants?

17. What might happen if a person is stuck in the oral or anal stage of development?

18. How might the crisis of "trust versus mistrust" affect later life?

19. How might the crisis of "autonomy versus shame and doubt" affect later life?

20. How do behaviourists explain the development of emotions and personality?

21. Why does "working model" arise from cognitive theory instead of from the other theories?

22. According to humanism, how might caregivers' needs affect their response to an infant?

23. How does evolution explain the parent–child bond?

24. Why is allocare necessary for survival of the human species?

25. What are the advantages and disadvantages of non–maternal infant care?

26. Compare costs and benefits of infant care by relatives versus centre daycare.

27. Why is it difficult to draw conclusions about infant daycare?

28. What are the benefits and problems for infants if their mothers are employed?

APPLICATIONS

1. One cultural factor influencing infant development is how infants are carried from place to place. Ask four mothers whose infants were born in each of the past four decades how they transported them—front or back carriers, facing out or in, strollers or carriages, in car seats or on mothers' laps, and so on. Why did they choose the mode(s) they chose? What are their opinions and yours on how that cultural practice might affect infants' development?

2. Observe synchrony for three minutes. Ideally, ask the parent of an infant under 8 months of age to play with the infant.

If no infant is available, observe a couple as they converse. Note the sequence and timing of every facial expression, sound, and gesture of both partners.

3. Telephone or do Internet research on several daycare centres to try to assess the quality of care they provide. Ask about such factors as adult/child ratio, group size, and training for caregivers of children of various ages. Is there a minimum age? Why or why not? Analyze the answers, using Table 4.4 as a guide.

>>ONLINE CONNECTIONS

To accompany your textbook, you have access to a number of online resources, including LearningCurve, which is an adaptive quizzing program; critical thinking questions; and case studies. For access to any of these links, go to www.worthpublishers.com/launchpad/bergerchuang1e. In addition to these resources, you'll find links to video clips, personalized study advice, and an e-Book. Among the videos and activities available online are the following:

- *Attachment Behaviors in the Strange Situation.* You'll get a chance to watch—and take your best guess about attachment states—as some infants are left in the company of strangers.

- *Self-Awareness and the Rouge Test.* A variety of videos showcase the development of self-awareness in young children.

Early Childhood

From ages 2 to 6 years, young children spend most of their waking hours discovering, creating, laughing, and imagining, as they acquire the skills they need. They chase each other and attempt new challenges (developing their bodies); they play with sounds, words, and ideas (developing their minds); and they invent games and dramatize fantasies (learning social skills and morals)—all under the guidance of their families and communities.

These years have been called the preschool years, but that has become a misnomer. Although still called preschoolers, many 2- to 6-year-olds are in school, learning and playing. Indeed, they learn while playing—imagination and fantasy make these years prime time for new ideas, language advances, and informal education. Consequently, this period is best called early childhood, a joyful time not only for young children, but also for anyone who joins them.

CHAPTER OUTLINE

EARLY CHILDHOOD:
Body and Mind

chapter 5

- Does obesity in early childhood have lasting impacts?
- To what extent are emotions rooted in a child's brain?
- How do children learn about the world around them?
- What are the developmental impacts of bilingualism?
- Does preschool attendance give children an educational advantage?

My oldest brother, Sam, and his wife, Kelly, have four children: three girls and a boy. The two youngest, Brenna and Kaitlyn, are 2½ years apart. When Kaitlyn was about 1½, she started trying to follow her big sister's example. Even though Brenna was 4 years old at the time and much more developmentally advanced, Kaitlyn, like many younger siblings, wanted to be "just like her sister."

Kaitlyn did her best to walk and talk like Brenna, and to jump as high and run as fast as her sister. She even wanted to wear Brenna's clothes, which didn't come close to fitting her. Although it was clear to everybody around Kaitlyn that it was developmentally impossible for her to be just like her older sister, that didn't stop Kaitlyn from trying.

It didn't help matters when people would stop my brother and ask if the two girls were twins, even though Kaitlyn was half the size of Brenna and their facial features were not at all similar. Perhaps this reflects the power of Kaitlyn's desire to be like her sister! ●

—Susan Chuang

DO YOU REMEMBER TRYING TO IMITATE AN OLDER sibling, or maybe an adult you loved and admired? Young children try, fail, and try again. This is how they become skilled and wise. Eventually they learn that growing up takes time, that there are always differences between individuals, and that although our aspirations are unlimited, our bodies are not. During early childhood, advances in body and brain, and the need for protection and education, are evident. This chapter describes amazing physical growth, brain maturation, social judgment, and a language explosion.

Size and Balance These cousins are only four years apart, but note the doubling in leg length and marked improvement in balance. The 2-year-old needs to plant both legs in the sand, while the 6-year-old cavorts on one foot.

Motor Skills Children learn whatever motor skills their culture teaches, including cutting sausage with a knife and fork. Unlike this child in Germany, some never master this skill, because about one-third of adults worldwide eat directly with their hands.

Body Changes

In early childhood, as in infancy, the body and brain develop according to influential epigenetic forces. Biology interacts with culture as children eat, grow, and play.

Growth Patterns

Comparing a toddling, unsteady 1-year-old with a cartwheeling 6-year-old makes some differences obvious. During early childhood, children slim down as the lower body lengthens, and fat decreases as children develop more muscle mass. The average body mass index (BMI, the ratio of weight to height) is lower at ages 5 and 6 years than at any other time of life. Gone are the toddler's protruding belly, round face, short limbs, and large head.

The centre of gravity moves from the chest to the belly, enabling cartwheels, somersaults, and many other motor skills. The joys of dancing, gymnastics, and pumping a swing become possible. Toddlers often tumble, unbalanced—fortunately, they are close to the floor and thus don't have too far to fall. Kindergartners race and rarely slip.

Increases in weight and height accompany this growth. Over each year of early childhood, well-nourished children gain about 2 kilograms and grow about 7 centimetres. By age 6, the average child in a developed nation

- weighs between 18 and 22 kilograms
- is at least 100 centimetres tall
- has adult-like body proportions (legs constitute about half the total height).

Improved Motor Skills

As the body gains strength, children develop motor skills, both gross motor skills (evident in activities such as skipping) and fine motor skills (evident in activities such as drawing). Mastery depends on maturation and practice; some 6-year-olds can ice skate or print legibly—but most cannot.

All, however, are physically active, practising whatever skills their culture and their friends value. If adults provide safe spaces, time, and playmates, skills develop. Children learn best from peers who do whatever the child is ready to try—from catching a ball to climbing a tree.

Nutritional Challenges

Nutrition at this age is very important for brain development. Because of this period of synaptic activity (which is discussed in greater detail later on), young children need high levels of fat in their diets. Up until 2 years of age, about 50 percent of their total calories should be dedicated to fat (e.g., whole milk). After about 2 years of age, the dietary fat should be reduced to no more than 30 percent of total calories, such as 1 or 2 percent cow's milk (Zero to Three, 2013).

Over the centuries, families encouraged eating, protecting children against famine. Today, 2- to 6-year-olds in developed nations may be at greater nutritional risk than children of any other age because they may eat too much of the wrong foods. However, in the poorest nations, infant and early childhood malnutrition contributes to one-third of all child deaths (UNICEF, 2008) and slows later growth, including growth of the brain.

OVERWEIGHT The cultural practice of encouraging children to eat has turned from protective to destructive. One example is Brazil, where 30 years ago the most common nutritional problem was under-nutrition; now, it is over-nutrition (Monteiro et al., 2004), with low-income Brazilians being particularly vulnerable (Monteiro et al., 2007). In almost every nation, 4-year-olds are more often overweight than 2-year-olds. This suggests that habits, not genetics, are the problem.

Obesity in Canada, a joint report by the Public Health Agency of Canada (PHAC) and the Canadian Institute for Health Information (2011), noted that childhood obesity has been proven to increase the risk of obesity among adults, which in turn can lead to the early development of serious medical conditions such as Type 2 diabetes, heart disease, and high blood pressure. The report also estimated that the total economic costs of obesity in Canada range from $4.6 billion to $7.1 billion annually.

Although obesity rates in Canada are lower than in the United States (between 2007 and 2009, 34 percent of Americans were obese compared with 24 percent of Canadians), a recent report from Statistics Canada and the U.S. Centers for Disease Control and Prevention indicated that Canada seems to be catching up, especially when it comes to rates of childhood obesity (Shields et al., 2011). Figure 5.1 shows that obesity rates in Canada increased significantly between 2000 and 2011. Also, according to the Government of Canada (2013a), over the last 25 years, Canada's obesity rate has almost tripled among children and youth.

What is most disconcerting is that childhood obesity seems to have dangerous effects on a person's physical, emotional, and social well-being for years to come. Heart disease and diabetes are becoming epidemic as overweight children become overweight adults (Saul, 2008). A medical report predicted that by 2020, 228 million adults worldwide will have diabetes (more in India than in any other nation) because of unhealthy eating habits acquired in childhood. Children who are obese are more likely to suffer from low self-esteem, negative body image, and depression. They are also more likely to be teased and bullied by their peers (Government of Canada, 2013a).

Victory! Well, maybe not quite yet, but he's on his way. This boy participates in a British initiative to combat childhood obesity. Mother and son are exercising together in Liverpool Park in an effort to develop healthy lifestyles.

◆ ESPECIALLY FOR Nutritionists
A parent complains that she prepares a variety of vegetables and fruits, but her 4-year-old wants only French fries and cake. What should you advise? (see response, page 179) ➞

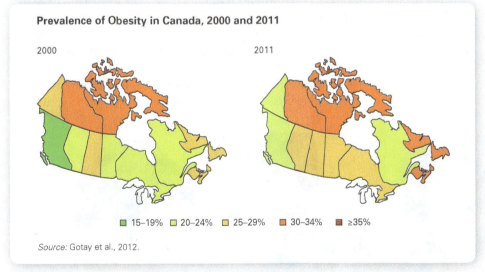

Prevalence of Obesity in Canada, 2000 and 2011

2000   2011

■ 15–19% ■ 20–24% ■ 25–29% ■ 30–34% ■ ≥35%

Source: Gotay et al., 2012.

FIGURE 5.1 A Growing Problem A 2013 study at the University of British Columbia found that, on average, between one-quarter and one-third of Canadians are obese, depending on the region (Gotay et al., 2013). Rates of obesity are highest in the Atlantic provinces, Nunavut, and the Northwest Territories. These maps show a general, countrywide rise in obesity rates between 2000 and 2011. What could be some reasons for this upward trend?

"I'm not hungry. I ate with Rover."

Eat Your Veggies On their own, children do not always eat wisely.

✦ **ESPECIALLY FOR Teachers** You know that young children are upset if forced to eat a food they hate, but you have eight 3-year-olds with eight different food preferences. What do you do? (see response, page 181) →

✦ **ESPECIALLY FOR Immigrant Parents** You and your family eat with chopsticks at home, but you want your children to feel comfortable in Western culture. Should you change your family's eating customs? (see response, page 182) →

Same Situation, Far Apart: Eager Eaters Preschoolers generally eat whatever they get. These are the fortunate ones, enjoying cut-up fruit and vegetables *(left)*, and sharing a fresh fruit snack with a friend *(right)*.

Appetite decreases between 1 and 6 years of age; young children need fewer calories per kilogram. In addition, many children today get much less exercise than their grandparents did. They rarely help on the farm, walk to school, or play in playgrounds. Yet many adults still threaten and bribe their children to overeat ("Eat your dinner and you can have ice cream"). Most parents falsely think that relatively thin children are less healthy than relatively heavy ones (Laraway et al., 2010).

NUTRITIONAL DEFICIENCIES Although most children consume more than enough calories, they do not always obtain adequate iron, zinc, and calcium. For example, children now drink less milk, which means weaker bones later on. Another problem is sugar. Many customs entice children to eat sweets—in birthday cake, holiday candy, desserts, and other treats. Carbohydrates such as breads also contain sugar, and so the total caloric intake of sugar becomes problematic.

Products advertised as containing 100 percent of daily vitamin requirements are sometimes misconstrued as a balanced, varied diet. In fact, healthy food is the best source of nutrition. Children who eat more vegetables and fewer fried foods usually gain bone mass but not fat, according to a study that controlled for gender and income (Wosje et al., 2010).

In developing nations, the lack of micronutrients is often severe due to a lack of variety of healthy foods. Studies have explored the effect of providing supplements, with mixed results. Providing micronutrients as part of fortified foods seems to have the best results (Ramakrishnan et al., 2011).

ALLERGIES Unfortunately, many parents face challenges in ensuring that their children are fed well nutritionally. Allergies are one such challenge. Between 3 to 8 percent of all young children have a food allergy, usually to a healthy, common food.

Diagnostic standards for food allergies vary (which explains the range of estimates). Treatment varies even more (Chafen et al., 2010). Some experts advocate avoiding the offending food. Many parents withhold their child's first taste of peanut butter until after age 3 years. Others suggest building up tolerance, such as by giving babies a tiny bit of peanut butter (Reche et al., 2011). Many public schools and daycares are nut-free environments, where no child ever brings a peanut butter sandwich for lunch.

Since allergies are so common among young children, in 2012 the Government of Canada began to enforce stronger labelling regulations for food products containing

allergens. The new regulations require food manufacturers to include clearer and more comprehensive labels on their packaging so that consumers can avoid products with ingredients that might make them ill. In drawing up the regulations, the government identified a list of 10 "priority allergens" that are most likely to cause serious reactions among Canadian consumers: peanuts, tree nuts, milk, eggs, seafood, soy, wheat, sesame seeds, mustard, and sulphites. The government also clarified its labelling requirements for gluten-free products to benefit the 1 percent of Canadians who have celiac disease (Health Canada, 2012a).

OBSESSIONS Feeding young children a varied diet is also complicated by the strong preferences that many of them have for routines. In some families, children are accustomed to having an after-school snack, regardless of whether they are actually hungry or not.

Similarly, some children insist on certain foods, prepared and served in a particular way. This rigidity, known as **just right,** is held strongly by many children because they have a desire for continuity and sameness. This occurs around age 3 (Evans & Leckman, 2006; Pietrefesa & Evans, 2007). Even familiar foods may be rejected if presented in a new way.

After age 5, rigidity fades (see Figure 5.2). The best reaction may be patience: A young child's insistence on a particular routine, a favourite cup, or a preferred cereal can be accommodated for a year or two. For children, routines need to be simple, clear, and healthy; then they can be accommodated until the child is ready to change.

ORAL HEALTH Too much sugar and too little fibre cause another common problem, tooth decay, which affects one-third of all young Canadian children (Ontario Dental Association, 2008). Soft drinks and fruit drinks are prime causes; even diet soft drinks contain acid that makes decay likely (Holtzman, 2009). Health Canada notes that breast milk and fruit juice can also lead to tooth decay in young children since the sugars in these foods combine with the bacteria in tooth plaque to create an acid that damages tooth enamel (Health Canada, 2009). This is one reason why toothbrushing and trips to the dentist should begin even before age 3 (Mofidi et al., 2009).

Avoidable Injuries

Worldwide, injuries cause millions of premature deaths among adults as well as children. Not until age 40 does any specific disease overtake accidents as a cause of mortality (World Health Organization, 2010). Two- to 6-year-olds are at a greater risk for injury than slightly older children because of their limited physical coordination and cognitive abilities to judge whether activities are safe.

In Canada, unintentional injuries kill more children and youth (ages 1–14 years) than all diseases combined. Each year on average, almost 300 children die and 21 000 are hospitalized from unintentional injuries, which costs the health-care system about $4 billion annually in direct and indirect costs (Fuselli et al., 2011). The leading cause of fatal injuries in Canada for children aged 1 to 4 is motor vehicle accidents; drowning is the second leading cause of death (PHAC, 2009). In terms of non-fatal injuries, many lead to lifelong impairments such as blindness, restricted mobility, and developmental delays as a result of brain and spinal-cord injuries.

just right
The tendency of children to insist on having things done in a particular way. This can include clothes, food, bedtime routines, and so on.

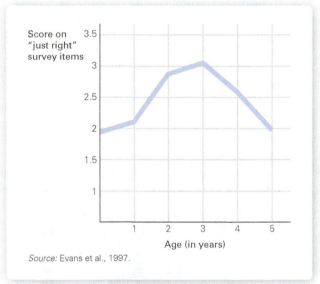

Source: Evans et al., 1997.

FIGURE 5.2 **Young Children's Insistence on Routine** This chart shows the average scores of children (who are rated by their parents) on a survey indicating the child's desire to have certain things—including food selection and preparation—done "just right." Such strong preferences for rigid routines tend to fade after age 5.

A VIEW FROM SCIENCE

Eliminating Lead

Lead was targeted as a poison a century ago (Hamilton, 1914). The symptoms of plumbism, as lead poisoning is called, were obvious—intellectual disability, hyperactivity, and even death if blood lead levels reached 70 micrograms per decilitre.

The lead industry defended the heavy metal as an additive, arguing that low levels were harmless and that parents needed to prevent their children from eating chips of lead paint (which taste sweet). Developmental scientists noted that the correlation between lead exposure and the symptoms mentioned above does not prove causation. Children with high levels of lead in their blood were often from low-SES families: Malnutrition, inadequate schools, family conditions, or a host of other reasons not related to lead could reduce their IQs (Scarr, 1985).

Consequently, lead remained a major ingredient in paint (it speeds drying) and in gasoline (it raises octane) for most of the twentieth century. The fact that babies in lead-painted cribs, preschoolers living near traffic, and children in lead-painted homes were often mentally challenged and hyperactive was still claimed to be correlation, not causation.

Finally, chemical analysis of blood and teeth, better intelligence tests, and careful longitudinal and replicated research proved that lead was indeed a poison, even at relatively low levels (Needleman et al., 1990, Needleman & Gatsonis, 1990). In Canada, the federal government began reducing lead levels in paint in 1976, and today lead is no longer used in household paints. The Canadian government outlawed leaded gas for automobiles in 1990. Yet, some lead sources are still unregulated, resulting in high levels in drinking water and jet fuel. Some people feel that may be harmless. However, pediatricians have set the acceptable level, formerly 40 micrograms per decilitre of blood, at 10 micrograms or less. One team contends that even 5 micrograms per decilitre is too much (Cole & Winsler, 2010), especially in a young child whose brain is rapidly developing.

The result of policies and regulations to protect against the dangers of lead is that contemporary children in North America have much lower levels of lead in their blood. According to the Canadian Health Measures Survey, lead levels in the blood of Canadians aged 6–79 years have declined more than 70 percent since the 1970s (Statistics Canada, 2011c). Even so, 100 percent of Canadians still have some lead in their blood (Statistics Canada, 2013b). Children aged 3 to 5 years have slightly higher levels of lead than those aged 6 to 11 years.

In addition to governments implementing laws and policies to reduce exposure to lead, parents can take action as well. Specifics include increasing children's consumption of calcium, wiping window ledges clean of dust, testing drinking water, replacing old windows, and making sure children do not swallow peeling chips of lead-based paint (still found in old buildings) (Dilworth-Bart & Moore, 2006; Nevin et al., 2008).

As well, every young child should be tested—only a pinprick of blood is needed. Repeated testing may be required if a child's lead level is initially found to be high. Once the source (old paint, lead in the soil, glazed dishes, home medicines) is identified and eliminated, blood lead levels fall and the brain recovers.

Remember from Chapter 1 that scientists use data collected for other reasons to draw new conclusions. This is the case with lead. About 15 years after the sharp decline in the number of preschool children with high blood lead levels, the rate of violent crime committed by teenagers and young adults fell sharply. Year-by-year correlations are apparent.

A scientist comparing these two trends concluded that some teenagers commit impulsive, violent crimes because their brains were poisoned by lead when they were preschoolers. The correlation is found in every nation that has reliable data on lead and crime—Canada, the United States, Germany, Italy, Australia, New Zealand, France, and Finland (Nevin, 2007). Not everyone is convinced, but the research shows that, although correlation does not prove causation, it can suggest causes that no one imagined before.

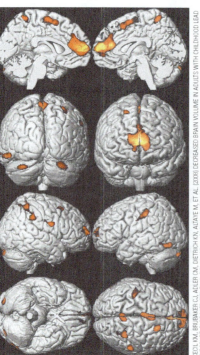

CECIL KM, BRUBAKER CJ, ADLER CM, DIETRICH KN, ALTAYE M, ET AL (2008) DECREASED BRAIN VOLUME IN ADULTS WITH CHILDHOOD LEAD EXPOSURE PLOS MED 5(5): E112 DOI 10.1371/JOURNAL.PMED.0050112

Toxic Shrinkage A composite of 157 brains shows reduced volume because of high lead levels. The red and yellow hotspots are all areas that are smaller than in a normal brain. No wonder lead-exposed children have multiple intellectual and behavioural problems.

The Canadian Paediatric Society (CPS) has pointed out that death rates from unintentional injuries among children and teens are three to four times higher in Aboriginal communities than elsewhere in Canada. Among Aboriginal children younger than 10 years of age, the leading causes of death due to injuries are fires and motorized vehicle accidents, including those involving snowmobiles and ATVs (Banerji, 2012). These disproportionately high rates have led the CPS to make six specific recommendations to reduce the number of deaths among Aboriginal children:

1. *Focus on surveillance*: Involve better data collection and research.

2. *Improve education*: Share information through conferences, public debates, and meetings with community members.

3. *Strengthen advocacy*: Cooperate among federal, provincial, and territorial governments in developing a national injury-prevention strategy.

4. *Reduce barriers*: Make particular efforts to reduce rates of poverty and substandard housing and increase access to drug and alcohol rehabilitation programs.

5. *Evaluate initiatives*: Measure the impact of injury-prevention programs.

6. *Provide resources*: Have effective funding for injury-prevention programs and research.

Note that throughout this discussion, we have been referring to these injuries as "unintentional," not "accidental." Even though such injuries are not deliberate, public health experts do not call them "accidents." The word implies that such an injury is random and unpredictable. Instead of *accident prevention,* health workers seek **injury control** (or **harm reduction**). Serious injury is unlikely if a child falls on a safety surface instead of on concrete, if a car seat protects the body in a crash, if a bicycle helmet cracks instead of a skull, or if pills are in a bottle with a child-resistant cap.

ENVIRONMENTAL HAZARDS Less obvious than unintentional injuries are dangers from pollutants that harm young, growing brains and bodies more than older, developed ones. For example, in India, one city of 14 million (Kolkata, formerly Calcutta) has such extensive air pollution that childhood asthma rates are soaring and lung damage is prevalent. In these circumstances, supervision is not enough: Regulation makes a difference. In the Indian city of Mumbai (formerly Bombay), air pollution has been reduced and children's health has been improved through several measures, including an extensive system of public buses that use clean fuels (Bhattacharjee, 2008).

A study in western Canada (Clark et al., 2010) examined the health impacts of air pollution. Some suspected pollutants, such as car and truck exhaust, were proven to be harmful to children, but others, such as woodsmoke, were not. Much more research on pollutants in food and water is needed.

HARM REDUCTION Three levels of harm reduction apply to every childhood health and safety issue:

- **Primary prevention** structures the environment to make harm less likely, reducing everyone's risk of sickness, injury, or death. Universal immunization and less pollution are examples of primary prevention.

CHIEN-MIN CHUNG / GETTY IMAGES

Could Your Child Do This? If acrobatics was your family's profession and passion, you might encourage your toddler to practise headstands, and years later, your child could balance on your head. Everywhere, young children try to do whatever their parents do.

injury control (or harm reduction) Practices that are aimed at anticipating, controlling, and preventing dangerous activities; these practices reflect the beliefs that accidents are not random and that injuries can be made less harmful if proper controls are in place.

RESPONSE FOR Teachers (from page 178) Remember to keep food simple and familiar. Offer every child the same food, allowing refusal but no substitutes—unless for all eight. Children do not expect school and home routines to be identical; they eventually taste whatever other children enjoy. ●

primary prevention Actions that change overall background conditions to prevent some unwanted event or circumstance, such as injury, disease, or abuse.

secondary prevention
Actions that avert harm in a high-risk situation, such as stopping a car before it hits a pedestrian or installing traffic lights at dangerous intersections.

tertiary prevention
Actions, such as immediate and effective medical treatment, that are taken after an adverse event (such as illness, injury, or abuse) occurs and that are aimed at reducing the harm or preventing disability.

RESPONSE FOR Immigrant Parents (from page 178) Children develop the motor skills that they see and practise. They will soon learn to use forks, spoons, and knives. Do not abandon chopsticks: Children can learn several ways of doing things, and the ability to eat with chopsticks is a social asset. ●

Same Situation, Far Apart: Keeping Everyone Safe Preventing unintentional injury to children requires action by adults and children. In North America, adults passed laws and bought safety seats—and here a young boy buckles up his stuffed toy for safety *(left)*. In France *(right)*, teachers stop cars while children hold hands to cross the street—so no daydreaming or rebellious partners run off.

- **Secondary prevention** is more specific, averting harm in high-risk situations or for vulnerable individuals. For instance, for children who are genetically predisposed to obesity, secondary prevention might mean exclusive breastfeeding for 6 months, no soft drinks or sweets in the kitchen for anyone, and frequent play outside.

- **Tertiary prevention** begins after harm has occurred, limiting the potential damage. For example, if a child falls and breaks an arm, a speedy ambulance and a sturdy cast are tertiary prevention.

How would these three levels apply to preventing child deaths from drowning? Tertiary prevention might be immediate mouth-to-mouth resuscitation when a submerged child is pulled from the water; secondary prevention would have parents put life jackets on children before taking them onto motor boats; and primary prevention might be laws that swimming pools be enclosed by a locked fence on all four sides.

Tertiary prevention is most visible, but primary prevention is most effective (Cohen et al., 2010). Harm reduction begins long before any particular child or parent does something foolish. For developmentalists, a systems approach helps pinpoint effective prevention.

When a child is seriously injured, analysis can find causes in the microsystem, exosystem, and macrosystem. For example, if a child pedestrian is hit by a car, the analysis would note the nature of the child (young boys are hit more often than older girls) and the possible lack of parental supervision (microsystem); the local speed limit, sidewalks, and traffic lights (exosystem); and the regulations regarding drivers, cars, and roadways (macrosystem).

Researchers seek empirical data in any scientific approach. For example, the rate of childhood poisoning has decreased since pill manufacturers adopted bottles with safety caps—a useful fact when anyone complains about the inconvenience.

Some adults say that children today are overprotected, with fewer swings and jungle gyms, mandated car seats, and nut-free schools. Statistics—not anecdotes and memories ("I loved the metal monkey bars, and I am still alive")—are needed, otherwise cultural assumptions may overtake effective injury control. Without evidence, people disagree as to when protection becomes overprotection, as the following explains.

OPPOSING PERSPECTIVES

Safety Versus Freedom

How far should schools go to accommodate children with allergies? My friend has a child with a peanut allergy, and she expects the school to go peanut free for him. On the one hand, it seems selfish to go to that extent for one child (or a few children). Wouldn't a peanut-free area be enough? What about children with other food allergies? Should the school become egg-free as well? On the other hand, this kid can die if exposed to peanuts. Isn't a little inconvenience worth saving his life? And is separating the child from everyone else discrimination? Will this cause bullying and other emotional problems? Is there a way to protect this child without disrupting everyone?

—Edited entry from an online parenting forum

Sara Shannon's daughter Sabrina was a 13-year-old high school student with severe peanut, dairy, and soy allergies in Pembroke, Ontario. During the school year, Sara usually packed Sabrina's lunch at home, but on September 29, 2003, Sabrina told her mom not to bother. She wanted to try the french fries in the school cafeteria. They weren't fried in peanut oil, Sabrina said, so they should be okay.

Sabrina had the fries for lunch and almost immediately experienced an allergic reaction. Short of breath and disoriented, she walked to the school office, where she collapsed before staff could administer the anti-allergy drug epinephrine. By the time an ambulance arrived, Sabrina's body was in what doctors call anaphylactic shock. Her heart stopped beating temporarily, and by the next day she was dead.

The coroner determined that Sabrina's allergic reaction was probably the result of cross-contamination—the tongs used to serve the fries had also been used to serve poutine. Minute traces of the milk curds in the poutine were enough to send the young girl's body into severe shock.

Sabrina's untimely and tragic death made her parents resolve to do whatever they could to ensure that no other child would suffer a similar fate. Soon they were joined by families of other children with allergies, and together they formed organizations that lobbied provincial politicians.

As a direct result, in 2005 the Ontario government passed a law called An Act to Protect Anaphylactic Pupils: Sabrina's Law. This was the first piece of legislation in the world designed to shield children with serious allergies from contamination threats at school. It has served as a model for laws and policy directives in several Canadian provinces. For example, Manitoba passed a similar law in 2008, and Alberta issued an Allergy and Anaphylaxsis Policy Advisory in 2007.

In the United States, several states now have laws or policy guidelines that clearly outline steps and procedures to make schools safer for children with severe allergies. In 2011, the U.S. federal government passed the Food Allergy and Anaphylaxsis Management Act (FAAMA), which identifies a

Protecting Children Jamie Nackan-April from Toronto, Ontario, has multiple food allergies. She is one of the many children who benefit from Sabrina's Law. Allergy groups are calling for clearer food labelling to help identify all ingredients to avoid potentially dangerous reactions.

set of "voluntary allergy management guidelines" for schools. (Smith, 2011).

Although these initiatives have saved children's lives, they have also created controversy. Some parents feel that the rights of the majority are being compromised for the sake of a minority. Although the number of children with food allergies has definitely risen over the last several years, they still make up less than 5 percent of the total under-18 population (Branum & Lukacs, 2008).

Most of the controversy centres on so-called "nut-free schools," where administrators have banned peanuts and other allergens from school cafeterias and from packed lunches that students bring from home. For example, in March 2011, parents in Edgewater, Florida protested outside the local public school after administrators not only declared the school a nut-free zone, but also directed students to wash their hands and rinse their mouths twice a day before entering the classroom, and brought a peanut-sniffing dog into the school over the spring break (Liston, 2011).

What do developmentalists think of this? Dr. Nicholas Christatis, a Harvard professor and social scientist, was quoted in *Time* magazine in 2009 criticizing some of the more extreme precautions schools have taken as a form of "societal hysteria." "There are some kids with severe allergies," said Dr. Christatis, "and they need to be taken seriously, but the problem with a disproportionate response is that it feeds the hysteria" (Sharples, 2009).

Dr. Robert Wood of the Johns Hopkins Children's Center also cautioned against allowing a few controversial examples to detract from the sensible approach most schools are taking in protecting allergic students: "There are definitely situations where we see a fear of the allergy that develops far out of proportion to the true risk, but for the vast majority of schools, things are mostly on balance and in perspective" (Sharples, 2009).

It's important to note that none of the measures such as Sabrina's Law in Canada or FAAMA in the United States specifically mandates nut-free zones or schools. Sabrina's Law has two major provisions:

- Every school board must establish and maintain an anaphylaxis policy.

- School principals must develop individual safety plans for allergic students.

It is up to the individual boards and principals to decide exactly how to implement these directives.

An issue such as this, which pits individual safety against the right of people to eat what they please, will probably never be resolved to everyone's satisfaction. Opinions are influenced not only by whether one's child has food allergies, but also by cohort, culture, and personality. Perhaps the best way to close this particular discussion is with a comment from Sabrina Shannon's mother, Sara.

"We have to make sure this doesn't happen again," Sara told an interviewer in regard to Sabrina's death. "When everything is done, everything is in place, every procedure, every emergency plan, then if a child dies, we can say, 'There was nothing we could do.' But when we know there is something we can do to prevent this, we can't live in a world of denial" (Smith, 2011).

KEY Points

- Young children continue to grow and develop motor skills, eating and playing actively.

- Hazards include eating too much of the wrong foods, environmental chemicals that are linked to diabetes and other health problems later on, and food allergies.

- Young children's natural energy and sudden curiosity make them vulnerable to injury.

- Primary and secondary prevention of harm begin long before injury, with restrictions on lead and other pollutants (primary) and measures to reduce harm to young children (secondary).

Brain Development

As with motor skills, the brains of young children show impressive growth, but are not nearly as developed as they will be later on. By age 2, most neurons are connected to other neurons and substantial pruning has occurred. The 2-year-old's brain already is 75 percent of adult weight; the 6-year-old's brain is 90 percent of adult weight. (Figure 5.3 shows the major structures of the brain.)

The Maturing Cortex

Since most of the brain is already present and functioning by age 2, what is still developing? The most important parts!

Although the 2-year-olds of other primates are more developed than human children in some ways (e.g., climb trees better, walk faster), and although many animals have abilities that people lack (e.g., a dog's sense of smell), young humans have intellectual capacities far beyond those of any other animal. Human brains continue to develop at least until early adulthood (Konner, 2010).

Considered from an evolutionary perspective, human brains have allowed the species to develop "a mode of living built on social cohesion, cooperation and efficient planning ... survival of the smartest," which seems more accurate than survival of the fittest

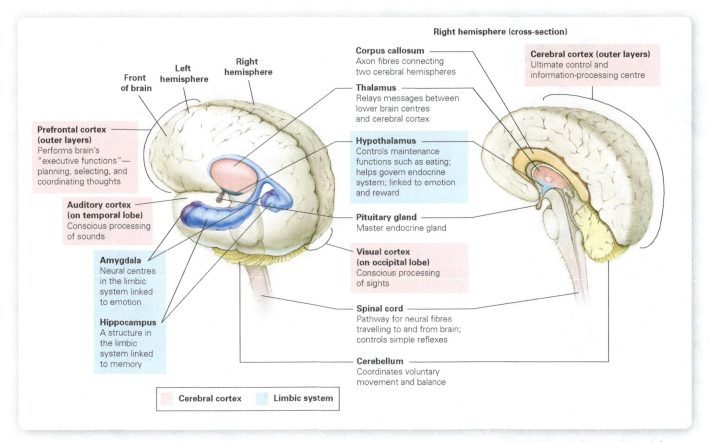

Right hemisphere (cross-section)

Front of brain

Left hemisphere

Right hemisphere

Prefrontal cortex (outer layers)
Performs brain's "executive functions"— planning, selecting, and coordinating thoughts

Auditory cortex (on temporal lobe)
Conscious processing of sounds

Amygdala
Neural centres in the limbic system linked to emotion

Hippocampus
A structure in the limbic system linked to memory

Corpus callosum
Axon fibres connecting two cerebral hemispheres

Thalamus
Relays messages between lower brain centres and cerebral cortex

Hypothalamus
Controls maintenance functions such as eating; helps govern endocrine system; linked to emotion and reward

Pituitary gland
Master endocrine gland

Visual cortex (on occipital lobe)
Conscious processing of sights

Spinal cord
Pathway for neural fibres travelling to and from brain; controls simple reflexes

Cerebellum
Coordinates voluntary movement and balance

Cerebral cortex (outer layers)
Ultimate control and information-processing centre

■ **Cerebral cortex**   ■ **Limbic system**

FIGURE 5.3 Connections A few of the dozens of named parts of the brain are shown here. Although each area has particular functions, the entire brain is interconnected. The processing of emotions, for example, occurs primarily in the limbic system, but many other brain areas are involved, including the amygdala, hippocampus, and hypothalamus.

(Corballis, 2011, p. 194). Those functions of the brain that distinguish us from apes begin in infancy but develop notably after age 2 years, enabling quicker, better coordinated, and more reflective thought (Johnson, 2010; Kagan & Herschkowitz, 2005).

Between the ages of 2 and 6 years, neurological increases are especially notable in the cortex regions, where planning, thinking, social awareness, and language occur. Elephants, crows, chimpanzees, and dolphins have all surprised researchers with their intelligence, but none come close to *Homo sapiens* in the relative size of the cortex or its capacity for social understanding (Corballis, 2011). For example, researchers gave a series of tests to 106 chimpanzees, 32 orangutans, and 105 human 2½-year-olds. The young humans were similar to chimpanzees on tasks of physical cognition, but scored significantly higher than both chimpanzees and orangutans on social cognition tasks such as pointing or following someone's gaze (Herrmann et al., 2007).

One part of the cortex in particular is much larger in humans than in any other creature. That is the *prefrontal cortex*, a brain area right above the eyes that is called the *executive* of the brain because planning, prioritizing, and reflection occur there. It is the prefrontal cortex that, for instance, allows young children to begin to plan ahead as well as to think about experiences they have had, for instance deciding who they want at their birthday party or what they liked best about a summer trip. The prefrontal cortex is very limited in infancy, begins to function in early childhood, and continues to develop for many more years (Johnson, 2010).

Speed of Thought

Most of the increases in brain weight after infancy are the result of **myelination.** *Myelin* (sometimes called the *white matter* of the brain) is a fatty coating on the axons that speeds signals between neurons (see Figure 5.4). Although myelination continues for years, the effects are especially apparent in early childhood (Silk & Wood, 2011).

myelination
The process by which axons become coated with myelin, a fatty substance that speeds the transmission of nerve impulses from neuron to neuron.

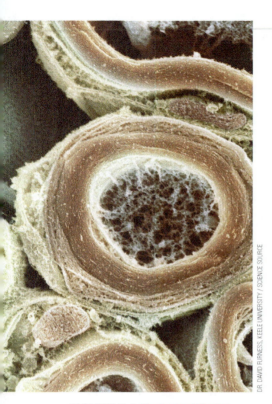

DR. DAVID FURNESS, KEELE UNIVERSITY / SCIENCE SOURCE

FIGURE 5.4 Faster and Faster Myelination is a lifelong process. Shown here is a cross-section of an axon (dark middle) coated with many layers of Schwann cells, as more and more myelin wraps around the axon throughout childhood. Age-related slowdowns in adulthood are caused by gradual disappearance of myelin layers.

perseveration
The tendency to persevere in, or stick to, one thought or action for a long time.

✦ ESPECIALLY FOR Early Childhood Teachers You know you should be patient, but you feel your frustration rising when your young charges dawdle as they walk to the playground a block away. What should you do? (see response, page 189) ➔

corpus callosum
A long, thick band of nerve fibres that connects the left and right hemispheres of the brain and allows communication between them.

Speed of thought from axon to neuron becomes pivotal when several thoughts and actions must occur in rapid succession. By age 6, most children can see an object and immediately name it, catch a ball and throw it, and write their ABCs in proper sequence, to name a few accomplishments. In fact, rapid naming of letters and objects—possible only when myelination is extensive—is a crucial indicator of later reading ability (Shanahan & Lonigan, 2010).

Of course, adults must be patient when listening to young children talk, helping them get dressed, or watching them write each letter of their names. Everything is done more slowly by 6-year-olds than by 16-year-olds because the younger children's brains have less myelination and experience, which slows information processing.

IMPULSIVENESS AND PERSEVERATION The young child's inability to speedily combine thoughts is evident when both action and reflection are needed. Neurons have only two kinds of impulses: on–off, or activate–inhibit. Each is signalled by biochemical messages from dendrites to axons to neurons. A balance of activation and inhibition is needed for thoughtful children, who neither leap too quickly nor hesitate too long.

Many young children have not yet found the balance. They are impulsive, going from one activity to another. That explains why many 3-year-olds cannot stay quietly on one task, even in "circle time" in preschool, where each child is told to sit in place, not talking or touching anyone else. Others persevere in, or stick to, one thought or action, often repeating the behaviours at inappropriate times, called **perseveration.** Impulsiveness and perseveration are opposite manifestations of a prefrontal cortex that is responsible for action control such as planning, coordinating action sequences, or focusing on mental goals (Perner & Lang, 2002; Verbruggen & Logan, 2008).

SHAPES AND COLOURS Perseveration gradually declines in every child. Consider a series of experiments in which 3-year-olds consistently make a mistake that they will no longer make by age 5. Children are given a set of cards with clear outlines of trucks or flowers, some red and some blue. They are asked to "play the shape game," putting trucks in one pile and flowers in another. Three-year-olds do this correctly. Then they are asked to "play the colour game," sorting the cards by colour. Most fail. Instead they sort by shape, as they had done before. This basic test has been replicated in many nations; 3-year-olds usually perseverate, getting stuck in their initial sorting pattern.

When this result was first obtained, researchers thought that 3-year-olds might not know colours. To test this possibility, some other 3-year-olds were asked to sort by colour. Most did that correctly. Then, when asked to play "the shape game," they still sorted by colour. Even with a new set of cards, such as yellow and green or rabbits and boats, 3-year-olds sort as they did originally, either by colour or shape. Most 5-year-olds can make the switch.

Researchers are looking into many possible explanations for this result (Marcovitch et al., 2010; Müller et al., 2006; Yerys & Munakata, 2006). All agree, however, that something in the brain matures between ages 3 and 5 to enable children to switch their way of sorting objects.

Connecting Hemispheres

One part of the brain that grows and myelinates rapidly during early childhood is the **corpus callosum,** a long, thick band of nerve fibres that connects the left and right sides of the brain. Growth of the corpus callosum makes communication between hemispheres more efficient, allowing children to coordinate the two sides of the brain or body. Failure of the corpus callosum to mature results in serious disorders;

this is one of several possible causes of autism (Frazier & Hardan, 2009), discussed in Chapter 7.

The two sides of the body and of the brain are not identical. Typically, the brain's left half controls the body's right side, as well as areas dedicated to logical reasoning, detailed analysis, and the basics of language; the brain's right half controls the body's left side, with areas dedicated to emotions, creativity, and appreciation of music, art, and poetry. This left–right distinction has been exaggerated, however (Hugdahl & Westerhausen, 2010), as both sides of the brain are involved in almost every skill. Nonetheless, each side specializes, being dominant for certain functions—the result of **lateralization,** literally, "sidedness," which advances with maturation of the corpus callosum (Boles et al., 2008). Lateralization is genetic and present at birth, but practice and time are needed before children can efficiently coordinate hands, feet, ears, and so on.

Some research a decade ago found that, relatively speaking, the corpus callosum was thicker in females than in males, a finding that led to speculation about women's superior emotional understanding. However, research using more advanced techniques now finds that this sex difference is far from universal. Some individual males and females have notably thicker corpus callosa than others, but gender does not seem relevant (Savic, 2010).

Although gender does not seem to affect thickness of the corpus callosum, handedness might. Left-handed people tend to have thicker corpus callosa than right-handed people, perhaps because they need to vary the interaction between the two sides of their bodies, depending on the task. For example, most left-handed people brush their teeth with their left hand because that is easier, but they shake hands with their right hand because that is what the social convention requires. Left-handed children need to learn when to use their non-dominant hand—with scissors that are not specially designed for left-handed people, for instance.

Often cultures assume everyone should be right-handed, an example of the difference-equals-deficit error. For example, many letters and languages are written from left to right, which is easier for right-handed people. In some Asian and African cultures, it is an insult to give someone anything with the left hand. Fortunately, acceptance of left-handedness is more widespread now than a century ago. About 13 percent of adults in Canada and 10 percent of adults in Great Britain and the United States now identify themselves as left-handed, compared to only 3 percent in 1900 (McManus et al., 2010).

Developmentalists advise against switching a left-handed child, not only because this causes adult–child conflicts and brain confusion, but also because left-handed people may have an advantage in creativity and rapid use of the entire brain. Dan Aykroyd, Michelangelo, Marshall McLuhan, Marie Curie, Jimi Hendrix, Celine Dion, Paul McCartney, Chris Bosch, and Sidney Crosby, as well as four of the past six U.S. presidents (Ronald Reagan, Jimmy Carter, Bill Clinton, and Barack Obama) were or are lefties. However, this link of left-handedness and creativity is still up for debate and does not discount that right-handed individuals are also creative.

STOCKBYTE / GETTY IMAGES

✦ **ESPECIALLY FOR Neurologists**
Why do many experts think that identifying the limbic system as the regulator of emotions is an oversimplified explanation of brain function? (see response, page 189) ➝

lateralization
Literally, "sidedness," referring to the specialization in certain functions by each side of the brain, with one side dominant for each activity. The left side of the brain controls the right side of the body, and vice versa.

Smarter than Most? Beware of stereotypes. This student is a girl, Asian, left-handed, and attending a structured school (note the uniform). Each of these four characteristics may lead some to conclude that she is more, or less, intelligent than other 7-year-olds. But all children have the potential to learn: Specific teaching, not innate characteristics, is crucial.

Emotions and the Brain

Now that we have considered the prefrontal cortex and the corpus callosum, we turn to the major brain region for emotions, sometimes called the **limbic system.** Emotional expression and emotional regulation advance during early childhood (more about that in the next chapter), and crucial to that advance are three major areas of the limbic system—the amygdala, the hippocampus, and the hypothalamus.

The **amygdala** is a tiny structure deep in the brain, named after the Greek word for almond because it is about the same shape and size. It registers emotions, both positive and negative, especially fear (Kolb & Whishaw, 2008). Increased amygdala activity is one reason some young children have terrifying nightmares or sudden terrors, overwhelming the prefrontal cortex and disrupting reason. Children may refuse to enter an elevator, or will hide when they hear thunder. Specifics depend on the child's innate temperament as well as on past social experiences (Tarullo et al., 2011).

Another structure in the brain's limbic system, the **hippocampus,** is located right next to the amygdala. A central processor of memory, especially memory for locations, the hippocampus responds to the anxieties of the amygdala by summoning memory. A child can remember, for instance, whether previous elevator riding was scary or fun. Memories of location are fragile in early childhood because the hippocampus is still developing.

The interaction of the amygdala and the hippocampus is sometimes helpful, sometimes not; fear can be constructive or destructive (LaBar, 2007). Studies performed on some animals show that when the amygdala is surgically removed, the animals are fearless in situations that should scare them; for instance, a cat will stroll nonchalantly past monkeys—something no normal cat would do (Kolb & Whishaw, 2008). With humans, if the amygdala is less connected to the other parts of the brain, young children are likely to be depressed, presumably because emotions are more overwhelming when the rest of the brain is disengaged (Luking et al., 2011).

A third part of the limbic system, the **hypothalamus,** responds to signals from the amygdala (arousing) and to signals from the hippocampus (usually dampening) by producing cortisol and other hormones that activate parts of the brain and body (see Figure 5.3). Ideally, this hormone production occurs in moderation (Tarullo & Gunnar, 2006).

limbic system
The major brain region crucial to the development of emotional expression and regulation; its three main areas are the amygdala, the hippocampus, and the hypothalamus, although recent research has found that many other areas of the brain are involved with emotions.

amygdala
A tiny brain structure that registers emotions, particularly fear and anxiety.

hippocampus
A brain structure that is a central processor of memory, especially memory for locations.

hypothalamus
A brain area that responds to the amygdala and the hippocampus to produce hormones that activate other parts of the brain and body.

Good Excuse It is true that emotional control of selfish instincts is difficult for young children because the prefrontal cortex is not yet mature enough to regulate some emotions. However, family practices can advance social understanding.

"I would share, but I'm not there developmentally."

As the limbic system develops, young children watch their parents' emotions closely (the social referencing described in Chapter 4). If a parent looks worried when entering an elevator, the child may fearfully cling to the parent when the elevator moves. If this sequence recurs often enough, the child's amygdala may become hypersensitive to elevators, as fear joins the hippocampus in remembering a specific location, and the result is increased cortisol. If, instead, the parent seems calm and makes elevator riding fun (letting the child push the buttons, for instance), the child will overcome initial feelings of fear, and the child might run to the elevator, happily pushing buttons.

Knowing the varieties of fears and joys is helpful if a teacher takes a group of young children on a trip. To stick with the elevator example, one child might be terrified while another child might rush forward, pushing the close button before the teacher enters. Every experience (elevators, fire engines, animals at the zoo, a police officer) is likely to trigger a range of emotions, without much reflection, in a group of 3-year-olds.

KEY Points

- The prefrontal cortex develops in early childhood and beyond, allowing the planning and analyzing that comprise executive processing.
- Myelination speeds mental processing, which eventually reduces impulsivity and perseveration.
- Emotional regulation requires coordination of several brain areas, including the amygdala, the hippocampus, and the hypothalamus.
- Brain maturation of young children is more advanced, especially in social understanding, than in other animals, but each child's particular culture and experience have a notable impact.

Thinking During Early Childhood

You have just learned that every year of early childhood brings more advanced motor skills, further brain development, and better control of impulses. All these affect cognition, as first described by Jean Piaget and Lev Vygotsky, already mentioned in Chapter 1.

Piaget: Preoperational Thought

Early childhood is the time of **preoperational intelligence,** the second of Piaget's four periods. He called early childhood thinking *pre*operational because children do not yet use logical operations (reasoning processes) (Inhelder & Piaget, 1964).

However, preoperational children are past sensorimotor intelligence because they can think in symbols, not just senses and motor skills. In **symbolic thought,** an object or word can stand for something else, including something pretended, or something not seen. For instance, toddlers often hold a block or hairbrush to their ear and pretend they are talking with someone. Symbolic thought allows for the language explosion (detailed later in this chapter), when children can talk about thoughts and memories.

Symbolic thought explains **animism,** the belief of many young children that natural objects (such as a tree or a cloud) are alive, and that non-human animals have the same characteristics as the child. For example, when my niece Kaitlyn was 2 years old, we went to an aquarium store to look at the fish. She pointed at one and

preoperational intelligence
Piaget's term for cognitive development between the ages of about 2 and 6; it includes language and imagination (which involve symbolic thought), but logical, operational thinking is not yet possible.

symbolic thought
The concept that an object or word can stand for something else, including something pretended or something not seen. Once symbolic thought is possible, language becomes much more useful.

animism
The belief that natural objects and phenomena are alive.

 **Susan's** STORY

asked me, "Why is this fish sad? Is it because he's not with his mommy?" The fish she pointed to had a mouth that sloped downwards as if it were frowning.

Preoperational thought is symbolic and magical, not logical and realistic. Animism gradually disappears as the mind becomes more mature and the child has more experiences of what is real and what is not (Kesselring & Müller, 2011).

OBSTACLES TO LOGIC Piaget described symbolic thought as characteristic of preoperational thought, and also described four limitations that make logic difficult until about age 6: centration, focus on appearance, static reasoning, and irreversibility.

Centration is the tendency to focus on one aspect of a situation to the exclusion of all others. Young children may, for example, sort blocks by colour (grouping blue blocks together and red ones in another pile). However, if you ask them to sort by colour and shape, putting the blue square blocks together in one pile and the blue triangle blocks in another, and the same for green, they would not be able to do it.

The block example illustrates a particular type of centration that Piaget called **egocentrism**—literally, "self-centredness." Egocentric children contemplate the world primarily from their personal perspective. Egocentrism is not selfishness. Consider, for example, a 3-year-old who chose to buy a model car as a birthday present for his mother: His "behaviour was not selfish or greedy; he carefully wrapped the present and gave it to his mother with an expression that clearly showed that he expected her to love it" (Crain, 2005, p. 108).

A second characteristic of preoperational thought is a **focus on appearance** to the exclusion of other attributes. Preschoolers are easily tricked by the outward appearance of things. In preoperational thought, a girl given a short haircut might worry that she has turned into a boy, and young children wearing the hats or shoes of a grown-up believe they themselves are grown up.

Third, preoperational children use **static reasoning,** believing that the world is unchanging, always in the state in which they currently encounter it. For instance, many children cannot imagine that their own parents were ever children. If they are told that their grandmother is their mother's mother, they still do not understand that people change with maturation. One preschooler told his grandmother to tell his mother to never spank him, because "she has to do what her mother says."

The fourth characteristic of preoperational thought is **irreversibility.** Preoperational thinkers fail to recognize that reversing a process sometimes restores whatever existed before. A young child might cry because her mother put lettuce on her sandwich. Overwhelmed by her desire to have things "just right," she might reject the food even after the lettuce is removed because she believes that what is done cannot be undone.

CONSERVATION AND LOGIC Piaget highlighted the many ways in which preoperational intelligence overlooks logic. A famous set of experiments involved **conservation,** the notion that the amount of something remains the same (is conserved) despite changes in its appearance.

Suppose two identical glasses contain the same amount of milk. If you ask a child to confirm that both glasses have the same amount, he or she will acknowledge that they do. But if you then take one of the glasses of milk and pour the milk into another glass that is taller and thinner, the child will insist that the narrower glass (with the higher level) has more milk. (See Figure 5.5 for other examples.)

All four characteristics of preoperational thought are evident in this mistake. Young children fail to understand conservation of liquids because they focus (*centre*) on what they see (*appearance*), noticing only the immediate (*static*) condition. It does not occur to them that they could reverse the process and re-create the level of a moment earlier (*irreversibility*).

---

centration
A characteristic of preoperational thought whereby a young child focuses (centres) on one idea, excluding all others.

egocentrism
Piaget's term for young children's tendency to think about the world entirely from their own personal perspective.

focus on appearance
A characteristic of preoperational thought whereby a young child ignores all attributes that are not apparent.

static reasoning
A characteristic of preoperational thought whereby a young child thinks that nothing changes. Whatever is now has always been and always will be.

irreversibility
A characteristic of preoperational thought whereby a young child thinks that nothing can be undone. A thing cannot be restored to the way it was before a change occurred.

conservation
The principle that the amount of a substance remains the same (i.e., is conserved) even when its appearance changes.

✦ **ESPECIALLY FOR Early Childhood Teachers** How might research on conservation help adults when feeding young children? (see response, page 193) ➡

COURTESY OF KATHLEEN BERGER

Demonstration of Conservation Sarah, here at age 5 ¾, demonstrates Piaget's conservation-of-liquids experiment. First, she examines both short glasses to be sure they contain the same amount of milk. Then, after the contents of one are poured into the tall glass and she is asked which has more, she points to the tall glass, just as Piaget would have expected. Later she added, "It looks like it has more because it's taller."

Piaget's original tests of conservation required children to respond verbally to an adult's questions. Later research has found that when the tests of logic are simplified or made playful, young children may succeed. In addition, researchers must consider children's eye movements or gestures, which may reveal children's thoughts before they can articulate them in words (Goldin-Meadow, 2009).

As with sensorimotor intelligence in infancy, Piaget underestimated what children could understand. Nonetheless, he was a pioneer in recognizing several crucial ways in which children's thought patterns are unlike those of adults.

FIGURE 5.5 Types of Conservation
According to Piaget, until children grasp the concept of conservation at (he believed) about age 6 or 7, they cannot understand that the transformations shown here do not change the total amount of liquid, checkers, clay, and wood.

Tests of Various Types of Conservation

Type of Conservation	Initial Presentation	Transformation	Question	Preoperational Child's Answer
Volume	Two equal glasses of liquid.	Pour one into a taller, narrower glass.	Which glass contains more?	The taller one.
Number	Two equal lines of checkers.	Increase spacing of checkers in one line.	Which line has more checkers?	The longer one.
Matter	Two equal balls of clay.	Squeeze one ball into a long, thin shape.	Which piece has more clay?	The long one.
Length	Two sticks of equal length.	Move one stick.	Which stick is longer?	The one that is farther to the right.

CORBIS RF / AGE FOTOSTOCK

Learning to Tie Shoes Could you describe how to tie shoes? The limitations of verbal tests of cognitive understanding are apparent in many skills.

OBSERVATION QUIZ

What three sociocultural factors make it likely that this child will learn? (see answer, page 194) →

zone of proximal development (ZPD) Vygotsky's term for the intellectual arena where new cognitive and physical skills can be mastered.

scaffolding Temporary support that is tailored to a learner's needs and abilities and aimed at helping the learner master the next task in a given learning process.

overimitation The tendency of children to copy an action that is not a relevant part of the behaviour to be learned; common among 2- to 6-year-olds when they imitate adult actions that are irrelevant and inefficient.

Vygotsky: Social Learning

For decades, the magical, illogical, and self-centred aspects of early childhood cognition dominated research; scientists were understandably influenced by Piaget. His description of egocentrism was confirmed daily by anecdotes of young children's behaviour. Vygotsky emphasized the influence of culture, acknowledging that the culturally specific nature of experience is an integral part of how the person thinks and acts, (Gauvain et al., 2011).

CHILDREN AND MENTORS Vygotsky believed that every aspect of children's cognitive development is embedded in a social context (Vygotsky, 1934/1987). Children are curious and observant. They ask questions—about how machines work, why weather changes, where the sky ends—and seek answers from more knowledgeable mentors. These answers are affected by the mentors' perceptions and assumptions—that is, their culture.

As you remember from Chapter 1, children learn through *guided participation*, as older and more skilled mentors teach them. Parents are the first guides, although many teachers, other family members, and peers are mentors as well. For example, the verbal proficiency of children in daycare centres is affected by the language of their playmates, who teach vocabulary without consciously doing so (Mashburn et al., 2009).

According to Vygotsky, children learn because their mentors do the following:

- Present challenges.
- Offer assistance (without taking over).
- Add crucial information.
- Encourage motivation.

Overall, the ability to learn from mentors indicates intelligence, according to Vygotsky: "What children can do with the assistance of others might be in some sense even more indicative of their mental development than what they can do alone" (1934/1987, p. 5).

SCAFFOLDING AND OVERIMITATION Vygotsky believed that each individual learns within their **zone of proximal development (ZPD),** an intellectual arena where new ideas and skills can be mastered. *Proximal* means "near," so the ZPD includes the ideas children are close to understanding and the skills they are close to attaining but not yet able to master independently. For example, a parent might hold her child's hands to help the child walk or hold the back of a bicycle seat as the child learns to ride the bike.

How and when children learn depends, in part, on the wisdom and willingness of mentors to provide **scaffolding,** or temporary sensitive support, to help them within their developmental zone. Good mentors provide plenty of scaffolding, encouraging children to look both ways before crossing the street (while holding the child's hand) or letting them stir the cake batter (perhaps the adult's hand covers the child's hand on the spoon handle, in guided participation).

Young children also imitate habits and customs that are meaningless, a trait called **overimitation,** evident in humans but not in other animals. This stems from the child's eagerness to learn from mentors, allowing "rapid, high-fidelity intergenerational transmission of cultural forms" (Nielsen & Tomaselli, 2010, p. 735). Children's reasons for imitating one person versus another can vary from seeking approval to trying to fit in with the group.

Overimitation was demonstrated in an experiment with 2- to 6-year-olds, 16 from Bushman communities in South Africa and Botswana and 16 from Australia. Australian adults often scaffold with words and actions, but Bushman adults rarely do so. The researchers expected the Australian children to follow adult demonstrations, as they had been taught. They did not expect the Bushman children to do so.

One by one some of the children observed an adult perform irrelevant actions, such as waving a red stick above a box three times and then using that stick to push down a knob to open the box, which could be easily opened by pulling a knob. Then children were given the stick and the box. No matter what their cultural background, the children followed the adult example, waving the stick three times.

Other children did not see the demonstration. When they were given the stick and the box, they simply pulled the knob. Then they observed an adult do the stick-waving opening and they copied those inefficient actions—even though they already knew the easy way to open the box. Apparently, children are universally predisposed to learn from others via observation if not deliberately taught.

Children's Theories

Piaget and Vygotsky recognized that children work to understand their world. No contemporary developmental scientist doubts that. The question now is: When and how do children acquire their impressive knowledge? Part of the answer is that children do not simply gain words, skills, and concepts—they develop theories to help them understand and remember.

THEORY-THEORY Humans of all ages want explanations. **Theory-theory** refers to the idea that children naturally construct theories to explain whatever they see and hear. In other words, the theory about how children think is that they construct a theory, as do all humans:

> We search for causal regularities in the world around us. We are perpetually driven to look for deeper explanations of our experience, and broader and more reliable predictions about it. … Children seem, quite literally, to be born with … the desire to understand the world and the desire to discover how to behave in it.
>
> *[Gopnik, 2001, p. 66]*

According to theory-theory, the best explanation for cognition in young children is that humans always seek reasons, causes, and underlying principles to make sense of their experiences. That requires curiosity and thought, connecting bits of knowledge and observations, which is what young children do.

Exactly how do children seek explanations? They ask questions, and, if not content with the answers, they develop their own theories. This is particularly evident in children's understanding of God and religion. One child thought his grandpa died because God was lonely; another thought thunder occurred because God rearranged the furniture.

In one study, Mexican-American mothers kept detailed diaries of every question their 3- to 5-year-olds asked and also what they themselves responded (Kelemen et al., 2005). Most of the questions were about human behaviour and characteristics (see Figure 5.6); for example, "Why do you give my mother a kiss?" "Why

✦ **ESPECIALLY FOR Teachers**
Sometimes your students cry, curse, or quit. How would Vygotsky advise you to proceed? (see response, page 195) →

RESPONSE FOR Early Childhood Teachers (from page 190) Since appearance is crucial, when you are giving drinks to more than one child, all the cups should be the same size. Children will also be happier with two very small crackers rather than one bigger one or with a scoop of ice cream in a small bowl rather than the same-sized scoop in a large one. ●

theory-theory
The idea that children attempt to explain everything they see and hear.

FIGURE 5.6 Questions, Questions
Parents found that most of their children's questions were about human behaviour—especially the parents' behaviour toward the child. Children seek to develop a theory to explain things, so the question "Why can't I have some candy?" is not satisfactorily answered by "It's almost dinnertime."

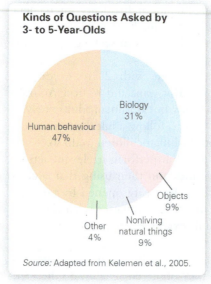

Kinds of Questions Asked by 3- to 5-Year-Olds

- Biology 31%
- Human behaviour 47%
- Other 4%
- Nonliving natural things 9%
- Objects 9%

Source: Adapted from Kelemen et al., 2005.

is my brother bad?" "Why do women have breasts?" Fewer questions were about non-living things ("Why does it rain?") or objects ("Why is my daddy's car white?").

Children seem to wonder about the underlying purpose of whatever they observe, although parents usually respond as if children were seeking scientific explanations. An adult might interpret a child's "Why?" to mean "What causes X to happen?" when the child intended "Why?" to mean "Tell me more about X" (Leach, 1997).

For example, if a child asks why women have breasts, adults might talk about hormones and maturation, but a child-centred response would be that breasts are for feeding babies. From a child's egocentric perspective, any query includes "How does this relate to me?" Accordingly, an adult might add that the child got his or her first nourishment from the mother's breast.

A series of experiments further explored when and how 3-year-olds understand other people's intent, which provided some support for theory-theory (Williamson et al., 2008). Children seem to figure out *why* adults act as they do before deciding to copy those actions. If an adult intended to accomplish something and succeeded, a child is likely to follow the example, but if the same action and result seemed inadvertent or accidental, the child is less likely to copy it. So, these children made a distinction between purposeful and perchance actions.

Indeed, even when asked to repeat something ungrammatical that an adult says, children are likely to correct the grammar based on their theory that the adult intended to speak grammatically but failed to do so (Over & Gattis, 2010). This is another example of a general principle: Children develop theories about intentions before they employ their impressive ability to imitate; they do not mindlessly copy whatever they observe.

ANSWER TO OBSERVATION QUIZ (from page 192) Motivation (children like to learn new things); human relationships (note the physical touching of father and son); and materials (the long laces make tying them easier). ●

theory of mind
A person's theory of what other people might be thinking. In order to have a theory of mind, children must realize that other people are not necessarily thinking the same thoughts that they themselves are. That realization is seldom achieved before age 4.

THEORY OF MIND Human mental processes—thoughts, emotions, beliefs, motives, and intentions—are among the most complicated and puzzling phenomena that we encounter every day. Adults wonder why people fall in love with a particular persons, or why they vote for a candidate, or why they make foolish choices—from taking on a huge mortgage to buying an overripe cucumber. Children are puzzled about a playmate's unexpected anger, a sibling's generosity, or an aunt's too-wet kiss.

To know what goes on in another's mind, people develop a *folk psychology*, which includes a set of ideas about other people's thinking called **theory of mind.** Theory of mind is an emergent ability, slow to develop but typically beginning in most children at about age 4 (Sterck & Begeer, 2010).

Realizing that thoughts do not reflect reality is beyond very young children, but it occurs to them sometime after age 3. They then realize that people can be deliberately deceived or fooled—an idea that requires some theory of mind.

In one of several false-belief tests that researchers have developed, a child watches a doll named Max put a puppy into a red box. Then Max leaves and the child sees the puppy taken out of the red box and put in a blue box. When Max returns, the child is asked, "Where will Max look for the puppy?" Most 3-year-olds confidently say, "In the blue box," believing Max would know and act in accordance with their newly acquired knowledge; most 6-year-olds correctly say, "In the red box." This pattern is found in a dozen nations (Wellman et al., 2001). Indeed, 3-year-olds almost always confuse what they recently learned with what they once thought and what someone else might think. Another way of describing this is to say that they are "cursed" by their own knowledge (Birch & Bloom, 2003), too egocentric to grasp others' perspectives.

The development of theory of mind can be seen when young children try to escape punishment by lying. Their facial expression often betrays them. Parents sometimes say, "I know when you are lying," and, to the consternation of most 3-year-olds, parents are usually right.

In one experiment, 247 children, aged 3 and 5, were left alone at a table that had an upside down cup that covered dozens of candies (Evans et al., 2011). The children were told not to peek, but more than half of them did (specifically, 49 percent of the 3-year-olds and 70 percent of the 5-year-olds), spilling the candies onto the table. They could not put them back to hide that the fact that they had peeked. The examiner returned, asking how the candies got on the table. Only one-fourth of the participants (more often the younger ones) told the truth. The rest lied, with increasing skill. The 3-year-olds typically told hopeless lies (e.g., "The candies got out by themselves"); the 4-year-olds told unlikely lies (e.g., "Other children came in and knocked over the cup"). Some of the 5-year-olds, however, told plausible lies (e.g. "My elbow knocked over the cup accidentally").

This particular study was done in Beijing, China, but the results seem universal: Older children are better liars. Beyond the age differences, the experimenters found that the more logical liars were also more advanced in theory of mind and executive functioning (Evans et al., 2011), which indicates a more mature prefrontal cortex (see Figure 5.7).

Brain and Context

Many scientists have found that theory of mind correlates with maturity of the prefrontal cortex and advances in executive processing (Liu et al., 2011; Mar, 2011). The brain connection was further supported by research on 8- to 16-year-olds. Their readiness to lie did *not* correlate with age or brain maturation (they were old enough to realize that a lie was possible, but whether they actually lied depended on their expectations and values). If they did lie, their executive abilities correlated with the sophistication of their lies (Evans & Lee, 2011).

Context and experience are relevant as well (Sterck & Begeer, 2010). Language proficiency helps, especially if mother–child conversations involve thoughts and wishes (Ontai & Thompson, 2008). Siblings help, too. As brothers and sisters argue, agree, compete, and cooperate, and as older siblings fool younger ones, it dawns on 3-year-olds that not everyone thinks as they do. Egocentrism is somewhat modified. By age 5, children with older siblings know what words and actions will gain parental sympathy to protect themselves against their older siblings, as well as how to persuade their younger brothers and sisters to give them a toy. As one expert stated, "Two older siblings are worth about a year of chronological age" (Perner, 2000, p. 383).

Finally, culture and context matter for theory of mind. A meta-analysis of 254 studies done in China and North America reported that Chinese children were about six months ahead of Canadian and U.S. children in development of theory of mind (Liu et al., 2008). A Canadian study found that children were slower by a few months if they often watched television (Mar et al., 2010). Everywhere, however, sometime between ages 2 and 6, children realize that not everyone knows what they know.

✦ **ESPECIALLY FOR Social Scientists** Can you think of any connection between Piaget's theory of preoperational thought and 3-year-olds' errors in the theory-of-mind task from Figure 5.7? (see response, page 197) ➤

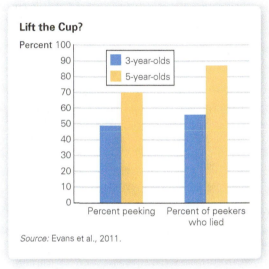

Lift the Cup?

Source: Evans et al., 2011.

FIGURE 5.7 Better with Age? Could an obedient and honest 3-year-old become a disobedient and lying 5-year-old? Apparently yes, as the proportion of peekers and liars in this study more than doubled over those two years. Does maturation make children more able to think for themselves or less trustworthy?

RESPONSE FOR Teachers (from page 193) Use guided participation and scaffold the instruction so your students are not overwhelmed. Be sure to provide lots of praise and days of practice. If emotion erupts, do not take it as an attack on you. ●

> **KEY Points**
>
> - Piaget believed that preoperational children can use symbolic thought but are illogical and egocentric, limited by appearance and immediate experience.
> - Vygotsky realized that children are influenced by their social contexts, including their parents and other mentors and the cultures in which they live.
> - In the zone of proximal development, children are ready to move beyond their current understanding, especially if deliberate or inadvertent scaffolding occurs.
> - Children use their cognitive abilities to develop theories about their experiences, as is evident in theory of mind, which appears between ages 3 and 5.
> - In all of cognitive development, family interactions guide and advance learning.

Language Learning

Language is the premier cognitive accomplishment of early childhood. Two-year-olds use short, telegraphic sentences ("Want cookie," "Where Daddy go?"), but 6-year-olds seem able to understand and discuss almost anything (see At About This Time).

A Sensitive Time

Brain maturation, myelination, scaffolding, and social interaction make early childhood ideal for learning language. As you remember from Chapter 1, scientists once thought that early childhood was a *critical period* for language learning—the *only* time when a first language could be mastered and the best time for learning a second or third language. It is true that in early childhood, children organize words and sounds into meaning (theory-theory), and for that reason teachers and parents should speak and listen to children many hours each day. However, many people learn languages after age 6; the critical-period hypothesis is false (Singleton & Muñoz, 2011). Instead,

AT ABOUT THIS TIME
Language in Early Childhood

Characteristic or Achievement in First Language	Age			
	2 years	3 years	4 years	5 years
Vocabulary	100–2000 words	1000–5000 words	3000–10 000 words	5000–20 000 words
Sentence length	2–6 words	3–8 words	5–20 words	Some seem unending ("… and … who … and … that … and …")
Grammar	Plurals Pronouns Nouns Verbs Adjectives	Conjunctions Adverbs Articles	Dependent clauses Tags at sentence end ("… didn't I?"; "… won't you?")	Complex May use passive voice ("Man bitten by dog") May use subjunctive ("If I were …")
Questions	"What's that?"	"Why?"	"Why?" "How?" "When?"	About social differences (male–female, old–young, rich–poor) and other issues

early childhood is a *sensitive period* for language learning—for rapidly and easily mastering vocabulary, grammar, and pronunciation. Young children are called "language sponges" because they soak up every drop of language they encounter.

Language learning is an example of dynamic systems, in that every part of the developmental process influences every other part. To be specific, there are "multiple sensitive periods … auditory, phonological, semantic, syntactic, and motor systems, along with the developmental interactions among these components" (Thomas & Johnson, 2008, p. 2), all of which facilitate language learning.

One of the valuable (and sometimes frustrating) traits of young children is that they talk a lot—to adults, to each other, to themselves, to their toys—unfazed by misuse, mispronunciation, stuttering, or other impediments to fluency. Language comes easily for young children partly because they are not self-critical about what they say. Egocentrism has advantages; this is one of them. Children believe they know more than they do (Marazita & Merriman, 2011), and they readily and confidently talk about it. For example, one 3-year-old said that a toy lion was a mother. Even when told by an adult that a lion can't be a mother because it has a mane, the three-year-old insisted that this one was a mother with a mane.

The Vocabulary Explosion

The average child knows about 500 words at age 2 and more than 10 000 at age 6 (Herschensohn, 2007). That's more than six new words a day. Precise estimates of vocabulary size vary; some children learn four times as many words as others. However, vocabulary always builds quickly and comprehension is more extensive than speech.

FAST-MAPPING After painstakingly learning one word at a time between 12 and 18 months of age, children develop an interconnected set of categories for words, a kind of filing cabinet or mental map, which makes speedy vocabulary acquisition possible. The process is called **fast-mapping** (Woodward & Markman, 1998). Rather than figuring out the exact definition after hearing a word used in several contexts, children hear a word once and quickly stick it into a category (like a folder) in their mental language filing cabinet. That quick-sticking is fast-mapping.

Language mapping is not precise. For example, children quickly map new animal names close to animal names they already know, without having all the details. Thus, *tiger* is easy to map if you know *lion,* but a leopard might be called a tiger. A trip to the zoo facilitates fast-mapping of animal names, if zoos scaffold learning by placing similar animals near each other. So does a picture book, if a mentor points to the tiger's stripes and the leopard's spots.

Fast-mapping begins even before age 2, and it accelerates over childhood, as each new word makes it easier to map other words (Gershkoff-Stowe & Hahn, 2007). Generally, the more linguistic clues children have, the better their fast-mapping is (Mintz, 2005).

An experiment in teaching the names of parts of objects (e.g., the spigot of a faucet) found that children learned much better if the adults named the object that had the part and then spoke of the object in the possessive (e.g., "See this butterfly? Look, this is the butterfly's thorax") (Saylor & Sabbagh, 2004). It is easier to map a new word when it is connected to a familiar one.

RESPONSE FOR Social Scientists
(from page 195) According to Piaget, preschool children focus on appearance and on static conditions (so they cannot mentally reverse a process). Furthermore, they are egocentric, believing that everyone shares their point of view. No wonder they believe that Max would look for the puppy in the blue box instead of in the red one. ●

fast-mapping
The speedy and sometimes imprecise way in which children learn new words by tentatively placing them in mental categories according to their perceived meaning.

DEA / DIEGO MROSSI / AGE FOTOSTOCK

Horse or Camel? These children might fast-map and call it a horse since it is horse-sized, horse-coloured, and has a horse-like head and legs. However, as in this example, fast-mapping can be misleading.

WORDS AND THE LIMITS OF LOGIC Closely related to fast-mapping is a phenomenon called *logical extension:* After learning a word, children use it to describe other objects in the same category. One child told her father she had seen some "Dalmatian cows" on a school trip to a farm. He remembered that she had petted a Dalmatian dog the weekend before.

Bilingual children who do not know a word in the language they are speaking often insert a word from the other language. Soon they know who understands which language—and make no substitutions when speaking to a monolingual person.

Some words are particularly difficult—*who/whom, have been/had been, here/there, yesterday/tomorrow.* More than one child has awakened on Christmas morning and asked, "Is it tomorrow yet?" A child told to "stay there" or "come here" may not follow instructions because the terms are confusing. It might be better to say "Stay on that bench" or "Come hold my hand."

Extensive study of children's language abilities finds that fast-mapping is only one of many techniques that children use to learn language. When a word does not refer to an object on the mental map, children use other ways to master it (Carey, 2010). If a word does not refer to anything the child can see or otherwise sense or act on, it may be ignored.

LISTENING, TALKING, AND READING Literacy is crucial for children. As a result, researchers have conducted studies to discover what activities and practices promote literacy. A meta-analysis of about 300 studies analyzed which activities in early childhood aided reading a few years later in elementary school. Both vocabulary and attention to the sounds of words (phonics) predicted fluent reading a few years later (Shanahan & Lonigan, 2010). Five specific strategies and experiences were particularly effective for young children of all incomes and ethnicities:

1. *Code-focused teaching.* In order for children to learn to read, they must "break the code" from spoken to written words. It is helpful for children to learn the letters and sounds of the alphabet (e.g., "A, Alligators all around" or "C is for cat").

2. *Book-reading.* Vocabulary as well as familiarity with print increase when adults read to children, allowing questions and conversation.

3. *Parent education.* When teachers and other professionals teach parents how to stimulate cognition (as in the book-reading above), children become better readers.

4. *Language enhancement.* Within each child's zone of proximal development, mentors can expand vocabulary and grammar, based on what the child knows and experiences.

5. *Preschool programs.* Children learn from teachers and other children.

ACQUIRING BASIC GRAMMAR We noted in Chapter 3 that the *grammar* of language includes the structures, techniques, and rules that are used to communicate meaning. By age 3, children understand the basics. English-speaking children know word order (subject/verb/object), saying, "I eat apple," not any of the other possible sequences of those three words. They use plurals; tenses (past, present, and future); and nominative, objective, and possessive pronouns (*I/me/mine* or *my*). Some 3-year-olds even use articles (*the, a, an*) correctly, although proper article use in English is bewilderingly complex. Every language has both easy and difficult aspects that native speakers eventually learn. Learning each aspect of language (grammar, vocabulary, pronunciation, etc.) follows a particular developmental path.

One reason for variation in language learning is that several parts of the brain are involved, each myelinating at a different rate. Further, many genes and alleles affect comprehension and expression. In general, genes affect *expressive* (spoken or written) language more than *receptive* (heard or read) language. Thus, some children are relatively talkative or quiet because they inherit that tendency, but experience (not genes) determines what they understand (Kovas et al., 2005).

Sometimes children apply the rules of grammar when they should not, an error called **overregularization.** For example, English-speaking children quickly learn to add *s* to form the plural: Toddlers follow that rule when they ask for two *cookies* or more *blocks.* Soon they apply this to nonsense words. If preschoolers are shown a drawing of an abstract shape, are told it is called a *wug,* and are then shown two of these shapes, they say there are two *wugs.* In keeping with the distinction between reception and expression, very young children realize words have a singular and a plural before they produce the words (Zapf & Smith, 2007). By age 4, many children overregularize that final *s,* talking about *foots, tooths,* and *mouses.* This is evidence of increasing knowledge. Many children first say words correctly, repeating what they have heard. Later, when they grasp the grammar and try to apply it, they overregularize, assuming that all constructions follow the regular path (Ramscar & Dye, 2011).

Learning Two Languages

Canada is a bilingual country with two official languages: English and French. About 58 percent of the total population is anglophone, while about 22 percent is francophone (Corbeil & Blaser, 2009). While most children learn one of the country's official languages, some receive a bilingual education.

Although there are no official national records on the number of bilingual schools in Canada, it is estimated that about 357 000 students participate in French immersion programs (Allen, 2009). Nationwide, fewer than 10 percent of eligible students are enrolled in French-immersion programs, with the highest enrolment rates being in Quebec and New Brunswick (37 and 26 percent, respectively) (Canadian Council on Learning, 2007).

Data from the Canadian Youth in Transition Survey, a longitudinal survey designed to study the transitions that youth make between education, training, and work, indicated that by age 21, 29 percent of the participants were bilingual (able to have a conversation in both English and French). However, this differs significantly by mother tongue. Specifically, bilingualism accounts for 65 percent of francophone youth, whereas only 18 percent of non-francophones are bilingual.

Learning two languages is also apparent with language-minority children. These children speak a language that is not their nation's dominant one but often learn English or French in school. The mother tongue of 20 percent of Canadians is not English or French or one of the Aboriginal languages. Chinese is now the third largest mother-tongue group in Canada, at 3.3 percent of the population. It is a mark of Canada's cultural diversity that the country is now home to people who speak about 200 different languages as their native tongue (Corbeil & Blaser, 2009). These children learn English or French

Some immigrant school-age children are immersed in a language that is neither there mother tongue nor the language most commonly spoken in their new community, thus learning a third language. For example, immigrant school-age children make up more than 25 percent of French immersion students in urban areas like Toronto and Vancouver (McMullen, 2004). Even though newcomer children are less likely to be enrolled in French-immersion schools than non-immigrant children, some findings report that immigrant English as Second Language (ESL) students enrolled in French immersion perform as well as their anglophone classmates. Also, those immigrant children who have already developed literacy in their native

overregularization
The application of rules of grammar even when exceptions occur, making the language seem more "regular" than it actually is.

✦ **ESPECIALLY FOR Immigrant Parents** You want your children to be fluent in the language of your family's new country, even though you do not speak that language well. Should you speak to your children in your native tongue or in the new language? (see response, page 201) →

language often perform even better than Anglophone students in French-immersion schools (Hurd, 1993; Swain et al., 1990).

HOW AND WHY Some worry that young children taught two languages might become only *semi*-lingual, not bilingual, and "at risk for delayed, incomplete, and possibly even impaired language development" (Genesee, 2008, p. 17). Others argue that "there is absolutely no evidence that children get confused if they learn two languages" (Genesee, 2008, p. 18). This second position has more research support. Soon after the vocabulary explosion, children who have heard two languages since birth usually master two distinct sets of words and grammar, along with each language's pauses, pronunciations, intonations, and gestures (Genesee & Nicoladis, 2007).

No doubt early childhood is the best time to learn a language or languages. Neuroscience finds that in young bilingual children, both languages exist in the same areas of their brains, yet they manage to keep them separate in practice. This separation allows them to activate one language and temporarily inhibit the other, experiencing no confusion when they speak to a monolingual person (Crinion et al., 2006). They may be a millisecond slower to respond if they must switch languages, but Canadian researchers have consistently found that their brains function better overall and may even have some resistance to Alzheimer's disease in old age (Bialystok et al., 2009; Gold et al., 2013).

Another factor that supports young children learning a second language is that it is easier for children to learn the pronunciation of a new language than it is for adults. Although almost all children have pronunciation difficulties even in their first language, they are usually unaware of their mistakes and gradually echo precisely whatever accent they hear. Mispronunciation does not impair fluency since children understand what they are hearing even if they cannot yet pronounce it.

In early childhood, children transpose sounds (*magazine* becomes *mazagine*), drop consonants (*truck* becomes *ruck*), and convert difficult sounds to easier ones (*father* becomes *fadder*). When I was a student teacher for a kindergarten class, the librarian was reading an alphabet book to the class. For each letter, she asked the class to think of other words. When she got to "W," there was a very long pause. Then a child raised his hand, and said with great excitement, "Wobot!" The whole class cheered and clapped at the excellent answer. Although the answer was wrong (robot), the adults all cheered with the class, too.

To speak well, young children need to be "bathed in language," as some early childhood educators express it. They need to listen and speak in every situation, just as a person taking a bath is surrounded by water. Television is a poor teacher because children need personalized, responsive instruction in the zone of proximal development. In fact, young children who watch the most television tend to be delayed in language learning (Harrison & McLeod, 2010).

Susan's STORY ▶

Smiling Faces Everyone in this group is an immigrant, born far from their current home in North America. Jean Luc Dushime escaped the 1994 genocide in Rwanda, central Africa, when he was 14. He eventually adapted to his new language, climate, surroundings, and culture. Today, he helps immigrant children make the same transition.

LANGUAGE LOSS AND GAINS Schools in all nations stress the dominant language, and language-minority parents fear that their children will make a *language shift,* becoming more fluent in the school language than in their home language. Language shift occurs everywhere—some First Nations children in Canada shift to English (Allen, 2007), as do some Chinese-speaking children in Canada and the United States—but not always (Zhang, 2010). The attitudes and practices of parents and the community are crucial.

Remember that young children are preoperational: They centre on the immediate status of their language (not on its global usefulness or past traditions) and on appearance more than substance. No wonder many shift toward the language of the dominant culture.

Since language is integral to culture, if a child is to become fluently bilingual, everyone who speaks with the child should show evident appreciation of both cultures (Pearson, 2008; Snow & Kang, 2006).

Becoming a **balanced bilingual,** speaking two languages so well that no audible hint suggests the other language, is accomplished by millions of young children in many nations, to their cognitive and linguistic benefit (Bialystok & Viswanathan, 2009; Pearson, 2008). Yet language loss is a valid fear. Millions of children either abandon their first language or do not learn the second as well as they might. Although skills in one language can be transferred to benefit the acquisition of another, transfer is not automatic or inevitable (Snow & Kang, 2006). Scaffolding is needed.

The basics of language learning—the naming and vocabulary explosions, fast-mapping, overregularization, extensive practice—apply to every language a young child learns. Young children's vocabulary in two languages is directly connected to how much they hear. If a child is to become a balanced bilingual, that child needs to hear twice as much talk as usual (Hammer et al., 2011). The same practices can make a child fluently trilingual, as some 5-year-olds are. One parent might talk and read to a child in French, for instance, another in English, while the child plays with Chinese-speaking friends at preschool.

Bilingual children and adults are advanced in theory of mind and executive functioning, probably because they need to be more reflective and strategic when they speak. However, sheer linguistic proficiency does not necessarily lead to cognitive advances (Bialystock & Barac, 2012). Simply learning new words and grammar (many preschools teach songs in a second language) does not guarantee a child will learn to understand and appreciate other cultures.

balanced bilingual
A person who is fluent in two languages, not favouring one over the other.

KEY Points

- Children learn language rapidly during early childhood.
- Fast-mapping is one way children learn. Errors in precision, overregularization, and mispronunciation are common and are not problematic at this age.
- Vocabulary advances, particularly if a child is "bathed in language," hearing many words and concepts.
- Young children can learn two languages almost as easily as one, if adults talk frequently, listen carefully, and value both languages.

Early Childhood Education

A hundred years ago, children had no formal education until Grade 1, which is why young children were *pre*schoolers. Today, virtually every nation has some program of early childhood education (Britto et al., 2011). In some countries, most 3- to 6-year-olds are in school, not only because of changing family patterns, but also because school facilitates the rapid development and great learning potential of the early years (Hyson et al., 2006).

Homes and Schools

Young children learn both at home and at school. In addition, there are a variety of school options for children in the early years. A robust research conclusion is that quality matters. If the home environment is poor, a good preschool program aids health, cognition, and social skills (Hindman et al., 2010). However, if a family

RESPONSE FOR Immigrant Parents (from page 199) Children learn by listening, so it is important to speak with them often. You might prefer to read to your children, sing to them, and converse with them primarily in your native language and find a good preschool where they will learn the new language. Try not to restrict speech in either tongue. ●

"We teach them that the world can be an unpredictable, dangerous, and sometimes frightening place, while being careful not to spoil their lovely innocence. It's tricky."

Tricky Indeed Young children are omnivorous learners, picking up certain habits, curses, and attitudes that adults would rather not transmit. Deciding what to teach—by actions more than words—is essential.

provides extensive learning opportunities and encouragement, the quality of the preschool is less crucial.

It is difficult to judge the quality of homes and schools in North America because of the wide variability and fragmentation of public and private schools (Pianta et al., 2009) and the changing configuration of home care. It is a mistake to conclude that care by the mother is better than care by another relative—or vice versa.

Educational institutions for young children are referred to by various names (preschool, nursery school, daycare, pre-primary, pre-K) or structures (public, private, centre, family), but these labels are not a reliable indicator of quality (Fuligni et al., 2009). Each early childhood educational program (and sometimes each teacher) emphasizes different skills, goals, and methods (Chambers et al., 2010; Walsh & Petty, 2007).

We will now consider two general categories of early childhood education: child-centred and teacher-directed. Remember, however, that the quality of the home and the effectiveness of the teachers have more impact on young children than does the label or professed philosophy of the program.

Child-Centred Programs

Many programs are called *developmental,* or *child-centred,* because they stress children's development and growth. Teachers in such programs believe children need to follow their own interests rather than adult directions. For example, they agree that children should be allowed to select many of their own activities from a variety of learning areas that the teacher has prepared (Lara-Cinisomo et al., 2011). The physical space and the materials (such as dress-up clothing, art supplies, puzzles, blocks, other toys) are arranged to allow self-paced exploration.

Most child-centred programs encourage artistic expression (Lim, 2004). Some educators argue that young children "are all poets" in that they are gifted in seeing the world more imaginatively than older people do. According to advocates of child-centred programs, this peak of creative vision should be encouraged; children are given many opportunities to tell stories, draw pictures, dance, and make music for their own delight.

Child-centred programs are often influenced by Piaget, who emphasized that each child will discover new ideas, and by Vygotsky, who thought that children learn from other children, with adult guidance (Bodrova & Leong, 2005). Trained teachers are crucial: A child-centred program requires appropriate activities for each child and teachers who guide and scaffold so that each child advances (Dominguez et al., 2010).

MONTESSORI SCHOOLS One type of child-centred school was founded a hundred years ago, when Maria Montessori opened nursery schools for poor children in Rome. She believed that children needed structured, individualized projects to give them a sense of accomplishment. They completed puzzles, used sponges and water to clean tables, traced shapes, and so on.

Tibetan Boy, Indian School, Italian Style Over the past half-century, as China increased its control of Tibet, thousands of refugees fled to northern India. Tibet traditionally had no preschools, but young children adapt quickly, as here in Ladakh, India. This Tibetan boy is working a classic Montessori board.

Contemporary **Montessori schools** still emphasize individual pride and achievement, presenting many literacy-related tasks (such as outlining letters and looking at books) to young children (Lillard, 2005). Specific materials differ from those that Montessori developed, but the underlying philosophy is the same. Children seek out learning tasks; they do not sit quietly in groups while a teacher instructs them. That makes Montessori programs child-centred.

This philosophy seems to work. A study of 5-year-olds in inner-city Milwaukee, Wisconsin, who were chosen by lottery to attend Montessori programs found that they became better at pre-reading and early math tasks, as well as at developing a theory of mind, than their peers in other schools (Lillard & Else-Quest, 2006). The probable explanation: Their gains in self-confidence, curiosity, and exploration transferred into more academic tasks.

Montessori schools
Schools that offer early childhood education based on the philosophy of Maria Montessori (an Italian educator more than a century ago). It is child-centred, emphasizing individual achievement and providing a variety of literacy-related tasks.

Reggio Emilia
A famous program of early childhood education that originated in the town of Reggio Emilia, Italy; it encourages each child's creativity in a carefully designed setting.

REGGIO EMILIA Another form of early-childhood education is **Reggio Emilia,** named after the town in Italy where it began. In Reggio Emilia schools, children are encouraged to master skills that are not usually taught in North American schools until age 7 or so, such as writing and using tools (hammers, knives, and so on).

In Reggio schools, there is no large-group instruction, with lessons in, say, forming letters or cutting paper. Instead, the belief is that every child is creative and full of potential (Gandini et al., 2005), with personal learning needs and artistic drive. Measurement of achievements, such as testing to see whether children have learned their letters, is not part of the core belief that each child should explore and learn in his or her own way (Lewin-Benham, 2008).

Appreciation of the arts is evident. Every Reggio Emilia school has a studio and an artist, as well as physical space, to encourage creativity. Reggio Emilia schools have a large central room with many hubs of activity and a low child/adult ratio. Children's art is displayed on white walls and hung from high ceilings, and floor-to-ceiling windows open to a spacious, plant-filled playground. Big mirrors are part of the school's decor—again, with the idea

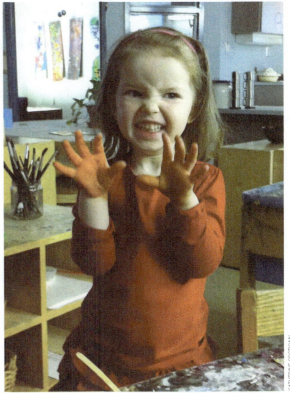

Encouraging Creativity How can Claire Costigan, a 3-year-old from British Columbia, seem so pleased that her hands are orange? The answer lies in her daycare, which promotes creativity and play.

of fostering individuality and expression. The curious little scientist is encouraged with materials to explore. The Reggio Emilia inspiration has been adopted in many schools across Canada.

Teacher-Directed Programs

Unlike child-centred programs, teacher-directed preschools stress academics, often taught by one adult to the entire group. The curriculum includes learning the names of letters, numbers, shapes, and colours according to a set timetable; every child naps, snacks, and goes to the bathroom on schedule as well. Children learn to sit quietly and listen to the teacher. Praise and other reinforcements are given for good behaviour, and time outs (brief separation from activities) are imposed to punish misbehaviour.

In teacher-directed programs, the serious work of schooling is distinguished from the unstructured play of home (Lara-Cinisomo et al., 2011). Many teacher-directed programs were inspired by behaviourism, which emphasizes step-by-step learning and repetition, with reinforcement (praise, gold stars, prizes) for accomplishment. Another inspiration for teacher-directed programs comes from research finding that children who have not learned basic vocabulary and listening skills by kindergarten often fall behind in primary school. In Canada, many provincial and territorial ministries of education mandate that preschoolers learn particular concepts, an outcome best achieved by teacher-directed learning (Bracken & Crawford, 2010).

Support for the importance of learning basic skills early on comes from a study by Elisa Romano from the University of Ottawa and her colleagues. They examined the long-term effects of school readiness using two Canadian surveys, the National Longitudinal Survey of Children and Youth (NLSCY) and the Montreal Longitudinal Experimental Preschool Study (MLEPS). In their first study with the NLSCY, they examined data on 1521 children in kindergarten and compared math and reading outcomes for these same children three years later. Findings revealed that kindergarten math, reading, and attention skills were significantly predictive of Grade 3 math and reading achievement. The researchers also discovered that some socioemotional behaviours such as hyperactivity/impulsivity, prosocial behaviour, and anxiety/depression were also significant predictors of Grade 3 math and reading outcomes (Romano et al., 2010).

Head Start
The most widespread early-childhood education program in the United States, begun in 1965 and funded by the federal government.

HEAD START Since 1965, millions of young children in the United States have received a "head start" on their formal education to help foster better health and cognition before Grade 1. The federal government funds a massive program for 4-year-olds called **Head Start.**

The goals for Head Start have changed over the decades, from lifting families out of poverty to promoting literacy, from providing dental care and immunizations to teaching standard English. Although initially most Head Start programs were child-centred, they have become increasingly teacher-directed as waves of legislators have approved and shaped them. Children have benefitted, learning whatever is stressed by their program. For example, many low-income 3- and 4-year-olds in the United States are not normally exposed to math. When a Head Start program engaged children in a board game with numbers, their mathematical understanding advanced significantly (Siegler, 2009).

Like the United States, Canadian provinces and territories have developed their own comprehensive school preparation programs for low-income families. No standard or unified legislation exists for these programs. However, in 1995, the Canadian government established the Aboriginal Head Start program, which was designed to aid the children of First Nations, Inuit, and Métis families living in urban centres or large northern communities by preparing them for school.

Modelled on the American system, the Aboriginal Head Start programs are also community based. They involve preschool children (younger than 6 years old) in various activities that are built around six key components:

- culture and language
- education
- health promotion
- nutrition
- social support
- parental involvement.

This last component is particularly important. Programs are designed to help parents strengthen the type of parenting skills and family relationships that will contribute to their children's overall healthy development. Some programs require parents to participate at least 10 hours a month, but many sites report that parents often devote more than the required 10 hours to their Head Start activities (Williams, n.d.).

There is no systematic, pre-set curriculum for the children, but rather a more culturally meaningful program that supports the Aboriginal culture and language. Children may learn how to identify the days of the week, numbers, and colours, all in their native language, and may do so with the help of drummers, traditional storytellers, and Elders who drop by to share with them the traditional teachings of their people. In this way, the Aboriginal programs strive to instill children with a sense of pride in their identity, a desire to learn, and increased confidence. As Mindy Sinclair, an early childhood education coordinator with the Peguis First Nation noted, "If the children understand their culture, then they understand themselves" (Health Canada, 2010).

AP / GETTY IMAGES

Learning from One Another Every nation creates its own version of early education. In this scene at a nursery school in Kuala Lampur, Malaysia, the students work together to learn a new game.

OBSERVATION QUIZ

What seemingly universal aspects of childhood are visible in this photograph? (see answer, page 206) →

✦ **ESPECIALLY FOR Teachers** What should parents look for when trying to find a preschool program? (see response, page 207) →

RON BULL / TORONTO STAR VIA GETTY IMAGES

First Nations School Students and teachers participate in a big circle of story-telling and playing music at the First Nations School in Toronto, Ontario. The Toronto District School Board recognizes the school as a Cultural Survival School, offering programs for students in kindergarten to Grade 8. Aboriginal values, spirituality, culture, and language are integrated into the school curriculum.

THE NEED FOR STRUCTURE IN CLASSROOMS Many developmentalists resist legislative prescriptions regarding what 3- and 4-year-olds should learn. Some teachers want to do whatever they believe is best, resulting in a variety of strategies. However, this may confuse children and parents. Differences may reflect culture, not what is best for children or what is consistent based on theory and research.

This was apparent in a detailed study in the Netherlands, where native-born Dutch teachers emphasized individual achievement (child-centred) more than did the teachers from the Caribbean or Mediterranean, who stressed proper behaviour and group learning (teacher-directed) (Huijbregts et al., 2009). Teachers of either background who had worked together for years shared more beliefs and practices than new teachers did (Huijbregts et al., 2009). Hopefully, they had learned from one another.

As many studies have shown, children can learn whatever academic and social skills they are taught. Those who attended preschool are usually advanced in cognitive skills because those skills are taught (Camilli et al., 2010; Chambers et al., 2010). No matter what the curriculum, all young children need personal attention, consistency, and continuity. This is one of many reasons that parents and teachers should communicate and cooperate in teaching young children, a strategy Head Start has emphasized from the early days.

Long-Term Gains from Intensive Early Childhood Programs

This discussion of various programs with fluctuating philosophies, practices, and child participation may give the impression that the research is mixed. That is the wrong impression. It is true that specifics are debatable, but empirical evidence and longitudinal evaluation has convinced most developmentalists that preschool education has many benefits if it is sufficiently intensive and employs effective teachers.

The evidence comes from three intensive programs that enrolled children full-time for years, sometimes beginning with home visits in infancy, sometimes continuing in after-school programs through Grade 1. One program, called Perry (or High/Scope), was developed in Michigan (Schweinhart & Weikart, 1997); another, called Abecedarian, got its start in North Carolina (Campbell et al., 2001); a third, called Child–Parent Centers, began in Chicago (Reynolds, 2000).

All three programs compared experimental groups of children with matched control groups, and all reached the same conclusion: Early intensive education can have substantial long-term benefits that become most apparent when the children are in Grade 3 or later. Children in these three programs scored higher on math and reading achievement tests at age 10 than did other children from the same backgrounds, schools, and neighbourhoods. They were also less likely to be placed in special education classes or to repeat a year of school compared with other children from the same neighbourhoods.

Further, in adolescence, the children who had undergone intensive preschool education had higher aspirations, possessed a greater sense of achievement, and were less likely to have been abused. As young adults they were more likely to attend college and less likely to go to jail, more often paying taxes rather than being on welfare (Reynolds & Ou, 2011; Schweinhart et al., 2005). Early education affected every aspect of their adult lives, as "early cognitive and scholastic advantages lead to social and motivational gains that culminate in enhanced well-being" (Reynolds & Ou, 2011, p. 578) (see Figure 5.8).

All three research projects found that providing direct cognitive training (rather than simply letting children play), with specific instruction in various school-readiness skills, was useful as long as each child's needs and talents were considered—a circumstance made possible because the child/adult ratio was low. The curricular approach was a combination of child-centred and teacher-directed. Teachers were

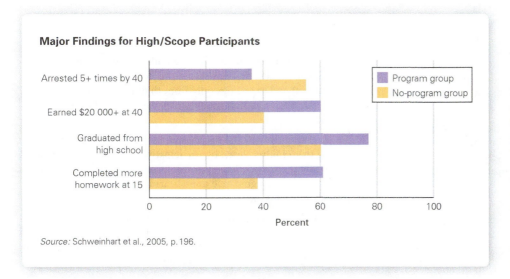

Major Findings for High/Scope Participants

Source: Schweinhart et al., 2005, p.196.

FIGURE 5.8 **And in Middle Age**
Longitudinal research found that two years in the intensive High/Scope preschool program changed the lives of dozens of children from impoverished families. The program had a positive impact on many aspects of their education, early adulthood, and middle age. (This graph does not illustrate another intriguing finding: The girls who attended High/Scope fared much better than the boys.)

encouraged to involve parents in their child's education, and each program included strategies to ensure this home–school connection.

These programs were expensive (ranging from $5000 to $17 000 annually per child in 2010 dollars). From a developmental perspective, the decreased need for special education and other social services eventually made such programs a wise investment, perhaps saving $4 for every dollar spent (Barnett, 2007). The benefits to society over the child's lifetime, including increased employment and reduced crime, are much more than that.

In fact, the greatest lifetime return came from boys from high-poverty neighbourhoods in the Chicago preschool program, with a social benefit over the boys' lifetime more than 12 times the cost (Reynolds et al., 2011). The problem is that the costs are immediate and the benefits long term; without a developmental perspective, some legislators and voters are unwilling to fund expensive intervention programs that do not pay off until a decade or more later.

In conclusion, we know much more today than in the past about what children can learn, and there is no doubt that 2- and 3-year-olds are capable of learning languages, concepts, and much else. A hundred years ago, that was not understood, and Piaget was considered a leader in recognizing the abilities of the child. Now Piaget's thinking has been eclipsed by new research: What a child learns before age 6 is pivotal for later schooling and adult life.

This theme continues in the next chapter, on the interaction between children and all the systems that surround them.

RESPONSE FOR Teachers (from page 205) Suggest that parents look at the people more than the program. Advise parents to look at the teacher–student ratio, the physical space, and the engagement of students. ●

KEY Points

- Young children can learn a great deal before kindergarten, either in a child-centred or teacher-directed preschool, or in an excellent home setting.

- Montessori and Reggio Emilia schools advance children's learning. Both emphasize individual accomplishments and child development.

- Teacher-directed programs stress readiness for school, emphasizing letters and numbers that all children should understand.

- Head Start and other programs advance learning for low-income children. Longitudinal research finds that some of the benefits are evident in adulthood.

SUMMARY

Body Changes

1. Children continue to gain weight and add height during early childhood. Many adults overfeed children, not realizing that young children are naturally quite thin.

2. Many young children consume too much sugar and too little calcium and other nutrients. One consequence is poor oral health. Children need to brush their teeth and visit the dentist years before their permanent teeth erupt.

3. Gross motor skills continue to develop; clumsy 2-year-olds become agile 6-year-olds who move their bodies well, guided by their culture. By playing with other children in safe places, they practise the skills needed for formal education.

4. Unintentional injuries cause more preventable deaths than diseases do. Young children are more likely to suffer a serious injury or premature death than are older children. Close supervision and public safeguards can protect young children from their own eager, impulsive curiosity. Pollutants hamper development, with lead proven to impair the brain and motor skills.

5. Injury control occurs on many levels, including long before and immediately after each harmful incident. Primary prevention protects everyone. Secondary and tertiary prevention also save lives.

Brain Development

6. The brain continues to grow in early childhood, reaching 75 percent of its adult weight at age 2 and 90 percent by age 5. Lateralization becomes evident.

7. Myelination is substantial during early childhood, speeding messages from one part of the brain to another. The corpus callosum becomes thicker and functions much better. Maturation of the prefrontal cortex, known as the executive of the brain, reduces both impulsivity and perseveration.

8. The expression and regulation of emotions are fostered by several brain areas collectively called the limbic system, including the amygdala, the hippocampus, and the hypothalamus.

Thinking During Early Childhood

9. Piaget stressed the egocentric and illogical aspects of thought during the play years; he called thinking at this stage preoperational because young children often cannot yet use logical operations. They sometimes focus on only one thing (centration) and see things only from their own viewpoint (egocentrism), remaining stuck on appearances and current reality.

10. Vygotsky stressed the social aspects of childhood cognition, noting that children learn by participating in various experiences, guided by more knowledgeable adults or peers who scaffold to aid learning. Such guidance assists learning within the zone of proximal development.

11. Children develop theories to explain human behaviour. One theory about children's thinking is called theory-theory—the hypothesis that children develop theories because people innately seek explanations for everything they observe.

12. In early childhood, children develop a theory of mind—an understanding of what others may be thinking. Notable advances in theory of mind occur at around age 4. Theory of mind is partly the result of brain maturation, but culture and experiences also have an impact.

Language Learning

13. Language develops rapidly during early childhood, a sensitive period but not a critical one for language learning. Vocabulary increases dramatically, with thousands of words added between ages 2 and 6. In addition, basic grammar is mastered.

14. Many children learn to speak more than one language, gaining cognitive as well as social advantages. Ideally, children become balanced bilinguals, equally proficient in two languages, by age 6.

Early Childhood Education

15. Organized educational programs during early childhood advance cognitive and social skills. Many child-centred programs are inspired by Piaget and Vygotsky. Behaviourist principles led to many specific practices of teacher-directed programs.

16. Many types of preschool programs are successful. It is the quality of early education—whether at home or at school—that matters.

KEY TERMS

amygdala (p. 188)
animism (p. 189)
balanced bilingual (p. 201)
centration (p. 190)
conservation (p. 190)
corpus callosum (p. 186)
egocentrism (p. 190)
fast-mapping (p. 197)
focus on appearance (p. 190)

Head Start (p. 204)
hippocampus (p. 188)
hypothalamus (p. 188)
injury control (or harm reduction) (p. 181)
irreversibility (p. 190)
just right (p. 179)
lateralization (p. 187)
limbic system (p. 188)

Montessori schools (p. 203)
myelination (p. 185)
overimitation (p. 192)
overregularization (p. 199)
perseveration (p. 186)
preoperational intelligence (p. 189)
primary prevention (p. 181)
Reggio Emilia (p. 203)

scaffolding (p. 192)
secondary prevention (p. 182)
static reasoning (p. 190)
symbolic thought (p. 189)
tertiary prevention (p. 182)
theory of mind (p. 194)
theory-theory (p. 193)
zone of proximal development (ZPD) (p. 192)

WHAT HAVE YOU LEARNED?

1. How are growth rates, body proportions, and motor skills related during early childhood?

2. Why might lower-income children be more vulnerable to nutritional problems?

3. What factors help children develop their motor skills?

4. Why do public health workers prefer to speak of "injury control" rather than "accident prevention"?

5. What are the six recommendations to reduce the number of deaths among Aboriginal children?

6. What are the differences among the three levels of harm reduction?

7. What changes in the brain's functioning are evident between ages 2 and 6 years?

8. Why is myelination important for thinking and motor skills?

9. How does the prefrontal cortex affect impulsivity and perseveration?

10. What is the function of the corpus callosum?

11. Why might left-handed children have thicker corpus callosa than right-handed children?

12. What role do the amygdala, hippocampus, and hypothalamus play in the expression and regulation of emotions?

13. In what way does symbolic thought advance cognition?

14. What barriers to logic exist at the preoperational stage? How might these affect children's thinking?

15. According to Vygotsky, what should parents and other caregivers do to encourage children's learning?

16. How does scaffolding increase a child's zone of proximal development?

17. What does the idea of theory-theory suggest about how children think?

18. What factors spur the development of theory of mind?

APPLICATIONS

1. Keep a food diary for 24 hours, writing down what you eat, how much, when, how, and why. Then think about nutrition and eating habits in early childhood. Did your food habits originate in early childhood, in adolescence, or at some other time? Explain.

2. Obtain permission and then observe young children play. Note the motor skills that the children demonstrate, including abilities and inabilities, and keep track of age and sex. What differences do you see among the children?

3. Replicate one of Piaget's conservation experiments. The easiest one is conservation of liquids (illustrated in Figure 5.5). Work with a child under age 5 who tells you that two identically shaped glasses contain the same amount of liquid. Then carefully pour one glass of liquid into a taller, narrower glass. Ask the child which glass now contains more or if the glasses contain the same amount.

>>ONLINE CONNECTIONS

To accompany your textbook, you have access to a number of online resources, including LearningCurve, which is an adaptive quizzing program; critical thinking questions; and case studies. For access to any of these links, go to www.worthpublishers.com/launchpad/bergerchuang1e. In addition to these resources, you'll find links to video clips, personalized study advice, and an e-Book. Among the videos and activities available online are the following:

- *Brain Development in Early Childhood.* Animations illustrate the macroscopic and microscopic changes as children's brains grow.

- *Stolen Childhoods.* Some children, because of poverty or abuse, never have the opportunities for schooling and nurture that many of us take for granted. Children in a variety of difficult circumstances, from sex workers to workers in carpet factories, tell their stories in a variety of video clips.

CHAPTER OUTLINE

EARLY CHILDHOOD:
Psychosocial Development

WHAT WILL YOU KNOW?

- Why do 2-year-olds have more sudden tempers, tears, and terrors than 6-year-olds?
- How important is play in a child's development?
- Is it better for parents to be strict disciplinarians or to let children do whatever they want?
- How do children know the difference between right and wrong?
- Do maltreated children always become abusive adults?

I t was a hot summer afternoon. My thirsty 3- and 4-year-olds were with me in the kitchen, which was in one corner of our living/dining area. The younger one opened the refrigerator and grabbed a bottle of orange juice. The sticky bottle slipped, shattering on the floor. My stunned daughters looked at me, at the shards, at the spreading juice with extra pulp. I picked them up and plopped them on the couch.

"Stay there until I clean this up," I shouted.

They did, wide-eyed at my fury. As they watched me pick, sweep, and mop, I understood how parents could hit their kids. By the end of this chapter, I hope you also realize how a moment like this—in the summer heat, with two small children, and unexpected and difficult work—can turn a loving, patient parent into something else. It is not easy, day after day, being the guide and model that parents should be. ●

—Kathleen Berger

FORTUNATELY, IN SUCH TRYING CIRCUMSTANCES, a number of safeguards prevent serious maltreatment (a belief children should not be hit, an understanding that accidents do happen) and keep parents from taking their frustrations out on their children. Many aspects of psychosocial development—as children learn to manage their emotions, as parents learn to guide their children, as the microcosm (beliefs) and macrocosm (household income) influence adult–child interaction—affect how well children develop from ages 2 to 6. This chapter describes all that.

Emotional Development

Children gradually become more capable in every aspect of their lives, including learning when and how to express emotions (Buckley & Saarni, 2009; Denham et al., 2003; Morrison et al., 2010). Controlling the expression of emotions, called **emotional regulation,** is the pre-eminent psychosocial accomplishment between ages 2 and 6 (Eisenberg et al., 2004).

Such regulation is very difficult in infancy, but when the emotional hot spots of the limbic system connect to the maturing prefrontal cortex, children become more aware of their reactions and better able to control them. Emotional regulation is a lifelong necessity and no one does it perfectly all the time.

Initiative Versus Guilt

During Erikson's third developmental stage, **initiative versus guilt,** children acquire many skills and competencies. *Initiative* can mean several things, such as saying something new, extending an ability, or beginning a project. Depending on the outcome (especially reactions from other people), children feel proud or guilty.

Usually, North American parents encourage enthusiasm, effort, and pride in their 3- to 6-year-olds. When parents criticize and hinder children from exploring their environment, children may become dependent, lack initiative, and fail to learn emotional regulation (Morris et al., 2007).

PROTECTIVE OPTIMISM Children's beliefs about their worth are connected to parental confirmation, especially when parents remind their children of their positive accomplishments ("You helped Daddy sweep the sidewalk? You made it very clean.") (Reese et al., 2007). Remember that Erikson described *autonomy* at age 2, often expressed as stubbornness, and nicknamed the terrible twos. By age 3, autonomy is better regulated, soon becoming initiative, as children are eager to learn new skills (Rubin et al., 2009).

Over the next several months, children develop a **self-concept,** which is the cognitive ability to understand that they are separate from others. For example, young children are given choices: "Water or juice?" "Blue pyjamas or red ones?" The act of choosing makes children believe they are independent agents (Kim & Chu, 2011). In North America, self-concept quickly includes gender and size. Girls are usually happy to be girls, and boys to be boys; both are glad they aren't babies. "Crybaby" is an insult, while praise for being "a big kid" is welcomed.

Erikson recognized that young children are not accurate in their assessment of themselves. They believe that they are strong, smart, and good-looking—and thus that any goal is achievable. Whatever they are (self-concept) is thought to be good. For instance, young children may believe that their school is the best and they feel sorry for children who go to a different school.

At this age, a positivity bias encourages children to try unfamiliar activities, make friends, begin school, and so on (Boseovski, 2010). They learn to pour juice, zip pants, or climb trees, undeterred by overflowing glasses, stuck zippers, or a perch too high. Faith in themselves helps them persist.

BRAIN MATURATION The new initiative that Erikson describes benefits from myelination of the limbic system, growth of the prefrontal cortex, and a longer attention span, all made possible by the neurological maturation described in Chapter 5. Emotional and cognitive maturation develop together, each enabling the other to advance (Bell & Calkins, 2012).

Normally, neurological advances in the prefrontal cortex at about age 4 or 5 make children less likely to throw a temper tantrum, engage in a physical attack,

emotional regulation
The ability to control when and how emotions are expressed.

initiative versus guilt
Erikson's third psychosocial crisis, in which children undertake new skills and activities and feel guilty when they do not succeed at them.

✦ **ESPECIALLY FOR Teachers** One of your students tells you about playing, sleeping, and talking with an imaginary friend. Does this mean that the child is emotionally disturbed? (see response, page 214) →

self-concept
A person's understanding of who he or she is, incorporating self-esteem, physical appearance, personality, and various personal traits, such as gender and size.

A Young Poet This girl is the winner of a national poetry contest. How might that affect her self-concept?

ENIGMA / ALAMY

or burst into giggles (Kagan & Herschkowitz, 2005). Throughout early childhood, behaviours such as violent outbursts, uncontrolled crying, and terrifying phobias (irrational, crippling fears) diminish. The capacity for self-control—such as not opening a present immediately if asked to wait and not expressing disappointment at an undesirable gift—becomes more evident (Carlson, 2003; Grolnick et al., 2006).

In one study, researchers asked children to wait 8 minutes while their mothers did some paperwork before opening a wrapped present that was in front of them (Cole et al., 2011). The children used strategies such as distractions and private speech. Keisha was one of the study participants:

> "Are you done, Mom?" … "I wonder what's in it"… "Can I open it now?" Each time her mother reminds Keisha to wait, eventually adding, "If you keep interrupting me, I can't finish and if I don't finish …" Keisha plops in her chair, frustrated. "I really want it," she laments, aloud but to herself. "I want to talk to Mommy so I won't open it. If I talk, Mommy won't finish. If she doesn't finish, I can't have it." She sighs deeply, folds her arms, and scans the room. … the research assistant returns. Keisha looks at her mother with excited anticipation. Her mother says, "OK, now." Keisha tears open the gift.
>
> [Cole et al., 2011, p. 59]

Ukrainian Pride All ethnic groups celebrate and have pride in their culture. This 9-year-old girl from Lethbridge, Alberta, proudly wears the clothing of her Ukrainian heritage as she celebrates mass at Saint Volodymyr Ukrainian Catholic Church.

Motivation

Motivation (the impulse that propels someone to act) comes either from a person's own desires or from the social context. **Intrinsic motivation** occurs when people do something for the joy of doing it: A musician might enjoy making music, even when no one else hears. Thinking back to your own childhood, did you have a hobby you loved, one that your parents didn't have to force you to pursue? That's another example of intrinsic motivation. **Extrinsic motivation** comes from outside the person, when people do something to gain praise (or some other reinforcement), such as a musician playing for applause or money.

Encouraging intrinsic motivation is crucial in teaching young children (Cheng & Yeh, 2009). Preschool children are often intrinsically motivated. They wake up eager to start playing and practising, whether or not someone else wants them to. Praise and prizes might be appreciated, but that's not why children work at what they do. When playing a game, they might not keep score; the fun is in the activity (intrinsic), not the winning.

It is only when others impose an external reward, for example by making the game competitive with prizes and trophies to be won, that children who were initially intrinsically motivated become extrinsically motivated. With extrinsic motivation, children often lose their pure love for the game. Personal joy and interest are soon replaced by a desire for the rewards.

intrinsic motivation
A drive, or reason to pursue a goal, that comes from inside a person, such as the need to feel smart or competent.

extrinsic motivation
A drive, or reason to pursue a goal, that arises from the need to have one's achievements rewarded from outside, perhaps by receiving material possessions or another person's esteem.

AN EXPERIMENT IN MOTIVATION In a classic experiment, preschool children were given markers and paper and assigned to one of three groups that received, respectively: (1) no award, (2) an expected award (they were told *before* they had drawn anything that they would get a certificate), and (3) an unexpected award (*after* they had drawn something, they were told, "You were a big help," and got a certificate) (Lepper et al., 1973).

✦ **ESPECIALLY FOR College and University Students** Is extrinsic or intrinsic motivation more influential in your study efforts? (see response, page 216) →

RESPONSE FOR Teachers (from page 212) No, unless the student is over age 10. In fact, imaginary friends are quite common, especially among creative children. The child may be somewhat lonely, though; you could help him or her find a friend. ●

Later, observers noted how often children in each group chose to draw when they were no longer part of a group. Those who received the expected award were less likely to draw than those who were unexpectedly rewarded. The interpretation was that extrinsic motivation (condition 2) undercut intrinsic motivation.

This research triggered a flood of studies seeking to understand whether, when, and how positive reinforcement should be given. The consensus is that praising or paying a person after an accomplishment sometimes encourages that behaviour. However, if payment is promised in advance, that extrinsic reinforcement may backfire (Cameron & Pierce, 2002; Deci et al., 1999; Gottfried et al., 2009).

Praise is effective if connected to the particular production, not to a general trait ("you did a good drawing," not "you are a great artist"), because then the child believes that effort paid off, which motivates a repeat performance (Zentall & Morris, 2010).

Same Situation, Far Apart: Overwhelming Emotions The days of early childhood are filled with terrors and tantrums because children have not yet learned how to use their words and logic to control their world. The result is futile protest: The North American mother *(top)* is not about to give her daughter what she wants, and this Japanese big brother (age 4, *bottom*) watches his sister's reaction after he moves the book away from her. Both children are likely to keep crying.

Culture and Emotional Control

Although there is considerable variation within, as well as among, cultures, national emphases on regulating emotions seem to include the following (Chen, 2011; Harkness et al., 2011; Miller, 2004; Stubben, 2001):

- fear (United States)
- anger (Puerto Rico)
- pride (China)
- selfishness (Japan)
- impatience (many Native American communities)
- disobedience (Mexico)
- erratic moods (the Netherlands).

Control strategies vary as well (Matsumoto, 2004). Peers, parents, and strangers sometimes ignore emotional outbursts, sometimes deflect them, sometimes punish them, and so forth. Shame is used when social reputation is a priority. Indeed, in some cultures, "pride goeth before a fall" and people who "have no shame" are considered mentally ill (Stein, 2006).

Cultural differences are also apparent in emotional expression: Children may be encouraged to laugh, cry, and yell, or to hide their emotions (Kim et al., 2008). Some adults guffaw, slap their knees, and stomp their feet for joy; others cover their mouths with their hands if a smile spontaneously appears. Children learn to do the same.

Finally, temperaments vary, which makes people within the same culture unlike one another: "Cultures are inevitably more complicated than the framework that is supposed to explain them" (Harkness et al., 2011, p. 92). Nonetheless, parents everywhere teach emotional regulation as their context expects. Unfortunately, children of parents who suffer from mental illness such as depression, bipolar disorder, or schizophrenia are less able to regulate their emotions (Kovacs et al., 2008).

A VIEW FROM SCIENCE

Sex Differences in Emotional Regulation

Biologically, the differences between males and females are minor, at least until puberty. Only one gene (SRY) on one of the 46 chromosomes (the Y) causes the difference in genitals. Most aspects of physical and cognitive growth are the same for all children. When differences appear, they are in averages, not absolutes. For example, girls average slightly more body fat than boys, but many boys weigh more than the average girl.

This overlapping of characteristics is one of two crucial points that scientists stress when they consider sex differences. Beyond anatomy, it is never true that all the boys have one trait and none of the girls do, or vice versa. The sexes overlap; they are not opposites.

The second crucial point is that both nature and nurture are connected to every difference that is found between boys and girls. For instance, even the fact that girls have more body fat than boys may seem to be nature, but among poor families in India, girls have less fat than boys, on average. The reason is cultural: When food is scarce, boys are better fed.

Now to emotional regulation. On average, young girls are advanced in controlling their emotions, particularly anger, compared with boys. One study traced externalizing and internalizing emotions from early to middle childhood. Researchers gave 5-year-olds two toy figures, told them the beginning of a hypothetical story about two children interacting with each other, and then had the children enact the scene with the toys (Zahn-Waxler et al., 2008). For example, the children were told that the two toy children (named Mark and Scott for the boys, Mary and Sarah for the girls) started yelling at each other. The 5-year-olds were asked to show what happened next.

Many boys showed Mark and Scott hitting and kicking. Boys whose externalizing behaviour worsened between ages 5 and 9 (as rated by teachers and parents) were the most likely to dramatize such attacks at age 5. By contrast, 5-year-old girls often had Mary and Sarah discuss the conflict or change the subject. Curiously, those 5-year-old girls who had Mary and Sarah engage in "reparative behaviour" (repairing the relationship, such as having Mary hug Sarah and say, "I'm sorry") were more likely to be disruptive at age 8 than the other girls were. Their quickness to repair the conflict may have signalled too much guilt or shame, which would sometimes erupt later on.

The authors of the study wrote:

> Gender-role stereotypes or exaggerations of masculine qualities (e.g., impulsive, aggressive, uncaring) and feminine qualities (submissive, unassertive, socially sensitive) are reflected not only in the types of problems males and females tend to develop but also in different forms of expression.

> [Zahn-Waxler et al., 2008, p. 114]

These researchers suggest that extreme externalization or extreme internalization predict future psychopathology. Because of gender differences, mistreated boys are likely to externalize and mistreated girls to internalize. By age 5, without emotional regulation, maltreated boys throw and hit, and maltreated girls sob uncontrollably or hide.

Later you will read that men are more likely to become antisocial or schizophrenic, while women are more likely to be overwhelmed by anxiety or depression. Perhaps as a result, females have more suicide attempts, but males more often kill themselves—typically without the warnings that suicidal females often provide. Is that culture or hormones?

In the study of 5-year-olds, above, why didn't more boys have Mark and Scott discuss their conflict? Does emotional regulation appear more quickly in young girls because their parents teach them to restrain their impulse to hit? Or does the prenatal testosterone in those boys' brains make them more violent at age 5?

Cute or Shy? Girls and women are often expected to be reticent. They cling more to their mothers in kindergarten, they wait to be asked to dance or date, and they talk less in co-ed groups. Are these cultural differences or genetic differences?

psychopathology
An illness or disorder of the mind.

externalizing problems
Difficulty with emotional regulation that involves expressing powerful feelings through uncontrolled physical or verbal outbursts, as by lashing out at other people or breaking things.

internalizing problems
Difficulty with emotional regulation that involves turning one's emotional distress inward, by feeling excessively guilty, ashamed, or worthless.

RESPONSE FOR College and University Students (from page 213) Each is important. Extrinsic motivation includes parental pressure and the need to get a good job after graduation. Intrinsic motivation includes the joy of learning. Have you ever taken a course that was not required and was said to be difficult? That was intrinsic motivation. ●

Seeking Emotional Balance

At every age, in all cultures, caregivers try to prevent **psychopathology,** an illness or disorder (*-pathology*) of the mind (*psycho-*). Although symptoms and diagnoses are influenced by culture—rebellion is expected in some cultures and considered pathological in others—impaired emotional regulation universally signals mental imbalance. Parents guide young children toward "an optimal balance" between emotional expression and emotional control (Blair & Dennis, 2010; Trommsdorff & Cole, 2011).

EXTERNALIZING AND INTERNALIZING PROBLEMS Without adequate regulation, emotions can be overwhelming. Intense reactions occur in two opposite ways, as you might expect from the activate–inhibit nature of neurons.

Some people have **externalizing problems:** Their powerful feelings burst out uncontrollably. They externalize rage, for example, by lashing out or breaking things. Without emotional regulation, an angry child might flail at another person or lie down screaming and kicking. By age 5, children usually have learned more self-control, perhaps pouting, but not hitting and screaming.

Other people have **internalizing problems:** They are fearful and withdrawn, turning distress inward. Emotions may be internalized via headaches or stomach aches. Although the cause is psychological, the ache is real.

Again, with maturity, the extreme fears of some 2-year-olds (e.g., terror of the bathtub drain or of a stranger on crutches) diminish. The fear isn't gone, but expression is better regulated: A child may be afraid of kindergarten, for instance, but bravely lets go of mother's or father's hand anyway.

KEY Points

- Emotional regulation is the crucial psychosocial task in early childhood.
- Erikson thought young children are naturally motivated to take initiative, with joy at new tasks, yet vulnerable to feeling guilty.
- Brain maturation and family guidance help children regulate their emotions, avoiding either extreme externalizing or internalizing reactions in a culturally appropriate way.
- Young girls are less aggressive and more advanced in controlling their emotions, but virtually all sex differences are in averages, not absolutes.
- Controlling emotions is influenced by both genetics and culture. Difficulties in controlling emotions can lead to externalizing and internalizing problems.

Gender Development

Biology determines whether a child is male or female. As you remember from Chapter 2, at about 8 weeks after conception, the SRY gene on the Y chromosome directs the reproductive organs to develop externally, and then male hormones exert subtle internal control over the brain, body, and later behaviour. Without that SRY gene, the fetus develops female organs, which produce other hormones that affect the brain and behaviour.

It is possible for sex hormones to be unexpressed prenatally, in which case the child does not develop like the typical boy or girl (Hines, 2010). However, that is very rare. Most children are male or female in all three ways: chromosomes, genitals, and hormones. That is their nature, but obviously nurture affects their sexual development from birth until death.

During early childhood, sex patterns and preferences become important to children and apparent to adults. At age 2, children consistently apply gender labels (*Ms.,* *Mr., boy, girl*). By age 4, children are convinced that certain toys (such as dolls or trucks) and roles (not just Daddy or Mommy, but also nurse, teacher, police officer, and soldier) are best for one sex or the other. Dynamic systems theory helps us realize that such preferences are affected by many developmental aspects of biology and culture, changing as humans grow older (Martin & Ruble, 2010).

Sex and Gender

Scientists distinguish **sex differences,** which are biological differences between males and females, from **gender differences,** which are culturally prescribed roles and behaviours. In theory, this seems straightforward, but as with every nature–nurture distinction, the interaction between sex and gender makes it difficult to tease the two apart (Hines, 2004).

Many studies in different countries, including Kenya, Nepal, Belize, and Samoa, have found that children undergo three stages in understanding gender (Munroe et al., 1984). The first stage is reached in the first year of life. During this first year, infants can make gender distinctions, correctly labelling themselves as a boy or girl, as well as labelling the gender of others. This first step is called **gender identity.**

But, being able to identify one's gender does not mean that toddlers have a full understanding of gender. For example, one little girl said she would grow a penis when she got older, and one little boy offered to buy his mother one. Ignorance about biology was demonstrated by a 3-year-old who went with his father to see a neighbour's newborn kittens. Returning home, the child told his mother that there were three girl kittens and two boy kittens. "How do you know?" she asked. "Daddy picked them up and read what was written on their tummies," he replied.

At about age 4, children reach the next step, **gender stability.** At this stage, children believe that a person will stay the same gender over his or her lifetime (Slaby & Frey, 1975). However, children at this age do not understand that gender is independent of physical appearance, such as type of clothing or haircut. They think that a girl who looks like a boy has become a boy, and vice versa.

sex differences
Biological differences between males and females, in organs, hormones, and body shape.

gender differences
Differences in the roles and behaviours that are prescribed by a culture for males and females.

gender identity (early childhood)
The ability of children to make gender distinctions by accurately labelling themselves as a boy or girl.

gender stability
The ability of children to understand that their gender is stable over time and will not change.

At the Beach What do you do at the beach? It may depend on gender. Girls may be more likely to run along the beach holding hands, while boys may be more likely to dig in the sand using construction tools.

When children truly believe that gender cannot change, regardless of outward appearances, they have reached the final stage, **gender constancy.** This occurs around the age of 5 or 6, similar to when children also have an understanding of conservation.

Theories of Gender Development

In recent years, sex and gender issues have become increasingly complex. Individuals may be lesbian, gay, bisexual, transsexual, mostly straight, or totally heterosexual (Thompson & Morgan, 2008). But around age 5 many children are quite rigid in their ideas of male and female. Already by age 3, most boys reject pink toys and most girls prefer them (LoBue & DeLoache, 2011). In early childhood programs, girls tend to play with girls, and boys with boys. Despite their parents' and teachers' wishes, children say, "No girls [or boys] allowed."

A dynamic systems approach reminds us that attitudes, roles, and even the biology of gender differences and similarities change from one developmental period to the next; theories about how and why this occurs change as well (Martin & Ruble, 2010). Nonetheless, it is useful to review the six theories described in Chapter 1 to understand the range of explanations for the apparent sexism of many 5-year-olds.

PSYCHOANALYTIC THEORY Freud (1938) called the period from about ages 3 to 6 the **phallic stage,** named after the phallus, the Greek word for "penis." At about 3 or 4 years of age, said Freud, boys become aware of their male sexual organ. They masturbate, fear castration, and develop sexual feelings toward their mother. This makes every young boy jealous of his father—so jealous, according to Freud, that every son wants to replace his father. Freud called this the **Oedipus complex,** after Oedipus of Greek mythology. Abandoned as an infant and raised in a distant kingdom, Oedipus returned to his birthplace and, without realizing it, killed his father and married his mother. When he discovered the horror, he blinded himself.

Freud believed that this ancient story dramatizes emotions that all boys feel about their parents—both love and hate. Every male feels guilty about his unconscious incestuous and murderous impulses. In self-defence, boys develop a powerful conscience called the **superego,** which is quick to judge and punish. This marks the beginning of morality, according to psychoanalytic theory, which contends that a boy's fascination with superheroes, guns, kung fu, and the like arises from his unconscious impulse to kill his father. According to this theory, adult man's homosexuality, homophobia, or obsession with punishment is explained by an imperfectly resolved phallic stage.

Freud offered several descriptions of the moral development of girls. One centres on the **Electra complex** (also named after a figure in classical mythology). The Electra complex is similar to the Oedipus complex in that the little girl wants to eliminate the same-sex parent (her mother) and become intimate with the opposite-sex parent (her father). That may also lead girls to develop a superego.

According to psychoanalytic theory, at the phallic stage children cope with guilt and fear through **identification;** that is, they try to become like the same-sex parent. Consequently, young boys copy their father's mannerisms, opinions, and actions, and girls copy their mother's. Both sexes exaggerate the male or female role.

Many social scientists from the mid-twentieth century onward believe that Freud's explanation of sexual and moral development "flies in the face of sociological and historical evidence" (David et al., 2004, p. 139). Accordingly, I learned in graduate school that Freud was unscientific. However, as explained in Chapter 1, developmental scientists seek to connect research, theory, and experience. My own experience has made me rethink my rejection of Freud.

gender constancy
The ability of children to understand that gender cannot change, regardless of their outside appearance, such as cutting their hair or wearing a dress.

phallic stage
Freud's third stage of development, when the penis becomes the focus of concern and pleasure.

Oedipus complex
The unconscious desire of young boys to replace their fathers and win their mothers' exclusive love.

superego
In psychoanalytic theory, the judgmental part of the personality that internalizes the moral standards of the parents.

Electra complex
The unconscious desire of girls to replace their mothers and win their fathers' exclusive love.

identification
An attempt to defend one's self concept by taking on the behaviours and attitudes of someone else.

Kathleen's STORY

It began with a conversation with my eldest daughter, Bethany, when she was about 4 years old:

Bethany: When I grow up, I'm going to marry Daddy.
    Me: But Daddy's married to me.
Bethany: That's all right. When I grow up, you'll probably be dead.
    Me: [*Determined to stick up for myself*] Daddy's older than me, so when I'm dead, he'll probably be dead, too.
Bethany: That's OK. I'll marry him when he gets born again.

I was dumbfounded, without a good reply. I had no idea where she had gotten the concept of reincarnation. Bethany saw my face fall, and she took pity on me:

Bethany: Don't worry, Mommy. After you get born again, you can be our baby.

The second episode was a conversation I had with my daughter Rachel when she was about 5:

Rachel: When I get married, I'm going to marry Daddy.
    Me: Daddy's already married to me.
Rachel: [*With the joy of having discovered a wonderful solution*] Then we can have a double wedding!

The third episode took the form of a "valentine" left on my husband's pillow on February 14th by my daughter Elissa (see image). Finally, when my youngest daughter Sarah, turned 5, she also said she would marry my husband. I told her she couldn't, because he was married to me. Her response revealed one more hazard of watching TV: "Oh, yes, a man can have two wives. I saw it on television."

A single example (or four daughters) does not prove that Freud was correct. But his theory may have some merit, as seen in the previous anecdotes.

Pillow Talk Elissa placed this artwork on my husband's pillow. My pillow, beside it, had a less colourful, less elaborate note—an afterthought. It read "Dear Mom, I love you too."

OTHER THEORIES OF SEX-ROLE DEVELOPMENT Although the psychoanalytic theory of early sex-role development is the most elaborate, there are many other theories that explain the young child's sex and gender awareness. We describe here the five other theories first mentioned in Chapter 1.

Learning theory teaches that virtually all roles, values, and behaviours are learned. To behaviourists, gender distinctions are the product of ongoing reinforcement and punishment, as well as social learning. Parents, peers, and teachers tend to reward behaviour that is "gender appropriate" more than behaviour that is "gender inappropriate" (Berenbaum et al., 2008). For example, adults compliment a girl when she wears a dress but not when she wears pants (Ruble et al., 2006), and a boy who asks for a train and a doll for his birthday is more likely to get the train. Boys are rewarded for boyish requests, not for girlish ones.

According to *social learning theory,* children model themselves after people they perceive to be nurturing, powerful, and yet similar to themselves. For young children, those people are usually their parents. As it happens, adults are the most sex-typed of their entire lives when they are raising young children. If ever a working woman is going to leave the labour market to take care of her home and children, it is when her children are infants and preschool age.

Furthermore, although national or provincial/territorial policies (e.g., subsidizing preschool) have an effect on gender roles, and many fathers are involved caregivers, in every nation women do much more child care, housecleaning, and meal preparation than men do (Hook, 2010). Children follow those examples, unaware that the examples they see are caused partly by their very existence: Before children are born, many couples share domestic work.

gender schema
A child's cognitive concept or general belief about sex differences, which is based on his or her observations and experiences.

Cognitive theory offers an alternative explanation for the strong gender identity that becomes apparent at about age 5. Remember that cognitive theorists focus on how children understand various ideas. A **gender schema** is the child's understanding of gender differences in the context of the gender norms and expectations of their culture (Kohlberg et al., 1983; Martin et al., 2011; Renk et al., 2006). Young children have many gender-related experiences but not much cognitive depth. They tend to see the world in simple terms. For this reason, their gender schemas categorize male and female as opposites. Nuances, complexities, exceptions, and gradations about gender (as well as about everything else) are beyond them.

Furthermore, as children try to make sense of their culture, they encounter numerous customs, taboos, and terminologies that enforce gender norms. Remember that for preoperational children, appearance is crucial. When they see men and women cut their hair, use cosmetics, and dress in distinct, gender-typed ways, static preoperational thinking makes them conclude that what they see is permanent and irreversible.

Systems theory teaches that mothers and fathers play an important role in developing their children's understanding of gender. The clothing colours that parents pick for their sons (usually blue) or daughters (usually pink and purple), the toys they buy them, and the activities they teach them provide clues about how to behave. If fathers are more traditional (acting as the primary breadwinner and expecting their wives to take care of the children), they may not do any of the cooking, cleaning, or caregiving. They may also teach their sons to behave in a similar fashion and insist that their daughters help the mother. On the other hand, fathers who share the household chores and caregiving duties with their spouses are more likely to have daughters who are not limited by gender roles in choosing a career.

Humanism stresses the hierarchy of needs, beginning with survival, then safety, then love and belonging. The final two—respect and self-actualization—are not priorities for people until the earlier ones are satisfied. Ideally, babies have all their basic needs met, and toddlers learn to feel safe, which puts preschoolers at the "love and belonging" stage. They seem to strive for admiration from the group of peers they belong to even more than for the love of their parents. Therefore, the girls want to be one of the girls and the boys to be one of the boys.

In a study of slightly older children, participants wanted to be identified as male or female, not because they disliked the other sex, but because same-sex groups satisfied their need to belong (Zosuls et al., 2011). This theory explains cultural differences in the strength of sexism, in that male/female divisions are much more dominant in some places than others. Specifics will vary (boys holding hands with boys is taboo or expected, depending on local customs), but everywhere young children try to belong by conforming to gender norms.

Evolutionary theory holds that sexual attraction is crucial for humankind's most basic urge, to reproduce. For this reason, males and females try to look attractive to the other sex, walking, talking, and laughing in gendered ways. If girls see their mothers wearing makeup and high heels, they want to do likewise. According to evolutionary theory, the species' need to reproduce is part of everyone's genetic impulses, so young boys and girls practise becoming attractive to the other sex. This ensures that they will be ready after puberty to find each other, and a new generation will be born.

WHAT IS BEST? Each of the major developmental theories strives to explain the sex and gender roles that young children express, but no consensus has been reached (as we saw was the case with emotional regulation in this chapter and language development in Chapter 5). The theories all raise important questions: What gender patterns *should* parents and caregivers teach? Should every child learn to combine the best masculine and feminine characteristics (called *androgyny*), thereby causing gender stereotypes to eventually disappear as children become more mature, as happens with their belief in Santa Claus and the tooth fairy? Or should male–female distinctions be encouraged as essential for the human family? Answers vary among developmentalists as well as among parents and cultures.

> ## KEY Points
>
> - Sex differences are biological differences between males and females, while gender differences are culturally prescribed roles and behaviours.
> - Young children learn gender identify during the first year of life; however, they do not have a full understanding of gender until later.
> - Theorists refer to attitudes, roles, and biology to explain sex-role development.

Play

Play is timeless and universal—apparent in every part of the world for thousands of years. Many developmentalists believe that play is the most productive as well as the most enjoyable activity that children undertake (Elkind, 2007; Frost, 2009; Smith, 2010). Whether play is essential for normal growth or is merely a fun activity that has developmental benefits is somewhat controversial (Pellegrini, 2011). There are echoes of this controversy in the variations in preschool education that were explained in Chapter 5. Some educators want children to focus on reading and math skills; others predict emotional and academic problems for children who rarely play (Hirsh-Pasek et al., 2009; Pellegrini, 2009; Rubin et al., 2009).

Play is so universally valued that the United Nations has explicitly recognized it as a specific right for all children. Article 31 of its Convention on the Rights of the Child states: "Parties recognize the right of the child to rest and leisure, to engage in play and recreational activities appropriate to the age of the child and to participate freely in cultural life and the arts" (United Nations Human Rights, 1990).

Same Situation, Far Apart: Culture Clash? Both children wear Muslim headwear. Although he is in Noida, India, and she is in an alley in Pakistan, both carry universal toys—a toy car and a bride doll, identical to those found in any city in Canada.

It is worth noting that when the province of Ontario implemented a full-day kindergarten program for 4- and 5-year-olds in 2010, the curriculum was entirely play-based. Activities include both child-initiated play and more structured play-based learning opportunities meant to develop literacy, numeracy, language acquisition, and social and problem-solving skills (Ontario Ministry of Education, 2010).

Playmates and Friendships

Young children play best with *peers,* that is, people of about the same age and social status. Two-year-olds are not yet good playmates: They might throw a ball and expect another child to throw it back, but most other 2-year-olds will keep it. By contrast, most 6-year-olds are quite skilled: They can gain entry to a peer group, manage conflict, take turns, find friends, and keep playmates. Over those years, social play with peers teaches emotional regulation, empathy, and cultural understanding (Göncü & Gaskins, 2011).

Through friendships, young children are able to learn and master age-graded tasks as friendships provide a forum for learning and refining of socioemotional skills. Through these peer interactions, children learn to cooperate and understand different perspectives; friendships also meet the needs for intimacy (Rubin et al., 1998).

For young children, friendships are typically play-oriented dyads that socialize children into group life (Hartup & Stevens, 1997). By age 5 or 6, children have a more complex understanding of friendship that includes mutual trust and support, and being able to count on their friend over time, which are important aspects of distinguishing between friends and peers (Hay et al., 2004). As Canadian researcher Kenneth Rubin (2004) stated, at all ages, individuals engage in more complicated social activity, talk, task orientation, cooperation, negotiation, prosocial activity, positive affect, and effective conflict management with their friends than with non-friends.

Whether playing with peers or friends, there is a tendency for sex segregation early in life. Children prefer to interact with peers of their own sex; this is called **sex homophily.** By preschool, about half of children's interactions are only with the same sex, while less than 10 percent of interactions are with only other-sex peer (Fabes et al., 2003). These segregated styles of interactions have important consequences for development (Leaper, 1994; Maccoby, 1998). For example, boys' interactions are rougher and more active (Fabes et al., 2003), whereas girls focus more on cooperation (Maccoby, 1990). So, do children seek same-sex peers because of sex homophily or because they share the same interests in toys and activities (activity homophily)?

There is evidence that children use both the gender of their peers as well as their shared interests when deciding whether they will play with them. As children play together, they reinforce the expected levels of engagement in gender-typed activities, which, in turn, further strengthens the tendencies for sex-segregation (Martin et al., 2013).

There is an obvious task for parents: to find playmates for their children who can later become friends. Even the most playful parent is outmatched by a child at negotiating the rules of tag, at play-fighting, at pretending to be on a picnic, or at slaying dragons. Specifics vary, but "play with peers is one of the most important areas in which children develop positive social skills" (Xu, 2010, p. 496).

Cultural Differences in Play

All young children play, and a child playing is a sign of healthy development (Gosso, 2010). Children create dramas that reflect their culture and they play games passed down from older generations. Chinese children fly kites, Inuit children tell dreams and stories, Lapp children pretend to be reindeer, Cameroon children hunt mice, and

sex homophily
A preference to interact with one's own sex.

so on. All children also play in ways that are similar in every culture, such as throwing and catching; pretending to be adults; and drawing with chalk, markers, sticks, and other instruments. Everywhere, play is the prime activity of young children.

Although play is universal, not only do specifics differ but so do frequency and playmates. When adults are concerned with basic survival, they rarely play with their children. Children play with each other instead, but they do not spend as much time playing as children in less impoverished communities (Kalliala, 2006; Roopnarine, 2011).

As children grow older, play becomes more social, influenced not only by the availability of playmates, but also by the physical setting (a small playroom, a large park, a wild hillside). One developmentalist bemoans the twenty-first century's "swift and pervasive rise of electronic media" and adults who lean "more toward control than freedom." He praises children who find places to play independently and who "conspire [in finding] ways to elude adult management" (Chudacoff, 2011, p. 98). This opinion may be extreme, but it is echoed in more common concerns.

Play Ball! In every nation, young children play with balls, but the specific games they play vary with the culture. Soccer is the favourite game in many countries, including Brazil, where these children are practising their dribbling on Copacabana Beach in Rio de Janeiro.

Before the electronic age, young children played outside with neighbourhood children, often of both sexes and several ages. The youngest children learned from the older ones. American sociologist Mildred Parten (1932) was one of the first to describe the development of social play from ages 1 to 6. She distinguished five kinds of play, each more advanced than the previous one:

1. *Solitary play:* A child plays alone, unaware of any other children playing nearby.
2. *Onlooker play:* A child watches other children play.
3. *Parallel play:* Children play with similar objects in similar ways, but not together.
4. *Associative play:* Children interact, sharing material, but their play is not reciprocal.
5. *Cooperative play:* Children play together, creating dramas or taking turns.

As already mentioned, play is affected by culture and context, and both of these have changed since Parten's day. Many Asian parents teach 3-year-olds to take turns, share, and otherwise cooperate. On the other hand, many North American children, at age 6 and older, engage in parallel play, especially in school, where each child has a desk. Given all the social, political, and economic changes over the past century, various forms of social play (not necessarily in Parten's sequence) may be age-appropriate (Xu, 2010).

Active Play

Children need physical activity to develop muscle strength and control. Peers provide an audience, role models, and sometimes competition. For instance, running skills develop best when children chase or race each other, not when a child runs alone. Gross motor play is favoured among young children, who enjoy climbing, kicking, and tumbling (Case-Smith & Kuhaneck, 2008).

Active social play—not solitary play—correlates with peer acceptance and a healthy self-concept (Nelson et al., 2008; Smith, 2010) and may help regulate emotions (Sutton-Smith, 2011)—something adults might remember when they wish their children were immobile and quiet. Among non-human primates, deprivation of social play warps later life, rendering some monkeys unable to mate, to make friends, or even to survive with other monkeys (Herman et al., 2011; Palagi, 2011).

Active play advances planning and self-control. Two-year-olds merely chase and catch each other, but older children keep the interaction fair, long-lasting, and fun. In tag, for instance, they set rules (adjusted to location) and each child decides how far to venture from base. If one child is "It" for too long, another child (often a friend) makes himself easy to be caught.

ROUGH-AND-TUMBLE PLAY The most common form of active play is called **rough-and-tumble** because it looks quite rough and because the children seem to tumble over one another. The term was coined by British scientists who studied primates in East Africa (Blurton-Jones, 1976). They noticed that monkeys often chased, attacked, rolled over in the dirt, and wrestled quite roughly, but without hurting one another. If a young monkey wanted rough-and-tumble play, all it had to do was come close, catch the eye of a peer, and then run a few metres. The invitation was almost always accepted, with a *play face* (smiling, not angry). Puppies, kittens, and chimps do the same thing.

When the scientists returned to London, they saw that human youngsters, like baby monkeys, also enjoy rough-and-tumble play (Pellegrini & Smith, 2005). They chase, wrestle, and grab each other, developing games like tag and cops and robbers, with play faces, lots of running, and various conventions, expressions, and gestures that children use to signify "just pretend."

Rough-and-tumble play happens everywhere (although "cops and robbers" can be "robots and humans" or one of many other iterations). It is particularly common among young males (human and otherwise) who are friends, playing in ample space with minimal supervision (Berenbaum et al., 2008; Hassett et al., 2008).

Many scientists think that rough-and-tumble play helps the prefrontal cortex develop, as children learn to regulate emotions, practise social skills, and strengthen their bodies (Pellegrini et al., 2007; Pellis & Pellis, 2011). Indeed, some believe that play in childhood, especially rough-and-tumble play between boys and their fathers, may prevent antisocial behaviour later on (Wenner, 2009).

DRAMA AND PRETENDING Another major type of active play is sociodramatic play, in which children act out various roles and plots. Through **sociodramatic play** children

- explore and rehearse social roles
- learn how to explain their ideas and convince playmates to agree
- practise emotional regulation by pretending to be afraid, angry, brave, and so on
- develop self-concept in a non-threatening context.

Sociodramatic play builds on pretending, which emerges in toddlerhood. But preschoolers do more than pretend; they combine their own imagination with that of others, advancing in theory of mind as they do so (Kavanaugh, 2011). The beginnings of sociodramatic play are illustrated by this pair, a 3-year-old girl and a 2-year-old boy. The girl wants to act out the role of a baby, and she persuades a boy in her nursery school to join her.

> **Boy:** Not good. You bad.
> **Girl:** Why?
> **Boy:** 'Cause you spill your milk.
> **Girl:** No. 'Cause I bit somebody.
> **Boy:** Yes, you did.

rough-and-tumble play
Play that mimics aggression through wrestling, chasing, or hitting, but in which there is no intent to harm.

sociodramatic play
Pretend play in which children act out various roles and themes in stories that they create.

MIKE GOLDWATER / ALAMY

A Toy Machine Gun These boys in Liberia are doing what young children everywhere do—following adult example. Whenever countries are at war, children play solders, rebels, heroes, or spies.

Girl: Say, "Go to sleep. Put your head down."
Boy: Put your head down.
Girl: No.
Boy: Yes.
Girl: No.
Boy: Yes. Okay, I will spank you. Bad boy. *[Spanks her, not hard]*
Girl: No. My head is up. *[Giggles]* I want my teddy bear.
Boy: No. Your teddy bear go away.
  [At this point she asked if he was really going to take the teddy bear away.]

[Garvey, 1977, quoted in Cohen, 2006, p. 72]

Note the social interaction in this form of play. The girl directed and played her part, sometimes accepting what the boy said and sometimes not. The boy took direction, yet also made up his own dialogue and actions ("Bad boy").

Older children are much more elaborate in their sociodramatic play, evident in four boys, about age 5, in a daycare centre in Finland. Joni plays the role of the evil one who menaces the other boys; Tuomas directs the drama and acts in it as well.

Tuomas: And now he [*Joni*] would take me and would hang me. … This would be the end of all of me.
Joni: Hands behind.
Tuomas: I can't help it. I have to. *[The two other boys follow his example.]*
Joni: I would put fire all around them.
  [All three brave boys lie on the floor with hands tied behind their backs. Joni piles mattresses on them, and pretends to light a fire, which crackles closer and closer.]
Tuomas: Everything is lost.
  [One boy starts to laugh.]
Petter: Better not to laugh, soon we will all be dead. … I am saying my last words.
Tuomas: Now you can say your last wish. … And now I say I wish we can be terribly strong.
  [At that point, the three boys suddenly gain extraordinary strength, pushing off the mattresses and extinguishing the fire. Good triumphs over evil, but not until the last moment, because, as one boy explains, "Otherwise this playing is not exciting at all."]

[adapted from Kalliala, 2006, p. 83]

Good versus evil is a favourite theme of boys' sociodramatic play. In contrast, girls often act out domestic scenes. Such gender differences are found in many cultures. In the same daycare centre where Joni piles mattresses on his playmates, the girls say their play is "more beautiful and peaceful … [but] boys play all kinds of violent games" (Kalliala, 2006, p. 110).

Although gender differences in sociodramatic play are found universally, the prevalence of such play varies. Some cultures find it frivolous and discourage it, while in other cultures parents teach toddlers to be lions, or robots, or ladies drinking tea, and children develop elaborate and extensive play (Kavanaugh, 2011).

The New Media

As mentioned above, one of today's great challenges is the influence of electronic media. All media—television, the Internet, electronic games, and so on—*can* be harmful, especially when the content is violent (Anderson et al., 2007, 2008; Bailey et al., 2010; Gentile et al., 2007; Smyth, 2007).

Electronic media for young children has become a multi-million-dollar industry, seeking profit through the education and entertainment of billions of young viewers (Steemers, 2010). Some children learn from educational videos, especially if adults watch with them and reinforce the lessons. However, children rarely select educational programs over fast-paced cartoons, in which everyone hits, shoots, and kicks.

The problem is not only that violent media teach aggression, but also that even nonviolent media take time from constructive interaction and creative play. Social interaction among family members is reduced when a TV is on, whether or not anyone is watching (Kirkorian et al., 2009).

The 2007–2009 Canadian Health Measures Survey (CHMS) indicates that Canadian children 6- to 19-years of age spend 62 percent of their waking hours in sedentary pursuits. Of this 8.6 hours per day (on average), as much as 6 hours is spent on screen time, such as television, computer, and/or smart phones (Active Healthy Kids Canada, 2011).

The Canadian Paediatric Society (2008) strongly discourages any screen time for children younger than 2 years of age, and recommends limiting older children to 1 to 2 hours a day. Similarly, six major organizations in the United States (the American Psychological Association, the American Academy of Pediatrics, the American Medical Association, the American Academy of Child and Adolescent Psychiatry, the American Academy of Family Physicians, and the American Psychiatric Association) recommend no electronic media at all for children under age 2 and strict limitations after that.

Using the Quebec Longitudinal Study of Child Development, Pagani and her colleagues (2010) investigated how early childhood television exposure influenced Grade 4 outcomes, including those for academic, psychosocial, and lifestyle pursuits. They found that every additional hour of television viewing beyond two hours per day at 29 months of age corresponded to a 7 percent decrease in classroom engagement and a 6 percent decrease in math achievement. It also was associated with a 10 percent greater likelihood of being victimized by classmates, a 13 percent decrease in engaging in physical activity on the weekends, a 9 percent decrease in activities needing physical effort, and an increase of 9 and 10 percent in the consumption of soft drinks and snacks, respectively.

Perhaps as a result of these last factors, each hour of viewing also correlated to a 5 percent increase in body mass index (Pagani et al., 2010). Such findings suggest that early television exposure can have serious long-term negative consequences for children.

KEY Points

- All children everywhere in every era play during early childhood, which makes some developmentalists think play is essential for healthy development.
- The specific forms of play vary by culture, gender, and parental example.
- Playmates of the same age foster emotional regulation.
- Rough-and-tumble play and sociodramatic play both help children with socialization, with boys and girls often creating distinct imaginary dramas.
- Young children are powerfully influenced by television, the Internet, video games, and other electronic media, which can take time away from physical activity and creative play.

The Role of Caregivers

We have seen that young children's emotions and actions are affected by many factors, including brain maturation, culture, and peers. Now we focus on another primary influence on young children: their caregivers.

All children need parents who care about them because, no matter what the parenting style, parental involvement plays an important role in the development of both social and cognitive competence (Parke & Buriel, 2006). As more and more children spend long hours during early childhood with other adults, alternate caregivers become pivotal as well.

Caregiving Styles

Although thousands of researchers have traced the effects of parenting on child development, the work of one person, more than 50 years ago, continues to be influential. In her original research, Diana Baumrind (1967, 1971) studied 100 preschool children, all from California and almost all middle-class European-Americans. (The cohort and cultural limitations of this sample were not obvious at the time.)

Baumrind found that parents differed on four important dimensions:

1. *Expressions of warmth.* Some parents are warm and affectionate; others, cold and critical.
2. *Strategies for discipline.* Parents vary in how they explain, criticize, persuade, and punish.
3. *Communication.* Some parents listen patiently; others demand silence.
4. *Expectations for maturity.* Parents vary in how much responsibility and self-control they expect.

BAUMRIND'S FOUR STYLES OF CAREGIVING On the basis of the dimensions listed above, Baumrind identified four parenting styles (summarized in Table 6.1).

- **Authoritarian parenting.** The authoritarian parent's word is law (e.g., my way or the highway) and not to be questioned. Misconduct brings strict punishment, usually physical. Authoritarian parents set down clear rules and hold high standards. They do not expect children to offer opinions; discussion about emotions is especially rare. (One adult from such a family said that "How do you feel?" had only two possible answers: "Fine" and "Tired.") Authoritarian parents seem cold, rarely showing affection.

authoritarian parenting
An approach to child-rearing that is characterized by high behavioural standards, strict punishment of misconduct, and little communication.

TABLE 6.1 Characteristics of Parenting Styles Identified by Baumrind

Style	Warmth	Discipline	Expectations of Maturity	Communication Parent to Child	Child to Parent
Authoritarian	Low	Strict, often physical	High	High	Low
Permissive	High	Rare	Low	Low	High
Authoritative	High	Moderate, with much discussion	Moderate	High	High
Neglecting-rejecting	Low	Rare	Low	Low	Low

permissive parenting
An approach to child-rearing that is characterized by high nurturance and communication but little discipline, guidance, or control.

authoritative parenting
An approach to child-rearing in which the parents set limits and enforce rules but are flexible and listen to their children.

rejecting-neglecting parenting
An approach to child-rearing in which the parents are indifferent toward their children and unaware of what is going on in their children's lives.

- **Permissive parenting.** Permissive parents (also called *indulgent parents*) make few demands, hiding any impatience they feel. Discipline is lax, partly because they have low expectations for maturity. Instead, permissive parents are highly nurturing and accepting, listening to whatever their offspring say, and supporting their decisions.

- **Authoritative parenting.** Authoritative parents set limits, but they are flexible. They encourage maturity, but they usually listen and forgive (not punish) if the child falls short. There is verbal give-and-take, taking the child's interests and opinions into consideration. Authoritative parents consider themselves as kind but firm guides, not authorities (like authoritarian parents) and not friends (like permissive parents).

- **Rejecting-neglecting parenting.** Rejecting-neglecting parents are disengaged, neither demanding nor responsive. Neglectful parents are unaware of their children's behaviour; they seem not to care. They have low expectations, and do not monitor or support their children. They may actively reject their children, or else entirely neglect their parenting responsibilities.

The following long-term effects of parenting styles have been reported in many nations (Baumrind, 2005; Baumrind et al., 2010; Chan & Koo, 2011; Huver et al., 2010; Rothrauff et al., 2009).

- *Authoritarian* parents raise children who become conscientious, obedient, and quiet but not especially happy. Such children tend to feel guilty or depressed, internalizing their frustrations and blaming themselves when things don't go well. As adolescents, they sometimes rebel, leaving home before age 20.

- *Permissive* parents raise unhappy children who lack self-control, especially in the give-and-take of peer relationships. Inadequate emotional regulation makes them immature and impedes friendships, which is the main reason for their unhappiness. They tend to continue to live at home, still dependent, in early adulthood.

- *Authoritative* parents raise children who are successful, articulate, happy with themselves, and generous with others. These children are usually liked by teachers and peers, especially in cultures that value individual initiative (e.g., North America).

- *Rejecting-neglecting* parents raise children who are immature, sad, lonely, and at risk of injury and abuse.

PROBLEMS WITH BAUMRIND'S STYLES Baumrind's classification is often criticized. Problems include the following:

- Her participants were not diverse in SES, ethnicity, or culture.
- She focused more on adult attitudes than on adult actions.
- She overlooked children's temperament, which affects the adult's parenting style.

- Her classifications did not capture the complexities of parenting; for example, she did not recognize that some "authoritarian" parents are also affectionate.

- Her classifications were mutually exclusive, but in reality parents use various "types" of parenting, depending on the situation at hand.

- She did not realize that some "permissive" parents provide extensive verbal guidance.

We now know that children's temperament and the culture's standards powerfully affect caregivers, as do the consequences of parenting style (Cipriano & Stifter, 2010).

Moving beyond Baumrind's dimensions, University of Toronto researchers Maayan Davidov and Joan Grusec (2006) focused on two features of positive parenting—responsiveness to distress, and warmth—and the effects of these features on children's socioemotional functioning. They found that both mothers' and fathers' responsiveness to their children's distress was linked to their children's negative affective regulation. Mothers' responsiveness to distress, but not fathers', was shown to also increase children's empathy and prosocial responses. Maternal warmth was linked to children's better regulation of positive affect, but paternal warmth was not. Another study of parenting at age 2 and children's competence in kindergarten (including emotional regulation and friendships) found multiple developmental pathways, with the best outcomes dependent on both the child and the adult (Blandon et al., 2010).

Also focusing on the emotional dimensions of parenting, Janet Strayer and William Roberts (2004) found that Canadian children were more likely to be angrier with mothers and fathers who were less empathic and warm, and had more age-*inappropriate* maturity demands. Children's anger was also linked to fathers who were more authoritarian and mothers who were more likely to use anxiety and guilt control.

Such studies suggest that certain aspects of parenting, like responsiveness to the child's distress and who the parent is (e.g., mother, father), can make unique contributions to the child's development.

Cultural Variations

The significance of context is particularly obvious when children of various ethnic groups are compared. It may be that certain alleles are more common in children of one group or another, and that affects their temperament. However, much more influential are the attitudes and actions of adult caregivers. As Kagicibasi (1996) argued, children from more interdependent cultures, where relationships and the group's needs are placed ahead of individual needs, may interpret high parental control as normal, and not as rejecting or harsh.

PARENTAL INFLUENCE North American parents of Chinese, Caribbean, or African heritage are often stricter, or more authoritarian, than those of European backgrounds, yet their children develop better than if the parents were easygoing (Chao, 2001; Parke & Buriel, 2006). Latino parents are sometimes thought to be too intrusive, other times too permissive—but their children seem to be happier than the children of North American parents who behave the same way (García & García, 2009; Ispa et al., 2004; Moreno, 1991). A three-way interaction seems to influence the outcome of any parenting style: the child's temperament, the parent's personality, and the social context.

In 1995, Chao examined Chinese-American and European-American mothers of children aged 2- to 5-years-old in terms of their child-rearing beliefs. She discovered that the way Chinese-American and European-American mothers defined independence in their children differed significantly. For Chinese-Americans, the

"He's just doing that to get attention."

Pay Attention Children develop best with lots of love and attention. They shouldn't have to ask for it!

idea of self-reliance and becoming a contributing member of society was appealing. European-American mothers, in contrast, defined independence as the child's own growing sense of individuality, self-expression, and separateness from the parents in action and in thought (Chao, 1995). Ten years later, Chuang's (2006) study of Chinese-Canadian mothers found that the two definitions were relevant, as these mothers defined independence as both self-reliance and separateness from the parents.

In another study of 1477 instances in which Mexican-American mothers of 4-year-olds tried to get their children to do something they were not doing, most of the time the mothers simply uttered a command and the children complied (Livas-Dlott et al., 2010). This simple strategy, with the mother asserting authority and the children obeying without question, might be considered authoritarian. However, almost never did the mothers use physical punishment or even harsh threats when the children did not immediately do as they were told—which happened 14 percent of the time. For example,

> Hailey [a 4-year-old] decided to look for another doll and started digging through her toys, throwing them behind her as she dug. Maricruz [the mother] told Hailey she should not throw her toys. Hailey continued to throw toys, and Maricruz said her name to remind her to stop. Hailey continued her misbehavior, and her mother repeated "Hailey" once more. When Hailey continued, Maricruz raised her voice but calmly directed, "Hailey, look at me." Hailey continued but then looked at Maricruz as she explained, "You don't throw toys; you could hurt someone." Finally, Hailey complied and stopped.
>
> *[Livas-Dlott et al., 2010, p. 572]*

Note that the mother's first three efforts failed, and then a look accompanied by an inaccurate explanation (in that setting, no one could be hurt) succeeded. The researchers explained that these Mexican-American families do not fit any of Baumrind's categories; respect for adult authority does not mean a hostile mother–child relationship. Instead, the relationship shows evident *cariño* (caring) (Livas–Dlott et al., 2010).

A study in Hong Kong found that almost all parents believed that young children need strong guidance, including physical punishment. But most classified themselves as authoritative, not authoritarian, because they listened to their children and adjusted their expectations when needed (Chan et al., 2009).

A multicultural study of Canadian parents used parent and teacher ratings of child behaviour to determine if there were cultural differences in terms of parenting and child behaviour. Using teacher ratings of student behaviour, parental harshness was positively related to child aggression in European-Canadian families but negatively related in South Asian-Canadian families. In contrast, when parent ratings of behaviour were used, parental harshness was positively related to children's aggression for all ethnic groups, although the strength of the relationship varied across ethnic groups (Ho et al., 2008).

In general, multicultural and international research has found that particular discipline methods and family rules are less important than warmth, support, and concern. Children from every ethnic group and every country benefit if they believe that they are appreciated; children everywhere suffer if they feel rejected and unwanted (Gershoff et al., 2010; Khaleque & Rohner, 2002).

Given a multicultural and multicontextual perspective, developmentalists hesitate to recommend any particular parenting style (Dishion & Bullock, 2002; J. G. Miller, 2004). That does not mean that all families function equally well—far from it. Signs of trouble include a child's anxiety, aggression, and inability to play with others. Ineffective, neglectful parents are one cause of such trouble, but not the only one. Another cause, child maltreatment, is discussed at the end of this chapter.

WHAT ABOUT TEACHERS? When Baumrind did her original research, 2- to 5-year-olds were cared for, almost exclusively, by their parents. Now most young children have teachers and other caregivers who can likewise be authoritative, authoritarian, permissive, or neglectful (Ertesvåg, 2011).

Although all four styles are possible for caregivers who watch only one child, almost no teacher is permissive or neglectful. They couldn't be. Allowing a group of 2- to 5-year-olds to do whatever they want would result in chaos, conflict, and perhaps danger. Young children are not so adept at emotional regulation and impulse control that several of them can safely play together, unguided or unsupervised, for long.

However, teachers can be authoritarian, setting down the law with no exceptions, or authoritative, setting flexible guidelines. Teachers with more education tend to be authoritative, responding to each child, listening and encouraging language, and so on. This fosters more capable children, which is one reason why teacher education is a measure used to indicate the quality of educational programs (Barnett et al., 2010; Norris, 2010).

In general, young children learn more from authoritative teachers because the teachers are perceived as warmer and more loving. In fact, one study found that, compared with children who had authoritarian teachers, those children whose teachers were child-centred, non-controlling, and very supportive scored higher on school-readiness measures (Barbarin et al., 2010).

KEY Points

- Baumrind identified four styles of caregiving: authoritarian, permissive, authoritative, and rejecting-neglecting. Each of these styles has specific effects on child development.
- Parenting styles differ according to the child's temperament and cultural variations.
- Teaching style and the caregiving style of daycare providers can also affect child development.

Moral Development

Children develop increasingly complex moral values, judgments, and behaviours as they mature. Social bonds (Chapter 4), theory of mind (Chapter 5), as well as the emotional and social maturation just described, are the foundations for morality.

Piaget thought that moral development began when children learned games with rules, which he connected with concrete operational thought at about age 7 (Piaget, 1932/1997). We now know that Piaget was mistaken: Both games with rules and moral development are evident much earlier. Some precursors of morality appear in infancy (Narvaéz & Lapsley, 2009).

Many developmentalists believe that children's attachment to their parents, and then to others, is the beginning of morality. According to evolutionary theory, humans protect, cooperate, and even sacrifice for one another precisely because

> our bodies are rather defenseless against the elements and even more vulnerable against possible predators. Thus, to survive, people have long needed to rely on coordination and cooperation.
>
> *[Dunning, 2011, pp. 1–2]*

With maturity and adult guidance, children develop guilt (as Erikson explained) and self-control. That helps them behave in ethical ways (Kochanska et al., 2009; Konner, 2010).

In contrast, Elliot Turiel's moral development theory (1979, 1983, 2008b) focused on the belief that as children interact with their social environment, they form their own ideas in an attempt to understand the events, people, and interactions around them. According to this social domain theory, children develop three separate and distinct domains of social knowledge:

Social Domain Theorist Elliot Turiel teaches courses on human development at the University of California. His research focuses on social and moral development.

JOSHUA TURIEL

- The *moral domain* deals with issues about rights, justice, and the welfare of others, such as when a child realizes it is wrong to hit someone.

- The *social conventional domain* deals with arbitrary but commonly agreed-upon rules, such as raising your hand in class or the need to be punctual for classes or appointments.

- The *personal domain* deals with matters of individual choice and preferences, such as the clothes you wear or your choice of leisure activities.

Children as young as two-and-a-half have been found to understand the difference between right and wrong and to have some sense of the difference between what is morally wrong and conventionally incorrect (Smetana, 1981).

Nature and Nurture

Many parents, teachers, and other adults consider morality as perhaps more important than any other advance already described (e.g., physical strength, motor skills, intelligence, language). Conflicting perspectives by scholars in many social sciences persist on how children internalize standards, develop virtues, and avoid vices:

- The "nature" perspective suggests that morality is genetic, an outgrowth of natural bonding, attachment, and cognitive maturation. That would explain why young children help and defend their parents, no matter what the parents do, and punish other children who violate moral rules. Even infants have a sense of what is fair and not, expecting adults to reward effort (Sloane et al., 2012).

- The "nurture" perspective contends that culture is crucial to the development of morality. That would explain why young children emulate people who follow the rules of their community, even if the actual behaviour is not innately good or bad.

Both nature and nurture are always influential, but developmentalists disagree about which is more important for morality (Killen & Smetana, 2007; Krebs, 2008; Narvaez & Lapsley, 2009; Turiel, 2006). That debate cannot be settled here; readers are encouraged to explore the issue further. However, here we explore two moral issues that arise from age 2 to age 6: children's aggression and adult's disciplinary practices. Nature and nurture are evident in both.

Empathy and Antipathy

Moral emotions are evident as children play with one another. With increasing social experiences and decreasing egocentrism, children develop **empathy,** an understanding of other people's feelings and concerns, and **antipathy,** dislike or even hatred.

PROSOCIAL ACTIONS Scientists studying young humans and other primates report spontaneous efforts to help others who are hurt, crying, or in need of help. Empathy is a necessary emotion to **prosocial behaviour,** extending helpfulness and kindness without any obvious benefit to oneself (Roberts & Strayer, 2008; Warneken & Tomasello, 2009). Expressing concern, offering to share, and including a shy child in a game or conversation are examples of prosocial behaviour among young children. So is the story of Jack who, at age 3, showed empathy when he refused to bring snacks with peanuts to school because another boy had to sit alone during snack because he was allergic to nuts. Jack wanted to sit with him (Lovecky, 2009).

Emotional regulation, moral development, and the emergence of empathy are nowhere more apparent than in the way children play with one another. Rough-and-tumble play, for instance, teaches children not to hurt their playmates; socio-dramatic play teaches children to take turns; and children learn to share art supplies, construction materials, and toys when engaged with other children (Peterson & Flanders, 2005; Utendale & Hastings, 2011). While sharing a crayon is hard at age 2, most 5-year-olds do it easily. Much depends on the child's family and preschool education: Children learn the balance between giving and taking. The result is more prosocial actions as children mature (Ramani et al., 2010).

Prosocial behaviour seems to result more from empathy than from cognition, more from emotional understanding than from theory of mind (Eggum et al., 2011). However, prosocial reactions are not automatic. Some children avoid contact with the person in need, which illustrates the importance of emotion development and regulation in the development of prosocial behaviour and the critical influence of cultural norms (Trommsdorff & Cole, 2011).

Some researchers have found a link between children's quality of attachment in infancy and their empathic responses as preschoolers. For example, children with secure attachment (whose parents were responsive and sensitive to their needs) showed more emotional and behavioural empathic responses to their peers' distress than did children with insecure–avoidant histories (Kestenbaum et al., 1989). Thus, children's internal working model, as discussed in Chapter 5, serves as the prototype for their later relationships with peers.

Also, researchers in Canada and the United States have examined the influence of parenting on children's prosocial behaviours. They found that authoritative parents are more likely to have children engage in prosocial behaviours, whereas these behaviours may be undermined by authoritarian parenting (Hastings et al., 2005; Kochanska, 1991). Authoritative parents may model prosocial behaviours for their children by showing concern and affection for others, which reinforces their children's own positive feelings for other people. In contrast, when authoritarian parents demonstrate a lack of concern for, or outright hostility toward others, these parents make it difficult for their children to see the value of prosocial activities.

ANTISOCIAL ACTIONS Antipathy can lead to **antisocial behaviour,** such as deliberately or unintentionally hurting another person, including people who have done no harm. Antisocial actions include verbal insults, social exclusion, and physical assaults (Calkins & Keane, 2009). A 4-year-old who is antisocial might look another child in the eye, scowl, and then kick him hard without provocation.

---

empathy
The ability to understand the emotions and concerns of another person, especially when they differ from one's own.

antipathy
Feelings of dislike or even hatred for another person.

prosocial behaviour
Actions that are helpful and kind but that are of no obvious benefit to the person doing them.

antisocial behaviour
Actions that are deliberately hurtful or destructive to another person.

instrumental aggression
Hurtful behaviour that is intended to get something that another person has and to keep it.

reactive aggression
An impulsive retaliation for another person's intentional or accidental action, verbal or physical.

relational aggression
Non-physical acts, such as insults or social rejection, aimed at harming the social connection between the victim and other people.

bullying aggression
Unprovoked, repeated physical or verbal attack, especially on victims who are unlikely to defend themselves.

Not surprisingly, given the moral sensibilities of young children, 5-year-olds already judge whether another child's aggression is justified or not (Etchu, 2007). As with adults, self-defence is more readily forgiven than is a deliberate, unprovoked attack. However, do not assume that bullies realize when they are wrong: At every age, aggressors feel they had a reason to do what they did.

Researchers recognize four general types of aggression, all evident in early childhood (see Table 6.2). **Instrumental aggression** is common among 2-year-olds, who often want something and try to get it without thinking. The aggressive reaction of the other child—crying, hitting, and resisting the grab of the instrumentally aggressive child—is also more typical at age 2 than earlier or later.

Reactive aggression is common among young children as well; almost every child reacts in an aggressive way when attacked. Children are less likely to respond with physical aggression as they develop emotional control and theory of mind (Olson et al., 2011).

Relational aggression (usually verbal) destroys the target child's self-esteem and disrupts the victim's social networks. The impact of this type of aggression becomes more hurtful as children mature. A young child might tell another, "You can't be my friend" or "You are fat," hurting another's feelings.

The fourth and most ominous type is **bullying aggression.** The intent of this form of aggression is to dominate someone else. This behaviour is not only destructive for the victims in the form of depression and low self-concept, but for bullies who will learn behaviour patterns that will have negative consequences in adulthood (see an in-depth discussion of bullying in Chapter 8).

All forms of aggression usually become less common from age 2 to 6, as the brain matures and empathy increases. Parents, peers, and preschool teachers are all pivotal mentors in this process. It is a mistake to expect children to regulate their emotions without guidance. It is also a mistake to punish aggressors too harshly because that may remove them from their zone of proximal development, where they can learn to regulate their anger.

A team of Canadian researchers (Côté et al., 2006) was the first to explore the differences between typical and atypical patterns of physical aggression among toddlers and the way these patterns might predict future aggressive behaviour. Using Canada's National Longitudinal Survey of Children and Youth, the researchers followed more than 10 000 children from the age of 2 to the age of 11. They discovered that the children fell into three distinct groups in terms of their use of physical aggression.

TABLE 6.2 The Four Forms of Aggression

Type of Aggression	Definition	Comments
Instrumental aggression	Hurtful behaviour that is aimed at gaining something (such as a toy, a place in line, or a turn on the swing) that someone else has	Often increases from age 2 to 6; involves objects more than people; quite normal; more egocentric than antisocial.
Reactive aggression	An impulsive retaliation for a hurt (intentional or accidental) that can be verbal or physical	Indicates a lack of emotional regulation, characteristic of 2-year-olds. A 5-year-old can usually stop and think before reacting.
Relational aggression	Non-physical acts, such as insults or social rejection, aimed at harming the social connections between the victim and others	Involves a personal attack and thus is directly antisocial; can be very hurtful; more common as children become socially aware.
Bullying aggression	Unprovoked, repeated physical or verbal attack, especially on victims who are unlikely to defend themselves	In both bullies and victims, a sign of poor emotional regulation; adults should intervene before the school years. (Bullying is discussed in Chapter 8.)

Pat, Pinch, or Poke Toddlers bite, hit, grab, and pull hair. By age 4 or 5—as a result of brain maturation, theory of mind, emotional regulation, and interactions with caregivers—children are more aware. Some, like the girl in the photo on the left, are deliberately prosocial, while others, like the boy in the photo on the right, are deliberately antisocial.

The first group—about one-third of the children—rarely used physical aggression as toddlers and almost never as preadolescents. Just over half of the children fell into the second group. They used physical aggression occasionally in toddlerhood and infrequently at age 11. The third group, about one-sixth of the children, used physical aggression frequently both as toddlers and as preadolescents.

The researchers concluded that the typical developmental pattern for physical aggression was of declining use over time. However, the third group, mostly boys from disadvantaged families, showed a stable or increased use of this behaviour, presumably because they had not learned other effective behavioural strategies that would limit their use of physical aggression (Côté et al., 2006).

Two explanations for children at risk of aggressive behaviour are biologically linked. First, some researchers have found that neurological deficits (acquired in utero or in infancy) may hinder children's ability to learn alternative strategies that would inhibit physical aggression (Moffitt, 2003; Tremblay et al., 2004). Second, some parents may hand down to their children genetic characteristics that do not facilitate learning of emotional regulation or inhibit the use of overt aggression (Arseneault et al., 2003; Dionne et al., 2003; Weaver et al., 2004).

Discipline

Ideally, adults guide children toward good behaviour and internalized standards of morality so that children behave well and never need to be disciplined. But this ideal is not realistic: Misbehaviour cannot always be prevented.

Lest anyone imagine that, with benevolent parents, children will always be good, consider a study of mothers and 3-year-olds during late afternoon (a stressful time). Conflicts (including verbal disagreements) arose about every two minutes (Laible et al., 2008). Here is one example that began with an activity recommended for every parent; the mother was about to take her daughter for a walk:

> **Child:** I want my other shoes.
> **Mother:** You don't need your other shoes. You wear your Pooh sandals when we go for a walk.
> **Child:** Noooooo.
> **Mother:** [*Child's name*]! You don't need your other shoes.
> **Child:** [*Cries loudly*]

✦ **ESPECIALLY FOR Parents of 3-Year-Olds** How could a parent compromise with a child who wants to wear "other shoes"? (see response, page 237) →

Mother: No, you don't need your other shoes. You wear your Pooh sandals when we go for a walk.

Child: Ahhhh. Want pretty dress. [*Crying*]

Mother: Your pretty dress!

Child: Yeah.

Mother: You can wear them some other day.

Child: Noooooo. [*Crying*]

[from Laible et al., 2008, pp. 442–443]

In this study, children who were securely attached at age 1 (an indication of responsive parenting) had as many conflicts as those who were insecurely attached. Obviously, good parenting does not always produce good children, if the latter are defined as children who are peaceful and obedient.

However, unlike in the snippet above, the mothers of securely attached children were more likely to compromise and explain (Laible et al., 2008). Is that the best response? Should the mother have offered reasons why the other shoes were not appropriate, or should she have let her daughter wear them? Alternatively, what if the mother had slapped the child for crying, or said, "I don't want to walk with you if you fuss"?

PHYSICAL PUNISHMENT Many adults remember receiving such punishment and think it works. Initially, they seem to be correct: Physical punishment (called *corporal punishment* because it hurts the body) succeeds at the moment—spanking stops misbehaviour. But, this is not a good solution.

Longitudinal research finds that children who are physically punished are more likely to become bullies, delinquents, and then abusive adults, as well as slower to learn in school (Straus & Paschall, 2009). Although some adults believe that physical punishment will "teach a lesson" of obedience, the lesson that children learn is that "might makes right." When they become bigger and stronger, they use corporal punishment on others. Parents who hit were usually hit themselves.

Debate continues about the effectiveness of physical punishment. Physical punishment is common worldwide, yet 24 countries have legislation that bans it (Zolotor & Puzia, 2010). Although spanking in North America has declined since 1975, almost 80 percent of the parents in one American study reported that they still discipline their preschool children in this way.

Many studies of children from all types of families find that physical punishment of young children correlates with delayed theory of mind and increased aggression (Olson et al., 2011). To prove cause without a doubt would require parents of monozygotic twins to raise them identically except that one twin would be spanked often and the other never. Of course, that is unethical as well as impossible.

Many developmentalists wonder why parents would take the chance administering physical punishment, knowing its consequences for child development. While many parents do absolutely refrain from spanking their children, they may routinely use other disciplinary techniques that can be equally harmful to child development (Larzelere et al., 2010). Let us consider some of those alternatives.

PSYCHOLOGICAL CONTROL Another common method of discipline is called **psychological control,** in which children's shame, guilt, and gratitude are used to control their behaviour (Barber, 2002). Psychological control may reduce academic achievement and emotional intelligence, just as spanking is thought to do (Alegre, 2011).

Consider the results of a study of an entire cohort (the best way to obtain an unbiased sample) of children born in Finland (Aunola & Nurmi, 2004). Their parents were asked 20 questions about their approach to child-rearing. The following four

◆ **ESPECIALLY FOR Parents** Suppose you agree that spanking is destructive, but you sometimes get so angry at your child's behaviour that you hit him or her. Is your reaction appropriate? (see response, page 238) ➞

psychological control
A disciplinary technique that involves threatening to withdraw love and support and that relies on a child's feelings of guilt and gratitude to the parents.

items, which the parents rated from 1 ("Not at all like me") to 5 ("Very much like me"), measured psychological control:

1. "My child should be aware of how much I have done for him/her."
2. "I let my child see how disappointed and shamed I am if he/she misbehaves."
3. "My child should be aware of how much I sacrifice for him/her."
4. "I expect my child to be grateful and appreciate all the advantages he/she has."

The higher the parents scored on these four measures of psychological control, the lower the children's math scores—and this connection grew stronger over time. Surprisingly, math achievement suffered most if parents were also high in affection (e.g., they frequently hugged their children) (Aunola & Nurmi, 2004). One explanation is that affection increased the child's fear of disappointing the parent, which made it more difficult for the child to learn.

Other research also finds that psychological control can depress children's achievement, creativity, and social acceptance (Soenens & Vansteenkiste, 2010). Compared to corporal punishment, children punished with psychological control seem less likely to be physical bullies but more likely to be relationally aggressive (Kuppens et al., 2009), depressed, and anxious (Gershoff et al., 2010).

TIME OUT The disciplinary technique most often used in North America is the **time out,** in which an adult requires a misbehaving child to sit quietly, without toys or playmates, for a short time (Barkin et al., 2007). Time out is favoured by many experts in North American education. For example, in the large, longitudinal evaluation of Head Start highlighted in Chapter 5, an increase in time outs and a decrease in spankings were considered signs of improved parental discipline (U.S. Department of Health and Human Services, 2010).

However, research on the effectiveness of the time out is confounded by the many ways it is used. Some parents angrily put the child in a corner, yelling at him or her to stay there until the parent is no longer angry. The effect is similar to corporal punishment: The child feels rejected. To be effective, a time out must be brief; one minute for each year of the child's age is suggested. As with every form of discipline, the parents' own emotional state and the child's temperament need to be considered.

EXPLANATION Another alternative to physical punishment is *induction*, in which the parents talk extensively with the misbehaving child, helping the child understand why his or her behaviour was wrong. Ideally, parents listen as children articulate their emotions and then encourage the children to imagine what they might have done instead of what they did.

Conversation helps children internalize standards, but induction takes time and patience. Since 3-year-olds confuse causes with consequences, they cannot answer "Why did you do that?" or appreciate a lengthy explanation of why a behaviour was wrong. Simple induction ("You made him sad") may be more appropriate.

RESPONSE FOR Parents of 3-Year-Olds (from page 235) Remember, authoritative parents listen but do not usually give in. A parent could ask why the child did not want the Pooh sandals (ugly, too tight, old?) and explain why the "other shoes" were not appropriate (raining, save for special occasions, hard to walk in). A promise for the future (e.g., "Let's save your other shoes and pretty dress for the birthday party tomorrow") might stop the "Noooo." ●

time out
A disciplinary technique in which a child is separated from other people and activities for a specified time.

Bad Boy or Bad Parent? For some children and in some cultures, sitting alone is an effective form of punishment; for others, it produces an angry child.

OPPOSING PERSPECTIVES

Is Spanking OK?

Some parents and researchers believe that children should never be spanked, while others believe there is a role for spanking. Worldwide, cultural differences in child discipline are apparent. For example, only half as many Canadian parents as U.S. parents slap, pinch, or smack their children (Oldershaw, 2002). Yet, the Criminal Code of Canada supports using reasonable force to punish children. Section 43 states that: "Every schoolteacher, parent or person standing in the place of a parent is justified in using force by way of correction toward a pupil or child, as the case may be, who is under his care, if the force does not exceed what is reasonable under the circumstances." By contrast, physical punishment by anyone—parent, teacher, sibling, stranger—is illegal in many other developed nations (including Austria, Croatia, Cyprus, Denmark, Finland, Germany, Israel, Italy, Norway, New Zealand, and Sweden). It is considered a violation of human rights (Bitensky, 2006).

Research finds that many methods of discipline, including spanking, affect the child's later levels of anxiety and aggression (Gershoff et al., 2010). Further complications can occur. Children vary in temperament; some may suffer from corporal punishment and some may not care at all. Parents vary in personality; some spank while out of control and others do not.

Opinions about discipline are clouded by past experiences and cultural norms, making it hard for opposing perspectives to be understood. For example, while one person may suggest putting hot sauce on a child's tongue as punishment for forbidden speech such as curses or sexual slang (Whelchel, 2005), another may consider this "plain mean & a newer version of old abuse tactics that our parents used to use" (Patterson, 2007).

As mentioned, cultures differ regarding which punishments are thought appropriate for which misdeeds. Harmful effects are reduced if a child does not feel unfairly disciplined

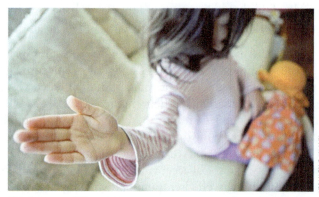

The Impact of Spanking Does spanking lead to increased aggression? The research is mixed, however it appears that the effects of spanking depend on the child and the family context.

because the particular punishment is the norm within their group (Vittrup & Holden, 2010). The parents' underlying attitude may be crucial. One study of African-American mothers found that if they disapproved of spanking but did it nonetheless, their children were likely to be depressed. However, their children were not harmed if mothers who spanked were convinced that spanking was what they should do (McLoyd et al., 2007). Similarly, Chinese-American parents who used physical punishment and shame raised children who were relatively happy and well-adjusted if the parents used those methods because they agreed with the Chinese ideology that led to them (Fung & Lau, 2009).

It is evident that there are many perspectives about corporal punishment. Many developmentalists are convinced that alternatives to spanking are better for the child as a safeguard against abuse. But a dynamic-systems view considers discipline as one aspect of a complex situation.

RESPONSE FOR Parents (from page 236) No. If you spank your child, you might seriously hurt him or her, and the child will associate anger with violence. You would do better to control your anger and develop other strategies for discipline and for prevention of misbehaviour. ●

KEY Points

- Children often advance in moral development during early childhood, usually gaining empathy as their theory of mind advances and emotions become better regulated.

- New empathy usually helps a child act prosocially, share, take turns, and so on.

- Children can also increasingly develop antipathy, which leads some to be aggressive without a self-protective reason (i.e., bullies), unlike those with instrumental or reactive aggression.

- Parents, guided by their culture, teach morality in many ways, including the strategies they choose for discipline.

- Every means of punishment may have long-term effects, with physical punishment especially criticized for encouraging aggression.

Child Maltreatment

We have reserved the most disturbing topic, child maltreatment, for the end of this chapter. The assumption throughout has been that parents and other adults seek the best for young children, and that their disagreements (e.g., what to feed them, how to discipline, what kind of early education to provide) arise from contrasting ideas about what is best.

However, the sad fact is that not everyone seeks the best for children. Sometimes parents harm their own offspring. Often the rest of society ignores the preventive and protective measures that could stop much maltreatment. Lest we become part of the problem, not part of the solution, we first need to recognize child neglect and abuse.

Maltreatment Noticed and Defined

Until about 1960, people thought child maltreatment was a rare, sudden attack by a disturbed stranger. Today we know better, thanks to a pioneering study based on careful observation of the "battered child syndrome" in one Boston hospital (Kempe & Kempe, 1978). Maltreatment is neither rare nor sudden, and the perpetrators are usually one or both of the child's parents. In these instances, maltreatment is often ongoing, and the child has no protector, which may make the maltreatment more damaging than a single incident, however injurious.

With this recognition came a broader definition: **Child maltreatment** now refers to all intentional harm to, or avoidable endangerment of, anyone under 18 years of age. Thus, child maltreatment includes both **child abuse,** which is deliberate action that is harmful to a child's physical, emotional, or sexual well-being, and **child neglect,** which is failure to meet a child's basic physical or emotional needs. **Reported maltreatment** means that the authorities have been informed. In Canada, the provinces and territories are responsible for protecting and supporting children at risk of abuse and neglect. **Substantiated maltreatment** means that a reported case has been investigated and verified.

child maltreatment
Intentional harm to or avoidable endangerment of anyone under 18 years of age.

child abuse
Deliberate action that is harmful to a child's physical, emotional, or sexual well-being.

child neglect
Failure to meet a child's basic physical, educational, or emotional needs.

reported maltreatment
Harm or endangerment about which someone has notified the authorities.

substantiated maltreatment
Harm or endangerment that has been reported, investigated, and verified.

Frequency of Maltreatment

How common is maltreatment? No one knows. Not all cases are noticed; not all noted cases are reported and not all reports are substantiated. The number of investigations for reported cases of child maltreatment in Canada rose sharply in the five-year period between 1998 and 2003, from 135 261 to 235 315. In 2008, it is estimated that about 235 842 investigations were reported in Canada (see Figure 6.1). Of those, about 36 percent were substantiated and 26 percent of the cases had children at risk (see Figure 6.2) (PHAC, 2010).

How maltreatment is defined by legislation and the level of public and professional awareness of the problem can influence the level of reporting. For example, the Canadian Incidence Study of Reported Child Abuse and Neglect reported that the average annual caseload in 2008 varied among provinces and territories. Based on the child population of 15 years or younger, the territories together

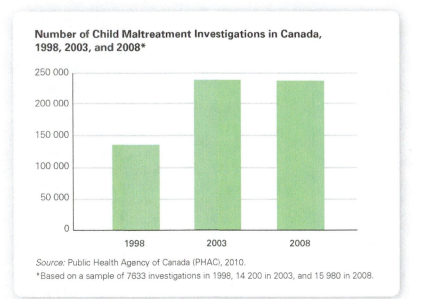

Number of Child Maltreatment Investigations in Canada, 1998, 2003, and 2008*

Source: Public Health Agency of Canada (PHAC), 2010.

*Based on a sample of 7633 investigations in 1998, 14 200 in 2003, and 15 980 in 2008.

FIGURE 6.1 **Levelling Off** Though the number of investigations for child maltreatment in Canada rose dramatically between 1998 and 2003, since then they seem to have levelled off.

OBSERVATION QUIZ

How would you explain the changes in rates of maltreatment-related investigations in Canada from 1998 to 2008? (see answer, page 241) ➡

FIGURE 6.2 Still Far Too Many
Although these rates are estimates and there have been changes in practices with how investigations are conducted, the number of children who have been maltreated is alarming.

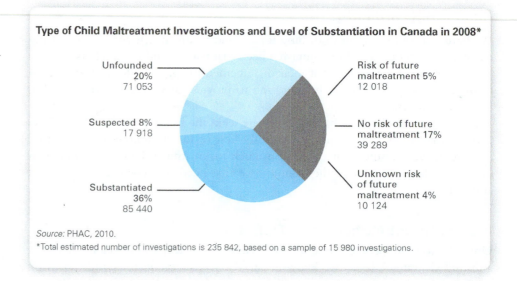

Type of Child Maltreatment Investigations and Level of Substantiation in Canada in 2008*

Unfounded 20%
71 053

Suspected 8%
17 918

Substantiated 36%
85 440

Risk of future maltreatment 5%
12 018

No risk of future maltreatment 17%
39 289

Unknown risk of future maltreatment 4%
10 124

Source: PHAC, 2010.

*Total estimated number of investigations is 235 842, based on a sample of 15 980 investigations.

had the highest level of reporting (11.67 percent), with British Columbia having the second highest rate (4 percent). The Atlantic provinces had the lowest level of reporting, at 1.54 percent. Generally, Aboriginal children were at greater risk of maltreatment (18 percent) as compared to their non-Aboriginal peers (2.31 percent) (PHAC, 2010).

The number of substantiated victims is much lower than the number of reported victims primarily because the same child is often reported several times, leading to one substantiated case. Also, substantiation requires proof—obvious evidence (broken bones, severe malnutrition) or reliable witnesses.

Often the first sign of maltreatment is delayed development, such as slow growth, immature communication, lack of curiosity, or unusual social interactions. Anyone familiar with child development can observe a young child and notice such problems. Maltreated children often seem fearful, startled by noise, defensive and quick to attack, and confused between fantasy and reality. Table 6.3 lists signs of child maltreatment, both neglect and abuse. None of these signs are proof that a child has been abused, but whenever any of them occurs, it signifies trouble.

Noticing children who are maltreated is only part of the task; we also need to notice the conditions and contexts that make abuse or neglect more likely (Daro, 2009). Poverty, social isolation, and inadequate support (public and private) for caregivers are among them. From a developmental perspective, immaturity of the caregiver is a risk factor: Maltreatment is more common if parents are younger than 20 or if families have several children under age 6.

Consequences of Maltreatment

The impact of any child-rearing practice is affected by the cultural context. Certain customs (such as circumcision, pierced ears, and spanking) are considered abusive in some cultures but not in others; their effects on children vary accordingly. Children suffer most if their parents seem to love them less when compared with the love they witness in neighbourhood families. For example, if a parent forbids something other children have (from candy to cellphones) or punishes more severely or not at all, children might feel unloved.

Although culture is always relevant, as more longitudinal research is published, the effects of maltreatment are proving to be devastating and long lasting. The physical and academic impairment from maltreatment is relatively easy to notice—a nurse sees that a child is bruised and broken, a teacher sees that a child is hungry, sleepy, or

✦ **ESPECIALLY FOR Nurses** While weighing a 4-year-old, you notice several bruises on the child's legs. When you ask about them, the child says nothing and the parent says the child bumps into things. What should you do? (see response, page 243) ➞

TABLE 6.3 Signs of Maltreatment in Children Aged 2 to 10

Injuries that do not fit an "accidental" explanation, such as bruises on both sides of the face or body; burns with a clear line between burned and unburned skin; "falls" that result in cuts, not scrapes

Repeated injuries, especially broken bones not properly tended (visible on X-ray)

Fantasy play, with dominant themes of violence or sexual knowledge

Slow physical growth, especially with unusual appetite or lack of appetite

Ongoing physical complaints, such as stomach aches, headaches, genital pain, sleepiness

Reluctance to talk, to play, or to move, especially if development is slow

No close friendships; hostility toward others; bullying of smaller children

Hypervigilance, with quick, impulsive reactions, such as cringing, startling, or hitting

Frequent absence from school

Frequent changes of address

Turnover in caregivers who pick up child, or caregiver who comes late, seems high

Expressions of fear rather than joy on seeing the caregiver

ANSWER TO **OBSERVATION QUIZ**
(from p. 239) Changes in rates might be due to changes in awareness of the problem, in legislation, in definitions of the problem, and/or in the actual rate of maltreatment. ●

failing despite ability. However, when researchers follow maltreated children over the years, enduring deficits in social skills seem even more crippling than physical or academic ones. To be specific, many studies have found that mistreated children typically regard other people as hostile and exploitative; hence, these children are less friendly, more aggressive, and more isolated than other children. The earlier abuse starts and the longer it continues, the worse children's peer relationships become (Scannapieco & Connell-Carrick, 2005).

Child neglect is three times more common than overt abuse. Research shows that children who were neglected experience even greater social deficits than abused ones because they were unable to relate to anyone, even in infancy (Stevenson, 2007). The best cure for a mistreated child is a warm and enduring friendship, but maltreatment makes this unlikely.

Adults who were severely maltreated (physically, sexually, or emotionally) often engage in self-destructive behaviours such as drug or alcohol abuse, eating disorders, or violence. They also may repeatedly enter unhealthy relationships, or sabotage their own careers. In addition, they have a much higher risk of emotional disorders and suicide attempts, even after other risk factors (e.g., poverty) are taken into account (Afifi et al., 2008).

Finding and keeping a job is a critical aspect of adult well-being; adults who were maltreated suffer in this way as well. One study (Currie & Widom, 2010) matched 807 children who had experienced substantiated abuse with other children from the same neighbourhood, and of the same sex, ethnicity, and SES. About 35 years later, the employment rate for those who had been mistreated was 14 percent lower than the rate for those who had not been abused. The researchers concluded that abused and neglected children experience large and enduring economic consequences (Currie & Widom, 2010). In this study, the women were more impaired than the men: It may be that self-esteem, emotional stability, and social skills are even more important for female than for male employees.

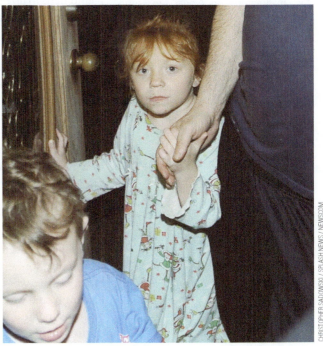

Abuse Victim? Anna (shown here), age 5, told the school nurse she was sunburned because her mother, Patricia, took her to a tanning salon. Patricia said Anna was gardening in the sun; Anna's father and brother (also shown here) said all three waited outside the salon while Patricia tanned inside. The story led to an arrest for child endangerment, a court trial, and a media frenzy.

CHRISTOPHER SADOWSKI / SPLASH NEWS / NEWSCOM

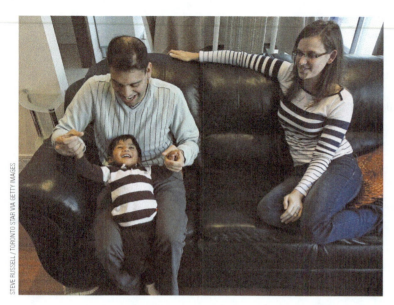

Learning to Trust Owen, adopted from India, laughs and plays with his parents in Toronto, Ontario. Amy, his mother, spent eight months in Bangalore, India, with her husband Trevor's family while the adoption was being processed. Amy spent weeks holding Owen, until finally, after seven months, he responded by holding on to her too.

permanency planning
An effort by child welfare authorities to find a long-term living situation that will provide stability and support for a maltreated child. A goal is to avoid repeated changes of caregiver or school, which can be particularly harmful to the child.

kinship care
A form of foster care in which a relative of a maltreated child, usually a grandparent, becomes the approved caregiver.

Three Levels of Prevention, Revisited

Just as with injury control, there are three levels of prevention of maltreatment. The ultimate goal is *primary prevention,* which focuses on the macrosystem and exosystem. Examples of primary prevention include increasing stable neighbourhoods and family cohesion, and decreasing financial instability, family isolation, and adolescent parenthood.

Secondary prevention involves spotting warning signs and intervening to keep a risky situation from getting worse (Giardino & Alexander, 2011). For example, insecure attachment, especially of the disorganized type (described in Chapter 4), is a sign of a disrupted parent–child relationship. Secondary prevention includes home visits by helpful nurses or social workers, as well as high-quality daycare that gives vulnerable parents a break while teaching children how to make friends and resolve conflicts.

Tertiary prevention includes everything that limits harm after maltreatment has already occurred. Reporting and substantiating abuse are only the first steps. Often the caregiver needs help to provide better care. Sometimes the child needs another home. If hospitalization is required, that signifies failure: Intervention should have begun much earlier. At that point, treatment is very expensive, harm has already been done, and hospitalization itself further strains the parent–child bond (Rovi et al., 2004).

Children need caregivers they trust, in safe and stable homes, whether they live with their biological parents, a foster family, or an adoptive family. Whenever a child is legally removed from an abusive or neglectful home and placed in foster care, **permanency planning** must begin, to find a family to nurture the child until adulthood. Permanency planning is a complex task. Parents are reluctant to give up their rights to the child; foster parents hesitate to take a child who is hostile and frightened; maltreated children need intensive medical and psychological help but foster care agencies are slow to pay for such services.

The most common type of foster care in North America is **kinship care** (see Chapter 4), in which a relative (most often the grandmother) takes over child-rearing from parents who are either abusive or simply unable to give their children the care they need. Unfortunately, kinship care typically receives fewer services and adds stress to the lives of the adults involved, a topic further discussed in Chapter 15 (Sakai et al., 2011). While adults argue about parental rights, criminal charges, and cultural differences, the immediate needs of the child may be ignored. A good treatment plan requires cooperation among social workers, judges, and psychologists, as well as the caregivers themselves (Edwards, 2007). Governments have to ensure that children who are taken from their parents' care—for whatever reason—do not get lost in the bureaucracy.

One tragic case in point involved a young First Nations boy from Norway House in Manitoba. Jordan River Anderson was born with a rare muscular disorder that meant he had very complex medical needs. Realizing they couldn't care for him themselves, Jordan's parents placed him with a child welfare agency shortly after his birth, and he was immediately admitted into a Winnipeg hospital. In the meantime, his family and the welfare agency worked to find him a foster home that could meet both his medical needs and give him the benefits of growing up in a positive family environment.

Shortly after his second birthday, the doctors were ready to release Jordan from hospital, but at that point the provincial and federal governments, who share jurisdiction for First Nations people, began a dispute over who should pay for Jordan's foster care. The dispute dragged on for more than two years as officials argued over the cost of installing a special ramp and the price of a showerhead. Shortly after Jordan's fifth birthday, he accidently pulled out his breathing tube and died in hospital (Lavallee, 2005).

This tragedy led to the establishment of Jordan's Principle, a measure meant to resolve jurisdictional disputes between the federal and provincial/territorial governments that involve services provided to First Nations children. Under this principle, whenever a dispute arises between two levels of government or between two departments of the same government over which should pay for services for a First Nations child, the government or department of first contact is required to pay until the dispute has been resolved. Under a private member's motion, Jordan's Principle was unanimously supported by the House of Commons in 2007 (Aboriginal Affairs and Northern Development Canada, 2013).

As detailed many times in this chapter, caring for young children—from making sure they brush their teeth to guiding their emotions—is not easy. Parents shoulder most of the burden, and their love and protection usually result in strong and happy children. Sadly, parents do not always get the help they need, and children sometimes suffer.

◆ **RESPONSE FOR Nurses** (from page 240) Any suspicion of child maltreatment must be reported, and these bruises are suspicious. Someone in authority must find out what is happening so that the parent as well as the child can be helped. →

KEY Points

- The source of child maltreatment is often the family system and the cultural context, not a disturbed stranger.
- Child maltreatment includes both abuse and neglect, with neglect more common and perhaps more destructive.
- Maltreatment can have long-term effects on cognitive and social development, depending partly on the child's personality and on cultural values.
- Prevention can be primary (laws and practices that protect everyone), secondary (protective measures for high-risk situations), and tertiary (reduction of harm after maltreatment has occurred).

SUMMARY

Emotional Development

1. Learning to regulate and control emotions is crucial during early childhood. Emotional regulation is made possible by maturation of the brain, particularly of the prefrontal cortex, as well as by experiences with parents and peers.

2. In Erikson's psychosocial theory, the crisis of initiative versus guilt occurs during early childhood. Children normally feel pride, sometimes mixed with feelings of guilt. Shame is also evident, particularly in some cultures.

3. Both externalizing and internalizing problems indicate impaired self-control. Some emotional problems that indicate psychopathology are first evident during these years, with boys more often manifesting externalizing behaviours and girls exhibiting internalizing behaviours.

Gender Development

4. Even 2-year-olds correctly use sex-specific labels. Young children become aware of gender differences in clothes, toys, playmates, and future careers.

5. Freud emphasized that children are attracted to the opposite-sex parent and eventually seek to identify, or align themselves, with the same-sex parent. Behaviourists hold that gender-related behaviours are learned through reinforcement and punishment (especially for males) and social modelling.

6. Cognitive theorists note that simplistic preoperational thinking leads to gender schemas and therefore stereotypes. Systems theory teaches that parents' expectations and views will affect their children's understanding of gender roles. Humanists stress the powerful need of all humans to belong to their group.

Evolutionary theory contends that sex and gender differences are crucial for the survival and reproduction of the species.

7. All six theories of sex-role development are plausible. Deciding what gender patterns parents and caregivers should teach is determined by parenting/caregiving style and culture.

Play

8. All young children enjoy playing—preferably with other children of the same sex, who teach them lessons in social interaction that their parents do not.

9. Active play takes many forms, with rough-and-tumble play fostering social skills and sociodramatic play developing emotional regulation.

10. Children are prime consumers of many kinds of media. The problems that arise from media exposure include increased aggression and less creative play.

The Role of Caregivers

11. Baumrind identified four classic styles of parenting: authoritarian, permissive, authoritative, and rejecting-neglecting. Generally, children are more successful and happy when their parents express warmth and set guidelines, characteristic of authoritative parenting.

12. Child temperament and culture play a role in parenting style.

Moral Development

13. The sense of self and the social awareness of young children become the foundation for morality, influenced by both nature and nurture.

14. Children from a young age have an understanding of the difference between morality and social conventions.

15. Prosocial emotions lead to caring for others; antisocial behaviour includes instrumental, reactive, relational, and bullying aggression.

16. Parental punishment can have long-term consequences, with both corporal punishment and psychological control teaching lessons that few parents want their children to learn.

17. Time out or parents explaining the situation is more appropriate and associated with more positive outcomes.

Child Maltreatment

18. Child maltreatment includes ongoing abuse and neglect, usually by a child's own parents. Physical abuse is the most obvious form of maltreatment, but neglect is more common and may be more harmful.

19. Health, learning, and social skills are all impeded by abuse and neglect, not only during childhood but also decades later.

20. Tertiary prevention may include placement of a child in foster care, such as kinship care. Permanency planning is needed: Frequent changes are harmful to children.

KEY TERMS

antipathy (p. 233)
antisocial behaviour (p. 233)
authoritarian parenting (p. 227)
authoritative parenting (p. 228)
bullying aggression (p. 234)
child abuse (p. 239)
child maltreatment (p. 239)
child neglect (p. 239)
Electra complex (p. 218)
emotional regulation (p. 212)
empathy (p. 233)
externalizing problems (p. 216)

extrinsic motivation (p. 213)
gender constancy (p. 218)
gender differences (p. 217)
gender identity (early childhood) (p. 217)
gender schema (p. 220)
gender stability (p. 217)
identification (p. 218)
initiative versus guilt (p. 212)
instrumental aggression (p. 234)
internalizing problems (p. 216)

intrinsic motivation (p. 213)
kinship care (p. 242)
Oedipus complex (p. 218)
permanency planning (p. 242)
permissive parenting (p. 228)
phallic stage (p. 218)
prosocial behaviour (p. 233)
psychological control (p. 236)
psychopathology (p. 216)
reactive aggression (p. 234)
rejecting-neglecting parenting (p. 228)

relational aggression (p. 234)
reported maltreatment (p. 239)
rough-and-tumble play (p. 224)
self-concept (p. 212)
sex differences (p. 217)
sex homophily (p. 222)
sociodramatic play (p. 224)
substantiated maltreatment (p. 239)
superego (p. 218)
time out (p. 237)

WHAT HAVE YOU LEARNED?

1. How might positivity bias lead to a child's acquisition of new skills and competencies?

2. What are examples of intrinsic versus extrinsic motivations for reading a book?

3. What is the connection between psychopathology and emotional regulation?

4. What does psychoanalytic theory say about the origins of sex differences and gender roles?

5. What do behaviourists say about the origins of sex differences and gender roles?

6. How does evolutionary theory explain why children follow gender norms?

7. In what ways might playing with peers teach emotional regulation, empathy, and cultural understanding?

8. How is the development of social play affected by culture?

9. Why might children's muscle strength and control develop better when playing with peers than when playing alone?

10. What do children learn from rough-and-tumble play?

11. What do children learn from sociodramatic play?

12. Why might North American child professionals advise no or limited electronic media for young children?

13. Describe the characteristics of the parenting style that seems to promote the happiest, most successful children.

14. What did Piaget believe about the moral development of children? How might evolutionary theory explain moral development?

15. What is the nature perspective on how people develop morals? What is the nurture perspective?

16. How might children develop empathy and antipathy as they play with one another?

17. What is the connection between empathy and prosocial behaviour?

18. What are the similarities and differences among the four kinds of aggression?

19. How does moral development relate to discipline?

20. Why have many nations made corporal punishment illegal?

21. When is a time out an effective punishment and when is it not?

22. What are the advantages and disadvantages of using induction as punishment?

23. Why might poverty, isolation of parents, and lack of good child care contribute to child maltreatment?

24. Why is it difficult to know exactly how often childhood maltreatment occurs?

25. What are the short-term and long-term consequences of childhood maltreatment?

26. What are the three levels of prevention of maltreatment? Give examples of each.

APPLICATIONS

1. Children's television programming is rife with stereotypes about ethnicity, gender, and morality. Watch an hour of children's TV, especially on a Saturday morning, and describe the content of both the programs and the commercials. Draw some conclusions about stereotyping in the material you watched, citing specific evidence (rather than merely reporting your impressions).

2. Gender indicators often go unnoticed. Go to a public place (park, restaurant, busy street) and spend at least 10 minutes recording examples of gender differentiation, such as articles of clothing, mannerisms, interaction patterns, and activities.

Quantify what you see, such as baseball hats on eight males and two females. Or (better, but more difficult) describe four male–female conversations, indicating gender differences in length and frequency of talking, interruptions, vocabulary, and so on.

3. Ask three parents how they were punished as a child, for what misdeeds, and by whom. Then ask them what punishments they use with their own children. Ask them how they feel the way they were punished as children has affected the way they punish their children.

>>ONLINE CONNECTIONS

To accompany your textbook, you have access to a number of online resources, including LearningCurve, which is an adaptive quizzing program; critical thinking questions; and case studies. For access to any of these links, go to www.worthpublishers.com/launchpad/bergerchuang1e. In addition to these resources, you'll find links to video clips, personalized study advice, and an e-Book. Among the videos and activities available online is the following:

- *Children at Play*. Watch video clips of children at play, identify the types of play you see, and review how each type contributes to children's development.

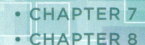
IV

Middle Childhood

Middle childhood, between the ages of 6 and 11 years, is when most children experience good health and steady growth as they master new athletic skills, learn thousands of words, and become less dependent on families. Usually they appreciate their parents, make new friends, and proudly learn about their country and religion. Life is safe and happy; the possible dangers of adolescence (drugs, sex, violence) are not yet on the horizon.

However, these years are not without challenges. Some children hate school; some live in destructive families; some have no permanent home. Others contend with obesity, asthma, learning disabilities, or bullies. The next two chapters celebrate the joys and discuss the difficulties of ages 6 to 11.

part

CHAPTER OUTLINE

MIDDLE CHILDHOOD:
Body and Mind

WHAT WILL YOU KNOW?

- Why have child obesity rates skyrocketed over the last 20 years?
- Why are math concepts difficult at age 4 but much easier at age 8?
- What is the most effective way to teach a child a new language?
- Are schools in Canada similar to schools in other nations?
- What causes a child to have autism spectrum disorder?

During one of our Christmas holidays, my oldest brother, Sam, brought his family from Nevada to our home in Brampton, Ontario. Sam's 10-year-old son, David, was a chess enthusiast who had been well schooled by his father. Sam never showed David any leniency on the chessboard, and this forced David to improve his skills in the ongoing quest to finally win a game against his dad. By the time David reached his 10th birthday, he could hold his own against his father at chess, and even beat him on a semi-regular basis.

My youngest brother, Andy, had heard about David's growing skill at chess. Andy was in his 30s at this point and took great pride in his chess abilities. This led him, on the last night of the holidays, to challenge his 10-year-old nephew to a game of chess.

Everyone gathered around the kitchen table to watch the game unfold. Young David seemed to employ an odd strategy, moving his line of pawns to create a zigzag pattern on the board.

"What's he doing?" someone asked. Andy, the boy's opponent, just shook his head and laughed.

"Nothing," he said. "It doesn't mean a thing."

But a few minutes later, David respectfully announced "Checkmate," stunning his uncle and the rest of us.

Convinced the first game was a fluke, Andy demanded a rematch. When David declined, his uncle insisted.

"One more game," he said. "And if you beat me again, I'll call you 'Chess Master.'"

So they played again with the same result: The 10-year-old defeated the man in his thirties. David left that night as "Chess Master," with Andy marvelling over the skill and poise shown by his much younger opponent. ●

—Susan Chuang

THIS CHAPTER DESCRIBES NOT ONLY THE ADVANCEMENTS OF children's cognitive abilities during middle childhood, but also other developments such as health and language. There are similarities among children, but also differences—in size, health, learning ability, and more. At the end of this chapter, we focus on children with special needs.

Health and Sickness

Genetic and environmental factors safeguard **middle childhood** (about ages 6 to 11 years), the period after early childhood and before adolescence. One explanation comes from the evolutionary perspective: Genes protect children who have already survived the hazards of birth and early childhood so they can live long enough to reproduce (Konner, 2010). This evolutionary explanation may not be accurate, but for whatever reason, fewer fatal diseases or accidents resulting in death occur from age 6 to age 11 than at any other period of life (see Figure 7.1).

Slower Growth, Greater Strength

Unlike infants or adolescents, school-age children's growth is slow and steady. Self-care is easy—from brushing their new teeth to dressing themselves, from making their own lunch to walking with friends to school. Once at school, brain maturation allows most of them to sit at their desks or tables and learn without too much difficulty.

Muscles, including the heart and lungs, become strong. With each passing year, children can run faster and exercise longer (Malina et al., 2004). As long as school-age children get enough food, they continue to grow 5 centimetres or more each year.

Medical Care

Immunization has reduced deaths dramatically, and throughout childhood, lethal accidents and fatal illnesses are far less common than a few years ago. For example, in Canada, before immunizations were introduced, about 9000 people, many of them young children, contracted diphtheria over any given five-year period. However, between 2000

middle childhood
The period between early childhood and early adolescence, approximately from ages 6 to 11.

FIGURE 7.1 Death in Middle Childhood Is Rare Schoolchildren are remarkably hardy, as measured in many ways. These charts show that death rates for 5- to 14-year-olds are lower than those for children younger than 5 or older than 14, and are much lower than those for adults.

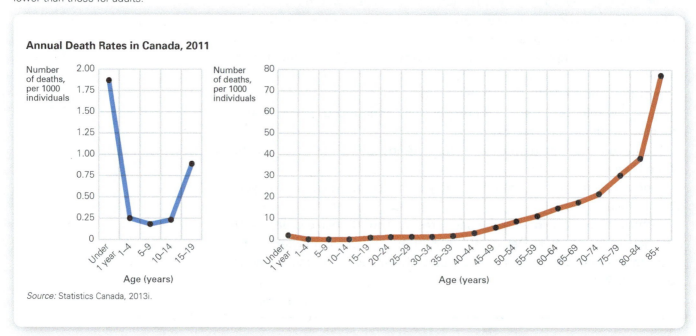

Annual Death Rates in Canada, 2011

Source: Statistics Canada, 2013i.

and 2004 (well after the introduction of the diphtheria vaccine), only one case of diphtheria was reported in Canada (Public Health Agency of Canada, 2011b).

Furthermore, better medical care (diagnostic and preventative) has meant fewer children suffer with chronic conditions such as hearing impairments or anemia—both of which are half as frequent in middle childhood as they were two decades ago. Fewer children breathe second-hand smoke: Cotinine (a biomarker that reveals inhaled nicotine) in children's blood declined by 28 percent in just one decade (1994–2004) (Morbidity and Mortality Weekly Report, July 11, 2008).

For all children, establishing good health habits in childhood protects health in adolescence and adulthood. This is especially important for children with serious, chronic conditions (such as diabetes, phenylketonuria [PKU], epilepsy, cancer, asthma, and sickle-cell anemia) who, as teenagers, may become rebellious and ignore special diets, pills, warning signs, and doctors (Dean et al., 2010; Suris et al., 2008).

Unfortunately, children in poor health for economic or social reasons are vulnerable throughout their lives. For low-income children, particularly, having a parent who is attentive and responsive (not only regarding health) makes a decided difference for adult health (Miller et al., 2011).

Physical Activity

The level of physical activity of children in middle childhood affects both their mental and physical health. The Health Behaviour in School-Aged Children Study (HBSC) examined the number of youth between the ages of 10 and 16 in 34 countries who engage in at least 60 minutes of physical activity a day for five or more days per week. Looking specifically at the data for 11-year-olds, youth from Ireland (31 percent of girls and 43 percent of boys), Austria (30 percent and 40 percent respectively), and Spain (26 percent and 41 percent respectively) fared best in the study. The least active groups were from the Russian Federation (11 percent of girls and 17 percent of boys), Denmark (10 percent and 16 percent respectively), and Italy (7 percent and 10 percent respectively). Canada ranked eleventh of the 34 countries, with 21 percent of 11-year-old girls and 31 percent of boys reporting at last one hour of daily physical activity. In addition, the results indicated that physical activity significantly decreases between ages 11 and 15 years (Currie et al., 2012).

Ian Janssen from Queen's University, Ontario, and his international collaborators examined the data from an earlier version of this study. They found that lower physical activity and a greater amount of time spent watching television were associated with a greater likelihood of becoming overweight (Janssen et al., 2005).

Beyond the sheer fun of playing, some benefits of physical activity are immediate. For example, a Canadian study found that 6- and 7-year-olds who felt victimized by peers improved academically if they played sports (Perron et al., 2011). Active play contributes to the following:

- better overall health
- less obesity
- appreciation of cooperation and fair play, especially when playing games with rules
- improved problem-solving abilities
- respect for teammates and opponents of many ethnicities and nationalities.

DAVID MERCADO / REUTERS / CORBIS

Expert Eye–Hand Coordination The specifics of motor-skill development in middle childhood depend on the culture. These flute players are carrying on the European Baroque musical tradition that thrives among the Guarayo people of Bolivia.

OBSERVATION QUIZ
Why do you think that level of physical activity decreases after age 11? (see answer, page 253) →

Playing sports during middle childhood also has risks:

- loss of self-esteem (teammates and coaches are sometimes cruel)
- injuries (sometimes serious, including concussions)
- reinforcement of prejudices (especially against the other sex)
- increased stress (evidenced by altered hormone levels, insomnia).

Where can children reap the benefits and avoid the hazards of active play? There are three possibilities: neighbourhoods, schools, and sports leagues.

Why Helmets? Children participating in organized sports, such as these 6- to 8-year-old male and female hockey players in Vancouver, BC, need to take precautions to avoid injuries. The emphasis at this age is on skill development and having fun. Young children are not allowed to body check, and at all ages they wear helmets to protect against potential concussions.

✦ ESPECIALLY FOR Physical Education Teachers A group of parents of Grade 4 and 5 students has asked for your help in persuading the school administration to sponsor a competitive sports team. How should you advise the group to proceed? (see response, page 255) →

Idyllic Two 8-year-olds, each with a 6-year-old sister, are daydreaming or exploring in a very old tree beside a lake in Denmark—what could be better?

NEIGHBOURHOOD GAMES Neighbourhood play is flexible. Rules and boundaries are adapted to the context (out of bounds is "past the tree" or "behind the parked truck"). Street hockey, touch football, tag, hide-and-seek, and dozens of other running and catching games go on forever—or at least until dark. The play is active, interactive, and inclusive—ideal for children of both sexes and several ages. It also teaches ethics. One scholar notes:

> Children play tag, hide and seek, or pickup basketball. They compete with one another but always according to rules, and rules that they enforce themselves without recourse to an impartial judge. The penalty for not playing by the rules is not playing, that is, social exclusion. ...
>
> *[Gillespie, 2010, p. 398]*

Unfortunately, "not playing" is not only a consequence of ignoring the rules, but also of not having the time or a place to play. Parks and empty fields are increasingly scarce. A century ago, 90 percent of the world's children lived in rural areas; now most live in cities or at the city's edge.

To make matters worse, many parents keep their children inside because they fear "stranger danger"—although one expert writes that "there is a much greater chance that your child is going to be dangerously overweight from staying inside than that he is going to be abducted" (quoted in Layden, 2004, p. 86). Homework and video games compete with outdoor play, especially in North America. According to an Australian scholar,

> Australian children are lucky. Here the dominant view is that children's after school time is leisure time. In the United States, it seems that leisure time is available to fewer and fewer children. If a child performs poorly in school, recreation time rapidly becomes remediation time. For high achievers, after school time is often spent in academic enrichment.
>
> *[Vered, 2008, p. 170]*

Canada and the United States are not the worst-offending nations in terms of using after-school time as study time instead of play time. South Korea, in particular, is known for the intensity of "shadow education," which is extra tutoring that parents find for their children, hoping to improve their test grades later on (Lee & Schouse, 2011).

ORGANIZED SPORT Schools in North America often have after-school sports teams, which offer additional opportunities for activity, as do private or non-profit clubs and organizations.

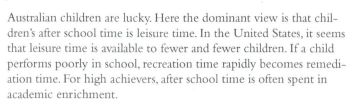

The organization known as Physical and Health Education Canada recommends that children receive at least 150 minutes of physical education (PE) a week. In reality, however, only 47 percent of parents report that their children receive enough activity through physical education classes at school (Canadian Fitness and Lifestyle Research Institute [CFLRI], 2011c).

Paradoxically, school exercise may actually improve academic achievement (Carlson et al., 2008), partly because of the increased blood flow to the brain. The Centers for Disease Control recommends that children be active (i.e., not sit on the sidelines awaiting a turn) for at least half of the time in their physical education classes (Khan et al., 2009). Many schools do not reach this goal.

About 75 percent of Canadian children engage in organized sports or physical activities (CFLRI, 2011a). The organized sport that parents sign their children up for varies depending on the family's culture and socioeconomic status. For example, some children join hockey leagues, others learn to play basketball or soccer, and others take karate or swimming lessons.

Unfortunately, children from low-SES families or with disabilities are less likely to belong to local clubs and teams, yet they would benefit most from the strength, activity, and teamwork of organized play. Even when joining is free, these children are less likely to be involved in extracurricular activities of any kind, and as a result, they do not reap the benefits of a more active lifestyle (Dearing et al., 2009). It is worth noting that Canadian children from higher-income families have a 25 percent higher participation rate than their peers from lower-income families (CFLRI, 2011b).

"Just remember, son, it doesn't matter whether you win or lose—unless you want Daddy's love."

ANSWER TO **OBSERVATION QUIZ**
(from page 251) Older children tend to spend more time on screen-related activities (texting, emailing, playing video games, watching movies/videos, etc.), which decreases the amount of time they spend on physical activity. ●

A VIEW FROM SCIENCE

Canadian Kids Get an "F" in Physical Activity

In the past several years, many scientific studies have established strong links between physical activity in middle childhood and the improved functioning of young bodies and minds (Bürgi et al., 2011; Davis et al., 2007). Demonstrated benefits include

- improved motor skills
- better aerobic fitness
- improved cognitive functions
- higher self-esteem.

Specifically, moderate to intense levels of physical activity have been shown to lower blood pressure and reduce body fat. Physically active children also appear to experience fewer problems with their mental health (Biddle & Asare, 2011).

With these proven benefits in mind, it is alarming that researchers have also documented steep declines over the last 50 years in physical activity levels among children in Canada and other countries. For example, data from the research organization Active Healthy Kids Canada (AHKC) show that from 2000 to 2010, the number of children who played outside after school dropped by 14 percent (AHKC, 2012b).

The Canadian Fitness & Lifestyle Research Institute (2011b) reported that in 2010, outdoor play was greater among boys than girls, and almost twice as high among 5- to 12-year-olds as among 13- to 17-year-olds (see Figure 7.2). In addition, children of younger parents were more likely to play outdoors and participate in unorganized physical activity and sport than were children of older parents.

Health Canada and the World Health Organization both recommend that 5- to 11-year-olds get at least 60 minutes of moderate to vigorous physical activity a day in order to enjoy the physical, mental, and emotional benefits outlined above (Tremblay et al., 2011). Sadly, very few Canadian children meet this minimum standard.

AHKC issues an annual bulletin in the form of a report card on activity levels of Canadian children. In 2012, the news was so dismal that AHKC entitled its report *Is Active Play Extinct?* and illustrated it with photographs of dinosaur skeletons juxtaposed with such childhood relics as paddle balls, skipping ropes, and hula hoops. For the sixth straight year, AHKC assigned Canadian children a grade of "F" in the category of physical activity (AHKC, 2012b).

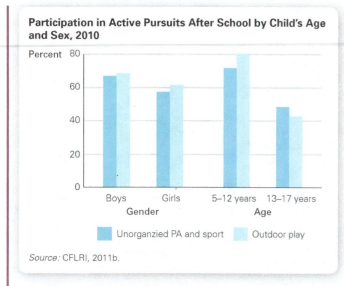

Participation in Active Pursuits After School by Child's Age and Sex, 2010

Source: CFLRI, 2011b.

FIGURE 7.2 Older Kids Play Less Boys and girls of all ages participate in organized physical activities at a similar rate, however there are age and gender differences in terms of participation in unorganized physical activity and sport and outdoor play, as shown in this graph. What effects might this result have on physical and mental development in middle childhood?

The data reported do indeed tell a grim story. Only 7 percent of Canadian children get the recommended 60 minutes of physical activity a day. This means the vast majority—93 percent—fail to meet even the minimum guidelines established by Health Canada. In fact, almost half of all Canadian children—46 percent—spend less than three hours a week in physical activity. This decline in physical activity correlates closely with rising rates of childhood obesity and the chronic diseases associated with these conditions, such as diabetes, heart disease, and high blood pressure (Anderson et al., 2006; Lambourne & Donnelly, 2011).

What has caused this remarkable falling off in activity levels among Canadian schoolchildren? According to the AHKC report, the two main reasons are

- safety concerns that lead to overprotective parenting
- dramatic increases in screen time for children and youth.

Even though Canadian crime rates are no higher today than in the 1970s, parents are more aware of cases of child assault and abduction due to greater media exposure (AHKC, 2012a; Silver, 2007). As a result, many parents have developed a "better safe than sorry" attitude. Whereas in past decades they allowed their children to play unsupervised for hours in empty lots or neighbourhood parks, today's parents take a much more cautious approach, encouraging their children to stay inside where they are easier to monitor.

Children's attraction to screen time means that most are only too happy to comply with the wishes of overly protective parents. One study indicates that Canadian children in Grades 6 to 12 spend an average of 7 hours and 48 minutes a day in front of the screens of their computers, televisions, video games, and smart phones (Leatherdale & Ahmed, 2011).

The result of parental worries over safety and their children's fascination with electronic media is that Canadian kids spend about 63 percent of their free time being sedentary, getting no exercise at all. In fact, on weekends, when they have an abundance of time to spend as they please, they are actually less active than during the week (Garriguet & Colley, 2012).

Both AHKC (2012b) and the Heart and Stroke Foundation of Canada (2011) make a number of recommendations that they hope will reverse declining rates of physical activity among children:

- Provide greater access to playing fields, natural areas, and parks, along with equipment such as balls and skipping ropes to encourage active play.
- Encourage children to engage in modes of active transportation such as walking, cycling, and in-line skating or skateboarding. Facilitate this through improvements to sidewalks, bike lanes, and pedestrian crosswalks.
- Support school environments that encourage healthy activity through physical education programs.
- Put in place household rules and limits to discourage excessive amounts of screen time, and provide time for active sport and play.

As Dr. Mark Tremblay, director of the Healthy Active Living and Obesity Research Group at the Children's Hospital of Eastern Ontario, noted, all children, regardless of age, should be engaged in regular forms of active play, where they can run, climb, jump, or cartwheel in open and safe places with their friends, like their parents once did. Active play not only improves children's motor function, but also their levels of creativity, decision making, problem solving, and social skills (AHKC, 2012a).

Health Problems

Although few children are seriously ill during middle childhood, many have at least one chronic condition that might interfere with school, play, or friendship. Individual, family, and contextual influences interact with one another in the causes and treatments of every illness. To illustrate the dynamic interactions of every health condition, we focus on two examples: obesity and asthma.

CHILDHOOD OBESITY **Body mass index (BMI)**, as mentioned in Chapter 5, is the ratio of weight to height. **Childhood overweight** is usually defined as having a BMI above the 85th percentile, and **childhood obesity** as having a BMI above the 95th percentile of children of the same age (Barlow & the Expert Committee, 2007).

Childhood obesity is increasing worldwide, having more than doubled since 1980 in all three nations of North America (Canada, the United States, and Mexico) (Ogden et al., 2011). Statistics Canada reports that about one-third of 5- to 17-year-olds were classified as overweight or obese in 2009 to 2011. In addition, at ages 5 to 11 years, significantly more males than females were classified as obese (Roberts et al., 2012) (see Figure 7.3).

Childhood obesity is linked to asthma, high blood pressure, and elevated cholesterol (especially LDL, the "lousy" cholesterol). According to the Canadian Diabetes Association (2012), 95 percent of children with Type 2 diabetes—a disease once thought to be an adult problem that has been increasing in children and youth over the past few decades—are overweight. Being overweight can affect children in other ways as well. As excessive weight builds, school achievement often decreases, self-esteem falls, and loneliness rises (Harrist et al., 2012). If obese children stay heavy, they become adults who are less likely to marry, attend college or university, or find work that reflects their ability (Han et al, 2011; Sobal & Hanson, 2011).

There are hundreds if not thousands of contributing factors for childhood obesity, from the cells of the body to the norms of the society (Harrison et al., 2011). More than 200 genes affect weight by influencing activity level, food preference, body type, and metabolism (Gluckman & Hanson, 2006). Having two copies of an allele called FTO increases the likelihood of both obesity and diabetes (Frayling et al., 2007).

But we cannot solely blame genes for today's increased obesity, since genes change little from one generation to the next (Harrison et al., 2011). Rather, family practices and eating habits have changed. Obesity is more common in infants who are not breastfed, in preschoolers who watch TV and drink soft drinks, and in school-age children who are driven to school, sleep too little, and rarely play outside (Hart et al., 2011; Institute of Medicine, 2006; Rhee, 2008).

During middle childhood, children themselves may contribute to their weight gain by pestering parents for calorie-dense foods. In addition, social practices and policies have an impact (Branca et al., 2007): Communities and nations determine the quality of school lunches; the location of vending machines and fast-food restaurants; the prevalence of parks, bike paths, and sidewalks; and the subsidies for corn oil and sugar.

One particular culprit is advertising for candy, cereal, and fast food (Linn & Novosat, 2008); the rate of childhood obesity correlates with how often children see food commercials (Lobstein & Dibb, 2005). As one researcher at the Université du Québec à Montréal reported, the various advertising strategies used by companies have increased children's temptation as marketers have given products effective appeal—they seduce (Laperrière, 2009). Such advertising is illegal or limited on children's television in some countries.

Since every system (bio-, micro-, macro-, and exo-) is relevant, it is not surprising that parents blame genes or outsiders, while medical professionals and political

body mass index (BMI)
A person's weight in kilograms divided by the square of height in metres.

childhood overweight
A child having a BMI above the 85th percentile.

childhood obesity
A child having a BMI above the 95th percentile.

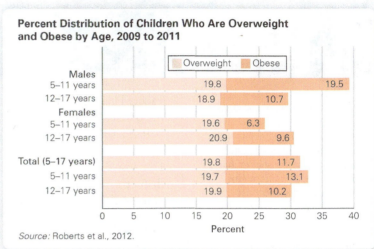

Source: Roberts et al., 2012.

FIGURE 7.3 Different for Boys and Girls Obesity rates are higher for males than females, especially those ages 5 to 11 years.

✦ **ESPECIALLY FOR Teachers** You are concerned about a child in your class who is overweight. What can you do to help? (see response, page 257) →

RESPONSE FOR Physical Education Teachers (from page 252) Discuss with the parents their reasons for wanting the team. Children need physical activity, but some aspects of competitive sports are better suited to adolescents and adults than to children. ●

Same Situation, Far Apart: Healthy Eating Children have small stomachs, so they enjoy frequent snacks more than big meals. Yet snacks are often poor sources of nutrition. Culture can also play a role in the snacks that children eat. Here, a boy from Alberta eats cotton candy, while Japanese children eat takoyaki (an octopus dumpling).

asthma
A chronic disease of the respiratory system in which inflammation narrows the airways from the nose and mouth to the lungs, causing difficulty in breathing. Signs and symptoms include wheezing, shortness of breath, chest tightness, and coughing.

leaders blame parents. The media contend that advertisements are only suggestions and parents or children are to blame if they follow harmful suggestions.

Rather than trying to zero in on any single factor, a dynamic-systems approach is needed: Many factors, over time, make a child overweight (Harrison et al., 2011). The answer to the first "What Will You Know?" question at the beginning of this chapter is precisely that: There are many reasons for childhood obesity and they are all interrelated.

ASTHMA **Asthma** is a chronic inflammatory disorder of the airways that makes breathing difficult. Although asthma affects people of every age, rates are highest among school-age children and have been increasing in most countries for decades (Cruz et al., 2010).

In Canada, asthma is one of the most common chronic childhood diseases (Garner & Kohen, 2008). After increasing steadily for several decades, the childhood asthma rate in Canada has levelled off and even declined slightly over the past few years (see Figure 7.4). Statistics Canada reports that asthma rates for children between the ages of 2 and 7 years rose from 11 percent in 1995 to as high as 13 percent in 2001, but then fell to 10 percent in 2009 (Thomas, 2010).

Many researchers are looking for the causes of asthma. A few alleles have been identified as contributing factors, but none acts in isolation (Akinbami et al., 2010; Bossé & Hudson, 2007). Several aspects of modern life—carpets, pollution, pets inside the home, airtight windows, parental smoking, cockroaches, less outdoor play—also contribute to the increased rates of asthma (Tamay et al., 2007), but again no single factor is the cause.

FIGURE 7.4 A Change for the Better As this bar graph shows, asthma rates among Canadian children peaked around the year 2001 and have dropped somewhat since then. Environmental factors that may have influenced this decline include a four-fold decrease between 2000 and 2008 in the number of children aged 1 to 11 who were exposed to cigarette smoke at home (Thomas, 2010).

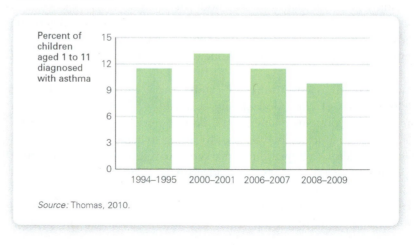

Percent of children aged 1 to 11 diagnosed with asthma

Source: Thomas, 2010.

Some experts suggest a *hygiene hypothesis*, proposing that "the immune system needs to tangle with microbes when we are young" (Leslie, 2012, p. 1428). Parents are so worried about viruses and bacteria that they overprotect their children, preventing minor infections and diseases that would strengthen their immunity. This hypothesis is supported by data showing that (1) first-born children develop asthma more often than later-born ones, perhaps because parents are more protective of first children than of later ones; (2) children growing up on farms have less asthma and other allergies, perhaps because they are exposed to more viruses and bacteria; and (3) children born by C-section (very sterile) have more asthma. However, none of those prove the hygiene hypothesis. Perhaps children living on farms are protected by drinking unpasteurized milk, by spending more time outdoors, or by genes that are more common in farm families (von Mutius & Vercelli, 2010).

The incidence of asthma increases as nations get richer, as seen dramatically in Brazil and China. Better hygiene is one explanation, but so is increasing urbanization, which correlates with more cars, more pollution, more allergens, and better medical diagnosis (Cruz et al., 2010). One review of the hygiene hypothesis notes that "the picture can be dishearteningly complex" (Couzin-Frankel, 2010, p. 1168)

PREVENTION OF HEALTH PROBLEMS The three levels of prevention (discussed in Chapters 5 and 6) apply to every health problem, including the two just reviewed: obesity and asthma.

Primary prevention requires changes in the entire society. Better ventilation of schools and homes, less pollution, fewer cockroaches, fewer antibiotics, and more outdoor play would benefit everyone. ParticipACTION's "Bring Back Play" initiative to promote outdoor play use is an example of primary prevention if it makes everyone more likely to be active.

Secondary prevention decreases illness among high-risk children. If asthma or obesity runs in the family, then breastfeeding for a year, regular and sufficient sleep, and low-fat diets would help prevent some illness. Annual checkups by the same pediatrician—who tests vision, hearing, weight, posture, blood pressure, and more—can spot potential problems while secondary prevention is still possible.

Finally, *tertiary prevention* treats problems after they appear. For asthma, for instance, that means prompt use of injections and inhalers. Even if tertiary prevention does not halt a condition, it can reduce the burden on the child.

RESPONSE FOR Teachers (from page 255) You could incorporate lessons about healthy snacks and exercise levels into the school day for the whole class so the child doesn't feel singled out. Children who learn about health from their teachers may then ask their parents for opportunities to exercise, to join a sports team, and so on. ●

Prevalence of Asthma The use of asthma inhalers by children in school is quite common. The causes of asthma are still unknown, although researchers point to genetic factors, parental smoking, house pets, pollution, and lack of exposure to viruses and bacteria as possible factors.

KATHY MCLAUGHLIN / THE IMAGE WORKS

Cognition in Middle Childhood

Learning is rapid in childhood. Young children's brains are continually growing and their cognitive abilities become more sophisticated. As you read at the beginning of this chapter, by age 11 some children can beat their elders at chess, while others play music that adults pay to hear, publish poems, or solve complex math problems in their heads. In fact, during these years, children can learn almost anything. Adults need to decide how and what to teach. Theories and practices differ, as you will see.

Piaget and Middle Childhood

concrete operational thought
Piaget's term for the ability to reason logically about direct experiences and perceptions.

Piaget called the cognition of middle childhood **concrete operational thought,** characterized by concepts that enable children to use logic. Operational comes from the Latin word *operare*, "to work; to produce."

By calling this period "operational," Piaget emphasized productive thinking. The 6- to 11-year-old school-age child, no longer limited by egocentrism and static reasoning, performs logical operations. However, thinking at this stage is concrete—that is, logic is applied to visible, tangible, real things, not to abstractions, which are understood at the next stage, formal operations.

classification
The logical principle that things can be organized into groups (or categories or classes) according to some characteristic they have in common.

A HIERARCHY OF CATEGORIES An example of concrete thinking is **classification,** the organization of things into groups (or *categories* or *classes*) according to some characteristic that they share. For example, children may sort their building blocks by shapes (squares, triangles, rectangles) or sort their Smarties by colour before eating them. Other common classes are people and animals. Each class includes some elements and excludes others, and each is part of a hierarchy.

Piaget devised many experiments to reveal children's understanding of classification. For example, in one study, an examiner showed a child a bunch of nine flowers—seven yellow daisies and two white roses (revised and published in Piaget et al., 2001). The examiner made sure the child knew the words "flowers," "daisies," and "roses." Then the examiner asked, "Are there more daisies or more flowers?" Until about age 7, most children say, "More daisies." Young children offer no justification for their answers, but some 6- or 7-year-olds explain that "there are more yellow ones than white ones" or that "because daisies are daisies, they aren't flowers" (Piaget et al., 2001). By age 8, most children can classify correctly: "More flowers than daisies," they say, and they can explain why they think so.

✦ **ESPECIALLY FOR Teachers** How might Piaget's and Vygotsky's ideas help in teaching geography to a class of Grade 3 students? (see response, page 260) ➡

MATH CONCEPTS Another logical concept is *seriation*, the understanding that things can be arranged in a logical series, such as from smallest to biggest. Seriation is crucial for using the alphabet or the number sequence (not merely memorizing, which younger children can do). By age 5 years, most children can count up to 100, but they cannot correctly estimate where any particular two-digit number would be placed on a line that starts at 0 and ends at 100. Generally, children can do this by age 8 (Meadows, 2006).

Concrete operational thinking allows children to understand math operations. For example, once children understand conservation (explained in Chapter 5), they realize that $12 + 3 = 3 + 12$, and that 15 is always 15. Reversibility allows the realization that if $5 \times 3 = 15$, then 15 divided by 3 must be 5.

Although Piaget was mistaken, there is no sudden shift between preoperational and concrete operational logic, his experiments revealed that, after about age 6, children use mental categories and subcategories more flexibly and inductively. They are less egocentric and more advanced as thinkers, and are operational in ways that younger children are not (Meadows, 2006).

Science Project Concrete operational 12-year-olds, like the girls shown here in a Toronto-area school, can be logical about anything they see, hear, or touch. Their science experiment—figuring out how to carry construction materials from the ground to the roof of the school—involves building elevators from Popsicle sticks, straws, tape, glue, and wood. As they work together to solve this problem, the girls discover what works and what doesn't, document why, and make changes as a result of their discoveries.

Vygotsky and Middle Childhood

Like Piaget, Vygotsky felt that educators should consider thought processes, not just the outcomes. He recognized that younger children are confused by some concepts that older children understand because they have not yet learned to process the ideas.

THE ROLE OF INSTRUCTION Unlike Piaget, Vygotsky regarded instruction as crucial to cognitive development (Vygotsky, 1934/1994). He thought that experts such as teachers and parents who have more advanced skills and knowledge can help children transition from potential development to actualization. Through the use of guided participation and scaffolding, children move through the zone of proximal development to eventually acquire the necessary skills and knowledge, as explained in Chapters 1 and 5.

Confirmation of the role of social interaction and instruction comes from children who, because of their school's entry-date cut-off, begin kindergarten when they are relatively young or old, not quite 5 or almost 6. Achievement scores of those 6-year-olds who began school relatively young, and thus already had a year of Grade 1, far exceed those of 6-year-olds who were born only one month later but had just completed kindergarten (Lincove & Painter, 2006; National Institute of Child Health and Human Development, 2007). Obviously, children learn a great deal from time in school.

Remember that Vygotsky believed education occurs everywhere—not only in school—through social interaction and technology. Children teach one another as they play together. They learn from people they see in the neighbourhood, from having dinner with their families, from television and computers, and from every other daily experience. In other words, children's cognitive development and learning is shaped by the everyday activity of their culture. And their culture influences what and how they learn.

An example of knowledge acquired from the social context comes from children in the northeast Indian district of Varanasi, many of whom have an extraordinary sense of spatial orientation—such as knowing whether they are facing north or south even when they are inside a room with no windows. In one experiment, after Varanasi children were blindfolded, spun around, and led to a second room, many of them knew which way they were facing (Mishra et al., 2009). This skill was learned during early childhood because people in that culture refer to the compass orientation to name the location of objects and so on. (Although the specifics differ, a cultural equivalent might be to say that the dog is sleeping southeast, not that the dog is sleeping by the door).

This amazing sense of direction, or any other skill learned in childhood, does not automatically transfer from one context to another. The blindfolded children retained their excellent sense of direction in this experiment, but a child from Varanasi might become disoriented in the tangle of mega-city streets—still knowing where north is, but not knowing how to get downtown. In addition, a child who is logical about math may not be logical about family relationships.

In North America, as in many parts of the world, adults are particularly concerned that 6- to 11-year-olds learn academic skills and knowledge. For this, Vygotsky's emphasis on mentoring is insightful. For instance, a large study of reading and math achievement of Grade 3 and 5 children found that high-scoring children usually had three sources of cognitive stimulation:

- their families (parents read to them daily when they were toddlers)
- preschool programs (children were involved with a variety of learning activities)
- Grade 1 (teachers emphasized literacy, with sensitivity to individual needs).

Although low-SES children were less likely to have all three experiences, the achievement scores of those few low-SES children who did have these mentoring advantages were higher than the average of high-SES children who did not have all three advantages (Crosnoe et al., 2010). In other words, active mentoring trumped socioeconomic status.

In addition, culture affects mentors and methods. This was evident in a study of 80 Mexican-American children in California (Silva et al., 2010). Half were from families where indigenous Indian learning was the norm: Children from that culture are expected to learn by watching others and to help each other if need be. The other half were from families more acculturated to U.S. norms; the children were accustomed to direct instruction, not observational learning. They expected to learn from adults and then to work on their own, without collaborating with their peers.

Researchers compared children from both backgrounds in a study in which children waited passively while a teacher taught their sibling how to make a toy. If they tried to help their brother or sister (more common among the indigenous children), they were prevented from doing so. A week later, the children were given an opportunity to make the toy themselves. The children from indigenous Indian backgrounds were better at it, which emphasizes that they learned more from observation than did the other children.

RESPONSE FOR Teachers (from page 258) Here are two of the most obvious ways. (1) Use logic. Once children can grasp classification and class inclusion, they can understand cities within provinces, provinces within countries, and countries within continents. Organize your instruction to make logical categorization easier. (2) Make use of children's need for concrete and personal involvement. You might have the children learn first about their own location, then about the places where relatives and friends live, and finally about places beyond their personal experience (via books, photographs, videos, and guest speakers). ●

The Importance of Formal Instruction Many child vendors, like this boy selling combs and other grooming aids on the streets of Manaus, Brazil, understand basic math and the give-and-take of social interaction. However, deprived of formal education, they know little or nothing about history and literature.

Information Processing and the Brain

As you learned in Chapter 1 the *information-processing perspective* is more recent than either Piaget's or Vygotsky's theories. Information processing benefits from technology, which allows more detailed data and analysis than was possible 50 years ago, particularly in neuroscience (Miller, 2011).

Rather than describing broad stages (Piaget) or contexts (Vygotsky), this perspective was inspired by the knowledge of how computers work. As a result, many information-processing researchers describe each small increment of input, processing, and output.

CONNECTING PARTS OF THE BRAIN Recall that the maturing corpus callosum connects the hemispheres of the brain, enabling balance and two-handed coordination, while myelination speeds up thoughts and behaviour. The prefrontal cortex—the executive part of the brain—begins to plan, monitor, and evaluate. All of these neurological developments continue in middle childhood and beyond.

Increasing maturation results, by 7 or 8 years of age, in a "massively interconnected" brain (Kagan & Herschkowitz, 2005, p. 220). Such connections are crucial for the complex tasks that children must master (M. H. Johnson et al., 2009). In fact, for many activities, children use more parts of their brains than adults do, thus requiring more connections (M. H. Johnson et al., 2009).

One example of a complex task that children must master is learning to read. Reading is not instinctual: Our ancestors never did it. The brain has no areas dedicated to reading, the way it does for talking, gesturing, or face recognition (Gabrieli, 2009). So, how do humans read without brain-specific structures? The answer is the interconnections between parts of the brain that deal with sounds, vision, comprehension, and so on, all coordinated by the prefrontal cortex.

Interconnections are needed for many social skills as well—deciding whom to trust, figuring out what is fair, interpreting ambiguous gestures and expressions. Younger children are not proficient at this. That's why they are told, "Don't talk to strangers," whereas adults use judgment to decide which strangers merit which interactions.

SPEED OF THOUGHT **Reaction time** is how long it takes the brain to respond to a stimulus; specifically, how quickly an impulse travels from one neuron to another to allow thinking to occur. Reactions are quicker with each passing year of childhood because increasing myelination and sequences of action reduce reaction time. Speedy reactions allow faster and more efficient learning. For example, school achievement requires quick coordination of multiple tasks within the brain. The result is a child who can listen to the teacher and read notes on the board or the overhead at the same time during a lesson, for example.

Indeed, reaction time relates to every intellectual, motor, and social skill, in school or not. A simple example is being able to kick a speeding soccer ball toward a teammate; a more complex example is being able to determine when to utter a witty remark and when to stay quiet. Young children find both impossible; fast-thinking older children sometimes succeed. By early adolescence, reaction time is quicker than at any later time—few adults can beat a teenager at a video game.

reaction time
The time it takes to respond to a stimulus, either physically (with a reflexive movement such as an eyeblink) or cognitively (with a thought).

PAY ATTENTION Neurological advances allow children to do more than think quickly. As the brain matures, it allows children to pay special attention to the most important elements of their environment. A crucial step in information processing occurs before conscious awareness, as the brain responds to input by deciding if it merits consideration.

Selective attention is the ability to concentrate on some stimuli while ignoring others. This improves markedly at about age 7. Older children learn to notice various stimuli (which is one form of attention) that younger children do not (such as the small difference in the appearance of the letters b, p, and d) and to select the best response when several possibilities conflict (such as when a c sounds like an s or a k) (Rueda et al., 2007).

In the classroom, selective attention allows children to listen, answer questions, and follow instructions for a class activity while ignoring distractions (all difficult at age 6, easier by age 10). At home, children can watch their favourite television show and tune out their parents when they are telling them to clean up their toys (although not for long, since most parents have a way of making themselves heard!).

selective attention
The ability to concentrate on some stimuli while ignoring others.

Indeed, selective attention underlies all the abilities that gradually mature during the formative years. Networks of collaborating cortical regions (M. H. Johnson et al., 2009) are required because attention involves not just one brain function, but three: alerting, orienting, and executive control (Posner et al., 2007).

LEARNING STRATEGIES One of the leaders of the information-processing perspective is Robert Siegler, who has studied the day-by-day details of children's understanding of math (Siegler & Chen, 2008). Remember that some logical ideas explained by Piaget relate to math understanding, but information-processing research finds that those ideas do not necessarily lead to proficient calculations.

Siegler has shown that a child attempts, ignores, half-uses, abandons, and finally adopts new and better strategies to solve math problems. Siegler compares the acquisition of knowledge to waves on a beach when the tide is rising. There is substantial ebb and flow as information is processed (Thompson & Siegler, 2010).

A practical application of the idea that knowledge comes in waves is that children need a lot of practice to master a new idea or strategy. Just because a child says a correct answer one day does not mean that the achievement is permanent. Lapses, earlier mistakes, and momentary insights are all part of the learning process—and adults need to be patient as well as consistent in what they teach.

MEMORY One foundation of new learning appears to be memory, which allows children to connect various aspects of past knowledge. Memory is now often studied with an information-processing approach. Input, storage, and retrieval underlie the increasing cognitive abilities of the schoolchild. Each of the three major steps in the memory process—sensory memory, working memory, and long-term memory—is affected by maturation and experience.

Sensory memory (also called the *sensory register*) is the first component of the human information-processing system. It stores incoming stimuli for a split second after they are received, with sounds being retained slightly longer than sights. To use terms explained in Chapter 3, *sensations* are retained for a moment, and then some become perceptions. This first step of memory is already quite good in early childhood, improves slightly until about age 10 years, and remains adequate until late adulthood.

Once some sensations become perceptions, the brain selects those perceptions that are meaningful and transfers them to working memory for further analysis. This is called *selective memory,* the result of selective attention as just described. It is in **working memory** (formerly called *short-term memory*) that current, conscious mental activity occurs. Processing, not mere exposure, is essential for getting information into working memory, which is why working memory improves markedly in middle childhood (Cowan & Alloway, 2009).

As Siegler's waves metaphor suggests, memory strategies do not appear suddenly. Gradual improvement occurs from toddlerhood through adolescence (Schneider & Lockl, 2008) (see Table 7.1). Children develop strategies to increase working memory (Camos & Barrouillet, 2011), and they use these strategies occasionally at first, then consistently over time.

Cultural differences are evident here as well, with children learning ways to master whatever their culture expects. For example, many Muslim children are taught to memorize all 80 000 words of the Quran, and they develop strategies to remember long passages—strategies that non-Muslim children may not know. On

sensory memory
The component of the information-processing system in which incoming stimulus information is stored for a split second to allow it to be processed. (Also called the *sensory register*.)

working memory
The component of the information-processing system in which current conscious mental activity occurs. (Formerly called *short-term memory*.)

Remembering their Lines These six girls are rehearsing for their Chatham, Ontario, school's production of *Annie*. The girls, ages 9 to 11 years, have a very large capacity for long-term memory—they use a variety of strategies to remember the lines and lyrics of the play.

TABLE 7.1 Advances in Memory from Infancy to Age 11

Child's Age	Memory Capabilities
Under 2 years	Infants remember actions and routines that involve them. Memory is implicit, triggered by sights and sounds (an interactive toy, a caregiver's voice).
2–5 years	Words are now used to encode and retrieve memories. Explicit memory begins, although children do not yet use memory strategies. They remember things by rote (their phone number, nursery rhymes) without truly understanding them.
5–7 years	Children realize that some things should be remembered, and they begin to use simple strategies, primarily rehearsal (repeating an item again and again). This is not a very efficient strategy, but with enough repetition, automatization occurs.
7–9 years	Children use new strategies if they are taught them. They use visual clues (remembering how a particular spelling word looks) and auditory hints (rhymes, letters), which provide evidence of the development of brain functions called the visual–spatial sketchpad and phonological loop. Children now benefit from the organization of things to be remembered.
9–11 years	Memory becomes more adaptive and strategic as children become able to learn various memory techniques from teachers and other children. They can organize material themselves, developing their own memory aids.

Source: Based on Meadows, 2006.

the other hand, drawing faces is forbidden in Islam, while it is a valued skill among other groups—and those children develop strategies to improve their work, such as learning the ratio of distance between the forehead, eyes, mouth, and chin.

Finally, information from working memory may be transferred to **long-term memory,** to store it for minutes, hours, days, months, or years. The capacity of long-term memory—how much can be crammed into one brain—is very large by the end of middle childhood. Together with sensory memory and working memory, long-term memory organizes ideas and reactions, with more effective brain functioning over the years of middle childhood (Wendelken et al., 2011).

Crucial to long-term memory is not merely storage (how much material has been deposited) but also retrieval (how readily past learning can be brought into working memory). For everyone, at every age, retrieval is easier for some memories (especially memories of vivid, emotional experiences) than for others. And for everyone, long-term memory is imperfect: We all forget and distort memories.

KNOWLEDGE As information-processing researchers have found, the more people know, the more they can learn. Having an extensive **knowledge base,** or a broad body of knowledge in a particular subject, makes it easier to master new, related information.

Three factors facilitate increases in the knowledge base: past experience, current opportunity, and personal motivation. Because of motivation, children's knowledge base is not always what their parents or teachers would like. Lack of motivation helps explain why some students don't remember what they learned in science class but do remember the scores for their favourite hockey team.

Specific examples of the results of motivation on the knowledge base include that many schoolchildren memorize words and rhythms of hit songs, know plots and characters of television programs, and can recite the names and histories of hockey players—yet they may not know whether World War I occurred in the nineteenth or twentieth century, or whether Afghanistan is in Asia or Africa.

long-term memory
The component of the information-processing system in which virtually limitless amounts of information can be stored indefinitely.

◆ **ESPECIALLY FOR Teachers** How might your understanding of memory help you teach a 2000-word vocabulary list to a class of Grade 4 students? (see response, page 264) →

knowledge base
A body of knowledge in a particular area that makes it easier to master new information in that area.

This provides a clue for teachers: New concepts are learned best if they are connected to personal and emotional experiences (Schneider & Lockl, 2008; Wittrock, 1974/2010). Parents likewise need to do more than tell children what they want them to know; they need to be actively involved with them.

CONTROL PROCESSES The mechanisms that combine memory, processing speed, and the knowledge base are **control processes;** they regulate the analysis and flow of information within the system. Control processes include emotional regulation (part of impulse control, explained in Chapter 9) and selective attention, explained earlier in this chapter.

Equally important is **metacognition,** sometimes defined as "thinking about thinking." Metacognition is the ultimate control process because it allows a person to evaluate a cognitive task, determine how to accomplish it, monitor performance, and then make adjustments.

Metacognition and other control processes improve with age and experience. For instance, in one study, children took a fill-in-the-blank test and indicated how confident they were of each answer. Then they were allowed to delete some questions, making the remaining ones count more. Already by age 9, the children were able to estimate correctness; by age 11, they were skilled at knowing what to delete (Roebers et al., 2009). That is metacognition, knowing which of one's ideas are solid and which are shaky.

Long-term memory is imperfect. Gradually children become more adept at differentiating what they know with certainty and what they only imagine. Unlike younger children who sometimes can't distinguish dreams from reality, older children use control processes to know that a certain thought was just a hope, fantasy, or dream.

Control processes can allow knowledge in one domain to transfer to another domain. This is the case for bilingual children, who learn to switch from one language to another. They are advanced not only in language, but also in other measures of executive control (Bialystok, 2010).

Information processing improves spontaneously during childhood, but children can learn explicit strategies and memory methods, as mentioned earlier. Table 7.1 notes memory improvements from birth to age 11 years. How much of this improvement involves metacognition? Sometimes teaching of memory is explicit, more so in some countries (e.g., Germany) than in others (e.g., the United States) (Bjorklund et al., 2009). Often children with special needs require help learning control processes (Riccio et al., 2010). Genes matter as well. Children with the long allele of dopamine D4 benefit from knowing how well they are doing in each learning task—that seems to help them control their effort. Children without that allele are not affected by immediate feedback (Kegel et al., 2011).

control processes
Mechanisms (including selective attention, metacognition, and emotional regulation) that combine memory, processing speed, and knowledge to regulate the analysis and flow of information within the information-processing system. (Also called *executive processes*.)

metacognition
"Thinking about thinking," or the ability to evaluate a cognitive task to determine how best to accomplish it, and then to monitor and adjust one's performance on that task.

RESPONSE FOR Teachers (from page 263) Children this age can be taught strategies for remembering by making links between working memory and long-term memory. You might break down the vocabulary list into word clusters grouped according to root words, make connections to the children's existing knowledge, use applications, or (as a last resort) focus on first letters or rhymes. Active, social learning is useful; perhaps groups of students could write a story each day that incorporates 15 new words. Each group could read its story aloud to the class. ●

KEY Points

- Piaget recognized concrete operational thought, when children can use logic regarding their actual (concrete) experiences.
- Vygotsky stressed the importance of social instruction to help schoolchildren learn.
- Information-processing theorists note children's step-by-step learning.
- Brain advances during middle childhood allow for faster reactions, selective attention, broader knowledge base, and development of control processes.
- All aspects of memory (sensory, working, and long-term) improve in middle childhood, making metacognition possible.

Language Advances

By age 6, children have mastered the basic vocabulary and grammar of their first language. Many also speak a second language fluently. These linguistic abilities form a strong knowledge base, enabling some school-age children to learn up to 20 new words a day and to apply complex grammar rules. Here are some specifics.

Vocabulary

By age 6, children know the names of thousands of objects, and they use many parts of speech—adjectives and adverbs as well as nouns and verbs. As Piaget recognized, they soon become more flexible and logical; they can understand prefixes, suffixes, compound words, phrases, metaphors, and figures of speech. This is a major accomplishment.

The humourist James Thurber remembered "the enchanted private world of [his] early boyhood":

> In this world, businessmen who phoned their wives to say they were tied up at the office sat roped to their swivel chairs, and probably gagged, unable to move or speak except somehow, miraculously, to telephone. … Then there was the man who left town under a cloud. Sometimes I saw him all wrapped up in the cloud and invisible. … At other times it floated, about the size of a sofa, above him wherever he went … [I remember] the old lady who was always up in the air, the husband who did not seem able to put his foot down, the man who lost his head during a fire but was still able to run out of the house yelling.
>
> *[Thurber, 1999, p. 40]*

Adults may not realize that some figures of speech, or even words, are culture-specific. For example, Canadians are known for saying "eh," particularly at the end of sentences, to mean "right?" or "you know what I mean." Similarly, Canadians, as well as others, have their own set of metaphors connected with ice hockey. "They were ready to drop the gloves" indicates that two people have reached a crisis point in their argument. "She stickhandled that situation very well" tells us that this woman has finely tuned diplomatic skills. In an article in *The New Yorker*, Canadian writer Adam Gopnik even used a hockey metaphor to describe the political savvy of the country's prime minister: "[Stephen] Harper is no pylon, as Canadians call a hapless defenseman whom you can go around at will" (Gopnik, 2009).

Because school-age children are able to create as well as understand metaphors, asking them to do so reveals emotions that might not be expressed in other ways. For instance, one 11-year-old said that his asthma is like

> a jellyfish, which has a deadly sting and vicious bite and tentacles which could squeeze your throat and make your bronchioles get smaller and make breathing harder. Or like a boa constrictor squeezing life out of you.
>
> *[quoted in Peterson & Sterling, 2009, p. 97]*

That boy felt that he alone had to fight his disease, which he considered evil and dangerous—and beyond help from his parents. Other children in the same study had more benign metaphors. This suggests a strategy for teachers who want to know how a child feels about something: Ask for a metaphor.

✦ **ESPECIALLY FOR Parents** You have had an exhausting day but are setting out to buy groceries. Your 7-year-old son wants to go with you. Should you explain that you are so tired that you want to make a quick solo trip to the supermarket this time? (see response, page 267) →

RADIUS IMAGES / PHOTOLIBRARY

Homework This 7-year-old is learning vocabulary related to science as she does an experiment with her father. Children learn most of their vocabulary with friends and family, not in class.

Adjusting to the Context

pragmatics
The practical use of language that includes the ability to adjust language communication according to audience and context.

One aspect of language that advances markedly in middle childhood is **pragmatics,** the practical use of language, which includes the ability to use words and other devices to communicate well with varied audiences in different contexts. As children master pragmatics, they become more adept in all domains.

LEARNING THE CODES Mastery of pragmatics allows children to change styles of speech, or "codes," depending on their audience. Each code includes many aspects of language—tone, pronunciation, gestures, sentence length, idioms, vocabulary, and grammar. Sometimes the switch is between formal code (used in academic contexts) and informal code (used with friends); sometimes it is between standard (or proper) speech and dialect or vernacular (used on the street). Many children use code in text messaging, with numbers (411), abbreviations (LOL), and emoticons (:-D), as well as with spellings that teachers might mark as wrong but which actually are right in context (r u ok?).

Children need instruction from teachers to become fluent in the formal code because the logic of grammar (whether *who* or *whom* is correct or when a sentence is incomplete) is almost impossible to deduce. Peers teach the informal code, with curses, slang, gestures, and alternate grammar.

Code changes are particularly obvious when children speak one language at home and another at school. Every nation includes many such children; most of the world's 6000 languages are not school languages. In Canada, more than 200 languages were reported as the home or mother language in the 2011 census. Specifically, 20 percent of the Canadian population, or more than 6 million people, speak a home language other than English or French (Statistics Canada, 2012a). This includes more than 200 000 people who speak an Aboriginal language (Langlois & Turner, 2012). Similarly, English is the language of instruction in Australia, but 17 percent of Australian children speak one of 246 other languages at home (Centre for Community Child Health, 2009).

Choice of Language Like children everywhere, these siblings, from Bordeaux, France, are texting their friends. What abbreviation do you think they use for LOL? (EDR, which stands for "*écroulé de rire,*" or "falling down laughing.) For L8R? (A+, which stands for "*À plus,*" or "See you soon.")

BSIP / SCIENCE SOURCE

LEARNING ANOTHER LANGUAGE The questions of when, how, to whom, and even whether schools should provide second-language instruction are answered in different ways from country to country. Some countries teach several languages throughout elementary school, while others punish children who utter any word that is not in the majority language.

immersion
A strategy in which instruction in all school subjects occurs in a second language that a child is learning.

bilingual schooling
A strategy in which school subjects are taught in both the learner's original language and the second language.

ESL (English as a second language)
An approach to teaching English in which all children who do not speak English are placed together in an intensive course to learn basic English so that they can be educated in the same classroom as native English speakers. (Also known as *EAL, English as an alternative language,* or *ELL, English Language Learning.*)

In some European countries, such as Sweden, Denmark, and the Netherlands, almost every child speaks two languages by age 10. In Africa, children who are talented and fortunate enough to reach high school often speak three languages. In Canada, about 15 percent of youths 15 to 19 years of age can speak both official languages. In the United States, less than 5 percent of children under age 11 study a language other than English in school (Robelen, 2011).

How do children learn a second language in school? One option is **immersion,** in which instruction occurs entirely in the new language. Another approach is the opposite: Teach in the children's first language for several years, and then teach the second language as a foreign tongue. Between these extremes lies **bilingual schooling,** with instruction in two languages.

In North America, there are **ESL (English as a second language)** programs for students whose first language is not English. In these programs, non–English speakers are taught together intensively and exclusively in English to prepare them for classes with native English speakers. More recently, some have re-termed ESL to EAL, *English as an alternative language*, or ELL, *English Language Learning*, as English may in fact be someone's third or fourth language.

In middle childhood, children sometimes successfully master a second language and sometimes fail: The research is not clear as to which approach is best (Gandara & Rumberger, 2009). Success is affected by context: Home literacy (frequent reading, writing, and listening in any language), cultural values, national attitudes and policies, and the teacher's warmth and skills all make a difference. Success is also affected by personality, ability, expectations, background, and SES.

RESPONSE FOR Parents (from page 265) Your son would understand your explanation, but you should take him along if you can do so without losing patience. While shopping, you can teach vocabulary (does he know pimientos, pepperoni, polenta?), categories (root vegetables, freshwater fish), and math (which size box of cereal is cheaper?). ●

> ## KEY Points
>
> - Language continues to develop rapidly during middle childhood.
> - Because children are now more logical, they can understand metaphors, prefixes, suffixes, and formal codes.
> - Social acceptance is crucial; pragmatics is evident as children learn the informal code.
> - Children advance in two languages if motivation is high and instruction is individualized.

Teaching and Learning

As we have just described, 6- to 11-year-olds are great learners. They use logic, develop strategies, accumulate knowledge, and expand vocabulary. Children are given new responsibilities and knowledge in middle childhood because that is when the human brain is ready.

Traditionally, children were taught domestic tasks and agriculture at home, but now more than 95 percent of the world's 7-year-olds are instructed in academics

All the Same These five children all speak a language other than English at home and are now learning English as a new language at school.

AP PHOTO / DANIEL SHANKEN

"The path to becoming an astronaut is rougher than I thought."

at school (Cohen & Malin, 2010). This is true even in developing nations. In 2010, for instance, India passed a law providing free education (no more school fees) to all 6- to 14-year-olds, regardless of caste or income. India now has over 100 million young children in school. Internationally, quality and content vary markedly, but most 7-year-olds have some formal education.

Schools Around the World

Although literacy and numeracy (reading and math) are goals for all children almost everywhere, curricula vary by nation, by community, and by subject. In France in 2000, for example, children had physical education for three hours and arts instruction for more than two hours each week (Marlow-Ferguson, 2002). By contrast, half of all U.S. 18- to 24-year-olds say they had no arts education in childhood, either in school or anywhere else (Rabkin & Hedberg, 2011).

Educational practices also differ radically even between nations that are geographically close. For example, in Germany the average school child studies science three times more often than in the Netherlands (Snyder & Dillow, 2010).

hidden curriculum
The unofficial, unstated, or implicit rules and priorities that influence the academic curriculum and every other aspect of learning in a school.

THE HIDDEN CURRICULUM Variation is even greater in aspects of the **hidden curriculum,** which refers to implicit values and assumptions evident in course selection, schedules, teacher characteristics, discipline, teaching methods, sports competition, student government, extracurricular activities, and so on. Even within countries, such practices differ. Children from a higher SES are more likely to know about and abide with the "unwritten rules" of the hidden curriculum than their classmates from a lower SES (Apple, 1975).

Whether students should be quiet or talkative in class is part of the hidden curriculum, taught to students from kindergarten on. In some countries, students are expected to stand when called on by the teacher and rarely participate in class discussions. In others, students remain seated when responding to the teacher and are more likely to speak spontaneously during discussions.

Same Situation, Far Apart: Spot the Hidden Curriculum Literacy is central to the curriculum for schoolchildren everywhere, no matter how far apart they live. However, the hidden curriculum is different in the North American classroom *(left)*, where children read illustrated stories, and in Ethiopia, where this boy is memorizing his holy book *(right)*.

A curriculum of social values is expressed in the school's physical setting, which might include spacious classrooms, wide hallways, and large, grassy playgrounds—or cramped, poorly equipped rooms and cement play yards or play streets. In some countries, school is outdoors. In spite of the fact that there may be no chairs, desks, or books, children are gathered together under a tree, sitting around their teacher. What is the hidden curriculum there?

INTERNATIONAL TESTING Over the past two decades, more than 50 nations have participated in massive tests of educational achievement. The results of these tests are carefully studied by political leaders: if achievement rises, the national economy advances—a sequence that seems causal, not merely correlational (Hanushek & Woessmann, 2009). Better-educated adults become more productive and healthier workers.

Science and math are tested in the **Trends in Math and Science Study (TIMSS).** The main test of reading is the **Progress in International Reading Literacy Study (PIRLS).** Both of these tests have been given several times, with East Asian nations usually at the top, the United States rising, and Canada somewhere behind the U.S. (see Tables 7.2 and 7.3). Most developing nations do not give these tests, but when they do, scores are low.

Many experts wonder what factors produce higher achievement. Teachers are thought to be crucial. For example, Finland, which scores high on many tests, allows only the top 3 percent of high school graduates to enter teachers' colleges. Then they are given five years of free college education, including a Master's degree in education theory and practice, as well as advanced training in an academic discipline.

Finnish teachers are also granted more autonomy within their classrooms than is typical in other systems, and they have time and are encouraged to collaborate with colleagues (Sahlberg, 2011). Buildings are designed to foster such collaboration, with comfortable teachers' lounges. Teachers might be the reason for Finland's success, or it may be something more basic regarding Finland's size, population, culture, or history.

Trends in Math and Science Study (TIMSS)
An international assessment of the math and science skills of Grade 4 and Grade 8 students. Although the TIMSS is very useful, different countries' scores are not always comparable because sample selection, test administration, and content validity are hard to keep uniform.

Progress in International Reading Literacy Study (PIRLS)
Inaugurated in 2001, a planned five-year cycle of international trend studies in the reading ability of Grade 4 students.

TABLE 7.2 TIMSS Ranking and Average Scores of Math Achievement for Grade 4 Students, 2011

Rank*	Country	Score
1.	Singapore	606
2.	Korea	605
3.	Hong Kong	602
4.	Chinese Taipei	591
5.	Japan	585
6.	N. Ireland	562
7.	Belgium	549
8.	Finland	545
9.	England	542
10.	Russia	542
11.	United States	541
12.	Netherlands	540
	Canada (Quebec)	533
	Germany	528
	Canada (Ontario)	518
	Australia	516
	Italy	508
	Sweden	504
	New Zealand	486
	Iran	431
	Yemen	248

*The top 12 groups are listed in order, but after that not all the jurisdictions that took the test are listed. Some nations have improved over the past 15 years (notably, Hong Kong, England) and some have declined (Austria, Netherlands), but most continue about where they have always been.

Sources: Mullis et al., 2012a; Provasnik et al., 2012.

TABLE 7.3 PIRLS Distribution of Reading Achievement

Country	Score
Hong Kong	571
Russia	568
Finland	568
Singapore	567
N. Ireland	558
United States	556
Denmark	554
Chinese Taipei	553
Ireland	552
England	552
Canada	548
Italy	541
Germany	541
Israel	541
New Zealand	531
Australia	527
Poland	526
France	520
Spain	513
Iran	457
Colombia	448
Indonesia	428
Morocco	310

Source: Mullis et al., 2012b.

"Big deal, an A in math. That would be a D in any other country."

In one study that examined the impact of teachers on their students' achievement, TIMSS experts videotaped 231 math classes in three nations—Japan, Germany, and the United States (Stigler & Hiebert, 2009). The U.S. teachers presented math at a lower level than did their German and Japanese counterparts, with more definitions but less connection to what the students had already learned. Teachers seemed disinterested and few students were engaged. By contrast, the Japanese teachers were excited about math instruction, working collaboratively and structuring lessons so that the children developed proofs and alternative solutions, alone and in groups. Teachers used social interaction and followed an orderly sequence (lessons built on previous knowledge). Such teaching reflected all three theories of cognition: problem solving from Piaget, collaborative learning from Vygotsky, and sequencing from information processing. Remember that Japanese students excel on the TIMSS, which suggests that all three theories may be relevant.

GENDER DIFFERENCES IN SCHOOL PERFORMANCE In addition to marked national, ethnic, and economic differences, gender differences in achievement scores are often reported. The PIRLS finds girls ahead of boys in verbal skills in every country, and, traditionally, the TIMSS has found boys ahead of girls in math and science. However, the most recent TIMSS results indicate that gender differences in math have narrowed or disappeared. In Grade 4, there were no significant differences in results for boys and girls in 26 of the 50 participating countries, while boys did slightly better in 20 countries and girls did significantly better in the remaining 4 countries (Mullis et al., 2012a). Such results lead to a gender-similarities hypothesis, that males and females are similar in cognition, with minimal exceptions (Hyde et al., 2008).

Academic achievement also differs by age. While girls usually have higher grades overall, at puberty girls' achievement dips, especially in science. Many reasons for these differences have been suggested (Halpern et al., 2007). For instance, girls in elementary school see their teachers, who are usually female, teaching all subjects and they feel or are encouraged by them. However, as they get older, they may have more male teachers teaching science and math and conclude that women don't

Chance or Design? These Grade 3 students are using dice to play a game to help them learn and practise multiplication.

need expertise in calculus or biology (Weisgram et al., 2010). For that reason, their motivation may falter in science and math.

Research on Grade 5 students with high IQs found an intriguing gender difference: When academic material became confusing, girls were less likely to persevere, but boys enjoyed the challenge (Dweck, 2007). Such discrepancies could be explained by nature or nurture.

However, do not make too much of these explanations for gender differences in school achievement. When scores are compared, gender differences are tiny compared with SES or national ones. The huge difference in test results between Hong Kong and Yemen (667 and 224) dwarfs the 10-point gender divide. International differences are usually explained as rooted in educational practices, national values, and economic wherewithal. Such factors are relevant within countries as well, as we shall now see.

Education In Canada

Unlike most nations, Canada does not have a national department of education to set and administer policies across the country. This is because section 23 of the Constitution Act, 1867 gives sole authority for education to the individual provinces and territories, stating that "in and for each province, the legislature may exclusively make laws in relation to education." The funding for education at both the primary and secondary level comes from a mixture of federal transfer payments and provincial or territorial and local taxes. In every province and territory, primary schooling is administered by local school boards.

Across the country, education is free and attendance is compulsory from about the age of 6 to 16, except in Manitoba, New Brunswick, and Ontario, where students must attend until they are 18. The federal government is in charge of funding the education of First Nations students in Canada.

PROVINCIAL AND TERRITORIAL RESPONSIBILITIES Since each province or territory is completely autonomous in regard to educational matters, each has the authority to develop its own curriculum, set standards for teacher training, and approve textbooks and other instructional materials. Each province or territory has also established a series of standardized tests to measure student achievement.

As a result of each province or territory developing its own policy independently of others, there are some notable differences in primary education across Canada. For example, provinces and territories differ in the extent to which they fund full-day kindergarten classes. In 2010, British Columbia, Ontario, and Prince Edward Island began ambitious programs for funding full-day classes, while New Brunswick and Nova Scotia have had full-day programs since the 1990s. Quebec and the Yukon also offer full-day kindergarten, while the Northwest Territories offers mostly full-day programs. In Alberta, Manitoba, Newfoundland and Labrador, Nunavut, and Saskatchewan, most kindergarten programs are still offered on a half-day basis.

Advocates of full-day kindergarten maintain that such programs improve literacy and numeracy and ease the transition to Grade 1 (Pelletier, 2012). As well, parents often favour full-day classes because they eliminate the need for daycare. At the same time, some researchers have questioned the costs involved with such programs (estimates for Ontario's program are $1.5 billion a year), and they ask whether the positive effects are long-term or merely fleeting (DeCicca, 2007).

Other interprovincial/territorial differences in primary education include the extent to which each province funds denominational schools. For example, British Columbia has a single public school system, while Ontario, Saskatchewan,

Newfoundland and Labrador, Quebec, Northwest Territories, Yukon, and Alberta fully fund both public and Catholic school boards. In addition, only five provinces fund private schools; in all other provinces and territories, private schools must raise money for most of their operating expenses through tuition fees. Finally, there are provincial differences in when elementary school ends, ranging from Grade 5 (New Brunswick), to Grade 6 (Alberta), to Grade 7 (British Columbia), to Grade 8 (Ontario).

Despite these differences in approach, the overall expectations that the provinces and territories set for their students and the achievement levels these students reach are remarkably similar across the country, as we shall now see.

NATIONAL STANDARDS Since Canada has no federal department of education, the government does not administer or sponsor any kind of national test to measure student achievement. However, the Council of Ministers of Education, Canada (CMEC), an intergovernmental organization whose membership consists of the ministers and deputy ministers of education from all the provinces and territories, does administer one such test. Every three years since 2007, the Pan-Canadian Assessment Program (PCAP) has tested the achievement of Grade 8 students in reading, mathematics, and science. It is hoped that by studying the results of this test, the education ministers can identify and remedy any gaps or challenges that may exist in their respective systems (CMEC, 2011).

The PCAP does not test every Grade 8 class in the country. Rather, certain schools and certain classes within those schools are randomly chosen each time the test is given to provide a comprehensive sampling. Figure 7.5 shows provincial results for the PCAP's mathematics assessment in 2010.

FIGURE 7.5 Differences Between Provinces and Territories Students in Quebec and Ontario scored above the Canadian mean score, while students from the Yukon, Manitoba, and Prince Edward Island scored well below it. How might ministers of education from each province and territory involved in PCAP use the assessment results to guide their educational policies?

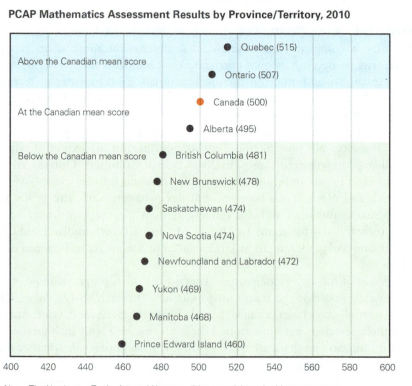

Note: The Northwest Territories and Nunavut did not participate in this assessment.
Source: CMEC, 2011.

The CMEC is also involved with administering the Organisation for Economic Co-operation and Development's (OECD) **Programme for International Student Assessment (PISA)** test, which measures achievement levels in reading, math, and science for 15-year-old students in 65 countries around the world. Some evidence that Canada's elementary school system does a good job of preparing students for secondary school is evident in Canada's consistently high placement in the country-by-country rankings of the PISA results. For instance, in 2009, Canada finished in the top 10 in all three categories, placing 6th in reading, 10th in math, and 8th in science (OECD, 2010b).

Programme for International Student Assessment (PISA)
An international assessment program that measures achievement in reading, math, and science for 15-year-olds.

ABORIGINAL EDUCATION The recent history of primary education among Aboriginal peoples (First Nations, Inuit, and Métis) in Canada has been marked by two ongoing struggles: the struggle to regain control over their children's education and the struggle to ensure that the quality of that education is at least on a par with that enjoyed by other Canadian children.

Today, most on-reserve First Nations children attend band-operated elementary schools staffed by First Nations teachers and administrators. About 500 of the 614 federally recognized First Nations have this type of school, where there is an emphasis on native language and culture in addition to the regular provincial curriculum (Reed et al., 2011). The situation is similar for Inuit students. In Nunavut, the territory's Education Act stipulates that the public school curriculum must be based on "Inuit societal values and the principles and concepts of Inuit Quajimajutuqangit [traditional teachings]" (Nunavut Department of Education, 2008).

Most Métis children go to non-Aboriginal public schools, but more and more of these schools in areas with significant Métis populations are implementing curricula that recognize Métis culture and history. As well, many school boards in these areas are giving Métis parents a greater chance than in the past to express their concerns and aspirations for their children (Reed et al., 2011).

It was not always so. Unfortunately in the twentieth century, most of the education of Aboriginal children in Canada took place under the shadow of the residential school system and the many abuses—physical, sexual, psychological, and cultural—associated with it. To understand the extent of the disaster that residential schools represented to Aboriginal peoples, keep in mind that First Nations and Inuit societies had their own well-developed educational systems in place before the arrival of European explorers and settlers. Each of these systems wasm to some extent, adapted to the local geography and climate, but they all shared two basic principles. Aboriginal children learned by watching the way other people in the community practised their skills and then imitating them, and by listening carefully to the traditional stories and teachings of their elders. Values associated with such learning systems included cooperation, respect, humility, and consensus-based decision making (McCue, 2012).

Most of these traditional systems disappeared after the establishment of residential schools in the late nineteenth century. Many of the schools were some distance away from the reserve or local community, which meant that the children who attended them were separated from their families for months or years at a time. Although the federal government funded the schools, Christian churches ran most of them. The teachers were often priests or ministers whose stated objective was to "civilize" the children in their care and assimilate them into the dominant culture of the time. In these schools, the teachers punished the children for speaking their own language, for practising their own religion, and for taking part in cultural ceremonies such as dancing, drumming, or smudging.

The developmental damage many of these children suffered was severe. Separation from their families deprived Aboriginal children of their parents' love and example.

Not only did this mean that the children themselves developed emotional problems, but they also had difficulties relating to their own children later on. In this way, the damage has continued for generations. In addition to these obvious impacts, thousands of well-documented cases of physical and sexual abuse have surfaced over the years. In some cases, the abuse was so severe that children died or committed suicide as a result of it. Some researchers estimate that as many as 3000 Aboriginal children died in residential schools (Canadian Press, 2013).

Although many Aboriginal parents and community leaders complained about the schools from the very beginning, nothing substantive happened to change the system until after the 1960s. It was only in 1960 that First Nations won the right to vote in federal elections, and this encouraged a political movement among First Nations and Inuit leaders to acquire the rights of full citizenship. Education became a focus of this movement, most forcefully expressed in the National Indian Brotherhood's 1972 publication called "Indian Control of Indian Education." This document had a strong influence on government policy in the following years, resulting in the eventual closing of the residential schools, which were replaced by new schools on reserves and in Inuit communities. To a large extent, these new schools were staffed by Aboriginal teachers. The curricula focused on the children maintaining knowledge of Aboriginal languages and traditions.

Today, however, many of the statistics associated with Aboriginal schooling are still so troubling that educators often refer to an "Aboriginal education gap" in Canada. For example, according to a report by the Canadian Council on Learning (CCL), in 2006,

- 40 percent of Aboriginal people aged 20 to 24 did not have a high school diploma, while the dropout rate for non-Aboriginal people was only 13 percent
- only 8 percent of Aboriginal people had completed a university degree, while the rate for non-Aboriginals was 23 percent (CCL, 2009).

There can be little doubt that high school and university attainment rates are directly linked to achievements at the elementary school level. It seems more than likely that part of the discrepancy that now exists between achievement levels of Aboriginal primary students and their non-Aboriginal peers is a direct result of the funding gap between these two groups of students. On-reserve First Nations students at the primary level are funded by the federal government, while students in non-Aboriginal schools get their funds from the provincial or territorial government. As of 2012, and depending on the province, First Nations students were receiving anywhere from 25 to 40 percent less money per capita than their non-Aboriginal peers (Sniderman, 2012).

Groups such as the Assembly of First Nations have been working with the federal government to equalize funding for Aboriginal students, but no comprehensive solution has emerged so far. Some on-reserve schools have taken the initiative to join the closest non-Aboriginal school board to put their students on an equal financial footing, but this is only a patchwork solution at best.

The need to equalize funding for all Aboriginal students is urgent if only because Aboriginal peoples are the youngest and fastest-growing demographic in Canada. Children under age 14 account for 28 percent of the Aboriginal population, compared with 17 percent among the non-Aboriginal population (Statistics Canada, 2013a). In 2010, the Centre for the Study of Living Standards in Ottawa estimated that if Aboriginal children had the same education rates as their non-Aboriginal peers, this would boost the Canadian economy by about $170 billion over the next 15 years (Sharpe & Arsenault, 2010). No doubt it would also improve the overall quality of life for many Aboriginal children and their communities.

Measuring the Mind

An underlying question is: Who should be taught in which way? Some children are ahead of others even before they enter school. Such early advances typically increase with age. Differential susceptibility and individual capacity mean that strategies, pacing, and curriculum details need to be tailored to the particular nature of the child (Kegel et al., 2011). One example is that reading scores rise with early phonic instruction for low-scoring children, but not for high-scoring ones (Sonnenschein et al., 2010). Another example is special education (discussed soon), which may be needed when a child's ability seems greater than achievement. But how should cognitive ability be assessed?

APTITUDE, ACHIEVEMENT, AND IQ *In theory,* **aptitude** is the potential to master a specific skill or to learn a certain body of knowledge. Intellectual aptitude is often measured by **intelligence quotient (IQ) tests.** Alfred Binet developed IQ tests in 1904 because he saw that children who did not achieve in school were beaten, shamed, and excluded. He wondered if their aptitude rendered them unable to achieve at grade level. Since IQ tests identified those children with lower aptitude, they could be protected from being abused as a result of their inability to achieve. Binet's tests were revised and published as the Stanford-Binet IQ tests, now in their fifth edition, and used in more than 1000 published studies in 2012.

Originally, an IQ score was literally a quotient: Mental age (the age of a typical child who had reached the tested child's intellectual level) was divided by chronological age (the tested child's actual age), and the result of that division (the quotient) was multiplied by 100. If mental age was the same as chronological age, the quotient would be 1, and the child's IQ would be 100, exactly average. The current method of calculating IQ is more complicated, but an IQ of 100 is still considered average.

In theory, achievement is learning that has occurred, not learning potential (aptitude). **Achievement tests** compare scores to norms established for each grade. For example, children of any age whose reading is typical of the average Grade 3 student are said to be at the Grade 3 level in reading achievement.

The words *in theory* precede the definitions of aptitude and achievement. Although potential and accomplishment are supposed to be distinct, IQ and achievement scores are strongly correlated for individuals, for groups of children, and for nations (Lynn & Mikk, 2007). Binet assumed that some children did not achieve much because of their low IQ, but perhaps low achievement was a cause (not just a result) of low IQ. Or perhaps some third factor (such as malnutrition) decreases both IQ and achievement.

Moreover, people once thought that aptitude was a fixed characteristic, present at birth—but this is not the case. Children with a low IQ can become above average, or even gifted. Indeed, the average IQ scores of entire nations have risen substantially— a phenomenon called the Flynn effect, named after James Flynn, the researcher who first described this increase in nation after nation. At first Flynn's conclusion was doubted, but the data have convinced the skeptics. The rise in intelligence may be the result of worldwide improvements in education and nutrition (Flynn, 1999, 2007).

MULTIPLE INTELLIGENCES Social scientists agree that the IQ score is only a snapshot—a static view of a dynamic, developing brain. Beyond the fact that IQ scores change, a more fundamental question is whether any single test can measure the complexities of cognitive development. This criticism has been targeted particularly at IQ tests when the underlying assumption is that there is one general thing called *intelligence* (often referred to as *g*, for general intelligence).

aptitude
The potential to master a specific skill or to learn a certain body of knowledge.

intelligence quotient (IQ) test
A test designed to measure intellectual aptitude, or ability to learn in school. Originally, intelligence was defined as mental age divided by chronological age, multiplied by 100—hence the term *intelligence quotient,* or *IQ.*

achievement test
A measure of mastery or proficiency in reading, mathematics, writing, science, or some other subject.

multiple intelligences
The idea that human intelligence is comprised of a varied set of abilities rather than a single, all-encompassing one.

✦ **ESPECIALLY FOR Teachers** What are the advantages and disadvantages of using Gardner's idea of multiple intelligences to guide your classroom curriculum? (see response, page 280) ➞

Children may instead inherit a set of abilities, some high and some low, rather than a general intellectual ability (e.g., Q. Zhu et al., 2010). Two leading developmentalists, Robert Sternberg and Howard Gardner, are among those who believe that humans have **multiple intelligences,** not just one (Furnham, 2012).

Robert Sternberg (1996) described three distinct types of intelligence: academic, measured by IQ and achievement tests; creative, evidenced by imaginative endeavours; and practical, seen in everyday problem solving. In contrast, Howard Gardner originally (1983) described seven intelligences: linguistic, logical–mathematical, musical, spatial, bodily–kinesthetic (movement), interpersonal (social understanding), and intrapersonal (self-understanding), each associated with a region of the brain. He has since added two more: naturalistic (understanding nature, as in biology or farming) and existential (thinking about life and death) (Gardner, 1999, 2006; Gardner & Moran, 2006).

Although every normal (not severely brain damaged) person has some of all nine intelligences, Gardner believes each individual has highs and lows. For example, someone might be gifted spatially but not linguistically (a visual artist who cannot describe her work), or might have interpersonal but not naturalistic intelligence (an astute clinical psychologist whose houseplants die).

Gardner's theory has been influential in education, especially the education of children (e.g., Armstrong, 2009; Rettig, 2005), when teachers allow children to demonstrate knowledge in their own ways—demonstrating their understanding of history with a drawing rather than an essay, for instance. Some children may learn by listening, others by looking, others by doing—an idea that led to research on learning styles.

Similarly, Sternberg believes that matching instruction to a person's analytic, creative, or practical ability advances his or her comprehension. However, these applications may not be supported by scientific research (Almeida et al., 2010; Pashler et al., 2008). Debate continues about whether intelligence is general or multiple, whether learning styles are relevant to achievement, and what the educational implications of aptitude and achievement scores might be (Furnham, 2012).

CULTURAL VARIATIONS One final criticism of IQ testing arises from two aspects of the life-span perspective: multicultural and multicontextual understanding. Every test reflects the culture of the people who create, administer, and take it. Some experts try to use tests that are culture-free, such as by asking children to identify shapes, draw people, repeat stories, hop on one foot, name their classmates, sort objects, and much more. However, even with such tests, culture is relevant. For example, researchers report that Sudanese children averaged 40 points lower when IQ testing required them to write with pencils, which they had not done before (Wicherts et al., 2010).

The IQ tests considered most accurate (the WISC [Wechsler Intelligence Scale for Children] and the Stanford-Binet) rely on one professional testing one child. The professional is trained to encourage without giving answers, and the report includes any specifics (for example, that this child was not feeling well) that might affect the score.

Yet remember that children reflect the hidden curricula. In some cultures, individuals are taught to consider themselves part of a group, and the intellectually gifted are particularly adept at working with others. In such cultures, a child's intellect may be more evident in social interaction, not in isolation. In Africa, for instance, testing an isolated child's IQ might not indicate potential (Nsamenang, 2004). Furthermore, if some children have been taught to be quiet and respectful, they might not readily answer questions posed by an unfamiliar professional. As a result, their IQ would not reflect their potential.

KEY Points

- Children worldwide attend school, but curricula, teaching methods, settings, and much else differ from one country to another.
- International tests of achievement usually find children in East Asian nations scoring far above Canadian children, and above children in many other countries.
- Since education is a provincial/territorial rather than a federal responsibility in Canada, some regional differences are evident in approaches to primary education.
- On the whole, Aboriginal students lag behind their non-Aboriginal peers, partly because of funding differences and the historical legacy of residential schools.
- IQ tests are designed to measure aptitude and other tests measure achievement, but both are affected by culture and by assumptions about intelligence.

Children with Special Needs

Many children have learning patterns that respond best to targeted education. Although some differences among children are harmless, others indicate disorders that need to be recognized to help children learn. Before leaping from diagnosis to special education, however, we need to understand three concepts: *comorbidity, multifinality,* and *equifinality* (Cicchetti & Toth, 2009).

Many disorders are **comorbid,** which means that at least two problems occur in the same person. A child may need special help to overcome one problem, but that help needs to take into account other problems that the child might have.

Multifinality means that one cause can have many (multiple) final manifestations. The same genes or past trauma may produce a child who is easily angered (conduct disorder) or quick to cry (major depression).

Equifinality (equal in final form) means that one symptom can have many causes. For instance, a 6-year-old who does not talk may be autistic, hard of hearing, developmentally disabled, or electively mute. Comorbidity, multifinality, and equifinality are reasons to be cautious before leaping from symptom to cure.

To illustrate all three concepts, we focus here only on attention deficit and bipolar disorders, learning disabilities, and autism spectrum disorders.

Attention Deficit Hyperactivity, Bipolar, and Disruptive Mood Dysregulation Disorders

Attention deficit hyperactivity disorder and bipolar disorder are discussed together because they are often comorbid and confused with one other (Miklowitz & Cicchetti, 2010). Disruptive mood dysregulation disorder is a new diagnosis that helps resolve this confusion.

ATTENTION DEFICIT HYPERACTIVITY DISORDER Perhaps 10 percent of all young children have **attention deficit hyperactivity disorder (ADHD),** which means they have difficulty paying attention and may also be filled with uncontrollable urges to be active or to act out impulsively. A typical child with ADHD, when made to sit down to do homework, might look up, ask questions, think about playing, get a drink, fidget, squirm, tap the table, jiggle his or her legs, and go to the bathroom—and then start the whole sequence again. Not surprisingly, such children tend

comorbid
The presence of two or more disease conditions at the same time in the same person.

multifinality
A basic principle of developmental psychopathology that holds that one cause can have many (multiple) final manifestations.

equifinality
A basic principle of developmental psychopathology that holds that one symptom can have many causes.

attention deficit hyperactivity disorder (ADHD)
A condition in which a person not only has great difficulty concentrating for more than a few moments but also is inattentive, impulsive, and overactive.

Almost Impossible The concentration needed to do homework is almost beyond Clint, age 11, who takes medication for attention deficit hyperactivity disorder (ADHD). Note his furrowed brow, resting head, and sad face.

bipolar disorder
A condition characterized by extreme mood swings, from euphoria to deep depression, not caused by outside experiences.

✦ **ESPECIALLY FOR Health Workers** Parents ask that some medication be prescribed for their child in kindergarten, who they say is much too active for them to handle. How do you respond? (see response, page 281) ➡

to have academic difficulties; they are less likely to graduate from high school and college (Loe & Feldman, 2007).

The number of children diagnosed with ADHD has increased in recent decades. For instance, the rate of diagnosis in the United States has increased from 5 percent in 1980 to about 10 percent currently. The rate has doubled in Europe as well (e.g., Hsia & Maclennan, 2009; van den Ban et al., 2010). About twice as many boys as girls have ADHD (National Center for Health Statistics, 2011).

Diagnosis is a problem, since some adults are quick to blame children's (especially boys') behaviour on a disorder. Experts say that ADHD should be diagnosed only when it is apparent in at least two places (e.g., home and school) and when it does not improve with consistent structure and guidance. A first step is for parents and teachers to learn how to provide that guidance (Subcommittee on ADHD, 2011).

BIPOLAR DISORDER **Bipolar disorder** is characterized by extreme mood swings, from euphoria to deep depression, that are not linked to external circumstances. Children with bipolar disorder experience at least one episode of grandiosity. They might believe, for instance, that they are the smartest person in the school, a genius destined to save the entire world. At other times, the same child might be severely depressed, unwilling or unable to read, play, or go to school (Miklowitz & Cicchetti, 2010).

One U.S. study reported that medical visits for youth under age 18 with a primary diagnosis of bipolar disorder increased 40-fold between 1995 and 2003, a period when adult diagnoses of bipolar merely doubled (Moreno et al, 2007). Such a rapid increase suggested to critics that childhood bipolar disorder was a diagnosis in the mind of the observer, not in the moods of the child. Others suggested that the rapid increase in diagnosis was the result of earlier misdiagnosis, not current overdiagnosis (Miklowitz & Cicchetti, 2010; Santosh & Canagaratnam, 2008).

OPPOSING PERSPECTIVES

Drugs for Children

ADHD is the most common diagnosis for children in North America. Using psychoactive drugs to treat children with ADHD and other disorders, such as depression, anxiety, developmental delay, autism spectrum disorder, and bipolar disorder, is a highly controversial but widespread practice. For example, In Canada, prescriptions for antidepressants among children increased by 75 to 80 percent between 1997 and 2003 before tapering off, partly in response to Health Canada's warning of a possible increase in suicide attempts by users of paroxetine, a particular type of antidepressant (Mitchell et al., 2008; Oberlander & Miller, 2011). Before the drop-off in 2003, about 2 percent of Canadian children were prescribed some form of antidepressant (Korenblum, 2004; Oberlander & Miller, 2011).

The drug most commonly prescribed in middle childhood is methylphenidate, sold under the name of Ritalin and used to treat ADHD. Ritalin is a type of drug known as a psychostimulant. It may seem odd to prescribe a stimulant

to children who are already hyperactive, but Ritalin stimulates the brain to cause the release of the neurotransmitter dopamine, which allows the executive centre of the brain in the prefrontal cortex to function in a normal fashion.

Much of the North American public is suspicious of any childhood psychiatric medicine (dosReis & Myers, 2008; McLeod et al., 2004; Rose, 2008), partly because many have been inadequately tested for children and are prescribed "off label"—they have not been approved for patients of that age or for the particular condition for which they have been prescribed. That suspicion affects attitudes toward drug use for children.

One small study of parents whose children were diagnosed with ADHD found that about 20 percent believed drugs should never be used for children (dosReis et al., 2009). A large study found that only about half (56 percent) of the parents of U.S. children who are diagnosed with ADHD give them medication every day (Scheffler et al., 2009).

The opposite perspective comes from professionals who find that medication helps schoolchildren with emotional problems, particularly ADHD (Epstein et al., 2010; King et al., 2009; Scheffler et al., 2009). Many educators and psychiatrists consider it tragic that only half of the children diagnosed with ADHD take medication of any kind for it (National Center for Health Statistics, 2011). They argue that if a child had Type 1 diabetes, parents would give insulin; so, logically, when a child has an emotional illness, parents should give medicine if it helps.

Some parents agree with that perspective. The same study that found 20 percent of parents were always opposed to drugs also found 29 percent who believed that drugs were necessary and who blamed doctors for waiting too long to prescribe (dosReis et al., 2009).

Although many drugs help children with their immediate problems, the long-term effects of drug use are a major concern. Three questions are often raised:

1. Will children who take drugs become adolescent addicts?

2. Will height be stunted?

3. Will medication cause other psychiatric disorders?

The answer to all three is no, according to scientific longitudinal studies. In fact, childhood medication for children who are unable to function normally reduces the risk of later illegal drug use and of other disorders, and does not make children shorter than their genes destined them to be (Biederman et al., 2009, 2010; Faraone & Wilens, 2003).

The rate of developing another psychiatric disorder is compared not with the overall average, but with the rate in children who have the same initial psychological problems but are not medicated. This is important because the incidence of pathology for young children who have special needs is higher than average, no matter what treatment they are given (Geller et al., 2008; Loe & Feldman, 2007; Molina et al., 2009).

There is another issue, however. As more drugs are prescribed, more abuse of those drugs occurs. Ritalin in particular is sometimes taken illegally by teenagers who want an extra boost (Setlik et al., 2009). Either they get the drug from someone who actually has ADHD, or they pretend to have ADHD themselves, or they buy it illegally.

Finally, although many children benefit from drug use in the short term, there is scant evidence that long-term use has any benefits (Sroufe, 2012). Indeed, Health Canada has warned of possible cardiac risks to people taking ADHD drugs for longer periods of time (Health Canada, 2006).

As you see, neither side has all the evidence in its favour. Since psychoactive drugs, taken daily from childhood on, add to the profits of drug manufacturers, some people suspect that money contaminates the research. No one disputes that, when children have special needs, parents and teachers need support and training. People on both sides also agree that drugs are not a lifelong solution. Whether short-term use in childhood is a benefit depends on many specifics, about which adults disagree.

DISRUPTIVE MOOD DYSREGULATION DISORDER Although professionals agreed that the rapid increase in the rates of childhood bipolar disorder were a result of misdiagnoses, they could not ignore the fact that many children were being brought to pediatricians and psychologists by parents (or referred by teachers) because they were too often rageful and irritable, even on their best days. These weren't just children going through a difficult phase, but children who were chronically angry, and whose behaviour was occurring at home, at school, and for months on end. The new edition of the DSM-5 includes a new type of depressive disorder, **disruptive mood dysregulation disorder (DMDD),** to describe the behaviour of these children. These are children who may scream over a dropped ice cream cone, or throw a remote control across the room rather than share it—and who look sad or angry when they are not losing their temper. These behaviours may not be precursors of adult bipolar disorder, but may instead predict later anxiety and depressive disorders, now apparent in a storm of unregulated feeling.

disruptive mood dysregulation disorder (DMDD)
A condition in which a child has chronic irritability and anger that culminates in frequent tantrums that are inappropriate to the circumstances and to the child's age.

DISTINGUISHING BETWEEN DISORDERS Bipolar disorder is extremely difficult to differentiate from other psychiatric illnesses in youth (Phillips, 2010). Many children diagnosed with either ADHD or bipolar disorder may be more accurately diagnosed with the other. It is hoped that the new DMDD diagnosis will result in more accurate diagnosis and effective treatment.

Go Team Remember that abnormality is normal. Which of these boys has been diagnosed with a serious disability? Michael, second from the right, has bipolar disorder.

specific learning disorder
A marked deficit in a particular area of learning that is not caused by an apparent physical disability, by another disorder, or by an unusually stressful home environment. Commonly referred to as *learning disability*.

dyslexia
Unusual difficulty with reading; thought to be the result of some neurological underdevelopment.

RESPONSE FOR Teachers (from page 276) The advantages are that all the children learn more aspects of human knowledge and many can develop their talents. Art, music, and sports should be an integral part of education, not just a break from academics. The disadvantage is that they take time and attention away from reading and math, which might lead to less proficiency in those subjects on standardized tests. ●

Both ADHD and bipolar disorder are more common in children whose parents have a disorder, sometimes the same disorder as the child. Parents of children with ADHD often have learning disabilities, whereas parents of children with bipolar disorder are likely to have mood disturbances. This suggests a genetic link as well as multifinality.

Both disorders are related to unusual brain patterns. Children with either disorder are less able than the average child to distinguish emotions when looking at faces. That much is true for both disorders, but activation of distinct parts of the amygdala differs between the two (Brotman et al., 2008, 2010).

Treatment involves (1) counselling and training for the family and the child; (2) showing teachers how to direct attention and increase structure to help the children learn; and, if that does not help, (3) medication to stabilize moods for bipolar children and to calm children with ADHD. Ongoing monitoring is crucial because some drugs help children with ADHD but harm those with bipolar disorder. In addition, each child responds differently to each drug, and responses change with time.

Specific Learning Disorders

The DSM-5 diagnosis of **specific learning disorder** now combines diagnoses of deficits in the perception or processing of information; such difficulty is commonly referred to as a *learning disability*. Many children have a specific learning disorder that leads to difficulty in mastering a particular skill that other people acquire easily. Indeed, according to Gardner's view of multiple intelligences, almost everyone has a specific inadequacy or two. Perhaps one person is clumsy (low in kinesthetic intelligence), while another sings loudly but off key (low in musical intelligence). Most such learning disabilities are not debilitating (the off-key singer learns to be quiet in chorus), but every schoolchild is expected to learn reading and math. Disabilities in either of these two subjects often undercut academic achievement and make a child feel inadequate, ashamed, and stupid.

Data from the 2002/2003 National Longitudinal Survey of Children and Youth (NLSCY) reported that about 4 percent of Canadian children from 8 to 11 years of age were diagnosed with a learning disability in 2002 (Milan et al., 2006). The most commonly diagnosed learning disability is **dyslexia,** unusual difficulty with reading. No single test accurately diagnoses dyslexia (or any learning disability) (Riccio & Rodriguez, 2007).

Early theories hypothesized that visual difficulties—for example, reversals of letters (reading *was* instead of *saw*) and mirror writing (*b* instead of *d*)—were the cause of dyslexia. We now know that more often dyslexia originates with speech and hearing difficulties (Gabrieli, 2009).

A decade ago, dyslexia was diagnosed when a child's reading achievement was far below that child's intellectual potential—that is, scores on achievement tests were lower than IQ. Now fMRI brain scans reveal that children of all intellectual levels (from genius to disabled) can have neurological problems that make reading difficult (Tanaka et al., 2011). It is no longer necessary to wait until tests reveal low achievement.

Learning to Make Sounds Most children teach themselves to talk clearly, but some need special help—as this 5-year-old does. Mirrors, mentoring, and manipulation may all be part of speech therapy.

Dyscalculia is unusual difficulty with math. The root cause is neurological, and although dyslexia and dyscalculia can be comorbid, each is a separate disorder originating from a different part of the brain, and each requires targeted education (Butterworth et al., 2011). Often computer programs as well as various auditory and visual treatments help. One strategy that is not effective and that can, in effect, be dangerous is simply waiting for a child to outgrow a learning disability. Many children who have learning problems develop behaviour problems as well.

dyscalculia
Unusual difficulty with math, probably originating from a distinct part of the brain.

Autism Spectrum Disorder

Of all special needs children, those with **autism spectrum disorder (ASD)** are perhaps the most troubling, not only because their problems are severe, but also because the causes of and treatments for ASD are hotly disputed. Most children with ASD can be identified in the first year of life, but some seem quite typical at first and then display signs of the disorder later on.

The Centers for Disease Control and Prevention (CDCP) report that ASD affects about 1 in every 88 children in the United States (three times as many boys as girls and more European-Americans than Latino-, Asian-, or African-Americans) (CDCP, 2013). In Canada, there is no national system in place to provide accurate data about the prevalence of autism spectrum disorder. However, a 2012 report from the National Epidemiological Database for the Study of Autism in Canada discovered increased rates of ASD diagnoses among children in Prince Edward Island, Newfoundland and Labrador, and southeastern Ontario. Depending on the age group and region, these increases varied from 39 to 204 percent (NEDSAC, 2012).

autism spectrum disorder
A developmental disorder marked by difficulty with social communication and interaction—including difficulty seeing things from another person's point of view—and restricted, repetitive patterns of behaviour, interests, or activities.

SYMPTOMS The two signs of autism spectrum disorder are (1) problems in social interaction and the social use of language, and (2) restricted, repetitive patterns of behaviour. Children with any form of ASD find it difficult to understand the emotions of others, which makes them feel alien, like "an anthropologist on Mars," as Temple Grandin, an educator and writer with ASD, expressed it (quoted in Sacks, 1995). Consequently, they do not want to talk, play, or otherwise interact with anyone, and they are especially delayed in developing a theory of mind (Senju et al., 2010).

Some children with autism spectrum disorder never speak, rarely smile, and often play for hours with one object (such as a spinning top or a toy train). Others are

RESPONSE FOR Health Workers (from page 278) Medication helps some hyperactive children, but not all. It might be useful for this child, but other forms of intervention should be tried first. Refer parents to an expert in early childhood for an evaluation and recommendations. Behaviour-management techniques geared to the particular situation, not medication, will be the first strategy. ●

called "high-functioning" and are extremely talented in some specialized area, such as drawing or geometry. Such high-functioning children are still said by some to have Asperger syndrome, but most clinicians and the DSM-5 consider this a part of the autism spectrum. Many are brilliant in unusual ways (Dawson et al., 2007), including Grandin, a well-respected expert on animal care (Grandin & Johnson, 2009).

Far more children have ASD now than in 1990, either because the incidence has increased or because more children receive the diagnosis. You read that currently in the United States about 1 child in 88 has ASD. Some other estimates put the number even higher—perhaps 1 child in 40. Underlying that estimate is the reality that no measure diagnoses ASD definitively: Many people are socially inept and poor at communication—do they all have ASD? No; for a diagnosis of autism spectrum disorder, a person's symptoms must be severe enough to significantly impact their ability to function.

PHANIE / SCIENCE SOURCE

Precious Gifts Many children with ASD are gifted artists. This boy attends a school in Montmoreau, France, that features workshops in which children with ASD develop social, play, and learning skills.

TREATMENT Some children with ASD are on special diets, take vitamin supplements, or are on medication. One drug in particular, risperidone, relieves some symptoms (although research finds side effects, including weight gain), but no biochemical treatment has proven successful at relieving the disorder itself. As you already know, medication use is controversial: Whether a child takes risperidone depends on many factors other than symptoms (Arnold et al., 2010; Rosenberg et al., 2010).

Some parents of children with ASD reported that they first noticed their infant's lack of social responses after vaccinations and believe thimerosal, an antiseptic containing mercury that was once used in immunizations, was the cause. No scientist who examines the evidence agrees: Extensive research has disproven this hypothesis many times (Offit, 2008). Thimerosal was removed from vaccines a decade ago, but the rate of ASD is still rising.

Doctors fear that parents who cling to this hypothesis and forgo routine vaccinations for their children are not only wrong, but are also harming millions of other children. Indeed, in North America, the 2012 rate of whooping cough was higher than in any year since 1960. Babies younger than 2 months have died of whooping cough because they are too young to be immunized and because older children whose parents do not vaccinate them spread contagious diseases.

One popular treatment for ASD is putting the child in a hyperbaric chamber to breathe more concentrated oxygen than is found in everyday air. Two studies of hyperbaric treatments—both with randomized participant selection and with control groups—reported contradictory results, either benefits (Rossignol et al., 2009) or no effect (Granpeesheh et al., 2010). Part of the problem may be multifinality and equifinality. Children with ASD share core symptoms (equifinality), but they differ in causes, from genes to birth trauma, from prenatal toxic substances to postnatal chemicals, and those same causes sometimes have other outcomes (multifinality).

Many behavioural methods to improve talking and socialization have been tried, with mixed results (Granpeesheh et al., 2009; Hayward et al., 2009; Howlin et al., 2009). Many clinicians use a mix of behaviour analysis, sensory play, and communication therapy to help children with ASD develop imaginative play, cognitive flexibility, and an understanding of the feelings of others. Early and individualized education of the child and parents sometimes succeeds, although special education is not a panacea, as you will now see.

Special Education in Canada

Developmentalists are well aware that physical, cognitive, and psychosocial development interact to affect each child's behaviour. That means doctors, parents, teachers, and policy-makers need to work collaboratively for each child. However, this does not necessarily occur. Special education is one example.

CHANGING POLICIES In the past in North America, children with disabilities were educated in separate schools or classrooms, if at all. Starting in the 1960s, in Canada and the United States, school administrators and government officials began to recognize that all students had the right to be educated in a common environment. One groundbreaking piece of legislation was the 1975 Education of All Handicapped Children Act in the United States, which stipulated that children with special needs must be educated in the **least restrictive environment (LRE)** (Edmunds & Edmunds, 2008). This national law meant that every state in the country had to adjust its educational practices in regard to children with disabilities.

In Canada, even though there is no federal department of education, every province and territory has adopted policies that to a large extent mirror those of the U.S. law when it comes to instructing children with special needs in an LRE. Most of the time, this has meant placing these children with other children in a regular class, also called "mainstreaming," rather than in a special classroom or school. Sometimes children are sent to a resource room, with a teacher who provides targeted tutoring. Other times, students attend an inclusion class, which means that children with special needs are included in the general classroom, with appropriate aids and services (Kalambouka et al., 2007). Table 7.4 describes how provincial and territorial departments of education define the concept of an LRE in their respective statements of philosophy regarding the education of students with special needs.

least restrictive environment (LRE) A legal requirement that children with special needs be assigned to the most general educational context in which they can be expected to learn.

TABLE 7.4 Description of Least Restrictive Environments (LRE), by Province and Territory

Province or Territory	Description of LRE
Alberta	"… regular classrooms in neighbourhood schools … first placement option."
British Columbia	"… equitable access to learning by all students."
Manitoba	"… students with special learning needs in regular classroom settings."
New Brunswick	"… with same-age peers in most enabling environments."
Newfoundland and Labrador	"… programming is delivered with age peers except where compelling reasons exist."
Northwest Territories	"… whenever possible, access to an education program in a classroom setting."
Nova Scotia	"… within regular instructional settings with their peers in age."
Nunavut	"… equal access for all students to educational programs offered in regular classroom settings with their peers."
Ontario	"… integration as the first consideration."
Prince Edward Island	"… most enabling environment that allows opportunities to interact with peers."
Quebec	"… a view to facilitating their learning and social integration."
Saskatchewan	"… students with exceptional needs … should experience education … in inclusive settings."
Yukon	"… in the least restrictive and most enabling environment to the extent that is considered practicable."

Sources: Edmunds & Edmunds, 2008; Saskatchewan Education, 2000.

response to intervention (RTI)
An educational strategy that uses early intervention to help children who demonstrate below-average achievement. Only children who are not helped are designated for more intense measures.

individual education plan (IEP)
A document that specifies educational goals and plans for a child with special needs.

A recent strategy in both Canada and the United States is called **response to intervention (RTI)** (Fletcher & Vaughan, 2009; Shapiro et al., 2011). All children who demonstrate below average achievement are given some special intervention. Most of them improve. For those who do not, more intervention occurs. Only if repeated intervention fails is the child referred for testing.

Professionals use a battery of tests (not just IQ or achievement tests) to decide whether a child needs special education. If so, they discuss an **individual education plan (IEP)** with the parents to specify educational goals for the child. The IEP goes by different names in different parts of Canada: individual program plan (IPP) in Alberta and Nova Scotia; personal program plan (PPP) in Saskatchewan; and individual services support plan (ISSP) in Newfoundland and Labrador. However, the intent and format of the document is similar from province to province. According to the Ontario Ministry of Education, an IEP is

> a written plan describing the special education program and/or services required by a particular student. It identifies learning expectations that are modified from or alternative to the expectations given in the curriculum policy document for the appropriate grade and subject or course, and/or any accommodations and special education services needed to assist the student in achieving his or her learning expectations. … The IEP is *not* a daily lesson plan itemizing every detail of the student's education.

Teaching strategies to assist students with disabilities may include using special resources such as videos, audiotapes, and simplified reading materials. Accommodating students includes giving them extra time for their tests or assignments, or assigning them scribes to take notes for them in class (Ontario Ministry of Education, 2000).

PREVALENCE AND ACCESS Since there is no federal department of education in Canada, this country lacks statistics on the overall number of students with disabilities. However, reports from the United States have revealed two important statistics:

- The number of students receiving special education services has increased every year since 1976–1977.

- In 2010, the number of 3- to 21-year-olds being served by special education was about 13 percent of the student population.

All Together Now Kiemel Lamb *(top centre)* leads children with ASD in song, a major accomplishment. For many of them, music is soothing, but words are difficult and hand-holding in a group is almost impossible.

Most experts think that similar trends and statistics apply in Canada (Edmunds & Edmunds, 2008). According to a 2006 Statistics Canada Survey, learning disabilities, which include ADHD and dyslexia/dyscalculia, are by far (81 percent) the most frequently reported condition requiring special education services (Kohen et al., 2006). In specific populations, rates of learning disabilities can be higher. For example, a report on students with special needs in First Nations schools in British Columbia concluded that almost one-third of the First Nations student population have been identified with moderate to severe special needs (Auerbach, 2007).

CULTURAL DIFFERENCES Developmentalists consider a child's biological and brain development as the starting point for whatever special assistance will allow each child to reach full potential. Then home and school practices are crucial. In regard to access to special education services, almost one-third of Canadian children with disabilities experience some sort of difficulty in getting the help they require. Problems range from insufficient staffing levels, to difficulties with assessment, to communication problems between parents and teachers and school administrators (Kohen et al., 2006).

At times, the problems parents experience in getting what they consider necessary services for their children have erupted into national controversies. Consider the case of Jeffrey Moore, a child with dyslexia attending a British Columbia grade school in the early 1990s. Every week in Grade 1, Jeffrey received two 40-minute sessions with a tutor and three 30-minute sessions with a learning-assistance teacher in addition to his regular class time. A psychologist said it would benefit Jeffrey to receive additional assistance at a reading-assistance centre in North Vancouver. During a financial crisis, the North Vancouver school district closed the centre. Several years later the Supreme Court of Canada ruled that this closing effectively discriminated against Jeffrey as a student with special needs. Reacting to the ruling, the *Globe and Mail* accused the court of opening a "Pandora's box" that would force public schools to "bleed" funds from other programs to support those for children with special needs. Where do we draw the line between what is merely "beneficial" and what is "required" (*Globe and Mail*, 2012)?

These are North American controversies. Other countries have quite different policies and approaches toward special education. For instance, in Finland almost every child is recognized as having some special educational needs, but almost no child is labelled or removed from the class for that reason. Instead, every teacher works to help each child with his or her special needs (Sahlberg, 2011).

GIFTED AND TALENTED Questions surrounding access and funding are also apparent for the 2 percent of school-age children who are unusually gifted. In Canada, most provinces and territories have systems in place for identifying and educating gifted children. How they do it varies tremendously. Should such children be accelerated, skipped, segregated, enriched, or left alone?

In the past, such children were simply put ahead a grade or more, but that left them socially isolated. One gifted student remembers:

> Nine-year-old little girls are so cruel to younger girls. I was much smaller than them, of course, and would have done anything to have a friend. Although I could cope with the academic work very easily, emotionally I wasn't up to it. Maybe it was my fault and I was asking to be picked on. I was a weed at the edge of the playground.
>
> *[Rachel, quoted in Freeman, 2010, p. 27]*

Lifelong problems occurred for this girl partly because she skipped two grades. She still thinks it might have been her fault that she was a weed, not a flower.

Currently, the most common solution for gifted children is to teach them all together, either in a separate classroom within a school or in a separate school, such as the Westmount Charter School in Calgary, Alberta, which caters exclusively to the gifted. Ideally, the children are neither bored nor lonely because each is challenged and appreciated. Their brains develop as well. A child's brain is quite plastic, and all children learn whatever their context teaches.

Some parents, however, experience problems in trying to place their children in gifted programs, even when the children have been assessed as gifted. Access problems are especially evident in times of financial restraint. During economic recessions, governments often cut education funding, and school boards in turn look for staff and programs to cut. Gifted programs, like special education programs, often suffer from these financial cuts.

Another issue that has repeatedly dogged gifted programs is their perceived tendency to favour students from higher-SES families and more privileged ethnic groups. One mother expressed her frustration in trying to find a diversified environment for her gifted middle-school child in this way: "I looked at every program in town and, frankly, they were all little white boys. We live in [ethnically diverse] Toronto. I don't see the point of that" (Pearce, 2012).

Such concerns are not abstract. One Canadian report indicated that in the Ottawa-Carleton area, 4 percent of schoolchildren have been assessed as gifted (which surpasses the North American average by 2 percentage points), while in neighbouring Renfrew County, the average was only 0.2 percent (Mendleson, 2009). No one really believes that living in the nation's capital makes kids smarter than their peers in other areas. Instead, the question may be whether coming from politically well-connected families gives them better access to special services.

DIFFERENCE AS THE RULE Scholars all find "much heterogeneity and diversity of high human potential in terms of varied developmental niches, trajectories, and pathways" (Dai, 2010, p. 121). With so many complexities, some nations and school systems avoid special education of the gifted, or of any child with special needs, at least until high school or post-secondary education.

China insists that effort, not innate ability, leads to excellence, and thus all children are educated together. In many nations of Asia and Africa, every child is expected to help his or her classmates, so separating out gifted students or those with disabilities would undercut education. This sometimes occurs in North America as well. For instance, Fern Hill School, a private school with campuses in Oakville and Burlington, Ontario, no longer assigns the gifted designation to any of its students. When asked why, one school administrator stressed that all children have talents (Pearce, 2012). A leading U.S. educator suggests that we

> give up the notions of 'the normal,' 'the disabled,' and 'the gifted' as they are typically applied in schools, especially for the purposes of classification and grouping, and simply accept difference as the rule.
>
> *[Borland, 2003, p. 121]*

Considering development in body and mind during middle childhood, differences abound—in size, health, skill, logic, intelligence, language, and more. The next chapter describes other major differences in family structures and social contexts. What are the implications? Answers are suggested at the end of Chapter 8.

KEY Points

- Emotional and behavioural disorders in childhood are difficult to diagnose and treat, in part because of multifinality and equifinality.
- In diagnosis of special needs, bipolar disorder is often confused with attention deficit hyperactivity disorder, although the treatment for the two differs.
- Learning disabilities are common, with dyslexia and dyscalculia being problematic in school.
- Children with autism spectrum disorder have difficulty with social interaction, language, and creative play.

SUMMARY

Health and Sickness

1. Middle childhood is a time of steady growth and few serious illnesses, thanks to genes and medical advances.

2. Physical activity aids health and joy. However, current social and environmental conditions make informal neighbourhood play scarce, school physical education less prevalent, and sports leagues less welcoming.

3. Childhood obesity and asthma are increasing worldwide. Although genes are part of the cause, public policies (e.g., food advertising, pollution standards) and family practices also have an impact.

Cognition in Middle Childhood

4. According to Piaget, middle childhood is the time of concrete operational thought, when egocentrism diminishes and logical thinking begins. School-age children can understand classification and conservation.

5. Vygotsky stressed the social context of learning, including the specific lessons of school and learning from peers and adults. Culture affects what children learn and how they learn.

6. An information-processing approach examines each step of the thinking process, focusing especially on brain processes, which continue to mature. Notable advances occur in reaction time, allowing faster and better coordination of many parts of the brain.

7. Memory begins with information that reaches the brain from the sense organs. Then, selection processes allow some information to reach working memory. Finally, long-term memory stores images and ideas indefinitely.

8. Selective attention, a broader knowledge base, logical strategies for retrieval, and faster processing advance every aspect of memory and cognition. Control processes, including metacognition, are crucial.

Language Advances

9. Language learning advances in many practical ways, including expansion of vocabulary and understanding of metaphors.

10. Children excel at pragmatics, often using one code with their friends and another in school. Many children become fluent in the school language while speaking their first language at home.

Teaching and Learning

11. Experts agree that primary education should be universal. Reading is assessed internationally with the PIRLS, and math and science with the TIMSS. On both, children in East Asia excel.

12. In Canada, where education is a provincial/territorial responsibility, the Pan-Canadian Assessment Program is a nationally administered test that measures the achievement of Grade 8 students in reading, mathematics, and science.

13. IQ tests are designed to quantify intellectual aptitude. Most such tests emphasize language and logic and predict school achievement. Critics contend that traditional IQ tests assess too narrowly because people have multiple types of intelligence.

14. Achievement tests measure accomplishment, often in specific academic areas. Aptitude and achievement are correlated, both for individuals and for nations.

Children with Special Needs

15. Many children have special educational needs. Among the more common causes are attention deficit hyperactivity disorder (ADHD), in which children have problems with inattention, impulsiveness, and overactivity; bipolar disorder, characterized by marked mood swings; specific learning disorders; and autism spectrum disorder.

16. All special needs are partly genetic, but family and school factors can make the problems better or worse. Treatments include medication, targeted education, and family training—some of which can be controversial.

17. In North America, about 13 percent of school-age children receive special education services, with an individual education plan (IEP) and assignment to the least restrictive environment (LRE), usually the regular classroom.

KEY TERMS

achievement test (p. 275)

aptitude (p. 275)

asthma (p. 256)

attention deficit hyperactivity disorder (ADHD) (p. 277)

autism spectrum disorder (p. 281)

bilingual schooling (p. 266)

bipolar disorder (p. 278)

body mass index (BMI) (p. 255)

childhood obesity (p. 255)

childhood overweight (p. 255)

classification (p. 258)

comorbid (p. 277)

concrete operational thought (p. 258)

control processes (p. 264)

disruptive mood dysregulation disorder (DMDD) (p. 279)

dyscalculia (p. 281)

dyslexia (p. 280)

equifinality (p. 277)

ESL (English as a second language) (p. 266)

hidden curriculum (p. 268)

immersion (p. 266)

individual education plan (IEP) (p. 284)

intelligence quotient (IQ) test (p. 275)

knowledge base (p. 263)

least restrictive environment (LRE) (p. 283)

long-term memory (p. 263)

metacognition (p. 264)

middle childhood (p. 250)

multifinality (p. 277)

multiple intelligences (p. 276)

pragmatics (p. 266)

Programme for International Student Assessment (PISA) (p. 273)

Progress in International Reading Literacy Study (PIRLS) (p. 269)

reaction time (p. 261)

response to intervention (RTI) (p. 284)

selective attention (p. 261)

sensory memory (p. 262)

specific learning disorder (learning disability) (p. 280)

Trends in Math and Science Study (TIMSS) (p. 269)

working memory (p. 262)

WHAT HAVE YOU LEARNED?

1. How does the physical growth of the school-age child compare with that of the younger child? What abilities emerge as a result of these changes?

2. How have children's medical care and health habits changed over the past few decades?

3. What are the main advantages and disadvantages of physical play during middle childhood?

4. What are the short-term and long-term effects of childhood obesity?

5. What roles do nature and nurture play in childhood asthma?

6. Why did Piaget call cognition in middle childhood concrete operational thought?

7. According to Vygotsky, where and how does cognitive development occur?

8. Why does quicker reaction time improve the ability to learn?

9. How might a lack of selective attention affect a child's ability to learn?

10. What aspects of memory improve markedly during middle childhood?

11. Why might having an extensive knowledge base make it easier for children to learn new, related information?

12. How might metacognitive skills help a student?

13. How is the understanding of vocabulary and metaphors affected by a child's age?

14. Why would a child's linguistic code be criticized by teachers but admired by friends?

15. How might a hidden curriculum affect how well a child learns in school?

16. What are two common international tests of achievement? Why are these tests given?

17. What gender differences are found in educational tests and school grades?

18. What is the difference between aptitude and achievement? Why might this difference be in theory only?

19. What are some of the differences in education policies across Canada?

20. What are the findings from the most recent PCAP?

21. What historical factors influence the implementation of Aboriginal education?

22. Why should education funding for Aboriginal students be equalized to that of other students in Canada?

23. Why might it be important for teachers to know about the theory of multiple intelligences?

24. In what ways might a child's culture affect the results of an IQ test?

25. Why might a child with ADHD have difficulty learning?

26. What are the signs of bipolar disorder?

27. What are dyslexia and dyscalculia?

28. What are the signs of autism spectrum disorder?

29. Describe LRE and RTI. How might each of these strategies help students with special needs?

30. How and why might SES and ethnic group affect a child being designated as gifted?

31. Why might boards or governments choose not to separate gifted children or children with disabilities from other students?

APPLICATIONS

1. Developmental psychologists believe that every teacher should be skilled at teaching children with a wide variety of needs. Does the teacher-training curriculum at your university reflect this goal? Should all teachers take the same courses or should some teachers be specialized? Give reasons for your opinions.

2. Internet sources vary in quality on any topic, but this may be particularly true of websites designed for parents of children with special needs. Pick one childhood disability or disease and find several web sources devoted to that condition. How might parents evaluate the information provided?

3. Obtain permission to visit a local elementary school and observe. Look for the hidden curriculum. For example, do the children line up? Why or why not? When and how? Does gender, age, ability, or talent affect the grouping of children or the selection of staff? What is on the walls? Are parents involved? If so, how? For everything you observe, speculate about the underlying assumptions.

4. Obtain permission to interview a 7- to 11-year-old child to find out what he or she knows and understands about mathematics. Relate both correct and incorrect responses to the logic of concrete operational thought.

>>ONLINE CONNECTIONS

To accompany your textbook, you have access to a number of online resources, including LearningCurve, which is an adaptive quizzing program; critical thinking questions; and case studies. For access to any of these links, go to www.worthpublishers.com/launchpad/bergerchuang1e. In addition to these resources, you'll find links to video clips, personalized study advice, and an e-Book. Among the videos and activities available online are the following:

- *Conservation.* Watch clips of children of various ages participating in Piaget's classic conservation tasks.

- *Theory of Mind.* Can someone else see what you're thinking? Video clips demonstrate children replicating the classic theory of mind experiments.

MIDDLE CHILDHOOD:
Psychosocial Development

8 chapter

WHAT WILL YOU KNOW?

■ Why do children collect worthless things, like pebbles or unusable stamps?

■ Do children always suffer if their parents divorce?

■ Why are friends (more than teachers or parents) the best defence against bullies?

■ Is it morally right for a child to lie to protect another child who has done something wrong?

 student of mine drove to a gas station to get a flat tire fixed. She wrote:

> As I pulled up, I saw a very small boy sitting at the garage door. I imagined him to be about 8 or 9 years old, and wondered why he was sitting there by himself. He directed me to park, and summoned a man who looked at my tire and spoke to the boy in a language I did not understand. This little boy then lifted my car with a jack, removed all the bolts, and fixed the flat. I was in shock. When I paid the man (who was his father), I asked how long his son had been doing this. He said about three years.
>
> *[adapted from Tiffany, personal communication, March 15, 2008]*
> —*Kathleen Berger*

Adults like Tiffany are often shocked to learn that many of the world's children are forced to work, in spite of the United Nations' declaration that children have the right

> to be protected from economic exploitation and from performing any work that is likely to be hazardous or to interfere with the child's education, or to be harmful to the child's health or physical, mental, spiritual, moral, or social development.
>
> *[Convention on the Rights of the Child]*

The International Labour Organization (ILO) of the United Nations estimated that this right was violated for 153 million 5- to 14-year-olds worldwide, with 115 million of them (4.3 percent of all children) engaged in hazardous work (Diallo et al., 2010).

Changing tires is not considered hazardous, but did it "interfere with the child's education" or harm him? The answer is not obvious. With almost every aspect of middle childhood, specific details are crucial. ●

ALL CHILDREN NEED FRIENDS, FAMILIES, AND SKILLS, but specifics matter: Some peers are destructive, some families are dysfunctional, and some skills should not be learned. This chapter describes issues that affect children's physical, mental, spiritual, moral, and social development. You will learn that child labour, peer culture, bullying, single-parent families, poverty, divorce, and so on are harmful sometimes, but not always. We begin with the children themselves, and then discuss families, peers, and morality.

AT ABOUT THIS TIME
Signs of Psychosocial Maturation over the Years of Middle Childhood

Children responsibly perform specific chores.

Children make decisions about a weekly allowance.

Children can tell time, and they have set times for various activities.

Children have homework, including some assignments over several days.

Children are less often punished physically than when they were younger.

Children try to conform to peers in clothes, language, and so on.

Children voice preferences about their after-school care, lessons, and activities.

Children are responsible for younger children, pets, and, in some places, work.

Children strive for independence from parents.

The Nature of the Child

As explained in the previous chapter, steady growth, brain maturation, and intellectual advances make middle childhood a time when children gain independence and autonomy (see At About This Time). They acquire an increasing ability to regulate themselves, to take responsibility, and to exercise self-control—all strengths that make this a period of positive growth (Huston & Ripke, 2006).

One result is that school-age children can care for themselves. They not only feed themselves, but also make their snacks; they not only dress themselves, but also pack their suitcases; and they not only walk to school, but also organize games with friends. They venture outdoors alone. Boys are especially likely to put some distance between themselves and their home, engaging in activities without their parents' awareness or approval (Munroe & Romney, 2006). This budding independence fosters growth.

Industry and Inferiority

Although adults have always taught 6- to 11-year-olds the skills they will need later on, it was not until developmentalists focused on the characteristics of these children that it became clear why they are such great learners. More than people of any other age, school-age children are industrious, practising whatever skills their culture values, or busy with their own activities. At the same time, they are much more vulnerable to criticism than are younger children.

industry versus inferiority
The fourth of Erikson's eight psychosocial crises, during which children attempt to master many skills, developing a sense of themselves as either industrious or inferior, competent or incompetent.

ERIKSON'S INSIGHTS The tension between productivity and incompetence is the fourth psychosocial crisis, **industry versus inferiority,** as described by Erik Erikson. He noted that during these years, the child "must forget past hopes and wishes, while his exuberant imagination is tamed and harnessed to the laws of impersonal things," and he becomes "ready to apply himself to given skills and tasks" (Erikson, 1963, pp. 258, 259).

Learning to read and add numbers can be a painstaking and boring process. For instance, slowly sounding out "Jane has a dog" or writing "3 + 4 = 7" for the hundredth time is not exciting. Yet children are intrinsically motivated to read a page, finish a worksheet, memorize a spelling word, colour a map, and so on. Similarly, they enjoy collecting, categorizing, and counting whatever they accumulate—perhaps stamps, stickers, stones, or seashells. That is industry. Children are able to do more complex tasks and look for ways to master new skills.

Overall, children judge themselves as either *industrious* or *inferior*—deciding whether they are competent or incompetent, productive or useless, winners or losers.

Being productive is intrinsically joyous, and it fosters the self-control that is a crucial defense against emotional problems (Bradley & Corwyn, 2005).

Parents who are supportive of their children's attempts and initiatives help them master skills and develop a sense of confidence in themselves. In contrast, parents who provide little or no encouragement to their children run the risk of instilling feelings of inferiority and helplessness in them.

A sense of industry may be a defence against early substance use as well. In a longitudinal study in Arizona of 509 Grade 3 and 4 students over a five-month period, an increasing number tried, or were expecting to try, alcohol (from 58 to 72 percent) and cigarettes (from 18 to 23 percent) (Jones, 2011). These children were aged 9 and 10, yet many already wanted the drugs that adolescents use. But here is the crucial finding: The children most likely to anticipate smoking or drinking were those who increasingly felt inferior, not industrious (Jones, 2011). For example, they did not agree that they "stick with things until they are finished" and they were not proud of what they did.

FREUD ON LATENCY Sigmund Freud described this period as **latency,** a time when emotional drives are quiet and unconscious sexual conflicts are submerged. Some experts complain that "middle childhood has been neglected at least since Freud relegated these years to the status of an uninteresting 'latency period'" (Huston & Ripke, 2006, p. 7).

But in one sense, at least, Freud was correct: Sexual impulses are quiet. Even when children were betrothed before age 12 (rare today, but not uncommon in earlier centuries), the couple had little interaction. Everywhere, boys and girls in middle childhood choose to be with others of their own sex. Indeed, boys who scrawl "Girls stay out!" on their clubhouses and girls who complain that "boys stink" are typical.

The Need to Celebrate No matter where they live, 6- to 11-year-olds seek to understand and develop whatever skills are valued by their culture. They do so in active, industrious ways, as described in every theory. This is illustrated here, as friends in Assam, northeastern India, usher in spring with a Bihu celebration. Soon they will be given sweets and tea, which is the sociocultural validation of their energy, independence, and skill.

latency
Freud's term for middle childhood, during which children's emotional drives and psychosexual needs are quiet (latent). Freud thought that sexual conflicts from earlier stages are only temporarily submerged, bursting forth again at puberty.

Self-Concept

As children mature, they develop their *self-concept,* which is how they perceive themselves, including intelligence, personality, abilities, gender, and ethnic background. As you remember, the very notion that they are individuals is a discovery in toddlerhood, and a positive, global self-concept is typical in early childhood.

That global self-acceptance changes in middle childhood. Self-concept gradually becomes more specific and logical, as one might expect, given increases in cognitive development and social awareness. Children begin to view themselves as being in specific domains (e.g., as students, as athletes). As one group of researchers explains, "The cognitive ability to combine specific behavioral features of the self (I can run fast and throw far) into higher order generalizations … (I am athletic) appears in middle childhood …" (Pfeifer et al., 2010, p. 144).

As self-concept becomes more specific and logical, it also incorporates influences from peers and the overall society. For example, some 6-year-olds from minority ethnic groups are unaware of prejudice against their group; by age 11, they are aware, usually taking pride in their self-concept as a member of an ethnic minority in defence against specific insults they have heard (Garcia Coll & Marks, 2009).

COMPARED WITH OTHERS The schoolchild's self-concept no longer mirrors the parents' perspective. Every theory and every observer notes that children become more concerned with the opinions of their peers as they age from 6 to 11.

During preadolescence, "the peer group exerts an increasingly salient socializing function" (Thomaes et al., 2010, p. 812). Research in many nations has found that teaching anxious children to confide in friends as well as to understand their own emotions helps them develop a better self-concept (Siu, 2007). Afterschool activities, particularly sports, can provide a foundation for friendship and realistic self-esteem, helping children develop a self-concept as industrious, not inferior. However, the influence of peers does not mean that parents are irrelevant. For example, parental attachment still mitigates low self-esteem at age 10 and 12 (Kerns et al., 2011).

Parents, peers, older children, and even strangers become potential critics. Children depend on **social comparison,** comparing themselves with other people, as they develop their self-concept (Carpendale & Lewis, 2004; Davis-Kean et al., 2009). Ideally, children develop feelings of self-esteem, competence, and individuality during middle childhood as they begin comparing themselves with peers (Ripke et al., 2006). Yet some children—especially those from minority ethnic or religious groups—become newly aware of prejudices they need to overcome (Kiang & Harter, 2008; McKown & Strambler, 2009). Children also become aware of gender discrimination as they compare themselves with peers of the other sex. For example, girls complain that they are not allowed to play tougher sports and boys complain that teachers favour the girls (Brown et al., 2011).

For all children, increasing self-understanding and social awareness come at a price. Self-criticism and self-consciousness rise from ages 6 to 11. By middle childhood the earlier overestimate of their ability decreases while self-esteem falls (Davis-Kean et al., 2009). In addition, partly because children think concretely during middle childhood, materialism increases and appearances matter. Attributes that adults might find superficial become important to children, which makes self-esteem more fragile and more dependent on externals (Chaplin & John, 2007). For example, insecure 10-year-olds might covet the latest shoes, cellphones, and so on. They also might criticize the way their parents dress, or talk, or style their hair.

CULTURE AND SELF-ESTEEM High self-esteem is neither universally valued nor universally criticized. Although many North American parents praise their children and want them to be proud of themselves, this is a cultural view, not a universal one (Yamaguchi et al., 2007). Many other cultures expect children to be modest,

social comparison
The tendency to assess one's abilities, achievements, social status, and other attributes by measuring them against those of other people, especially one's peers.

Same Situation, Far Apart: Helping at Home While household chores may differ in different countries, children everywhere often help out at home, as these children from North America and China do.

not prideful. For example, Australians say that "tall poppies" are cut down, and the Japanese discourage social comparison aimed at making oneself feel superior. Interestingly, research finds that very high self-esteem in middle childhood can undercut effort and empathy and thus work against healthy development (Reijntjes et al., 2011; Menon et al., 2007).

Culture seems to be more relevant than objective accomplishment in developing self esteem. For example, Japanese children excel at math on the TIMSS, but only 17 percent are confident of their math ability (Snyder & Dillow, 2010). In Ontario, 33 percent of those taking the TIMSS are confident of their math ability, and those who enjoy math and are confident in their abilities have higher levels of achievement (Mullis et al., 2012a). In contrast, in Estonia low self-esteem correlates with high academic achievement (Pullmann & Allik, 2008).

Resilience and Stress

Young children depend on their families for many things, including food, emotional support, learning, and life itself. Then "experiences in middle childhood can sustain, magnify, or reverse the advantages or disadvantages that children acquire in the preschool years" (Huston & Ripke, 2006, p. 2).

Supportive families continue to be protective, but children may escape destructive family influences by finding their own niche in the larger world. Some children break free, seemingly unscathed by early experiences. They have been called "resilient" or even "invincible." **Resilience** has been defined as "a dynamic process encompassing positive adaptation within the context of significant adversity" (Luthar et al., 2000, p. 543). Note the three parts of this definition:

resilience
The capacity to adapt well to significant adversity and to overcome serious stress.

1. Resilience is *dynamic,* not stable: It may be evident at one age but not a later one.

2. Resilience is a *positive adaptation* to stress. For example, if home problems lead a child to greater involvement with schoolwork and school friends, that is positive adaptation.

3. Adversity must be *significant.* Some adversities are comparatively minor (large class size, poor vision) and some are major (victimization, neglect). Children cope with all kinds of adversities, but not all coping is resilient.

Over the past six decades, researchers across the globe have been exploring resilience in children who have faced adversity. In Canada, Michael Ungar and Linda Liebenberg are directors of the Resilience Research Centre at Dalhousie University in Nova Scotia, where they have been examining children's responses to different types of stress in various cultures and countries.

In a 2008 review of the resilience literature, Ungar (2008) found that the term had different meanings depending on its context. Specifically, resilience

- describes a group of characteristics that allow certain children to grow up successfully despite being born into difficult circumstances

- refers to a child's ability to demonstrate competence under stress

- is the ability to recover from traumatic experiences.

In studying 1500 children around the world, Ungar concluded that culture and context are important factors in determining a child's ability to deal with stress. As an example, he quotes Mani, a young Innu woman from Sheshatshkiu in Newfoundland and Labrador, who made the following comments in response to her cousin's suicide:

> My coping skills were tested and it was hard. … I never knew that kind of devastation existed in my own family members. I didn't know how to react or respond.

I didn't know the difference between what was real and wasn't real. I just couldn't get myself to speak or think. It was a scary time for us and the scars will live on. We did receive lots of support from community leaders, workers, and members. It was kind of nice how my whole family were together like that. … Our family needs to stay together and focused now. I need them to balance their lives and mine.

[Ungar, 2008]

TABLE 8.1 Dominant Ideas About Resilience, 1965–Present

1965	All children have the same needs for healthy development.
1970	Some conditions or circumstances—such as "absent father," "teenage mother," "working mom," and "daycare"—are harmful for every child.
1975	All children are *not* the same. Some children are resilient, coping easily with stressors that cause harm in other children.
1980	Nothing inevitably causes harm. Both maternal employment and preschool education, once thought to be risks, are often helpful.
1985	Factors beyond the family, both in the child (low birth weight, prenatal alcohol exposure, aggressive temperament) and in the community (poverty, violence), can be very risky for children.
1990	Risk–benefit analysis finds that some children are "invulnerable" to, or even benefit from, circumstances that destroy others.
1995	No child is invincibly resilient. Risks are always harmful—if not in education, then in emotions; if not immediately, then long term.
2000	Risk–benefit analysis involves the interplay among many biological, cognitive, and social factors, some within the child (genes, disability, temperament), the family (function as well as structure), and the community (including neighbourhood, school, place of worship, and culture).
2008	Focus on strengths, not risks. Assets in child (intelligence, personality), family (secure attachment, warmth), community (schools, after-school programs), and nation (income support, health care) must be nurtured.
2010	Strengths vary by culture and national values. Both universal ideals and local variations must be recognized and respected.
2012	Genes as well as cultural practices can be either strengths or weaknesses; differential sensitivity means identical stressors can benefit one child and harm another.

Note that Mani received support from her community and family, which was crucial to her resilient response to this crisis. Note too that even with such support and her determination to cope, Mani realizes that "the scars will live on."

Indeed, current thinking about resilience (see Table 8.1), with insights from dynamic-systems theory, suggests that, although some children cope better than others, none are unaffected by their past (Jenson & Fraser, 2006; Luthar et al., 2003). Sensitivity is affected by genes, early child-rearing, preschool education, and sociocultural values. Thus, a child's traits alone are not enough to ensure resilience; instead, protective factors (such as parents, teachers, extended family, and the community) that are embedded in the child's environment and culture are also important.

CUMULATIVE STRESS One important discovery is that accumulated stresses over time, including minor ones (called "daily hassles"), are more devastating than an isolated major stress. Almost every child can withstand a single stressful, momentary event, but repeated stresses make resilience difficult (Jaffee et al., 2007).

Another example comes from children who survived Hurricane Katrina, in Louisiana. Years after the hurricane, about half were resilient but the other half (especially those in middle childhood) were still traumatized. The incidence of serious psychological problems was affected more by ongoing problems—frequent moves, changes in caregivers, disruption of schooling—than by the hurricane itself (Kronenberg et al., 2010; Viadero, 2007).

An international example of resilience comes from Sri Lanka, where many children have been exposed to war, the 2004 tsunami, poverty, deaths of relatives, and relocation. The accumulated stresses, more than any single problem, increased pathology and decreased achievement. Researchers point to "the importance of multiple contextual, past, and current factors in influencing children's adaptation" (Catani et al., 2010, p. 1188).

COGNITIVE COPING Coping measures reduce the impact of repeated stress. One factor is the child's own interpretation of events. For example, cortisol levels increased in low-income children *if* they interpreted events connected to their family's poverty as a personal threat and *if* the family lacked order and routines (thus increasing daily hassles) (Chen et al., 2010). When low-income children did not take things personally and their family was not chaotic, more were resilient. As you remember from Chapter 7, low income in childhood was less likely to harm later health *if* the child's mother was affectionate and supportive (Miller et al., 2011). This applies to psychosocial health as well as physical health. The effects last a lifetime.

Many adults who did not consider themselves poor as children nonetheless were poor, as measured by their family's annual income. Because they did not know they were poor, they were not burdened by their poverty.

In general, a child's interpretation of a family situation (poverty, divorce, and so on) determines how that context affects him or her (Olson & Dweck, 2008). Some children consider the family they were born into a temporary hardship; they look forward to the day when they can leave childhood behind. Other children experience *parentification*: They act as parents, taking on the roles and responsibilities that are traditionally associated with adults (Hooper, 2007). When this happens, it can interfere with or halt a child's own development.

Researchers have noted two distinct types of parentification:

1. *emotional*, in which children try to respond to the emotional demands of their parents and siblings, for example, by being the peacemaker in the family

2. *practical*, in which children do all the household's daily chores, such as cooking meals, cleaning up, and paying bills.

Emotional parentification almost always has a destructive effect on children's development. Spending long periods as their parent's confidante can mean children suppress their own emotional needs, and this can cripple their ability to develop adult relationships (Earley & Cushway, 2002; Jurkovic et al., 2001).

Practical parentification has milder effects on a child's development. As mentioned in Chapter 1 in the discussion on family systems theory, the actions of one family member always affect the other members. If a child takes on more household responsibilities, this may reduce the parents' anxieties. Consequently, the child may feel a sense of accomplishment as the parents' stress levels decrease (Jurkovic & Casey, 2000; Minuchin et al., 1967).

ESCAPING FAMILY STRESSES A 40-year study in Hawaii began with children born into poverty, often to parents who were alcoholic or mentally ill. Many of these children showed signs of deprivation when they were infants (low weight, medical problems, and so on). Experts predicted a troubled future for them. But that did not necessarily happen.

One such infant was Michael, born preterm, weighing just over 2 kilograms. His parents were low-income teenagers; his father was absent for the first two years of his life, returning to impregnate Michael's mother again and again and again. When Michael was 8, both parents left him and three younger siblings with his grandparents. Yet Michael ultimately became a successful, happy, loving adult (E. Werner, 1979).

Michael was not the only resilient one. Amazingly, about one-third of the high-risk Hawaiian babies coped well. By middle childhood, they had discovered ways to avoid family stresses, to achieve in school, to make good friends, and to find adult mentors. As adults, they left family problems behind (many moved far away) and established their own healthy relationships (E. Werner & Smith, 1992, 2001).

As was true for many of these children, school and then college can be an escape. An easygoing temperament and a high IQ help children cope with adversity, but they are not essential. For the Hawaiian children, "a realistic goal orientation, persistence, and 'learned creativity' enabled ... a remarkable degree of personal, social, and occupational success," even for those with learning disabilities (E. Werner & Smith, 2001, p. 140).

Learning as Lifeline Originally from Libya—where bombs, guns, and death were common—this boy's family escaped to a refugee camp in Tunisia. The adults suffer from crowding and deprivation, but some children are resilient—especially with the help of a caring teacher and regular schooling.

REUTERS / ANIS MILI

SOCIAL SUPPORT AND RELIGIOUS FAITH Social support is a major factor that strengthens the ability to deal with stress, especially for minority children who are aware of prejudice against them (Gillen-O'Neel et al., 2011). Compared with the homebound lives of younger children, the expanding social world of middle childhood allows new possibilities. Relatives, teachers, peers, pets, community programs, libraries, and concerts all help children cope with stress (Bryant & Donnellan, 2007). One study concludes:

> When children attempt to seek out experiences that will help them overcome adversity, it is critical that resources, in the form of supportive adults or learning opportunities, be made available to them so that their own self-righting potential can be fulfilled.
>
> *[Kim-Cohen et al., 2004, p. 664]*

A specific example is seen in a study of refugee children in Alberta. Fantino and Colak (2001) recount the story of 11-year-old Sanela, who lost her father in the Yugoslav wars of the 1990s. She later immigrated to Canada with her mother and two younger siblings. Since her mother was seriously ill and used a wheelchair, Sanela was responsible for taking care of her brother and sister. At the same time, she had to learn a new language and adapt to life in Canada.

In the beginning, Sanela had nightmares so vivid they kept her terrified for days at a time. She refused to talk about the war, her father, or her homeland. It was only after receiving extensive settlement support and counselling and being connected to a Canadian "host friendship" family that Sanela began to show a sense of relief and some signs of optimism about her future.

Aside from social support services, children may also make use of religion to bolster their resilience. Religion often provides support via adults from the same faith group (P. E. King & Furrow, 2004). Church involvement particularly helps African-American children in communities characterized by social stress and racial prejudice (Akiba & Garcia Coll, 2004). The help occurs in three ways: practical (a church or temple becomes a second home, with many activities); social (children use slightly older believers as role models); and cognitive (concepts of sin, grace, and salvation help children make sense of what they see) (Mattis & Mattis, 2011). Faith is psychologically protective when it helps children reinterpret their experiences (Crawford et al., 2006).

Same Situation, Far Apart: Praying Hands Differences are obvious between the Northern Indian girls entering their Hindu school and the West African boy in a Christian church, even in their clothes and hand positions. But underlying similarities are more important. In every culture, many 8-year-olds take comfort from prayer.

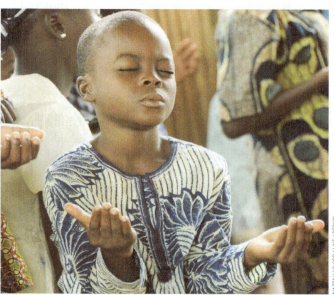

Prayer may also foster resilience. In one study, adults were required to pray for a specific person for several weeks. Their attitude about that person changed (Lambert et al., 2010). Ethics precludes such an experiment with children, but it is known that children often pray, expecting that prayer will make them feel better, especially when they are sad or angry (Bamford & Lagattuta, 2010). As you now know, expectations and interpretations can be powerful.

KEY Points

- In middle childhood, children seek to be industrious, actively mastering various skills.
- Social comparison helps children refine their self-concept.
- Resilient children cope well with major adversities.
- Schools, places of worship, and many other institutions help children deal with difficult family conditions.

Families and Children

No one doubts that genes affect personality as well as ability, that peers are vital, and that schools and cultures influence what, and how much, children learn, as well as how they feel about themselves. Some researchers have even suggested that genes, peers, and communities have so much influence that parenting has little impact— unless it is grossly abusive (Harris, 1998, 2002; McLeod et al., 2007). But parents are instrumental in creating the environment that allows their children to thrive, and as such play an important role in their children's lives.

As an example, Midgett and his colleagues (2002) examined the relationship between parent–child interactions, achievement, and self-esteem among Grade 4 and Grade 7 Canadian students. Although there seems to be a relationship between self-esteem and achievement, this relationship disappears once family factors are considered, indicating the importance of parenting.

Shared and Non-shared Environments

Environmental influence on any two children comes either from factors that are shared (both children experience the same environment) or factors that are not shared. For example, all the children raised in one home might be said to share the same parents, and children who grow up in separate nations might have non-shared cultural influences.

Many studies have found that children are less affected by *shared environment* than by *non-shared environment*. A formula for the influences on a child is $G + Shared\ E + Non\text{-}shared\ E$, which is read as genes plus home environment plus non-home environment. Research that applied this formula to twins, full and half siblings, and stepchildren found that most personality traits and intellectual characteristics are the product of genes plus non-shared environments, with little left over for the shared influences, such as those for siblings growing up together.

Even psychopathology (Burt, 2009) and sexual orientation (Långström et al., 2010) arise primarily from genes and non-shared environment. Parenting does not make a child heterosexual or homosexual: Identical twins usually have the same sexual orientation, but if they do not, it seems to be because of non-shared factors.

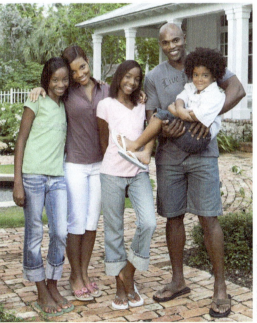

Family Unity Even though these siblings are being raised together, they do not share the same environment. Age, genes, resilience, and gender have an impact on how children deal with adverse and stressful events.

MASTERFILE / RADIUS IMAGES

Since shared environment has little impact, does this mean that parents are merely caretakers, providing basic care (food, shelter) with little influence on children's personality, intellect, and so on, no matter what rules, routines, or responses they provide? No! Recent findings reassert parental influence. The formula and calculation of shared and non-shared influences was correct, but the definition of *Shared E* was based on a false assumption: Siblings raised together do *not* share the same environment.

For example, if relocation, divorce, unemployment, or a new job occurs in a family, the impact on each child depends on that child's age, genes, resilience, and gender. Thus, moving to another town might disturb a 9-year-old girl more than her baby brother because she must leave friends behind; divorce often harms boys more than girls because it weakens connections with their father; and poverty may hurt children of one age more than another.

The variations just mentioned do not apply equally to all siblings: *Differential sensitivity* means that one child is more affected, for better or worse, than the other (Pluess & Belsky, 2010). Even if siblings are raised together, the mix of parental personality, genes, age, and gender may lead one child to become antisocial, another to have a personality disorder, and a third to be resilient (Beauchaine et al., 2009).

In addition to variations within the home, parents choose for their children many outside, non-shared influences, such as school and neighbourhood. Those choices sometimes affect each child differently (Simpkins et al., 2006). For instance, perhaps the oldest child attended the nearby public school and then family income shifted so that a younger sibling attended a private school 10 kilometres away. School would be a non-shared influence on these two children, with the parents playing a pivotal role in the choice of school.

Even identical twins, with the same genes, age, and sex, may not share their home or school environment (Caspi et al., 2004). For example, one mother spoke of her monozygotic daughters:

> Susan can be very sweet. She loves babies … she can be insecure … she flutters and dances around. … There's not much between her ears. … She's exceptionally vain, more so than Ann. Ann loves any game involving a ball, very sporty, climbs trees, very much a tomboy. One is a serious tomboy and one's a serious girlie girl. Even when they were babies I always dressed one in blue stuff and one in pink stuff.
>
> *[quoted in Caspi et al., 2004, p. 156]*

✦ **ESPECIALLY FOR Scientists** How would you determine whether parents treat all their children the same way? (see response, page 302) →

Even though the mother from the beginning dressed her daughters differently, how the girls reacted, their personalities, their personal preferences, and their activities would then encourage or discourage the environment the mother was creating for them.

Family Structure and Family Function

Family structure refers to the legal and genetic connections among people living in the same household. **Family function** refers to how a family cares for its members. The data affirm that parents are crucial for family function, determining non-shared as well as shared environments. Does it matter what structure the family has? Are some family structures more supportive of parents and children, enabling well-functioning families? What is a dysfunctional, or a well-functioning, family?

Part of the answer is known. No matter what the structure, one family function is crucial: People need family love and encouragement. Beyond that, needs vary by age. As you have seen, infants need responsive caregiving, frequent exposure to language, and social interaction; preschoolers need encouragement and guidance. Later chapters of this text describe the needs of adolescents and adults.

family structure
The legal and genetic relationships among relatives living in the same home; includes nuclear family, extended family, stepfamily, and so on.

family function
The way a family works to meet the needs of its members. Children need families to provide basic material necessities, to encourage learning, to help them develop self-respect, to nurture friendships, and to foster harmony and stability.

During middle childhood, children need five things from their families:

1. *Physical necessities.* Although children in middle childhood eat, dress, and go to sleep without help, families furnish food, clothing, and shelter.

2. *Learning.* These are prime learning years: Families choose schools, help with homework, and encourage education.

3. *Self-respect.* Families give each child a way to shine. Especially if academic success is elusive, opportunities in sports, the arts, and so on are crucial.

4. *Peer relationships.* Families foster friendships via play dates, group activities, school choice, and classroom support.

5. *Harmony and stability.* Families provide protective, predictable routines within a home that is a safe haven for everyone.

Now consider the tire-changing boy from the opening story of this chapter. To decide whether that young tire-changer should be helping his father would require finding out whether his life situation satisfies the five needs that are thought to be universal during middle childhood. Are his material needs met, is he learning in school, does he have friends, is he proud of himself, is his work keeping his family harmonious and stable? If the answer to these questions is yes, then Tiffany's understandable shock, or the father's acceptance of child labour, may reflect their cultures, not the boy's welfare.

CONTINUITY AND CHANGE No family always functions perfectly, but children worldwide fare better in families than in other institutions (such as group residences), and best if families provide the five functions listed above. Item five, harmony and stability, is especially crucial in middle childhood: Children like continuity, not change; peace, not conflict. To some degree, this is unique to middle childhood. Indeed, a decade or so later, emerging adults enjoy new places, seek challenges, and provoke arguments with friends and family. University students sometimes study in other nations or stay up all night debating issues with friends—not something young children do. Adults may not recognize a child's wish for continuity. Parents often move to a "better" neighbourhood during these years, thinking they are securing a better life for their children. However, children may feel vulnerable as a result of moving, not protected.

The importance of continuity is evident from the findings of a study from Japan (Tanaka & Nakazawa, 2005). The researchers began with the knowledge that children benefit from living with their fathers. Father absence correlates with poverty and divorce, both also harmful. Given that, the researchers wanted to learn how children would be affected if the father's absence did *not* correlate with low income and hostile mother–father interaction. Accordingly, they sought to replicate prior father-absence investigations by studying children of happily married couples in which the fathers were gainfully employed and supporting the family, but nonetheless absent.

An opportunity for such research arose in Japan because many Japanese corporations transfer employees from one location to another to help them understand how the company functions. Some families moved with the father, while others did not. As a result, researchers were able to study two similar groups of children, with only one major difference between the groups: whether the father was present or absent every day.

The hypothesis was that children who moved with their fathers would benefit because his daily presence would help them with self-esteem, homework, and therefore school achievement. However, the opposite turned out to be true. Although the mothers who moved with their husbands were happier, the schoolchildren who moved were more depressed and their school achievement suffered. It seems that the benefit of father presence was undermined by the stress of change.

What Must She Leave Behind? In every nation, children are uprooted from familiar places as a result of adult struggles and/or aspirations for a better life. This girl is leaving a settlement in the Gaza Strip, due to the Israeli–Palestinian conflict that has disrupted millions of lives. Worldwide, children suffer most from relocation.

AMIT SHABI / LAIF / REDUX

RESPONSE FOR Scientists (from page 300) Proof is very difficult when human interaction is the subject of investigation, since random assignment is impossible. Ideally, researchers would find identical twins being raised together and would then observe the parents' behaviour over the years. ●

nuclear family
A family that consists of a father, a mother, and their biological children under age 18.

Same Situation, Far Apart: Happy Families The children in both photos are about 4 years old. Mia *(left)* lives with her parents in Toronto. Here, her father is picking her up from her day-care centre. The youngest child in the Balmedina family *(right)* lives with his nuclear family in the Philippines. Even though these families live in different countries, they share the same family structure.

MILITARY FAMILIES North American children in military families face particular challenges in terms of the fifth point on the list of family functions, stability. Military parents repeatedly depart and return, and families typically relocate every few years (Riggs & Riggs, 2011; Titus, 2007). Generally, adults are happy when a soldier comes home safely, but even a safe return may disrupt the children's lives. Military children experience emotional problems and a decrease in achievement with each change (Hall, 2008).

For that reason, since 1991, the Canadian Forces (CF) and the Canadian/Military Family Resource Centres (C/MFRCs) have partnered together to try to deliver responsible services and support to CF families. Currently there are 32 C/MFRCs across Canada, five in the United States, and six more overseas. These centres are designed to provide various educational and support services to meet the unique needs of these families, especially in regard to stressful situations that may arise from a parent's deployment overseas.

Specifically, such support includes information on issues such as the emotional cycle family members are likely to experience when a parent is deployed; preparing for departure; dealing with the absence; preparing for the return; and creating a new family routine after the return (National Defence and the Canadian Armed Forces, 2013).

The same underlying principles apply to non-military families. Remember that children need stability in their lives. If an out-of-work parent finds a job far away, or if circumstances make it easier to leave a destructive neighbourhood, an inferior school, or a crowded extended family, most family members may rejoice—but not necessarily the 6- to 11-year-olds. This, of course, does not preclude such moves, but disrupted children need special attention and support.

DIVERSITY OF STRUCTURES Worldwide, two cohort factors—more single-parent households and fewer children per family—have changed families from what they were a few decades ago. Table 8.2 describes various family structures that exist around the world.

In Canada, about 80 percent of children aged 14 and under live in two-parent homes, most often with their biological parents, an arrangement called a **nuclear family.** Most parents in a nuclear family are married (64 percent). However, in Canada, the percentage of couples living in a common-law arrangement has been increasing steadily in recent years, from 13 percent in 2006 to 16 percent in 2011 (Statistics Canada, 2012e) (see Figure 8.1).

The number of same-sex couples is also increasing in Canada. Since Canada legalized same-sex marriage in 2005, these couples are now included in the census

TABLE 8.2 Types of Family Structures

Two-Parent Families

- **Nuclear family.** Named after the nucleus (the tightly connected core particles of an atom), the nuclear family consists of a man and a woman and their biological offspring under 18 years of age.

- **Step-parent family.** When children from a former relationship live with the new couple, it creates a step-parent family. If the step-parent family includes children born to two or more couples (such as children from the spouses' previous marriages and/or children of the new couple), that is called a *blended family.*

- **Adoptive family.** In this type of family, couples or single people adopt one or more children from their country or from foreign countries.

- **Grandparents alone.** Grandparents take on parenting for some children when biological parents are absent (dead, imprisoned, sick, addicted, etc.).

- **Same-sex parents.** Some two-parent families are headed by a same-sex couple, whose legal status, in terms of their relationship with one another and their role as parents (married, step-, adoptive) varies.

Single-Parent Families

One-parent families are increasing, but they average fewer children than two-parent families.

- **Single mother or father.** Children may live with mothers or fathers who have never been married, or are separated, divorced, or widowed. Most children live with a female single parent.

- **Grandparent alone.** Sometimes a single grandparent (usually the grandmother) becomes the sole caregiving adult for a child.

More Than Two Adults

- **Extended family.** Some children live with a grandparent or other relatives, as well as with one or both of their parents. This pattern is most common with infants but occurs in middle childhood as well.

category of "married couples." Overall, between 2006 and 2011, the number of same-sex married couples in Canada nearly tripled, increasing by a rate of 182 percent (Statistics Canada, 2012). As of 2011, same-sex couples accounted for 0.8 percent of all Canadian couples, and 9.4 percent of those couples had children. Even though same-sex couples are more likely to be male (55 percent) than female (46 percent), about 80 percent of same-sex couples who have children are female (Statistics Canada, 2012).

Almost 1 in 5 Canadian children (19 percent) currently live in a **single-parent family.** By far, most of these children (82 percent) live with a female single parent. Overall, the number of single-parent families increased by 8 percent in the five-year period between 2006 and 2011 (Statistics Canada, 2012).

Two-parent and single-parent structures are often contrasted with the **extended family,** a family that includes non-parental adults, usually grandparents and often aunts, uncles, and cousins, all under one roof. In 2011, about 3 percent of private households in Canada consisted of extended families, also called *multi-generational households* (Statistics Canada, 2012). Infants are more likely to live in extended families than older children are. Extended families save on housing costs and child care, which makes them more common among low-income households.

The distinction between one-parent, two-parent, and extended families is not as simple in practice as on paper. Many young parents live near relatives who provide meals, emotional support, money, and child care, functioning as an extended family. Similarly, extended families can be like nuclear families, especially in developing nations: Some families are considered extended because they share a roof, but they create separate living quarters for each set of parents and children (Georgas et al., 2006).

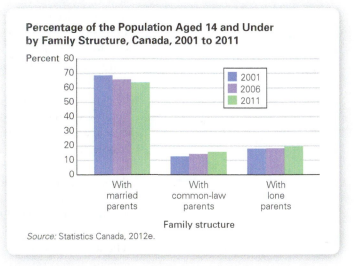

Percentage of the Population Aged 14 and Under by Family Structure, Canada, 2001 to 2011

Source: Statistics Canada, 2012e.

FIGURE 8.1 Common Family Structures in Canada This graph shows the most common family structures for children under 14 years of age in Canada from 2001 to 2011. Note that while the percentage of married couples steadily decreased during this period, the percentage of common-law parents saw a corresponding and significant increase.

single-parent family
A family that consists of only one parent and his or her biological children under age 18.

extended family
A family of three or more generations living in one household.

Connecting Family Structure and Function

Structure influences but does not determine function. Which structures make it more likely that the five family functions (necessities, learning, self-respect, friendship, harmony/stability) will occur?

BENEFITS OF NUCLEAR FAMILIES In general, nuclear families function best; children in the nuclear structure tend to achieve higher grades in school and have fewer psychological problems. A scholar who summarized dozens of studies concluded, "Children living with two biological married parents experience better educational, social, cognitive, and behavioural outcomes than do other children" (Brown, 2010, p. 1062). Does this mean that parents should all marry and stay married? Developmentalists are not that prescriptive because some of the benefits are correlates, not causes.

Many advantages of nuclear families begin before the wedding because education, earning potential, and emotional maturity all make it more likely that people will marry, have children, and stay married. Thus, brides and grooms bring personal assets to their new family. In other words, there is a correlation between child success and married parents partly because of who marries, not because of the fact of marriage itself.

To some extent, however, marriage in itself does benefit children. The selection effects noted earlier are not the entire story (Amato, 2005; Brown, 2010). Ideally, mutual affection between spouses encourages them to become wealthier and healthier than either would be alone, and that helps their children. Furthermore, the *parental alliance,* in which the mother and father support each other in their commitment to the child, decreases neglect and abuse and increases the likelihood that children have someone to read to them, check homework, invite friends over, buy new clothes, and save for their future.

In fact, a broad survey of parental contributions to college and university tuition found that the highest contributions came from nuclear families. These results might be expected when two-parent families are compared with single and divorced parents because one-parent families average less income. However, even when the income of remarried and nuclear parents is taken into consideration, remarried parents contribute less, on average, to the college or university tuition of stepchildren (Turley & Desmond, 2011). This suggests that the benefits of nuclear families continue for decades, even after children are grown.

FUNCTION OF OTHER TWO-PARENT FAMILIES Although nuclear families may be the ideal, they certainly are not the only way to raise healthy and happy children. The advantages of two-parent families are not limited to biological parents, whose genetic connection to their children partially explains their commitment.

Same-sex parents typically function very well for children, often better than the average nuclear family. Studies on how same-sex couples function are reassuring, but because same-sex marriage is relatively recent and not an option in many countries, the ideal studies—longitudinal research on a large sample, with valid comparisons to male/female families of the same age, marital status, and education—have not yet been published. Keep in mind that for decades, some female/female couples have raised children, usually the biological child of one mother who has custody after divorce. In general, their offspring develop well, emotionally and intellectually (Biblarz & Stacey, 2010).

The *step-parent structure* has advantages and disadvantages. The primary advantage is financial, especially when compared with the average single-parent family. However, some biological fathers who do not have custody and some stepfathers who are not genetically related to their stepchildren are reluctant to provide the formal and informal financial support that children need (Meyer et al., 2011). Furthermore, the other biological parent, as well as the children themselves, may make it difficult for the non-custodial or step-parent to develop a parental relationship with the child. On the other hand, many *step-parent families* function well. For example, when children are younger than 2 years and a new step-parent forms a supportive relationship with the biological parent, the children usually thrive (Ganong et al., 2011).

Income and intimacy aside, another disadvantage of step-families is in meeting the fifth family function listed earlier—providing harmony and stability. Instability is typical: Not only does remarriage usually entail moving to a new home, but also older stepchildren leave home sooner than older biological children, new babies arrive more often, and marriages are more likely to dissolve (Teachman, 2008).

Harmony may also be absent, especially if the child's loyalty to both biological parents is undermined by ongoing disputes between them. A solid parental alliance is more difficult to form when it includes three adults—two of whom disliked each other enough to divorce, and a third who is a newcomer to the child's life.

Another version of a two-parent family occurs when grandparents are full-time caretakers for children without parents present (called a *skipped-generation family,* the most common form of foster care). The hope is that grandparents provide excellent care since they are experienced, mature, and devoted to their grandchildren. Those characteristics may be present, but skipped-generation families average lower incomes, more health problems, and less stability than other two-parent families (Arber & Timonen, 2012). In Canada in 2011, about 0.5 percent of children 14 and under were living in a skipped-generation household (Statistics Canada, 2012e).

Adequate health care and schooling for children is particularly difficult in skipped-generation families, partly because many of these children have special needs due to the circumstances that led them to live with the grandparents in the first place. Although skipped-generation families need extra help, they are less likely to receive it (Baker & Mutchler, 2010).

Finally, *adoptive families* typically function well for children, although they can vary tremendously in their ability to meet the needs of children. Many of the children in such families pose special challenges, particularly at puberty and later. Support from agencies and communities is needed, but not always available.

SINGLE-PARENT FAMILIES On average, the single-parent structure functions less well because income and stability are lower. Most single parents fill many roles—including wage earner, daughter or son (single parents often depend on their own parents), and lover (many seek a new partner)—and this makes it hard to provide steady emotional and academic support for their children and to meet their children's needs.

Family and community support for single parents make a difference. Some support programs help single parents access education, legal assistance, or financial counselling, which can help with their overall well-being. Although income support is crucial, it is also critical that support programs address the problems of loneliness, social isolation, and lack of parenting support. However, single parents who need help the most often seem least likely to receive it (Harknett & Hartnett, 2011).

On the other hand, millions of children raised by single parents are well loved and nurtured. It is important to keep in mind that single parents are a diverse group, and most are not depressed or in poor health. Remember that difference is not always deficit; good caregiving is more difficult in the single parent structure, but it is far from impossible.

KIMBERLY P. MITCHELL / MCT / NEWSCOM

Building a Blended Family Tom and Jakey expect a happy future as husband and wife. They plan to wed in three months, move into their new house (behind them) and lead a happy, blended family with his smiling daughters, Simone (17) and Shayla (12), now swinging her son, Nathaniel (5). However, blended families often experience challenges as step-parents try to establish relationships with stepchildren.

✦ **ESPECIALLY FOR Single Parents** You have heard that children raised in one-parent families may have difficulty establishing intimate relationships as adolescents and adults. What can you do about this possibility? (see response, page 306) →

CULTURE AND FAMILY STRUCTURE Cultural variations in the support provided for various family structures make it hard to conclude that a particular structure is always best. For example, many French parents are unmarried. Some might assume that an unmarried mother is also a single mother. However, French unmarried mothers generally live with their children's fathers. French cohabiting parents separate less often than do married parents in North America, which suggests more stability in the average French cohabiting family than in the average married structure in North America. An analysis of 27 countries found that for women in particular, social context had a major impact on their happiness (Lee & Ono, 2012), which probably would affect their ability to parent successfully.

For children in North America, the cohabiting structure is more challenging than marriage because cohabiting parents separate more often than married parents do (Musick & Bumpass, 2012). This is one example of a general truth: Function is affected by national mores (S. L. Brown, 2004; Gibson-Davis & Gassman-Pines, 2010).

Ethnic norms matter as well. Single parenthood is more accepted among African-Americans (60 percent of African-American 6- to 11-year-olds live with only one parent). Consequently, relatives and friends routinely help single parents, who might be more isolated and dysfunctional if they were of another ethnicity (Cain & Combs-Orme, 2005; Taylor et al., 2008).

Another family structure that has emerged in Canada and some other countries is that of the **astronaut family** in which family members live in different and often widely separated countries across the globe. A common example of astronaut families consists of Chinese parents (from Hong Kong, Taiwan, or mainland China) and their children (known as *satellite* or *parachute* children) who have emigrated from their home country for the sake of economic or educational opportunities abroad. At some point, the father or mother or both return to the home country to pursue their careers (Man, 1994, 2013).

For example, a couple with two children may leave Hong Kong for Vancouver, where the parents work for several years before the father (the "astronaut") returns to Hong Kong to establish a business there. If the mother and father both return, the children may be left with grandparents in Vancouver, or, if they are old enough, they may be left on their own while they finish university and begin their careers. Typically, parents will travel frequently between their home and adopted countries to maintain family ties.

Astronaut families differ from single-parent or cohabiting-parent families in that the structure of the astronaut family exists primarily in response to economic pressures: The parents are trying to find the best jobs available and to enhance their children's own career opportunities. However, astronaut families do place certain pressures on children, especially on those in middle childhood. Although the family as a whole may enjoy economic benefits, children may feel emotionally deprived if they are separated from their parents, especially from their mother, for long periods of time.

In discussing various and different family structures, it is important not to conclude that one is better than another. Contrary to the averages, thousands of nuclear families are dysfunctional, thousands of step-parents provide excellent care, thousands of cohabiting couples are great parents, and thousands of single-parent families are wonderful. Structure and culture tend to protect or undercut healthy function, many parents overcome structural challenges, and many families of all types provide school-age children with the support and encouragement they need.

French Bliss Healthy twins (Layanne and Rayanne) are born in Paris to thrilled parents. As is common in France, these parents are not married.

OWEN FRANKEN / CORBIS

astronaut family A family where members live in different countries; children in such families are known as *satellite* or *parachute* children.

RESPONSE FOR Single Parents (from page 305) Do not get married mainly to provide a second parent for your child. If you were to do so, things would probably get worse rather than better. Do make an effort to have friends of both sexes with whom your child can interact. ●

Family Challenges

Two factors interfere with family function in every structure, ethnic group, and nation: low income and high conflict. Many families experience both poverty and acrimony because financial stress increases conflict and vice versa (McLanahan, 2009).

POVERTY Suppose a 6-year-old boy spills his milk, as every 6-year-old sometimes does. In a well-functioning, two-parent family, one parent guides him to mop up the spill while the other parent pours more milk, perhaps encouraging family harmony by saying, "Everyone has an accident sometimes."

What if the 6-year-old lives with a single parent struggling with overdue rent, unemployment, and an older child who wants money for a school trip? What if the child spilled the last of the milk and there is no money left this month to buy more? Shouting, crying, and accusations are almost inevitable. As in this example, poverty makes anger spill over when the milk does.

Family income correlates with structure. Many low-income adults are reluctant to marry until both spouses have good jobs, so the married structure is less common as income falls. Since conflicts about money are a major reason for divorce, if such parents do marry, then low income makes divorce more likely.

Family function is also affected by income: Obviously money is needed for the first of the five functions listed earlier—physical necessities—and it has an influence on functions 2 through 5 as well. Since most funds for schools in North America come from local property taxes, *learning* is affected by neighbourhood affluence. Since *self-esteem* may benefit from costly sports and arts programs, poverty reduces that as well. *Friendship* is limited if children have many tasks to do at home, and poor families *move* more often.

The effects of poverty on children are cumulative; most children are resilient if income drops for a year, but an entire childhood in poverty is difficult to overcome. Low SES may be especially damaging during middle childhood (Duncan et al., 2010). Several researchers have developed the *family-stress model,* which holds that the crucial question about any risk factor (such as low income, divorce, single parenthood, or unemployment) is whether it increases stress. Thus, poverty is less stressful *if* low income is temporary and the family's net worth (home ownership, investments, and so on) buffers the strain (Yeung & Conley, 2008). However, ongoing economic hardship increases stress, and adults may become tense and hostile (Conger et al., 2002; Parke et al., 2004). Thus, the *reaction* to poverty, not the sheer monthly income, is crucial.

Reaction to wealth may also be harmful. Children in high-income families develop more than their share of developmental problems, such as depression, eating disorders, and drug addiction. One reason may be parental pressure, causing children to develop externalizing and internalizing problems (see Chapter 6) (Ansary & Luthar, 2009).

Some intervention programs aim to teach parents to be more encouraging and patient (McLoyd et al., 2006). In low-income families, however, this focus may be misplaced. Poverty itself—with attendant problems such as inadequate schools, poor health, and the threat of homelessness—causes stress (Duncan et al., 2010).

Remember the dynamic-systems perspective described in Chapter 1? That perspective applies to poverty: Multi-generational research finds that poverty is both a cause and a symptom—parents with less education and immature emotional control are more likely to have difficulty finding employment and raising their children, and then low income adds to those difficulties (Schofield et al., 2011).

If that is so, more income might improve family functioning. Some support for this idea comes from research indicating that children in single-mother households do much better if their father pays child support, even if he is not actively involved in the child's daily life (Huang, 2009). Children also do much better in countries that subsidize single parents (e.g., Austria and Iceland). These countries have smaller achievement gaps between low- and middle-SES children on the TIMSS.

These findings are suggestive, but controversial and value-laden. Some developmentalists report that raising income does not, by itself, improve parenting (L. M. Berger et al., 2009). Using government funds to raise incomes of families living in poverty has become particularly controversial in Canada, where rates of childhood poverty remain disturbingly high, as explained in Chapter 3. This is especially true among Aboriginal peoples in this country. A 2013 joint report from the Canadian Centre for Policy Alternatives and Save the Children noted that although in 2009 the overall childhood poverty rate was 17 percent, it was significantly higher for Aboriginal children, at 40 percent. Moreover, when just status First Nations children were considered, it climbed to 50 percent (Macdonald & Wilson, 2013). The poverty rate for Aboriginal children also varied by region, and was highest in the Prairies. In Manitoba, 52 percent of Aboriginal children were living in poverty, and in Saskatchewan the rate was 55 percent (see Figure 8.2).

As you read in Chapter 7, many experts have called for closing the "education gap" that exists between Aboriginals and non-Aboriginals as one means of alleviating childhood poverty on reserves and in other Aboriginal communities. Figure 8.3 gives just one example, from British Columbia, of how wide this gap can be in middle childhood.

A Canadian Centre for Policy Alternatives (CCPA) report makes a number of recommendations for eliminating poverty among Aboriginal children, some of which involve increasing government funding for various programs. For example, the report suggests that if the government increased Aboriginal Affairs and Northern Development Canada's budget by 11 percent, the worst child poverty among status First Nations children could be completely eliminated (Macdonald & Wilson, 2013). This is a worthy goal, the price does not seem prohibitive, and as noted in Chapter 7, some experts believe that doing so could boost the Canadian economy by about

FIGURE 8.2 From Bad to Worse?
The overall poverty rate for Canadian children is bad enough at 17 percent. Canada is ranked 25th out of 30 industrialized countries tracked by the Organisation for Economic Co-operation and Development. However, for Aboriginal children in Canada, the poverty rate is even worse, at 40 percent. And as this map shows, regional variations mean that in provinces such as Manitoba and Saskatchewan, the rate exceeds 50 percent. What the map does not show is that the poverty rate specifically for on-reserve First Nations children in those two provinces is an astounding 62 and 64 percent, respectively. How can such rates be acceptable in a wealthy nation like Canada?

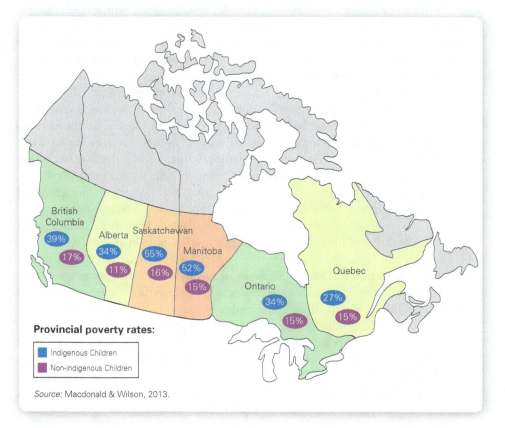

Source: Macdonald & Wilson, 2013.

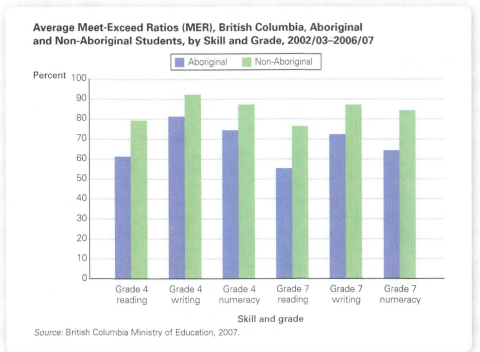

Average Meet-Exceed Ratios (MER), British Columbia, Aboriginal and Non-Aboriginal Students, by Skill and Grade, 2002/03–2006/07

Source: British Columbia Ministry of Education, 2007.

FIGURE 8.3 Why Have Aboriginal Students Fallen Behind? This graph clearly illustrates what experts call "the Aboriginal education gap." It shows meet-exceed ratios for Aboriginal and non-Aboriginal students in British Columbia primary schools between 2002 and 2007. (Meet-exceed ratios are a commonly used summary statistic for standardized test scores). In each of the three tested areas, Aboriginal students lagged well behind their peers.

OBSERVATION QUIZ
What do you think are some of the reasons for the Aboriginal education gap? (see answer, page 311) →

$170 billion over the next 15 years (Sharpe & Arsenault, 2010). The question remains whether the political willpower and popular support exist to achieve such a goal.

CONFLICT There is no controversy about conflict. Every researcher agrees that family conflict harms children, especially when adults fight about child-rearing. Such fights are more common in stepfamilies, divorced families, and extended families. Of course, nuclear families are not immune: Children suffer especially if their parents abuse each other or if one parent walks out, leaving the other distraught.

The impact of genes on children's reactions to conflict was explored in a longitudinal study of family conflict in 1734 married parents, each with a twin who was also a parent and part of the research. The twins' husbands or wives, and an adolescent from each family, were also studied. Genetics as well as conflict could be analyzed, since 388 of the pairs of twins were monozygotic and 479 were dizygotic. Each adolescent was compared with a cousin, who had half (if the parent was monozygotic) or a quarter (if the parent was dizygotic) of the same genes (Schermerhorn et al., 2011).

Participants consisted of 5202 individuals, one-third of them adult twins, one-third of them spouses of twins, and one-third adolescents with a twin parent. Conflict was assessed with a well-known questionnaire that included items such as, "We fight a lot in our family."

The researchers found that although genes had some effect, conflict itself was the main influence on the child's well-being. For example, whether teenagers became delinquent depended less on the genes they inherited than on the conflict in their families. Open conflict was especially detrimental, leading to externalizing problems in the boys and internalizing problems in the girls.

Simple disagreement (assessed by both members of each couple) did not do much harm to the child—unless the dispute erupted into open conflict (such as yelling in front of the children) or divorce (Schermerhorn et al., 2011).

Even though conflict had a greater impact than genes, one measure did show genetic influence—the adolescents' (not the parents') estimate of how much conflict the family had. From this, the researchers suggest that some teenagers, for temperamental reasons, are more sensitive to conflict than others.

OPPOSING PERSPECTIVES

Divorce for the Sake of the Children

Opposing perspectives on divorce begin with three facts:

1. About 40 percent of Canadian marriages end in divorce. The divorce and remarriage rate in the United States is even higher: Almost half of all marriages end in divorce.

2. On average, children fare best, emotionally and academically, with married parents.

3. Divorce tends to impair children's academic achievement and psychosocial development for years, even decades.

A simple conclusion from these three facts might be that every couple should marry before they have children, and that no married couple should divorce. That is the perspective taken by many adults. But the opposite side—that divorce often benefits children, especially in high-conflict marriages—has proponents as well.

Opinions are strongly influenced by each person's past history and cultural values. For example, married parents who stay together are much more negative about divorce than are divorced adults. Adults whose parents divorced tend to have a much more positive take on divorce than adults whose parents stayed together (Moon, 2011).

Some argue that attitudes toward marriage account for the problem of high divorce rates (Cherlin, 2009). North American culture idealizes both marriage and personal freedom. As a result, many young adults assert their independence by marrying "for love." Then, when they are overwhelmed by child care and financial stress, romance fades, the marriage becomes strained, and they divorce.

Often the happiest time is right after the wedding, before children are born; the least happy time is when the children are infants or young teenagers. Marriage happiness dips during children's infancy and rises when the children are self-sufficient adults. Financial and caregiving strains are greatest when children are younger than 5 years of age. Many couples meet that challenge by both working shifts, so one parent is always home. That solution has one hazard: Divorce is more common in such families. Divorce rates are also higher in younger marriages and in marriages between people who recently met.

Because marriage remains the ideal, divorced adults often blame their former mate or their own poor decision for the breakup. They may then enter into a second marriage—which may lead to another divorce. If they have children in each relationship, these children in particular are likely to suffer. In addition, encouraging unmarried parents to wed may be shortsighted because such marriages are at high risk of divorce (Brown, 2010). Indeed, at least one longitudinal study of unwed mothers found that those who married were eventually worse off than those who did not (Lichter et al.,

2006). Research on unwed parents finds that many consider marriage a much riskier commitment than child-bearing (Gibson-Davis, 2011).

Scholars now describe marriage and divorce as a process, with transitions and conflicts before and after the formal events (Magnuson & Berger, 2009; Potter, 2010). As you remember, resilience is difficult when a child must contend with repeated changes and ongoing hassles. All couples experience some disagreement and conflict, which are not harmful if the conflict is resolved in a healthy way. How parents deal with conflict is critical in the relationship as well as to the well-being of the children. There is a greater likelihood of marital stability if the couple supports each other during personal difficulties (Pasch & Bradbury, 1998). Unfortunately, when there is marital conflict, children are often at risk for adjustment difficulties (Grych & Fincham, 1990).

Children's emotional reactions and coping behaviours are also impacted by the emotionality of their parents' conflicts (e.g., positive emotions, anger, sadness, fear) (Cummings et al., 2002). Coping is particularly hard when children are at a developmental transition, such as entering Grade 1 or beginning puberty, and when their parents involve them in the conflict.

Looking internationally, it is noteworthy that divorce is rare in some nations, especially in the Middle East and Africa. In those regions, adults expect marriages to endure, so in-laws help troubled couples stay together. Are children better off because of that? Maybe not. In fact, more child abuse and less child education characterize low-divorce nations. But again, linking these outcomes is a leap, not supported by data.

Given all of this, young adults may avoid marriage to avoid divorce. This strategy is working—the age at first marriage is increasing, which is one reason the divorce rate is falling even faster than the marriage rate (Amato, 2010). Is this a problem or a solution?

On the one hand, marriages need not be satisfying to the parents in order to function well for the children—an argument against divorce. But a pro-divorce argument arises from other research. If a marriage is harmful to family harmony, then divorce may help the children. This is especially true if both divorced parents are warm, attentive, and involved with their children, separating their interpersonal relationship from their parenting roles (Vèlez et al., 2011).

Can any conclusion be drawn by developmental study as to whether divorce is good for the children? As with many other issues, the answer depends on careful analysis, case by case.

KEY points

- Parents influence their children's development primarily in non-shared ways that differ for each child.
- During middle childhood, families ideally provide basic necessities and foster learning opportunities, self-respect, friendships, harmony, and stability.
- Every family structure can support child development, but children from nuclear families, on average, are most likely to develop well.
- Family poverty and conflict are usually harmful to 6- to 11-year-olds, although genes and culture can provide some protection.
- When parents are stressed by poverty, divorce, or anything else, they are less likely to nurture children well.

The Peer Group

Peers become increasingly important in middle childhood. Younger children learn from their friends, but egocentrism buffers them from rejection. By age 8, however, children are very aware of their classmates' opinions, judgments, and accomplishments. Social comparison, already explained at the beginning of this chapter, is one consequence of concrete operational thought.

The Culture of Children

Peer relationships, unlike adult–child relationships, involve partners who negotiate, compromise, share, and defend themselves as equals. Consequently, children learn social lessons from one another that grown-ups cannot teach. Adults sometimes command obedience, sometimes are playfully docile, but they are always much older and bigger, with the values and experiences of their own cohort, not the child's.

Child culture includes the particular rules and behaviours that are passed down to younger children from slightly older ones; it includes not only fashions and gestures, but also values and rituals. Jump-rope rhymes, nursery games, insults, and superstitions are often part of the peer culture. Throughout the world, the child culture encourages independence from adults. Classmates pity those (especially boys) whose parents kiss them ("mama's boy"), tease children who please the teachers ("teacher's pet," "suck-up"), and despise those who betray children to adults ("tattletale," "snitch," "rat").

As a result of this search for independence from adults, a clash sometimes develops between the generations. For example, children may refuse to wear the clothes their parents buy for them because they are too loose, too tight, too long, too short, or wrong in colour, style, brand, or some other aspect that adults ignore. Children view all of these issues as personal preferences, and think that adults should have no say over such matters. Such cohort differences may be multiplied if grandparents are involved: They may be shocked at what their grandchildren wear, say, or do.

The culture of children is not always benign. For instance, children might learn swear words and slang from their friends at school—expressions that may not be appreciated by their parents. In addition, in seeking independence from parents, children may find friends who defy authority (J. Snyder et al., 2005), sometimes harmlessly (passing a note during class), sometimes not (shoplifting, cigarette smoking).

KIDSTOCK / BLEND IMAGES / GETTY IMAGES

How to Play Boys teach each other the rituals and rules of engagement. The bigger boy shown here could hurt the smaller ones, but he won't; their culture forbids it in such situations.

child culture
The particular habits, styles, and values that reflect the set of rules and rituals that characterize children as distinct from adult society.

Pity the Teacher The culture of children encourages pranks, jokes, and the defiance of authorities at school. At the same time, as social cognition develops, many children secretly feel empathy for their teachers.

FRIENDSHIP AND SOCIAL ACCEPTANCE Children want to be liked; they learn faster as well as feel happier when they have friends. Indeed, if they had to choose between being friendless but popular (looked up to by many peers) or having close friends but being unpopular (ignored by most classmates), most would prefer to have friends. This is particularly true for children younger than 10 years of age; in early adolescence, popularity may become the priority (LaFontana & Cillessen, 2010).

Friendships become more intense and intimate as social cognition and effortful control advance. By the end of middle childhood, friends demand more of each other, including loyalty. It can be devastating when a friendship ends, partly because making new friends is difficult. Gender differences persist in activities (girls converse more, boys play active games), but both boys and girls want best friends. Having no close friend at age 11 predicts depression at age 13 (Brendgen et al., 2010).

Most children learn how to be a good friend. For example, when Grade 5 children were asked how they would react if other children teased their friend, almost all said they would ask their friend to do something fun with them and would reassure the friend that "things like that happen to everyone" (Rose & Asher, 2004).

Older children tend to choose best friends whose interests, values, and backgrounds are similar to their own. By the end of middle childhood, close friendships are almost always between children of the same sex, age, ethnicity, and socioeconomic status. This occurs not because children become more prejudiced over the course of middle childhood (they do not), but because they seek friends who understand and agree with them. Remember: Children at this age seek harmony, not conflict.

POPULAR AND UNPOPULAR CHILDREN It seems universally true that children seek close friends, but we need to consider how culture and cohort affect and influence what qualities children deem as desirable. Academic achievement is valued in middle childhood. For example, one longitudinal study in Canada found that among francophone children from ages 7 to 10, higher-achieving children had more friends, as well as classmates who wanted to be their friends. They were not usually the most popular children, but their friends were themselves high achievers (Véronneau et al., 2010). Academic achievement is less admired if a particular child is the only one who attains it in their peer group.

In North America, shy children are not popular; but when Xinyin Chen was a professor at Western University in London, Ontario, he and his colleagues found that in Shanghai, China, shy children were respected and often were popular (X. Chen et al., 1992). That is a cultural difference, but a cohort difference occurred over 12 years in Shanghai. As assertiveness became more valued in Chinese culture, a survey from the same schools found that shy children were less popular than their shy predecessors had been (X. Chen et al., 2005). A later third study found that, in rural China, shyness was still valued and predicted adult adjustment (X. Chen et al., 2009). Obviously, cohort and context matter.

Over the years of middle childhood, two types of popular children and three types of unpopular children become apparent (see Figure 8.4). Throughout childhood, children who are kind, trustworthy, and cooperative are well liked. The second type of popular children emerges around Grade 5, when children who are "athletic, cool, dominant, arrogant, and … aggressive" are sometimes popular (Cillessen & Mayeux, 2004, p. 147; Rodkin & Roisman, 2010).

As for the three types of unpopular children, some are *neglected,* but not actively rejected by peers. They are ignored, but not shunned. The neglected child does not enjoy school but is psychologically unharmed, especially if the child has a supportive family and outstanding talent (e.g., in music or the arts) (Sandstrom & Zakriski, 2004).

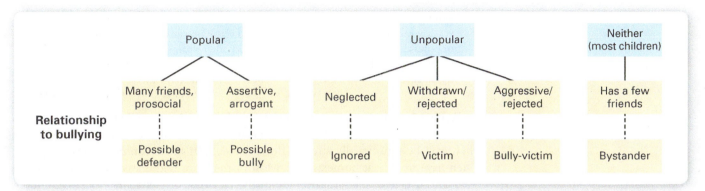

The other two types of unpopular children may be psychologically harmed. Specifically, they are at increased risk of depression and uncontrolled anger over the years of middle childhood. One type of unpopular child is **aggressive-rejected,** disliked because he or she is antagonistic and confrontational; the other type is **withdrawn-rejected,** disliked because he or she is timid and anxious. Children of these two types have much in common, often misinterpreting social situations, lacking emotional regulation, and experiencing mistreatment at home. They may become bullies or victims, a topic discussed next.

Bullying

From a developmental perspective, childhood bullying is connected to many other aspects of aggression, including maltreatment and delinquency (discussed in Chapters 6 and 10). Here we focus on bullies and victims in school.

Bullying is defined as repeated, systematic attacks intended to harm those who are unable or unlikely to defend themselves. It occurs in every nation, in every community, and in every kind of school (public or private, progressive or traditional, large or small). Although adults are often unaware of it, children recognize it as common. As one girl said, "There's a little bit of bully in everyone" (Guerra et al., 2011, p. 303).

Bullying may be of four types:

- *physical* (hitting, pinching, or kicking)
- *verbal* (teasing, taunting, or name-calling)
- *relational* (destroying peer acceptance and friendship)
- *cyberbullying* (using electronic means to harm another).

The first three types of bullying are common in primary school and may begin even earlier, in preschool. Cyberbullying is a particularly devastating form of relational bullying, more common in secondary school than in primary school. It is discussed in Chapter 9.

A key word in the definition of bullying is *repeated*. Almost everyone experiences an isolated attack or is called a derogatory name at some point in middle childhood. Victims of bullying, however, endure hurtful experiences again and again—being forced almost daily to hand over lunch money, laugh at insults, perform degrading acts, and so on—with no one defending them. Victims tend to be "cautious, sensitive, quiet … lonely and abandoned at school. As a rule, they do not have a single good friend in their class" (Olweus et al., 1999, p. 15).

Some adults think that victims have particular physical characteristics that make them prone to bullying, but this is not usually true. Victims are chosen because of their personality and isolation; they may be teased about their appearance, but it is their emotional vulnerability that attracts the bully. As one boy said,

> You can get bullied because you are weak or annoying or because you are different. Kids with big ears get bullied. Dorks get bullied. You can also get bullied because

FIGURE 8.4 Popularity Most children are neither popular nor unpopular, and the arrogant popular type is not usually evident until the end of middle childhood. The relationship to bullying is shown as a dotted line because these types of children are not always involved in bullying—it depends on the school culture.

aggressive-rejected
Someone rejected by peers because of antagonistic, confrontational behaviour.

withdrawn-rejected
Someone rejected by peers because of timid, withdrawn, and anxious behaviour.

bullying
Repeated, systematic efforts to inflict harm through physical, verbal, or social attack on a weaker person.

you think too much of yourself and try to show off. Teacher's pet gets bullied. If you say the right answer too many times in class you can get bullied. There are lots of popular groups who bully each other and other groups, but you can get bullied within your group too. If you do not want to get bullied, you have to stay under the radar, but then you might feel sad because no one pays attention to you.

[quoted in Guerra et al., 2011, p. 306]

Remember the three types of unpopular children? Neglected children are not victimized; they are ignored, "under the radar." However, if their family is supportive, they may be emotionally strong (Bowes et al., 2010). In contrast, rejected victims often have trouble at home as well. Most of them are withdrawn-rejected, but some are aggressive-rejected. The latter are **bully-victims** (or *provocative victims*) (Unnever, 2005), "the most strongly disliked members of the peer group," with neither friends nor sympathizers (Sandstrom & Zakriski, 2004, p. 110). One study found that teachers tend to mistreat bully-victims, making their problems worse (Khoury-Kassabri, 2009).

Unlike bully-victims, most bullies are *not* rejected. Although some have low self-esteem, others are proud; they bully because they are pleased with themselves and they find bullying cool (Guerra et al., 2011). Often bullies have a few admiring friends. Typically bullying is a social event, as bullies show off their power (not true for cyberbullying, but very true for physical bullying).

Bullies usually pick victims who are already rejected by most classmates (Veenstra et al., 2010), who have no friends to stick up for them, and who cannot fight back effectively. This is true for all forms of bullying, relational as well as physical, for both sexes. However, there are some sex differences in bullying type. Boy bullies are often big; they use physical aggression on smaller, weaker boys. Girl bullies are often sharp-tongued, preferring verbal aggression such as spreading rumours; they harass shyer, more soft-spoken girls.

Remember the latency period, in which children are involved with others of their own sex, both as friends and as victims. Bullies generally turn on their own, seeking admiration from other boys or other girls. Occasionally, boys accept other boys who bully girls, but girls almost never bully boys in middle childhood. This changes at puberty: Boys are no longer admired for bullying girls, but girls are allowed to bully boys, perhaps as a defence against (or expression of?) sexual feelings (Veenstra et al., 2010).

bully-victim
Someone who attacks others and who is attacked as well. (Also called a *provocative victim* because the child does things that elicit bullying.)

Who Suffers More? The 12-year-old girl and the 10-year-old boy both seem to be bullying younger or smaller children, but their attacks differ. Some developmentalists think a verbal assault is more painful than a physical one because it lingers for years.

CAUSES AND CONSEQUENCES OF BULLYING When a toddler is aggressive, parents, teachers, and peers usually teach the child to rein in those impulses and develop emotional regulation and effortful control (Chapter 6). However, the opposite may occur if families create insecure attachment, provide a stressful home life, are ineffective at discipline, or include hostile siblings (Granic & Patterson, 2006). In these cases, young children can become more aggressive.

Peers are influential as well. Some peer groups approve of bullying, and children in those groups entertain their classmates by mocking, excluding, punching, and insulting each other (N. E. Werner & Hill, 2010). On the other hand, when students themselves disapprove of bullying, its incidence is reduced (Guerra & Williams, 2010).

Young bullies and victims sometimes escape serious depression or other harm. Both bullies and victims can be identified in Grade 1 and need active guidance and remediation before their behaviour patterns become truly destructive (Leadbeater & Hoglund, 2009). Unless bullies are deterred, they and their victims risk lower school achievement and relationship difficulties later on. Bystanders who witness bullying suffer as well, experiencing physical and emotional trauma as a result of the experience (Ma et al., 2009; Monks & Coyne, 2011; Nishina & Juvonen, 2005; Rivers et al., 2009).

CAN BULLYING BE STOPPED? Most victimized children find ways to halt ongoing bullying—by ignoring, retaliating, defusing, or avoiding. A study of older children who were bullied in one year but not in the next indicated that finding new friends was crucial (P. K. Smith et al., 2004). Friendships help individual victims, but what can be done to halt bullying altogether? We know what does *not* work: increasing students' awareness, instituting zero tolerance for fighting, or putting troubled students together in a therapy group or a classroom (Baldry & Farrington, 2007; Monks & Coyne, 2011). This last measure tends to make daily life easier for some teachers, but it increases aggression.

Think Pink Students in this Peterborough, Ontario, school are raising awareness for Anti-Bullying Pink Shirt Day. This day, celebrated in schools across Canada, was initiated as a result of a student being bullied in Nova Scotia for wearing a pink shirt. Students send powerful messages to bullies by wearing pink shirts, making posters, and discussing ways to address bullying.

We also know that each specific school, with its teachers, students, and practices, can make much more difference than the macrosystem can (such as a provincial policy against bullying or a national value). For example, a study of more than 1000 schools in Columbia (where guerilla and paramilitary troops have fought for decades) found that regional poverty, population density, and homicide rate did not correlate with bullying nearly as much as did hostility and lack of empathy within each school (Chaux et al., 2009).

Empathy can be taught via cooperative learning, friendship encouragement, and school pride. A "whole school" approach—including all teachers and bystanders, parents and aides, bullies and victims—seems to be most effective. For example, a study of children with high self-esteem found that when the overall school climate seemed to encourage learning and cooperation, children with high self-esteem were unlikely to be bullies; yet when the school climate was hostile, those with high self-esteem were often bullies (Gendron et al., 2011).

Peers are crucial: If they are taught to notice bullying, become aware of it, and yet do nothing (some anti-bullying programs don't teach them what to do), that is of no help. However, if peers empathize with victims and refuse to admire bullies, that reduces classroom aggression (Salmivalli, 2010).

Programs and initiatives designed to change the entire school culture are credited with recent successful efforts to decrease bullying in schools in England (e.g., Cross et al., 2010), in Canada (reported by National Crime Prevention Centre, 2013), throughout Norway, in Finland (Kärnä et al., 2011), and in the United States (Allen, 2010; Limber, 2011). A review of all research on successful ways to halt bullying finds the following (Berger, 2007):

● Everyone in the school must change, not just the identified bullies.

● Intervention is more effective in the earlier grades.

● Evaluation is critical: Programs that initially appear to be good might not work.

This final point merits special emphasis. Longitudinal research finds that some programs reduce bullying and others increase it. Results depend on the age of the children, the strategies employed, and the outcome measures used (peer reports, teacher reports, suspensions, etc.). Objective follow-up suggests that, although well-intentioned efforts sometimes fail, bullying can be reduced.

There can be little doubt that bullying is a significant social problem in North America (Craig & Pepler, 2007). A survey by the World Health Organization ranked Canada 26th and 27th out of 35 industrialized nations on measures regarding bullying and victimization, respectively (Craig & Harel, 2004). Such results have led a coalition of academics and non-governmental organizations in Canada to set up an umbrella organization called PREVNet (Promoting Relationships and Eliminating Violence Network) to formulate a national strategy to deal with the problem of bullying in schools. Codirected by Debra Pepler (York University) and Wendy Craig (Queen's University), PREVNet's three key messages are

1. Bullying is wrong and hurtful to victims.

2. Bullying is a relationship problem that is destructive.

3. It is everybody's responsibility to promote positive relationships and eliminate violence.

✦ **ESPECIALLY FOR Parents of an Accused Bully** Another parent has told you that your child is a bully. Your child denies it and explains that the other child doesn't mind being teased. What should you do? (see response, page 318) →

Empathy Building Look at their facial expressions, not just their matching hats and gloves. For this 9-year-old sister and 7-year-old brother, moral development in the form of caring for one another is apparent.

> **KEY Points**
>
> • Schoolchildren want and need friends to encourage and support them and to convey the culture of children.
>
> • Some children are popular while others are not, primarily as a result of their behaviour and degree of conformity.
>
> • Bullying is common in middle childhood, occurring in every school, in every country.
>
> • Bullying can be reduced by an effort that engages everyone in a school—children, teachers, parents, and principal—to change the school culture so that empathy and friendship increase.

Children's Moral Values

Although the origins of morality are debatable (see Chapter 6), researchers have found significant evidence showing that even very young children understand moral issues, that is, the difference between right and wrong. Ages 7 to 11 are

> years of eager, lively searching on the part of children … as they try to understand things, to figure them out, but also to weigh the rights and wrongs. … This is the time for growth of the moral imagination, fueled constantly by the willingness, the eagerness of children to put themselves in the shoes of others.
>
> [Coles, 1997, p. 99]

This optimistic assessment seems validated by detailed research. In middle childhood, children are quite capable of making moral judgments, differentiating universal principles from mere conventional norms (Turiel, 2008a). Empirical studies show that throughout middle childhood, children readily suggest moral arguments to distinguish right from wrong (Killen, 2007).

Many forces drive children's growing interest in such issues. Three of them are (1) peer culture, (2) personal experience, and (3) empathy. As already explained, part of the culture of children involves moral values, such as being loyal to friends and protecting children from adults. A child's personal experiences also matter. For example, children in multi-ethnic schools are better able to use principles to argue against prejudice than are children who attend homogeneous schools (Killen et al., 2006).

Empathy becomes stronger in middle childhood because children are more aware of one another. This increasing perception can backfire, however. One example was just described: Bullies become adept at picking victims who are rejected by classmates, and then others admire the bullies (Veenstra et al., 2010). However, the increase in empathy during middle childhood at least allows the *possibility* of moral judgment that notices, and defends, children who are unfairly rejected.

Obviously, ethical advances are not automatic. Children who are slow to develop theory of mind—which, as you remember from Chapter 5, is affected by family and culture—are also slow to develop empathy (Caravita et al., 2010). In addition, the authors of a study of 7-year-olds conclude that "moral *competence* may be a universal human characteristic, but that it takes a situation with specific demand characteristics to translate this competence into actual prosocial performance" (van IJzendoorn et al., 2010, p. 1). In other words, school-age children can think and act morally, but they do not always do so.

Moral Reasoning

Much of the developmental research on children's moral thinking began with Piaget's descriptions of the rules used by children as they play (Piaget, 1932/1997). This led to Lawrence Kohlberg's description of cognitive stages of morality (Kohlberg, 1963).

KOHLBERG'S LEVELS OF MORAL THOUGHT Kohlberg described three levels of moral reasoning and two stages at each level (see Table 8.3), with parallels to Piaget's stages of cognition (see also Table 1.5).

- **Preconventional moral reasoning** is similar to preoperational thought in that it is egocentric; children seek pleasure and avoid pain rather than focusing on social concerns.

- **Conventional moral reasoning** parallels concrete operational thought in that it relates to specific practices: Children try to follow societal norms, that is, what parents, teachers, and friends do.

- **Postconventional moral reasoning** uses formal operational thought; people use logic in developing a personal moral code, questioning "what is" in order to decide "what should be."

According to Kohlberg, cognition advances morality. During early and middle childhood, children's answers shift from being preconventional to conventional: Concrete thought and peer experiences help children move past the first two stages (level I) to the next two stages (level II). Postconventional reasoning does not appear until later, if at all.

Kohlberg posed moral dilemmas to school-age boys (and eventually girls, teenagers, and adults). The story of a poor man named Heinz, whose wife was dying,

Showing Empathy When he was 6 years old, Canadian Ryan Hreljac began collecting money to build a well that would provide Ugandan villagers with clean drinking water. His original fundraising drive has evolved into a foundation that has built more than 700 wells in 16 countries. Here he is shown with Environment Minister Rona Ambrose at a conference in Mexico in 2006. What role would empathy play in Ryan's decision to become involved with such projects?

FRED CHARTRAND / CP IMAGES

preconventional moral reasoning Kohlberg's first level of moral reasoning, emphasizing rewards and punishments.

conventional moral reasoning Kohlberg's second level of moral reasoning, emphasizing social rules.

postconventional moral reasoning Kohlberg's third level of moral reasoning, emphasizing moral principles.

> ### TABLE 8.3 Kohlberg's Three Levels and Six Stages of Moral Reasoning
>
> **Level I: Preconventional Moral Reasoning**
> The goal is to get rewards and avoid punishments; this is a self-centred level.
>
> - *Stage one: Might makes right* (a punishment-and-obedience orientation). The most important value is to maintain the appearance of obedience to authority, avoiding punishment while still advancing self-interest. Don't get caught!
>
> - *Stage two: Look out for number one* (an instrumental and relativist orientation). Each person tries to take care of his or her own needs. The reason to be nice to other people is so that they will be nice to you.
>
> **Level II: Conventional Moral Reasoning**
> Emphasis is placed on social rules; this is a parent- and community-centred level.
>
> - *Stage three: Good girl and nice boy.* Proper behaviour pleases other people. Social approval is more important than any specific reward.
>
> - *Stage four: Law and order.* Proper behaviour means being a dutiful citizen and obeying the laws set down by society, even when no police are nearby.
>
> **Level III: Postconventional Moral Reasoning**
> Emphasis is placed on moral principles; this level is centred on ideals.
>
> - *Stage five: Social contract.* Obey social rules because they benefit everyone and are established by mutual agreement. If the rules become destructive or if one party doesn't live up to the agreement, the contract is no longer binding. Under some circumstances, disobeying the law is moral.
>
> - *Stage six: Universal ethical principles.* Universal principles, not individual situations (level I) or community practices (level II), determine right and wrong. Ethical values (such as "life is sacred") are established by individual reflection and may contradict egocentric (level I) or social and community (level II) values.

RESPONSE FOR Parents of an Accused Bully (from page 316) The future is ominous if the concern is justified. Your child's denial is a sign that there is a problem. (An innocent child would be worried about the misperception instead of categorically denying that any problem exists.) You might ask the teacher what the school is doing about bullying. Family counselling might help. Since bullies often have friends who egg them on, you may need to monitor your child's friendships. Talk matters over with your child. Ignoring the situation might lead to heartache later on. ●

was one such dilemma. A local druggist sold the only cure for 10 times what it cost to make:

> Heinz went to everyone he knew to borrow the money, but he could only get together about half of what it cost. He told the druggist that his wife was dying and asked him to sell it cheaper or let him pay later. But the druggist said "no." The husband got desperate and broke into the man's store to steal the drug for his wife. Should the husband have done that? Why?
>
> *[Kohlberg, 1963, p. 19]*

Kohlberg judged moral development not by answers, but by the *reasons* for the answers. Thus, the why is crucial. For instance, someone might say that the husband should steal the drug because he needs his wife to care for him (preconventional), or because people will blame him if he lets his wife die (conventional), or because human life is more important than obeying the law (postconventional).

CRITICISMS OF KOHLBERG Kohlberg has been criticized for not appreciating cultural or gender differences or the cognitive advancement of young children from early on. He valued abstract justice more than family or cultural loyalty: Not every culture agrees (Sherblom, 2008). Furthermore, his original participants were all boys, which has led to criticisms of gender bias (e.g., Gilligan, 1982).

Some developmentalists maintain that children are actually capable of postconventional moral reasoning at much younger ages than Kohlberg believed. This argument was made most notably by Turiel, who worked with Kohlberg for several years, first as a graduate student at Yale University in 1960 and later as a professor at Harvard. In his own research, Turiel tried to show empirically when young people pass from conventional (stage 4) to postconventional (stage 5) moral reasoning. He found that they actually make this transition while still in early childhood, not in adolescence, as Kohlberg had thought. This discovery led Turiel to formulate the social domain theory, discussed in Chapter 6 (Chuang, private communication, 2013).

Turiel argued that even children as young as 2 or 3 years of age can distinguish between different kinds of moral *transgressions* because of the experiences they have either as direct participants or witnesses. As children interact with their social environment, they interpret and make meaning of these experiences. They can see that not all transgressions are of the same kind. Transgressions that involve issues of justice, rights, and welfare (morality) are obviously different from those that are based in the social order (social conventions). For instance, stealing another child's chocolate bar (a moral transgression) is quite a different matter from wearing pyjamas to school (which violates a social convention).

Many other researchers have conducted experiments that seem to substantiate Turiel's theory. For example, Judi Smetana (1981) asked 2- and 4-year-old children which type of transgression they thought should be punished more severely, one that violated moral or social conventions, giving them examples of each. Most of the children believed that moral transgressions deserved a greater punishment than social transgressions.

In one respect, however, Kohlberg was undeniably correct: Children use their intellectual abilities to justify their moral actions. The role of cognition was evident when trios of 8- to 18-year-olds (the children in each trio were about the same age) were asked to decide how to divide a sum of money with another trio of children. Some groups chose to share equally; other groups were more selfish. There were no age differences in the actual decisions, but there were age differences in the arguments voiced. Older children suggested more complex rationalizations for their choices, both selfish and altruistic (Gummerum et al., 2008).

A VIEW FROM SCIENCE

Developing Moral Values

Many adults wonder how best to instill moral values in children. The first thought is to punish immoral behaviour, the authoritarian approach explained in Chapter 6. However, that stops overt behaviour but not covert actions. Ideally children should internalize standards, doing the right thing even when being caught is unlikely.

As noted above, Turiel believed that even very young children can understand the difference between right and wrong and distinguish among transgressions that violate a moral code, those that violate social conventions, and those that violate a personal standard. By middle childhood, children should be using their cognitive advances to develop their own moral code. In other words, they should avoid stealing because they believe it is wrong, not because they are afraid of being punished if caught. How do they learn that?

Parents and other adults sometimes lecture children, sometimes hope children will follow the adult's example, and sometimes discuss issues, expressing opinions but also listening to their children. What works? A detailed examination of the effect of conversation on morality began with an update on one of Piaget's moral issues: whether *retribution* (hurting the transgressor) or *restitution* (restoring what was lost) is best when someone does something wrong. Piaget

believed that restitution was the more advanced punishment; he also found that between ages 8 and 10, children progress from retribution to restitution (Piaget, 1932/1937).

Following Piaget's hypothesis, researchers asked 133 9-year-olds a question:

Late one afternoon there was a boy who was playing with a ball on his own in the garden. His dad saw him playing with it and asked him not to play with it so near the house because it might break a window. The boy didn't really listen to his dad, and carried on playing near the house. Then suddenly, the ball bounced up high and broke the window in the boy's room. His dad heard the noise and came to see what had happened. The father wonders what would be the fairest way to punish the boy. He thinks of two punishments. The first is to say: "Now, you didn't do as I asked. You will have to pay for the window to be mended, and I am going to take the money from your pocket money." The second is to say: "Now, you didn't do as I asked. As a punishment you have to go to your room and stay there for the rest of the evening." Which of these punishments do you think is the fairest?

[Leman & Björnberg, 2010, p. 962]

The 9-year-olds were split equally, half choosing retribution (go to his room) and half choosing restitution (pay for the window). Then the researchers paired 48 of them with a child who answered the other way, and each pair was asked to talk together to try to reach agreement. Six pairs were boy–boy, six were boy–girl with the boy favouring restitution, six were boy–girl with the girl favouring restitution, and six were girl–girl. As a control, the rest of the children were not paired and did not discuss the dilemma.

The conversations typically took only five minutes, and the retribution side was more often chosen—which Piaget would consider a moral backslide. However, when the children were queried again two weeks and eight weeks later,

their responses changed toward the more advanced, restitution thinking (see Figure 8.5). This occurred even for the children who had not been paired to discuss the problem, but it was particularly true for the children who had engaged in conversation.

The main conclusion from this study was that children's "conversation on a topic may stimulate a process of individual reflection that triggers developmental advances" (Leman & Björnberg, 2010, p. 969). Raising moral issues, and letting children talk about them, may advance their understanding of morality.

Source: Leman & Björnberg, 2010.

FIGURE 8.5 Benefits of Time and Talking The graph on the left shows that most children, immediately after their initial punitive response, became even more likely to seek punishment rather than to repair damage. However, after some time and reflection, they affirmed the response Piaget would consider more mature. The graph on the right indicates that children who had talked about the broken window example moved toward restorative justice even in examples they had not heard before, which was not true for those who had not talked about the first story.

What Children Value

Many lines of research have shown that children begin to develop their own morality early on, guided by peers, parents, and culture (Turiel, 2006). Some prosocial values are evident in early childhood. Among these are caring for close family members, cooperating with other children, and not hurting anyone intentionally (Eisenberg et al., 2006).

As children become more aware of themselves and others in middle childhood, they realize that one person's values may conflict with another's. Concrete operational cognition, which gives children the ability to use logic about what they see, propels them to think and act ethically (Turiel, 2006), and to recognize immorality in their peers (Abrams et al., 2008) and, later, in their parents, themselves, and their culture. During middle childhood, morality can be scaffolded just as cognitive skills are, with mentors—peers or adults—structuring moral dilemmas to advance moral understanding (Nucci & Turiel, 2009; Turner & Berkowitz, 2005).

As children learn to make moral distinctions, another domain of knowledge develops, the *psychological* or *personal domain* (see Chapter 6). This domain involves preferences and choices that are purely personal, such as what to eat or wear, and that children tend to think should be outside the jurisdiction of adult authority (Smetana, 2002). Issues of personal freedom often spark intergenerational conflicts between children and parents. Choices that seem strictly personal to children may strike their parents more as involving issues of safety or social conventions. For instance, in Canada, parents may want their 10-year-old son to wear a warm parka in winter, whereas the son may prefer to wear his favourite jean jacket instead.

In a study on Taiwanese-Canadian mothers of young children (4 to 6 years old), Chuang (2006) asked mothers if it was important for their children to make their own decisions. Most mothers agreed that it was important for their children's sense of independence to do things on their own. These mothers listed various issues that they allowed their children to decide about by themselves. However, the mothers also listed these same issues as points of contention when asked what conflicts they had with their children. Similar findings have been noted in studies of children and youths of European and African-American descent (e.g., Nucci & Smetana, 1996; Smetana, 2002; Smetana et al., 2003).

The moral lesson of this chapter, then, is that the psychosocial development of children must be carefully assessed, child by child. As you have seen, self-esteem is a positive attribute that may become destructive if it is too high; married-couple families are usually good for children but not always; friends protect victims, but sometimes they encourage bullies. As with all of development, individual children, families, and cultures vary, and that must be taken into account before conclusions are drawn.

KEY Points

- During middle childhood, children are intensely concerned about moral issues.
- Kohlberg believed that cognition and morality advance together, as children gradually become less self-centred and more concerned about universal principles.
- Children learn from the morality and customs of their peers and may choose loyalty to friends over cultural or familial values.
- Ongoing conversation and discussion seems to be the best way for children to internalize a moral perspective.

SUMMARY

The Nature of the Child

1. All theories of development acknowledge that school-age children become more independent and capable in many ways.

2. Erikson emphasized industry, when children busily strive to master various tasks. If they are unable to do so, they feel inferior. Freud described a latency period, when psychosexual needs are quiet.

3. Children develop their self-concept during middle childhood, basing it on a more realistic assessment of their competence than they had in earlier years.

4. Children need to develop pride in themselves and in their background, although very high self-esteem is not valued in every culture.

5. Both daily hassles and major stresses take a toll on children, with accumulated stresses more likely to impair development than any single event on its own. The child's interpretation of the situation and the availability of supportive adults, peers, and institutions aid resilience.

Families and Children

6. Families influence children in many ways, as do genes and peers. Although most siblings share a childhood home and parents, each sibling experiences different (non-shared) circumstances within the family.

7. The five functions of a supportive family are to satisfy children's physical needs; to encourage learning; to nurture friendships; to foster self-respect; and to provide a safe, stable, and harmonious home.

8. The most common family structure worldwide is the nuclear family, usually with other relatives nearby. Other two-parent families include adoptive, same-sex, grandparent, and step-parent families, each of which often functions well for children. However, each also has vulnerabilities.

9. Generally, it seems better for children to live with two parents rather than one because a parental alliance can support children's development. Single-parent families tend to be less stable, with changes in where they live and who belongs to the family. Children are stressed by new circumstances and conditions, especially in middle childhood.

10. Income affects family function. Poor children are at greater risk for emotional and behavioural problems because the stresses that often accompany poverty hinder effective parenting. High income may be stressful as well. No matter what the family SES, instability and conflict are harmful.

The Peer Group

11. Peers teach crucial social skills during middle childhood. Each cohort of children has a culture, passed down from slightly older children. Close friends are wanted and needed.

12. Popular children may be cooperative and easy to get along with or may be competitive and aggressive. Much depends on the age and culture of the children.

13. Rejected children may be neglected, aggressive, or withdrawn. Aggressive and withdrawn children have difficulty with social cognition; their interpretation of the normal give-and-take of childhood is impaired.

14. Bullying of all sorts—physical, verbal, relational, and cyber—is common, with long-term consequences for both bullies and victims. Bullies themselves may be admired, which makes their behaviour more difficult to stop.

15. Overall, a multifaceted, long-term, whole-school approach, with parents, teachers, and bystanders working together, seems the best way to halt bullying. Careful evaluation is needed to discover if a particular strategy changes the school culture.

Children's Moral Values

16. School-age children seek to differentiate right from wrong. Peer values, cultural standards, and family practices are all part of their personal morality.

17. Kohlberg described three levels of moral reasoning, each related to cognitive maturity. His theory has been criticized for focusing too much on abstractions.

18. When values conflict, children often choose loyalty to peers over adult standards of behaviour. When children discuss moral issues with other children, they develop more thoughtful answers to moral questions.

KEY TERMS

aggressive-rejected (p. 313)
astronaut family (p. 306)
bullying (p. 313)
bully-victim (p. 314)
child culture (p. 311)

conventional moral reasoning (p. 317)
extended family (p. 303)
family function (p. 300)
family structure (p. 300)

industry versus inferiority (p. 292)
latency (p. 293)
nuclear family (p. 302)
postconventional moral reasoning (p. 317)

preconventional moral reasoning (p. 317)
resilience (p. 295)
single-parent family (p. 303)
social comparison (p. 294)
withdrawn-rejected (p. 313)

WHAT HAVE YOU LEARNED?

1. How do Erikson's stages of cognition for school-age children and for preschool children differ?

2. How does a school-age child develop a sense of self?

3. Why is social comparison particularly powerful during middle childhood?

4. What factors help a child become resilient?

5. Why and when might minor stresses be more harmful than major stresses?

6. How might a child's interpretation of events help him or her cope with repeated stress?

7. Give examples of how siblings raised together may not share the same environment.

8. What is the difference between family structure and family function?

9. Why is a harmonious, stable home particularly important during middle childhood?

10. Describe the characteristics of four different family structures.

11. What are the advantages for children in a nuclear family structure?

12. What are the advantages and disadvantages of a step-parent family?

13. List three reasons why the single-parent structure might function less well than other family structures.

14. In what ways are family structure and family function affected by culture?

15. Using the family-stress model, explain how low family income might affect family function.

16. How does what children wear reflect the culture of children?

17. In what ways are friendships at the end of middle childhood different from those at the beginning of middle childhood?

18. How is a child's popularity affected by culture and the child's age?

19. What are the similarities and differences between boy bullies and girl bullies?

20. List at least three causes and three consequences of bullying.

21. How might bullying be reduced?

22. Using Kohlberg's levels of moral reasoning, explain how cognition advances morality.

23. What are the main criticisms of Kohlberg's theory of moral development?

APPLICATIONS

1. Go someplace where school-age children congregate (such as a schoolyard, a park, or a community centre) and use naturalistic observation for at least half an hour. Make sure to obtain permission to observe the children. Describe what popular, average, withdrawn, and rejected children do. Note at least one potential conflict. Describe the sequence and the outcome.

2. Focusing on verbal bullying, describe at least two times when someone said something hurtful to you and two times when you said something that might have been hurtful to someone else. What are the differences between the two types of situations?

3. How would your childhood have been different if your family structure had been different, such as if you had (or had not) lived with your grandparents, if your parents had (or had not) gotten divorced, if you had (or had not) been adopted?

>> ONLINE CONNECTIONS

To accompany your textbook, you have access to a number of online resources, including LearningCurve, which is an adaptive quizzing program; critical thinking questions; and case studies. For access to any of these links, go to www.worthpublishers.com/launchpad/bergerchuang1e. In addition to these resources, you'll find links to video clips, personalized study advice, and an e-Book. Among the videos and activities available online is the following:

■ *Moral Reasoning.* This activity reviews Kohlberg's theory of age-related changes in moral reasoning. Was he right? You can decide as you watch footage of people solving the famous Heinz dilemma.

Adolescence

One observer said adolescence is like "starting turbo-charged engines with an unskilled driver" (Dahl, 2004, p. 17). Would you ride with an unskilled driver? I did. When my daughter Bethany had her learner's permit, I sought to convey confidence. Not until I heard a terrified "Mom! Help!" did I grab the wheel to avoid hitting a subway kiosk. I should have intervened sooner, but it is hard to know when adult-size children need their mothers. Bethany was an adolescent, neither child nor adult, sometimes wanting independence, sometimes not.

–Kathleen Berger

It used to be easier to parent a teenager. A century ago, puberty didn't begin until age 15 or so. Soon after that, most girls married and most boys found work. It is said that *adolescence begins with biology and ends with society*. If so, then a hundred years ago adolescence lasted a few months. Currently, it lasts a decade or more, and for our purposes we define adolescence as lasting from about age 11 to age 18. Indeed, the period that was once considered late adolescence (from age 18 to adulthood) is now considered a separate period, called *emerging adulthood* in this book and others.

Understanding adolescence is more than an abstract challenge: Those turbo-charged engines need skilled guidance. Get ready to grab the wheel.

CHAPTER OUTLINE

ADOLESCENCE:
Body and Mind

9

WHAT WILL YOU KNOW?

- What makes a particular child reach puberty early or late?
- Why do adolescents starve themselves?
- How can teenagers be both logical and impulsive?
- Why does bullying increase in middle school?

Several years ago, a couple approached me for help with their only child, a daughter who was 16 years old. When I met with the girl and asked why she was refusing to go to school (or even leave the family's apartment), she began pinching her arms and said, "I'm fat. Can't you see how fat I am?"

I was surprised; she was probably a size 2 at the most.

"Look at the dark circles under my eyes," she added. There were no dark circles.

Underneath the girl's rebellion were some serious family issues. The family had immigrated to Canada when the girl was in Grade 9. After arriving, the teen befriended someone online. The parents became concerned about the online connection, so the following year they sent her back to their home country, China, to a remote place with limited or no Internet access. However, having been away from China for one year resulted in it being too difficult for her to catch up academically with her peers. A year later, the teen came back to Canada. Unfortunately, she lost interest in school and her grades suffered.

There were other problems too. The teen confided in her mom that she liked a boy. Fearful of what might transpire, the mother secretly asked her daughter's friends for the boy's phone number. She then called him and asked what his intentions were and if he liked her daughter. The daughter found out about this through her friends, to her horror and embarrassment. She confronted her mother, who then denied this incident.

The moving back and forth between Canada and China, along with feeling betrayed by her mother, were the real causes of this girl's rebellion. I met with her and her parents many times, and the mother apologized and asked for forgiveness. During one of our conversations, I mentioned the importance of school and that perhaps the teen would consider coming to my university. Seven years later she contacted me, stating that she had applied to an undergraduate program at my university. She studied hard and received an entrance scholarship. When we talk about the past today, she laughs and says she can't believe how immature she was at 16. She also states that her relationship with her parents is much better, and she is happy.

The reality that children grow into men and women is no shock to any adult. However, teenagers are often surprised, and sometimes even shocked, at the physical changes that occur during puberty. As at all stages of development, parents continue to play an important role in their youth's development. ●

—Susan Chuang

THIS CHAPTER DESCRIBES GROWING BODIES AND CHANGING MINDS. It all begins with hormones, but other invisible changes may be even more potent—such as the timing of neurological maturation that does not yet allow adolescents to realize that their minor imperfections are insignificant.

Puberty

Puberty refers to the years of rapid physical growth and sexual maturation that end childhood, producing a person of adult size, shape, and sexuality. The forces of puberty are released by a cascade of hormones that produce external growth and internal changes, including heightened emotions and sexual desires.

This process normally starts between ages 8 and 14 and follows the sequence outlined in At About This Time. Most physical growth and maturation end about four years after the first signs appear, although some individuals add height, weight, and muscle until age 20 or so.

For girls, the observable changes of puberty usually begin with nipple growth. Soon a few pubic hairs are visible, then peak growth spurt, widening of the hips, the first menstrual period **(menarche),** full pubic-hair pattern, and breast maturation (Susman et al., 2010). The average age of menarche among normal-weight girls is about 12 years, 8 months (Rosenfield et al., 2009), although variation in timing is quite normal.

For boys, the usual sequence is growth of the testes, initial pubic-hair growth, growth of the penis, first ejaculation of seminal fluid **(spermarche),** appearance of facial hair, peak growth spurt, deepening of the voice, and final pubic-hair growth (Biro et al., 2001; Herman-Giddens et al., 2001; Susman et al., 2010). The typical age of spermarche is just under 13 years, close to the age for menarche.

Unseen Beginnings

Just described are the visible changes of puberty, but the entire process begins with an invisible event: a marked hormonal increase. Throughout adolescence, hormone levels correlate with physiological changes and self-reported developments (Shirtcliff et al., 2009).

Hormones are body chemicals that regulate hunger, sleep, moods, stress, sexual desire, immunity, reproduction, and many other bodily reactions, including puberty. The process begins deep within the brain when biochemical signals from the hypothalamus signal another brain structure, the **pituitary.**

puberty
The time between the first onrush of hormones and full adult physical development. Puberty usually lasts three to five years. Many more years are required to achieve psychosocial maturity.

menarche
A girl's first menstrual period, signalling that she has begun ovulation. Pregnancy is biologically possible, but ovulation and menstruation are often irregular for years after menarche.

spermarche
A boy's first ejaculation of sperm. Erections can occur as early as infancy, but ejaculation signals sperm production. Spermarche may occur during sleep (in a "wet dream") or via direct stimulation.

hormone
An organic chemical substance that is produced by one body tissue and conveyed via the bloodstream to another to affect some physiological function.

pituitary
A gland in the brain that responds to a signal from the hypothalamus by producing many hormones, including those that regulate growth and that control other glands, among them the adrenal and sex glands.

AT ABOUT THIS TIME
The Sequence of Puberty

Girls	Approximate Average Age*	Boys
Ovaries increase production of estrogen and progesterone**	9	
Uterus and vagina begin to grow larger	9½	Testes increase production of testosterone**
Breast "bud" stage	10	Testes and scrotum grow larger
Pubic hair begins to appear; weight spurt begins	11	
Peak height spurt	11½	Pubic hair begins to appear
Peak muscle and organ growth; hips become noticeably wider	12	Penis growth begins
Menarche (first menstrual period)	12½	Spermarche (first ejaculation); weight spurt begins
First ovulation	13	Peak height spurt
Voice lowers	14	Peak muscle and organ growth; shoulders become noticeably broader
Final pubic-hair pattern	15	Voice lowers; visible facial hair
Full breast growth	16	
	18	Final pubic-hair pattern

*Average ages are rough approximations, with many perfectly normal, healthy adolescents as much as three years ahead of or behind these ages.

**Estrogens and testosterone influence sexual characteristics, including reproduction. Charted here are the increases produced by the gonads (sex glands). The ovaries produce estrogens and the testes produce androgens, especially testosterone. Adrenal glands produce some of both kinds of hormones (not shown).

The pituitary produces hormones that stimulate the **adrenal glands,** located above the kidneys, which produce more hormones. Many hormones that regulate puberty follow this route, known as the **HPA (hypothalamus–pituitary–adrenal) axis** (see Figure 9.1).

The **HPG (hypothalamus–pituitary–gonad) axis** is another hormonal sequence. In adolescence, gonadotropin-releasing hormone (GnRH) is released by the hypothalamus, causing the pituitary to release gonadotropins (LH & FSH), which in turn activate the gonads. As a result, the gonads enlarge and increase their production of sex hormones, chiefly **estradiol** in girls and **testosterone** in boys.

These sex hormones affect the body's shape and function, producing additional hormones that regulate stress and immunity (E. A. Young et al., 2008). *Estrogens* (including estradiol) are female hormones, and *androgens* (including testosterone) are male hormones, although the adrenal glands produce both hormones in both sexes.

A dramatic increase in estrogens or androgens at puberty produces mature ova or sperm, released in menarche or spermarche. This same hormonal rush awakens

adrenal glands
Two glands, located above the kidneys, that produce hormones (including the "stress hormones" epinephrine [adrenaline] and norepinephrine).

HPA (hypothalamus–pituitary–adrenal) axis
A sequence of hormone production that originates in the hypothalamus, moves to the pituitary, and then ends in the adrenal glands.

HPG (hypothalamus–pituitary–gonad) axis
A sequence of hormone production that originates in the hypothalamus, moves to the pituitary, and then ends in the gonads.

estradiol
A sex hormone, considered the chief estrogen. Females produce much more estradiol than males do.

testosterone
A sex hormone, the best known of the androgens (male hormones); secreted in far greater amounts by males than by females.

FIGURE 9.1 Biological Sequence of Puberty Puberty begins with a hormonal signal from the hypothalamus to the pituitary gland. The pituitary, in turn, signals the adrenal glands and the ovaries or testes to produce more of their hormones.

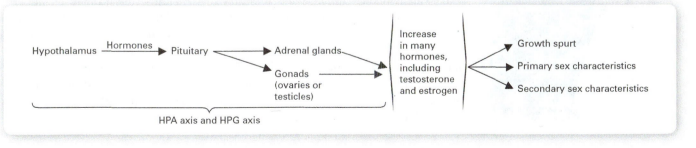

Puberty and Appearance Teenagers are often preoccupied with appearance as their bodies go through changes in puberty.

primary sex characteristics
The parts of the body that are directly involved in reproduction, including the vagina, uterus, ovaries, testicles, and penis.

secondary sex characteristics
Physical traits that are not directly involved in reproduction but that indicate sexual maturity, such as a man's beard and a woman's breasts.

Both 12 The ancestors of these 12-year-old boys came from northern Europe and West Africa, respectively. Their genes have dictated some differences between them, including the timing of puberty.

interest in sex and makes reproduction biologically possible, although peak fertility occurs four to six years later.

Hormonal increases affect psychopathology in sex-specific ways (Naninck et al., 2011; Steiner & Young, 2008). Psychological disorders in both sexes increase at adolescence, but males are twice as likely as females to become schizophrenic, whereas females are twice as likely to become depressed. This greater likelihood of psychopathology is also influenced by other psychological and environmental factors, such as stressful experiences.

Sexual Maturation

The body characteristics that are directly involved in conception and pregnancy are called **primary sex characteristics.** During puberty, every primary sex organ (the ovaries, the uterus, the penis, and the testes) increases dramatically in size and matures in function. By the end of the process, reproduction is possible.

At the same time as maturation of the primary sex characteristics, secondary sex characteristics develop. **Secondary sex characteristics** are bodily features that do not directly affect fertility (hence they are secondary) but that visually signify masculinity or femininity. One secondary characteristic is shape. At puberty, males widen at the shoulders and grow about 13 centimetres taller than females, whereas girls develop breasts and a wider pelvis. Breasts and broad hips are often considered signs of womanhood, but neither is required for conception; thus, they are secondary, not primary, sex characteristics.

Age and Puberty

Parents often have a very practical concern: When will adolescence begin? Some fear *precocious puberty* (sexual development before age 8) or very late puberty (after age 16), but both are rare (Cesario & Hughes, 2007). Quite normal are increased hormones at any time from ages 8 to 14, with the precise age affected by genes, gender, body fat, and stress.

GENES AND GENDER About two-thirds of the variation in age of puberty is genetic, evident not only in families but also in ethnic groups (Ge et al., 2007; Susman et al., 2010; van den Berg & Boomsma, 2007). For instance, northern European girls reach menarche at 13 years, 4 months, on average; southern European girls do so at 12 years, 5 months (Alsaker & Flammer, 2006). The average age of first menarche is 13 years in Australia and Russia; 13 years, 2 months in Norway; 12 years, 3 months in Greece; and 13 years, 3 months in Finland (Al-Sahab et al., 2010; Steingraber, 2007).

Research in the United States indicates that African-Americans reach puberty about seven months earlier than European- or Hispanic-Americans, whereas Chinese-Americans average several months later. In Canada, results from the National Longitudinal Survey of Children and Youth (NLSCY) indicated regional differences in the age of onset of menarche: Girls in British Columbia reached menarche at the youngest age (11 years, 5 months), while girls Ontario reached this stage at the oldest age (13 years, 9 months). The average age of menarche in Canada is 12.72 years (Al-Sahab et al., 2010).

Genes on the sex chromosomes have a marked effect. In height, the average girl is about two years ahead of the average boy. However, the female height spurt occurs before menarche, whereas for boys the increase in height is relatively late, occurring after spermarche (Hughes & Gore, 2007). Thus, when it comes to hormonal and sexual changes, girls are only a few months ahead of boys.

BODY FAT Another major influence on the onset of puberty is body fat, at least in girls. Heavy girls reach menarche years earlier than malnourished ones do. Most girls must weigh at least 45 kilograms before they experience their first period (Berkey et al., 2000).

Worldwide, urban children are more often overfed and underexercised compared with rural children. That is probably why puberty starts earlier in the cities of India and China than it does in more remote villages, a year earlier in Warsaw than in rural Poland, and earlier in Athens than in other parts of Greece (Malina et al., 2004).

Body fat also explains why youth reach puberty at age 15 or later in some parts of Africa, although their genetic relatives in North America mature much earlier. Similarly, malnutrition may explain why puberty began at about age 17 in sixteenth-century Europe. Puberty has occurred at younger ages every century since then. This is one result of the *secular trend:* More food has allowed biological advances. Over most of the twentieth century, each generation experienced puberty a few weeks earlier and grew a centimetre or so taller than did the preceding one (Floud et al., 2011).

One hormone causes increased body fat and then triggers puberty: **leptin,** which stimulates the appetite. Leptin levels in the blood show a natural increase over childhood, peaking at puberty (Rutters et al., 2008). Curiously, leptin affects appetite in females more than it does in males (Geary & Lovejoy, 2008), and body fat is more closely connected to the onset of puberty in girls than in boys. In fact, the well-established finding that body fat precipitates puberty may not be true for boys in nations where malnutrition is rare: One study found that, unlike girls, U.S. boys who are heavy in childhood reach puberty later, not earlier, than others (J. M. Lee et al., 2010).

leptin
A hormone that affects appetite and is believed to affect the onset of puberty. Leptin levels increase during childhood and peak at around age 12.

Too Early, Too Late

Few adolescents care about speculation regarding hormones or evolution. Only one aspect of pubertal timing matters to them: their friends' schedules. No one wants to be first or last; every adolescent wants to hit puberty "on time." Research finds that a wise hope since, for both sexes, early and late puberty increase the rate of almost every adolescent problem.

Teen Development Although this Australian girl looks physically mature, in reality she is only 13 years old and lacks social maturity.

GIRLS Think about the early-maturing girl. If she has visible breasts at age 10, boys tease her. She will need to fit her developing body into a school chair designed for smaller children; she might hide her breasts in bulky sweaters; she might also refuse to undress for gym. Early-maturing girls tend to have lower self-esteem, more depression, and poorer body image than do other girls (Compian et al., 2009). Sometimes early-maturing girls have older boyfriends, which gains them status—but also increases their risk of drug and alcohol use, eating disorders, relational bullying, and victimization of physical violence (from that same boyfriend) (DeRose et al., 2011; Schreck et al., 2007).

Delayed puberty in girls can be hereditary, but it can also be due to malnutrition, chromosomal abnormalities, genetic disorders, or illness. If puberty is delayed, girls may become distressed by the differences in their bodies compared to others.

BOYS There was a time when early-maturing boys became leaders in high school and successful men later in life (M. C. Jones, 1965; Taga et al., 2006). Since about 1960, however, the risks associated with early male maturation have outweighed the benefits.

SHARONLEIGHTPHOTOGRAPHY.BLOGSPOT.COM / GETTY IMAGES

♦ **ESPECIALLY FOR Parents Worried About Early Puberty** Suppose your cousin's 9-year-old daughter has just had her first period, and your cousin blames hormones in the food supply for this "precocious" puberty. Should you change your young daughter's diet? (see response, page 334) →

For the past few decades, early-maturing boys have been more aggressive, law-breaking, and alcohol-abusing than later-maturing boys (Biehl et al., 2007; Lynne et al., 2007). As a result, they have more trouble with parents, schools, and the police. Speed of change adds to the problems. If puberty is both early and quick, boys are likely to become depressed (Mendle et al., 2010). In adolescence, male depression may appear as anger: The flailing, fuming 12-year-old boy may actually be more sad than mad. Boys who reach puberty late may also have problems, becoming more anxious, depressed, and afraid of sex than other boys (Lindfors et al., 2007).

A VIEW FROM SCIENCE

Stress and Puberty

Stress affects the sexual reproductive system by *hastening* (not delaying) the hormonal onset of puberty and by making reproduction more difficult in adulthood. Thus puberty arrives earlier if a child experiences, for instance, problems at school, social challenges, low SES, or family instability, such as divorce.

The connection between stress and puberty is provocative. Is stress really a cause of earlier puberty? Perhaps it is only a correlate, and a third variable is the underlying reason why children under stress experience earlier puberty.

A logical third variable would be genes. For instance, mothers who are genetically programmed for early menarche may also be more likely to have early sex. That would make them vulnerable to teenage pregnancy, and if they marry while they are immature, the marriages would likely be turbulent. The fact that their children experience early puberty would then be the result not of the conflicted marriage, but of genes, inherited from their mother.

However, although genes affect age of puberty, careful research finds that stress is in fact a cause, not merely a correlate, of early menarche. It seems that stress hormones, particularly cortisol, directly cause early puberty. For example, in one research study, a group of sexually abused girls began puberty 7 months earlier, on average, than did a matched comparison group. The stress and trauma that the girls faced in their earlier years influenced the timing of puberty (Trickett et al., 2011).

One longitudinal study followed 756 children from infancy to adolescence. Those who were harshly treated (rarely hugged and often spanked) in childhood also had earlier puberty. This study also found that harsh parenting correlated with earlier puberty for daughters, not sons—especially if those daughters cried a lot as infants, which suggests that they were sensitive to stress (Belsky et al., 2007). This means that genes probably have some impact, via differential sensitivity (see Chapter 1). In this study, nature influenced earlier puberty only for some children, and only when nurture was stressful.

A follow-up study of the same girls at age 15, controlling for genetic inheritance, found that harsh treatment in childhood not only speeded up puberty, but also increased sexual risk. The girls who had been harshly treated had more sex partners, pregnancies, and sexual infections, but they did *not* take more risks overall: They were not more likely to use drugs or commit crimes (Belsky et al., 2010), which suggests that stress targets sexual hormones more than other genetic or environmental factors that increase adolescent rebellion.

So why is stress a cause of early puberty? One explanation comes from evolutionary theory:

> Maturing quickly and breeding promiscuously would enhance reproductive fitness more than would delaying development, mating cautiously, and investing heavily in parenting. The latter strategy, in contrast, would make biological sense, for virtually the same reproductive-fitness-enhancing reasons, under conditions of contextual support and nurturance.
>
> *[Belsky et al., 2010, p. 121]*

This evolutionary explanation seems in accord with the existing evidence (Ellis et al., 2011). In stressful times in the past, for species survival, stressed adolescents needed to replace themselves before they died. Of course, natural selection would postpone puberty during extreme famine (so that pregnant girls or their newborns would not die of malnutrition).

However, natural selection would favour genes that hastened puberty for well-fed girls whose families and tribes were in conflict. In that case, a new generation could be born before too many of the older generation were killed. By contrast, in more peaceful times and families, puberty could occur later, allowing children to benefit from years of nurturance from their parents and grandparents. For that reason, genes could have evolved to respond differentially to war and peace—again, differential sensitivity.

Today this evolutionary explanation no longer applies. However, the genome has been shaped over millennia; change takes centuries.

Growing Bigger and Stronger

For every child, puberty begins a **growth spurt**—an uneven jump in the size of almost every body part. Growth proceeds from the extremities to the core (the opposite of the earlier proximodistal growth). Thus, fingers and toes lengthen before hands and feet, hands and feet before arms and legs, arms and legs before the torso. Many pubescent children are temporarily big-footed, long-legged, and short-waisted.

SEQUENCE: WEIGHT, HEIGHT, AND MUSCLES As the bones lengthen and harden (visible on X-rays) children eat more and gain weight. Exactly when, where, and how much weight they gain depends on heredity, hormones, diet, exercise, and gender. For instance, at age 17, the average girl has twice the percentage of body fat as her male classmate, whose increased weight is mostly muscle (Roche & Sun, 2003).

A height spurt follows the weight spurt. Then, a year or two later, a muscle spurt occurs. Thus, the pudginess and clumsiness of early puberty are usually gone by late adolescence.

Lungs triple in weight; consequently, adolescents breathe more deeply and slowly. The heart doubles in size as the heart beat slows, decreasing the pulse rate while increasing blood pressure (Malina et al., 2004). Red blood cells increase in both sexes, but dramatically more so in boys, which aids oxygen transport during intense exercise. Endurance improves: Some teenagers can run for long distances or dance for hours.

Both weight and height increase *before* muscles and internal organs: Athletic training and weight lifting should be tailored to an adolescent's size the previous year to protect immature muscles and organs. Sports injuries are the most common school accidents. Injuries increase at puberty, partly because the height spurt precedes increases in bone mass, making young adolescents particularly vulnerable to fractures (Mathison & Agrawal, 2010).

Only one organ system, the lymphoid system (which includes the tonsils and adenoids), *decreases* in size, so teenagers are less susceptible to respiratory ailments. Consequently, mild asthma often disappears at puberty (Busse & Lemanske, 2005), and teenagers have fewer colds than younger children do. This is aided by growth of the larynx, which gives deeper voices to both sexes, dramatically noticeable in boys.

SKIN AND HAIR Because of the increased hormones, the fatty acid composition of perspiration changes into more "adult" body odour. Secretion of oils from the skin also increases, which results in a greater susceptibility to acne.

Hair also changes. During puberty, hair on the head and limbs becomes coarser and darker. New hair grows under arms, on faces, and over sex organs. For males, visible facial and chest hair is sometimes considered a sign of manliness, although hairiness in either sex depends on genes as well as on hormones.

To become more attractive, many teenagers spend considerable time, money, and thought on their head hair—growing, gelling, shaving, curling, straightening, highlighting, brushing, combing, styling, dyeing, wetting, drying, and so forth. If parents dislike the styling choices their teens make, hair can become a point of contention, and for the teens, a sign of independence.

growth spurt
The relatively sudden and rapid physical growth that occurs during puberty. Each body part increases in size on a schedule: Weight usually precedes height, and growth of the limbs precedes growth of the torso.

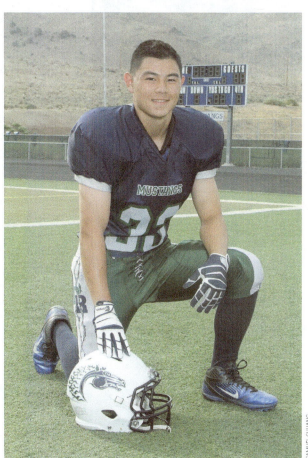

SAMUEL CHUANG

Bigger and Stronger During puberty, teenage boys first gain weight, then grow taller, and then develop muscle mass; young adolescents, such as Susan's nephew, David Chuang, from Reno, Nevada, emerge as promising athletes.

PURESTOCK / GETTY IMAGES

I Covered That Teachers everywhere complain that students are falling asleep in class. Maybe schedules, not disinterest or lack of motivation, are to blame.

circadian rhythm
A day–night cycle of biological activity that occurs approximately every 24 hours (*circadian* means "about a day").

✦ **ESPECIALLY FOR Parents of Teenagers** Why would parents blame adolescent moods on hormones? (see response, page 336) →

RESPONSE FOR Parents Worried About Early Puberty (from page 332) Probably not. If she is overweight, her diet should change, but the hormone hypothesis is speculative. Genes are the main factor; she shares only one-eighth of her genes with her cousin. ●

Body Rhythms

The brain of every living creature responds to the environment with natural rhythms that rise and fall by the hours, days, and seasons. Some *biorhythms* are on a day–night cycle of biological activity that occurs approximately every 24 hours; this cycle is called the **circadian rhythm** (*circadian* means "about a day").

The hypothalamus and the pituitary regulate the hormones that affect biorhythms of stress, appetite, sleep, and so on. Hormones of the HPA axis at puberty cause a *phase delay* in sleep–wake cycles, making many teens wide awake and hungry at midnight but half asleep with little appetite or energy all morning. By contrast, many older adults are naturally alert in the morning and sleepy at night because of their circadian rhythms.

Biology (circadian rhythms) and culture (socializing with friends and technology) work in opposite directions, making teenagers increasingly sleep-deprived with each year of high school (Carskadon, 2011). Not only does insufficient sleep decrease learning and well-being, but so does an uneven sleep schedule (more sleep on weekends, erratic bedtimes) (Fuligni & Hardway, 2006; Holm et al., 2009). Parents who yell at their wide-awake teenagers to turn off the bedroom light at midnight often must also drag those same children out of bed at 6 A.M. to get ready for school. Many high schools begin before 8 A.M., even though the evidence indicates that a later start time improves adolescent learning (Kirby et al., 2011).

Research indicates that 25 percent of Canadians are sleep-deprived, while 60 to 70 percent of Canadian students report being very sleepy during their morning classes (Douglas Mental Health University Institute, 2012). Sleepy teenagers are more likely doze in school, fall asleep while driving, develop eating and mood disorders (depression, conduct disorder, anxiety), have poor relationships with their parents, and abuse substances (partly to wake up or sleep). These problems risk jeopardizing their future health, increasing the likelihood of future obesity, diabetes, and heart disease. (Mueller et al., 2011; Patrick & Schulenberg, 2011; Roenneberg et al., 2012).

KEY Points

- Hormones begin the sequence of biological changes known as puberty, affecting every body function, including appetite, sleep, and reproductive potential.
- Although many similarities are evident in how boys and girls experience puberty, timing differs, with girls beginning between 6 months and 2 years ahead of boys, depending on the specific pubertal characteristic.
- The onset of puberty depends on genes, gender, body fat, and stress, with the normal hormonal changes beginning at any time from 8 to 14 years.
- Puberty changes every part of the body and every aspect of sexuality; weight gain precedes increases in height, muscles, and sexuality.

Nutrition

All the changes of puberty depend on adequate nourishment, yet many adolescents do not consume enough vitamins or minerals. Teenagers often skip breakfast, eat at midnight, guzzle down soft drinks, and munch on salty, processed snacks. One reason is that their hormones affect their diurnal rhythms, including their appetites; another reason is that they seek independence by eating what they want, when they want.

In 2004, the Canadian government created its first national survey of Canadians' eating habits since the 1970s. The Canadian Community Health Survey (CCHS) queried more than 35 000 people and asked them to recall what and when they had eaten in the last 24 hours. The findings were not promising, especially among adolescents. About 62 percent of girls and 68 percent of boys between the ages of 9 and 13 did not meet Canada's Food Guide's recommendation for at least five daily servings of fruit and vegetables. The Food Guide also recommends a daily serving of 100 to 300 grams of cooked meat or alternatives such as beans or eggs. According to the survey, 14 to 18 percent of girls aged 9 to 18 ate less than 100 grams of meat or other protein sources per day (Garriguet, 2004).

Diet Deficiencies

Deficiencies of iron, calcium, zinc, and other minerals are especially common after puberty. Anemia, which is a deficiency of iron, is more likely among adolescent girls than among people of any other age or gender. This is partly because adolescents of both sexes in every nation do not eat enough iron-rich foods either because they are not able to afford them or because they choose to eat iron-poor chips, sweets, and fries instead. Coffee, tea, and soft drinks also reduce iron absorption. In addition, for girls, menstruation depletes iron. Boys, who naturally require more iron to be healthy, may also be iron-deficient if they push their bodies in physical labour or sports: Muscles need iron for growth and strength.

STEPHAN GLADIEU / GETTY IMAGES

Diet Worldwide, adolescent obesity is increasing. However, these girls are addressing their weight challenges by eating balanced meals, restricting fat consumption, and walking more than 10 000 steps a day. For people who are used to eating poorly, this way of eating takes some getting used to.

Similarly, although the daily recommended intake of calcium for teenagers is 1300 milligrams, the average North American teen consumes less than 500 milligrams a day. Although Canada's Food Guide recommends that 10- to 16-year-olds have three to four servings of high-calcium products such as milk, cheese, or yogourt per day, the 2004 CCHS found that 61 percent of boys and 83 percent of girls in this age bracket did not meet the minimum recommended servings.

While teens' consumption of milk products is down, the CCHS also found that their intake of soft drinks and other sugary drinks is higher than it should be:

> Fewer than 10 percent of children aged 1 to 3 had a regular soft drink the day before the CCHS interview, but at ages 14 to 18, the percentages were 53 percent for boys and 35 percent for girls. Boys' average daily consumption of regular soft drinks climbs from 68 grams at ages 4 to 8 to 376 grams at ages 14 to 18; among girls, the rise is from 47 to 179 grams. Moreover, among soft drink consumers, average daily intake is slightly more than 200 grams at ages 1 to 3, but at ages 14 to 18, 715 grams for boys and 514 grams for girls.
>
> *[Garriguet, 2008, p. 3]*

OBSERVATION QUIZ
How can schools help teens to eat properly? (see answer, page 337) ➔

Such data led one researcher, Susan Whiting of the University of Saskatchewan, to tell the CBC, "You don't want people to be too complacent about these drinks. I think other research shows that if it gets out of hand, these sugary beverages can make a big impact on weight" (CBC News, 2012). Too many soft drinks and too little calcium between the ages of 10 and 20, when about half of adult bone mass is acquired, also means that many contemporary teenagers will develop osteoporosis (fragile bones), a major cause of disability in late adulthood.

body image
A person's idea of how his or her body looks.

RESPONSE FOR Parents of Teenagers (from page 334) Hormones disrupt adolescents' circadian rhythms, which in turn can lead to sleep deprivation and mood swings. ●

anorexia nervosa
An eating disorder characterized by severe calorie restriction and the fear of being fat. Affected individuals undereat, or overeat and then over-exercise or purge, depriving their vital organs of nutrition. Anorexia can be fatal.

Effects of Anorexia Elize, seen here at age 20, has been suffering from anorexia since she was 18 after she went on a diet to lose weight. She eats no more than 1200 calories per day. Some clinicians suggest that starving oneself is a destructive way to avoid the womanly body that develops at puberty.

FRED DUFOUR / AFP / GETTY IMAGES

bulimia nervosa
An eating disorder characterized by binge eating and subsequent purging, usually by induced vomiting and/or use of laxatives.

Body Image

One reason for poor nutrition among teenagers is anxiety about **body image**—that is, a person's idea of how his or her body looks. Few teenagers welcome every physical change in their bodies. Instead, they exaggerate imperfections (as did the girl in the story that opens this chapter) and sacrifice future health to improve current body image.

Girls diet because they want to be thinner (Halpern et al., 2005). Boys want to look taller and stronger, a concern that increases from ages 12 to 17 (D. Jones & Crawford, 2005). In both sexes and in adolescents of all ethnicities, dissatisfaction with body image is linked to low self-esteem (van den Berg et al., 2010).

Thus, as the hormones of puberty awaken sexual interest, both sexes become less happy with their own bodies and more superficial in their evaluation of the other sex. This is true worldwide. A longitudinal study in Korea found that, as in the West, body image dissatisfaction began in early adolescence and increased until age 15 or so (Kim & Kim, 2009).

Eating Disorders

One result of dissatisfaction with body image is that many teenagers, mostly girls, eat erratically or ingest drugs (especially diet pills) to lose weight; others, mostly boys, take steroids to increase muscle mass. Eating disorders are rare in childhood but increase dramatically at puberty, accompanied by distorted body image, food obsession, and depression (Bulik et al., 2008; Hrabosky & Thomas, 2008).

Adolescents sometimes switch from obsessive dieting to overeating and back again. Obesity, which is a problem at every age, is discussed primarily in other chapters. Here we describe two other eating disorders that are common in adolescence and early adulthood.

ANOREXIA Some young women (and occasionally men) suffer from **anorexia nervosa,** a disorder characterized by severe calorie restriction, or a cycle of bingeing followed by purging, that can lead to death by organ failure or suicide for between 5 and 20 percent of sufferers. If a person's body mass index (BMI) is 17 or lower, and if she or he has a fixation with weight—believing that she or he is overweight despite all evidence to the contrary—anorexia is suspected. Anorexia was undiagnosed until about 1950, when some high-achieving, upper-class young women became so emaciated that they died. Soon anorexia became evident among younger women (the rate spikes at puberty and again in emerging adulthood), among men (especially wrestlers, runners, and dancers), and in every nation and ethnic group (Chao et al., 2008).

According to DSM-5, anorexia is officially diagnosed when three symptoms are present:

1. significantly low body weight for developmental stage (BMI of 17 or lower)

2. intense fear of weight gain

3. disturbed body perception and denial of the problem.

Certain alleles increase the risk of anorexia (J. K. Young, 2010), but context is crucial. The disorder seems related to cultural pressure to be thin.

BULIMIA About three times as common as anorexia is **bulimia nervosa,** sometimes called the *binge–purge syndrome*. People with bulimia overeat compulsively, wolfing down thousands of calories within an hour or two, and then purge by vomiting or using laxatives or diuretics. They may also engage in excessive exercise.

Most bulimics are close to normal in weight and are unlikely to starve. However, they risk serious health problems, including damage to their gastrointestinal systems and cardiac arrest from electrolyte imbalance (Shannon, 2007). They also risk compulsion and depression, including thoughts of suicide (Parylak et al., 2011).

According to DSM-5, 1 to 3 percent of female teenagers and young adults are clinically bulimic. They have the following three symptoms:

1. bingeing and purging at least once a week for three months

2. uncontrollable urges to overeat

3. sense of self inordinately tied to body shape and weight.

In addition to anorexia nervosa and bulimia, DSM-5 now includes a new diagnostic category, binge-eating disorder, which allows some individuals, whose condition was previously considered non-specific or undefined, to develop a clearer understanding of their symptoms and behaviours.

People with an eating disorder tend to be perfectionists at school or at work and to have low self-esteem and an inaccurate body image. Although the precise causes of developing an eating disorder are unclear, several factors have been linked to these disorders.

The way society views attractiveness and the implicit message that thinness is desirable may be one factor. Also, young people who have an immediate family member with an eating disorder sometimes develop a similar disorder, which implies a genetic link (Bulik et al., 2005). Lastly, people with other emotional or psychological disorders, especially substance abuse, personality disorders, or affective disorders such as depression are much more likely to develop an eating disorder (K. A. Langlois et al., 2012).

ANSWER TO **OBSERVATION QUIZ**
(from page 335) Schools could offer healthy choices such as water rather than soft drinks, and healthy snacks and meals in the cafeteria. In addition, schools could start the morning later to be more in line with students' sleeping patterns. ●

KEY Points

- Adolescent diets are often deficient, especially in calcium and iron.
- Body-image worries are common, leading many adolescent girls to skip eating for a day and many boys to take steroids.
- Some adolescents develop serious eating disorders, starving themselves (anorexia nervosa) or bingeing and purging (bulimia nervosa).

Thinking, Fast and Slow

Body changes in adolescence are dramatic, but even more life-changing are the intellectual advances during adolescence. Teenagers no longer think like children, but they do not yet think like adults. We begin with the neurological changes of adolescence, and then explore the cognitive and social factors that maturation brings.

Brain Development

Like the other parts of the body, different parts of the brain grow at different rates (Blakemore, 2008). The limbic system, including the amygdala (where intense fear and excitement originate) matures before the prefrontal cortex (where planning, emotional regulation, and impulse control occur). As a result, the instinctual and emotional areas of the adolescent brain develop ahead of the reflective, analytic areas. Furthermore, pubertal hormones target the amygdala directly, whereas the cortex responds more to age and experience than to hormones. These neurobehavioural changes have been linked with youths' increased behaviours in risk taking, sensation seeking, and recklessness (Dahl, 2004).

This is evident via brain scans. Emotional control, revealed by fMRI studies, is not fully developed until adulthood (Luna et al., 2010). When compared with 18- to 23-year-olds, 14- to 15-year-olds show heightened arousal in the brain's reward centres, making them seek excitement and pleasure (van Leijenhorst et al., 2010).

CAUTION NEEDED The fact that the frontal lobes (prefrontal cortex) are the last to mature may explain something that has long bewildered adults: Many adolescents are driven by the excitement of new experiences and sensations—forgetting the caution that their parents have tried to instill (Steinberg, 2008).

Laurence Steinberg is a noted expert on adolescent thinking. He is also a father.

> When my son, Benjamin, was 14, he and three of his friends decided to sneak out of the house where they were spending the night and visit one of their girlfriends at around two in the morning. When they arrived at the girl's house, they positioned themselves under her bedroom window, threw pebbles against her windowpanes. … The boys set off the house's burglar alarm, which activated a siren and simultaneously sent a direct notification to the local police station, which dispatched a patrol car. When the siren went off, the boys ran down the street and right smack into the police car, which was heading to the girl's home. … One of the boys was caught by the police and taken back to his home, where his parents were awakened and the boy questioned.
>
> … After his near brush with the local police, Ben had returned to the house out of which he had snuck, where he slept soundly until I awakened him with an angry telephone call, telling him to gather his clothes and wait for me in front of his friend's house. On our drive home, after delivering a long lecture about what he had done and about the dangers of running from armed police in the dark when they believe they may have interrupted a burglary, I paused.
>
> "What were you thinking?" I asked.
>
> "That's the problem, Dad," Ben replied, "I wasn't."
>
> [Steinberg, 2004, pp. 51, 52]

Same People, But Not the Same Brain These brain scans are part of a longitudinal study that repeatedly compares the proportion of grey matter from childhood through adolescence. Grey matter is reduced as white matter increases, in part because pruning during the teen years (the last two pairs of images here) allows intellectual connections to build. As the authors of one study that included this chart explain, teenagers may "look like an adult, but cognitively they are not there yet" (K. Powell, 2006, p. 865).

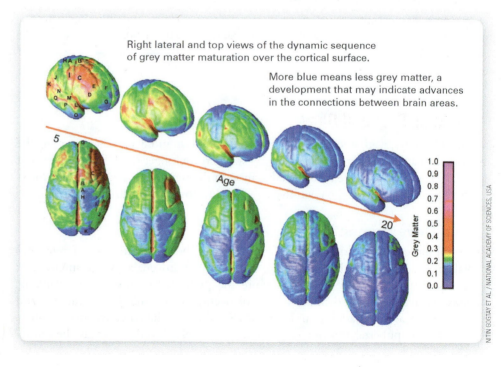

Right lateral and top views of the dynamic sequence of grey matter maturation over the cortical surface.

More blue means less grey matter, a development that may indicate advances in the connections between brain areas.

Age

Grey Matter

1.0 0.9 0.8 0.7 0.6 0.5 0.4 0.3 0.2 0.1 0.0

NITIN GOGTAY ET AL / NATIONAL ACADEMY OF SCIENCES, USA

Steinberg agrees with his son. As he expresses it, "The problem is not that Ben's decision-making was deficient. The problem is that it was nonexistent" (Steinberg, 2004, p. 52). Steinberg points out a characteristic of adolescent thought: When emotions are intense, especially when friends are nearby, the logical part of the brain shuts down.

This neurological shutdown is not reflected in questionnaires that ask teenagers to respond to hypothetical dilemmas. On those tests, most teenagers think carefully and answer correctly. They have been taught the risks of sex and drugs in biology or health classes in school, and they circle the right answers on multiple-choice tests. However,

> the prospect of visiting a hypothetical girl from class cannot possibly carry the excitement about the possibility of surprising someone you have a crush on with a visit in the middle of the night. It is easier to put on a hypothetical condom during an act of hypothetical sex than it is to put on a real one when one is in the throes of passion. It is easier to just say no to a hypothetical beer than it is to a cold frosty one on a summer night.
>
> *[Steinberg, 2004, p. 53]*

Brain immaturity is not the origin of every "troublesome adolescent behavior," but it is true that teenage brains have underdeveloped "response inhibition, emotional regulation, and organization" (Sowell et al., 2007, p. 59) because their prefrontal cortexes are immature.

The normal sequence of brain maturation (limbic system at puberty, then prefrontal cortex by the earlier 20s) combined with the early onset of puberty means that, for contemporary teenagers, emotions rule behaviour for years (Blakemore, 2008). The limbic system, unchecked by the slower-maturing prefrontal cortex, makes powerful sensations—loud music, speeding cars, strong drugs—compelling.

It is not that the prefrontal cortex shuts down completely. In fact, it continues to mature throughout childhood and adolescence, and, when they think about it, adolescents are able to assess risks better than children are (Pfeiffer et al., 2011). However, *when they think about it* is crucial. The thoughtful parts of the adolescent brain are less synchronized with the limbic system than they were earlier in life, and thus emotions from the amygdala are less modulated than they once were (Pfeiffer et al., 2011). The balance and coordination among the various parts of the brain is off-kilter, not the brain itself (Casey et al., 2011).

When stress, arousal, passion, sensory bombardment, drug intoxication, or deprivation is extreme, the adolescent brain is flooded with impulses. Teenagers brag about being so drunk they were "wasted," "bombed," "smashed"—a state most adults try to avoid and would be ashamed to admit. Unlike adults, some teenagers choose to spend a night without sleep, go through a day without eating, exercise in pain, or play hockey after a mild concussion.

RISK AND REWARD Every decision, from whether to eat a peach to when and where to enrol in college or university, requires balancing risk and reward, caution and attraction. For everyone, experiences, memories, emotions, and the prefrontal cortex help in choosing to avoid some actions and perform others. Neurological research finds that the reward parts of adolescents' brains (the parts that respond to excitement and pleasure) are far stronger than the inhibition parts (the parts that urge caution) (Van Leijenhorst et al., 2010). The parts of the brain dedicated to analysis may be immature until years after the first hormonal rushes and sexual urges.

With regard to risk, by far the most common cause of teenage death is automobile accidents, and this is true despite teens having quicker reflexes

Same Situation, Far Apart: Danger Ahead They may be far apart in culture, but both think like the teenagers they are. Jumping from a bridge in Bangladesh, he ignores the risk; at the wheel in North America, she ignores the road.

ZAYAN,1904 / GETTY IMAGES

YELLOW DOG PRODUCTIONS / GETTY IMAGES

and better vision than older people. A Statistics Canada report notes that of all the Canadians who were killed in motor-vehicle accidents over one five-year period, almost one-quarter (24 percent) were aged 15 to 24 (Statistics Canada, 2012d).

Thoughtless impulses and poor decisions, rather than problems with reflexes or vision and hearing, are almost always to blame for these accidents. A major problem today is teens texting and talking on cellphones while driving. This has become such a problem in Canada that six provinces—Newfoundland and Labrador, Nova Scotia, Quebec, Ontario, British Columbia, and Saskatchewan—have passed laws restricting hand-held cellular phone use while driving. In addition, Transport Canada recommends a total ban on cellphone use by drivers (Huang et al., 2010).

Extensive research reveals that four measures have saved hundreds of lives of teenage drivers: (1) requiring more time between issuing a learner's permit and granting a full licence, (2) no driving at night, (3) no teenage passengers, and (4) a zero-alcohol policy for young drivers (Fell et al., 2011).

Thinking About Oneself

During puberty, young people focus on themselves, in part because maturation of the brain heightens self-consciousness (Sebastian et al., 2008). It is typical for young adolescents to think deeply (but not always realistically) about their own emotions about adults, education, friends, and the future. One reason adolescents spend so much time talking on the phone, emailing, and texting is that they like to ruminate about each nuance of whatever they have done, might have done, and could do: "He said, she said, and I should've said."

EGOCENTRISM Young adolescents not only think intensely about themselves, they also think about what others think about them. Together, these two aspects of thought are called **adolescent egocentrism,** first described by David Elkind (1967). Egocentrism dominates in early adolescence, but it appears at times throughout the teen years, especially when the young person enters a new school or new peer group or goes off to college or university.

In egocentrism, adolescents regard themselves as unique, special, and much more socially significant (i.e., noticed by everyone) than they actually are. Egocentrism creates an **imaginary audience** in the minds of many adolescents. They believe they are at centre stage, with all eyes on them, and they imagine how others might react to their appearance and behaviour. The imaginary audience can cause teenagers to enter a crowded room as if they are the most attractive human beings alive. Take the case of Edgar, as described by his older sister:

> Now in the 8th grade, Edgar has this idea that all the girls are looking at him in school. He got his first pimple about three months ago. I told him to wash it with my face soap but he refused, saying, "Not until I go to school to show it off." He called the dentist, begging him to approve his braces now instead of waiting for a year. The perfect gifts for him have changed from action figures to a bottle of cologne, a chain, and a fitted baseball hat like the rappers wear.
>
> *[adapted from Eva, personal communication, 2007]*

The reverse is also possible: Unlike with Edgar, egocentrism might cause adolescents to avoid scrutiny lest someone notice a blemish on their chin or make fun of their braces.

Egocentrism also leads adolescents to interpret everyone else's behaviour as if it were a judgment on them. A stranger's frown or a teacher's critique could make a teenager conclude that "No one likes me" and then deduce that "I am unlovable" or even to claim that "I can't leave the house." More positive casual reactions—a smile from a sales clerk or an extra-big hug from a younger brother—could lead to "I am great" or "Everyone loves me," with similarly distorted self-perception. Given

◆ **ESPECIALLY FOR Parents Worried About Their Teenager's Risk Taking** You remember the risky things you did at the same age, and you are alarmed by the possibility that your child will follow in your footsteps. What should you do? (see response, page 344) ➞

adolescent egocentrism
A characteristic of adolescent thinking that leads young people (ages 10 to 13) to focus on themselves to the exclusion of others.

imaginary audience
The other people who, in an adolescent's egocentric belief, are watching and taking note of his or her appearance, ideas, and behaviour. This belief makes many teenagers very self-conscious.

Look at Me Egocentrism can cause teenagers to dye their hair blue, wax their eyebrows, or wear a checked shirt over stripes to call attention to themselves.

PICTURE PARTNERS / ALAMY

the rapid mood changes of adolescence, such conclusions are usually short-lived and susceptible to reversal with another offhand remark.

Elkind named several aspects of adolescent egocentrism, including the **personal fable** and the **invincibility fable,** which often appear together (Alberts et al., 2007). The *personal fable* is the belief that one is unique and destined to have a heroic, fabled, even legendary life. Some 12-year-olds plan to star in the NBA, or become billionaires, or cure cancer. In some adolescent minds, there is no contradiction between the personal fable and *invincibility,* the idea that, unless fate wills it, they will not be hurt by fast driving, unprotected sex, or addictive drugs. If they take risks and survive without harm, they feel invincible, not relieved.

Formal Operational Thought

In his theory of cognitive development, Jean Piaget described a shift in adolescence from concrete operational thought to what he called **formal operational thought.** Adolescents begin to consider abstractions and can make "assumptions that have no necessary relation to reality" (Piaget, 1972, p. 148).

One way to distinguish formal from concrete thinking is to compare curricula in primary school and high school. For example in math, younger children multiply real numbers, such as $4 \times 3 \times 8$; adolescents multiply abstract (algebraic) numbers, such as $(2x)(3y)$ or $(25xy^2)(3zy^3)$. In social studies, younger children learn about other cultures by reading about daily life or experiencing aspects of the culture themselves—drinking goat's milk or building an igloo, for instance. Adolescents can hypothesize how gross national product and fertility rate might affect global politics.

PIAGET'S EXPERIMENTS Piaget and his colleagues devised a number of tasks to assess formal operational thought (Inhelder & Piaget, 1958). In one experiment (diagrammed in Figure 9.2), children of many ages balance a scale by hooking weights onto the scale's arms. To master this task, they must realize that the weights' heaviness and distance from the centre interact reciprocally to affect balance.

personal fable
An aspect of adolescent egocentrism characterized by an adolescent's belief that his or her thoughts, feelings, and experiences are unique, and more wonderful or awful than anyone else's.

invincibility fable
An adolescent's egocentric conviction that he or she cannot be overcome or even harmed by anything that might defeat a normal mortal, such as unprotected sex, drug abuse, or high-speed driving.

formal operational thought
In Piaget's theory, the fourth and final stage of cognitive development, characterized by more systematic logical thinking and by the ability to understand and systematically manipulate abstract concepts.

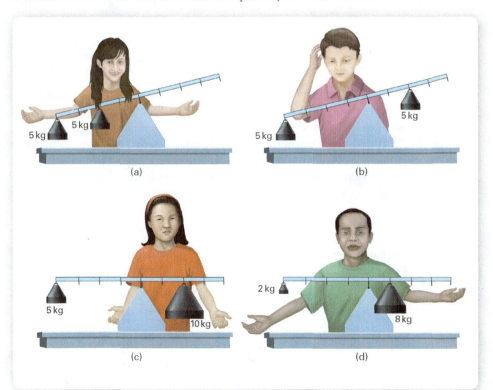

FIGURE 9.2 How to Balance a Scale Piaget's balance-scale test of formal reasoning, as it is attempted by *(a)* a 4-year-old, *(b)* a 7-year-old, *(c)* a 10-year-old, and *(d)* a 14-year-old. The key to balancing the scale is to make weight times distance from the centre equal on both sides of the centre; the realization of that principle requires formal operational thought.

Scientific Reasoning Jordan Hikowitz, also known as Doctor Mad Science, is an 11-year-old science sensation from Richmond Hill, Ontario. He conducts experiments, films them, and posts them online for millions to view. Here, he creates a liquid lava lamp.

hypothetical thought
Reasoning that includes propositions and possibilities that may not reflect reality.

The concept of balancing (that a heavy weight close to the centre could be balanced by a lighter weight farther from the centre on the other side) was completely beyond the 3- to 5-year-olds. By age 7, children could balance the scale by putting the same amount of weight on each arm, but they didn't realize that the distance from the centre mattered. By age 10, children thought about location, but used trial and error, not logic. Finally, by about age 13 or 14, some children hypothesized and tested the reciprocal relationship between weight and distance and developed the correct formula (Piaget & Inhelder, 1969). In all of Piaget's experiments, "in contrast to concrete operational children, formal operational adolescents imagine all possible determinants … [and] systematically vary the factors one by one, observe the results correctly, keep track of the results, and draw the appropriate conclusions" (P. H. Miller, 2011, p. 57).

HYPOTHETICAL-DEDUCTIVE REASONING One hallmark of formal operational thought is the capacity to think of possibility, not just reality. "Here and now" is only one of many alternatives, including "there and then," "long, long ago," "nowhere," "not yet," and "never." As Piaget said:

> The adolescent … thinks beyond the present and forms theories about everything, delighting especially in considerations of that which is not.
>
> *[Piaget, 1972, p. 148]*

Adolescents are primed to engage in **hypothetical thought,** reasoning about *if–then* propositions that do not reflect reality. For example, consider this question (adapted from De Neys & Van Gelder, 2009):

> If all mammals can walk,
> And whales are mammals,
> Can whales walk?

Younger adolescents often answer "No!" They know that whales swim, not walk, so the logic escapes them. Some adolescents answer "Yes." They understand the concept of *if:*

> *Possibility* no longer appears merely as an extension of an empirical situation or of action actually performed. Instead, it is *reality* that is now secondary to *possibility.*
> *[Inhelder & Piaget, 1958, p. 251; emphasis in original]*

deductive reasoning
Reasoning from a general statement, premise, or principle, through logical steps, to figure out (deduce) specifics. (Also called *top-down reasoning*.)

inductive reasoning
Reasoning from one or more specific experiences or facts to reach (induce) a general conclusion. (Also called *bottom-up reasoning*.)

In developing the capacity to think hypothetically, adolescents gradually become capable of **deductive reasoning,** or *top-down reasoning.* Deductive reasoning begins with an abstract idea and then uses logic to draw specific conclusions (Galotti, 2002; Keating, 2004). By contrast, during the primary school years, children accumulate facts and personal experiences (the knowledge base), asking what and why. The result is **inductive reasoning,** or *bottom-up reasoning,* with many specific examples leading to general conclusions (see Figure 9.3).

FIGURE 9.3 Bottom Up or Top Down? Children, as concrete operational thinkers, are likely to draw conclusions on the basis of their own experiences and what they have been told. This is called inductive, or bottom-up, reasoning. Adolescents can think deductively, from the top down.

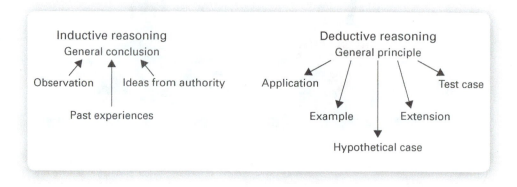

Two Modes of Thinking

The fact that adolescents and adults *can* use hypothetical-deductive reasoning does not necessarily mean that they *do* use it (Kuhn & Franklin, 2006). Adolescents particularly find it much easier and quicker to forget about logic and instead to follow their impulses.

In adolescence, abstract logic is counterbalanced by the increasing power of intuitive thinking. A **dual-process model** of adolescent cognition has been formulated (Albert & Steinberg, 2011). Various scholars choose different terms and sometimes distinct definitions of the two processes of thinking, such as: intuitive and analytic, implicit and explicit, creative and factual, contextualized and decontextualized, unconscious and conscious, hot and cold, gist and quantitative, emotional and intellectual, experiential and rational, and system 1 and system 2.

The thinking described by the first half of each pair (intuitive, implicit, creative, contextualized, unconscious, hot, gist, emotional, experiential, system 1) is preferred in everyday life. Sometimes, however, circumstances and experience compel people to use the second mode, when deeper thought is demanded. Because of the discrepancy between the maturation of the limbic system and the prefrontal cortex, adolescents are particularly likely to use intuition, not analysis (Gerrard et al., 2008). **Intuitive thought** begins with a belief, assumption, or general rule (called a *heuristic*) rather than with logic. Intuition is quick and powerful; it feels "right." **Analytic thought** is the formal, logical, hypothetical-deductive thinking as described by Piaget. It involves rational analysis of many factors whose interactions have to be calculated, as in the scale-balancing problem.

When the two modes of thinking conflict, people sometimes use one mode and sometimes the other. Experiences and role models influence the choice. For example, one study found that when adolescents enter a multicultural high school, some rely on old stereotypes and others reassess their thoughts to consider new perspectives. Which of these two modes of thinking predominates depends on the students' specific experiences and on the attitudes of the adults in the school (Crisp & Turner, 2011).

COMPARING INTUITION AND ANALYSIS Paul Klaczynski conducted dozens of studies comparing the thinking of children, young adolescents, and older adolescents (usually 9-, 12-, and 15-year-olds) (Holland & Klaczynski, 2009; Klaczynski, 2001, 2011; Klaczynski et al., 2009). In one, he presented 19 logical problems, for example:

> Timothy is very good-looking, strong, and does not smoke. He likes hanging around with his male friends, watching sports on TV, and driving his Ford Mustang convertible. He's very concerned with how he looks and with being in good shape. He is a high school senior now and is trying to get a college scholarship.
>
> Based on this [description], rank each statement in terms of how likely it is to be true. … The most likely statement should get a 1. The least likely statement should get a 6.
>
> _____ Timothy has a girlfriend.
> _____ Timothy is an athlete.
> _____ Timothy is popular and an athlete.
> _____ Timothy is a teacher's pet and has a girlfriend.
> _____ Timothy is a teacher's pet.
> _____ Timothy is popular.

PHOTO BY JOHN GIBBINS, SAN DIEGO UNION-TRIBUNE / ZUMA PRESS © 2009

Impressive Thinking "Correlating Genetic Signature with Surface Sugar Expression in Vibrio vulnificus" is the title of Shilpa Argade's winning science project about a sometimes deadly bacteria. Like many other high school seniors, she is capable of deductive reasoning.

dual-process model
The notion that two networks exist within the human brain, one for emotional and one for analytical processing of stimuli.

intuitive thought
Thought that arises from an emotion or a hunch, beyond rational explanation, and is influenced by past experiences and cultural assumptions.

analytic thought
Thought that results from analysis, such as a systematic ranking of pros and cons, risks and consequences, and possibilities and facts. Analytic thought depends on logic and rationality.

RESPONSE FOR Parents Worried About Their Teenager's Risk Taking (from page 340) It is normal to be concerned about your child's behaviour. However, it is important to understand that you won't be able to control your teenager. Set reasonable limits, and when the opportunity arises, be ready to listen and communicate. ●

In ranking these statements, most adolescents (73 percent) made at least one analytic error, ranking a double statement (e.g., popular *and* an athlete) as more likely than a single statement included in it (popular *or* an athlete). They intuitively jumped to the more inclusive statement, rather than sticking to logic. In many other studies, adults often make the same mistake (Kahneman, 2011).

Klaczynski found that almost all adolescents were analytical and logical on some of the 19 problems but not on others. Logical thinking improved with age and education, although not with IQ. In other words, being smarter as measured by an intelligence test did not advance logic as much as did having more experience, in school and in life. Klaczynski (2001) concluded that, even though teenagers *can* use logic, "most adolescents do not demonstrate a level of performance commensurate with their abilities" (p. 854).

PREFERRING EMOTIONS What would motivate adolescents to use—or fail to use—their formal operational thinking? Klaczynski's participants had all learned the scientific method in school, and they knew that scientists use empirical evidence and deductive reasoning. But they did not always think like scientists. Why not?

Dozens of experiments and extensive theorizing have found some answers (Albert & Steinberg, 2011; Kahneman, 2011). Essentially, analytic thought is more difficult than intuition, and it requires examination of comforting, familiar prejudices.

Once people of any age reach an emotional conclusion (sometimes called a "gut feeling"), they resist changing their minds. As people gain experience in making decisions and thinking things through, they become better at knowing when analysis is needed (Milkman et al., 2009).

For example, in contrast to younger students, older adolescents are more suspicious of authority and more likely to consider mitigating circumstances when judging the legitimacy of a rule (Klaczynski, 2011). Both suspicion of authority and awareness of context signify advances in reasoning, but both also complicate simple issues.

BOB BOUGHNER / CHATHAM DAILY NEWS / QMI AGENCY

Robot Competition This robot is about to compete in the Annual Robotics Olympic challenge in Dresden, Ontario. Breanne, a 14-year-old from Chatham, Ontario, designed this robot to compete in a number of activities such as steeple chase, relay races, and weightlifting.

KEY points

- Uneven brain development characterizes adolescence, with the limbic system developing faster than the prefrontal cortex.

- Young adolescents are often egocentric, thinking of themselves as invincible and performing for an imaginary audience.

- Adolescents are also capable of logical, hypothetical thought, what Piaget described as formal operational thinking.

- Both emotional intuition and logical analysis are stronger in adolescence than earlier in life. Adolescents usually prefer the former because it is faster and easier.

Teaching and Learning

What does our knowledge of adolescent thought imply about education? Which curricula and school structures (single-sex or co-ed, large or small, public or private) are best for 11- to 18-year-olds? Adolescents differ: "Some students thrive at school, enjoying and benefitting from most of their experiences there; others muddle along and cope as best they can with the stress and demands of the moment; and still others find school an alienating and unpleasant place to be ..." (Eccles & Roeser, 2011, p. 225).

Given personal and cultural variations, no specific school curriculum, structure, or teaching method is best for everyone. Various scientists, nations, schools, and teachers try many strategies. To analyze these, we begin with definitions and facts.

Definitions and Facts

Each year of schooling advances human potential, as recognized by leaders and scholars in every nation and discipline. As you have read, adolescents are capable of deep and wide-ranging thought, no longer limited by personal experience; yet they are often egocentric, impulsive, and intuitive. The quality of education matters: A year can propel thinking forward or can have little impact (Hanushek & Woessmann, 2010).

Secondary education—traditionally Grades 7 through 12 (Grade 11 in Quebec)—denotes the school years after elementary or grade school (known as primary education) and before college or university (known as tertiary education, or more commonly as post-secondary). Often two levels of secondary education are provided: **middle school,** for 10- to 13-year-olds (Grades 6, 7, and 8), and high school, for Grades 9 to 12. As the age of puberty has decreased, middle schools have replaced junior high schools, which were for students in Grades 7, 8, and 9.

SECONDARY EDUCATION Secondary education is important to adults' health. Data on almost every ailment, from every nation and ethnic group, confirm that high school graduation correlates with better health. Some of the reasons are only indirectly related to education (e.g., income and place of residence), but even when such factors are taken into account, health improves with education. Even such a seemingly unrelated condition as serious hearing loss in late adulthood is twice as common among those who never graduated from high school as it is among high school graduates (National Center for Health Statistics, 2010).

Secondary education is also important for a nation's economic growth, since that growth depends on highly educated workers. Partly because political leaders recognize that educated adults advance national wealth and health, every nation is increasing the number of students in secondary schools. Education is compulsory until at least age 12 almost everywhere (UNESCO, 2008), and several national leaders advocate compulsory education until age 18 or high school graduation, whichever comes first.

MIDDLE SCHOOL Middle school is a challenging time for students. The average grades on report cards fall, achievement tests show less learning each year, students are less motivated to study and learn, and behavioural problems rise. Do these middle school experiences matter for later achievement? One team believes so: "Long-term academic trajectories—the choice to stay in school or to drop out and the selection in high school of academic college-prep courses versus basic-level courses—are strongly influenced by experience in grades 6–8" (Snow et al., 2007, p. 72).

Puberty itself is part of the problem. At least for other animals, especially when under stress, learning slows down at puberty (McCormick et al., 2010). The same is probably true for humans, who experience biological and psychological stresses during puberty. However, many experts do not believe stresses of puberty are the main reasons learning suffers in early adolescence. Instead, they blame the organizational structure of many middle schools (Meece & Eccles, 2010). To be specific, unlike in primary school, where each teacher is responsible for one classroom of children, middle school teachers are not connected to any small group. Instead, they specialize in an academic subject, taught to hundreds of students each year. This makes them

secondary education
Literally, the period after primary education (elementary or grade school) and before tertiary education (college or university). It usually occurs from about age 12 to 18, although there is some variation by school and by nation.

middle school
A school for children in the grades between elementary and high school. Middle school usually begins with Grade 6 and ends with Grade 8.

✦ **ESPECIALLY FOR Middle School Teachers** You think your lessons are interesting, but many of your students seem disinterested, distract their fellow classmates, or simply tune you out. What do you do? ➞

Same Situation, Far Apart: Different Learning Young adolescents around the globe, such as these in Canada *(left)* and Pakistan *(right)*, attend middle school, but what they learn differs. Many North American schools encourage collaboration and hands-on learning (these girls are building roller coasters), whereas many south Asian schools stress individual writing.

impersonal and distant: Students learn less and risk more because no one teacher is aware of their actions (Crosnoe et al., 2004). It is ironic that just when egocentrism leads young people to feelings of shame or fantasies of stardom (the imaginary audience), many middle schools require them to change rooms, teachers, and classmates every 40 minutes or so. That makes public acclaim and personal recognition difficult.

Since public acclaim is elusive, many middle school students seek acceptance from their peers. Bullying increases, appearance becomes important, status symbols are displayed (from gang colours to expensive shoes), and sexual conquests are flaunted, with boys bragging and girls gaining status if they are dating an older person. Values change too: In Grade 4 the "coolest" peers are good students; by Grade 8, cool peers are not involved in school and are likely to be antisocial (not kind, antagonistic to adults) (Galván et al., 2011). Of course, much depends on the cultural context, but almost every middle school student seeks peer approval in ways that adults disapprove of (Véronneau & Dishion, 2010).

Motivation

A cognitive perspective on development highlights the academic disengagement typical of many middle school students, and tries to understand its causes and seek effective prevention. Some reasons have already been suggested: puberty, alienation from teachers, reliance on peers. But an additional reason may be adolescents' assumptions about their potential and how to achieve what they wish.

entity approach to intelligence
An approach to understanding intelligence that sees ability as innate, a fixed quantity present at birth; those who hold this view do not believe that effort enhances achievement.

If they believe in the **entity approach to intelligence** (i.e., that ability is innate, a fixed quantity present at birth), then they think it is hopeless to study, especially in subjects that do not come easily. All they can do is accept their deficiencies, such as for math, or writing, or languages. They are convinced that they are incapable of mastering particular skill sets and this will never change, making comments such as, "I'm just not good at math." This entity belief reduces stress but also reduces achievement.

incremental approach to intelligence
An approach to understanding intelligence that holds that intelligence can be directly increased by effort; those who subscribe to this view believe they can master whatever they seek to learn if they pay attention, participate in class, study, complete their homework, and so on.

By contrast, if students believe in the **incremental approach to intelligence** (i.e., that ability increases if they work on it), then they will pay attention, participate in class, study, complete their homework, and so on. That is called *mastery motivation*.

This is not just a hypothesis. In the first year of middle school, students with entity beliefs tend not to be academically successful, whereas those with mastery motivation show achievement gains (Blackwell et al., 2007). In one study, some students in their first year of middle school took part in a program in which they were taught eight lessons designed to convey the idea that being smart was incremental. For instance, they were taught ways to "Grow Your Intelligence," as one segment of the program was called. Those students gained—especially if they had formerly held the entity theory of intelligence—while students in other classes did not (Blackwell et al., 2007).

Teachers themselves were surprised at the effect. Among the typical comments was a teacher explaining that a boy

> who never puts in any extra effort and doesn't turn in homework on time, actually stayed up late working for hours to finish an assignment early so I could review it and give him a chance to revise it. He earned a B+ ... he had been getting C's and lower.
>
> *[quoted in Blackwell et al., 2007, p. 256]*

The concept that skills and intelligence can be mastered motivates the learning of social skills as well as academic subjects (Olson & Dweck, 2008). This makes it particularly important in adolescence, when peers are so important.

The contrast between the entity and incremental approaches is apparent not only for individual adolescents, but also for teachers, parents, schools, and cultures. If a school is structured so that children individually compete with each another rather than in cooperative groups, then individuals who score low are likely to cope by endorsing the entity theory (Eccles & Roeser, 2011). By contrast, when teachers and students are supportive of each other's learning, the belief in mastery is evident. (Patrick et al., 2011).

According to international comparisons, educational systems that track students into higher or lower classes, that expel students who are not learning, and that allow competition between schools for the brightest students (all reflecting entity, not incremental, theory) are also school systems with lower average achievement and a larger gap between the scores of students at the highest and lowest score quartiles (Organisation for Economic Co-operation and Development [OECD], 2011).

Before assuming that all middle school students are disengaged, remember that adolescents vary in every aspect of development, including motivation. A study of student emotional and academic engagement from Grade 5 to Grade 8 found that, as expected, the overall direction was less engagement. Yet, a distinct group (about 18 percent) was highly engaged throughout, and only a few (about 5 percent) decreased drastically in engagement from Grades 5 to 8. The disengaged students were more often minority boys from low-income families (Li & Lerner, 2011). That finding should alert teachers to choose those young boys for various roles and responsibilities—engaging them before they have a chance to disengage.

School Transitions

Every transition is stressful. The most difficult times are the first year of middle school, the first year of high school, and the first year of college or university. The larger and less personal the new institution is, and the more egocentric the student is, the more difficult the transition.

STRANGERS IN SCHOOLS When students enter a new school with classmates and customs unlike those in their old school, they often feel alienated, fearing failure (Benner & Graham, 2007). This is especially true for students entering large schools from more intimate ones. Some research suggests that school enrolment should be 600 or fewer students, although many urban high schools boast more than 1000 students. When schools are that large, many students are strangers to each other. In addition, for most (though not all) students, engagement decreases as school size increases (Weiss et al., 2010). However, school size may be less problematic than school organization, such as having many different students for each teacher (too impersonal) and weak school norms, loyalty, and spirit (a problem for large schools) (Gottfredson & DiPietro, 2011).

The transition to a new school is even more challenging for immigrant students. In a study of 125 Canadian youths (aged 11 to 19 years) from immigrant families in five provinces (Alberta, British Columbia, Nova Scotia, Ontario, and Quebec), students cited several challenges in adjusting to their new school environment. Most prominent among these challenges were the structure of the school (i.e., having to rotate from classroom to classroom), class assignments such as group projects, and their inability to speak either official language (English or French) (Chuang & Canadian Immigrant Settlement Sector Alliance, 2009).

RESPONSE FOR Middle School Teachers (from page 345) Students need both challenge and involvement; avoid lessons that are too easy or too passive. Create small groups; assign oral reports, debates, role-plays, and so on. Remember that adolescents like to hear each other's thoughts and their own voices. ●

Another important problem is *stereotype threat,* the anxiety-producing idea that other people are judging you in stereotyped ways (Aronson & Dee, 2012). Stereotype threat may be disconnected from actual stereotyping, as it describes a person's own perceived fear that other people are judging him or her as deficient for being black or white, male or female, rich or poor. This idea is further explained in Chapter 11.

A study of the transition from middle to high school confirmed that personal relationships are crucial in helping students adapt to unfamiliar circumstances: Students are less likely to drop out if they have friends in the new school and teachers who encourage learning. School policies (e.g., class placement, group discussions) can facilitate such relationships (Langenkamp, 2010).

Students already at risk of emotional problems may suffer more than others because of the transition; anxiety, depression, and quitting may result. Worse psychological disorders may occur. As one expert notes, "Depression, self-injury behavior, substance abuse, eating disorders, bipolar disorder, and schizophrenia have striking developmental patterns corresponding to transitions in early and late adolescence" (Masten, 2004, p. 310).

Of course, transitions are not the only cause of adolescent pathology; hormones, body changes, sexual experiences, family conflict, and cultural expectations also contribute. In addition, puberty may activate genes that predispose a person to mental disorders (Erath et al., 2009), and the sequence of brain development may cause emotional difficulties. Nonetheless, for many reasons, adolescent newcomers to a school community need extra support to learn well.

cyberbullying
Bullying that occurs when one person spreads insults or rumours about another by means of technology (e.g., emails, text messages, or cell-phone videos).

Cyberbullying This high school student, Yuriko, suffered severe depression as a result of cyberbullying, the effects of which may be worse in Japan than in other countries because social reputation is so crucial.

REUTERS / YURIKO NAKAO

To eliminate one transition, some school systems and even some countries (e.g., Finland) have children attend the same institution from Grade 1 through Grades 8 and 9. In Canada and the United States, districts vary in terms of when and whether children leave primary school. When the move occurs early, after Grade 4 (as opposed to after Grade 5, 6, or 7), or not until after Grade 8, children seem to learn more (Schwartz et al., 2011).

Some small private schools eliminate transitions by having one school from kindergarten through Grade 12. This may facilitate learning, or it may make it more difficult for graduates to adjust to college or university, to the workplace, or to a new community.

BULLYING Bullying decreases each year of elementary school, perhaps because students learn from classmates and teachers that there are better ways to interact with other children. However, many studies find that bullying increases in the first year of middle school and again in the first year of high school. This occurs between the sexes as well as within them, with girls likely to bully other girls they perceive as sexual rivals, and boys likely to bully other boys they perceive as weaker. Beyond that, students new to a larger school may feel they need to assert themselves. Some students, especially bully-victims (see Chapter 8), engage in or are victims of bullying that uses technology, called **cyberbullying** (Tokunaga, 2010). In many ways, cyberbullying is similar to other forms of harassment—academically harmful to everyone, undermining learning in bullies, bystanders, and particularly in victims (Marsh et al., 2010; Schneider et al., 2011; P. K. Smith et al., 2008). It is another form of relational bullying, designed to harm social interactions, with girls being cyberbullies as often as boys.

Although the causes of all forms of bullying seem similar, each carries its own sting. All bullying is harmful when the self-image is forming, the imaginary audience is looming, and impulsive thinking supersedes analytic thinking. However, cyberbullying—which allows rumours and insults to spread far and wide, with immediate reach, day and night, guided by impulses that can be actualized at the touch of button (Englander et al., 2009)—may be especially harmful. The ease of posting photos makes it even worse: It is hard to deny visual evidence of oneself drunk, naked, or crying.

All forms of bullying are affected by the school climate. When students consider their school a good place to be—with supportive teachers, friendly students, opportunities for growth (clubs, sports, theatre, music), and so on—those with high self-esteem are not only less likely to engage in cyberbullying, but they also disapprove of it (Gendron et al., 2011). That reduces the incidence overall. However, when the school climate is negative, those with high self-esteem are often bullies themselves (Gendron et al., 2011).

OPPOSING PERSPECTIVES

Misconceptions about Bullying

Amanda Todd was born on November 26, 1996. She committed suicide on October 10, 2012, one month shy of her 16th birthday. But one month before this terrible end, Amanda powerfully chronicled her tragic life events on YouTube.

Amanda was twelve years old when she was befriended by a boy online. Flattered by his comments, Amanda lifted up her top and flashed the person via her webcam. This single moment of indiscretion followed her for three years before she ended her life. In Gillian Shaw's interview with Amanda Todd's mother for the *Vancouver Sun,* Carol Todd stated,

> The Internet stalker she flashed kept stalking her. Every time she moved schools he would go undercover and become a Facebook friend. What the guy did was he went online to the kids who went to (the new school) and said that he was going to be a new student—that he was starting school the following week and that he wanted some friends and could they friend him on Facebook.

The cyberstalker then sent the video and pictures of Amanda to everybody at her new school—students, parents, and teachers. Amanda was taunted, beaten, and could not escape the cyberstalker until she unfortunately took matters into her own hands. Sadly, Amanda is not unique; many have been the victims of bullying. These cases raise questions for educators, researchers, and social policy-makers about how to deal with bullying and cyberbullying.

PREVNet is a network of 69 Canadian researchers and 55 national youth-serving organizations working together to stop bullying in Canada and promote safe and healthy relationships for all children and youth. As discussed in Chapter 8, PREVNet's three core beliefs are that: (1) bullying is wrong and hurtful, (2) bullying is a relationships problem, and (3) promoting relationships and eliminating violence are everybody's responsibilities (PREVNet.ca, n.d.).

As PREVNet has reported, ongoing misunderstanding and misconceptions about bullying hinder the efforts being made to eliminate bullying. First, bullying does cause serious harm, and it has short-term as well as long-term effects. Those who are bullied tend to suffer more headaches, stomachaches, depression, and anxiety. Mental health issues have been found to extend for many years. Both children who have been bullied and those who bully are more likely to have lower academic performance, miss school, or commit suicide.

Another misconception about bullying is that children who bully will grow out of it. Childhood bullies who are not identified early and do not receive intervention are more likely to bully in adolescence and adulthood. Their bullying behaviour progresses into more sophisticated forms over time as their thinking and social skills develop, and they become even more aware of their victims' vulnerabilities. These behaviours include sexual and work harassment, dating violence, marital abuse, child abuse, and elder abuse.

Children who are victimized cannot stop the bullying on their own. Due to the victim's vulnerable position in the relationship, adult intervention is required to correct the power imbalance. Children and parents may even need to report bullying to various adults in authority, such as a teacher or principal.

Along similar lines, telling children to fight back may worsen the situation. Research has shown that children who use aggressive strategies to combat their victimizer tend to experience longer and more severe bullying interactions. As a result, all adults, including parents, teachers, and other adults in the community, are responsible for supporting children in developing effective social skills and learning to respect each other, regardless of ethnicity, gender, or citizenship (PREVNet.ca, n.d.).

Succeeding in High School

"What do you want to be when you grow up?" is a question often asked of children. Younger children often aspire to a career that fewer than one in a million will obtain—rock star, sports hero, prime minister—and adults smile at such fantasies. By the teen years, however, more practical concerns arise, specifically what jobs are available, and how enjoyable, remunerative, and demanding each is. The question becomes hard to answer.

MEASURING PRACTICAL COGNITION Employers hope their future employees will have learned in secondary school how to think, explain, write, concentrate, and get along with other people. Those skills are hard to measure, especially on the two international tests described in Chapter 7, the PIRLS and the TIMSS.

The PISA (Programme for International Student Assessment), also mentioned in Chapter 7, was designed to measure the cognitive abilities needed in adult life. The PISA is taken by 15-year-olds, an age chosen because many students that age are close to the end of their formal school career. On this test, the questions are written to be practical, measuring knowledge that might apply at home or on the job, as students deal with everyday problems and challenges (PISA, 2009). For example, among the math questions is this one:

Robert's mother lets him pick one candy from a bag. He can't see the candies. The number of candies of each color in the bag is shown in the following graph.

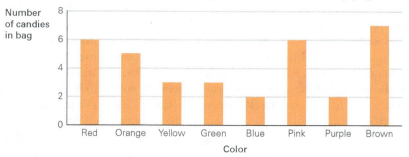

What is the probability that Robert will pick a red candy?

A. 10%   B. 20%   C. 25%   D. 50%

For that and the other questions on the PISA, the calculations are quite simple—most 10-year-olds can do them; no calculus, calculators, or complex formulas are needed. However, the reasoning may be challenging and many students do not know how to read a graph. Half of the 15-year-olds worldwide answered that question incorrectly (the answer is B).

In 2009, on the PISA overall (reading, science, and math), China, Finland, and Korea were at the top; Canada was close to the top; and the United States scored near average (see Table 9.1 for math scores). Analysis of nations and scores on the PISA finds four factors that correlate with high achievement (OECD, 2010a, p. 6):

1. Leaders, parents, and citizens overall value education, with individualized approaches to learning so that all students learn what they need.

2. Standards are high and clear, so every student knows what he or she must do, with a focus on the acquisition of complex, higher order thinking skills.

3. Teachers and administrators are valued, given considerable discretion in determining content and sufficient salary as well as time for collaboration.

4. Learning is prioritized across the entire system, with high-quality teachers working in the most challenging environments.

TABLE 9.1 Math Scores on the PISA, 2009/2006

Nation	Score	Nation	Score	Nation	Score
China Shanghai	600/n/a	Denmark	503/513	Greece	466/459
Singapore	562/n/a	Norway	498/490	Israel	447/442
Hong Kong	555/547	France	497/496	Turkey	445/424
South Korea	546/547	Austria	496/505	Uruguay	427/427
Chinese Taipei	543/549	Poland	495/495	Romania	427/415
Finland	541/548	Sweden	494/502	Chile	421/411
Switzerland	534/530	Czech Republic	493/510	Thailand	419/417
Japan	529/523	United Kingdom	492/495	Mexico	419/406
Canada	527/527	Hungary	490/491	Argentina	388/381
Netherlands	526/531	Ireland	487/501	Jordan	387/384
New Zealand	519/522	United States	487/474	Brazil	386/370
Belgium	515/520	Portugal	487/466	Colombia	381/370
Australia	514/520	Spain	483/480	Indonesia	371/391
Germany	513/504	Italy	483/462	Tunisia	371/365
Iceland	507/506	Russia	468/476		

Source: PISA, 2009.

Practical Knowledge Tested by the PISA The PISA is taken by 15-year-olds in many nations. Questions are designed to measure practical applications of school knowledge in science, reading, and math. National variations are more closely tied to educational practices and values at school and home, not to geography, genes, or immigration. For instance, the Netherlands and Norway are close on the map but not in math achievement, and, although most East Asian nations do very well, Thailand scores low. Also note that nations with a higher proportion of immigrants (e.g., Canada) or very few immigrants (e.g., Japan) seem to do equally well.

DROPOUT RATES Indications from the PISA and from international comparisons of high school dropout rates suggest that secondary education can be improved for those who do not go to college or university. Surprisingly, students who are capable of passing their classes drop out as often as those who are less capable, at least as measured on IQ tests.

Persistence, engagement, and motivation seem more crucial for high school success than is intellectual ability (Archambault et al., 2009). One study that measured engagement and motivation reported developmental differences: Students were most motivated and engaged in primary school, somewhat engaged in college or university, but least engaged in secondary school (Martin, 2009).

According to a study conducted in 2002, Canada has been more successful at reducing dropout rates than many other developed countries. Canada's dropout rate was almost 4 points lower than the average for the 25 OECD industrialized countries (see Figure 9.4). Except for Great Britain, Canada had the lowest dropout rate among the G7 nations that year.

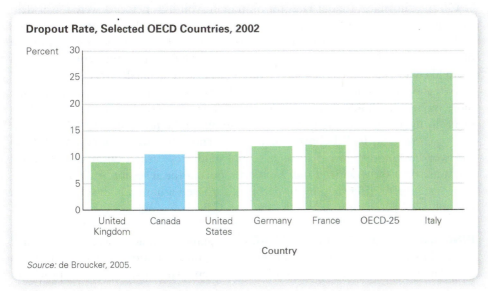

Dropout Rate, Selected OECD Countries, 2002

Source: de Broucker, 2005.

FIGURE 9.4 **International Comparisons** A study from 2002 showed Canada was doing relatively well internationally with respect to dropout rates. Just under 11 percent of Canadians aged 20 to 24 had not finished high school, while the average rate for 25 OECD countries was 14.7 percent.

FIGURE 9.5 Cause for Hope?
According to Statistics Canada, the nation's dropout rate has declined steadily since the academic year 1990–1991. By 2011–2012, the overall rate had fallen to 7.8 percent. Dropout rates have been consistently lower for females than for males.

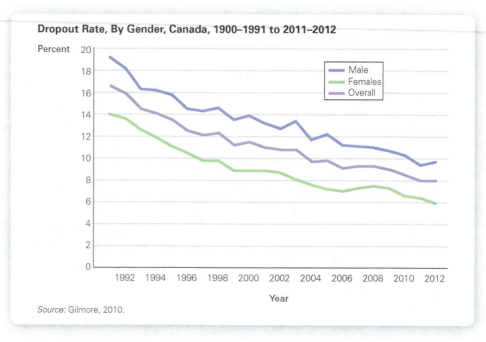

Dropout Rate, By Gender, Canada, 1900–1991 to 2011–2012

Source: Gilmore, 2010.

According to Statistics Canada, the high school dropout rate decreased significantly over the last 20 years—from nearly 17 percent in 1991 to about 8 percent in 2012 (see Figure 9.5) (Gilmore, 2010). That's the good news. The bad news is that rates for certain groups remain unacceptably high. As the graph in Figure 9.5 shows, male Canadians are more likely to drop out than young women (by more than 4 percentage points on average over the 20-year period), and for different reasons. Men often stated that they didn't find school engaging or that they wanted to start earning money. Women, on the other hand, usually left because of family or personal circumstances (J. W. Bowlby & McMullen, 2002).

Generally, Canadian dropout rates tend to be somewhat higher in rural areas, in Quebec, and in the Western provinces of Manitoba, Saskatchewan, and Alberta. However, between 2007 and 2010, the three territories had the highest dropout rates in Canada by far: 16 percent in the Yukon, 30 percent in the Northwest Territories, and 50 percent in Nunavut (Gilmore, 2010). As noted in Chapter 7, this reflects the generally high dropout rate among Aboriginal peoples in Canada, which in 2006 reached 40 percent.

On the plus side, dropout rates for immigrant youth (6 percent) were lower than for Canadian-born youth (9 percent). One reason for this discrepancy may be the high value that immigrant parents and their children place on education as a means of improving their economic status (Abada et al., 2008). Immigrant families are also more likely to live in big cities, where dropout rates are generally lower.

Two good reasons for getting a high school diploma are that graduates usually make more money than students who drop out, and they also have better rates of employment during tough economic times. For example, in the fiscal year 2009/2010, even those people who had dropped out of high school but were employed full time and worked longer hours than high school graduates earned on average $70 less per week than the graduates did. Moreover, during the recession of 2008 to 2009, employment rates decreased by 10 percent for those without a high school diploma but only by 4 percent for graduates (Statistics Canada, 2013g).

INNOVATIVE PROGRAMS IN CANADA In high schools across Canada, guidance counsellors work to support students in realizing their vocations. Their goal is try to find ways to keep students in school and help them plan for the future. As provinces

✦ **ESPECIALLY FOR High School Teachers** You are much more interested in the nuances and controversies than in the basic facts of your subject, but you know that your students need to learn the required curriculum and their final grades will have a major impact on their futures. What should you do? (see response, page 355) ➡

and territories acknowledge the individual differences among students, innovative programs are being developed that are customized to students' strengths and learning needs. These governmental efforts are aimed at increasing graduation rates.

As an example, Alberta Education identified the outcomes for students' programs of study in consultation with educators, business, industry, and other community organizations. While these outcomes are established at the provincial level and applied to all students, how they are implemented is individualized to each student or group of students. For example, the Career and Technology Studies (CTS) program has been designed around career pathways. Currently, there are five clusters: (1) business, administration, finance, and information technology; (2) health, recreation, and human services; (3) media, design, and communication arts; (4) natural resources; and (5) trades, manufacturing, and transportation. Students can take other courses that will enhance not only their academic skills and learning, but also their competencies in the workforce, thus increasing chances of their success in transitioning into employment or other education (college, university) and training opportunities (Alberta Education, 2013).

In Ontario, high schools are partnering with local communities, employers, colleges, universities, and training centres to foster students' interests. For example, students can enrol in programs such as specialist high skills majors, cooperative education, and dual credit programs.

Specialist high skills majors are 8 to 10 courses in a specific field, such as the economic sector, agriculture, or information technology. Along with their coursework, students complete industry certifications (including first aid and CPR qualifications), and learn important job skills. Students who choose this track include those who want to do an apprenticeship, training, or workforce program, or attend college or university. The program gives students an opportunity to identify and explore potential careers early on.

Cooperative education is similar to the specialist high skills majors as it combines both classroom and workplace learning. However, in this track, students complete at least two co-op courses toward their degree. The co-op course is monitored by a cooperative education teacher, and students follow a curriculum outline. Here, students field-test their career options and gain valuable hands-on learning.

Same Situation, Far Apart: How to Learn Developmental psychologists find that adolescents learn best when they are actively engaged with ideas. Khalid, a Grade 12 student in Toronto, is motivated in a hands-on co-op program where he works with luxury and performance cars. In contrast, these girls from Kabul, Afghanistan, are motivated in a more traditional classroom, where they are reciting lessons.

Aboriginal Education Native language teacher Annie Boulanger works with Amanda, a Grade 12 student, in Winnipeg, Manitoba. The Children of the Earth school encourages and supports the study of Aboriginal languages.

Lastly, the dual credit programs provide opportunities for students to earn both their high school diploma as well as credits toward a college diploma or apprenticeship certification. Students in this track participate in college courses. This track is especially meaningful for students who may be at risk of not graduating from high school or those who had left high school but are now deciding to return (Ontario Ministry of Education, 2012).

Alberta and Ontario are just two examples of provinces whose ministries of education are building meaningful learning experiences for students, which will ease their transition to the next stage of their lives, whether it be post-secondary education or the workplace.

THE COLLEGE- OR UNIVERSITY-BOUND STUDENT Although many Canadian students enter university or college directly from high school, some take an additional year of high school (called the "victory lap"), while others return years later to upgrade their skills and knowledge.

What are the rates of registration in universities and colleges? Data from the Postsecondary Student Information System (PSIS) includes information from 1992 to 2007 for universities and 2000 to 2006 for colleges across Canada. In 2006, over 1.6 million students were registered in colleges and universities, with about 400 000 graduating that year. The majority of the students (75 percent) were between the ages of 17 and 27. There was little gender difference by age for both college and university graduates (Dale, 2013).

Aboriginal youth are one of the fastest growing age groups in Canada; there are more than 560 000 Aboriginal youth under the age of 25. However, only 8 percent of Aboriginals complete a university degree, one third of the Canadian average (Association of Universities and Colleges of Canada, 2013). As a result, Canada's universities have launched an online program specifically for Aboriginal students to provide them with better access to information about various relevant programs and services on campuses nationwide. The Association of Universities and Colleges of Canada developed the searchable database, which includes information about 286 academic programs designed for Aboriginal students. It also includes other useful information about financial assistance, housing, counselling, cultural activities, availability of Elders, and gathering spaces and mentoring.

Praising Adolescent Cognition

It is easy to conclude that adolescent thinking is immature and self-absorbed. No wonder secondary schools have difficulty imparting information and students are disengaged. However, we should not close this chapter on that note.

BENEFITS OF ADOLESCENT BRAIN DEVELOPMENT With increased myelination and slower inhibition, reactions become lightning fast; such speed is valuable in cognition as well as in other domains. For instance, adolescent athletes are potential superstars, not only quick but fearless as they steal a base, skate at full speed to the net, tackle a fullback, or race when their lungs feel about to burst. Ideally, coaches have the wisdom to channel such bravery.

Furthermore, as the reward areas of the brain activate and the production of certain mood-enhancing neurotransmitters increases, teenagers become happier. Reaction to a new love, or a first job, or even an A on a term paper can be ecstasy, a joy to be cherished in memory for life.

Before another wave of pruning (at about age 18), and before the brain becomes fully mature (at about age 25), "young brains have both fast-growing synapses and sections that remain unconnected" (Ruder, 2008, p. 8). This allows new connections to facilitate acquisition of new ideas, words, memories, personality patterns, and dance steps. As we have seen, adolescents can think abstractly, analytically, hypothetically, and logically—as well as personally, emotionally, intuitively, and experientially.

Synaptic growth enhances moral development as well. Adolescents question their elders and seek to forge their own standards. In short, several aspects of adolescent brain development can be positive. The fact that the prefrontal cortex is still developing "confers benefits as well as risks. It helps explain the creativity of adolescence and early adulthood, before the brain becomes set in its ways" (Monastersky, 2007, p. A-17).

Even those aspects of adolescent thinking that could be considered negative, such as a tendency toward intuitive thinking and egocentrism, may have their advantages. At every age, the best thinking may be "fast and frugal" (Gigerenzer, 2008). Weighing alternatives, and thinking of possibilities, is sometimes paralyzing. Few adolescents have that problem.

As for egocentrism, it protects the self each time an individual enters a new environmental context or life situation (Schwartz et al., 2008). Young adolescents who feel psychologically invincible (not harmed by others' judgments) tend to be resilient and less likely to be depressed (Hill et al., 2012).

Of course, if a criticism from a peer cuts too deep, friends and family need to help the young person gain perspective, but difficult experiences build resilience as long as they are not overwhelming (Seery, 2011). All the sudden and erratic body changes of puberty that we have described are easier if a person feels special and strong.

WHAT ADULTS CAN DO Does learning during adolescence matter when considering the entire life span? For individuals, the answer is a resounding yes. Not only health, but also almost every other indicator of a good life—high income, stable marriage, successful children, satisfying work—correlates with education.

For society, the answer is yes as well. Nations gain from the quality of secondary education. For example, the cognitive skills that boost economic development are creativity, flexibility, and analytic ability; they allow innovation and mastery of new technology. When nations raise their human capital by having more adults with those skills, their economies prosper (Cohen & Soto, 2007).

Those cognitive abilities that nations need in the twenty-first century are exactly what adolescents can develop—with proper education and guidance. The potential is there; what will we do about it?

RESPONSE FOR High School Teachers (from page 352) Use a variety of strategies to teach the information your students need to master as a foundation for the exciting and innovative topics you want to teach. This will help your students feel a personal connection to the information, they may learn more, and student achievement should improve. ●

KEY Points

- Secondary education is crucial for personal health and for national economic development.

- Many students become alienated from learning during middle school; middle schools are not usually organized to encourage relationships between teachers and students.

- Transitions to new schools are always challenging, as illustrated by the increase in bullying, especially cyberbullying, as middle school begins.

- International tests such as the PISA indicate that Canadian students are achieving well in math, reading, and science.

- Adolescents are capable of intense learning of new ideas and of questioning traditional beliefs.

SUMMARY

Puberty

1. Puberty refers to the various changes that transform a child's body into an adult one. A sequence of biochemical signals from the hypothalamus to the pituitary gland to the adrenal glands (the HPA axis) increases production of testosterone, estrogen, and various other hormones, which in turn causes the body to develop.

2. Sexual characteristics differentiate males from females at adolescence, not only in reproductive potential, but also in body shape, breasts, voice, body hair, and so on.

3. Puberty most often begins between ages 10 and 13. Genes, gender, body fat, and family stress all contribute to this variation in timing, with girls generally beginning puberty before boys.

4. Adolescents who reach puberty earlier or later than their friends experience additional stresses. Generally (depending on culture, community, and cohort), early-maturing girls and late-maturing boys have a particularly difficult time.

5. The growth spurt is an acceleration of growth in every part of the body. Peak weight usually precedes peak height, which is then followed by peak muscle growth.

6. Hormones regulate daily and seasonal body rhythms. In adolescence, these may result in sleep deprivation because high schools open early and the natural circadian rhythm keeps teenagers wide awake at night.

Nutrition

7. Many adolescents are very concerned about body image, especially how they think they look to other adolescents. They may diet irrationally instead of eating a balanced diet, which can often result in calcium and iron deficiency.

8. Although anorexia and bulimia are often not diagnosed until early adulthood, their precursors are evident during puberty. The origins are genetic and familial as well as cultural.

Thinking, Fast and Slow

9. Various parts of the brain mature during puberty and in the following decade. The regions dedicated to emotional arousal (including the limbic system) mature before those that regulate and rationalize emotion (the prefrontal cortex). Consequently, many adolescents are quick to react, take risks, and learn.

10. Cognition in early adolescence may be egocentric, a kind of self-centred thinking. Adolescent egocentrism gives rise to the personal fable, the invincibility fable, and the imaginary audience.

11. Formal operational thought is Piaget's term for the last of his four periods of cognitive development, in which adolescents are no longer earthbound and concrete in their thinking. They prefer to speculate instead of focusing on reality. They develop hypotheses and explore, using deductive reasoning.

12. Intuitive thinking also becomes stronger during adolescence. Few teenagers always use logic, although they are capable of doing so.

Teaching and Learning

13. Secondary education—after primary education (grade school) and before tertiary education (college or university)—correlates with the health and wealth of individuals and nations.

14. In middle school, many students tend to be bored, difficult to teach, and hurtful to one another. One reason may be that middle schools are not structured to accommodate egocentrism or intuitive thinking.

15. Cyberbulling and many forms of psychopathology increase during school transitions, which are particularly difficult in adolescence, when young people must also adjust to biological and family changes.

16. The PISA, an international test for high school students, is designed to measure the cognitive abilities that students will need in adult life.

KEY TERMS

adolescent egocentrism (p. 340)
adrenal glands (p. 329)
analytic thought (p. 343)
anorexia nervosa (p. 336)
body image (p. 336)
bulimia nervosa (p. 337)
circadian rhythm (p. 334)
cyberbullying (p. 348)
deductive reasoning (p. 342)

dual-process model (p. 343)
entity approach to intelligence (p. 346)
estradiol (p. 329)
formal operational thought (p. 341)
growth spurt (p. 333)
hormone (p. 328)
HPA (hypothalamus–pituitary–adrenal) axis (p. 329)

HPG (hypothalamus–pituitary–gonad) axis (p. 329)
hypothetical thought (p. 342)
imaginary audience (p. 340)
incremental approach to intelligence (p. 346)
inductive reasoning (p. 342)
intuitive thought (p. 343)
invincibility fable (p. 341)
leptin (p. 331)
menarche (p. 328)

middle school (p. 345)
personal fable (p. 341)
pituitary (p. 328)
primary sex characteristics (p. 330)
puberty (p. 328)
secondary education (p. 345)
secondary sex characteristics (p. 330)
spermarche (p. 328)
testosterone (p. 329)

WHAT HAVE YOU LEARNED?

1. What visible changes take place in puberty?

2. How do hormones affect the physical and psychological aspects of puberty?

3. What is the crucial difference between primary sex characteristics and secondary sex characteristics? Give examples of each.

4. What are the gender differences in the growth spurt?

5. What is the connection between body fat and onset of puberty in girls? In boys?

6. Why might early puberty be difficult for girls?

7. What problems are common among early-maturing boys?

8. What problems result from the growth spurt sequence (weight, then height, then muscles)?

9. How do the skin and hair change during puberty?

10. Why might some high schools decide to adopt later start times?

11. What problems might occur if adolescents do not get enough iron or calcium?

12. Why is body image often distorted in adolescence?

13. List the symptoms of anorexia and of bulimia.

14. Why does the limbic system develop before the prefrontal cortex, and what are the consequences?

15. How does adolescent egocentrism differ from early childhood egocentrism?

16. How might the invincibility fable explain why adolescents reveal personal information on social media websites?

17. What are the characteristics of formal operational thinking?

18. What is the difference between inductive reasoning and deductive reasoning?

19. How might intuition and analysis lead to opposite conclusions?

20. What mode of thinking—intuitive or analytic—do most people prefer, and why?

21. Why have most junior high schools disappeared?

22. What characteristics of middle schools make them more difficult for students than elementary schools?

23. What is the connection between school climate and bullying?

24. How might a school that believes in the incremental approach to intelligence structure itself to increase student motivation?

25. Why are transitions from one school to another a particular concern for educators? What steps can they take to ease transitions?

26. List five benefits of adolescent brain development.

27. Why is high school achievement likely to advance the national economy?

APPLICATIONS

1. Visit a Grade 5, 6, or 7 class. Note variations in the size and maturity of the students. Do you see any patterns related to gender, ethnicity, body fat, or self-confidence?

2. Interview two to four of your friends who are in their late teens or early 20s about their memories of menarche or spermarche, including their memories of others' reactions. Analyze the connections between body changes and emotional reactions.

3. Talk to a teenager about politics, families, school, religion, or any other topic that might reveal the way that young person thinks. Do you hear any characteristics of adolescent cognition, such as egocentrism, intuitive thinking, or formal thought? Cite examples.

4. Think of a life-changing decision you have made. How did logic and emotion interact? What might have changed if you had given the matter more thought—or less?

>>ONLINE CONNECTIONS

To accompany your textbook, you have access to a number of online resources, including LearningCurve, which is an adaptive quizzing program; critical thinking questions; and case studies. For access to any of these links, go to www.worthpublishers.com/launchpad/bergerchuang1e. In addition to these resources, you'll find links to video clips, personalized study advice, and an e-Book. Among the videos and activities available online are the following:

- *The Timing of Puberty.* Too early? Too late? Teens tell their own stories about the impact of pubertal timing. The video also reviews physical changes and gender differences in maturation.

- *Brain Development: Adolescence.* There's a lot going on in a teenager's brain! Animations and illustrations highlight that development and its effect on behaviour.

CHAPTER OUTLINE

ADOLESCENCE:
Psychosocial Development

10

WHAT WILL YOU KNOW?

- Why do many teenagers find it hard to achieve sexual identity?
- How could adolescent rebellion be considered a good sign?
- Who is the best source for sex education during adolescence?
- Is adolescent suicide rare, common, or an epidemic?
- When does drug use become drug abuse?

In a study that focused on immigrant youth in Canada (Chuang, 2010), I talked to 125 newcomers from five provinces (Alberta, British Columbia, Nova Scotia, Ontario, and Quebec). The youths ranged in age from 11 to 19 years. They came from 30 countries, and were attending either middle school or high school.

I wanted to hear about their experiences in Canada and how they coped with their challenges. In one focus group of girls from Ontario, an 18-year-old African girl talked about her experience at school. She began by saying, "I went to my science class. My teacher was like, 'Oh, tell me the story about Africa.' So I was telling her about (Africa) and everything ... ."

The group was impressed that a science teacher was interested in learning about this girl's culture and country. But then the girl said tearfully, "And suddenly she was like, 'Oh, do African people sleep in trees?'"

"Why would you even say that?" the girl cried. "You are my teacher!" She told us that because of this experience, she would never take another science class. After the focus group, I encouraged her not to let this one offensive comment limit her academic future. She agreed.

Unfortunately, I was not able to follow up with her, but I do hope she was able to develop a strong social network to cope with such challenges. As you will learn in this chapter, peers become increasingly important to adolescents as they try to develop a sense of their own identity. ●

—Susan Chuang

THIS CHAPTER DESCRIBES THE TEENAGER'S SEARCH FOR IDENTITY, which is often a mixture of personal preferences, parental pressure, and teenage rebellion, always within cultural contexts. Adults and peers influence adolescents, who often resist parts of their familial and cultural heritage while accepting other parts. One important topic is romance; many adolescents try to discern and express their gender identity via partners, aspirations, and sexuality.

Dangers lurk during these years as well. A few adolescents plunge into despair and attempt suicide; most experiment with drugs and defy rules. We'll cover all these topics while tracing the journey of 11- to 18-year-olds through the psychosocial maze from childhood to adulthood.

Identity

Psychosocial development during adolescence is often considered the search for self-understanding. Self-expression and self-concept become increasingly important, as the egocentrism described in Chapter 9 illustrates. Each young person wants to know "Who am I?"

According to Erik Erikson, life's fifth psychosocial crisis is **identity versus role confusion:** Negotiating the complexities of finding one's own identity is the primary task of adolescence (Erikson, 1968). He said this crisis is resolved with **identity achievement,** when adolescents have reconsidered the goals and values of their parents and culture, accepting some and discarding others, and discerning their own identity. The result is neither wholesale rejection nor unquestioning acceptance of social norms (Côté, 2009).

Not Yet Achieved

Erikson's insights have inspired thousands of researchers. Notable among them was James Marcia, who described and measured four specific ways in which young people cope with this stage of life: (1) role confusion, (2) foreclosure, (3) moratorium, and (4) identity achievement (Marcia, 1966). The first three will be described here.

First, however, you need to know about a historical change. Over the past half-century, major psychosocial shifts have lengthened the duration of adolescence and made identity achievement more complex (Côté, 2006; Kroger et al., 2010; Meeus, 2011). Although Marcia's way stations on the road to identity achievement still seem evident, the path is longer and more circuitous. Indeed, several aspects of the identity search, especially for sexual and vocational identity, have become more arduous than when Erikson wrote about them. Adolescents still seek identity, but developmentalists believe that this crisis is rarely resolved by age 18: Studies of adults reveal that identity is a lifelong process (Meeus, 2011).

Role confusion is the opposite of identity achievement. Characterized by lack of commitment to any goals or values, role confusion is sometimes called *identity diffusion* to emphasize that some adolescents seem diffuse, unfocused, and unconcerned about their future (Phillips & Pittman, 2007). Even common social demands—such as putting away clothes, making friends, completing school assignments, and thinking about a post-secondary education or career—are beyond role-confused adolescents. Instead, they might sleep too much, immerse themselves in video games or mind-numbing television, and turn from one flirtation to another. Their thinking is disorganized, they procrastinate, and they avoid issues and actions (Côté, 2009).

Identity **foreclosure** occurs when young people accept traditional values (Marcia, 1966; Marcia et al., 1993). They might follow roles and customs transmitted from their parents or culture, rarely exploring alternatives. Or they might foreclose on an oppositional, *negative identity*—the direct opposite of whatever their parents

---

identity versus role confusion Erikson's term for the fifth stage of development, in which the person tries to figure out "Who am I?" but is confused as to which of many possible roles to adopt.

identity achievement Erikson's term for the attainment of identity, or the point at which a person understands who he or she is as a unique individual, in accord with past experiences and future plans.

role confusion A situation in which an adolescent does not seem to know or care what his or her identity is. (Sometimes called *identity* or *role diffusion*.)

foreclosure Erikson's term for premature identity formation, which occurs when an adolescent adopts his or her parents' or society's roles and values wholesale, without questioning or analysis.

want—again without thoughtful questioning. Foreclosure is comfortable. For many, it is a temporary shelter, a time for commitment to a particular identity, which will be followed by more exploration (Meeus, 2011).

A more mature shelter is **moratorium,** a time out that includes some exploration, either in breadth (trying many things) or in depth (examining one path after making a tentative commitment) (Meeus, 2011). Societies provide many opportunities for moratoria, such as post-secondary education or volunteering overseas, allowing adolescents to postpone identity achievement. Moratorium is most common at about age 19, although it can occur earlier or later (Kroger et al., 2010).

moratorium
An adolescent's choice of a socially acceptable way to postpone making identity-achievement decisions. Going to college or university is a common example.

Five Arenas of Identity Formation

Erikson's (1968) view on identity versus role confusion is claimed to be the cornerstone of his theory. Individuals struggle to develop a sense of wholeness, connecting their views of self in childhood to their views of self in adulthood and the self as perceived by others. Thus, identity is formed through exchanges with others, which then become integrated in the formation of one's sense of self (Sneed et al., 2006).

Erikson (1968) highlighted four aspects of identity: religious, political, vocational, and sexual. Although terminology and timing have changed—for example, the process of identity formation has been found to be a lifelong process—each still merits examination. Also, with the increased numbers of immigrant youth globally, many researchers have been exploring a fifth aspect of identity formation, ethnic identity, which we will also discuss.

Same Situation, Far Apart: Exploring Religious Identity
An Orthodox Jewish boy lighting Hanukkah candles in Israel *(left)* and teenagers in Alberta with Bishop Fred Henry of the Catholic Diocese of Calgary *(right)* are much alike, despite distance and appearance. For many teenagers, religion provides meaning as well as coping skills (King & Roeser, 2009).

RELIGIOUS IDENTITY Some theorists believe that people categorize themselves (as well as others) into groups based on various characteristics, like religion. Burris and Jackson (2000) contend that "religion has been numbered—along with gender, ethnicity, and nationality—among the core social categories around which an individual's social identity is organized" (p. 257). More than 80 percent of people in

ROB HOWARD / CORBIS

A Religious Life These young adolescents in Ethiopia are studying to be monks. Will the rituals and beliefs provide them with a way to achieve identity?

Champion of Girls' Rights Malala Yousafzai, a 16-year-old Pakistani girl, receives the 2013 International Children's Peace Prize in The Hague, the Netherlands.

ROBIN UTRECHT / XINHUA / LANDOV

the world follow one of the five major religions: Judaism, Christianity, Islam, Hinduism, or Buddhism (Kriger & Seng, 2005).

Past parental practices influence adolescents' religious identity. Some adolescents may question specific beliefs as their cognitive processes allow more reflection, but few have a crisis of faith unless unusual circumstances propel it (King & Roeser, 2009). In fact, some adolescents may turn to religion in ways that their parents do not anticipate. For example, a Muslim girl raised in a non-traditional home might start to wear a headscarf, or a Catholic boy might study for the priesthood, or a Baptist teenager might join a Pentecostal youth group. Usually religious exploration is part of the search for identity—a process that currently lasts long past the teen years (Alisat & Pratt, 2012).

POLITICAL IDENTITY As with religion, parents influence the development of their children's political identity, even when that political identity is a disinterest in politics—not the political identity that Erikson anticipated. Like their parents, teenage children may proudly say they do not care about politics—a stance that is likely to continue into adulthood (Côté, 2009). For example, in Canada, young people are generally less interested in politics and less likely to vote than older adults, particularly if they live in an urban centre (Blais & Loewen, 2011).

Other teenagers become very politically engaged. The case of Malala Yousafzai is only one such example. Malala is a schoolgirl who was shot by the Taliban in Swat, Pakistan, for campaigning for a girl's right to attend school and receive an education. Another example is youth involvement in the democracy movement that has gained momentum in several Arab countries in North Africa and the Middle East. For instance, in both Egypt and Tunisia, more than half the population is less than 30 years of age, and in both these countries (Tunisia in 2011 and Egypt in 2012) dictators were forced to give way to democratically elected governments. As more and more young people join the democracy movement, they organize their own factions, such as "Youth for Change," and use social media such as Facebook and Twitter to draw their peers into political activism and to swell the numbers attending political demonstrations (Lange, 2011).

A word here about political and religious extremism. People who are relatively young (under age 30) are often on the front lines of revolutions or are disciples within groups that their elders consider cults. Fanatical political and religious movements have much in common: The age range of most new adherents is one of them (L. L. Dawson, 2010). However, adolescents are rarely drawn to these groups unless personal loneliness or family background (such as a parent's death caused by an opposing group) compels them. It is a myth that every teenager is potentially a suicide bomber or willing martyr.

The topic of political identity brings up the subject of *identity politics*, the tendency to identify with and vote for people of one's own race, religion, ethnicity, or sex (Bernstein, 2005; McClain et al., 2009).

Hope and Anger Adolescents and young adults everywhere demonstrate against adult authority as they seek to establish their political identity, with varied strategies and results. In Cairo's Tahrir Square *(left)*, this young man flashes the peace sign hours before President Mubarak's resignation. The 2011 "Arab Spring" in other nations was not as successful. French students *(right)* protest cuts in high school staff, but their demands were resisted by the government. Worldwide, social change is fuelled by youthful aspirations—sometimes leading to victory, sometimes to despair.

Identity politics is more like foreclosure than achievement because it precludes questioning and rational analysis. The identity politics that seems most attractive to youth is generational: They might reject an older member of their race, religion, or ethnic group in favour of a candidate of a different race, religion, or ethnicity who is under age 30 and who shares their views on topics such as interracial dating, gay marriage, and economic inequality.

VOCATIONAL IDENTITY Vocational identity means envisioning oneself as a worker in a particular occupation. Decades ago, it was thought that a person would hold this occupation for life. Once adolescents established a vocational identity, it would help them determine what courses to take in high school and whether to aim for college or university. Today, however, most workers do not hold the same job throughout their lives. According to Human Resources and Skills Development Canada, most Canadians will have about three careers and eight jobs over their lifetime (Feigelsohn, 2013). As a result, definitive early vocational identity is no longer a realistic, or necessary, goal.

This does not mean, however, that beginning to establish career goals and a vocational identity are irrelevant. As explained in Chapter 9, adolescents are more likely to be engaged in their education if they believe that they are learning skills they will need. A specific vocational identity takes years to establish, but wanting to become a self-sufficient adult motivates many young people.

Some adolescents may begin to establish their vocational identity through part-time employment. Finding a job may be a challenge, though. In Canada in 2012, the gap between youth (15 to 24 years of age) and adult employment rates was the widest in 35 years. The youth unemployment rate was just over 14 percent, compared with 6 percent for adults. This was largely because employment rates for young people had still not returned to the rates that existed before the economic recession that began in 2008 (Bernard, 2013).

Even for teenagers who do find part-time employment, the benefits may be questionable. Working over vacations or for a few hours during the school week may provide teenagers with wages and a sense of pride. However, if teens work too many hours, grades fall, since work hours interfere with homework, extra help, and school attendance. In addition, adolescents who work more than 20 hours a week during the school year tend to quit school, fight with parents, smoke cigarettes, and hate

Same Situation, Far Apart: Gender Identity Around the world, clothing, behaviour, and appearance are used to express gender identity; however, the specific ways in which gender identity is expressed vary from place to place. For instance, these girls from Guelph, Ontario, *(left)* have uncovered heads, unlike the girls from Indonesia *(right)* whose heads are covered. However, the ways that girls everywhere laugh together and hold each other may be universal.

gender identity (adolescence)
A person's acceptance of the roles and behaviours that society associates with the biological categories of male and female.

ethnic identity
The extent to which a person identifies with a particular ethnic group's roles and behaviours. (Also known as *ethnocultural identity* or *cultural identity.*)

their jobs—in adulthood as well as adolescence (Staff & Schulenberg, 2010). Only a tiny and shrinking minority—alienated from school but appreciated, mentored, and promoted at work—benefit from intense teenage employment.

GENDER IDENTITY As stated in Chapter 6, for social scientists *sex* and *sexual* refer to biological characteristics, whereas *gender* refers to cultural and social attributes. The distinction between biology and culture is not always obvious, since the body is affected by behaviour and vice versa. Nonetheless, today Erikson's term *sexual identity* has been replaced by **gender identity** (Denny & Pittman, 2007), which refers primarily to a person's self-definition of male or female.

Gender identity often (but not always) begins with the person's biological sex and leads to a gender role, one that society considers appropriate for that gender. Gender roles once meant that only men were employed; they were breadwinners (good providers) and women were housewives (married to their houses). When women entered the labour market in large numbers in the 1970s, gender roles expanded but remained distinct, as with secretary/businessman, nurse/doctor, pink collar/blue collar. Now vocational roles are increasingly unisex.

It is apparent that gender identity is much more complicated than once thought (Perry & Pauletti, 2011). An increasing number of adolescents feel that they do not identify with their biological sex. In some places, it may be possible for these children to be treated as a member of the opposite sex by adopting different clothing and friends—or even, in adolescence, by trying hormone treatments. But others may not be able to transition to another gender as easily and may suffer from feeling they do not match their biological sex. These children may be diagnosed with gender dysphoria, a new DSM-5 diagnosis that describes the distress individuals may feel as a consequence of feeling that they are in "the wrong body."

ETHNIC IDENTITY Especially today and in a country like Canada, many researchers contend that another aspect of identity development that needs to be considered is **ethnic identity,** sometimes referred to as *ethnocultural identity* or *cultural identity.* Canada has the second-highest percentage of immigrants as compared to its total population of any country in the world (after Australia), and is home to people with more than 200 different ethnic origins (Statistics Canada, 2008a).

Many researchers have examined the ways in which new immigrants re-create their personal identity in their new home country. Ethnic identity in its most basic sense is usually a combination of a person's self-concept as a member of a social group or groups and the emotional significance that attaches to that membership

(Tajfel & Turner, 1986). Thus, ethnic identity includes both personal and group identities that develop over time.

John Berry of Queen's University and his colleagues studied the way that ethnic identity is modified in young people by the experience of immigration to a new country. The researchers examined more than 5000 youths from 13 immigrant-receiving countries, and found four types of ethnic-identity formation (Berry et al., 2006):

1. an *integrated identity* in which youths maintain their heritage identity while incorporating aspects of the settlement, or new country, identity

2. a *separated identity* in which youths maintain their heritage identity while rejecting the settlement identity

3. a *national identity* in which youths reject their heritage identity and replace it with the settlement identity

4. a *diffuse identity* in which youths reject both their heritage and their settlement identity.

Berry's study revealed that most youths prefer an integrated identity if only because it is the most adaptive of the four types (Sam & Virta, 2001; Stuart & Ward, 2011). It is also a type of ethnic identity that is well received in a country like Canada, where legislation such as the Multiculturalism Act and the Canadian Charter of Rights and Freedoms guarantee the rights of all individuals to their own identity (Bourhis et al., 1997).

FRANCES ROBERTS / ALAMY

Instant Connections Having friends of the same ethnicity—who support one another while understanding the historical, practical, and social customs and challenges of the ethnic group—helps adolescents achieve ethnic identity.

KEY Points

- As Erikson famously recognized, adolescents experience an identity crisis, asking "Who am I?"

- Identity achievement is arduous and takes years to accomplish. Researchers stress that identity formation is a lifelong process.

- Many adolescents experience role confusion or sidestep the anxiety via foreclosure or moratoria.

- In establishing religious and political identity, adolescents often follow parental examples.

- Achieving vocational and gender identity today is more complicated than it was 50 years ago, partly because the number of careers options, as well as the variety of gender identities, have increased.

- Ethnic identity needs to be included in an understanding of identity formation, especially among visible minority immigrants. It is complex and varied, as individuals need to take into consideration their native and host country's cultural beliefs and values.

Relationships with Others

Adolescence is often characterized as a time for personal rebellion. That perspective overlooks the reality that most teenagers are powerfully influenced by many people. Social influences include teachers, grandparents, and other relatives, as well as popular musicians, actors, sports stars, and other luminaries. Here we focus on the two most powerful influences, parents and peers.

Not only are parents and peers impactful social influences, but each also affects the other. When adolescents have a supportive, affectionate relationship with their parents, they tend to have similar relationships with their peers; when they fight with their parents, they are likely to fight with peers. This anger spillover is reciprocal though less common (Chung et al., 2011); a conflict with a friend makes it likely that a teen will soon conflict with a parent.

Parents

Parent–adolescent relationships affect every aspect of adolescent development. Disputes are common because the adolescent's drive for independence, arising from biological as well as psychological impulses, clashes with the parents' desire to maintain control (Eisenberg et al., 2008; Laursen & Collins, 2009). Normally, parent–adolescent conflict, especially between mothers and daughters, peaks in early adolescence. It usually manifests as **bickering**—repeated, petty arguments (more nagging than fighting) about routine, day-to-day concerns such as cleanliness, clothes, chores, and schedules (Eisenberg et al., 2008).

bickering
Petty, peevish arguing, usually repeated and ongoing.

"So I blame you for everything—whose fault is that?"

Some bickering may indicate a healthy family, since close relationships almost always include conflict (Smetana et al., 2004). One of the reasons for conflict is that the two generations may have different interpretations of the same situation. As you read in Chapter 5, there are areas of a teenager's life that he or she believes are "off limits" to parents and their rules. If parents encroach on a teen's personal preferences and choices, this will lead to conflicts and disagreements. For example, a teen's messy room is a common battlefield. Parents focus on issues such as health and sanitation (perhaps there are dirty plates among the clothes) or on keeping order in the house (a social convention). On the other hand, the teen may believe that the bedroom is personal space and therefore beyond the parents' authority (Smetana et al., 2003).

There may be a discrepancy in the way parents and youths view each other's intentions. Parents sometimes think their offspring have more negative thoughts than other children have, and adolescents imagine much more intrusive control than the parents intend (Sillars et al., 2010). Both generations would benefit if they were more explicit. For instance, if the argument is only about the dirty socks on the floor, the solution is easy: The teenager can put them in the laundry. However, if the fight is not really about socks but about parents dictating personal habits, of course the child resists.

These parent–adolescent conflicts are common in many families around the world, including youth of Arab, Croatian, East Asian, and South Asian backgrounds in Canada (Gonsalves & Chuang, 2010; Samarin & Chuang, 2012), as well as various ethnic groups in the United States (Fuligni, 1998) and other countries. This finding emphasizes that developing one's independence is not a cultural artifact, but developmental and relevant for all.

With time, parents gradually grant more autonomy, and positive relationships typically return to preadolescent levels (Collins & Laursen, 2004). By age 18, many teenagers appreciate their parents, who have learned to allow more independence (Masche, 2010).

OPPOSING PERSPECTIVES

Honour Killing or Domestic Violence?

Sometimes, the search for adolescent independence results in more significant family conflict than bickering. After repeated arguments with her father, 16-year-old Ontario schoolgirl Aqsa Parvez left home and went to live with family friends. Aqsa's father, Muhammad, was a strict Muslim who had immigrated to Canada from Pakistan. The youngest of eight children, Aqsa refused to wear the hijab, or traditional headscarf of Muslim women, and she posted photos of herself on Facebook and announced her intention of getting a part-time job. All these signs of independence enraged Aqsa's father.

On the morning of December 10, 2007, Aqsa's father and brother, Waqas, picked up Aqsa from the school bus stop and drove her home so she could collect some clothes and other belongings. Later that morning, Mr. Parvez called the police and told them that he had killed his daughter. Aqsa was taken to Toronto's Sick Children's Hospital where she died that afternoon from what the doctors called "neck compression" or strangulation.

The murder of this healthy, outgoing teenager by her own father shocked and bewildered the Canadian public. In many Western countries like Canada, the belief exists that adolescents will challenge their parents to further develop their sense of independence, a necessity for psychological well-being. Indeed, Sigmund Freud's daughter Anna, herself a prominent psychoanalyst, once wrote that adolescent resistance to parental authority is "welcome … beneficial … inevitable" (A. Freud, 1958/2000, p. 263).

In an attempt to understand how a father could feel justified in killing his own child, the press identified Aqsa's murder as an "honour killing." According to this view, the father's narrow interpretation of Islam convinced him that Aqsa's rebellion had dishonoured the entire family. He told his wife, "My community will say, 'You have not been able to control your daughter.' This is my insult. She is making me naked."

Aqsa's mother told the police: "This is the way it's done in Pakistani culture. Either they kill the girl or turn her out of the house."

This idea—that Aqsa's murder was a religious duty her father had to perform—took such hold in the public mind that the term "honour killing" came to be freely used every time a Muslim man murdered his child or wife. In fact, the *National Post* began to keep a tally sheet of honour killings in Canada and announced in 2011 that it had counted 15 such cases over the last several years. Some commentators referred to Aqsa's murder as "death by culture," the implication being

that the culture in question was backward, inflexible, and inhumane.

"What happens," a columnist for the *Globe and Mail* asked, "when large groups of immigrants cling to values and beliefs that diverge so sharply from the mainstream? And can we still rely on the passage of time to smooth the differences away?" (Wente, 2010).

Many in the Canadian Muslim community resisted the idea that Aqsa's murder had anything to do with Islam as a religion. For instance, Dr. Jasmine Zine, from the Department of Sociology at Wilfrid Laurier University, argued that characterizing Aqsa's death as an honour killing was little more than "a validation for Islamophobia and xenophobic political agendas" (Zine, 2008). It would be more accurate, in Dr. Zine's view, to understand this killing as an example of the domestic violence that is endemic to Canadian society as a whole.

In a case study/information kit developed for the Canadian Council of Muslim Women, Dr. Zine and Dr. Zabedia Nazim, also from Wilfrid Laurier University, cited a 2009 Statistics Canada report on family violence as evidence that such father–daughter violence is hardly exclusive to the Muslim community (CCMW, 2010):

- Nearly 53 400 children and youth were the victims of a police-reported assault in 2007. About 30 percent of the assaults were committed by a family member.

- When children and youth were victims of family violence, a parent was identified as the abuser in nearly 6 in 10 incidents.

- Homicides of children and youth (under the age of 18) represented about 9 percent of all homicides in 2007. Most child and youth homicide victims were killed by someone they knew.

- Parents were the perpetrators in most child and youth homicides committed by family members. Fathers (54 percent) were more likely than mothers (34 percent) to be the perpetrators.

Whatever the root causes of the Aqsa Parvez tragedy, a multicultural perspective has shown that what adolescents and parents expect from each other does vary by culture (Brown & Bakken, 2011). However, the fact remains that on the rare occasions when intergenerational conflict degenerates into extreme violence, this may have more to do with personal factors (genes) than with social and religious influences (culture).

CLOSENESS WITHIN THE FAMILY Family closeness has four aspects:

1. communication (Do family members talk openly with one another?)

2. support (Do they rely on one another?)

3. connectedness (How emotionally close are they?)

4. control (Do parents encourage or limit adolescent autonomy?)

No developmentalist doubts that the first two, communication and support, are helpful, and perhaps essential. Patterns set in place during childhood continue, ideally buffering some of the turbulence of adolescence (Cleveland et al., 2005; Laursen & Collins, 2009). As you saw in earlier chapters, communication leads to more pro-social behaviour and positive parent–child relationships, aiding development at every age. Regarding the other two aspects, connectedness and control, consequences vary and observers differ in what they see.

How do you react to this example, written by a student?

> I got pregnant when I was sixteen years old, and if it weren't for the support of my parents, I would probably not have my son. And if they hadn't taken care of him, I wouldn't have been able to finish high school or attend college. My parents also helped me overcome the shame that I felt when … my aunts, uncles, and especially my grandparents found out that I was pregnant.

> *[L., personal communication]*

This student was grateful to her parents, but others might wonder whether her early motherhood gave her parents too much control, requiring dependency instead of autonomy. If so, the emotional closeness that seems helpful may in fact not be. A longitudinal study of pregnant adolescents found that most (but not all) young mothers and their children fared best if the teen's parents did not take over child care (Borkowski et al., 2007). Taking over meant taking too much control and implied that the mother was incapable of mothering.

A related issue is **parental monitoring**—that is, parental knowledge about each child's whereabouts, activities, and companions. Some adolescents happily tell parents about their activities, whereas others are secretive (Vieno et al., 2009). Most are selective, omitting things their parents would not approve of (Brown & Bakken, 2011).

Monitoring is a good sign if it indicates mutual trust (Kerr et al., 2010). When parental knowledge is the result of a warm, supportive relationship, children are likely to become confident, well-educated adults, avoiding drugs and risky sex (G. M. Barnes et al., 2006; Fletcher et al., 2004). However, monitoring may be harmful when it derives from suspicion.

A breakdown in parent–youth relationships may be due to too much criticism and control, which might stop dialogue instead of improving communication and support (Tilton-Weaver et al., 2010). Overly restrictive and controlling parenting correlates with many adolescent problems, including depression (Brown & Bakken, 2011).

Finding the right balance between freedom and control has the added complication of the particular personality of the child. As one scholar notes, "deft parental steering" is useful, but if "an adolescent is engaged in more than minor delinquent behavior, a much more structured and rule-based approach may be needed" (Capaldi, 2003, pp. 175–176).

In Chapter 6, you learned that authoritative parenting is usually best for children and that uninvolved parenting is worst. This holds true for adolescents. Although teenagers may say they no longer need their parents, neglect is always destructive.

One example is Joy. When she was 16, her stepfather said: "Teens all around here [are] doing booze and doing drugs … . But my Joy here ain't into that stuff" (quoted

parental monitoring
Parents' ongoing awareness of what their children are doing, where, and with whom.

in C. Smith & Lundquist, 2005, p. 10). In fact, however, Joy was smoking pot, drinking alcohol, and having sex with her boyfriend. She said she

> overdosed on a bunch of stuff once, pills or some prescription of my mom's—I took the whole bottle. It didn't work. I just went to sleep for a long time … . They never found out … pretty pitiful.
>
> *[quoted in C. Smith & Lundquist, 2005, p. 12]*

Peer Power

Adolescents rely on peers to help them navigate the physical changes of puberty, the intellectual challenges of high school, and the social changes of leaving childhood. Peers are much more useful for these three challenges than parents are. For instance, adolescents rely on friends to hear every detail of a romantic interaction, providing an audience and advice, to soften breakups and encourage new loves (Mehta & Strough, 2009). Friends are usually of the same sex and same sexual orientation, but not necessarily so; the crucial factor is that the friend is willing to listen and encourage.

PEER PRESSURE Friendships are important at every stage, but during early adolescence, peers have increased power because popularity is also coveted (LaFontana & Cillessen, 2010). All children, each in their own way, seek their peers' acceptance. Peer power can lead to constructive, destructive, or neutral behaviour.

Adults sometimes fear **peer pressure,** that is, that peers will push an adolescent to try drugs, break the law, or do other things the child would never do. It is true that young people *can* lead one another into trouble. Collectively, peers sometimes provide **deviancy training,** whereby one person shows another how to circumvent adult restrictions (Dishion et al., 2001). There is a developmental progression here: For example, the combination of problem behaviour, school marginalization, and low academic performance at age 11 leads to gang involvement two years later, deviancy training two years after that, and violent behaviour at age 18 or 19 (Dishion et al., 2010). However, innocent teens are not routinely corrupted by deviant friends.

Generally, friends encourage socially desirable behaviours (Berndt & Murphy, 2002), such as playing sports, studying, quitting smoking, or applying to college or university. Peers are more helpful than harmful (Audrey et al., 2006; Nelson & DeBacker, 2008), especially in early adolescence, when biological and social stresses can be overwhelming. In later adolescence, teenagers are less susceptible to peer pressure, either positive or negative (Monahan et al., 2009).

✦ **ESPECIALLY FOR Parents of a Teenager** Your 13-year-old comes home after a sleepover at a friend's house with a new, weird hairstyle. What do you say and do? (see response, page 370) →

peer pressure
Encouragement to conform to one's friends or contemporaries in behaviour, dress, and attitude; usually considered a negative force, as when adolescent peers encourage one another to defy adult authority.

deviancy training
Destructive peer support in which one person shows another how to rebel against authority or social norms.

Same Situation, Far Apart: Friends Together Teenagers in North America *(left)* and in Sudan *(right)* prefer to spend their free time with peers, not with adults. Generational loyalty is stronger during these years than during any other stage of life.

clique
A group of adolescents made up of close friends who are loyal to one another while excluding outsiders.

crowd
A larger group of adolescents who have something in common but who are not necessarily friends.

CROWDS AND CLIQUES To understand the role of peers, it is useful to examine how adolescents organize themselves. A cluster of close friends who are loyal to one another and who exclude outsiders is called a **clique**. A larger group of adolescents who share common interests is a **crowd**. Cliques and crowds provide control, guidance, and support via comments, exclusion, and admiration (B. Brown & Larson, 2009).

A crowd may exhibit small signs of identity (a certain brand of backpack, a particular greeting) that adults do not notice but that members of other crowds do (Strouse, 1999). Crowds may be based on some personal characteristic or activity—such as the "brains," "jocks," "skaters," or "goths"—or they may be based on ethnicity. In large schools with many ethnic groups, ethnic crowds attract those who seek to avoid isolation while establishing their identity—a difficult process (Kiang et al., 2010). At the same time, students of all groups explore their relationships with other groups.

Crowds encourage certain values. For instance, one U.S. study found that "tough" and "alternative" crowds felt that teenagers should question every adult rule, whereas the "prep" crowd thought that parental authority was usually legitimate (Daddis, 2010). A study in Finland found that students with the highest grades were dismissive of those who devoted themselves to sports or those who were disaffected from school, who reciprocated by disliking the honours crowd (Laursen et al., 2010).

To further understand the impact of peers, two concepts are helpful: *selection* and *facilitation*. Teenagers select a clique whose values and interests they share, abandoning former friends who follow other paths. Peers then facilitate constructive or destructive behaviours. It is easier to do the right thing ("Let's study together for the chem exam") or the wrong thing ("Let's all skip school on Friday") if close friends are doing it, too.

Both selection and facilitation can work in any direction. One teenager joins a clique whose members smoke cigarettes and drink beer, and together they take the next step, perhaps sharing a joint. Another teenager chooses friends who enjoy math puzzles, and they might all enrol in calculus together. As one student explains,

> [companionship] makes me excited about calculus. That is a hard class, but when you need help with calculus, you go to your friends. You may think no one could be excited about calculus, but I am. Having friends in class with you definitely makes school more enjoyable.
>
> *[Hamm & Faircloth, 2005, p. 72]*

Thus, adolescents select and then facilitate, choose and are chosen. Happy, energetic, and successful teens have close friends who themselves are high achievers, with no major emotional problems. The opposite also holds: Those who are drug users and alienated from school choose compatible friends and support one another in continuing on that path (Crosnoe & Needham, 2004; Kiuru et al., 2010).

RESPONSE FOR Parents of a Teenager (from page 369) Remember: Communicate, do not control. Let your child talk about the meaning of the hairstyle. Remind yourself that a hairstyle in itself is harmless. Don't say "What will people think?" or "Are you on drugs?" or anything that might give your child reason to stop communicating. ●

KEY Points

- Adolescents are influenced by many other people, especially in the years right after puberty begins when independence is particularly difficult.
- Parents and their adolescents often bicker. Mutual communication and support are important. Closeness and control are more controversial.
- Parental monitoring is usually an element of a close, involved parent–child relationship, but may be a sign of suspicion and secrecy.
- Peer influences are typically positive, although peers sometimes provide training and encouragement for deception and deviancy.

Sexual Interactions

As explained in Chapter 9, the hormones of puberty awaken sexual interest. Adolescent sexual interactions are not only normal, they are joyous and instructive, preparing young people for healthy adult relationships. Of course, teenage romance is complicated and early sex is problematic, as soon described. But first, let us celebrate: Teenagers today are sexually healthier than teenagers a few decades ago.

- *In general, there has been a downward trend in teen births around the world.* For example, between 1960 and 2010, the adolescent birth rate in China was cut in half (reducing the United Nations' projections of the world's population in 2050 by about 1 billion). In Canada between 1996 and 2006, the teen pregnancy rate declined by 37 percent, continuing a long-term downward trend evident since the 1970s. However, between 2006 and 2010, the national teen pregnancy rate edged slightly upwards, and four provinces experienced increases of more than 15 percent (McKay, 2013). Curiously, most experts feel the economic recession had a lot to do with the upsurge. According to Alex McKay, research coordinator for the Sex Information and Education Council of Canada: "Young women who feel optimistic about their futures with respect to access to education and career tend not to get pregnant. Young women who are starting to feel discouraged about their employment and education opportunities are more likely to get pregnant. That is a straightforward correlation that persists wherever in the Western world you go" (Bielski, 2013).

- *The use of protection has risen.* Contraception, particularly condom use among adolescent boys, has increased markedly everywhere since 1990 (Santelli & Melnikas, 2010). In Canada, among males aged 15 to 24 with just one sexual partner, condom use increased from 59 percent in 2003 to 67 percent in 2010 (Rotermann, 2012).

- *The teen abortion rate is down.* From 2001 to 2010, the teenage abortion rate in Canada decreased by more than 24 percent, from 19.4 per 1000 to 14.7 (McKay, 2013).

For all these, cohort is crucial. For most of the twentieth century, North American youth reported sexual activity at younger and younger ages. For the most part, this trend has either reversed or stabilized. In Canada, the percentage of 15- to 17-year-olds reporting having sexual intercourse remained relatively stable between 1996 and 2010, and was consistently lower than the rates for 18- to 19-year-olds (see Figure 10.1) (Rotermann, 2012).

During the same period, the double standard (with boys expected to be more sexually active than girls) decreased, and today boys and girls are quite similar in reported sexual activity. Both sexes are much more knowledgeable about sexual matters, which may be the underlying reason for all the trends reported above.

COURTESY RICHARD RONAY

Watch Me Fall Adolescent boys in a skate park were videotaped in two circumstances: with an attractive female stranger sitting on a bench nearby and with no one watching. (The camera was hidden.) The boys took more risks, and fell more often, with the female observer present (Ronay & von Hippel, 2010).

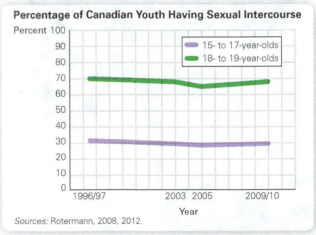

Percentage of Canadian Youth Having Sexual Intercourse

Percent 100

- 15- to 17-year-olds
- 18- to 19-year-olds

Sources: Rotermann, 2008, 2012.

FIGURE 10.1 Rates of Sexual Intercourse The percentage of 15- to 17-year-olds reporting ever having sexual intercourse has remained relatively stable between 1996 and 2010. For 18- to 19-year-olds during the same period, the percentage decreased slightly and then increased slightly.

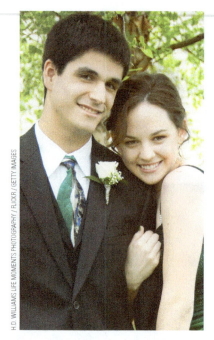

Romance By the end of high school, romantic partnerships often form, as shown with this couple going to prom together.

Romance

Decades ago, Australian researcher Dexter Dunphy (1963) described the sequence of male–female relationships during childhood and adolescence:

1. Groups of friends, exclusively one sex or the other
2. A loose association of girls and boys, with public interactions within a crowd
3. Small mixed-sex groups of the advanced members of the crowd
4. Formation of couples, with private intimacies.

Dunphy recognized, and later data from many nations confirm, that culture affects the timing and manifestation of each step, but not the sequence. Youth worldwide (and even the young of other primates) avoid the other sex in childhood and are attracted to them after puberty, with romantic partnerships gradually forming. This universal pattern suggests that physiological maturation governs this sequence.

In modern developed nations, where puberty begins with hormones at about age 10 and enduring partnerships occur much later, each of Dunphy's four stages typically lasts several years. Early, exclusive romances are more often a sign of social trouble than maturity, especially for girls (Eklund et al., 2010; Hipwell et al., 2010).

ROMANCE AND SEXUAL INTERCOURSE Contrary to adult fears, many teenage romances do not include sexual intercourse. When and with whom a person becomes sexually active depends on a cascade of factors, including age at puberty, parenting practices, peer pressure, culture, and dating relationships (Longmore et al., 2009). In British Columbia in 2008, even though one-third of all high school students said they were sexually experienced by Grade 10, another one-third of graduating students were virgins (Saewyc et al., 2008). These trends were similar in the United States. Norms vary markedly from crowd to crowd, school to school, city to city, and country to country. For instance, less than half as many high school students in San Francisco as in Philadelphia say they are currently sexually active (20 versus 45 percent) (Morbidity & Mortality Weekly Report [MMWR], June 8, 2012).

Regarding sex-related impulses, some experts believe that boys are more influenced by hormones and girls by culture (Baumeister & Blackhart, 2007). Perhaps. It does seem true that girls are more concerned than boys about the depth of the romance (Zani & Cicognani, 2006). Girls hope their partners say, "I'll love you forever"; boys like to hear, "I want you now."

However, everyone is influenced by biology, hormones, society, and culture. All adolescents have sexual interests (biology), which produce behaviours that teenagers in other nations would not engage in (culture) (Moore & Rosenthal, 2006).

Same Situation, Far Apart: Shared Joy Adults sometimes call teenage romances "puppy love," as if couples were too immature and playful to experience true affection. Some adults assume that lust, not love, connects teen boys and girls. But as these couples in North America (left) and Estonia (right) show, strong emotional connections supersede sexual contact.

SAME-SEX ROMANCES **Sexual orientation** refers to the direction of a person's erotic desires. One meaning of *orient* is to "turn toward"; thus, sexual orientation refers to whether a person is sexually and romantically attracted to people of the other sex, the same sex, or both sexes. That basic orientation seems primarily biological, but obviously culture is involved as well.

It is not known how many adolescents are romantically oriented toward people of their own sex, partly because sexual orientation can be strong, weak, acted upon, secretive, or unconscious. Relying on self-reports is bound to underestimate prevalence. One thing is clear: Increasing numbers of young adults are lesbian, gay, bisexual, and transexual. Many are supported by family, friends, and changing cultural norms and attitudes (see Figure 10.2).

Research in the United States indicates that boys who identify as male and girls who identify as female (no issue with gender identity), and who are attracted to people of their same sex, develop happily as long as society accepts them. However, many gay youth hide or deny their orientation by dating members of the other sex. Binge drinking, drug addiction, and suicidal thoughts are more common among this group, with bisexual youth and youth who are confused about their sexuality being particularly vulnerable (MMWR, June 10, 2011; Reiger & Savin Williams, 2012).

sexual orientation
A term that refers to whether a person is sexually and romantically attracted to others of the same sex, the opposite sex, or both sexes.

Who and Where? This Ontario teen won the right to take his boyfriend to his school prom, and is making a speech at the gay pride parade in Halifax, Nova Scotia. This parade would not have occurred 50 years ago.

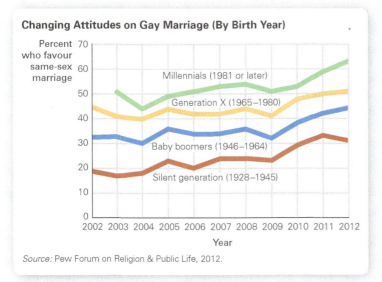

Changing Attitudes on Gay Marriage (By Birth Year)

Percent who favour same-sex marriage

- Millennials (1981 or later)
- Generation X (1965–1980)
- Baby boomers (1946–1964)
- Silent generation (1928–1945)

Year: 2002 2003 2004 2005 2006 2007 2008 2009 2010 2011 2012

Source: Pew Forum on Religion & Public Life, 2012.

FIGURE 10.2
Young and Old
All generations show increasing support for same-sex marriage over time, and each succeeding generation shows a higher rate of support than the previous generation.

What Next? Sherry, with her 11-month-old daughter, Alyssa, is a teen mom in Ontario. Teenage parents face numerous challenges. This child will reach puberty before Sherry is 30 and faces an increased risk of depression, delinquency, and another teen pregnancy.

Possible Problems

As you read, teen births and abortions are declining worldwide. Furthermore, adolescents are more informed about sexuality than they were a few generations ago, and, at least in North America, the rate of teenage intercourse is lower in the twenty-first century than it was at the end of the twentieth. However, several problems are apparent.

ADOLESCENT PREGNANCY Poverty and lack of education correlate with teenage pregnancy and a host of problems for both teenage mothers and their babies (Santelli & Melnikas, 2010). These problems begin even before birth. No matter what their SES, younger pregnant teenagers are often malnourished and postpone prenatal care (Borkowski et al., 2007). If a pregnant teenager is under 16 (most are not), complications—including spontaneous or induced abortion, high blood pressure, stillbirth, preterm birth, and a low-birth-weight newborn—are more likely.

The risks to the mother decrease after age 16, but the children of young parents (even as "old" as 17 or 18) have more medical, educational, and social problems. From a developmental perspective, each child is born not only to the mother but also to the family. In previous generations, more family support was forthcoming. Since most teen mothers were married, most fathers were legally committed to the children of teenage mothers. Furthermore, unlike in the current job market, most such fathers could find employment. In addition, 50 years ago few grandmothers on either side of the family were in the labour force; they often helped with child care. Currently, some unmarried fathers and some employed grandmothers are committed to the children of teenage mothers, but on average family support is much less available than it once was.

child sexual abuse
Any erotic activity that arouses an adult and excites, shames, or confuses a child, whether or not the victim protests and whether or not genital contact is involved.

SEXUAL ABUSE **Child sexual abuse** is defined as any activity (including fondling and photographing) that sexually stimulates an adult and that involves a juvenile. The most common time for sexual abuse, which is often committed by family members, is when the first signs of puberty occur, with girls particularly vulnerable, although boys are also at risk.

Prevalence studies find national variations in sexual assault rates. In Canada, sexual assault is the second most common type of violence committed against children that is reported to the police. While both girls and boys are vulnerable to sexual abuse, 82 percent of child sex abuse victims were female. Children ages 12 to 14 years reported the highest rates of sexual abuse. (See Figure 10.3 for Canadian abuse data.)

Relatively low child sexual abuse rates are reported from Asia, and relatively high rates are reported for girls in Australia and boys in Africa (Stoltenborgh et al., 2011). A study of the general population in England found that 2.8 percent of women and 0.8 percent of men had experienced unwanted intercourse before adulthood (Bebbington et al., 2011). International differences are affected by definitions and by the cultural willingness of adults to report past abuse (Hillberg et al., 2011). However, researchers worldwide agree that sexual abuse is not uncommon, that it is more likely than other forms of maltreatment to occur across the SES spectrum, that rates increase at puberty, and that it is equally prevalent among all ethnic groups.

Child sexual abuse is often rationalized by the abuser as relatively harmless, especially if it does not include intercourse or if a young teenager does not object. Yet research finds that the victims may be affected for many years. No matter what criteria are used, developmentalists conclude that the long-term harm from child sexual abuse is worse than the harm from other forms of maltreatment that are more obvious.

Remember that the HPA (hypothalamus–pituitary–adrenal) system regulates puberty and many other physiological responses. Many abuse victims show signs of a breakdown in the HPA regulatory system, which alters their cortisol responses. That produces heightened stress reactions in early adolescence, but then abnormally low stress responses in adulthood (Trickett et al., 2011).

Other research found that girls who have been sexually abused tend to experience earlier puberty, partly because of the dysregulation of the HPA axis (Mendle et al., 2011). As you remember from Chapter 9, early puberty for girls often leads to many other problems. Another study found that childhood sexual abuse correlates, in adulthood, with difficulty recognizing and expressing emotions, yet feeling depressed overall (Thomas et al., 2011).

Many studies indicate that the emotional consequences of childhood sexual abuse—night terrors, dangerous risk taking, serious addiction, suicidal

FIGURE 10.3 Rates of Sexual Assault This graph shows that the rates of sexual assault are higher for females than for males at all ages. The rates are highest for females ages 12 to 17 years.

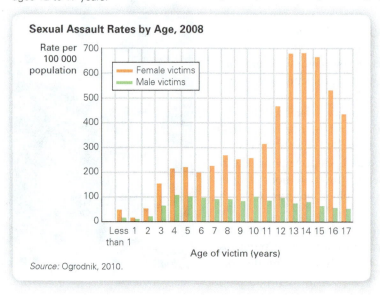

Sexual Assault Rates by Age, 2008

Rate per 100 000 population

Female victims
Male victims

Age of victim (years)

Source: Ogrodnik, 2010.

depression—may linger for life. This may be the worst consequence of all: The brains of sex abuse victims may be forever changed, causing distressing flashbacks (such as nightmares of a man suddenly entering the bedroom), impulses (such as the urge to suffocate a lover), and fears (such as fear of being alone) that never disappear.

A VIEW FROM SCIENCE

Consequences of Sexual Abuse

Puberty not only increases the odds of sexual abuse, but it can also make the emotional consequences worse because young adolescents have not yet developed a firm sense of their identity (Graber et al., 2010). For example, an 11-year-old girl who is sexually abused might conclude that she is a bad person because she attracts sexual attention, or that all men are abusive, or that her value as a human being depends on her sexuality.

The long-term harm from abuse varies depending on the victim, the family, and the community, as well as whether the abuse was an isolated instance or continued for years (more common). Nonetheless, virtually every adolescent problem—including early pregnancy, drug abuse, eating disorders, and suicide—is more frequent in those who have been sexually abused.

Consider what you have just read about the importance of supportive family and helpful peers, and then think of how sexual abuse undercuts those connections. Typically, abuse occurs at home, is perpetrated by an adult, and is allowed to continue by people who are supposed to protect the child.

For example, two sisters, La Tanya and Tichelle, were repeatedly sexually abused by their mother's live-in boyfriend. When they told their mother, she threw him out—only to let him back in again and again. The mother bought a lock for the girls' bedroom door, but the abuser broke the lock, not once but three times. Rescue finally came when a school social worker suspected that something was wrong, and La Tanya told her what was happening at home. The abuser was arrested, convicted, and sentenced to 85 years in prison. Later, the mother said that not making him leave permanently was the greatest mistake of her life (Bazelon, 2006).

The consequences extend far beyond the event. Young people who are sexually exploited typically fear sex and devalue themselves for their remaining lifetimes. Those two girls did manage to find outside help, but even as adults they are plagued by their former abuse. For example, La Tanya has nightmares that cause her to wake up and compulsively check all the locks.

La Tanya and Tichelle are just two cases. In other instances, no long-term consequences are apparent, especially when the abuse stops quickly and the child feels protected.

Remember from Chapter 1 that a single case is not conclusive. Scientific research is needed on a group of victims, ideally over several years with a control group. At least one such study has been conducted—a 23-year study of 84 reported victims (aged 6 to 16, all girls) of child sex abuse (Trickett et al., 2011). To isolate the effects of abuse, the researchers also traced the development of girls from similar backgrounds (SES, ethnicity, and so on) who were not sexually abused.

Sadly, after confidential interviews, 14 of those initially selected for the control group were found also to have been sexually abused, although that had not been reported to authorities. Other studies have also found that sexual abuse often goes unreported. Those participants who had not reported their abuse were excluded from the final comparison group.

Although both victims and controls moved residences frequently in adolescence and adulthood (including some who went to homeless shelters and some who moved in with distant relatives, leaving no forwarding addresses), the researchers were extraordinarily dedicated. They maintained contact with almost all the participants, keeping in touch (e.g., sending them birthday cards) even when funding temporarily stopped (Trickett et al., 2011).

Thus, because many guidelines for good longitudinal research were followed, the results of this study are probably valid—and definitely tragic. Although prosecutors often centre on immediate biological harm (infections, pregnancy, physical abuse), this study found that long-term cognitive and psychosocial effects of sex abuse were much worse than biological harm.

To be specific, school achievement and language development were impaired for life. Intellectual problems were apparent throughout adolescence (often years after police action stopped the abuse). In adulthood, many former victims suffered new physical and sexual abuse, severe depression, drug addiction, and obesity.

This study also found that harm extended to the next generation. Some of the 84 women had children, who also experienced cognitive and emotional problems. Of their 78 babies, three died in infancy, and nine were permanently removed from their mothers. These rates were many times higher than those for the control group, who themselves had higher rates of child death or foster care than the national averages—probably because they and the abuse victims were often from dysfunctional neighbourhoods.

Only the most severely abused or neglected children are removed from their parents. Many others suffer while remaining with their mothers. The fact that nine of the surviving children were removed indicates that many of the other 66 children were also impaired by having mothers who had been sexually abused.

sexually transmitted infection (STI)
An infection spread by sexual contact; includes syphilis, gonorrhea, genital herpes, chlamydia, and HIV. (Formerly called *sexually transmitted disease* or *venereal disease*.)

INFECTIONS AND DISEASES Teen pregnancy, abortions, and sexual abuse are less common than they were a decade ago, perhaps because sex education is earlier and more relevant than it was. However, one major problem of teenage sex shows no signs of abating: **sexually transmitted infections (STIs).** Worldwide, sexually active teenagers have higher rates of the most common STIs—gonorrhea, genital herpes, and chlamydia—than do sexually active people of any other age group (World Health Organization [WHO], 2005). In Canada, youth ages 15 to 24 years experience some of the highest STIs rates of any age group (Public Health Agency of Canada, 2008).

STIs were earlier called *sexually transmitted diseases* (STDs) or *venereal disease* (VD), terms that referred to any infection transmitted through sexual contact. One reason for the name change is that diseases may be long-lasting, caused partly by factors that are hard to avoid (such as cancer or heart disease), whereas infections are transmitted from one person to another and are more likely to be cured if treated promptly. There are hundreds of STIs, each with distinct symptoms, treatment, and consequences (James, 2007). By calling them infections, perhaps people will be more likely to seek diagnosis and treatment.

Those who have sexual intercourse before age 16 are twice as likely to become infected as are those who begin sexual activity after age 19 (Ryan et al., 2008). One reason is biological. Fully developed women have some natural biological defences against STIs; this is less true for pubescent girls (WHO, 2005). In addition, if symptoms appear, teens are reluctant to seek diagnosis or alert their partners. Infections continue and spread as a result. In cultures or families in which teenage sex is forbidden, adolescents avoid treatment for STIs until pain requires it.

Condom use, which can protect against STIs, varies internationally. French 15-year-old teenagers are among the most likely to use condoms, as well as other protective measures simultaneously (called dual use). One reason may be that most French high schools (including Catholic ones) provide free, confidential medical care and condoms; by contrast, providing either one is illegal at many U.S. schools. The emphasis of sex education in France is on health protection, not sex avoidance. Fifteen-year-old teens in the United States are least likely to use condoms (68 percent), while teens in Canada are more likely to do so (78 percent) (Higgins & Cooper, 2012; Nic Gabhainn et al., 2009) (see Table 10.1). According to a Statistics Canada report, in 2009/2010, 68 percent of Canadian youth aged 15 to 24 said that they used condoms the last time they had intercourse, up from 62 percent in 2003 (Rotermann, 2012). Among those most reluctant to carry condoms or find treatment for STIs are adolescents with same-sex partners whose community considers their sexuality shameful.

TABLE 10.1 Condom Use Among 15-Year-Olds (Grade 10) in 2009

Country	Sexually Active (% of total)	Used Condom at Last Intercourse (% of those sexually active)
Canada	23	78
England	29	83
France	20	84
Israel	14	72
Russia	33	75
United States	41	68

Sources: MMWR, June 4, 2010; Nic Gabhainn et al., 2009.

PSYCHOSOCIAL PROBLEMS Sexual health is multi-faceted, involving physical, emotional, mental, and social aspects of a person's well-being (WHO, 2013b). So it is not surprising that early intercourse presages psychosocial problems later on. A study of 3923 adult women in the United States found that those who *voluntarily* had sex before age 16 were more likely to divorce later on, whether or not that early sex resulted in pregnancy and whether or not they married their first sexual partner. The same study found that adolescents of any age whose first sexual experience was unwanted (either "really didn't want" or "had mixed feelings about") were also more likely to later divorce (Paik, 2011).

Sex Education

Many adolescents have strong sexual urges but minimal logic about pregnancy and disease. That might be expected, given the power of intuitive thought and the differential maturation of the limbic system and prefrontal cortex. They do not know what is normal and what is dangerous, and they do not think logically unless they must.

Without guidance, millions of teenagers worry that they are oversexed, undersexed, or deviant, unaware that thousands, maybe millions, of people are just like them. As a result, "students seem to waffle their way through sexually relevant encounters driven both by the allure of reward and the fear of negative consequences" (Wagner, 2011, p. 193). Obviously, they have much to learn. Where do they learn it?

LEARNING FROM PARENTS Home is where sex education begins. Every study finds that explicit parental communication is influential (Longmore et al., 2009). Ideally, parents are the best sex educators because they know their children well and can have private conversations that allow teens to ask personal questions. However, many parents wait too long to discuss sex, are silent about crucial aspects, and know little about their adolescents' romances. For example, one study showed that most parents of 12-year-old girls did not know if their daughters had hugged or kissed a boy "for a long time" or hung out with older boys (signs that sex information is urgently needed) (O'Donnell et al., 2008).

What exactly should parents tell their children? That is the wrong question, according to a longitudinal study of thousands of adolescents. A more relevant question might be "How exactly should parents talk to their children?" The study showed that teenagers tended to ignore parental lectures, for instance, in which they were warned to stay away from sex. Adolescents were more likely to remain virgins if they had a warm relationship with their parents—specific information was less important than was open communication (Deptula et al., 2010).

LEARNING FROM PEERS Adolescent sexual behaviour is strongly influenced by peers, especially when parents are silent, forbidding, or vague. Many younger adolescents discuss details of romance and sex with other members of their clique, seeking advice and approval (Laursen & Mooney, 2007).

Often the boys brag and the girls worry. Sometimes two inexperienced partners teach each other. However, the lessons from a sexual partner are more about pleasure and techniques than about consequences and protection. Only about half of U.S. adolescent couples discuss how they will avoid pregnancy and disease before they have sex (Ryan et al., 2007).

LEARNING FROM THE MEDIA Another source of sex information is the media. Sexual content appears almost seven times per hour on the TV shows most watched by teenagers (Steinberg & Monahan, 2011). That content is almost always enticing: Almost never does a television character develop an STI, deal with an unwanted pregnancy, or mention (much less use) a condom. Print media that teenagers read is no better. One study found that men's magazines convince teenage boys that manliness means many sexual conquests (Ward et al., 2011).

The impact of exposure to sex on TV, in film, and in music is controversial (Collins et al., 2011; Steinberg & Monahan, 2011). Although there is a correlation between adolescent exposure to media sex and adolescent sexual initiation, that correlation may reflect selection, not cause. Perhaps teenagers watch sexy TV because they are sexually active, not vice versa. One analysis concludes that "the most important influences on adolescents' sexual behavior may be closer to home than Hollywood" (Steinberg & Monahan, 2011, p. 575).

✦ **ESPECIALLY FOR Sex Educators**
Suppose adults in your community never talk to their children about sex or puberty. Is that a mistake? (see response, page 380) ➡

LEARNING AT SCHOOL Most northern European nations begin sex education in elementary school, and by middle school students learn about sexual responsibility, masturbation, same-sex romance, and oral and anal sex—subjects rarely covered in Canadian and U.S. classes. Rates of teenage pregnancy in most European nations are lower than those in North America; perhaps curriculum is the reason.

"Smirking or non-smirking?"

Many North American sex educators wish teachers would be more forthcoming about sex. However, probably the entire culture, not just the curriculum, is relevant. Within Canada, the curriculum for sex education varies from province to province. At present, Quebec is the only province that does not have mandatory sex education in school, although it has recently moved to reinstate mandatory sex education classes (Feldman, 2011). In the other provinces, changes to the curriculum are highly controversial. For example, Ontario has the oldest sex education curriculum in the country, introduced in 1998. A planned revision to the curriculum for Grades 1 to 8 was cancelled by the provincial government in 2010 after religious groups complained that it would introduce children to concepts, such as masturbation and same-sex relationships, that they were too young to handle (Carlson, 2011). A coalition of health and education experts continues to push the provincial government to update its outdated sex education curriculum (Brown, 2013).

The reality is that in the Internet age, many children and teens go online to learn about sex, often viewing pornography, which may not be the best way to develop a comprehensive knowledge and healthy attitudes about this realm of human experience. One commentator noted:

> In the fifth grade, my friends and I had a special afternoon tradition. When school let out at 3:30, we would walk to Katherine's house (a pseudonym), raid her fridge, go upstairs to her bedroom, lock the door and watch Internet pornography. Where were Katherine's parents? They were at work. But it wouldn't have mattered. When they were around, we just turned off the sound, or read erotic literature on a website called *Kristen Archives*. This is how we gained the indispensable knowledge that some women like to be ravished by farmhands, and others, by farm animals. The year was 1999. We had not yet sat through our first sex-ed class [in Ontario], but when we did, almost two years later, it was spectacularly disappointing. We had seen it all, and now we were shading in a diagram of the vas deferens.
>
> [Teitel, 2013]

Online pornography presents all sorts of challenges, but one question it raises is how society will deliver to its youth an alternative way of learning about sex, and about the joys, the dangers, and the responsibilities that go with it. It remains to be seen how provincial and territorial boards of education will meet the challenges posed by the "learning experiences" teenagers can access on the Internet and social media such as Facebook, Twitter, and Flickr.

According to a controlled nationwide study of sex education in the United Kingdom, whether or not an adolescent becomes sexually active depends more on family, peers, and culture than on information from classes (Allen et al., 2007). The success of sex education is measured not by whether adolescents can learn facts (most pass multiple-choice tests), but by whether their knowledge affects their behaviour (Kirby & Laris, 2009).

> ## KEY ρoints
>
> - Adolescent sexual interactions are healthier than they were a few decades ago, with fewer unwanted pregnancies, fewer abortions, and more contraception use.
> - Biological impulses at puberty lead to sexual interest, but culture strongly affects behaviour, including whether a teenager becomes sexually active and with whom.
> - Adolescents benefit from parental discussion of sexual matters, but many parents are unable or hesitant to talk openly and honestly about sex with their children.
> - Sex education varies dramatically from nation to nation, and in Canada, from one province or territory to another.

Emotions: Sadness and Anger

Adolescence is usually a wonderful time, perhaps better for current teenagers than for any prior generation. Nonetheless, troubles plague about 20 percent of today's adolescents. Distinguishing between normal moodiness and serious pathology is complex. Adolescent emotions change day to day, even minute by minute. For a few, negative emotions become intense, chronic, or even deadly.

Depression

The general trend from late childhood through adolescence is toward less confidence, with more moments of emotional despair and anger than earlier—as well as more moments of happiness (Neumann et al., 2011). A dip in self-esteem at puberty is found for children of every ethnicity and gender (Fredricks & Eccles, 2002; Greene & Way, 2005; Kutob et al., 2010). Some studies report rising self-esteem thereafter, but variations are many, as are individual differences.

On average, self-esteem is lower in girls compared to boys, lower in Asian-Americans compared to African-Americans, and lower in younger adolescents compared to older adolescents (Bachman et al., 2011). Many studies report a gradual rise in self-esteem from early adolescence through at least age 30, but all find notable variability as well as some continuity, as you would expect since genes remain the same even as age increases. That means that seriously depressed adolescents cannot be promised "you'll feel better soon"—depression lightens, but it rarely disappears (Huang, 2010).

Adolescents of any background with low self-esteem often turn to drugs, sex, self-harm, and dieting—all of which deepen depression (Biro et al., 2006; Trzesniewski et al., 2006). Some communities have lower rates of depression because they promote strong and supportive relationships between teenagers and adults; studies find that parents, as well as peers, affect self-esteem (Hall-Lande et al., 2007). One factor in an individual's level of self-esteem may be the adolescents' own neurological propensity (differential sensitivity again).

One of the first major surveys on depression in children in Canada was conducted by the Ontario Child Health Study on youths aged 6 to 16 in the late 1980s. Findings indicated that depression rates ranged by age from 2.7 to 7.8 percent. More recently, based on Statistics Canada's *Canadian Community Health Survey—Mental Health and Well-being* (2003), Cheung and Dewa (2006) reported that for adolescents

RESPONSE FOR Sex Educators (from page 378) Ideally, parents should talk to their children about sex, presenting honest information and listening to the child's concerns. However, many parents find it very difficult to do this because they feel embarrassed. ●

clinical depression
Feelings of hopelessness, lethargy, and worthlessness that last two weeks or more.

rumination
Repeatedly thinking and talking about past experiences; can contribute to depression.

suicidal ideation
Thinking about suicide, usually with some serious emotional and intellectual or cognitive overtones.

parasuicide
Any potentially lethal action against the self that does not result in death. (Also called *attempted suicide* or *failed suicide*.)

aged 15 to 18, the lifetime prevalence rate for depression was just under 8 percent. More females (11 percent) were depressed than males (4 percent). Also, teenagers living in the Maritimes had lower rates of depression than Ontario teens, while for those in British Columbia, the rates were higher. These gender and regional differences may be the result of variations in health care systems across the country that affect the accessibility of mental health services (Cheung & Dewa, 2006).

CLINICAL DEPRESSION Some adolescents sink into **clinical depression,** a feeling of a deep sadness and hopelessness that disrupts all normal, regular activities. The origins and causes, such as alleles and early care, predate adolescence. Then puberty—with its myriad physical and emotional ups and downs—plunges some into despair. The rate of clinical depression more than doubles during this time, to an estimated 15 percent, affecting about 1 in 5 girls and 1 in 10 boys.

It is not known whether the reasons for these gender differences are primarily biological, psychological, or social (Alloy & Abramson, 2007). Obviously, sex hormones differ, but girls also experience social pressures from their families, peers, and cultures that boys do not. Perhaps the combination of biological and psychosocial stresses causes some to slide into depression.

Genes also play a factor. For instance, adolescent girls are especially likely to be depressed if their mothers are belligerent, disapproving, and contemptuous. However, some girls seem genetically protected. They have equally difficult mothers, but they escape depression, probably because they are innately less vulnerable (Whittle et al., 2011).

One study found that the short allele of the serotonin transporter promoter gene (5-HTTLPR) increased the rate of depression among girls everywhere but increased depression among boys only if they lived in communities of low SES (Uddin et al., 2010). It is not surprising that certain genes make depression more likely, but the gender-specific neighbourhood correlation is puzzling. Perhaps boys are more likely to become depressed if they see no job prospects, and that is more likely in economically disadvantaged neighbourhoods.

A cognitive explanation has been offered for gender differences in depression. **Rumination**—talking about, remembering, and mentally replaying past experiences—is more common among girls than boys. If unpleasant incidents are replayed, rumination may lead to depression (Ayduk & Kross, 2008).

Adolescent depression is expressed in many ways, including eating disorders, school alienation, and sexual risk taking, all already discussed. In addition, an increasing number of depressed adolescents turn to self-harm, specifically cutting themselves to draw blood, or burning themselves to relieve anxiety. Cutting and burning are not intended as suicide attempts; they temporarily halt the unbearable emotions that triggered self-abuse. However, such actions may become addictive, leading to deeper depression. That deeper depression is linked to suicide (Asarnow et al., 2011).

SUICIDE Serious depression can lead to thoughts about killing oneself (called **suicidal ideation**). Suicidal ideation can in turn lead to **parasuicide,** also called *attempted suicide* or *failed suicide.* It includes any deliberate self-harm that could have been lethal. *Parasuicide* is the best word to use because "failed" implies that death is success. "Attempt" is likewise misleading because, especially in adolescence, the difference between attempted and completed suicide is often luck, timing, and medical response. Depression and parasuicide are more common among females, but completed suicide is higher for males (except in China). A major reason for the greater percentage of males who complete suicide has to do with the method: Males typically jump from high places or shoot themselves (immediately lethal), whereas females often swallow pills or cut their wrists (allowing time for possible intervention or second thoughts).

Another explanation is that girls talk about their emotions, allowing friends and families to help them. Boys withdraw; their warning signs are less obvious.

Suicide is the second leading cause of death among Canadian teenagers, next to accidents. In 2009, almost one-quarter (23 percent) of all deaths among 15- to 19-year-olds was the result of suicide (Statistics Canada, 2012f). Some gender differences were evident in this age group: The suicide rate for boys was 145 per 100 000, whereas for girls it was considerably less, at 57 per 100 000 (Statistics Canada, 2012g, 2012h). These statistics represent a fluctuation in suicide rates for youth aged 15 to 19 between 2005 and 2009, from 213 deaths in 2005 to 185 deaths in 2007 to 202 deaths in 2009, per 1000 youth. Over these same five years, rates steadily decreased for children aged 10 to 14 years, from 43 deaths to 25 deaths per 1000 (Statistics Canada, 2014b).

Youths from low-income families are at higher risk for suicide than youths from higher-SES families (Cheung & Dewa, 2006), though wealth and education do not decrease the incidence of suicide. One possibility is that adolescents from high-SES families may not know how to cope with a failing grade or a broken relationship. Rates of suicide are also higher for gay adolescents who have been rejected by family (Saewyc, 2011). There are regional differences in suicide, too. As is the case with depression, in British Columbia the rate of suicidal youths is higher than in Ontario (Cheung & Dewa, 2006). Alarmingly, the suicide rates for Aboriginal youth are about five to seven times higher than non-Aboriginal youth. More specifically, Inuit youth have the highest suicide rates in the world, at about eleven times the national average (Health Canada, 2013).

Many people mistakenly think suicide is more frequent in adolescence for four reasons:

1. The rate, low as it is, is far higher than it appeared to be decades ago.

2. Statistics on "youth" often include emerging adults, aged 18 to 25, whose suicide rates are higher than those of adolescents.

3. Adolescent suicides capture media attention, and people of all ages make a logical error (called base rate neglect), noticing the published cases and not considering the millions of non-suicidal youth.

4. Parasuicide may be more common in adolescence than later.

Because they are more emotional than analytical, adolescents are particularly affected when they hear about a suicide, either via media reports or from peers (Insel & Gould, 2008). That makes them susceptible to **cluster suicides,** a term for several suicides within a group over a brief span of time—a few weeks or months. If a high school student's "tragic end" is sentimentalized, that elicits suicidal ideation among his or her peers. Media attention increases the risk.

Delinquency and Disobedience

Like low self-esteem and suicidal ideation, bouts of anger are common in adolescence. In fact, the moody adolescent could be both depressed and delinquent because externalizing and internalizing behaviour are more closely connected in adolescence than at any other age (Loeber & Burke, 2011). That is why teenagers jailed for assault (externalizing) are suicide risks (internalizing).

Externalizing actions are obvious. Many adolescents slam doors, defy parents, and complain to friends about parents or teachers. Some teenagers—particularly boys— act out by breaking laws. They steal, damage property, or injure others.

Before further discussing juvenile rebellion, we should emphasize that adolescents who commit serious crimes are unusual. Most teenagers usually obey the law, with moments of hot anger (loud profanity) or minor rebellion (smoking a joint),

✦ **ESPECIALLY FOR Journalists** You just heard that a teenage girl jumped off a tall building and died. How should you report the story? (see response, page 383) →

cluster suicides
Several suicides committed by members of a group within a brief period.

but nothing more. Dozens of longitudinal studies confirm that increased anger after puberty is normal, but anger is usually expressed in acceptable ways. For a few, anger explodes: Teens break something or hurt someone. And a few of that few have been aggressive throughout childhood, becoming worse after puberty.

BREAKING THE LAW Both the prevalence (how widespread) and the incidence (how frequent) of crime increase during adolescence and continue at high levels in emerging adulthood. Arrest statistics in every nation reflect this, although some nations have much higher arrest rates overall than others.

In Canada in 2006, 180 000 youth were implicated with violating the Criminal Code, which does not include traffic tickets. The rate was 6885 per 100 000, an increase of 3 percent over the previous year. However, 60 percent of these youths were not formally charged (Taylor-Butts & Bressan, 2008). As you can see in Table 10.2, Canadian youths committed 9560 violent offences (e.g., physical and sexual assault, robbery) and 1052 drug offences in 2010/2011.

CAUSES OF DELINQUENCY Two clusters of factors, one from childhood (primarily brain-based) and one from adolescence (primarily contextual), predict delinquency. Knowing this allows prevention to focus on causes.

The first of these clusters includes a short attention span, hyperactivity, inadequate emotional regulation, slow language development, low intelligence, early and severe malnutrition, autistic tendencies, maternal cigarette smoking, and being the victim of severe child abuse, especially if it includes blows to the head. Most of these factors are more common among boys than girls, which may be one reason why females account for only about 5 percent of the inmates in Canadian correctional facilities.

Any of these signs of neurological impairment (either inborn or caused by early experiences) increases the risk that a child will become a **life-course-persistent offender** (Moffitt et al., 2001). As the term implies, a life-course-persistent offender is someone who breaks the law before and after adolescence, as well as during it.

The second cluster of factors that predict delinquency encompasses risk factors that are primarily psychosocial. They include having deviant friends; having few connections to school; living in a crowded, violent, unstable neighbourhood; not having a job; using drugs and alcohol; and having close relatives (especially older siblings) in jail. These factors are more prevalent among low-income, urban adolescents, but are certainly not exclusive to them. At any income level, an adolescent who experiences several of these risks is likely to become an **adolescence-limited offender,** someone whose criminal activity starts at puberty and stops by age 21 (Moffitt, 2003). Adolescence-limited offenders break the law with their friends, facilitated by their chosen antisocial clique. More boys than girls are in this group, but some law-breaking cliques include both sexes (the gender gap in law-breaking is narrower in late adolescence than earlier or later) (Moffitt et al., 2001).

The criminal records of both types of teenagers may be similar. However, if adolescence-limited delinquents can be protected from various snares (e.g., quitting school, entering prison, drug addiction, early parenthood), they may outgrow their criminal behaviour. This is confirmed by other research: Few delinquent youth who are not imprisoned continue breaking the law in early adulthood (Monahan et al.,

---

TABLE 10.2 Youth Admissions to Correctional Services, by Most Serious Offence

Most serious offence	2010/2011
Total admissions of most serious offence	43 344
Total violent offences	9 560
Assault level 2	2 335
Common assault	2 395
Sexual assault	439
Robbery	2 512
Other violent offences	1 909
Total property offences	8 002
Break and enter	2 712
Theft $5000 and under	2 099
Theft over $5000	442
Possession stolen goods	978
Mischief	1 264
Other property offences	507
Other criminal code	5 084
Total other offences	3 300
Drug-related offences	1 052
Youth Criminal Justice Act (VJCA) and Young Offenders Act (YOA)	2 007
Other federal offences	6
Provincial and Municipal offences	235

Source: Statistics Canada, 2012k.

---

life-course-persistent offender
A person whose criminal activity typically begins in early adolescence and continues throughout life; a career criminal.

adolescence-limited offender
A person whose criminal activity stops by age 21.

✦ **ESPECIALLY FOR Police Officers** You see some 15-year-olds drinking beer in a local park when they belong in school. What do you do? (see response, page 384) ➡

2009). This does not mean that adolescence-limited law-breaking should be ignored. Antisocial behaviour is dangerous, especially to other adolescents, who are victimized three times as often as adults (Baum, 2005). Fortunately, maturation puts an end to adolescence-limited law-breaking.

By contrast, life-course-persistent offending begins in childhood and continues in adulthood with more crime, less education, lower income, unhappy marriages, and violence (Huesmann et al., 2009). It extends to the next generation: If life-course-persistent offenders have children, those children are likely to become lawbreakers themselves, partly for genetic reasons but primarily because they will have been mistreated by their parents before and after birth.

One way to prevent adolescent crime is to analyze earlier behaviour patterns and stop delinquency before the police become involved. Three pathways can be seen:

1. Stubbornness can lead to defiance, which can lead to running away—runaways are often victims as well as criminals (e.g., prostitutes, petty thieves).

2. Shoplifting can lead to arson and burglary.

3. Bullying can lead to assault, rape, and murder.

Each of these pathways demands a different response. The rebelliousness of the stubborn child can be channelled or limited until more maturation and less impulsive anger prevail. Those on the second pathway require stronger human relationships and moral education.

Those on the third pathway present the most serious problem. Bullies need to be stopped and helped in early childhood, as already discussed. If that does not occur, and a teenager is still a bully, intense treatment may deflect the pattern. If that does not occur, and a teenager is convicted of assault, rape, or murder, then arrest, conviction, and jail might be the only options. In all cases, intervention is more effective earlier than later (Loeber & Burke, 2011).

As you can see in Figure 10.4, both the crime rate and crime severity for Canadian youths ages 12 to 17 years decreased steadily over the 10-year period from 2001 to 2011. Although these data are solid, explanations are not. Possibilities include fewer

RESPONSE FOR Journalists (from page 381) Since teenagers seek admiration from their peers, be careful not to glorify the victim's life or death. Facts are needed, as is, perhaps, the inclusion of warning signs that were missed or cautions about alcohol abuse. Avoid prominent headlines or anything that might encourage another teenager to do the same thing. ●

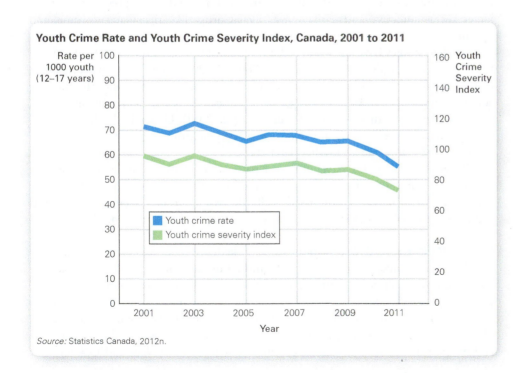

Youth Crime Rate and Youth Crime Severity Index, Canada, 2001 to 2011

Source: Statistics Canada, 2012n.

FIGURE 10.4 Good News? Youth crime has been steadily declining in Canada for several years. According to Statistics Canada, both the youth crime rate, which measures the volume of youth crime, and youth crime severity, a measure of the seriousness of youth crime, fell 10 percent in 2011, continuing a downward trend evident over the last decade. One reason for the continued decline may be that starting in 2003, when the Youth Criminal Justice Act was passed, the rate of youths diverted from the formal justice system has continually exceeded the rate of youths formally charged.

school dropouts (more education means less crime); wiser judges (using community service and drug treatment to prevent escalation); better policing (arrests for misdemeanors are up, alerting parents); smaller families (parents attend more to each child); better contraception and legal abortion (wanted children less often become criminals); more immigrants (who are more law-abiding); less lead damage (reducing impulsivity); and stricter drug laws (binge drinking and use of drugs are down).

KEY Points

- The emotions of adolescents often include marked depression and anger, sometimes pathological, sometimes not.
- Clinical depression is more common in teenage girls than boys; experts disagree as to whether this is primarily caused by hormones, rumination, or society.
- Breaking the law is common among adolescents, with more arrests during these years than later.
- Some offenders are adolescence-limited—they stop breaking the law at adulthood; some are life-course-persistent—they become criminal adults.

Drug Use and Abuse

RESPONSE FOR Police Officers (from page 382) Avoid both extremes: Don't let them think this situation is either harmless or horrifying. You might call their parents and discuss the situation. ●

Adolescents enjoy doing something forbidden. Moreover, their hormonal surges and brain patterns increase the reward sensations produced by drugs. But their developing bodies and brains make drug use particularly hazardous.

Variations in Drug Use

Most teenagers try *psychoactive drugs,* which are drugs that affect the mind. Although police officers are concerned primarily with the legal issues of drug use, developmentalists are more concerned that cigarettes, alcohol, and many prescription medicines are as addictive and damaging as illegal drugs like marijuana, cocaine, and heroin.

Canadian studies have shown that the three most popular drugs among youth are tobacco, alcohol, and cannabis (Vega et al., 2002). In 2012, Statistics Canada reported that, among youths aged 15 to 24, use of cannabis was three times higher than among adults 25 and older, and use of drugs such as cocaine, speed, hallucinogens, ecstasy, and heroin was five times higher (Health Canada, 2011). Generally, both the prevalence and incidence of drug use increase every year from age 10 to 25, and then decrease. Use before age 18 predicts later abuse.

The exception to this developmental pattern is inhalants (fumes from aerosol containers, cleaning fluid, etc.), which are used more by younger adolescents, partly because they can be easily purchased. Sadly, the youngest adolescents are least able, cognitively, to analyze risks, and parents rarely suspect a drug problem.

VARIATIONS BY REGION Nations vary markedly in drug use. Consider the most common drugs: alcohol and tobacco. In most European nations, alcohol is widely used, even by children. In contrast, in much of the Middle East, alcohol use is illegal and teenagers almost never drink. In many Asian nations, anyone may smoke anywhere; in the United States, smoking is forbidden in many schools and public places, but advertised widely; in Canada, cigarette smoking is forbidden in schools and public places, and cigarette advertising is outlawed. Canadian and U.S. teens of

A Man Now This boy in Tibet is proud to be a smoker—in many Asian nations, smoking is considered manly.

both sexes smoke fewer cigarettes than Western European teens, and Canadian teens smoke less than U.S. teens. Even within Canada, cigarette smoking varies by region. For example, in 2010–2011, about 9 percent of youth in Ontario in Grades 6 to 9 had tried smoking cigarettes, compared to 24 percent of youth in Quebec (Health Canada, 2012b).

VARIATIONS BY GENERATION AND GENDER The specifics of use and abuse vary historically and culturally, partly because each generation develops a distinct pattern to differentiate itself from the earlier cohorts and other cultures. Use of drugs has decreased or stayed the same in Canada since 2004 (as Figure 10.5 shows).

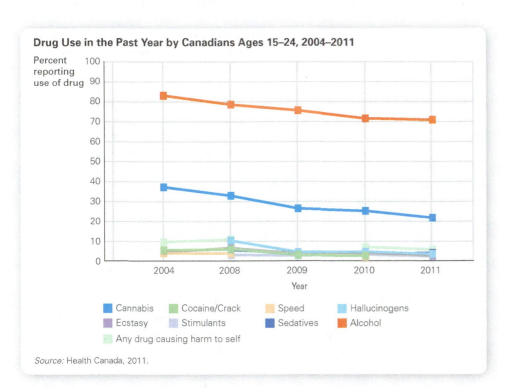

Drug Use in the Past Year by Canadians Ages 15–24, 2004–2011

Legend:
- Cannabis
- Cocaine/Crack
- Speed
- Hallucinogens
- Ecstasy
- Stimulants
- Sedatives
- Alcohol
- Any drug causing harm to self

Source: Health Canada, 2011.

FIGURE 10.5 Drug use in Canada The Canadian Alcohol and Drug Use Monitoring Survey (CADUMS) is an ongoing survey of Canadians aged 15 years and older about their alcohol and drug use. As the graph indicates, the use of all drugs by 15- to 24-year-olds has decreased since 2004.

OBSERVATION QUIZ
Which of the drugs listed here do you think are relatively more accessible to youth, and subject to more lenient possessions laws? (see answer, page 386) →

With some exceptions, adolescent boys use more drugs, and use them more often, than girls do, especially outside North America. An international survey of 13- to 15-year-olds in 131 nations found that more boys are smokers (except in a few European nations), including three times as many boys as girls in Southeast Asia (Warren et al., 2006). According to another international survey of 31 nations, almost twice as many boys as girls have tried marijuana (26 percent versus 15 percent) (ter Bogt et al., 2006).

These gender differences are reinforced by social constructions about proper male and female behaviour. In Indonesia, for instance, 38 percent of the boys smoke cigarettes, but only 5 percent of the girls do. One Indonesian boy explained, "If I don't smoke, I'm not a real man" (quoted in Ng et al., 2007).

A recent report from the Canadian Centre on Substance Abuse found few gender differences in alcohol or cannabis use among Canadian students aged 12 to 18; however, more males report drinking and consuming cannabis before driving (Young et al., 2011). In addition, young men are more likely to report risky drinking (defined as four or more drinks for women, and five or more drinks for men on one occasion) than are women: 62.9 percent compared to 50.1 percent (Canadian Centre on Substance Abuse, 2013).

Harm from Drugs

Many teenagers believe that adults exaggerate the evils of drug use and think it hypocritical that a parent who has cocktails before dinner or beer with lunch would dare prohibit adolescent drug use. Nonetheless, developmentalists see both immediate and long-term harm when teenagers use drugs.

Addiction and brain damage are among the consequences of drug use that appear to be more pronounced in adolescents than in adults, a difference that has been linked to brain maturation (Moffitt et al., 2006). Few adolescents notice when they move past *use* (experimenting) to *abuse* (experiencing harm) and then to *addiction* (needing the drug to avoid feeling nervous, anxious, or in pain). They do not know or care that every psychoactive drug excites the limbic system and interferes with the prefrontal cortex. Drug users are thus more emotional (specifics vary, from ecstasy to terror, paranoia to rage) than they otherwise would be, as well as less reflective. Every hazard of adolescence—including car crashes, unsafe sex, and suicide—is more common among teens who have taken a psychoactive drug.

In terms of specific drugs, a negative effect of *tobacco* that impacts teens in particular is that it impairs digestion and nutrition, slowing down growth. Abuse of tobacco occurs with bidis, cigars, pipes, and chewing tobacco, as well as with cigarettes. In India, widespread tobacco use is one reason for chronic undernutrition (Warren et al., 2006). Since internal organs continue to mature after the height spurt, cigarette-smoking teenagers who appear full-grown may damage their developing hearts, lungs, brains, and reproductive systems.

Alcohol is the most frequently abused drug in North America. Heavy drinking impairs memory and self-control by damaging the hippocampus and the prefrontal cortex, perhaps distorting the reward circuits of the brain permanently (Guerri & Pascual, 2010). Although some specifics of the impact of alcohol on the adolescent brain are still unknown, there is no doubt that alcohol affects adolescents more than adults because of their brain immaturity (Chin et al., 2010).

Like many other drugs, alcohol allows momentary denial of problems: Worries seem to disappear when a person is under the influence. When ignored, problems get worse and more alcohol is needed—a vicious cycle that often leads to addiction.

✦ **ESPECIALLY FOR Parents Who Drink Socially** You have heard that parents should allow their children to drink at home, to teach them to drink responsibly and not get drunk elsewhere. Is that wise? (see response, page 388) ➜

SPENCER PLATT / GETTY IMAGES

How to Escape Imagine living where these boys do, on the streets of Tegucigalpa, the capital city of Honduras, the nation with the highest murder rate in the world. What would stop you from doing what they do—sniff paint thinner for a dangerous moment of joy?

Denial is a problem for all alcoholics, but particularly for teenagers who have not yet learned that they cannot drive, write, or even think after several drinks.

Similarly, *marijuana* seems harmless to many teenagers, partly because users seem more relaxed than inebriated. A girl named Johanna said:

> I started off using about every other weekend, and pretty soon it increased to three to four times a week. … I started skipping classes to get high. I quit soccer because my coach was a jerk. My grades dropped, but I blamed that on my not being into school. … Finally, some of my friends cornered me and told me how much I had changed, and they said it started when I started smoking marijuana. They came with me to see the substance-abuse counselor at school.
>
> *[Bell, 1998, p. 199]*

Johanna's future was in jeopardy. Adolescents who regularly smoke marijuana are more likely to drop out of school, become teenage parents, and be unemployed. Marijuana affects memory, language proficiency, and motivation (Lane et al., 2005)— all of which are especially crucial during adolescence. An Australian study found that even occasional marijuana use (once a week) before age 20 affected development up to 10 years later (Degenhardt et al., 2010).

These are correlations, which, as you know, do not reveal causation. Is it possible that adolescents who are not particularly clever or ambitious choose to smoke marijuana, rather than vice versa? Is some third variable (such as hostile parents) the cause of both academic problems and drug use, rendering the correlation deceptive? This seems plausible because drug-using adolescents often distrust their parents, injure themselves, hate their schools, and break the law.

These questions led to the hypothesis that the psychic strains of adolescence lead to drug use, not vice versa. In fact, however, longitudinal research suggests that drug use *causes* more problems than it solves, often *preceding* anxiety disorders, depression, and rebellion (Chassin et al., 2009; Meririnne et al., 2010).

Marijuana use is particularly common among wealthier adolescents, who then become less motivated to achieve in school and more likely to develop other problems (Ansary & Luthar, 2009). Rather than lack of ambition leading to marijuana use, marijuana itself destroys ambition.

Preventing Drug Abuse: What Works?

Drug abuse is a progression, beginning with a social occasion and ending alone. The first use usually occurs with friends, which leads adolescents to believe that occasional use is an expression of friendship or generational solidarity. Few adolescent drug users are addicts, and, for those who are, usually they and their friends are unaware of it. However, the younger a person is when beginning occasional drug use, the more likely addiction will eventually occur. That may not persuade young adolescents, who, as you remember, think they are invulnerable exceptions to any rule.

With harmful drugs, as with many other aspects of life, each generation prefers to learn things for themselves. A common phenomenon is **generational forgetting,** the idea that each new generation forgets what the previous generation learned (Chassin et al., 2009; Johnston et al., 2010). Mistrust of the older generation, added to loyalty to one's peers, leads not only to generational forgetting, but also to a backlash. If adults say something is forbidden, that is a reason to try it.

Some antidrug curricula and advertisements using scare tactics (such as the one that showed eggs being broken into a hot frying pan while an announcer intoned, "This is your brain on drugs") have the opposite effect than intended, increasing rather than decreasing drug use. One reason may be that such advertisements make drugs seem exciting; another may be that adolescents recognize the exaggeration. Similarly, anti-smoking announcements produced by cigarette companies (such as one that showed a clean-cut young person advising viewers to think before they started smoking) actually increased use (Strasburger et al., 2009).

Changing the social context has an impact. For example, Aboriginal people in North America are significantly more likely to smoke than the general population. This is due to availability of inexpensive cigarettes (tax-exempted), relatively poor SES status, greater difficulties in accessing quality health care, and environmental factors (Samji & Wardman, 2009; Wardman & Khan, 2005).

All the research confirms that parents are influential, yet many parents are unaware of their children's drug use, so their educational efforts may be too late, too general, or too naive. When parents forbid smoking in their homes, fewer adolescents smoke (Messer et al., 2008); when parents are careful with their own drinking, fewer teenagers abuse alcohol (Van Zundert et al., 2006). When parents provide guidance about drinking, teenagers are less likely to get drunk or use other substances (Miller & Plant, 2010). In addition, growing up with two married parents reduces cigarette and alcohol use, even when other influences (such as parental smoking and family income) are taken into account (Brown & Rinelli, 2010). The probable reasons include better parent–child monitoring: Usually at least one of the parents is aware of what the child is doing.

It is apparent that, although puberty is a universal biological process, its effects vary widely. Sharply declining rates of teenage pregnancy, abortions, suicides, homicides, and use of several legal and illegal drugs are evident in many nations. Changing times bring new iterations of the identity crisis. Human growth starts with genes when a single sperm penetrates a single ovum, but it certainly is not wholly determined by biology. This will be even more apparent in the next five chapters: By the end of adolescence a person has completed body growth but not development. No adult of any age is unchanged over the past five years, and no one will be the same five years hence.

generational forgetting The idea that each new generation forgets what the previous generation learned. As used here, the term refers to knowledge about the harm drugs can do.

RESPONSE FOR Parents Who Drink Socially (from page 386) No. Alcohol is particularly harmful for young brains. Children who are encouraged to drink with their parents are more likely to drink when no adults are present. Instead, ensure that children understand the risks associated with drinking. ●

KEY Points

- Many adolescents try psychoactive drugs; however, alcohol and marijuana use are most common among Canadian youth.
- Countries vary tremendously in the legality and availability of drugs.
- Adolescents are often unaware of the dangers of drugs, which are particularly harmful to the developing brain and body.
- Drug use is highest among Canadian youth as compared to other age groups.
- Some educational measures to halt adolescent drug use are not effective, but parental example and changing the social context have reduced prevalence.

SUMMARY

Identity

1. Adolescence is a time for self-discovery. According to Erikson, adolescents seek their own identity, sorting through the traditions of their families and cultures.

2. Many young adolescents foreclose on their options without exploring possibilities, experience role confusion, or reach moratorium. Identity achievement takes longer for contemporary adolescents than it did half a century ago, when Erikson first described it.

3. Identity achievement occurs in many domains, including religion, politics, vocation, sex, and ethnicity. Each of these remains important over the life span, but timing, contexts, and terminology have changed since Erikson and Marcia first described the domains of identity achievement.

4. Immigrant youths undergo one of four potential ethnic identities: integrated, separated, national, and diffuse.

Relationships with Others

5. Parents continue to influence their growing children, despite bickering over minor issues. Ideally, communication and warmth remain high within the family, whereas parental control decreases and adolescents develop independence.

6. There are cultural differences in the timing of conflicts and particulars of parental monitoring. Too much parental control, with psychological intrusiveness, is harmful, as is neglect. Parents need to find a balance between granting freedom and providing guidance.

7. Family closeness has four aspects, including communication, support, connectedness, and control.

8. Peers and peer pressure can be beneficial or harmful, depending on particular friends, cliques, and crowds. Adolescents select their friends, including friends of the other sex, who then facilitate constructive and/or destructive behaviour such as deviancy training.

9. Crowds and cliques are evident in high schools; they are necessary to help adolescents develop their values and life habits. Peers may be particularly crucial for ethnic-minority and immigrant adolescents, who need to establish their own ethnic identity.

Sexual Interactions

10. Current youth may have healthier sexual relationships than did youth a generation ago. Teen pregnancy and abortion are lower, contraception use is higher, and sexual intercourse, at least in North America, occurs at later ages.

11. Puberty triggers sexual interest, but cultures and crowds have a major influence on how, when, and to whom those interests are expressed. Early, exclusive sexual relationships are a sign of emotional immaturity.

12. Some youth are oriented toward same-sex romance; others have sexual relationships with both sexes. Depending on the family, culture, and cohort, sexual-minority youth may experience depression and other problems.

13. Problems with adolescent sexuality include adolescent pregnancy (especially for Canadian teens who are discouraged about their future career and educational opportunities) and STIs (higher in adolescence than later).

14. Sexual abuse is more likely to occur in early adolescence than at other ages, and it can permanently harm a victim's brain and psychological development. Girls are most often the victims; the perpetrators are most often family members.

15. Incident rates of teen pregnancy, abortions, intercourse, and sexual abuse are declining, although sexually transmitted infections are the highest among Canadian youth. STIs can have long-term effects but culture and religion may prevent youth from seeking treatment.

16. Sex education occurs in many ways, with parents the most powerful influence but often the least informed. Schools vary in scope and success of sex education.

Emotions: Sadness and Anger

17. A few adolescents become seriously depressed. Many adolescents (especially girls) think about suicide, and some attempt it. Few adolescents actually kill themselves; most who do so are boys. However, the exception is Aboriginal youth who have one of the highest rates of suicide in the world.

18. Law-breaking and momentary rage are common, although few adolescents commit serious crimes.

19. There are different groups of youth offenders: life-course-persistent offenders who continue to be delinquent into adulthood; and adolescence-limited offenders who start and stop their delinquent behaviours in adolescence.

20. Youths' childhood experiences, family relationships, and environment are determinants of the extent of the youths' delinquent tendencies.

Drug Use and Abuse

21. Most adolescents experiment with drugs, especially alcohol and tobacco, although such substances impair growth of the body and the brain. National culture has a powerful influence on which specific drugs are used as well as on the frequency of use. Age, gender, community, and parental factors are also influential.

22. Prevention and moderation of adolescent drug use and abuse are possible. Anti-drug programs and messages need to be carefully designed to avoid a backlash or generational forgetting. Other factors to consider when trying to decrease drug use and abuse include availability, family and community environments, SES, and accessibility to quality health care.

KEY TERMS

adolescence-limited offender (p. 382)
bickering (p. 366)
child sexual abuse (p. 374)
clinical depression (p. 380)
clique (p. 370)
cluster suicides (p. 381)

crowd (p. 370)
deviancy training (p. 369)
ethnic identity (p. 364)
foreclosure (p. 360)
gender identity (adolescence) (p. 364)
generational forgetting (p. 388)

identity achievement (p. 360)
identity versus role confusion (p. 360)
life-course-persistent offender (p. 382)
moratorium (p. 361)
parasuicide (p. 380)
parental monitoring (p. 368)

peer pressure (p. 369)
role confusion (p. 360)
rumination (p. 380)
sexual orientation (p. 373)
sexually transmitted infection (STI) (p. 376)
suicidal ideation (p. 380)

WHAT HAVE YOU LEARNED?

1. What are the differences between identity achievement and role confusion?

2. What role do parents play in religious and political identity?

3. What are the pros and cons of teens having part-time jobs while in school?

4. In what crucial way do the terms "sexual identity" and "gender identity" differ?

5. What are the roles of parents, peers, and society in helping an adolescent develop an ethnic identity?

6. Why do parents and adolescents often bicker?

7. What four factors affect family closeness? Why is each factor important?

8. How and when can peer pressure be helpful and how can it be harmful?

9. What evidence is there that teenagers today are sexually healthier than teenagers a few decades ago?

10. What are Dunphy's four stages of male–female relationships?

11. What factors influence sexual activity? Explain.

12. What risks are associated with teenage pregnancy, for both the mother and the child?

13. Why is it harmful for a young adolescent and an adult to have sex?

14. Among sexually active people, why do adolescents have more STIs than adults?

15. In terms of learning about sex from parents, what seems to be the most influential factor?

16. Why might peers be an unreliable source of information about sex?

17. Why is it difficult to know what influence the media has on adolescents having sex?

18. What are the variations in sex education in schools, and how does this affect adolescent sexual behaviour?

19. What gender differences are evident in depression, and why?

20. What gender differences are evident in suicide, and why?

21. What factors make serious delinquency more likely, and what factors decrease the risk?

22. What variations in adolescent drug use are evident? Why?

23. Why are psychoactive drugs particularly destructive in adolescence?

24. What works and does not work in reducing adolescent drug use?

APPLICATIONS

1. Teenage cliques and crowds may be more important in large high schools than elsewhere. Interview people who spent their teenage years in schools of various sizes, or in another nation, about the peer relationships in their high schools. Describe and discuss any differences you find.

2. Locate a news article about a teenager who committed suicide. Can you find evidence in the article that there were warning signs that were ignored? Does the report inadvertently encourage cluster suicides?

3. Cultures have different standards for drug use among children, adolescents, and adults. Interview three people from different cultures (not necessarily from different nations; each occupation, generation, or religion can be said to have a culture) about their culture's drug-use standards. Ask your respondents to explain the reasons behind the cultural standards.

>>ONLINE CONNECTIONS

To accompany your textbook, you have access to a number of online resources, including LearningCurve, which is an adaptive quizzing program; critical thinking questions; and case studies. For access to any of these links, go to www.worthpublishers.com/launchpad/bergerchuang1e. In addition to these resources, you'll find links to video clips, personalized study advice, and an e-Book. Among the videos and activities available online is the following:

- *Who Am I?* This video reviews pathways to identity achievement and Marcia's dimensions of exploration and commitment. Teens talk about identity. The embedded questionnaire lets you gauge your progress in identity formation.

Adulthood

We now begin the sixth part of this text. These three chapters cover 47 years (ages 18 to 65), when bodies mature and people develop areas of expertise as they contribute to the workforce.

No decade of adulthood is exclusively linked to any one event: Adults at many ages can get stronger or weaker, learn and produce, nurture friendships and marriages, and care for children and aging relatives. Many may experience hiring and firing, wealth and poverty, births and deaths, weddings and divorces, windfalls and disasters, and illness and recovery. Adulthood is punctuated by many events, some joyful and some sorrowful.

There are some chronological norms, noted in these chapters. Early in adulthood, few people are married or settled in a career; later, many have partners and offspring. Expertise at a particular job is also more likely at age 50 than 20.

Developmental history is always relevant: Adults are guided by nature and nurture as they choose partners, activities, communities, and habits. The experience of adulthood is not the same everywhere. In some nations and cultures, dominant influences are families, economics, and past history; in others, genetic heritage and personal choice are the focus. Of course, it is a matter of degree.

The following three chapters describe adulthood: the universals, the usual, and the diverse.

CHAPTER OUTLINE

EMERGING ADULTHOOD:
Body, Mind, and Social World

WHAT WILL YOU KNOW?

- Why have birth rates fallen so dramatically in North America and around the world?
- How can imagining other people's stereotypes be harmful?
- Does cohabitation precede, ruin, or substitute for marriage?
- Is independence from parents a sign of healthy adulthood?

The years from ages 18 to 25 were once merely part of adulthood; then were distinguished as late adolescence, youth, or early adulthood; and now they are often labelled emerging adulthood. In emerging adulthood, many people seek higher education and explore their identity by postponing marriage or partnership, parenthood, and career.

I experienced this myself. Between ages 18 and 25, I attended four colleges or universities, changed majors five times, rejected marriage proposals from four young men, lived in ten places, and started several jobs—none lasting more than 18 months. After that period of rapid change, I stayed put for 30 years—one husband, one city, one street, one career.

Similar patterns occur everywhere. Although few have as many options as I did, youth in many nations gain more education and choose to marry later than previous generations did, if at all. ●

—Kathleen Berger

EMERGING ADULTHOOD IS A WORLDWIDE STAGE OR PROCESS (Arnett et al., 2011). As always, culture, context, and cohort are influential, but few people have settled down by age 18. Although 18-year-olds are no longer adolescents in body, mind, or social context, they are also not yet adults as traditionally defined.

emerging adulthood
The period of life between the ages of 18 and 25. Emerging adulthood is now widely thought of as a separate developmental stage.

Focus on Education This emerging-adult couple, posing in front of the stadium in Beijing, China, has just started dating. Their primary focus at this age is on their education.

Biosocial Development

Biologically, the years from ages 18 to 25 are prime time for hard physical work and successful reproduction. However, the fact that young adults can carry rocks, plow fields, and reproduce more easily than older adults is no longer universally admired.

If a contemporary young couple had a baby every year, their neighbours would be more surprised than approving. In fact, large families have become so unusual that they are sometimes the focus of TV reality shows. Today, during emerging adulthood, societies, families, and young adults themselves expect more education, later marriage, and fewer children than was true as recently as 50 years ago (see At About This Time). More people are pursuing post-secondary education, and the median age for family commitment is at the end of emerging adulthood. It is also important to note that many people do not follow this normative path. Sometimes such expectations are thought to be exclusive to the middle class in advanced nations, but the trends are apparent everywhere.

<table>
<tr><td colspan="2">AT ABOUT THIS TIME
Following Certain Patterns, by Average Age:</td></tr>
<tr><td>Age 17–18</td><td>Graduate from high school (about 74 percent graduate*)</td></tr>
<tr><td>Age 18–19</td><td>Enrol in college or university (about 79 percent enrol[†])</td></tr>
<tr><td>Age 22</td><td>Earn college or university degree (about 53 and 65 percent graduate from universities and colleges, respectively[†])</td></tr>
<tr><td>Age 25</td><td>Steady employment in chosen field (rate fluctuates, depends on economy)</td></tr>
<tr><td>Age 28</td><td>Women's first child (for those who will have children[‡]; about 20 percent will not)</td></tr>
<tr><td>Age 29</td><td>Women's first marriage[§]</td></tr>
<tr><td>Age 31</td><td>Men's first marriage[§]</td></tr>
</table>

*Council of Ministers of Education, Canada, 2008.
[†]Statistics Canada, 2008b.
[‡]Employment and Social Development Canada, n.d.[a].
[§]Employment and Social Development Canada, n.d.[c].

Peak Performance
Because this is a soccer match, of course we see skilled feet and strong legs—but also notice the arms, torsos, and feats of balance. Deniz Naki (age 21) and Luis Gustavo (age 23) are German soccer team members and are in better shape than most emerging adults, but imagine these two a decade earlier (at age 11 and 13) or later (at age 31 and 33) and you will realize why, physiologically, one's early 20s are considered the prime of life.

Strong and Active Bodies

Health does not change significantly in early adulthood, except maybe to improve with advanced technology and research. Every human body system—including the digestive, respiratory, circulatory, and sexual-reproductive systems—functions optimally at the beginning of adulthood. In a recent Canadian national survey, *Health Profile,* 68.4 percent of young adults (age 20 to 34) reported that their physical health was either very good or excellent (Statistics Canada, 2013k).

Specifics confirm the health of emerging adults. Serious diseases are usually not yet apparent, and some childhood ailments are outgrown. For example, childhood asthma disappears as often as it continues. Although many emerging adults continue the poor health habits they had as adolescents, the trend is toward better diets and regular exercise, and that improves mental as well as physical health (Walsh, 2011).

However, this does not mean that serious health problems from childhood disappear or that new health concerns do not emerge. A comprehensive review of many studies finds that low birth weight, undernutrition in infancy, and rapid weight gain in early childhood tend to result in shorter height, reduced body functioning, and higher risk of disease in early adulthood (Victora et al., 2008). In a Canadian survey in which only 5.8 percent of young adults rated their health as fair or poor, 9.7 percent reported they had asthma, 2.5 percent said they had arthritis, 2.1 percent had high blood pressure, and 0.9 percent had diabetes. In addition, 7.7 percent had moderate or severe pain or discomfort, and 8.9 percent had pain or discomfort that prevented activities (Statistics Canada, 2013k).

Fortunately, severe health problems are usually kept in check during early adulthood, when the immune system is strong (Grubeck-Loebenstein, 2010). For instance, between 2005 and 2009, 346 330 Canadians died of cancer, but only 1400 (0.4 percent) were age 15 to 29 years (Canadian Cancer Society's Advisory Committee on Cancer Statistics, 2013). Death from heart disease is equally rare for emerging adults.

For most emerging adults, teeth have no new cavities, heart rate is steady, the brain functions well, and lung capacity is sufficient. Many diagnostic tests, such as PSAs (for prostate cancer), mammograms (for breast cancer), and colonoscopies (for colon cancer) are not usually recommended until decades later, unless risk factors are present. Death from any disease is rare, although, as discussed later, death from accidents, suicide, and homicide increase, and psychosocial problems may occur.

Fertility, Then and Now

Dramatic fertility shifts have been observed around the world over the past 50 years. For example, average births per woman over this time period declined from 7 to 1.5 in Iran, 8 to 4 in Kenya, 6 to 2 in South America, and 5 to 1.5 in East Asia. For the world as a whole, the birth rate from 1960 to 2010 fell from 4.9 to 2.45 (United Nations, 2011). Similarly, Canada's fertility rate in 2011 was 1.63, a significant decrease from 3.81 in 1960, and the lowest rate in North America (see Figure 11.1).

The sexual-reproductive system is at its strongest during emerging adulthood. Moreover miscarriage is less common, and serious birth complications are unusual. Historically, most couples had their first child as teenagers. Many had a second and a third child before age 25. Today, 29 is the average age for a *first* birth in Canada (Employment and Social Development Canada, n.d.[a]), with first births occurring even later in some other countries.

DELAYING PREGNANCY Many emerging adults who have sex know that they are not prepared for parenthood, mentally, emotionally, or financially, and use contraception to avoid pregnancy. Although no contraception is always successful, long-acting contraception (implant, IUD, Depo-Provera) almost never fails (about 1 failure in 400 women), whereas shorter-acting measures (pill, patch, or ring) fail for 1 in 20 women (Winner et al., 2012). Failure rates are higher in adolescents than in emerging adults.

Largely as a result of the use of contraception, the birth rate has fallen—a trend for all women under age 40, with a particularly strong drop for those ages 20 to 24 (Livingston, 2011). This does not mean that parenthood is not important to young adults and those in their late 20s. Even compared with 13 years ago, more people in this age range hope to become good parents, while fewer say that having a successful marriage is one of the most important things in their life (Wang & Taylor, 2011).

SEXUALLY TRANSMITTED INFECTIONS As mentioned in Chapter 10, sexually transmitted infections are on the rise worldwide, with half of all new cases occurring in people younger than 26 (Gewirtzman et al., 2011). In Canada in 2008, the

Years of Practice People of any age can begin ballet lessons or any other physical activity, but mastery requires a decade or more. Russian ballet dancers begin intensive practice in childhood, hoping for the fame achieved by Yulia Tikka, here at age 23 in her prime. Her solo career will soon end; superstars in almost every demanding athletic activity slow down by age 30.

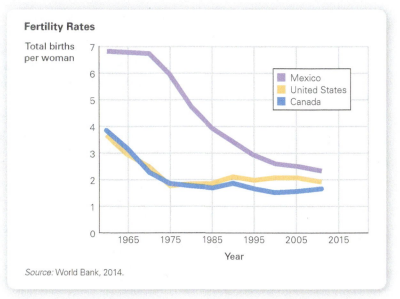

Fertility Rates

Total births per woman

Source: World Bank, 2014.

FIGURE 11.1 Fertility Rates Are Dropping In all three North American countries, fertility rates have fallen dramatically since the 1960s. What might be some reasons for the decreasing rate in Canada? What implications might this have for national policies on the economy and immigration?

highest rates of all types of infections were found in those younger than age 30 (Public Health Agency of Canada, 2008). This trend is also seen in the United States, Australia, and the United Kingdom.

Young adults are the prime vectors (those who spread disease) for HIV/AIDS as well. The Public Health Agency of Canada reports that HIV is acquired primarily by men having sex with men (46.7 percent), by use of infected needles (16.9 percent), and through heterosexual contact with those from a non-prevalent HIV region (17.6 percent) or prevalent HIV region (14.9 percent).

Beginning in emerging adulthood, rates of HIV diagnosis/people living with HIV begin to increase. Between 1985 and 2012, about 26 percent of positive HIV tests in Canada were for males under the age of 29 years, and about 37 percent were for females of that same age group (PHAC, 2012a).

It is important to note that the majority of positive HIV test reports are for those over the age of 30. In addition, since 2010, the AIDS epidemic has been slowing, largely because young people are protecting themselves against HIV (World Health Organization [WHO] UNAIDS, 2011). Protection includes fewer sex partners, later sex, more condom use, provision of sterile needles to intravenous drug users, and voluntary circumcision among young adult men (WHO UNAIDS, 2011).

Taking Risks

Remember that each developmental period brings gains and losses, and any specific age-related characteristic can be a blessing or a burden. One example is risk taking, with emerging adults particularly likely (bravely or foolishly) to take risks. In addition to age, risk taking is affected by gender, genes, hormones, and culture. Young North American males who are genetically impulsive are often remarkably brave and foolhardy.

BENEFITS AND LIABILITIES Societies, as well as individuals, benefit from this characteristic of emerging adults. Enrolling in college or university, moving to a new city or country, getting married, having a baby—all are risky. So is starting a business, becoming a firefighter, entering an athletic contest, enlisting in the army, and rescuing a stranger. Without emerging adults, all those activities would occur less often.

Yet risk taking is often destructive. Although their bodies are strong and their reactions quick, emerging adults have more accidents that send them to emergency rooms than do people of any other age (except for falls in the elderly). Because of their good overall health, usually they are stitched, casted, medicated, stabilized, and discharged in short order.

The low rate of serious disease between ages 18 and 25 is counterbalanced by a high rate of severe injuries and violent deaths, with males at least twice as vulnerable as females. (Sometimes the ratio is as high as 5:1, depending on which nation and which type of violent death is analyzed.) For both sexes, age is always a factor in suicide, self-destructive behaviours, homicide, and accidents. More people are murdered during emerging adulthood than at any other period. Many specific types of accidental death are also more frequent during these years, including drug overdose, motor vehicle crashes, and drowning. Among the destructive risks more common in emerging adulthood are

- unprotected sex with a new partner
- driving fast without a seat belt
- abusing drugs
- addictive gambling.

✦ **ESPECIALLY FOR Nurses** When should you discuss the possibility of an STI with a patient? (see response, page 400) ➜

People behave this way partly for the rush of adrenalin (Cosgrave, 2010). Ironically, warning emerging adults about the risks may lead to a backlash—some subsequently *increase* their risk taking in order to defy death and aging (Popham et al., 2011a).

RISKY SPORTS Many young adults seek the rush of risk taking in recreational activities. They climb mountains, swim in oceans, run in pain, play past exhaustion, and so on. Skydiving, bungee-jumping, pond-swooping, parkour, potholing (in caves), waterfall kayaking, and many more activities have been invented to satisfy the joy of risk. Serious injury is not the goal, of course, but high risk adds to the challenge (Brymer, 2010).

Competitive **extreme sports** (such as *freestyle motocross*—riding a motorcycle off a ramp, catching "big air," doing tricks while falling, and hoping to land upright) are thrilling for some emerging adults. They find golf, bowling, and so on too tame (Breivik, 2010). As one researcher concluded about dirt-bikers (off-road motorcyclists), particularly from ages 18 to 24 there may be a developmental lag between impulse control and cognitive evaluation of risk (Dwane, 2012). The thrill overwhelms reason.

This is clearer with an example. Travis Pastrana won the 2006 X Games MotoX Freestyle event at age 22 with a double backflip because, as he explained, "The two main things are that I've been healthy and able to train at my fullest, and a lot of guys have had major crashes this year" (Higgins, 2006, D7). Four years later, in 2010, he set a new record for leaping through big air in an automobile, driving over the ocean from a ramp on the California shore to a barge more than 76 metres out. He crashed into a barrier on the boat, emerging ecstatic and unhurt, to the thunderous cheers of thousands of other young adults (Roberts, 2010). In 2011, a broken foot and ankle made him temporarily halt extreme sports—but soon he was back risking his life to the acclaim of his cohort, winning races rife with flips and other hazards.

DRUG ABUSE The same impulse that is admired in extreme sports can lead to behaviours that are clearly destructive, not only for individuals but for the community. The most studied of these is drug abuse, which can involve dozens of substances—both legal and illegal (Maisto et al., 2011).

extreme sports
Forms of recreation that include apparent risk of injury or death and are attractive and thrilling as a result.

Travis Could Crash But he didn't. The possibility of death is what makes thousands watch Travis Pastrana perform his risky stunts, as here in Sydney, Australia.

Risks During Post-Secondary Education Alcohol and drug use can be a risky part of the college or university experience for emerging adults. Alcohol use during Spring Break in Florida is common, as shown in this photo. Drinking large quantities in a short time can be dangerous.

drug abuse
The ingestion of a drug to the extent that it impairs the user's biological or psychological well-being.

◆ **ESPECIALLY FOR Substance Abuse Counsellors** What three possible explanations can you think of for the more precipitous drop in the use of illegal drugs compared with legal ones? (see response, page 402) ➡

RESPONSE FOR Nurses (from page 398) Always. Maintain a professional, rather than judgmental, attitude, and be aware that education, gender, self-confidence, and income do not necessarily mean that a given patient is free of an STI. ●

By definition, **drug abuse** occurs whenever a person uses a drug that harms physical, cognitive, or psychosocial well-being. Occasional smoking can be abuse, as can alcohol bingeing or heavy drinking (5 or more drinks on one occasion). In 2011, a national survey found that 17.4 percent of Canadians aged 12 and over stated that they had engaged in binge drinking at least once a month for one year. Men generally reported higher rates than women, with the highest reports of heavy drinking coming between the ages of 18 to 34 (Statistics Canada, 2013d). Even one-time use can be abusive, if, for instance, it leads to driving while drunk, walking into traffic while hallucinating, being arrested for cocaine use, and so on.

More often, abusers are also addicts: They need the drug to feel okay, and they become chronic users. Drug addiction and abuse are more common during emerging adulthood than at any other age (Johnston et al., 2010). Part of the attraction of drugs for this age group is in their abuse, specifically in taking a drug to feel dizzy, out-of-body, or high. It adds to the thrill if authority figures disapprove. Buying, carrying, and using an illegal drug, knowing that arrest is possible, are all exciting. So is selling: Most street sellers of drugs are relatively young—they often quit, go to prison, or are killed before middle age. Illegal drug use peaks at about age 20 and declines sharply after that (see Figure 11.2).

Surprisingly, drug abuse is more common among college and university students than among their contemporaries who are not in post-secondary education. Alcohol abuse is rampant in colleges and universities, with 25 percent of young men and 5 percent of young women reporting that they consumed 10 or more drinks in a row at least once in the previous two weeks (Johnston et al., 2009). Such excesses arise from the same drive as extreme sports or other risks—with the same potential consequence: death.

FIGURE 11.2 Substance Abuse by Age As you can see, emerging adults are the biggest substance abusers, but illegal drug use drops much faster than cigarette use or binge drinking. This figure depicts drug use in one nation (the United States in 2008), but the same trends are universal.

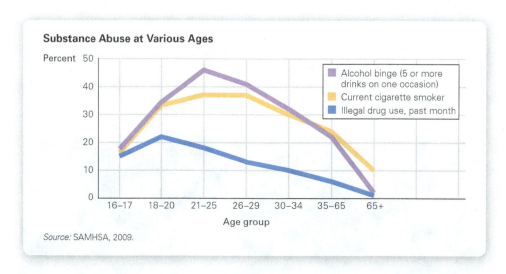

Source: SAMHSA, 2009.

KEY ℘oints

- Young adults are usually healthy and at peak reproductive potential.
- Many emerging adults use a form of contraception to avoid pregnancy.
- Sexually transmitted infections are more common among emerging adults.
- Emerging adults are risk takers, sometimes risking their life.
- Drug abuse and addiction are more common during emerging adulthood than in any other period.

Cognitive Development

As you remember, each of the four periods of child and adolescent development is characterized by major cognitive advances, each described by Piaget. Piaget believed that the fourth stage, *formal operational thought,* continued throughout life. However, some recent scholars contend that adult thought differs from adolescent thinking: It is more practical, more flexible, and better able to coordinate objective and subjective perspectives. This may constitute a major advance, combining a new ordering of formal operations with a necessary subjectivity (Sinnott, 1998).

Postformal Thought

Many developmentalists believe that Piaget's fourth stage, formal operational thought, is inadequate to describe adult cognition. Some have proposed a fifth stage, called **postformal thought,** characterized by "problem finding," not just "problem solving." At this stage a person is more open to ideas and less concerned with absolute right and wrong (Yan & Arlin, 1995).

As a group of scholars explained, in postformal thought "one can conceive of multiple logics, choices, or perceptions … in order to better understand the complexities and inherent biases in 'truth'" (Griffin et al., 2009, p. 173). That is more typical of adult thought than adolescent thought; hence the idea that a fifth stage exists.

COMBINING EMOTIONS AND LOGIC As you read in Chapter 9, adolescents use two modes of thought (dual processing, called by various names). They use formal analysis to learn science, distill principles, develop arguments, and resolve the world's problems; in the other mode, they think spontaneously and emotionally. However, they rarely coordinate both types of thinking and prefer the quick, impulsive, intuitive thought.

Postformal thinkers are less impulsive than adolescents. They do not wait for someone to present a problem to solve or for circumstances to require a reaction. They take a more flexible and comprehensive approach, using forethought, noting difficulties, and anticipating problems, not denying, avoiding, or procrastinating. As a result, postformal thought is more practical as well as more creative and imaginative than thinking in previous cognitive stages (Wu & Chiou, 2008).

postformal thought
A proposed adult stage of cognitive development, following Piaget's four stages. Postformal thought goes beyond adolescent thinking by being more practical, more flexible, and more dialectical (i.e., more capable of combining contradictory elements into a comprehensive whole).

✦ **ESPECIALLY FOR Someone Who Has to Make an Important Decision** Which is better: to go with your gut feelings or to consider pros and cons as objectively as you can? (see response, page 403) →

CRAIG GLOVER / THE LONDON FREE PRESS / QMI AGENCY

Crammed Together Students eat and study in cafeterias at Western University before final exams, making cramming a social experience. This is contrary to what scientific evidence has shown is the best way to learn— through *distributed practice,* which means studying consistently throughout the semester, not bunching it all at the end. Is cramming simply the result of poor time management or is it a rational choice?

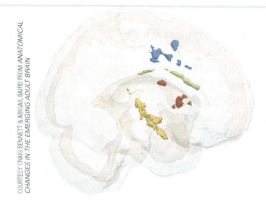

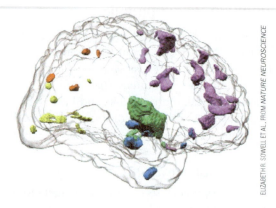

Thinking Away from Home Entering a residence at college or university means experiencing new foods, new friends, and new neurons. A longitudinal study of 18-year-old students at the beginning and end of their first year in a post-secondary institution found increases in the brain areas that integrate emotion and cognition—namely, the cingulate cortex *(blue and yellow),* caudate nucleus *(red),* and insula *(orange).* Researchers also studied one-year changes in the brains of students over age 25 at the same institution and found no dramatic growth.

More Purple Means More Planning Shown here are the areas of one person's brain changes from age 14 to age 25. The frontal cortex *(purple)* demonstrated many changes in particular parts, as did the areas for processing speech *(green and blue)*—a crucial aspect of young adult learning. Areas for visual processing *(yellow)* showed less change. Researchers now know that brains mature in many ways between adolescence and adulthood; scientists are not yet sure of the cognitive implications.

RESPONSE FOR Substance Abuse Counsellors (from page 400) Legal drugs could be more addictive, or the thrill of illegality may diminish with age, or the fear of arrest may increase. In any case, treatment for young-adult substance abusers may need to differ from that for older ones. ●

REALLY A STAGE? Piaget's notion that the final, and best, thinking is formal operational, achieved at adolescence, has come under especially heavy criticism, with some data finding that adults do not usually reach formal operations. As mentioned, others argue that formal operational thought does not adequately capture the level of adult cognition. Similarly, problems arise with postformal thought. Attempts to measure it empirically are not very successful: Many other variables in addition to intellectual maturation affect how adults think (Cartwright et al., 2009).

Some cognitive scientists, especially those who take an information-processing perspective, think that all stage theories of cognition are mistaken; others, especially those influenced by Vygotsky, think that formal and postformal thought are more affected by culture than by maturation. Certainly, if *stage* means reaching a new set of abilities (such as the verbal explosion that distinguishes sensorimotor from preoperational thought), then adulthood has no cognitive stages. Rather than a fifth stage, adult thinking is like adolescent thinking in many ways. For instance, the same two processes that were described in Chapter 9 (intuitive and analytic, or system 1 and system 2) are evident throughout adulthood (Kahneman, 2011).

Nonetheless, the prefrontal cortex is not fully mature until the early 20s, and new dendrites and even new neurons grow throughout adulthood. This neurological maturation enables adults to think in ways that adolescents do not. One lead researcher concludes that adult thinking can be ordered in terms of increasing levels of complexity and integration (Labouvie-Vief et al., 2009). For instance, research on people aged 13 to 45 found that logical skills improved from adolescence to emerging adulthood and then stayed steady, as might be expected, as analytic thought becomes established (Demetriou & Bakracevic, 2009).

That same study found that social understanding continued to advance beyond early adulthood (Demetriou & Bakracevic, 2009). Social understanding includes knowing how best to interact with other people: making and keeping good friends, responding to social slights, helping others effectively, and so on. It makes sense that social cognition continues to improve, since cohort changes, cultural variations, and genetic uniqueness combine to make this the most complex type of thought.

Another study found that college students who have friends from other backgrounds are more likely to think in postformal ways (Galupo et al., 2010). The researchers believe that having friends with varied cultural perspectives advances postformal thought. A third study found that students' concepts of God became more complex theologically when they were more capable of postformal thinking (Benovenli et al., 2011).

Overall, many scholars find that thinking changes both qualitatively and quantitatively during adulthood (Bosworth & Hertzog, 2009). The term *fifth stage* may be a misnomer, but emerging adults can, and often do, reach a new cognitive level when their brains and life circumstances allow it.

Countering Stereotypes

Most North Americans say that they are not prejudiced, and their behaviour reveals no bias—at least in explicit tests in a research laboratory; however, studies reveal implicit biases. For instance, one study that examined reaction times when viewing photos of African-Americans and European-Americans revealed an implicit bias against African-Americans (Baron & Banaji, 2006). Thus, many adults have both unconscious prejudice and conscious tolerance—a combination of emotion and reason that illustrates dual processing. Ideally, cognitive flexibility allows people to recognize their underlying emotional biases and then to change their behaviour to be in accord with their rational thought. This is difficult without the intellectual openness and flexibility that characterize emerging adults.

A notable example of implicit prejudice, and then the ability to overcome it, occurs with **stereotype threat,** first named by an African-American scholar who called it a "threat in the air" (Steele, 1997). Stereotype threat begins with the thought that other people hold unspoken prejudices against one's social group, and then that thought becomes a threat which produces anxiety. In reality, those other people may not hold those stereotypes (that's why the threat is "in the air"), but the mere possibility that they do undermines cognition (Inzlicht & Schmader, 2012). For example, if a person imagines that someone else (or even people in general) holds the stereotype that members of a particular group are stupid, lazy, oversexed, or somehow inferior because of ethnicity, sex, age, or appearance, then the mere awareness of the *possibility* of being stereotyped will make that person feel anxious. That anxiety hijacks cognition, disrupting memory, logic, and so on (Schmader, 2010).

Stereotype threat may interfere with emerging adults in many ways. For instance, if young people fear that leaving home will expose them to prejudice, they might not live in residence at college or university. That will limit their exposure to other opinions. Perhaps the most widely known example of stereotype threat is reduced performance by students on tests if they think that others expect them to do poorly. This finding has been replicated in laboratory studies, in real classrooms, and during standardized tests.

Stereotype threat does not only have negative effects on individuals but also can boost performance, in a stereotype boost. Shih and his colleagues (1999) reported that Asian-American women achieved higher test scores when their Asian identity was cued, but did worse when their gender identity was cued, as compared to a control group.

RESPONSE FOR Someone Who Has to Make an Important Decision (from page 401) Both are necessary. Mature thinking requires a combination of emotions and logic. Take your time (don't just act on your first impulse) and talk with people you trust. Ultimately, you will have to live with your decision, so do not ignore either intuitive or logical thought. ●

stereotype threat
The possibility that one's appearance or behaviour will be misread to confirm another person's oversimplified, prejudiced attitudes.

The Threat of Bias If students fear that others expect them to do poorly in school because of their ethnicity or gender, they might not identify with academic achievement and therefore do worse on exams than they otherwise would have.

A VIEW FROM SCIENCE

Undercutting Stereotype Threat

One statistic has troubled social scientists for decades: African-American men have lower grades in high school, drop out more often, and earn only half as many college degrees as their genetic peers, African-American women. And African-American women themselves do less well than women of other ethnic groups. This disparity has many possible causes, with most scientists blaming the current context and historical past discrimination (Arnett & Brody, 2008).

Claude Steele, the African-American man who first described stereotype threat, reasoned that when African-American males become aware of the stereotype that they are poor scholars, they become anxious. That anxiety reduces their ability and motivation to focus on schoolwork. Then, if they underachieve, they might dismiss academics to protect their pride, which leads to disengagement from studying and even lower achievement (Steele, 1997).

Hundreds of studies show that almost all humans can be harmed by stereotype threat: Women underperform in math, older people are more forgetful, bilingual students stumble while speaking English, and every member of a stigmatized minority in every nation performs less well if they think others are judging them unfairly.

Margaret Walsh and her colleagues from Memorial University in Newfoundland explored the influence of gender labelling (i.e., identifying whether a character was female, male, or gender neutral) and gender stereotype threat in mathematical problem solving among males and females (1999). For example, the problem-solving questions included different gender labels such as "Mr. Mason" or "Ms. Mason" or "the Masons," while the rest of the question was the same. In one experiment, middle-school children who were tested with male-labelled characters had higher scores than those who had questions that were either female-labelled or gender neutral. Moreover, students who had lower mathematical performance in class did best on questions with female-labelled characters, whereas those who were doing well in class did best on questions with male-labelled characters. This gender label influence is believed to reflect an emotional reaction to gender labelling (framing) that can either enhance or inhibit mathematical reasoning ability.

In another experiment, students wrote a version of the Standardized Achievement Test (SAT) that had been modified in terms of both gender labelling and gender stereotype threat. Gender labelling modifications to the questions did not account for gender differences in achievement. However, female students scored lower when they believed that the test had previously shown gender differences. There was no difference in achievement when women were told that the test was comparing Canadian and American students (Walsh et al., 1999).

Even those sometimes thought to be on top—white men—do less well in math if they think they will be negatively compared with Asian-American men (stereotyped as innately skilled in math), and they do less well in basketball if they think they will be compared with African-American men (again stereotyped as innately skilled) (Schmader et al., 2008). When athletes of any ethnicity unexpectedly underperform because of stress (called choking), stereotype threat may be the cause (Hill et al., 2010).

Can stereotype threat be eliminated, or at least reduced? One group of researchers developed a hypothesis that stereotype threat will decrease and academic achievement will increase for African-American college students if they *internalize* (believe wholeheartedly, not just intellectually) that intelligence is plastic, not the unchangeable product of genes and gender. Using a clever combination of written materials, mentoring, and video performing, these scientists convinced an experimental group of students at Stanford University that their ability and hence their achievement depended on their personal efforts. Some of the students were African-American, some were European-American.

The hypothesis: Convincing college students that intellectual ability could be improved by hard work (the incremental, not the entity, theory of intelligence described in Chapter 9) would encourage them to study and prevent choking under pressure (as when taking exams). The intervention succeeded for the African-Americans: They earned higher grades. The European-American students were not affected; apparently, stereotype threat had not impaired their achievement (Aronson et al., 2002).

This experiment has intrigued thousands of researchers. They realized that this study required replication, since the participants were only 79 students at a highly selective university. Might other stereotyped groups respond differently?

Soon this study was replicated with many other groups, often but not always targeting young adults. The results confirm, again and again, that stereotype threat is pervasive and debilitating, but that it can be alleviated (Inzlicht & Schmader, 2012; Mangels et al., 2012; Rydell & Boucher, 2010). It is activated especially when someone reminds a person of the stereotype (e.g., "This test will reveal whether women are inferior in math ability"), but it disappears if a person internalizes the notion that the stereotype is irrelevant (e.g., "My math ability depends only on me and is not affected by gender").

The Effects of College or University

A major reason that emerging adulthood has become a new period of development, when people postpone the usual markers of adult life (marriage, a steady job), is that many older adolescents seek education, choosing to postpone traditional adult responsibilities.

MASSIFICATION Tertiary (or post-secondary) education improves health and wealth. In Canada, completing a post-secondary program significantly increases earnings. For example, a trades or college graduate earns $7200 more than a high school graduate, and a university graduates earns $23 000 more (Employment and Social Development Canada, 2008). Similarly, U.S. census data indicate that a college degree adds about $20 000 per year to a worker's salary. This is averaged over a lifetime—often more apparent in middle age than right after university or college.

As mentioned above, university or college graduates are also healthier, living about 10 years longer than those without a high school diploma. An Organisation for Economic Co-operation and Development international study exploring health survey data from Australia, Canada, England, and Korea indicated a correlation between better education and lower rates of obesity. Each additional year of education was associated with a lower rate of obesity for men and women in Canada, Australia, England, and for women in Korea, particularly for tertiary education (Devaux et al., 2011).

To improve health and increase productivity, every nation has increased the number of students enrolled in college and university. This has led to **massification,** the idea that tertiary education could benefit everyone (the masses) (Altbach et al., 2010). The United States was the first major nation to accept that idea, establishing thousands of institutions of higher learning and boasting millions of college students by the middle of the twentieth century. The United States no longer leads in massification, however. More than half of all 25- to 29-year-olds in Canada, Korea, Russia, and Japan are university graduates. The United States ranks twelfth on that measure, with only one-third (32 percent) of U.S. 25- to 29-year-olds having at least a bachelor's degree (Aud et al., 2012; Montgomery & Williams, 2010; UNESCO, 2009).

Massification has expanded in Asia and Africa, where university and college enrolment has more than tripled in the past several decades (Altbach et al., 2010). Thirty years ago, many wealthy and capable students in developing nations travelled to the West to earn university and college degrees. Such students often returned to their home nations as professors, bringing new perspectives to their classrooms. A global shift is under way: Hundreds of new universities have opened in Asia, Africa, and the Middle East. Many undergraduates now remain in their own nations to continue their studies. As a result, there are far more university students in China and in India than in North America. Of course, the total population of those nations is larger than that of North America, but these numbers are part of a global trend.

✦ **ESPECIALLY FOR Those Considering Studying Abroad** Given the effects of college and university, would it be better for a student to study abroad in the first year or last year of post-secondary education? (see response, page 407) →

massification
The idea that establishing higher learning institutions and encouraging college and university enrolment could benefit everyone (the masses), leading to marked increases in the number of emerging adults in post-secondary institutions.

Education in Process These students, checking the Internet on the steps in San Miguel de Allende in Mexico, illustrate why some scholars claim that college and university students learn more from each other than from their professors.

JEREMY WOODHOUSE / AGE FOTOSTOCK

POST-SECONDARY EDUCATION AND COGNITION For developmentalists interested in cognition, the crucial question is not about the three issues already mentioned: wealth, health, and massification. Instead, the question is: "Does a college or university education advance critical thinking and postformal thought?" Past research finds that the answer is yes.

According to one classic study (Perry, 1981, 1999), thinking progresses through nine levels of complexity over the four years that lead to a bachelor's degree. A first-year student may think with simplistic dualism (right or wrong, yes or no, success or failure) and gradually progress to recognizing the validity of many perspectives (see Table 11.1). Other research has confirmed Perry's conclusions. In general, the more years of higher education a person pursues, the deeper and more postformal that person's reasoning becomes (Pascarella & Terenzini, 1991).

TABLE 11.1 Perry's Scheme of Cognitive and Ethical Development During College and University

First-Year Students	Position 1	Authorities know, and if we work hard, read every word, and learn right answers, all will be well.
Dualism modified	Transition	But what about those others I hear about? And different opinions? And uncertainties? Some of our own authorities disagree with each other or don't seem to know, and some give us problems instead of answers.
	Position 2	True authorities must be right; the others are frauds. We remain right. Others must be different and wrong. Good authorities give us problems so we can learn to find the right answer by our own independent thought.
	Transition	But even good authorities admit they don't know all the answers yet!
	Position 3	Then some uncertainties and different opinions are real and legitimate temporarily, even for authorities. They're working on them to get to the truth.
	Transition	But there are so many things they don't know the answers to! And they won't for a long time.
Relativism discovered	Position 4a	Where authorities don't know the right answers, everyone has a right to his or her own opinion; no one is wrong!
	Transition	Then what right have they to grade us? About what?
	Position 4b	In certain courses, authorities are not asking for the right answer. They want us to think about things in a certain way, supporting opinion with data. That's what they grade us on.
	Position 5	Then all thinking must be like this, even for them. Everything is relative but not equally valid. You have to understand how each context works. Theories are not truth but metaphors to interpret data with. You have to think about your thinking.
	Transition	But if everything is relative, am I relative, too? How can I know I'm making the right choice?
	Position 6	I see I'm going to have to make my own decisions in an uncertain world with no one to tell me I'm right.
	Transition	I'm lost if I don't. When I decide on my career (or marriage or values), everything will straighten out.
Commitments in relativism developed	Position 7	Well, I've made my first commitment!
	Transition	Why didn't that settle everything?
	Position 8	I've made several commitments. I've got to balance them—how many, how deep? How certain, how tentative?
	Transition	Things are getting contradictory. I can't make logical sense out of life's dilemmas.
Graduating Students	Position 9	This is how life will be. I must be wholehearted while tentative, fight for my values yet respect others, believe my deepest values are right yet be ready to learn. I see that I shall be retracing this whole journey over and over—but, I hope, more wisely.

Sources: Perry, 1981, 1999.

Which aspect of college or university is the primary catalyst for such growth? Is it the challenging academic work, the professors' lectures, the peer discussions, the new setting, or living away from home? All are possibilities. Perry found that the college or university experience itself causes this progression, as peers, professors, books, and class discussion stimulate new thoughts. Every scientist finds that social interaction and intellectual challenge advance thinking.

College and university students expect classes and conversations to further their intellectual depth—which is exactly what occurs (Kuh et al., 2005). This is not surprising, since colleges and universities were designed to foster intellectual growth.

Professors may also advance in their own thinking as they teach and learn, passing those advances on to their students. For example, one of the leading thinkers in postformal thought is Jan Sinnott, a professor and former editor of the *Journal of Adult Development*. She describes the first course she taught:

> I did not think in a postformal way. … Teaching was good for passing information from the informed to the uninformed. … I decided to create a course in the psychology of aging … with a fellow graduate student. Being compulsive graduate students had paid off in our careers so far, so my colleague and I continued on that path. Articles and books and photocopies began to take over my house. And having found all this information, we seem to have unconsciously sworn to use all of it. …
>
> Each class day, my colleague and I would arrive with reams of notes and articles and lecture, lecture, lecture. Rapidly! … The discussion of death and dying came close to the end of the term (naturally). As I gave my usual jam-packed lecture, the sound of note-taking was intense. But toward the end of the class … an extremely capable student burst into tears and said she had to drop the class. … Unknown to me, she had been the caretaker of an older relative who had just died in the past few days. She had not said anything about this significant experience when we lectured on caretaking. … How could she? … We never stopped talking. "I wish I could tell people what it's really like," she said.
>
> [Sinnott, 2008, pp. 54–55]

Sinnott changed her lesson plan. In the next class, the student told her story.

> In the end, the students agreed that this was a class when they … synthesized material and analyzed research and theory critically.
>
> [Sinnott, 2008, p. 56]

Sinnott still lectures and gives multiple-choice exams, but she also includes personal stories. She combines analysis and emotion; she includes the experiences of her students. Her teaching became postformal, flexible, and responsive.

CURRENT CONTEXTS You may have noticed that Perry's study was first published in 1981. Hundreds of other studies have also found that a college or university education deepens cognition, but most of that research also occurred in the twentieth century. Since cohort and culture are crucial, you may wonder if those conclusions still hold.

An impressive twenty-first-century longitudinal study of U.S. college students found that their growth in critical thinking, analysis, and communication over the four years of college was only half as much as it was among college students two decades earlier (Arum et al., 2011). The results of that study were published in a provocative book titled *Academically Adrift*. Among the findings is that 45 percent of college students made no significant advances at all in the first two years (Arum & Roksa, 2011). The reasons are many: Students study less, academic expectations are reduced, and fewer students enrol in classes that require reading 40 pages a week or writing 20 pages a semester. Administrators hope for intellectual growth, but rigorous classes are often cancelled or not required.

RESPONSE FOR Those Considering Studying Abroad (from page 405) Since one result of college or university is that students become more open to other perspectives while developing their commitment to their own values, foreign study might be most beneficial after several years of post-secondary education. If they study abroad too early, some students might be either too narrowly patriotic (they are not yet open) or too quick to reject everything about their national heritage (they have not yet developed their own commitments). •

OPPOSING PERSPECTIVES

What Is the Purpose of Post-Secondary Education?

Underlying the debate about standards and massification are opposite opinions about the purpose of higher education. Developmentalists, most professors, and many college and university graduates believe that personal and intellectual growth is the goal. However, others believe that acquiring specific skills and knowledge is more important. Many contemporary students seem to agree (see Figure 11.3).

In 2011/2012, 1 144 812 Canadian students were enrolled in university and 664 733 in college (Statistics Canada, 2012l). In 2011, 245 235 Canadian university students and 179 226 Canadian college students graduated (Statistics Canada, 2012m). Despite rising tuition fees, the proportion of Canadians aged 25 to 64 receiving a post-secondary certificate, diploma, or degree increased from 53 percent to 61 percent from 2001 to 2006 (Yuen, 2010).

Notably, although university enrolment has been steadily increasing over the years for most Canadians, for one segment of the population the increase has been much less. The Association of Universities and Colleges of Canada (AUCC) reports that the proportion of Aboriginal Canadians with a university degree is significantly lower than non-Aboriginal Canadians. For example, from 1981 to 2006, the Aboriginal university attainment rate went from 2 percent to 7.7 percent; by comparison, the rate increased from 8.1 percent to 23.4 percent for non-Aboriginals (AUCC, 2011).

AUCC (2011) reports that the increased number of students in higher education is a result of Canada's demand for a highly skilled and educated labour force—in other words, it is a requirement of future employment. About 60 to 80 percent of the jobs in business and finance, art, culture and recreation, health, engineering and applied sciences, social and legal professions, and teaching are filled by university graduates. Moreover, up to 40 percent of the people in management positions (not including food and retail management) have university degrees. In the last 20 years, there were 1.5 million new jobs for professional and management positions, of which 1.3 million were filled by university graduates.

Employers often want workers with advanced skills, specific knowledge, and practical experience with technology. Canadian colleges and universities have responded to these demands by modifying and creating new programs that meet the needs of the community and students. Universities have also enhanced their quality of education by integrating more interactive and engaging learning experiences, and more and more colleges and universities are collaborating to provide dual degree and certificate programs. These changes have

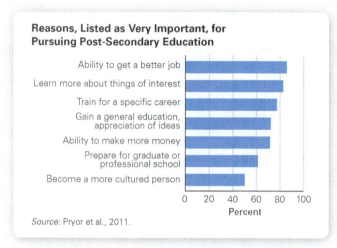

Reasons, Listed as Very Important, for Pursuing Post-Secondary Education

Source: Pryor et al., 2011.

FIGURE 11.3 Cohort Shift Students in 1980 thought new ideas and a philosophy of life were prime reasons to go to college or university—they were less interested in jobs, careers, and money than were students in 2011.

been shown to increase students' academic performance, knowledge acquisition, and skills development (AUCC, 2011).

Changes have also been seen in students' fields of study. In the early 1990s, enrolment shifted from arts and science majors to various professional and science-based majors. For example, from 1992 to 1997, enrolment decreased in liberal arts and sciences, the social sciences, English, and history, while the fields of computer science, biology and biomedical sciences, communication, and journalism experienced increased enrolment. The fastest enrolment growth between 2002 and 2007 was in physical sciences, health professions, and biology and biomedical sciences (see Figure 11.4).

Opposing views of the purpose of college and university are evident between present-day students ("Will that be on the test?") and faculty who were educated decades ago ("Better to thirst for knowledge than to know the answers"), and between current political leaders (who are concerned with students getting jobs) and traditional scholars (who are more focused on personal and intellectual growth). These issues are debated everywhere, even in nations that seem to regiment higher education. For instance, a new Chinese university (called South University of Science and Technology of China, SUSTC) is designed to encourage analysis and critical thinking, a deliberate contrast to the emphasis on knowledge and skills in other Chinese institutions.

SUSTC does not require prospective students to take the national exam (*Gao Kao*); instead, creativity and a passion for learning are the admission criteria (Stone, 2011). SUSTC faculty are supposed to nurture curiosity and evoke questions, not lecture. After waiting a year to see how the first group of students performed, the Chinese government accredited SUSTC in April 2012 (Huang, 2012).

Besides gaining employment, college and university graduates have higher income advantages, are less likely to face long periods of low income, and are less likely to experience labour disruptions. If they do face labour disruptions, the length of time is shorter than those with no degree. Graduates also help their co-workers—a "spill over" effect—by sharing their skills, knowledge, and expertise with less-educated workers.

As compared to high school graduates, students in and completing college and university are also more likely to have healthier and longer lives and to smoke and abuse drugs and alcohol less. They are more socially active in volunteering, more engaged in social and political activities, and more likely to share and promote educational, health, and social values to their children and their children's children (AUCC, 2011).

The question remains: Is the purpose of post-secondary education to learn skills or to advance postformal thought? Currently, students and the workforce seem to want a combination of both, and colleges and universities are trying to respond to that demand.

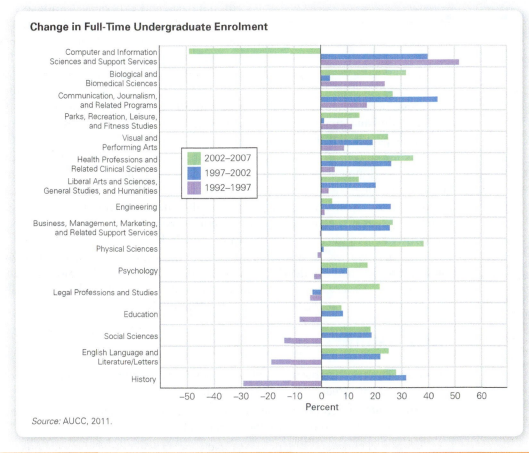

Change in Full-Time Undergraduate Enrolment

Legend:
- 2002–2007
- 1997–2002
- 1992–1997

Source: AUCC, 2011.

FIGURE 11.4 Shifting Demand in Canada As this graph clearly shows, student demand for certain university courses and programs has changed over time. What selection criterion did you use in choosing your own course of study: intellectual growth or skills acquisition?

THE EFFECTS OF DIVERSITY At least one characteristic of the twenty-first-century university scene bodes well for cognitive growth—the diversity of the student body. People learn when they interact with others who disagree with them. Those who are most likely to be postformal thinkers are also those with the most friends from other backgrounds (Galupo et al., 2010).

The most obvious increased diversity is gender: In 1970, two-thirds of college and university students were male; now in every developed nation (except Germany), more than half (56.5 percent in Canada) are female. Moreover, majors that were traditionally male (math, physics) now include many women. That means almost every college and university student hears academic insights and opinions from the other sex.

✦ **ESPECIALLY FOR High School Teachers** One of your brightest students doesn't want to go to college or university. She would rather keep serving in a restaurant, where she makes good money in tips. What do you say? (see response, page 410) →

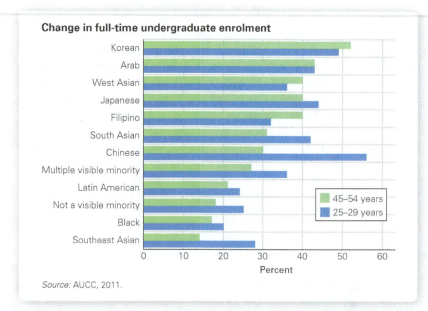

Change in full-time undergraduate enrolment

Source: AUCC, 2011.

FIGURE 11.5 Where Are They Coming From? In 2008, students from 200 foreign countries were registered in Canadian universities. China has been the top source for foreign students since 2001, and in 2008 France overtook the United States as the second most common source. Other main sources included India and South Korea.

RESPONSE FOR High School Teachers (from page 409) Even more than ability, motivation is crucial for post-secondary success, so don't insist that she attend college or university immediately. Since your student has money and a steady job (prime goals for today's college- or university-bound youth), she may not realize what she would be missing. Ask her what she hopes for, in work and lifestyle, in the decades ahead. ●

Ethnic, economic, religious, and cultural diversity are also evident. Although in Canada and the United States the modal students are mostly still European-Canadian/American, aged 18 to 22, attending full-time, the trend for the past 50 years has been toward more students who are non-European and older than 24, and who attend part-time. In fact, in Canada, visible minorities are much more likely to have completed a university degree than non-visible minorities (AUCC, 2011) (see Figure 11.5).

Discussion among people of different backgrounds, ages, and experiences leads to intellectual challenge and deeper thought. Thus, the increased diversity of the student body may enhance learning (Bowman, 2011; Loes et al., 2012). Colleges and universities that make use of their diversity—via curriculum, class assignments, discussions, cooperative education, learning communities, and so on—help students stretch their understanding, not only of differences and similarities among people, but also of themselves.

Attending university or college does not automatically produce a leap ahead in cognitive development or in appreciation of differing political, social, and religious views. Skeptical readers might question the data that link university and college graduation to wealthier, wiser, and happier adults. Such skepticism is warranted since correlation does not equal causation: Student characteristics before college or university may be a third variable that explains these links.

However, when selection is taken into account, college and university attendance still seems to aid cognitive development (Pascarella, 2005). Even the critics agree that some students at every institution advance markedly in critical thinking and analysis because of their post-secondary experience (Arum & Roksa, 2011).

KEY Points

- Adult cognition has been described as postformal, a fifth stage, although not every scholar agrees with that description.
- As the prefrontal cortex matures, thinking in adulthood becomes more flexible, and better able to combine emotions and analysis.
- College and university attendance is rapidly increasing in developing nations, as it is apparent that tertiary education improves health, productivity, and income.
- College and university education advances thought, not only through academic work, but also via the diversity of the student body.

Psychosocial Development

A theme of human development is that continuity and change are evident throughout a lifetime. In emerging adulthood, the legacy of early development is apparent amidst new achievement. As you remember, Erikson recognized this ongoing process in describing the fifth of his eight stages, *identity versus role confusion*. The identity crisis begins in adolescence, but it is not usually resolved then.

Identity Achieved

Erikson believed that the outcome of earlier crises provides the foundation for each new stage. He associated each stage with a particular virtue and type of psychopathology, as shown in Table 11.2. He also thought that earlier crises could re-emerge, taking a specific form at each stage. The identity crisis is an example.

Worldwide, adults ponder all five arenas of identity—religious, sex/gender roles, political, ethnic, and vocational—trying to reconcile plans for the future with beliefs acquired in the past. Their new cognitive abilities, combining emotional and rational thinking, aid in identity integration and achievement. Now we will focus specifically on ethnicity and vocation, two identities that were described in Chapter 10 but that are especially significant in emerging adulthood.

ETHNIC IDENTITY Identity development, especially the development of ethnic and racial identity, now continues long past adolescence (Whitbourne et al., 2009). This extended search is often the result of new challenges that emerging adults face.

The most basic challenge is how to identify oneself amidst a multi-ethnic society. In Canada, just over one-quarter of 15- to 24-year-olds are of Aboriginal, African, Caribbean, Arabic, Asian, or Latino heritage (Statistics Canada, 2006). Many of them identify as Canadians but also as something else, as they have parents or earlier ancestors who come from different ethnic backgrounds.

Whether one's heritage is mixed or not or considered minority or not, ethnicity is a significant aspect of a person's identity (Phinney, 2006). During late adolescence and early adulthood, people are more likely to be proud, or at least accepting, of their ethnic background than younger adolescents are (Worrell, 2008).

More than any other age group, as they leave their childhood homes to enrol in colleges or universities or to find work, emerging adults have friends and acquaintances of many backgrounds. Typically, they have both positive and negative experiences related to their ethnic background, developing a strong sense of ethnic identity—true for college and university students of every group (Syed & Azmitia, 2010).

It may be a mistake if emerging adults either assimilate (accepting the host culture, rejecting their native heritage) or become alienated (isolated and antagonistic). Those who resist both assimilation

Just Like Me Emerging adults of every ethnicity take pride in their culture. In Japan, adulthood begins with a celebration at age 20, to the evident joy of these young women on Coming of Age Day, a national holiday.

ISSEI KATO / REUTERS

TABLE 11.2 Erikson's Eight Stages of Development

Stage	Virtue/Pathology	Possible in Emerging Adulthood If Not Successfully Resolved
Trust vs. mistrust	Hope/withdrawal	Suspicious of others, making close relationships difficult
Autonomy vs. shame and doubt	Will/compulsion	Obsessively driven, single-minded, not socially responsive
Initiative vs. guilt	Purpose/inhibition	Fearful, regretful (e.g., very homesick in college or university)
Industry vs. inferiority	Competence/inertia	Self-critical of any endeavour, procrastinating, perfectionistic
Identity vs. role diffusion	Fidelity/repudiation	Uncertain and negative about values, lifestyle, friendships
Intimacy vs. isolation	Love/exclusivity	Anxious about close relationships, jealous, lonely
Generativity vs. stagnation	Care/rejection	[In the future] Fear of failure
Integrity vs. despair	Wisdom/disdain	[In the future] No "mindfulness," no life plan

Source: Erikson, 1982.

and alienation fare best: They are most likely to maintain their ethnic identity, deflect stereotype threat, and become good students (Rivas–Drake & Mooney, 2009).

University or college classes, especially in history, ethnic studies, and sociology, attract many emerging adults who want to learn more about their culture. In addition, extracurricular groups help solidify identity because students encounter others of similar backgrounds who confront the same issues, as well as youth of other backgrounds as they join teams, political committees, special interest groups, and so on.

VOCATIONAL IDENTITY Establishing a vocational identity is considered part of growing up, not only by developmental psychologists, but also by emerging adults themselves (Arnett, 2004). As already noted, many young adults go to college or university to prepare for work. Emerging adulthood is a critical time for the acquisition of resources—including the education, skills, and experience needed for career and family success (Tanner et al., 2009).

Preparation for lifetime work may include taking temporary jobs. Between ages 18 and 27, the average U.S. worker holds eight jobs, with college-educated workers changing jobs more often than those who are less educated (U.S. Bureau of the Census, 2011). This illustrates the exploration that is part of the identity search. Another way to explore is to take vocational aptitude tests, or a variety of courses, or to use Holland's six categories (first mentioned in Chapter 9) to figure out how one's personal preferences mesh with a considered vocation (Holland, 1997) (see Figure 11.6).

None of this is guaranteed to make vocational choice easy. For most emerging adults, "the process of identifying with society's work ethic, the core of this issue

FIGURE 11.6 Happy at Work John Holland's six-part diagram is used to help jobseekers realize that income and benefits are not the only goals of employment. Workers have healthier hearts and minds if their job fits their personal preferences.

OBSERVATION QUIZ
Based on Holland's diagram in Figure 11.6, which category do you best fit in? Is this category consistent with your major/area of study? (see answer, page 414) ➡

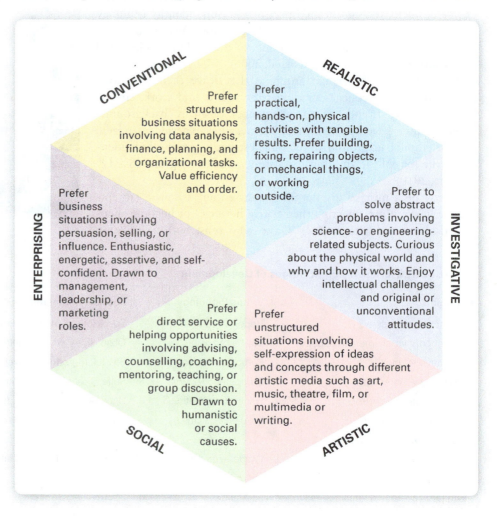

- **CONVENTIONAL** Prefer structured business situations involving data analysis, finance, planning, and organizational tasks. Value efficiency and order.
- **REALISTIC** Prefer practical, hands-on, physical activities with tangible results. Prefer building, fixing, repairing objects, or mechanical things, or working outside.
- **INVESTIGATIVE** Prefer to solve abstract problems involving science- or engineering-related subjects. Curious about the physical world and why and how it works. Enjoy intellectual challenges and original or unconventional attitudes.
- **ARTISTIC** Prefer unstructured situations involving self-expression of ideas and concepts through different artistic media such as art, music, theatre, film, or multimedia or writing.
- **SOCIAL** Prefer direct service or helping opportunities involving advising, counselling, coaching, mentoring, teaching, or group discussion. Drawn to humanistic or social causes.
- **ENTERPRISING** Prefer business situations involving persuasion, selling, or influence. Enthusiastic, energetic, assertive, and self-confident. Drawn to management, leadership, or marketing roles.

[identity achievement] in Erikson's scheme, continues to evolve throughout early adulthood" (Whitbourne et al., 2009, p. 1329). The young worker is not yet climbing, rung-by-rung, a chosen career ladder.

Many developmentalists wonder whether achieving a single vocational identity is still possible and desirable. Especially for young people, hiring and firing sometimes seems disconnected from education, skills, or aspirations. Commitment to a particular career may limit rather than increase vocational success.

Flexibility seems especially needed for the current generation. Sébastien LaRochelle-Côté, labour statistician from Statistics Canada, reported that young people tend to experience difficulty in finding employment in the aftermath of recessions. They are also at a higher risk for job losses than older people are (LaRochelle-Côté & Gilmore, 2009; Fong, 2012). For example, in 2009, about 5.2 million Canadians between the ages of 18 to 31 experienced employment instability (LaRochelle-Côté, 2013). According to LaRochelle-Cote (2013) some of the reasons for their instability included

● being employed in temporary jobs (part-time or full-time) (56 percent)

● working in a permanent job but in a part-time capacity (26 percent)

● being unemployed, out of the labour force, and not attending school (19 percent).

Recent recessions have affected a disproportionate number of younger workers in terms of job loss. In 2012, the unemployment rate of youths aged 15 to 24 was 14.3 percent compared with a rate of 6 percent for workers aged 25 to 54 and for those 55 and older (Bernard, 2013).

Personality in Emerging Adulthood

Continuity and change are evident in personality as well as identity (McAdams & Olson, 2010). Of course, the genetic roots of temperament and the early childhood influences on personality endure. If self-doubt, anxiety, depression, and so on are present in childhood and adolescence, they are often still evident years later. Traits present at age 5 or 15 do not disappear by age 25.

Yet personality is not static. After adolescence, new characteristics may appear and negative traits diminish. Emerging adults make choices that break with the past. This age period is now characterized by years of freedom from a settled lifestyle, which allows shifts in attitude and personality.

A crucial factor found in many studies is whether the person thrives in high school and college or university. This is affected *by* personality, but also *affects* personality (Klimstra et al., 2012). In other words, college or university success can improve personality.

Same Situation, Far Apart: Connecting with Their Generation Neither of these young women considers her job a vocation, but both are gaining useful skills and knowledge. The DJ *(left)* mixes music for emerging adults who crowd thousands of clubs in China to drink, dance, and socialize; the Apple Store employee *(right)* works to meet the booming young-adult demand for the latest and greatest in technology.

INCREASING HAPPINESS Psychological research finds both continuity and improvement in attitudes. For example, one longitudinal study found that 17-year-olds who saw life in positive terms maintained their outlook as time went on, while those who were negative often changed for the better (Blonigen et al., 2008). Another longitudinal study of 3912 U.S. students indicated that those who lived away from home showed the largest gains in well-being, but all were happier than they had been in high school (Schulenberg et al., 2005).

This positive trend of increasing happiness has become more evident over recent decades, perhaps because young adults are more likely to make their own life decisions (Twenge et al., 2008). Logically, one might expect that the many stresses and transitions of emerging adulthood would reduce self-esteem, but that is not what the research finds. For instance, a team of researchers followed 404 young adults in western Canada, repeatedly surveying them from ages 18 to 25. These emerging adults reported increasing self-esteem over time (Galambos et al., 2006). Although psychopathology may also increase during these years, most emerging adults do not develop serious disorders (Twenge et al., 2010). Instead, most enjoy their new maturity and independence.

ANSWER TO **OBSERVATION QUIZ** (from page 412) The category that you fit in will depend on how you define your identity. This will include taking future job opportunities, interests, skills, and experience into account. ●

WORRISOME CHILDREN GROW UP The research just cited about rising self-esteem came from several studies of North American youth. However, similar conclusions can be drawn from a European longitudinal study that began with 4-year-olds who were high in one or the other of two traits known to have strong genetic roots: shyness and aggression. These 38 children were extremely shy or aggressive at age 4 and continued to exhibit those undesirable traits throughout childhood. This is not surprising because the same genetic, familial, and cultural influences that were present at age 4 were present every later year (Asendorpf et al., 2008).

By early adulthood, those early traits were still evident, but neither was as extreme nor debilitating as earlier. Continuity could be seen, especially for those who had been aggressive 4-year-olds. At age 25, they had more conflicts with their parents and friends. They were more likely to have quit school—two-thirds had dropped out of high school, compared with one-third of their non-aggressive peers. By age 23, half had been arrested at least once, another sign of their aggressive temperament.

Yet, unexpectedly, these aggressive emerging adults had as many friends as their average peers did. They sought more education and rated themselves as quite conscientious. Their arrests were usually adolescent-limited, for minor offences: Only one had been sent to prison, and only one other had been arrested several times.

A closer examination of their school records found that behaviour, not ability, caused their childhood teachers to fail them. That proved harmful; many had to repeat grades. In high school, they were older than their classmates, often rebelled against restrictions and assumptions, and ultimately quit. But they still enjoyed learning and were intellectually capable.

That explained some seemingly surprising outcomes: As emerging adults, most of the formerly aggressive children were developing well, with social and vocational lives that were normal for their cohort. Many had put their childhood problems behind them; some were employed and others had enrolled in college or university.

As for those formerly shy 4-year-olds, outcomes were good. Evidence of their earlier temperament was that they were cautious, reserved adults. For example, they were slower than average to secure a job, choose a career, or find a romance. However, there were few signs of internalizing problems (Asendorpf et al., 2008). The participants were neither more anxious nor more depressed than their peers, and their self-esteem was similar. They had many friends and saw them often. Their delayed employment and later partnership were in keeping with the patterns of successful emerging adults. The shyness that was considered a handicap in childhood had become an asset in adulthood.

SERIOUS PSYCHOLOGICAL DISORDERS The general trends toward better health and rising self-esteem do not mean that every emerging adult is healthy and happy, however. Indeed, the rate of emotional disorders also rises toward the end of adolescence and in the first years of adulthood (Kessler et al., 2007).

The most troubling increase is in *schizophrenia,* rare before the mid-teens but showing a peak of new cases diagnosed at about age 21. Men are more likely to develop this disorder than women. Schizophrenia is certainly partly genetic and biochemical, but both physiological maturation and psychological stresses cause this increase in diagnosis in emerging adulthood.

A combination of medical and psychological interventions can reduce the impairment, but consequences of the disorder may remain throughout life. Those who are not diagnosed with schizophrenia but who have schizoid symptoms—such as distorted thinking, lack of energy, and flat affect (i.e., not particularly happy or sad at various experiences)—are at higher risk of later psychological disorders (Rössler et al., 2011). After age 30, however, few people are newly diagnosed with this disorder: Emerging adulthood is the usual time when symptoms become overpowering.

Severe *anxiety* and *depression* are not unusual during adolescence and emerging adulthood, especially for young women. The anxiety that is particularly likely to be diagnosed at about age 20 is social phobia, the fear of other people. Without treatment, anxiety and depression restrict an emerging adult's later development, as they make it much more difficult to succeed in college or university or to find a mate.

Many believe that ongoing psychological vulnerability, combined with the need to establish one's own identity apart from the family, is the reason why many mental illnesses become more pronounced in adolescence and emerging adulthood (O'Neil et al., 2011), though there are certainly biological causes as well (Trudeau et al., 2012). Family communication and guidelines during adolescence can reduce the rate of these internalizing disorders. As a result of their more positive mental health, individuals will be less likely to drop out of school and more likely to have higher attainment levels, which in turn can lead to higher income. On the other hand, mental illness is linked to an increased risk of certain physical health problems, such as chronic respiratory conditions and heart disease (Canadian Mental Health Association (Ontario), 2009; Himelhoch et al., 2004; McIntyre et al., 2006).

It is important to acknowledge that mental health and mental illness are not the opposite of each other; when mental health increases, mental illness does not necessarily decrease (Keyes, 2007). Instead, individuals who believe they have a purpose in life, good relations with others, experience personal growth, feel a sense of belonging, and can contribute to society have positive mental health. This will provide individuals with meaningful and productive lives, regardless of whether they have mental illness or mental health problems (Keyes, 2007; Pape & Galipeault, 2002).

PLASTICITY In the research just discussed as well as in other research, plasticity is evident. Personality is not fixed by age 5, or 15, or 20, as it was once thought to be. Emerging adults are open to experiences (a reflection of their adventuresome spirit), which allows personality shifts and eagerness for more education (McAdams & Olson, 2010; Tanner et al., 2009). The trend is toward less depression and more joy, along with more insight into the self (Galambos et al., 2006; McAdams et al., 2006).

Going to college or university, leaving home, paying one's way, stopping drug abuse, moving to a new city, finding satisfying work and performing it well, making new friends, committing to a partner—each of these might alter a person's life course. Each of these is more common from ages 18 to 25 than at any other time of life. The feeling of self-efficacy builds with each successful accomplishment, giving people the confidence and courage to modify whatever destructive traits they may have.

Total transformation does not occur since genes, childhood experiences, and family circumstances affect people all their lives. Nor do new experiences always result in desirable changes. Cohort may be important: Perhaps rising self-esteem as reported in longitudinal research reflects historical conditions at the end of the twentieth century. Perhaps the current economic downturn may soon cause the self-esteem of the average emerging adult to fall. But there is no doubt that personality *can* shift after adolescence.

Increased well-being and maturation may explain another shift: Emerging adults seem to become less self-centred and more caring of others (Eisenberg et al., 2005; Padilla-Walker et al., 2008). This can be seen as the foundation of the next psychosocial stage of development.

Intimacy

intimacy versus isolation
The sixth of Erikson's eight stages of development. Adults seek someone with whom to share their lives in an enduring and self-sacrificing commitment. Without such commitment they risk profound loneliness and isolation.

In Erikson's theory, after achieving identity, people experience the sixth developmental crisis, **intimacy versus isolation.** This crisis arises from the powerful desire to share one's personal life with someone else. Without intimacy, adults are lonely and isolated. Erikson explains:

> The young adult, emerging from the search for and the insistence on identity, is eager and willing to fuse his identity with others. He is ready for intimacy, that is, the capacity to commit himself to concrete affiliations and partnerships and to develop the ethical strength to abide by such commitments, even though they call for significant sacrifices and compromises.
>
> *[Erikson, 1963, p. 263]*

The urge for social connection is a powerful human impulse, one reason our species has thrived. Other theorists use different words (*affiliation, affection, interdependence, communion, belonging, bonding, love*) for the same human need.

There is no doubt that all adults seek friends, lovers, companions, and partners. Having close friends in early adulthood correlates with close relationships earlier in life and helps in other aspects of current life—including the ability to do well in college or university (Pettit et al., 2011).

All intimate relationships (friendship, family ties, and romance) have much in common—both in the psychic needs they satisfy and in the behaviours they require (Reis & Collins, 2004). Intimacy progresses from attraction to close connection to ongoing commitment. Each relationship demands some personal sacrifice, including vulnerability that brings deeper self-understanding and shatters the isolation caused by too much self-protection. As Erikson explains, to establish intimacy, the emerging adult must

> face the fear of ego loss in situations which call for self-abandon: in the solidarity of close affiliations [and] sexual unions, in close friendship and in physical combat, in experiences of inspiration by teachers and of intuition from the recesses of the self. The avoidance of such experiences ... may lead to a deep sense of isolation and consequent self-absorption.
>
> *[Erikson, 1963, pp. 163–164]*

According to a more recent theory, an important aspect of close human connections is "self-expansion," the idea that each of us enlarges our understanding, our experiences, and our resources through our intimate friends and lovers (Aron et al., 2005). Without that, we are not only lonely, we are also likely to get sick, feel tired, and eat and drink too much (Cacioppo & Cacioppo, 2012; Miller, 2011).

Contemporary emerging adults often gain friends as they transition from their childhood family and move away from their neighbourhood to their adult community. This leads to wider social networks and expanded understanding, one reason for the adult cognition explained earlier. Intimacy needs remain; the way they are satisfied differs. A specific example is the use of social networking, texting, email, video chatting, and so on. Although older adults once thought that technology would lead to social isolation, the opposite seems more likely: Most emerging adults connect often with many friends, face to face and online. The result is emotional health and well-being. As one study concludes, social networking sites help youth maintain psychosocial connections with their peers in a mobile world (Manago et al., 2012).

ROMANTIC PARTNERS Love, romance, and commitment are all of primary importance for emerging adults, although many specifics have changed. One dramatic change in Canada is that most people in their 20s are not married: The proportion of adults who are single, as well as the average age of marriage, have been rising for the past 30 years. For women in Canada, the average age at first marriage has increased from 22.5 years in 1972 to 29.1 years in 2008. For Canadian men over the same period, the average age went up from 24.9 years to 31.1 years (Employment and Social Development Canada, n.d.[c]). Most emerging adults are postponing, not abandoning, marriage.

Observers note two new sexual interaction patterns. One is "hooking up" (when two people have sex without any interpersonal relationship), and the other is "friends with benefits" (when two people are friends, sometimes having sex, but not in a dating relationship). Sometimes casual sex is a step toward a more serious relationship. As one U.S. sociologist explains, "despite the culture of divorce, Americans remain optimistic about, and even eager to enter, marriages" (Hill, 2007, p. 295).

The relationship between love and marriage is obviously not only a personal one. It reflects era and culture, with three distinct patterns evident (Georgas et al., 2006):

1. In about one-third of the world's families, love does not bring about marriage; parents do. They arrange marriages that will join two families together.

2. In another one-third of families, adolescents meet only a select group, for example, people of the same ethnicity, religion, or social class. If they decide to marry someone from that pre-selected group, the man asks the woman's father for "her hand in marriage." For these couples, parents supervise premarital interactions, usually bestowing their blessing. That was a traditional pattern: If parents did not approve, young people parted sorrowfully or eloped.

3. The final pattern is relatively new, although it is the dominant one in developed nations today. Young people socialize with hundreds of other young people, mostly unknown to their parents. They sometimes hook up, they sometimes develop serious relationships, but they often do not marry until they are able, financially and emotionally, to be independent.

Suggesting "one-third" for each of these patterns is a rough approximation. In former times, most marriages were of the first type; young people almost never met anyone unknown to their parents or thought of marrying without advance approval (Apostolou, 2007). Currently, in developing nations, practice often blends the first two types. For example, most brides in modern India believe they have a choice, but many meet their future husbands shortly before the wedding via parental arrangement. The young man or woman can veto the match, but they rarely do so (Desai & Andrist, 2010).

Parents are peripheral for the last one-third. A young person's choices tilt toward personal qualities observable at the moment—physical appearance, personal hygiene, personality, sexuality, a sense of humour—and not to qualities more important to parents, such as religion, ethnicity, or long-term stability.

For Western emerging adults, love is considered a prerequisite for marriage. Once love has led to commitment, sexual exclusiveness is expected. A survey asked 14 121 adults of many ethnic groups and sexual orientations to rate (on a scale from 1 to 10, 10 being the highest) how important money, race, commitment, love, and faithfulness

Much in Common Emerging adults seek partners who are like them. These two Canadians, Josh and Hui, are of Chinese ancestry. They share an understanding of cultural expectations, including food preferences, jokes, and sayings.

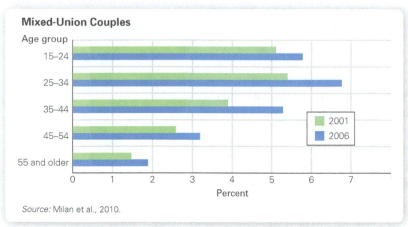

Mixed-Union Couples

Source: Milan et al., 2010.

FIGURE 11.7 Mixing It Up This chart clearly shows the development of two recent trends in Canada: The number of mixed-union couples is on the rise, and mixed unions are more common among young adults than any other age group. As immigration rates continue to go up, will these trends continue or change?

were for a successful marriage or a serious long-term relationship (Meier et al., 2009). Faithfulness was the most important of all (rated 10 by 89 percent) and love was almost as high (rated 10 by 86 percent). By contrast, most thought being the same race did not matter much (57 percent rated it very low, at 1, 2, or 3). Money, while important to many, was not nearly as crucial as love and fidelity.

This survey was conducted in North America, but emerging adults worldwide now share similar values. For instance, emerging adults in Kenya also reported that love was the prime reason for sex and marriage; money was less important (S. Clark et al., 2010). The international question is whether love precedes marriage, as most Westerners believe, or follows it, as was expected in the past.

LOVE AND ETHNICITY In 2006, 3.9 percent of all married and common-law couples in Canada were in mixed unions, that is, the partners were from different ethnocultural backgrounds. This marked a 33 percent increase in mixed-union couples from 2001, an increase due at least in part to the influx of immigrants over the same period.

As you can see in Figure 11.7, mixed-union couples were most common among young adults (aged 25 to 34) and then among 15- to 24-year-olds. Japanese-Canadians had the highest rate of mixed-union marriages, at 74 percent, and Chinese-Canadians were among the lowest at 17.4 percent (Milan et al., 2010). Mixed-union couples are also common in the United States, where 15 percent of all marriages were officially counted as inter-ethnic (Passel et al., 2010).

When it comes to romance, ethnicity may be a bond. The reasons for romances within groups involve not rejection of other groups so much as bonding with co-ethnics over matters of daily life—habits of speech, food preferences, jokes, and so on. People in inter-ethnic marriages bond for other reasons, for instance, because of political, religious, or economic values, which overcome their ethnic differences.

Thus, emerging adults usually choose mates like themselves. That is particularly true for South Asians and Chinese living in Canada (Milan et al., 2010). These two groups are the largest visible minority groups in Canada. As a result, these populations may have a higher likelihood of meeting with and interacting with people within the same group.

FINDING EACH OTHER As already explained, the traditional way to find marriage partners was through the parents, or within a very narrow social circle. But many of today's emerging adults range far from home and would resist any parental matchmaking. Instead, they must find partners among many thousands of possible mates— not an unmixed blessing.

Many websites now allow people to post their photos and personal information on the Internet, sharing the details of their daily lives and romantic involvement with thousands of others. This seems to be a wonderful innovation, as "the potential to reach out to nearly 2 billion other people offers several opportunities to the relationship-seeker that are unprecedented in human history" (Finkel et al., 2012, p. 4). Most emerging adults use such social networks, some of which pre-select potential mates (by religion, age, education, orientation, hobbies, and so on).

One potential problem with this is **choice overload,** when too many options are available. Choice overload increases doubts after a selection is made (people wonder if another choice would have been better). Some people, feeling overloaded, freeze; they are unable to choose (Iyengar & Lepper, 2000; Reutskaja & Hogarth, 2009). Having many complex options, such as partner selection, each requiring assessment of future advantages and disadvantages, makes choice overload likely (Scheibehenne et al., 2010). Successful matches require face-to-face interactions over time to discern compatibility, as was the case for couples before the Internet (Finkel et al., 2012).

It is logical that too many choices make marriage commitment difficult, but choice overload studies have not focused scientifically on mate selection. Instead, research has compared having a few choices or many when choosing jams, or cars, or apartments. It is possible that similar doubts might emerge if a person has too many possible mates, but more research needs to be done.

We already know one problem is that having too many choices slows down analysis. If people feel rushed, they are more likely to regret their choice later on (Inbar et al., 2011). This might be why couples slow down the selection process by postponing marriage and living together instead.

LIVING TOGETHER A new form of mating for contemporary emerging adults is **cohabitation,** living together in a romantic partnership without being married. Marked national differences are apparent in acceptance and timing of cohabitation.

Currently, most emerging adults in Canada, the United States, northern Europe, England, and Australia live unmarried with a partner for at least a few months. Some think of their living together as a prelude to marriage, others as a test of compatibility, and still others as a way to have an intimate relationship while saving money. By contrast, in some regions—Sweden, France, Jamaica, and Puerto Rico among them—cohabitation is more often a substitute for, not merely a prelude to, marriage. In still other nations—including Japan, Ireland, and Italy—cohabitation is not the norm, neither as a prelude nor as an enduring state; in those areas, cohabitation is unusual.

choice overload
Having so many options that a thoughtful choice becomes difficult, and regret after making a choice is more likely.

cohabitation
An arrangement in which two people live together in a committed romantic relationship but are not formally married.

Cohabitation Toronto FC (Major League Soccer) player Danny Koevermans and his common-law wife Marijke are raising their two daughters together. Cohabitating couples are increasingly common in North America and in other countries around the world. Here, they enjoy family time on the boardwalk in Toronto.

VINCE TALOTTA / TORONTO STAR VIA GETTY IMAGES

In Canada in 2006, common-law couples made up 18.4 percent of all couples in the country. However, in Quebec, the cohabitation rate was much higher, at 34.6 percent. Not only was the Quebec rate higher than in any other Canadian province or territory, but it also far exceeded rates in many other countries, including Sweden, Finland, and New Zealand, where cohabitation is widely practised (see Table 11.3). Why is this so? According to a Statistics Canada report from 2007, the main reason may be historical:

> The popularity of common-law unions in Quebec is rooted in the Quiet Revolution. Throughout the 1960s and 1970s, a new "mode de vie" emerged in Quebec which reflected a declining influence of the Catholic church on family life. At the same time, greater access to contraception, the women's movement, and more liberal divorce laws contributed to the decline in marriage and the growth of common-law unions in Quebec.
>
> [Milan et al., 2007]

Research from 27 nations finds that acceptance of cohabitation within the nation affects the happiness of those who cohabit. Within those 27 nations, among the married and cohabitants, demographic differences (such as education, income, age, and religion) affect happiness, as one might expect, but it is remarkable that national attitudes permeate such a personal experience (Lee & Ono, 2012).

Although there are practical reasons for cohabitation—it saves money and postpones commitment—no research from any nation has yet found that it improves psychosocial development later in life. Thus, the research suggests caution—that neither the popularity of cohabitation, nor the immediate happiness of those who move in together, is proof that cohabitation is beneficial over the long term.

Family Forces

It is hard to overestimate the importance of the family at any period of the life span. Although made up of individuals, a family is much more than the individuals who belong to it. In dynamic synergy, children grow, adults find support, and everyone is part of a family ethos that gives meaning to, and provides models for, hope and action.

TABLE 11.3 Proportion of Common-Law Couples in Quebec, Canada, and Other Selected Countries

Countries	Percentage of all couples	Reference year
Quebec	34.6	2006
Sweden	25.4	2005
Finland	23.9	2006
New Zealand	23.7	2006
Denmark	22.2	2007
Iceland	19.9	2006
Canada	18.4	2006
United Kingdom	15.5	2004
Australia	14.8	2006
Ireland	14.1	2006
Other provinces and territories	13.4	2006

Source: Milan et al., 2007.

LINKED LIVES Emerging adults are said to set out on their own, leaving their parents and childhood home behind. They strive for independence and postpone establishing new family commitments. From that one might conclude that they no longer need family support and guidance. However, this would be incorrect.

The data show that parents continue to be crucial for adult children—perhaps even more so now than for previous generations since fewer contemporary young adults have completed their education or have new families and high-paying jobs. They rely on their parents, who often are deeply concerned about their welfare.

All members of each family have **linked lives,** meaning that the experiences and needs of individuals at one stage of life are affected by those at other stages (Macmillan & Copher, 2005). We have seen this in earlier chapters: Each newborn affects every family member of every age, and growing children are affected by their parents' relationship, even if the children are not directly involved in domestic disputes, financial stresses, parental alliances, and so on.

A strong linkage between emerging adults and their parents in the twenty-first century may seem counterintuitive, as emerging adults are striving for independence and cohort changes are notable. Nonetheless, many studies have found family congruence in attitudes, aspirations, and actions. As already noted, political and religious loyalties often link the generations. For instance, a detailed Dutch study found substantial agreement between parents and their adult children on issues that might, in theory, be contentious—such as cohabitation, same-sex partnerships, and divorce. Some generational differences appeared, but when parents were compared with their own children (not young adults in general), similar attitudes were apparent. Adult children who still lived with their parents (about one-fourth of the sample) were more likely to agree with their parents than were adults who lived apart from them, but all groups showed intergenerational convergence (Bucx et al., 2010).

Extensive research also confirms that family patterns persist, affecting every adult as well as every child. For example, early attachment between infant and caregiver influences that child's future relationships, including friendships, romantic partnerships, and parenthood. Securely attached infants are more likely to become happily married adults; avoidant infants hesitate to marry. Some insecure infants marry early, but they are more likely to divorce. In addition, adults who were securely attached infants are more likely to have secure relationships with their own children. Of course, plasticity is evident throughout life; early attachment affects adult relationships, but it does not determine them.

NATIONAL DIFFERENCES Is living with parents as an emerging adult the key to strong relationships? Apparently, it depends on the economy and on the culture. Almost all unmarried young adults in Italy and Japan remain in their childhood home, and in those nations both generations seem content with that arrangement. Half of the young adults in England live with their parents, but friction often arises (Manzi et al., 2006).

According to a recent Statistics Canada analysis of 2011 census data, 42.3 percent of Canadians aged 20 to 29 were living in their parents' home, either because they had never moved out or because they had returned home. Adult children who move out of their parents' home and then move back are referred to as **boomerang children.** There were some differences in those 20- to 29-year-olds who were living in their parents' home, depending on age, gender, and region. For example, young men ages 20 to 24 were more likely to live with their parents (63.3 percent) as compared to young women (55.2 percent). In addition, Ontario had the highest proportion of young adults living with their parents in Canada, at 50.6 percent. Although the overall percentage has changed little since 2006, it represents a significant increase over previous decades: In 1991 the figure was 32.1 percent, and in 1981 it was 26.9 percent (Statistics Canada, 2013e) (see Figure 11.8).

linked lives
Lives in which the success, health, and well-being of each family member are connected to those of other members, including members of another generation, as in the relationship between parents and children.

✦ **ESPECIALLY FOR Family Therapists** Emerging-adult children who live with their parents do so primarily for financial reasons, yet you have learned that families often function better when young adults live on their own. What would you advise? (see response, page 423) →

boomerang children
Adult children who move out of their parents' home at some point in time before moving back.

FIGURE 11.8 Stay-at-homes Partly for economic reasons, partly because of cultural norms, the number of young people living in the parental home in Canada has been increasing over the past several decades. Although many more people in their younger twenties live at home, rates for those aged 25 to 29 have also gone up.

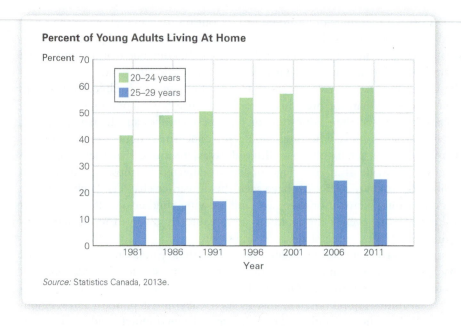

Percent of Young Adults Living At Home

Source: Statistics Canada, 2013e.

Young adults live at home for various reasons, but primarily for financial or emotional support. This does not mean that the young people are the only ones to benefit from such an arrangement, since they often contribute in various ways to the household economy and the family's sense of well-being.

Some North Americans believe that dependence on parents is not healthy for young adults. However, not all North Americans agree. As explained earlier, *familism* is a strong value among many cultures. Closer relationships between parents and their adult children are increasingly common and welcomed among North Americans of all ethnicities. As two experts in human development write, "with delays in marriage, more Americans choosing to remain single, and with high divorce rates, a tie to a parent may be the most important bond in a young adult's life" (Fingerman & Furstenberg, 2012).

In order for relationships to stay strong, it is important that emerging adults and their parents share the same assumptions and guidelines. What those assumptions are often depends on culture. What is expected in, say, Cambodia, would be unacceptable in, say, Colombia. Chinese young adults expect their parents and friends to comment on their romantic partners; North American adults know they must *not* do so. Compared with their North American contemporaries, Chinese emerging adults

Living With Parents It is not unusual for emerging-adult children to live at home with their parents. Thierry, from Saint Lambert, Quebec, is seen here with his parents, Ian and Mireille. The arrangement provides many financial and family benefits.

are about twice as likely to stop dating someone if their parents disapprove (Zhang & Kline, 2009).

Cultural differences aside, parents encourage young adults in every nation to do well in school and to get good jobs, partly to make their families proud, partly so they will be able to care for their relatives when necessary, partly to help secure their own future, and partly so they can be satisfied in their own lives.

ALL TOGETHER NOW When we look at actual lives, not the cultural ideal of independence or interdependence, all emerging adults have much in common, including close family connections and a new freedom from parental limits (Georgas et al., 2006). It is a mistake to assume that emerging adults in Western nations abandon their parents. Just the opposite: Some studies find that family relationships *improve* when young adults leave home (Smetana et al., 2004).

Regarding the overall experiences of emerging adults, this stage of life has many critical opportunities, since "decisions made during the transition to adulthood have a particularly long-lasting influence on the remainder of the life course because they set individuals on paths that are sometimes difficult to change" (Thornton et al., 2007, p. 13). Fortunately, most emerging adults, like humans of all ages, have strengths as well as liabilities. Many survive risks, overcome substance abuse, combat loneliness, and deal with other problems through further education, friends, family, and maturation. If they postpone marriage, prevent parenthood, and avoid a set career (all characteristic of 18- to 25-year-olds) until their identity is firmly established and their education complete, they may be ready for joyful adult commitments and responsibilities.

Same Situation, Far Apart: Dedication Is Universal The activities and clothing of these Acadia University students in their dorm room *(left)* and the young mother in the doorway of her Rajastan, India, home *(right)* are typical of emerging adults: These young women are all active, healthy, and working for their futures, within the norms of their cultures.

RESPONSE FOR Family Therapists (from page 421) Remember that family function is more important than family structure. Sharing a home can work out well if contentious issues—like sexual privacy, money, and household chores—are clarified before resentments arise. Encourage emerging adults and their parents to explore assumptions and guidelines. ●

KEY Points

- Many emerging adults continue their identity search, especially for vocational and ethnic identity.

- Personality shows continuity and change in emerging adulthood, with many people gradually becoming happier. Another smaller group develops serious disorders.

- Marriage is often postponed, but intimacy needs are met in other ways.

- Computer matches and cohabitation have become the norm in North America, each with obvious advantages but also troublesome disadvantages.

- Intergenerational bonds continue to be important in every culture, with many parents helping their emerging adult children, financially and emotionally.

SUMMARY

Biosocial Development

1. Emerging adults usually have strong and healthy bodies. Death from disease is rare.

2. The sexual-reproductive system reaches a peak during these years, but most current emerging adults postpone child-bearing. The results include both increased use of contraception and higher rates of sexually transmitted infections and viruses.

3. Willingness to take risks is characteristic of emerging adults. This allows positive behaviours, such as entering college or university, meeting new people, volunteering for difficult tasks, and finding new jobs. It may also lead to destructive actions, such as unprotected sex, drug use, and an increase in injuries.

4. Extreme sports are attractive to some emerging adults, who find the risk of serious injury thrilling.

Cognitive Development

5. Adult thinking is more flexible and better able to coordinate the objective and the subjective. Some scholars consider this development a fifth stage of cognition, referred to as postformal thought.

6. Whether or not a fifth stage exists, there is no doubt that maturation of the prefrontal cortex allows more advanced thought.

7. The flexibility of young-adult cognition allows people to re-examine stereotypes from their childhood. This may decrease stereotype threat, which impairs adult performance if left unchecked.

8. Worldwide there are far more college and university students, especially in Asia and Africa, than there were a few decades ago, as massification has become an accepted goal.

9. Everywhere, students' backgrounds and current situations are more diverse, which advances postformal thinking. Practical, vocational skills are also valued.

Psychosocial Development

10. Identity continues to be worked out in emerging adulthood. Ethnic identity is particularly important in multi-ethnic cultures, not only for people of mixed and minority backgrounds, but also for those in the majority.

11. The current economic situation makes achieving vocational identity even more problematic than a decade ago. The average emerging adult changes jobs several times.

12. Personality traits from childhood do not disappear in emerging adulthood, but many people learn to modify or compensate for whatever negative traits they have. New experiences—such as moving away from home and going to college or university—allow some plasticity in personality.

13. The need for social connections and relationships is ongoing and lasting. In earlier times, and in some cultures currently, emerging adults followed their parents' wishes in seeking marriage partners. Today's emerging adults are more likely to choose their own partners and postpone marriage.

14. Cohabitation is the current norm for emerging adults in many nations. Nonetheless, marriage to partners of similar backgrounds still seems to be the goal.

15. Family members continue to be important to emerging adults. Parental support—financial as well as emotional—may be more crucial than in earlier times.

KEY TERMS

boomerang children (p. 421)

choice overload (p. 419)

cohabitation (p. 419)

drug abuse (p. 400)

emerging adulthood (p. 395)

extreme sports (p. 399)

intimacy versus isolation (p. 416)

linked lives (p. 421)

massification (p. 405)

postformal thought (p. 401)

stereotype threat (p. 403)

WHAT HAVE YOU LEARNED?

1. What advantages do emerging adults have in terms of their health?

2. Biologically, why is emerging adulthood the best time to have a baby?

3. Why do many emerging adults choose to delay parenthood?

4. Why has the AIDS epidemic slowed in recent years?

5. What are the pros and cons of risk taking in emerging adulthood?

6. Why are emerging adults more likely than people of other ages to take part in risky sports?

7. Why is drug abuse common among emerging adults?

8. What are the differences between formal operational thought and postformal thought?

9. How is adult thinking different from adolescent thinking?

10. In what ways does cognition continue to change throughout adulthood?

11. How does flexible thinking affect social understanding?

12. How do current college and university enrolment patterns differ from those of 50 years ago?

13. According to Perry, how does students' thinking change during their college or university career? What factors explain this change?

14. Why are some current researchers criticizing college and university education?

15. In what way does diversity affect college and university students' learning?

16. How does ethnic pride change from early adolescence to adulthood?

17. Why might vocational identity be an outdated social construction?

18. What is the general trend of self-esteem during emerging adulthood?

19. What reassurance might you offer the parents of an aggressive teen and of a shy teen as their children enter emerging adulthood?

20. What factors might explain personality shifts—both positive and negative—after adolescence?

21. In what three main ways do young adults meet their need for intimacy?

22. In what three main ways do emerging adults meet their romantic partners?

23. How has social networking changed the process of mate selection?

24. Why do many emerging adults cohabit instead of marrying?

25. Why do people assume that emerging adults are not influenced by their parents?

26. What surprises have emerged from studies of the attitudes of emerging adults and their parents?

27. Why might family relationships sometimes improve when young adults leave home?

APPLICATIONS

1. Describe an incident during your emerging adulthood when taking a risk could have led to disaster. What were your feelings at the time? What would you do if you knew that a child of yours was about to do the same thing?

2. Read a biography or autobiography that includes information about the person's thinking from adolescence through adulthood. How did personal experiences, education, and maturation affect the person's reactions and analysis?

3. Only a few statistics regarding historical and national changes in admission of college and university students of both sexes and various backgrounds are reported here. Compare your country, province, or territory with another, using current as well as historical date. Discuss causes and implications of differences.

4. Talk to three people you would expect to have contrasting views on love and marriage (differences in age, gender, upbringing, experience, and religion might affect attitudes). Ask each the same questions and then compare their answers.

>>ONLINE CONNECTIONS

To accompany your textbook, you have access to a number of online resources, including LearningCurve, which is an adaptive quizzing program; critical thinking questions; and case studies. For access to any of these links, go to www.worthpublishers.com/launchpad/bergerchuang1e. In addition to these resources, you'll find links to video clips, personalized study advice, and an e-Book. Among the videos and activities available online are the following:

■ *Transition to Parenthood*. Videos of couples in various stages of parenthood highlight the physical, emotional, social, household, and vocational changes that accompany this new responsibility.

■ *Homosexuality: Genes Versus Environment*. What makes someone gay? This video shows how the nature–nurture debate plays out when applied to this question.

CHAPTER OUTLINE

ADULTHOOD:
Body and Mind

WHAT WILL YOU KNOW?

- Why don't people feel as old as they are?
- Why are lung cancer rates decreasing in North American men but increasing in North American women?
- Do adults increase their levels of cognitive abilities and knowledge from age 25 to age 65?
- Is everyone an expert in something?

Jenny was in her early 30s, a star in my human development class. She told the class that she was divorced, raising her son, daughter, and two orphaned nephews in public housing in the south Bronx. She spoke eloquently and enthusiastically about free activities for her children—public parks, museums, the zoo, Fresh Air Fund camp. We were awed by her creativity and energy.

A year later, Jenny came to my office to speak privately. She said she was four weeks pregnant. The father, Billy, was a married man. He had told her he would not leave his wife but that he would pay for an abortion. She loved him and feared he might end their relationship if she did not terminate the pregnancy. She wanted to talk to me first.

I learned more. She was not opposed to abortion; her 7-year-old son needed speech therapy; she thought she was too old to have another infant; she was a carrier for sickle-cell anemia, which had complicated her most recent pregnancy; her crowded apartment was no longer "babyproof" since her youngest child was 7.

Jenny was about to graduate with honours and had found a job that would enable her family to leave their dangerous neighbourhood. She was eager to get on with her life. After a long conversation, she thanked me profusely—even though I had only asked questions, provided facts, and listened.

Then she surprised me: "I'll have the baby," she said. "Men come and go, but children are always with you." I thought she would come to a different conclusion. We all make decisions about our bodies and our futures based on the values that shape our lives, ideally after discussing facts and implications with someone we trust. ●

—*Kathleen Berger*

Adulthood covers four decades, from ages 25 to 65. Concerns about health, career, and family arise throughout adulthood. This chapter explains facts about sex, reproduction, aging, and more, and then goes on to describe adult thinking processes. Cognition helps adults sort through facts, emotions, and values, leading to sometimes unexpected thoughts and personal decisions.

Expertise is described in this chapter. Jenny was the expert about her own circumstances, as will become clear at the end of this chapter, when you learn what happened to her.

Senescence

Everyone ages. As soon as growth stops, **senescence,** a gradual physical aging over time, begins. Senescence affects every part of the body, visible and invisible.

In some cultures, aging is devalued and senescence has a negative connotation, but aging can be positive. From a developmental perspective, every period of life is multidirectional. Our scientific study of life-span development helps us understand the gains and losses of adulthood.

The Experience of Aging

Although we are all aging, senescence often goes unacknowledged until late in adulthood. Typically, 30- to 65-year-olds feel 5 to 10 years younger than their chronological age and think that "old" describes people significantly older than they themselves are currently (see Figure 12.1) (Pew Research Center, 2009a). Other research confirms that most adults feel strong, capable, healthy, and "in their prime." At least three aspects of body functioning protect adults from recognizing senescence: organ reserve, homeostasis, and allostasis.

Organ reserve is a characteristic of every organ that allows normal functioning throughout the adult years. Because organ reserve is built into the human body, people rarely notice that their hearts, lungs, and so on are losing capacity. That reserve power decreases each year, but it usually does not matter because people rarely need to depend on it. Bodies function well throughout middle age unless major stress has caused too much extra strength to ebb away. Furthermore, all the parts of the body work in harmony. **Homeostasis**—a balance among various parts of the body systems—keeps every physical function connected to every other. The result is that few adults are aware of their aging organs. For instance, when people exercise, the muscles require more oxygen, so heart rate increases and breathing quickens to bring in more air to the lungs and then oxygen to the bloodstream. Age reduces this process: Vital capacity (the amount of air expelled after a deep breath) decreases about 4 percent per decade (faster for smokers), and breathing becomes quicker and shallower as people age, but homeostasis keeps sufficient oxygen in the blood (P. S. Timiras & De Martinis, 2007). Marked shortness of breath is a sign of illness, not aging.

Related to homeostasis is **allostasis,** a dynamic body adjustment over time that affects overall physiology. The main difference between homeostasis and allostasis is time: Homeostasis requires an immediate response from the body systems, whereas allostasis requires longer-term adjustment.

For example, how much a person eats daily is affected by many factors related to appetite—that is the homeostatic set point. An empty stomach triggers hormones, stomach pains, digestion, and so on, that lead a person to eat again.

---

senescence
A gradual physical decline related to aging. Senescence occurs in everyone and in every body part, but the rate of decline is highly variable within and between persons.

organ reserve
The extra capacity built into each organ, such as the heart and lungs, that allows a person to cope with extraordinary demands or to withstand organ strain.

homeostasis
The adjustment of all the body's systems to keep physiological functions in a state of equilibrium, moment by moment. As the body ages, it takes longer for these homeostatic adjustments to occur, so it becomes harder for older bodies to adapt to stress.

allostasis
A dynamic body adjustment, related to homeostasis, that over time affects overall physiology. The main difference is that while homeostasis requires an immediate response, allostasis requires longer-term adjustment.

FIGURE 12.1 Not Old Yet When people are asked when someone is "old," answers depend on how old they themselves are. As this graph shows, the older the person, the older the age that he or she considers "old."

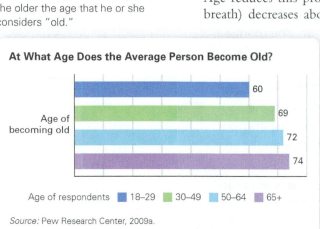

At What Age Does the Average Person Become Old?

Age of becoming old	
	60
	69
	72
	74

Age of respondents ■ 18–29 ■ 30–49 ■ 50–64 ■ 65+

Source: Pew Research Center, 2009a.

If an overweight person begins a serious diet, rapid weight loss soon triggers short-term, homeostatic reactions, making it harder to lose weight (Tremblay & Chaput, 2012).

Eating is related to a broader human need: how emotionally satisfied or distressed a person is. Many people overeat when they are upset or celebrating, and they eat less when they have recently exercised—those responses could be considered part of homeostasis as well. Our bodies are designed to be comfortable, with many mechanisms to relieve the pain of hunger, low oxygen, thirst, and so on. Those reactions are short term—if a person is hungry for a long time, the body adjusts. Feeding a starving person a heavy meal might result in vomiting or diarrhea, as a result of homeostasis.

Over the years, allostasis becomes crucial: If a person overeats or starves day after day, the body suffers. In medical terminology, that person has an increased allostatic load; the short-term equilibrium (homeostasis) may impair long-term health. Obesity is one cause of diabetes, heart disease, high blood pressure, and so on—which are all the result of physiological adjustment (allostasis) (Sterling, 2012).

Thus, overeating and underexercising require not just adjustment for each moment (homeostasis), but also adjustment over decades. One heavy meal reduces appetite for the next few hours (homeostasis); years of obesity put increasing pressure on the allostatic system, so a new stress (such as running up three flights of stairs) may cause a major breakdown (such as a heart attack).

Since momentary stresses that become ongoing habits increase the allostatic load, the solution is to choose patterns that gradually become habits and decrease stress over the years—enjoying nature, or jogging, or socializing, or yoga, or prayer, or simply watching a beautiful sunset. Homeostasis will make such activities part of the daily rhythm: That is why a runner who is immobilized will feel unhappy. These joys, day after day, will improve long-term health by lightening the allostatic load.

Sex and Fertility

Most 60-year-olds can usually do almost everything 30-year-olds can do, and they are often unaware of doing anything less well. However, they do notice changes in the sexual reproductive system. Arousal, orgasm, fertility, and menopause are all affected by age.

SEXUAL RESPONSIVENESS Sexual arousal occurs more slowly with age, and orgasm takes longer. These slowdowns are counterbalanced, however, by reduced anxiety, longer lovemaking, and better communication, as partners become more familiar with their own bodies and those of their partners. Any distress that exists is less connected to age than to troubled relationships, irrational fears, and unrealistic expectations (Duplassie & Daniluk, 2007; L. Siegel & Siegel, 2007).

According to a study of couples conducted in North America in the early 1990s, most adults of all ages enjoy "very high levels of emotional satisfaction and physical pleasure from sex within their relationships" (Laumann & Michael, 2000, p. 250). That study found that men and women were likely to be extremely satisfied with sex if they were in a committed, monogamous relationship—a circumstance more likely between ages 25 and 65 than earlier or later. Frequency of intercourse correlated with age, but not necessarily with satisfaction.

Strangers No More Leanne Kennedy *(right)* was dying from kidney failure, barely surviving with daily dialysis. She had been on the waiting list for a donor kidney for four years. Her fiancé, Shawn Stefanovic, offered his kidney—no match. Then Stuart Kilgannan *(left),* Shawn's best man, offered his. It was a match! How could the new couple repay him? "Name a baby after me," he said.

CATERS NEWS AGENCY / NEWSCOM / CS9

Same Situation, Far Apart: Physical Closeness Whether in Thailand *(left)* or North America *(right)*, at every age couples delight in being close to each other, physically and emotionally.

OBSERVATION QUIZ
What are some of the signs of closeness in these photos? (See answer, page 432). ➡

infertility
The inability to conceive a child after trying for at least a year.

REPRODUCTION Bearing many children was crucial for societies and individuals in former centuries. Historically, pregnancy was welcomed, partly to compensate for the infants and teenagers who died. In Chapter 11, you learned that fertility peaks in the late teens and early 20s. However, with increasing numbers of women attaining higher levels of education and being career-oriented, childbirth is more likely to be delayed to their late 20s or later. Earlier pregnancy is often not desired, even though conception becomes increasingly difficult with each passing year of adulthood.

Although **infertility** is still generally defined as the inability to conceive after a year of trying, age is now considered as a factor. For example, the Government of Canada considers women older than 35 infertile if they are unable to conceive after 6 months of trying (Government of Canada, 2013b).

About one in six Canadian couples experience infertility, a rate that has doubled since the 1980s (Government of Canada, 2013b). The cause of a couple's infertility may be traced to either partner or to both. Out of every 10 times, three times the cause is in the man, four times the cause is in the woman, two times the cause is a mix of factors in both the man and the woman, and one time no specific cause can be found.

The most common cause of male infertility is a low sperm count. Conception is most likely if a man ejaculates more than 20 million sperm per millilitre of semen, two-thirds of them mobile and viable, because each sperm's journey through the cervix and uterus is aided by millions of fellow travellers. In most men, about 100 million sperm reach maturity each day after about 75 days of development. Anything that impairs body functioning over that 75-day period (e.g., fever, radiation, prescription drugs, time in a sauna, excessive stress, environmental toxins, drug abuse, alcoholism, cigarette smoking) can reduce sperm number, shape, and motility (activity) and make conception less likely.

Age also reduces sperm count. Men older than 45 take five times as many months to impregnate a woman as do men who are younger than 25 (Hassan & Killick, 2003). (This study controlled for frequency of sex and age of the woman.) Pollution and stress, both of which accumulate with age, are factors too. Those factors may be the reason the number of viable sperm varies by geographic location—higher in southern France than in Paris, higher in New York than in California, higher in

Finland than in Sweden—although the interpretation and even the validity of such data are debatable (Merzenich et al., 2010).

Even more than for men, age slows down every step of female reproduction—ovulation, implantation, fetal growth, labour, and birth. Female fertility is also affected by anything that impairs physical functioning—including several diseases, smoking, extreme dieting, and obesity. Many infertile women have had pelvic inflammatory disease (PID). Unless properly diagnosed and treated, PID creates scar tissue that blocks fallopian tubes, preventing the sperm from reaching an ovum.

For both sexes, STIs interfere with healthy reproduction. Since the number of past partners increases with age, this may lead to greater chance of exposure to STIs, which may be another reason that age correlates with infertility.

The Government of Canada (2013b) has several recommendations for ways to increase fertility. These include eating a healthy diet, getting regular exercise, quitting smoking, decreasing alcohol consumption, and finding ways to decrease stress levels. Other suggestions are to ensure optimal timing of sexual intercourse, to take hormonal drugs to correct imbalances, and to have surgery to repair any damaged reproductive organs.

CULTURE AND INFERTILITY Infertility occurs everywhere, but the impact depends on the culture. In some nations, Nigeria among them, a woman is not considered fully a woman until she bears a child. There, each year of infertility is a sad one (Hollos et al., 2009). In other nations, such as Germany, being childless by choice is an accepted, even admired, condition (Sobotka & Testa, 2008).

Currently in Canada and the United States, about 15 percent of all adult couples are infertile, some because they postponed child-bearing. Another 15 percent of couples choose not to have children. Among the remaining 70 percent, about half become pregnant as desired and about half become pregnant by mistake (i.e., mistimed, not necessarily unwanted). Wanting a baby is also affected by the economy. In fact, since the financial crisis began in 2007 in the U.S. and in 2008 in Canada, birth rates have decreased each year in both countries (Milan, 2013).

Although birth rates overall have declined in recent years, in many nations the birth rate among older women has increased. Despite the fact that the risk of infertility and birth complications increase with age, in 2009, 11 969 babies were born in Canada to women 40 years and older (Statistics Canada, 2009), with most babies and mothers quite healthy. A major reason for the increased birth rate after age 35 is that many older infertile couples seek medical assistance. It is no longer unusual for a couple to be married and childless for a decade or more, and then to have twins.

FERTILITY RESTORED In the past 40 years, advances in medicine have solved about half of all fertility problems. Surgery can repair male or female reproductive systems, and *assisted reproductive technology* (ART) helps many couples overcome various fertility obstacles (Sharif & Coomarasamy, 2012). For instance, drugs can precipitate ovulation, often of several ova. Or ova can be surgically removed from an ovary and fertilized in a glass lab dish. This is **in vitro fertilization (IVF)**—*in vitro* literally means "in glass." One standard procedure, called *intra-cytoplasmic sperm injection* (ICSI), is to insert a single sperm into each healthy ovum to overcome low sperm count.

IVF zygotes begin to duplicate in the glass dish, and at the 4- or 8-cell stage, technicians insert one or several of them into the mother's womb. Most do not implant and grow, but some do. A total of 8195 IVF treatment cycles were performed in Canada in 2005. For women under 35, the success rate was 32 percent, for women aged 35–39, the rate was 24 percent, and for women 40 and older, the live birth rate was 12 percent. Less than 2 percent had complications (IVA.ca, 2007). Since the first

in vitro fertilization (IVF)
A technique in which ova (egg cells) are surgically removed from a woman and fertilized with sperm in a laboratory. After the original fertilized cells (the zygotes) have divided several times, they are inserted into the woman's uterus.

Her Parents' Love New parents Jhian and Nawwaf show off their baby girl, Wateen, at the Royal Victoria Hospital in Montreal. Wateen is one of many babies successfully conceived using in vitro fertilization.

ANSWER TO **OBSERVATION QUIZ** (from page 430) Signs of closeness include arms around each other; bodies nestled together; inclining of heads toward each other and/or looking at each other; smiles; and relaxed faces. ●

"test-tube" baby was born in 1973, IVF has produced 4 million babies worldwide. Between 1 and 3 percent of all newborns in developed nations and thousands more in developing nations are now conceived via IVF.

Millions of formerly childless couples, either infertile or same-sex, have become parents. Their children are not necessarily their genetic offspring. Many families adopt. In addition, donated sperm have been used for decades, resulting in millions of babies born after *intrauterine insemination* (formerly called *artificial insemination*). Donor ova and donor wombs (when an IVF embryo is implanted in a woman who did not provide the ovum) are also increasingly common.

Birth defects and later illnesses increase slightly with IVF (Kalra & Barnhart, 2011; C. Williams et al., 2010), but the risk is small: About 97 percent of all IVF newborns have no apparent defects. Not small, however, is the risk of prematurity and low birth weight. A Canadian meta-analysis indicated that IVF singleton babies are at higher risk for two factors: preterm birth and low birth weight (McDonald, Han, et al., 2009). In the United States, about half of all IVF babies are low-birth-weight twins or triplets (Centers for Disease Control and Prevention, 2011).

The Aging Brain

Like every other part of the body, the brain also slows down with age. Neurons fire more slowly, and messages sent from the axon of one neuron are not picked up as quickly by the dendrites of other neurons. One result is that reaction time lengthens. In addition, multitasking becomes harder, processing takes longer, and complex working-memory tasks (e.g., repeating eight numbers in sequence, adding the first four, deleting the fifth one, subtracting the next two, and multiplying the total by the last one—all in your head) become much more difficult (Fabiani & Gratton, 2009).

A few individuals (less than 1 percent of those under age 65) experience significant brain loss with age; they "encounter a catastrophic rate of cognitive decline, passing through … the dementia threshold" (Dangour et al., 2007, p. 54). But for most adults, brain changes do not correlate with intellectual power (Greenwood & Parasuraman, 2012). Adults can perform the brain equivalent of a marathon—one reason that judges and many world leaders are usually at least 50 years old. Their thinking has benefited from their experience.

If severe brain loss occurs before late adulthood, the cause is not normal senescence but one of the following:

- *Drug abuse.* All psychoactive drugs harm the brain, especially prolonged, excessive use of alcohol, which can cause Wernicke-Korsakoff syndrome ("wet brain").
- *Poor circulation.* Everything that impairs blood flow—such as hypertension (high blood pressure) and heavy cigarette smoking—also impairs cognition.
- *Viruses.* The blood–brain barrier keeps most viruses away, but a few—including HIV and the prion that causes bovine spongiform encephalopathy ("mad cow disease")—can destroy neurons.
- *Genes.* About 1 in 1000 people inherits a dominant gene for Alzheimer's disease, which destroys memory. Other uncommon genes also affect the brain.

Later in this chapter, we will describe adult cognitive development. Intellectual abilities can rise, fall, zigzag, or stay the same, partly dependent on specifics of each individual's life. This again illustrates the life-span perspective: Intelligence is multidirectional, multicultural, multicontextual, and plastic, but overall quite steady.

Sense Organs

Although brain changes are usually insignificant until late adulthood, significant sensory changes occur in almost everyone. Each sense becomes less acute with age. Specifics of which part of vision, hearing, and so on changes depend on genes, experience, and programmed senescence, which vary by particulars. For example, with sight, peripheral (sidelong) vision ages faster than frontal vision, perception of some colours fades more quickly than that of others, and nearsightedness decreases as farsightedness increases. This explains why, compared with 20-year-olds, 40-year-olds often hold their newspapers, books, or tablets farther away (the print is blurry at a closer reading distance). The eyes take longer to adjust to darkness or glare, making driving at night more dangerous. Note, however, that some people who were previously nearsighted can now see well while driving without glasses—an age-related improvement.

Variable losses also occur in hearing, which is most acute at about age 10. Sounds at high frequencies (e.g., the voice of a small child) become inaudible sooner than do sounds at low frequencies (e.g., a low booming voice).

For contemporary middle-aged adults, hearing loss is rarely problematic before age 65. However, in one recent study of 1512 teenagers, almost one-third reported early symptoms of hearing loss (ringing, muffled sounds, temporary deafness) after listening to music on their headphones. Most routinely set the volume to decibel levels known to damage the sensitive hairs of the inner ear (Vogel et al., 2010). In future generations, then, middle-aged adults might have significant hearing problems.

The senses of taste and smell, as well as one's balance, are also affected by age throughout adulthood. The variations are usually not noticeable to the individual, but they are detectable in laboratory measurements.

Gains and Losses In his 20s, Phil Collins was the drummer for the band Genesis, becoming a star solo singer and songwriter by age 30. A mid-life ear infection and a spinal injury resulted in major sensory loss, making drumming impossible and causing him to retire from music. Most adults are neither so impaired nor so successful, but a combination of gains and losses occurs between ages 25 and 65 for everyone.

Physical Appearance

As you have just read, the invisible changes of senescence do not affect daily life for most contemporary adults. However, visible changes may be disconcerting. In an age-conscious society, no one wants to look old, yet everyone ages.

SKIN AND HAIR The first visible changes are in the skin, which becomes dryer and rougher. Collagen, a component of the body's connective tissue, decreases by about 1 percent every year after age 20 (M. L. Timiras, 2007). Skin becomes thinner and less flexible; the cells just beneath the surface are more variable; wrinkles appear, particularly around the eyes. Diet has an effect (fat slows down wrinkling), but aging is apparent in every layer of the skin for everyone (Nagata et al., 2010).

Especially on the face (exposed to sun, rain, heat, cold, and pollution), the skin loses firmness and elasticity (Whitbourne, 2008). These changes are almost imperceptible, but if you meet a typical pair of siblings, aged 18 and 28, you can tell by their skin which one is older. By age 60, all faces are wrinkled—some much more so than others. The smooth, taut, flexible young face has disappeared.

Hair usually turns grey and thins, first at the temples by age 40, and then over the rest of the scalp. This does not affect health, but since hair is a visible sign of aging, adults often spend money and time on colouring, thickening, styling, and more. Body hair (on the arms, legs, and pubic area) also becomes thinner and lighter. An occasional thick, unwanted hair may appear on the chin, inside the nose, or somewhere else on the body.

SHAPE AND AGILITY The body also changes shape between ages 25 and 65. A "middle-age spread" increases waist circumference; all the muscles weaken; pockets of fat settle on the abdomen, upper arms, buttocks, and chin; people stoop slightly when they stand (Whitbourne et al., 2008).

By late middle age, back muscles, connective tissue, and bones lose density, making the vertebrae in the spine shrink. People lose about 2 to 3 centimetres of height by age 65. That loss occurs not in leg bones but in the trunk, with compression of the space between spinal discs (Tilling et al., 2006)—another reason that waists widen.

Agility is also reduced. Consequently, rising from sitting on the floor, twisting in a dance, or even walking "with a spring in your step" is harder. The joints lose flexibility; stiffness is more evident; bending is harder, especially by middle age.

The aging of the body is most evident in sports that require strength, agility, and speed: Gymnasts, boxers, and basketball players benefit from youth. Of course, the intellectual and emotional gains of adulthood may compensate for the physiological slowdowns: Some 30-year-olds are better athletes than their younger teammates.

Declining Hormones

Over the decades of adulthood, the level of hormones in the bloodstream decreases, altering sleep patterns, appetite, and the appearance changes just noted. The decline in sex hormones, which occurs suddenly in women and more gradually in men, is the hormonal change that adults notice most, since it affects desire and behaviour.

menopause
The time in middle age, usually around age 50, when a woman's menstrual periods cease and the production of estrogen, progesterone, and testosterone drops. Strictly speaking, menopause is dated one year after a woman's last menstrual period, although many months before and after that date are considered part of the period of menopause.

MENOPAUSE For women, ovulation and menstruation stop at **menopause,** when estrogen levels fall. This occurs naturally between ages 42 and 58 (the average age is 51). Genes are an important influence on a woman's age at menopause (Morris et al., 2011).

Common symptoms of menopause are disturbances of body temperature—hot flashes (feeling hot), hot flushes (looking hot), and cold sweats (feeling chilled). Other symptoms include increased osteoporosis (fragile bones) and neurocognitive disorders. However, these symptoms vary by ethnicity. No marked disturbances are reported by 40 percent of Asian-Americans, 25 percent of European- and Hispanic-Americans, and 15 percent of African-Americans. The psychological consequences of menopause vary as well. Some menopausal women find a new zest for life; others become depressed. One woman said menopause is "somewhere between a taboo and a joke" (Duffy et al., 2011, p. 497).

The historical Western notion that menopausal women "temporarily lose their minds" (Neugarten & Neugarten, 1986) contrasts with the traditional view among Hindi women in India that menopause represents liberation (Menon, 2001). The latter reaction is becoming more common in North America as well, as women typically are less depressed and less anxious five years after menopause than five years before (Gibson et al., 2012).

hormone replacement therapy (HRT)
Taking hormones (in pills, patches, or injections) to compensate for hormone reduction. HRT is most common in women at menopause or after removal of the ovaries, but it is also used by men to help restore their decreased testosterone level. HRT has some medical uses but also carries health risks.

Over the past 30 years, millions of women undergoing **hormone replacement therapy (HRT)** took hormone supplements, usually estrogen combined with progesterone, to alleviate common menopause symptoms. In addition, correlational studies originally found that heart disease, strokes, and neurocognitive disorders occurred less often with estrogen, which prompted many women to use HRT for decades.

Researchers now believe that a third variable, SES, was the reason HRT-takers experienced less disease. Women with more education and income were more likely to use HRT and to be healthier overall. In fact, in controlled longitudinal studies, the U.S. Women's Health Initiative found that taking estrogen for 10 years or more *increased* the risk of heart disease, stroke, and breast cancer and had no effect on the most common types of neurocognitive disorders (U.S. Preventive Services Task Force, 2002).

When that result was publicized, millions of women around the world stopped HRT—but that may have been an overreaction, and the fear of increased disease may be greater than the research warrants (Cumming et al., 2011; Powledge, 2007; Sturdee & Pines, 2011). Instead, the risk of increased disease seems to depend on whether HRT consists of estrogen only or of estrogen and progesterone, and level of risk depends on the age of the woman taking HRT and the length of time on HRT.

A medical review stresses the variability of risk, complaining that the early presentation of the Women's Health Initiative results may have disadvantaged nearly a decade of women who may have unnecessarily suffered severe menopausal symptoms (Sturdee & Pines, 2011). Estrogen may aid cognition, if not prevent neurocognitive disorders (Erickson & Korol, 2009; Greenwood & Parasuraman, 2012), and risks and benefits vary from person to person (Stevenson et al., 2011).

A *hysterectomy* (surgical removal of the uterus) usually includes removal of the ovaries, which causes sudden menopause if the woman has not already experienced it naturally. About 320 per 100 000 Canadian women in 2011 had a hysterectomy (Statistics Canada, 2013d). Rates vary by cohort, region, and nation. For example, Saskatchewan has the highest rate of hysterectomies in Canada, at 469 per 100 000 women, followed by Nova Scotia at 411. The lowest provincial rate in Canada is in British Columbia, at 285. Hysterectomy rates are falling in many places as the risks of surgery and the benefits of estrogen, when naturally produced by the ovaries, become better known.

ANDROPAUSE? Hormone replacement for men is likewise controversial. The debate begins by asking whether men undergo anything like menopause. Some suggest that many men experience an age-related reduction of testosterone that decreases sexual desire, erections, and muscle mass (Harrison, 2011). But many doctors think that the term **andropause** (or *male menopause*) is misleading because it implies a sudden drop in reproductive ability or hormones. That does not occur; many men produce viable sperm throughout their lives. Sexual inactivity and anxiety cause a reduction in testosterone—a phenomenon similar to menopause but with a psychological, not physiological, cause. As one review explains, "Retirement, financial problems, unresolved anger, and dwindling social relationships can wreak havoc on some men's sense of masculinity and virility" (L. Siegel & Siegel, 2007, p. 239).

To combat a decline in testosterone, some men choose HRT, in their case taking testosterone (some women also take smaller amounts of testosterone to increase their sexual desire). Doctors are understandably cautious about prescribing HRT to men, as they are with women; supplemental hormones may be harmful (Bhasin, 2007; Moffat, 2005; Sokol, 2009). Overdoses of testosterone by athletes have led to sudden cardiac arrest. Yet low testosterone correlates with increased risk of heart disease (Kaushik et al., 2010). This debate is not settled, but all the evidence finds that adult health, for both men and women, depends more on habits than on hormones.

andropause
A term coined to signify a drop in testosterone levels in older men, which normally results in reduced sexual desire, erections, and muscle mass. (Also called *male menopause*.)

KEY Points

- Aging is universal, but the meaning of senescence depends on the individual and on cultural factors.

- Fertility decreases with time. Many infertile couples use assisted reproductive technology, especially IVF.

- Brains, muscles, and the senses are notably affected by age, but few adults in developed nations are debilitated by these changes.

- Menopause is universal, but reactions to it vary. Experts do not agree about the existence of andropause or about the use of hormonal supplements.

Health Habits and Age

Each person's routines of daily life powerfully affect their susceptibility to diseases and chronic conditions; this applies both to current routines and to those that have been in place since childhood. It is particularly true for problems associated with aging—from arthritis to varicose veins.

Consider cancer, the leading cause of death for adults aged 25 to 65. The risk of cancer increases with every year of life, but lifestyle, not age, is usually the underlying cause. According to one estimate, 30 percent of cancer cases are caused by smoking, 30 percent by diet, and 5 percent by inactivity (Willett & Trichopoulos, 1996).

Of course, the specific lifestyle effects on susceptibility vary with each disease, even each type of cancer, and uncontrollable factors, primarily genetic, play a major role in some diseases and a minor role in others. However, people can cut in half their overall morbidity and mortality during adulthood (ages 25 to 65) if they have healthy habits.

To clarify this, it is important to know the various ways in which health is measured:

- *Mortality* means death.
- *Morbidity* means disease, the rates of which depend partly on diagnosis.
- *Disability,* the usual result of morbidity, is the inability to do something that people usually can do. For example, one form of morbidity is glaucoma; this could mean serious disability if a person can see only shapes, but less serious disability if the person cannot read without glasses.
- *Vitality*—also known as life force, or *joie de vivre*—may be the most important, but it is the most difficult to measure. Some people with morbid conditions that increase disability and the risk of mortality are nonetheless happy and active.

The goal of good health habits is not only to reduce illness, but also to increase wellness so that adults can live for decades at full vitality.

Tobacco and Alcohol

Many teenagers believe that smoking and drinking make them cool and signify maturity. Nicotine also provides an energy boost, which seems to be an indicator of health. Accordingly, many young people pick up those habits as soon as they can, legally or not.

Even though many people eventually quit smoking, they are still at greater risk for developing cancer. We now know that cancer deaths reflect smoking patterns of years earlier. Canadian men have been quitting smoking for decades. As a result, the incidence of lung cancer among men levelled off in the 1980s and then began declining (see Figure 12.2). Conversely, smoking among women has increased over

✦ **ESPECIALLY FOR Doctors and Nurses** If you had to choose between recommending various screening tests and recommending various lifestyle changes to a 35-year-old, which would you choose? (see response, page 438) →

FIGURE 12.2 Gender Differences As this graph shows, the death rate due to lung cancer has been decreasing steadily for males since the 1980s. In contrast, the death rate increased for females over the same time frame, and has now levelled off.

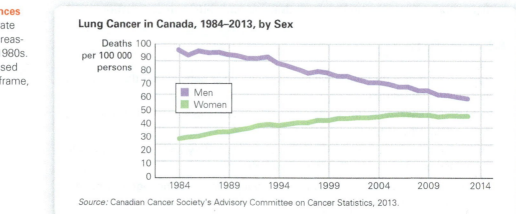

Lung Cancer in Canada, 1984–2013, by Sex

Source: Canadian Cancer Society's Advisory Committee on Cancer Statistics, 2013.

time. As a result, lung cancer rates for women started increasing in 1982 and then went up significantly, by a rate of 1.1 percent a year between 1998 and 2007, before levelling off. Even so, the incidence of lung cancer is still higher among Canadian men (60 per 100 000) than women (47 per 100 000) (Canadian Cancer Society's Advisory Committee on Cancer Statistics, 2013).

While rates of smoking and lung cancer deaths are decreasing in countries such as Canada and the United States, they are rising in other countries, such as China, India, and Indonesia, especially among women. For instance, in these countries, more than half of the men are smokers as are just less than 10 percent of the women. The World Health Organization calls tobacco the single largest preventable cause of death and chronic disease (Blas & Kurup, 2010).

The harm from cigarettes is dose-related: Each puff, each day of smoking, each breath of secondhand smoke makes cancer, heart disease, stroke, and emphysema more likely. No such linear harm results from drinking alcohol. In fact, alcohol can be beneficial: People who drink wine, beer, or spirits *in moderation*—no more than two drinks a day—live longer than abstainers. The primary reason is that alcohol reduces coronary heart disease and strokes. It increases HDL (high-density lipoprotein), the "good" form of cholesterol, and reduces LDL (low-density lipoprotein), the "bad" cholesterol that causes clogged arteries and blood clots. It also lowers blood pressure and glucose (Klatsky, 2009).

However, moderation is impossible for some. Alcoholics may find it easier to abstain than to have one, and only one, drink a day. Higher amounts of drinking destroys brain cells; contributes to osteoporosis; decreases fertility; accompanies many suicides, homicides, and accidents; destroys families; and increases the risk of 60 diseases, not only of the liver but also of the breasts, stomach, and throat (Hampton, 2005).

Alcoholism increases with poverty and causes disproportionate harm in poorer countries (Grimm, 2008) because prevention, treatment, and enforcement strategies have not caught up with abuse. In general, low-income nations have more abstainers as well as more abusers, while more affluent nations have more moderate drinkers (Blas & Kurup, 2010).

Homeostasis and allostasis may be factors: Poverty reduces the sources of pleasure and increases stress, so temporary joy comes from smoking and drinking. But then more nicotine and alcohol become needed because of homeostasis, and, over the long term, addiction begins, joy declines, and life ends (Sterling, 2012). Momentary vitality becomes morbidity and then mortality.

Guess His Age A man puffs on a bidi, a flavoured cigarette, in Bangalore, India. He looks elderly but is actually middle-aged (about age 40). He is at risk of being among the 1 million Indians who die each year of smoking-related causes.

Overeating

Metabolism decreases by one-third between ages 20 and 60, which means that adults need to eat less and move more each year. Few adults do so; instead, obesity increases with each decade of adulthood until old age.

A WORLDWIDE PROBLEM Obesity is now recognized as a major health problem in many nations. Cultural solutions—a national diet that emphasizes less meat and more vegetables as in China, or fewer fast-food restaurants and more leisurely dining as in France, or more olive oil and less corn oil as in Greece—are beyond the scope of this book. Although one might hope that globalization would lead to these or other improvements in eating habits in Canada and the United States, the opposite seems true: Fast-food restaurants are proliferating in these and most other nations.

Statistics Canada reports that in 2012, 60 percent of males 18 years and older were either overweight or obese, as were 45 percent of women. Overall, slightly more than 18 percent of adult Canadians qualified as obese. The authors of this report caution that these are self-reported figures, and that the actual rates of obesity and overweight are probably higher (Statistics Canada, 2013f).

OCEAN / CORBS

Bad Habits This office worker is eating cake made with white flour, butter, and sugar. More adult deaths occur as a consequence of chronic unhealthy snacking than of drug addiction. However, it is far easier to recognize others' destructive habits than to change one's own bad behaviours.

RESPONSE FOR Doctors and Nurses (from page 436) Much depends on the specific patient. However, far more people develop disease or die because of years of poor health habits than because of various illnesses not spotted in time. With some exceptions, age 35 is too early to detect incipient cancers or circulatory problems, but it is prime time for stopping cigarette smoking, curbing alcohol abuse, and improving exercise and diet. ●

Just Give Me the Usual Even bad habits can feel comfortable—that's what makes them habits.

BRUCE ERIC KAPLAN / THE NEW YORKER COLLECTION / CARTOONBANK.COM

"The fresh mountain air is starting to depress me."

In the United States, the rates are even more alarming. There, 65 percent of adults are overweight, with a body mass index (BMI) above 25. More than half of those overweight people are obese (with a BMI of 30 or more), and 6 percent overall are morbidly obese (with a BMI of 40 or more) (Flegal et al., 2012). Rates in the other North American nation, Mexico, are also high.

Excess weight increases the risk of every chronic disease, but the most glaring example is diabetes, which affects twice as many North Americans currently as it did 40 years ago (Taubes, 2009). The direct cause is insulin resistance (where the body fails to respond to its own insulin), which, left untreated, can lead to death. Diabetes also causes eye, heart, and foot problems.

Sadly, partly because of how they are treated, obese adults avoid socializing, exercising, and going for medical checkups. As a result, their morbidity increases far more than their weight alone would predict (Puhl & Heuer, 2010).

SOLUTIONS TO THE OBESITY EPIDEMIC Stopping any addiction is difficult because long-standing habits are embedded in each adult's daily life. Diets—there are hundreds of them—work if they reduce calories and involve exercise, but they need to be maintained for decades, a daunting task. Sustained counselling and encouragement from health practitioners is time-consuming but effective in the long run. However, many people seek a quick, effective weight-loss method instead.

Diet drugs are one traditional option; however, many have been found to cause cardiovascular and digestive problems, or to lead to addiction. Gastric bypass surgery causes dramatic weight loss in many patients, but as with all surgical procedures, there are risks. The risks may be worth it though, since morbidly obese people have higher death rates without surgery than with it (Schauer et al., 2010).

Drugs and surgery are not enough: Patients must change their lifestyle to accommodate new eating habits and exercise. People who are highly motivated and long past adolescence and emerging adulthood are much more likely to follow through with those required lifestyle changes. For those morbidly obese teenagers who undergo surgery, the adjustments may be particularly difficult (Widhalm et al., 2011).

Developmentalists emphasize that early prevention is more effective than medical remedies. You have already read that babies born underweight often become fat children, who may become overweight adults. At that point, the stigma and discrimination experienced by obese people can have an adverse effect on their health, both psychological as well as physical (Puhl & Heuer, 2010).

Inactivity

Regular exercise protects against illness even if a person is overweight or a smoker. When any habit changes for the better, a daily hour of exercise is the best predictor of maintaining the change (Shai & Stampfer, 2008). Specific benefits of exercise include lower blood pressure, stronger hearts and lungs, and reduced risk of almost every disease, including depression, diabetes, osteoporosis, heart disease, arthritis, and even cancer. By contrast, sitting for long hours correlates with almost every unhealthy condition, especially heart disease and diabetes, both of which carry additional health hazards beyond the disease itself. Even a little movement—gardening, light housework, walking up the stairs or to the bus—helps.

Walking briskly for 30 minutes a day, five days a week, is a reasonable goal. More intense exercise (e.g., swimming, jogging, bicycling) is ideal. It is possible to exercise too much, but almost no adult aged 25 to 65 does. In fact, one study that used objective assessment of adult movement (electronic monitors) found that less than 5 percent of adults in the United States and England exercise even 30 minutes per day (Weiler et al., 2010). Self-reports put the number at about 30 percent.

In 2010, about 52 percent of Canadians aged 12 and older reported that they were moderately active during their leisure time, which was equivalent to walking at least 30 minutes a day or engaging in a one-hour exercise class at least three times per week. Walking was the most popular form of exercise (70 percent). Males were more likely to report being at least moderately active than women (54.9 percent versus 49.4 percent) (Statistics Canada, 2011e).

The close connection between exercise and health, both physical and mental, is well known, as is the influence of family, friends, and neighbourhoods. Exercise-friendly communities have lower rates of obesity, hypertension, and depression (Lee et al., 2009). This is not merely a correlation but a cause: People who are more fit are likely to resist disease and to feel healthier as they age (Carnethon et al., 2003; Shirom et al., 2008).

Researchers are now trying to pin down specifics. Does the type of exercise matter (walking, gardening, swimming, running)? Is half an hour each day better than four hours on the weekend? These are unanswered questions, but no one doubts that adults should be active, year in, year out. Maintaining any healthy habit is the hardest part, as the following explains.

Hope It Helps Sitting on an exercise ball instead of a chair may help this woman increase her balance and strengthen the core muscles in her back and stomach. She can also lie on the ball to stretch out her back or do ab crunches to further strengthen her core.

A VIEW FROM SCIENCE

A Habit Is Hard to Break

Every adult knows that smoking cigarettes, abusing alcohol, overeating, and remaining sedentary are harmful, yet many have at least one destructive habit. Why don't we all shape up and live right? Breaking New Year's resolutions; criticizing people whose bad habits are not our own; feeling guilty for consuming sweets, salt, fried foods, cigarettes, or alcohol; buying gym memberships that go unused or exercise equipment that becomes dust-gathering sculptures—these behaviours are common.

Social scientists have focused on this conundrum (Conner, 2008; Shumaker et al., 2009). They have found that changing a habit is a long, multi-step process: Ignoring that reality is one reason habits continue, because strategies that work at one stage fail at another. One list of these steps is as follows:

1. denial
2. awareness
3. planning
4. implementation
5. maintenance.

The first step, *denial,* occurs because all bad habits exist for good reasons. For example, most cigarette smokers begin as teenagers because they seek social acceptance and/or weight control—both especially important to adolescents. Warnings about mortality in the distant future seem irrelevant. Then nicotine creates addiction: Without the drug, smokers become anxious, confused, angry, and depressed—no wonder some smokers deny the harm of smoking since the pain of not smoking is more evident to them.

In fact, with many life-threatening addictions, hearing that death might result leads to *more* smoking, drinking, and so on, not less (Ben-Zur & Zeidner, 2009; Martin & Kamins, 2010). A theory, called *terror management theory,* explains that people reduce fear by doing exactly what they have been warned not to do.

Denial reduces stress, which leads people to deny what is obvious to others. They say, "I only drink on weekends," or "It's genetic," or "Other people eat more." Ideally, denial crumbles and the person moves to the next stage.

Awareness must be attained by the individual. Others help, not by accusing but by listening, either via *motivational interviewing* (encouraging the individual to describe the reasons why change is needed) or via *acceptance and commitment therapy* (recognizing the emotional aspects of the habit). Both motivational interviewing and commitment therapy begin with the person's own values. This is crucial: Adults rebel when others tell them what to do, think, or believe (Bricker & Tollison, 2011).

Planning occurs only after the person is aware of the problem and wants to solve it. Planning is specific, with a set date for quitting and strategies to overcome obstacles. Care is needed at this step because humans tend to underestimate the power of their own impulses; this is true for smokers, dieters, and addicts of all kinds.

Such underestimating was evident in a particular experiment. Researchers gave students who were entering or leaving a college cafeteria their choice of several packaged snacks, promising them about $10 (and the snack) if they did not eat it for a week. Those who were entering, presumably aware of the demands of hunger and less certain of their ability to shrug off cravings, planned to avoid temptation by choosing a healthy snack. Most of them (61 percent) earned the money. However, those leaving the cafeteria apparently underestimated the power of hunger and overestimated their ability to battle cravings. They chose a more tempting snack and later ate it; only 39 percent earned the money (Nordgren et al., 2009). Planning has to take into account a person's weakest moments: Most planners are too optimistic; counsellors can help turn awareness into a solid plan.

Implementation is quitting a harmful habit according to plan. One crucial factor is gathering social support, such as by (1) letting others know the date and the plan, (2) finding a buddy, or (3) joining a group (e.g., Weight Watchers, Alcoholics Anonymous, or SmokEnders). Engaging all three forms of social support is even better yet, since private efforts often fail.

Willpower is like a muscle: Putting too much stress on it for too long will make it break, but gradual strengthening is possible (Vohs & Baumeister, 2013). That means implementation is most successful when tackling one habit at a time: Quitting cigarettes when starting a diet is almost impossible; this double-barrelled approach is usually short-lived.

Maintenance is the most important step, yet the one that most people ignore. Although quitting may be difficult, many addicts experience the pain of quitting, get past the pain, and then relapse, only to quit again and again. Dieters gain and lose weight so often that this phenomenon has a name—*yo-yo dieting*. That same phenomenon is part of every addiction: Maintaining a good habit requires intense, individualized attention (Ridenour et al., 2012).

Maintenance is destroyed by overconfidence. People forget the power of temptation. The recovered alcoholic goes out with friends who drink, planning to order only juice; the dieter buys ice cream to offer to guests or for the rest of the family; the person who joined the gym skips a day, promising to make up for it the following day. Such actions are far more dangerous than people realize because they add stress. For instance, the dinner guests might not eat all the ice cream, and later, the stress of having resisted it earlier finally makes the ice cream all the more irresistible.

In another study, dieters who were given a stressful task (remembering a nine-digit number) entered a room that had been set, seemingly at random, either with some tempting foods or with a scale and a diet book. They were then asked to taste a milkshake to give their opinion of the particular drink; they were also told they could take a tiny sip or drink as much as they wanted. Those who saw eating clues drank more than those who saw dieting clues (Mann & Ward, 2007), unaware that stress made them vulnerable.

This is an example of *attention myopia,* when resolve (maintenance ability) momentarily fades. Attention myopia occurs with many self-control efforts: People temporarily lose focus on the goal of halting aggression, curbing lust, stopping drug abuse, and so on (Giancola et al., 2010). Many people who restart a bad habit cite a specific stress—from a bitter divorce to a bothersome toothache—that makes them lose focus. Sooner or later every adult is stressed and habits reappear, unless maintenance strategies are ongoing.

Accumulating Stressors

Stress is part of life, from birth to death. Between ages 25 and 65, everyone experiences major stress (e.g., the death of a family member), minor stress (e.g., a snowstorm), and daily hassles (e.g., traffic jams).

stressor
Any situation, event, experience, or other stimulus that causes a person to feel stressed. Many circumstances become stressors for some people but not for others.

FROM STRESS TO STRESSOR Not every stress becomes a **stressor,** however. A stressor is any experience, circumstance, or condition that negatively affects a person. How people cope with stresses, making some become stressors and others not, affects their health.

Particularly if organ reserves are depleted or allostatic load is high, the physiological toll of major and minor stressors lowers immunity, increases blood pressure, speeds up the heart, reduces sleep, and produces many other reactions that lead to serious illness. A comprehensive review finds that stress clearly affects the whole body and that the best coping measures vary for each illness and each person (Aldwin, 2007). For instance, some patients recover better from surgery if they know details of their vital signs and healing; others just need to know that doctors are working to make them better.

For some, reactions to stressors can cause more stressors. For example, a longitudinal study of married couples in their 30s found that, if the husband's health deteriorated, the chance of divorce increased. This was apparent with all couples, but it was particularly evident for well-educated European-Americans (Teachman, 2010). One possible explanation is that these couples were less accustomed to stress and thus less able to cope. Those best able to deal with stress are those who have had some, but not too much, trauma in their lives (Seery, 2011).

AGE AND GENDER Psychologists distinguish between two major ways of coping. In **problem-focused coping,** people attack their problems (e.g., confront a difficult boss, move out of a noisy neighbourhood). In **emotion-focused coping,** people change their emotions (e.g., from anger to acceptance). In general, younger adults and adults of higher SES are more likely to attack problems, whereas older adults and those of lower SES try to accept them (Aldwin, 2007). This may indicate that those who are poorer and older believe that there is not much they can do to change their circumstances. A pessimistic attitude about the future is more common the less money one has (Robb et al., 2009).

Sex hormones may also affect responses to stress. Men are inclined to be problem-focused, reacting in a "fight-or-flight" manner. Their sympathetic nervous system (faster heart rate, increased adrenaline) prepares them for attack or escape. Their testosterone rises when they attack and decreases if they fail. On the other hand, women are more emotion-focused. They "tend and befriend"—that is, seek the reassurance of other people when they are under pressure. In reaction to stress, their bodies produce oxytocin, a hormone that leads them to seek confidential and caring interactions (S. E. Taylor, 2006; S. E. Taylor et al., 2000). This gender difference explains why a woman might get upset if a man doesn't want to talk about his problems. By contrast, a man might be annoyed if a woman just talks, not appreciating his advice about how to confront and solve the problem.

Adults of both sexes and of every age and income level use both strategies, depending on the situation. The worst situation is to have no strategy at all—denying a problem until it escalates and takes a physical toll. One study found that when both spouses in a marriage avoid either strategy and instead suppress justifiable anger, their death rate is twice as high as when at least one partner expresses anger (Harburg, 2008). With age and experience, adults may learn to respond wisely, as age brings a more positive attitude toward life. Then stresses do not become stressors (Charles & Carstensen, 2010).

Age brings another advantage. Emerging adulthood is a time of heightened aggravations (Aldwin, 2007). Once life settles down, some stresses (dating, job hunting, moving) are less frequent. Adults are more capable of arranging their lives to minimize the occurrence of stressors (Aldwin, 2007).

SES and Health Habits

Money and education protect health in every nation. According to Statistics Canada, less-educated people live two to three years fewer than their well-educated peers (Greenberg & Normandin, 2011). Similarly, an economist who analyzed historical U.S. data determined that after age 35, the average life span increases by 1.7 years for each year of education (Lleras-Muney, 2005).

It is not obvious why this connection is so strong. Does education teach better health habits? Does income result in better medical care? Does high IQ added to high family SES in childhood allow more education, followed by living in better

problem-focused coping
A strategy to deal with stress by tackling a stressful situation directly.

emotion-focused coping
A strategy to deal with stress by changing feelings about the stressor rather than changing the stressor itself.

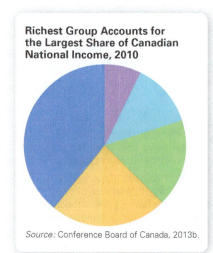

Richest Group Accounts for the Largest Share of Canadian National Income, 2010

Source: Conference Board of Canada, 2013b.

FIGURE 12.3 Richer/Poorer One way to track income inequality is by dividing the population into five groups (quintiles), and then calculating each group's share of income. If each group has the same share of the nation's total income—i.e., 20 percent—then the distribution is equal. As this graph shows, the richest income group in Canada has by far the largest share of the total national income. This group was also the only group to increase its share of the national income over the last 20 years; every other group has lost share (Conference Board of Canada, 2013b).

neighbourhoods, with less pollution and more opportunities to walk, bike, and play outside? Are wealthy people better able to insulate themselves from stressors because they can hire people to help them?

For whatever reason, the differences are dramatic. The 10 million U.S. residents with the highest SES outlive—by an average of about 30 years—the 10 million with the lowest SES (C. J. L. Murray et al., 2006). Recent data find the SES gap widening in the United States (Olshansky et al., 2012).

Although not as glaring as in the U.S., Canada's income disparity is also at a record high. A recent report from the Conference Board of Canada (2013b) noted that not only did income inequality increase between 1990 and 2010, but since 1990, the richest group of Canadians has increased its total share of national income, while the poorest and middle-income groups have lost share (see Figure 12.3). A Montreal study that examined the social inequalities in health found an 11-year difference in life expectancy between those who lived in the poorest neighbourhoods and those in the richest neighbourhoods (Agence de la santé et des services sociaux de Montréal, 2011).

SES is protective between nations as well as within them: Rich nations have less disease, injury, and death. For example, a baby born in 2010 in northern Europe can expect to live to age 79; in sub-Saharan Africa, to 55 (United Nations, 2012).

DISEASES OF AFFLUENCE Certain diseases, including diabetes, lung cancer, and breast cancer, were once called *diseases of affluence* because they were more common among the rich than the poor (Hu, 2011; Krieger, 2002, 2003) and in wealthier groups within each nation—Japanese-Canadians more than Filipino-Canadians, for instance. However, when smoking became less expensive (between 1920 and 1950), fast food more available, and illness better diagnosed, the diseases of affluence did not correlate with wealth at all; they were more common among the poor.

Distinguishing the effects of income, education, cohort, and culture is difficult because, as you remember from Chapter 1, all these factors overlap. For example, currently, African-American women are more likely to die of breast cancer than are women of other U.S. ethnic groups, but medical researchers are not sure why (DeSantis et al., 2011). The reason could be genetic, but it could also be a lower quality of health care, poorer eating habits, more stress, or an avoidance of doctors.

A recently proposed hypothesis is that low SES in the United States (and possibly in other parts of North America) leads to poor health habits—overeating, smoking, drinking—as ways of coping with stress; such practices impair physical health while reducing depression and anxiety. This may begin prenatally: A poor pregnant woman, worried about how she will provide for her baby, is less likely to follow good nutritional and sleep routines. Wealthier adults, on the other hand, tend to avoid poor lifestyle habits and are generally in better physical health, but, ironically, accumulation of stress may lead to higher rates of mental disorders among them (Jackson, 2012). Whether it is the case that the wealthy actually have higher rates of depression and anxiety, or rather that the data merely reflect a higher rate of diagnosis and therapy seeking, is not known.

HEALTH OF IMMIGRANTS Data on immigrants complicate the connection between SES and health. Recent immigrants to both Canada and the United States tend to be healthier yet poorer than the native born: They have less heart disease, drug abuse, obesity, and so on than do their wealthier co-ethnics (Garcia Coll & Marks, 2011).

One suggested explanation is that healthy people are more likely to emigrate; then their good health protects them even though they may be poor. Or, as Morton Beiser at the University of Toronto has noted, immigrants are healthier primarily because Canada has selection criteria that emphasize good health, and all potential immigrants must undergo a comprehensive medical screening (Beiser, 2005). All this may be true; however, the data find that the "healthy migrant" theory is not sufficient to explain immigrant health (Bates et al., 2008; Garcia Coll & Marks, 2011). Perhaps psychological or ethnic influences in low-SES cultures foster good health habits that continue after emigration.

> ## KEY Points
>
> - Mortality is increasingly uncommon in adulthood (ages 25 to 65): morbidity, disability, and loss of vitality remain problems.
> - Smoking always harms health, but the effect of alcohol is harder to assess as it is beneficial in moderation and lethal in excess.
> - Obesity and inactivity are increasing worldwide, leading to higher rates of many diseases, especially diabetes.
> - People of different ages, genders, and incomes cope with stressors in varying ways.

What Is Adult Intelligence?

You just read that both education and intelligence, measured by IQ tests, might explain why high-SES adults are healthier than those of low SES. But is there such a thing as "intelligence"? You read in Chapter 7 that intelligence in childhood correlates with school achievement, itself controversial. However, what about intellectual development over the years of adulthood?

One leading theoretician, Charles Spearman (1927), proposed a single entity that he called **general intelligence (g)**. Although g cannot be measured directly, it can be inferred from various abilities, such as vocabulary, memory, and reasoning. Most experts who agree with Spearman contend that children gain in ability as they mature, and thus scores on intelligence tests take a child's age into account. Once a person reaches adulthood, an IQ score indicates whether that adult is a genius, average, or below average, no matter what the person's age. The same IQ test is taken at age 18 or 88.

The belief that g exists still influences thinking and testing on intelligence. Many neuroscientists seek genetic underpinnings for the intellectual differences among adults. However, efforts to find specific genes or abilities that comprise g have not succeeded (Deary et al., 2010; Haier et al., 2009). Some researchers believe g does not exist.

general intelligence (g) The idea of g assumes that intelligence is one basic trait, underlying all cognitive abilities. According to this concept, people have varying levels of this general ability.

Adult Intelligence The achievements of Jane Goodall *(left)* and Ellen Johnson-Sirleaf *(right)* are indicators of the success that is possible later in life.

Research on Age and Intelligence

Research on intelligence over the years of adulthood has reached conflicting conclusions (Hertzog, 2011). Cross-sectional studies find that intellectual ability peaks in adolescence and then gradually declines. Typical 50-year-olds score lower on IQ tests than typical 25-year-olds do, and 50-year-olds score higher than typical 75-year-olds do. However, when longitudinal research is conducted, testing the same people again and again as they age, scores improve—at least until late adulthood. Those 50-year-olds score higher than they did at age 25. How could this be?

THE FLYNN EFFECT The most plausible hypothesis for the divergence between the conclusions of cross-sectional and longitudinal research begins with a fact: For most of the past century, each generation was healthier and better educated than the previous one.

In many nations, the typical 75-year-old had never attended college or university, but now a typical 25-year-old has some college or university education. Furthermore, 25-year-olds have had better childhood health (vaccines, nutrition) and more information (via television and computers) available to them. That affects intelligence; younger cohorts would therefore have higher IQ scores on cross-sectional research.

The same factors explain the results of longitudinal research. Contemporary 75-year-olds have experienced those advantages as they aged, being better informed about the world than they were as children. For that reason, longitudinal research would find them scoring higher than they did 50 years ago. Powerful evidence supporting this explanation comes from test scores in many nations (Dickinson & Hiscock, 2010). In every country where data allow a valid comparison, more recent cohorts outscore previous generations tested at the same age. This is called the **Flynn effect.**

As a result it is unfair—and scientifically invalid—to compare IQ scores of a cross section of adults of various ages. Older adults will score lower, but that does not mean they have lost intellectual power; quite the opposite is the case. (This may not be true for the oldest adults, however; more on that in Chapter 14).

CROSS-SEQUENTIAL RESEARCH Scientists now realize that neither cross-sectional nor longitudinal research is completely accurate to ascertain age changes, since historical conditions change as well (Hertzog, 2011). The best way to understand the effects of time without the confounding complications of contextual changes is to combine the two. One scholar famously pioneered this combination.

As an undergraduate in the middle of the twentieth century, K. Warner Schaie began to study adult intelligence. For his doctoral dissertation, he tested 500 adults, aged 20 to 50, on five standard primary mental abilities thought to be the foundation of intelligence: (1) verbal meaning (vocabulary), (2) spatial orientation, (3) inductive reasoning, (4) number ability, and (5) word fluency (rapid verbal associations). Schaie's initial cross-sectional results showed a gradual, age-related decline in these five abilities, as others had found before him. He had read that longitudinal research found an increase in IQ, so he planned to retest his population seven years later.

He then had a brilliant idea: He would not only retest his initial participants, he would also test a new young group who were the same age as his earlier sample had been. By comparing the scores of the retested individuals with their own earlier scores *and* with the scores of a new group who were the same age as his first group had been, he hoped to learn more about age and intelligence. His results surprised the experts; he discovered cohort effects that few people had imagined earlier.

For example, each successive cohort scored higher in verbal memory and inductive reasoning, but scored lower in number ability than adults who had been tested

Flynn effect
The rise in average IQ scores that has occurred over the decades in many nations.

✦ **ESPECIALLY FOR Older Brothers and Sisters** If your younger siblings mock your ignorance of current TV shows and beat you at the latest video games, does that mean your intellect is fading? (see response, page 447) →

seven years earlier at the same age. That led to the hypothesis that classroom teaching affected ability: The curriculum in many U.S. schools had shifted by mid-century to emphasize reading, writing, and self-expression, not math.

Schaie found that one correlate of higher ability was intellectual complexity at work and at home, both of which tended to peak in middle age, from ages 39 to 53. Because of complexity, women of earlier cohorts, who often stayed home or had less challenging jobs, lost IQ in mid-life, but this did not occur for contemporary women.

Schaie conducted the first massive *cross-sequential research*. Cross-age comparisons allowed analysis of potential influences, including retesting, cohort differences, experience, education, and gender. Ten times over more than five decades, Schaie and his colleagues have tested a new group and retested his earlier participants (Schaie, 2005). The results of this project, known as the **Seattle Longitudinal Study,** confirmed and extended what others had found: People improve in most mental abilities during adulthood. As Figure 12.4 shows, each particular ability at each age and for each gender has a distinct pattern. All abilities gradually improve and then eventually decline. Men are initially better with numbers and women with words, and that gap narrows with age.

Many other researchers have reported similar results (Alwin, 2009). For example, Paul Baltes (2003) tested hundreds of older Germans in Berlin and found that only at age 80 did every cognitive ability show age-related declines. As noted earlier in this chapter, for some people aging impairs the brain, reducing cognition. But more often adult IQ increases, or at least stays the same.

Components of Intelligence: Many and Varied

Developmentalists are now looking closely at patterns of cognitive gains and losses over the adult years. These patterns vary markedly; intelligence often rises and falls within the same person, as "vast domains of cognitive performance … may not follow a common, age-linked trajectory of decline" (Dannefer & Patterson, 2008, p. 116).

As you read in Chapter 7, many psychologists envision multiple intellectual abilities (Roberts & Lipnevich, 2012). One influential proposal—Gardner's theory of nine multiple intelligences, with its many implications for childhood education—was explained in Chapter 7. We now consider two other proposals in detail.

Seattle Longitudinal Study
The first cross-sequential study of adult intelligence. This study began in 1956; the most recent testing was completed in 2013.

FIGURE 12.4 Age Differences in Intellectual Abilities Cross-sectional data on intellectual abilities at various ages show much steeper declines. Longitudinal research, in contrast, shows more notable rises. Because Schaie's research is cross-sequential, the trajectories it depicts are more revealing: None of the average scores for the five abilities at any age is above 55 or below 35. Because the methodology takes into account the cohort and historical effects, the age-related differences from ages 25 to 60 are very small.

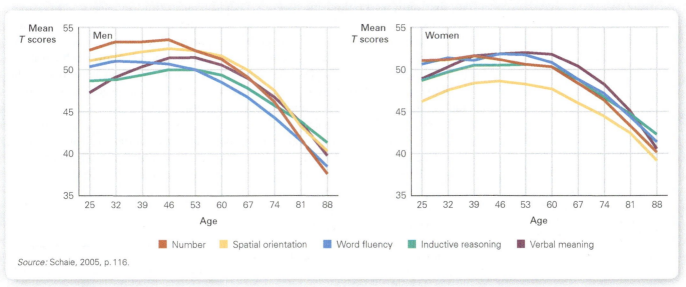

Source: Schaie, 2005, p. 116.

Think Before Acting Both these adults need to combine fluid and crystallized intelligence, insight and intuition, logic and experience. One *(left)* is a surgeon, studying X-rays before picking up her scalpel. The other *(right)* is the executive director of a community organization in Mississauga, Ontario, and a part-time doctoral student at the University of Guelph, reading about a new resource for immigrant parents of young children.

fluid intelligence
Those types of basic intelligence that make learning of all sorts quick and thorough. Abilities such as short-term memory, abstract thought, and speed of thinking are all usually considered part of fluid intelligence.

crystallized intelligence
Those types of intellectual ability that reflect accumulated learning. Vocabulary and general information are examples. Some developmental psychologists think crystallized intelligence increases with age, while fluid intelligence declines.

FLUID AND CRYSTALLIZED INTELLIGENCE In the 1960s, leading personality researcher Raymond Cattell teamed up with a graduate student, John Horn, to study intelligence tests. They concluded that adult intelligence is best understood if various measures are grouped into two categories: fluid and crystallized (Horn & Cattell, 1967).

As its name implies, **fluid intelligence** is like water, flowing to its own level no matter where it happens to be. Fluid intelligence is quick and flexible, enabling people to learn anything, even things that are unfamiliar and unconnected to what they already know. Curiosity, learning for the joy of it, and the thrill of discovering something new are marks of fluid intelligence (Silvia & Sanders, 2010).

People high in fluid abilities can draw inferences, understand relations between concepts, and quickly process new ideas and facts. They are fast and creative with words and numbers and enjoy intellectual puzzles. The kind of question that tests fluid intelligence among Western adults might be like these:

What comes next in each of these two series?
4 9 1 6 2 5 3
V X Z B D★

Puzzles are often used to measure fluid intelligence, with speedy solutions earning bonus points (as on many IQ tests). Efficient working memory—with immediate recall of nonsense words, of numbers, of a sentence just read—is a crucial aspect of fluid intelligence.

A study of adults aged 34 to 83 found that stresses and stressors did not vary by age, but did vary by fluid intelligence. People high in fluid intelligence were more often exposed to stress but were less likely to suffer from it: They used their intellect to turn potential stressors into positive experiences (Stawski et al., 2010). Fluid intelligence is associated with openness to new experiences and overall brain health (Batterham et al., 2009; Silvia & Sanders, 2010), which may contribute to an ability to detoxify stress. That may be one reason why high fluid intelligence in emerging adulthood leads to longer life and higher IQ later in adulthood.

By contrast, the accumulation of facts, information, and knowledge as a result of education and experience is called **crystallized intelligence.** Size of vocabulary, knowledge of chemical formulas, and memory for dates all indicate crystallized intelligence. Tests to measure this intelligence might include questions like these:

What is the meaning of the word *misanthrope?*
Who would hold a harpoon?
What was Sri Lanka called in 1950?§

★The fluid intelligence answers are 6 and F; other answers are possible.
§The crystallized intelligence answers might be: someone who dislikes people; a fisherman who caught whales or swordfish in the past; Ceylon.

Although questions that test for crystallized intelligence seem to measure education more than aptitude, these two are connected, especially in adulthood. Intelligent adults read widely, think deeply, and remember what they learn: Crystallized intelligence reflects fluid intelligence. Consequently, many researchers consider years of education a rough indication of IQ.

Age complicates the calculation of adult IQ. Scores on items measuring fluid intelligence decrease with age since everything in the brain as well as the body slows down. However, if a person continues to read and think, scores on items measuring crystallized intelligence increase. These two clusters, changing in opposite directions, make a person's IQ score (composed of diverse subtests) fairly steady from ages 30 to 70, even though particular abilities change.

Barring pathology, the brain slowdown is rarely apparent until massive declines in fluid intelligence begin to affect crystallized intelligence, perhaps at age 70 or so. It may be foolish to try to measure *g*, a single omnibus intelligence, because both fluid and crystallized intelligence need to be measured separately.

When thinking about age changes in fluid and crystallized intelligence, note the connection between speed and IQ. Many items that test fluid intelligence are timed, with extra points for quick answers. In a culture that values youth, abilities that favour the young (e.g., fast reaction time, capacious short-term memory) are central to success on psychometric intelligence tests, whereas the strengths of older adults (e.g., emotional regulation and the upholding of traditional values) are not.

Thus, fluid intelligence is valued in a youth-oriented culture more than crystallized intelligence. A word often used to describe a highly intelligent person is *quick,* whereas a less intelligent person is called *slow*—exactly what happens with age. Perhaps the assumptions that led to the creation of IQ tests are faulty when applied to adults.

THREE FORMS OF INTELLIGENCE: STERNBERG Robert Sternberg (1988, 2003) agrees that the notion of a single intelligence score is misleading. As first mentioned in Chapter 7, Sternberg proposed three fundamental forms of intelligence: analytic, creative, and practical. Each can be tested.

Analytic intelligence includes all the mental processes that foster academic proficiency. It draws on abstract planning, strategy selection, focused attention, memory, and information processing, as well as on verbal and logical skills. Strengths in those areas are particularly valuable for younger adults in higher education and job training. Multiple-choice tests and brief essays that call forth remembered information, with one and only one right answer, indicate analytic intelligence.

Creative intelligence involves the capacity to be intellectually flexible and innovative. Creative thinking is divergent rather than convergent, valuing unexpected, imaginative, and unusual thoughts rather than standard and conventional ones. Sternberg developed tests of creative intelligence that include writing a short story titled "The Octopus's Sneakers" or planning an advertising campaign for a new doorknob. High scores are earned by those with many unusual ideas.

Practical intelligence involves the capacity to adapt to the demands of a given situation. This includes an accurate grasp of the expectations and needs of the people involved and an awareness of the particular skills that are called for, along with the ability to use these insights effectively. If employers want to assess practical intelligence, they might test workers with a case study or see how they function on the job. Practical intelligence is sometimes called *tacit intelligence* because it is not obvious on tests. Instead it comes from "the school of hard knocks" and is sometimes called "street smarts" rather than "book smarts."

Practical intelligence is needed in adulthood. It allows a person to manage the conflicting personalities in a family or to convince members of an organization

RESPONSE FOR Older Brothers and Sisters (from page 444) No. While it is true that each new cohort might be smarter than the previous one in some ways, cross-sequential research suggests that you are smarter than you used to be. ●

analytic intelligence
A form of intelligence that involves such mental processes as abstract planning, strategy selection, focused attention, and information processing, as well as verbal and logical skills.

creative intelligence
A form of intelligence that involves the capacity to be intellectually flexible and innovative.

practical intelligence
The intellectual skills used in everyday problem solving. (Sometimes called *tacit intelligence*.)

✦ **ESPECIALLY FOR Prospective Parents** What types of intelligence are most needed for effective parenting? (see response, page 450) →

Smart Farmer This creative field trip is to a wheat field, where children study grains that will become bread. Farmers like this one use every kind of intelligence. To succeed they need to decide what crops and seed varieties to plant, to anticipate market prices, and to analyze soil, fertilizer, pests, and so on.

Same Situation, Far Apart: Men at Work The bean merchant in Nairobi, Kenya *(left)*, and the construction supervisor in Beijing, China *(right)*, have much in common: They are high in practical intelligence and they love their jobs. Context is crucial to their success since, if they traded places, each would be lost at first. However, practical intelligence could save the day—a few months of intensive instruction might enable each to master his new role.

(e.g., a business, a social group, or a school) to do something. Ideally, practical intelligence gradually builds over the years, as people learn from experience. Flexibility is also needed, as you will soon see in the discussion of expertise (K. Sloan, 2009).

Without practical intelligence, a solution found by analytic intelligence is doomed to fail because people resist academic brilliance as unrealistic and elite. Similarly, a stunningly creative idea may be rejected as ridiculous without practical intelligence.

Sternberg believes that each of these three forms of intelligence is useful; adults ideally deploy the strengths and guard against the limitations of each. Choosing which type of intelligence to use takes wisdom, which Sternberg has added as a fourth ingredient of successful intelligence. He writes:

> One needs creativity to generate novel ideas, analytical intelligence to ascertain whether they are good ideas, practical intelligence to implement the ideas and persuade others of their value, and wisdom to ensure that the ideas help reach a common goal.
>
> *[Sternberg, 2012, p. 21]*

Think about these intelligences cross-culturally. Each type might be more appreciated in some situations than in others. For example, analytic individuals would do well in college or university but might be seen as arrogant and be criticized for being the "elite" when in a different environment. Creative individuals are critical of tradition and would be tolerated only in some political environments (Sternberg, 2006b). Practical intelligence might be particularly needed when traditional customs and practices no longer seem useful.

The fact that those who do well in college or university might not adapt well to life outside of school raises the question—what do adults need to do in order to succeed? In a knowledge economy, analytic intelligence may be crucial … or may not be. Opposing perspectives on this are illustrated by asking, "What makes a good parent?"

OPPOSING PERSPECTIVES

What Makes a Good Parent?

Tests of good infant care have been developed, based primarily on analytic, not practical, child-rearing (e.g., McCall et al., 2010). One of the most common scales is the *Knowledge of Infant Development Inventory* (KIDI) (MacPhee, 1981). KIDI measures how much caregivers know about infant senses, motor skills, and communication—such as at what age an infant is expected to sit up or whether parents should talk to pre-verbal babies.

Such knowledge seems helpful. For example, mothers and fathers who score higher on the KIDI are less depressed and more likely to provide responsive baby care (Howard, 2010; Zolotor et al., 2008). Many researchers believe that knowledge of infant development causes (not merely correlates with) good care.

Should we worry when mothers do not know about their babies' growth? Perhaps. For instance, in one study only 29 percent of immigrant mothers knew that 2-month-olds can distinguish one speech sound from another, an item on the KIDI. The researchers suggest that those mothers are less able to advance their infants' language and social skills, hindering future development (Bornstein & Cote, 2007).

The opposing perspective suggests that knowledge of infant development does not matter in caregiving. A study supporting this view found that an immigrant child's later cognitive development was best predicted not by KIDI scores or other measures of parenting, but by parents' SES and language use. In this longitudinal study, the mothers' KIDI scores did not predict later school success for Asian-American or Latino children, but it did for European-American children (Han et al., 2012).

In another study, researchers provided supportive, encouraging visitors to low-income, unmarried mothers—many of whom did not plan or want their babies. Compared with a control group with no visits, and even compared with mothers in the intervention group who had relatively few home visits, mothers who were visited 30 or more times became better infant caregivers. However, both before and after many visits, the KIDI scores of the mothers were low. The authors of the study wrote:

> A significant impact of this intervention was its effect on the mothers' ability to create home environments more suitable for the needs of their infants ... despite lack of measurable change in mothers' knowledge of infant development.
>
> *[Katz et al., 2011, p. S81]*

In other words, advances in practical skills, not analytic ones, made a difference.

Knowledge may not be the only way to improve parenting. Instead, warmth and patience, responsiveness (without expecting an infant to reciprocate), mental health, or social support networks may be more critical than knowledge.

Part of the underlying reason why tests of knowledge do not always predict good parenting is that cultures vary in what they believe about infant development. For example, an anthropologist studied the Ache in Paraguay. They were respectful and deferential to her on repeated visits, until she and her husband

> arrived at their study site in the forest of Paraguay with their infant daughter in tow. The Ache greeted her in a whole new way. They took her aside and in friendly and intimate but no-nonsense terms told her all the things she was doing wrong as a mother. ... "This older woman sat with me and told me I *must* sleep with my daughter. They were horrified that I brought a basket with me for her to sleep in." Here was a group of forest hunter-gatherers, people living in what Westerners would call basic conditions, giving instructions to a highly educated woman from a technologically sophisticated culture.
>
> *[Small, 1998, p. 213]*

How important to quality care is accurate knowledge of child development? The way knowledge is interpreted and used by parents is complicated by various factors such as culture and SES, as we have just read. In the end, the most important aspect of good parenting may not be information, and the sign of an intelligent adult may be something other than analytic intelligence. What we do know about child care is that parents need to be continually responsive and sensitive to their children's development, both of which require creative and practical intelligence.

Keep Him Close Mothers everywhere keep their toddlers nearby, but it is particularly important in an environment where poisonous spiders and plants thrive. This Ache mother is required to use analytic intelligence (e.g., to assess danger), as well as creative and practical intelligence (e.g., to keep her child safe).

RESPONSE FOR Prospective Parents (from page 447) Because parenthood demands flexibility and patience, Sternberg's practical intelligence or Gardner's social understanding is probably most needed. Anything that involves finding a single correct answer, such as analytic intelligence or number ability, would not be much help. ●

> ## KEY points
>
> - Cross-sectional research shows declines in the IQ scores of adults, longitudinal research shows increases, and cross-sequential research shows cohort effects.
> - Worldwide improvements in health and education have advanced adult intelligence.
> - Fluid intelligence declines with age; crystallized intelligence advances.
> - Analytic, creative, and practical intelligence are each more important in certain contexts and cultures than in others.

Selective Gains and Losses

Aging neurons, cultural pressures, historical conditions, and past schooling all affect adult cognition, as just reviewed. None of these is under direct individual control. However, adults can choose what abilities to nurture. For example, many adults use calculators instead of paper-and-pencil (or mental) calculations to do math. If adults threw out their calculators, would their math skills improve? Probably. But most adults would not choose to do so.

Optimization with Compensation

selective optimization with compensation

The theory, developed by Paul and Margret Baltes, that people try to maintain a balance in their lives by looking for the best way to compensate for physical and cognitive losses and to become more proficient in activities they can already do well.

Paul and Margret Baltes (1990) developed a theory, called **selective optimization with compensation,** to describe the general process of systematic function (P. B. Baltes, 2003) as older adults maintain a balance in their lives. The idea is that people seek to *optimize* their development, looking for the best ways to *compensate* for losses and to become more proficient at activities they want to perform well.

Selective optimization helps explain the variations in intellectual abilities just reviewed. As other research has found, when older adults are motivated to do well, few age-related deficits are apparent. However, compared with younger adults, older adults are typically less motivated to put forth their best effort when the task at hand is not particularly engaging (Hess et al., 2009). Often people prefer the easy way over the way that will challenge their intellect.

SPECIALIZED LEARNING Specialization works as follows. Suppose a man who was interested in one area of the world noticed that aging affected his vision and memory. He might compensate by buying reading glasses, increasing the type size on his computer, and keeping a file or notebook for whatever he reads about that area, sometimes rereading it. He might be selective, skipping over most of the news about other parts of the world. In that way, he would still know more about his particular specialty (optimization) than anyone else.

Selective optimization with compensation may be particularly crucial on the job, as older workers notice that some tasks now take longer or are more difficult for them to do. If they use compensation strategies, they are more likely to see opportunities for continued growth and improvement, making the job more interesting to them (Zacher & Frese, 2011).

An example that may be familiar to everyone is multi-tasking, which becomes more difficult with every passing decade (Reuter-Lorenz & Sylvester, 2005). "I can't do everything at once" is more often said by adults than by teenagers because adults have learned to be selective, compensating for slower thinking by concentrating on one task at a time. Resources—of the brain as well as material resources—may be increasingly limited with age, but compensation allows optimal functioning (Freund, 2008).

Selective optimization with compensation applies to every aspect of life, from choosing friends to playing baseball. Each adult seeks to maximize gains and minimize losses, choosing to practise some abilities and ignore others. Choices are critical because every ability can be enhanced or diminished, depending on how, when, and why a person uses it. It is possible to "teach an old dog new tricks," but adults need to choose and practise the tricks.

Particularly relevant may be the selection of cognitive abilities. As Baltes and Baltes (1990) explain, selective optimization means that each person optimizes some intellectual abilities and neglects others. If the ignored abilities are the ones measured by IQ tests, then IQ scores fall. This would occur even though other abilities increase.

SELECTION AND ACTION Selective optimization is the probable explanation for the continued intellectual ability of adults. However, the concept is most easily demonstrated by brain activity that involves the motor system, not disembodied thinking (Beilock, 2010). For example, experienced typists scan more letters at a time to compensate for slower finger action, chefs prepare more foods in advance to avoid having multiple pots on the stove at once, and servers in restaurants use downtime to clear tables and prepare for new customers. Each of these occupations has been studied, with efficiency more apparent in experienced workers because of compensatory moves.

The most frequently studied action-based compensation is that of professional sports players, probably because optimal performance is worth millions (Ajemian et al., 2010). Athletes need to practise and warm up to activate the neurological connections in their brains that allow the quick and precise movements to hit a baseball, throw a basketball, hit a hockey puck, and so on. If they are not selective in their neurological activity and they allow interference from memory or emotion, they risk failure.

Thus, when star athletes are asked the secret of their success, they often do not know or remember because memory and emotion must shut down in order for professional expertise to focus solely on performance. According to a cognitive psychologist, "That's why they usually thank God or their moms. They don't know what they did, so they don't know what else to say" (Beilock, quoted in Bascom, 2012, p. 22).

Expert Cognition

Everyone can develop expertise, specializing in activities that are personally meaningful—whether that be car repair, gourmet cooking, illness diagnosis, or fly fishing. As people develop expertise in some areas, they pay less attention to others. For example, some adults develop expertise in cooking rather than gardening, or in music versus dance, or in one style of music over another.

Culture and context guide all of us in selecting areas of expertise. Many adults born 60 years ago are much better than more recent cohorts at writing letters with distinctive but legible handwriting. Because of their childhood culture, they selected and practised penmanship, became expert in it, and maintained that expertise. On the other hand, younger adults grew up with various technological devices; some older adults are still cautious in programming everything from smart phones to video screens.

Experts, as cognitive scientists define them, are not necessarily those with rare and outstanding proficiency. Although sometimes the term *expert* connotes an extraordinary genius, to researchers it means more—and less—than that. An **expert** is notably more accomplished, proficient, and knowledgeable in a particular skill, topic, or task than the average person (Charness & Krampe, 2008; Ericsson, 2009).

Expertise is not innate, nor does it always correlate with basic abilities (such as the five abilities measured in the Seattle Longitudinal Study). However, genetic predispositions may incline a person to be better at some skills than others. Expert language interpreters, for instance, might have been born with brain capacity to

expert
One who is notably more accomplished, proficient, and/or knowledgeable in a particular skill, topic, or task than the average person.

expertise
Accomplishment at a particular skill or in-depth knowledge of a particular subject that is greater than that of the average person.

Experts All Every adult is an expert. Shown here *(clockwise from top left):* a Borek (a Turkish delicacy) baker at the market, a connoisseur evaluating the bouquet of a costly red wine, a musician playing the didgeridoo, and a professor in her biology lab. Most of us would be inept and bewildered in those roles. Students likely also know a great deal about some things that are unfamiliar to others—electronic music, artistic makeup, Italian cuisine, professional baseball, and more.

understand dialect, but they also need years of training and experience to become expert (Golestani et al., 2011).

An expert is not simply someone who knows more about something, or who has done it often. At a certain tipping point, accumulated knowledge, practice, and experience become transformative, changing the brain, putting the expert in a different league (Ericsson, 2009; Wan et al., 2011). The quality as well as the quantity of cognition is advanced. Expert thought is: (1) intuitive, (2) automatic, (3) strategic, and (4) flexible, as we now describe.

INTUITIVE Novices follow formal procedures and rules. Experts rely more on their past experiences and on immediate contexts. Their actions are therefore more intuitive and less stereotypic. The role of experience and intuition is evident, for example, during surgery. Outsiders might think medicine is straightforward, but experts understand the reality:

> Hospitals are filled with varieties of knives and poisons. Every time a medication is prescribed, there is potential for an unintended side effect. In surgery, collateral damage is inherent. External tissue must be cut to allow internal access so that a diseased organ may be removed, or some other manipulation may be performed to return the patient to better health.
>
> *[Dominguez, 2001, p. 287]*

In one study, many surgeons saw the same videotape of a gall-bladder operation and were asked to talk about it. The experienced surgeons anticipated and described problems twice as often as did the residents (who had also removed gallbladders, just not as many) (Dominguez, 2001). Data on physicians indicate that the single most important question to ask a surgeon is, "How often have you performed this operation?" The novice, even with the best, most recent training, is less skilled than the expert.

Another study found that the number of years since a doctor was in medical school correlated *negatively* with proficiency (Choudhry et al., 2005). Obviously, when experience leads to habits that should change because of more recent advances, then simply having done something the same old way a thousand times does not mean that the task is performed better than it is by someone who uses a better technique, learned recently and performed only 50 times. Intuition arises from practice, but practice does not always lead to intuition.

A different experiment that studied the relationship between expertise and intuition centred on predicting winners of several soccer matches, either instantly or after two minutes. College students who were avid fans made more accurate predictions when they had two minutes of unconscious thought (they were required to perform difficult math calculations and then give their answer) compared with when they had two minutes to mull over their choice (see Figure 12.5). In this, intuition trumped conscious thought. When given the same task, college students who didn't care much about soccer (the non-experts) did worse overall, as expected, but the surprising result is that intuition didn't help at all: They did worst of all when they had two minutes of the same math problems that helped the experts (Dijksterhuis et al., 2009).

This experiment suggests that intuition, here occurring unconsciously, helps experts but not non-experts. The latter gain nothing from thinking it over, either consciously or not.

AUTOMATIC Automatic processing is thought to be a crucial reason why expert chess and Go (a Chinese board game that requires the use of strategy) players are much better at the game than are novices. They see a configuration of game pieces and automatically encode it as a whole, rather than analyzing it bit by bit.

A study of expert chess players (aged 17 to 81) found minor age-related declines, but expertise was much more important than age. This was particularly apparent for speedy recognition that the king was threatened: Older experts did it almost as quickly (within a fraction of a second) as younger experts, despite far steeper, age-related declines on standard tests of memory and speed (Jastrzembski et al., 2006).

Many elements of expert performance are automatic. The complex action and thought required for performance have become routine, making it appear that most aspects of the task are performed instinctively. Experts process incoming information more quickly and analyze it more efficiently than do non-experts. They then act in well-rehearsed ways that make their efforts appear unconscious.

In fact, some automatic actions are no longer accessible to the conscious mind. For example, adults are much better at tying their shoelaces than children are (adults can do it in the dark), but they are much worse at describing how they do it (McLeod et al., 2005). When experts think, they engage in automatic weighting of various non-verbalized factors (Dijksterhuis et al., 2009). This is apparent if you are an experienced driver and have attempted to teach someone else to drive. Excellent drivers who are inexperienced instructors find it hard to recognize or verbalize things that have become automatic—such as noticing pedestrians and cyclists on the far side of the road, or feeling the car shift gears as it heads up an incline, or hearing the tires lose traction on a bit of sand. Yet such factors differentiate the expert from the novice.

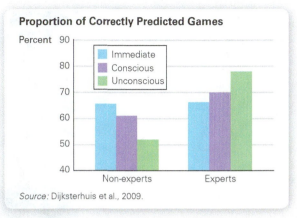

Proportion of Correctly Predicted Games

Source: Dijksterhuis et al., 2009.

FIGURE 12.5 If You Don't Know, Don't Think! Undergraduates at the University of Amsterdam were asked to predict winners of four World Cup soccer matches in one of three conditions: (1) immediate—as soon as they saw the names of the nations that were competing in each of the contests, (2) conscious—after thinking for two minutes about their answers, and (3) unconscious—after two minutes of solving distracting math tasks. The experts were better at predicting winners after unconscious processing, but the non-experts became less accurate when they thought about their answers, either consciously or unconsciously.

automatic processing
Thinking that occurs without deliberate, conscious thought. Experts process most tasks automatically, saving conscious thought for unfamiliar challenges.

Checkmate Automatic processing has allowed this young woman *(right)* to develop expertise in chess at a very young age. A 12-year-old chess prodigy, she is seen here challenging older players on Main Street, in Vancouver.

This may explain why, despite powerful motivation, quicker reactions, and better vision, teenagers have far more car accidents than middle-aged drivers do. Sometimes teenage drivers deliberately take risks (speeding, running a red light, etc.), but more often they simply misjudge and misperceive conditions that a more experienced driver would automatically notice.

Automaticity is particularly crucial if a person's conscious mind is focused on something else, which is why many regions place restrictions on the number and age of passengers teen drivers are allowed to drive with (Zernike, 2012). Having passengers in the vehicle can be distracting, especially for new drivers. By contrast, adult drivers automatically ignore passengers when their unconscious alert system signals that focused attention is needed.

The relationship among expertise, age, and automaticity is not straightforward. Time is only one of the essential requirements for expertise. Not everyone becomes an expert over time (depending on the task), but everyone needs months—or even years—of deliberate practice to develop expertise (Ericsson et al., 2006).

Some researchers think practice must be extensive—several hours a day for at least 10 years (Charness et al., 1996; Ericsson, 1996)—but that may be true in only some areas, not all. Circumstances, training, talent, ability, practice, and age all affect expertise, which means that experts in one specific field are often quite inexpert in other areas.

STRATEGIC The third characteristic of experts is that they have more and better strategies, especially when problems are unexpected (Ormerod, 2005). Indeed, strategy may be the most crucial difference between a skilled person and an unskilled one. Expert chess players not only have general strategies for winning, but they also have specific plans for the possibilities after a move—that is their specialty (Bilalić et al., 2009).

Similarly, a strategy used by expert team leaders in the military and in civilian life is ongoing communication and reminders, especially during slow times. Consequently, when stress builds, no team member misinterprets the rehearsed plans, commands, and requirements. You have likely witnessed the same phenomenon in expert professors: They put well-developed strategies in place during the early weeks to avoid problems later on.

An intriguing study of age and strategy in job effectiveness comes from an occupation most everyone is familiar with: driving a taxi. In major cities, taxi drivers must find the best route (factoring in traffic, construction, time of day, and many other details), all while knowing where new passengers are likely to be found, as well as how to relate to customers, some of whom might want to chat, others not.

Research in London, England—where taxi drivers have to learn the layout of 25 000 streets and the locations of thousands of places of interest, and pass stringent examinations (Woollett et al., 2009)—found not only that the drivers became more expert with time, but also that their brains adjusted to the need for particular knowledge. In fact, some regions of English taxi drivers' brains (areas thought to help with spatial representation) were more extensive and active than those of an average person (Woollett et al., 2009). On ordinary IQ tests, their scores were typical, but in navigating London, expertise was apparent. Other studies also show that people become more expert, and that their brains adapt, as they practise various skills (Park & Reuter-Lorenz, 2009).

Of course, strategies themselves need to be updated as situations change—and no chess game, or battle, or class is exactly like another. The monthly fire drill required by some schools, the standard lecture given by some professors, and the routine safety instructions read by airline attendants before takeoff become less effective than when they were first used. People tune them out.

In one study, pilots and non-pilots listened to air traffic control messages that described a flight path while referring to a chart of the airspace. They read back (or repeated) each message and then answered a question about the route. If allowed to take notes while listening to the messages, pilots' read-back proficiency did not decline with age, as it did for non-pilots. In fact, the researchers found no differences in the read-back proficiency among pilots of three age groups: 22 to 40, 50 to 59, and 60 to 76. However, if not allowed to take notes, the accuracy of the read-backs declined with age, for both pilots and non-pilots (Morrow et al., 2003). For pilots, then, note-taking was a strategy that compensated for age.

This does not mean, of course, that strategy always overcomes age deficits. In another study of pilots (aged 19 to 79) conducted with a flight simulator, the decision of whether to land in the fog involved more risk with increasing age, not the other way around. Older adult pilots had some strengths—they were quicker to begin necessary actions needed for a safe landing in difficult weather—but the older pilots had slower processing skills. When confronted with many indicators of weather and flight, they were less skilled than their younger colleagues at the necessary split-second judgments required in this simulation (Kennedy et al., 2010).

FLEXIBLE Finally, perhaps because they are intuitive, automatic, and strategic thinkers, experts are also more flexible. The expert artist, musician, or scientist is creative and curious, deliberately experimenting, enjoying the challenge when things do not go according to plan (Csikszentmihalyi, 1996).

Consider the expert surgeon who takes the most complex cases and prefers unusual patients over typical ones because operating on them might bring sudden, unexpected complications. Compared with the novice, the expert surgeon is not only more likely to notice telltale signs (an unexpected lesion, an oddly shaped organ, a rise or drop in a vital sign) that may signal a problem, but is also more flexible and more willing

Flexible Expert Although there are many things to pay attention to this 911 operator in Chatham-Kent Police headquarters in Ontario needs to be flexible in her thinking to accommodate each caller's physical and emotional situation.

DIANA MARTIN / CHATHAM DAILY NEWS / QMI AGENCY

to deviate from standard textbook procedures if those procedures prove ineffective (Patel et al., 1999).

Similarly, experts in all walks of life adapt to individual cases and exceptions—like an expert chef who adjusts ingredients, temperature, technique, and timing as a dish develops, tasting to see if a little more ginger is needed, seldom following a recipe exactly. Standards are high: Some chefs throw food in the garbage rather than serve a dish that many people would happily eat. Expert chess players, auto mechanics, and violinists are similarly aware of nuances that might escape the novice.

Jenny, Again

The research on expertise focuses on job-related learning, but the most important aspect of adult life may be responding to other people—especially children and partners. Years of experience in human relationships may sometimes make adults more intuitive, automatic, strategic, and flexible. For example, many parents find themselves less anxious about their second or third baby than their first, and grandparents may be more responsive and patient with children than they were as parents.

Kathleen's STORY ▶

A dispassionate analysis of Jenny's situation, from this chapter's opening story, would conclude that another baby—with no marriage, no job, and an apartment in the south Bronx—would doom her to poor health, poor prospects, and a depressing life. This is not a stereotype: The data show that lifelong poverty is the usual future for low-income mothers who have another child, out-of-wedlock, with another man.

But statistics do not reflect Jenny's intelligence, creativity, and practical expertise. She already knew how to access social support, evident by her seeking help. She was not daunted by her poverty; remember, she found many free activities for her children to enjoy, including sending them on vacation in the country. She was exceptional, but not unique: Many low-income people overcome the potential stressors of poverty (Chen & Miller, 2012).

Jenny used her knowledge well. She asked Billy, the father of the child, to be tested for sickle-cell anemia (results were negative), and she knew she should be honest with him. She told him she would have the baby, which was not his choice but one he admired. She continued to encourage her children in public school and established friendships with some of their teachers, who in turn gave them special attention.

After she had the baby (a healthy, full-term girl), she interviewed for a city job tutoring children in her home; that way, she could earn money while caring for her newborn. I brought baby clothes to her apartment one day and noticed that her framed Bronx Community College associate's degree diploma wasn't displayed anywhere; she explained that she took it off the wall, fearing that the job agency might think she was overqualified. That was expertise: She got the tutoring job.

When her baby was a little older, Jenny headed back to college, earning her BA on a full scholarship. Her professors recognized her intelligence: She was chosen to give the student speech at graduation. She then found work as a receptionist in a city hospital, a job that provided daycare and health benefits. That allowed her to move her family to a better neighbourhood of the Bronx.

Billy would sometimes visit Jenny and his daughter. His wife became suspicious and hired a detective to follow him—and then gave him an ultimatum: Stop seeing Jenny or obtain a divorce. At that point, it was very obvious that Jenny had some insight into human relations that I did not recognize in my office years earlier—because Billy chose divorce and then married her. Within a few years, Jenny, Billy, and the children moved to Florida, where she got a master's degree (she phoned me to say she was assigned my textbook to read) and then a professional job in the school system.

The last time I saw her, I learned that she bikes, swims, and gardens every day. I met her son: He had earned a PhD in psychology, and both her daughters are also college graduates.

Not everyone becomes an expert in human relations. But one lesson from this chapter is that health, intelligence, and even wisdom may improve over the years of adulthood. As further explained in Chapter 13, adult choices made, and relationships tended, make a difference—true for Jenny and for us all.

KEY points

- Adults compensate for deficits, selecting what particular skills and abilities to optimize.
- Expertise is developed over the years as adults become more intuitive, automatic, strategic, and flexible in their thinking and actions regarding what task they have chosen as their specialty.
- Some people become experts in human relations, able to accurately assess their own abilities and the motivations of other people.

SUMMARY

Senescence

1. Senescence causes a universal slowdown during adulthood, but aging is often imperceptible because organ reserve maintains capacity. The entire body adjusts to changes in the short term (homeostasis) and the long term (allostasis).

2. Sexual satisfaction may improve with age, but infertility becomes more common. Sperm count gradually decreases in men, and every step of female reproduction—ovulation, implantation, fetal growth, labour, and birth—slows down. For both sexes, STIs interfere with healthy reproduction. Overall good health, especially sexual health, correlates with fertility.

3. A number of assisted reproductive technology (ART) procedures, including in vitro fertilization (IVF), offer potential answers to infertility. Donor sperm, donor ova, and/or donor wombs have helped millions of infertile couples become parents.

4. The brain slows down and begins a gradual decline. The brain benefits from measures to improve overall health, especially exercise, and is harmed by most psychoactive drugs.

5. Senescence is apparent in the senses, notably vision and hearing. Everyone becomes more far-sighted and less able to hear high-frequency sounds as they age.

6. Appearance also changes with age, as evident in less elastic skin, more wrinkles, less hair, and more fat. Ease of movement decreases as people become less agile.

7. At menopause, ovulation ceases and estrogen is markedly reduced. Hormone production declines more gradually in men. For both sexes, hormone replacement therapy (HRT) should be used cautiously, if at all.

Health Habits and Age

8. Mortality, morbidity, disability, and vitality are all measures of health, each overlapping but distinct. During adulthood (ages 25 to 65), mortality is unusual in developed nations, unless drug abuse (including smoking and drinking) is severe.

9. Adults in North America smoke cigarettes much less often than they once did, and rates of lung cancer and other diseases are falling, largely for that reason. Alcohol abuse remains a major health problem worldwide.

10. Good health habits include exercising regularly and maintaining a healthy weight. On both these counts, today's adults are less healthy than prior generations. This is especially true in North America.

11. People experience many stresses over the 40 years of adulthood. They use various coping measures, both problem-focused and emotion-focused, to prevent stresses from becoming stressors. Low income correlates with many measures of poor health.

What Is Adult Intelligence?

12. It was traditionally assumed that there is one general intelligence (*g*), measurable by IQ tests. Cross-sectional research found that *g* decreased over adulthood. However, longitudinal research found that IQ scores increased in adulthood, particularly in tests of vocabulary. In addition, researchers found that average IQ scores increased over the twentieth century, perhaps due to education and health.

13. Much depends on how intelligence is defined and measured. Crystallized intelligence, reflecting accumulated knowledge, increases, but fluid, flexible reasoning declines in adults.

14. Sternberg proposed three fundamental forms of intelligence: analytic, creative, and practical. Cultural values encourage development of some cognitive abilities more than others. Each person responds to these cultural priorities, which may not be reflected in IQ scores.

Selective Gains and Losses

15. As people grow older, they select certain aspects of their lives to focus on, optimizing development in those areas and compensating for declines in others. Applied to cognition,

this means that people become selective experts in whatever intellectual skills they choose to develop. Meanwhile, abilities that are not exercised may fade.

16. In addition to being more experienced, experts are better thinkers than novices because they are more intuitive; their cognitive processes are automatic, often seeming to require little conscious thought; they use more and better strategies to perform whatever task is required; and they are more flexible in their thinking.

17. Experienced adults may surpass younger adults if they specialize and harness their efforts, compensating for any deficits that may appear. According to a study of taxi drivers in London, England, brains grow to support selective expertise.

KEY TERMS

allostasis (p. 428)
analytic intelligence (p. 447)
andropause (p. 435)
automatic processing (p. 453)
creative intelligence (p. 447)
crystallized intelligence (p. 446)

emotion-focused coping (p. 441)
expert (p. 451)
expertise (p. 451)
fluid intelligence (p. 446)
Flynn effect (p. 444)
general intelligence (*g*) (p. 443)
homeostasis (p. 428)

hormone replacement therapy (HRT) (p. 434)
in vitro fertilization (IVF) (p. 431)
infertility (p. 430)
menopause (p. 434)
organ reserve (p. 428)
practical intelligence (p. 447)

problem-focused coping (p. 441)
Seattle Longitudinal Study (p. 445)
selective optimization with compensation (p. 450)
senescence (p. 428)
stressor (p. 440)

WHAT HAVE YOU LEARNED?

1. How often and why do people lose significant brain function before age 65?

2. How do vision and hearing change during adulthood?

3. What visible changes take place in the skin and hair between ages 25 and 65?

4. What visible changes take place in body shape between ages 25 and 65?

5. What aspects of body functioning keep adults from recognizing that their bodies are working less well over time?

6. How are men and women affected by the changes in sexual responsiveness with age?

7. What are some of the factors that diminish fertility?

8. How have advances in medicine helped people with fertility problems?

9. What are the advantages and disadvantages of HRT for women?

10. Why do many doctors consider the term *andropause* misleading?

11. What changes in tobacco use have occurred, where, and with what consequences?

12. How does obesity affect health and well-being?

13. What are some solutions to obesity? What drawbacks are there to these solutions?

14. What diseases and conditions are less likely in people who exercise every day?

15. In what different ways do men and women deal with stress? What biological factors help explain these differences?

16. Why have traditional diseases of affluence become more common among the poor?

17. Why does health vary between and within SES and ethnic groups?

18. What differing opinions exist about *g*?

19. What does cross-sectional research on IQ scores throughout adulthood usually find? What does longitudinal research on IQ scores throughout adulthood usually find?

20. Why do cross-sectional and longitudinal studies of intelligence reach different conclusions?

21. How does cross-sequential research control for cohort effects?

22. How is fluid intelligence different from crystallized intelligence?

23. What are Sternberg's three fundamental forms of intelligence?

24. What is the basic idea of selective optimization with compensation?

25. What might a person do to optimize ability in some area not discussed in the book, such as playing the flute, growing tomatoes, or building a cabinet?

26. How do athletes compensate for the physical losses that come with age?

27. What factors contribute to expertise?

28. Using a specific example, demonstrate how an expert's intuition might aid ability.

29. How does automatic thinking lead to expert performance?

30. Why might strategy be the most important difference between a skilled person and an unskilled one?

31. Give an example of how an expert in a profession of your choice might think flexibly.

APPLICATIONS

1. Guess the ages of five people you know and then ask them how old they are. Analyze the clues you used for your guesses and the people's reactions to your question.

2. Find a speaker willing to come to your class who is an expert on weight loss, adult health, smoking, or drinking. Write a one-page proposal explaining why you think this speaker would be good and what topics he or she should address. Give this proposal to your instructor, with contact information for your speaker. The instructor can call the potential speakers, thank them for their willingness, and decide whether to actually invite them to speak.

3. The importance of context and culture is illustrated by the things that people think are basic knowledge. Choose a partner, and each of you write four questions that you think are hard but fair as measures of general intelligence. Then give your test to your partner and answer the four questions that person has prepared for you. What did you learn from the results?

4. Skill at video games is sometimes thought to reflect intelligence. Interview three or four people who play such games. What abilities do they think video games require? What do you think these games reflect in terms of experience, age, and motivation?

>>ONLINE CONNECTIONS

To accompany your textbook, you have access to a number of online resources, including LearningCurve, which is an adaptive quizzing program; critical thinking questions; and case studies. For access to any of these links, go to www.worthpublishers.com/launchpad/bergerchuang1e. In addition to these resources, you'll find links to video clips, personalized study advice, and an e-Book. Among the videos and activities available online are the following:

■ *Brain Development: Middle Adulthood.* Animations show age-related loss of brain volume and compensatory increase in the size of the ventricles and the volume of cerebrospinal fluid.

■ *Development of Expertise.* Expertise involves analytic, creative, and practical intelligence, but what makes it happen? Research shows that talent is not enough—practise, practise, practise!

CHAPTER OUTLINE

ADULTHOOD:
Psychosocial Development

WHAT WILL YOU KNOW?

- Do adults keep the personality traits they had as infants?
- When is it better to divorce than to stay married?
- When is it better to be unemployed than to have a job?

I broke two small bones in my pelvis—a mishap I caused myself: I was rushing, wearing smooth-soled shoes, carrying papers, in the rain, after dark, stepping up a curb. I fell hard on the sidewalk. That led to a 911 call, an ambulance, five hospital days, five rehab days, heartfelt admiration for the physical therapists who got me walking, and deep appreciation of colleagues who taught my classes for two weeks.

I mention that minor event because it spotlights generativity. My four children, adults now, cared for me far beyond what I thought I needed. The two nearby daughters, Elissa and Sarah, got to the emergency room within an hour; Rachel flew in from Minnesota and bought me new shoes with slip-proof treads; Bethany drove down from Connecticut with planters, dirt, flowers, and trees to beautify my home. They brought me books and a computer, questioned nurses and doctors, phoned insurance companies, filled prescriptions, arranged taxis, pushed my wheelchair, and did laundry, shopping, cooking, and cleaning.

It was hard for me to accept help. I had told my friends that I wanted no visitors. One said, "You can't move, you are stuck in bed, I am coming." I'd planned to immediately return to the classroom because I thought my students needed me. But after several days in the hospital, I realized I needed them as much as, or more than, they needed me. ●

—*Kathleen Berger*

IN ADULTHOOD, WE INCREASINGLY SEE THAT GENERATIVITY IS MUTUAL: People need to receive help as well as to give it. That is a theme of this chapter, which focuses on the many interactions that mark adult lives: partnering, parenting, and mentoring. Each individual is unique, charting his or her own path, but always helped by others. We begin, then, with the personality traits that endure. We continue with some of the ways people support each other, and we end with the complexities of combining work and family.

Personality Development in Adulthood

A mixture of genes, experiences, and contexts results in personality, which includes each person's unique actions and attitudes. Continuity is evident: Few people develop characteristics that are the opposite of their childhood temperament. But personality can change as people deal with adversity and challenge.

Theories of Adult Personality

To organize the discussion of this mix of embryonic beginnings, childhood experiences, and adulthood contexts, we begin with theories.

ERIKSON AND MASLOW Erikson originally envisioned eight stages of development, three of which occur after adolescence. He is praised as "the one thinker who changed our minds about what it means to live as a person who has arrived at a chronologically mature position and yet continues to grow, to change, and to develop" (Hoare, 2002, p. 3).

Erikson's early stages, described in previous chapters, are each tied to a particular chronological period. But late in his life, Erikson stressed that adult stages do not occur in lockstep. Adults of many ages can be in the fifth stage, *identity versus role confusion,* or in any of the three adult stages—*intimacy versus isolation, generativity versus stagnation,* and *integrity versus despair* (McAdams, 2006) (see Table 13.1). He saw adulthood as the continuation of identity seeking via exploration of intimacy and generativity, a vision confirmed by current research (Beaumont & Pratt, 2011).

Similarly, Abraham Maslow (1954) refused to link chronological age and adult development when he described a *hierarchy of needs* with five stages achieved in sequence (see Chapter 1, Figure 1.11). Completion of each stage allows a person to move ahead.

TABLE 13.1 Erikson's Stages of Adulthood

Unlike Freud or other early theorists who thought adults simply worked through the legacy of their childhood, Erikson described psychosocial needs after puberty in half of his eight stages. His most famous book, *Childhood and Society* (1963), devoted only two pages to each adult stage, but published and unpublished elaborations in later works led to a much richer depiction (Hoare, 2002).

Identity Versus Role Confusion
Although Erikson originally situated the identity crisis during adolescence, he realized that identity concerns could be lifelong. Identity combines values and traditions from childhood with the current social context. Since contexts keep evolving, many adults reassess all types of identity (sexual/gender, vocational/work, religious/spiritual, political, and ethnic).

Intimacy Versus Isolation
Adults seek intimacy—a close, reciprocal connection with another human being. Intimacy is mutual, not self-absorbed, which means that adults need to devote time and energy to one another. This process begins in emerging adulthood and continues throughout life. Isolation is especially likely when divorce or death disrupts established intimate relationships.

Generativity Versus Stagnation
Adults need to care for the next generation, either by raising their own children or by mentoring, teaching, and helping others. Erikson's first description of this stage focused on parenthood, but later he included other ways to achieve generativity. Adults extend the legacy of their culture and their generation with ongoing care, creativity, and sacrifice.

Integrity Versus Despair
When Erikson himself was in his 70s, he decided that integrity, with the goal of combatting prejudice and helping all humanity, was too important to be left to the elderly. He also thought that each person's entire life could be directed toward connecting a personal journey with the historical and cultural purpose of human society, the ultimate achievement of integrity.

As an example, people who are in Maslow's third level (*love and belonging,* similar to Erikson's *intimacy versus isolation*) seek to be loved and accepted by partners, family members, and friends. Without affection, people might stay stuck at this level. By contrast, those who experience abundant love are able to move to the next level, *success and esteem.* The dominant need at this fourth stage is to be respected and admired.

For humanists like Maslow, these five drives characterize all people, with most adults seeking love or respect (levels three and four). Unless mired in poverty or war, people move past Maslow's lower two stages (safety and basic needs) by adulthood.

Other theorists agree, sometimes describing *affiliation* and *achievement,* sometimes using other labels. We will soon use Erikson's terms, *intimacy* and *generativity,* as a scaffold to describe these two universal needs. Every theory of adult personality recognizes that both are important in adulthood.

Risk Taking Generally, risk taking decreases with age, but modern technology allows older adults to put their bodies on the line. This middle-aged man chases tornados with a "Doppler on wheels."

midlife crisis
A supposed period of unusual anxiety, radical self-examination, and sudden transformation that was once widely associated with middle age, but that actually had more to do with developmental history than with chronological age.

THE MIDLIFE CRISIS No current theorist sets chronological boundaries for specific stages of adult development. Middle age, if it exists, can begin at age 35 or 50. This contradicts the theory of the **midlife crisis,** thought to be a time of anxiety and radical change as age 40 approaches. Men, in particular, were said to leave their wives, buy red sports cars, and quit their jobs because of midlife panic. The midlife crisis was popularized by Gail Sheehy (1976), who called it "the age 40 crucible," and by Daniel Levinson (1978), who said men experienced

> tumultuous struggles within the self and with the external world. … Every aspect of their lives comes into question, and they are horrified by much that is revealed. They are full of recriminations against themselves and others.
>
> *[Levinson, 1978, p. 199]*

However, no large study over the past three decades has found evidence of a normative midlife crisis (Austrian, 2008). In hindsight, it is easy to see where Sheehy and Levinson went astray. Levinson studied just 40 men, all from one cohort, and the data were then analyzed by men who were also middle-aged, which introduced bias into the analysis. Sheehy summarized social scientists' research and then supplemented it by interviewing people she specifically chose. Neither Sheehy nor Levinson used replicated, multi-method, longitudinal research, the bedrock of developmental science.

The initial research on midlife crises was conducted in the early 1970s. Men who reached age 40 during that time period were affected by historic upheavals in their families. Many began marriages and careers in the 1950s with particular expectations of their children, wives, and careers. Instead, the first wave of feminism took place when they reached middle age. As a result, women's views of family and career changed dramatically. Although the researchers concluded that the men were experiencing a crisis as a result of their age, in fact it was as a result of historical circumstances.

Regardless, the concept of midlife crisis continues to be referenced in popular movies, books, and songs. A 2013 Google search found more than 19 million hits for "midlife crisis." In popular culture, midlife crisis is used to explain almost every aspect of adult personality, health, careers, and relationships. However, the reality is that as we get older, we must inevitably deal with loss, failure, and relationship problems. Most people who reach age 40 do not have a midlife crisis.

Personality Traits

Remember from Chapter 4 that each baby has a distinct temperament. Some are shy, others outgoing; some are frightened, others fearless. Such traits are affected by experiences, but they begin with genes.

THE BIG FIVE Temperament does not vanish: Researchers find substantial, even astonishing, coherence in personality throughout life. There are hundreds of examples. One recent study found, for instance, that temperament at age 3 predicted gambling problems at age 32 (Slutske et al., 2012).

Longitudinal, cross-sectional, and multicultural research has identified five clusters of personality traits that appear in every culture and era, called the **Big Five** (to remember the Big Five, the acronym OCEAN is useful):

- *Openness:* imaginative, curious, artistic, creative, open to new experiences
- *Conscientiousness:* organized, deliberate, conforming, self-disciplined
- *Extroversion:* outgoing, assertive, active
- *Agreeableness:* kind, helpful, easygoing, generous
- *Neuroticism:* anxious, moody, self-punishing, critical.

Each person's personality is somewhere between extremely high and extremely low on each of these five. The low end might be described, in the same order as above, with these five adjectives: *closed, careless, introverted, hard to please,* and *placid.*

These five clusters not only affect career choices and health habits, as expected, but also much more. Adults choose their social context, or **ecological niche,** selecting vocations, hobbies, mates, and neighbourhoods at least in part because of personality traits. Even the decision to retire and the reaction to retirement are related to the Big Five (Robinson et al., 2010).

Among the factors linked to the Big Five are education (conscientious people have higher rates of post-secondary graduation), marriage (extroverts are more likely to marry), divorce (more often for neurotics), fertility (lower for women in recent cohorts who are more conscientious), IQ (higher in people who are more open), verbal fluency (again, associated with openness and extroversion), and even political views (conservatives are less open) (Duckworth et al., 2007; Gerber et al., 2011; Jokela, 2012; Pedersen et al., 2005; Silvia & Sanders, 2010).

International research confirms that all human personality traits (there are hundreds of them) can be grouped in the Big Five. Of course, personality and behaviour are influenced by many other factors, not only gender and cohort as seen above, but also culture. It would be foolish to predict college or university graduation or voting behaviour or anything else *solely* on a person's rank on the Big Five.

Indeed, anyone might act in uncharacteristic ways if circumstances are dramatically altered—perhaps by unexpected divorce, recovery from addiction, forced emigration, treated depression, or a sudden disabling disease (Mroczek et al., 2006). Events influence traits, although the specific impact is always affected by personality (Specht et al., 2011). Nature and nurture interact, each affecting the other.

Thus, new events sometimes bring out old personality patterns. People might divorce and then remarry someone like the old partner, for instance, or find a new job that reflects their personality rather than change their personality to fit the job. In general, people are most comfortable when their personality fits with their partners, their neighbours, and their careers. For instance, one study found that

Big Five
The five basic clusters of personality traits that remain quite stable throughout adulthood: openness, conscientiousness, extroversion, agreeableness, and neuroticism.

ecological niche
The particular lifestyle and social context that adults settle into because it is compatible with their individual personality needs and interests.

✦ **ESPECIALLY FOR Immigrants and Children of Immigrants**
Poverty and persecution are the main reasons some people leave their home for another country, but personality is also influential. Which of the Big Five personality traits do you think is most characteristic of immigrants? (see response, page 467) ➡

Personality Endures Fearfulness is one of the personality traits most likely to endure from childhood through late adulthood. Some children are terrified by Disney movies and fairy tales. Others enjoy the thrill of fear.

Young Stephen King

people high in neuroticism tend to work in hazardous conditions—and then complain about it (Sutin & Costa, 2010).

Even happiness seems a matter of personality more than circumstances. Adults who experience things that temporarily make them overjoyed (e.g., winning a lottery) or depressed (e.g., losing a loved one) often revert to the level of happiness they had before that event. Personality trumps experience (Gilbert, 2006).

Same Situation, Far Apart: Scientists at Work Most scientists are open-minded and conscientious (two of the Big Five personality traits). Culture and social context are crucial, however. The doctor in North America *(left)* focuses on research, while the doctor in Tanzania *(right)* treats patients.

CULTURE, AGE, AND CONTEXT Many researchers who study personality find that people adapt to their culture, expressing personality traits differently in, say, Egypt or Ecuador (Church, 2010). Traits that are considered pathological in one place (such as neuroticism in North America) tend to be modified as people mature within that community (L. A. Clark, 2009). By contrast, traits that are valued (such as conscientiousness) endure.

That is exactly what was found in a massive longitudinal study of midlife North Americans (called MIDUS). Agreeableness and conscientiousness increased slightly overall while neuroticism decreased, as did openness and extroversion (which may be more appreciated in the young than the old) (see Figure 13.1) (Lachman & Bertrand, 2001). This pattern was also found in other research (Allemand et al., 2008; Donnellan & Lucas, 2008).

Since cultural values interact with personality traits, it should also be noted that the terms used to describe personality are not neutral. For instance, "open" seems a positive trait and "closed" seems negative. But instead of closed, perhaps another term, such as *traditional,* might be a more accurate descriptor.

The relationship between enduring personality and changing context was evident in a longitudinal study that tracked women in the United States from ages 20 to 70 (George et al., 2011). When women were in college in the 1950s, they expected to become wives and mothers, not employees. In the 1960s, the culture shifted—and so did the women. Most entered the workforce, learning new skills and gaining confidence. Nonetheless, personality endured, evident in the jobs they found. For example, those high in extroversion might work in sales and management; those high in conscientiousness might become nurses or accountants.

The relationship between personality and context are evident not only in careers, but also in family structure. For both men and women born in 1920, those high in openness had about the same number of children as those low in that trait. For those born in 1960, however, the more open a person was, the fewer children he or she had. They were open to non-traditional life patterns, which for some meant having no children (Jokela, 2012).

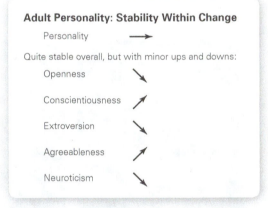

FIGURE 13.1 Trends, Not Rules Overall stability, with some marked individual variation, is the main story for the Big Five over the decades of adulthood. In addition, each of the traits tends to shift slightly, as depicted here.

OPPOSING PERSPECTIVES

Local Context Versus Genes

Some people believe that personality is so powerfully shaped by regional culture that a baby will have a different personality if born and raised in, say, Canada or Mexico. The opposite hypothesis is that personality is innate, fixed at birth, and impervious to social pressures with only minor, temporary impact from culture.

Evidence for the second hypothesis includes the fact that the same Big Five traits are found in many nations, with similar age-related trends. Supposed national differences in personality may instead be unfounded stereotypes (McCrae & Terracciano, 2006).

Further evidence that personality is inborn, not made by context, is the stability of personality throughout adulthood (B. W. Roberts et al., 2006; Specht et al., 2011). Extroverted emerging adults become outgoing seniors, with many friends from early adulthood and with more new friends along the way. Other traits likewise endure, in new forms.

Other research, however, finds that culture and events change personality. For example, according to some social scientists, Asian cultures encourage a sixth personality dimension, called *dependence on others,* which should be added to the Big Five when studying Asians (Hofstede, 2007; Okazaki et al., 2009; Suh et al., 2008).

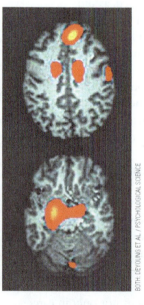

BOTH: DEYOUNG ET AL / PSYCHOLOGICAL SCIENCE

Asian children who seem low on this trait are encouraged by their culture to increase it, so cooperation is more common among Asian adults than among children. Since we now know that brain structures respond to experience, the childhood context—such as a preschool that teaches sharing and group cohesion—may cause an enduring, neurological change.

When Asian adults emigrate to a culture in which that trait is less valued, they may be considered too docile and overly concerned with blending in. This would not be true for Asians who emigrated as babies and were raised in the individualistic culture, unless their parents were strongly opposed to new cultural influences and raised their children as they themselves had been raised. Clinicians find that personality tests developed for native-born North Americans do not properly assess the personality traits of Asian-Americans who grew up in Asia (Okazaki et al., 2009).

Another example of personality change is in the Big Five trait of openness. Cultures differ in the extent to which they consider openness desirable. In some cultures, openness is prized as an indication of intelligence and willingness to learn. Children who ask questions in class are appreciated. However, in some places interpersonal harmony is more valued than individual initiative (Church, 2010). For instance, one group of researchers concluded: "Openness is not commonly used as a distinct dimension in the taxonomy of personality traits in Chinese culture" (Cheung et al., 2008, p. 103). In this case, children are discouraged from impulsively "interrupting" with questions.

The idea that context shapes personality is highlighted in a U.S. study that found that the Big Five scores differ among adults in the 50 states (Rentfrow et al., 2008). According to the answers of 619 397 respondents to an Internet survey that asked questions about their traits, New Yorkers are highest in openness, New Mexicans highest in conscientiousness, North Dakotans highest in both extroversion and agreeableness, and West Virginians highest in neuroticism. Lowest in these five are, in the same order, residents of North Dakota, Alaska, Maryland, Alaska (again), and Utah.

This suggests that local norms, institutions, history, and geography also have an impact on personality. For example, residents of Utah include Mormons (a culture that does

Active Brains, Active Personality The hypothesis that individual personality traits originate in the brain was tested by scientists who sought correlates between brain activity (shown in red) and personality traits. People high in four of the Big Five (conscientiousness, extroversion, agreeableness, neuroticism—but not openness) activated brain regions known for comparable characteristics. Here are two side views *(left)* and a top and bottom view *(right)* of brains of people high in neuroticism. Regions sensitive to stress, depression, threat, and punishment (yellow bull's eyes) were more active than in the low neurotic individuals (Deyoung et al., 2010).

not use drugs, has large families, and are generally in good health) and awesome mountains. That might make them less anxious and more serene, resulting in low levels of neuroticism. In contrast, New York is multi-ethnic because it has always been an international arrival city (Ellis Island and the Statue of Liberty are in the harbour), which might encourage openness. The authors of this study suggest that many aspects of adults' lives, including criminal behaviour, morbidity, education, and political preference, spring from regional differences in personality (Rentfrow, 2010).

Before concluding that environment shapes personality, however, consider the opposite idea—that personality is innate. This could also spring from the same U.S. data. Perhaps adults move to wherever they feel appreciated for who they are. For example, a North Dakotan who, unlike his neighbours, is high in openness might relocate to New York. If many people moved because of their personality, then regional or national differences would appear as people go where their inborn temperament is valued.

A decades-long study in Finland indeed found that personality often leads to relocation (Jokela et al., 2008; Silventoinen et al., 2008). Finns with an outgoing personality (high in extroversion, or sociability) were likely to move from isolated rural areas to urban ones.

A consensus regarding the relationship between culture, geography, genes, and personality has not yet emerged (Church, 2010). As you see, both opposing views make sense: More longitudinal research is needed.

KEY Points

- Adults seek intimacy and generativity (Erikson) or love and respect (Maslow).
- The Big Five personality traits (openness, conscientiousness, extroversion, agreeableness, neuroticism) are evident worldwide.
- Adult personality shows both continuity with childhood temperament and change in reaction to life circumstances.
- Personality traits affect adults' choices of partners, jobs, and life patterns.

RESPONSE FOR Immigrants and Children of Immigrants (from page 464) Extroversion and neuroticism, according to one study (Silventoinen et al., 2008). Because these traits decrease over adulthood, fewer older adults emigrate. ●

Intimacy

Every adult experiences the crisis Erikson called *intimacy versus isolation,* seeking to connect with other people. Specifics vary. Some adults are distant from their parents but close to partners and friends; others rely on family members but not on non-relatives. The need for intimacy is universal yet dynamic: Each adult regulates closeness and reciprocity, combining friends, acquaintances, and relatives (Lang et al., 2009).

Everyone is part of a **social convoy,** a group of people who "provide a protective layer of social relations to guide, encourage, and socialize individuals as they go through life" (Antonucci et al., 2001, p. 572). The term *convoy* originally referred to a group of travellers in hostile territory, such as soldiers marching across unfamiliar terrain. Individuals were strengthened by the convoy, sharing difficult conditions and defending one another.

As people move through life, their social convoy metaphorically functions as those earlier convoys did (Crosnoe & Elder, 2002; Lang et al., 2009). Paradoxically, current changes in the historical context (globalization, longevity, and ethnic and sexual diversity) make intimacy more vital. Humans need social convoys (Antonucci et al., 2007).

social convoy
Collectively, the family members, friends, acquaintances, and even strangers who move through life with an individual.

Friends and Acquaintances

Friends are crucial members of the social convoy, partly because they are chosen for the traits that make them reliable fellow travellers. They are usually about the same age, with similar experiences and values. Mutual loyalty and aid are expected from friends: A relationship that is imbalanced (one person always giving, the other always taking) over the years is likely to end because both parties are uneasy. Of course, sometimes a friend needs care and cannot reciprocate at the time. Friends

REZA / GETTY IMAGES

Shared Genes, Different History
These four generations of one family in rural China illustrate historical shifts in social relationships. The great-grandmother's social convoy was confined to close family members, a marked contrast to her great-granddaughter, who has many friends from work and school.

consequential strangers
People who are not in a person's closest friendship circle but nonetheless have an impact.

provide practical help and useful advice when serious problems—death of a family member, personal illness, job loss—arise.

FRIENDSHIP AND HUMAN DEVELOPMENT A comprehensive study found that friendships improve with age. To be specific, adolescents and young adults consider a significant minority of their friendships *ambivalent* or *problematic.* By adulthood, most friendships are rated *close,* few are ambivalent, and almost none are problematic (Fingerman et al., 2004).

Close friends offer companionship, information, and laughter in daily life. They encourage one another during challenging periods, helping with mental health. One reason depression seems to decrease with age is that friends are more carefully selected, and friendships are more nourished, so that friends become more supportive over time.

Friends help with details of physical health as well, encouraging one another to eat better, quit smoking, exercise, and so on. The reverse is also true: If someone gains weight over the years of adulthood, his or her best friend is likely to do so as well. In fact, although most adults keep their friends for decades, health habits are one reason some adults change friends (O'Malley & Christakis, 2011). For instance, a friendship between a chain smoker and someone who quit smoking is likely to fray.

If an adult has no friends, health suffers (Couzin, 2009). This seems as true in developing nations as in developed ones. Universally, humans are healthier with supportive friends and relatives, and sicker when they are socially isolated (Kumar et al., 2012).

ACQUAINTANCES In addition to friends, hundreds of other acquaintances provide information, support, social integration, and new ideas (Fingerman, 2009). Neighbours, co-workers, store clerks, the local police officer, members of a religious or community group, and so on are **consequential strangers,** defined as people who are not in a person's closest convoy but who nonetheless have an impact.

Among the consequential strangers in your life might be

- dog owners you meet when you walk your dog
- the barber or hair stylist who regularly cuts your hair
- the coffee shop staff from whom you buy a muffin every day
- your friend's parents.

A consequential stranger may also be an actual stranger, such as someone who sits next to you on an airplane, or directs you when you are lost, or gives you a seat on the bus. Such acquaintances differ from most close friends and family members in that they include people of diverse religions, ethnic groups, ages, and political opinions (Fingerman, 2009). The Internet has strengthened friendships and added more consequential strangers to many people's lives (Stern & Adams, 2010; Wang & Wellman, 2010).

Regular acquaintances are part of each person's peripheral social network. With age, the number of such peripheral friends decreases. For example, one study found that the average emerging adult had 16 peripheral friends, but the average middle-aged adult had 12 (Zhang et al., 2011). The same study also found, however, that people who were high in the temperamental characteristic of dependence on others (or *interdependence,* suggested as a sixth trait added to the Big Five) did not follow the usual pattern of having fewer peripheral friends as they aged. In fact, they were likely to add people to their social network, not lose them (Zhang et al., 2011).

The composition of social networks varies by culture. In many African nations, everyone in the community is in the peripheral network. They might stop by, unannounced, to visit, which in other cultures might be considered rude. Another cultural difference is whether family members are considered friends. For example, one study found that in both Germany and Hong Kong, adults had about the same number of intimates, but the Germans tended to include more non-family friends, whereas the Chinese included more family members (Fung et al., 2008).

Family Bonds

Close friends often are referred to as being "like a sister" or "my brother." Such terms reflect the assumption that family connections are intimate. As just mentioned, this is more reflective of some cultures than of others, but family relationships are crucial for many adults, usually more so as they age.

Which particular family members become intimates varies for many reasons, as one might expect. One intriguing study of the population of Denmark found that twins married less often than single-born adults. According to the researchers, twins may be less likely to need another close companion (not needing a spouse since they have each other), but if they married, they were less likely to divorce because they knew how to get along with another person (Petersen et al., 2011).

ADULT CHILDREN AND THEIR PARENTS Although most adults in modern societies leave their parents' homes to establish their own households, a study of 7578 adults in seven nations found that physical separation did not necessarily weaken family ties. In fact, these authors concluded that intergenerational relationships are becoming stronger, not weaker, as more adult children live apart from their parents (Treas & Gubernskaya, 2012). This bond is sometimes financial as well as emotional. In many nations, young adults who leave home to find work send most of their salary back home. Personal goals are sacrificed for family concerns, and "collectivism often takes precedence and overrides individual needs and interests" (Wilson & Ngige, 2006, p. 248).

Other research points to the fact that the relationship between parents and adult children tends to be less affectionate if they live together (Ward & Spitze, 2007). This may be correlation rather than cause, since intergenerational living may come about when either the parents or the children are unable to live independently.

Overall, parents usually provide more financial and emotional support to their adult children than vice versa, although most children rally if necessary. In assessing intimacy, it should be noted that whenever adult children have serious financial, legal, or marital problems, most parents try to help. This has always been evident for young, single adults, but the economic recession has led to an increasing number of 25- to 34-year-olds living with their parents.

SIBLINGS AND OTHER RELATIVES With adulthood often comes marriage and childbearing, both of which can potentially increase the closeness between siblings or enhance previous difficulties (Conger & Little, 2010). The potential for closeness is greater when nieces and nephews are born. Parents want their children to know their aunts, uncles, and cousins, and that reduces sibling distance. Furthermore, adulthood frees siblings from forced cohabitation and rivalry, allowing them to differ without fighting.

Competition Among Siblings
Fernando *(left)* and Humberto *(right)* Campana are designers from Brazil, shown here at an exhibit of their work in Spain. As with many siblings, competition and collaboration have inspired them all their lives.

STEFANO G. PAVESI / CONTRASTO / REDUX

FIGURE 13.2 **From Rival to Friend**
Adolescents are not usually close to their siblings, but that often changes with time. By late adulthood, brothers and sisters usually consider one another among their best friends.

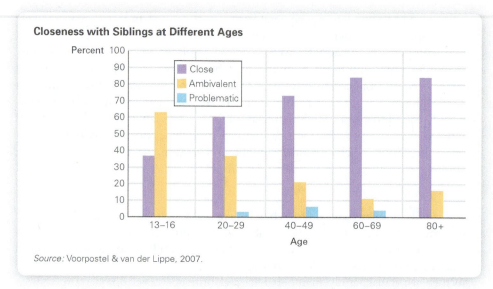

Closeness with Siblings at Different Ages

Percent

- Close
- Ambivalent
- Problematic

Age: 13–16, 20–29, 40–49, 60–69, 80+

Source: Voorpostel & van der Lippe, 2007.

Adult siblings often help one another, providing practical support (especially between brothers) and emotional support (especially between sisters) (see Figure 13.2) (Voorpostel & van der Lippe, 2007). For example, a middle-aged woman who lived thousands of kilometres from her four siblings said

> I have a good relationship with my brothers. … Every time I come, they are very warm and loving, and I stayed with my brother for a week. … Sisters is another story. Sisters are best friends. Sisters is like forever. When I have a problem, I phone my sisters. When I'm feeling down, I phone my sisters. And they always pick me up.
>
> *[quoted in Connidis, 2007, p. 488]*

In several South Asian nations, brothers are obligated to bestow gifts on their sisters, who in turn are expected to cook for and nurture their brothers (Conger & Little, 2010). Such patterns may impede individual growth, but they reduce poverty and strengthen family bonds. By encouraging siblings to care for one another, they satisfy intimacy needs.

A large study in the Netherlands found a curious relationship between closeness to parents and closeness among siblings. As expected, when adult women were close to their parents, they also were close to their siblings. To some extent, this was true for the men as well. However, those brothers who were distant from their parents tended to be closer than average to their siblings, as if to compensate. One family link becomes stronger because another one is weak (Voorpostel & Blieszner, 2008).

Family Harmony It is not easy to craft and sell stringed instruments, especially in the mountains of Northern Italy. However, this father and son team is successful, partly because they support each other.

DIEGO CERVO / BLEND IMAGES RM / GETTY IMAGES

GETTING ALONG Time and again, researchers have found that adults who have separate households from other adults in their family are nevertheless profoundly affected by their relationships with these family members. Such relationships can be supportive, as mentioned above, or destructive. Often they are both; ambivalence in parent–child relationships is more likely than placid harmony (Bojczyk et al., 2011; Reid & Reczek, 2011). Parental satisfaction is strongly affected by the adult lives of their children, with the most troubled children having more impact on parental well-being than the happy, successful ones (Fingerman et al., 2012).

In one international study, older adults (average age of 77) were asked how they got along with a particular child (average age of 53) (Silverstein et al., 2010). Answers were clustered into four groups: *amicable* (close, got along well, high communication), *detached* (distant, low communication), *disharmonious* (conflict, critical, arguing), and *ambivalent* (both close and critical, high communication).

All of the six nations studied had some elders in each of the four clusters, with amicable relationships being the most common. National differences were evident in the frequency of each cluster, with England and Norway being the most amicable, Germany and Spain the most detached, and Israel the most ambivalent. No nation had many disharmonious relationships, but the United States had more (20 percent) than the other five nations (Silverstein et al., 2010). Frail and dependent elders were more likely to experience friction, even though they often lived with their children. Close and affectionate family relations were most likely when the government provided many services (e.g., health care, senior residences). This suggests again that emotional intimacy is a distinct need for adults, independent of practical necessity.

Back to the interplay of friends and relatives: In every nation, most family members support each other. However, some adults stay distant from their blood relatives because they find them toxic. Such adults may become **fictive kin** in another family. They are not technically related (hence fictive), but are accepted and treated like a family member (hence kin). If adults have difficult relationships with their original family or if they are far from home, fictive kin can be a lifeline (Ebaugh & Curry, 2000; Heslin et al., 2011; Kim, 2009; Muraco, 2006).

Committed Partners

As detailed earlier, people in many nations take longer than previous generations did to publicly commit to one long-term romantic partner. Nonetheless, although specifics differ (marriage at age 20 is late in some cultures and far too early in others), adults everywhere seek long-term partners to help meet their needs for intimacy as well as to raise children, share resources, and provide care when needed.

Recent longitudinal Canadian data indicate that in 1961, married couples represented 91.6 percent of census families, but by 2011, this proportion had significantly declined to 67.0 percent. This decrease may be partly due to the increased number of common-law couples, from 5.6 percent in 1981 to 16.7 percent in 2011 (Milan & Bohnert, 2012).

In other nations, less than 2 percent of the population stays single for life. However, cohort matters. In Canada after the Depression, in the first couple of years of World War II (1940–1942), and immediately after the war, the marriage rate was at a high of 11 marriages per 1000 people. The rate then declined steadily (down to about 7 marriages per 1000 in the 1960s) until the 1970s, when the rate increased to 9.2 marriages per 1000. Rates then continued to decline, down to 4.4 in 2008 (see Figure 13.3).

MARRIAGE AND HAPPINESS From a developmental perspective, marriage is a useful institution. Adults thrive if another person is committed to their well-being; children benefit when they have two parents who are legally as well as emotionally dedicated to them; and societies are stronger if individuals form families.

From an individual perspective, the consequences are more mixed. There is no doubt that a satisfying marriage improves health, wealth, and happiness, but some marriages are not satisfying (Fincham & Beach, 2010). Generally, married people are a little happier, healthier, and richer than never-married ones—but not by much.

fictive kin
Someone who becomes accepted as part of a family to which he or she has no blood relation.

Same Situation, Far Apart: Happily Married Sarah and Alex *(top)* met online in North America and now enjoy a face-to-face connection. This couple in Siberia *(bottom)* lives on a farm and endures cold winters and hard work. Although the couples met in different ways, they are both committed to making a life together.

DAVE REEDE / AGSTOCK IMAGES / CORBIS

AKG-IMAGES / MARK DEFRAEYE / NEWSCOM

FIGURE 13.3 Changing Marriage Rates Marriage serves important social and economic roles in Canadian society. This graph shows the changes in marriage rates since 1921. The rate of 4.4 marriages per 1000 people in 2008 is the lowest rate seen in the last hundred years.

OBSERVATION QUIZ

What are some possible reasons for the increase in marriage rates in the 1940s and again in the 1970s? (see answer, page 474) →

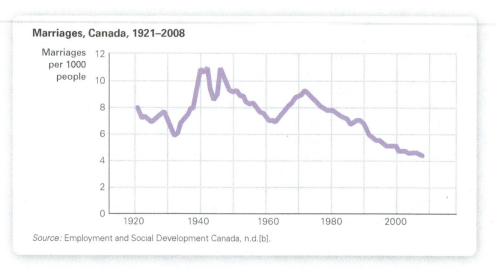

Marriages, Canada, 1921–2008

Marriages per 1000 people

Source: Employment and Social Development Canada, n.d.[b].

A 16-nation survey over 20 years ago found one nation (Portugal) where single people were happier than married ones, another (France) where both groups were equally content, and several where married adults were only slightly more often "very happy" than never-married adults. The largest differences were in the United States, where more married than single adults were "very happy" (37 versus 26 percent) (Inglehart, 1990).

Another large longitudinal study of married adults found that

> there were as many people who ended up less happy than they started as there were people who ended up happier than they started (a fact that is particularly striking given that we restricted the sample to people who stayed married).
>
> *[Lucas et al., 2003, p. 536]*

Thus, most adults marry and expect ongoing happiness because of it, but some will be disappointed (Coontz, 2005). Those who never marry can be quite happy as well (DePaulo, 2006).

Cohabitation historically has led to less happy adults than has marriage, especially for women. However, this also is changing by cohort and varies by culture, with some places finding few significant differences between cohabiting and married couples, or between men and women (Stavrova et al., 2012). Researchers now realize that cohabiters who expect to marry are quite different from those who choose to live together without expectation of marriage. If the latter couple eventually marries, their chances of a happy marriage are less than average (Sassler et al., 2012).

One Love, Two Homes Their friends and family know that Jonathan and Diana are a happy British couple, together day and night, year after year. But one detail distinguishes them from most couples: Each owns a house. They commute 16 kilometres to be LAT, living apart together.

For many cohabiters, living together is the first step in commitment and mutual trust. The next step is the wedding, and then each year of marriage increases their public and personal commitment to each other. Divorce becomes less likely, and many signs indicate that they are a couple, not just two individuals. For instance, they have more children than cohabiters who did not intend to marry, the man earns more than comparable unmarried men, and the woman spends more time on household tasks (Kuperberg, 2012).

A sizable number of adults have found a third way to have a steady romantic partner, called *living apart together* (LAT). They have separate residences, but especially when the partners are older than 30, LATs may be committed to each other, perhaps functioning as a couple for decades (Duncan & Phillips, 2010).

There are many ways to understand love, cross-culturally and over time (Sternberg & Weis, 2006). Robert Sternberg developed one useful construct when he wrote that love has three parts: passion, intimacy, and commitment.

Among twenty-first-century North Americans, passion is usually first, then shared confidences create intimacy, and finally commitment leads to an enduring relationship. When all three are evident, that is consummate love—an ideal sometimes, but not always, attained in marriage (Sternberg, 2006a).

PARTNERSHIPS OVER THE YEARS Not surprisingly, a meta-analysis of 93 studies found that personal well-being is affected by the quality of the marriage as well as vice versa, especially for people married eight years or longer (Proulx et al., 2007). The long-term nature of a relationship is affected by many factors, including the childhood experiences of both partners (Overbeek et al., 2007), economic instability (decreasing happiness), and the partners' personalities (agreeable people are usually happy; neurotic ones are usually not).

The passage of time also makes a difference. For instance, the honeymoon period tends to be happy, but soon frustration increases because conflicts arise (see At About This Time). Intimate partner violence is more likely in the first years of a relationship than later on (H. K. Kim et al., 2008). Partnerships (including heterosexual married couples, committed cohabiters, same-sex couples, and LAT couples) tend to be less happy when the first child is born, and again when children reach puberty (Umberson et al., 2010). Divorce risk rises and then falls as marriage progresses.

Gradually, after a decade or two of declining satisfaction, partnerships improve (Scarf, 2008). Part of the explanation is that many unhappy relationships end after a few years; this is particularly true for cohabiters, who have fewer barriers to separation. Generally, those who continue to be committed learn to appreciate each other, avoiding the flash points that previously caused fights.

Contrary to outdated impressions, the **empty nest** (the time when parents are alone again after their children have moved out and launched their own lives) often improves a relationship (Gorchoff et al., 2008). Simply spending time together, without interruptions from infants, demands from children, or rebellions from teenagers, improves intimacy as partners can focus on each other's needs. However, if couples have stayed together because of the children, the empty nest stage can become a time of conflict or divorce.

When all the children have become independent, long-term partnerships often benefit financially. The money spent on children is reduced when they become self-supporting. Many middle-aged couples finally have fewer expenses, so they can afford to be generous to themselves and their offspring. Another financial advantage is seniority: If one or both members of a couple have a steady job, income and security are likely to increase over time. Contemporary couples fight more about money than anything else; middle age reduces that friction.

Aside from the impact of freedom and income, some troubled relationships rebound to earlier levels of satisfaction as mates learn to understand and forgive one

empty nest
The time in the lives of parents when their children have left the family home to pursue their own lives.

At About This Time
Marital Happiness over the Years

Interval After Wedding	Characterization
First 6 months	Honeymoon period—happiest of all
6 months to 5 years	Happiness dips; divorce is more common now than later in marriage
5 to 10 years	Happiness holds steady
10 to 20 years	Happiness dips as children reach puberty
20 to 30 years	Happiness rises when children leave the nest
30 to 50 years	Happiness is high and steady, barring serious health problems

ANSWER TO OBSERVATION QUIZ
(from page 472) The fluctuations in the rates of marriages over the years are most likely due to historical events. For example, the increased number of marriages in the 1940s is due to the end of World War II, and the increase in the 1970s is due to the large number of baby boomers reaching adulthood. ●

another (Fincham et al., 2007). However, much depends on context: The process of forgiveness can help or harm a relationship, depending on the characteristics of the relationship (McNulty & Fincham, 2012). Shared backgrounds, values, and interests (homogamy) reduce conflict, whereas different backgrounds (heterogamy) raise issues that were not expected.

Marriages among people of different ethnic groups increased more than 20-fold from 1960 to 2000 (Lee & Bean, 2007). Such marriages have a higher risk of divorce, not only because of tensions from the outside culture, but also because of clashes in assumptions and habits between the partners (Burton et al., 2010; Fu & Wolfinger, 2011). On the other hand, as you learned in Chapter 1, SES may be more crucial than race: If a couple have ancestors from different continents, but have similar levels of education and family income and are acculturated to the same culture, they may be more compatible than some same-race couples.

Time may help repair a relationship, but sometimes new stressors occur. Economic stress causes marital friction no matter how many years a couple has been together (Conger et al., 2010), and contextual factors can undermine a couple's willingness to communicate and compromise (Karney & Bradbury, 2005). A long-standing relationship might crumble, especially under the weight of major crises—particularly financial (such as a foreclosed home, a stretch of unemployment) or relational (such as demanding in-laws or an extramarital affair).

Every generality obscures specifics. Some long-term marriages are happy; others are not. Marriage has never been magical: It does not always make adults joyful or children successful (Acs, 2007; Foster & Kalil, 2007). As you remember from the discussion of family structure in Chapter 8, correlation is not causation. Some husbands and wives consider each other best friends, while others do not.

Why Marry? Because many young people question the need for a wedding, marriage rates are down overall, but countries that allow same-sex couples to wed find a sudden increase. Paula Barrero *(centre)* and Blanca Mejias *(right)* were married by the Reverend Cheri DiNovo *(left)* at Emmanuel-Howard Park United Church in Toronto.

GAY AND LESBIAN PARTNERS Almost everything just described applies to gay and lesbian partners as well as to heterosexual ones (Biblarz & Savci, 2010; Herek, 2006). Some same-sex couples are faithful and supportive of each other; their emotional well-being thrives on their intimacy. Others are conflicted, with problems of finances, communication, and domestic abuse resembling those in heterosexual marriages.

Political and cultural contexts for same-sex couples are changing markedly. Many nations, including Canada and Spain, and an increasing number of U.S. states, as well as the District of Columbia, recognize same-sex marriage. Many other nations and U.S. states are ambivalent, and most countries, as well as many states, explicitly outlaw same-sex marriage.

According to Statistics Canada, the last census reported 64 575 same-sex couple families, of which 21 015 were married couples and the others were common-law couples. In total, same-sex couples accounted for 0.8 percent of all couples in Canada in 2011, up from 0.5 in 2001 (see Table 13.2) (Statistics Canada, 2012e). Same-sex marriage was legalized in Canada in 2005.

Current research with a large, randomly selected sample of people in gay or lesbian marriages in North America is not yet available. Many studies are designed to prove that same-sex marriage is, or is not, beneficial. That makes it difficult to draw objective conclusions. However, a review of 15 years of same-sex marriages in Denmark, Sweden, and Norway found that neither the greatest fears nor the greatest hopes for such unions are realized (Biblarz & Stacey, 2010).

DIVORCE AND SEPARATION Throughout this text, developmental events that seem isolated, personal, and transitory are shown to be interconnected and socially mediated, and to have enduring consequences. Relationships never improve or end

TABLE 13.2 Distribution (Number and Percentage) and Percentage Change of Couple Families by Opposite-Sex or Same-Sex Status, Canada, 2001 to 2011 Table Summary

Couple/family	2001 Number	2001 Percent	2006 Number	2006 Percent	2011 Number	2011 Percent	Percent change 2006 to 2011
All couples	7 059 830	100.0	7 482 775	100.0	7 861 860	100.0	5.1
Opposite-sex couples	7 025 630	99.5	7 437 430	99.4	7 797 280	99.2	4.8
Married	5 901 425	83.6	6 098 445	81.5	6 272 935	79.8	2.9
Common-law	1 124 200	15.9	1 338 980	17.9	1 524 345	19.4	13.8
Same-sex couples	34 200	0.5	45 345	0.6	64 575	0.8	42.4
Married	N/A	N/A	7 465	0.1	21 015	0.3	181.5
Common-law	34 200	0.5	37 885	0.5	43 560	0.6	15.0

Source: Statistics Canada, 2012e.

in a vacuum; they are influenced by the social and political context (Fine & Harvey, 2006). Divorce, separation, and the end of a cohabiting relationship are all affected by time and circumstances (see Table 13.3).

Divorce occurs because at least one half of a couple believes that he or she would be happier not married. According to General Social Survey data, 7 percent of the total Canadian population aged 15 and older in 2006 was divorced. In addition, about 13 percent of the population had experienced at least one divorce, and nearly half had remarried (Beaupré, 2008).

The divorce rate in Canada peaked at 50.6 percent in 1987 after a change in the Divorce Act in 1986 allowed individuals to file for divorce after one year of separation (instead of three years). Since 2008, the divorce rate has ranged between 35 to 42 percent. For example, in 2008, 40.7 percent of marriages were projected to end in divorce. The highest divorce rate was in the Yukon (59.7 percent) and the lowest was in Newfoundland and Labrador (25.0 percent) (Employment and Social Development Canada, n.d.[b]). With each subsequent marriage, the odds of divorce increase.

Typically, people divorce because some aspects of the marriage have become difficult to endure, yet divorce often presents a new set of challenges, including reduced income, lost friendships (many couples have only other couples as friends), and weakened relationships with the children. Weakened relationships occur immediately—usually custodial parents become stricter and non-custodial parents feel excluded—and also when the children become adults (Kalmijn, 2010; Mustonen et al., 2011).

Family problems arise not only with children, but also with other relatives. The divorced adult's parents may be financially supportive, but they may also be emotionally critical that their child's marriage did not work out. Some married adults have good relationships with some of their in-laws; this almost always disappears when the couple splits, a loss of part of the social convoy.

Although divorce is finalized on a particular day, from a developmental perspective it is a process that begins years before the official decree and reverberates for decades after (Amato, 2010). Income, family welfare, and self-esteem are lower among the formerly married than among people of the same age who are still married or who have always been single.

Some research finds that women suffer from divorce more than men do (their income, in particular, is lower), but men's intimacy needs are especially at risk. Some husbands rely on their wives for companionship and social interaction; they

The Marriage Option Canada legalized same-sex marriage in July 2005. The years from 2006 to 2011 represent the first five-year period for which Statistics Canada recorded same-sex unions. Canada was the fourth country in the world to legalize marriage between members of the same sex, after the Netherlands, Belgium, and Spain.

TABLE 13.3 Factors That Make Divorce More Likely

Before Marriage

Divorced parents

Either partner under age 21

Family opposed

Cohabitation before marriage

Previous divorce of either partner

Large discrepancy in age, background, interests, values (heterogamy)

During Marriage

Divergent plans and practices regarding child-bearing and child rearing

Financial stress, unemployment

Substance abuse

Communication difficulties

Lack of time together

Emotional or physical abuse

Unsupportive relatives

In the Culture

High divorce rate in cohort

Weak religious values

Laws that make divorce easier

Approval of remarriage

Acceptance of single parenthood

"But you knew I was addicted to bad men when you married me."

are unaccustomed to inviting friends over or chatting on the phone. Divorced fathers are often lonely, alienated from their adult children and grandchildren (Lin, 2008a).

If divorce ends an abusive, destructive relationship (as it does about one-third of the time), it usually benefits at least one spouse and the children (Amato, 2010). Furthermore, developing stronger and warmer parent–child relationships after a divorce helps children cope, not only immediately but also for years later (Vélez et al., 2011).

RE-PARTNERING Divorce is most likely within the first five years after a wedding, and cohabitation usually ends even sooner, with half of cohabiting relationships ending before two years (Kennedy & Bumpass, 2008). (These data are for the United States; intimate partnerships typically last longer elsewhere.)

Usually, both former partners in a severed relationship attempt to re-establish friendships and resume dating. Often they marry again, especially if they are young men. Women with children are less likely to remarry, but when they do, often their new husbands also have children from a previous marriage (Goldscheider & Sassler, 2006). About half of all North American marriages are remarriages for at least one partner.

Divorced adults who do not plan to remarry often develop new romantic partnerships, on average within two years of divorce. Rates of re-partnering vary depending on several factors: Rates are higher among those with more education, higher among those with more income, and lower among those who are already parents. Ethnicity is also a factor—in the United States, African-Americans, especially those with less than a high school education, are least likely to remarry (McNamee & Raley, 2011).

Initially, remarriage restores intimacy, health, and financial security. For remarried fathers, bonds with their new stepchildren or with a new baby may replace strained relationships with their children from the earlier marriage. Divorce usually increases depression and loneliness; re-partnering brings relief.

Most remarried adults are quite happy immediately after the wedding (Blekesaune, 2008). However, their happiness may not endure. Remember that personality tends to change only slightly over the life span; people who were chronically unhappy in their first marriage may also become unhappy in their second. Stepchildren add unexpected stresses (Sweeney, 2010), and stepparents have difficulty letting the spouse's former mate continue to care for their own children (Gold, 2010). One theory is that because expectations are not clear about the proper role of step-parents, adults fight about what they expect each other to do or not do (Pollet, 2010).

Remember, however, that each cohort develops in a distinct historical period, and the context of divorce has changed over the past decades. As more people separate or divorce, more people find suitable new partners and more stepchildren and step-parents have friends who have experienced the same problems and who can help with adjustment.

One specific cohort change is that contemporary adults have more friends of both sexes than was true 50 years ago. If they get divorced, that friendship network may buffer them from the loneliness and loss of intimacy that divorced adults once experienced. Research on older adults who are divorced makes staying married seem best, on average, but that research may not predict the future for 30-year-olds who cohabit, marry, divorce, or remarry.

KEY 𝒫oints

- Friends and consequential strangers are part of the social convoy that helps adults navigate happily through the years.

- Family connections remain important, especially between parent and adult child and between siblings.

- Happiness in marriage ebbs and flows, with highs in the first months of a new relationship and lows when children are very young.

- Divorce is almost always difficult; remarriage can bring new happiness and new problems.

Generativity

According to Erikson, after the stage of *intimacy versus isolation* comes the stage of **generativity versus stagnation,** when adults seek to be productive in a caring way. Without generativity, adults experience "a pervading sense of stagnation and personal impoverishment" (Erikson, 1963, p. 267).

Adults satisfy their need to be generative in many ways, especially through art, caregiving, and employment. Of these three, the link between artistic expression and generativity has been least studied (although creativity is recognized as an avenue for self-expression, as we will see in the next chapter). Here we explore what has been learned about the two other generative activities: caregiving and employment. Balancing care and employment to achieve generativity is not easy, as we also discuss.

Parenthood

Although generativity can take many forms, its chief form is establishing and guiding the next generation, usually through parenthood (Erikson, 1963). Many adults pass along their values as they respond to the hundreds of requests and unspoken needs of their children each day, thus becoming generative.

Parenting has been discussed many times in this text, primarily with a focus on its impact on children. Now we concentrate on the adult half of this interaction—the impact of parenting on the parents themselves. Bearing and rearing children are labour-intensive expressions of generativity, "a transformative experience" with more costs than benefits when children are young (Umberson et al., 2010). Indeed, having a child is perhaps the most stressful experience in a family's life (McClain, 2011).

Adults who choose parenthood willingly cope with the many stresses that come with that role. As Erikson (1963) says, "The fashionable insistence on dramatizing the dependence of children on adults often blinds us to the dependence of the older generation on the younger one" (p. 266).

generativity versus stagnation The seventh of Erikson's eight stages of development. Adults seek to be productive in a caring way, perhaps through art, caregiving, and employment.

Caregiving Dads Fathers are often caregivers for their young children. Most developmentalists think that men have always nurtured their children, although in modern times employed mothers have made caregiving more crucial for men.

NICOLE HILL / RUBBERBALL / CORBIS

Four Generations of Caregiving
These four women, from the great-grandmother to her 17-year-old great-granddaughter, all care for one another. Help flows to whoever needs it, not necessarily to the oldest or the youngest—although everyone cares for the youngest family member, the boy in front.

Children sometimes reorder adult perspectives, as adults become less focused on their personal identity or intimate relationships. One sign of a good parent is the parent's realization that the infant's cries are communicative, not selfish, and that adults need to care for children more than vice versa (Katz et al., 2011). This generative response does not always happen in the way that developmentalists would prefer. For example, a study of 91 gang members who became fathers found that almost all of them expressed new pride and priorities, but few quit their gangs and law-breaking ways (Moloney et al., 2009).

Every parent is tested by the dynamic experience of raising children. Many parents learn that, just when adults think they have mastered the art of parenting, children become older, thus presenting new challenges. Over the decades of family life, babies arrive and older children grow up, financial burdens shift, income almost never seems adequate, and, if the family includes several children, seldom is every child thriving. Illness and disability require extra care.

Problems and stresses increase as family size increases. This is true worldwide, at least until the children are grown (Margolis & Myrskylä, 2011). As already mentioned, adult children usually bring their parents more joy than distress, but if even only one of them is troubled, middle-aged and older parents are less happy (Fingerman et al., 2012).

Chapter 8 explained that children can develop well in any family structure—nuclear or extended; heterosexual or same-sex; single-parent, two-parent, or grandparent. Can adults also thrive in any kind of parenting relationship? Roughly one-third of all North American adults become step-parents, adoptive parents, or foster parents. These non-biological parents have abundant opportunities for generativity, but they also experience distinct vulnerabilities as they meet the challenges of each of these routes to parenthood.

Grandparenthood can be another source of generativity and intimacy, depending on national policies and customs, gender, parent–child relationships, and the financial resources of both adult generations. Most adults become grandparents in their 50s or 60s, and grandparenthood continues for decades. Worldwide, grandparents believe their work includes helping their grandchildren, especially if the middle generation is in crisis, such as experiencing divorce or illness (Herlofson & Hagestad, 2012). This topic is discussed in detail in Chapter 15, which presents the experiences of many older adults who have grandchildren of various ages and needs.

FOSTER CHILDREN Parent-child attachment does not depend on biology. Some people become parents to foster children, who may have spent their early years with their birth parents. These children may remain attached to their biological parents—even if they were not ideally generative—for example, if they were neglectful or abusive. This can impede connection to foster parents. Furthermore, a secure new attachment is hampered if both adult and child know that their connection can be severed for reasons unrelated to caregiving quality or relationship strength. Such separations often occur with foster children who may be moved from one foster home to another, or back to the birth parent, for reasons unrelated to the adequacy of the foster parents (Pew Commission on Children in Foster Care, 2004). As a result, adults who are not the birth parents face the dilemma of "whether to 'love' the children or maintain a cool, aloof posture with minimal sensitive or responsive interactions" (St. Petersburg–USA Orphanage Research Team, 2008, p. 15). A loving bond is better for both the foster parent and the child, but if that forms, separation is painful to both.

STEP-PARENTING Adults become step-parents when they marry someone who had children from a previous relationship. It can be challenging for step-parents to form connections with stepchildren. For example, children may be jealous that they no longer have their custodial parent's sole attention; they may resent an outsider's interference; and/or they may feel that that they are betraying their non-custodial parent by forming a close connection with a step-parent. In addition, step-parents may have unrealistic expectations about the kind of relationship they will form with their stepchildren (Ganong et al., 2011).

Yet, children may benefit from a step-parent's love, guidance, and perspective. For example, studies have shown that many men become "social fathers," providing fatherly care to children who are not their genetic progeny, benefitting both generations (Bzostek, 2008). The personality of the adults and the nature of the new marriage determine step-parents' connection with their stepchildren and affect whether a family will weather storms (Ganong & Coleman, 2004).

ADOPTION Most adoptions in Canada are "open," which means that the adoptive parents and the birth mother have a relationship with each other and exchange information. The amount of information that is exchanged depends mostly on the closeness of the relationship between the two parties. The advantages of an open adoption are that the birth mother has more input into the adoption process, and the needs of the child are more readily met.

In any given year, there are about 78 000 children in Canada waiting for adoption. In addition, about 2000 international children are adopted in Canada every year. Most overseas adoptions are not open since the birth parents are mostly not involved in the adoption process, and are often not known. As of 2010, the most common country from which children were adopted was China (see Table 13.4). Other countries from which Canadians adopted children include Haiti, the United States, Vietnam, and Russia (Adoption Council of Canada, 2011). One reason for the popularity of adoptions from China is the large number of baby girls available for adoption due to that country's one-child-per-couple policy. In recent years, it's become more difficult to adopt from China due to new restrictions and income requirements.

TABLE 13.4	International Adoptions to Canada: Top 10 Source Countries, 2008–2010		
	2008	2009	2010
China	431	451	472
Haiti	147	141	172
U.S.	182	253	148
Vietnam	111	159	139
Russia	91	121	102
South Korea	98	93	98
Philippines	118	86	88
Ethiopia	187	170	63
Colombia	53	41	62
India	54	59	55
All countries	1 915	2 122	1 946

Source: Adoption Council of Canada, 2011.

Strong parent–child bonds often develop with adoption, especially when children are adopted as infants. Secure attachments can also develop if adoption occurs when the children are older (ages 4 to 7), especially when the adopting mother was strongly attached to her own mother (Pace et al., 2011). However, children who spend their early years in an institution may never have been attached to anyone, and that makes it more difficult for the adoptive parent. Such children are often mistrustful of all adults and fearful of loving anyone (St. Petersburg–USA Orphanage Research Team, 2008).

Strong bonds may be stressed in adolescence, when teenagers may want to know more about their genetic and ethnic roots. One college student who feels well loved and cared for by her adoptive parents explains:

> In attempts to upset my parents sometimes I would (foolishly) say that I wish I was given to another family, but I never really meant it. Still when I did meet my birth family I could definitely tell we were related—I fit in with them so well. I guess I have a very similar attitude and make the same faces as my birth mother! It really makes me consider nature to be very strong in personality.

[April, 2012, personal communication]

Attitudes in the larger culture often increase tensions between adoptive parents and children. For example, the mistaken notion that the "real" parents are the biological ones is a common social construction that hinders a secure attachment.

An important factor to consider when adopting children from overseas or from North America is race. Adoptive children are often of a different race and/or culture than their adoptive parents. It is helpful to expose adopted children who are of a different ethnicity to experiences, customs, and history unique to that ethnicity, to help children establish their ethnic identity.

All the details already explained in this text, from the Brazelton Neonatal Behavioral Assessment Scale (Chapter 2) to the first words (Chapter 3), from theory of mind (Chapter 5) to learning to read (Chapter 7), are accomplishments celebrated by an astute parent—no matter how parenting came about. For this, continuity of care is crucial because knowing a particular child well is essential in interpreting those first mispronounced words, understanding early emotional expressions, and knowing when to help with schoolwork. Good parents are intensely committed to a particular, unique human being—and from that commitment both the joys and the concerns of parenting arise.

Caregiving

Erikson (1963) wrote that a mature adult needs to feel needed. Some caregiving requires meeting physical needs—feeding, cleaning, and so on—but much of it involves fulfilling another person's psychological needs. One study concludes:

> The time and energy required to provide emotional support to others must be reconceptualized as an important aspect of the *work* that takes place in families … Caregiving, in whatever form, does not just emanate from within, but must be managed, focused, and directed so as to have the intended effect on the care recipient.
>
> [Erickson, 2005, p. 349]

Thus, caregiving includes responding to the emotions of people who need a confidant, a cheerleader, a counsellor, or a close friend. Parents and children care for one another, as do partners. Often neighbours, friends, and more distant relatives are caregivers as well.

kinkeeper
A caregiver who takes responsibility for maintaining communication among family members.

Most extended families include a **kinkeeper,** a caregiver who takes responsibility for maintaining communication. The kinkeeper gathers everyone for holidays; spreads the word about anyone's illness, relocation, or accomplishments; buys gifts for special occasions; and reminds family members of one another's birthdays and anniversaries (Sinardet & Mortelmans, 2009). Guided by their kinkeeper, all the family members become more generative.

Fifty years ago, kinkeepers were almost always women, usually the mother or grandmother of a large family. Now families are smaller and gender equity is more evident, so some men or young women can be kinkeepers. Generally, however, the kinkeeper is still a middle-aged or older mother with several adult children. This role may seem burdensome, but caregiving provides both satisfaction and power (Mitchell, 2010). The best caregivers share the work; shared kinkeeping is an example of generativity.

sandwich generation
The generation of middle-aged people who are supposedly "squeezed" by the needs of the younger and older members of their families. In reality, some adults do feel pressured by these obligations, but most are not burdened by them, either because they enjoy fulfilling them or because they choose to take on only some of them or none of them.

CARING FOR OLDER AND YOUNGER GENERATIONS Because of their position in the generational hierarchy, many middle-aged adults are expected to help both the older and younger generations. They have been called the **sandwich generation,** a term that evokes an image of a layer of filling pressed between two slices of bread. This analogy suggests that the middle generation is squeezed between the needs of younger and older relatives. This sandwich metaphor is vivid, but it gives a false impression (Grundy & Henretta, 2006).

Caregiving is beneficial because people feel useful when they help one another. Far from being squeezed, older adults are *less* likely to be depressed if they are supporting their adult children than when they are distant from them (Byers et al., 2008). On their part, many grown children get pleasure from helping their parents. For instance, researchers find that young adults often help their parents understand current culture and technological change, providing information and insight.

Many middle-aged adults have their parents living with them along with their children—three generations. Of Canadian families with children aged 14 and under, 4.8 percent had at least one grandparent living with them (Statistics Canada, 2012e). Culture, and not caring for aged parents, is often a key factor in three- or four-generational living arrangements (Statistics Canada, 2004). In 2004, multi-generational family arrangements were most common among Aboriginal people and recent immigrants. For example, almost one in every 10 grandchildren in Nunavut lived with at least one grandparent.

Because of better health and vitality throughout life, many adults do not need to provide extensive physical care for older generations. Specifics of elder care differ (see Table 13.5). As we will explain in detail in Chapter 15, in developed nations when elders need care, it is typically provided by a spouse or a paid caregiver. Adult children and grandchildren are part of the caregiving team, but not the major providers.

For a minority of adults—usually middle-aged women—providing care for an elderly relative affects sibling relationships, marriages, or employment. For example, although siblings usually become closer in adulthood, a caregiving burden can disrupt that. If an elderly parent needs care, one sibling usually becomes the chief caregiver, potentially causing resentment. Husbands and wives can become resentful, too, if care of one spouse's elderly relatives is not what the other spouse anticipated. As explained next, cultures differ radically on caregiving expectations, and husbands and wives may have been raised with opposite assumptions.

CULTURE AND FAMILY CAREGIVING Family bonds depend on many factors, including childhood attachments, cultural norms, and the financial and practical resources of each generation. Some cultures assume that elderly parents should live with their children; others believe that elders should live alone as long as possible and then enter a care-providing residence (Parveen & Morrison, 2009; Ron, 2009). Cultures also differ as to whether sons or daughters should provide more help and whether divorced, step-, or distant parents deserve care.

In North America, Western Europe, and Australia, older adults cherish their independence and dread burdening their children. Even frail parents seek to maintain autonomy, feeling that moving in with their children is a sign of failure. By contrast, in nations where interdependence is a desirable personality trait, living with family does not necessarily signify a problem (Harvey & Yoshino, 2006).

Caregiving This grandfather is helping care for his grandchild in Indonesia. Multi-generational families are common in many countries.

Elder Care Connections between middle-aged adults and their parents vary a great deal from family to family, cohort to cohort, and place to place. For instance, these data, which are from the United States, indicate more contact and help provided to the wife's parents than to the husband's. However, in many Asian nations, connections are stronger to the husband's parents than the wife's.

TABLE 13.5 Contacts and Help Provided by Middle-Aged Couples to Parents and In-Laws

	Phone Calls per Month	Visits per Month	Minutes of Help per Week
Wife to own parents	11	6	120
Husband to wife's parents	8	5	70
Total to wife's parents	19	11	190
Husband to own parents	7	4	100
Wife to husband's parents	5	4	58
Total to husband's parents	12	8	158

Source: E. Lee et al., 2003.

Ethnic variations are evident in how close family members are expected to be. Generally, ethnic minorities are more closely connected to family members than are ethnic majorities in that they see each other more often and share food, money, and so on. However, although people may assume that closeness means affection, for minorities particularly, closeness sometimes increases conflict (Voorpostel & Schans, 2011). Ethnic variation is also evident in arrangements for caring for older family members. For instance, most elderly Chinese have their own homes; however, if they live with an adult child, in mainland China it is usually with a son, but in Taiwan it is usually with a daughter (Chu et al., 2011).

Lowered Expectations It was once realistic for adults to expect to be better off than their parents had been, but hard times have reduced the socioeconomic status of many adults.

Employment

Besides family caregiving, the other major avenue for generativity is employment. Most of the social science research on jobs has focused on economic productivity, an important issue but not central to our study of human development. Social scientists, in economics and in other disciplines, are beginning to include working as part of broader psychological theory and practice (Blustein, 2006).

As is evident from many of the terms used to describe healthy adult development, such as *generativity, success and esteem, instrumental,* and *achievement,* adults have many psychosocial needs that employment can fill. The converse is also true: Unemployment is associated with higher rates of child abuse, alcoholism, depression, and many other social and mental health problems (Freisthler et al., 2006; Wanberg, 2012). In addition, a longitudinal Canadian study indicated that unemployed men and women had an elevated risk of mortality from accidents, violence, and chronic diseases (Mustard, Bielecky, et al., 2013). Another study found that American adults who can't find work are 60 percent more likely to die than other people their age, especially if they are younger than 40 (Roelfs et al., 2011).

WORKING FOR MORE THAN MONEY Income pays living expenses, but it also does far more than that. It allows people to buy items that they desire, move to safer neighbourhoods, and live healthier and safer lives. However, to understand human development, we must go beyond income and consider the generative aspects of work—and there are many. Work provides a structure for daily life, a setting for human interaction, and a source of social status and fulfillment. In addition, work meets generativity needs by allowing people to do the following:

- develop and use their personal skills
- express their creative energy
- help and advise co-workers as a mentor or friend
- support the education and health of their families
- contribute to the community by providing goods or services.

The pleasure of "a job well done" is universal, as is the joy of having supportive supervisors and friendly co-workers. Job satisfaction correlates more strongly with challenge, creativity, productivity, and relationships among employees than with high pay or easy work (Pfeffer, 2007). Workers quit their jobs more often because of unpleasant social interactions at the workplace than because of dissatisfaction with wages or benefits (LeBlanc & Barling, 2004). These facts highlight the distinction between the **extrinsic rewards of work**—which are the tangible benefits such as

extrinsic rewards of work The tangible benefits, usually in the form of compensation (e.g., salary, health insurance, pension), that one receives for doing a job.

salary, health insurance, and pension—and the **intrinsic rewards of work**—which are the intangible gratifications of actually doing the job. Generativity is intrinsic.

A developmental view finds that extrinsic rewards tend to be more important at first, when young people enter the workforce and begin to establish their careers (Kooij et al., 2011). After a few years, in a developmental shift as an individual ages, the intrinsic rewards of work become more important" (Sterns & Huyck, 2001).

The power of intrinsic rewards explains why older employees display, on average, less absenteeism, less lateness, and more job commitment than do younger workers (Landy & Conte, 2007). A crucial factor may be that in many jobs, older employees have more control over what they do, as well as when and how they do it. Autonomy reduces strain and increases dedication and vitality. Autonomy is also seen as an important part of intrinsic motivation (Ryan & Deci, 2000).

Another crucial factor is family support. Family members being appreciative and helpful regarding a worker's job requirements benefits the person's health. Satisfaction at work spills over to satisfaction at home and vice versa. For example, when health impairs a husband's ability to work, divorce is more likely (Teachman, 2010).

The Changing Workplace

Obviously, work is changing in many ways. Globalization means that each nation exports what it does best (and cheapest) and imports what it needs. Specialization, interdependency, and international trade are increasing. Advanced nations are shifting from industry-based economies to information and service economies; poorer nations are shifting from subsistence agriculture to industry. Although every change has implications for human development, we focus here on only three—diversity among workers, job changes, and alternate schedules.

DIVERSITY Dramatic changes have occurred in who has a job and what they do. This is true in every nation, but we provide statistics for Canada as an obvious example. About 40 years ago, women accounted for 39.1 percent of the labour force; in 2009, women accounted for 58.3 percent of the Canadian workforce (Statistics Canada, 2011f). In 1996, 10 percent of the labour force belonged to a visible minority group; by 2006, this had increased to 15 percent (Martel et al., 2012). Of this group, an increasing number were born in Canada rather than having immigrated here.

In terms of salary, in 1980, recent immigrants earned much less than their Canadian-born peers; immigrant men and women earned 85 cents on the dollar. By 2005, the discrepancy had increased even more—immigrant men and women were making 63 and 56 cents respectively for each dollar Canadian-born workers were making.

On average over this 25-year period, immigrants' pay decreased even though their educational attainment was higher than that of their counterparts. Low-paying jobs such as those of clerks, taxi drivers, and cashiers are more likely among immigrants with university degrees. The major reasons for these discrepancies include the person's lack of proficiency in English as well as lack of recognition of their credentials from back home.

Immigrants from different countries experience different rates of employment in Canada (see Figure 13.4). From 2001 to 2006, immigrants born in Southeast Asia experienced similar employment and unemployment rates as the Canadian-born population. On the other hand, immigrants born in Africa faced difficulties in the workforce, regardless of when they came to Canada. For example, in 2006, the jobless rate for African-born immigrants was 21 percent, more than four times the rate of Canadian-born peers (Statistics Canada, 2010b).

As mentioned above, diversity in the workplace also exists in terms of who does what job. Historically, specific occupations have been far more segregated by sex and ethnicity than they are today; for example, male nurses and female police officers

intrinsic rewards of work
The intangible gratifications (e.g., job satisfaction, self-esteem, pride) that come from within oneself as a result of doing a job.

◆ **ESPECIALLY FOR Entrepreneurs**
Suppose you are starting a business. In what ways would middle-aged adults be helpful to you? (see response, page 487) →

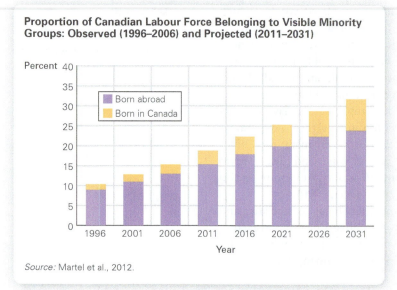

Proportion of Canadian Labour Force Belonging to Visible Minority Groups: Observed (1996–2006) and Projected (2011–2031)

Source: Martel et al., 2012.

FIGURE 13.4 Diversity at Work
The Canadian labour force is becoming increasingly diverse, thanks in large part to high immigration rates from Asia and Africa. Ideally, all adults would have jobs that complement their individual abilities, but that is not yet the case. The next challenge is for women and people of all ethnic groups to be proportionally distributed in various vocations, management positions, and workplaces.

Global Labour Market These hundreds of trainees in India hope for a steady job, responding to North American callers who are confused about their computers, bills, or online orders. For millions of educated but unemployed Indians, this aspect of the global labour market may be their best hope.

were very rare in 1960 but are much more common today. Employment discrimination in gender and ethnicity is still present—but to a much smaller degree.

CHANGING JOBS One recent change in the labour market is that resignations, firings, and hirings occur more often. Temporary employees are also more common, as are career and job changes. It is estimated that Canadian workers will have, on average, about three careers and eight jobs over their employment life (Human Resources and Skills Development Canada, 2011). Similarly, between the ages of 23 and 44, the average worker in the United States has seven different employers, with men somewhat more likely to change jobs than women (U.S. Bureau of the Census, 2011b). Sometimes jobs are lost because employers downsize, reorganize, relocate, outsource, or merge. Sometimes adults choose to quit because of dissatisfaction or frustration.

No matter the reason for job loss, when it occurs social connections to consequential strangers are broken and workers suffer. These human costs are confirmed by longitudinal research: People who frequently changed jobs by age 36 were three times more likely to have various health problems by age 42 (Kinnunen et al., 2005). This study controlled for smoking and drinking; if it had not, the health impact would have been even greater, since poor health habits correlate with job instability.

As adults grow older, job changes become increasingly stressful, for several reasons (Rix, 2011):

1. Seniority brings higher salaries, more respect, and greater expertise; workers who leave a job they have had for years lose these advantages.

2. Many skills required for employment were not taught decades ago, and many employers are reluctant to hire and train older workers.

3. Age discrimination is illegal, but workers are convinced that it is common, especially after age 50. Even if this is not true, we know from stereotype threat that it undercuts success in job searches.

4. Relocation reduces both intimacy and generativity.

From a developmental perspective, this last factor is crucial. Imagine that you are a middle-aged adult who has always lived in Toronto, and your employer goes out of business. You try to find work, but no one hires you, partly because there are many people also seeking employment. Would you move a thousand kilometres to Calgary, where the unemployment rate is lower?

If you were unemployed and in debt, and a new job was guaranteed, you might leave your friends and your community. But would your spouse and children quit their jobs, schools, and social networks to move with you? For you and everyone in your family, moving means losing intimacy.

Such difficulties are magnified for immigrants. Many depend on other immigrants for housing, work, and social support (García Coll & Marks, 2011). That meets some intimacy and generativity needs, but obviously any move decreases a person's chance to have friends, family, and employment that enhance psychological and physical health.

A VIEW FROM SCIENCE

Accommodating Diversity

Accommodating the various sensitivities and needs of a diverse workforce requires far more than reconsidering the cafeteria menu and the holiday schedule. Private rooms for breastfeeding, revised uniform guidelines, better office design, and new management practices may be required. Exactly what is needed depends on the particular culture of the workers: Some are satisfied with conditions that others would reject. For example, one study found that U.S. employees were stressed when they had little control over their work or when they had direct confrontations with their supervisors, whereas employees in China were most stressed by the possibility of negative job evaluations and indirect conflicts with co-workers (C. Liu et al., 2007).

Some words, policies, jokes, or mannerisms may seem innocuous to people of one group but toxic to people of another group. Researchers have begun to explore *micro-aggressions*—small things unnoticed by the majority person that seem aggressive to the minority person (Sue, 2010).

Micro-aggressions can be detected by people who identify with a particular ethnic group, or by people of a particular age, sexual orientation, or religion. For example, one research group found that older workers were particularly likely to experience micro-aggression at their workplace, but that some young men also noticed micro-aggressions aimed at them (Chou & Choi, 2011). Comments about "senior moments" or being "colour blind" or the "fair sex" or "the model minority" can be perceived as aggressive, even though the person making such comments is convinced that they are helpful, not hurtful.

Consider one study in detail. African-Americans and European-Americans read transcripts of discussions among hiring teams who were supposedly analyzing job applicants (Salvatore & Shelton, 2007). The applicants listed experiences or memberships that alerted the readers about their race. The transcripts were designed to show one of three possibilities: (1) that the hiring teams judged applicants fairly, regardless of race; (2) that the teams were clearly racist; or (3) that a minority applicant was rejected with reasons that seemed plausible though not entirely convincing.

After reading the transcripts, the participants took a test that required mental concentration. The performance of the European-Americans was impaired after they read the blatantly racist responses, but not after they read the more subtle ones. The opposite was true for the African-Americans—their intellectual sharpness was not affected by the clearly racist responses, but was hindered by the ambiguous ones.

The experimenters believe that this result shows that the African-Americans were not surprised by overt racism, so processing the racist transcripts did not require much mental energy. However, more subtle prejudice did trouble them because considerable mental effort was required for them to decide whether racism was a factor. That result alerts every worker and employer to be aware not only of racist or sexist remarks but also of inadvertent comments or behaviours that might be interpreted as prejudicial.

WORK SCHEDULES No longer does work always follow a 9-to-5, Monday-through-Friday schedule. In Canada, only about one-third of all employees work on that traditional schedule. The service sector of the economy often includes evening, night, and weekend work, and service jobs are increasing as manufacturing and agriculture jobs decrease. In Canada, about two-thirds of all workers have non-standard schedules. In Europe, the proportion of employees on non-standard work schedules varies from 25 percent in Sweden to 40 percent in Italy (Presser et al., 2008) (see Figure 13.5). In developing nations, most workers have non-standard hours.

One crucial variable for job satisfaction is whether employees can choose their own hours, particularly when it comes to working overtime. Workers who volunteer for paid overtime are usually satisfied, but workers who are required to work overtime are not (Beckers et al., 2008). This is true no matter how experienced the workers are, what their occupation is, or where they live. For instance, a nationwide study of 53 851 American nurses, ages 20 to 59, found that *required* overtime was one of the few factors that reduced job satisfaction in every cohort (Klaus et al., 2012). Similarly, a study of office workers in China found that the extent of required overtime correlated with less satisfaction and poorer health (Houdmont et al., 2011). Apparently, although work (paid or unpaid) is satisfying to every adult, working too long and not by choice undercuts the psychological and physical benefits.

Work Schedules These two skilled technicians are working on an oil rig south of Fort McMurray. Despite high pay, their jobs are hard to fill because they must spend days and even years far from their homes and families.

European Employees on Non-standard Work Schedules

Source: Presser et al., 2008.

FIGURE 13.5 Non-standard Hours
The traditional work schedule—Monday to Friday, 9:00 A.M. to 5:00 P.M.—is best for workers and their families. Employers and consumers, however, would prefer to have workers on the job on weekends and during evening and night shifts. European nations tilt toward the standard schedule, although percentages vary by nation.

flextime
An arrangement in which work schedules are flexible so that employees can balance personal and occupational responsibilities.

telecommuting
Working at home and keeping in touch with the office via computer and telephone.

Weekend work, especially with mandatory overtime, is particularly difficult for parent–child relationships because normal rhythms of family life are negatively affected by irregular schedules (Hook, 2012). Some nations, including Canada and many countries in Europe, impose limits on what employers can demand of employees who are parents (Gornick & Meyers, 2003).

One attempt to provide more worker choice is **flextime,** which gives employees some choice in the particular hours they work. Some form of flextime is available in over three-quarters of Canadian and American businesses. **Telecommuting,** when an employee works from home and uses video-conferencing and online communication to keep in touch with the office, is also becoming more common. These options are offered primarily for office and professional jobs.

Such schedules have many advantages for employees and employers. However, while they allow workers to have the benefits of greater family enrichment, the concurrent demands of family life and work can increase stress (Bianchi & Milkie, 2010; Golden et al., 2006).

In theory, part-time work and self-employment might allow adults to balance conflicting demands. But reality does not conform to the theory. In many nations (except the Netherlands, where half the workers are part time), part-time work is typically underpaid, without benefits such as health care (in the United States) or pensions (in many nations). Thus, workers avoid it if possible.

About one-third of all working couples who have young children and nonstandard schedules choose to have one parent at home while the other is at work. Mothers, particularly, are likely to rearrange meal and sleeping schedules so that they spend time with their children (Hook, 2012). However, night work and other nonstandard work schedules, especially when combined with overwork, correlate with personal, relational, and child-rearing difficulties (K. D. Davis et al., 2008; H. Liu et al., 2011).

Combining Intimacy and Generativity

Adult development depends on particulars of job, home, and personality that affect the ability to balance intimacy and generativity (Voydanoff, 2007). Employment contributes to adult psychosocial health, but other factors are important as well: Some adults are happy without a job, especially if others in their household are employed, with adequate income.

A large study of adult Canadians found that about half of the variation in their distress was related to employment (working conditions, support at work, occupation, job security), but at least as much was related to family (having children younger than age 5, support at home) and feeling personally competent (Marchand et al., 2012).

To find an ideal balance, at least three factors are helpful: adequate income, chosen schedules, and social support. For new parents in Canada, employment insurance (EI) is key. EI provides benefits for mothers and fathers who are expecting, will be giving birth, are adopting a child, or are caring for a newborn. A maximum of 35 weeks of parental benefits is available to biological or adoptive parents, which can be shared between the two parents. To be eligible, the parent must have paid EI premiums, accumulated at least 600 hours of insurable employment,

and had his or her normal weekly earnings reduced by more than 40 percent (Government of Canada, 2014).

When parents have children, they adjust their work and child-care hours, usually with the mother cutting back on employment, but not always—sometimes the father has fewer labour market hours and the mother has more. When mothers work full time, often fathers spend far more time with their children, and mothers do less housework (Abele & Volmer, 2011).

In many ways, family members adjust to one another's employment, helping everyone cope. They may recognize that men, women, and children can be better off with today's dual-income families and variable schedules, in spite of the challenges that these present (Bianchi & Milkie, 2010).

From a developmental perspective, it is clear that intimacy and generativity continue to be important to adults, as they always have been. As you will see in Chapters 14 and 15, many perspectives are possible on late adulthood as well. Some view the last years of life with dismay, while others consider them the golden years. Neither view is quite accurate.

Same Situation: Far Apart: Mothers at Work Mothers have always worked while tending their babies—be it in the fields, as this Hmong woman from Vietnam *(left)* still does, or at home *(right)*, where this North American woman checks her email. In many countries, work is now less physical and more cognitive, allowing many mothers to enter the labour market.

RESPONSE FOR Entrepreneurs (from page 483) Middle-aged adults are beneficial as employees and as customers. Middle-aged workers are steady, with few absences and good "people skills," and they like to work. In addition, household income is likely to be higher at about age 50 than at any other time, so middle-aged adults will probably be able to afford your products or services. ●

KEY Points

- Adults strive to meet their generativity needs, primarily through raising children, caring for others, and being productive members of society.
- Parenthood of all kinds is difficult yet rewarding, with foster, step-, and adoptive parents facing additional challenges.
- Caregivers are generative, with each adult caring for other family members.
- Employment ideally aids generativity, via productivity and social networks.
- Many parents seek to combine child-rearing and employment, with mixed success, depending on the specifics of employment and family life.

SUMMARY

Personality Development in Adulthood

1. The personality of adults remains quite stable, although many adults become more mature, as described by Erikson and Maslow. The midlife crisis is more myth than fact, more a cohort effect than a universal experience.

2. The Big Five personality traits—openness, conscientiousness, extroversion, agreeableness, and neuroticism—characterize personality at every age, with each person relatively high or low on each of these five. Adults choose their particular ecological niche based partly on personality. Culture and context affect everyone.

3. Although chosen careers and partners typically reinforce existing personality traits, unexpected events (e.g., a major illness or financial windfall) can temporarily disrupt personality.

Intimacy

4. Intimacy is a universal human need, satisfied in diverse ways, with friends and family, romantic partners, and consequential strangers. Each person has a social convoy of other people with whom he or she travels through life.

5. Friends are crucial for buffering stress and sharing secrets, for everyday companionship and guidance. This is true for both sexes.

6. Family members have linked lives, continuing to affect one another as they all grow older. Parents and adult children are less likely to live together than in earlier times, but family members are often mutually supportive, emotionally and financially.

7. Marriage typically occurs later now than it did in earlier decades, and cohabitation and living apart together are sometimes alternatives to, sometimes preludes to, marriage. Most adults still

seek a romantic partner (same sex or other sex) with whom to share life.

8. Divorce can be difficult for both partners and their family members, not only immediately but for years before and after the event.

9. Remarriage is common, especially for men. This solves some of the problems (particularly financial and intimacy troubles) of divorced adults, but the success of second marriages varies.

Generativity

10. Adults seek to feel generative, achieving, successful, and instrumental—all words used to describe a major psychosocial need that each adult meets in various ways.

11. Parenthood is a common expression of generativity. Even wanted and planned-for biological children pose challenges; foster children, stepchildren, and adoptive children bring additional stresses and joys.

12. Caregiving is more likely to flow from the older generations to the younger ones, so the "sandwich generation" metaphor is misleading. Many families have a kinkeeper, who aids generativity within the family.

13. Employment brings many rewards to adults, particularly intrinsic benefits such as pride and friendship. Changes in employment patterns—including job switches, shift work, and the diversity of fellow workers—can affect other aspects of adult development.

14. Combining work schedules, caregiving requirements, and intimacy needs is not easy; consequences are mixed. Some adults benefit from new patterns within the labour market; others find that the demands of work impair family well-being.

KEY TERMS

Big Five (p. 464)
consequential strangers (p. 468)
ecological niche (p. 464)
empty nest (p. 473)

extrinsic rewards of work (p. 482)
fictive kin (p. 471)
flextime (p. 486)

generativity versus stagnation (p. 477)
intrinsic rewards of work (p. 483)
kinkeeper (p. 480)

midlife crisis (p. 463)
sandwich generation (p. 480)
social convoy (p. 467)
telecommuting (p. 486)

WHAT HAVE YOU LEARNED?

1. Describe the two basic needs of adulthood.

2. Explain how the midlife crisis might reflect cohort rather than maturational changes.

3. Give examples to demonstrate how each of the Big Five personality traits might influence an adult's choice of jobs, mates, and neighbourhoods.

4. Explain the concept of "social convoy."

5. What roles do friends play in a person's life?

6. What are the differences between friends and consequential strangers?

7. What is the usual relationship between adult children and their parents? What factors might explain this relationship?

8. What usually happens to sibling relationships over the course of adulthood?

9. Why do people have fictive kin?

10. What needs do long-term partners meet?

11. How and why does marital happiness change from the wedding to old age?

12. What evidence is there that political and cultural attitudes toward same-sex partnerships are changing?

13. What are the usual consequences of divorce?

14. Many people who re-partner are happy at first, but their happiness may not last. Why might this be the case?

15. What is the basic idea of generativity?

16. In what ways does parenthood satisfy an adult's need to be generative?

17. What factors might make it difficult for foster children and foster parents to bond?

18. How might each of the Big Five personality traits make it easier or more difficult to develop positive relationships with stepchildren?

19. What are the benefits of open adoption?

20. Women are more often kinkeepers and caregivers than are men. How is this role both a blessing and a burden?

21. Why are middle-aged adults sometimes called the "sandwich generation"? Why might this metaphor create a false impression?

22. What are the advantages and disadvantages of familism? Of individualism?

23. What are some extrinsic and intrinsic rewards of work?

24. What are the advantages of greater ethnic diversity at work?

25. List four reasons why changing jobs is stressful.

26. What innovations in work scheduling have helped families? What innovations have hurt families?

27. Why, overall, might men and women be happier with current employment patterns than earlier ones?

APPLICATIONS

1. Describe a relationship that you know of in which a middle-aged person and a younger adult learned from each other.

2. Did your parents' marital and employment status affect you? How would you have fared if they had chosen other marriage or work patterns?

3. Imagine becoming a foster or adoptive parent yourself. What do you see as the personal benefits and costs?

4. Ask several people how their personalities have changed in the past decade. The research suggests that changes are usually minor. Is that what you found?

>>ONLINE CONNECTIONS

To accompany your textbook, you have access to a number of online resources, including LearningCurve, which is an adaptive quizzing program; critical thinking questions; and case studies. For access to any of these links, go to www.worthpublishers.com/launchpad/bergerchuang1e. In addition to these resources, you'll find links to video clips, personalized study advice, and an e-Book. Among the videos and activities available online is the following:

- *Caregivers Between Generations: What Is the "Sandwich Generation"?* In this short video, two experts discuss the realities and stresses of caring for impaired elders.

Late Adulthood

What emotions do you anticipate as you read about late adulthood? Sadness, depression, resignation, sympathy, sorrow? Expect instead surprise and joy. You will learn that many older adults are active, alert, and self-sufficient; that marked intellectual decline is unusual; and that even at age 90 or 100 people are quite happy. That does not mean mindless contentment. Earlier personality and social patterns continue; the complexities of human life are evident. Joy is mixed with sorrow, and poverty, loneliness, and chronic illness are always difficult. However, most older adults, most of the time, are active and independent.

Unfortunately, late adulthood, more than any other part of life, is a magnet for misinformation and prejudice. If your first thought was a sad one as you approached these chapters, you are one of many. Why? Think about that as you read.

CHAPTER OUTLINE

LATE ADULTHOOD:
Body and Mind

14

WHAT WILL YOU KNOW?

- What percentage of older people are in nursing homes?
- At what age is it no longer possible to learn new things?
- Is forgetting names the first sign of neurocognitive disorder?
- Is wisdom always, sometimes, or never characteristic of the elderly? The young?

took Asa, age 1, to the playground. One mother, watching her son, warned me that the sandbox would be crowded before long because the children from a nearby daycare centre would soon arrive. I asked questions, and to my delight she explained details of the centre's curriculum, staffing, scheduling, and tuition as if I were Asa's mother, weighing my options for next year.

Soon I realized she probably was merely being polite, because a girl too young to be graciously ageist glanced at me and asked:

"Is that your grandchild?"

I nodded.

"Where is the mother?" was her next question.

Later that afternoon came the final blow. As I opened the gate for a middle-aged man, he said, "Thank you, young lady." I don't think I look old, but no one would imagine I was young. That "young lady" was benevolent, but it made me realize that my pleasure at the first woman's words was a sign of my own, self-deceptive prejudice. ●

—*Kathleen Berger*

Now we begin our study of the last phase of life, from age 65 or so until death. This chapter starts by exploring the prejudices that surround aging. Then we describe biosocial changes—in the senses, the vital organs, and especially the mind.

Prejudice and Predictions

Prejudice about late adulthood is common among people of all ages, including young children and older adults. That is a reflection of **ageism,** the idea that age determines who you are. Ageism can target people of any age. Why do people accept it, especially in regard to the old?

ageism
A prejudice whereby people are categorized and judged solely on the basis of their chronological age.

Same Situation, Far Apart: Agile, Balanced, and Old Not every older adult can spin wool or traverse a tight rope, like this Moroccan woman *(left)* and Korean man *(right)*. Arthritic fingers or unsteady feet may render this impossible. But these two prove that stereotypes and generalities are false.

One expert contends that "there is no other group like the elderly about which we feel free to openly express stereotypes and even subtle hostility. ... [M]ost of us ... believe that we aren't really expressing negative stereotypes or prejudice, but merely expressing true statements about older people when we utter our stereotypes" (Nelson, 2011, p. 40). As mentioned above, even older people express these stereotypes. If an older person forgets something, he or she might claim a "senior moment," not realizing the ageism of that reaction. When hearing an ageist phrase, such as "second childhood," or a patronizing compliment, such as "spry" or "having all her marbles," elders themselves miss the insult. The expert believes that a major problem is that ageism is institutionalized in our culture, evident in the media, employment, and retirement communities.

Another reason people accept ageism is that it often seems complimentary ("young lady") or solicitous (Bugental & Hehman, 2007). However, the effects of ageism, whether benevolent or not, are insidious. They seep into the older person's feelings of competence; the resulting self-doubt fosters anxiety, morbidity, and even mortality. As one author writes, stereotyping makes ageism "a social disease, much like racism and sexism ... [causing] needless fear, waste, illness, and misery" (Palmore, 2005, p. 90).

Believing the Stereotype

When families are confronted with racism or sexism, parents teach their children to recognize and counter bias, while encouraging them to be proud of who they are. However, when children believe an ageist idea, few people teach them otherwise. Later on, their longstanding prejudice is very difficult to change, undercutting their own health and intellect (Golub & Langer, 2007).

The positive and negative stereotypes that people hold can have either beneficial or detrimental effects on their own cognitive and physical development. According to stereotype embodiment theory, ageist stereotypes can

- become internalized across the life span
- operate unconsciously
- become self-referential
- influence a person's future pathways by having psychological, behavioural, and physiological effects on him or her (Levy, 2009).

Having positive or negative age stereotypes can influence people's actions in an unconscious way. In one study, seniors who were subliminally exposed to negative stereotypes of the elderly, later gave handwriting samples that were noticeably shaky and "senile" looking, whereas those who were exposed to positive images had handwriting that appeared confident and "wise" (Levy, 2000).

Rothermund (2005) found that people who thought of certain behaviours as characteristic of the "typical old person" tended to incorporate those characteristics into their own self-views five years later. They internalized certain age stereotypes, which then affected their behaviour.

Some studies have reported that age stereotypes create expectations that act as self-fulfilling prophecies. This can then have a direct influence on a senior's health. For example, stereotypes that suggest cognitive decline is inevitable could influence whether seniors believe that a healthy diet can have positive effects on their future well-being, or whether any attempt to improve their health will be futile (Levy & Myers, 2004).

AGEIST ELDERS Most people older than 70 think they are doing better than other people their age—who, they believe, have worse problems and are too self-absorbed (Cruikshank, 2009; Townsend et al., 2006). Asked how old they feel, typical 80-year-olds take a decade or more off their age (Pew Research Center, 2009). Yet if most 80-year-olds feel like they are 70, then that feeling is, in fact, typical for 80-year-olds. In this example, older people reject their own ageist stereotype of 80-year-olds, although they feel the same way most 80-year-olds actually do. This is illogical, but in an ageist culture, thinking you feel younger than your chronological age is self-protective. Indeed "feeling youthful is more strongly predictive of health than any other factors including commonly noted ones like chronological age, gender, marital status and socioeconomic status" (Barrett, 2012, p. 3).

Stereotype threat (discussed in Chapter 11) can be as debilitating for the aged as for other groups (Hummert, 2011). For instance, if the elderly fear they are losing their minds, that fear itself may undermine cognitive competence (Hess et al., 2009).

The effect of internalized ageism was apparent in a classic study (Levy & Langer, 1994). The researchers selected three groups. Two were chosen because they might have been less exposed to ageism: residents of China, since older people are traditionally respected and honoured there, and North Americans who had been deaf throughout their lives. The third group was composed of North Americans with typical hearing, who presumably had listened to ageist comments all their lives. In each of these three groups, half the participants were young and half were old.

Memory tests were given to everyone, six clusters in all. Elders in all three groups (Chinese, Americans who are deaf, and Americans who can hear) scored lower than their younger counterparts. This was expected; age differences are common in laboratory tests of memory.

The purpose of this study, however, was not to replicate earlier research, but to see if ageism affected memory. It did. The gap in scores between younger and older North Americans who could hear (those most exposed to ageism) was double that between younger and older North Americans who were deaf, and five times wider than the age gap in the Chinese. Ageism undercut ability, a conclusion also found in many later studies (Levy, 2009). Sadly, later studies have found that, with modernization, many Asian cultures have become more ageist than they were when this earlier research occurred (Nelson, 2011).

When older people believe that they are independent and in control of their own lives, despite the ageist assumptions of others, they are likely

✦ **ESPECIALLY FOR** Young Adults
Should you always speak louder and slower when talking to a senior citizen? (see response, page 496) ➡

Not Yet When should aging people retire? In his younger years, Canadian actor Christopher Plummer played the lead male role, that of Baron von Trapp, in the classic movie *The Sound of Music*. Here, at the age of 80, he accepts an Oscar for best supporting actor for his role in the film *Beginners*.

DOUG PETERS / PA PHOTOS / LANDOV

ASHLEY COOPER / CORBIS

Slowing Down? Lest you think that bikes are only for children, an extensive study of five European nations (Germany, Italy, Finland, Hungary, and the Netherlands) found that 15 percent of Europeans *older than 75* ride their bicycles every day (Tacken & van Lamoen, 2005). This 75-year-old man from London, England, is not letting age slow him down, either. Rather than driving to his destination, he hopped on his bike and is, in fact, travelling faster than the cars on his right, stuck in traffic.

RESPONSE FOR Young Adults (from page 495) No. Some seniors hear quite well, and they would resent it. ●

to be healthier—mentally, as well as physically—than other people their age. Of course, some elders need special care. If an older person struggling with a heavy bag is offered a helping hand, it might be appreciated. But do not assume help is needed.

Elders must find a way to balance knowing when to persist and do things for themselves and when to seek assistance (Lachman et al., 2011). For instance, at a restaurant, older people should feel no shame in asking a younger dinner companion to read the fine print of a menu, but that younger person should not spontaneously offer to cut the elder's steak.

AGEISM LEADING TO ILLNESS Ageism impairs daily life. For example, it prevents depressed older people from seeking help because they resign themselves to infirmity. Could that, as well as a greater reluctance among men than women to ask for help, be why elderly men between the ages of 85 and 89 have the highest suicide rate of any age and either gender (Statistics Canada, 2012h)?

Ageism also leads others to undermine the vitality and health of the aged. For instance, health professionals are less aggressive in treating disease in older patients, researchers testing new prescription drugs enrol few older adults (who are most likely to use those drugs), and caregivers diminish independence by helping the elderly too much (Cruikshank, 2009; Herrera et al., 2010; Peron & Ruby, 2011–2012). A lack of understanding of changing physical needs may also undermine the health of the aged. One specific example is sleep.

The day–night circadian rhythm diminishes with age: Many older people wake before dawn and are sleepy during the day. Older adults spend more time in bed, take longer to fall asleep, and wake frequently (about 10 times per night) (Ayalon & Ancoli-Israel, 2009). They also are more likely to nap. All this is normal: If they choose their own sleep schedules, elders are less likely to feel tired than are young adults. However, if ageism, which leads people to believe that the patterns of the young are ideal, results in distress over normal elderly sleep patterns, doctors might prescribe narcotics, or elders might drink alcohol to put themselves to sleep. These can overwhelm an aging body, causing heavy sleep, confusion, nausea, depression, and unsteadiness.

Ageism may also be a contributing factor to a lower level of exercise among the elderly. In Canada, only 11 percent of those aged 60 to 79 meet recommended guidelines for exercise (2½ hours a week of moderate-to-vigorous physical activity), compared with 19 percent for adults aged 18 to 39 (Statistics Canada, 2013c). Part of the reason for this low level of exercise is that many activities are geared to the young. Team sports are organized for children, teenagers, and young adults; traditional dancing assumes a balanced sex ratio (which does not exist among the elderly); many yoga, aerobic, and other classes are paced and designed for young adults; bike paths are scarce, and many bikes are designed for speed, not stability.

Added to that, self-imposed ageism leads the elderly to exercise less, which increases stiffness and reduces range of motion while impairing circulation, digestion, and thinking. Balance is decreased, necessitating a slower gait, a cane, or a walker (Newell et al., 2006). Thus, internalized as well as externalized ageism makes people sick.

None of the normal changes of senescence requires that exercise stop, although some adjustments may be needed (more walking, less sprinting). Health is protected by activity, but ageism in one's culture, caregivers, and the elderly themselves leads to inaction, then stagnation, and then poor health. Indeed, the passive, immobile elder is at increased risk of virtually every illness.

ELDERSPEAK People's stereotypes of the elderly are evident in **elderspeak,** or the way they talk to the old (Nelson, 2011). Like baby talk, elderspeak uses simple and short sentences, slower talk, higher pitch, louder volume, and frequent repetition. Ironically, elderspeak reduces communication. Higher frequencies are harder for the elderly to hear, stretching out words makes comprehension worse, shouting causes stress and anxiety, and simplified vocabulary reduces the precision of language.

elderspeak
A condescending way of speaking to older adults that resembles baby talk, with simple and short sentences, exaggerated emphasis, repetition, and a slower rate and a higher pitch than used in normal speech.

DESTRUCTIVE PROTECTION Some younger adults and the media discourage the elderly from leaving home. For example, whenever an older person is robbed, raped, or assaulted, sensational headlines add to fear and, consequently, to ageism. In fact, street crime targets young not older adults (see Figure 14.1). The homicide rate (the most reliable indicator of violent crime, since reluctance to report is not an issue) of those over age 65 is one-half the rate for those aged 18 to 24 (Statistics Canada, 2013m). Telling older adults to stay home is shortsighted and prevents them from enjoying the benefits of activities outside the home.

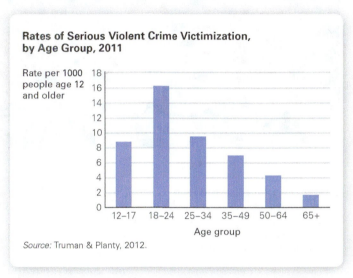

Rates of Serious Violent Crime Victimization, by Age Group, 2011

Source: Truman & Planty, 2012.

FIGURE 14.1 Victims of Crime
As people grow older, they are less likely to be crime victims. These figures come from personal interviews in which respondents were asked whether they had been the victim of a violent crime—assault, sexual assault, rape, or robbery—in the past several months. Personal interviews yield more accurate results than official crime statistics because many crimes are never reported to the police.

The Demographic Shift

Demography is the science that describes populations, including population by cohort, age, gender, or region. When certain subpopulations become significantly greater or smaller than in past years, this is a **demographic shift.** In an earlier era, there were 20 times more children than older people, and only 50 years ago, the world had 7 times more people under age 15 than over age 64. No longer.

demographic shift
A shift in the proportions of the populations of various ages.

THE WORLD'S AGING POPULATION The United Nations estimates that nearly 8 percent of the world's population in 2010 was 65 or older, compared with only 2 percent a century earlier. This number is expected to double by the year 2050. Already 13 percent in the United States are that age, as are 14 percent in Canada and Australia, 20 percent in Italy, and 23 percent in Japan (United Nations, 2012).

Demographers often depict the age structure of a population as a series of stacked bars, one bar for each age group, with the bar for the youngest at the bottom and the bar for the oldest at the top. Historically, the shape was a *demographic pyramid*. Like a wedding cake, it was widest at the base, and each higher level was narrower than the one beneath it, for three reasons—none currently true:

1. More children were born than the replacement rate of one per adult, so each new generation had more people than the previous one.

2. Many babies died, which made the bottom bar much wider than later ones.

3. Serious illness was usually fatal, reducing the size of each older group.

Sometimes unusual events caused a deviation from this wedding-cake pattern. For example, the Great Depression and World War II reduced births. Then postwar prosperity and the soldiers' return caused a baby boom between 1946 and 1964, just when infant survival increased. The mushrooming birth and survival rates led many demographers to predict a population explosion, with mass starvation by 2000 (Ehrlich, 1968).

That fear evaporated as new data emerged. Birth rates fell and a "green revolution" doubled the food supply. Now people worry about another demographic shift: fewer babies and more elders, affecting world health and politics (Albert &

Same Situation, Far Apart: Keep Smiling Good humour seems to be a cause of longevity, and vice versa. This is true for both sexes, including the British men on Founder's Day *(left)* and the two Indian women on an ordinary sunny day in Dwarka *(right).*

Freedman, 2010). Early death is uncommon; demographic stacks have become rectangles, not pyramids.

The demographic revolution is ongoing, although not yet starkly evident everywhere. Most nations still have more people under age 15 than over age 64. Worldwide, children outnumber elders more than 3 to 1. United Nations predictions for 2015 are for 1 877 551 000 people younger than 15 and 602 332 000 older than 64. Not until 2065 is the ratio projected to be 1 to 1 (United Nations, 2012).

According to Canada's 2011 National Household Survey, the aging population (65 and older) make up 12.9 percent (4 551 535) of the population; 33.6 percent of this population are immigrants. Over 10 percent are visible minorities, with Chinese (141 650) and South Asians (130 115) the two largest visible minority senior groups (Statistics Canada, 2014d). While about 76.8 percent speak at least one of the official languages, those who do not pose additional challenges for families, communities, and health professionals, who may require translators' assistance in order to provide adequate and meaningful care and support to the older population (Statistics Canada, 2014a).

STATISTICS THAT FRIGHTEN Unfortunately, demographic data are sometimes reported in ways designed to alarm. For instance, have you heard that people aged 80 and up are the fastest-growing age group? That is true but misleading.

In 2013 in Canada, there were more than 1.4 million people aged 80 and older. Statistics Canada (2013h) estimates that this number could more than double—to 3.3 million—by 2036. Stating the numbers this way can trigger ageist fears of a nation burdened by hungry hoards of frail and confused elders.

But stop and think. According to Statistics Canada, the Canadian population as a whole will also grow over that period, from 33.7 million to about 43.8 million. The percent of residents 80 and older will double, increasing between 2009 and 2036 from 3.8 percent to 7.5 percent (Statistics Canada, 2010d). That proportion will be far from overwhelming for the other 92.5 percent of the population.

dependency ratio
A calculation of the number of self-sufficient, productive adults compared with the number of dependents (children and the elderly) in a given population.

Demographers and politicians sometimes report the **dependency ratio,** estimating the proportion of the population that *depends* on care from others. This ratio is calculated by dividing the number of dependants (defined as those under age 15 or over age 64) by the number of people in the middle, aged 15 to 64. The highest dependency ratio is in Uganda, with more than one dependant per adult (more than 1:1); the lowest is in Bahrain, with one dependant per three adults (1:3). Most nations, including Canada and the United States, have a dependency ratio of about 1:2 (United Nations, 2012).

But the calculation of the dependency ratio assumes that older adults are dependent. Most elders are fiercely independent; they are care*givers* not care receivers. In 2007, about one in four caregivers were seniors themselves, with one-third over the age of 75 (Statistics Canada, 2008c). Only 10 percent of those over age 64 are dependent on others for basic care, and those "others" are usually relatives, not unrelated taxpayers.

YOUNG, OLD, AND OLDEST Almost everyone overestimates the population in nursing homes because people tend to notice only the frail, not recognizing the rest. This is a characteristic of human thought—the memorable case is thought to be typical—that feeds ageism rather than reflecting reality.

Gerontologists distinguish among the *young-old,* the *old-old,* and the *oldest-old.* The **young-old** are the largest group of older adults. They are healthy, active, financially secure, and independent. Few people notice them or realize their age. The **old-old** suffer some losses in body, mind, or social support, but they proudly care for themselves. Only the **oldest-old** are dependent, and they are the most noticeable.

Many of the young-old are aged 65 to 75, old-old 75 to 85, and oldest-old over 85, but age itself does not indicate dependency. An old-old person can be 65 or 100. For well-being and independence, attitude is more important than age (O'Rourke et al., 2010a).

Ongoing Senescence

The reality that most people over age 64 are quite capable of caring for themselves does not mean that they are unaffected by time. The processes of senescence, described in Chapter 12, continue throughout life. Good health habits slow down aging but do not stop it.

THEORIES OF AGING Why don't people stay young? Hundreds of theories and thousands of scientists have sought to understand why aging occurs. To simplify, these theories can be understood in three clusters: wear and tear, genetic adaptation, and cellular aging.

The oldest, most general theory of aging is known as **wear and tear.** This theory contends that the body wears out, part by part, after years of use. Organ reserve and repair processes are exhausted as the decades pass (Gavrilov & Gavrilova, 2006).

Is this true? For some body parts, yes. Athletes who put repeated stress on their shoulders or knees often have chronically painful joints by middle adulthood; workers who inhale asbestos and smoke cigarettes destroy their lungs. However, many body functions benefit from use. Exercise improves heart and lung functioning; tai chi improves balance; weight training increases muscles; sexual activity stimulates the sexual-reproductive system; foods that require intestinal activity benefit the digestive system. In many ways, people are more likely to "rust out" from disuse than to wear out. Thus, although the wear-and-tear theory applies to some body parts, it does not explain aging overall.

A second cluster of theories focuses on genes (Sutphin & Kaeberlein, 2011). Humans may have a **genetic clock,** a mechanism in the DNA of cells that regulates life, growth, and aging. Just as genes start puberty at about age 10, genes may switch on aging. For instance, when a person is injured, aging genes spread the damage, so that an infection spreads rather than being halted and healed (Borgens & Liu-Snyder, 2012).

Evidence for genetic aging comes from premature aging. For example, children born with Hutchinson-Gilford syndrome (a genetic disease also called *progeria*) stop growing at about age 5 and begin to look old, with wrinkled skin and balding heads.

young-old
Healthy, vigorous, financially secure older adults (generally, those aged 60 to 75) who are well integrated into the lives of their families and communities.

old-old
Older adults (generally, those older than 75) who suffer from physical, mental, or social deficits.

oldest-old
Elderly adults (generally, those older than 85) who are dependent on others for almost everything, requiring supportive services such as nursing homes and hospital stays.

wear and tear
A view of aging as a process by which the human body wears out because of the passage of time and exposure to environmental stressors.

✦ **ESPECIALLY FOR Biologists** What are some immediate practical uses for research on the causes of aging? (see response, page 501) →

genetic clock
A purported mechanism in the DNA of cells that regulates the aging process by triggering hormonal changes and controlling cellular reproduction and repair.

A Trick Question How old is he? His strong muscles and body's flexibility make him comparable to a fit 30-year-old. However, the placement of this photo should give you a clue that this man is a senior.

cellular aging
The ways in which molecules and cells are affected by age. Many theories aim to explain how and why aging causes cells to deteriorate.

Hayflick limit
The number of times a human cell is capable of dividing into two new cells. The limit for most human cells is approximately 50 divisions, an indication that the life span is limited by our genetic program.

calorie restriction
The practice of limiting dietary energy intake (while consuming sufficient quantities of vitamins, minerals, and other important nutrients) for the purpose of improving health and slowing down the aging process.

These children die in their teens of heart diseases typically found in people five times their age.

Other genes seem to allow an extraordinarily long and healthy life. People who live far longer than the average usually have alleles that other people do not (Halaschek-Wiener et al., 2009; Sierra et al., 2009).

Hundreds of genes hasten aging of one body part or another, such as genes for hypertension or many forms of cancer. Certain alleles—SIR2, def-2, among them—directly accelerate aging and death (Finch, 2010).

Other alleles are protective. For instance, allele 2 of ApoE aids survival. Of men in their 70s, 12 percent have ApoE2, but of men older than 85, 17 percent have it. This suggests that men with allele 2 are, for some reason, more likely to survive. However, another common allele of the same gene, ApoE4, increases the risk of death by heart disease, stroke, neurocognitive disorder, and—if a person is HIV-positive—by AIDS (Kuhlmann et al., 2010).

Why would human genes promote human aging? Evolutionary theory provides an explanation (Hughes, 2010). Societies need young adults to produce the next generation and then need the elders to die (leaving their genes behind) so that the new generation can thrive. Thus, genetic aging may seem harsh to older individuals, but it is actually benevolent for communities.

The third cluster of theories examines **cellular aging,** focusing on molecules and cells (Sedivy et al., 2008). Toxic substances damage cells over time, so minor errors in copying accumulate (remember, cells replace themselves many times). Over time, imperfections proliferate. The job of the cells of the immune system is to recognize pathogens and destroy them, but the immune system weakens with age as well as with repeated stresses and infections (Wolf, 2010).

Eventually, the organism can no longer repair every cellular error, resulting in senescence. This process is first apparent in the skin, an organ that replaces itself often. The skin becomes wrinkled and rough, eventually developing "age spots" as cell rejuvenation slows down. Cellular aging also occurs inside the body, notably in cancer, which involves duplication of rogue cells. Every type of cancer becomes more common with age because the body is increasingly less able to control the cells.

Even without specific infections, healthy cells stop replicating at a certain point. This is referred to as the **Hayflick limit,** named after the scientist who discovered this phenomenon. Leonard Hayflick believes that the Hayflick limit, and therefore aging, is caused by a natural loss of molecular fidelity—that is, by inevitable errors in transcription as each cell reproduces itself. He believes that aging is a natural process built into the very cells of our species, affected by stress, drugs, and so on (Hayflick, 2004).

One cellular change over time occurs with *telomeres*—stretches of DNA at the ends of chromosomes that protect the cell's genetic blueprint. As cells divide, telomeres get shorter. Eventually, at the Hayflick limit, the telomere is gone and cell duplication stops.

Telomere length is about the same in newborns of both sexes and all ethnic groups, but by late adulthood, telomeres are longer in women than in men, and longer in European-Americans than in African-Americans (Aviv, 2011). There are many possible explanations, but cellular aging theorists consider this one reason why women outlive men and European-Americans outlive African-Americans.

CALORIE RESTRICTION Aging slows down in most living organisms with **calorie restriction,** which is drastically reducing daily calories while maintaining ample vitamins, minerals, and other important nutrients. The benefits of calorie restriction have been demonstrated by research with dozens of creatures, from fruit flies to chimpanzees. Generally, compared with no restrictions, keeping non-humans on a restricted diet after puberty results in less aging and longer life (sometimes twice as long), as well as stronger hearts, less disease, and better cognition (Bendlin et al., 2011). However, specifics of diet and timing may be crucial. That may explain, for instance, why some research on monkeys finds that calorie restriction extends life, but other studies do not (Mattison et al., 2012). Much remains to be understood; calorie restriction is a fact in search of a theory, as "the molecular mechanisms by which such a simple intervention has such a stunning effect has eluded researchers for decades" (Masoro & Austad, 2011, p. xi).

Application of calorie restriction to humans is controversial. Controlled experiments with people would be unethical as well as impossible since researchers would have to find hundreds of people, half of whom would be randomly assigned to eat much less than usual, whereas the other half would eat normally. For both groups, periodic checks would ascertain whether they were sticking to their diets and would measure dozens of biomarkers in the blood, urine, heart rate, breathing, and so on.

The researchers would exclude anyone younger than 21 or potentially pregnant since undereating would be particularly harmful to them. They would warn the participants that calorie restriction reduces the sex drive, causes temporary infertility, weakens bones and muscles, affects moods, decreases energy, and probably affects other body functions.

As a result, studies of the effects of calorie restriction on humans have been limited. Researchers have studied populations from places such as Okinawa, Denmark, and Norway, where wartime brought severe calorie reduction plus healthy diets (mostly fresh vegetables). The result was a markedly lower death rate (Fontana et al., 2011). In addition, studies have been conducted with volunteers (not random participants) who choose to reduce their calories. Currently, more than 1000 North Americans belong to the Calorie Restriction Society, voluntarily eating only 1000 nutritious calories a day, none of them buttered or fried. One leader of this group is Michael Rae, from Calgary. He explained:

> Aging is a horror and it's got to stop right now. People are popping antioxidants, getting face-lifts, and injecting Botox, but none of that is working. At the moment, C.R. [calorie restriction] is the only tool we have to stay younger longer.
> *[quoted in Hochman, 2003, p. A9]*

Preliminary data on practitioners of calorie restriction find some health improvements as a result of calorie restriction, but also find somewhat different responses than for non-humans. Scientists are trying to find some easier way—perhaps a drug or nutrient—that would achieve the same result as calorie restriction, halting genetic or cellular aging (Barzilai & Bartke, 2009; Beil, 2011).

All the theories of aging, and all the research on calorie restriction, have not led to any simple way to stop senescence. Most scientists are skeptical, not only of calorie restriction but of what people are willing to give up for a longer life. More than ever, scientists recommend exercise, a moderate diet, and staying away from harmful drugs (especially cigarettes).

Selective Optimization

Social scientists have another goal, not of adding years to life but adding life to years. One method is called *selective optimization with compensation* (see Chapter 12). The hope is that the elderly will compensate for any impairments of senescence and will excel (optimize) at whatever specific tasks they select. We will look at three examples: sex, driving, and the senses. All three involve personal choice, societal practices, and technological options, but here each is used to illustrate one of these three dimensions of the compensation process.

RESPONSE FOR Biologists (from page 499) Although ageism and ambivalence limit the funding of research on the causes of aging, many scientists believe that research on cell aging and on the immune system will benefit people of all ages. Such applications include prevention of AIDS, cancer, intellectual decline, and physical damage from pollution. ●

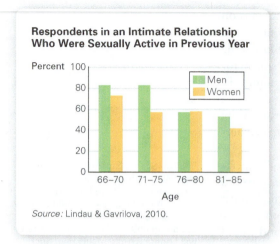

Respondents in an Intimate Relationship Who Were Sexually Active in Previous Year

Source: Lindau & Gavrilova, 2010.

FIGURE 14.2 Intimate Relations
Older adults who consider their health good (most of them) were asked if they had had sexual intercourse within the past year. If they answered yes, they were considered sexually active. As the graph shows, more than 50 percent of adults aged 66 to 80 had had sexual intercourse. For many elders, sexual affection is expressed in many more ways than intercourse, and it continues throughout life.

INDIVIDUAL COMPENSATION: SEX Most people are sexually active throughout adulthood. Some continue to have intercourse long past age 65 (see Figure 14.2) (Lindau & Gavrilova, 2010). However, on average, intercourse becomes less frequent than it was earlier, often stopping completely. Nonetheless, sexual satisfaction within long-term relationships increases past middle age (Heiman et al., 2011). How could that be?

Many older adults reject the idea that intercourse is the only or even the optimal measure of sexual activity. Instead, if sexual desire remains, then cuddling, kissing, caressing, and fantasizing become more important. Is that optimization, compensation, or both? Desire correlates with sexual satisfaction and quality of life in late adulthood more than frequency of intercourse does (Chao et al., 2011). Indeed, a five-nation (United States, Germany, Japan, Brazil, and Spain) study found that kissing and hugging, not intercourse, predicted happiness in long-lasting romances (Heiman et al., 2011).

The research finds that older women, more often than older men, say they have no sexual desire, and, on average, women stop intercourse earlier than men. This is primarily because of a lack of partner availability—there are more older women than older men—not biology. However, elders who feel sexual desire tend to be happier and healthier than those who do not (Ambler et al., 2012).

After divorce or death of a partner, selectivity is evident. Some of the elderly prefer to consider sex a thing of the past, some cohabit, some begin LAT (living apart together) with a new partner but without marriage or leaving their own home, and some remarry. That is selective optimization—each older person choosing whether and how to be sexual.

SOCIAL COMPENSATION: DRIVING A life-span perspective reminds us that "aging is a process, socially constructed to be a problem" (Cruikshank, 2009, p. 8). The process is biological, but the problem begins in the social world. That means selective optimization with compensation is needed by families and societies, too. One example is driving. With age, sign reading takes longer, head turning is reduced, reaction time slows, and night vision worsens. The elderly compensate: Many drive slowly and avoid night driving.

Although drivers compensate, few societies do. If an older adult causes a crash, age is blamed rather than other factors, such as the law (Satariano, 2006). Laws are often lax; many jurisdictions renew licences without testing, even at age 80. If testing is required, it often focuses on knowing the rules of the road or being able to read with glasses, not on the characteristics that correlate with accidents. For instance, when vision is tested, it is usually to gauge a person's face-front reading ability, yet peripheral vision is a stronger predictor of accidents (Johnson & Wilkinson, 2010; Wood, 2002).

Beyond more effective retesting, there are many other things that societies can do. Larger-print signs before an exit, mirrors that replace the need to turn the neck, illuminated side streets and driveways, non-glaring headlights and hazard flashes, and warnings of ice or fog ahead would reduce accidents. Well-designed cars, roads, signs, lights, tests, as well as appropriate laws and enforcement, would allow for selective optimization; competent elderly drivers could thus maintain independence, and dangerous drivers (of all ages) could be kept off the road.

TECHNOLOGICAL COMPENSATION: THE SENSES Every sense becomes slower and less sharp with each passing decade (Meisami et al., 2007). This is true for touch (particularly in the fingers), taste (particularly for sour and bitter), smell, and pain, as well as for sight and hearing. Yet in the twenty-first century, hundreds of

(a)

(b)

(c)

(d)

Through Different Eyes These photographs depict the same scene as it would be perceived by a person with (a) normal vision, (b) cataracts, (c) glaucoma, or (d) macular degeneration.

ALL PHOTODISC / GETTY IMAGES

manufactured devices compensate for sensory loss, from eyeglasses (first invented in the thirteenth century) to tiny video cameras worn on the head that connect directly to the brain, allowing people whose eyes no longer see to process images (not yet commercially available).

Only 10 percent of people of either sex over age 65 see well without glasses (see Table 14.1), but selective compensation allows almost everyone to use their remaining sight quite well. Changing the environment—brighter lights, large and darker print—is a simple first step. Corrective lenses and magnifying glasses can also help. For those who are totally blind, dogs, canes, and audio devices have for decades allowed mobility and cognition.

Similarly, by age 90, the average man is almost deaf, as are about half of the women. For all sensory deficits, an active effort to compensate—not accept—is needed. Unfortunately, ageism leads many elders to avoid bifocals and hearing aids, squinting and mishearing, until blindness or deafness is imminent (Meisami et al., 2007).

TABLE 14.1 Common Vision Impairments Among the Elderly

- *Cataracts.* As early as age 50, about 10 percent of adults have cataracts, a thickening of the lens, causing vision to become cloudy, opaque, and distorted. By age 70, 30 percent do. Cataracts can be removed in outpatient surgery and replaced with an artificial lens.

- *Glaucoma.* About 1 percent of those in their 70s and 10 percent in their 90s have glaucoma, a buildup of fluid within the eye that damages the optic nerve. The early stages have no symptoms, but the later stages cause blindness, which can be prevented if an ophthalmologist or optometrist treats glaucoma before it becomes serious. People with diabetes may develop glaucoma as early as age 40.

- *Macular degeneration.* About 4 percent of those in their 60s and about 12 percent over age 80 have a deterioration of the retina, called macular degeneration. An early warning occurs when vision is spotty (e.g., some letters missing when reading). Again, early treatment—in this case, medication—can restore some vision, but without treatment, macular degeneration is progressive, causing blindness about five years after it starts.

PETER CHRISTOPHER / ALAMY

No Quitter When hearing fades, many older people avoid social interaction. Not so for this man, who wears a hearing aid that is quite discreet.

Ageism also affects the use or non-use of technological possibilities by society. Few designers and engineers create innovations that compensate for sensory losses, although the technology is available. Look around at the built environment (stores, streets, schools, and homes); notice the print on medicine bottles; listen to the public address systems in train stations; ask why most homes have entry stairs and narrow bathrooms, why most buses and cars require a big step up to enter. Just about everything, from airplane seats to fashionable shoes, is designed for able-bodied, sensory-acute adults. Many disabilities would disappear with better design (Satariano, 2006).

Sensory loss need not lead to morbidity or senility, but without compensation, it can result in less movement and reduced intellectual stimulation. Consequently, illness increases and cognition declines as the senses become less acute.

> ### KEY Points
>
> - Ageism is stereotyping based on age, a prejudice that leads to less competent and less confident elders.
> - Demographic changes have resulted in more elders and fewer children in every nation.
> - There are many theories of aging, but beyond good health habits, calorie restriction is the only way proven to extend life for some creatures—but not yet proven in humans.
> - Elders need not be dependent if they themselves, and others, compensate for whatever difficulties they have.
> - Every sense becomes less acute with age, but technology provides many remedies—if individuals and societies take advantage of them.

Cognition

Ageism impairs elders in many ways, but the most insidious, and most feared, involves the mind, not the body. As with many stereotypes, it begins with a half-truth and stops there. Many adults in their 70s show evidence of age-related decline, but some continue to maintain very high levels of cognitive performance (Nyberg & Bäckman, 2011). The fear is worse than the facts, but the fear itself makes compensation less likely.

The Aging Brain

New neurons form and dendrites grow in adulthood—a fact that 10 years ago surprised many scientists who thought brain growth stopped in childhood. However, that good news is tempered by another fact—growth is slow. Just like the legs, the heart, and every other part of the body, the brain becomes less efficient as people grow older (Park & Reuter-Lorenz, 2009).

SLOWER AND SMALLER Senescence reduces production of neurotransmitters—glutamate, acetylcholine, serotonin, and especially dopamine—that allow a nerve impulse to jump quickly across the synaptic gap from one neuron to another. Neural fluid decreases, myelination thins, and cerebral blood circulates more slowly. The result is an overall brain slowdown, evident in reaction time, moving, talking, and thinking. Deterioration of cognition correlates with slower walking as well as with almost every kind of physical disability (Kuo et al., 2007; Salthouse, 2010).

Brain slowdown can be a severe drain on the intellect because speed is crucial for many aspects of cognition. In fact, some experts believe that speed is the *g* mentioned in Chapter 12, the intellectual ability that underlies all other aspects of intelligence.

Although all scientists agree that reduced speed is a component of late-life cognition, other factors may be more important, especially when individuals, not group averages, are examined (Zimprich & Martin, 2009). For example, brain aging is evident in size as well as in speed. Some areas shrink more than others, among them the hippocampus (crucial for memory) and the prefrontal cortex (necessary for planning, inhibiting unwanted responses, and coordinating thoughts) (Kramer et al., 2006; Rodrigue & Kennedy, 2011).

In every part of the brain, the volume of grey matter (crucial for processing new experiences) is reduced. As a consequence, many people must use their cognitive reserve to understand events (Park & Reuter-Lorenz, 2009). White matter typically is reduced overall as well, but white matter lesions, or areas of greater intensity, increase: Bright white spots appear on MRIs after age 50 or so. These markedly increase the time it takes for a thought to be processed in the brain (Rodrigue & Kennedy, 2011).

VARIATION IN BRAIN EFFICIENCY As is the case with changes to every other organ, all these aspects of brain senescence vary markedly from individual to individual. Although variability is obvious, the reasons are not. Higher education and vocational challenge correlate with less decline, either because keeping the mind active is protective or because such people began late adulthood with more robust and flexible minds (Gow et al., 2011; Salthouse, 2010).

Exercise, nutrition, and normal blood pressure are powerful influences on brain health, and all predict intelligence in old age. In fact, some experts contend that with good health habits and favourable genes, no intellectual decrement will occur (Greenwood & Parasuraman, 2012).

USING MORE OF THE BRAIN A curious finding from PET and fMRI scans is that, compared with younger adults, older adults use more parts of their brains, including both hemispheres, to solve problems. This may be selective compensation: Using only one brain region may be inadequate, so the older brain automatically activates more parts.

Consequently, on many tasks, older adults are as intellectually sharp as they always were. However, in performing difficult tasks that require younger adults to use all their cognitive resources, older adults are less proficient, perhaps because they already are using their brains to maximum capacity (Cappell et al., 2010).

Brain shrinkage interferes with multi-tasking. No one is intellectually as efficient with two tasks as with one, but young children and older adults are particularly affected when they are given several tasks at once (Krampe et al., 2011) (see

Mind Over Matter Hazel McCallion was 89 years old when she was sworn in for her twelfth term as mayor of Mississauga, Ontario, in 2010. First elected to that position in 1978, she earned the nickname "Hurricane Hazel" for her strong, outspoken style. One of Canada's longest-serving mayors, she was born and educated in Quebec and worked in the corporate world until 1967, when she decided to dedicate her career to politics.

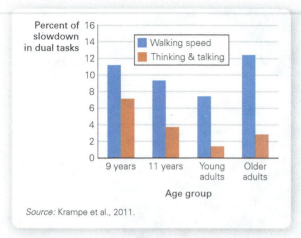

Source: Krampe et al., 2011.

FIGURE 14.3 One Task at a Time
Doing two things at once impairs performance. In this study, researchers compared the speed of a sensorimotor task (walking) and a cognitive task (naming objects within a category—for example, colours, spices, insects, crimes, four-legged animals). The participants did each task separately first, and then they did both at once. The latter resulted in performance losses across the board. Note, however, that the eldest seemed to safeguard verbal fluency (only a 3 percent slowdown) at the expense of significantly slower walking.

OBSERVATION QUIZ
How much were the 9-year-olds affected by doing both tasks at once? (see answer, page 508) ➔

Recognition At every age, recognition memory is much better than recall. Chances are that few high school classmates could describe how Kathleen looked back then, but all of them could point out her picture among the hundreds of photos in their yearbook.

Figure 14.3). Recognizing this, many elders are selective. In daily life, suppose that a grandfather is interrupted by a grandchild's questions while reading the newspaper, or that a grandmother is getting dressed when someone asks her to choose which bus to take. Most likely the grandfather will put down the newspaper and then answer, and the grandmother will first dress and then decide on transportation.

Information Processing After Age 65

Given the complexity and diversity of late life cognition, we need to examine specifics to combat general stereotypes. For this, the information-processing approach is useful, with details of input (sensing), memory (storage), programming (control), and output.

INPUT Processing information requires that sensations precede perception, yet as you just read, no sense is as sharp at age 65 as at age 15. Glasses and hearing aids mitigate most severe sensory losses, but more subtle deficits also impair cognition. Information must cross the *sensory threshold,* the divide between what is sensed and what is not, in order to be perceived. Sensory losses may not be recognized because the brain automatically fills in missed sights and sounds. People of all ages believe they look at the eyes of their conversation partner, yet a study that examined gaze-following found that older adults were less adept at knowing where someone was looking (Slessor et al., 2008). That creates a disadvantage in social interactions. Another study found that already by age 50, adults were less adept at reading emotions by looking at the eyes (Pardini & Nichelli, 2009).

Acute hearing is also needed to detect nuances of emotion. Older adults are less able to decipher the emotional content in speech, even when they hear the words correctly (Dupuis & Pichora-Fuller, 2010). Similarly, for older adults, understanding speech is impaired when vision is impaired (Tye-Murray et al., 2011), probably because we all watch lips and facial expressions to assist in understanding. Thus, small sensory losses—not noticed by the person or family but inevitable with age—impair cognition.

MEMORY The second step of information processing is memory. Remember stereotype threat: If older people suspect their memory is fading, anxiety itself impairs memory, a phenomenon more apparent among those with more education (Hess et al., 2009), probably because they are quicker to notice it.

Here again, specifics are important to fight stereotypes. Some aspects of memory remain strong throughout late adulthood, including vocabulary, whereas others do not, such as memory for names. Thus, a person who cannot recall a name should not conclude that memory, overall, is fading.

One memory deficit is *source amnesia*—forgetting the origin of a fact, idea, or snippet of conversation. Source amnesia is particularly problematic with the information bombardment of television, radio, print, and the Internet. Elders may believe a rumour or political advertisement if they forget the source (Jacoby & Rhodes, 2006). Compensation would mean deliberate attention to the reason behind the message before accepting a televised ad or a con man's promises.

Working memory, the memory of information held in the brain for a moment before processing (evaluating, calculating, and inferring), shrinks with age. Speed is critical here: Older individuals take longer to perceive and process sensations, and this reduces working memory because some items fade before they can be evaluated. A common test of working memory is repeating a string of digits backwards, but if the digits are said quickly, a slow-thinking person may not be able to process each number and properly hold them all in memory. Speed of processing would explain why memory for vocabulary (especially recognition memory, not recall) is often unaffected by age. For instance, speed is irrelevant in deciding if *chartreuse* is a colour or an animal.

Some research finds that when older people take their time and concentrate, their working memory may be as good as ever. For example, a study of reading ability found that although older people reread phrases more than younger people did, when allowed ample time the old and young were equally accurate in reading comprehension (Stine-Morrow et al., 2010). For testing memory, not only time but also motivation and context are crucial. Almost invariably, realistic circumstances (as when people are quizzed at home instead of in a university laboratory) result in better results on memory tests.

IN DAILY LIFE **Ecological validity** is the idea that ability should be measured in everyday tasks and circumstances, not as laboratory tests assess it. Ecological validity is particularly significant for the elderly, who are disadvantaged by traditional testing (Marsiske & Margrett, 2006).

Ecological validity in measuring the intellect begins with arranging the testing conditions so that optimal performance is assessed. For example, older adults are at their best in the early morning, when adolescents are half asleep. If both groups are tested at 8 A.M., or at 2 P.M., comparisons would reflect time of day, not just mental ability. Similarly, if basic intellectual ability is assessed via a timed test, then faster thinkers (usually young) would seem more capable than slower thinkers (usually old), even if the slower ones were more accurate, given a few more seconds to think.

A more fundamental ecological issue regards what should be assessed: pure, abstract thinking or practical, contextual thought. Traditional tests measure fluid cognitive abilities that are valued by the young, but the elderly are more adept at problem solving and emotional regulation. Those practical abilities may improve with age but are not traditionally measured.

Awareness of the need for ecological validity has helped scientists restructure research on memory, finding fewer deficits than originally thought. However, some tests may still overestimate or underestimate ability. For instance, how should we test long-term memory? We know that people of all ages misremember and that few early memories are verifiable. Many older people recount vivid and detailed memories of events that occurred decades ago. That is an impressive intellectual feat—if the memories are accurate.

It is impossible to be totally objective in assessing memory. We know, at least, that stereotypes must be avoided, and global assessments are too simplistic. Not only do individuals vary, but some kinds of memory show marked age-related loss, and other kinds do not. Names are harder to recall than actions: Grandpa can still swim, ride a bike, and drive a car, even if he cannot name a province or territory's premier.

The final ecological question is "What is memory for?" Older adults usually think they remember well enough and, unless they develop a brain condition such as Alzheimer's disease (soon to be described), they are correct: They remember how to live their daily lives, happily and independently.

CONTROL PROCESSES Instead of the analysis and forethought that characterize executive function, the elderly tend to rely on prior knowledge, general principles, familiarity, and rules of thumb in their decision making (Peters et al., 2011). They are less likely to use analytic reasoning and more likely to base conclusions on personal and emotional experience. As you remember from the discussion of dual processing in Chapter 9, experiential thinking is not always faulty, but sometimes analytical thinking is needed to control the impulses that arise from past experience.

ecological validity
The idea that cognition should be measured in settings that are as realistic as possible and that the abilities measured should be those needed in real life.

Thus, the underlying impairment of cognition in late adulthood may be in *control processes,* which, as you read in Chapter 7, are the various methods used to regulate the analysis and flow of information from all parts of the brain. These include memory and retrieval strategies, selective attention, and rules or strategies for problem solving, all part of what is considered *executive function.* Control processes depend on the prefrontal cortex, which shrinks with age.

As mentioned, one control process is retrieval, which is crucial for analysis. Analysis involves retrieving thoughts and memories of past events and then recognizing the similarities and differences between these experiences and new challenges. Without access to these previous instances, the benefits of past experiences fade for elders.

Inadequate control processes may explain why many older adults have extensive vocabularies (measured by written tests) but limited fluency (when they write or talk), why they are much better at recognition than recall, why tip-of-the-tongue forgetfulness is common, and why spelling is poorer than pronunciation.

In a study that illustrated strategic retrieval, adults of varying ages were given props for 30 odd and memorable actions, such as kissing an artificial frog or stepping into a large plastic bag (Thomas & Bulevich, 2006). They were asked to perform 15 of these actions (and they did them), and they were told to *imagine* doing the other 15. Two weeks later, participants read a list of 45 actions (15 done, 15 imagined, and 15 new). They were asked which were performed, which were imagined, and which were new. Half the participants just read the list and answered performed/imagined/new; the other half were first guided in memory strategies that might help (asked to remember sensations, such as the feel of the frog as they kissed it).

Among the half who merely read the list, the younger adults assigned 78 percent of the items to the correct categories, whereas the older adults were correct only 52 percent of the time. As for the half who were taught memory strategies, the younger adults still got 78 percent correct, but the older ones were correct 66 percent of the time (Thomas & Bulevich, 2006). Thus, guidance in retrieval strategies was more helpful to the old than to the young.

Many gerontologists think elders would benefit from using control strategies, as in this example. Unfortunately, even though "a high sense of control is associated with being happy, healthy, and wise," many older adults resist suggested strategies because they believe that declines are "inevitable or irreversible" and that no strategy could help (Lachman et al., 2009, p. 144). Efforts to improve their use of control strategies are often discouraging (McDaniel & Bugg, 2012).

Don't Forget As a retrieval strategy, this shop owner posts dozens of reminders for herself on the wall.

AP PHOTO / SALISBURY DAILY TIMES, BRICE STUMP

ANSWER TO OBSERVATION QUIZ (from page 506) Nine-year-olds were the only group to slow down significantly in both tasks. Impairment was about 11 percent in walking and 7 percent in naming within a category. ●

✦ **ESPECIALLY FOR People Who Are Proud of Their Intellect** What can you do to keep your mind sharp all your life? (see response, page 510) ➡

OUTPUT The final step in information processing is output. In the Seattle Longitudinal Study (described in Chapter 12), the measured output of all five primary mental abilities—verbal meaning, spatial orientation, inductive reasoning, number ability, and word fluency—declined, beginning at about age 60. This was particularly notable in the subtests affected by spatial perception and processing speed (Schaie, 2005). Similar results are found in many tests of cognition. Thus, the usual path of cognition in late adulthood is gradual decline, at least in output (Salthouse, 2010).

Overall, note that output is usually measured by various tests of production, validated by comparing the output of older adults with that of younger adults. As detailed in Chapters 7 and 12, intelligence tests were initially designed to measure success in school. Many of the questions are quite abstract, and many are timed, since speed of thinking correlates with intelligence for younger adults. A smart person is said to be a "quick" thinker, the opposite of someone who is "slow." But abstractions and speed are exactly the aspects of cognition that fade most with age. Perhaps ecological validity, already described regarding memory tests, is especially crucial for output. Thus training that considers individual interests and abilities might increase the intellect. This possibility is being explored by many scientists, as the following describes.

A VIEW FROM SCIENCE

Learning Late in Life

Many people have tried to improve the intellectual abilities of older adults by teaching or training them in various tasks (Lustig et al., 2009; Stine-Morrow & Basak, 2011). Success has been reported in specific abilities.

Dr. Reza Naqvi of the University of Toronto reviewed more than 5000 studies from as far back as the 1960s and concluded that brain exercises based on computer programs or memory games were more effective than medications and vitamin supplements in maintaining older adults' cognitive health (Naqvi et al., 2013). For example, in one part of the Seattle Longitudinal Study, 60-year-olds who had lost some spatial understanding had five sessions of personalized training and practice. They returned to the skill level of 14 years earlier (Schaie, 2005).

Another group of researchers (Basak et al., 2008) targeted control processes. Volunteers, with an average age of 69 and no signs of neurocognitive disorder (all similar in cognition before the study began), were divided into an experimental group and a control group (all similar in cognition before the study began). None were video-game players. They took a battery of cognitive tests to measure executive function.

The experimental group was then taught to play a video game, set to begin at the easiest level. Participants enjoyed the game and tried to improve. After each game, they were told their score, and another game began—more challenging in pace and memory if the earlier game was too easy. After 20 hours of training over several weeks, the original battery of tests was given again. The experimental group improved, compared with the control group, in mental activities that were *not* exactly the ones taught by the video game.

Similar results have been found in many other training programs involving the young-old who are taught a specific

Excited Neurons Energetic activities director Cyndi Bolen *(left)* joins one of the oldest residents of this nursing home, Mildred Secrest *(right)*, in a Wii Sports bowling game. Playing video games with Cyndi gives Mildred an opportunity to exercise her mind and body and to escape the social isolation often experienced by elders. How did Mildred do? Great! See how thrilled she was when she got a spare!

skill. This has led to a conclusion now accepted by almost all researchers: People younger than 80 can learn almost any cognitive skill if the educational process is carefully targeted to the individual's motivation and ability.

What about the old-old? Learning is more difficult, but possible. One careful experiment improved visual working memory in healthy people in their 80s (Buschkuehl et al., 2008). However, the benefits were no longer apparent a year later. It seems that learning is possible in late adulthood, but the older a person is, the more difficult and less comprehensive that learning will be (Stine-Morrow & Basak, 2011). Apparently, ongoing practice is particularly important for the old-old (Buschkuehl et al., 2008).

Many developmentalists are suspicious of the simple "use it or lose it" hypothesis, especially when it leads to many of the elderly doing newspaper puzzles (crosswords, mazes, Sudoku) to supposedly prevent neurocognitive impairment. However, they are not about to tell older people to stop trying to learn new skills. One researcher concluded, "[A]lthough my professional opinion is that … the mental-exercise hypothesis is more of an optimistic hope than an empirical reality, my personal recommendation is that people should behave as if it is true" (Salthouse, 2006, p. 84).

Screen to Brain Although elders are least likely to have an Internet connection at home, they may be most likely to benefit from it, whether they videoconference with grandchildren or play video games. Family joy and mental flexibility correlate with a long and happy life.

RESPONSE FOR People Who Are Proud of Their Intellect (from page 508) You might be inclined to answer "Use it or lose it" or "Do crossword puzzles," but that is not necessarily the correct answer. No specific brain activity has been proven to prevent brain slowdown. Overall health is good for the brain as well as for the body, so exercise, a balanced diet, and well-controlled blood pressure are some smart answers. ●

KEY Points

- The brain slows down in late adulthood, which impairs cognition.
- Variation is evident in late-life intellectual ability, not only among people but also among abilities, with vocabulary particularly likely to stay or increase, and speed of thought and spatial abilities particularly likely to decrease.
- Memory for names and places fades more quickly than memory overall.
- Impairment in control processes—especially retrieval strategies—may underlie the cognitive deficits of old age.

Aging and Disease

As you read in Chapter 12, with each passing decade reaction time slows, the senses become less acute, organ reserves are depleted, and homeostasis takes longer. Skin, hair, and body shape show unmistakable senescence, while every internal organ—especially the heart and the brain—ages.

Primary and Secondary Aging

primary aging
The universal and irreversible physical changes that occur in all living creatures as they grow older.

secondary aging
The specific physical illnesses or conditions that become more common with aging but are caused by health habits, genes, and other influences that vary from person to person.

Gerontologists distinguish between **primary aging,** which involves universal changes that occur with the passage of time, and **secondary aging,** the consequences of particular inherited weaknesses, chosen health habits, and environmental conditions. One explains:

> Primary aging is defined as the universal changes occurring with age that are not caused by diseases or environmental influences. Secondary aging is defined as changes involving interactions of primary aging processes with environmental influences and disease processes.

> [Masoro, 2006, p. 46]

Primary aging does not directly cause illness, but it increases the impact of every secondary factor—cigarette smoking, viruses, obesity, and stress—and it makes almost every disease more likely. For example, with age, the heart pumps more slowly and the vascular network is less flexible, increasing the risk of stroke and heart attack. The lungs take in and expel less air with each breath so that blood oxygen is reduced and chronic obstructive pulmonary disease is more common. Digestion slows and the kidneys are less efficient, risking problems if people become dehydrated because they drink less to reduce incontinence, which itself is caused by an aging renal/urinary system.

Furthermore, healing takes longer if an illness or an accident occurs (Arking, 2006). For example, young adults who contract pneumonia usually recover in a few weeks, but in the very old the strain of pneumonia over several days can overwhelm a weakened body. Indeed, pneumonia is a leading cause of death for the oldest-old.

Medical intervention affects the old differently than the young, reducing the effectiveness of drugs, surgery, and so on. For instance, anaesthesia may damage an older person's brain or may cause the heart to stop. Temporary hallucinations and delirium after surgery are far more common for the old than for the young (Strauss, 2012).

A surprising example of the effects of age comes from medication that reduces hypertension. If systolic blood pressure is above 140, and diet and exercise do not lower it, drugs not only reduce it but also make strokes and heart attacks less likely for middle-aged adults. However, the same drugs for the same blood pressure are counterproductive for the oldest-old. For them, mild hypertension (140–160) may be protective because their slower homeostasis does not quickly respond to a sudden dip in blood pressure. That can be fatal (Beckett et al., 2008).

A developmental view of the relationship between primary and secondary aging harkens back to the lifelong toll of stress, as explained in Chapter 12. *Allostatic load* is measured by 10, or even 16, biomarkers—including cortisol, C-reactive protein, systolic and diastolic blood pressure, waste-hip ratio, and insulin resistance. All of these indicate stress on the body, and such stress, if ongoing, harms health.

Thus, measurement of allostatic load assesses the combined, long-term effect of many indicators, none necessarily dangerous alone. If many of these biomarkers are outside the normal range, people become sick and die, especially when aging already has reduced organ reserve (see Figure 14.4). In this way, lifelong responses to stress create a biological burden, a load that becomes lethal.

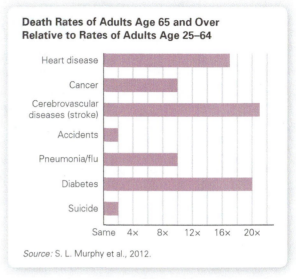

Death Rates of Adults Age 65 and Over Relative to Rates of Adults Age 25–64

Source: S. L. Murphy et al., 2012.

FIGURE 14.4 More Years to Live
Even compared with a decade ago, fewer people die before age 65, which means that, for many causes, death is far more likely in old age. Most of the underlying conditions for these diseases were present in middle age.

compression of morbidity
A shortening of the time a person spends ill or infirm, accomplished by postponing illness.

osteoporosis
Fragile bones that result from primary aging, which makes bones more porous, especially if a person is at genetic risk.

Compression of Morbidity

Ideally, prevention of the diseases of the old begins in childhood and continues throughout life, so societies need to recognize that public health and aging efforts are not only for the older adults of today but also for the future elder generations (Albert & Freedman, 2010). Illness can be delayed, and its severity can be limited by having established good childhood habits. Delayed illness is an example of **compression of morbidity,** which is reducing (compressing) sickness before death. There is good news here. In recent years, morbidity has been successfully compressed. For instance, unlike 30 years ago, most people diagnosed with cancer, diabetes, or a heart condition continue to be independent for decades (Hamerman, 2007).

Compression of morbidity is a social and psychological blessing as well as a personal, biological one. A healthier person remains alert and active—in other words, experiences the optimal aging of the young-old, not the dependence of the oldest-old. Improved prevention, diagnosis, and treatment mean less pain, more mobility, better vision, stronger teeth, sharper hearing, clearer thinking, and enhanced vitality.

The importance of compression of morbidity is apparent with **osteoporosis** (fragile bones), which occurs because primary aging makes bones more porous, especially if a person is at genetic risk (North American women of European descent are more vulnerable, genetically, than women of other ethnic groups). A fall that would have merely bruised a young person may result in a broken wrist or hip in an elder. That leads to morbidity, sometimes for months, especially when hospitalization and bed rest cause infections and stress.

How can morbidity from osteoporosis be compressed? First, through better health habits earlier in life. Tobacco and alcohol weaken bones, as do low calcium and insufficient weight-bearing exercise. With strong bones, a fall does not cause a break. Second, through the use of special equipment, such as shoes, canes, and so on. These aids help elders strengthen their muscles and improve their balance, so morbidity does not even begin. Third, by becoming less fearful and fatalistic. By old age, the most common liability from a fall is fear. A prospective longitudinal study of Dutch elders (Stel et al., 2004) found that one-third of those who fell became overcautious, reducing their activity. That inactivity made all their organs less efficient. Ironically, only 6 percent of the falls for these elders resulted in serious injury, but the 94 percent with less serious injuries often moved less. That increased their morbidity.

This applies to every kind of primary aging. If the elderly selectively remedy whatever challenges their primary aging presents, morbidity will be compressed.

Moving Along Her stiffening joints have made a walker necessary, but this elderly woman in Gujarat, India, is maintaining her mobility by going for a stroll every day.

Neurocognitive Disorders

The patterns of cognitive aging challenge another assumption: that older people always lose the ability to think and remember. That is not true. Many older people are less sharp than they were, but are still quite capable of intellectual activity. Others experience serious decline.

The Ageism of Words

It is undeniable that the rate of neurocognitive disorders increases with every decade after age 70. To understand that and prevent the worst of it, caution is needed in using words. Formerly, *senility* was used to mean severe mental impairment, which implied that old age always brings intellectual failure—an ageist myth; *senile* simply means "old." *Dementia* was a more precise term than *senility* for irreversible, pathological loss of brain functioning, but dementia also has inaccurate connotations. The DSM-5 now describes **neurocognitive disorder (NCD),** either *major neurocognitive disorder* or *mild neurocognitive disorder,* depending on the severity of symptoms.

Memory impairment is common in every cognitive disorder, although symptoms of neurocognitive disorders include many more problems, especially in learning new material, using language, moving the body, and responding to people. Practical challenges include getting lost, becoming confused about using common objects like a telephone or toothbrush, or having extreme emotional reactions.

The lines between normal age-related problems, mild disorder, and major disorder are not clearly defined, and the symptoms vary depending on the specifics of brain loss and context. Variation is evident in origin as well: More than 70 diseases can cause neurocognitive disorder, each with particular symptoms, sequence, and severity. Making distinctions more difficult is that the former word—*dementia*—is still often used in research, and the inaccurate word—*senility*—is used in common speech.

The problem of ageist terminology has been recognized internationally. In Japanese, the traditional word for neurocognitive disorder was *chihou,* translated as "foolish" or "stupid." As more people reached old age, the Japanese decided on a new word, *ninchihou,* which means "cognitive syndrome" (George & Whitehouse, 2010). That is similar to the changes in English terminology over the past decades, from *senility* to *dementia* to *neurocognitive disorder.*

Mild and Major Impairment

Many instances of memory loss are not necessarily ominous signs of severe loss to come. Older adults who have significant problems with memory, but who still function well at work and home, might be diagnosed with *mild NCD,* formerly called *mild cognitive impairment (MCI).* Although some of these adults will develop major

neurocognitive disorder (NCD)
Impairment of intellectual functioning caused by organic brain damage or disease. NCD may be diagnosed as major or mild, depending on the severity of symptoms. It becomes more common with age, but it is abnormal and pathological even in the very old.

disorders, about half will be mildly impaired for decades or will regain cognitive abilities (Lopez et al., 2007; Salthouse, 2010).

Many tests are designed to measure mild loss, including one that takes less than 10 minutes—the quick MCI (Qmci) (O'Caoimh et al., 2013). The problem with every test is that scores are affected by many factors, with no universally accepted cut-off between normal, mild, and major impairment.

Many scientists seek biological indicators (called "biomarkers"), such as substances in the blood or cerebrospinal fluid, or brain indicators (as found in brain scans) that predict major memory loss. However, although abnormal scores on many tests (biological, neurological, or psychological) indicate possible problems, an examination of 24 such measures found no single test, and no combination of tests, to be 100 percent accurate (Ewers et al., 2012).

The final determinant of neurocognitive disorders is the clinical judgment of a professional who considers all the symptoms and markers—everything from uncontrolled impulses to memory lapses. Any diagnosis may focus too much on losses and not enough on individual strengths. As the previous sections on brain aging and information processing explain, no very old person is as intellectually sharp as they once were, so almost everyone could be considered mildly impaired. Opinions are always subjective; objective data can be discounted or overemphasized by both professionals and patients. That obviously complicates diagnosis.

Prevalence of NCD

According to the Alzheimer Society of Canada, in 2011, 747 000 Canadians were living with some form of cognitive impairment, including NCD, which accounted for about 14.9 percent of Canadians aged 65 and older (Alzheimer Society of Canada, 2012). (Figure 14.5 shows the predicted number of new cases of NCD in Canada each year until 2038.) Rates of NCD vary by nation, from about 2 to 25 percent of elders, with an estimated 35 million people affected worldwide (Kalaria et al., 2008; WHO, 2012). Developing nations have lower rates, but that may be because millions of people in the early stages are not counted or because health care overall is poor.

How would poor health care lead to less, not more, impairment? Because many people die before any neurocognitive problems are apparent. People with diabetes, Parkinson's disease, strokes, and heart surgery are more likely to lose intellectual capacity in old age, but in poor nations many people with those conditions die before age 70.

Improvements in health care can reduce cognitive impairment. The three ideal goals of public health are said to be better physical health, less mental disorder, and longer lives. That is becoming a reality in some nations. In England and Wales, the rate of NCD for people over age 65 was 8.3 percent in 1991 but only 6.5 percent in 2011 (Matthews et al., 2013). Sweden had a similar decline (Qiu et al., 2013). In China, rates were much higher in rural areas than in urban ones, probably because rural Chinese had less education (Jia et al., 2014) and, thus, less understanding about how to stay healthy. A comparable survey has not been done in North America, but some signs suggest improvement.

Of course, reduction in rate does not necessarily mean reduction in number, since more people live to old age. In England over the past 20 years, the number of people

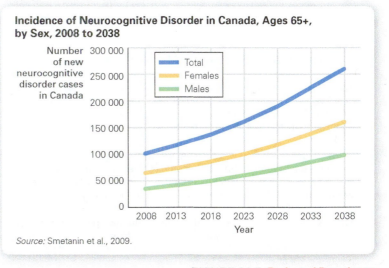

Incidence of Neurocognitive Disorder in Canada, Ages 65+, by Sex, 2008 to 2038

Number of new neurocognitive disorder cases in Canada

Source: Smetanin et al., 2009.

FIGURE 14.5 **Projected Prevalence** The number of new cases of neurocognitive disorder in 2038 among Canadians 65 years and older is expected to be about 2.2 times that of the number of cases in 2013, with a much higher prevalence rate in females than in males.

with NCD has stayed about the same (Matthews et al., 2013) even while the rate has declined.

Genetics and social context affect rates, but it is not known by how much (Bondi et al., 2009). For example, more older women than older men are diagnosed with neurocognitive disorders, which may be genetic, educational, or stress-related. Or it may be simply that women live longer than men (Alzheimer's Association, 2012).

Now consider some specific types of age-related neurocognitive disorders.

ALZHEIMER'S DISEASE In 1906, a physician named Dr. Alois Alzheimer performed an autopsy on a patient who had lost her memory. He found unusual material in her brain, but he was uncertain whether it specified a distinct disease (George & Whitehouse, 2010). Others, convinced that he had discovered a disease, named it after him. In the past century, millions of people in every large nation have been diagnosed with **Alzheimer's disease (AD),** now formally referred to as *major or mild NCD due to Alzheimer's disease.* (See Table 14.2 for the stages of Alzheimer's disease.) In China, for example, 5.7 million people have Alzheimer's disease (K.Y. Chan et al., 2013).

As Dr. Alzheimer discovered, autopsies reveal that some aging brains have many *plaques* and *tangles* in the cerebral cortex. These abnormalities destroy the ability of neurons to communicate with one another, causing severe cognitive loss. **Plaques** are clumps of a protein called *beta-amyloid,* found in tissues surrounding the neurons; **tangles** are twisted masses of threads made of a protein called *tau* within the neurons. A normal brain contains some beta-amyloid and some tau, but in brains with AD these plaques and tangles proliferate, especially in the hippocampus, the brain structure crucial for memory. Forgetfulness is the dominant symptom; working memory disappears first.

Although finding massive brain plaques and tangles at autopsy proves that a person diagnosed with NCD had Alzheimer's disease, between 20 and 30 percent of cognitively normal elders have, at autopsy, the same level of plaques in their brains as people who had been diagnosed with AD (Jack et al., 2009). Possibly the elders who had not been diagnosed with NCD had compensated by using other parts of their brains; possibly they were in the early stages, not yet suspected of having AD; possibly plaques are a symptom, not a cause.

Alzheimer's disease is partly genetic. If it develops in middle age, the affected person either has trisomy-21 (Down syndrome) or has inherited one of three genes: amyloid precursor protein (APP), presenilin 1, or presenilin 2. For these people, the disease progresses quickly, reaching the last phase within three to five years.

Most cases begin much later, at age 75 or so. Many genes have some impact, including SORL1 and ApoE4 (allele 4 of the ApoE gene). People who inherit one copy of ApoE4 have about a 50/50 chance of developing AD. Those who inherit two copies almost always develop the disorder if they live long enough.

VASCULAR NCD The second most common cause of neurocognitive disorder is a *stroke* (a temporary obstruction of a blood vessel in the brain) or a series of strokes, called *transient*

Alzheimer's disease (AD)
The most common cause of neurocognitive disorder, characterized by gradual deterioration of memory and personality and marked by the formation of plaques of beta-amyloid protein and tangles of tau in the brain. (Previously referred to as *senile dementia of the Alzheimer's type.*)

plaques
Clumps of a protein called *beta-amyloid,* found in brain tissues surrounding the neurons; a normal brain contains some beta-amyloid protein, but in brains of people with Alzheimer's disease these plaques proliferate, especially in the hippocampus, a brain structure crucial for memory.

tangles
Twisted masses of threads made of a protein called *tau* within the neurons of the brain; a normal brain contains some tau, but in brains of people with Alzheimer's disease these tangles proliferate, especially in the hippocampus, a brain structure crucial for memory.

TABLE 14.2 The Progression of Alzheimer's Disease

Stage 1. People in the first stage forget recent events or new information, particularly names and places. For example, they might forget the name of a famous film star or how to get home from a familiar place. This first stage is similar to mild cognitive impairment—even experts cannot always tell the difference.

Stage 2. Generalized confusion develops, with deficits in concentration and short-term memory. Speech becomes aimless and repetitious, vocabulary is limited, words get mixed up. Personality traits are not curbed by rational thought. For example, suspicious people may decide that others have stolen the things that they themselves have mislaid.

Stage 3. Memory loss becomes dangerous. Although people at stage 3 can care for themselves, they might leave a lit stove or hot iron on or might forget whether they took essential medicine and thus take it twice—or not at all.

Stage 4. At this stage, full-time care is needed. People cannot communicate well. They might not recognize their closest loved ones.

Stage 5. Finally, people with AD become unresponsive. Identity and personality have disappeared. Death comes 10 to 15 years after the first signs appear.

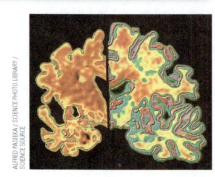

The Alzheimer's Brain This computer graphic shows a vertical slice through a brain ravaged by Alzheimer's disease *(left)* compared with a similar slice of a normal brain *(right)*. The diseased brain is shrunken as a result of the degeneration of neurons.

ALFRED PASIEKA / SCIENCE PHOTO LIBRARY / SCIENCE SOURCE

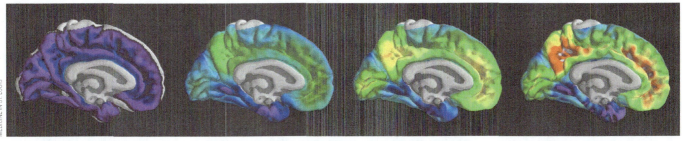

(a) Non-carriers   (b) Pre-symptomatic   (c) Mild symptoms   (d) Alzheimer's disease

ischemic attacks (TIAs, or ministrokes). The interruption in blood flow reduces oxygen, destroying part of the brain. Symptoms (blurred vision, weak or paralyzed limbs, slurred speech, and mental confusion) suddenly appear.

In a TIA, symptoms may vanish quickly, unnoticed. However, unless it is recognized and preventive action is taken, another is likely. Repeated TIAs produce a type of NCD sometimes called **vascular neurocognitive disorder.** The progression of vascular NCD differs from Alzheimer's disease, but the final result is similar (see Figure 14.6).

Neurocognitive disorders caused by vascular disease are apparent in many of the oldest-old worldwide. Vascular NCD is more common than Alzheimer's disease for those over age 90 but not for the young-old. Vascular NCD correlates with the ApoE4 allele (Cramer & Procaccio, 2012), and for some of the elderly it is caused by surgery that requires general anaesthesia. They may suffer a ministroke, which, added to reduced cognitive reserve, damages the brain (Stern, 2013).

FRONTAL LOBE DISORDERS Several types of neurocognitive disorders are called **frontal lobe disorders,** or *frontotemporal lobar degeneration.* (Pick's disease is the most common form). These disorders are particularly likely to occur at relatively young ages (under age 70), unlike Alzheimer's disease and vascular NCD, which typically begin later (Seelaar et al., 2011).

In frontal lobe disorders, parts of the brain that regulate emotions and social behaviour (especially the amygdala and prefrontal cortex) deteriorate. Emotional and personality changes are the main symptoms (Seelaar et al., 2011). A loving father with frontal lobe degeneration might reject his children, or a formerly astute business-woman might invest in a hare-brained scheme.

Frontal lobe problems may be worse than more obvious types of neurocognitive disease in that compassion, self-awareness, and judgment fade in a person who otherwise seems typical. One wife, Ruth French, was furious because her husband

> threw away tax documents, got a ticket for trying to pass an ambulance, and bought stock in companies that were obviously in trouble. Once a good cook, he burned every pot in the house. He became withdrawn and silent, and no longer spoke to his wife over dinner. That same failure to communicate got him fired from his job.
>
> *[Grady, 2012, p. A1]*

Finally, he was diagnosed with frontal lobe disorder. Ruth asked him to forgive her fury. It is not clear that he understood either her anger or her apology.

Hopeful Brains Even the brain without symptoms *(a)* might eventually develop Alzheimer's disease, but people with a certain dominant gene definitely will. They have no symptoms *(b)* in early adulthood, some symptoms *(c)* in middle adulthood, and stage five Alzheimer's disease *(d)* before old age. Research has led to the discovery of early markers (such as those shown here) that predict the disease. As scientists detect early signs, they hope to determine a treatment to halt brain destruction before it starts.

vascular neurocognitive disorder
A form of neurocognitive disorder characterized by sporadic and progressive loss of intellectual functioning caused by repeated infarcts, or temporary obstructions of blood vessels, which prevent sufficient blood from reaching the brain.

frontal lobe disorder
Deterioration of the amygdala and frontal lobes that may be the cause of 15 percent of all neurocognitive disorders. (Also called *frontotemporal lobar degeneration.*)

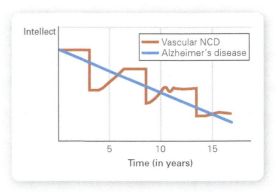

FIGURE 14.6 The Progression of Alzheimer's Disease and Vascular Neurocognitive Disorder Cognitive decline is apparent in both Alzheimer's disease (AD) and vascular neurocognitive disorder. However, the pattern of decline for each disease is different. People with AD show steady, gradual decline, while those who suffer from vascular NCD get suddenly much worse, improve somewhat, and then experience another serious loss.

Although there are many forms and causes of frontal lobe disorders—including a dozen or so alleles—they usually progress rapidly, leading to death in about five years.

OTHER DISORDERS Many other brain diseases begin with impaired motor control (shaking when picking up a coffee cup, falling when trying to walk), not with impaired thinking. The most common of these is **Parkinson's disease,** the cause of about 3 percent of all cases of NCD (Aarsland et al., 2005).

Parkinson's disease starts with rigidity or tremor of the muscles as dopamine-producing neurons degenerate, affecting movement long before cognition. Younger adults with Parkinson's disease usually have sufficient cognitive reserve to avoid major intellectual loss, although about one-third have mild impairment (Gao et al., 2013). Older people with Parkinson's develop cognitive problems sooner (Pfeiffer, 2012). If people with Parkinson's live 10 years or more, major neurocognitive impairment almost always occurs (Pahwa & Lyons, 2013).

Another 5 to 15 percent of Canadians with NCD suffer from an excess of **Lewy bodies:** deposits of a particular kind of protein in their brains. Lewy bodies are also present in Parkinson's disease, but in Lewy body disease they are more numerous and dispersed throughout the brain, interfering with communication between neurons.

As a result, movement and cognition are both impacted, although motor effects are less severe than in Parkinson's disease and memory loss is not as dramatic as in Alzheimer's disease (Bondi et al., 2009). The main symptom is loss of inhibition: A person might gamble or become hypersexual.

Comorbidity is common with all these disorders. For instance, most people with Alzheimer's disease also show signs of vascular impairment (Doraiswamy, 2012). Parkinson's disease, Alzheimer's disease, and Lewy body disease can occur together: People who have all three experience more rapid and severe cognitive loss (Compta et al., 2011).

Some other types of NCD begin in middle age or even earlier, caused by Huntington disease, multiple sclerosis, a severe head injury, or the last stages of syphilis, AIDS, or bovine spongiform encephalitis (BSE, or mad cow disease). Repeated blows to the head, even without concussions, can cause chronic traumatic encephalopathy (CTE), which first causes memory loss and emotional changes, and eventually further cognitive loss (Voosen, 2013). Although the rate of systemic brain disease increases dramatically with every decade after age 60, brain disease can occur at any age, as revealed by the autopsies of a number of young professional athletes. For athletes, prevention includes better helmets and fewer body blows.

Parkinson's disease
A chronic, progressive disease that is characterized by muscle tremor and rigidity and sometimes cognitive impairment; caused by reduced dopamine production in the brain.

Lewy bodies
Deposits of a particular kind of protein in the brain that interfere with communication between neurons; Lewy bodies cause neurocognitive disorder.

Healing Doll This Japanese robotic doll, Yumel, is purchased not only for children but also for the elderly, for social and therapeutic purposes. Owners cuddle with and talk to these dolls, which have a vocabulary of 1200 phrases, sing lullabies, and can even be programmed to sleep or wake up at the same time as their owners, saying "good morning" or inviting the elderly to go to sleep, as the doll's eyes close. Interacting with dolls such as these may affect an owner's brain chemistry and slow down neurocognitive disorder.

Preventing Impairment

Since aging increases the rate of cognitive impairment, slowing down senescence may postpone major neurocognitive disorders, and ameliorating mild losses may prevent worse ones. That may have occurred in the decreasing rates of major NCD documented in England (Matthews et al., 2013).

Epigenetic research is particularly likely to lead to better prevention, because "the brain contains an epigenetic 'hotspot' with a unique potential to not only better understand its most complex functions, but also to treat its most vicious diseases" (Gräff et al., 2011, p. 603). Genes are always influential. Some are expressed, affecting development, and some are latent unless circumstances change. The reasons are epigenetic: Factors beyond the genes are crucial (Issa, 2011; Skipper, 2011).

The most important non-genetic factor is exercise. Because brain plasticity continues throughout life, exercise that improves blood circulation not only prevents cognitive loss but also builds capacity and repairs damage. The benefits of exercise have been repeatedly cited in this text. Now we simply emphasize that physical exercise—even more than good nutrition and mental exercise—prevents, postpones, and slows cognitive loss of all kinds (Erickson et al., 2012; Gregory et al., 2012; Lövdén et al., 2013).

Medication to prevent stroke also protects against neurocognitive disorders. In a Finnish study, half of a large group of older Finns were given drugs to reduce lipids (primarily cholesterol) in their system. Years later, fewer of them had developed NCD than did a comparable group who were not given the drug (Solomon et al., 2010).

Avoiding specific pathogens is critical. For example, beef can be tested to ensure that it does not have BSE, condoms can protect against AIDS, and syphilis can be cured with antibiotics. For most neurocognitive disorders, however, despite the efforts of thousands of scientists and millions of older people, no foolproof prevention or cure has been found. Avoiding toxic substances (lead, aluminum, copper, and pesticides) and adding supplements (hormones, aspirin, coffee, insulin, antioxidants, red wine, blueberries, and statins) have been tried as preventative measures but have not proven effective in controlled, scientific research.

Lost Memories This man, who is in the last stage of Alzheimer's disease, no longer remembers his daughter and is often unresponsive when she visits.

Thousands of scientists have sought to halt the production of beta-amyloid and have had some success in mice but not yet in humans. One current goal is to diagnose Alzheimer's disease 10 or 15 years before the first outward signs appear in order to prevent brain damage. That is one reason for the interest in mild neurocognitive disorders: They often (though not always) progress to major problems. If it were known why some mild losses do not lead to major ones, a means of prevention might be found.

Among professionals, hope is replacing despair. Earlier diagnosis seems possible; many drug and lifestyle treatments are under review (Hampel et al., 2012; Lane et al., 2011). The first step, however, in prevention and treatment of NCD is to improve overall health. High blood pressure, diabetes, arteriosclerosis, and emphysema all impair cognition, because they disrupt the flow of oxygen to the brain. Each type of neurocognitive disorder, each slowdown, and every chronic disease interact, so progress in one area may reduce incidence and severity in another. A healthy diet, social interaction, and, especially, exercise decrease cognitive impairment of every kind, affecting brain chemicals and encouraging improvement in other health habits.

Reversible Neurocognitive Disorder?

Sometimes memory and other problems are not the result of a neurocognitive disorder. Older people may be thought to be permanently "losing their minds," when in fact a reversible condition is at fault. This highlights the importance of an accurate diagnosis.

DEPRESSION AND ANXIETY The most common reversible condition that is mistaken for neurocognitive disorder is depression. Normally, older people tend to be quite happy; frequent sadness or anxiety is not normal. Ongoing, untreated depression increases the risk of NCD (Y. Gao et al., 2013).

Ironically, people with untreated anxiety or depression may exaggerate minor memory losses or refuse to talk. Quite the opposite reaction occurs with early Alzheimer's disease, when victims are often surprised when they cannot answer questions, or with Lewy body or frontal lobe disorders, when people talk without thinking.

Specifics provide other clues. People with neurocognitive loss might forget what they just said, heard, or did because current brain activity is impaired, but they might repeatedly describe details of something that happened long ago. The opposite may be true for emotional disorders, when memory of the past is impaired but short-term memory is not.

NUTRITION Malnutrition and dehydration can also cause symptoms that may seem like brain disease. The aging digestive system is less efficient but needs more nutrients and fewer calories. This requires new habits, less fast food, and more grocery money (which many do not have). Some elderly people deliberately drink less because they want to avoid frequent urination, yet adequate liquid in the body is needed for cell health. Since homeostasis slows with age, older people are less likely to recognize and remedy their hunger and thirst, and thus may inadvertently impair their cognition.

Additionally, several specific vitamins, including antioxidants (C, A, E) and vitamin B-12, have been suggested as a means of decreasing the rate of neurocognitive disorders. Conversely, high levels of homocysteine (from animal fat) seem to increase NCD (Perez et al., 2012; Whalley et al., 2013). Obviously, any food that increases the risk of heart disease also increases the risk of stroke and hence vascular disease. In addition, some prescribed drugs destroy certain nutrients, although specifics require more research (Jyrkkä et al., 2012).

Indeed, well-controlled longitudinal research on the relationship between particular aspects of nutrition and NCD has not been done. It is known, however, that people who already suffer from NCD tend to forget to eat or choose unhealthy foods, which hastens their mental deterioration. It is also known that alcohol abuse interferes with nutrition, directly (reducing eating and hydration) and indirectly (by destroying some vitamins).

polypharmacy
A situation in which elderly people are prescribed several medications. The various side effects and interactions of those medications can result in symptoms of neurocognitive disorder.

POLYPHARMACY At home as well as in the hospital, most elderly people take numerous drugs—not only prescribed medications, but also over-the-counter preparations and herbal remedies—a situation known as **polypharmacy** (Hajjar et al., 2007). Excessive reliance on drugs can occur as a result of doctor's orders as well as a lack of patient knowledge.

Unfortunately, recommended doses of many drugs are determined primarily by clinical trials with younger adults, for whom homeostasis usually eliminates excess medication (Herrera et al., 2010). When homeostasis slows down, excess may linger. In addition, most trials to test the safety of a new drug exclude people who have more than one disease. That means drugs are not tested on many of the elderly who will use them, so recommended dosages may not be appropriate for them.

The average elderly person in Canada sees a doctor several times a year. Typically, each doctor follows "clinical practice guidelines," which are recommendations for one specific condition. A "prescribing cascade" (when many interacting drugs are prescribed) may occur. In one disturbing case, a doctor prescribed medication to raise his patient's blood pressure, and another doctor, noting the raised blood pressure, prescribed a drug to lower it (McLendon & Shelton, 2011–2012). Usually, doctors ask patients what medications they are taking and why, which could prevent such an error. However, people who are sick and confused may not give accurate responses.

Another problem is that people of every age forget when to take which drugs (before, during, or after meals? after dinner or at bedtime?), a problem multiplied as more drugs are prescribed (Bosworth & Ayotte, 2009). Short-term memory loss makes this worse. Even when medications are taken as prescribed and the right dose reaches the bloodstream, drug interactions can cause confusion and memory loss. Cognitive side effects can occur with almost any drug, but, in particular, drugs intended to reduce anxiety and depression often affect memory or reasoning.

Finally, following recommendations from the radio, friends, and television ads, many of the elderly try supplements, compounds, and herbal preparations that contain mind-altering toxic substances. Some of the elderly believe that only illegal drugs are harmful to the mind; clearly, this is not the case.

OPPOSING PERSPECTIVES

Too Many Drugs or Too Few?

The case for medication is persuasive. Thousands of drugs have been proven effective, many of them responsible for longer and healthier lives. It is estimated that, on doctor's orders, 20 percent of older people take 10 or more drugs on a regular basis (Boyd et al., 2005). Common examples of life-saving drugs are insulin to halt the ravages of diabetes, statins to prevent strokes, and antidepressants to reduce despair.

In addition, many older people take supplements, drink alcohol, and swallow vitamins and other non-prescription drugs daily. The combination of doctor-ordered and self-administered drugs may lengthen life, but they may do the opposite. For example, Audrey, a 70-year-old widow

was covered with large black bruises and burns from her kitchen stove. Audrey no longer had an appetite, so she ate little and was emaciated. One night she passed out in her driveway and scraped her face. The next morning, her neighbor found her face down on the pavement in her nightgown.

Audrey couldn't be trusted with the grandchildren anymore, so family visits were fewer and farther between. She rarely showered and spent most days sitting in a chair alternating between drinking, sleeping, and watching television. She stopped calling friends, and social invitations had long since ceased.

Audrey obtained prescriptions for Valium, a tranquilizer, and Placidyl, a sleep inducer. Both medications, which are addictive and have more adverse effects in patients over age 60, should be used only for short periods of time. Audrey had taken both medications for years at three to four times the prescribed dosage. She mixed them with large quantities of alcohol. She was a full-fledged addict ... close to death.

Her children knew she had a problem, but they ... couldn't agree among themselves on the best way to help her. Over time, they became desensitized to the seriousness of her problem—until it progressed to a dangerously advanced stage. Luckily for Audrey, she was referred to a new doctor who recognized her addiction. ... Once Audrey was in treatment and weaned off the alcohol and drugs, she bloomed. Audrey's memory improved; her appetite returned; she regained her energy; and she started walking, swimming and exercising every day.

Now, a decade later, Audrey plays an important role in her grandchildren's lives, gardens, and she lives creatively and with meaning.

[Colleran & Jay, 2003, p. 11]

Audrey is a stunning example of the danger of ageist assumptions—her children did not realize that she was capable of an intellectually and socially productive life—as well as of polypharmacy.

The solution seems simple: Discontinue drugs. However, that may increase both disease and neurocognitive disorders. One expert criticizes polypharmacy but adds that "underuse of medications in older adults can have comparable adverse effects on quality of life" (Miller, 2011–2012, p. 21).

For instance, untreated diabetes and hypertension cause cognitive loss. Lack of drug treatment for those conditions may be one reason why low-income elders experience more illness, more neurocognitive disease, and earlier death than do high-income elders: The poor are less likely to obtain medical care or to be able to afford drugs that might improve their health.

Obviously, money complicates the issue: Prescription drugs are expensive, which increases profits for drug companies, but they can also reduce surgery and hospital stays, thus saving money. As one observer notes, the discussion about spending for prescription drugs is highly polarized, emotionally loaded, with little useful debate. A war is waged over the cost of prescriptions for older people, and it is a "gloves-off, stab-you-in-the-guts struggle to the death" (Sloan, 2011–2012, p. 56).

Which is it—too many drugs or too few? Any general answer may be too glib, since specifics depend on the health and values of each patient as well as on caregivers—some who are antidrug, and others who want drugs to control symptoms (e.g., insomnia, anger, sadness) that the elderly person might prefer not to medicate. Which is better: to be suspicious of every drug, herb, or supplement or to hope that some medication will protect or restore health?

The current policy is to let the doctor and the patient decide. Even family members are not consulted or informed unless the patient agrees. That seems like a wise protection of privacy. But remember Audrey.

New Cognitive Development

You have learned that most older adults maintain adequate intellectual power. Some losses—in rapid reactions, for instance—are quite manageable, and only a minority of elders develops NCD. But the life-span perspective holds that gains as well as losses occur at every period. Are there cognitive gains in late adulthood? Yes! New depth, enhanced creativity, and even wisdom are possible.

Erikson and Maslow

Both Erik Erikson and Abraham Maslow were particularly interested in the elderly, interviewing older people to understand their views. Erikson's final book, *Vital Involvement in Old Age* (Erikson et al., 1986), written when he was in his 90s, was based on responses from other 90-year-olds—the cohort who had been studied since they were babies in Berkeley, California.

Erikson found that many older people gained interest in the arts, in children, and in human experience as a whole. He said elders are "social witnesses," aware of the interdependence of the generations as well as of all of human experience. His eighth stage, *integrity versus despair*, is the time when life comes together in a "re-synthesis of all the resilience and strengths already developed" (Erikson et al., 1986, p. 40).

Maslow maintained that older adults are more likely than younger people to reach the highest stage of development, **self-actualization.** Remember that Maslow rejected an age-based sequence of life, refusing to confine self-actualization to the old. Some youth might already be self-actualizers and some elders might still be at earlier steps of Maslow's hierarchy, seeking love or success. However, Maslow also believed that life experience helps people move forward, so more of the old reach the final stage.

The stage of self-actualization is characterized by aesthetic, creative, philosophical, and spiritual understanding (Maslow, 1970). A self-actualized person might have a deeper spirituality than ever; or might be especially appreciative of nature; or might find life more amusing, laughing often at himself or herself. Studies of centenarians find that they often have a deep spiritual grounding and a surprising sense of humour—surprising, that is, if one has the ageist view that older people have little to laugh about.

self-actualization
The final stage in Maslow's hierarchy of needs, characterized by aesthetic, creative, philosophical, and spiritual understanding.

Aesthetic Sense and Creativity

For many, old age can be a time of emotional sensory awareness and enjoyment (R. N. Butler et al., 1998). For that reason, some of the elderly take up gardening, bird watching, sculpting, painting, or making music, even if they have never done so before.

An example of late creative development is the American artist Anna Moses, who was a farm wife in rural New York. For most of her life, she expressed her artistic impulses by stitching quilts and embroidering in winter, when farm work was slow. At age 75, arthritis made needlework impossible, so she took to "dabbling in oil." Four years later, three of her paintings, displayed in a local drugstore, caught the eye of a New York City art dealer who happened to be driving through town. He bought them, drove to her house, and bought 15 more. The following year, at age 80, "Grandma Moses" had a one-woman show, receiving international recognition for her unique "primitive" style. She continued to paint for 20 years, changing her style considerably over that time. Anna Moses died at age 101.

Other well-known artists continue in late adulthood, sometimes producing their best work. Michelangelo painted the awe-inspiring frescoes in the Sistine Chapel at age 75; Verdi composed the opera *Falstaff* when he was 80; Frank Lloyd Wright completed the design of New York City's Guggenheim Museum when he was 91.

In a study of extraordinarily creative people, almost none felt that their ability, their goals, or the quality of their work had been much impaired by age. The leader of that study observed, "In their seventies, eighties, and nineties, they may lack the fiery ambition of earlier years, but they are just as focused, efficient, and committed as before … perhaps more so" (Csikszentmihalyi, 1996, p. 503).

Creativity and the Mind Creative activity may improve the intellect, especially when it involves social activity. Both the man playing the sousaphone in a band in Cuba *(left)* and the woman in a ceramics class in France *(right)* are gaining much more than the obvious lung or hand exercise.

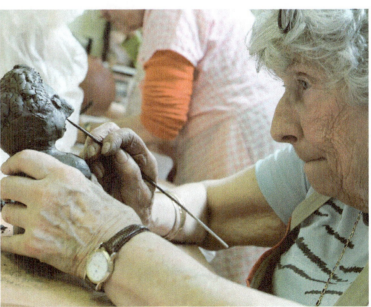

The creative impulse is one that family members and everyone else should encourage in the elderly, according to many professionals. Expressing one's creativity and aesthetic sense is said to aid in social skills, resilience, and even brain health (McFadden & Basting, 2010).

The same can be said for the **life review,** in which elders provide an account of their personal journey by writing or telling their story. They want others to know their history, telling not solely about themselves but also about their family, cohort, or ethnic group. A leading gerontologist wants us to listen:

> We have been taught that this nostalgia represents living in the past and a preoccupation with self and that it is generally boring, meaningless, and time-consuming. Yet as a natural healing process it represents one of the underlying human capacities on which all psychotherapy depends. The life review should be recognized as a necessary and healthy process in daily life as well as a useful tool in the mental health care of older people.
>
> *[R. N. Butler et al., 1998, p. 91]*

Wisdom

In a massive international survey of 26 nations, at least one on each inhabited continent, researchers found that most people everywhere agree that wisdom is a characteristic of the elderly (Löckenhoff et al., 2009). One reviewer contends that "wise elders might become a valuable asset for a more just and caring future society" (Ardelt, 2011, p. 287). Yet another reviewer offers a different opinion: The idea that older people are wise is a "hoped-for antidote to views that have cast the process of aging in terms of intellectual deficit and regression" (Labouvie-Vief, 1990, p. 52). Contrary to people's wishes and opinions, most objective research finds that wisdom does not necessarily increase with age. Starting at age 25 or so, some adults of every age are wise, but most, even at age 80, are not (Ardelt, 2011).

An underlying research quandary is that a universal definition of wisdom is elusive: Each culture and each cohort has its own concept, with fools sometimes seeming wise (as in many Shakespearean plays). Older and younger adults differ in how they make decisions; one interpretation of these differences is that the older adults are wiser, but not every younger adult would agree (Worthy et al., 2011).

One summary describes wisdom as an "expert knowledge system dealing with the conduct and understanding of life" (P. B. Baltes & Smith, 2008, p. 58). Several factors just mentioned, including the ability to put aside one's personal needs (as in self-actualization), self-reflective honesty (as in integrity), and perspective on past living (the life review), are considered part of wisdom. If this is true, the elderly have a head start in becoming wise, particularly if they have dedicated their lives to the "understanding of life," are willing and able to learn from their experiences, and have become more mature and integrated in the process (Ardelt, 2011, p. 283). Probably for that reason, philosophers, psychologists, and the general public connect wisdom with old age: That may be why popes and Supreme Court judges are usually quite old.

The popular consensus may be grounded in reality. Two psychologists explain:

> Wisdom is one domain in which some older individuals excel. … [They have] a combination of psychosocial characteristics and life history factors, including openness to experience, generativity, cognitive style, contact with excellent mentors, and some exposure to structured and critical life experiences.
>
> *[P. B. Baltes & Smith, 2008, p. 60]*

These researchers posed life dilemmas to adults of various ages and asked others (who had no clue as to how old the participants were) to judge whether the responses were wise. They found that wisdom is rare at any age, but, unlike physical strength and cognitive quickness, wisdom does not fade with maturity. Thus, some people of every age were judged as wise.

Similarly, the author of a detailed longitudinal study of 814 people concludes that wisdom is not reserved for the old, and yet humour, perspective, and altruism increase over the decades, gradually making people wiser. He then wrote:

> To be wise about wisdom we need to accept that wisdom does—and wisdom does not—increase with age. ... Winston Churchill, that master of wise simplicity and simple wisdom, reminds us, "We are all happier in many ways when we are old than when we are young. The young sow wild oats. The old grow sage."
>
> *[Vaillant, 2002, p. 256]*

The Centenarians

If age brings integrity, creativity, and maybe even wisdom, then the oldest-old should excel in many ways and those who reach age 100 and beyond should be best of all. Is there any evidence that this is true?

OTHER PLACES, OTHER STORIES In the 1970s, three remote places—one in the Republic of Georgia, one in Pakistan, and one in Ecuador—were in the news because many vigorous old people were found to live there, with several over 100 years old. One researcher described people 90 and older:

> Most of the aged work regularly. ... Some even continue to chop wood and haul water. Close to 40 percent of the aged men and 30 percent of the aged women report good vision; that is, that they do not need glasses for any sort of work, including reading or threading a needle. Between 40 and 50 percent have reasonably good hearing. Most have their own teeth. Their posture is unusually erect, even into advanced age. Many take walks of more than two miles a day and swim in mountain streams.
>
> *[Benet, 1974]*

A more comprehensive study (Pitskhelauri, 1982) found that the lifestyles in all three of these regions were similar in four ways:

1. *Diet.* People ate mostly fresh vegetables and herbs, with little meat or fat. They thought it better to be a little bit hungry than too full.

2. *Work.* Even the very old did farm work, household tasks, and child care.

3. *Family and community.* The elderly were well integrated into families of several generations and interacted frequently with friends and neighbours.

4. *Exercise and relaxation.* Most took a walk every morning and evening (often up and down mountains), napped midday, and socialized in the evening.

Perhaps these factors—diet, work, social interaction, and exercise—lengthened life.

THE TRUTH ABOUT LIFE AFTER 100 Insights gained from the studies of the three regions famous for long-lived humans have been questioned because many of those studied lacked verifiable birth or marriage records. Their claims of being centenarians are now thought to have been exaggerated, and researchers who believed them are thought to have been too eager to accept the idea that life would be long and wonderful if only the ills of modern civilization could be avoided (Thorson, 1995).

As for preventing the ills of old age, it does seem that exercise, diet, and social integration add a few years to the average life, but not decades. It is important to distinguish the *average* life span from the *maximum*.

maximum life span
The oldest possible age that members of a species can live under ideal circumstances. For humans, that age is approximately 122 years.

average life expectancy
The number of years the average newborn in a particular population group is likely to live.

Genes seem to bestow on every species an inherent **maximum life span,** defined as the oldest possible age for members of that species (Wolf, 2010). Under ideal circumstances, the maximum that rats live seems to be 4 years; rabbits, 13; tigers, 26; house cats, 30; brown bats, 34; brown bears, 37; chimpanzees, 55; Indian elephants, 70; finback whales, 80; humans, 122; lake sturgeon, 150; giant tortoises, 180.

Maximum life span is quite different from **average life expectancy,** which is the average life span of individuals in a particular group. In human groups, average life expectancy varies a great deal, depending on historical, cultural, and socioeconomic factors as well as on genes (Sierra et al., 2009). Recent increases in life expectancy are attributed to the reduction in deaths from adult diseases (heart attack, pneumonia, cancer, childbed fever).

In Canada from 2007 to 2009, average life expectancy at birth was about 79 years for men and 83 years for women. That is much longer than from 1980 to 1982, when the average life expectancy for men was 72 years and for women 79 years (Statistics Canada, 2012c). How long can average life expectancy keep increasing?

Gerontologists are engaged in a debate as to whether the average life span will keep rising and whether the maximum is genetically fixed and our society has just about reached that (Couzin-Frankel, 2011b, p. 549). The longest well-documented life ended at age 122, when Jeanne Calment died in southern France in 1997. No one has yet been proven to have outlived her, despite documented birth dates for a billion people who have died since then.

Everyone agrees, however, that the last years of life can be good ones. Those who study centenarians find many quite happy (Jopp & Rott, 2006). Jeanne Calment enjoyed a glass of red wine and some olive oil each day. "I will die laughing," she said.

Disease, disability, depression, and neurocognitive disorder may eventually set in; studies disagree about how common these problems are past age 100. Some studies find a higher rate of physical and mental health problems before age 100 than after. For example, in Sweden, where medical care is free, researchers found that centenarians were less likely to take antidepressants, but more likely to use pain medication, than those who were aged 80 or so (Wastesson et al., 2012).

Could centenarians be happier than octogenarians, as these Swedish data suggest? That is not known. However, it is true that more and more people live past 100, and many of them are energetic, alert, and optimistic (Perls, 2008; Poon, 2008). Social relationships in particular correlate with robust mental health (Margrett et al., 2011). Centenarians tend to be upbeat about life. Whether their attitude is justified is not

Guess Their Age America's Besse Cooper *(left)* was 114 and Japan's Jiroemon Kimura *(right)* was 112 when these photos were taken. Besse was believed to be the oldest person in the world when she died at age 116 in 2012, and Jiroemon, who died in 2013, also at the age of 116, was the first man verified to have lived so long. Some of the reasons for longevity are visible: genes (note their smooth skin), caregivers (note Besse's carefully coiffed hair and Jiroemon's pristine white shirt), technology (glasses and hearing aid), and attitude (proud smiles). Not visible is their independence (Besse lived alone on a Georgia farm from ages 67 to 105) or many descendants (over 60 for Jiroemon).

clear. Remember, however, that ageism affects all of us. As explained in the beginning of this chapter, ageism shortens life and makes the final years less satisfying. Don't let it. As thousands of centenarians demonstrate, a long life can be a happy one.

KEY Points

- Old age may be a time of integrity and self-actualization, although this is not always the case.
- Many older people are more creative than they were earlier in life, enjoying art and music.
- Wisdom is thought to correlate with experience, although research finds that some people are wise long before old age, and most people are never wise.
- The number of centenarians is increasing, as the average but not the maximum life span increases; some of those over age 100 are active, independent, and happy.

Religious Devotion Many of the oldest men of Mali are revered for their spirituality, as this elder Muslim is.

SEAN CAFFREY / LONELY PLANET IMAGES / GETTY IMAGES

SUMMARY

Prejudice and Predictions

1. Contrary to ageist stereotypes, most older adults are happy, quite healthy, and active. Benevolent as well as dismissive ageism reduces health and self-image, as elderspeak illustrates.

2. An increasing percentage of the population is older than 64, but the numbers are sometimes presented in misleading ways. Currently, about 14 percent of people in Canada are elderly, and most of them are self-sufficient and productive.

3. Gerontologists distinguish the young-old, the old-old, and the oldest-old, according to each age group's relative degree of dependency. Only 10 percent of those over age 64 are dependent on others for basic care, and those "others" are usually relatives, not unrelated taxpayers.

4. Sexual intercourse occurs less often, driving a car becomes more difficult, and all the senses become less acute with age. However, selective optimization with compensation can mitigate almost any loss. A combination of personal determination, adjustment by society, and technological devices is needed.

Cognition

5. Brain scans and measurements show that the speed of processing slows down, parts of the brain shrink, and more areas of the brain are activated in older people.

6. Memory is affected by aging, but specifics vary. As the senses become dulled, some stimuli never reach the sensory memory. Working memory shows notable declines with age because slower processing means that some thoughts are lost.

7. Control processes are less effective with age, as retrieval strategies become less efficient. Anxiety may prevent older people from using the best strategies for cognitive control. Ecologically valid, real-life measures of cognition are needed.

Aging and Disease

8. Primary aging happens to everyone, reducing organ reserve in body and brain. Secondary aging depends on the individual's past health habits and genes. The combination of primary and secondary aging eventually causes morbidity, disability, and mortality.

Neurocognitive Disorders

9. Neurocognitive disorders (NCDs), formerly (and now informally) called dementia, are characterized by cognitive loss—at first minor lapses, then more serious impairment, and, finally, such major losses that even recognition of family members, or remembering how to eat or talk, may fade.

10. The most common cause of cognitive loss among the elderly is Alzheimer's disease, an incurable ailment that worsens over time, as plaques and tangles increase.

11. Vascular neurocognitive disorders result from a series of ministrokes (transient ischemic attacks, or TIAs) that occur when impairment of blood circulation destroys portions of brain tissue.

12. Other NCDs, including frontal lobe disorders and Lewy body disease, also become more common with age. Several other types of neurocognitive disorder can occur in early or middle adulthood. One is Parkinson's disease, which begins with loss of muscle control. Parkinson's disease can also cause neurocognitive problems, particularly in the old.

13. Neurocognitive disorder is sometimes mistakenly diagnosed when individuals are suffering from a reversible problem, such as anxiety, depression, and polypharmacy.

New Cognitive Development

14. Many people become more interested and adept in creative endeavours, as well as more philosophical, as they grow older.

The life review is a personal reflection that many older people undertake, remembering earlier experiences, putting their entire lives into perspective, and achieving integrity or self-actualization.

15. Wisdom does not necessarily increase as a result of age, but some elderly people are unusually wise or insightful.

16. It was once believed that many people in certain parts of the world lived long past 100 as a result of moderate diet, exercise, hard work, and respect for the aged. Such reports are now thought to have been exaggerated.

17. The number of centenarians is increasing, and many of them are quite healthy and happy. The personality and attitudes of the very old suggest that long-term survival may be welcomed more than feared.

KEY TERMS

ageism (p. 493)

Alzheimer's disease (AD) (p. 514)

average life expectancy (p. 524)

calorie restriction (p. 500)

cellular aging (p. 500)

compression of morbidity (p. 511)

demographic shift (p. 497)

dependency ratio (p. 498)

ecological validity (p. 507)

elderspeak (p. 497)

frontal lobe disorder (p. 515)

genetic clock (p. 499)

Hayflick limit (p. 500)

Lewy bodies (p. 516)

life review (p. 522)

maximum life span (p. 524)

neurocognitive disorder (NCD) (p. 512)

oldest-old (p. 499)

old-old (p. 499)

osteoporosis (p. 511)

Parkinson's disease (p. 516)

plaques (p. 514)

polypharmacy (p. 518)

primary aging (p. 510)

secondary aging (p. 510)

self-actualization (p. 520)

tangles (p. 514)

vascular neurocognitive disorder (p. 515)

wear and tear (p. 499)

young-old (p. 499)

WHAT HAVE YOU LEARNED?

1. What are the similarities and differences among ageism, racism, and sexism?

2. In what ways do older adults perpetuate ageism?

3. How does ageism affect older adults' mental and physical health?

4. In what ways does elderspeak reduce communication?

5. Give an example of how protecting older adults might actually lead to more harm.

6. Why is the increasing number of older people less problematic than it was once thought to be?

7. What are the differences among young-old, old-old, and oldest-old?

8. What are the differences in the sleep patterns of the old and the young?

9. What problems associated with aging do older drivers experience? How do they compensate for these problems? What other measures would help them (and all other drivers)?

10. What changes occur in the sense organs in old age, and how can their effects be minimized?

11. What changes in the brain occur with age?

12. Why is multi-tasking particularly difficult in late adulthood?

13. How does sensory loss affect cognition?

14. Which kinds of things are harder to remember with age? Which kinds of memories seem well preserved with age?

15. How are control processes affected by age?

16. Why is ecological validity especially important for testing cognition and abilities?

17. What is the difference between primary aging and secondary aging?

18. How is compression of morbidity good for society as well as for the individual?

19. Why is falling a serious health problem in old age?

20. Why has the language surrounding neurocognitive disorder changed in recent years?

21. What proof is there that Alzheimer's disease is partly genetic?

22. Why are most people unaware of the early stages of vascular NCD?

23. In what ways is frontal lobe disorder more challenging than Alzheimer's disease?

24. What effect does a person's age have on the progression of Parkinson's disease?

25. Why is an excess of Lewy bodies sometimes mistaken for Parkinson's disease?

26. How successful are scientists at preventing neurocognitive disorders?

27. Why is accurate diagnosis important when older people have cognitive difficulties?

28. Why is overmedication more likely for older people than younger adults?

29. According to Erikson, what gains may be evident in older people? What gains may be evident according to Maslow?

30. What are the purpose and benefits of the life review?

31. What factors are considered part of wisdom, and how do these relate to aging?

32. What lifestyle factors might result in increased energy, alertness, and optimism in centenarians?

APPLICATIONS

1. Analyze websites that have information about aging for evidence of ageism, anti-aging measures, and exaggeration of longevity.

2. Ask five people of various ages if they want to live to age 100 and record their responses. Would they be willing to eat half as much, exercise much more, experience weekly dialysis, or undergo other procedures in order to extend life? Analyze the responses.

3. Visit someone in the hospital. Note all the elements in the environment—such as noise, lights, schedules, and personnel— that might cause an elderly patient to seemingly have a neurocognitive disorder.

>>ONLINE CONNECTIONS

To accompany your textbook, you have access to a number of online resources, including LearningCurve, which is an adaptive quizzing program; critical thinking questions; and case studies. For access to any of these links, go to www.worthpublishers.com/launchpad/bergerchuang1e. In addition to these resources, you'll find links to video clips, personalized study advice, and an e-Book. Among the videos and activities available online is the following:

- *Alzheimer Disease.* This activity includes videos and animations that outline the progressive course of Alzheimer's disease, as well as the types and limits of treatments.

CHAPTER OUTLINE

15

LATE ADULTHOOD:
Psychosocial Development

WHAT WILL YOU KNOW?

- Do older people become more depressed as time goes by?
- Do the elderly hope to move to a distant, warm place?
- What do adult children owe their elderly parents?
- Is home care better than nursing home care?

My parents grew up together in the same small town in Taiwan. Shortly after they married, they immigrated to Canada. My father is a family physician. To be accredited in Canada, he completed his residency in Ottawa, where my two older brothers were born, and another year in New Brunswick, where I was born. The family moved a couple more times before settling just outside Toronto, and it was there that my younger brother was born. Thus, my parents had four children in their first five years in Canada.

With four young children, my parents finally settled down, and my father opened up a family practice where he continues to work. They had been living in the same house for almost 40 years and were hap-pily married for almost 49 years, until my mother unexpectedly passed away in November 2013. But like any couple, they had their ups and downs. My father has always used his sense of humour to keep peace in the household. Once he got my mother to laugh, she couldn't stay upset for very long; luckily it was easy to make her laugh.

My mother had her own sense of humour. "Your father is the head of the household," she told my brothers and me once. We just laughed—we couldn't believe she said that with a straight face.

Then she said, "But I am the neck that turns him."

Together for Almost 50 Years
Susan's parents—the best parents in the world—spent many years together in Taiwan and Canada. Together they experienced many successes and challenges across the various developmental stages.

As they grew older, my parents spent most of their time together. Their roles and responsibilities in the family changed over time, especially for my mother. She was a stay-at-home mom until all of us were in middle school, and then she enjoyed a successful career as a real estate agent. At the same time, she continued to study theology, became an ordained minister, and volunteered as a pastor for various churches over the years.

After my mother retired, my father continued to work, although the hours were fewer than before. Together they enjoyed more relaxing moments, reminiscing about their childhoods and their lives with one another, and spending time with the family, including grandchildren. My father has also spent more time reading, updating his knowledge on medical issues, learning Hebrew, and studying the Bible. ●

—Susan Chuang

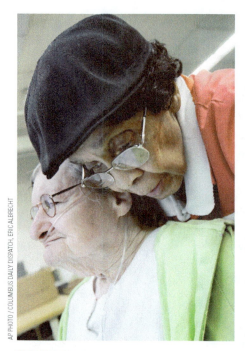

Still Helping Virginia Ryder, seen here helping Betty Baldwin, is a lifelong helper. She cared for younger children when she was an adolescent, and she has been a senior companion for the past 19 years, often for younger people. She is 89 years old.

THE TOPIC OF THIS CHAPTER IS THE VARIABILITY and complexity of development in later life. Some of the elderly are frail, lonely, and vulnerable to abuse, because of either private circumstances or public failures. For most, however, psychosocial development includes working and socializing, concern for others, and self-care.

As the number of elderly people continues to increase in North America, it is important to understand the theories of late adulthood and how factors such as age, gender, and sociocultural contexts may affect aging, geographical distribution, and political activism. Understanding how older adults spend their time and the types of social relationships they have also provides great insight into this stage of life.

Theories of Late Adulthood

Development in late adulthood may be more diverse than at any other age: Some elderly people run marathons and lead nations, whereas others can no longer walk or talk. Moreover, individuals vary within themselves in almost every measure from day to day, with some days much better than others (Krenk et al., 2012). Many social scientists try to understand the significance and origin of these variations and to describe the general course of old age.

Some theories of late adulthood have been called *self theories* because they focus on individuals' perceptions of themselves and their ability to meet challenges to their identity. Other theories are called *stratification theories* because they describe the ways in which societies place people on a particular life path.

Self Theories

It can be said that people become more truly themselves as they grow old, an idea captured by Anna Quindlen:

It's odd when I think of the arc of my life from child to young woman to aging adult. First I was who I was, then I didn't know who I was, then I invented someone and became her, then I began to like what I'd invented, and finally I was what I was again. It turned out I wasn't alone in that particular progression.

[Quindlen, 2012, ix]

The essential self is protected and rediscovered, despite all the changes that may occur. **Self theories** emphasize how people negotiate their personal challenges (Sneed & Whitbourne, 2005). Such negotiation is particularly crucial when older adults are confronted with multiple challenges like illness, retirement, and the death of loved ones.

A central idea of self theories is that each person ultimately depends on himself or herself. As one woman explained:

> I actually think I value my sense of self more importantly than my family or relationships or health or wealth or wisdom. I do see myself as on my own, ultimately. … Statistics certainly show that older women are likely to end up being alone, so I really do value my own self when it comes right down to things in the end.
>
> *[quoted in J. Kroger, 2007, p. 203]*

Studies of personality over the life span confirm the continuity of self. An individual's high or low level on each of the Big Five personality traits (see Chapter 13) tends to remain the same, not only throughout the earlier adult years, but even when people are in their 80s (Mõttus et al., 2012).

INTEGRITY The most comprehensive self theory was from Erik Erikson. His eighth and final stage of development is called **integrity versus despair,** a period in which older adults seek to integrate their unique experiences with their vision of community (Erikson et al., 1986). The word *integrity* is often used to mean honesty, but it also means a feeling of being whole, not scattered, and comfortable with oneself. (*Integrity* comes from the same root word as *integer,* a math term meaning "a whole number, not a fraction.")

As an example of integrity, many older people express pride and contentment regarding their personal history. They are proud of their past, even when it includes events that an outsider might not consider worthy of pride—such as skipping school, taking drugs, or escaping arrest. Psychologists sometimes call this the *"sucker to saint" phenomenon*—that is, people interpret their experiences as signs of their nobility (saintliness), not their stupidity (Jordan & Monin, 2008).

As Erikson (1963) explains it, such self-glorifying distortions are far better than losing hope, or "feeling that the time is now short, too short for the attempt to start another life" (p. 269). As with every crisis, tension occurs between the two opposing aspects of development. Past crises, particularly Erikson's fifth crisis of *identity versus role confusion,* reappear when the usual pillars of the self-concept (such as employment or good looks) crumble. One 70-year-old said, "I know who I've been, but who am I now?" (quoted in J. Kroger, 2007, p. 201).

This tension helps advance the person toward a more complete self-concept. In this last stage,

> life brings many, quite realistic reasons for experiencing despair: aspects of the present that cause unremitting pain; aspects of a future that are uncertain and frightening. And, of course, there remains inescapable death, that one aspect of the future which is both wholly certain and wholly unknowable. Thus, some despair must be acknowledged and integrated as a component of old age.
>
> *[Erikson et al., 1986, p. 72]*

That integration of death and the self is an important accomplishment of this stage. The life review (explained in Chapter 14) and the acceptance of death (to be explained in the Epilogue) are crucial aspects of the integrity envisioned by Erikson (Zimmermann, 2012).

self theories
Theories of late adulthood that emphasize the core self, or the search to maintain one's integrity and identity.

integrity versus despair
The final stage of Erik Erikson's developmental sequence, in which older adults seek to integrate their unique experiences with their vision of community.

AP PHOTO / JEFF MOORE, POOL

Fiercely Independent In the first half of his life, Nelson Mandela led the fight against apartheid in his native South Africa—until he was convicted of sabotage and sentenced to life in prison. Remarkably, he stayed true to his beliefs; released 27 years later to lead once again, he was elected president and served from 1994 to 1999. Still his true self, he next formed The Elders and pledged to be "a fiercely independent force for good." Pictured here at age 92, he sat with two other Elders, Desmond Tutu (72) and Jimmy Carter (79). Mandela died 3 years later, at age 95, on December 5, 2013.

HOLDING ON TO ONE'S SELF Most older people consider their personalities and attitudes quite stable over their life span, even as they acknowledge the physical changes of their bodies (Fischer et al., 2008). One 103-year-old woman observed, "My core has stayed the same. Everything else has changed" (quoted in Troll & Skaff, 1997, p. 166). Sometimes it is a struggle to maintain a strong sense of self. As bodies and social relationships change, adults may need to revise their self theory about their identity.

The need to maintain the self may explain behaviour that younger people might consider foolish. For example, many elders hate to give up driving a car because the independence that driving offers them has become an integral part of their view of self, especially for men (Davidson, 2008, p. 46). Also, objects and places become more precious in late adulthood than they were earlier, as people seek a way to hold on to identity (J. Kroger, 2007; Whitmore, 2001).

The tendency to cling to familiar possessions may be problematic if it leads to **compulsive hoarding.** While younger relatives may complain that the accumulation of old papers, furniture, and mementos takes up space and is a fire hazard, for the elderly, compulsive hoarding can be seen as maintaining the self: Possessions become a part of self-expression, and the elderly resist self-destruction (Ayers et al., 2010).

Similarly, many older people refuse to move from drafty and dangerous dwellings into smaller, safer apartments because abandoning familiar places means abandoning personal history. Likewise, they may avoid surgery or reject medicine because they fear anything that might distort their thinking or emotions: Their priority is self-protection, even if it means shortening life (S. W. Miller, 2011–2012).

The need to preserve one's self explains why many of the elderly strive to maintain childhood cultural and religious practices. For instance, grandparents may painstakingly teach a grandchild a language that is rarely used in their current community, or encourage the child to repeat rituals and prayers they themselves learned as children. In cultures that emphasize youth and novelty, the elderly worry that their old values will be lost and, thus, that they themselves will disappear from memory.

The importance of self-validation is particularly apparent among older immigrants. Many grew up with customs unlike those where they and their descendants now live. They may become depressed if they think their culture is not appreciated and struggle to reconcile their traditional values with those of their children (Abu-Bader et al., 2011; H. Y. Lee et al., 2011).

THE POSITIVITY EFFECT As you remember from Chapter 14, some people cope successfully with the changes of late adulthood through *selective optimization with compensation*. This is central to self theories. Individuals set their personal goals, assess their own abilities, and figure out how to accomplish those goals despite limitations. For some people, simply maintaining identity correlates with well-being (Ebner et al., 2006).

One strategy for selective optimization is known as the **positivity effect.** Elderly people are more likely to perceive, prefer, and remember positive images and experiences than negative ones (Carstensen et al., 2006). Compensation occurs via selective recall: Unpleasant experiences are reinterpreted as inconsequential. For example, with age, stressful events (economic loss; serious illness; the death of friends, family, or, in the future, oneself) are less likely to be considered central to one's identity. That enables the elderly to be unperturbed by much of what happens; they maintain emotional health via positive self-perception (Boals et al., 2012).

The positivity effect is evident in many nations. After taking into account income, education, and gender, adults everywhere report gradually increasing happiness from age 50 on (Blanchflower et al., 2008).

---

compulsive hoarding
The urge to accumulate and hold on to familiar objects and possessions, sometimes to the point of their becoming health and/or safety hazards. This impulse tends to increase with age.

positivity effect
The tendency for elderly people to perceive, prefer, and remember positive images and experiences more than negative ones.

A VIEW FROM SCIENCE

No Regrets

Many researchers have studied the positivity effect. They have found not only that a positive world view usually increase with age but also that it correlates with believing that life is meaningful (Hicks et al., 2012). Those elders who are highest in positivity (e.g., feeling happy, not frustrated or depressed) are likely to agree strongly that their life has a purpose (e.g., "I have a system of values that guides my daily activities" and "I am at peace with my past") (Hicks et al., 2012).

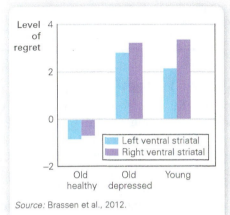

Level of regret

■ Left ventral striatal
■ Right ventral striatal

Old healthy Old depressed Young

Source: Brassen et al., 2012.

FIGURE 15.1 Let Bygones Be Bygones Young adults, depressed older adults, and emotionally healthy older adults played a computer game in which they could continue opening a series of boxes that they hoped would have money in them or risk finding a cartoon picture of the devil, which caused them to lose all their money and ended the game. Young adults and depressed older adults who discovered, at the end of a round, that they could have opened more boxes safely were more disappointed than were emotionally healthy, older adults. This was evident in their behaviour—they took more risks in subsequent rounds—and in increased activity in areas of the brain (the ventral striatal) that are activated when a person feels regret.

Researchers have measured expressed attitudes and memories as well as brain and body reactions to disappointment. For example, Brassen and colleagues (2012) explored the reactions of adults of various ages to questions such as "When something doesn't happen as you wish, are you likely to take a greater risk the next time, or are you likely to let go of your disappointment?" Emerging adults might take a greater risk, but emotionally healthy older adults are not likely to. The emotionally healthy elderly react to disappointment by letting it go and thinking positively about going forward (see Figure 15.1).

In this and many other experiments, older adults are found to be able to let bygones be bygones, leading to greater emotional well-being from middle age onward and fewer experiences of anger. In this particular study, the brain activity and heart rate of healthy older adults (average age 66) show a different response to disappointment.

This study also included a group of older adults who had been diagnosed with late-life depression. Their brains, bodies, and behaviour were more like those of the younger adults. The researchers concluded that those who are emotionally healthy have reduced responses to regretful events.

Other research has also found that depressed older adults are neurologically impaired, particularly in the anterior cingulate cortex, a brain region crucial for processing conflicting emotions and thoughts (Ochsner et al., 2009). Because of the positivity effect, anger, sadness, and disappointment are limited in healthy older people—and they are happier because of it.

The positivity effect is not always dramatic. Consider the details of a different study (Werheid et al., 2010). In four experiments, a total of 132 individuals—60 young (average age 25) and 72 old (average age 66)—looked at photographs of happy, neutral, or angry faces. They were then shown the same faces and an equal number of new faces either one day later (experiments 1, 2, and 3) or two weeks later (experiment 4), and were asked which faces they had seen before.

All four experiments showed the positivity effect somewhat, but not dramatically. For instance, in the first experiment, the older adults were slightly better than the younger ones at recognizing happy faces (74 versus 70 percent) and worse at recognizing angry faces (81 versus 84 percent) or neutral faces (65 versus 69 percent). They were also likely to mistakenly claim that the new happy faces were familiar (22 versus 7 percent).

The presence of even a mild positivity effect suggests that elders ignore or move past certain negative realities, such as expressions of anger and frustration. For example, adults in one study were asked about recent instances of personal confrontation (Sorkin & Rook, 2006). More than one-third (39 percent) of the adults older than 65 could not think of any negative social exchanges. Of those who remembered unpleasant encounters, most of the elders, unlike the younger participants, said that their primary goal after the event was to maintain goodwill. Only a few sought to change the other person's behaviour (see Figure 15.2).

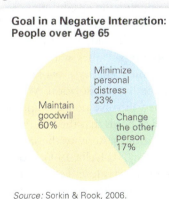

Goal in a Negative Interaction: People over Age 65

Maintain goodwill 60%
Minimize personal distress 23%
Change the other person 17%

Source: Sorkin & Rook, 2006.

FIGURE 15.2 Keep the Peace When someone does something mean or unpleasant, what is your goal in your interaction with that person? If your goal is to maintain goodwill, as was the case for a majority of older adults studied, you are likely to be quicker to forgive and forget.

Since their goal was to achieve harmony, the elderly were more likely to compromise instead of insist that they were correct. This led to a happier outcome. As the researchers stated,

> [p]articipants whose primary coping goal was to preserve goodwill reported the highest levels of perceived success

and the least intense and shortest duration of distress. In contrast, participants whose … goal was to change the other person reported the lowest levels of perceived success and the most intense and longest lasting distress.

[Sorkin & Rook, 2006, p. 723]

Stratification Theories

stratification theories
Theories that emphasize that social forces, particularly those related to a person's social stratum or social category, limit individual choices and affect a person's ability to function in late adulthood because past stratification continues to limit life in various ways.

A second set of theories, called **stratification theories,** emphasizes societal forces that place each person in a social strata or level. Such stratification makes it difficult for a person to earn more income, have better health, or live longer than people of their group. Stratification begins from day one, as babies are conceived in societies that are already stratified, or differentiated, by various dimensions such as gender, ethnicity, and SES (Lynch & Brown, 2011).

The problem with stratification is that it results in inequality for reasons beyond the individual. As the decades of life go by, stratification by age, gender, ethnicity, and income become increasingly burdensome, causing double, triple, or even quadruple jeopardy. We describe each of these in turn.

IMAGINECHINA / AP IMAGES

Respected Twins Ageism takes many forms. Some cultures are youth-oriented, devaluing the old, while others are the opposite. These twin sisters were born in rural China in 1905. Pictured here, at age 103, they were venerated for their experience and wisdom.

disengagement theory
The view that aging makes a person's social sphere increasingly narrow, resulting in role relinquishment, withdrawal, and passivity.

activity theory
The view that elderly people want and need to remain active in social spheres—with relatives, friends, and community groups—and become withdrawn only unwillingly, as a result of ageism.

STRATIFICATION BY AGE Ageism is, of course, stratification by age. Age affects a person's life in many ways, including income and health. For example, seniority builds in the workplace, increasing income up to a certain point; then employment may stop when a person reaches a given age, with that person perhaps earning a pension but never as much income as before.

This is just one example of the many ways in which industrialized nations segregate elderly people, gradually shutting them out of the mainstream of society as they grow older (Achenbaum, 2005). That harms all generations because it limits social experiences: Younger as well as older people have a narrower perspective on life if they interact only with people their own age.

The most controversial version of age-stratification theory is **disengagement theory** (Cumming & Henry, 1961). This theory holds that, as people age, traditional roles become unavailable or unimportant, the social circle shrinks, co-workers stop asking for help, and adult children turn away to focus on their own children. According to this theory, disengagement is a mutual process, chosen by both older and younger generations. Children want to be with other children, adults with other adults, and older adults with one another or by themselves. Thus, younger people disengage from the old, who themselves voluntarily disengage from younger adults. They relinquish past roles, withdrawing from life's action.

Disengagement theory provoked a storm of protest because people feared it justified ageism and social isolation. Many gerontologists insisted that older people need and want new involvements. Some developed an opposing theory, called **activity theory,** which holds that the elderly seek to remain active with relatives, friends, and community groups. Activity theorists contend that if the elderly disengage, they do so unwillingly (J. R. Kelly, 1993; Rosow, 1985).

Later research has found that elders who are more active are happier, intellectually more alert, and less depressed. This is true at younger ages as well, although some studies find that activity is particularly likely to correlate with high functioning at older ages (Bielak, 2010; Bielak et al., 2012).

Both disengagement and activity theories need to be applied with caution, however. Disengagement in one aspect of life (e.g., retiring from employment) does not necessarily mean disengagement overall: Many retirees disengage from work but find new roles and activities to participate in (Freund et al., 2009). The positivity effect, just described, may mean that an older person disengages from emotional events that cause anger, regret, and sadness, while actively enjoying other experiences (Brassen et al., 2012).

A cautionary note comes from research in China. One study found that among the Chinese young-old, activity correlated with health, particularly if the activities involved social interactions. But among the oldest-old, activity did not correlate with longevity: For some of the oldest Chinese, disengagement was more closely associated with health (R. Sun & Liu, 2008). Both theories—that all the elderly want to withdraw and that they all should stay active—may arise from cultural stereotypes.

Never Too Old One would not expect an 80-year-old to skydive, but that is exactly what this active Israeli woman did!

STRATIFICATION BY GENDER Feminist theory draws attention to stratification that puts males and females on separate tracks through life. From pink or blue blankets for newborns' bassinets to flowers or stripes for nursing home bedsheets, gender is signalled throughout life. These signals alert everyone—caregivers, family members, and strangers—to treat males and females differently. Such stratification, when combined with ageism, makes people expect older women to be, for instance, either warm and giving (grandmotherly, providing kindness and cookies) or sickly and dependent. Older men might be seen, for example, as elder statesmen or as grumpy and curmudgeonly.

The implications of gender divergence are illustrated by a study of caregiving among older married couples. Both sexes provided care if their spouse became needy, but they did so in opposite ways: Women quit their jobs, whereas men worked longer. To be specific, employed women whose husbands needed care were five times more likely to retire than were other employed women. By contrast, employed husbands whose wife needed care retired only half as often as other men (Dentinger & Clarkberg, 2002).

Note, however, that both partners sacrifice. Men stayed on the job so they could keep insurance and hire household help, and women quit to provide personal care. Both sexes followed the gender stratification of decades earlier: Women were socialized to be caregivers, and men's employment patterns (not part-time, more seniority) typically included higher salaries and better insurance than women's patterns (more interruptions, and hence less pay and benefits). In this situation, past stratification disadvantages the older women: Their caregiving response leads to poverty and loneliness.

Irrational, gender-based fear may also lead to unequal experiences for older men and women. For example, because adult children want to protect their mothers, they are more likely to persuade their widowed mothers to live with them than they are their widowed fathers, thus limiting their mothers' independence. The children's fear for the mother's safety is not based on evidence. Men living alone are more likely than women to have a sudden health crisis and are more likely to be the victim of a violent crime (5 percent versus 2 percent) (P. Klaus, 2005).

A Nobel Prize Winner As a younger adult, author Alice Munro won three Governor General Awards (in 1968, 1978, and 1986), then as an older adult she won two Giller Prizes (in 1998 and 2004) and the Mann Booker International Prize (in 2009). In 2013, at the age of 82, she became the 13th woman, and 1st Canadian woman, to win the Nobel Prize in literature, in 2013. She was named "master of the contemporary short story."

In another example of stratification, women typically marry men a few years older than they are and then outlive them. Especially if they lived in rural areas (as most North Americans did until about 1950), married women often relied on their husbands to drive, to manage money, and to keep up with politics. Then, if the husband died, past gender stratification led to isolation, poverty, and dependence among the oldest-old widows.

Men, too, may be harmed. For instance, boys are taught that males are stoic, repressing emotions and avoiding medical care. Is that why, in every nation, adult women outlive men? This could be biological (protective hormones), but it could result from lifelong stratification, making men more vulnerable in old age.

STRATIFICATION BY ETHNICITY Like age and gender, ethnic background affects every aspect of development throughout life, including education, health, place of residence, and employment. Stratification theory suggests that these factors accumulate, creating large discrepancies by old age that leave ethnic minority seniors at risk of becoming marginalized (National Advisory Council On Aging, 2005).

When one considers Canadian seniors, stratification by ethnicity is probably most evident among immigrants, especially those who arrived recently, and among Aboriginal peoples. In 2006, about 30 percent of Canadian seniors were immigrants, many of them from visible minorities (Ng, 2010). Aboriginal peoples accounted for 1 percent of Canada's seniors (Chief Public Health Officer, 2010).

Common problems faced by ethnic minority and Aboriginal seniors include greater rates of poverty and illness and, for Aboriginal peoples, shorter life expectancies. In 2001, 13 percent of Aboriginal seniors, compared to 7 percent of non-Aboriginal seniors, were living in low-income households. Similarly, 50 percent of Aboriginal seniors not living with family were in low-income situations compared to 40 percent of non-Aboriginal seniors in the same living situation (Chief Public Health Officer, 2010). This income discrepancy is largely due to higher levels of unemployment among the Aboriginal population, higher percentages of Aboriginals working part time, lower levels of participation in the labour force (i.e., employed or looking for work), and lower wages for those employed (Turcotte & Schellenberg, 2006).

Higher poverty rates are also present among elderly immigrants, particularly those who are recent immigrants as compared to those who have been in the country longer than 10 years (Eigersma, 2010). For example, in 2003, 26 percent of recent immigrant seniors were in the lowest income quartile compared with 12 percent of long-term immigrant seniors and 15 percent of non-immigrant seniors (Eigersma, 2010). Statistics Canada reports that, in general, recent immigrant seniors experience higher unemployment rates, lower earnings, and greater difficulties in matching their qualifications to their employment (Turcotte & Schellenberg, 2006). Difficulties in finding a suitable job consequently impair new immigrants' efforts to accumulate sufficient funds for retirement. As well, when recent immigrants do retire, they are often ineligible for Old Age Security benefits since that program requires a 10-year residency in Canada before a person can collect benefits (Eigersma, 2010; Jackson, 2001). In a culture where workers are expected to retire and live on pension income, many older immigrants (without a host country work history) are left unemployed, poor, and lonely.

A particular form of ethnic stratification may affect immigrant elders who find themselves dependent on their adult children within a culture stratified against both the old and the immigrant. Many traditional cultures expect younger generations to care for the elderly personally, but North American families tend to be nuclear families, not extended ones.

For some cultures, the traditional notion of adult children caring for their aging parents remains strong. In some Chinese families, for example, the thought of placing

♦ ESPECIALLY FOR Social Scientists
The various social science disciplines tend to favour different theories of aging. Can you tell which theories would be more acceptable to psychologists and which to sociologists? (see response, page 538) ➔

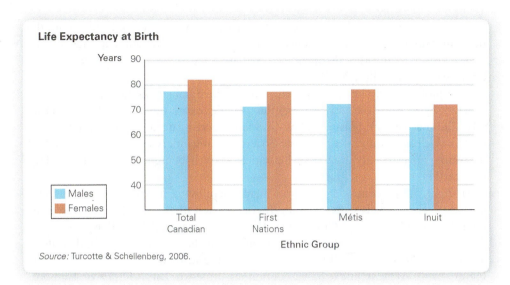

Life Expectancy at Birth

Years

Males
Females

Total Canadian | First Nations | Métis | Inuit

Ethnic Group

Source: Turcotte & Schellenberg, 2006.

FIGURE 15.3 Lower Life Expectancies While the life expectancies of Aboriginal peoples have improved over time, they remain lower than that of the total population.

OBSERVATION QUIZ
Which Aboriginal group has the lowest life expectancy? Why might this be the case? (see answer, page 539) ➔

an ailing and aged parent in a nursing home may conflict with their sense of responsibility. One recent response to this problem has been the appearance of ethnoculturally focused nursing homes such as the Yee Hong Geriatric Care Centre that services the Chinese community in Mississauga, Ontario. About 10 Asian-focused nursing homes now exist in Canada, mainly for the Chinese and South Asian communities, but demand far outstrips availability. The average wait time for a space in a mainstream seniors' facility in Ontario is 113 days; at the Yee Hong Centre, it can take 10 years to find a place (Bascaramurty, 2012).

Since poverty often has negative impacts on a person's health, it comes as no surprise that in 2001—the same year that 13 percent of Aboriginal seniors, compared to 7 percent of non-Aboriginal seniors, were living in low-income households—only 24 percent of non-reserve Aboriginal seniors reported that their health was very good to excellent (O'Donnell & Tait, 2003), compared to 36.4 percent among seniors in the general population (Statistics Canada, 2002). In 2003—the same year that 26 percent of recent immigrant seniors were in the lowest income quartile compared with 12 percent of long-term immigrant seniors and 15 percent of non-immigrant seniors—only 28 percent of recent immigrant seniors reported that their health was very good to excellent, compared with 36 percent of long-term immigrants and 38 percent of non-immigrant seniors (Turcotte & Schellenberg, 2006).

A 2008 report for Statistics Canada found discrepancies in the mortality rates among various ethnic groups but especially for Aboriginal peoples. First Nations, Métis, and Inuit had substantially higher mortality rates than non-Aboriginal Canadians (see Figure 15.3). The highest rate of all was among registered Indians, a subgroup of First Nations (Wilkens et al., 2008). Another government report found that compared with other Canadian seniors, Aboriginal seniors tend to have double or triple the prevalence of certain chronic conditions that often end in death, such as heart disease, hypertension, diabetes, and arthritis (Health Canada in collaboration with the Interdepartmental Committee on Aging and Seniors Issues, 2002). Remember that living in poverty can place repeated stresses on a person that result in conditions such as hypertension and obesity as well as the other 8 to 14 indicators of allostatic load. Over the years, this can take a toll on a person's health and well-being.

STRATIFICATION BY SES Finally, the pivotal influence on the well-being of the elderly may be financial, not directly gender, ethnicity, or age. Income correlates with those three but is not caused by them (Bird et al., 2010). A child of a family with low SES will have less education, worse health, and a poorer work history (and thus more unemployment, fewer benefits, no pensions). He or she will experiences stress of all kinds, accumulating disadvantages that are increasingly limiting as the years go by (Bowen & González, 2010).

The problem may begin even before birth, since epigenetic factors—themselves affected by maternal health—shape the genetic expression (Shanahan & Hofer, 2011). Those who are born into low-SES families risk late-life illnesses, such as diabetes, as well as disabilities. Obviously, poverty among elders should be alleviated, but mitigating poverty early in life may be critical for well-being in late adulthood (Herd et al., 2011).

In 2010, 5.3 percent of seniors in Canada were living in poverty—that is, below what Statistics Canada calls the Low-Income Cut-Off (LICO) (see the discussion on LICO in Chapter 1) (Conference Board of Canada, 2013a). This represents a significant decrease in the LICO rate among Canadian seniors over the last almost 40 years; in 1976, almost 30 percent of seniors found themselves below LICO (see Figure 15.4). At least one expert, economics professor Lars Osberg of Dalhousie University, has hailed this drop in poverty rates among seniors as "the major success story of Canadian social policy in the twentieth century" (Osberg, 2001).

Perhaps the main reason for the decrease was the institution of the Canada Pension Plan and Quebec Pension Plan in 1966. Canadian seniors can also access two other government transfer programs:

1. *Old Age Security.* Almost all Canadians older than 65 receive OAS, which is an income supplement that averages about $450 a month.

2. *Guaranteed Income Supplement.* This provides additional funds to low-income seniors who are enrolled in OAS and meet certain other requirements.

In addition, some seniors have access to their own savings or private pension plans that they enrolled in at work.

Despite the drop in poverty rates among seniors, one group that remains vulnerable to low income in old age is women, especially those older than 75 and who have been widowed or are living alone for other reasons. Women often receive less than men from government pension plans because the benefits are usually linked to a person's employment history. In the period between 2006 and 2010, the number of Canadian seniors living below LICO increased by about 160 000, and 60 percent of them were women (Conference Board of Canada, 2013a).

One important financial problem for the elderly is that inflation makes retirement income worth less than half of what it was when that money was first set aside. Those

RESPONSE FOR Social Scientists (from page 536) In general, psychologists favour self theories, and sociologists favour stratification theories. Of course, each discipline respects the other, but each believes that its perspective is more honest and accurate. ●

FIGURE 15.4 Low-Income Rates Among Seniors The number of seniors living below LICO has decreased dramatically since the 1970s, largely because of payments from the Canada Pension Plan and Quebec Pension Plan, as well as from private pension plans.

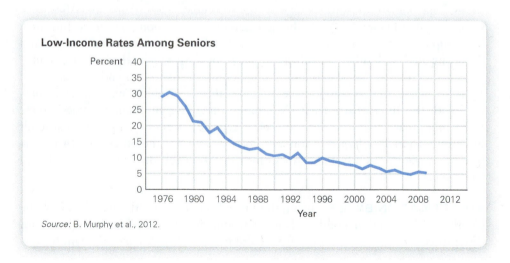

Low-Income Rates Among Seniors

Source: B. Murphy et al., 2012.

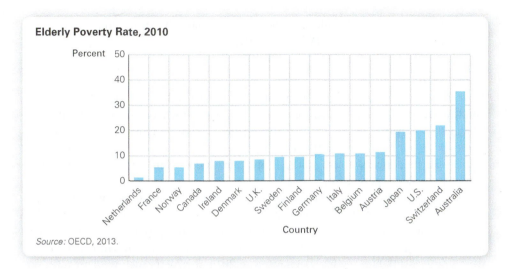

Elderly Poverty Rate, 2010

Source: OECD, 2013.

FIGURE 15.5 **When Below Average Is a Good Thing** Canada has done relatively well in reducing poverty rates among its seniors population compared with other industrialized countries in the Organisation for Economic Co-operation and Development (OECD). On average, 12.8 percent of people over the age of 65 in OECD countries live in poverty, which is defined as having an income below half the national median. Canada's poverty rate is 7.2 percent.

middle-aged adults who have adequate savings for retirement are in the minority: Typically, they are already wealthy, another example of SES stratification.

Internationally, stratification by income for the elderly varies a great deal (see Figure 15.5). Some nations provide free health care and heavily subsidized senior residences for everyone. One of these is Denmark, which also has the highest proportion of happy seniors. By contrast, other nations provide nothing at all, expecting family members to care for the elderly. In several Asian nations, it is illegal for adult children not to provide for their parents.

This is a developmental issue to which applying a cross-cultural approach would be useful. Every nation has had unexpectedly large increases in the number of older adults, and every nation is cutting government assistance to the economically disadvantaged. The resulting dilemma is more economically disadvantaged elders than in the past. Some nations have found better solutions than others, but nations can learn from one another.

ANSWER TO **OBSERVATION QUIZ** (from page 537) The Inuit. They are less likely to have access to health care services; their rates of smoking are higher than those of other populations; they are more likely to live in poorer conditions (crowded homes, unsafe drinking water); their levels of education are lower, which correlates with health and well-being, and so on. ●

KEY Points

- Self theories of late adulthood stress that people try to remain themselves, achieving integrity and not despairing.
- The positivity effect protects the self, as elders take pleasure and pride in who they are.
- The disengagement theory holds that as people age, they relinquish past roles and withdraw from life's action.
- Activity theory suggests that, if the aged disengage, it is not by choice. Contrary to disengagement theory, it suggests societies should encourage activity in old age.
- Gender, ethnicity, and economic strata all place people on particular paths for life: This stratification may be particularly harmful in late adulthood.

Activities in Late Adulthood

Many elders complain that they do not have enough time each day to do all they want to do. This might come as a surprise to younger adults, who see few grey hairs at sports events, political rallies, job sites, or midnight concerts. In fact, most college and university students consider the elderly to be relatively passive and inactive, with plenty of time on their hands (Wurtele, 2009). Wrong.

Paid Work

Developmentalists are aware of the significant physical and psychological impacts that employment has on individuals and their families (Moen & Spencer, 2006). Work provides social support and status, boosting self-esteem. For many people, employment allows generativity and is evidence of productivity, effectiveness, and independence—all cherished Western values (Tornstam, 2005). Many elders are reluctant to give that up (see Figure 15.6).

Of course, many elders work because they need the money, increasingly so as pensions and investments shrink or disappear in the economic recession. This shrinkage is global. For example, riots and strikes in France, aimed at stopping the government from changing the age at which French citizens are granted government pensions, were unsuccessful. The age had been 60; as of 2011, it is 62. French workers must stay on the job longer now.

Participation in the labour force after age 60 is higher among non-unionized low-wage workers (who need the income) and professionals (who welcome the status) than among those in between. Many older adults who have pensions work part time (Rix, 2011); some employers offer phased retirement (called "bridge work"). Older workers are also more likely to become self-employed, with small businesses or consulting work.

RETIREMENT Are all older adults healthier and happier when they are employed? Not necessarily, although some people thought so, warning about "the presumed traumatic aspects of retirement" (Tornstam, 2005, p. 19). In 2011, the Canadian Parliament passed the Keeping Canada's Economy and Jobs Growing Act and amended the Canadian Human Rights Act to prohibit mandatory retirement. Now those Canadian workers older than 65 who wish to continue working may do so. If they are terminated, they must receive severance pay regardless of their age and pension eligibility (Human Resources and Skills Development Canada, 2012).

Canadian workers approach retirement in a number of ways. Some retire as soon as they can, while others keep working as long as they are able. Some choose a third path and ease their way into retirement by working part time for several years. One recent government survey found that those seniors who fully retired from work reported worse general health, with more chronic health issues and less physical activity, than seniors who continued to work either full or part time (Park, 2011).

FIGURE 15.6 **Along with Everyone Else** Although younger adults might imagine that older people stop work as soon as they can, this is clearly not the case for everyone.

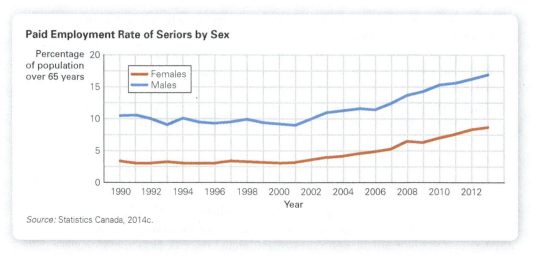

Paid Employment Rate of Seniors by Sex

Source: Statistics Canada, 2014c.

It is important to remember, however, that poor health may have influenced people's decision to retire in the first place. For example, about 25 percent of full retirees stated that their health was the primary reason for retiring. About 40 percent of those who chose to keep working did so for financial reasons. More than one-third of these senior workers still had a mortgage on their homes, compared with one-quarter of the partially retired and only 11 percent of the fully retired (Park, 2011).

There is no doubt that employment and retirement can both cause distress. Planning and income are often inadequate; married couples may disagree as to who should retire, when retirement should begin, and how their lives should be restructured (Moen et al., 2005). Many retirees live longer than they expected, not having anticipated inflation, lost pensions, and increased health costs. After retirees' initial activities—completing long-postponed projects (anything from travelling to China to painting the porch)—their goals need to be flexible to change with the aging process (Nimrod, 2007).

Same Situation, Far Apart: Satisfying Work In Nice, France, two paleontologists *(left)* examine a skull bone, and in Tofino, on Vancouver Island a First Nations artist *(right)* carves an eagle from yellow cedar.

VOLUNTEER WORK Volunteering offers some of the benefits of paid employment (generativity, social connections, less depression) and, consequently, is related to well-being in later life (Morrow-Howell & Freedman, 2006–2007). Is the connection between well-being and volunteering merely an "idea"? No; empirical data confirm the benefits. Longitudinal and cross-sectional research have found a strong link between health and volunteering (Cutler et al., 2011). It is true that volunteers are typically healthy and socially active *before* they volunteer as well as after, but helping other people itself aids well-being.

Even though Canadian seniors are less likely to volunteer than the younger cohort aged 15 to 24 (36 percent versus 58 percent), those seniors who do volunteer average far more hours annually (218 hours versus 130, respectively) (see Figure 15.7). As self theory would predict, volunteer work attracts older people who always were strongly committed to their community and had more social contacts (Pilkington et al., 2012). Those who volunteer earlier in adulthood are more likely to continue volunteering in old age, becoming "mentors, guides, and repositories of experience" for younger people (Settersten, 2002, p. 65). Because of their age and experience,

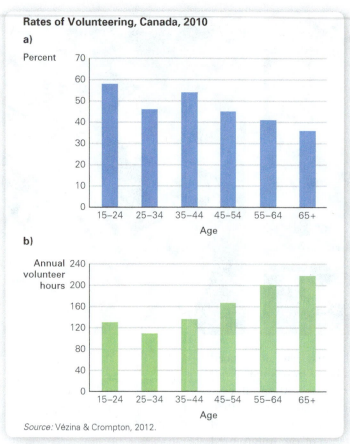

Rates of Volunteering, Canada, 2010

a)

FIGURE 15.7 Older Volunteers
As you can see, older adults volunteer with non-profit and charitable organizations less often than do those younger than them (a); however, the average number of volunteer hours is higher among seniors than in any other cohort (b).

Source: Vézina & Crompton, 2012.

senior volunteers tend to be "top volunteers," defined as the top 25 percent of volunteers who put in 171 hours or more a year; in 2007, they accounted for 78 percent of total volunteering hours in Canada (Hall et al., 2009).

Seniors tend to focus their volunteer efforts in particular areas. In 2007, they logged more volunteering hours than any other age group working with religious organizations, hospitals, and social services organizations. In a government survey, they mentioned many reasons for volunteering their time, but the most common was that they believed it made a significant contribution to their community. They also reported that volunteering motivated them to build their social networks, that their friends volunteered, and that they wanted to meet people. Many also wished to continue using the skills and experience that they had spent years acquiring at work and at home (National Seniors Council, 2010).

Culture or national policy affects volunteering: Nordic elders (in Sweden and Norway) volunteer more often than Mediterranean ones (in Italy and Greece), differences that persist when illness is taken into account (Erlinghagen & Hank, 2006). The microsystem also has an effect. Being married to a volunteer makes it more likely that a person will volunteer also.

In light of the benefits, why are more elders not volunteering? Four possible explanations:

1. *Social culture.* Ageism may discourage meaningful volunteering. Many volunteer opportunities are geared toward the young, who are attracted to intense, short-term experiences. A week of building a house during reading week or two years of teaching in a developing nation are not designed for older volunteers (Morrow-Howell & Freedman, 2006–2007).

2. *Organizations.* Institutions lack recruitment, training, and implementation strategies for attracting older volunteers. For instance, they may have systemic language and culture barriers that prevent people from volunteering; they may not be located in barrier-free buildings; there may be a lack of access to public transportation for those older adults who no longer drive; or the organizations may not allow the flexible schedule that older adults require in order to accommodate travel, health concerns, medical appointments, and so on (Cook & Speevak Sladowski, 2013).

3. *The elderly themselves.* Older people may find it difficult to identify volunteer opportunities that suit their skills and circumstances. They may be reluctant to ask for accommodations to address their changing abilities. If they are not comfortable with technology, they may be intimidated by technology that they would use to carry out their volunteer work (Cook & Speevak Sladowski, 2012).

4. *The science.* The problem may lie not with the people but with the definitions used in the research that tracks volunteerism. Surveys of volunteer work ignore daily caregiving and informal helping. Activities such as babysitting grandchildren, caring for an ill relative, and shopping for an infirm neighbour are not counted. If they were, the rates of volunteering among elders would be shown to be much higher.

Home Sweet Home

One of the favourite activities of many retirees is caring for their homes. Typically, both men and women do more housework and meal preparation (eating less fast food and more fresh ingredients) after retirement (Luengo-Prado & Sevilla, 2013). Both sexes also do yard work, redecorate, build shelves, and rearrange furniture. Challenging hobbies, home repair projects, and gardening activities all correlate with less neurocognitive disorder and longer life (E. Kröger et al., 2008; Paganini-Hill et al., 2011).

Gardening is popular: Tending flowers, herbs, and vegetables is particularly beneficial during late adulthood because it is a productive activity that not only involves exercise but often promotes social interaction (Schupp & Sharp, 2012). Even the oldest-old benefit from caring for a plant on a windowsill.

In keeping up with household tasks and maintaining their property, many older people demonstrate that they prefer to **age in place,** rather than moving to another residence. That is the preference of most baby boomers as well: 83 percent of those aged 55 to 64 prefer to stay in their own homes when they retire (Koppen, 2009). If they must move, most older adults want to remain in their familiar neighbourhood, perhaps in a smaller apartment with an elevator, but not in a different city or province/territory. In fact, they are wise: Elders fare best when they are surrounded by friends and acquaintances, people who are difficult to replace. Gerontologists recognize that disrupting or altering social connections may be detrimental, particularly for women and those who are the frailest (Berkman et al., 2011).

In a 2011 review, Herbert Northcott and Courtney Petruik from the University of Alberta examined the geographic mobility of elderly Canadians. They found that most Canadian seniors do age in place, choosing not to move for long periods of time in their older years. Statistics indicate that in 2006, more than 70 percent of the older population had not moved in the last five years. Of the small percentage of Canadian seniors who did move, many moved locally, to neighbouring cities, towns, or villages (Northcott & Petruik, 2011).

Many seniors own their homes outright, having paid off their mortgages. For them, home ownership is a powerful motivator to stay in place. At least one Canadian researcher has found that older adults are generally not motivated to use their house for equity, either for moving to another place or for general spending (Ostrovsky, 2004). This finding agrees with research on elders in the United States and Europe. Seniors who do move may move for other reasons, such as poor health.

With the aging population increasing, houses are being built or remodelled to suit people with obvious visual, hearing, or motor difficulties as well as those for whom age has made it more difficult to reach high shelves, climb steep stairs, or respond to the doorbell. **Universal design,** which is the design of physical space and common tools (from computer screens to screwdrivers) so that people of all ages and all levels of ability can use them, is an emerging field.

Sometimes a neighbourhood or an apartment complex becomes a **naturally occurring retirement community (NORC),** a neighbourhood where people who moved in as young adults never move out. Many elderly people in NORCs are content to live alone. They stay on after their children have moved away or their partners have died, in part because they know the community and have friends there (C. C. Cook et al., 2007).

To age in place successfully, elderly people need many community services (K. Black, 2008). Aging in place does not mean seniors need to be left alone; it means that care should come to them (Golant, 2008).

age in place
Remaining in the same home and community in later life, adjusting but not leaving when health fades.

universal design
Designing physical space and common tools that are suitable for people of all ages and all levels of ability.

naturally occurring retirement community (NORC)
A neighbourhood or apartment complex whose population is mostly retired people who moved to the location as younger adults and never left.

Religious Involvement

Older adults attend fewer religious services than do the middle-aged, but faith and praying increase with age. The elderly are more likely than younger adults to believe in God and an afterlife. This may be part of a universal process that benefits their development.

In his later years, Maslow reassessed his final level, *self-actualization*. He suggested a sixth, more spiritual level, which he called *self-transcendence* (Koltko-Rivera, 2006)—not usually attained until late in life. This stage is echoed in the views of at least one gerontologist, who believes that an "increasing feeling of cosmic communion" comes with age and that older people are better able to see beyond their own immediate needs and to care about other people, ask enduring questions, and emphasize spiritual needs (Tornstam, 2005, p. 41).

Religious practices of all kinds are linked with physical and emotional health (Idler, 2006). Social scientists have found several reasons for this: (1) religious prohibitions encourage health (e.g., less drug use); (2) beliefs give meaning to life and death, thus reducing stress; and (3) joining a faith community increases social relationships (Atchley, 2009). In fact, a nearby house of worship, where not only their volunteer efforts but also their mere presence is valued, is one reason why elders prefer to age in place.

One Canadian study followed more than 12 000 people over the course of 14 years to track the connection between spirituality—specifically, attendance at religious services—and major depression. The researchers found that those who went to services on a monthly basis tended to be older, female, and married, and that they had a 22 percent lower risk of depression than those who did not attend. Their conclusion? Attending religious services at least once a month served as a protective factor against major depression (Balbuena et al., 2013).

Religious identity and religious institutions are especially important for older members of minority groups, many of whom feel a stronger commitment to their religious heritage than to their national or cultural background. For example, elderly Ethiopians, Iraqis, and Turks tend to focus on their Muslim, or Christian, or Jewish faith rather than on their nationality (Gelfand, 2003). For all elderly people, no matter what their particular faith or ethnicity, psychological health depends on feeling that they are part of traditions that were handed down by their ancestors and will be carried on by their descendants.

Political Activism

In some respects, elderly people are not politically active. Few older people turn out for massive rallies, sign petitions, search for information on a political issue, or boycott or choose a product for ethical reasons (Turcotte & Schellenberg, 2006), and only about 8.6 percent of Canadians aged 55 and older reported being involved in political parties and campaigns. However, the performance rate for younger adults in this regard is even worse. Only 5.1 percent of people aged 25 to 54 were involved with a political party or group (Statistics Canada, 2011d).

By other measures, however, elder adults are more politically active than people of any other age. In Canada's 2008 general election, only 58.8 percent of registered voters cast a vote. But according to that year's General Social Survey, 89.4 percent of respondents aged 55 and older reported that they had voted in the election, compared with 75.8 percent of respondents aged 25 to 54, and 55.9 percent of those aged 18 to 24 (Statistics Canada, 2011d).

✦ ESPECIALLY FOR Religious Leaders Why might the elderly have strong faith but poor attendance at places of worship? (see response, page 548) ➡

Standing Up for His Rights Most of the elderly avoid political demonstrations, but at an all-candidates meeting in Calgary in 2013, a group of seniors takes the time to question mayoral hopefuls on everything from a lack of seniors' housing to the city's plans for a $52 million tax surplus.

The elderly are also more likely than younger adults to keep up with the news. In 2003, 89 percent of seniors reported that they followed news and current affairs daily, compared to 68 percent for those between 25 and 54 years of age. This was true regardless of seniors' education levels (Turcotte & Schellenberg, 2006).

CARP (formerly the Canadian Association of Retired Persons) is a national, non-partisan, non-profit organization that is committed to helping older adults in Canada. Founded in 1985 by Lilian and Murray Morgenthau, CARP's mission is based on the three ABCs: advocacy, benefits, and community. CARP promotes social change by protecting the interests, rights, and quality of life for Canadians as they age. Over the years, the organization has advocated on behalf of seniors for financial security, equitable accessibility to health care, and freedom from discrimination (CARP, 2014).

CARP
A Canadian organization that advocates for Canadians as they age. It was originally called the Canadian Association of Retired Persons, but now only the initials CARP are used, since members need not be retired.

KEY Points

- The elderly remain active in many ways, sometimes staying in the labour force when it is not financially necessary.

- Volunteering is an example of an activity that benefits individual health as well as the community.

- Retirement sometimes improves health and leads to more active involvement with home, neighbourhood, and religion.

- Compared with young adults, the elderly are more likely to be informed about current events and to vote.

Friends and Relatives

Humans are social animals, dependent on one another for survival and drawn to one another for joy. This is as true in late life as in infancy and at every stage in between. Remember from Chapter 13 that every person travels the life course in the company of other people, who make up the social convoy (Antonucci et al., 2007). Given that, it is not surprising that friends are particularly important in old age. Bonds formed over a lifetime allow people to share triumphs and tragedies with others who understand past victories and defeats. Siblings, old friends, and spouses are ideal convoy members.

Long-Term Partnerships

Spouses buffer each other against the problems of old age, thus extending life. This was one conclusion from a meta-analysis of dozens of studies with a combined total of 250 000 participants (Manzoli et al., 2007). Married older adults are healthier, wealthier, and happier than unmarried people their age. Of course, as self theories contend, the dominant influence on each person's sense of well-being is his or her own past well-being, not that of his or her partner. However, longitudinal research finds that spouses continue to affect each other, even in late adulthood: One older partner who is healthy and happy improves the other's well-being (Ruthig et al., 2012).

Elderly divorced people are lower in health and happiness than are those who are still married, although some argue that income and personality are the reasons, not marital status (Manzoli et al., 2007). Obviously, not every marriage is good for every older person: About one in every six long-term marriages is not satisfying, in which case the relationship increases neither health nor happiness (Waldinger & Schulz, 2010).

Same Situation, Far Apart: Partners Whether in the living room of their home in Canada *(left)* or at a seniors centre in the Philippines *(right)*, elderly people are more likely to be happy when they are with one another than when they are alone.

A Morning Kiss Ralph Young awakens Ruth with a kiss each day, as he has for most of the 78 years of their marriage. The only major separation occurred when he was a soldier in World War II; then he wrote to her every day. Here they are both 99, "more in love than ever." They had no children, so parental alliance did not bring them closer, but they did enjoy many things together—vacations, square dancing, and listening to country music on the radio.

Nonetheless, happiness typically increases with the length as well as the quality of an intimate relationship—an association more apparent in longitudinal than in cross-sectional research (Proulx et al., 2007; Scarf, 2008). A lifetime of shared experiences—living together, raising children, and dealing with financial and emotional crises—brings partners closer.

In general, older couples have learned how to disagree. They consider their conflicts to be discussions, not fights. That is not unusual. In one U.S. study of long-lasting marriages, 86 percent of the partners surveyed thought their relationship was about equal in give-and-take (Gurung et al., 2003). Similar results were found in a comparison of couples in various European nations. Objectively, wives were less equal in some nations (e.g., Portugal) than others (e.g., France), but subjectively they felt fairly treated (M. Braun et al., 2008).

Outsiders might judge many long-term marriages as unequal, since one or the other spouse usually provides most of the money, or needs most of the care, or does most of the housework. Yet such disparities do not seem to bother older partners, who typically accept each other's frailties and dependencies, remembering times (perhaps decades ago) when the situation was reversed.

Given the importance of relationship building over the life span, it is not surprising that elders who are disabled (e.g., have difficulty walking, bathing, and performing other activities of daily life) are less depressed and anxious if they are in a close marital relationship (Mancini & Bonanno, 2006). A couple can achieve selective optimization with compensation: The one who is bedbound but cognitively alert can keep track of what the one who is mobile but experiences confusion is supposed to do, for instance.

Besides caregiving, sexual intimacy is another major aspect of long-lasting marriages. As already noted in Chapter 14, younger adults tend to measure sexual activity by frequency of orgasm. By that measure, sexual activity decreases with each decade (Lindau & Gavrilova, 2010). Remember, however, that diversity is common among older adults: Some are no longer interested in sexual intimacy whereas others enjoy frequent sexual interaction, hugging and caressing as well as, for some, having intercourse.

For most older couples, sexual interaction remains important (Johnson, 2007). This is true whether a couple is married or not married; a couple may cohabit, or, as discussed in Chapter 13, they may live apart together (LAT). Many elders—especially those who are divorced or widowed—live apart from their sexual partner, not only because they want to age in place but also because they want independent relationships with their own children or parents (Strohm et al., 2009), a topic discussed next.

Relationships with Younger Generations

In past centuries, many adults died before their grandchildren were born. By contrast, some families currently span five generations, consisting of elders and their children, grandchildren, great-grandchildren, and great-great-grandchildren. The result is "longer years of 'shared lives' across generations" (Bengtson, 2001, p. 6).

Since the average couple now has fewer children, the *beanpole family,* representing multiple generations but with only a few members in each, is becoming more common (see Figure 15.8) (Murphy, 2011). Some members of the youngest generation have no cousins, brothers, or sisters but a dozen elderly relatives. Intergenerational relationships are becoming more important as many grandparents have only one or two grandchildren.

Although elderly people's relationships with members of younger generations are usually positive, they can also include tension and conflict. In some families, intergenerational respect and harmony abound whereas in others, members of one generation never see members of another. Each culture and, indeed, each family, have patterns and expectations for how the younger and oldest generations interact (Herlofson & Hagestad, 2011). Some conflict is commonplace.

For the most part, however, family members tend to support one another. As you remember, *familism* prompts siblings, cousins, and even more distant relatives to care for one another as adulthood unfolds. One manifestation of familism is **filial responsibility,** the obligation of adult children to care for their aging parents. This does not always work out well for either generation, but filial responsibility is a value in every nation, stronger in some cultures than in others (Saraceno, 2010).

When parents need caregiving, adult children often sacrifice to provide it. More often, though, the older generation gives to their adult children. This can strain a long-lasting marriage. One mother describes her daughter's circumstances and the stress it has placed on her and her husband:

> When my daughter divorced, they nearly lost the house to foreclosure, so I went on the loan and signed for them. But then again they nearly foreclosed, so my husband and I bought it. … So now I have to make the payment on my own house and most of the payment on my daughter's house, and that is hard. … I am hoping to get that money back from our daughter, to quell my husband's sense that the kids are all just taking and no one is giving back. He sometimes feels used and abused.

[quoted in Meyer, 2012, p. 83]

Emotional support and help with managing life may be more crucial and complex than financial assistance, sometimes increasing when money is less needed (Herlofson & Hagestad, 2012). One complexity is that some elders resent exactly the same supportive behaviours that other elders expect from their children—such as visiting frequently, giving presents, or cleaning the refrigerator—and some children resent

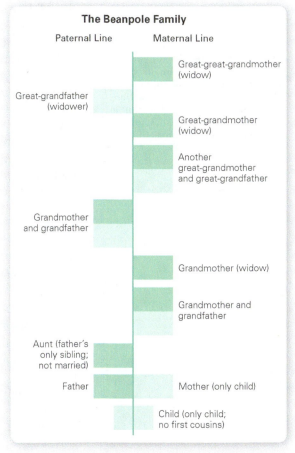

FIGURE 15.8 **Many Households, Few Members** The traditional nuclear family consists of two parents and their children living together. Today, as couples have fewer children, the beanpole family is becoming more common. This kind of family has many generations, each typically living in its own household, with only a few members in each generation.

filial responsibility
The obligation of adult children to care for their aging parents.

help that the parents give. For instance, when a grandmother suggests that the baby's bathwater is too hot, a daughter may take this as a global criticism of her ability to care for her child (Roiphe, 2009).

A longitudinal study of attitudes found no evidence that recent changes in family structure (including divorce) reduce the sense of filial responsibility (Gans & Silverstein, 2006). In fact, younger cohorts (born in the 1950s and 1960s) endorsed *more* responsibility toward older generations, notwithstanding the sacrifices involved, than did earlier cohorts (born in the 1930s and 1940s). Likewise, almost all elders believe the older generation should help the younger ones, although specifics vary by culture (Herlofson & Hagestad, 2012).

In Canada and many other countries, every generation values independence. That is why, after midlife and especially after the death of their own parents, members of the older generation are *less* likely to say that children should provide substantial care for their parents and are more likely to strive to be helpful to their children. The authors of the longitudinal study just mentioned conclude that, as adults become more likely to receive than to give intergenerational care, "reappraisals are likely the result of altruism (growing relevance as a potential receiver) or role loss (growing irrelevance as a provider)" (Gans & Silverstein, 2006, p. 974). Adults of all ages like to be needed, not needy.

This may be less true in Asian cultures. Often the first-born son encourages his elderly parents to move in with him and they expect to do so. Indeed, a study in rural China found depression more common among the elderly people whose daughters took care of them instead of their daughters-in-law (Cong & Silverstein, 2008). Asian daughters-in-law seem to experience frustrations and joys in caregiving similar to those of European-American daughters (Pinquart & Sörensen, 2011).

TENSIONS BETWEEN OLDER AND YOUNGER ADULTS A good relationship with successful grown children enhances a parent's well-being. By contrast, a poor relationship makes life worse for everyone. Ironically, conflict is more likely in emotionally close relationships than in distant ones (Silverstein et al., 2010), especially when either generation becomes dependent on the other (Birditt et al., 2009).

It is a mistake to think of the strength of the relationship as merely the middle generation paying back the older one for past sacrifices when they were children or young adults. Instead, family norms—either for intergenerational support or for independence—seem to predict how family members interact in late adulthood (Bucx et al., 2012; Henretta et al., 2011). Extensive research has found that relationships between parents and adult children are affected by many factors:

- Assistance arises both from need and from the ability to provide.
- Frequency of contact is related to geographical proximity, not affection.
- Love is influenced by the interaction remembered from childhood.
- Sons feel stronger obligation; daughters feel stronger affection.

Members of each generation tend to overestimate how much they contribute to the other (Lin, 2008b; Mandemakers & Dykstra, 2008). As already noted, contrary to popular perceptions, financial assistance and emotional support flow more often from the older generation down instead of from the younger generation up, although much depends on who needs what (Silverstein, 2006). Only when elders become frail (discussed later) are they more likely to receive family assistance than to give it.

GRANDCHILDREN Most (80 percent of women and 74 percent of men) Canadians older than 65 are grandparents; over the next decade or so, a significant number of baby boomers will become grandparents, too. Some have coined a new term to

"They grow up too fast."

Twenty-First-Century Pacifier These grandmothers remember when infants were calmed or distracted by rattles or soothers. Now, parents give their anxious children smart phones or other digital devices to keep them occupied and quiet in their strollers.

describe this next stage of life for those born between 1946 and 1964: They will be known as "grandboomers" ("Grandparenting," 2005). Personality, background, and past family interactions all influence the nature of the grandparent–grandchild relationship, as does the child's personality.

As with parents and children, the relationship between grandparents and grandchildren depends partly on the age of the grandchildren. One of my college students realized this when she wrote:

> Brian and Brianna are twins and are turning 13 years old this coming June. Over the spring break my family celebrated my grandmother's 80th birthday and I overheard the twins talking about how important it was for them to still have grandma around because she was the only one who would give them money if they really wanted something their mom wasn't able to give them. … I lashed out … how lucky we were to have her around and that they were two selfish little brats. She's the rock of the family and "the bank" is the least important of her attributes. …
>
> [Giovanna, 2010]

In developed nations, grandparents fill one of four roles:

1. *Remote grandparents* (sometimes called *distant grandparents*) are emotionally distant from their grandchildren. They are esteemed elders who are honoured, respected, and obeyed, expecting to get help whenever they need it.

2. *Companionate grandparents* (sometimes called *"fun-loving" grandparents*) entertain and "spoil" their grandchildren—especially in ways, or for reasons, that the parents would not.

3. *Involved grandparents* are active in the day-to-day lives of their grandchildren. They live near them and see them daily.

4. *Surrogate parents* raise their grandchildren, usually because the parents are unable or unwilling to do so.

Currently, in developed nations, most grandparents are companionate, partly because all three generations expect them to be beloved older companions rather than authority figures. Contemporary elders are usually proud of their grandchildren and care about their well-being but also enjoy their own independence. They provide babysitting and financial help but not advice or discipline (May et al., 2012). If grandparents become too involved and intrusive, parents tend to be forgiving but not appreciative (Pratt et al., 2008).

◀ **Kathleen's STORY**

Same Situation, Far Apart: Happy Grandfathers No matter where they are, grandparents and grandchildren often enjoy each other's company, partly because conflict is less likely, as grandparents are usually not as strict as parents are.

Such generative distance is not possible for grandparents who become surrogates when the biological parents are incapable of parenting; what results is a family structure called *skipped generation* because the middle generation is absent. Social workers often seek grandparents for kinship foster care, which works for the children as well as or better than foster care by strangers, but may be difficult for the older generation for many reasons:

- Both old and young are sad about the missing middle generation.
- Difficult grandchildren (such as drug-affected infants and rebellious school-age boys) are more likely to live with grandparents.
- Surrogate grandparents tend to be the most vulnerable elders, almost always grandmothers not grandfathers, already affected by past poverty.

For all these reasons, in North America and Europe, grandparents who are totally responsible for their grandchildren experience more illness, depression, and marital problems than do other elders (Hank & Buber, 2009; S. J. Kelley & Whitley, 2003). Stresses of all kinds abound, including worries about the children under their care (Shakya et al., 2012).

As for children of skipped-generation families, they are less likely to graduate from high school than are children from the same SES and ethnic groups who grow up in other family structures (Monserud & Elder, 2011). This has lifelong consequences, including unrealized potential, reduced lifetime earnings, poor health, increased unemployment, delinquency and crime, substance abuse, early child-bearing, and increased marital instability (Dryfoos, 1990; Human Resources Development Canada, Applied Research Branch, Strategic Policy, 2000; OECD, 2006). In addition, those who do not complete high school have a life expectancy 9.2 years less than that of graduates (Levin, 2005).

Before concluding that grandparents raising children without the parents is always problematic for all three generations, we need to consider the circumstances. For instance, in China, many rural grandparents become full-time caregivers because the middle generation is working in the cities, unable to bring children with them. The working parents typically make sure the grandparents want the caregiver role and then make sure to send money, as well as to visit when they can. For those grandparents, caring for their grandchildren actually improves their physical and psychological health (Baker & Silverstein, 2012).

The fact that grandparenting is not always wonderful should not obscure the more typical situation: Most grandparents enjoy their role, gain generativity from it, and are appreciated by younger family members (C. L. Kemp, 2005; Thiele & Whelan, 2008). In most conditions, grandparenting benefits all three generations. Some grandparents are rhapsodic and spiritual about the experience. One writes:

> Not until my grandson was born did I realize that babies are actually miniature angels assigned to break through our knee-jerk habits of resistance and to remind us that love is the real reason we're here.
>
> *[M. Golden, 2009, p. 125]*

On the other side of the equation, even young adult grandchildren who are international students living thousands of kilometres away from their grandparents often express warmth, respect, and affection for at least one of them (usually their maternal grandmother) (A. C. Taylor et al., 2005).

Friendship

Recent widowhood or divorce is almost always difficult, but elderly people who have spent a lifetime without a spouse or a partner usually have friendships, activities, and social connections that keep them busy and happy (DePaulo, 2006). A study of 85 single elders found that their level of well-being was similar to that of people in long-term equitable marriages, and they were happier than either recent widows or married adults in unequal marriages (Hagedoorn et al., 2006).

This does not mean that loners are happy, however. All the research finds that older adults need at least one close companion. For many (especially husbands), their intimate friend is also a spouse; for others, the friend is another relative; for still others, it is an unrelated member of their social convoy.

Older adults may not recognize the need for a confidant until a relationship is severed. For example, one man consulted a therapist because he was unexpectedly depressed after retiring. He quit work when he chose to do so, expecting to be happy. The therapist noted, "For over forty years, he had car-pooled with another man who worked in the same office. They traveled to and from work; an hour's drive each way. They had spent ten hours each week together, for over forty years, sharing their lives, hopes, dreams, and demons" (Rosowsky, 2007, p. 39). Once the problem was recognized, the man initiated get-togethers with his friend, and his depression lifted.

There is a lesson here: Many people do not realize the importance of social relationships until those relationships end. Quality (not quantity) of friendship is crucial, especially among the oldest-old (Krause, 2006). A study of widows found that those who fared best increased their contact with close friends after the death of their spouses (Zettel & Rook, 2004). Successful aging requires that people not be socially isolated. For contemporary elders, does this mean that they should begin social networking on their computers? Maybe, but not everyone agrees, as explained in the following.

Close Friends Late adulthood poses many challenges, from taking care of one's health to deciding how to spend one's money and time. Having fun with friends, as this group exploring small islets within British Columbia's Desolation Sound is doing, helps older adults feel less alone.

OPPOSING PERSPECTIVES

Social Networking, for Good or Ill

Older people text, tweet, post, and stream less than younger ones. Compared with emerging adults, older adults own fewer computers, are less connected to the Internet, and avoid social networking. One statistic makes the point: In Canada in 2012, 98.6 percent of all 16- to 24-year-olds had used the Internet in the past 12 months for personal reasons, but only 47.5 percent of those 65 years or older had (Statistics Canada, 2013l).

Older adults may not realize what they are missing: Seniors are significantly less likely than other age groups to realize that a lack of broadband access is a major disadvantage across a range of situations, such as making travel arrangements, researching investments, banking electronically, or accessing government services, with only one elder in nine considering lack of Internet connection "a major disadvantage" (A. Smith, 2010).

Age-related conditions, such as arthritis or macular degeneration, can partially explain reduced online activity among seniors. Canadian researchers such as Wendy Young at Memorial University of Newfoundland are exploring ways

of helping elders with conditions such as these to use digital devices. As Young stressed, many elderly are less likely to leave their homes, so online social interactions are becoming increasingly meaningful for this population. Assisting them with the ability to text, email, and access social networking sites such as Facebook, Twitter, LinkedIn, and Pinterest would decrease their likelihood of becoming socially isolated and depressed (Canadian Institutes of Health Research, 2013).

In fact from 2010 to 2012, the rates of social networking among those 65 and older increased by 60 percent, while rates for 16- to 24-year-olds rose only 2.6 percent (see Figure 15.9) (Statistics Canada, 2013m). As one newspaper reported,

Richard Bosack joined Facebook on Thursday, after his buddy Ray Urbans recommended the ubiquitous social networking site a few days earlier. Bosack is 89. Urbans is 96. … The hottest growth segment in online social networking sites is guys like Richard and Ray and their lady friends. That's right. Grampy and Grammy are down with "the Face."

[Gregory, 2010]

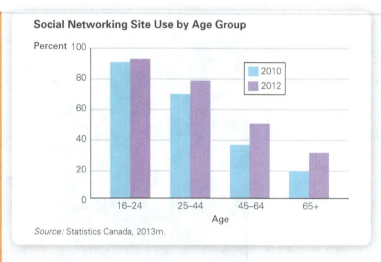

Social Networking Site Use by Age Group

Source: Statistics Canada, 2013m.

FIGURE 15.9 **A Narrowing Gap** The digital age gap was once especially apparent for social networking. Facebook, Twitter, LinkedIn, online dating, and so on are populated by millions of 16- to 24-year-olds, with fewer participants in every older cohort. While the gap still exists, use of social media by those 65 and older is increasing at a rate greater than that of any other cohort and four times that of the average: 60 percent compared to 15 percent.

From a developmental perspective, this may be good news. Elders who have strong social networks, close friends, and cognitively stimulating activities tend to live long and healthy lives. Involved, interacting elders are more cogent and happier than their relatively lonely and isolated peers. Internet use and social networking correlate with more frequent contact with friends, family, and community organizations (Hogeboom et al., 2010; Lewis & Ariyachandra, 2011).

Analysis of the characteristics of those who are not involved in social networking finds that old age itself is the characteristic they have most in common but that shyness and loneliness are also typical (Sheldon, 2012). Those who are networking are also less shy and less lonely—could that be cause, not merely correlation?

Pause to appreciate the scope of the historical change in social networking. A few decades ago, social networks were maintained through direct contact. Neighbours were *neighbourly*, a word that means "friendly and helpful." Everyone

Staying Connected Rosie Chapman's Facebook page allows her to stay connected with friends, family, and community. In an age when people may be less neighbourly, technology allows her to feel less alone that she might otherwise feel.

shopped, worshipped, studied, and played at the same places as everyone else, so they saw one another often. People always answered their phones and doorbells and complained if their friends did not "stay in touch," which once meant literally touching, with a hug or a handshake. Today, most adults would be upset if a friend stopped by unannounced, although one study found that those over age 80 would not mind (Felmlee & Muraco, 2009).

Many elders today have dozens of face-to-face friends, as they did a few decades ago, but no online friends. Are they missing something? For younger adults, Internet use correlates with more offline friends, partly because friendships seem strengthened through online contact (Wang & Wellman, 2010). This could happen for the aged as well.

Then why is social networking a topic for "opposing perspectives" instead of celebration, with suggestions as to how to get more of the elderly online? Three reasons:

1. Older adults' first reaction to social media is negative. They worry especially about privacy.

2. Social networking may increase prejudice.

3. Virtual activism and involvement may decrease community activism.

First, privacy concerns. As you have read, many elders are fiercely independent, and they fear that social networking will make them vulnerable to strangers who want to sell them something, alter their habits, or change their lives (Sheldon, 2012). This concern is also expressed by people of all other ages; perhaps the elders, as a cohort, are more aware of the need for personal privacy than younger adults are.

Second, with wider access, people become more exclusive and selective about their contacts, lists, and news sources—screening out anything that might not be in line with their preconceived notions. Yet on blogs, in chat rooms, and on YouTube, much more so than in newspapers and magazines, rumours and prejudices become viral, infecting thousands before anyone discovers a hoax, lie, or distortion. Reflection, analysis, and contrary opinions are more necessary than ever, yet with aging, the prefrontal cortex that enables such thinking shrinks. Remember that source amnesia is a particular problem with age, so bias might increase as more elderly go online.

Third, although social networking increases the frequency of contact with friends, it may also decrease true intimacy and commitment. Writer Malcolm Gladwell (2010) explains:

> The platforms of social media are built around weak ties. ... Facebook is a tool for effectively managing your acquaintances, for keeping up with the people you would not otherwise be able to stay in touch with.
>
> *[p. 42]*

Weak ties, Gladwell contends, do not spur people to action; instead, they encourage comfort, lip service, and passivity—thus maintaining the status quo.

"I used to call people, then I got into e-mailing, then texting, and now I just ignore everyone."

Two eminent scholars, Thomas Sander and Robert Putnam (2010), fear that social networking will weaken social involvement. They hope that "technological innovators may yet master the elusive social alchemy that will enable online behavior to produce real and enduring civic effects" (p. 15), but they do not see it thus far. Furthermore, they note that posts on Twitter, or "tweets," "convey people's meal and sock choices, instant movie reactions, rush-hour rants, and occasionally even their profound reflections." They "remain agnostic ... about whether [these] replace traditional social ties" (p. 15).

Two other social scientists conclude: "Changing social connectivity is, after all, neither a dystopian loss nor a utopian gain but an intricate, multifaceted, fundamental social transformation" (Wang & Wellman, 2010, p. 1164). Apparently all of us—old and young alike—are in the thralls of this transformation. Opinions differ as to the outcome.

KEY Points

- Long-term partnerships are beneficial, as research finds that married people tend to have longer, healthier, and happier lives than unmarried ones.
- Adults who have never married tend to have strong social connections with friends, sometimes faring better than those who have been divorced or widowed.
- Children and grandchildren are important parts of the social network for many elders, who more often give care than receive it from the younger generations.
- Familism, not only in filial obligation but also in older parents caring for the younger generations, is apparent in every culture, expressed in divergent ways.

The Frail Elderly

Now that we have dispelled stereotypes by describing aging adults who are active and enjoy supportive friends and family, we can turn to the **frail elderly**—those who are infirm, very ill, seriously disabled, and/or cognitively impaired. They are not the majority, but they are also not rare: eventually about one-third of older people will be frail for at least a year before they die.

frail elderly
People older than 65, and often older than 85, who are physically infirm, very ill, or cognitively disabled.

Activities of Daily Life

The crucial indicator of frailty, according to insurance standards and medical professionals, is the inability to perform the tasks of self-care to maintain independence. Gerontologists often assess five physical **activities of daily life (ADLs):** eating, bathing, toileting, dressing, and moving (transferring) from a bed to a chair.

Equally important may be the **instrumental activities of daily life (IADLs),** which require intellectual competence and forethought. Indeed, problems with IADLs often precede problems with ADLs since planning and problem solving help frail elders maintain self-care. It is more difficult to list IADLs because they vary from culture to culture. In developed nations, IADLs may include evaluating nutrition, preparing income tax forms, using modern appliances, and keeping appointments (see Table 15.1). In rural areas of other nations, feeding the chickens, cultivating the garden, mending clothes, getting water from the well, and making dinner might be considered IADLs.

Everywhere, the inability to perform IADLs makes people frail, even if they can perform all five ADLs. In 2003, the Canadian Community Health Survey reported that only 6 percent of senior men and 7 percent of senior women who were living in private households needed some level of assistance with their daily living (ADLs) (Gilmour & Park, 2006). As both a cause and a consequence, more of the elderly are living in the community rather than in assisted-care facilities.

WHOSE RESPONSIBILITY? There are marked cultural differences in care for the frail elderly, as already mentioned. As is true in many non-Western cultures, there is a strong cultural ideology in many African and Asian nations that values filial responsibility. As an example, India passed a law in 2007 making it a crime to neglect one's elderly parents, and in 2012 the Chinese government revised the Law of Protection of Rights and Interests of the Aged to make it mandatory for adult children to visit and support their aged parents. The law specifically states that family members must visit their parents who are 60 and older "often," although "often" has not been defined.

Chinese courts have not hesitated to enforce the new law. For example, the People's Court in Beitang district ordered a woman and her husband to visit the woman's

TABLE 15.1 Instrumental Activities of Daily Life

Domain	Exemplar Task
Managing medical care	Keeping current on check-ups, including teeth and eyes
	Assessing supplements as good, worthless, harmful
Food preparation	Evaluating nutritional information on food labels
	Preparing and storing food to eliminate spoilage
Transportation	Comparing costs of car, taxi, bus, and train
	Determining quick and safe walking routes
Communication	Knowing when and whether to use landline, cell, texting, mail, email
	Programming speed dial for friends, emergencies
Maintaining household	Following instructions for operating an appliance
	Keeping safety devices (fire extinguishers, CO_2 alarms) active
Managing one's finances	Budgeting future expenses (housing, utilities, etc.)
	Completing timely income tax returns

77-year-old mother at least twice a month and on at least two of China's national holidays. If they fail to do so, the couple may be fined (Agence France Presse, 2013).

This new law has come into force as China faces the implications of a growing and significant older population; almost 14 percent of the country's population is older than 60. At 194 million, China's senior population is more than 5.5 times greater than Canada's total population.

Demographics have changed in developed nations. Gerontologists note that one middle-aged couple, neither with siblings, might be responsible for four elderly parents and eight grandparents—fewer if some died, but more if some divorced and remarried. At least one of those 12, and maybe several, are likely to need intense caregiving.

PREVENTING FRAILTY Governments, families, and aging individuals all have a role to play in preventing frailty. To take a simple example, leg muscles weaken in everyone in old age, but the individual, the social network, and the larger community all influence whether weakened leg muscles lead to frailty. Fear of falling might make a person walk rarely, preferring to stay in bed. Other people might encourage frailty: Perhaps an overly solicitous caregiver brings meals and an adult child buys a large-screen TV with remote control for the bedroom. The macrosystem and exosystem play a role too: The physical environment might make walking outside hazardous or the home might have been constructed with many stairs.

Getting Around This man's weakened leg muscles don't mean a loss of independence. With his mobile wheelchair and his chihuahua by his side, he heads out every day for exercise, fresh air, and social interaction.

To prevent frailty, the person could exercise daily, first in bed, then lying on the floor, then with machines to increase strength and daily excursions. Family members, friends, and volunteers could walk with that leg-weakened person on pathways that the local government has built to be safe and pleasant. Someone could make sure the person has a sturdy walker, and public funds could underwrite the purchase. Personal trainers and/or physical therapists could help, paid by the individual, the family, or public health care. Thus, all three—the elder, the family, and the community—could prevent or at least postpone frailty.

Consider another example, this one not theoretical:

> A 70-year-old Hispanic man came to his family doctor following a visit to his family in Colombia, where he had appeared to be disoriented (he said he believed he was in the United States, and he did not recognize places that were known to be familiar to him) and he was very agitated, especially at night. An interview with the patient and a family member revealed a history that had progressed over the past six years, at least, of gradual worsening cognitive deficit which that family had interpreted as part of normal aging. Recently his symptoms had included difficulty operating simple appliances, misplacement of items, and difficulty finding words, with the latter attributed to his having learned English in his late 20s. … [His] family had been very protective and increasingly had compensated for his cognitive problems.
>
> … He had a lapse of more than five years without proper control of his medical problems [hypertension and diabetes] because of difficulty gaining access to medical care. …
>
> Based on the medical history, a cognitive exam … and a magnetic resonance imaging of the brain … the diagnosis of moderate Alzheimer's disease was made. Treatment with ChEI [cholinesterase inhibitors] was started. … His family noted that his apathy improved and that he was feeling more connected with the environment.

[Griffith & Lopez, 2009]

In this example, you can see that both the community (those five years without treatment for hypertension and diabetes, both known to impair cognition) and the family (making excuses, protecting him) contributed to his reaching a stage of neurocognitive disorder that could have been delayed, if not prevented altogether.

The man himself was not blameless. If he had recognized his condition, he would have realized that travelling to Colombia was the worst thing he could do: Disorientation of place is an early symptom of neurocognitive disorder, and changing one's physical (or geographic) location can make the problem worse. With many neurocognitive disorders, which cause severe IADL disability, as well as with all other kinds of physical and mental impairment, delay, moderation, and sometimes prevention are possible.

Caring for the Frail Elderly

The caregiver of a married frail elderly person is usually the spouse, who is also elderly (Pinquart & Sörensen, 2011). If an impaired person has no partner, usually siblings or adult daughters become caregivers. Less often, sons and daughters-in-law or adult grandchildren provide care.

Using a representative sample of 300 Quebec elders living at home, Réjean Hébert and colleagues at the University of Sherbrooke found that 70 to 80 percent of care for home-based, elders with disabilities was provided by informal caregivers such as family members (Hébert et al., 2001). This finding was extended to the country as a whole by a more recent report from Statistics Canada, which noted that in 2007 almost 70 percent of eldercare in Canada was provided by close family members (Cranswick & Dosman, 2008). Since women tend to live longer than men, caregivers most commonly reported caring for their mothers (37 percent—a rate three times more often than for their fathers) (see Figure 15.10).

Sometimes—usually when the elderly person needs extensive daily care—home health aides or nursing homes (which will be discussed later) are used. Families are still needed to coordinate, supplement, and sometimes fund the care. Professional caregivers are not a substitute for family care; instead they are part of a team that is necessary when family members are overwhelmed.

Remember diversity, however, especially in attitudes, beliefs, and cultural practices. In northern European nations, most elder care is provided through a social safety net of senior daycare centres, senior homes, and skilled nurses. In some cultures, an older

Caregiving Family support is evident here, as *(left)* the older sister (Lillian, age 75) escorts the younger sister (Julia, age 71) to the doctor and as *(right)* Susan's father feeds her mother at a surprise family reunion that Susan organized. This event lifted Susan's mother's spirits, improved her appetite, and created wonderful memories for the whole family.

person who is dying is taken to a hospital; in other cultures, such intervention is seen as interference with the natural order. As mentioned earlier in the chapter, traditionally in Asian nations, a son's wife provides elder care. In a 1990s study in South Korea, for instance, 80 percent of those with neurocognitive disorder were cared for by daughters-in-law and only 7 percent by spouses. In contrast, among Americans of Korean descent with neurocognitive disorder, 19 percent were cared for by daughters-in-law and 40 percent by spouses, with some of the rest in nursing homes (which almost never happened in Korea) (Youn et al., 1999). That is changing, in Korea and in other Asian nations.

Even with professional help, family caregivers experience substantial stress, although according to a longitudinal study, the stress is less when they receive practical help as well as emotional encouragement from other family members, even as the frail person's needs increase (Roth et al., 2005). Conversely, without help, family caregivers experience less health and more depression. The stress is manifest in various illnesses, in part because the immune system weakens. This is particularly true when caregivers themselves are old (Lovell & Wetherell, 2011). After listing the problems and frustrations of caring for someone who is mentally incapacitated but physically strong, the authors of one overview note:

> The effects of these stresses on family caregivers can be catastrophic. ... They may include increased levels of depression and anxiety as well as higher use of psychotropic medicine such as tranquilizers, poorer self-reported health, compromised immune function, and increased mortality.
>
> *[Gitlin et al., 2003, p. 362]*

Even in ideal circumstances with cultural and community support, family caregiving can result in problems. For instance, if one adult child is the primary caregiver, other siblings may feel relief, and if the caregiver requests their help, they may resent being told what to do. On the other hand, if the parent develops a closer relationship with the primary caregiver, the other siblings may experience jealousy. In addition, care receivers and caregivers may disagree about schedules, menus, doctor visits, and so on. Resentments on both sides can disrupt mutual affection and appreciation.

In every culture, emotional and physical needs, as well as expectations, vary because of past experiences and current personalities. Some older people would rather accept help from a paid stranger than from a son or a daughter; others insist on the opposite. Some families admire caregivers and help them often; others isolate and resent them. A tradition of caregiving may explain why at least one study found that caregiving African-Americans are less depressed than caregivers of other ethnicities (Roth et al., 2008). As always, ethnic generalities may obscure many individual variations: Some caregivers of every group feel burdened by the role; others are uplifted.

Developmentalists are trained to see "change over time," as Chapter 1 explains. From a life-span perspective, frailty should be anticipated and postponed, and potential challenges, such as caregiver exhaustion, should be addressed early on. However, in many nations, public policy and cultural values create situations that place undue burdens of elder care on the family (Seki, 2001).

Developmentalists, concerned about the well-being of people of all ages, advocate more help for families caring for frail elders at home (see Fortinsky et al., 2007; Stone, 2006). Spouses, in particular, need some relief from full responsibility, including more

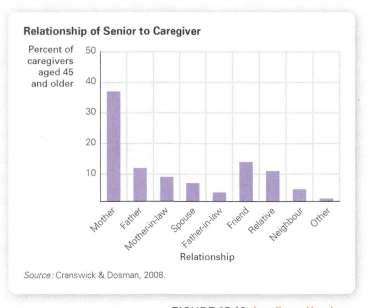

Relationship of Senior to Caregiver

Percent of caregivers aged 45 and older

Source: Cranswick & Dosman, 2008.

FIGURE 15.10 Lending a Hand
Caregivers over the age of 45 usually take care of frail parents, spouses, and in-laws, but they may also care for friends, neighbours, other relatives, and others.

✦ **ESPECIALLY FOR** Those Uncertain About Future Careers Would working in a nursing home be a good career for you? (see response, page 560) ➡

free time (via professional providers or family members who take over on a regular basis) and better medical attention (usually with visiting nurses who provide medical and psychological care for both caregiver and care receiver). Such measures can make home care tolerable, even fulfilling, for caregivers. Fortunately, these developmental concerns are now shared by many members of the public: Elderly people are far more likely to age in place than was true 20 years ago, and help is more available (Lovell & Wetherell, 2010).

ELDER ABUSE When caregiving results in resentment and social isolation, the risk of depression, poor health, and abuse (of either the frail person or the caregiver) escalates (Smith et al., 2011). The World Health Organization (WHO) defines elder abuse as: "A single, or repeated act, or lack of appropriate action, occurring within any relationship where there is an expectation of trust that causes harm or distress to an older person" (WHO, 2002). Abuse is likely if the *caregiver* suffers from emotional problems or substance abuse, if the *care receiver* is frail and demanding, and if *care location* is an isolated place where visitors are few and far between.

Elder abuse can take several forms. Caregivers may resort to overmedication, locked bedroom doors, and physical restraints to cope with difficult patients. The next step may be improper feeding or rough treatment. In other cases, abuse may be financial more than physical—the spending of the elder's pension cheque, for example.

Typically, abuse begins gradually and can continue for years without anyone realizing it. Abuse is generally not the result of one factor but of a combination of factors that can be heightened and complicated by various life events. Employment and Social Development Canada (2013) has noted some risk factors:

- a change in lifestyle (like retirement)
- employment or financial difficulties
- disputes over property/money
- physical illness
- mental/psychiatric illness
- addictions
- lack of adequate supports
- isolation
- changing relationships with family and/or friends
- declining independence.

Extensive public and personal safety nets for the frail elderly are needed. Most social workers and medical professionals are alert to the possibility of elder abuse and are suspicious if an elder is unexpectedly quiet, losing weight, or injured. However, when elder abuse is financial, bankers, lawyers, and investment advisors may not be able to recognize it nor are they obligated to respond (S. L. Jackson & Hafemeister, 2011).

A major problem is awareness: Professionals and relatives alike hesitate to criticize a family caregiver who is spending the pension cheque, disrespecting the elder, or simply not responding as quickly and carefully as the elder wishes. At what point does this become abuse? This is an issue for all cultures, incomes, and families.

Sometimes the caregiver becomes the victim, cursed at or even attacked by the confused elderly person. As with other forms of abuse, the dependency of the victim makes prosecution difficult (Mellor & Brownell, 2006).

Researchers find that about 5 percent of elders say they are abused and that up to 25 percent of all elders are vulnerable but do not report abuse (Cooper et al., 2008).

Elders who are mistreated by family members are often ashamed to admit it, so the actual rate of abuse is probably close to 25 percent. Accurate incidence data are complicated by lack of consensus regarding standards of care: Some elders feel abused, but caregivers disagree. It is known that elders who are mistreated are more likely to be depressed and ill, but neither of these conditions proves abuse (Dong et al., 2011).

LONG-TERM CARE At some point, elders may require a level of care that is too great for their caregivers at home. Long-term care, for example in nursing homes, is one option—though it is feared by many. Some families feel shame if they place an elderly relative in an institution. Others are concerned that institutions are dehumanizing. Some institutions *are* dehumanizing. One 61-year-old woman with cerebral palsy, who spent time in a nursing home, said:

> I would rather die than have to exist in such a place where residents are neglected, ignored, patronized, infantilized, demeaned; where the environment is chaotic, noisy, cold, clinical, even psychotic.
>
> *[quoted in W. H. Thomas, 2007, p. 159]*

Helping Out A volunteer at a nursing home in Haiti cuts and styles this woman's hair. She is one of a network of caregivers who help the elderly live their lives with pride and dignity.

Among the signs of a humane setting are provisions for independence; individual choice—for example, in terms of what to eat, where to walk, and whether to have a pet; and privacy. Activities should be engaging, not demeaning. For example, at one time, playing Bingo was a common activity in many nursing homes, but many of today's elderly find the idea of playing the game ageist (Baker, 2007).

The training and the workload of the staff, especially of the aides who provide the most frequent and most personal care, are crucial: Such simple tasks as helping a frail person out of bed can be done clumsily, painfully, or skillfully. The difference depends on proficiency, experience, and patience—all possible with a sufficient number of well-trained and well-paid staff with a low turnover rate. Currently, however, most front-line workers have little training, low pay, and many patients—and almost half leave each year (Golant, 2011).

Quality care is much more labour-intensive and expensive than most people realize. In Canada, nursing home care is subsidized nationwide; however, residents must also contribute to some of the costs. Some provinces, for example Ontario, require a co-payment from residents, with the amount depending on the type of accommodation, such as a semi-private room, and length of stay (a long-term stay in a basic room is about $55 per day). In British Columbia, nursing home residents pay a fee of up to 80 percent of their after-tax income. In 2010, the minimum client rate was $894 per month. In Quebec, the rate for a room with three or more people was about $34 per day (Senioropolis.com, n.d).

In North America and particularly in western Europe, good private nursing-home care is available for those who can afford it. There are also non-profit homes subsidized by religious organizations. In North America, the trend over the past 20 years has been toward fewer nursing-home residents, and those few are usually over 80 years old, frail and confused, with several medical problems (Moore et al., 2012). Another trend is toward smaller nursing homes with more individualized care, with nurses and aides working more closely together (Sharkey et al., 2011), as well as nursing homes with more homelike surroundings.

Although 90 percent of elders are independent and community dwelling at any given moment, half of them will need nursing-home care at some point, usually for less than a month as they recuperate from hospitalization. Some need such care for more than a year, and only a few will need it for 10 years or more (Stone, 2006).

assisted living
A living arrangement for elderly people that combines privacy and independence with medical supervision.

RESPONSE FOR Those Uncertain About Future Careers (from page 557) It may be a good career choice. The demand for good workers will increase as the population ages, and the working conditions will improve. An important problem is that the quality of nursing homes varies, so you need to make sure you work in one whose policies incorporate the view that the elderly can be quite capable, social, and independent. ●

Same Situation, Far Apart: Diversity Continues No matter where they live, elders thrive with individualized care and social interaction, as apparent here. Martina McGoey *(left)*, Bernice Walker *(middle)*, and Peggy McCruer *(right)* take part in an exercise class at the Riverside Senior Living Centre, in Toronto, and an elderly chess player in a senior residence in Kosovo *(far right)* contemplates protecting his king. Both photos show that these elders maintain their individuality.

ALTERNATIVE CARE Most elder-care arrangements that include special services, such as home care, aging in place, and NORCs, are less costly and more individualized than nursing homes. Another alternative is **assisted living,** an arrangement that combines some of the privacy and independence of home life with some of the medical supervision of a nursing home (Imamoglu, 2007).

An assisted-living residence typically provides a private room or apartment for each person, allowing pets and furnishings just as in a traditional home. Services might include one communal meal per day, special bus trips and activities, and optional arrangements for household cleaning and minor repairs. Usually, medical assistance is readily available—from daily supervision of pill taking to emergency help, with a doctor and ambulance provided when necessary.

Assisted-living facilities range from group homes for three or four elderly people to large apartment or townhouse developments for hundreds of residents (Golant, 2011). Almost every province and territory, and almost every nation, has its own standards for assisted-living facilities, but many such places are unlicensed. Some regions of the world (e.g., northern Europe) have many assisted living options, while others (e.g., sub-Saharan Africa) have almost none.

Another form of alternative care is sometimes called *village care.* Although not really a village, it is so named because of the African proverb "It takes a whole village to raise a child." The idea is that if elderly people who live near one another all pool their resources, they can stay in their homes but also have special assistance when they need it. Such communities require that the elderly contribute financially and that they be relatively competent, so village care is not suited for everyone. However, for some it is ideal (Scharlach et al., 2012).

Overall, as with many other aspects of aging, the emphasis in living arrangements is on selective optimization with compensation. Elders need to live in settings that allow them to be at their best, safe and respected, in control of as much of their own lives as possible. Depending not only on the specifics of ADLs and IADLs, but also on the personality of the elder and the depth of the social network, many housing solutions are possible. One expert explains: "There is no one-size-fits-all set of optimum residential activities, experiences, and situations" (Golant, 2011).

We close with an example of family care and nursing-home care at their best. A young adult named Rob related that his 98-year-old great-grandmother "began to fail. We had no idea why and thought, well, maybe she is growing old" (quoted in

L. P. Adler, 1995, p. 242). All three younger generations of the family conferred and reluctantly decided that it was time to move the matriarch from her suburban home, where she had lived for decades, into a nearby nursing home. She reluctantly agreed.

Fortunately, this nursing home encouraged independence and did not assume that decline is always a sign of "final failing." The doctors there discovered that the woman's heart pacemaker was not working properly. Rob tells what happened next:

> We were very concerned to have her undergo surgery at her age, but we finally agreed. … Soon she was back to being herself, a strong, spirited, energetic, independent woman. It was the pacemaker that was wearing out, not Great-grandmother.
>
> *[quoted in L. P. Adler, 1995, p. 242]*

This story contains a lesson repeated throughout this book. When a toddler does not talk, or a preschooler grabs a toy, or a teenager gets drunk, or an emerging adult takes dangerous risks, or a newlywed contemplates divorce, or an older person seems to be failing, one might conclude that such problems are normal for that particular age. There is truth in that: Each of these is more common at those stages. But each of these behaviours should also alert caregivers to encourage talking, sharing, moderation, caution, or self-care. The life-span perspective holds that, at every age, people can be "strong, spirited, and energetic" if all of us do our part.

KEY Points

- The frail elderly are unable to perform activities of daily life (ADLs) such as feeding, dressing, and bathing themselves.
- Instrumental activities of daily life (IADLs) require intellectual competence and may be more crucial for independent living than ADLs.
- Caregiving of the frail elderly can be depressing or satisfying, depending partly on support from professionals, family members, and the care receiver.
- Professional help, in assisted-living facilities or nursing homes, can be beneficial or dehumanizing.

SUMMARY

Theories of Late Adulthood

1. Self theories hold that adults make personal choices in ways that allow them to become fully themselves. One such theory arises from Erikson's last stage, integrity versus despair, in which individuals seek integrity that connects them to the human community.

2. Research finds substantial continuity over adulthood in the Big Five personality traits. The positivity effect and a tendency toward self-actualization also can be seen as part of the drive to become more oneself.

3. Compulsive hoarding can be understood as an effort to hold onto the self, keeping objects from the past that others might consider worthless.

4. Stratification theories maintain that social forces—such as ageism, racism, and sexism—limit personal choices throughout

the life span, keeping people on a particular level or stratum of society.

5. Age stratification can be blamed for the disengagement of older adults. Activity theory counters disengagement theory, stressing that older people need to be active.

6. Because of earlier discrimination and past experiences—in health, education, and employment—people who are from low-income backgrounds, especially if they are from minority ethnic groups, have a more difficult old age. This does not seem true if they reach very old age, 90 and older.

Activities in Late Adulthood

7. At every age, employment can provide social and personal satisfaction as well as needed income. However, retirement may be welcomed by the elderly, if they remain active in other ways.

8. Some elderly people perform volunteer work and are active politically—writing letters, voting, staying informed. These activities enhance health and well-being and benefit the larger society.

9. Common among retirees are an increase in religious activity (but not attendance at places of worship) and a wish to age in place. Many of the elderly engage in home improvement or redecoration, preferring to stay in their own homes and attend their local house of worship.

Friends and Relatives

10. A romantic partner is the most important member of a person's social convoy. Older adults in long-standing marriages tend to be satisfied with their relationships and to safeguard each other's health. As a result, married elders tend to live longer, happier, and healthier lives than unmarried ones.

11. Elders who have never married tend to have many friends. Everyone needs someone who is a close confidant.

12. Relationships with adult children and grandchildren are usually mutually supportive, although conflicts arise as well. Financially, elders more often support the younger generations than vice versa.

13. Most of the elderly prefer to maintain their independence, living alone, but some become surrogate parents, raising their grandchildren. This adds stress to the older generation, especially when it occurs suddenly because the middle generation is unfit or unable to care for the children.

The Frail Elderly

14. Most elderly people are self-sufficient, but some eventually become frail. They need help with their activities of daily life, either with physical tasks (such as eating and bathing) or with instrumental ones (such as completing income taxes and comparing transportation options).

15. Care of the frail elderly is usually undertaken by adult children or spouses, who are often elderly themselves. Most families have a strong sense of filial responsibility, although elder abuse may occur when the stress of care is great and social support is lacking.

16. Nursing homes, assisted living, and professional home care are of varying quality and availability. Each of these arrangements can provide necessary and beneficial care, but they do not always do so. Good care for the frail elderly involves a combination of professional and family support, recognizing diversity in needs and personality.

KEY TERMS

activities of daily life (ADLs) (p. 554)
activity theory (p. 534)
age in place (p. 543)
assisted living (p. 560)
CARP (p. 545)

compulsive hoarding (p. 532)
disengagement theory (p. 534)
filial responsibility (p. 547)
frail elderly (p. 553)
instrumental activities of daily life (IADLs) (p. 554)

integrity versus despair (p. 531)
naturally occurring retirement community (NORC) (p. 543)
positivity effect (p. 532)

self theories (p. 531)
stratification theories (p. 534)
universal design (p. 543)

WHAT HAVE YOU LEARNED?

1. What do self theories seek to explain?

2. Explain Erikson's eighth stage, integrity versus despair, as it relates to late adulthood.

3. How are behaviours such as refusing to give up driving and compulsive hoarding examples of older adults maintaining the self?

4. Explain the connection between the positivity effect and well-being.

5. What do stratification theories seek to explain?

6. Give examples to demonstrate how both the disengagement theory and the activity theory might apply to older adults.

7. How is gender stratification evident in the way that older men and women take care of one another?

8. In what ways might stratification by ethnicity exacerbate the problems that older adults experience?

9. How has the LICO rate among Canadian seniors changed over the last almost 40 years, and what accounts for this change?

10. Why would a person choose not to retire?

11. What are some benefits of volunteering, and what can be done to encourage more volunteerism among older adults?

12. What are the benefits and liabilities for elders who want to age in place?

13. How do religion and religious institutions fulfill the needs of the elderly?

14. How does the political activism of older and younger adults differ?

15. In what ways might long-term partners protect one another against the problems of old age?

16. In what ways do older and younger generations support one another?

17. Choose one factor that impacts relationships between parents and adult children and explain how it might affect the relationship.

18. Which type of grandparenting seems to benefit both generations the most? Explain.

19. Why is it important for older adults to have close companions?

20. What are ADLs and IADLs? Why is it important to consider both when discussing frailty?

21. What problems might arise in caring for a frail elderly person? What measures might help caregivers?

22. What factors might increase the likelihood of elder abuse?

23. What criteria would you use when evaluating a nursing home?

24. When might assisted living be a good option for elderly people and when might village care be a good option?

APPLICATIONS

1. Attitudes about disabilities are influential. Visit the disability office on your campus, asking both staff and students what they see as the effects of attitude on the performance of all students. How do your findings relate to the elderly?

2. People of different ages, cultures, and experiences vary in their values regarding family caregiving, including the need for safety, privacy, independence, and professional help. Find four people whose backgrounds (age, ethnicity, SES) differ. Ask their opinions on family caregiving and analyze the results.

3. Visit a nursing home or assisted-living residence in your community. Record details about the physical setting, the social interactions of the residents, and the activities of the staff. Would you like to work or live in this place? Why or why not?

>>ONLINE CONNECTIONS

To accompany your textbook, you have access to a number of online resources, including LearningCurve, which is an adaptive quizzing program; critical thinking questions; and case studies. For access to any of these links, go to www.worthpublishers. com/launchpad/bergerchuang1e. In addition to these resources, you'll also find links to video clips, personalized study advice, and an e-Book. Among the videos and activities available online is the following:

■ *Grandparents as Parents.* In text and video, find out how elders cope with this growing phenomenon and how it affects grandparents and grandchildren.

EPILOGUE:
Death and Dying

WHAT WILL YOU KNOW?

- Why is death a topic of hope, not despair?
- What is the difference between a good death and a bad one?
- How does mourning help with grief?

My husband, Martin, died 10 years ago. The immediate cause was an infection, which was exacerbated by steroids, which helped him breathe and which he needed because he had lung cancer, which occurred because he was a lifelong smoker. I blame both of us—me because I never convinced him to quit smoking, him because he never quit. I blame the U.S. Army, too, because they gave him free cigarettes when he was a 17-year-old recruit. And I blame our culture because boys smoke to act like men. I even blame Hitler, already dead when Martin enlisted, but Martin had grown up wanting to join the army to fight him.

My search for causes—steroids, addiction, him, me, the military, machismo, Hitler—arises from anger and guilt, not from acceptance of death as a natural part of the life span. I have kept fresh flowers on our mantle next to his urn for 10 years now: Martin would have laughed at that and insisted that I stop being so foolish. ●

—Kathleen Berger

THIS CHAPTER IS ABOUT DEATH. DYING IS A process that begins with personal choices (such as smoking cigarettes) and social contexts (such as the army). Culture is always influential. Blame is irrational; bereavement takes many forms. Foolishness is not unusual. When author Joan Didion's husband died, she described a "year of magical thinking," including keeping his shoes in the closet because he would need them if he came back (Didion, 2005).

Thanatology is the study of all this. Perhaps surprisingly, thanatology is neither morbid nor gloomy. Rather, as the three sections of this chapter detail, *hope* in death, *choices* in dying, and *affirmation* of life are the themes of thanatology.

thanatology
The study of death and dying, especially of the social and emotional aspects.

Death and Hope

A multicultural life-span perspective reveals that reactions to death are filtered through many cultural prisms and are affected by historical changes (see Table EP.1) and regional variations, as well as by the age of both the dying and the bereaved. We will examine some of these differences.

TABLE EP.1 How Death Has Changed in the Past 100 Years

Death occurs later. A century ago, the average life span worldwide was less than 40 years. Half of the world's babies died before age 5. Now newborns are expected to live to age 79; in many nations, elderly people age 85 and over are the fastest-growing age group.

Dying takes longer. In the early 1900s, death was usually fast and unstoppable; once the brain, the heart, or other vital organs failed, the rest of the body quickly followed. Now death can often be postponed through medical intervention: Hearts can beat for years after the brain stops functioning, respirators can replace lungs, and dialysis can do the work of failing kidneys. As a result, dying is often a lengthy process.

Death often occurs in hospitals. A hundred years ago, death almost always occurred at home, with the dying person surrounded by familiar faces. Now many deaths occur in hospitals, surrounded by medical personnel and technology.

The main causes of death have changed. People of all ages once died of infectious diseases (tuberculosis, typhoid, smallpox), and many women and infants died in childbirth. Now disease deaths before age 50 are rare, and almost all newborns (99 percent) and their mothers (99.99 percent) live, unless the infant is very frail or medical care of the mother is grossly inadequate.

And after death ... People once knew about life after death. Some believed in heaven and hell; others, in reincarnation; others, in the spirit world. Many prayers were repeated—some on behalf of the souls of the deceased, some for remembrance, some to the dead asking for protection. Believers were certain that their prayers were heard. Today's young adults are aware of cultural and religious diversity, which makes them question what earlier generations believed, raising doubts that never occurred to their ancestors.

Source: Adapted from Kastenbaum, 2006.

You will see that one emotion is constant: hope. It appears in many ways: hope for life after death, hope that the world is better because someone lived, hope that death occurred for a reason, hope that survivors rededicate themselves.

Cultures, Epochs, and Death

Few people in developed nations have actually witnessed someone die. This was not always the case. Those who reached age 50 in 1900 in North America and who had had 20 classmates in their high school class would have already seen at least six of their classmates die. The survivors would have visited and reassured several of their friends dying at home, promising to see them in heaven. Shared religious beliefs led almost everyone to believe in life after death.

Now fewer people die before old age, and those who do usually die suddenly and unexpectedly, most often in motor vehicle collisions. Ironically, death has become more feared as it has become less familiar (Carr, 2012). Accordingly, we begin by describing various responses to death, to help each of us find the hope that death can provide.

ANCIENT TIMES One of the signs of a "higher" animal is reacting with sorrow when death occurs. Elephants and chimpanzees have done that for hundreds of thousands of years. Jane Goodall reported that when the chimp Flo died, Flo's older daughter was away, so Flo's youngest son (Flint), alone, became "hollow-eyed, gaunt, and utterly depressed, huddled in the vegetation near where Flo had died" (Goodall, 2000, p. 224). Within weeks, he was also dead.

Humans have developed ways to deal with their grief. Paleontologists believe that 100 000 years ago, the Neanderthals buried their dead with tools, bowls, or jewellery, signifying belief in an afterlife (Hayden, 2012). The date is controversial: Burial could have begun 200 000 years ago or only 20 000 years ago, but it is certain that by 5000 years ago death had become an occasion for hope, mourning, and remembrance. Two ancient Western civilizations with written records—Egypt and Greece—had elaborate death rituals, described here to help us see what is universal and what is unique about the human response to death.

The ancient Egyptians built magnificent pyramids, refined the science of mummification, and scripted written instructions (called the Book of the Dead) to aid the soul (*ka*), personality (*ba*), and shadow (*akh*) in reuniting after death, blessing and protecting the living (Taylor, 2010). The fate of a dead Egyptian depended partly on his or her actions while alive, partly on the circumstances of death, and partly on proper burial by the family. That made death a reason to live morally and to honour the past. The Egyptians believed that if a dead person was not appropriately cared for after death, the living would suffer.

For the ancient Greeks, continuity between life and death was an evident theme, with hope for this world and the next. The fate of a dead person depended on past good or evil deeds. A few would have a blissful afterlife, a few were condemned to torture (in Hades, a form of hell), and most would exist in a shadow world until they were reincarnated to live another life.

Three themes are apparent in all the known ancient cultures, not only those of Greece and Egypt, but also in the Mayan, Chinese, and African cultures:

- Actions during life were thought to affect destiny after death.
- An afterlife was more than a hope; it was assumed.
- Mourners responded to death with specific prayers and offerings, in part to prevent the spirit of the dead person from haunting and hurting them.

CONTEMPORARY RELIGION AND DEATH Now let us look at contemporary religions. Each faith seems distinct. As one review states, "Rituals in the world's religions, especially those for the major tragic and significant events of bereavement and death, have a bewildering diversity" (Idler, 2006, p. 285). Some details illustrate this diversity.

According to many branches of Hinduism, a person should die on the floor, surrounded by family, who neither eat nor wash until the funeral pyre is extinguished. By contrast, among some (but not all) Christians, mourners gather at a family member's home or in a church, and share in the fellowship of food and drink, sometimes with music and dancing. In many Muslim and Hindu cultures, the dead person is bathed by the next of kin; among some Aboriginal peoples (e.g., the Navajo), no family member touches the dead person.

Although religions everywhere have specific beliefs and rituals, there is a great deal of diversity within each religion. For instance, some Buddhist rituals help believers accept a person's death and detach from grieving in order to escape the suffering that living without the person entails. Other rituals help people connect to the dead, part of the continuity between life and death (Cuevas & Stone, 2011). Beliefs and rituals vary by region, too. There are more than 600 First Nations bands in Canada, each with its own heritage: It is a mistake to assume that all First Nations peoples have the same customs.

Religious practices change as historical conditions do. One specific example comes from Korea. Traditionally, Koreans were opposed to autopsies because the body is considered a sacred gift from the parents. However, contemporary Koreans recognize that medical schools need bodies to autopsy in order to teach science to the next generation. This clash led to a new custom: a special religious service honouring the dead who give their body for medical education (J-T. Park et al., 2011). As medical schools instituted such ceremonies, the number of bodies donated for research in Korea rose dramatically.

Diversity is also evident in descriptions of life after death. Some religions believe in reincarnation—that a dead person is reborn, with the specific new life dependent on the person's past life. Other religions believe that souls are judged and then sent to heaven or hell. Still others contend that the spirits of the dead remain on earth, affecting the life of those still living. Finally, some religions hold that the dead live on only in memory, which leads to customs such as naming a baby after a dead person or honouring the dead on a particular memorial day.

The Western practice of building a memorial, dedicating a plaque, or naming a location for a dead person is antithetical to Eastern cultures, in which all signs of

Shared Grief When a 5-day-old baby died in Santa Rosa, Guatemala, the entire neighbourhood mourned as they watched a procession go by.

OBSERVATION QUIZ
What symbols do you notice in the photo that might help with grief? (see answer, page 569) →

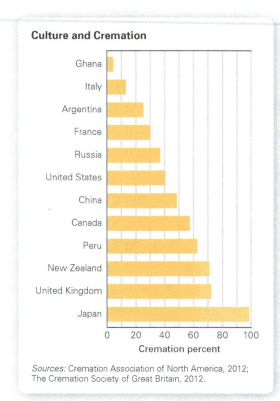

Culture and Cremation

Ghana
Italy
Argentina
France
Russia
United States
China
Canada
Peru
New Zealand
United Kingdom
Japan

0   20   40   60   80   100
Cremation percent

Sources: Cremation Association of North America, 2012; The Cremation Society of Great Britain, 2012.

FIGURE EP.1 We All Die ... But
What happens to the body depends on where we live and what our culture is. If a dead elder in Ghana were cremated, everyone would be shocked, as that practice is considered an insult that might harm the entire community. However, cremation would be assumed in Japan, where any other custom would be viewed as disrespectful to the community and to the deceased.

the dead are removed after proper prayers have been said, in order to allow the spirit to leave in peace. This difference in customs was evident when terrorist bombs in Bali, Indonesia, killed 38 Indonesians and 164 foreigners, mostly Australian and British. The Indonesians prayed intensely and then destroyed all reminders; the Australians raised money to build a memorial (de Jonge, 2011). Neither group understood the deep emotions of the other.

There are variations in what happens to a dead body. An open casket and then burial is traditional among Christians in North America. Caskets themselves can be luxurious, silk-lined, and protected from the elements with strong metal, or families can opt for a plain pine box (Sanders, 2010). By contrast, many Muslim groups believe that the body should return to the earth and thus be buried directly in the soil, not in a casket at all.

In most nations of Asia, from India in the west to Japan in the east, bodies are cremated and returned to the land or water, a practice that is becoming more common among other cultures, although regional variations exist (see Figure EP.1). Ashes may be interred next to buried coffins or may be scattered.

In some cultures, a home altar is created, where the living can commune with the spirits of the dead. Spirits not only hover in their special spot, but they also travel—especially during the Hungry Ghost Festival (in many East Asian nations), on the Day of the Dead (in many Latin American nations), or on All Souls' Day (in many European nations). All of these beliefs can change as cultures do. For instance, while every Chinese home once had an altar honouring the ancestors, currently most do not (Chan, 2011).

In recent decades, people everywhere have become less devout, a fact evident in surveys of religious beliefs as well as in attendance at religious services. And yet, people worldwide become more religious when confronted with their own or someone else's death, seeking reassurances of hope in an afterlife in the face of loss and potential despair. This is true even for people who do not consider themselves religious (Heflick & Goldenberg, 2012).

Regardless of the diversity of death customs and beliefs, death has always inspired strong emotions, many of which can be constructive or life-affirming. Paradoxically, the experience of death can often intensify one's positive aspect toward life and its meaningfulness. It is the *denial* of death that leads to despair (Wong & Tomer, 2011). This may explain why, in all faiths and cultures, death is considered a passage, not an endpoint, and a reason for families and communities to come together.

Understanding Death Throughout the Life Span

Thoughts about death are influenced by each person's cognitive maturation and past experiences. Here are some of the specifics.

A CHILD'S UNDERSTANDING OF DEATH Some adults think children are oblivious to death; others believe children understand death and should participate in funerals and other rituals, just as adults do (Talwar et al., 2011). You know from your study of childhood cognition that neither view is completely correct.

Children as young as 2 have some understanding of death, but their perspective differs from that of older people. One idea they find particularly incomprehensible is that the dead person or animal cannot come back to life; it takes a while for the reality of the situation to sink in. As a result, a child might not be sad initially when a person or animal dies but might later have moments of profound sorrow, when they realize that their loved one is not coming back.

In addition to sadness, a child who loses a friend, a relative, or a pet typically demonstrates loneliness, anger, and other signs of mourning, but adults cannot be certain how a particular child might react. For example, one 7-year-old boy seemed to take in stride the loss of three grandparents and an uncle within two years. However, he became extremely upset when his dog, Twick, died.

That boy's parents were taken aback by the depth of their son's emotions. They regretted that they had not taken him to the animal hospital to say goodbye to the dog. The boy angrily refused to go back to school, saying, "I wanted to see him one more time. … You don't understand. … I play with Twick every day" (quoted in K. R. Kaufman & Kaufman, 2006, pp. 65–66).

Because the loss of a particular companion is a young child's prime concern, it is not helpful to say that a dog can be replaced. Even a 1-year-old knows that a new puppy is not the same dog and might be upset or confused that an adult would think that it is. Nor should a child be told that Grandma is sleeping, that God wanted his or her sister in heaven, or that Grandpa went on a trip. The child may take such explanations literally, wanting to wake up Grandma, complain to God, or tell Grandpa to come home.

If a child realizes that adults are afraid to say that death has occurred, the child might conclude that death is so horrible that adults cannot talk about it—a terrifying conclusion. Even worse, they may feel that adults are not to be trusted, since they lie about important events (Doering, 2010).

Remember how cognition changes with development. Egocentric preschoolers may fear that they, personally, caused death and may be seriously troubled that their unkind words or thoughts killed someone. As children become concrete operational thinkers, they seek specific facts, such as exactly how a person died and where he or she is now. Adolescents may be self-absorbed, philosophical, or analytic—or all three at different moments.

At every age, questions should be answered honestly, in words the child can understand. In a study of 4- to 8-year-olds, those who knew more about the specifics of a loved one's death were less anxious about death and dying (Slaughter & Griffiths, 2007).

If a child encounters death, adults should listen with full attention, neither ignoring the child's concerns nor expecting adult-like reactions (Doering, 2010). Children are more impulsive than deliberate, as their limbic systems mature more rapidly than their prefrontal cortexes. They may seem happy one day and morbidly depressed the next. In addition, each child is affected by the attitudes of other family members. Even if a parent dies, some children cope well—if their caregiving adult is able to cope well (Melhem et al., 2011). In general, children neither forget nor dwell on the death of a loved one.

Children who themselves are fatally ill typically fear that death means being abandoned by beloved and familiar people (Wolchik et al., 2008). Consequently, parents are advised to stay with a dying child day and night, holding, reading, singing, and sleeping, always ensuring that the child is not alone.

UNDERSTANDING DEATH IN LATE ADOLESCENCE AND EMERGING ADULTHOOD "Live fast, die young, and leave a good-looking corpse" is advice often attributed to actor James Dean, who died in a car crash at age 24. At what stage would a person most likely agree? Emerging adulthood. Worldwide, teenagers and emerging adults control their death anxiety by taking risks and valuing friends, perhaps expecting to die long before old age (de Bruin et al., 2007; Luxmoore, 2012).

Terror management theory explains some illogical responses to death, including why young people take death-defying risks (Mosher & Danoff-Burg, 2007). By surviving, they prove to themselves that they will not die. Especially when people

ANSWER TO **OBSERVATION QUIZ** (from page 567) The white coffin indicates that the infant was without sin and will therefore be in heaven, and the red roses are a symbol of love. ●

terror management theory (TMT) The idea that people adopt cultural values and moral principles in order to cope with their fear of death. This system of beliefs protects individuals from anxiety about their mortality and bolsters their self-esteem, so they react harshly when other people go against any of the moral principles involved.

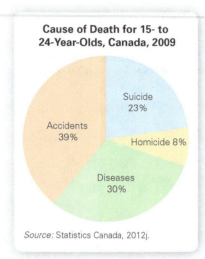

Cause of Death for 15- to 24-Year-Olds, Canada, 2009

Suicide 23%

Accidents 39%

Homicide 8%

Diseases 30%

Source: Statistics Canada, 2012j.

FIGURE EP.2 **Accidents Versus Diseases** In 2009, 5 times as many young adults in Canada died in accidents than died of the most common lethal disease (malignant neoplasms, or tumours), which took the life of 7.9% of all 15- to 24-year-olds (Statistics Canada, 2012j).

Kathleen's STORY

aged 15 to 24 have access to cars and guns, the developmental tendency toward risk taking can be deadly (see Figure EP.2). Cluster suicides, foolish dares, fatal gang fights, and drunk driving are all much more common in those younger than 25 than older.

As already noted, many studies have found that when health promotion messages explicitly link negative behaviours with death, it may ironically increase the likelihood of engaging in that behaviour (Goldenberg & Arndt, 2008); for example, it may increase smoking in teenagers and young adults who want to protect their pride and self-esteem while defying death and adults. Likewise, college students who heard about the fatal risks associated with binge drinking were more, not less, willing to binge (Jessop & Wade, 2008).

Other research in many nations has found that when adolescents and emerging adults thought about death, they sometimes tried to hold onto their self-esteem and faith in their cultural world views, which, to some extent, protected them from death-related anxiety (Maxfield et al., 2007). Some people distance themselves from people with diseases such as cancer to avoid anxiety about their own death; others avoid funerals and blame people who died in accidents that occurred through no fault of their own (Hirschberger, 2006; Renkema et al., 2008).

Teenagers who themselves are dying of a fatal disease tend to be saddened and shocked ("Why me?") at first, and then they try to live life to the fullest, proving that death cannot conquer them. One dying 17-year-old said

> don't be scared of death. Don't go and lock yourself in your little room, under your little bedcovers, and just sit there and cry and cry and cry. Don't do that because you're wasting time, and you're not only hurting yourself, you're hurting the people around you. … That's why never ever ever stop doing what you love. Just be yourself. Be normal. Don't shut them out, but bring them in—your loved ones, your friends.
>
> *[Kellehear & Ritchie, 2003, p. 21]*

UNDERSTANDING DEATH IN ADULTHOOD A shift in attitudes toward death occurs when adults become responsible for work and family. Death is no longer romanticized; it is to be avoided or at least postponed. Fear of death builds in early adulthood, reaching a lifetime peak in middle age.

Many adults stop taking addictive drugs, start wearing seat belts, and adopt other precautions when they become parents. One of my students eagerly anticipated the thrill of her first skydive. She reserved her spot on the plane and paid in advance. However, the day before the scheduled dive she learned she was pregnant. She forfeited the money and shopped for prenatal vitamins instead.

When adults hear about another's death, their reaction is closely connected to the person's age. Death in the prime of life is harder to accept than death in late adulthood.

To defend themselves against the fear of aging and untimely death, adults often ask for details about a person's death to convince themselves that their situation is different. Sometimes the deceased was much older and had been ailing; in that case, adults do not take the death personally. If the dead person was a contemporary or even younger, then adults seek to explain why that person's genes, or habits, or foolish behaviour is unlike their own.

In other situations, adults may not readily accept the death of others—even others who are ready to die. Thus, when Dylan Thomas was about age 30, he wrote his most famous poem, addressed to his dying father: "Do not go gentle into that good night/Rage, rage against the dying of the light" (D. Thomas, 1957).

Nor do adults readily accept their own death. A woman diagnosed at age 42 with a rare and almost always fatal cancer (a sarcoma) wrote:

I hate stories about people dying of cancer, no matter how graceful, noble, or beautiful. … I refuse to accept that I am dying; I prefer denial, anger, even desperation. … I resist the lure of dignity; I refuse to be graceful, beautiful, beloved.

[Robson, 2010, pp. 19, 27, 28]

Reactions to one's own mortality differ depending on developmental stage as well. In adulthood, from ages 25 to 65, terminally ill people worry about leaving something undone or abandoning family members, especially children.

One such adult was Randy Pausch, a 47-year-old professor and father of three young children. Ten months before he died of cancer in 2008, he delivered a famous last lecture, detailing his childhood dreams and saluting those who would continue his work. After advising his students to follow their own dreams, he concluded, "This talk is not for you, it's for my kids" (R. Pausch, 2007). Not surprisingly, that message was embraced by his wife, also in mid-adulthood, who wrote her own book titled *Dream New Dreams,* which deals with overcoming death by focusing on life (J. Pausch, 2012).

Attitudes about death are often irrational. Rationally, adults should work to change social factors that increase the risk of mortality—such as air pollution, junk foods, and unsafe transportation—and they should change their own life-shortening behaviours, such as smoking cigarettes, eating salty snacks, and having unsafe sex. Instead, many people react more strongly to events that rarely cause death, such as an avalanche, a mysterious poison, or a freak accident. For this reason, many more people are afraid of flying than of driving, when statistically more people are killed in Canada by motor vehicle collisions than die worldwide in airline crashes in a year (CBC News, 2013).

"For My Kids" Randy Pausch was a brilliant, innovative scientist who specialized in virtual reality research at Pittsburgh's Carnegie Mellon University. When he was diagnosed with terminal pancreatic cancer, he gave a talk titled "The Last Lecture: Really Achieving Your Childhood Dreams" that became famous worldwide. He devoted the final 10 months of his life to his family—his wife, Jai, and their children, Chloe, Dylan, and Logan.

ASSOCIATED PRESS

DEATH IN LATE ADULTHOOD In late adulthood, attitudes about death shift again. Anxiety decreases; hope rises (De Raedt et al., 2013). Life-threatening illnesses reduce life satisfaction more among the middle-aged than the elderly (Wurm et al., 2008). The irrational reactions of terror management theory are less prominent in late adulthood (Maxfield et al., 2007). Some older people are quite happy despite knowing that their remaining time is short.

This shift in attitudes is beneficial. Indeed, many developmentalists believe that one sign of mental health among older adults is acceptance of mortality and an increasing altruistic concern about those who will live on after them. As a result, older people write their wills, designate health care proxies, read scriptures, reconcile with estranged family members, and, in general, tie up all the loose ends that most young adults avoid (Kastenbaum, 2012). Sometimes middle-aged adults are troubled when their elderly parents allocate heirlooms, choose funeral music, or buy a burial plot, but all those actions might be developmentally appropriate toward the end of life.

Acceptance of death does not mean that the elderly give up on living. On the contrary, most try to maintain their health and independence. However, priorities

Same Situation, Far Apart: Death of a Holy Man Thousands attend the funeral of a religious leader, offering blessings and confirming their belief in life after death by doing so. That much is universal, but notice the many contrasts between the rituals for Catholic Archbishop Joseph Serge Miot and his vicar general Charles Benoit in Haiti *(left)* and the Buddhist monk Young Am in Korea *(right)*.

shift. In an intriguing series of studies (Carstensen, 2011), people were presented with the following scenario:

> Imagine that in carrying out the activities of everyday life, you find that you have half an hour of free time, with no pressing commitments. You have decided that you'd like to spend this time with another person. Assuming that the following three persons are available to you, with whom would you want to spend that time:
> ● a member of your immediate family
> ● the author of a book you have just read
> ● an acquaintance with whom you seem to have much in common?

Older adults, more than younger ones, choose the family member. The researchers explain that family becomes more important when death seems near. This is supported by a study of 329 people of various ages who had recently been diagnosed with cancer and a matched group of 170 people (of the same ages) who had no serious illness (Pinquart & Silbereisen, 2006). The most marked difference was between those with and without cancer, regardless of age (see Figure EP.3). Life-threatening illness, more common in late adulthood but not directly caused by age, seems to change attitudes about life, people, and death.

Would you spend a free half-hour with a family member, a book author, or an acquaintance?

Healthy people younger than 60
Healthy people age 60 or older
Young people with cancer
Older people with cancer

0   20   40   60   80   100
Percent choosing to spend time
with a family member

Source: Pinquart & Silbereisen, 2006.

FIGURE EP.3 **Turning to Family as Death Approaches** Both young and older people diagnosed with cancer (one-fourth of whom died within five years) were more likely to prefer to spend a free half-hour with a family member rather than with an unrelated person with whom they had a common interest. Among healthy people, there were significant age-related differences in choices.

Near-Death Experiences

Even coming close to death is often an occasion for hope. This is most obvious in what is called a *near-death experience,* in which a person almost dies but survives and reports having left his or her body and moved toward a bright white light while feeling peacefulness and joy. The following classic report is typical:

> I was in a coma for approximately a week. … I felt as though I were lifted right up, just as though I didn't have a physical body at all. A brilliant white light appeared. … The most wonderful feelings came over me—feelings of peace, tranquility, a vanishing of all worries.

> *[quoted in R. A. Moody, 1975, p. 56]*

Near-death experiences often include religious elements (angels have been seen, celestial music heard), and survivors often adopt a more spiritual, less materialistic view of life as a result (Vaillant, 2008). To some, near-death experiences prove that "Heaven is for real" (Burpo & Vincent, 2010). Most scientists are skeptical, claiming that "there is no evidence that what happens when a person really dies and 'stays dead' has any relationship to the experience reported by those who have recovered from a life-threatening, episode. In fact, it is difficult to imagine how there could ever be such evidence" (Kastenbaum, 2006, p. 448).

Nevertheless, a reviewer of near-death experiences is struck by the similarity of near-death experiences, and of religious beliefs about death itself, in many cultures. In every culture, although dying experience is varied, people tend to face similar realizations: (1) the limitations of social status, (2) the insignificance of material possessions, and (3) the narrowness of self-centredness (Greyson, 2009). Near-death experiences do this as well: Those who recall such moments seem more loving and hopeful than they were before.

KEY Points

- Since the mid-twentieth century, first-hand experience with death has become less common and therefore death less familiar. In the nineteenth century, everyone knew several people who died before age 40.

- Ancient cultures and current world religions have various customs about death, which help people live better lives as they respond to sorrow with hope.

- People react to death differently, depending on their developmental stage, with older adults less anxious than younger ones.

- Near-death experiences seem to make people more spiritual, less materialistic, and more appreciative of others.

Choices in Dying

Do you recoil at the thought of "choices in dying"? If so, you may be living in the wrong century. Every twenty-first-century death involves choices, beginning with risks taken or not. This is very apparent in accidents and most diseases. For example, heart disease and stroke, which accounted for 7 million and 6.2 million deaths respectively worldwide in 2011 (WHO, 2013c), involve a multitude of choices, not only in behaviours that increase risk but also after diagnosis—that is, whether medical treatment is provided and, if so, what, where, and when. Ideally, when confronted with a life-threatening illness, the patient decides. We now describe some of these choices.

A Good Death

People everywhere hope for a good death (Vogel, 2011), one that is

- at the end of a long life
- peaceful
- quick
- in familiar surroundings
- with family and friends present
- without pain, confusion, or discomfort.

Those six characteristics are accepted by almost everyone, but other aspects are less universal. Many would add that *control over circumstances* and *acceptance of the outcome* are also characteristic of a good death. However, it is important to note that this varies by culture and individuals. For example, some dying individuals willingly cede control to doctors or caregivers, and some fight every sign that death is near. Since individuals and cultures disagree on what is considered good, then the term "good death" can also be confusing (Bauer-Maglin & Perry, 2010).

Although aspects of a good death are culturally driven, a *bad death* (lacking the six characteristics above) is universally dreaded, particularly by the elderly. Many of them have known people who died in hospitals, semi-conscious, and alone. Sadly, even though most people would prefer to die at home (Canadian Institute for Health Information, 2007), about 65 percent of Canadian deaths in 2011 took place in hospitals (Statistics Canada, 2012i).

In some ways, modern medicine makes a good death more likely. The first item on the list has become the norm: Death usually occurs at the end of a long life. Younger people still get sick, but surgery, drugs, radiation, and rehabilitation typically mean that, in developed countries, the ill go to the hospital, are treated, and then return home.

In other ways, however, contemporary advances have made a bad death more likely. Instead of acceptance, which allows people to die peacefully at home with close friends, people attempt to fight death with surgery and drugs that prolong pain and confusion rather than restore health and comfort. Patients may become delirious or unconscious, unable to die in peace, and hospitals may exclude visitors at the most critical stage of patient illness.

The underlying problem may be medical care itself, so focused on life-saving that dying becomes victim to well-intentioned over-medicalization (Ashby, 2009). Fortunately, three factors that make a good death more likely have increased: honest conversation, the hospice, and palliative care.

HONEST CONVERSATION In about 1960, psychiatrist Elisabeth Kübler-Ross (1969, 1975) asked the administrator of a large Chicago hospital for permission to speak with dying patients. He informed her that no one in the hospital was dying! Eventually, she found a few terminally ill patients who, to everyone's surprise, wanted very much to talk.

From ongoing interviews, Kübler-Ross identified emotions experienced by dying people, which she divided into a sequence of five stages:

1. Denial ("I am not really dying.")
2. Anger ("I blame my doctors, or my family, or God for my death.")
3. Bargaining ("I will be good from now on if I can live.")
4. Depression ("I don't care about anything; nothing matters anymore.")
5. Acceptance ("I accept my death as part of life.")

Another set of stages of dying is based on Abraham Maslow's hierarchy of needs, discussed in Chapter 1 (Zalenski & Raspa, 2006):

1. Physiological needs (freedom from pain)
2. Safety (no abandonment)
3. Love and acceptance (from close family and friends)
4. Respect (from caregivers)
5. Self-actualization (appreciating one's unique past and present).

Maslow later suggested a possible sixth stage, *self-transcendence* (Koltko-Rivera, 2006), which emphasizes the acceptance of death.

Other researchers have *not* found sequential stages in dying people's approach to death. Remember the woman, cited earlier, who was dying of a sarcoma? She said that she would never accept death and that Kübler-Ross should have included desperation as a stage.

Many thanatologists find that the stages of denial, anger, and depression disappear and reappear, that bargaining is brief because it is fruitless, and that acceptance may never occur. Regarding Maslow, although all of his levels are important throughout the dying process, there is no set sequence.

Nevertheless, both lists remind caregivers that each dying person has emotions and needs that may be unlike those of another—or even unlike that same person's emotions and needs a few days or weeks earlier. Furthermore, a dying person's emotions may not be what family, medical personnel, and others might expect.

It is important for everyone—doctors, nurses, family, friends, and the patient—to know that a person is dying; then, care is more likely to improve rather than degrade (Lundquist et al., 2011). Unfortunately, even if a patient is terminally ill with incurable cancer, most doctors never ask what end-of-life care the patient wants. One study found that doctors discussed final care with their patients only 31 percent of the time. Those patients who did *not* have such a conversation (69 percent) experienced more pain and procedures, but not a longer life, than those who did discuss final care (Zhang et al., 2009).

As Kübler-Ross and others have discovered, most dying people want to spend time with loved ones and to talk honestly with medical and religious professionals. Human relationships are crucial: People continue to need each other (Planalp & Trost, 2008). Dying patients do not want to be cut off from daily life; they want to know what their relatives and friends are doing and how they are feeling.

However, avoid assumptions. Kübler-Ross also stressed that each person responds to death in his or her own way; some people do *not* want the whole truth, and some do *not* want many visitors. In some cultures, telling people they are dying is thought to destroy hope. Indeed, even maintaining human relationships via long, intimate conversations may be counter to certain religious beliefs, for instance, when the purpose of death is seen as relinquishing ties to this world (Baugher, 2008).

THE HOSPICE In 1950s London, England, Cecily Saunders opened the first modern **hospice,** where terminally ill people could spend their last days in comfort (Saunders, 1978). Thousands of other such places have opened in many nations, staffed by doctors, nurses, psychologists, social workers, clergy, music therapists, and so on who provide individualized care day and night. In addition, hundreds of thousands of hospice caregivers bring medication and care to dying people where they live, including in their home.

Hospice professionals relieve pain and discomfort, not only with drugs but also with massage, bathing, and so on. They avoid measures that merely delay death; their aim is to make dying easier. There are two principles of hospice care:

- Each patient's autonomy and decisions are respected. For example, pain medication is readily available, not on a strict schedule or at a minimal dosage.

- Family members and friends are counselled before the death, taught to provide care, and guided in mourning. Hospice personnel believe that the mourners' needs, both before and after the death, are as important as the needs of the patient.

Unfortunately, hospice care is far from universally available, even in wealthy nations, much less in developing ones (Kiernan, 2010). For example, hospice care is more common in England than in mainland Europe and more common in some Canadian provinces or territories than in others. Depending on their location, only 16 to 30 percent of Canadians who are dying have access to hospice services.

hospice
An institution or program in which terminally ill patients receive care to reduce suffering; family and friends of the dying are helped as well.

✦ **ESPECIALLY FOR Relatives of a Person Who Is Dying** Why would a healthy person want the attention of hospice caregivers? (see response, page 577) ➞

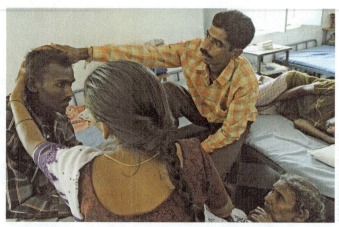

Same Situation, Far Apart: Getting Support People with amyotrophic lateral sclerosis (ALS), also referred to as Lou Gehrig's disease, require ongoing support, as this patient in Manitoba *(left)* is receiving, and often need hospice care, just as this man from India *(right)* is receiving. He is seen here with his family, in a Catholic hospice in Andhra Pradesh.

Financial challenges restrict the size and scope of hospice programs as well as access to them, especially for patients in remote or rural areas of Canada (Canadian Hospice Palliative Care Association [CHPCA], 2012). To date, only some Canadian provinces and territories have acknowledged that hospice palliative care is a core health service under their health plans. Other provinces or territories have placed this form of care within home care and other health service budgets. Such programs are more vulnerable to budget reductions (CHPCA, 2012). As a result, the costs of hospices are often shouldered by private donors, with family members also paying a portion of the costs.

Home hospice care is less expensive than care in a separate institution, but caregivers are needed, day and night. Hospice nurses often train family members to offer care, but not everyone has such family members available. In 2003, 23 percent of Canadians reported that they were caregivers for a family member or friend in the last year. This caregiving had certain negative consequences for the caregivers, including using up their personal savings (41 percent) and missing at least one month of work (22 percent). Other negative effects were reported in 2006, such as strains on mental health (41 percent) and physical health (38 percent). Some experts have estimated that in 2009 the replacement costs for such unpaid caregiving in Canada ranged between 25 and 26 billion dollars (CHPCA, 2012).

palliative care
Care designed not to treat an illness but to provide physical and emotional comfort to the patient and support and guidance to his or her family.

double effect
A situation in which an action (such as administering opiates) has both a positive effect (relieving a terminally ill person's pain) and a negative effect (hastening death by suppressing respiration).

PALLIATIVE CARE The same "bad death" conditions that inspired the hospice movement have led to **palliative care,** a medical specialty that focuses on the relief of pain and suffering, as well as emotional support to the patient and his or her family. Often powerful painkillers are given to the patient. These painkillers were once prescribed sparingly because of their addictive properties; however, palliative approaches came to view the risk of drug addiction as secondary to the greater goal of freedom from pain for the dying.

Morphine and other opiates do, however, have a **double effect:** They relieve pain (a positive effect), but they also slow down respiration (a negative effect). A painkiller that reduces both pain and breathing is considered acceptable in law, ethics, and medical practice. In England, for instance, although it is illegal to cause the death of a terminally ill patient (even one who repeatedly asks to die), it is legal to prescribe drugs that have a double effect. One-third of all English deaths include such drugs.

Deciding When Death Occurs

In earlier times, death occurred when an organ shut down, but not now. Breathing continues with respirators, stopped hearts are restarted, stomach tubes provide calories, and medication fights pneumonia. At what point, if ever, should such measures be halted so that death will occur?

Ethical dilemmas arise in almost every life-threatening condition. Treatments are avoided, started, or stopped, prolonging life, or hastening dying. This has fostered impassioned arguments about ethics, both among nations (evidenced by radically different laws) and within nations. Family members, religious advisers, doctors, and lawyers disagree among themselves and with one another (Ball, 2012; Engelhardt, 2012; Prado, 2008).

Historically, death was determined by listening to a person's heart: No heartbeat meant death. To make sure, a feather was put to the person's nose to detect respiration—a person who did not exhale was pronounced dead. Very rarely, but widely publicized when it happened, a person was declared dead when in fact he or she was alive.

Modern medicine has changed that: If an individual is still alive but not capable of breathing on his or her own, respirators can pump air into the lungs and life can continue. Many other life-support measures and medical interventions now circumvent the diseases and organ failures that once caused death. Checking breathing with feathers is a curiosity, thankfully never used today. But how can we know for sure when death has occurred?

In the late 1970s, a group of Harvard physicians concluded that when brain waves ceased, death occurred. This definition is now used worldwide (Wijdicks et al., 2010). However, many doctors now suggest that death can occur even if primitive brain waves continue (Kellehear, 2008; Truog, 2007) (see Table EP.2).

Some researchers attempt to distinguish between people who are in a permanent vegetative state (and thus will never regain the ability to think) and those who are in a coma but could recover. Many scientists seek to define death more precisely than was possible even 30 years ago. One crucial factor is whether the person could ever again be expected to breathe without a respirator, but that is hard to guarantee if "ever again" includes the distant future.

In 2008, the American Academy of Neurology gathered experts to conduct a meta-analysis of all the recently published studies regarding end-of-life brain functioning. They found 38 empirical articles. Two experts independently read each one, noting what measures were used to determine death and how much time was required between lack of brain function and the pronouncement of a person's death. They reached no consensus. Only two indicators of death were confirmed: Dead people no longer breathe spontaneously, and their eyes no longer respond to pain.

There is no definitive, instant test to indicate when a person is brain-dead (Wijdicks et al., 2010). Thus, family members may spend weeks, sometimes months or years, hoping for life long after medical experts believe no recovery is possible.

In October 2013, the Supreme Court of Canada dismissed an appeal by two Toronto doctors who wanted to stop treatment of a patient with severe brain damage, Hassan Rasouli, aged 61. Rasouli had developed meningitis and suffered brain damage after undergoing surgery to remove a brain tumour in 2010. He fell into a coma and was put on a ventilator. Parichehr Salasel, Rasouli's wife and a doctor herself, was his designated decision maker, and she refused permission to take him off the ventilator. She and her daughters maintained that Rasouli was in a "minimally conscious state"—that he did respond to stimulation and was capable of communicating with them.

Supreme Court Chief Justice Beverly McLachlin wrote in the majority opinion on the case, "By removing medical services that are keeping a patient alive,

RESPONSE FOR Relatives of a Person Who Is Dying (from page 575) Death affects the entire family, including children and grandchildren. I (Susan) learned this myself when my mother was dying. A hospice nurse not only gave her pain medication but also counselled me. At the nurse's suggestion, I asked for forgiveness. My mother indicated that there was nothing to forgive. We both felt a peace that would have eluded us without hospice care. ●

TABLE EP.2 Dead or Not? Yes, No, and Maybe

Brain death: Prolonged cessation of all brain activity with complete absence of voluntary movements; no spontaneous breathing; no response to pain, noise, and other stimuli. Brain waves have ceased; the electroencephalogram is flat; *the person is dead.*

Locked-in syndrome: The person cannot move, except for the eyes, but normal brain waves are still apparent; *the person is not dead.*

Coma: A state of deep unconsciousness from which the person cannot be aroused. Some people awaken spontaneously from a coma; others enter a vegetative state; *the person is not yet dead.*

Vegetative state: A state of deep unconsciousness in which all cognitive functions are absent, although eyes may open, sounds may be emitted, and breathing may continue; *the person is not yet dead.* The vegetative state can be *transient, persistent,* or *permanent.* No one has ever recovered after two years; most who recover (about 15 percent) improve within three weeks (Preston & Kelly, 2006). After sufficient time has elapsed, the person may, effectively, be dead, although exactly how many days that requires is not yet determined (Wijdicks et al., 2010).

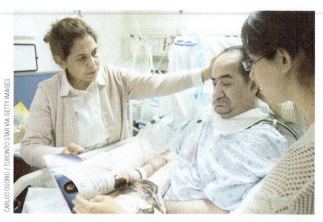

Life Support Issues Hassan Rasouli, pictured here with his wife *(left)* and daughter *(right)* in Sunnybrook Hospital, Toronto, developed an infection after surgery in 2010 and slipped into a coma. His doctors wanted to take him off life support, but his family refused. The case went to the Supreme Court of Canada, which ruled that doctors cannot unilaterally choose to end life support services for Rasouli.

passive euthanasia
A situation in which a seriously ill person is allowed to die naturally, through the cessation of medical intervention.

DNR (do not resuscitate) order
A written order from a physician (sometimes initiated by a patient's advance directive or by a health care proxy's request) that no attempt should be made to revive a patient if he or she suffers cardiac or respiratory arrest.

active euthanasia
A situation in which someone takes action to bring about another person's death, with the intention of ending that person's suffering.

physician-assisted suicide
A form of active euthanasia in which a doctor provides the means for someone to end his or her own life.

withdrawal of life support impacts patient autonomy in the most fundamental way." One legal expert said it appeared that the Court wanted to avoid giving doctors the right to make such decisions on their own, against the wishes of the patient's family (Mulholland, 2013).

ETHICAL QUANDARIES As you have read, death can be postponed with antibiotics and other drugs, surgery, respirators, and stomach tubes, which is partly why the average person today lives twice as long as the average person did a century ago. Yet many elderly people fear being kept alive too long when death is near. Their concerns raise ethical questions—especially when they are considering measures such as suicide and euthanasia.

In **passive euthanasia**, a person nearing death is simply allowed to die in due course. The chart of a patient may include a **DNR (do not resuscitate) order,** which instructs the medical staff not to restore breathing or restart the heart if breathing or pulsating stops. A DNR usually reflects the expressed wishes of the patient or health care proxy (discussed below).

Passive euthanasia is legal everywhere, but many emergency personnel start artificial respiration and stimulate hearts without taking time to read a person's chart to ascertain whether DNR has been chosen. Then the issue becomes more complex because removing life support may be considered active euthanasia.

Active euthanasia is deliberately doing something to cause a person's death, such as turning off a respirator before a person has been declared brain-dead or giving the person a lethal drug. Some physicians perform active euthanasia when confronted with three conditions: (1) suffering they cannot relieve, (2) illness they cannot cure, and (3) a patient who wants to die. Active euthanasia is legal under some circumstances in the Netherlands, Belgium, Luxembourg, and Switzerland, but it is illegal (yet rarely prosecuted) elsewhere.

Many people see a major moral distinction between active and passive euthanasia, although the final result is the same. A survey of physicians in the United States found that while a majority (69 percent) objected to active euthanasia, few (18 percent) objected to sedation that had a double effect. Even fewer (5 percent) objected to withdrawing life support when a patient was brain-dead (Curlin et al., 2008). A similar survey in seven other nations found wide variations within and among them, with some physicians saying they would never perform active euthanasia and others reporting they had done so (Löfmark et al., 2008).

In Canada, a 2013 survey carried out for LifeCanada by the Environics Research Group found that 55 percent of Canadians were in favour of legalizing active euthanasia compared with 40 percent who opposed such a measure. However, only 18 percent of those surveyed "strongly" supported euthanasia; the majority of those in favour said they "somewhat" supported it. Support was strongest in Quebec and among men; opposition was strongest among older Canadians, people without a high school education, and those in the lowest income bracket (Environics, 2013).

WHEN DOCTORS HELP PEOPLE DIE Between passive and active euthanasia is another end-of-life option: Someone may provide the means for an alert patient to end his or her own life. Some people advocate **physician-assisted suicide,** whereby a doctor provides lethal medication that a patient can then swallow in order to die. Acceptance of physician-assisted suicide varies markedly by culture, religion, education, and local values (Prado, 2008; Verbakel & Jaspers, 2010).

The Netherlands first permitted active euthanasia and physician-assisted suicide in 1980 and refined the law in 2002. The patient must be clear and aware in making the request, and the goal is to halt "unbearable suffering" (Buiting et al., 2009). Consequently, the physician's first response is to make the suffering bearable, usually by increasing or changing medication. However a qualitative analysis found that "fatigue, pain, decline, negative feelings, loss of self, fear of future suffering, dependency, loss of autonomy, being worn out, being a burden, loneliness, loss of all that makes life worth living, hopelessness, pointlessness, and being tired of living were constituent elements of unbearable suffering" (Dees et al., 2011, p. 727). Obviously, medication cannot alleviate all those.

Two other nations near the Netherlands—Belgium and Luxembourg—passed similar laws. Switzerland, on the other hand, has not passed regulations as to when doctors may, and may not, hasten death; however, it has explicitly declined to prosecute doctors who do so.

Voters in the state of Oregon approved physician-assisted suicide (but not other forms of active euthanasia) in 1994 and again in 1997, explicitly asserting that such deaths should be called "death with dignity," not suicide. The first such legal deaths occurred in 1998.

Oregon's law requires the following:

- The dying person must be an adult and an Oregon resident.
- The dying person must request the lethal drugs twice orally and once in writing.
- Fifteen days must elapse between the first request and the prescription.
- Two physicians must confirm that the person is terminally ill, has less than six months to live, and is competent (i.e., not mentally impaired or depressed).

The law also requires record-keeping and annual reporting.

Between 1998 and 2013, more than 190 000 people in Oregon died; 752 of those obtained prescriptions for lethal drugs and used them to die. As Table EP.3 shows, Oregon residents requested the drugs primarily for psychological, not biological, reasons—they were more concerned about their autonomy than their pain.

In 2013 alone, 122 Oregonians obtained lethal prescriptions, and 63 used them to die. Most of the rest died naturally, but some were still alive at the end of that year and thought they might use the drug in the future (according to data from previous years, about 10 percent of the people who obtain the prescription save it to use in the following year) (Oregon Public Health Division, 2014).

In Canada, the United Kingdom, Australia, and New Zealand, suicide is legal, but voluntary euthanasia and assisted suicide are not. There have been two high-profile Canadian court cases regarding the "right to die," the first involving Sue Rodriguez and the second involving Gloria Taylor. Both women suffered from amyotrophic lateral sclerosis (ALS). ALS eventually paralyzes muscles throughout the body, causing chronic pain and eventually death, but without affecting cognitive functioning.

In her 1993 case before the Supreme Court of Canada, Sue Rodriguez cited section 241(b) of the Canadian Charter of Rights and Freedoms, arguing that she had a right to "life, liberty, and security of the person." She interpreted this as her right to decide how, when, and under what circumstances she would die. Although the Supreme Court ruled against her, it did so by the narrowest of margins: the vote was five to four.

Almost 20 years later, Gloria Taylor also challenged the law against assisted suicide. Being unsuccessful in Canada, she ended up travelling to Switzerland, where a doctor aided her in committing suicide.

In the LifeCanada survey mentioned above, Canadians were almost twice as likely to support physician-assisted suicide as to oppose it (63 percent versus 32 percent),

TABLE EP.3 Oregon Residents' Reasons for Requesting Physician Assistance in Dying, 1998–2013

Reason	Patients Giving Reason (%)
Loss of autonomy	91
Less able to enjoy life	89
Loss of dignity	82
Loss of control over body	52
Burden on others	39
Pain	23

Source: Oregon Public Health Division, 2014.

Physician-Assisted Suicide
Dr. Donald Low was a Canadian micro-biologist known for his role in battling the outbreak of severe acute respiratory syndrome (SARS) in Toronto in 2003. He died September 18, 2013, from a brain tumour. Eight days before his death, he created a YouTube video in which he made an impassioned plea to legalize physician-assisted suicide for terminally ill patients in Canada. He said, "I'm going to die, but what worries me is how I'm going to die … I wish [assisted suicide opponents] could live in my body for 24 hours …" (Low, 2013).

but less than a third of those surveyed (29 percent) expressed strong support for such a law. The highest level of support for physician-assisted suicide was in British Columbia, where the Supreme Court had recently struck down a law against doctor-assisted deaths (Environics, 2013).

Some of the arguments raised in favour of legalizing euthanasia and assisted suicide are:

- each person's right to autonomy and freedom of choice
- the medical limitations on alleviating a patient's pain and suffering
- section 15 of the Canadian Charter of Rights and Freedoms, which has been interpreted to allow able-bodied people, but not those with physical limitations, to commit suicide.

Arguments against this legalization include:

- the belief that there is a fundamental societal value for the respect of life, and that killing another human being is intrinsically wrong
- the fear that legalizing euthanasia or assisted suicide may result in abuse of the law, and may make some people—for example, the disabled and very old—vulnerable to the "decision makers" (this is known as the "slippery slope" argument) (see Opposing Perspectives)
- the corresponding fear that this law may limit potential medical advances and research to improve care, since doctors may consider euthanasia an easier and quicker solution than healing or palliative care (Butler et al., 2013).

At present, it is difficult to tell how the law will evolve in Canada. As noted above, in October 2013, the British Columbia Court of Appeals overturned the earlier decision by the provincial Supreme Court that declared the law against physician-assisted suicide unconstitutional. The case appears to be headed once again to the Supreme Court of Canada; there are conflicting opinions over what the Court's decision might be this time around.

ADVANCE DIRECTIVES Many people hope to increase personal choice about death, opting for advance directives—a person's instructions regarding end-of-life medical care, written before such care is needed.

Some people try to exert control over their dying by creating a living will and/or assigning a health care proxy. Recognizing that individuals differ dramatically on specifics, hospitals and hospices strongly recommend both of these. Nonetheless, most people resist: A study of cancer patients in a leading hospital found that only 16 percent had living wills and only 48 percent had designated a proxy (Halpern et al., 2011).

A **living will** indicates what sort of medical intervention a person wants or does not want in the event that he or she becomes unable to express those preferences. Of course, if the person is conscious and lucid, hospital personnel ask about each specific procedure, often requiring written consent before surgery. The patient can override any instructions that he or she included in the living will. The reason a person might want to override earlier wishes is that living wills include phrases such as "incurable," "reasonable chance of recovery," and "extraordinary measures"; it is difficult to know what those phrases mean until a specific issue arises. Doctors and family members also disagree about what is "extraordinary" or "reasonable."

Some people designate a **health care proxy,** another person to make medical decisions for them if they become unable to do so. That seems logical, but

living will
A document that indicates what medical intervention an individual prefers if he or she is not conscious when a decision must be made.

health care proxy
A person chosen by an individual to make medical decisions if that individual becomes unable to do so.

OPPOSING PERSPECTIVES

The "Right to Die" or a "Slippery Slope"?

Many people fear that legalizing euthanasia or physician-assisted suicide will create a **slippery slope**—that is, they fear that hastening death at the request of the dying will cause society to slide toward killing people who are not ready to die—especially the disabled, the old, minorities, and the economically disadvantaged.

The 2002 revision of the Netherlands law allows euthanasia not only when a person is terminally ill but also when a person is chronically ill and in pain. Is this evidence of a slide? Some people think so, especially those who believe that God alone decides the moment of death, and that anyone who interferes is defying God.

An alternative opinion is expressed by this cancer specialist:

> To be forced to continue living a life that one deems intolerable when there are doctors who are willing either to end one's life or to assist one in ending one's own life is an unspeakable violation of an individual's freedom to live—and to die—as he or she sees fit. Those who would deny patients a legal right to euthanasia or assisted suicide typically appeal to two arguments: a "slippery slope" argument, and an argument about the dangers of abuse. Both are scare tactics, the rhetorical force of which exceeds their logical strength.
>
> *[Benatar, 2011, p. 206]*

A highly publicized Canadian case from the 1990s clearly illustrates the dangers inherent in the slippery slope, of sliding from assisting those who have definitely stated that they wish to die to making that decision for others who have not expressed any such desire.

Twelve-year-old Tracy Latimer lived with her parents on a Saskatchewan farm and suffered from a rare form of cerebral palsy. As a result, she had been in pain from the day of her birth. Although she was not terminally ill, Tracy was paraplegic, unable to walk or talk or feed herself, and suffered several seizures a day. She was scheduled to undergo hip surgery that would cause more pain and necessitate more surgery in the future.

On October 24, 1993, Tracy's father, Robert, placed her in the cab of his pickup truck, ran a hose from the tail pipe into the cab, and turned on the engine. Tracy died from carbon monoxide poisoning, and Robert Latimer was charged with murder. At trial, Latimer defended himself by stating that his only wish was to put Tracy out of her pain. He was convicted of second-degree murder and sentenced to 10 years in prison.

When Latimer appealed, the jury again convicted him but recommended a lighter sentence; the judge reduced his sentence to two years. The Crown appealed and the case eventually went to the Supreme Court of Canada, which affirmed both the original verdict and the 10-year sentence. In its decision, the Court stated that despite the extenuating circumstances, the 10-year prison sentence was not "cruel and unusual" for second-degree murder and therefore did not violate section 12 of the Charter of Rights and Freedoms (Butler et al., 2013).

The case clearly divided public opinion in Canada. Human rights advocates applauded the Supreme Court decision for protecting the rights of the disabled. However, a poll taken in 1999 showed that 73 percent of Canadians believed Latimer acted out of compassion over his daughter's suffering and should have received a lighter sentence (Ipsos, 1999).

Whatever one's opinion may be on this case, Tracy Latimer's death still informs the right-to-die debate in Canada.

---

unfortunately neither a living will nor a health care proxy guarantees that medical care will be exactly what a person would choose. For one thing, designated proxies often find it difficult to allow a loved one to die if there is any chance of recovery.

A larger problem is that few people—experts included—understand the risks, benefits, and alternatives to every medical procedure. That makes it difficult to decide for oneself, much less for a family member, exactly when the risks outweigh the benefits. Even people who have been married for years do not necessarily know their partner's wishes; husbands are more likely than wives to believe they know, but are less likely to be accurate (Zettel-Watson et al., 2008). In addition, family members may be on opposite sides when it comes to specifics.

A heartbreaking example occurred in the case of a Florida woman named Theresa (Terri) Schiavo. Terri was 26 years old when her heart suddenly stopped. Emergency personnel restarted it, but she fell into a deep coma. Like almost everyone her age, Terri had no advance directives. A court designated Michael, her husband of six years, as her health care proxy.

slippery slope
The argument that a given action will start a chain of events that will culminate in an undesirable outcome.

✦ **ESPECIALLY FOR People Without Advance Directives** Why do very few young adults have advance directives? (see response, page 582) ➞

RESPONSE FOR People Without Advance Directives (from page 581) Young adults usually do not have trouble doing future-oriented things such as getting a tetanus shot or enrolling in a pension plan, yet they tend to avoid thinking realistically about their own deaths. This attitude is emotional, not rational; the actual task of preparing advance directives is easy (the forms can be downloaded; no lawyer is needed). •

Michael attempted many measures to bring back his wife, but after 11 years he accepted her doctors' repeated diagnosis: Terri was in a persistent vegetative state. He petitioned to have her feeding tube removed. The court agreed, noting the testimony of witnesses who said that Terri had told them that she never wanted to be on life support. Terri's parents appealed the decision, but lost. They then pleaded with the public.

The Florida legislature responded, passing a law that required that the tube be reinserted. After three more years of legal wrangling, the U.S. Supreme Court ruled that the lower courts were correct. Then the U.S. Congress passed a law requiring that artificial feeding be continued, but that law was overturned as unconstitutional. The stomach tube was removed, and Terri died on March 31, 2005—although some maintained that she had really died 15 years earlier.

Partly because of the conflicts among family members, and between appointed judges and elected politicians, Terri's case caught media attention. Every North American newspaper and television station was following the case, inspiring vigils and protests. Lost in that blitz, though, are the thousands of other mothers and fathers, husbands and wives, sons and daughters, judges and politicians, doctors and nurses who struggle less publicly with similar issues.

Advance directives are intended to help caregivers avoid conflicts, but in any case, honest conversation is needed long before a crisis occurs (Sabatino, 2010). Dying is hard to talk about, much less accept. Thanatologists wish it were otherwise.

KEY Points

- Modern medicine has made some aspects of a good death more likely but has also added complexities, including the possibility of physician action to hasten death.
- Honest conversation, hospice care, and palliative medicine have all made dying easier than when almost everyone died alone, in hospitals.
- Determining when death has occurred, or when a dying person cannot recover, is not always simple.
- Living wills and health care proxies can prevent some family conflicts and help people die as they wish.

Affirmation of Life

Grief and mourning are part of living. Humans need relationships with many others in order to survive and thrive, but every person who reaches adulthood experiences the death of someone they know. Grief can turn into depression or can become a reason to live life more deeply.

Grief

grief
The deep sorrow that people feel at the death of another. Grief is personal and unpredictable.

Grief is the powerful sorrow that an individual feels at the death of another. It is a highly personal emotion, an anguish that overtakes daily life.

NORMAL GRIEF The first thing to understand about grief is that it is a normal human emotion, even when it leads to unusual actions and thoughts. Grief is manifest in uncontrollable crying, sleeplessness, and irrational and delusional thoughts—the "magical thinking" Joan Didion described after her husband's death:

Grief has no distance. Grief comes in waves, paroxysms, sudden apprehensions that weaken the knees and blind the eyes and obliterate the dailiness of life. … I see now that my insistence on spending that first night alone was more complicated than it seemed, a primitive instinct. … There was a level on which I believed that what had happened remained reversible. That is why I needed to be alone. … I needed to be alone so that he could come back. This was the beginning of my year of magical thinking.

[Didion, 2005, pp. 27, 32, 33]

Loneliness, denial, anger, and sorrow come in rapid waves after a loved one's death, and the normal human needs—to sleep, to eat—temporarily give way. Grief usually hits hardest in the first week after death and then lingers—with much dependent on mourning, soon to be discussed.

COMPLICATED GRIEF Sometimes grief takes a form that is not typical (Qualls & Kasl-Godley, 2010; van der Houwen et al., 2010). About 10 percent of all mourners experience what is known as **complicated grief,** a type of grief that impedes the person's future life (Neimeyer & Currier, 2009).

I saw this type of grief in my father. After my mother died, my brother and I tried to get him involved in activities that he could not participate in when our mother was alive and bedridden, to no avail. He became indifferent, and his self-care diminished. He died five months after my mother. Although his death was unexpected, it is not uncommon for widows and widowers to die within a year of losing their spouse if they have been married for a long time.

Another type of grief is is called **absent grief,** when a bereaved person does not seem to grieve. This may be a first reaction, as some people cannot face the reality of the death at first, but if it continues, absent grief can trigger physical or psychological symptoms—for instance, trouble breathing or walking, sudden panic attacks, or depression. If such disabilities appear for no reason, the underlying cause might be grief that was never expressed.

Absent grief may be more common in modern society than it was earlier. People who live and work where others may not know about their personal lives lack a sense of community or recognized customs to help them grieve. Indeed, for workers at large corporations or students in universities, grief becomes "an unwelcome intrusion (or violent intercession) into the normal efficient running of everyday life" (M. Anderson, 2001, p. 141). This leads to isolation—exactly the opposite of what bereaved people need.

Modern life also increases the incidence of **disenfranchised grief,** wherein the bereaved are not allowed to mourn publicly because of cultural customs or social restrictions. For instance, typically, only a current spouse or close blood relative decides on funeral arrangements, disposal of the body, and other matters. This may result in "gagged grief and beleaguered bereavement" for others who feel a powerful emotion but cannot express it (L. Green & Grant, 2008, p. 275). The deceased's unmarried lover, a divorced spouse, young children, and close friends at work may be excluded (perhaps by the relatives, either deliberately or through ignorance) from saying goodbye to the dying person, viewing the corpse, or participating in the aftermath of death. Parents may grieve the loss of a fetus or newborn, but others may dismiss their sorrow, saying, "You never knew that child; you can have another."

Another possible complication is **incomplete grief.** Murders and suicides often trigger police investigations and press reports, which interfere with the grief process. An autopsy undercuts grieving, particularly if it delays or threatens cultural or religious practices associated with the afterlife of the deceased. In addition, the inability to recover a body, as happens for soldiers who are missing in action or victims of a major flood or fire, may not allow grief to be expressed and then to dissipate.

Kathleen's STORY

complicated grief
A type of grief that impedes a person's future life, usually because the person clings to sorrow or is buffeted by contradictory emotions.

absent grief
A situation in which mourners do not grieve, either because other people do not allow grief to be expressed or because the mourners do not allow themselves to feel sadness.

disenfranchised grief
A situation in which certain people, although they are bereaved, are prevented from mourning publicly by cultural customs or social restrictions.

incomplete grief
A situation in which circumstances, such as a police investigation or an autopsy, interfere with the process of grieving.

PAUL CHIAASSON / CP IMAGES

Protecting the Survivors On the 20th anniversary of the killing rampage by a lone gunman of 14 women at Montreal's École polytechnique engineering school, a bouquet of 14 white roses is placed by the commemorative plaque. Thirteen other people were also wounded.

mourning
The ceremonies and behaviours that a religion or culture prescribes for people to employ in expressing their bereavement after a death.

Saying Goodbye At this Roman Catholic burial in Mbongolwane, South Africa, friends and neighbours gather to honour the dead person and to comfort his or her family members.

Sometimes events interrupt the responses of the community, for example, when a person dies on a major holiday, immediately after another death or disaster, or during wartime. In these cases, it is harder for the survivors to grieve because their social network is preoccupied with the larger event. For example, one widow whose husband died of cancer on September 10, 2001, complained, "People who attended the funeral talked only about the terrorist attack of September 11, and my husband wasn't given the respect he deserved" (quoted in Schachter, 2003, p. 20). Although she expressed concern for her husband, it is apparent that she herself needed sympathy.

Mourning

Grief splinters people into jumbled pieces, making them vulnerable. Mourning reassembles them, making them whole again and able to rejoin the larger community. To be more specific, **mourning** is the public and ritualistic expression of bereavement, the ceremonies and behaviours that a religion or culture prescribes to honour the dead. Some mourning rituals were described earlier in the chapter. Here we focus on the purposes of mourning.

HOW MOURNING HELPS Mourning customs are designed to move grief from loss toward reaffirmation (Harlow, 2005). Eulogies that emphasize the dead person's good qualities, and family and friends who attend wakes, funerals, or memorial services to honour the dead and comfort the survivors, are part of the reaffirmation process. If the deceased was a public figure, mourners may include thousands, even millions. They express their sorrow to one another, weep as they watch funerals on television, and pledge to affirm the best of the deceased.

© DAVID LARSEN / AFRICANPICTURES.NET / THE IMAGE WORKS

One function of mourning is to allow expression of grief publicly and thus limit acute personal grief. Examples include the Jewish custom of sitting shiva at home for a week, the three days of active sorrow among some Muslim groups, or 10 days of ceremonies beginning at the next full moon following a death in Hinduism. Memories often return on the anniversary of a death, so many cultures include annual rituals such as visiting a grave or lighting a candle.

For many people who are unaffiliated with a religious institution, funeral services or observances have been replaced with social gatherings or celebrations of life that have less traditional structures. Whatever one's custom or ideology, it remains important that people are able to mourn publicly and openly in the company of family, friends, or community. A deficit of mourning may undercut survivors' ability to respond to their loss in a healthful way.

SEEKING MEANING As you may remember, denial and anger appear first on Kübler-Ross's list of reactions to death; ideally, people eventually move on to acceptance. The need to find meaning in death may be crucial to the reaffirmation that follows grief. In some cases, this search starts with preserving memories: Displaying photographs and personal effects and telling anecdotes about the dead person are central to many memorial services.

Mourners may also be helped by strangers who have experienced a similar loss, especially when friends are unlikely to understand. This explains why groups have been organized for parents of murdered children, mothers whose adolescents were killed by drunk drivers, families and friends of people who committed suicide, children and teens who have experienced the death of a parent, sibling, or close friend, and so on.

Mourners sometimes want the broader community to know about a death. Obituaries are found in every major newspaper and on funeral homes' websites, and spontaneous memorials (graffiti, murals, stuffed animals, flowers) appear in public spaces, such as a spot on a roadside where a fatal crash occurred. This practice was once rare and discouraged, but no longer. Authorities realize that public commemoration aids grief and mourning, building community: Public markers of bouquets and so on are dismantled only when flowers fade and complaints are lodged after time has passed (Dickinson & Hoffmann, 2010).

Organizations devoted to causes such as fighting cancer and banning handguns find their most dedicated supporters among people who have lost a loved one to that particular circumstance. Often when someone dies, the close family designates a charity that is somehow connected to the deceased, inviting other mourners to make contributions.

In certain circumstances, to make a death meaningful, mourning may lead to public protest. For instance, when a truck killed a 9-year-old in Germany, neighbours and strangers blocked the street for days until new safeguards were installed. When a pregnant cyclist was killed by a turning truck in Toronto, other cyclists erected a "ghost bike," organized a memorial "ghost ride," and signed a petition urging the federal government to make truck side guards mandatory (CBC News, 2011b; Rulfs, 2011).

The impulse to seek meaning is not always constructive. A common impulse after death is for the survivors to assess blame—for medical measures not taken, laws not enforced, unhealthy habits not changed. The bereaved sometimes blame the dead person, sometimes themselves, and sometimes others. A desire for revenge or redress also sometimes arises, even leading to long-standing family feuds or legal disputes.

In general, the normal grief reaction is intense and irrational at first, but it gradually eases as time, social support, and traditions help with the initial outpouring of

Memorial Praying beside the ghost bike at the spot where an 18-wheeler killed cyclist Kathryn Rickson may help these two family members grieve and then recover. Grief is much less likely to destroy the survivors when markers or rituals are observed.

emotion and then with the search for meaning and reaffirmation. The individual may engage in *grief work,* experiencing and expressing strong emotions and then moving toward wholeness, which includes recognizing the larger story of human life and death.

Diversity of Reactions

Bereaved people depend on the customs and attitudes of their community, as well as on their social network, to guide them through their irrational thoughts and grief. Particulars depend on the specific culture. For example, mourners who keep the dead person's possessions, talk to the deceased, and frequently review memories are notably *less* well-adjusted 18 months after the death if they live in the United States but are *better* adjusted if they live in China. This country difference may be reflective of how Chinese social supports work. Grieving Chinese are supported and encouraged to outwardly show signs of grief and continued bonding with the deceased in the early months of bereavement. This social network and grieving process may then be a buffer for long-term distress among Chinese individuals (Lalande & Bonanno, 2006).

LEGACY OF EARLIER LOSS Childhood experiences also affect bereavement. A child who lost her parents might be more distraught decades later when someone else dies. Attachment history may also be important (Hansson & Stroebe, 2007). Older adults who were securely attached may be more likely to experience normal grief; those whose attachment was insecure-avoidant may have absent grief; and those who were insecure-resistant may become stuck, unable to find meaning in death and thus unable to reaffirm their own lives.

Reaffirmation does not mean forgetting the dead person; many *continuing bonds* are evident years after death (Stroebe et al., 2010). Although in Western nations having hallucinations of the dead person (seeing ghosts, hearing voices) is a sign of complicated grief, continuing bonds such as thinking about memories and seeing the dead person as a role model are linked to greater personal growth (Field & Filanosky, 2009). Often survivors write letters to the deceased person, or talk to them, or consider events—a sunrise, a butterfly, a rainstorm—as messages of comfort from the dead person.

A VIEW FROM SCIENCE

Making Meaning After a Death

Earlier studies overestimated the frequency of pathological grief. For obvious reasons, scientists usually began research on mourning with mourners—that is, with people who recently experienced the death of a loved one. They did not analyze mourners' personalities before the death, yet we now know that personality traits powerfully affect grief (Boyraz, 2012).

Furthermore, psychiatrists often studied people who needed psychological help, again for obvious reasons. Some patients experienced absent grief; others felt disenfranchised grief; some were overcome by unremitting sadness many months after the loss; still others could not find meaning in a violent, sudden, unexpected death. All these people consulted therapists, who often helped them and described the problems and the solutions.

Such mourners are *not* typical. Almost everyone experiences several deaths over a lifetime—of parents and grandparents, of a spouse or close friend. Most feel sadness at first but then resume their customary activities, functioning as well a few months later as they did before. Only a small subset, about 10 to 15 percent, exhibit extreme or complicated grief (Bonanno & Lilienfeld, 2008).

The variety of grief reactions was evident in a qualitative study in New Brunswick of 28 older Canadian widows (van den Hoonaard, 2002). The study explored the social meaning of widowhood and attitudes regarding future relationships from the perspective of women between the ages of 53 to 87 who had been widowed in the previous five years.

The majority of these women did not want to remarry. Many felt that they had already had the best possible husband. As had been found in a similar study of 319 widows and widowers in Detroit (Boerner et al., 2004, 2005), 15 of the 28 widows in New Brunswick had idealized the image of their husbands. One even claimed that her husband had been the "perfect man." This idealization of a past marriage is a normal phenomenon that other research finds connected to psychological health, not pathology (O'Rourke et al., 2010b).

Other New Brunswick widows did not wish to remarry because they did not want to suffer through the loss of another husband. Also, since many of these women were more likely to have been involved in "traditional" marriages (e.g., where the wife was responsible for household chores) in which they compromised their own priorities or scheduled their lives according to the wishes of their spouses, they did not want to involve themselves in a similar relationship.

Although many of the widows did not want to remarry, this did not mean that they wished to avoid social relationships with men. On the contrary, some wanted male companionship that was physical but not intimate—someone with whom they could go out to dinner, take dance classes, and so on.

The author of the New Brunswick study also interviewed 21 older widowers. Interestingly, all the men who participated were remarried widowers, whereas none of the widows had remarried at the time of the study. Like women, men had been concerned about entering a new relationship; they had worried about getting "trapped" by a new spouse or losing control in the relationship. However, men appeared to assume that it was important to re-partner and not to "wallow in grief." For women, re-partnering was not a priority.

Studies such as these emphasize the importance of better understanding how individuals make social meaning of their world after a significant other has passed away. Although the sample of widows and widowers was small in the New Brunswick study, the study's findings stress the continued complexities of social relationships in older adulthood.

Bereavement theory once held that mourners should grieve, then move on and realize that the dead person is gone forever. It was thought that if this did not happen, pathological grief could result, with the person either not grieving enough (absent grief) or grieving too long (incomplete grief). Current research finds a much wider variety of reactions.

PRACTICAL APPLICATIONS The research suggests that when someone is grieving, it is common to experience powerful, complicated, and unexpected emotions. To help the griever, a friend should listen and sympathize, never implying that the person is too grief-stricken or not grief-stricken enough.

A bereaved person *might or might not* want to visit the grave, light a candle, cherish a memento, pray, or sob. He or she may want to be alone or may want company. Those who have been taught to bear grief stoically may be doubly distressed if a friend advises them to cry but they cannot. Conversely, those whose cultures expect loud wailing may resent it if they are urged to hush.

Even absent grief—in which the bereaved person refuses to do any of these things—might be appropriate. So might be the opposite reaction, when people want to talk again and again about their loss, gathering sympathy, ascribing blame, and finding meaning.

It may help to express emotions through a variety of actions—by joining a bereavement group; protesting some policy; planting a garden; walking, running, or biking to raise money for a cause. Remember the 7-year-old boy whose grandparents, uncle, and dog (Twick) died? He wrote a memorial poem for Twick, which his parents framed and hung in the living room. That comforted him, and he agreed to return to school (K. R. Kaufman & Kaufman, 2006).

No matter what rituals are followed or what pattern is evident, the result may give the living a deeper appreciation of themselves and others. In fact, a theme frequently sounded by those who work with the dying and the bereaved is that death leads to a greater appreciation of life, especially of the value of intimate, caring relationships.

George Vaillant is a psychiatrist who studied a group of men from the time they were Harvard students through old age. He writes about funerals, "With tears of remembrance running down our cheeks. … Remembered love lives triumphantly today" (Vaillant, 2008, p. 133).

It is fitting to end this Epilogue, and this book, with a reminder of the creative work of living. As first described in Chapter 1, the study of human development is a science, with topics to be researched, understood, and explained. But the process of living is an art as well as a science, with strands of love and sorrow woven into each person's unique tapestry. Death, when it leads to hope; dying, when it is accepted; and grief, when it fosters affirmation—all add meaning to birth, growth, development, and love.

KEY Points

- Grief is an overpowering and irrational emotion, a normal reaction when a loved one dies.
- Grief can be complicated—continuing too long, or being absent, incomplete, or disenfranchised.
- Mourning is a social and cultural process to help people move past grief and reaffirm life.
- Among the common reactions to death are to assess blame for the death and to seek meaning in it. These can be either helpful or destructive.

SUMMARY

Death and Hope

1. Thanatology is the study of death and dying, a topic that has always led to strong emotions. Currently, fewer people have personally witnessed the dying process than in the past.

2. In ancient times, death was considered a connection between the living, the dead, and the spirit world. People respected the dead and tried to live their lives so that their own death and afterlife would be good.

3. Every religion includes rituals and beliefs about death. These vary a great deal, but all bring hope to the living and strengthen the community.

4. Death has various meanings, depending partly on the age of the person involved and whether that person is themselves dying or in mourning for someone else. For example, young children are more concerned about being separated from those they see every day whereas adults tend to worry about leaving something undone or abandoning family members, especially children.

5. Terror management theory finds that some emerging adults cope with anxiety about death by defiantly doing whatever is considered risky for their health. Adults are concerned about their own life plans; older adults are more accepting of death.

Choices in Dying

6. Everyone wants a good death, one that is painless and at the end of a long life. This may be more possible today than in earlier times. However, other aspects of a good death—quick, at home, surrounded by loved ones—may be less likely.

7. The emotions of people who are dying may change over time. Some may move from denial to acceptance, although stages of dying vary much more than originally proposed. Honest conversation helps many, but not all, dying persons.

8. Hospice caregivers meet the biological and psychological needs of terminally ill people and their families. This can occur at home or at a specific place. Palliative care relieves pain and other uncomfortable aspects of dying, and provides emotional support to patients and their families.

9. Drugs that produce a double effect—reducing pain as well as hastening dying—are acceptable to many. However, both passive and active euthanasia and physician-assisted suicide are controversial. A few nations allow some forms of these, but most do not.

10. Since 1980, death has been defined as occurring when brain waves stop; however, many modern measures can prolong life when no conscious thinking occurs. The need for a more precise, updated definition is apparent, but professionals are not sure what that new definition should be.

11. A living will and a health care proxy are recommended for everyone, although it is impossible to anticipate the possible interventions that may occur when someone is dying. Family members as well as professionals often disagree about specifics.

Affirmation of Life

12. Grief is overwhelming sorrow. It may be irrational and complicated, absent, or disenfranchised.

13. Mourning rituals channel human grief, helping people move to affirm life. Most people are able to do this.

KEY TERMS

absent grief (p. 583)

active euthanasia (p. 578)

complicated grief (p. 583)

disenfranchised grief (p. 583)

DNR (do not resuscitate) order (p. 578)

double effect (p. 576)

grief (p. 582)

health care proxy (p. 580)

hospice (p. 575)

incomplete grief (p. 583)

living will (p. 580)

mourning (p. 584)

palliative care (p. 576)

passive euthanasia (p. 578)

physician-assisted suicide (p. 578)

slippery slope (p. 581)

terror management theory (TMT) (p. 569)

thanatology (p. 565)

WHAT HAVE YOU LEARNED?

1. Why are people less familiar with death than they were 100 years ago? What impact might this have?

2. According to the ancient Egyptians and Greeks, what determined a person's fate after death?

3. What is one example of contrasting rituals about death?

4. What should parents remember when talking with children about death?

5. How does terror management theory explain young people's risk taking?

6. How does parenthood affect people's thoughts about their own death?

7. How do attitudes about death shift in late adulthood? What evidence is there of this shift?

8. In what ways do people change after a near-death experience?

9. What is a good death?

10. According to Kübler-Ross, what are the five stages of emotions associated with dying? Why doesn't everyone agree with Kübler-Ross's stages?

11. What are the guiding principles of hospice care, and why is each one important?

12. Why is the double effect legal everywhere, even though it speeds death?

13. What differences of opinion are there with respect to the definition of death?

14. What is the difference between passive and active euthanasia?

15. What are the four conditions of physician-assisted "death with dignity" in Oregon? Why is each condition important?

16. Why would a person who has a living will also need a health care proxy?

17. What is grief, and what are some of its signs?

18. List three types of complicated grief. Why is each type considered "complicated"?

19. What are the purposes of mourning?

20. How can a grieving person find meaning in death?

21. How might reactions such as talking to the deceased make it both easier and more difficult to adjust to the death of a loved one?

22. If a person still feels a loss six months after a death, is that pathological?

23. What should friends and relatives remember when helping someone who is grieving?

APPLICATIONS

1. Death is sometimes said to be hidden, even taboo. Ask 10 people if they have ever been with someone who was dying. Note not only the yes and no answers, but also the details and reactions. For instance, how many of the deaths occurred in hospitals?

2. Find quotes about death online or in a book such as *Bartlett's Familiar Quotations*. Do you see any historical or cultural patterns of acceptance, denial, or fear?

3. Every aspect of dying is controversial in modern society. Do an Internet search for a key term such as *euthanasia* or *grief*. Analyze the information and the underlying assumptions. What is your opinion, and why?

4. People of varying ages have different attitudes toward death. Ask people of different ages (ideally, at least one person younger than 20, one adult between 20 and 60, and one older person) what thoughts they have about their own death. What differences do you find?

>> ONLINE CONNECTIONS

To accompany your textbook, you have access to a number of online resources, including LearningCurve, which is an adaptive quizzing program; critical thinking questions; and case studies. For access to any of these links, go to www.worthpublishers.com/launchpad/bergerchuang1e. In addition to these resources, you'll also find links to video clips, personalized study advice, and an e-Book. Among the videos and activities available online are the following:

■ *Bereavement.* This in-depth activity covers the four stages of the grieving process and bereavement at different points in the life span. People share their personal experiences of loss.

■ *Preparing to Die.* Experts discuss the process of dying, and dying people tell their stories. Covers death at different ages, palliative and hospice care, and more.

GLOSSARY

A

absent grief A situation in which mourners do not grieve, either because other people do not allow grief to be expressed or because the mourners do not allow themselves to feel sadness.

acculturation The process of cultural and psychological change that occurs when individuals come into contact with a new culture.

achievement test A measure of mastery or proficiency in reading, mathematics, writing, science, or some other subject.

active euthanasia A situation in which someone takes action to bring about another person's death, with the intention of ending that person's suffering.

activities of daily life (ADLs) Typically identified as five tasks of self-care that are important to independent living: eating, bathing, toileting, dressing, and transferring from a bed to a chair. The inability to perform any of these tasks is a sign of frailty.

activity theory The view that elderly people want and need to remain active in social spheres—with relatives, friends, and community groups—and become withdrawn only unwillingly, as a result of ageism.

additive gene A gene that adds something to some aspect of the phenotype. Its contribution depends on additions from the other genes, which may come from either the same or the other parent.

adolescence-limited offender A person whose criminal activity stops by age 21.

adolescent egocentrism A characteristic of adolescent thinking that leads young people (ages 10 to 13) to focus on themselves to the exclusion of others.

adrenal glands Two glands, located above the kidneys, that produce hormones (including the "stress hormones" epinephrine [adrenaline] and norepinephrine).

age in place Remaining in the same home and community in later life, adjusting but not leaving when health fades.

age of viability The age (about 22 weeks after conception) at which a fetus may survive outside the mother's uterus if specialized medical care is available.

ageism A prejudice whereby people are categorized and judged solely on the basis of their chronological age.

aggressive-rejected Someone rejected by peers because of antagonistic, confrontational behaviour.

allele Any of the possible forms in which a gene for a particular trait can occur.

allocare Literally, "other-care"; the care of children by people other than the biological parents.

allostasis A dynamic body adjustment, related to homeostasis, that over time affects overall physiology. The main difference is that while homeostasis requires an immediate response, allostasis requires longer-term adjustment.

Alzheimer's disease (AD) The most common cause of neurocognitive disorder, characterized by gradual deterioration of memory and personality and marked by the formation of plaques of beta-amyloid protein and tangles of tau in the brain. (Previously referred to as *senile dementia of the Alzheimer's type*.)

amygdala A tiny brain structure that registers emotions, particularly fear and anxiety.

analytic intelligence A form of intelligence that involves such mental processes as abstract planning, strategy selection, focused attention, and information processing, as well as verbal and logical skills.

analytic thought Thought that results from analysis, such as a systematic ranking of pros and cons, risks and consequences, and possibilities and facts. Analytic thought depends on logic and rationality.

andropause A term coined to signify a drop in testosterone levels in older men, which normally results in reduced sexual desire, erections, and muscle mass. (Also called *male menopause*.)

animism The belief that natural objects and phenomena are alive.

anorexia nervosa An eating disorder characterized by severe calorie restriction and the fear of being fat. Affected individuals undereat, or overeat and then overexercise or purge, depriving their vital organs of nutrition. Anorexia can be fatal.

A-not-B error The tendency to reach for a hidden object where it was last found rather than in the new location where it was last hidden.

anoxia A lack of oxygen that, if prolonged, can cause brain damage or death.

antipathy Feelings of dislike or even hatred for another person.

antisocial behaviour Actions that are deliberately hurtful or destructive to another person.

Apgar scale A quick assessment of a newborn's body functioning. The baby's heart rate, respiratory effort, muscle tone, colour, and reflexes are given a score of 0, 1, or 2 twice—at one minute and five minutes after birth—and each time the total of all five scores is compared with the ideal score of 10 (which is rarely attained).

aptitude The potential to master a specific skill or to learn a certain body of knowledge.

assisted living A living arrangement for elderly people that combines privacy and independence with medical supervision.

asthma A chronic disease of the respiratory system in which inflammation narrows the airways from the nose and mouth to the lungs, causing difficulty in breathing. Signs and symptoms include wheezing, shortness of breath, chest tightness, and coughing.

astronaut family A family where members live in different countries; children in such families are known as *satellite* or *parachute* children.

attachment A bond that an infant forms with a caregiver; a tie that binds them together in space and endures over time.

attention deficit hyperactivity disorder (ADHD) A condition in which a person not only has great difficulty concentrating for more than a few moments but also is inattentive, impulsive, and overactive.

authoritarian parenting An approach to child-rearing that is characterized by high behavioural standards, strict punishment of misconduct, and little communication.

authoritative parenting An approach to child-rearing in which the parents set limits and enforce rules but are flexible and listen to their children.

autism spectrum disorder A developmental disorder marked by difficulty with social communication and interaction—including difficulty seeing things from another person's point of view—and restricted, repetitive patterns of behaviour, interests, or activities.

automatic processing Thinking that occurs without deliberate, conscious thought. Experts process most tasks automatically, saving conscious thought for unfamiliar challenges.

autonomy versus shame and doubt Erikson's second crisis of psychosocial development. Toddlers either succeed or fail in gaining a sense of self-rule over their actions and their bodies.

average life expectancy The number of years the average newborn in a particular population group is likely to live.

axon A fibre that extends from a neuron and transmits electrochemical impulses from that neuron to the dendrites of other neurons.

B

babbling The extended repetition of certain syllables, such as *ba-ba-ba,* that begins when babies are between 6 and 9 months old.

balanced bilingual A person who is fluent in two languages, not favouring one over the other.

behavioural teratogens Agents and conditions that can harm the prenatal brain, impairing the future child's intellectual and emotional functioning.

behaviourism A learning theory based on the idea that behaviours can be trained and changed in response to stimuli in the environment.

bickering Petty, peevish arguing, usually repeated and ongoing.

Big Five The five basic clusters of personality traits that remain quite stable throughout adulthood: openness, conscientiousness, extroversion, agreeableness, and neuroticism.

bilingual schooling A strategy in which school subjects are taught in both the learner's original language and the second language.

binocular vision The ability to focus the two eyes in a coordinated manner to see one image.

bipolar disorder A condition characterized by extreme mood swings, from euphoria to deep depression, not caused by outside experiences.

body image A person's idea of how his or her body looks.

body mass index (BMI) A person's weight in kilograms divided by the square of height in metres.

boomerang children Adult children who move out of their parents' home at some point in time before moving back.

Brazelton Neonatal Behavioral Assessment Scale (NBAS) A test often administered to newborns that measures responsiveness and records 46 behaviours, including 20 reflexes.

bulimia nervosa An eating disorder characterized by binge eating and subsequent purging, usually by induced vomiting and/or use of laxatives.

bullying Repeated, systematic efforts to inflict harm through physical, verbal, or social attack on a weaker person.

bullying aggression Unprovoked, repeated physical or verbal attack, especially on victims who are unlikely to defend themselves.

bully-victim Someone who attacks others and who is attacked as well. (Also called a *provocative victim* because the child does things that elicit bullying.)

C

Caesarean section (C-section) A surgical birth, in which incisions through the mother's abdomen and uterus allow the fetus to be removed quickly, instead of being delivered through the vagina.

calorie restriction The practice of limiting dietary energy intake (while consuming sufficient quantities of vitamins, minerals, and other important nutrients) for the purpose of improving health and slowing down the aging process.

CARP A Canadian organization that advocates for Canadians as they age. It was originally called the Canadian Association of Retired Persons, but now only the initials CARP are used, since members need not be retired.

carrier A person whose genotype includes a gene that is not expressed in the phenotype. Such an unexpressed gene occurs in half the carrier's gametes and thus is passed on to half the carrier's children, who will most likely be carriers, too. Generally, the characteristic appears in the phenotype only when such a gene is inherited from both parents.

case study An in-depth study of one person, usually requiring personal interviews to collect background information and various follow-up discussions, tests, questionnaires, and so on.

cellular aging The ways in which molecules and cells are affected by age. Many theories aim to explain how and why aging causes cells to deteriorate.

centration A characteristic of preoperational thought whereby a young child focuses (centres) on one idea, excluding all others.

centre daycare Child care that occurs in a place especially designed for the purpose, where several paid adults care for many children. Usually, the children are grouped by age, the daycare centre is licensed, and providers are trained and certified in child development.

cerebral palsy A disorder that results from damage to the brain's motor centres. People with cerebral palsy have difficulty with muscle control, so their speech and/or body movements are impaired.

child abuse Deliberate action that is harmful to a child's physical, emotional, or sexual well-being.

child culture The particular habits, styles, and values that reflect the set of rules and rituals that characterize children as distinct from adult society.

child maltreatment Intentional harm to or avoidable endangerment of anyone under 18 years of age.

child neglect Failure to meet a child's basic physical, educational, or emotional needs.

child sexual abuse Any erotic activity that arouses an adult and excites, shames, or confuses a child, whether or not the victim protests and whether or not genital contact is involved.

child-directed speech The high-pitched, simplified, and repetitive way adults speak to infants. (Also called *baby talk, motherese,* or *parentese.*)

childhood obesity A child having a BMI above the 95th percentile.

childhood overweight A child having a BMI above the 85th percentile.

choice overload Having so many options that a thoughtful choice becomes difficult, and regret after making a choice is more likely.

chromosome One of the 46 molecules of DNA (in 23 pairs) that each cell of the human body contains and that, together, contain all the genes. Other species have more or fewer chromosomes.

circadian rhythm A day–night cycle of biological activity that occurs approximately every 24 hours (*circadian* means "about a day").

classical conditioning A learning process in which a meaningful stimulus (such as the smell of food to a hungry animal) gradually comes to be connected with a neutral stimulus (such as a particular sound) that had no special meaning before the learning process began. (Also called *respondent conditioning.*)

classification The logical principle that things can be organized into groups (or categories or classes) according to some characteristic they have in common.

clinical depression Feelings of hopelessness, lethargy, and worthlessness that last two weeks or more.

clique A group of adolescents made up of close friends who are loyal to one another while excluding outsiders.

cluster suicides Several suicides committed by members of a group within a brief period.

cognitive theory A theory of human development that focuses on changes in how people think over time. According to this theory, our thoughts shape our attitudes, beliefs, and behaviours.

cohabitation An arrangement in which two people live together in a committed romantic relationship but are not formally married.

cohort A group defined by the shared age of its members, who, because they were born at about the same time, move through life together, experiencing the same historical events and cultural shifts.

comorbid The presence of two or more disease conditions at the same time in the same person.

complicated grief A type of grief that impedes a person's future life, usually because the person clings to sorrow or is buffeted by contradictory emotions.

compression of morbidity A shortening of the time a person spends ill or infirm, accomplished by postponing illness.

compulsive hoarding The urge to accumulate and hold on to familiar objects and possessions, sometimes to the point of their becoming health and/or safety hazards. This impulse tends to increase with age.

concrete operational thought Piaget's term for the ability to reason logically about direct experiences and perceptions.

conditioning According to behaviourism, the processes by which responses become linked to particular stimuli and learning takes place. The word "conditioning" is used to emphasize the importance of repeated practice, as when an athlete conditions his or her body to perform well by training for a long time.

consequential strangers People who are not in a person's closest friendship circle but nonetheless have an impact.

conservation The principle that the amount of a substance remains the same (i.e., is conserved) even when its appearance changes.

control processes Mechanisms (including selective attention, metacognition, and emotional regulation) that combine memory, processing speed, and knowledge to regulate the analysis and flow of information within the information-processing system. (Also called *executive processes.*)

conventional moral reasoning Kohlberg's second level of moral reasoning, emphasizing social rules.

corpus callosum A long, thick band of nerve fibres that connects the left and right hemispheres of the brain and allows communication between them.

correlation A number that indicates the degree of relationship between two variables, expressed in terms of the likelihood that one variable will (or will not) occur when the other variable does (or does not). A correlation indicates only that two variables are related, not that one variable causes the other to occur.

cortex The outer layers of the brain in humans and other mammals. Most thinking, feeling, and sensing involve the cortex.

cortisol The primary stress hormone; fluctuations in the body's cortisol level affect human emotion.

co-sleeping A custom in which parents and their children (usually infants) sleep together in the same room.

couvade Symptoms of pregnancy and birth experienced by fathers.

creative intelligence A form of intelligence that involves the capacity to be intellectually flexible and innovative.

critical period A time when a particular type of developmental growth (in body or behaviour) must happen if it is ever going to happen.

cross-sectional research A research design that compares groups of people who differ in age but are similar in other important characteristics.

cross-sequential research A hybrid research design in which researchers first study several groups of people of different ages (a cross-sectional approach) and then follow those groups over the years (a longitudinal approach). (Also called *cohort-sequential research* or *time-sequential research*.)

crowd A larger group of adolescents who have something in common but who are not necessarily friends.

crystallized intelligence Those types of intellectual ability that reflect accumulated learning. Vocabulary and general information are examples. Some developmental psychologists think crystallized intelligence increases with age, while fluid intelligence declines.

culture A system of shared beliefs, norms, behaviours, and expectations that persist over time and prescribe social behaviour and assumptions.

cyberbullying Bullying that occurs when one person spreads insults or rumours about another by means of technology (e.g., emails, text messages, or cellphone videos).

D

deductive reasoning Reasoning from a general statement, premise, or principle, through logical steps, to figure out (deduce) specifics. (Also called *top-down reasoning*.)

deferred imitation A sequence in which an infant first perceives something done by someone else and then performs the same action hours or even days later.

demographic shift A shift in the proportions of the populations of various ages.

dendrite A fibre that extends from a neuron and receives electrochemical impulses transmitted from other neurons via their axons.

dependency ratio A calculation of the number of self-sufficient, productive adults compared with the number of dependents (children and the elderly) in a given population.

dependent variable In an experiment, the variable that may change as a result of whatever new condition or situation the experimenter adds. In other words, the dependent variable depends on the independent variable.

developmental theory A group of ideas, assumptions, and generalizations that interpret and illuminate the thousands of observations that have been made about human growth. A developmental theory provides a framework for explaining the patterns and problems of development.

deviancy training Destructive peer support in which one person shows another how to rebel against authority or social norm

difference-equals-deficit error The mistaken belief that a deviation from some norm is necessarily inferior to behaviour or characteristics that meet the standard.

differential sensitivity The idea that some people are more vulnerable than others are to certain experiences, usually because of genetic differences.

disenfranchised grief A situation in which certain people, although they are bereaved, are prevented from mourning publicly by cultural customs or social restrictions.

disengagement theory The view that aging makes a person's social sphere increasingly narrow, resulting in role relinquishment, withdrawal, and passivity.

disorganized attachment A type of attachment that is marked by an infant's inconsistent reactions to the caregiver's departure and return.

disruptive mood dysregulation disorder (DMDD) A condition in which a child has chronic irritability and anger that culminates in frequent tantrums that are inappropriate to the circumstances and to the child's age.

distal parenting Caregiving practices that involve remaining distant from the baby, providing toys, food, and face-to-face communication with minimal holding and touching.

dizygotic twins Twins who are formed when two separate ova are fertilized by two separate sperm at roughly the same time. (Also called *fraternal twins*.)

DNA (deoxyribonucleic acid) The molecule that contains the chemical instructions for cells to manufacture various proteins.

DNR (do not resuscitate) order A written order from a physician (sometimes initiated by a patient's advance directive or by a health care proxy's request) that no attempt should be made to revive a patient if he or she suffers cardiac or respiratory arrest.

dominant–recessive pattern The interaction of a pair of alleles in such a way that the phenotype reveals the influence of one allele (the dominant gene) more than that of the other (the recessive gene).

double effect A situation in which an action (such as administering opiates) has both a positive effect (relieving a terminally ill person's pain) and a negative effect (hastening death by suppressing respiration).

doula A woman who helps with the birth process. Doulas are trained to offer support to new mothers, including massage and suggestions for breastfeeding positions.

Down syndrome A condition in which a person has 47 chromosomes instead of the usual 46, with three rather than two chromosomes at the 21st position. People with Down syndrome typically have distinctive characteristics, including atypical facial features (thick tongue, round face, slanted eyes), heart abnormalities, and language difficulties. (Also called *trisomy-21*.)

drug abuse The ingestion of a drug to the extent that it impairs the user's biological or psychological well-being.

dual-process model The notion that two networks exist within the human brain, one for emotional and one for analytical processing of stimuli.

dynamic-systems approach A view of human development as an ongoing, ever-changing interaction between a person's physical and emotional being and between the person and every aspect of his or her environment, including the family and society.

dyscalculia Unusual difficulty with math, probably originating from a distinct part of the brain.

dyslexia Unusual difficulty with reading; thought to be the result of some neurological underdevelopment.

E

ecological niche The particular lifestyle and social context that adults settle into because it is compatible with their individual personality needs and interests.

ecological validity The idea that cognition should be measured in settings that are as realistic as possible and that the abilities measured should be those needed in real life.

ecological-systems approach The view that in the study of human development, the person should be considered in all the contexts and interactions that constitute a life. (Later renamed *bioecological theory*.)

egocentrism Piaget's term for young children's tendency to think about the world entirely from their own personal perspective.

elderspeak A condescending way of speaking to older adults that resembles baby talk, with simple and short sentences, exaggerated emphasis, repetition, and a slower rate and a higher pitch than used in normal speech.

Electra complex The unconscious desire of girls to replace their mothers and win their fathers' exclusive love.

embryo The name for a developing human organism from about the third through the eighth week after conception.

embryonic period The stage of prenatal development from approximately the third through the eighth week after conception, during which the basic forms of all body structures, including internal organs, develop.

emerging adulthood The period of life between the ages of 18 and 25. Emerging adulthood is now widely thought of as a separate developmental stage.

emotional regulation The ability to control when and how emotions are expressed.

emotion-focused coping A strategy to deal with stress by changing feelings about the stressor rather than changing the stressor itself.

empathy The ability to understand the emotions and concerns of another person, especially when they differ from one's own.

empirical evidence Evidence based on data from scientific observation or experiments; not theoretical.

empty nest The time in the lives of parents when their children have left the family home to pursue their own lives.

entity approach to intelligence An approach to understanding intelligence that sees ability as innate, a fixed quantity present at birth; those who hold this view do not believe that effort enhances achievement.

epigenetic Referring to the effects of environmental forces on the expression of an individual's, or a species', genetic inheritance.

equifinality A basic principle of developmental psychopathology that holds that one symptom can have many causes.

ESL (English as a second language) An approach to teaching English in which all children who do not speak English are placed together in an intensive course to learn basic English so that they can be educated in the same classroom as native English speakers. (Also known as *EAL, English as an alternative language*, or *ELL, English Language Learning*.)

estradiol A sex hormone, considered the chief estrogen. Females produce much more estradiol than males do.

ethnic group People whose ancestors were born in the same region and who often share a language, culture, and religion.

ethnic identity The extent to which a person identifies with a particular ethnic group's roles and behaviours. (Also known as *ethnocultural identity* or *cultural identity*.)

experiment A research method in which the researcher tries to determine the cause-and-effect relationship between two variables by manipulating one (the independent variable) and then observing and recording the ensuing changes in the other (the dependent variable).

expert One who is notably more accomplished, proficient, and/or knowledgeable in a particular skill, topic, or task than the average person.

expertise Accomplishment at a particular skill or in-depth knowledge of a particular subject that is greater than that of the average person.

extended family A family of three or more generations living in one household.

externalizing problems Difficulty with emotional regulation that involves expressing powerful feelings through uncontrolled physical or verbal outbursts, as by lashing out at other people or breaking things.

extreme sports Forms of recreation that include apparent risk of injury or death and are attractive and thrilling as a result.

extremely low birth weight (ELBW) A body weight at birth of less than 1000 grams.

extrinsic motivation A drive, or reason to pursue a goal, that arises from the need to have one's achievements rewarded from outside, perhaps by receiving material possessions or another person's esteem.

extrinsic rewards of work The tangible benefits, usually in the form of compensation (e.g., salary, health insurance, pension), that one receives for doing a job.

F

family daycare Child care that includes several children of various ages and usually occurs in the home of a woman who is paid to provide it.

family function The way a family works to meet the needs of its members. Children need families to provide basic material necessities, to encourage learning, to help them develop self-respect, to nurture friendships, and to foster harmony and stability.

family structure The legal and genetic relationships among relatives living in the same home; includes nuclear family, extended family, stepfamily, and so on.

family systems theory A theory of human behaviour that focuses on the family as a unit or functioning system, with each member having a role to play and rules to respect.

fast-mapping The speedy and sometimes imprecise way in which children learn new words by tentatively placing them in mental categories according to their perceived meaning.

fetal alcohol syndrome (FAS) A cluster of birth defects, including abnormal facial characteristics, slow physical growth, and intellectual disabilities, that may occur in the child of a woman who drinks alcohol while pregnant.

fetal period The stage of prenatal development from the ninth week after conception until birth, during which the fetus grows in size and matures in functioning.

fetus The name for a developing human organism from the start of the ninth week after conception until birth.

fictive kin Someone who becomes accepted as part of a family to which he or she has no blood relation.

filial responsibility The obligation of adult children to care for their aging parents.

fine motor skills Physical abilities involving small body movements, especially of the hands and fingers, such as drawing and picking up a coin. (The word *fine* here means "small.")

flextime An arrangement in which work schedules are flexible so that employees can balance personal and occupational responsibilities.

fluid intelligence Those types of basic intelligence that make learning of all sorts quick and thorough. Abilities such as short-term memory, abstract thought, and speed of thinking are all usually considered part of fluid intelligence.

Flynn effect The rise in average IQ scores that has occurred over the decades in many nations.

focus on appearance A characteristic of preoperational thought whereby a young child ignores all attributes that are not apparent.

foreclosure Erikson's term for premature identity formation, which occurs when an adolescent adopts his or her parents' or society's roles and values wholesale, without questioning or analysis.

formal operational thought In Piaget's theory, the fourth and final stage of cognitive development, characterized by more systematic logical thinking and by the ability to understand and systematically manipulate abstract concepts.

frail elderly People older than 65, and often older than 85, who are physically infirm, very ill, or cognitively disabled.

frontal lobe disorder Deterioration of the amygdala and frontal lobes that may be the cause of 15 percent of all neurocognitive disorders. (Also called *frontotemporal lobar degeneration*.)

G

gamete A reproductive cell; that is, a sperm or an ovum that can produce a new individual if it combines with a gamete from the other sex to form a zygote.

gender constancy The ability of children to understand that gender cannot change, regardless of their outside appearance, such as cutting their hair or wearing a dress.

gender differences Differences in the roles and behaviours that are prescribed by a culture for males and females.

gender identity (adolescence) A person's acceptance of the roles and behaviours that society associates with the biological categories of male and female.

gender identity (early childhood) The ability of children to make gender distinctions by accurately labelling themselves as a boy or girl.

gender schema A child's cognitive concept or general belief about sex differences, which is based on his or her observations and experiences.

gender stability The ability of children to understand that their gender is stable over time and will not change.

gene A small section of a chromosome; the basic unit for the transmission of heredity. A gene consists of a string of chemicals that provide instructions for the cell to manufacture certain proteins.

general intelligence (*g*) The idea of *g* assumes that intelligence is one basic trait, underlying all cognitive abilities. According to this concept, people have varying levels of this general ability.

generational forgetting The idea that each new generation forgets what the previous generation learned. As used here, the term refers to knowledge about the harm drugs can do.

generativity versus stagnation The seventh of Erikson's eight stages of development. Adults seek to be productive in a caring way, perhaps through art, caregiving, and employment.

genetic clock A purported mechanism in the DNA of cells that regulates the aging process by triggering hormonal changes and controlling cellular reproduction and repair.

genome The full set of genes that are the instructions to make an individual member of a certain species.

genotype An organism's entire genetic inheritance, or genetic potential.

germinal period The first two weeks of prenatal development after conception, characterized by rapid cell division and the beginning of cell differentiation.

grammar All the methods—word order, verb forms, and so on—that languages use to communicate meaning, apart from the words themselves.

grief The deep sorrow that people feel at the death of another. Grief is personal and unpredictable.

gross motor skills Physical abilities involving large body movements, such as walking and jumping. (The word *gross* here means "big.")

growth spurt The relatively sudden and rapid physical growth that occurs during puberty. Each body part increases in size on a schedule: Weight usually precedes height, and growth of the limbs precedes growth of the torso.

H

Hayflick limit The number of times a human cell is capable of dividing into two new cells. The limit for most human cells is approximately 50 divisions, an indication that the life span is limited by our genetic program.

Head Start The most widespread early-childhood education program in the United States, begun in 1965 and funded by the federal government.

head-sparing A biological mechanism that protects the brain when malnutrition disrupts body growth. The brain is the last part of the body to be damaged by malnutrition.

health care proxy A person chosen by an individual to make medical decisions if that individual becomes unable to do so.

heritability A statistic that indicates what percentage of the variation in a particular trait within a particular population, in a particular context and era, can be traced to genes.

hidden curriculum The unofficial, unstated, or implicit rules and priorities that influence the academic curriculum and every other aspect of learning in a school.

hippocampus A brain structure that is a central processor of memory, especially memory for locations.

holophrase A single word that is used to express a complete, meaningful thought.

homeostasis The adjustment of all the body's systems to keep physiological functions in a state of equilibrium, moment by moment. As the body ages, it takes longer for these homeostatic adjustments to occur, so it becomes harder for older bodies to adapt to stress.

hormone An organic chemical substance that is produced by one body tissue and conveyed via the bloodstream to another to affect some physiological function.

hormone replacement therapy (HRT) Taking hormones (in pills, patches, or injections) to compensate for hormone reduction. HRT is most common in women at menopause or after removal of the ovaries, but it is also used by men to help restore their decreased testosterone level. HRT has some medical uses but also carries health risks.

hospice An institution or program in which terminally ill patients receive care to reduce suffering; family and friends of the dying are helped as well.

HPA (hypothalamus–pituitary–adrenal) axis A sequence of hormone production that originates in the hypothalamus, moves to the pituitary, and then ends in the adrenal glands.

HPG (hypothalamus–pituitary–gonad) axis A sequence of hormone production that originates in the hypothalamus, moves to the pituitary, and then ends in the gonads.

humanism A theory that stresses the potential of all human beings for good and the belief that all people have the same basic needs, regardless of culture, gender, or background.

hybrid theory A perspective that combines various aspects of different theories to explain how language, or any other developmental phenomenon, occurs.

hypothalamus A brain area that responds to the amygdala and the hippocampus to produce hormones that activate other parts of the brain and body.

hypothesis A specific prediction that can be tested.

hypothetical thought Reasoning that includes propositions and possibilities that may not reflect reality.

I

identification An attempt to defend one's self concept by taking on the behaviours and attitudes of someone else.

identity achievement Erikson's term for the attainment of identity, or the point at which a person understands who he or she is as a unique individual, in accord with past experiences and future plans.

identity versus role confusion Erikson's term for the fifth stage of development, in which the person tries to figure out "Who am I?" but is confused as to which of many possible roles to adopt.

imaginary audience The other people who, in an adolescent's egocentric belief, are watching and taking note of his or her appearance, ideas, and behaviour. This belief makes many teenagers very self-conscious.

immersion A strategy in which instruction in all school subjects occurs in a second language that a child is learning.

immunization A process that stimulates the body's immune system to defend against attack by a particular contagious disease. Immunization may be accomplished either naturally (by having the disease) or through vaccination (often by having an injection). (Also called *vaccination.*)

implantation The process, beginning about 10 days after conception, in which the developing organism burrows into the tissue that lines the uterus, where it can be nourished and protected as it continues to develop.

in vitro fertilization (IVF) A technique in which ova (egg cells) are surgically removed from a woman and fertilized with sperm in a laboratory. After the original fertilized cells (the zygotes) have divided several times, they are inserted into the woman's uterus.

incomplete grief A situation in which circumstances, such as a police investigation or an autopsy, interfere with the process of grieving.

incremental approach to intelligence An approach to understanding intelligence that holds that intelligence can be directly increased by effort; those who subscribe to this view believe they can master whatever they seek to learn if they pay attention, participate in class, study, complete their homework, and so on.

independent variable In an experiment, the variable that is introduced to see what effect it has on the dependent variable. (Also called *experimental variable.*)

individual education plan (IEP) A document that specifies educational goals and plans for a child with special needs.

inductive reasoning Reasoning from one or more specific experiences or facts to reach (induce) a general conclusion. (Also called *bottom-up reasoning.*)

industry versus inferiority The fourth of Erikson's eight psychosocial crises, during which children attempt to master many skills, developing a sense of themselves as either industrious or inferior, competent or incompetent.

infant mortality rate The rate, per 1000 live births, at which babies of less than one year of age die.

infertility The inability to conceive a child after trying for at least a year.

information-processing theory A perspective that compares human thinking processes, by analogy, to computer analysis of data, including sensory input, connections, stored memories, and output.

initiative versus guilt Erikson's third psychosocial crisis, in which children undertake new skills and activities and feel guilty when they do not succeed at them.

injury control (or harm reduction) Practices that are aimed at anticipating, controlling, and preventing dangerous activities; these practices reflect the beliefs that accidents are not random and that injuries can be made less harmful if proper controls are in place.

insecure-avoidant attachment A pattern of attachment in which an infant avoids connection with the caregiver, as when the infant seems not to care about the caregiver's presence, departure, or return.

insecure-resistant/ambivalent attachment A pattern of attachment in which an infant's anxiety and uncertainty are evident, as when the infant becomes very upset at separation from the caregiver and both resists and seeks contact on reunion.

instrumental activities of daily life (IADLs) Actions (e.g., budgeting and preparing food) that are important to independent living and that require some intellectual competence and forethought. The ability to perform these tasks may be even more critical to self-sufficiency than ADL ability.

instrumental aggression Hurtful behaviour that is intended to get something that another person has and to keep it.

integrity versus despair The final stage of Erik Erikson's developmental sequence, in which older adults seek to integrate their unique experiences with their vision of community.

intelligence quotient (IQ) test A test designed to measure intellectual aptitude, or ability to learn in school. Originally, intelligence was defined as mental age divided by chronological age, multiplied by 100—hence the term *intelligence quotient*, or *IQ*.

internalizing problems Difficulty with emotional regulation that involves turning one's emotional distress inward, by feeling excessively guilty, ashamed, or worthless.

intimacy versus isolation The sixth of Erikson's eight stages of development. Adults seek someone with whom to share their lives in an enduring and self-sacrificing commitment. Without such commitment they risk profound loneliness and isolation.

intrinsic motivation A drive, or reason to pursue a goal, that comes from inside a person, such as the need to feel smart or competent.

intrinsic rewards of work The intangible gratifications (e.g., job satisfaction, self-esteem, pride) that come from within oneself as a result of doing a job.

intuitive thought Thought that arises from an emotion or a hunch, beyond rational explanation, and is influenced by past experiences and cultural assumptions.

invincibility fable An adolescent's egocentric conviction that he or she cannot be overcome or even harmed by anything that might defeat a normal mortal, such as unprotected sex, drug abuse, or high-speed driving.

irreversibility A characteristic of preoperational thought whereby a young child thinks that nothing can be undone. A thing cannot be restored to the way it was before a change occurred.

J

just right The tendency of children to insist on having things done in a particular way. This can include clothes, food, bedtime routines, and so on.

K

kangaroo care A child-care technique in which a new mother holds the baby between her breasts, like a kangaroo that carries her immature newborn in a pouch on her abdomen.

kinkeeper A caregiver who takes responsibility for maintaining communication among family members.

kinship care A form of foster care in which a relative of a maltreated child, usually a grandparent, becomes the approved caregiver.

knowledge base A body of knowledge in a particular area that makes it easier to master new information in that area.

kwashiorkor A disease of chronic malnutrition during childhood, in which a protein deficiency makes the child more vulnerable to other diseases, such as measles, diarrhea, and influenza.

L

language acquisition device (LAD) Chomsky's term for a hypothesized mental structure that enables humans to learn language, including the basic aspects of grammar, vocabulary, and intonation.

latency Freud's term for middle childhood, during which children's emotional drives and psychosexual needs are quiet (latent). Freud thought that sexual conflicts from earlier stages are only temporarily submerged, bursting forth again at puberty.

lateralization Literally, "sidedness," referring to the specialization in certain functions by each side of the brain, with one side dominant for each activity. The left side of the brain controls the right side of the body, and vice versa.

learning theory A theory of human development that describes the laws and processes by which observable behaviour is learned.

least restrictive environment (LRE) A legal requirement that children with special needs be assigned to the most general educational context in which they can be expected to learn.

leptin A hormone that affects appetite and is believed to affect the onset of puberty. Leptin levels increase during childhood and peak at around age 12.

Lewy bodies Deposits of a particular kind of protein in the brain that interfere with communication between neurons; Lewy bodies cause neurocognitive disorder.

life review An examination of one's own role in the history of human life, engaged in by many elderly people.

life-course-persistent offender A person whose criminal activity typically begins in early adolescence and continues throughout life; a career criminal.

life-span perspective An approach to the study of human development that takes into account all phases of life, not just childhood or adulthood.

limbic system The major brain region crucial to the development of emotional expression and regulation; its three main areas are the amygdala, the hippocampus, and the hypothalamus, although recent research has found that many other areas of the brain are involved with emotions.

linked lives Lives in which the success, health, and well-being of each family member are connected to those of other members, including members of another generation, as in the relationship between parents and children.

little scientist The stage-five toddler (age 12 to 18 months) who experiments without anticipating the results, using trial and error in active and creative exploration.

living will A document that indicates what medical intervention an individual prefers if he or she is not conscious when a decision must be made.

longitudinal research A research design in which the same individuals are followed over time and their development is repeatedly assessed.

long-term memory The component of the information-processing system in which virtually limitless amounts of information can be stored indefinitely.

low birth weight (LBW) A body weight at birth of less than 2500 grams.

M

marasmus A disease of severe protein-calorie malnutrition during early infancy, in which growth stops, body tissues waste away, and the infant eventually dies.

massification The idea that establishing higher learning institutions and encouraging college and university enrolment could benefit everyone (the masses), leading to marked increases in the number of emerging adults in post-secondary institutions.

maximum life span The oldest possible age that members of a species can live under ideal circumstances. For humans, that age is approximately 122 years.

menarche A girl's first menstrual period, signalling that she has begun ovulation. Pregnancy is biologically possible, but ovulation and menstruation are often irregular for years after menarche.

menopause The time in middle age, usually around age 50, when a woman's menstrual periods cease and the production of estrogen, progesterone, and testosterone drops. Strictly speaking, menopause is dated one year after a woman's last menstrual period, although many months before and after that date are considered part of the period of menopause.

metacognition "Thinking about thinking," or the ability to evaluate a cognitive task to determine how best to accomplish it, and then to monitor and adjust one's performance on that task.

middle childhood The period between early childhood and early adolescence, approximately from ages 6 to 11.

middle school A school for children in the grades between elementary and high school. Middle school usually begins with Grade 6 and ends with Grade 8.

midlife crisis A supposed period of unusual anxiety, radical self-examination, and sudden transformation that was once widely associated with middle age, but that actually had more to do with developmental history than with chronological age.

mirror neurons Cells in an observer's brain that respond to an action performed by someone else in the same way they would if the observer had actually performed that action.

monozygotic twins Twins who originate from one zygote that splits apart very early in development. (Also called *identical twins*.)

Montessori schools Schools that offer early childhood education based on the philosophy of Maria Montessori (an Italian educator more than a century ago). It is child-centred, emphasizing individual achievement and providing a variety of literacy-related tasks.

moratorium An adolescent's choice of a socially acceptable way to postpone making identity-achievement decisions. Going to college or university is a common example.

motor skills The learned abilities to move some part of the body, in actions ranging from a large leap to a flicker of the eyelid. (The word *motor* here refers to movement of muscles.)

mourning The ceremonies and behaviours that a religion or culture prescribes for people to employ in expressing their bereavement after a death.

multifinality A basic principle of developmental psychopathology that holds that one cause can have many (multiple) final manifestations.

multiple intelligences The idea that human intelligence is comprised of a varied set of abilities rather than a single, all-encompassing one.

myelination The process by which axons become coated with myelin, a fatty substance that speeds the transmission of nerve impulses from neuron to neuron.

N

naming explosion A sudden increase in an infant's vocabulary, especially in the number of nouns, that begins at about 18 months of age.

naturally occurring retirement community (NORC) A neighbourhood or apartment complex whose population is mostly retired people who moved to the location as younger adults and never left.

nature A general term for the traits, capacities, and limitations that each individual inherits genetically from his or her parents at the moment of conception.

neurocognitive disorder (NCD) Impairment of intellectual functioning caused by organic brain damage or disease. NCD may be diagnosed as major or mild, depending on the severity of symptoms. It becomes more common with age, but it is abnormal and pathological even in the very old

neuron One of billions of nerve cells in the central nervous system, especially in the brain.

neurotransmitter A brain chemical that carries information from the axon of a sending neuron to the dendrites of a receiving neuron.

norm An average, or standard, measurement, calculated from the measurements of many individuals within a specific group or population.

nuclear family A family that consists of a father, a mother, and their biological children under age 18.

nurture A general term for all the environmental influences that affect development after an individual is conceived.

O

object permanence The realization that objects (including people) still exist even if they can no longer be seen, touched, or heard.

Oedipus complex The unconscious desire of young boys to replace their fathers and win their mothers' exclusive love.

oldest-old Elderly adults (generally, those older than 85) who are dependent on others for almost everything, requiring supportive services such as nursing homes and hospital stays.

old-old Older adults (generally, those older than 75) who suffer from physical, mental, or social deficits.

operant conditioning A learning process in which a particular action is followed either by something desired (which makes the person or animal more likely to repeat the action) or by something unwanted (which makes the action less likely to be repeated). (Also called *instrumental conditioning*.)

organ reserve The extra capacity built into each organ, such as the heart and lungs, that allows a person to cope with extraordinary demands or to withstand organ strain.

osteoporosis Fragile bones that result from primary aging, which makes bones more porous, especially if a person is at genetic risk.

overimitation The tendency of children to copy an action that is not a relevant part of the behaviour to be learned; common among 2- to 6-year-olds when they imitate adult actions that are irrelevant and inefficient.

overregularization The application of rules of grammar even when exceptions occur, making the language seem more "regular" than it actually is.

P

palliative care Care designed not to treat an illness but to provide physical and emotional comfort to the patient and support and guidance to his or her family.

parasuicide Any potentially lethal action against the self that does not result in death. (Also called *attempted suicide* or *failed suicide*.)

parental monitoring Parents' ongoing awareness of what their children are doing, where, and with whom.

parent–infant bond The strong, loving connection that forms as parents hold, examine, and feed their newborn.

Parkinson's disease A chronic, progressive disease that is characterized by muscle tremor and rigidity and sometimes cognitive impairment; caused by reduced dopamine production in the brain.

passive euthanasia A situation in which a seriously ill person is allowed to die naturally, through the cessation of medical intervention.

peer pressure Encouragement to conform to one's friends or contemporaries in behaviour, dress, and attitude; usually considered a negative force, as when adolescent peers encourage one another to defy adult authority.

perception The mental processing of sensory information when the brain interprets a sensation.

permanency planning An effort by child welfare authorities to find a long-term living situation that will provide stability and support for a maltreated child. A goal is to avoid repeated changes of caregiver or school, which can be particularly harmful to the child.

permissive parenting An approach to child-rearing that is characterized by high nurturance and communication but little discipline, guidance, or control.

perseveration The tendency to persevere in, or stick to, one thought or action for a long time.

personal fable An aspect of adolescent egocentrism characterized by an adolescent's belief that his or her thoughts, feelings, and experiences are unique, and more wonderful or awful than anyone else's.

phallic stage Freud's third stage of development, when the penis becomes the focus of concern and pleasure.

phenotype The observable characteristics of a person, including appearance, personality, intelligence, and all other traits.

physician-assisted suicide A form of active euthanasia in which a doctor provides the means for someone to end his or her own life.

pincer movement The use of the thumb and forefinger to pick up objects.

pituitary A gland in the brain that responds to a signal from the hypothalamus by producing many hormones, including those that regulate growth and that control other glands, among them the adrenal and sex glands.

plaques Clumps of a protein called *beta-amyloid,* found in brain tissues surrounding the neurons; a normal brain contains some beta-amyloid protein, but in brains of people with Alzheimer's disease these plaques proliferate, especially in the hippocampus, a brain structure crucial for memory.

plasticity The ability to be modified or changed.

polypharmacy A situation in which elderly people are prescribed several medications. The various side effects and interactions of those medications can result in symptoms of neurocognitive disorder.

positivity effect The tendency for elderly people to perceive, prefer, and remember positive images and experiences more than negative ones.

postconventional moral reasoning Kohlberg's third level of moral reasoning, emphasizing moral principles.

postformal thought A proposed adult stage of cognitive development, following Piaget's four stages. Postformal thought goes beyond adolescent thinking by being more practical, more flexible, and more dialectical (i.e., more capable of combining contradictory elements into a comprehensive whole).

postpartum depression The sadness and inadequacy felt by some new mothers in the days and weeks after giving birth.

practical intelligence The intellectual skills used in everyday problem solving. (Sometimes called *tacit intelligence*.)

pragmatics The practical use of language that includes the ability to adjust language communication according to audience and context.

preconventional moral reasoning Kohlberg's first level of moral reasoning, emphasizing rewards and punishments.

prefrontal cortex The area of the cortex at the very front of the brain that specializes in anticipation, planning, and impulse control.

preoperational intelligence Piaget's term for cognitive development between the ages of about 2 and 6; it includes language and imagination (which involve symbolic thought), but logical, operational thinking is not yet possible.

preterm birth A birth that occurs three or more weeks before the full 38 weeks of the typical pregnancy have elapsed—that is, at 35 or fewer weeks after conception.

primary aging The universal and irreversible physical changes that occur in all living creatures as they grow older.

primary prevention Actions that change overall background conditions to prevent some unwanted event or circumstance, such as injury, disease, or abuse.

primary sex characteristics The parts of the body that are directly involved in reproduction, including the vagina, uterus, ovaries, testicles, and penis.

problem-focused coping A strategy to deal with stress by tackling a stressful situation directly.

Programme for International Student Assessment (PISA) An international assessment program that measures achievement in reading, math, and science for 15-year-olds.

Progress in International Reading Literacy Study (PIRLS) Inaugurated in 2001, a planned five-year cycle of international trend studies in the reading ability of Grade 4 students.

prosocial behaviour Actions that are helpful and kind but that are of no obvious benefit to the person doing them.

protein-calorie malnutrition A condition in which a person does not consume sufficient food of any kind. This deprivation can result in several illnesses, severe weight loss, and even death.

proximal parenting Caregiving practices that involve being physically close to the baby, with frequent holding and touching.

pruning When applied to brain development, the process by which unused connections in the brain atrophy and die.

psychoanalytic theory A theory of human development that holds that irrational, unconscious drives and motives, often originating in childhood, underlie human behaviour.

psychological control A disciplinary technique that involves threatening to withdraw love and support and that relies on a child's feelings of guilt and gratitude to the parents.

psychopathology An illness or disorder of the mind.

puberty The time between the first onrush of hormones and full adult physical development. Puberty usually lasts three to five years. Many more years are required to achieve psychosocial maturity.

Q

qualitative research Research that considers qualities instead of quantities. Descriptions of particular conditions and participants' expressed ideas are often part of qualitative studies.

quantitative research Research that provides data that can be expressed with numbers, such as ranks or scales.

R

race A group of people regarded as distinct from other groups on the basis of appearance, typically skin colour. Social scientists think race is a misleading concept, as biological differences are not signified by outward appearance.

reaction time The time it takes to respond to a stimulus, either physically (with a reflexive movement such as an eyeblink) or cognitively (with a thought).

reactive aggression An impulsive retaliation for another person's intentional or accidental action, verbal or physical.

reflex An unlearned, involuntary action or movement in response to a stimulus. A reflex occurs without conscious thought.

Reggio Emilia A famous program of early childhood education that originated in the town of Reggio Emilia, Italy; it encourages each child's creativity in a carefully designed setting.

reinforcement A technique for conditioning a particular behaviour in which that behaviour is followed by something desired, such as food for a hungry animal or a welcoming smile for a lonely person.

rejecting-neglecting parenting An approach to child-rearing in which the parents are indifferent toward their children and unaware of what is going on in their children's lives.

relational aggression Non-physical acts, such as insults or social rejection, aimed at harming the social connection between the victim and other people.

REM (rapid eye movement) sleep A stage of sleep characterized by flickering eyes behind closed lids, dreaming, and rapid brain waves.

reminder session A perceptual experience that is intended to help a person recollect an idea, a thing, or an experience, without testing whether the person remembers it at the moment.

replication The repetition of a study, using different participants.

reported maltreatment Harm or endangerment about which someone has notified the authorities.

resilience The capacity to adapt well to significant adversity and to overcome serious stress.

response to intervention (RTI) An educational strategy that uses early intervention to help children who demonstrate below-average achievement. Only children who are not helped are designated for more intense measures.

role confusion A situation in which an adolescent does not seem to know or care what his or her identity is. (Sometimes called *identity* or *role diffusion*.)

rough-and-tumble play Play that mimics aggression through wrestling, chasing, or hitting, but in which there is no intent to harm.

rumination Repeatedly thinking and talking about past experiences; can contribute to depression.

S

sandwich generation The generation of middle-aged people who are supposedly "squeezed" by the needs of the younger and older members of their families. In reality, some adults do feel pressured by these obligations, but most are not burdened by them, either because they enjoy fulfilling them or because they choose to take on only some of them or none of them.

scaffolding Temporary support that is tailored to a learner's needs and abilities and aimed at helping the learner master the next task in a given learning process.

science of human development The science that seeks to understand how and why people of all ages and circumstances change or remain the same over time.

scientific method A way to answer questions that requires empirical research and data-based conclusions.

scientific observation A method of testing a hypothesis by unobtrusively watching and recording participants' behaviour in a systematic and objective manner—in a natural setting, in a laboratory, or in searches of archival data.

Seattle Longitudinal Study The first cross-sequential study of adult intelligence. This study began in 1956; the most recent testing was completed in 2013.

secondary aging The specific physical illnesses or conditions that become more common with aging but are caused by health habits, genes, and other influences that vary from person to person.

secondary education Literally, the period after primary education (elementary or grade school) and before tertiary education (college or university). It usually occurs from about age 12 to 18, although there is some variation by school and by nation.

secondary prevention Actions that avert harm in a high-risk situation, such as stopping a car before it hits a pedestrian or installing traffic lights at dangerous intersections.

secondary sex characteristics Physical traits that are not directly involved in reproduction but that indicate sexual maturity, such as a man's beard and a woman's breasts.

secure attachment A relationship in which an infant obtains both comfort and confidence from the presence of his or her caregiver.

selective attention The ability to concentrate on some stimuli while ignoring others.

selective optimization with compensation The theory, developed by Paul and Margret Baltes, that people try to maintain a balance in their lives by looking for the best way to compensate for physical and cognitive losses and to become more proficient in activities they can already do well.

self theories Theories of late adulthood that emphasize the core self, or the search to maintain one's integrity and identity.

self-actualization The final stage in Maslow's hierarchy of needs, characterized by aesthetic, creative, philosophical, and spiritual understanding.

self-awareness A person's realization that he or she is a distinct individual whose body, mind, and actions are separate from those of other people.

self-concept A person's understanding of who he or she is, incorporating self-esteem, physical appearance, personality, and various personal traits, such as gender and size.

self-righting The inborn drive to remedy a developmental deficit; literally, to return to sitting or standing upright after being tipped over. People of all ages have self-righting impulses, for emotional as well as physical imbalance.

senescence A gradual physical decline related to aging. Senescence occurs in everyone and in every body part, but the rate of decline is highly variable within and between persons.

sensation The response of a sensory system (eyes, ears, skin, tongue, nose) when it detects a stimulus.

sensitive period A time when a certain type of development is most likely to happen or happens most easily, although it may still happen later with more difficulty. For example, early childhood is considered a sensitive period for language learning.

sensorimotor intelligence Piaget's term for the way infants think—by using their senses and motor skills—during the first period of cognitive development.

sensory memory The component of the information-processing system in which incoming stimulus information is stored for a split second to allow it to be processed. (Also called the *sensory register*.)

separation anxiety An infant's distress when a familiar caregiver leaves, most obvious between 9 and 14 months.

sex differences Biological differences between males and females, in organs, hormones, and body shape.

sex homophily A preference to interact with one's own sex.

sexual orientation A term that refers to whether a person is sexually and romantically attracted to others of the same sex, the opposite sex, or both sexes.

sexually transmitted infection (STI) An infection spread by sexual contact; includes syphilis, gonorrhea, genital herpes, chlamydia, and HIV. (Formerly called *sexually transmitted disease* or *venereal disease*.)

shaken baby syndrome (SBS) A life-threatening injury that occurs when an infant is forcefully shaken back and forth, a motion that ruptures blood vessels in the brain and breaks neural connections.

single-parent family A family that consists of only one parent and his or her biological children under age 18.

slippery slope The argument that a given action will start a chain of events that will culminate in an undesirable outcome.

small for gestational age (SGA) Having a body weight at birth that is significantly lower than expected, given the time since conception. For example, a 2265-gram newborn is considered SGA if born on time but not SGA if born two months early. (Also called *small-for-dates*.)

social comparison The tendency to assess one's abilities, achievements, social status, and other attributes by measuring them against those of other people, especially one's peers.

social construction An idea that is based on shared perceptions, not on objective reality. Many age-related terms, such as childhood, adolescence, yuppie, and senior citizen, are social constructions.

social convoy Collectively, the family members, friends, acquaintances, and even strangers who move through life with an individual.

social learning The acquisition of behaviour patterns by observing the behaviour of others.

social learning theory An extension of behaviourism that emphasizes that other people influence each person's behaviour. The theory's basic principle is that even without specific reinforcement, every individual learns many things through observation and imitation of other people.

social referencing Seeking information about how to react to an unfamiliar or ambiguous object or event by observing someone else's expressions and reactions. That other person becomes a social reference.

social smile A smile evoked by a human face, normally first evident in infants about 6 weeks after birth.

sociodramatic play Pretend play in which children act out various roles and themes in stories that they create.

socioeconomic status (SES) A person's position in society as determined by income, wealth, occupation, education, and place of residence. (Sometimes called *social class*.)

specific learning disorder A marked deficit in a particular area of learning that is not caused by an apparent physical disability, by another disorder, or by an unusually stressful home environment. (Commonly referred to as *learning disability*.)

spermarche A boy's first ejaculation of sperm. Erections can occur as early as infancy, but ejaculation signals sperm production. Spermarche may occur during sleep (in a "wet dream") or via direct stimulation.

static reasoning A characteristic of preoperational thought whereby a young child thinks that nothing changes. Whatever is now has always been and always will be.

stem cells Cells from which any other specialized type of cell can form.

stereotype threat The possibility that one's appearance or behaviour will be misread to confirm another person's oversimplified, prejudiced attitudes.

still-face technique An experimental practice in which an adult keeps his or her face unmoving and expressionless in face-to-face interaction with an infant.

Strange Situation A laboratory procedure for measuring attachment by evoking infants' reactions to the stress of various adults' comings and goings in an unfamiliar playroom.

stranger wariness An infant's expression of concern—a quiet stare while clinging to a familiar person, or a look of fear—when a stranger appears.

stratification theories Theories that emphasize that social forces, particularly those related to a person's social stratum or social category, limit individual choices and affect a person's ability to function in late adulthood because past stratification continues to limit life in various ways.

stressor Any situation, event, experience, or other stimulus that causes a person to feel stressed. Many circumstances become stressors for some people but not for others.

stunting The failure of children to grow to a normal height for their age due to severe and chronic malnutrition.

substantiated maltreatment Harm or endangerment that has been reported, investigated, and verified.

sudden infant death syndrome (SIDS) The term used to describe an infant's unexpected death; when a seemingly healthy baby, usually between 2 and 6 months old, suddenly stops breathing and dies unexpectedly while asleep.

suicidal ideation Thinking about suicide, usually with some serious emotional and intellectual or cognitive overtones.

superego In psychoanalytic theory, the judgmental part of the personality that internalizes the moral standards of the parents.

survey A research method in which information is collected from a large number of people by interviews, written questionnaires, or some other means.

symbolic thought The concept that an object or word can stand for something else, including something pretended or something not seen. Once symbolic thought is possible, language becomes much more useful.

synapse The intersection between the axon of one neuron and the dendrites of other neurons.

synchrony A coordinated, rapid, and smooth exchange of responses between a caregiver and an infant.

T

tangles Twisted masses of threads made of a protein called *tau* within the neurons of the brain; a normal brain contains some tau, but in brains of people with Alzheimer's disease these tangles proliferate, especially in the hippocampus, a brain structure crucial for memory.

telecommuting Working at home and keeping in touch with the office via computer and telephone.

temperament Inborn differences between one person and another in emotions, activity, and self-regulation. It is measured by the person's typical responses to the environment.

teratogen Any agent or condition, including viruses, drugs, and chemicals, that can impair prenatal development, resulting in birth defects or complications.

terror management theory (TMT) The idea that people adopt cultural values and moral principles in order to cope with their fear of death. This system of beliefs protects individuals from anxiety about their mortality and bolsters their self-esteem, so they react harshly when other people go against any of the moral principles involved.

tertiary prevention Actions, such as immediate and effective medical treatment, that are taken after an adverse event (such as illness, injury, or abuse) occurs and that are aimed at reducing the harm or preventing disability.

testosterone A sex hormone, the best known of the androgens (male hormones); secreted in far greater amounts by males than by females.

thanatology The study of death and dying, especially of the social and emotional aspects.

theory of mind A person's theory of what other people might be thinking. In order to have a theory of mind, children must realize that other people are not necessarily thinking the same thoughts that they themselves are. That realization is seldom achieved before age 4.

theory–theory The idea that children attempt to explain everything they see and hear.

threshold effect A situation in which a certain teratogen is relatively harmless in small doses but becomes harmful once exposure reaches a certain level (the threshold).

time out A disciplinary technique in which a child is separated from other people and activities for a specified time.

transient exuberance The great but temporary increase in the number of dendrites that develop in an infant's brain during the first two years of life.

Trends in Math and Science Study (TIMSS) An international assessment of the math and science skills of Grade 4 and Grade 8 students. Although the TIMSS is very useful, different countries' scores are not always comparable because sample selection, test administration, and content validity are hard to keep uniform.

trust versus mistrust Erikson's first crisis of psychosocial development. Infants learn basic trust, if the world is a secure place where their basic needs (for food, comfort, attention, and so on) are met.

U

ultrasound An image of a fetus (or an internal organ) produced by using high-frequency sound waves. (Also called *sonogram*.)

universal design Designing physical space and common tools that are suitable for people of all ages and all levels of ability.

V

vascular neurocognitive disorder A form of neurocognitive disorder characterized by sporadic and progressive loss of intellectual functioning caused by repeated infarcts, or temporary obstructions of blood vessels, which prevent sufficient blood from reaching the brain.

very low birth weight (VLBW) A body weight at birth of less than 1500 grams.

W

wasting The tendency for children to be severely underweight for their age as a result of malnutrition.

wear and tear A view of aging as a process by which the human body wears out because of the passage of time and exposure to environmental stressors.

withdrawn-rejected Someone rejected by peers because of timid, withdrawn, and anxious behaviour.

working memory The component of the information-processing system in which current conscious mental activity occurs. (Formerly called *short-term memory*.)

working model In cognitive theory, a set of assumptions that the individual uses to organize perceptions and experiences. For example, a person might assume that other people are trustworthy and be surprised by an incident that suggests this working model of human behaviour was erroneous.

X

X-linked A gene carried on the X chromosome. If a male inherits an X-linked recessive trait from his mother, he expresses that trait because the Y from his father has no counteracting gene. Females are more likely to be carriers of X-linked traits but are less likely to express them.

XX A 23rd chromosome pair that consists of two X-shaped chromosomes, one each from the mother and the father. XX zygotes become females.

XY A 23rd chromosome pair that consists of an X-shaped chromosome from the mother and a Y-shaped chromosome from the father. XY zygotes become males.

Y

young-old Healthy, vigorous, financially secure older adults (generally, those aged 60 to 75) who are well integrated into the lives of their families and communities.

Z

zone of proximal development (ZPD) Vygotsky's term for the intellectual arena where new cognitive and physical skills can be mastered.

zygote The single cell that is formed from the fusing of two gametes, a sperm and an ovum.

REFERENCES

A

Aarnoudse-Moens, C. S. H., Smidts, D. P., Oosterlaan, J., Duivenvoorden, H. J., & Weisglas-Kuperus, N. (2009). Executive function in very preterm children at early school age. *Journal of Abnormal Child Psychology, 37,* 981–993.

Aarsland, D., Zaccai, J., & Brayne, C. (2005). A systematic review of prevalence studies of dementia in Parkinson's disease. *Movement Disorders, 20,* 1255–1263. doi:10.1002/mds.20527

Abada, T., Hou, F., & Ram, B. (2008). *Group differences in educational attainment among the children of immigrants* (Catalogue No. 11F0019M—No. 308). Retrieved from http://crcw.princeton.edu/migration/files/library/Group%20Differences%20in%20Educational%20Attainment%20Among%20the%20Children%20of%20Immigrants%20(2).pdf

Abel, E. L. (2009). Fetal alcohol syndrome: Same old, same old. *Addiction, 104,* 1274–1275. doi:10.1111/j.1360–0443.2008.02481.x

Abele, A. E., & Volmer, J. (2011). Dual-career couples: Specific challenges for work-life integration. In S. Kaiser, M. J. Ringlestetter, D. R. Elkhof, & M. Pina e Cunha (Eds.), *Creating balance? International perspectives on the work-life integration of professionals* (pp. 173–189). Heidelberg, Germany: Springer Berlin Heidelberg.

Aboriginal Affairs and Northern Development Canada. (2013). *Backgrounder: Implementation of Jordan's Principle in Saskatchewan.* Retrieved from http://www.aadnc-aandc.gc.ca/aiarch/mr/nr/s-d2009/bk000000451-eng.asp

Abrams, D., Rutland, A., Ferrell, J. M., & Pelletier, J. (2008). Children's judgments of disloyal and immoral peer behavior: Subjective group dynamics in minimal intergroup contexts. *Child Development, 79,* 444–461.

Abu-Bader, S. H., Tirmazi, M. T., & Ross-Sheriff, F. (2011). The impact of acculturation on depression among older Muslim immigrants in the United States. *Journal of Gerontological Social Work, 54,* 425–448. doi:10.1080/01634372.2011.560928

Achenbaum, W. A. (2005). *Older Americans, vital communities: A bold vision for societal aging.* Baltimore, MD: Johns Hopkins University Press.

Acs, G. (2007). Can we promote child well-being by promoting marriage? *Journal of Marriage and Family, 69,* 1326–1344.

Active Healthy Kids Canada (AHKC). (2011). *Don't let this be the most physical activity our kids get after school: The Active Healthy Kids Canada 2011 report card on physical activity for children and youth.* Retrieved from http://dvqdas9jty7g6.cloudfront.net/reportcard2011/ahkcreportcard20110429final.pdf

Active Healthy Kids Canada (AHKC). (2012a). *Active play: Fun and fundamental.* Retrieved from http://dvqdas9jty7g6.cloudfront.net/reportcards2012/ahkc2012-mattestory-final.pdf

Active Healthy Kids Canada (AHKC). (2012b). *Is active play extinct? The 2012 Active Healthy Kids Canada report card on physical activity for children and youth.* Retrieved from http://dvqdas9jty7g6.cloudfront.net/reportcards2012/AHKC%202012%20-%20Report%20Card%20Long%20Form%20-%20FINAL.pdf

Adam, E. K., Klimes-Dougan, B., & Gunnar, M. R. (2007). Social regulation of the adrenocortical response to stress in infants, children, and adolescents: Implications for psychopathology and education. In D. Coch, G. Dawson, & K. W. Fischer (Eds.), *Human behavior, learning, and the developing brain: Atypical development* (pp. 264–304). New York, NY: Guilford Press.

Adamson, L. B., & Bakeman, R. (2006). Development of displaced speech in early mother-child conversations. *Child Development, 77,* 186–200.

Adelson, N. (2007). Biomedical approach a poor fit with Aboriginal views on health and healing. *Canadian Psychiatry Aujourd'hui, 3.* Retrieved from http://publications.cpa-apc.org/browse/documents/142

Adler, L. P. (1995). *Centenarians: The bonus years.* Santa Fe, NM: Health Press.

Adolph, K. E., & Berger, S. E. (2005). Physical and motor development. In M. H. Bornstein & M. E. Lamb (Eds.), *Developmental science: An advanced textbook* (5th ed., pp. 223–281). Mahwah, NJ: Erlbaum.

Adolph, K. E., Vereijken, B., & Shrout, P. E. (2003). What changes in infant walking and why. *Child Development, 74,* 475–497.

Adoption Council of Canada. (2011, December 4). *Canadians go abroad to adopt 1,946 children in 2010.* Retrieved from http://www.adoption.ca/adoption-news?news_id=56

Afifi, T. O., Enns, M. W., Cox, B. J., Asmundson, G. J. G., Stein, M. B., & Sareen, J. (2008). Population attributable fractions of psychiatric disorders and suicide ideation and attempts associated with adverse childhood experiences. *American Journal of Public Health, 98,* 946–952. doi:10.2105/ajph.2007.120253

Agence de la santé et des services sociaux de Montréal. (2011). *2011 report of the Director of Public Health: Social inequalities in health in Montreal—Progress to Date.* Retrieved from http://publications.santemontreal.qc.ca/uploads/tx_asssmpublications/978-2-89673-131-2.pdf

Agence France Presse. (2013, July 2). Under China's new elderly rights law, women order to visit mother once every 2 months. *Huffington Post.* Retrieved from http://www.huffingtonpost.com/2013/07/02/china-elderly-rights-law_n_3531832.html

Ahmed, P., & Jaakkola, J. J. K. (2007). Maternal occupation and adverse pregnancy outcomes: A Finnish population-based study. *Occupational Medicine, 57,* 417–423. doi:10.1093/occmed/kqm038

Ainsworth, M. D. (1967). *Infancy in Uganda: Infant care and the growth of love.* Oxford, England: Johns Hopkins Press.

Ainsworth, M. D. S. (1973). The development of infant-mother attachment. In B. M. Caldwell & H. N. Ricciuti (Eds.), *Review of child development research* (Vol. 3, pp. 1–94). Chicago, IL: University of Chicago Press.

Ajemian, R., D'Ausilio, A., Moorman, H., & Bizzi, E. (2010). Why professional athletes need a prolonged period of warm-up and other peculiarities of human motor learning. *Journal of Motor Behavior, 42*, 381–388. doi:10.1080/00222895.2010.528262

Akiba, D., & García Coll, C. T. (2004). The development of children and families of color: Past issues and future directions. In T. B. Smith & P. S. Richards (Eds.), *Handbook of multicultural counseling: Internalizing & affirming diversity in counseling & psychology*. Boston: Allyn & Bacon.

Akinbami, L. J., Lynch, C. D., Parker, J. D., & Woodruff, T. J. (2010). The association between childhood asthma prevalence and monitored air pollutants in metropolitan areas, United States, 2001–2004. *Environmental Research, 110*, 294–301.

Al-Sahab, B., Ardern, C. I., Hamadeh, M. J., & Tamim, H. (2010). Age at menarche in Canada: Results from the National Longitudinal Survey of Children & Youth. *BMC Public Health, 10*(736). Retrieved from http://www.biomedcentral.com/content/pdf/1471-2458-10-736.pdf

Alasuutari, P., Bickman, L., & Brannen, J. (2008). Introduction: Social research in changing social conditions. In P. Alasuutari, L. Bickman, & J. Brannen (Eds.), *The SAGE Handbook of Social Research Methods* (pp. 1–8). London: Sage.

Albert, D., & Steinberg, L. (2011). Judgment and decision making in adolescence. *Journal of Research on Adolescence, 21*, 211–224. doi:10.1111/j.1532–7795.2010.00724.x

Albert, S. M., & Freedman, V. A. (2010). *Public health and aging: Maximizing function and well-being* (2nd ed.). New York: Springer.

Alberta Education. (2013). *Guide to education: ECS to grade 12*. Retrieved from http://www.education.alberta.ca/media/7044993/guidetoed2013.pdf

Alberts, A., Elkind, D., & Ginsberg, S. (2007). The personal fable and risk-taking in early adolescence. *Journal of Youth and Adolescence, 36*, 71–76.

Aldwin, C. M. (2007). *Stress, coping, and development: An integrative perspective* (2nd ed.). New York: Guilford Press.

Alegre, A. (2011). Parenting styles and children's emotional intelligence: What do we know? *The Family Journal, 19*, 56–62. doi:10.1177/1066480710387486

Alisat, S., & Pratt, M. W. (2012). Characteristics of young adults' personal religious narratives and their relation with the identity status model: A longitudinal, mixed methods study. *Identity, 12*, 29–52. doi:10.1080/15283488.2012.632392

Allemand, M., Zimprich, D., & Martin, M. (2008). Long-term correlated change in personality traits in old age. *Psychology and Aging, 23*, 545–557. doi:10.1037/a0013239

Allen, E., Bonell, C., Strange, V., Copas, A., Stephenson, J., Johnson, A., & Oakley, A. (2007). Does the UK government's teenage pregnancy strategy deal with the correct risk factors? Findings from a secondary analysis of data from a randomised trial of sex education and their implications for policy. *Journal of Epidemiology & Community Health, 61*, 20–27.

Allen, K. P. (2010). A bullying intervention system in high school: A two-year school-wide follow-up. *Studies In Educational Evaluation, 36*, 83–92.

Allen, M. (2009). *Youth bilingualism in Canada*. Retrieved from http://www.statcan.gc.ca/pub/81-004-x/2008004/article/10767-eng.htm#tphp

Allen, S. (2007). The future of Inuktitut in the face of majority languages: Bilingualism or language shift? *Applied Psycholinguistics, 28*, 515–536.

Alloy, L. B., & Abramson, L. Y. (2007). The adolescent surge in depression and emergence of gender differences: A biocognitive vulnerability-stress model in developmental context. In D. Romer & E. F. Walker (Eds.), *Adolescent psychopathology and the developing brain: Integrating brain and prevention science* (pp. 284–312). New York, NY: Oxford University Press.

Alm, B. (2007). To co-sleep or not to sleep. *Acta Pædiatrica, 96*, 1385–1386.

Almeida, L. S., Prieto, M. D., Ferreira, A. I., Bermejo, M. R., Ferrando, M., & Ferrandiz, C. (2010). Intelligence assessment: Gardner multiple intelligence theory as an alternative. *Learning and Individual Differences, 20*, 225–230.

Alsaker, F. D., & Flammer, A. (2006). Pubertal development. In S. Jackson & L. Goossens (Eds.), *Handbook of adolescent development* (pp. 30–50). Hove, East Sussex, UK: Psychology Press.

Altbach, P. G., Reisberg, L., & Rumbley, L. E. (2010, March/April). Tracking a global academic revolution. *Change: The Magazine of Higher Learning, 42*, 30–39.

Alwin, D. F. (2009). History, cohorts, and patterns of cognitive aging. In H. B. Bosworth & C. Hertzog (Eds.), *Aging and cognition: Research methodologies and empirical advances* (pp. 9–38). Washington, DC: American Psychological Association.

Alzheimer Society of Canada. (2012). *Facts about dementia*. Retrieved from http://www.alzheimer.ca/en/on/About-dementia/Dementias/What-is-dementia/Facts-about-dementia

Alzheimer's Association. (2012). 2012 Alzheimer's disease facts and figures. *Alzheimer's & Dementia: The Journal of the Alzheimer's Association, 8*, 131–168.

Amato, P. R. (2005). The impact of family formation change on the cognitive, social, and emotional well-being of the next generation. *Future of Children, 15*(2), 75–96.

Amato, P. R. (2010). Research on divorce: Continuing trends and new developments. *Journal of Marriage and Family, 72*, 650–666. doi:10.1111/j.1741–3737.2010.00723.x

Ambady, N., & Bharucha, J. (2009). Culture and the brain. *Current Directions in Psychological Science, 18*, 342–345. doi:10.1111/j.1467–8721.2009.01664.x

Ambler, D. R., Bieber, E. J., & Diamond, M. P. (2012). Sexual function in elderly women: A review of current literature. *Reviews in Obstetrics and Gynecology, 5*, 16–27.

Anderson, C. A., Gentile, D. A., & Buckley, K. E. (2007). *Violent video game effects on children and adolescents: Theory, research, and public policy*. New York, NY: Oxford University Press.

Anderson, C. A., Sakamoto, A., Gentile, D. A., Ihori, N., Shibuya, A., Yukawa, S., ... Kobayashi, K. (2008). Longitudinal effects of violent video games on aggression in Japan and the United States. *Pediatrics, 122*, e1067–1072. http://pediatrics.aappublications.org/cgi/content/abstract/122/5/e1067 doi:10.1542/peds.2008-1425

Anderson, L. B., Harro, M., Sardinha, L. B., Froberg, K., Ekelund, U., Brage, S., & Anderson, M. (2001). 'You have to get inside the person' or making grief private: Image and metaphor in the therapeutic reconstruction of bereavement. In J. Hockey (Ed.), *Grief, mourning, and death rituals* (pp. 135–143). Buckingham, England: Open University Press.

Anderssen, S. A. (2006). Physical activity and clustered cardiovascular risk in children: A cross-sectional study (The European Youth Heart Study). *The Lancet, 368*, 299–304. Retrieved from http://www.outdoorfoundation.org/pdf/PhysicalActivityAndCardio.pdf

Ansary, N. S., & Luthar, S. S. (2009). Distress and academic achievement among adolescents of affluence: A study of externalizing and internalizing problem behaviors and school performance. *Development and Psychopathology, 21*, 319–341. doi:10.1017/S0954579409000182

Antonucci, T. C., Akiyama, H., & Merline, A. (2001). Dynamics of social relationships in midlife. In M. E. Lachman (Ed.), *Handbook of midlife development* (pp. 571–598). New York, NY: Wiley.

Antonucci, T. C., Jackson, J. S., & Biggs, S. (2007). Intergenerational relations: Theory, research, and policy. *Journal of Social Issues, 63*, 679–693.

Aouizerat, B., Pearce, C. L., & Miaskowski, C. (2011). The search for host genetic factors of HIV/AIDS pathogenesis in the postgenome era: Progress to date and new avenues for discovery. *Current HIV/AIDS Reports, 8*, 38–44. doi:10.1007/s11904–010–0065–1

Apgar, V. (1953). A proposal for a new method of evaluation of the newborn infant. *Current Researches in Anesthesia and Analgesia, 32*, 260–267.

Apostolou, M. (2007). Sexual selection under parental choice: The role of parents in the evolution of human mating. *Evolution and Human Behavior, 28*, 403–409.

Apple, M. W. (1975). The hidden curriculum and the nature of conflict. In W. Pinar (Ed.), *Curriculum theorizing: The reconceptualists* (pp. 95–119). Berkeley, CA: McCutchan.

Arber, S., & Timonen, V. (2012). *Contemporary grandparenting: Changing family relationships in global contexts*. Chicago, IL: Policy Press.

Archambault, I., Janosz, M., Fallu, J.-S., & Pagani, L. S. (2009). Student engagement and its relationship with early high school dropout. *Journal of Adolescence, 32*, 651–670.

Ardelt, M. (2011). Wisdom, age, and well-being. In K. W. Schaie & S. L. Willis (Eds.), *Handbook of the psychology of aging* (7th ed., pp. 279–291). San Diego, CA: Academic Press.

Arking, R. (2006). *The biology of aging: Observations and principles* (3rd ed.). New York, NY: Oxford University Press.

Armstrong, T. (2009). *Multiple intelligences in the classroom* (3rd ed.). Alexandria, VA: Association for Supervision and Curriculum Development.

Arnett, J. J. (2004). *Emerging adulthood: The winding road from the late teens through the twenties*. New York, NY: Oxford University Press.

Arnett, J. J., & Brody, G. H. (2008). A fraught passage: The identity challenges of African American emerging adults. *Human Development, 51*, 291–293.

Arnett, J. J., Kloep, M., Hendry, L. B., & Tanner, J. L. (2011). *Debating emerging adulthood: Stage or process?* New York, NY: Oxford University Press.

Arnold, L. E., Farmer, C., Kraemer, H. C., Davies, M., Witwer, A., Chuang, S., ... Swiezy, N. B. (2010). Moderators, mediators, and other predictors of risperidone response in children with autistic disorder and irritability. *Journal of Child and Adolescent Psychopharmacology, 20*, 83–93. doi:10.1089/cap.2009.0022

Aron, A., McLaughlin-Volpe, T., Mashek, D., Lewandowski, G., Wright, S. C., & Aron, E. N. (2005). Including others in the self. *European Review of Social Psychology, 15*, 101–132.

Aronson, J., & Dee, T. (2012). Stereotype threat in the real world. In M. Inzlicht & T. Schmader (Eds.), *Stereotype threat: Theory, process, and application* (pp. 264–279). New York, NY: Oxford University Press.

Aronson, J., Fried, C. B., & Good, C. (2002). Reducing the effects of stereotype threat on African American college students by shaping theories of intelligence. *Journal of Experimental Social Psychology, 38*, 113–125.

Arseneault, L., Moffit, T. E., Caspi, A., Taylor, A., Rijsdijk, F. V., Jaffee, S. R., ... Measelle, J. R. (2003). Strong genetic effects on cross-situational antisocial behaviour among 5-year-old children according to mothers, teachers, examiner-observers, and twins' self-reports. *Journal of Child Psychology and Psychiatry, 44*, 832–848.

Arum, R., & Roksa, J. (2011). *Academically adrift: Limited learning on college campuses*. Chicago, IL: University of Chicago Press.

Arum, R., Roksa, J., & Cho, E. (2011). *Improving undergraduate learning: Findings and policy recommendations from the SSRC-CLA Longitudinal Project*. New York, NY: Social Science Research Council.

Asarnow, J. R., Porta, G., Spirito, A., Emslie, G., Clarke, G., Wagner, K. D., ... Brent, D. A. (2011). Suicide attempts and nonsuicidal self-injury in the treatment of resistant depression in adolescents: Findings from the TORDIA study. *Journal of the American Academy of Child and Adolescent Psychiatry, 50*, 772–781.

Asendorpf, J. B., Denissen, J. J. A., & van Aken, M. A. G. (2008). Inhibited and aggressive preschool children at 23 years of age: Personality and social transitions into adulthood. *Developmental Psychology, 44*, 997–1011.

Ashby, M. (2009). The dying human: A perspective from palliative medicine. In A. Kellehear (Ed.), *The study of dying: From autonomy to transformation* (pp. 76–98). New York, NY: Cambridge University Press.

Asia Pacific Foundation of Canada. (2012). *Immigrants by regional source as percentage of total ommigration*. Retrieved from http://www.asiapacific.ca/statistics/immigration/immigration-arrivals/immigrants-regional-source-percentage-total-immigration

Association of Universities and Colleges of Canada (AUCC). (2011). *Trends in higher education. Volume 1: Enrolment.* Retrieved from http://www.aucc.ca/wp-content/uploads/2011/05/trends-2011-vol1-enrolment-e.pdf

Association of Universities and Colleges of Canada (AUCC). (2013). Opening doors for Aboriginal students: New national database enhances access to university [Press release]. Retrieved from http://www.aucc.ca/media-room/news-and-commentary/aboriginal-database/

Atchley, R. C. (2009). *Spirituality and aging.* Baltimore, MD: Johns Hopkins University Press.

Atkinson, J., & Braddick, O. (2003). Neurobiological models of normal and abnormal visual development. In M. de Haan & M. H. Jackson (Eds.), *The cognitive neuroscience of development* (pp. 43–71). New York, NY: Psychology Press.

Aud, S., Hussar, W., Johnson, F., Kena, G., Roth, E., Manning, E., ... Zhang, J. (2012). *The condition of education 2012.* Washington, DC: U.S. Department of Education, National Center for Education Statistics.

Audrey, S., Holliday, J., & Campbell, R. (2006). It's good to talk: Adolescent perspectives of an informal, peer-led intervention to reduce smoking. *Social Science & Medicine, 63,* 320–334.

Auerbach, S. (2007). *Special needs students in First Nations schools: Inclusion in school based special education programs.* Retrieved from http://www.fnsa.ca/Attachments/Special%20Education/20072008/07%20SpEd%20Evaluation%20Report%20Revised.pdf

Aunola, K., & Nurmi, J.-E. (2004). Maternal affection moderates the impact of psychological control on a child's mathematical performance. *Developmental Psychology, 40,* 965–978.

Austrian, S. G. (2008). *Developmental theories through the life cycle* (2nd ed.). New York, NY: Columbia University Press.

Aviv, A. (2011). Leukocyte telomere dynamics, human aging and life span. In E. J. Masoro & S. N. Austad (Eds.), *Handbook of the biology of aging* (7th ed., pp. 163–176). San Diego, CA: Academic Press.

Ayalon, L., & Ancoli-Israel, S. (2009). Normal sleep in aging. In T. L. Lee-Chiong (Ed.), *Sleep medicine essentials* (pp. 173–176). Hoboken, NJ: Wiley-Blackwell.

Ayduk, Ö., & Kross, E. (2008). Enhancing the pace of recovery. *Psychological Science, 19,* 229–231. doi:10.1111/j.1467-9280.2008.02073.x

Ayers, C. R., Saxena, S., Golshan, S., & Wetherell, J. L. (2010). Age at onset and clinical features of late life compulsive hoarding. *International Journal of Geriatric Psychiatry, 25,* 142–149. doi:10.1002/gps.2310

B

Bachman, J. G., O'Malley, P. M., Freedman-Doan, P., Trzesniewski, K. H., & Donnellan, M. B. (2011). Adolescent self-esteem: Differences by race/ethnicity, gender, and age. *Self Identity, 10,* 445–473. doi:10.1080/15298861003794538

Bagner, D. M., Pettit, J. W., Lewinsohn, P. M., & Seeley, J. R. (2010). Effect of maternal depression on child behavior: A sensitive period? *Journal of the American Academy of Child and Adolescent Psychiatry, 49,* 699–707.

Bailey, K., West, R., & Anderson, C. A. (2010). A negative association between video game experience and proactive cognitive control. *Psychophysiology, 47,* 34–42. doi:10.1111/j.1469-8986.2009.00925.x

Baker, B. (2007). *Old age in a new age: The promise of transformative nursing homes.* Nashville, TN: Vanderbilt University Press.

Baker, J. P. (2000). Immunization and the American way: 4 childhood vaccines. *American Journal of Public Health, 90,* 199–207.

Baker, L., & Silverstein, M. (2012). The wellbeing of grandparents caring for grandchildren in rural China and the United States. In S. Arber & V. Timonen (Eds.), *Contemporary grandparenting: Changing family relationships in global contexts* (pp. 51–70). Bristol, UK: Policy Press.

Baker, L. A., & Mutchler, J. E. (2010). Poverty and material hardship in grandparent-headed households. *Journal of Marriage and Family, 72,* 947–962. doi:10.1111/j.1741-3737.2010.00741.x

Balbuena, L., Baetz, M., & Bowen, R. (2013). Religious attendance, spirituality, and major depression in Canada: A 14-year follow-up study. *Canadian Journal of Psychiatry, 58,* 225–232.

Baldry, A. C., & Farrington, D. P. (2007). Effectiveness of programs to prevent school bullying. *Victims & Offenders, 2,* 183–204. doi:10.1080/15564880701263155

Ball, H. (2012). *At liberty to die: The battle for death with dignity in America.* New York, NY: New York University Press.

Ball, H., Hooker, E., & Kelly, P. (2000). Parent-infant co-sleeping: Fathers' roles and perspectives. *Infant and Child Development, 9,* 67–74.

Baltes, P. B. (2003). On the incomplete architechture of human ontogeny: Selection, optimization and compensation as foundation of developmental theory. In U. M. Staudinger & U. E. R. Lindenberger (Eds.), *Understanding human development: Dialogues with lifespan psychology* (pp. 17–43). Dordrecht, The Netherlands: Kluwer.

Baltes, P. B., & Baltes, M. M. (1990). Psychological perspectives on successful aging: The model of selective optimization with compensation. In P. B. Baltes & M. M. Baltes (Eds.), *Successful aging: Perspectives from the behavioral sciences* (pp. 1–34). New York, NY: Cambridge University Press.

Baltes, P. B., Lindenberger, U., & Staudinger, U. M. (2006). Life span theory in developmental psychology. In R. M. Lerner (Ed.), *Handbook of child psychology: Vol. 1. Theoretical models of human development* (6th ed., pp. 569–664). Hoboken, NJ: Wiley.

Baltes, P. B., & Smith, J. (2008). The fascination of wisdom: Its nature, ontogeny, and function. *Perspectives on Psychological Science, 3,* 56–64.

Bamford, C., & Lagattuta, K. H. (2010). A new look at children's understanding of mind and emotion: The case of prayer. *Developmental Psychology, 46,* 78–92.

Bandura, A. (1977). *Social learning theory.* Englewood Cliffs, NJ: Prentice Hall.

Banerji, A. (2012). Preventing unintentional injuries in Indigenous children and youth in Canada. *Paediatrics & Child Health, 17,* 393.

Barbarin, O., Downer, J. T., Head, D., & Odom, E. (2010). Home-school differences in beliefs, support, and control during public pre-kindergarten and their link to children's kindergarten readiness. *Early Childhood Research Quarterly, 25,* 358–372. doi:10.1016/j.ecresq.2010.02.003

Barber, B. K. (Ed.). (2002). *Intrusive parenting: How psychological control affects children and adolescents.* Washington, DC: American Psychological Association.

Bargh, J. A., & McKenna, K. Y. A. (2004). The Internet and social life. *Annual Review of Psychology, 55,* 573–590. doi: 10.1146/annurev.psych.55.090902.141922

Bargh, J. A., McKenna, K. Y. A., & Fitzsimons, G. M. (2002). Can you see the real me? Activation and expression of the "true self" on the Internet. *Journal of Social Issues, 58,* 33–48. Retrieved from http://smg.media.mit.edu/personals/chi2004/private/papers/bargh.pdf

Barkin, S., Scheindlin, B., Ip, E. H., Richardson, I., & Finch, S. (2007). Determinants of parental discipline practices: A national sample from primary care practices. *Clinical Pediatrics, 46,* 64–69.

Barlow, S. E., & the Expert Committee. (2007). Expert committee recommendations regarding the prevention, assessment, and treatment of child and adolescent overweight and obesity: Summary report. *Pediatrics, 120*(Suppl. 4), S164–S192. doi:10.1542/peds.2007-2329C

Barnes, G. M., Hoffman, J. H., Welte, J. W., Farrell, M. P., & Dintcheff, B. A. (2006). Effects of parental monitoring and peer deviance on substance use and delinquency. *Journal of Marriage and Family, 68,* 1084–1104.

Barnett, M., Watson, R., & Kind, P. (2006). Pathways to barrel development. In R. Erzurumlu, W. Guido, & Z. Molnár (Eds.), *Development and plasticity in sensory thalamus and cortex* (pp. 138–157). New York, NY: Springer.

Barnett, W. S. (2007). The importance of demographic, social, and political context for estimating policy impacts: Comment on "Implementing New York's universal pre-kindergarten program". *Early Education and Development, 18,* 609–616.

Barnett, W. S., Epstein, D. J., Carolan, M. E., Fitzgerald, J., Ackerman, D. J., & Friedman, A. H. (2010). *The state of preschool 2010.* New Brunswick, NJ: National Institute for Early Education Research.

Baron, A. S., & Banaji, M. R. (2006). The development of implicit attitudes: Evidence of race evaluations from ages 6 and 10 and adulthood. *Psychological Science, 17,* 53–58.

Barr, R. G., Barr, M., Fujiwara, T., Conway, J., Catherine, N., Brant, R. (2009). Do educational materials change knowledge and behaviour about crying and shaken baby syndrome? A randomized controlled trial. *Canadian Medical Association Journal, 180,* 727–733. doi: 10.1503/cmaj.081419

Barrett, A. E. (2012). Feeling young—A prescription for growing older? *Aging Today, 33,* 3–4.

Barzilai, N., & Bartke, A. (2009). Biological approaches to mechanistically understand the healthy life span extension achieved by calorie restriction and modulation of hormones. *Journals of Gerontology Series A: Biological Sciences and Medical Sciences, 64A,* 187–191. doi:10.1093/gerona/gln061

Basak, C., Boot, W. R., Voss, M. W., & Kramer, A. F. (2008). Can training in a real-time strategy video game attenuate cognitive decline in older adults? *Psychology and Aging, 23,* 765–777. doi:10.1037/a0013494

Bascaramurty, D. (2012, January 27). Ethnic-focused nursing homes put a Canadian face on filial piety. *The Globe and Mail.* Retrieved from http://www.theglobeandmail.com/news/national/ethnic-focused-nursing-homes-put-a-canadian-face-on-filial-piety/article1359997/?page=all

Bascom, N. (2012, January 14). Brainy ballplayers: Elite athletes get their heads in the game. *Science News, 181,* 22–25.

Bates, L. M., Acevedo-Garcia, D., Alegria, M., & Krieger, N. (2008). Immigration and generational trends in body mass index and obesity in the United States: Results of the National Latino and Asian American Survey, 2002–2003. *American Journal of Public Health, 98,* 70–77. doi:10.2105/ajph.2006.102814

Bateson, P. (2005, February 4). Desirable scientific conduct. *Science, 307,* 645.

Batterham, P. J., Christensen, H., & Mackinnon, A. J. (2009). Fluid intelligence is independently associated with all-cause mortality over 17 years in an elderly community sample: An investigation of potential mechanisms. *Intelligence, 37,* 551–560.

Bauer, P. J., San Souci, P., & Pathman, T. (2010). Infant memory. *Wiley Interdisciplinary Reviews: Cognitive Science, 1,* 267–277.

Bauer-Maglin, N., & Perry, D. M. (2010). *Final acts: Death, dying, and the choices we make.* New Brunswick, NJ: Rutgers University Press.

Baugher, J. E. (2008). Facing death: Buddhist and western hospice approaches. *Symbolic Interaction, 31,* 259–284. doi:10.1525/si.2008.31.3.259

Baum, K. (2005). *Juvenile victimization and offending, 1993–2003* (NCJ 209468). Washington, DC: U.S. Department of Justice, Office of Justice Programs.

Baumeister, R. F., & Blackhart, G. C. (2007). Three perspectives on gender differences in adolescent sexual development. In R. C. M. E. Engels, M. Kerr, & H. Stattin (Eds.), *Friends, lovers, and groups: Key relationships in adolescence* (pp. 93–104). Hoboken, NJ: Wiley.

Baumrind, D. (1967). Child care practices anteceding three patterns of preschool behavior. *Genetic Psychology Monographs, 75,* 43–88.

Baumrind, D. (1971). Current patterns of parental authority. *Developmental Psychology, 4*(1, Pt. 2), 1–103.

Baumrind, D. (2005). Patterns of parental authority and adolescent autonomy. *New Directions for Child and Adolescent Development, 2005,* 61–69. doi:10.1002/cd.128

Baumrind, D., Larzelere, R. E., & Owens, E. B. (2010). Effects of preschool parents' power assertive patterns and practices on adolescent development. *Parenting: Science and Practice, 10,* 157–201. doi:10.1080/15295190903290790

Bayer, J. K., Hiscock, H., Hampton, A., & Wake, M. (2007). Sleep problems in young infants and maternal mental and physical health. *Journal of Paediatrics and Child Health, 43,* 66–73. doi:10.1111/j.1440-1754.2007.01005.x

Bazelon, E. (2006, April 30). A question of resilience. *New York Times Magazine.* Retrieved from http://www.nytimes.com/2006/04/30/magazine/30abuse.html?pagewanted=all

Beal, S. (1988). Sleeping position and sudden infant death syndrome. *Medical Journal of Australia, 149*, 562.

Beauchaine, T. P., Klein, D. N., Crowell, S. E., Derbidge, C., & Gatzke-Kopp, L. (2009). Multifinality in the development of personality disorders: A Biology × Sex × Environment interaction model of antisocial and borderline traits. *Development and Psychopathology, 21*, 735–770. doi:10.1017/S0954579409000418

Beaumont, S., & Pratt, M. (2011). Identity processing styles and psychosocial balance during early and middle adulthood: The role of identity in intimacy and generativity. *Journal of Adult Development, 18*, 172–183. doi:10.1007/s10804–011–9125–z

Beaupré, P. (2008). *I do… Take two? Changes in intentions to remarry among divorced Canadian during the past 20 years.* Retrieved from http://www.statcan.gc.ca/pub/89-630-x/2008001/article/10659-eng.htm

Beaupré, P., Dryburgh, H., & Wendt, M. (2010). *Making fathers "count."* Retrieved from http://www.statcan.gc.ca/pub/11-008-x/2010002/article/11165-eng.htm

Bebbington, P., Jonas, S., Brugha, T., Meltzer, H., Jenkins, R., Cooper, C., … McManus, S. (2011). Child sexual abuse reported by an English national sample: Characteristics and demography. *Social Psychiatry and Psychiatric Epidemiology, 46*, 255–262. doi:10.1007/s00127–010–0245–8

Beck, M. (2009, May 26). How's your baby? Recalling the Apgar score's namesake. *Wall Street Journal*, pp. D-1.

Beckers, D. G. J., van der Linden, D., Smulders, P. G. W., Kompier, M. A. J., Taris, T. W., & Geurts, S. A. E. (2008). Voluntary or involuntary? Control over overtime and rewards for overtime in relation to fatigue and work satisfaction. *Work & Stress, 22*, 33–50.

Beckett, N. S., Peters, R., Fletcher, A. E., Staessen, J. A., Liu, L., Dumitrascu, D., … Bulpitt, C. J. (2008). Treatment of hypertension in patients 80 years of age or older. *New England Journal of Medicine, 358*, 1887–1898. doi:10.1056/NEJMoa0801369

Beevar, D. S., & Beevar, R. J. (1998). *Pragmatics of human relationships.* Iowa City, IA: Geist & Russell.

Beil, L. (2011, June 4). Healthy aging in a pill. *Science News, 179*, 22–25.

Beilin, L., & Huang, R.-C. (2008). Childhood obesity, hypertension, the metabolic syndrome and adult cardiovascular disease. *Clinical and Experimental Pharmacology and Physiology, 35*, 409–411.

Beilock, S. (2010). *Choke: What the secrets of the brain reveal about getting it right when you have to* (1st Free Press hardcover ed.). New York, NY: Free Press.

Beiser, M. (2005). The health of immigrants and refugees in Canada. *Canadian Journal of Public Health, 96 Supplement 2*, S30–44.

Bell, A. F., White-Traut, R., & Medoff-Cooper, B. (2010). Neonatal neurobehavioral organization after exposure to maternal epidural analgesia in labor. *Journal of Obstetric, Gynecologic, & Neonatal Nursing, 39*, 178–190. doi:10.1111/j.1552–6909.2010.01100.x

Bell, A. M., & Robinson, G. E. (2011, June 3). Behavior and the dynamic genome. *Science, 332*, 1161–1162.

Bell, M. A., & Calkins, S. D. (2012). Attentional control and emotion regulation in early development. In M. I. Posner (Ed.), *Cognitive neuroscience of attention* (2nd ed., pp. 322–330). New York, NY: Guilford Press.

Bell, R. (1998). *Changing bodies, changing lives: A book for teens on sex and relationships* (Expanded 3rd ed.). New York, NY: Times Books.

Belle, D. (1990). Poverty and women's mental health. *American Psychologist, 45*, 385–389. doi:10.1037/0003-066X.45.3.385

Belsky, J., Bakermans-Kranenburg, M. J., & Van IJzendoorn, M. H. (2007). For better and for worse: Differential susceptibility to environmental influences. *Current Directions in Psychological Science, 16*, 300–304.

Belsky, J., & de Haan, M. (2011). Parenting and children's brain development: The end of the beginning. *Journal of Child Psychology and Psychiatry, 52*, 409–428. doi:10.1111/j.1469–7610.2010.02281.x

Belsky, J., Schlomer, G. L., & Ellis, B. J. (2012). Beyond cumulative risk: Distinguishing harshness and unpredictability as determinants of parenting and early life history strategy. *Developmental Psychology, 48*, 662–673. doi:10.1037/a0024454

Belsky, J., Steinberg, L., Houts, R. M., Halpern-Felsher, B. L., & The NICHD Early Child Care Research Network. (2010). The development of reproductive strategy in females: Early maternal harshness → earlier menarche → increased sexual risk taking. *Developmental Psychology, 46*, 120–128.

Benatar, D. (2011). A legal right to die: Responding to slippery slope and abuse arguments. *Current Oncology, 18*, 206–207.

Bendlin, B. B., Canu, E., Willette, A. A., Kastman, E. K., McLaren, D. G., Kosmatka, K. J., … Johnson, S. C. (2011). Effects of aging and calorie restriction on white matter in rhesus macaques. *Neurobiology of Aging, 32*, 2319.e1–11. doi:10.1016/j.neurobiolaging.2010.04.008

Benet, S. (1974). *Abkhasians: The long-living people of the Caucasus.* New York, NY: Holt, Rinehart & Winston.

Bengtson, V. L. (2001). Beyond the nuclear family: The increasing importance of multigenerational bonds (The Burgess Award Lecture). *Journal of Marriage & the Family, 63*, 1–16.

Benner, A. D., & Graham, S. (2007). Navigating the transition to multi-ethnic urban high schools: Changing ethnic congruence and adolescents' school-related affect. *Journal of Research on Adolescence, 17*, 207–220.

Benovenli, L., Fuller, E., Sinnott, J., & Waterman, S. (2011). Three applications of the theory of postformal thought: Wisdom, concepts of God, and success in college. In R. L. Piedmont & A. Village (Eds.), *Research in the social scientific study of religion* (Vol. 22, pp. 141–154). Leiden, The Netherlands: Brill.

Bentley, G. R., & Mascie-Taylor, C. G. N. (2000). Introduction. In G. R. Bentley & C. G. N. Mascie-Taylor (Eds.), *Infertility in the modern world: Present and future prospects* (pp. 1–13). Cambridge, England: Cambridge University Press.

Ben-Zur, H., & Zeidner, M. (2009). Threat to life and risk-taking behaviors: A review of empirical findings and explanatory models. *Personality and Social Psychology Review, 13*, 109–128. doi:10.1177/1088868308330104

Berenbaum, S. A., Martin, C. L., Hanish, L. D., Briggs, P. T., & Fabes, R. A. (2008). Sex differences in children's play.

In J. B. Becker, K. J. Berkley, N. Geary, E. Hampson, J. P. Herman, & E. Young (Eds.), *Sex differences in the brain: From genes to behavior* (pp. 275–290). New York, NY: Oxford University Press.

Berg, S. J., & Wynne-Edwards, K. E. (2002). Salivary hormone concentrations in mothers and fathers becoming parents are not correlated. *Hormones & Behavior, 42*, 424–436.

Berger, K. S. (2007). Update on bullying at school: Science forgotten? *Developmental Review, 27*, 90–126.

Berger, L. M., Paxson, C., & Waldfogel, J. (2009). Income and child development. *Children and Youth Services Review, 31*, 978–989.

Berkey, C. S., Gardner, J. D., Frazier, A. L., & Colditz, G. A. (2000). Relation of childhood diet and body size to menarche and adolescent growth in girls. *American Journal of Epidemiology, 152*, 446–452. doi:10.1093/aje/152.5.446

Berkman, L. F., Ertel, K. A., & Glymour, M. M. (2011). Aging and social intervention: Life course perspectives. In R. H. Binstock & L. K. George (Eds.), *Handbook of aging and the social sciences* (7th ed., pp. 337–351). San Diego, CA: Academic Press.

Berlin, L. J., Appleyard, K., & Dodge, K. A. (2011). Intergenerational continuity in child maltreatment: Mediating mechanisms and implications for prevention. *Child Development, 82*, 162–176. doi:10.1111/j.1467–8624.2010.01547.x

Bernard, A. (2013). *Unemployment dynamics among Canada's youth* (Catalogue No. 11–626–X—No. 024). Retrieved from http://www.statcan.gc.ca/pub/11-626-x/11-626-x2013024-eng.pdf

Bernard, K., & Dozier, M. (2010). Examining infants' cortisol responses to laboratory tasks among children varying in attachment disorganization: Stress reactivity or return to baseline? *Developmental Psychology, 46*, 1771–1778.

Berndt, T. J., & Murphy, L. M. (2002). Influences of friends and friendships: Myths, truths, and research recommendations. In R. V. Kail (Ed.), *Advances in child development and behavior* (Vol. 30, pp. 275–310). San Diego, CA: Academic Press.

Bernstein, M. (2005). Identity politics. *Annual Review of Sociology, 31*, 47–74. doi:10.1146/annurev.soc.29.010202.100054

Berry, J. W., Kim, U., Power, S., Young, M., & Bujaki, M. (1989). Acculturation attitudes in plural societies. *Applied Psychology, 38*, 185–206. doi:10.1111/j.1464–0597.1989.tb01208.x

Berry, J. W., Phinney, J. S., Sam, D. L., & Vedder, P. (2006). Immigrant youth: Acculturation, identity, and adaptation. *Applied Psychology: An International Review, 55*, 303–332. doi:10.1111/j.1464–.597.2006.00256.x

Best Start Resource Centre. (2009). *Preconception health: Awareness and behaviours in Ontario*. Toronto, ON: Author.

Bhasin, S. (2007). Approach to the infertile man. *Journal of Clinical Endocrinology & Metabolism, 92*, 1995–2004. doi:10.1210/jc.2007–0634

Bhattacharjee, Y. (2008, February 8). Choking on fumes, Kolkata faces a noxious future. *Science, 319*, 749.

Bialystok, E. (2010). Global-local and trail-making tasks by monolingual and bilingual children: Beyond inhibition. *Developmental Psychology, 46*, 93–105. doi:10.1037/a0015466

Bialystok, E., & Barac, R. (2012). Emerging bilingualism: Dissociating advantages for metalinguistic awareness and executive control. *Cognition, 122*, 67–73.

Bialystok, E., Craik, F. I. M., Green, D. W., & Gollan, T. H. (2009). Bilingual minds. *Psychological Science in the Public Interest, 10*, 89–129. doi:10.1177/1529100610387084

Bialystok, E., & Viswanathan, M. (2009). Components of executive control with advantages for bilingual children in two cultures. *Cognition, 112*, 494–500. doi:10.1016/j.cognition.2009.06.014

Bianchi, S. M., & Milkie, M. A. (2010). Work and family research in the first decade of the 21st century. *Journal of Marriage and Family, 72*, 705–725. doi:10.1111/j.1741–3737.2010.00726.x

Biblarz, T. J., & Savci, E. (2010). Lesbian, gay, bisexual, and transgender families. *Journal of Marriage and Family, 72*, 480–497. doi:10.1111/j.1741–3737.2010.00714.x

Biblarz, T. J., & Stacey, J. (2010). How does the gender of parents matter? *Journal of Marriage and Family, 72*, 3–22. doi:10.1111/j.1741–3737.2009.00678.x

Biddle, S. J. H., & Asare, M. (2011). Physical activity and mental health in children and adolescents: a review of reviews. *British Journal of Sports Medicine, 45*, 886–895.

Biederman, J., Monuteaux, M. C., Spencer, T., Wilens, T. E., & Faraone, S. V. (2009). Do stimulants protect against psychiatric disorders in youth with ADHD? A 10-year follow-up study. *Pediatrics, 124*, 71–78. doi:10.1542/peds.2008–3347

Biederman, J., Spencer, T. J., Monuteaux, M. C., & Faraone, S. V. (2010). A naturalistic 10-year prospective study of height and weight in children with attention-deficit hyperactivity disorder grown up: Sex and treatment effects. *The Journal of Pediatrics, 157*, 635–640.e631.

Biehl, M. C., Natsuaki, M. N., & Ge, X. (2007). The influence of pubertal timing on alcohol use and heavy drinking trajectories. *Journal of Youth and Adolescence, 36*, 153–167.

Bielak, A. A. M. (2010). How can we not 'lose it' if we still don't understand how to 'use it'? Unanswered questions about the influence of activity participation on cognitive performance in older age—A mini-review. *Gerontology, 56*, 507–519.

Bielak, A. A. M., Anstey, K. J., Christensen, H., & Windsor, T. D. (2012). Activity engagement is related to level, but not change in cognitive ability across adulthood. *Psychology and Aging, 27*, 219–228. doi:10.1037/a0024667

Bielski, Z. (2013, January 29). Why teen pregnancy is on the rise again in Canada (and spiking in these provinces). *The Globe and Mail*. Retrieved from http://www.theglobeandmail.com/life/health-and-fitness/health/why-teen-pregnancy-is-on-the-rise-again-in-canada-and-spiking-in-these-provinces/article7927983/

Bilalić, M., McLeod, P., & Gobet, F. (2009). Specialization effect and its influence on memory and problem solving in expert chess players. *Cognitive Science, 33*, 1117–1143. doi:10.1111/j.1551–6709.2009.01030.x

Birch, S. A. J., & Bloom, P. (2003). Children are cursed: An asymmetric bias in mental-state attribution. *Psychological Science, 14*, 283–286.

Bird, C. E., Seeman, T., Escarce, J. J., Basurto-Dávila, R., Finch, B. K., Dubowitz, T., ... Lurie, N. (2010). Neighbourhood socioeconomic status and biological 'wear and tear' in a nationally representative sample of US adults. *Journal of Epidemiology and Community Health, 64,* 860–865. doi:10.1136/jech.2008.084814

Birditt, K. S., Miller, L. M., Fingerman, K. L., & Lefkowitz, E. S. (2009). Tensions in the parent and adult child relationship: Links to solidarity and ambivalence. *Psychology and Aging, 24,* 287–295. doi:10.1037/a0015196

Birdsong, D. (2006). Age and second language acquisition and processing: A selective overview. *Language Learning, 56*(Suppl. 1), 9–49.

Birney, D. P., Citron-Pousty, J. H., Lutz, D. J., & Sternberg, R. J. (2005). The development of cognitive and intellectual abilities. In M. H. Bornstein & M. E. Lamb (Eds.), *Developmental science: An advanced textbook* (5th ed., pp. 327–358). Mahwah, NJ: Erlbaum.

Biro, F. M., McMahon, R. P., Striegel-Moore, R., Crawford, P. B., Obarzanek, E., Morrison, J. A., ... Falkner, F. (2001). Impact of timing of pubertal maturation on growth in black and white female adolescents: The National Heart, Lung, and Blood Institute Growth and Health Study. *Journal of Pediatrics, 138,* 636–643.

Biro, F. M., Striegel-Moore, R. H., Franko, D. L., Padgett, J., & Bean, J. A. (2006). Self-esteem in adolescent females. *Journal of Adolescent Health, 39,* 501–507.

Bitensky, S. H. (2006). *Corporal punishment of children: A human rights violation.* Boston, MA: Brill.

Bjorklund, D. F., Dukes, C., & Brown, R. D. (2009). The development of memory strategies. In M. L. Courage & N. Cowan (Eds.), *The development of memory in infancy and childhood* (2nd ed., pp. 145–175). New York, NY: Psychology Press.

Black, K. (2008). Health and aging-in-place: Implications for community practice. *Journal of Community Practice, 16,* 79–95.

Blackwell, L. S., Trzesniewski, K. H., & Dweck, C. S. (2007). Implicit theories of intelligence predict achievement across an adolescent transition: A longitudinal study and an intervention. *Child Development, 78,* 246–263. doi:10.1111/j.1467-8624.2007.00995.x

Blair, C., & Dennis, T. (2010). An optimal balance: The integration of emotion and cognition in context. In S. D. Calkins & M. A. Bell (Eds.), *Child development at the intersection of emotion and cognition* (pp. 17–36). Washington, DC: American Psychological Association.

Blais, A., & Loewen, P. (2011). *Youth electoral engagement in Canada.* Retrieved from http://www.elections.ca/res/rec/part/youeng/youth_electoral_engagement_e.pdf

Blakemore, S.-J. (2008). Development of the social brain during adolescence. *The Quarterly Journal of Experimental Psychology, 61,* 40–49.

Blanchflower, D. G., & Oswald, A. J. (2008). Is well-being U-shaped over the life cycle? *Social Science & Medicine, 66,* 1733–1749. doi:10.1016/j.socscimed.2008.01.030

Blandon, A. Y., Calkins, S. D., & Keane, S. P. (2010). Predicting emotional and social competence during early childhood from toddler risk and maternal behavior. *Development and Psychopathology, 22,* 119–132. doi:10.1017/S0954579409990307

Blas, E., & Kurup, A. S. (Eds.). (2010). *Equity, social determinants, and public health programmes.* Geneva, Switzerland: World Health Organization.

Blekesaune, M. (2008). Partnership transitions and mental distress: Investigating temporal order. *Journal of Marriage and Family, 70,* 879–890.

Blonigen, D. M., Carlson, M. D., Hicks, B. M., Krueger, R. F., & Iacono, W. G. (2008). Stability and change in personality traits from late adolescence to early adulthood: A longitudinal twin study. *Journal of Personality, 76,* 229–266.

Bloom, D. E. (2011, July 29). 7 billion and counting. *Science, 333,* 562–569.

Blum, D. (2002). *Love at Goon Park: Harry Harlow and the science of affection.* Cambridge, MA: Perseus.

Blurton-Jones, N. G. (1976). Rough-and-tumble play among nursery school children. In J. S. Bruner & A. Jolly (Eds.), *Play: Its role in development and evolution* (pp. 352–363). New York, NY: Basic Books.

Blustein, D. L. (2006). *The psychology of working: A new perspective for career development, counseling, and public policy.* Mahwah, NJ: Erlbaum.

Boals, A., Hayslip, B., Knowles, L. R., & Banks, J. B. (2012). Perceiving a negative event as central to one's identity partially mediates age differences in posttraumatic stress disorder symptoms. *Journal of Aging and Health, 24,* 459–474. doi:10.1177/0898264311425089

Bodrova, E., & Leong, D. J. (2005). High quality preschool programs: What would Vygotsky say? *Early Education and Development, 16,* 435–444.

Boerner, K., Schulz, R., & Horowitz, A. (2004). Positive aspects of caregiving and adaptation to bereavement. *Psychology and Aging, 19,* 668–675. doi:10.1037/0882-7974.19.4.668

Boerner, K., Wortman, C. B., & Bonanno, G. A. (2005). Resilient or at risk? A 4-year study of older adults who initially showed high or low distress following conjugal loss. *Journals of Gerontology: Series B: Psychological Sciences and Social Sciences, 60,* 67–73.

Bojczyk, K. E., Lehan, T. J., McWey, L. M., Melson, G. F., & Kaufman, D. R. (2011). Mothers' and their adult daughters' perceptions of their relationship. *Journal of Family Issues, 32,* 452–481. doi:10.1177/0192513x10384073

Boland, M. (2005). Exclusive breastfeeding should continue to six months. *Paediatrics and Child Health, 10,* 148.

Boles, D. B., Barth, J. M., & Merrill, E. C. (2008). Asymmetry and performance: Toward a neurodevelopmental theory. *Brain and Cognition, 66,* 124–139.

Bonanno, G. A., & Lilienfeld, S. O. (2008). Let's be realistic: When grief counseling is effective and when it's not. *Professional Psychology: Research and Practice, 39,* 377–378. doi:10.1037/0735-7028.39.3.377

Bondi, M. W., Salmon, D. P., & Kaszniak, A. W. (2009). The neuropsychology of dementia. In I. Grant & K. M. Adams (Eds.), *Neuropsychological assessment of neuropsychiatric and neuromedical disorders* (3rd ed., pp. 159–198). New York, NY: Oxford University Press.

Borgens, R. B., & Liu-Snyder, P. (2012). Understanding secondary injury. *The Quarterly Review of Biology, 87*, 89–127. doi:10.1086/665457

Borke, J., Lamm, B., Eickhorst, A., & Keller, H. (2007). Father-infant interaction, paternal ideas about early child care, and their consequences for the development of children's self-recognition. *Journal of Genetic Psychology, 168*, 365–379.

Borkowski, J. G., Farris, J. R., Whitman, T. L., Carothers, S. S., Weed, K., & Keogh, D. A. (2007). *Risk and resilience: Adolescent mothers and their children grow up.* Mahwah, NJ: Erlbaum.

Borland, J. H. (Ed.). (2003). *Rethinking gifted education.* New York, NY: Teachers College Press.

Bornstein, M. H., Arterberry, M. E., & Mash, C. (2005). Perceptual development. In M. H. Bornstein & M. E. Lamb (Eds.), *Developmental science: An advanced textbook* (5th ed., pp. 283–325). Mahwah, NJ: Erlbaum.

Bornstein, M. H., & Cote, L. R. (2007). Knowledge of child development and family interactions among immigrants to America: Perspectives from developmental science. In J. E. Lansford, K. Deater-Deckard, & M. H. Bornstein (Eds.), *Immigrant families in contemporary society* (pp. 121–136). New York, NY: Guilford Press.

Bornstein, M. H., Mortimer, J. T., Lutfey, K., & Bradley, R. (2011). Theories and processes in life-span socialization. In K. L. Fingerman (Ed.), *Handbook of life-span development* (pp. 27–56). New York, NY: Springer.

Boseovski, J. J. (2010). Evidence for "rose-colored glasses": An examination of the positivity bias in young children's personality judgments. *Child Development Perspectives, 4*, 212–218. doi:10.1111/j.1750–8606.2010.00149.x

Bossé, Y., & Hudson, T. J. (2007). Toward a comprehensive set of asthma susceptibility genes. *Annual Review of Medicine, 58*, 171–184.

Bosworth, H. B., & Ayotte, B. J. (2009). The role of cognitive and social function in an applied setting: Medication adherence as an example. In H. B. Bowsworth & C. K. Hertzog (Eds.), *Aging and cognition: Research methodologies and empirical advances* (pp. 219–239). Washington, DC: American Psychological Association.

Bosworth, H. B., & Hertzog, C. (2009). *Aging and cognition: Research methodologies and empirical advances.* Washington, DC: American Psychological Association.

Boudarbat, B., & Chernoff, V. (2009, October). *The determinants of education-job match among Canadian university students* (Discussion Paper No. 4513). Retrieved from http://ftp.iza.org/dp4513.pdf

Bourhis, R. Y., Moise, L. C., Perreault, S., & Senecal, S. (1997). Towards an interactive acculturation model: A social psychological approach. *International Journal of Psychology, 32*, 369–386. doi:10.1080/002075997400629

Bowen, M. E., & González, H. M. (2010). Childhood socioeconomic position and disability in later life: Results of the health and retirement study. *American Journal of Public Health, 100*(Suppl. 1), S197-S203. doi:10.2105/ajph.2009.160986

Bowes, L., Maughan, B., Caspi, A., Moffitt, T. E., & Arseneault, L. (2010). Families promote emotional and behavioural resilience to bullying: Evidence of an environmental effect. *Journal of Child Psychology and Psychiatry, 51*, 809–817. doi:10.1111/j.1469–7610.2010.02216.x

Bowlby, J. (1951). *Maternal care and mental health.* Geneva: World Health Organization.

Bowlby, J. (1969). *Attachment and loss. Vol. 1: Attachment.* London: Hogarth.

Bowlby, J. (1973a). *Attachment and loss. Vol. 2: Separation: Anxiety and anger.* New York: Basic Books.

Bowlby, J. (1973b). *Attachment and loss. Vol. 3: Loss: Sadness and depression.* New York: Basic Books.

Bowlby, J. (1988). *A secure base: Parent-child attachment and healthy human development.* Tavistock professional book. London: Routledge.

Bowlby, J. W., & McMullen, K. (2002). *At a crossroads: First results for the 18 to 20-year old cohort of the Youth in Transition Survey* (Catalogue No. 81–59-XIE). Retrieved from http://www.statcan.gc.ca/pub/81-591-x/81-591-x2000001-eng.pdf

Bowman, N. A. (2011). Promoting participation in a diverse democracy: A meta-analysis of college diversity experiences and civic engagement. *Review of Educational Research, 81*, 29–68. doi:10.3102/0034654310383047

Boyce, W. T., Essex, M. J., Alkon, A., Goldsmith, H. H., Kraemer, H. C., & Kupfer, D. J. (2006). Early father involvement moderates biobehavioral susceptibility to mental health problems in middle childhood. *Journal of the American Academy of Child and Adolescent Psychiatry, 45*, 1510–1520.

Boyd, C. M., Darer, J., Boult, C., Fried, L. P., Boult, L., & Wu, A. W. (2005). Clinical practice guidelines and quality of care for older patients with multiple comorbid diseases: Implications for pay for performance. *Journal of the American Medical Association, 294*, 716–724.

Boyraz, G., Horne, S. G., & Sayger, T. V. (2012). Finding meaning in loss: The mediating role of social support between personality and two construals of meaning. *Death Studies, 36*, 519–540.

Bracken, B. A., & Crawford, E. (2010). Basic concepts in early childhood educational standards: A 50-state review. *Early Childhood Education Journal, 37*, 421–430.

Bradley, R. H., & Corwyn, R. F. (2005). Productive activity and the prevention of behavior problems. *Developmental Psychology, 41*, 89–98.

Branca, F., Nikogosian, H., & Lobstein, T. (Eds.). (2007). *The challenge of obesity in the WHO European Region and the strategies for response.* Copenhagen, Denmark: WHO Regional Office for Europe.

Branum, A. M., & Lukacs, S. L. (2008, October). Food allergy among U.S. children: Trends in prevalence and hospitalizations. *NCHS Data Brief, 10.* Retrieved from http://www.cdc.gov/nchs/data/databriefs/db10.htm

Brassen, S., Gamer, M., Peters, J., Gluth, S., & Büchel, C. (2012, May 4). Don't look back in anger! Responsiveness to missed chances in successful and nonsuccessful aging. *Science, 336*, 612–614.

Braun, M., Lewin-Epstein, N., Stier, H., & Baumgärtner, M. K. (2008). Perceived equity in the gendered division of household labor. *Journal of Marriage and Family, 70*, 1145–1156.

Brazelton, T. B. (1978). The remarkable talents of the newborn. *Birth, 5*, 187–191. doi:10.1111/j.1523–536X.1978.tb01276.x

Breivik, G. (2010). Trends in adventure sports in a post-modern society. *Sport in Society: Cultures, Commerce, Media, Politics, 13*, 260–273. doi:10.1080/17430430903522970

Brendgen, M., Lamarche, V., Wanner, B., & Vitaro, F. (2010). Links between friendship relations and early adolescents' trajectories of depressed mood. *Developmental Psychology, 46*, 491–501.

Brenner, S., Kleinhaus, K., Kursmark, M., & Weitzman, M. (2009). Increased paternal age and child health and development. *Current Pediatric Reviews, 5*, 135–146.

Bretherton, I. (2010). Fathers in attachment theory and research: A review. *Early Child Development and Care, 180*, 9–23.

Bricker, J., & Tollison, S. (2011). Comparison of motivational interviewing with acceptance and commitment therapy: A conceptual and clinical review. *Behavioural and Cognitive Psychotherapy, 39*, 541–559. doi:10.1017/S1352465810000901

British Columbia Ministry of Education. (2007). *Aboriginal report 2002/03 to 2006/07: How are we doing?* Retrieved from http://www.bced.gov.bc.ca/abed/perf2007.pdf

Britto, P. R., Boller, K., & Yoshikawa, H. (2011). Quality of early childhood development programs in global contexts: Rationale for investment, conceptual framework and implications for equity. *Social Policy Report, 25*(2), 1–30.

Brody, G. H., Beach, S. R. H., Philibert, R. A., Chen, Y.-f., & Murry, V. M. (2009). Prevention effects moderate the association of 5-HTTLPR and youth risk behavior initiation: Gene × environment hypotheses tested via a randomized prevention design. *Child Development, 80*, 645–661. doi:10.1111/j.1467–8624.2009.01288.x

Bronfenbrenner, U., & Morris, P. A. (2006). The bioecological model of human development. In R. M. Lerner (Ed.), *Handbook of child psychology: Vol. 1. Theoretical models of human development* (6th ed., pp. 793–828). Hoboken, NJ: Wiley.

Bronte-Tinkew, J., Moore, K. A., Matthews, G., & Carrano, J. (2007). Symptoms of major depression in a sample of fathers of infants: Sociodemographic correlates and links to father involvement. *Journal of Family Issues, 28*, 61–99.

Brotman, M. A., Guyer, A. E., Lawson, E. S., Horsey, S. E., Rich, B. A., Dickstein, D. P., … Leibenluft, E. (2008). Facial emotion labeling deficits in children and adolescents at risk for bipolar disorder. *American Journal of Psychiatry, 165*, 385–389. doi:10.1176/appi.ajp.2007.06122050

Brotman, M. A., Rich, B. A., Guyer, A. E., Lunsford, J. R., Horsey, S. E., Reising, M. M., … Leibenluft, E. (2010). Amygdala activation during emotion processing of neutral faces in children with severe mood dysregulation versus ADHD or bipolar disorder. *American Journal of Psychiatry, 167*, 61–69. doi:10.1176/appi.ajp.2009.09010043

Brown, B. B., & Bakken, J. P. (2011). Parenting and peer relationships: Reinvigorating research on family–peer linkages in adolescence. *Journal of Research on Adolescence, 21*, 153–165. doi:10.1111/j.1532–7795.2010.00720.x

Brown, B. B., & Larson, J. (2009). Peer relationships in adolescence. In R. M. Lerner & L. D. Steinberg (Eds.), *Handbook of adolescent psychology: Vol. 2. Contextual influences on adolescent development* (3rd ed., pp. 74–103). Hoboken, NJ: Wiley.

Brown, C. S., Alabi, B. O., Huynh, V. W., & Masten, C. L. (2011). Ethnicity and gender in late childhood and early adolescence: Group identity and awareness of bias. *Developmental Psychology, 47*, 463–471. doi:10.1037/a0021819

Brown, I. (2009). *The boy in the moon: A father's search for his disabled son.* Toronto, ON: Random House Canada.

Brown, J. L., & Pollitt, E. (1996). Malnutrition, poverty and intellectual development. *Scientific American, 274*(2), 38–43.

Brown, L. (2013, June 3). Ontario health and education experts call on Queen's Park to update old sex education curriculum. *The Star.* Retrieved from http://www.thestar.com/news/canada/2013/06/03/ontario_health_and_education_experts_call_on_queens_park_to_update_old_sex_education_curriculum.html

Brown, S. L. (2004). Family structure and child well-being: The significance of parental cohabitation. *Journal of Marriage and Family, 66*, 351–367. doi:10.1111/j.1741–3737.2004.00025.x

Brown, S. L. (2010). Marriage and child well-being: Research and policy perspectives. *Journal of Marriage and Family, 72*, 1059–1077. doi:10.1111/j.1741–3737.2010.00750.x

Brown, S. L., & Rinelli, L. N. (2010). Family structure, family processes, and adolescent smoking and drinking. *Journal of Research on Adolescence, 20*, 259–273.

Bryant, A. S., Worjoloh, A., Caughey, A. B., & Washington, A. E. (2010). Racial/ethnic disparities in obstetric outcomes and care: Prevalence and determinants. *American Journal of Obstetrics and Gynecology, 202*, 335–343.

Bryant, B. K., & Donnellan, M. B. (2007). The relation between socio-economic status concerns and angry peer conflict resolution is moderated by pet provisions of support. *Anthrozoös, 20*, 213–223.

Bryant, G. A., & Barrett, H. C. (2007). Recognizing intentions in infant-directed speech: Evidence for universals. *Psychological Science, 18*, 746–751.

Brymer, E. (2010). Risk and extreme sports: A phenomenological perspective. *Annals of Leisure Research, 13*, 218–239.

Buckley, M., & Saarni, C. (2009). Emotion regulation: Implications for positive youth development. In M. J. Furlong, R. Gilman, & E. S. Huebner (Eds.), *Handbook of positive psychology in schools* (pp. 107–118). New York, NY: Routledge/Taylor & Francis.

Bucx, F., Raaijmakers, Q., & van Wel, F. (2010). Life course stage in young adulthood and intergenerational congruence in family attitudes. *Journal of Marriage and Family, 72*, 117–134.

Bucx, F., van Wel, F., & Knijn, T. (2012). Life course status and exchanges of support between young adults and parents. *Journal of Marriage and Family, 74*, 101–115. doi:10.1111/j.1741–3737.2011.00883.x

Bugental, D. B., & Hehman, J. A. (2007). Ageism: A review of research and policy implications. *Social Issues and Policy Review, 1*, 173–216.

Buiting, H., van Delden, J., Onwuteaka-Philpsen, B., Rietjens, J., Rurup, M., van Tol, D., … van der Heide, A. (2009). Reporting of euthanasia and physician-assisted suicide in the Netherlands: Descriptive study. *BMC Medical Ethics, 10,* 18. doi:10.1186/1472-6939–10–18

Bulik, C. M., Reba, L., Siega-Riz, A-M., & Reichborn-Kjennerud, T. (2005). Anorexia nervosa: Definition, epidemiology, and cycle of risk. *International Journal of Eating Disorders, 37,* 52–59.

Bulik, C. M., Thornton, L., Pinheiro, A. P., Plotnicov, K., Klump, K. L., Brandt, H., … Kaye, W. H. (2008). Suicide attempts in anorexia nervosa. *Psychosomatic Medicine, 70,* 378–383.

Bürgi, F., Meyer U., Granacher, U., Schindler, C., Marques-Vidal, P., Kriemler, S., & Puder, J. J. (2011). Relationship of physical activity with motor skills, aerobic fitness, and body fat in preschool children: A cross-sectional and longitudinal study (Ballabeina). *International Journal of Obesity, 35,* 937–944. doi: 10.1038/ijo.2011.54

Burpo, T., & Vincent, L. (2011). *Heaven is for real: A little boy's astounding story of his trip to heaven and back.* Nashville, TN: Thomas Nelson.

Burris, C. T., & Jackson, L. M. (2000). Social identity and the true believer: Responses to threatened self-stereotypes among the intrinsically religious. *British Journal of Social Psychology, 29,* 257–278.

Burt, S. A. (2009). Rethinking environmental contributions to child and adolescent psychopathology: A meta-analysis of shared environmental influences. *Psychological Bulletin, 135,* 608–637.

Burton, L. M., Bonilla-Silva, E., Ray, V., Buckelew, R., & Hordge Freeman, E. (2010). Critical race theories, colorism, and the decade's research on families of color. *Journal of Marriage and Family, 72,* 440–459. doi:10.1111/j.1741–3737.2010.00712.x

Buschkuehl, M., Jaeggi, S. M., Hutchison, S., Perrig-Chiello, P., Dapp, C., Muller, M., … Perrig, W. J. (2008). Impact of working memory training on memory performance in old-old adults. *Psychology and Aging, 23,* 743–753. doi:10.1037/a0014342

Bushnik, T. (2006). *Child care in Canada.* (Catalogue No. 89–599–MIE—No. 003). Retrieved from http://publications.gc.ca/Collection/Statcan/89-599-MIE/89-599-MIE2006003.pdf

Busse, William W., & Lemanske, R. F. (Eds.). (2005). *Lung biology in health and disease: Vol. 195. Asthma prevention.* Boca Raton, FL: Taylor & Francis.

Butler, M., Tiedmann, M., Nicol, J., & Valiquet, D. (2013). *Euthanasia and assisted suicide in Canada.* Retrieved from http://www.parl.gc.ca/Content/LOP/ResearchPublications/2010-68-e.htm

Butler, R. N., Lewis, M. I., & Sunderland, T. (1998). *Aging and mental health: Positive psychosocial and biomedical approaches* (5th ed.). Boston, MA: Allyn & Bacon.

Butterworth, B., Varma, S., & Laurillard, D. (2011, May 27). Dyscalculia: From brain to education. *Science, 332,* 1049–1053.

Byers, A. L., Levy, B. R., Allore, H. G., Bruce, M. L., & Kasl, S. V. (2008). When parents matter to their adult children: Filial reliance associated with parents' depressive symptoms. *The Journals of Gerontology Series B: Psychological Sciences and Social Sciences, 63,* 33–40.

Byers-Heinlein, K., Burns, T. C., & Werker, J. F. (2010). The roots of bilingualism in newborns. *Psychological Science, 21,* 343–348. doi:10.1177/0956797609360758

Bzostek, S. H. (2008). Social fathers and child well-being. *Journal of Marriage and Family, 70,* 950–961.

C

Cacioppo, J. T., & Cacioppo, S. (2012). The phenotype of loneliness. *European Journal of Developmental Psychology, 9,* 446–452. doi:10.1080/17405629.2012.690510

Cain, D. S., & Combs-Orme, T. (2005). Family structure effects on parenting stress and practices in the African American family. *Journal of Sociology & Social Welfare, 32,* 19–40.

Cairns, R. B., & Cairns, B. D. (2006). The making of developmental psychology. In R. M. Lerner (Ed.), *Handbook of child psychology: Vol. 1. Theoretical models of human development* (6th ed., pp. 89–165). Hoboken, NJ: Wiley.

Calkins, S. D., & Keane, S. P. (2009). Developmental origins of early antisocial behavior. *Development and Psychopathology, 21,* 1095–1109. doi:10.1017/S095457940999006X

Cameron, J., & Pierce, W. D. (2002). *Rewards and intrinsic motivation: Resolving the controversy.* Westport, CT: Bergin & Garvey.

Camilli, G., Vargas, S., Ryan, S., & Barnett, W. S. (2010). Meta-analysis of the effects of early education interventions on cognitive and social development. *Teachers College Record, 112,* 579–620.

Camos, V., & Barrouillet, P. (2011). Developmental change in working memory strategies: From passive maintenance to active refreshing. *Developmental Psychology, 47,* 898–904. doi:10.1037/a0023193

Campaign 2000. (2011). *Revisiting family security in insecure times: 2011 report card on child and family poverty in Canada.* Retrieved from http://campaign2000.ca/reportCards/national/2011EnglishRreportCard.pdf

Campbell, F. A., Pungello, E. P., Miller-Johnson, S., Burchinal, M., & Ramey, C. T. (2001). The development of cognitive and academic abilities: Growth curves from an early childhood educational experiment. *Developmental Psychology, 37,* 231–242.

Camras, L. A., & Shutter, J. M. (2010). Emotional facial expressions in infancy. *Emotion Review, 2,* 120–129. doi:10.1177/1754073909352529

Canadian Cancer Society's Advisory Committee on Cancer Statistics. (2013). *Canadian Cancer Statistics 2013: Special topic—Liver cancer.* Retrieved from http://www.cancer.ca/~/media/cancer.ca/CW/cancer%20information/cancer%20101/Canadian%20cancer%20statistics/canadian-cancer-statistics-2013-EN.pdf

Canadian Centre on Substance Abuse (CCSA). (2013). *Trends in drug use among youth.* Retrieved from http://www.ccsa.ca/2013%20CCSA%20Documents/CCSA-Trends-in-Drug-Use-Youth-2012-en.pdf

Canadian Council of Muslim Women (CCMW). (2010). *Being a Canadian Muslim woman in the 21st century; Module 6a: Violence against women & children: Media literacy case studies (The case of Aqsa Parvez).* Retrieved from http://ccmw.com/wp-content/uploads/2013/05/06-ccmw_being_muslim_toolkit_module6a.pdf

Canadian Council on Learning (CCL). (2007). *Lessons in learning: French-immersion education in Canada.* Retrieved from http://www.ccl-cca.ca/ccl/Reports/LessonsInLearning/LinL20070517_French_Immersion_programs.html

Canadian Council on Learning (CCL). (2009). *The state of Aboriginal learning in Canada: A holistic approach to measuring success.* Retrieved from http://www.ccl-cca.ca/pdfs/StateAboriginalLearning/SAL-FINALReport_en.pdf

Canadian Diabetes Association. (2012). *Children and type 2 diabetes.* Retrieved from http://www.diabetes.ca/diabetes-and-you/youth/type2/

Canadian Fitness & Lifestyle Research Institute (CFLRI). (2011a). *Getting kids active! 2010 Physical activity monitor: Facts and figures. Bulletin 2: Participation in sport among children and youth.* Available from http://www.cflri.ca/node/904

Canadian Fitness & Lifestyle Research Institute (CFLRI). (2011b). *Getting kids active! 2010 physical activity monitor: Facts and figures. Bulletin 4: Children's active pursuits during the after school period.* Available from http://www.cflri.ca/node/922

Canadian Fitness & Lifestyle Research Institute (CFLRI). (2011c). *Getting kids active! 2010 Physical activity monitor: Facts and figures. Bulletin 15: Opportunities at school to be active.* Available from http://72.10.49.94/node/1001

Canadian Hospice Palliative Care Association (CHPCA). (2012). *Fact sheet: Hospice palliative care in Canada.* Retrieved from http://www.chpca.net/media/7622/fact_sheet_hpc_in_canada_may_2012_final.pdf

Canadian Institute for Health Information (CIHI). (2007). *Health care use at the end of life in Western Canada.* Retrieved from https://secure.cihi.ca/free_products/end_of_life_report_aug07_e.pdf

Canadian Institute for Health Information (CIHI). (2009). *Too early, too small: A profile of small babies across Canada.* Retrieved from https://secure.cihi.ca/free_products/too_early_too_small_en.pdf

Canadian Institute for Health Information (CIHI). (2010). *Health care in Canada 2010.* Retrieved from https://secure.cihi.ca/free_products/HCIC_2010_Web_e.pdf

Canadian Institutes of Health Research. (2103). *Research profile: Growing older in a digital age.* Retrieved from http://www.cihr-irsc.gc.ca/e/46194.html

Canadian Mental Health Association (Ontario). (2009). *Connection between mental and physical health.* Retrieved from http://www.ontario.cmha.ca/fact_sheets.asp?cID=3963

Canadian Paediatric Society (CPS). (2008). *How to promote good television habits.* Retrieved from http://www.caringforkids.cps.ca/handouts/promote_good_television_habits

Canadian Press. (2013, February 18). *At least 3,000 died in residential schools, research shows.* Retrieved from http://www.cbc.ca/news/canada/story/2013/02/18/residential-schools-student-deaths.html

Canadian Psychological Association. (2000). *Canadian code of ethics for psychologists* (3rd ed.). Ottawa, ON: Author.

Capaldi, D. M. (2003). Parental monitoring: A person-environment interaction perspective on this key parenting skill. In A. C. Crouter &

A. Booth (Eds.), *Children's influence on family dynamics: The neglected side of family relationships* (pp. 171–179). Mahwah, NJ: Lawrence Erlbaum.

Cappell, K. A., Gmeindl, L., & Reuter-Lorenz, P. A. (2010). Age differences in prefontal recruitment during verbal working memory maintenance depend on memory load. *Cortex, 46,* 462–473. doi:10.1016/j.cortex.2009.11.009

Caravita, S. C. S., Di Blasio, P., & Salmivalli, C. (2010). Early adolescents' participation in bullying: Is ToM involved? *The Journal of Early Adolescence, 30,* 138–170. doi:10.1177/0272431609342983

Carey, S. (2010). Beyond fast mapping. *Language Learning and Development, 6,* 184–205. doi:10.1080/15475441.2010.484379

Carlson, K. B. (2011, October 8). Flash points in the sex-ed curricula across Canada. *The National Post.* Retrieved from http://news.nationalpost.com/2011/10/08/flash-points-in-the-sex-ed-curricula-across-canada/

Carlson, S. A., Fulton, J. E., Lee, S. M., Maynard, L. M., Brown, D. R., Kohl, H. W., III, & Dietz, W. H. (2008). Physical education and academic achievement in elementary school: Data from the early childhood longitudinal study. *American Journal of Public Health, 98,* 721–727. doi:10.2105/ajph.2007.117176

Carlson, S. M. (2003). Executive function in context: Development, measurement, theory and experience. *Monographs of the Society for Research in Child Development, 68*(3, Serial No. 274), 138–151.

Carnethon, M. R., Gidding, S. S., Nehgme, R., Sidney, S., Jacobs, D. R., Jr., & Liu, K. (2003). Cardiorespiratory fitness in young adulthood and the development of cardiovascular disease risk factors. *Journal of the American Medical Association, 290,* 3092–3100. doi:10.1001/jama.290.23.3092

CARP. (2014). *About CARP.* Retrieved from http://www.carp.ca/about-carp/

Carpendale, J. I. M., & Lewis, C. (2004). Constructing an understanding of mind: The development of children's social understanding within social interaction. *Behavioral and Brain Sciences, 27,* 79–96. doi:10.1017/S0140525X04000032

Carpenter, S. (2012, March 30). Psychology's bold initiative. *Science, 335,* 1558–1561.

Carr, D. (2012). Death and dying in the contemporary United States: What are the psychological implications of anticipated death? *Social and Personality Psychology Compass, 6,* 184–195. doi:10.1111/j.1751–9004.2011.00416.x

Carskadon, M. A. (2011). Sleep in adolescents: The perfect storm. *Pediatric Clinics of North America, 58,* 637–647.

Carstensen, L. (2011). *A long bright future: Happiness, health, and financial security in an age of increased longevity.* New York, NY: PublicAffairs.

Carstensen, L. L., Mikels, J. A., & Mather, M. (2006). Aging and the intersection of cognition, motivation, and emotion. In J. E. Birren & K. W. Schaie (Eds.), *Handbook of the psychology of aging* (6th ed., pp. 343–362). Amsterdam, The Netherlands: Elsevier.

Cartwright, K., Galupo, M., Tyree, S., & Jennings, J. (2009). Reliability and validity of the complex postformal thought questionnaire: Assessing adults' cognitive development. *Journal of Adult Development, 16,* 183–189. doi:10.1007/s10804–009–9055–1

Case-Smith, J., & Kuhaneck, H. M. (2008). Play preferences of typically developing children and children with developmental delays between ages 3 and 7 years. *OTJR: Occupation, Participation and Health, 28,* 19–29.

Casey, B. J., Jones, R. M., & Somerville, L. H. (2011). Braking and accelerating of the adolescent brain. *Journal of Research on Adolescence, 21,* 21–33. doi:10.1111/j.1532–7795.2010.00712.x

Caspi, A., Moffitt, T. E., Morgan, J., Rutter, M., Taylor, A., Arseneault, L., ... Polo-Tomas, M. (2004). Maternal expressed emotion predicts children's antisocial behavior problems: Using monozygotic-twin differences to identify environmental effects on behavioral development. *Developmental Psychology, 40,* 149–161.

Caspi, A., & Shiner, R. L. (2006). Personality development. In N. Eisenberg (Ed.), *Handbook of child psychology: Vol. 3. Social, emotional, and personality development* (6th ed., pp. 300–365). Hoboken, NJ: Wiley.

Cassia, V. M., Kuefner, D., Picozzi, M., & Vescovo, E. (2009). Early experience predicts later plasticity for face processing: Evidence for the reactivation of dormant effects. *Psychological Science, 20,* 853–859. doi:10.1111/j.1467–9280.2009.02376.x

Catani, C., Gewirtz, A. H., Wieling, E., Schauer, E., Elbert, T., & Neuner, F. (2010). Tsunami, war, and cumulative risk in the lives of Sri Lankan schoolchildren. *Child Development, 81,* 1176–1191. doi:10.1111/j.1467–8624.2010.01461.x

CBC News. (2011a, January 7). *Canada weighs in: CBC News special report on health and well-being.* Retrieved from http://www.cbc.ca/news/health/story/2010/12/15/f-canada-weighs-in.html

CBC News. (2011b, November 11). *'Ghost ride' held for killed cyclist.* Retrieved from http://www.cbc.ca/news/canada/toronto/ghost-ride-held-for-killed-cyclist-1.1057062

CBC News. (2012, June 18). *Children's pop consumption still rising.* Retrieved from http://www.cbc.ca/news/health/children-s-pop-consumption-still-rising-1.1225898

CBC News. (2013, August 1). *Is it safer to fly, drive or take the train?* Retrieved from http://www.cbc.ca/news/world/is-it-safer-to-fly-drive-or-take-the-train-1.1409337

CBS News. (2005, Feb 8). *World's smallest baby goes home: Cellphone-sized baby is discharged from hospital.* Retrieved from http://www.cbsnews.com/stories/2005/02/08/health/main672488.shtml

Centers for Disease Control and Prevention. (2013). *Autism spectrum disorders (ASDs).* Retrieved from http://www.cdc.gov/ncbddd/autism/facts.html

Centers for Disease Control and Prevention, American Society for Reproductive Medicine, Society for Assisted Reproductive Technology. (2011). *2009 assisted reproductive technology success rates: National summary and fertility clinic reports.* Atlanta, GA: U.S. Department of Health and Human Services.

Centre for Community Child Health and Telethon Institute for Child Health Research. (2009). *A snapshot of early childhood development in Australia: Australian Early Development Index (AEDI) national report 2009.* Retrieved from http://www.rch.org.au/aedi/media/Snapshot_of_Early_Childhood_DevelopmentinAustralia_AEDI_National_Report.pdf

Centre for Spatial Economics. (2010). *Early learning and care impact analysis.* Milton, ON: Author. Retrieved from http://ywcacanada.ca/data/research_docs/00000122.pdf

Cesario, S. K., & Hughes, L. A. (2007). Precocious puberty: A comprehensive review of literature. *Journal of Obstetric, Gynecologic, & Neonatal Nursing, 36,* 263–274.

Chafen, J. J. S., Newberry, S. J., Riedl, M. A., Bravata, D. M., Maglione, M., Suttorp, M. J., ... Shekelle, P. G. (2010). Diagnosing and managing common food allergies. *Journal of the American Medical Association, 303,* 1848–1856. doi:10.1001/jama.2010.582

Chakravarti, A. (2011, October 7). Genomics is not enough. *Science, 334,* 15.

Chambers, B., Cheung, A. C., Slavin, R. E., Smith, D., & Laurenzano, M. (2010). *Effective early childhood education programs: A systematic review.* Baltimore, MD: Johns Hopkins University, Center for Research and Reform in Education.

Champagne, F. A., & Curley, J. P. (2010). Maternal care as a modulating influence on infant development. In M. Blumberg, J. Freeman, & S. Robinson (Eds.), *Oxford handbook of developmental behavioral neuroscience* (pp. 323–341). New York, NY: Oxford University Press.

Chan, C. C. Y., Brandone, A. C., & Tardif, T. (2009). Culture, context, or behavioral control? English- and Mandarin-speaking mothers' use of nouns and verbs in joint book reading. *Journal of Cross-Cultural Psychology, 40,* 584–602. doi:10.1177/0022022109335184

Chan, K. Y., Wang, W., Wu, J. J., Liu, L., Theodoratou, E., Car, J., ... & Rudan, I. on behalf of the Global Health Epidemiology Reference Group (GHERG). (2013). Epidemiology of Alzheimer's disease and other forms of dementia in China, 1990—2010: A systematic review and analysis. *The Lancet 381,* 2016–2023. doi:10.1016/S0140–6736(13)60221–4

Chan, S. M., Bowes, J., & Wyver, S. (2009). Parenting style as a context for emotion socialization. *Early Education & Development, 20,* 631–656.

Chan, W. H. (2011). Reviving sociability in contemporary cultural practices and concepts of death in Hong Kong. In S. Conway (Ed.), *Governing death and loss: Empowerment, involvement and participation* (pp. 63–70). New York, NY: Oxford University Press.

Chao, J.-K., Lin, Y.-C., Ma, M.-C., Lai, C.-J., Ku, Y.-C., Kuo, W.-H., & Chao, I. C. (2011). Relationship among sexual desire, sexual satisfaction, and quality of life in middle-aged and older adults. *Journal of Sex & Marital Therapy, 37,* 386–403. doi:10.1080/0092623x.2011.607051

Chao, R. K. (1994). Beyond parental control and authoritarian parenting style: Understanding Chinese parenting through the cultural notion of training. *Child Development, 65,* 1111–1119.

Chao, R. K. (1995). Chinese and European American cultural models of the self reflected in mothers' childrearing beliefs. *Ethos, 23,* 328–354. doi:10.1525/eth.1995.23.3.02a00030

Chao, R. K. (2001). Extending research on the consequences of parenting style for Chinese Americans and European Americans. *Child Development, 72,* 1832–1843.

Chao, Y. M., Pisetsky, E. M., Dierker, L. C., Dohm, F.-A., Rosselli, F., May, A. M., & Striegel-Moore, R. H. (2008). Ethnic differences in weight control practices among U.S. adolescents from 1995 to 2005. *International Journal of Eating Disorders, 41*, 124–133.

Chaplin, L. N., & John, D. R. (2007). Growing up in a material world: Age differences in materialism in children and adolescents. *Journal of Consumer Research, 34*, 480–493.

Charles, S. T., & Carstensen, L. L. (2010). Social and emotional aging. *Annual Review of Psychology, 61*, 383–409. doi:10.1146/annurev.psych.093008.100448

Charness, N., & Krampe, R. T. (2008). Expertise and knowledge. In S. M. Hofer & D. F. Alwin (Eds.), *Handbook of cognitive aging: Interdisciplinary perspectives.* (pp. 244–258). Thousand Oaks, CA: Sage.

Charness, N., Krampe, R., & Mayr, U. (1996). The role of practice and coaching in entrepreneurial skill domains: An international comparison of life-span chess skill acquisition. In K. A. Ericsson (Ed.), *The road to excellence: The acquisition of expert performance in the arts and sciences, sports, and games* (pp. 51–80). Hillsdale, NJ: Erlbaum.

Chassin, L., Hussong, A., & Beltran, I. (2009). Adolescent substance use. In R. M. Lerner & L. D. Steinberg (Eds.), *Handbook of adolescent psychology: Vol. 1. Individual bases of adolescent development* (3rd ed., pp. 723–763). Hoboken, NJ: Wiley.

Chaux, E., Molano, A., & Podlesky, P. (2009). Socioeconomic, socio-political and socio-emotional variables explaining school bullying: A country-wide multilevel analysis. *Aggressive Behavior, 35*, 520–529. doi:10.1002/ab.20320

Chen, E., Cohen, S., & Miller, G. E. (2010). How low socioeconomic status affects 2-year hormonal trajectories in children. *Psychological Science, 21*, 31–37. doi:citeulike-article-id:6704024

Chen, E., & Miller, G. E. (2012). "Shift-and-persist" strategies: Why low socioeconomic status isn't always bad for health. *Perspectives on Psychological Science, 7*, 135–158. doi:10.1177/1745691612436694

Chen, X. (2011). Culture and children's socioemotional functioning: A contextual-developmental perspective. In X. Chen & K. H. Rubin (Eds.), *Socioemotional development in cultural context* (pp. 29–52). New York, NY: Guilford Press.

Chen, X., Cen, G., Li, D., & He, Y. (2005). Social functioning and adjustment in Chinese children: The imprint of historical time. *Child Development, 76,* 182–195.

Chen, X., Rubin, K. H., & Sun, Y. (1992). Social reputation and peer relationships in Chinese and Canadian children: A cross-cultural study. *Child Development, 63*, 1336–1343.

Chen, X., Wang, L., & Wang, Z. (2009). Shyness-sensitivity and social, school, and psychological adjustment in rural migrant and urban children in China. *Child Development, 80*, 1499–1513. doi: 10.1111/j.1467–8624.2009.01347.x

Chen, X. K., Wen, S. W., Krewski, D., Fleming, N., Yang, Q., & Walker, M. C. (2007). Paternal age and adverse birth outcomes: Teenager or 40+, who is at risk? *Human Reproduction, 23*, 1290–1296. doi:10.1093/humrep/dem403

Cheng, Y.-C., & Yeh, H.-T. (2009). From concepts of motivation to its application in instructional design: Reconsidering motivation from an instructional design perspective. *British Journal of Educational Technology, 40*, 597–605. doi:10.1111/j.1467–8535.2008.00857.x

Cherlin, A. J. (2009). *The marriage-go-round: The state of marriage and the family in America today.* New York, NY: Knopf.

Cheslack-Postava, K., Liu, K., & Bearman, P. S. (2011). Closely spaced pregnancies are associated with increased odds of autism in California sibling births. *Pediatrics, 127*, 246–253. doi:10.1542/peds.2010–2371

Cheung, A. H., & Dewa, C. S. (2006). Canadian Community Health Survey: Major depressive disorder and suicidality in adolescents. *Healthcare Policy, 2*, 76–89. doi:10.12927/hcpol.2007.18540

Cheung, F. M., Cheung, S. F., Zhang, J., Leung, K., Leong, F., & Huiyeh, K. (2008). Relevance of openness as a personality dimension in Chinese culture. *Journal of Cross-Cultural Psychology, 39*, 81–108. doi:10.1177/0022022107311968

Chief Public Health Officer. (2010). *The Chief Public Health Officer's report on the state of public health in Canada 2010: Growing older—Adding life to years.* Retrieved from http://www.phac-aspc.gc.ca/cphorsphc-respcacsp/2010/fr-rc/pdf/cpho_report_2010_e.pdf

Chin, V. S., Skike, C. E. V., & Matthews, D. B. (2010). Effects of ethanol on hippocampal function during adolescence: A look at the past and thoughts on the future. *Alcohol, 44*, 3–14.

Chomsky, N. (1968). *Language and mind.* New York, NY: Harcourt Brace & World.

Chomsky, N. (1980). *Rules and representations.* New York, NY: Columbia University Press.

Chou, R. J.-A., & Choi, N. G. (2011). Prevalence and correlates of perceived workplace discrimination among older workers in the United States of America. *Ageing and Society, 31*, 1051–1070.

Choudhry, N. K., Fletcher, R. H., & Soumerai, S. B. (2005). Systematic review: The relationship between clinical experience and quality of health care. *Annals of Internal Medicine, 142*, 260–273.

Christian, C. W., Block, R., & and the Committee on Child Abuse and Neglect. (2009). Abusive head trauma in infants and children. *Pediatrics, 123*, 1409–1411. doi:10.1542/peds.2009–0408

Chu, C. Y. C., Xie, Y., & Yu, R. R. (2011). Coresidence with elderly parents: A comparative study of southeast China and Taiwan. *Journal of Marriage and Family, 73*, 120–135.

Chuang, S. S. (2006). Taiwanese-Canadian mothers' beliefs about personal freedom for their young children. *Social Development, 15*, 520–536. doi:10.1111/j.1467–9507.2006.00354.x

Chuang, S. S. (2009). Transformation and change: Parenting in Chinese societies. In J. Mancini & K. A. Roberto (Eds.), *Pathways of development: Explorations of change* (pp. 191–206). Lanham, MA: Lexington Books.

Chuang, S. S. (2013). Fathering roles and responsibilities of contemporary Chinese fathers in Canada and China. In S. S. Chuang & C. S. Tamis-LeMonda (Eds.), *Gender roles in immigrant families* (pp. 27–42). New York, NY: Springer.

Chuang, S. S., & Canadian Immigrant Settlement Sector Alliance. (2009). *New start: Immigrant serving agencies' perspective on the issues and needs of immigrant and refugee children and youth in Canada.* Retrieved from http://www.isccalgary.ca/carestrategy/081109%20Access%20CISSA%20-%20ACSEI%20IRCY%20Discussion%20Paper.pdf

Chuang, S. S., & Moreno, R. P. (Eds.). (2011). *Immigrant children: Change, adaptation, and cultural transformation.* Lanham, MD: Lexington Books.

Chuang, S. S., & Su, Y. (2008). Transcending Confucian teachings on fathering: A sign of the times or acculturation? In S. S. Chuang & R. P. Moreno (Eds.), *On new shores: Understanding immigrant fathers in North America* (pp. 129–150). Lanham, MD: Lexington Books.

Chuang, S. S., & Su, Y. (2009). Says who? Decision-making and conflicts among Chinese-Canadian and Mainland Chinese parents of young children. *Sex Roles, 60,* 527–536.

Chuang, S. S., & Tamis-LeMonda, C. S. (Eds.). (2013). *Gender roles in immigrant families.* New York, NY: Springer Science+Business Media.

Chudacoff, H. P. (2011). The history of children's play in the United States. In P. Nathan & A. D. Pellegrini (Eds.), *The Oxford handbook of the development of play* (pp. 101–109). New York, NY: Oxford University Press.

Chung, G. H., Flook, L., & Fuligni, A. J. (2011). Reciprocal associations between family and peer conflict in adolescents' daily lives. *Child Development, 82,* 1390–1396. doi:10.1111/j.1467–8624.2011.01625.x

Church, A. T. (2010). Current perspectives in the study of personality across cultures. *Perspectives on Psychological Science, 5,* 441–449. doi:10.1177/1745691610375559

Cicchetti, D. (2003). Neuroendocrine functioning in maltreated children. In D. Cicchetti & E. Walker (Eds.), *Neurodevelopmental mechanisms in psychopathology* (pp. 345–365). New York, NY: Cambridge University Press.

Cicchetti, D., & Toth, S. L. (2009). The past achievements and future promises of developmental psychopathology: The coming of age of a discipline. *Journal of Child Psychology and Psychiatry, 50,* 16–25. doi:10.1111/j.1469–7610.2008.01979.x

Cillessen, A. H. N., & Mayeux, L. (2004). From censure to reinforcement: Developmental changes in the association between aggression and social status. *Child Development, 75,* 147–163.

Cipriano, E. A., & Stifter, C. A. (2010). Predicting preschool effortful control from toddler temperament and parenting behavior. *Journal of Applied Developmental Psychology, 31,* 221–230.

Claas, M. J., de Vries, L. S., Bruinse, H. W., van Haastert, I. C., Uniken Venema, M. M. A., Peelen, L. M., & Koopman, C. (2011). Neurodevelopmental outcome over time of preterm born children ≤750g at birth. *Early Human Development, 87,* 183–191.

Clark, L. A. (2009). Stability and change in personality disorder. *Current Directions in Psychological Science, 18,* 27–31.

Clark, N. A., Demers, P. A., Karr, C. J., Koehoorn, M., Lencar, C., Tamburic, L., & Brauer, M. (2010). Effect of early life exposure to air pollution on development of childhood asthma. *Environmental Health Perspectives, 118,* 284–290. doi:10.1289/ehp.0900916

Clark, S., Kabiru, C., & Mathur, R. (2010). Relationship transitions among youth in urban Kenya. *Journal of Marriage and Family, 72,* 73–88.

Cleveland, M. J., Gibbons, F. X., Gerrard, M., Pomery, E. A., & Brody, G. H. (2005). The impact of parenting on risk cognitions and risk behavior: A study of mediation and moderation in a panel of African American adolescents. *Child Development, 76,* 900–916.

Cohen, D. (2006). *The development of play* (3rd ed.). New York, NY: Routledge.

Cohen, D., & Soto, M. (2007). Growth and human capital: Good data, good results. *Journal of Economic Growth, 12,* 51–76. doi:10.1007/s10887–007–9011–5

Cohen, J. (2007a, September 7). DNA duplications and deletions help determine health. *Science, 317,* 1315–1317.

Cohen, J. (2007b, March 9). Hope on new AIDS drugs, but breast-feeding strategy backfires. *Science, 315,* 1357.

Cohen, J. E., & Malin, M. B. (Eds.). (2010). *International perspectives on the goals of universal basic and secondary education.* New York, NY: Routledge.

Cohen, L., Chávez, V., & Chehimi, S. (2010). *Prevention is primary: Strategies for community well-being* (2nd ed.). San Francisco, CA: Jossey-Bass.

Cohen, L. B., & Cashon, C. H. (2006). Infant cognition. In D. Kuhn & R. S. Siegler (Eds.), *Handbook of child psychology: Vol. 2. Cognition, perception, and language* (6th ed., pp. 214–251). Hoboken, NJ: Wiley.

Cole, C., & Winsler, A. (2010). Protecting children from exposure to lead: Old problem, new data, and new policy needs. *Social Policy Report, 24,* 3–29.

Cole, P. M., Armstrong, L. M., & Pemberton, C. K. (2010). The role of language in the development of emotion regulation. In S. D. Calkins & M. A. Bell (Eds.), *Child development at the intersection of emotion and cognition* (pp. 59–78). Washington, DC: American Psychological Association.

Cole, P. M., Tan, P. Z., Hall, S. E., Zhang, Y., Crnic, K. A., Blair, C. B., & Li, R. (2011). Developmental changes in anger expression and attention focus: Learning to wait. *Developmental Psychology, 47,* 1078–1089. doi:10.1037/a0023813

Coles, R. (1997). *The moral intelligence of children: How to raise a moral child.* New York, NY: Random House.

College of Midwives of Ontario. (n.d.). *The facts about home birth in Ontario.* Retrieved from http://www.durhammidwives.com/uploads/home-birth-sheet.pdf

Colleran, C., & Jay, D. (2003). Surviving addiction: Audrey's story. *Aging Today, 24*(1).

Collins, R. L., Martino, S. C., Elliott, M. N., & Miu, A. (2011). Relationships between adolescent sexual outcomes and exposure to sex in media: Robustness to propensity-based analysis. *Developmental Psychology, 47,* 585–591. doi:10.1037/a0022563

Collins, W. A., & Laursen, B. (2004). Parent-adolescent relationships and influences. In R. M. Lerner & L. D. Steinberg (Eds.), *Handbook of adolescent psychology* (2nd ed., pp. 331–361). Hoboken, NJ: Wiley.

Compian, L. J., Gowen, L. K., & Hayward, C. (2009). The interactive effects of puberty and peer victimization on weight concerns and depression symptoms among early adolescent girls. *The Journal of Early Adolescence, 29,* 357–375. doi:10.1177/0272431608323656

Compta, Y., Parkkinen, L., O'Sullivan, S. S., Vandrovcova, J., Holton, J. L., Collins, C., ... Revesz, T. (2011). Lewy- and Alzheimer-type pathologies in Parkinson's disease dementia: Which is more important? *Brain, 134,* 1493–1505. doi:10.1093/brain/awr031

Conboy, B. T., & Thal, D. J. (2006). Ties between the lexicon and grammar: Cross-sectional and longitudinal studies of bilingual toddlers. *Child Development, 77,* 712–735.

Conference Board of Canada. (2012). *Infant mortality.* Retrieved from http://www.conferenceboard.ca/hcp/details/health/infant-mortality-rate.aspx

Conference Board of Canada. (2013a). *Elderly poverty.* Retrieved from http://www.conferenceboard.ca/hcp/details/society/elderly-poverty.aspx

Conference Board of Canada. (2013b). *Income inequality.* Retrieved from http://www.conferenceboard.ca/hcp/details/society/income-inequality.aspx

Cong, Z., & Silverstein, M. (2008). Intergenerational support and depression among elders in rural China: Do daughters-in-law matter? *Journal of Marriage and Family, 70,* 599–612.

Conger, K. J., & Little, W. M. (2010). Sibling relationships during the transition to adulthood. *Child Development Perspectives, 4,* 87–94.

Conger, R. D., Conger, K. J., & Martin, M. J. (2010). Socioeconomic status, family processes, and individual development. *Journal of Marriage and Family, 72,* 685–704. doi:10.1111/j.1741-3737.2010.00725.x

Conger, R. D., Wallace, L. E., Sun, Y., Simons, R. L., McLoyd, V. C., & Brody, G. H. (2002). Economic pressure in African American families: A replication and extension of the family stress model. *Developmental Psychology, 38,* 179–193.

Conner, M. (2008). Initiation and maintenance of health behaviors. *Applied Psychology, 57,* 42–50.

Connidis, I. A. (2007). Negotiating inequality among adult siblings: Two case studies. *Journal of Marriage and Family, 69,* 482–499.

Cook, C. C., Martin, P., Yearns, M., & Damhorst, M. L. (2007). Attachment to "place" and coping with losses in changed communities: A paradox for aging adults. *Family & Consumer Sciences Research Journal, 35,* 201–214.

Cook, S. L., & Speevak Sladowski, P. (2013, February). *Volunteering and older adults.* Retrieved from http://volunteer.ca/content/volunteering-and-older-adults-final-report

Cooke, L. P., & Baxter, J. (2010). "Families" in international context: Comparing institutional effects across Western societies. *Journal of Marriage and Family, 72,* 516–536. doi:10.1111/j.1741-3737.2010.00716.x

Coon, C. S. (1962). *The origin of races.* New York, NY: Knopf.

Coontz, S. (2005). *Marriage, a history: From obedience to intimacy or how love conquered marriage.* New York, NY: Viking.

Cooper, C., Selwood, A., & Livingston, G. (2008). The prevalence of elder abuse and neglect: A systematic review. *Age and Ageing, 37,* 151–160. doi:10.1093/ageing/afm194

Corballis, M. C. (2011). *The recursive mind: The origins of human language, thought, and civilization.* Princeton, NJ: Princeton University Press.

Corbeil, J.-P., & Blaser, C. (2009). *2006 Census: The evolving linguistic portrait, 2006 Census: Highlights* (Catalogue No. 97-555-XWE2006001). Available from http://www12.statcan.ca/census-recensement/2006/as-sa/97-555/index-eng.cfm

Corda, L., Khanapure, A., & Karoshi, M. (2012). Biopanic, advanced maternal age and fertility outcomes. In M. Karoshi, S. Newbold, C. B-Lynch, & L. Keith (Eds.), *A textbook of preconceptional medicine and management* (pp. 3–18). Carlisle, UK: Sapiens.

Cosgrave, J. F. (2010). Embedded addiction: The social production of gambling knowledge and the development of gambling markets. *Canadian Journal of Sociology, 35,* 113–134.

Côté, J. E. (2006). Emerging adulthood as an institutionalized moratorium: Risks and benefits to identity formation. In J. J. Arnett & J. L. Tanner (Eds.), *Emerging adults in America: Coming of age in the 21st century* (pp. 85–116). Washington, DC: American Psychological Association.

Côté, J. E. (2009). Identity formation and self-development in adolescence. In R. M. Lerner & L. D. Steinberg (Eds.), *Handbook of adolescent psychology: Vol. 1. Individual bases of adolescent development* (3rd ed., pp. 266–304). Hoboken, NJ: Wiley.

Côté, S., Vaillancourt, T., LeBlanc, J. C., Nagin, D. S., & Tremblay, R. E. (2006). The development of physical aggression from toddlerhood to pre-adolescence: A nation wide longitudinal study of Canadian children. *Journal of Abnormal Child Psychology, 34,* 71–85.

Côté, S. M., Borge, A. I., Geoffroy, M.-C., Rutter, M., & Tremblay, R. E. (2008). Nonmaternal care in infancy and emotional/behavioral difficulties at 4 years old: Moderation by family risk characteristics. *Developmental Psychology, 44,* 155–168.

Council of Ministers of Education, Canada (CMEC). (2008). *Education in Canada.* Retrieved from http://www.cmec.ca/Publications/Lists/Publications/Attachments/64/Education-in-Canada2008.pdf

Council of Ministers of Education, Canada (CMEC). (2011). *PCAP-2010: Report on the Pan-Canadian assessment of mathematics, science, and reading.* Retrieved from http://www.cmec.ca/Publications/Lists/Publications/Attachments/274/pcap2010.pdf

Couperus, J. W., & Nelson, C. (2006). Early brain development and plasticity. In K. McCartney & D. Phillips (Eds.), *Blackwell handbook of early childhood development.* New York, NY: Blackwell Publishing.

Couzin, J. (2009, January 23). Friendship as a health factor. *Science, 323,* 454–457.

Couzin-Frankel, J. (2010, November 26). Bacteria and asthma: Untangling the links. *Science, 330,* 1168–1169.

Couzin-Frankel, J. (2011a, January 14). New high-tech screen takes carrier testing to the next level. *Science, 331,* 130–131.

Couzin-Frankel, J. (2011b, July 29). A pitched battle over life span. *Science, 333,* 549–550.

Cowan, N. (Ed.). (1997). *The development of memory in childhood.* Hove, East Sussex, UK: Psychology Press.

Cowan, N., & Alloway, T. (2009). Development of working memory in childhood. In M. L. Courage & N. Cowan (Eds.), *The development of memory in infancy and childhood* (2nd ed., pp. 303–342). New York, NY: Psychology Press.

Craig, W. M., & Harel, Y. (2004). Bullying, physical fighting and victimization. In C. Currie, C. Roberts, A. Morgan, R. Smith, W. Settertobulte, O. Samdal, & V. B. Rasmussen (Eds.), *Young people's health in context: Healthy behaviour in school-aged children (HBSC) study: International report from the 2001/2002 survey* (pp. 133–44). Retrieved from http://www.who.int/immunization/hpv/target/young_peoples_health_in_context_who_2011_2012.pdf

Craig, W. M., & Pepler, D. J. (2007). Understanding bullying; From research to practice. *Canadian Psychology, 48,* 86–93. doi:10.1037/cp2007010

Crain, W. C. (2005). *Theories of development: Concepts and applications* (5th ed.). Upper Saddle River, NJ: Prentice Hall.

Cramer, S. C., & Procaccio, V. (2012). Correlation between genetic polymorphisms and stroke recovery: Analysis of the GAIN Americas and GAIN International Studies. *European Journal of Neurology, 19,* 718–724. doi:10.1111/j.1468–1331.2011.03615.x

Cranswick, K., & Dosman, D. (2008). *Eldercare: What we know today.* Retrieved from http://www.statcan.gc.ca/pub/11-008-x/2008002/article/10689-eng.pdf

Crawford, E., Wright, M. O. D., & Masten, A. S. (2006). Resilience and spirituality in youth. In E. C. Roehlkepartain, P. E. King, L. M. Wagener, & P. L. Benson (Eds.), *The handbook of spiritual development in childhood and adolescence* (pp. 355–370). Thousand Oaks, CA: Sage.

Cremation Association of North America. (2012). *Annual CANA statistics report 2011.* Retrieved from http://blcremationsystems.com/CANA_2011_Annual_Statistics_Report.pdf

Cremation Society of Great Britain. (2012). *Cremation statistics: National and international.* Available from http://www.srgw.demon.co.uk/CremSoc4/Stats/

Creswell, J. W. (2009). *Research design: Qualitative, quantitative, and mixed methods approaches* (3rd ed.). Thousand Oaks, CA: Sage.

Crinion, J., Turner, R., Grogan, A., Hanakawa, T., Noppeney, U., Devlin, J. T., … Price, C. J. (2006, June 9). Language control in the bilingual brain. *Science, 312,* 1537–1540.

Crisp, R. J., & Turner, R. N. (2011). Cognitive adaptation to the experience of social and cultural diversity. *Psychological Bulletin, 137,* 242–266. doi:10.1037/a0021840

Crosnoe, R., & Elder, G. H., Jr. (2002). Successful adaptation in the later years: A life course approach to aging. *Social Psychology Quarterly, 65,* 309–328.

Crosnoe, R., & Johnson, M. K. (2011). Research on adolescence in the twenty-first century. *Annual Review of Sociology, 37,* 439–460. doi:10.1146/annurev-soc-081309-150008

Crosnoe, R., Johnson, M. K., & Elder, G. H., Jr. (2004). Intergenerational bonding in school: The behavioral and contextual correlates of student–teacher relationships. *Sociology of Education, 77,* 60–81.

Crosnoe, R., Leventhal, T., Wirth, R. J., Pierce, K. M., Pianta, R. C., & NICHD Early Child Care Research Network. (2010). Family socioeconomic status and consistent environmental stimulation in early childhood. *Child Development, 81,* 972–987. doi:10.1111/j.1467–8624.2010.01446.x

Crosnoe, R., & Needham, B. (2004). Holism, contextual variability, and the study of friendships in adolescent development. *Child Development, 75,* 264–279.

Cruikshank, M. (2009). *Learning to be old: Gender, culture, and aging* (2nd ed.). Lanham, MD: Rowman & Littlefield.

Cruz, A. A., Bateman, E. D., & Bousquet, J. (2010). The social determinants of asthma. *European Respiratory Journal, 35,* 239–242. doi:10.1183/09031936.00070309

Csikszentmihalyi, M. (1996). *Creativity: Flow and the psychology of discovery and invention.* New York, NY: HarperCollins.

Cuevas, B. J., & Stone, J. I. (2007). *The Buddhist dead: Practices, discourses, representations.* Honolulu, HI: University of Hawaii Press.

Cuijpers, P., Brännmark, J. G., & van Straten, A. (2008). Psychological treatment of postpartum depression: A meta-analysis. *Journal of Clinical Psychology, 64,* 103–118.

Cumming, E., & Henry, W. E. (1961). *Growing old: The process of disengagement.* New York, NY: Basic Books.

Cumming, G. P., Currie, H. D., Panay, N., Moncur, R., & Lee, A. J. (2011). Stopping hormone replacement therapy: Were women ill advised? *Menopause International, 17,* 82–87. doi:10.1258/mi.2011.011103

Cummings, E. M., Goeke-Morey, M. C., Papp, L. M., & Dukewich, T. L. (2002). Children's responses to mothers' and fathers' emotionality and tactics in marital conflict in the home. *Journal of Family Psychology, 16,* 478–492.

Curlin, F. A., Nwodim, C., Vance, J. L., Chin, M. H., & Lantos, J. D. (2008). To die, to sleep: US physicians' religious and other objections to physician-assisted suicide, terminal sedation, and withdrawal of life support. *American Journal of Hospice and Palliative Medicine, 25,* 112–120. doi:10.1177/1049909107310141

Currie C., Zanotti, C., Morgan, A., Currie, D., de Looze, M., Roberts, C., … Barnekow, V. (Eds.). (2012). *Social determinants of health and well-being among young people: Health behaviour in school-aged children (HBSC) study: International report from the 2009/2010 survey (Health Policy for Children and Adolescents, No. 6).* Retrieved from http://www.euro.who.int/__data/assets/pdf_file/0003/163857/Social-determinants-of-health-and-well-being-among-young-people.pdf

Currie, J., & Widom, C. S. (2010). Long-term consequences of child abuse and neglect on adult economic well-being. *Child Maltreatment, 15,* 111–120. doi:10.1177/1077559509355316

Cutler, S. J., Hendricks, J., & O'Neill, G. (2011). Civic engagement and aging. In R. H. Binstock & L. K. George (Eds.), *Handbook of aging and the social sciences* (7th ed., pp. 221–233). San Diego, CA: Academic Press.

D

Daddis, C. (2010). Adolescent peer crowds and patterns of belief in the boundaries of personal authority. *Journal of Adolescence, 33*, 699–708.

Dahl, R. E. (2004). Adolescent brain development: A period of vulnerabilities and opportunities. Keynote address. In R. E. Dahl & L. P. Spear (Eds.), *Adolescent brain development: Vulnerabilities and opportunities* (Vol. 1021, pp. 1–22). New York, NY: New York Academy of Sciences.

Dai, D. Y. (2010). *The nature and nurture of giftedness: A new framework for understanding gifted education.* New York, NY: Teachers College Press.

Dale, M. (2013). *Trends in the age composition of college and university students and graduates.* Retrieved from http://www.statcan.gc.ca/pub/81-004-x/2010005/article/11386-eng.htm

Dalman, C., Allebeck, P., Gunnell, D., Harrison, G., Kristensson, K., Lewis, G., ... Karlsson, H. (2008). Infections in the CNS during childhood and the risk of subsequent psychotic illness: A cohort study of more than one million Swedish subjects. *American Journal of Psychiatry, 165*, 59–65.

Danel, I., Berg, C., Johnson, C. H., & Atrash, H. (2003). Magnitude of maternal morbidity during labor and delivery: United States, 1993–1997. *American Journal of Public Health, 93*, 631–634.

Dangour, A. D., Fletcher, A. E., & Grundy, E. M. D. (2007). *Ageing well: Nutrition, health, and social interventions.* Boca Raton, FL: CRC Press/Taylor & Francis.

Dannefer, D., & Patterson, R. S. (2008). The missing person: Some limitations in the contemporary study of cognitive aging. In S. M. Hofer & D. F. Alwin (Eds.), *Handbook of cognitive aging: Interdisciplinary perspectives* (pp. 105–119). Thousand Oaks, CA: Sage.

Daro, D. (2009). The history of science and child abuse prevention: A reciprocal relationship. In K. A. Dodge & D. L. Coleman (Eds.), *Preventing child maltreatment: Community approaches* (pp. 9–28). New York, NY: Guilford Press.

Darwin, C. (1859). *On the origin of species by means of natural selection.* London, England: J. Murray.

David, B., Grace, D., & Ryan, M. K. (2004). The gender wars: A self-categorization perspective on the development of gender identity. In M. Bennett & F. Sani (Eds.), *The development of the social self* (pp. 135–157). Hove, East Sussex, England: Psychology Press.

Davidov, M., & Grusec, J. E. (2006). Untangling the links of parental responsiveness to distress and warmth to child outcomes. *Child Development, 77*, 44–58.

Davidson, K. (2008). Declining health and competence: Men facing choices about driving cessation. *Generations, 32*(1), 44–47.

Davis, C. L., Tomporowski, P. D., Boyle, C. A., Waller, J. L., Miller, P. H., Naglieri, J. A., & Gregoski, M. (2007). Effects of aerobic exercise on overweight children's cognitive functioning: A randomized controlled trial. *Research Quarterly for Exercise and Sport, 78*, 510–519.

Davis, K. D., Goodman, W. B., Pirretti, A. E., & Almeida, D. M. (2008). Nonstandard work schedules, perceived family well-being, and daily stressors. *Journal of Marriage and Family, 70*, 991–1003.

Davis, R. N., Davis, M. M., Freed, G. L., & Clark, S. J. (2011). Fathers' depression related to positive and negative parenting behaviors with 1-year-old children. *Pediatrics, 127*, 612–618. doi:10.1542/peds.2010–1779

Davis-Kean, P. E., Jager, J., & Collins, W. A. (2009). The self in action: An emerging link between self-beliefs and behaviors in middle childhood. *Child Development Perspectives, 3*, 184–188. doi:10.1111/j.1750–8606.2009.00104.x

Dawson, L. L. (2010). The study of new religious movements and the radicalization of home-grown terrorists: Opening a dialogue. *Terrorism and Political Violence, 22*, 1–21.

Dawson, M., Soulières, I., Gernsbacher, M. A., & Mottron, L. (2007). The level and nature of autistic intelligence. *Psychological Science, 18*, 657–662.

de Broucker, P. (2005). *Without a paddle: What to do about Canada's young drop-outs.* Retrieved from http://cprn.org/documents/39460_en.pdf

de Bruin, W. B., Parker, A. M., & Fischhoff, B. (2007). Can adolescents predict significant life events? *The Journal of Adolescent Health, 41*, 208–210.

De Cock, K. M. (2011). Trends in global health and CDC's international role, 1961–2011. *MMWR, 60*(Suppl. 4), 104–111.

de Heering, A., de Liedekerke, C., Deboni, M., & Rossion, B. (2010). The role of experience during childhood in shaping the other-race effect. *Developmental Science, 13*, 181–187.

de Jonge, A., van der Goes, B. Y., Ravelli, A. C. J., Amelink-Verburg, M. P., Mol, B. W., Nijhuis, J. G., ... Buitendijk, S. E. (2009). Perinatal mortality and morbidity in a nationwide cohort of 529,688 low-risk planned home and hospital births. *BJOG: An International Journal of Obstetrics & Gynaecology, 116*, 1177–1184. doi:10.1111/j.1471–0528.2009.02175.x

de Jonge, H. M. C. (2011). Purification and remembrance: Eastern and western ways to deal with the Bali bombing. In P. J. Margry & C. Sánchez-Carretero (Eds.), *Grassroots memorials: The politics of memorializing traumatic death* (pp. 262–284). New York, NY: Berghahn Books.

De Neys, W., & Van Gelder, E. (2009). Logic and belief across the lifespan: The rise and fall of belief inhibition during syllogistic reasoning. *Developmental Science, 12*, 123–130.

De Raedt, R., Koster, E. H. W., & Ryckewaert, R. (2013). Aging and attentional bias for death related and general threat-related information: Less avoidance in older as compared with middle-aged adults. *The Journals of Gerontology, Series B: Psychological Sciences and Social Sciences, 68*, 41–48. doi:10.1093/geronb/gbs047

de Schipper, E. J., Riksen-Walraven, J. M., & Geurts, S. A. E. (2006). Effects of child-caregiver ratio on the interactions between caregivers and children in child-care centers: An experimental study. *Child Development, 77*, 861–874.

De Wals, P., Tairou, F., Van Allen, M. I., Uh, S-H., Lowry, R. B., Sibbald, B., ... & Niyonsenga, T. (2007). Reduction in neural-tube defects after folic acid fortification in Canada. *New England Journal of Medicine, 357*, 135–142. doi:10.1056/NEJMoa067103

Dean, A. J., Walters, J., & Hall, A. (2010). A systematic review of interventions to enhance medication adherence in children and adolescents with chronic illness. *Archives of Disease in Childhood, 95,* 717–723. doi:10.1136/adc.2009.175125

Dearing, E., Wimer, C., Simpkins, S. D., Lund, T., Bouffard, S. M., Caronongan, P., ... Weiss, H. (2009). Do neighborhood and home contexts help explain why low-income children miss opportunities to participate in activities outside of school? *Developmental Psychology, 45,* 1545–1562.

Deary, I. J., Penke, L., & Johnson, W. (2010). The neuroscience of human intelligence differences. *Nature Reviews Neuroscience, 11,* 201–211. doi:10.1038/nrn2793

DeCasper, A. J., & Fifer, W. P. (1980). Of human bonding: Newborns prefer their mother's voices. *Science, 208,* 1174–1176.

Deci, E. L., Koestner, R., & Ryan, R. M. (1999). A meta-analytic review of experiments examining the effects of extrinsic rewards on intrinsic motivation. *Psychological Bulletin, 125,* 627–668.

DeCicca, P. (2007). Does full-day kindergarten matter? Evidence from the first two years of schooling. *Economics of Education Review, 26,* 67–82.

Dees, M. K., Vernooij-Dassen, M. J., Dekkers, W. J., Vissers, K. C., & van Weel, C. (2011). 'Unbearable suffering': A qualitative study on the perspectives of patients who request assistance in dying. *Journal of Medical Ethics, 37,* 727–734. doi:10.1136/jme.2011.045492

Degenhardt, L., Coffey, C., Carlin, J. B., Swift, W., Moore, E., & Patton, G. C. (2010). Outcomes of occasional cannabis use in adolescence: 10-year follow-up study in Victoria, Australia. *The British Journal of Psychiatry, 196,* 290–295. doi:10.1192/bjp.bp.108.056952

Delaunay-El Allam, M., Soussignan, R., Patris, B., Marlier, L., & Schaal, B. (2010). Long-lasting memory for an odor acquired at the mother's breast. *Developmental Science, 13,* 849–863. doi:10.1111/j.1467–7687.2009.00941.x

Demetriou, A., & Bakracevic, K. (2009). Reasoning and self-awareness from adolescence to middle age: Organization and development as a function of education. *Learning and Individual Differences, 19,* 181–194.

Denham, S. A., Blair, K. A., DeMulder, E., Levitas, J., Sawyer, K., Auerbach-Major, S., & Queenan, P. (2003). Preschool emotional competence: Pathway to social competence. *Child Development, 74,* 238–256.

Denny, D., & Pittman, C. (2007). Gender identity: From dualism to diversity. In M. S. Tepper & A. Fuglsang Owens (Eds.), *Sexual health: Vol. 1. Psychological foundations* (pp. 205–229). Westport, CT: Praeger/Greenwood.

Dentinger, E., & Clarkberg, M. (2002). Informal caregiving and retirement timing among men and women: Gender and caregiving relationships in late midlife. *Journal of Family Issues, 23,* 857–879. doi:10.1177/019251302236598

DePaulo, B. M. (2006). *Singled out: How singles are stereotyped, stigmatized, and ignored and still live happily ever after.* New York, NY: St. Martin's Press.

Deptula, D. P., Henry, D. B., & Schoeny, M. E. (2010). How can parents make a difference? Longitudinal associations with adolescent sexual behavior. *Journal of Family Psychology, 24,* 731–739. doi:10.1037/a0021760

DeRose, L. M., Shiyko, M. P., Foster, H., & Brooks-Gunn, J. (2011). Associations between menarcheal timing and behavioral developmental trajectories for girls from age 6 to age 15. *Journal of Youth and Adolescence, 40,* 1329–1342. doi:10.1007/s10964–010–9625–3

Desai, S., & Andrist, L. (2010). Gender scripts and age at marriage in India. *Demography, 47,* 667–687.

DeSantis, C., Siegel, R., Bandi, P., & Jemal, A. (2011). Breast cancer statistics, 2011. *CA: A Cancer Journal for Clinicians, 61,* 408–418. doi:10.3322/caac.20134

Devaux, M., Sassi, F., Church, J., Cecchini, M., & Borgonovi, F. (2011). Exploring the relationship between education and obesity. *OECD Journal: Economic Studies, 2011,* 121–159. doi:10.1787/eco_studies-2011-5kg5825v1k23

DeYoung, C. G., Hirsh, J. B., Shane, M. S., Papademetris, X., Rajeevan, N., & Gray, J. R. (2010). Testing predictions from personality neuroscience. *Psychological Science, 21,* 820–828. doi:10.1177/0956797610370159

Diallo, Y., Hagemann, F., Etienne, A., Gurbuzer, Y., & Mehran, F. (2010). *Global child labour developments: Measuring trends from 2004 to 2008.* Geneva, Switzerland: International Labour Office, International Programme on the Elimination of Child Labour.

Diamond, A., & Amso, D. (2008). Contributions of neuroscience to our understanding of cognitive development. *Current Directions in Psychological Science, 17,* 136–141.

Diamond, L. M., & Fagundes, C. P. (2010). Psychobiological research on attachment. *Journal of Social and Personal Relationships, 27,* 218–225. doi:10.1177/0265407509360906

Diamond, M. E. (2007). Neuronal basis of perceptual intelligence. In F. Santoianni & C. Sabatano (Eds.), *Brain development in learning environments: Embodied and perceptual advancements* (pp. 98–108). Newcastle, UK: Cambridge Scholars.

Dick, D. M. (2011). Developmental changes in genetic influences on alcohol use and dependence. *Child Development Perspectives, 5,* 223–230. doi:10.1111/j.1750–8606.2011.00207.x

Dickinson, G. E., & Hoffmann, H. C. (2010). Roadside memorial policies in the United States. *Mortality, 15,* 154–167. doi:10.1080/13576275.2010.482775

Dickinson, M. D., & Hiscock, M. (2010). Age-related IQ decline is reduced markedly after adjustment for the Flynn effect. *Journal of Clinical and Experimental Neuropsychology, 32,* 865–870. doi:10.1080/13803391003596413

Didion, J. (2005). *The year of magical thinking.* New York, NY: Knopf.

DiGirolamo, A., Thompson, N., Martorell, R., Fein, S., & Grummer-Strawn, L. (2005). Intention or experience? Predictors of continued breastfeeding. *Health Education & Behavior, 32,* 208–226.

Dijksterhuis, A., Bos, M. W., van der Leij, A., & van Baaren, R. B. (2009). Predicting soccer matches after unconscious and conscious thought as a function of expertise. *Psychological Science, 20*, 1381–1387.

Dijksterhuis, A., & Nordgren, L. F. (2006). A theory of unconscious thought. *Perspectives on Psychological Science, 1*, 95–109. doi:10.1111/j.1745–6916.2006.00007.x

Dilworth-Bart, J. E., & Moore, C. F. (2006). Mercy mercy me: Social injustice and the prevention of environmental pollutant exposures among ethnic minority and poor children. *Child Development, 77*, 247–265. doi:10.1111/j.1467–8624.2006.00868.x

Dionne, G., Tremblay, R. E., Boivin, M., Laplante, D., & Pérusse, D. (2003). Physical aggression and expressive vocabulary in 19-month-old twins. *Developmental Psychology, 39*, 261–273.

Dishion, T. J., & Bullock, B. M. (2002). Parenting and adolescent problem behavior: An ecological analysis of the nurturance hypothesis. In J. G. Borkowski, S. Landesman Ramey, & M. Bristol-Power (Eds.), *Parenting and the child's world: Influences on academic, intellectual, and social-emotional development* (pp. 231–249). Mahwah, NJ: Erlbaum.

Dishion, T. J., Poulin, F., & Burraston, B. (2001). Peer group dynamics associated with iatrogenic effects in group interventions with high-risk young adolescents. In D. W. Nangle & C. A. Erdley (Eds.), *New Directions for Child and Adolescent Development: No. 91. The role of friendship in psychological adjustment* (pp. 79–92). San Francisco, CA: Jossey-Bass.

Dishion, T. J., Véronneau, M.-H., & Myers, M. W. (2010). Cascading peer dynamics underlying the progression from problem behavior to violence in early to late adolescence. *Development and Psychopathology, 22*, 603–619. doi:10.1017/S0954579410000313

Dobson, V., Candy, T. R., Hartmann, E. E., Mayer, D. L., Miller, J. M., & Quinn, G. E. (2009). Infant and child vision research: Present status and future directions. *Optometry & Vision Science, 86*, 559–560.

Doering, K. (2010). Death: The unwritten curriculum. *Encounter: Education for Meaning and Social Justice, 23*, 57–62.

Dominguez, C. O. (2001). Expertise in laparoscopic surgery: Anticipation and affordances. In E. Salas & G. A. Klein (Eds.), *Linking expertise and naturalistic decision making* (pp. 287–301). Mahwah, NJ: Erlbaum.

Dominguez, X., Vitiello, V. E., Maier, M. F., & Greenfield, D. B. (2010). A longitudinal examination of young children's learning behavior: Child-level and classroom-level predictors of change throughout the preschool year. *School Psychology Review, 39*, 29–47.

Dong, X., Simon, M. A., Beck, T. T., Farran, C., McCann, J. J., Mendes de Leon, C. F., ... Evans, D. A. (2011). Elder abuse and mortality: The role of psychological and social wellbeing. *Gerontology, 57*, 549–558.

Donnellan, M. B., & Lucas, R. E. (2008). Age differences in the Big Five across the life span: Evidence from two national samples. *Psychology and Aging, 23*, 558–566. doi:10.1037/a0012897

Doraiswamy, P. M. (2012). Silent cerebrovascular events and Alzheimer's disease: An overlooked opportunity for prevention? *American Journal of Psychiatry, 169*, 251–254. doi:10.1176/appi.ajp.2011.11121830

dosReis, S., Mychailyszyn, M. P., Evans-Lacko, S. E., Beltran, A., Riley, A. W., & Myers, M. A. (2009). The meaning of attention-deficit/hyperactivity disorder medication and parents' initiation and continuity of treatment for their child. *Journal of Child and Adolescent Psychopharmacology, 19*, 377–383. doi:10.1089/cap.2008.0118

dosReis, S., & Myers, M. A. (2008). Parental attitudes and involvement in psychopharmacological treatment for ADHD: A conceptual model. *International Review of Psychiatry, 20*, 135–141.

Douglas Mental Health University Institute. (2012). *Sleep and children: The impact of lack of sleep on daily life.* Retrieved from http://www.douglas.qc.ca/info/sleep-and-children-impact-of-of-sleep-on-daily-life

Douglas Mental Health University Institute. (2013). *Epigenetics: When the environment modifies the genes.* Retrieved from http://www.douglas.qc.ca/info/epigenetics

Doumbo, O. K. (2005, February 4). It takes a village: Medical research and ethics in Mali. *Science, 307*, 679–681.

Dowling, J. E. (2004). *The great brain debate: Nature or nurture?* Washington, DC: Joseph Henry Press.

Drover, J., Hoffman, D. R., Castañeda, Y. S., Morale, S. E., & Birch, E. E. (2009). Three randomized controlled trials of early long-chain polyunsaturated fatty acid supplementation on means-end problem solving in 9-month-olds. *Child Development, 80*, 1376–1384. doi:10.1111/j.1467–8624.2009.01339.x

Dryfoos, J. G. (1990). *Adolescents at risk: Prevalence and prevention.* New York, NY: Oxford University Press.

Duckworth, A. L., Peterson, C., Matthews, M. D., & Kelly, D. R. (2007). Grit: Perseverance and passion for long-term goals. *Journal of Personality and Social Psychology, 92*, 1087–1101.

Duffy, O., Iversen, L., & Hannaford, P. C. (2011). The menopause 'It's somewhere between a taboo and a joke'. A focus group study. *Climacteric, 14*, 497–505. doi:10.3109/13697137.2010.549974

Duncan, G. J., & Magnuson, K. (2007). Penny wise and effect size foolish. *Child Development Perspectives, 1*, 46–51.

Duncan, G. J., Ziol-Guest, K. M., & Kalil, A. (2010). Early-childhood poverty and adult attainment, behavior, and health. *Child Development, 81*, 306–325. doi:10.1111/j.1467–8624.2009.01396.x

Duncan, S., & Phillips, M. (2010). People who live apart together (LATs)—How different are they? *The Sociological Review, 58*, 112–134. doi:10.1111/j.1467–954X.2009.01874.x

Dunning, D. (2011). *Social motivation.* New York, NY: Psychology Press.

Dunphy, D. C. (1963). The social structure of urban adolescent peer groups. *Sociometry, 26*, 230–246.

Duplassie, D., & Daniluk, J. C. (2007). Sexuality: Young and middle adulthood. In M. S. Tepper & A. Fuglsang Owens (Eds.), *Sexual health: Vol. 1. Psychological foundations* (pp. 263–289). Westport, CT: Praeger/Greenwood.

Dupuis, K., & Pichora-Fuller, M. K. (2010). Use of affective prosody by young and older adults. *Psychology and Aging, 25*, 16–29. doi:10.1037/a0018777

Dwane, H. D. (2012). Self-control and perceived physical risk in an extreme sport. *Young Consumers: Insight and Ideas for Responsible Marketers, 13*, 62–73.

Dweck, C. S. (2007). Is math a gift? Beliefs that put females at risk. In S. J. Ceci (Ed.), *Why aren't more women in science?: Top researchers debate the evidence* (pp. 47–55). Washington, DC: American Psychological Association.

E

Earley, L., & Cushway, D. (2002). The parentified child. *Clinical Child Psychology and Psychiatry, 7*, 163–178. doi:10.1177/1359104502007002005

Earth Policy Institute. (2011). *Two stories of disease: Smallpox and polio.* Retrieved from http://www.earth-policy.org/data_highlights/2011/highlights19

Ebaugh, H. R., & Curry, M. (2000). Fictive kin as social capital in new immigrant communities. *Sociological Perspectives, 43*, 189–209.

Ebner, N. C., Freund, A. M., & Baltes, P. B. (2006). Developmental changes in personal goal orientation from young to late adulthood: From striving for gains to maintenance and prevention of losses. *Psychology and Aging, 21*, 664–678.

Eccles, J. S., & Roeser, R. W. (2011). Schools as developmental contexts during adolescence. *Journal of Research on Adolescence, 21*, 225–241. doi:10.1111/j.1532-7795.2010.00725.x

Edmunds, A., & Edmunds, G. (2008). *Special education in Canada.* Toronto, ON: McGraw-Hill Ryerson.

Edwards, J. L. P. (2007). Achieving timely permanency in child protection courts: The importance of frontloading the court process. *Juvenile and Family Court Journal, 58*, 1–37. doi:10.1111/j.1755-6988.2007.tb00136.x

Eggum, N. D., Eisenberg, N., Kao, K., Spinrad, T. L., Bolnick, R., Hofer, C., … Fabricius, W. V. (2011). Emotion understanding, theory of mind, and prosocial orientation: Relations over time in early childhood. *The Journal of Positive Psychology, 6*, 4–16. doi:10.1080/17439760.2010.536776

Ehrlich, P. R. (1968). *The population bomb.* New York, NY: Ballantine Books.

Eigersma, S. (2010). *Immigrant seniors: Their economic security and factors affecting their access to benefits.* Retrieved from http://www.parl.gc.ca/content/lop/researchpublications/07-45-e.htm

Einstein, A. (1954/1994). *Ideas and opinions.* New York: Modern Library.

Eisenberg, N., Cumberland, A., Guthrie, I. K., Murphy, B. C., & Shepard, S. A. (2005). Age changes in prosocial responding and moral reasoning in adolescence and early adulthood. *Journal of Research on Adolescence, 15*, 235–260.

Eisenberg, N., Fabes, R. A., & Spinrad, T. L. (2006). Prosocial development. In N. Eisenberg (Ed.), *Handbook of child psychology: Vol. 3. Social, emotional, and personality development* (6th ed., pp. 646–718). Hoboken, NJ: Wiley.

Eisenberg, N., Hofer, C., Spinrad, T. L., Gershoff, E. T., Valiente, C., Losoya, S., … Maxon, E. (2008). Understanding mother–adolescent conflict discussions: Concurrent and across-time prediction from youths' dispositions and parenting. *Monographs of the Society for Research in Child Development, 73*(2, Serial No. 290), vii-viii, 1–160.

Eisenberg, N., Spinrad, T. L., Fabes, R. A., Reiser, M., Cumberland, A., Shepard, S. A., … Thompson, M. (2004). The relations of effortful control and impulsivity to children's resiliency and adjustment. *Child Development, 75*, 25–46.

Eklund, J. M., Kerr, M., & Stattin, H. (2010). Romantic relationships and delinquent behaviour in adolescence: The moderating role of delinquency propensity. *Journal of Adolescence, 33*, 377–386.

Elder, G. H., Jr., & Shanahan, M. J. (2006). *The life course and human development* (6th ed.). Hoboken, NJ: Wiley.

Elkind, D. (1967). Egocentrism in adolescence. *Child Development, 38*, 1025–1034.

Elkind, D. (2007). *The power of play: How spontaneous, imaginative activities lead to happier, healthier children.* Cambridge, MA: Da Capo Press.

Ellis, B. J., Shirtcliff, E. A., Boyce, W. T., Deardorff, J., & Essex, M. J. (2011). Quality of early family relationships and the timing and tempo of puberty: Effects depend on biological sensitivity to context. *Development and Psychopathology, 23*, 85–99.

Else-Quest, N. M., Hyde, J. S., Goldsmith, H. H., & Van Hulle, C. A. (2006). Gender differences in temperament: A meta-analysis. *Psychological Bulletin, 132*, 33–72.

Employment and Social Development Canada. (2008, January). *Indicators of well-being in Canada: Special reports—What difference does learning make to financial security?* Retrieved from http://www4.hrsdc.gc.ca/.3ndic.1t.4r@-eng.jsp?iid=54#a2

Employment and Social Development Canada. (2013). *Elder abuse modules.* Retrieved from http://www.esdc.gc.ca/eng/seniors/funding/pancanadian/elder_abuse.shtml

Employment and Social Development Canada. (n.d.[a]). *Indicators of well-being in Canada: Family life—Age of mother at childbirth.* Retrieved from http://www4.hrsdc.gc.ca/.3ndic.1t.4r@-eng.jsp?iid=75

Employment and Social Development Canada. (n.d.[b]). *Indicators of well-being in Canada: Family life—Divorce.* Retrieved from http://www4.hrsdc.gc.ca/.3ndic.1t.4r@-eng.jsp?iid=76

Employment and Social Development Canada. (n.d.[c]). *Indicators of well-being in Canada: Family life—Marriage.* Retrieved from http://www4.hrsdc.gc.ca/.3ndic.1t.4r@-eng.jsp?iid=78

Engelberts, A. C., & de Jonge, G. A. (1990). Choice of sleeping position for infants: Possible association with cot death. *Archives of Disease in Childhood, 65*, 462–467.

Engelhardt, H. T., Jr. (2012). Why clinical bioethics so rarely gives morally normative guidance. In H. T. Engelhardt (Ed.), *Bioethics critically reconsidered* (pp. 151–174). New York: Springer.

Englander, E., Mills, E., & McCoy, M. (2009). Cyberbullying and information exposure: User-generated content in post-secondary education. *International Journal of Contemporary Sociology, 46*, 213–230.

Enserink, M. (2011, February 18). Can this DNA sleuth help catch criminals? *Science, 331*, 838–840.

Environics Research Group. (2013). *Canadians' attitudes towards end-of-life issues.* Retrieved from http://right2life.ca/wp-content/uploads/2012/09/Environics-LifeCanada-Euthansia-Report-2013-FINAL.pdf

Epps, C., & Holt, L. (2011). The genetic basis of addiction and relevant cellular mechanisms. *International Anesthesiology Clinics, 49,* 3–14.

Epstein, J. N., Langberg, J. M., Lichtenstein, P. K., Altaye, M., Brinkman, W. B., House, K., & Stark, L. J. (2010). Attention-deficit/hyperactivity disorder outcomes for children treated in community-based pediatric settings. *Archives of Pediatrics & Adolescent Medicine, 164,* 160–165. doi:10.1001/archpediatrics.2009.263

Erath, S. A., Keiley, M. K., Pettit, G. S., Lansford, J. E., Dodge, K. A., & Bates, J. E. (2009). Behavioral predictors of mental health service utilization in childhood through adolescence. *Journal of Developmental & Behavioral Pediatrics, 30,* 481–488.

Erdman, P., & Ng, K.-M. (Eds.). (2010). *Attachment: Expanding the cultural connections.* New York, NY: Routledge.

Erickson, K. I., & Korol, D. L. (2009). Effects of hormone replacement therapy on the brains of postmenopausal women: A review of human neuroimaging studies. In W. Chodzko-Zajko, A. Kramer, & L. Poon (Eds.), *Enhancing cognitive functioning and brain plasticity* (pp. 133–158). Champaign, IL: Human Kinetics.

Erickson, K. I., Miller, D. L., Weinstein, A. M., Akl, S. L., & Banducci, S. (2012). Physical activity and brain plasticity in late adulthood: A conceptual and comprehensive review. *Aging Research, 3,* 99–108. doi: http://dx.doi.org/10.4081/ar.2012.e6

Erickson, R. J. (2005). Why emotion work matters: Sex, gender, and the division of household labor. *Journal of Marriage and Family, 67,* 337–351.

Ericsson, K. A. (1996). The acquisition of expert performance: An introduction to some of the issues. In K. A. Ericsson (Ed.), *The road to excellence: The acquisition of expert performance in the arts and sciences, sports, and games* (pp. 1–50). Hillsdale, NJ: Erlbaum.

Ericsson, K. A. (2009). *Development of professional expertise: Toward measurement of expert performance and design of optimal learning environments.* New York, NY: Cambridge University Press.

Ericsson, K. A., Charness, N., Feltovich, P. J., & Hoffman, R. R. (Eds.). (2006). *The Cambridge handbook of expertise and expert performance.* New York: Cambridge University Press.

Erikson, E. H. (1963). *Childhood and society* (2nd ed.). New York, NY: Norton.

Erikson, E. H. (1968). *Identity: Youth and crisis.* New York, NY: Norton.

Erikson, E. H. (1982). *The life cycle completed: A review.* New York, NY: Norton.

Erikson, E. H., Erikson, J. M., & Kivnick, H. Q. (1986). *Vital involvement in old age.* New York, NY: Norton.

Erlinghagen, M., & Hank, K. (2006). The participation of older Europeans in volunteer work. *Ageing & Society, 26,* 567–584.

Ertesvåg, S. K. (2011). Measuring authoritative teaching. *Teaching and Teacher Education, 27,* 51–61.

Ertmer, D. J., Young, N. M., & Nathani, S. (2007). Profiles of vocal development in young cochlear implant recipients. *Journal of Speech, Language, and Hearing Research, 50,* 393–407. doi:10.1044/1092-4388(2007/028)

Etchu, K. (2007). Social context and preschoolers' judgments about aggressive behavior: Social domain theory. *Japanese Journal of Educational Psychology, 55,* 219–230.

EURO-PERISTAT, SCPE, EUROCAT, & EURONEOSTAT. (2008). *European perinatal health report.* Retrieved from http://www.europeristat.com/images/doc/EPHR/european-perinatal-health-report.pdf

Evans, A. D., & Lee, K. (2011). Verbal deception from late childhood to middle adolescence and its relation to executive functioning skills. *Developmental Psychology, 47,* 1108–1116. doi:10.1037/a0023425

Evans, A. D., Xu, F., & Lee, K. (2011). When all signs point to you: Lies told in the face of evidence. *Developmental Psychology, 47,* 39–49.

Evans, D. W., & Leckman, J. F. (2006). Origins of obsessive-compulsive disorder: Developmental and evolutionary perspectives. In D. Cicchetti & D. J. Cohen (Eds.), *Developmental psychopathology: Vol. 3. Risk, disorder, and adaptation* (2nd ed., pp. 404–435). Hoboken, NJ: Wiley.

Evans, D. W., Leckman, J. F., Carter, A., Reznick, J. S., Henshaw, D., King, R. A., & Pauls, D. (1997). Ritual, habit, and perfectionism: The prevalence and development of compulsive-like behavior in normal young children. *Child Development, 68,* 58–68.

Ewers, M., Walsh, C., Trojanowski, J. Q., Shaw, L. M., Petersen, R. C., Jack, C. R., Jr., ... & Hampel, H. (2012). Prediction of conversion from mild cognitive impairment to Alzheimer's disease dementia based upon biomarkers and neuropsychological test performance. *Neurobiology of Aging, 33,* 1203–1214. doi: 10.1016/j.neurobiolaging.2010.10.019

EXPRESS Group. (2009). One-year survival of extremely preterm infants after active perinatal care in Sweden. *Journal of the American Medical Association, 301,* 2225–2233. doi:10.1001/jama.2009.771

F

Fabes, R. A., Martin, C. L., & Hanish, L. D. (2003). Young children's play qualities in same-, other-, and mixed-sex peer groups. *Child Development, 74,* 921–932. doi:10.1111/1467-8624.00576

Fabiani, M., & Gratton, G. (2009). Brain imaging probes into the cognitive and physiological effects of aging. In W. Chodzko-Zajko, A. Kramer, & L. Poon (Eds.), *Enhancing cognitive functioning and brain plasticity* (pp. 1–13). Champaign, IL Human Kinetics.

Facebook Newsroom. (2012). *Key facts.* Retrieved from http://newsroom.fb.com/content/default.aspx?NewsAreaId=22

Fantino, A. M., & Colak, A. (2001). Refugee children in Canada: Searching for identity. *Child Welfare, 80,* 587–596.

Farahani, M., Subramanian, S. V., & Canning, D. (2009). The effect of changes in health sector resources on infant mortality in the short-run and the long-run: A longitudinal econometric analysis. *Social Science & Medicine, 68,* 1918–1925.

Faraone, S. V., & Wilens, T. (2003). Does stimulant treatment lead to substance use disorders? *Journal of Clinical Psychiatry, 64,* 9–13.

Fazzi, E., Signorini, S. G., Bomba, M., Luparia, A., Lanners, J., & Balottin, U. (2011). Reach on sound: A key to object permanence in visually impaired children. *Early Human Development, 87,* 289–296.

Feeley, N., Sherrard, K., Waitzer, E., & Boisvert, L. (2013). The father at the bedside: Patterns of involvement in the NICU. *Journal of Perinatal & Neonatal Nursing, 27,* 72–80. doi:10.1097/JPN.0b013e31827fb415

Feigelsohn, R. (2013, March 19). *Job hopping is the new career.* Retrieved from http://www.jobpostings.ca/career-planning/joblife/job-hopping-new-career

Feldman, C. (2011, March 28). Sex at school: Sex education in Quebec. *The Dominion.* Retrieved from http://www.dominionpaper.ca/articles/3939

Feldman, R. (2007). Parent-infant synchrony and the construction of shared timing; Physiological precursors, developmental outcomes, and risk conditions. *Journal of Child Psychology and Psychiatry, 48,* 329–354.

Feldman, R., Gordon, I., & Zagoory-Sharon, O. (2011). Maternal and paternal plasma, salivary, and urinary oxytocin and parent–infant synchrony: Considering stress and affiliation components of human bonding. *Developmental Science, 14,* 752–761. doi:10.1111/j.1467–7687.2010.01021.x

Fell, J. C., Todd, M., & Voas, R. B. (2011). A national evaluation of the nighttime and passenger restriction components of graduated driver licensing. *Journal of Safety Research, 42,* 283–290.

Felmlee, D., & Muraco, A. (2009). Gender and friendship norms among older adults. *Research on Aging, 31,* 318–344. doi:10.1177/0164027508330719

Fergusson, E., Maughan, B., & Golding, J. (2008). Which children receive grandparental care and what effect does it have? *Journal of Child Psychology and Psychiatry, 49,* 161–169.

Fewtrell, M., Wilson, D. C., Booth, I., & Lucas, A. (2011). Six months of exclusive breast feeding: How good is the evidence? *BMJ, 342.* doi:10.1136/bmj.c5955

Field, N. P., & Filanosky, C. (2009). Continuing bonds, risk factors for complicated grief, and adjustment to bereavement. *Death Studies, 34,* 1–29. doi:10.1080/07481180903372269

Finch, C. E. (2010). Evolution of the human lifespan and diseases of aging: Roles of infection, inflammation, and nutrition. *Proceedings of the National Academy of Sciences, 107*(Suppl. 1), 1718–1724. doi:10.1073/pnas.0909606106

Fincham, F. D., & Beach, S. R. H. (2010). Of memes and marriage: Toward a positive relationship science. *Journal of Family Theory & Review, 2,* 4–24. doi:10.1111/j.1756–2589.2010.00033.x

Fincham, F. D., Stanley, S. M., & Beach, S. R. H. (2007). Transformative processes in marriage: An analysis of emerging trends. *Journal of Marriage and Family, 69,* 275–292.

Fine, M. A., & Harvey, J. H. (2006). *Handbook of divorce and relationship dissolution.* Mahwah, NJ: Erlbaum.

Fingerman, K. L. (2009). Consequential strangers and peripheral ties: The importance of unimportant relationships. *Journal of Family Theory & Review, 1,* 69–86. doi:10.1111/j.1756–2589.2009.00010.x

Fingerman, K. L., Berg, C., Smith, J., & Antonucci, T. C. (2011). *Handbook of lifespan development.* New York: Springer.

Fingerman, K. L., Cheng, Y.-P., Birditt, K., & Zarit, S. (2012). Only as happy as the least happy child: Multiple grown children's problems and successes and middle-aged parents' well-being. *The Journals of Gerontology Series B: Psychological Sciences and Social Sciences, 67B,* 184–193. doi:10.1093/geronb/gbr086

Fingerman, K. L., & Furstenberg, F. F. (2012, May 30). You can go home again. *New York Times,* p. A29.

Fingerman, K. L., Hay, E. L., & Birditt, K. S. (2004). The best of ties, the worst of ties: Close, problematic, and ambivalent social relationships. *Journal of Marriage and Family, 66,* 792–808.

Finkel, E. J., Eastwick, P. W., Karney, B. R., Reis, H. T., & Sprecher, S. (2012). Online dating: A critical analysis from the perspective of psychological science. *Psychological Science in the Public Interest, 13,* 3–66. doi:10.1177/1529100612436522

Fischer, R. S., Norberg, A., & Lundman, B. (2008). Embracing opposites: Meanings of growing old as narrated by people aged 85. *International Journal of Aging and Human Development, 67,* 259–271.

Flegal, K. M., Carroll, M. D., Kit, B. K., & Ogden, C. L. (2012). Prevalence of obesity and trends in the distribution of body mass index among US adults, 1999–2010. *Journal of the American Medical Association, 307,* 491–497.

Flensborg-Madsen, T., Bay von Scholten, M., Flachs, E. M., Mortensen, E. L., Prescott, E., & Tolstrup, J. S. (2011). Tobacco smoking as a risk factor for depression. A 26-year population-based follow-up study. *Journal of psychiatric research, 45,* 143–149.

Fletcher, A. C., Steinberg, L., & Williams-Wheeler, M. (2004). Parental influences on adolescent problem behavior: Revisiting Stattin and Kerr. *Child Development, 75,* 781–796.

Fletcher, J. M., & Vaughn, S. (2009). Response to intervention: Preventing and remediating academic difficulties. *Child Development Perspectives, 3,* 30–37. doi:10.1111/j.1750–8606.2008.00072.x

Floud, R., Fogel, R. W., Harris, B., & Hong, S. C. (2011). *The changing body: Health, nutrition, and human development in the western world since 1700.* Cambridge, UK: Cambridge University Press.

Flynn, J. R. (1999). Searching for justice: The discovery of IQ gains over time. *American Psychologist, 54,* 5–20.

Flynn, J. R. (2007). *What is intelligence? Beyond the Flynn effect.* New York, NY: Cambridge University Press.

Fong, F. (2012, March 8). The plight of younger workers. *Observation, TD Economics.* Retrieved from http://www.td.com/document/PDF/economics/special/ff0312_younger_workers.pdf

Fontana, L., Colman, R. J., Holloszy, J. O., & Weindruch, R. (2011). Calorie restriction in nonhuman and human primates. In E. J. Masoro & S. N. Austad (Eds.), *Handbook of the biology of aging* (7th ed., pp. 447–461). San Diego, CA: Academic Press.

Forget-Dubois, N., Dionne, G., Lemelin, J.-P., Pérusse, D., Tremblay, R. E., & Boivin, M. (2009). Early child language mediates the relation between home environment and school readiness. *Child Development, 80,* 736–749.

Fortinsky, R. H., Tennen, H., Frank, N., & Affleck, G. (2007). Health and psychological consequences of caregiving. In C. M. Aldwin, C. L. Park, A. Spiro, III, & R. P. Abeles (Eds.), *Handbook of health psychology and aging* (pp. 227–249). New York, NY: Guilford Press.

Fortuna, K., & Roisman, G. I. (2008). Insecurity, stress, and symptoms of psychopathology: Contrasting results from self-reports versus interviews of adult attachment. *Attachment & Human Development, 10,* 11–28.

Foster, E. M., & Kalil, A. (2007). Living arrangements and children's development in low-income White, Black, and Latino families. *Child Development, 78,* 1657–1674.

Fox, N. A., Henderson, H. A., Rubin, K. H., Calkins, S. D., & Schmidt, L. A. (2001). Continuity and discontinuity of behavioral inhibition and exuberance: Psychophysiological and behavioral influences across the first four years of life. *Child Development, 72,* 1–21.

Frayling, T. M., Timpson, N. J., Weedon, M. N., Zeggini, E., Freathy, R. M., Lindgren, C. M., ... McCarthy, M. I. (2007, May 11). A common variant in the FTO gene is associated with body mass index and predisposes to childhood and adult obesity. *Science, 316,* 889–894.

Frazier, T. W., & Hardan, A. Y. (2009). A meta-analysis of the corpus callosum in autism. *Biological Psychiatry, 66,* 935–941.

Fredricks, J. A., & Eccles, J. S. (2002). Children's competence and value beliefs from childhood through adolescence: Growth trajectories in two male-sex-typed domains. *Developmental Psychology, 38,* 519–533.

Freeman, J. (2010). *Gifted lives: What happens when gifted children grow up?* New York, NY: Routledge.

Freisthler, B., Merritt, D. H., & LaScala, E. A. (2006). Understanding the ecology of child maltreatment: A review of the literature and directions for future research. *Child Maltreatment, 11,* 263–280. doi:10.1177/1077559506289524

Freud, A. (1958/2000). Adolescence. In J. B. McCarthy (Ed.), *Adolescent development and psychopathology* (Vol. 13, pp. 29–52). Lanham, MD: University Press of America.

Freud, S. (1935). *A general introduction to psychoanalysis* (J. Riviere, Trans.). New York, NY: Liveright.

Freud, S. (1938). *The basic writings of Sigmund Freud* (A. A. Brill, Trans.). New York, NY: Modern Library.

Freud, S. (1940/1964). An outline of psycho-analysis. In J. Strachey (Ed. and Trans.), *The standard edition of the complete psychological works of Sigmund Freud* (Vol. 23, pp. 144–207). London, England: Hogarth Press.

Freund, A. M. (2008). Successful aging as management of resources: The role of selection, optimization, and compensation. *Research in Human Development, 5,* 94–106.

Freund, A. M., Nikitin, J., & Ritter, J. O. (2009). Psychological consequences of longevity: The increasing importance of self-regulation in old age. *Human Development, 52,* 1–37.

Fries, A. B. W., & Pollak, S. D. (2007). Emotion processing and the developing brain. In D. Coch, G. Dawson, & K. W. Fischer (Eds.), *Human behavior, learning, and the developing brain. Typical development* (pp. 329–361). New York, NY: Guilford Press.

Frost, J. L. (2009). *A history of children's play and play environments: Toward a contemporary child-saving movement.* New York, NY: Routledge.

Fu, V. K., & Wolfinger, N. H. (2011). Broken boundaries or broken marriages? Racial intermarriage and divorce in the United States. *Social Science Quarterly, 92,* 1096–1117. doi:10.1111/j.1540–6237.2011.00809.x

Fuligni, A. J. (1998). Authority, autonomy, and parent-adolescent conflict and cohesion: A study of adolescents from Mexican, Chinese, Filipino, and European backgrounds. *Developmental Psychology, 34,* 782–792.

Fuligni, A. J., & Hardway, C. (2006). Daily variation in adolescents' sleep, activities, and psychological well-being. *Journal of Research on Adolescence, 16,* 353–378.

Fuligni, A. S., Howes, C., Lara-Cinisomo, S., & Karoly, L. A. (2009). Diverse pathways in early childhood professional development: An exploration of early educators in public preschools, private preschools, and family child care homes. *Early Education and Development, 20,* 507–526. doi:10.1080/10409280902783483

Fuller-Thomson, E. (2005). *Grandparents raising grandchildren in Canada: A profile of skipped generation families* (SEDAP Research Paper No. 132). Retrieved from http://socserv.mcmaster.ca/sedap/p/sedap132.pdf

Fung, H. H., Stoeber, F. S., Yeung, D. Y.-l., & Lang, F. R. (2008). Cultural specificity of socioemotional selectivity: Age differences in social network composition among Germans and Hong Kong Chinese. *Journals of Gerontology Series B: Psychological Sciences and Social Sciences, 63,* 156–164.

Fung, J. J., & Lau, A. S. (2009). Punitive discipline and child behavior problems in Chinese-American immigrant families: The moderating effects of indigenous child-rearing ideologies. *International Journal of Behavioral Development, 33,* 520–530. doi:10.1177/0165025409343749

Furnham, A. (2012). Intelligence and intellectual styles. In L-F. Zhang, R. J. Sternberg, & S. Rayner (Eds.), *Handbook of intellectual styles: Preferences in cognition, learning, and thinking* (pp. 173–192). New York, NY: Springer.

Fuselli, P., Groff, P., Nesdale-Tucker, R., Waldie, R., & Wanounou, A. (2011, January 18). The financial costs and prevention strategies of unintentional injuries. *Public Sector Digest.*

G

Gabrieli, J. D. E. (2009, July 17). Dyslexia: A new synergy between education and cognitive neuroscience. *Science, 325,* 280–283.

Gaertner, B. M., Spinrad, T. L., Eisenberg, N., & Greving, K. A. (2007). Parental childrearing attitudes as correlates of father involvement during infancy. *Journal of Marriage and Family, 69,* 962–976.

Galambos, N. L., Barker, E. T., & Krahn, H. J. (2006). Depression, self-esteem, and anger in emerging adulthood: Seven-year trajectories. *Developmental Psychology, 42,* 350–365.

Gallese, V., Fadiga, L., Fogassi, L., & Rizzolatti, G. (1996). Action recognition in the premotor cortex. *Brain, 119,* 593–609. doi:10.1093/brain/119.2.593

Galotti, K. M. (2002). *Making decisions that matter: How people face important life choices.* Mahwah, NJ: Erlbaum.

Galupo, M. P., Cartwright, K., & Savage, L. (2010). Cross-category friendships and postformal thought among college students. *Journal of Adult Development, 17,* 208–214. doi:10.1007/s10804–009–9089–4

Galván, A., Spatzier, A., & Juvonen, J. (2011). Perceived norms and social values to capture school culture in elementary and middle school. *Journal of Applied Developmental Psychology, 32,* 346–353.

Gandara, P., & Rumberger, R. W. (2009). Immigration, language, and education: How does language policy structure opportunity? *Teachers College Record, 111,* 750–782.

Gandini, L., Hill, L., Cadwell, L., & Schwall, C. (Eds.). (2005). *In the spirit of the studio: Learning from the atelier of Reggio Emilia.* New York, NY: Teachers College Press.

Gangestad, S. W., & Simpson, J. A. (2007). *The evolution of mind: Fundamental questions and controversies.* New York, NY: Guilford Press.

Ganong, L. H., & Coleman, M. (2004). *Stepfamily relationships: Development, dynamics, and interventions.* New York, NY: Kluwer Academic/Plenum.

Ganong, L. H., Coleman, M., & Jamison, T. (2011). Patterns of stepchild–stepparent relationship development. *Journal of Marriage and Family, 73,* 396–413. doi:10.1111/j.1741–3737.2010.00814.x

Gans, D., & Silverstein, M. (2006). Norms of filial responsibility for aging parents across time and generations. *Journal of Marriage and Family, 68,* 961–976.

Gao, Y., Huang, C., Zhao, K., Ma, L., Qiu, X., Zhang, L., ... & Xiao, Q. (2013). Depression as a risk factor for dementia and mild cognitive impairment: A meta-analysis of longitudinal studies. *International Journal of Geriatric Psychiatry, 28,* 441–449. doi:10.1002/gps.3845

García, F., & Gracia, E. (2009). Is always authoritative the optimum parenting style? Evidence from Spanish families. *Adolescence, 44,* 101–131.

García Coll, C. T., & Marks, A. K. (2009). *Immigrant stories: Ethnicity and academics in middle childhood.* New York, NY: Oxford University Press.

García Coll, C. T., & Marks, A. K. (2011). *The immigrant paradox in children and adolescents: Is becoming American a developmental risk?* Washington, DC: American Psychological Association.

Gardner, H. (1983). *Frames of mind: The theory of multiple intelligences.* New York, NY: Basic Books.

Gardner, H. (1999). Are there additional intelligences? The case for naturalist, spiritual, and existential intelligences. In J. Kane (Ed.), *Education, information, and transformation: Essays on learning and thinking* (pp. 111–131). Upper Saddle River, NJ: Merrill.

Gardner, H. (2006). *Multiple intelligences: New horizons in theory and practice* (Completely rev. and updated ed.). New York, NY: Basic Books.

Gardner, H., & Moran, S. (2006). The science of multiple intelligences theory: A response to Lynn Waterhouse. *Educational Psychologist, 41,* 227–232.

Garner, R., & Kohen, D. (2008). *Changes in the prevalence of asthma among Canadian children.* Retrieved from http://www.statcan.gc.ca/pub/82-003-x/2008002/article/10551-eng.htm

Garriguet, D. (2004). *Nutrition: Findings from the Canadian Community Health Survey: Overview of Canadians' eating habits.* Retrieved from http://publications.gc.ca/collections/Collection/Statcan/82-620-M/82-620-MIE2006002.pdf

Garriguet, D. (2008). *Beverage consumption of children and teens* (Catalogue no. 82–003-X). Retrieved from http://www.sugar.ca/english/pdf/garriguet_beverage_consumption_of_children_and_teens.pdf

Garriguet, D., & Colley, R. C. (2012). *Daily patterns of physical activity participation among Canadians* (Catalogue No. 82–003-X). Retrieved from http://www.statcan.gc.ca/pub/82-003-x/2012002/article/11649-eng.pdf

Gaskins, S. (1999). Children's daily lives in a Mayan village: A case study of culturally constructed roles and activities. In A. Göncü (Ed.), *Children's engagement in the world: Sociocultural perspectives* (pp. 25–60). New York, NY: Cambridge University Press.

Gauvain, M., Beebe, H., & Zhao, S. (2011). Applying the cultural approach to cognitive development. *Journal of Cognition and Development, 12,* 121–133. doi:10.1080/15248372.2011.563481

Gavrilov, L. A., & Gavrilova, N. S. (2006). Reliability theory of aging and longevity. In E. J. Masoro & S. N. Austad (Eds.), *Handbook of the biology of aging* (6th ed., pp. 3–42). Amsterdam, The Netherlands: Elsevier Academic Press.

Ge, X., Natsuaki, M. N., Neiderhiser, J. M., & Reiss, D. (2007). Genetic and environmental influences on pubertal timing: Results from two national sibling studies. *Journal of Research on Adolescence, 17,* 767–788.

Geary, N., & Lovejoy, J. (2008). Sex differences in energy metabolism, obesity, and eating behavior. In J. B. Becker, K. J. Berkley, N. Geary, E. Hampson, J. P. Herman, & E. Young (Eds.), *Sex differences in the brain: From genes to behavior* (pp. 253–274). New York, NY: Oxford University Press.

Gelfand, D. E. (2003). *Aging and ethnicity: Knowledge and services* (2nd ed.). New York, NY: Springer.

Geller, B., Tillman, R., Bolhofner, K., & Zimerman, B. (2008). Child bipolar I disorder: Prospective continuity with adult bipolar I disorder; characteristics of second and third episodes; predictors of 8-year outcome. *Archives of General Psychiatry, 65,* 1125–1133. doi:10.1001/archpsyc.65.10.1125

Gendron, B. P., Williams, K. R., & Guerra, N. G. (2011). An analysis of bullying among students within schools: Estimating the effects of individual normative beliefs, self-esteem, and school climate. *Journal of School Violence, 10,* 150–164. doi:10.1080/15388220.2010.539166

Genesee, F. (2008). Early dual language learning. *Zero to Three, 29,* 17–23.

Genesee, F., & Nicoladis, E. (2007). Bilingual first language acquisition. In E. Hoff & M. Shatz (Eds.), *Blackwell handbook of language development* (pp. 324–342). Malden, MA: Blackwell.

Genesee, F. H. (2009). Early childhood bilingualism: Perils and possibilities. *Journal of Applied Research on Learning, 2,* 1–21. Retrieved from http://www.ccl-cca.ca/pdfs/JARL/Jarl-Vol2Art2-Genesse_EN.pdf

Gentile, D. A., Saleem, M., & Anderson, C. A. (2007). Public policy and the effects of media violence on children. *Social Issues and Policy Review, 1,* 15–61.

Geoffroy, M. C., Séguin, J. R., Lacourse, E., Boivin, M., Tremblay, R. E., & Côté, S. M. (2012). Parental characteristics associated with childcare use during the first 4 years of life: Results from a representative cohort of Québec families. *Canadian Journal of Public Health, 103,* 76–80.

Georgas, J., Berry, J. W., van de Vijver, F. J. R., Kagitçibasi, Ç., & Poortinga, Y. H. (2006). *Families across cultures: A 30-nation psychological study.* Cambridge, UK: Cambridge University Press.

George, D., & Whitehouse, P. (2010). Dementia and mild cognitive impairment in social and cultural context. In D. Dannefer & C. Phillipson (Eds.), *The SAGE Handbook of Social Gerontology* (pp. 343–356). London, UK: SAGE.

George, L. G., Helson, R., & John, O. P. (2011). The "CEO" of women's work lives: How Big Five Conscientiousness, Extraversion, and Openness predict 50 years of work experiences in a changing sociocultural context. *Journal of Personality and Social Psychology, 101,* 812–830.

Gerber, A. S., Huber, G. A., Doherty, D., & Dowling, C. M. (2011). The Big Five personality traits in the political arena. *Annual Review of Political Science, 14,* 265–287. doi:10.1146/annurev-polisci-051010–111659

Gerrard, M., Gibbons, F. X., Houlihan, A. E., Stock, M. L., & Pomery, E. A. (2008). A dual-process approach to health risk decision making: The prototype willingness model. *Developmental Review, 28,* 29–61.

Gershkoff-Stowe, L., & Hahn, E. R. (2007). Fast mapping skills in the developing lexicon. *Journal of Speech, Language, and Hearing Research, 50,* 682–696.

Gershoff, E. T., Grogan-Kaylor, A., Lansford, J. E., Chang, L., Zelli, A., Deater-Deckard, K., & Dodge, K. A. (2010). Parent discipline practices in an international sample: Associations with child behaviors and moderation by perceived normativeness. *Child Development, 81,* 487–502. doi:10.1111/j.1467–8624.2009.01409.x

Gettler, L. T., & McKenna, J. J. (2010). Never sleep with baby? Or keep me close but keep me safe: Eliminating inappropriate safe infant sleep rhetoric in the United States. *Current Pediatric Reviews, 6,* 71–77.

Gewirtzman, A., Bobrick, L., Conner, K., & Tyring, S. K. (2011). Epidemiology of sexually transmitted infections. In G. Gross (Ed.), *Sexually transmitted infections and sexually transmitted diseases* (pp. 13–34). New York, NY: Springer.

Giancola, P. R., Josephs, R. A., Parrott, D. J., & Duke, A. A. (2010). Alcohol myopia revisited: Clarifying aggression and other acts of disinhibition through a distorted lens. *Perspectives on Psychological Science, 5,* 265–278. doi:10.1177/1745691610369467

Giardino, A. P., & Alexander, R. (2011). *Child maltreatment* (4th ed.). St. Louis, MO: G. W. Medical.

Gibson, C. J., Joffe, H., Bromberger, J. T., Thurston, R. C., Lewis, T. T., Khalil, N., & Matthews, K. A. (2012). Mood symptoms after natural menopause and hysterectomy with and without bilateral oophorectomy among women in midlife. *Obstetrics and Gynecology, 119,* 935–941. doi:10.1097/AOG.0b013e31824f9c14

Gibson-Davis, C. (2011). Mothers but not wives: The increasing lag between nonmarital births and marriage. *Journal of Marriage and Family, 73,* 264–278. doi:10.1111/j.1741–3737.2010.00803.x

Gibson-Davis, C. M., & Gassman-Pines, A. (2010). Early childhood family structure and mother–child interactions: Variation by race and ethnicity. *Developmental Psychology, 46,* 151–164. doi:10.1037/a0017410

Gigerenzer, G. (2008). Why heuristics work. *Perspectives on Psychological Science, 3,* 20–29.

Gilbert, D. (2006). *Stumbling on happiness.* New York, NY: Knopf.

Giles, A., & Rovee-Collier, C. (2011). Infant long-term memory for associations formed during mere exposure. *Infant Behavior and Development, 34,* 327–338.

Gillen-O'Neel, C., Ruble, D. N., & Fuligni, A. J. (2011). Ethnic stigma, academic anxiety, and intrinsic motivation in middle childhood. *Child Development, 82,* 1470–1485. doi:10.1111/j.1467–8624.2011.01621.x

Gilles, F. H., & Nelson, M. D. (2012). *The developing human brain: Growth and adversities.* London, UK: Mac Keith Press.

Gillespie, M. A. (2010). Players and spectators: Sports and ethical training in the American university. In E. Kiss & J. P. Euben (Eds.), *Debating moral education: Rethinking the role of the modern university* (pp. 293–316). Durham, NC: Duke University Press.

Gilligan, C. (1982). *In a different voice: Psychological theory and women's development.* Cambridge, MA: Harvard University Press.

Gilmore, J. (2010). *Trends in dropout rates and the labour market outcomes of young dropouts.* Available from http://www.statcan.gc.ca/pub/81-004-x/2010004/article/11339-eng.htm

Gilmour, H., & Park, J. (2006). Dependency, chronic conditions and pain in seniors. *Health Reports, 16* (Supplement), 21–31. Retrieved from http://www.statcan.gc.ca/pub/82-003-s/2005000/pdf/9087-eng.pdf

Gitlin, L. N., Belle, S. H., Burgio, L. D., Czaja, S. J., Mahoney, D., Gallagher-Thompson, D., ... Ory, M. G. (2003). Effect of multicomponent interventions on caregiver burden and depression: The REACH multisite initiative at 6-month follow-up. *Psychology & Aging, 18,* 361–374.

Gladwell, M. (2010, October 4). Small change: Why the revolution will not be tweeted. *The New Yorker, 86,* 42–49.

Globe and Mail. (2012, November 9). *Supreme Court ruling on special education opens Pandora's box.* Retrieved from http://www.theglobeandmail.com/globe-debate/editorials/supreme-court-ruling-on-special-education-opens-pandoras-box/article5169193/

Gluckman, P. D., & Hanson, M. A. (2006). *Developmental origins of health and disease.* Cambridge, England: Cambridge University Press.

Golant, S. M. (2008). Commentary: Irrational exuberance for the aging in place of vulnerable low-income older homeowners. *Journal of Aging & Social Policy, 20,* 379–397. doi:10.1080/08959420802131437

Golant, S. M. (2011). The changing residential environments of older people. In R. H. Binstock & L. K. George (Eds.), *Handbook of aging and the social sciences* (7th ed., pp. 207–220). San Diego, CA: Academic Press.

Gold, B. T., Kim, C., Johnston, N. F., Kryscio, R. J., & Smith, C. D. (2013). Lifelong bilingualism maintains neural efficiency for cognitive control in aging. *The Journal of Neuroscience, 33,* 387–396. doi: 10.1523/JNEUROSCI.3837–12.2013

Gold, J. M. (2010). Helping stepfathers "step away" from the role of "father": Directions for family intervention. *The Family Journal, 18,* 208–214. doi:10.1177/1066480710364498

Goldberg, W. A., Prause, J., Lucas-Thompson, R., & Himsel, A. (2008). Maternal employment and children's achievement in context: A meta-analysis of four decades of research. *Psychological Bulletin, 134,* 77–108.

Golden, M. (2009). Angel baby. In B. Graham (Ed.), *Eye of my heart: 27 writers reveal the hidden pleasures and perils of being a grandmother* (pp. 125–133). New York, NY: HarperCollins.

Golden, T. D., Veiga, J. F., & Simsek, Z. (2006). Telecommuting's differential impact on work-family conflict: Is there no place like home? *Journal of Applied Psychology, 91,* 1340–1350.

Goldenberg, J. L., & Arndt, J. (2008). The implications of death for health: A terror management health model for behavioral health promotion. *Psychological Review, 115,* 1032–1053. doi:10.1037/a0013326

Goldin-Meadow, S. (2006). Nonverbal communication: The hand's role in talking and thinking. In D. Kuhn & R. S. Siegler (Eds.), *Handbook of child psychology: Vol. 2. Cognition, perception, and language* (6th ed., pp. 336–369). Hoboken, NJ: Wiley.

Goldin-Meadow, S. (2009). How gesture promotes learning throughout childhood. *Child Development Perspectives, 3,* 106–111. doi:10.1111/j.1750–8606.2009.00088.x

Goldscheider, F., & Sassler, S. (2006). Creating stepfamilies: Integrating children into the study of union formation. *Journal of Marriage and Family, 68,* 275–291.

Goldstein, M. H., Schwade, J. A., & Bornstein, M. H. (2009). The value of vocalizing: Five-month-old infants associate their own noncry vocalizations with responses from caregivers. *Child Development, 80,* 636–644.

Golestani, N., Price, C. J., & Scott, S. K. (2011). Born with an ear for dialects? Structural plasticity in the expert phonetician brain. *The Journal of Neuroscience, 31,* 4213–4220. doi:10.1523/jneurosci.3891–10.2011

Golinkoff, R. M., & Hirsh-Pasek, K. (2008). How toddlers begin to learn verbs. *Trends in Cognitive Sciences, 12,* 397–403.

Golub, S. A., & Langer, E. J. (2007). Challenging assumptions about adult development: Implications for the health of older adults. In C. M. Aldwin, C. L. Park, A. Spiro, III, & R. P. Abeles (Eds.), *Handbook of health psychology and aging* (pp. 9–29). New York, NY: Guilford Press.

Göncü, A., & Gaskins, S. (2011). Comparing and extending Piaget's and Vygotsky's understandings of play: Symbolic play as individual, sociocultural, and educational interpretation. In P. Nathan & A. P. Pellegrini (Eds.), *The Oxford handbook of the development of play* (pp. 48–57). New York, NY: Oxford University Press.

Gonsalves, M., & Chuang, S. S. (2010, March). *Cultural and developmental issues in South Asian youth.* Poster presented at the National Metropolis Conference, Montreal, QC.

Goodall, J. (2000). *Through a window: My thirty years with the chimpanzees of Gombe* (1st Mariner Books ed.). Boston, MA: Houghton Mifflin.

Goodman, J. C., Dale, P. S., & Li, P. (2008). Does frequency count? Parental input and the acquisition of vocabulary. *Journal of Child Language, 35,* 515–531. doi:10.1017/S0305000907008641

Goodman, S. H., & Gotlib, I. H. (2002). *Children of depressed parents: Mechanisms of risk and implications for treatment.* Washington, DC: American Psychological Association.

Gopnik, A. (2001). Theories, language, and culture: Whorf without wincing. In M. Bowerman & S. C. Levinson (Eds.), *Language acquisition and conceptual development* (pp. 45–69). Cambridge, UK: Cambridge University Press.

Gopnik, A. (2009, September 7). Letter from Canada: The return of the native. *The New Yorker,* p. 29. Retrieved from http://archives.newyorker.com/?i=2009-09-07#folio=026

Gorchoff, S. M., John, O. P., & Helson, R. (2008). Contextualizing change in marital satisfaction during middle age: An 18-year longitudinal study. *Psychological Science, 19,* 1194–1200.

Gordis, E. B., Granger, D. A., Susman, E. J., & Trickett, P. K. (2008). Salivary alpha amylase-cortisol asymmetry in maltreated youth. *Hormones and Behavior, 53,* 96–103.

Gornick, J. C., & Meyers, M. (2003). *Families that work: Policies for reconciling parenthood and employment.* New York, NY: Russell Sage Foundation.

Gosso, Y. (2010). Play in different cultures. In P. K. Smith (Ed.), *Children and play: Understanding children's worlds* (pp. 80–98). Chichester, West Sussex, UK: Wiley-Blackwell.

Gotay, C. C., Iatzmarzyk, P. T., Janssen, I., Dawson, M. Y., Aminoltejari, K., & Bartley, N. L. (2012). Updating the Canadian obesity maps: An epidemic in progress. *Canadian Journal of Public Health, 104,* 64–68.

Gottfredson, D. C., & DiPietro, S. M. (2011). School size, social capital, and student victimization. *Sociology of Education, 84,* 69–89.

Gottfried, A. E., Marcoulides, G. A., Gottfried, A. W., & Oliver, P. H. (2009). A latent curve model of parental motivational practices and developmental decline in math and science academic intrinsic motivation. *Journal of Educational Psychology, 101,* 729–739.

Gottlieb, G. (1992). *Individual development and evolution: The genesis of novel behavior.* New York, NY: Oxford University Press.

Gottlieb, G. (2002). *Individual development and evolution: The genesis of novel behavior.* Mahwah, NJ: Erlbaum.

Gottlieb, G. (2007). Probabilistic epigenesis. *Developmental Science, 10,* 1–11.

Gottlieb, G. (2010). Normally occurring environmental and behavioral influences on gene activity. In K. E. Hood, C. T. Halpern, G. Greenberg, & R. M. Lerner (Eds.), *Handbook of developmental science, behavior, and genetics* (pp. 13–37). Malden, MA: Wiley-Blackwell.

Gough, M., & Killewald, A. (2011). Unemployment in families: The case of housework. *Journal of Marriage and Family, 73*, 1085–1100. doi:10.1111/j.1741–3737.2011.00867.x

Government of Canada. (2013a). *Childhood obesity.* Retrieved from http://healthycanadians.gc.ca/kids-enfants/obesity-obesite/risks-risques-eng.php?utm_campaign=CHS1213&utm_source=google_en&utm_content=ADV0096-12_sem-ad-1_en&utm_medium=cpc&utm_keyword=%2Bobesity%20%2Bchild

Government of Canada. (2013b). *Fertility.* Retrieved from http://healthycanadians.gc.ca/health-sante/pregnancy-grossesse/fert-eng.php

Government of Canada. (2014). *Employment Insurance Maternity and Parental Benefits.* Available from http://www.servicecanada.gc.ca/eng/sc/ei/benefits/maternityparental.shtml

Gow, A. J., Johnson, W., Pattie, A., Brett, C. E., Roberts, B., Starr, J. M., & Deary, I. J. (2011). Stability and change in intelligence from age 11 to ages 70, 79, and 87: The Lothian Birth Cohorts of 1921 and 1936. *Psychology and Aging, 26*, 232–240. doi:10.1037/a0021072

Graber, J. A., Nichols, T. R., & Brooks-Gunn, J. (2010). Putting pubertal timing in developmental context: Implications for prevention. *Developmental psychobiology, 52*, 254–262. doi:10.1002/dev.20438

Grady, D. (2007, February 6). Girl or boy? As fertility technology advances, so does an ethical debate. *New York Times,* pp. F5, F10.

Grady, D. (2012, May 5). When illness makes a spouse a stranger. *New York Times.* Retrieved from http://www.nytimes.com/2012/05/06/health/a-rare-form-of-dementia-tests-a-vow-of-for-better-for-worse.html?pagewanted=all

Gräff, J., Kim, D., Dobbin, M. M., & Tsai, L.-H. (2011). Epigenetic regulation of gene expression in physiological and pathological brain processes. *Physiological Reviews, 91*, 603–649. doi:10.1152/physrev.00012.2010

Grandin, T., & Johnson, C. (2009). *Animals make us human: Creating the best life for animals.* Boston: Houghton Mifflin Harcourt.

Grandparenting in the twenty-first century: The times they are a changin'. (2005). Ontario Health Promotion E-Bulletin: OHPE Bulletin 434. Retrieved from http://www.ohpe.ca/node/6892

Granic, I., & Patterson, G. R. (2006). Toward a comprehensive model of antisocial development: A dynamic systems approach. *Psychological Review, 113*, 101–131.

Granpeesheh, D., Tarbox, J., & Dixon, D. R. (2009). Applied behavior analytic interventions for children with autism: A description and review of treatment research. *Annals of Clinical Psychiatry, 21*, 162–173.

Granpeesheh, D., Tarbox, J., Dixon, D. R., Wilke, A. E., Allen, M. S., & Bradstreet, J. J. (2010). Randomized trial of hyperbaric oxygen therapy for children with autism. *Research in Autism Spectrum Disorders, 4*, 268–275.

Green, J. A., Whitney, P. G., & Potegal, M. (2011). Screaming, yelling, whining, and crying: Categorical and intensity differences in vocal expressions of anger and sadness in children's tantrums. *Emotion, 11*, 1124–1133. doi:10.1037/a0024173

Green, L., & Grant, V. (2008). "Gagged grief and beleaguered bereavements?" An analysis of multidisciplinary theory and research relating to same sex partnership bereavement. *Sexualities, 11*, 275–300. doi:10.1177/1363460708089421

Greenberg, L., & Normandin, C. (2011). *Disparities in life expectancy at birth* (Catalogue No. 82–624-X). Retrieved from http://www.statcan.gc.ca/pub/82-624-x/2011001/article/11427-eng.pdf

Greene, M. L., & Way, N. (2005). Self-esteem trajectories among ethnic minority adolescents: A growth curve analysis of the patterns and predictors of change. *Journal of Research on Adolescence, 15*, 151–178.

Greenhalgh, S. (2008). *Just one child: Science and policy in Deng's China.* Berkeley, CA: University of California Press.

Greenough, W. T., Black, J. E., & Wallace, C. S. (1987). Experience and brain development. *Child Development, 58*, 539–559.

Greenwood, P. M., & Parasuraman, R. (2012). *Nurturing the older brain and mind.* Cambridge, MA: MIT Press.

Gregory, S. M., Parker, B., & Thompson, P. D. (2012). Physical activity, cognitive function, and brain health: What is the role of exercise training in the prevention of dementia? *Brain Sciences, 2*, 684–708. doi:10.3390/brainsci2040684

Gregory, T. (2010, August 28). Grampy down with 'the Face': Social networking by seniors doubles over last year, survey says. *Chicago Tribune.* Retrieved from http://articles.chicagotribune.com/2010-08-28/news/ct-talk-social-mediaolder-adults-08220100827_1_social-networking-facebook-sites

Greyson, B. (2009). Near-death experiences and deathbed visions. In A. Kellehear (Ed.), *The study of dying: From autonomy to transformation* (pp. 253–275). New York, NY: Cambridge University Press.

Griffin, J., Gooding, S., Semesky, M., Farmer, B., Mannchen, G., & Sinnott, J. (2009). Four brief studies of relations between postformal thought and non-cognitive factors: Personality, concepts of god, political opinions, and social attitudes. *Journal of Adult Development, 16*, 173–182. doi:10.1007/s10804–009–9056–0

Griffith, P., & Lopez, O. (2009). Disparities in the diagnosis and treatment of Alzheimer's disease in African American and Hispanic patients: A call to action. *Generations, 33*(1), 37–46.

Grimm, D. (2008, May 16). Staggering toward a global strategy on alcohol abuse. *Science, 320*, 862–863.

Grivell, R. M., Reilly, A. J., Oakey, H., Chan, A., & Dodd, J. M. (2012). Maternal and neonatal outcomes following induction of labor: A cohort study. *Acta Obstetricia et Gynecologica Scandinavica, 91*, 198–203. doi:10.1111/j.1600–0412.2011.01298.x

Grobman, K. H. (2008). *Learning & teaching developmental psychology: Attachment theory, infancy, & infant memory development.* Retrieved from http://www.devpsy.org/questions/attachment_theory_memory.html

Grolnick, W. S., McMenamy, J. M., & Kurowski, C. O. (2006). Emotional self-regulation in infancy and toddlerhood. In L. Balter & C. S. Tamis-Lemonda (Eds.), *Child psychology: A handbook of contemporary issues* (2nd ed., pp. 3–25). New York, NY: Psychology Press.

Grossmann, K. E., Grossmann, K., & Waters, E. (Eds.). (2005). *Attachment from infancy to adulthood: The major longitudinal studies.* New York, NY: Guilford Press.

Grosvenor, T. (2003). Why is there an epidemic of myopia? *Clinical and Experimental Optometry, 86,* 273–275.

Grubeck-Loebenstein, B. (2010). Fading immune protection in old age: Vaccination in the elderly. *Journal of Comparative Pathology, 142*(Suppl. 1), S116–S119. doi:10.1016/j.jcpa.2009.10.002.

Grundy, E., & Henretta, J. C. (2006). Between elderly parents and adult children: A new look at the intergenerational care provided by the 'sandwich generation'. *Ageing & Society, 26,* 707–722.

Grych, J. H., & Fincham, F. D. (1990). Marital conflict and children's adjustment: A cognitive-contextual framework. *Psychological Bulletin, 108,* 267–290.

Guerra, N. G., & Williams, K. R. (2010). Implementing bullying prevention in diverse settings: Geographic, economic, and cultural influences. In E. Vernberg & B. Biggs (Eds.), *Preventing and treating bullying and victimization* (pp. 319–336). New York, NY: Oxford University Press.

Guerra, N. G., Williams, K. R., & Sadek, S. (2011). Understanding bullying and victimization during childhood and adolescence: A mixed methods study. *Child Development, 82,* 295–310. doi:10.1111/j.1467–8624.2010.01556.x

Guerri, C., & Pascual, M. (2010). Mechanisms involved in the neurotoxic, cognitive, and neurobehavioral effects of alcohol consumption during adolescence. *Alcohol, 44,* 15–26.

Gummerum, M., Keller, M., Takezawa, M., & Mata, J. (2008). To give or not to give: Children's and adolescents' sharing and moral negotiations in economic decision situations. *Child Development, 79,* 562–576.

Gunnar, M. R. (1998). Quality of early care and buffering of neuroendocrine stress reactions: Potential effects on the developing human brain. *Preventive Medicine, 27,* 208–211.

Guo, S., Padmadas, S. S., Zhao, F., Brown, J. J., & Stones, R. W. (2007). Delivery settings and caesarean section rates in China. *Bulletin of the World Health Organization, 85,* 755–762.

Gupta, R. C. (2011). *Reproductive and developmental toxicology.* Boston, MA: Elsevier/Academic Press.

Gurung, R. A. R., Taylor, S. E., & Seeman, T. E. (2003). Accounting for changes in social support among married older adults: Insights from the MacArthur Studies of Successful Aging. *Psychology & Aging, 18,* 487–496.

H

Hagedoorn, M., Van Yperen, N. W., Coyne, J. C., van Jaarsveld, C. H. M., Ranchor, A. V., van Sonderen, E., & Sanderman, R. (2006). Does marriage protect older people from distress? The role of equity and recency of bereavement. *Psychology and Aging, 21,* 611–620.

Haier, R. J., Colom, R., Schroeder, D. H., Condon, C. A., Tang, C., Eaves, E., & Head, K. (2009). Gray matter and intelligence factors: Is there a neuro-g? *Intelligence, 37,* 136–144.

Hajjar, E. R., Cafiero, A. C., & Hanlon, J. T. (2007). Polypharmacy in elderly patients. *American Journal of Geriatric Pharmacotherapy, 5,* 345–351. doi:10.1016/j.amjopharm.2007.12.002

Halaschek-Wiener, J., Amirabbasi-Beik, M., Monfared, N., Pieczyk, M., Sailer, C., Kollar, A., ... Brooks-Wilson, A. R. (2009). Genetic variation in healthy oldest-old. *PLoS ONE.* 2009/08/15. Retrieved from http://www.plosone.org/article/info:doi/10.1371/journal.pone.0006641

Hall, L. K. (2008). *Counseling military families: What mental health professionals need to know.* New York, NY: Taylor and Francis.

Hall, M., Lasby, D., Ayers, S., & Gibbons, W. D. (2009). *Caring Canadians, involved Canadians: Highlights from the 2007 Canada survey of giving, volunteering and participating* (Catalogue no. 71–542-XPE). Retrieved from http://www.statcan.gc.ca/pub/71-542-x/71-542-x2009001-eng.pdf

Hall-Lande, J. A., Eisenberg, M. E., Christenson, S. L., & Neumark-Sztainer, D. (2007). Social isolation, psychological health, and protective factors in adolescence. *Adolescence, 42,* 265–286.

Halpern, C. T., King, R. B., Oslak, S. G., & Udry, J. R. (2005). Body mass index, dieting, romance, and sexual activity in adolescent girls: Relationships over time. *Journal of Research on Adolescence, 15,* 535–559.

Halpern, D. F., Benbow, C. P., Geary, D. C., Gur, R. C., Hyde, J. S., & Gernsbacher, M. A. (2007). The science of sex differences in science and mathematics. *Psychological Science in the Public Interest, 8,* 1–51. doi:10.1111/j.1529–1006.2007.00032.x

Halpern, N. A., Pastores, S. M., Chou, J. F., Chawla, S., & Thaler, H. T. (2011). Advance directives in an oncologic intensive care unit: A contemporary analysis of their frequency, type, and impact. *Journal of Palliative Medicine, 14,* 483–489. doi:10.1089/jpm.2010.0397

Hamerman, D. (2007). *Geriatric bioscience: The link between aging and disease.* Baltimore, MD: Johns Hopkins University Press.

Hamerton, J. L., & Evans, J. A. (2005). Sex chromosome anomalies. In M. G. Butler & F. J. Meaney (Eds.), *Genetics of developmental disabilities* (pp. 585–650). Boca Raton, FL: Taylor & Francis.

Hamilton, A. (1914). Lead poisoning in the United States. *American Journal of Public Health, 4,* 477–480.

Hamm, J. V., & Faircloth, B. S. (2005). The role of friendship in adolescents' sense of school belonging. *New Directions for Child and Adolescent Development, 107,* 61–78.

Hammer, C. S., Jia, G., & Uchikoshi, Y. (2011). Language and literacy development of dual language learners growing up in the United States: A call for research. *Child Development Perspectives, 5,* 4–9. doi:10.1111/j.1750–8606.2010.00140.x

Hammond, C. J., Andrew, T., Mak, Y. T., & Spector, T. D. (2004). A susceptibility locus for myopia in the normal population is linked to the PAX6 gene region on chromosome 11: A genomewide scan of dizygotic twins. *American Journal of Human Genetics, 75,* 294–304.

Hampel, H., Lista, S., & Khachaturian, Z. S. (2012). Development of biomarkers to chart all Alzheimer's disease stages: The royal road to cutting the therapeutic Gordian Knot. *Alzheimer's & Dementia, 8,* 312–336. doi:10.1016/j.jalz.2012.05.2116

Hampton, T. (2005). Alcohol and cancer. *Journal of the American Medical Association, 294,* 1481. doi:10.1001/jama.294.12.1481-c

Han, E., Norton, E. C., & Powell, L. M. (2011). Direct and indirect effects of body weight on adult wages. *Economics & Human Biology, 9,* 381–392. doi:10.1016/j.ehb.2011.07.002

Han, W.-J., Lee, R., & Waldfogel, J. (2012). School readiness among children of immigrants in the US: Evidence from a large national birth cohort study. *Children and Youth Services Review, 34,* 771–782.

Hank, K., & Buber, I. (2009). Grandparents caring for their grandchildren: Findings from the 2004 Survey of Health, Ageing, and Retirement in Europe. *Journal of Family Issues, 30,* 53–73. doi:10.1177/0192513x08322627

Hannan, C., Buchanan, A. D., & Monroe, J. (2009). Maintaining the vaccine safety net. *Pediatrics, 124*(Suppl. 5), S571–572. doi:10.1542/peds.2009–1542U

Hansson, R. O., & Stroebe, M. S. (2007). *Bereavement in late life: Coping, adaptation, and developmental influences.* Washington, DC: American Psychological Association.

Hanushek, E. A., & Woessmann, L. (2009). *Do better schools lead to more growth? Cognitive skills, economic outcomes, and causation.* Bonn, Germany: Institute for the Study of Labor.

Hanushek, E. A., & Woessmann, L. (2010). *The high cost of low educational performance: The long-run economic impact of improving PISA outcomes.* Paris, France: OECD.

Harburg, E., Kaciroti, N., Gleiberman, L., Julius, M., & Schork, M. A. (2008). Marital pair anger-coping types may act as an entity to affect mortality: Preliminary findings from a prospective study (Tecumseh, Michigan, 1971–1988). *Journal of Family Communication, 8,* 44–61. doi:10.1080/15267430701779485

Hardy, C., & Bellamy, S. (2013). *Caregiver-infant attachment for Aboriginal families.* Retrieved from http://www.nccah-ccnsa.ca/Publications/Lists/Publications/Attachments/75/Infant%20Attachment%20Fact%20Sheet_English.pdf

Harjes, C. E., Rocheford, T. R., Bai, L., Brutnell, T. P., Kandianis, C. B., Sowinski, S. G., … Buckler, E. S. (2008, January 18). Natural genetic variation in Lycopene Epsilon Cyclase tapped for maize biofortification. *Science, 319,* 330–333.

Harkness, S., Super, C. M., & Mavridis, C. J. (2011). Parental ethnotheories about children's socioemotional development. In X. Chen & K. H. Rubin (Eds.), *Socioemotional development in cultural context* (pp. 73–98). New York, NY: Guilford Press.

Harknett, K. S., & Hartnett, C. S. (2011). Who lacks support and why? An examination of mothers' personal safety nets. *Journal of Marriage and the Family, 73,* 861–875. doi:10.1111/j.1741-3737.2011.00852.x

Harlow, H. (1958). The nature of love. *American Psychologist, 13,* 673–685.

Harlow, I. (2005). Shaping sorrow: Creative aspects of public and private mourning. In S. C. Heilman (Ed.), *Death, bereavement, and mourning* (pp. 33–52). New Brunswick, NJ: Transaction.

Harris, J. R. (1998). *The nurture assumption: Why children turn out the way they do.* New York, NY: Free Press.

Harris, J. R. (2002). Beyond the nurture assumption: Testing hypotheses about the child's environment. In J. G. Borkowski, S. Landesman Ramey, & M. Bristol-Power (Eds.), *Parenting and the child's world: Influences on academic, intellectual, and social-emotional development* (pp. 3–20). Mahwah, NJ: Erlbaum.

Harrison, J. (2011). 'Talking about my generation': A state-of-the-art review of health information for men in the andropause. *Health Information & Libraries Journal, 28,* 161–170. doi:10.1111/j.1471-1842.2011.00950.x

Harrison, K., Bost, K. K., McBride, B. A., Donovan, S. M., Grigsby-Toussaint, D. S., Kim, J., … Jacobsohn, G. C. (2011). Toward a developmental conceptualization of contributors to overweight and obesity in childhood: The Six-Cs model. *Child Development Perspectives, 5,* 50–58. doi:10.1111/j.1750–8606.2010.00150.x

Harrison, L. J., & McLeod, S. (2010). Risk and protective factors associated with speech and language impairment in a nationally representative sample of 4- to 5-year-old children. *Journal of Speech, Language, and Hearing Research, 53,* 508–529. doi:10.1044/1092-4388(2009/08-0086)

Harrist, A. W., Topham, G. L., Hubbs-Tait, L., Page, M. C., Kennedy, T. S., & Shriver, L. H. (2012). What developmental science can contribute to a transdisciplinary understanding of childhood obesity: An interpersonal and intrapersonal risk model. *Child Development Perspectives, 6,* 445–455. doi:10.1111/cdep.12004

Hart, C. N., Cairns, A., & Jelalian, E. (2011). Sleep and obesity in children and adolescents. *Pediatric Clinics of North America, 58,* 715–733.

Harter, S. (2006). The self. In N. Eisenberg (Ed.), *Handbook of child psychology: Vol. 3. Social, emotional, and personality development* (6th ed., pp. 505–570). Hoboken, NJ: Wiley.

Hartup, W., & Stevens, N. (1997). Friendships and adaptation in the life course. *Psychological Bulletin, 121,* 355–370. doi:10.1037/0033-2909.121.3.355

Harvey, C. D. H., & Yoshino, S. (2006). Social policy for family caregivers of elderly: A Canadian, Japanese, and Australian comparison. *Marriage & Family Review, 39,* 143–158.

Hassan, M. A. M., & Killick, S. R. (2003). Effect of male age on fertility: Evidence for the decline in male fertility with increasing age. *Fertility and Sterility, 79,* 1520–1527.

Hassett, J. M., Siebert, E. R., & Wallen, K. (2008). Sex differences in rhesus monkey toy preferences parallel those of children. *Hormones and Behavior, 54,* 359–364. doi:10.1016/j.yhbeh.2008.03.008

Hastings, P. D., Rubin, K. H., & DeRose, L. (2005). Links among gender, inhibition, and parental socialization in the development of prosocial behavior. *Merrill-Palmer Quarterly, 51,* 467–493.

Hawthorne, J. (2009). Promoting development of the early parent-infant relationship using the Neonatal Behavioural Assessment Scale. In J. Barlow & P. O. Svanberg (Eds.), *Keeping the baby in mind: Infant mental health in practice* (pp. 39–51). New York, NY: Routledge/Taylor & Francis Group.

Hay, D. F., Payne, A., & Chadwick, A. (2004). Peer relations in childhood. *Journal of Child Psychology & Psychiatry & Applied Disciplines, 45,* 84–108.

Hay, D. I. (2009). *Poverty reduction policies and programs.* Ottawa, ON: Canadian Council on Social Development.

Hayden, B. (2012). Neandertal social structure? *Oxford Journal of Archaeology, 31*, 1–26. doi:10.1111/j.1468–0092.2011.00376.x

Hayes, R. A., & Slater, A. (2008). Three-month-olds' detection of alliteration in syllables. *Infant Behavior & Development, 31*, 153–156.

Hayflick, L. (2004). "Anti-aging" is an oxymoron. *Journals of Gerontology: Series A: Biological Sciences and Medical Sciences, 59A*, 573–578.

Hayne, H., & Simcock, G. (2009). Memory development in toddlers. In M. L. Courage & N. Cowan (Eds.), *The development of memory in infancy and childhood* (2nd ed., pp. 43–68). New York, NY: Psychology Press.

Hayward, D. W., Gale, C. M., & Eikeseth, S. (2009). Intensive behavioural intervention for young children with autism: A research-based service model. *Research in Autism Spectrum Disorders, 3*, 571–580.

Hazlett, H. C., Poe, M. D., Gerig, G., Styner, M., Chappell, C., Smith, R. G., ... Joseph Piven, M. (2011). Early brain overgrowth in autism associated with an increase in cortical surface area before age 2 years. *Archives of General Psychiatry, 68*, 467–476.

Health Canada. (2005). *STOP fetal alcohol syndrome/fetal alcohol effects NOW!* [Pamphlet]. Ottawa, ON: Author.

Health Canada. (2006, May 26). *New cautions regarding heart-related risks for all ADHD drugs* [Advisory]. Retrieved from http://www.healthycanadians.gc.ca/recall-alert-rappel-avis/hc-sc/2006/13107a-eng.php

Health Canada. (2009). *Healthy living: Children.* Retrieved from http://www.hc-sc.gc.ca/hl-vs/oral-bucco/care-soin/child-enfant-eng.php

Health Canada. (2010). *Aboriginal Head Start on Reserve Program.* Retrieved from http://www.hc-sc.gc.ca/fniah-spnia/famil/develop/ahsor-papar-eng.php

Health Canada. (2011). *Major findings from the Canadian Alcohol and Drug Use Monitoring Survey (CADUMS) 2011.* Retrieved from http://www.hc-sc.gc.ca/hc-ps/drugs-drogues/stat/index-eng.php

Health Canada. (2012a). Harper government strengthens food allergen labelling regulations [Press release]. Retrieved from http://www.hc-sc.gc.ca/ahc-asc/media/nr-cp/_2011/2011_23-eng.php

Health Canada. (2012b). *Summary of results of the 2010–11 Youth Smoking Survey.* Retrieved from http://www.hc-sc.gc.ca/hc-ps/tobac-tabac/research-recherche/stat/_survey-sondage_2010-2011/result-eng.php

Health Canada. (2013). *First Nations & Inuit Health: Suicide prevention.* Retrieved from http://www.hc-sc.gc.ca/fniah-spnia/promotion/suicide/index-eng.php

Health Canada in collaboration with the Interdepartmental Committee on Aging and Seniors Issues. (2002). *Canada's aging population.* Retrieved from http://publications.gc.ca/collections/Collection/H39-608-2002E.pdf

Heart and Stroke Foundation of Canada. (2011). *Position statement: Physical activity, heart disease and stroke.* Retrieved from http://www.heartandstroke.com/atf/cf/{99452D8B-E7F1-4BD6-A57D-B136CE6C95BF}/PhysicalActivity4pager.pdf

Hébert, R., Dubuc, N., Buteau, M., Desrosiers, J., Bravo, G., Trottier, L., ... Roy, C. (2001). Resources and costs associated with disabilities of elderly people living at home and in institutions, *Canadian Journal on Aging, 20*, 1–22. doi: 10.1017/S0714980800012113

Heflick, N. A., & Goldenberg, J. L. (2012). No atheists in foxholes: Arguments for (but not against) afterlife belief buffers mortality salience effects for atheists. *British Journal of Social Psychology, 51*, 385–392. doi:10.1111/j.2044–8309.2011.02058.x

Heiman, J. R., Long, J. S., Smith, S. N., Fisher, W. A., Sand, M. S., & Rosen, R. C. (2011). Sexual satisfaction and relationship happiness in midlife and older couples in five countries. *Archives of Sexual Behavior, 40*, 741–753. doi:10.1007/s10508–010–9703–3

Henretta, J. C., Soldo, B. J., & Van Voorhis, M. F. (2011). Why do families differ? Children's care for an unmarried mother. *Journal of Marriage and Family, 73*, 383–395. doi:10.1111/j.1741–3737.2010.00813.x

Herd, P., Robert, S. A., & House, J. S. (2011). Health disparities among older adults: Life course influences and policy solutions. In R. H. Binstock & L. K. George (Eds.), *Handbook of aging and the social sciences* (7th ed., pp. 121–134). San Diego, CA: Academic Press.

Herek, G. M. (2006). Legal recognition of same-sex relationships in the United States: A social science perspective. *American Psychologist, 61*, 607–621.

Herlofson, K., & Hagestad, G. (2011). Challenges in moving from macro to micro: Population and family structures in ageing societies. *Demographic Research, 25*, 337–370.

Herlofson, K., & Hagestad, G. O. (2012). Transformations in the role of grandparents across welfare states. In S. Arber & V. Timonen (Eds.), *Contemporary grandparenting: Changing family relationships in global contexts* (pp. 27–49). Bristol, UK: Policy Press.

Herman, K. N., Paukner, A., & Suomi, S. J. (2011). Gene x environment interactions and social play: Contributions from rhesus macaques. In P. Nathan & A. D. Pellegrini (Eds.), *The Oxford handbook of the development of play* (pp. 58–69). New York, NY: Oxford University Press.

Herman-Giddens, M. E., Wang, L., & Koch, G. (2001). Secondary sexual characteristics in boys: Estimates from the National Health and Nutrition Examination Survey III, 1988–1994. *Archives of Pediatrics & Adolescent Medicine, 155*, 1022–1028.

Herrera, A. P., Snipes, S. A., King, D. W., Torres-Vigil, I., Goldberg, D. S., & Weinberg, A. D. (2010). Disparate inclusion of older adults in clinical trials: Priorities and opportunities for policy and practice change. *American Journal of Public Health, 100*, S105–112. doi:10.2105/ajph.2009.162982

Herrmann, E., Call, J., Hernàndez-Lloreda, M. V., Hare, B., & Tomasello, M. (2007, September 7). Humans have evolved specialized skills of social cognition: The cultural intelligence hypothesis. *Science, 317*, 1360–1366.

Herschensohn, J. R. (2007). *Language development and age.* New York, NY: Cambridge University Press.

Hertzog, C. (2011). Intelligence in adulthood. In R. J. Sternberg & S. B. Kaufman (Eds.), *The Cambridge handbook of intelligence* (pp. 174–190). New York, NY: Cambridge University Press.

Heslin, K. C., Hamilton, A. B., Singzon, T. K., Smith, J. L., Lois, N., & Anderson, R. (2011). Alternative families in recovery: Fictive kin relationships among residents of sober living homes. *Qualitative Health Research, 21,* 477–488.

Hess, T., Hinson, J., & Hodges, E. (2009). Moderators of and mechanisms underlying stereotype threat effects on older adults' memory performance. *Experimental Aging Research, 35,* 153–177.

Hess, T. M., Leclerc, C. M., Swaim, E., & Weatherbee, S. R. (2009). Aging and everyday judgments: The impact of motivational and processing resource factors. *Psychology and Aging, 24,* 735–740.

Hicks, J. A., Trent, J., Davis, W. E., & King, L. A. (2012). Positive affect, meaning in life, and future time perspective: An application of socioemotional selectivity theory. *Psychology and Aging, 27,* 181–189. doi:10.1037/a0023965

Higgins, J. A., & Cooper, A. D. (2012). Dual use of condoms and contraceptives in the USA. *Sexual Health, 9,* 73–80. doi:10.1071/SH11004

Higgins, M. (2006, August 7). A series of flips creates some serious buzz. *New York Times,* p. D7.

Higuchi, S., Matsushita, S., Muramatsu, T., Murayama, M., & Hayashida, M. (1996). Alcohol and aldehyde dehydrogenase genotypes and drinking behavior in Japanese. *Alcoholism: Clinical and Experimental Research, 20,* 493–497.

Hill, D. M., Hanton, S., Matthews, N., & Fleming, S. (2010). Choking in sport: A review. *International Review of Sport and Exercise Psychology, 3,* 24–39. doi:10.1080/17509840903301199

Hill, P. L., Duggan, P. M., & Lapsley, D. K. (2012). Subjective invulnerability, risk behavior, and adjustment in early adolescence. *The Journal of Early Adolescence, 32,* 489–501. doi:10.1177/0272431611400304

Hill, S. A. (2007). Transformative processes: Some sociological questions. *Journal of Marriage and Family, 69,* 293–298.

Hillberg, T., Hamilton-Giachritsis, C., & Dixon, L. (2011). Review of meta-analyses on the association between child sexual abuse and adult mental health difficulties: A systematic approach. *Trauma, Violence, & Abuse, 12,* 38–49. doi:10.1177/1524838010386812

Himelhoch, S., Lehman, A., Kreyenbuhl, J., Daumit, G., Brown, C., & Dixon, L. (2004). Prevalence of chronic obstructive pulmonary disease among those with serious mental illness. *American Journal of Psychiatry, 161,* 2317–2319.

Hindman, A. H., Skibbe, L. E., Miller, A., & Zimmerman, M. (2010). Ecological contexts and early learning: Contributions of child, family, and classroom factors during Head Start, to literacy and mathematics growth through first grade. *Early Childhood Research Quarterly, 25,* 235–250.

Hinds, D. A., Stuve, L. L., Nilsen, G. B., Halperin, E., Eskin, E., Ballinger, D. G., … Cox, D. R. (2005, February 18). Whole-genome patterns of common DNA variation in three human populations. *Science, 307,* 1072–1079.

Hines, M. (2004). *Brain gender.* Oxford, England: Oxford University Press.

Hines, M. (2010). Sex-related variation in human behavior and the brain. *Trends in Cognitive Sciences, 14,* 448–456.

Hipwell, A. E., Keenan, K., Loeber, R., & Battista, D. (2010). Early predictors of sexually intimate behaviors in an urban sample of young girls. *Developmental Psychology, 46,* 366–378.

Hirschberger, G. (2006). Terror management and attributions of blame to innocent victims: Reconciling compassionate and defensive responses. *Journal of Personality and Social Psychology, 91,* 832–844. doi:10.1037/0022-3514.91.5.832

Hirsh-Pasek, K., Golinkoff, R. M., Berk, L. E., & Singer, D. G. (2009). *A mandate for playful learning in preschool: Presenting the evidence.* New York, NY: Oxford University Press.

Ho, C., Bluestein, D. N., & Jenkins, J. M. (2008). Cultural differences in the relationship between parenting and children's behavior. *Developmental Psychology, 44,* 507–522.

Ho, E. S. (2010). Measuring hand function in the young child. *Journal of Hand Therapy, 23,* 323–328.

Hoare, C. H. (2002). *Erikson on development in adulthood: New insights from the unpublished papers.* New York, NY: Oxford University Press.

Hochman, D. (2003, November 23). Food for holiday thought: Eat less, live to 140? *The New York Times,* p. A9. Retrieved from http://query.nytimes.com/gst/health/article-page.html?res=9C0CE7DB123BF930A15752C1A9659C8B63

Hoffmann, R. (2008). *Socioeconomic difference in old age mortality.* New York, NY: Springer.

Hofstede, G. (2007). A European in Asia. *Asian Journal of Social Psychology, 10,* 16–21.

Hogeboom, D. L., McDermott, R. J., Perrin, K. M., Osman, H., & Bell-Ellison, B. A. (2010). Internet use and social networking among middle aged and older adults. *Educational Gerontology, 36,* 93–111. doi:10.1080/03601270903058507

Holden, C. (Ed.). (2010). Myopia out of control. *Science, 327,* 17. doi:10.1126/science.327.5961.17-c

Holland, J. D., & Klaczynski, P. A. (2009). Intuitive risk taking during adolescence. *Prevention Researcher, 16,* 8–11.

Holland, J. L. (1997). *Making vocational choices: A theory of vocational personalities and work environments* (3rd ed.). Odessa, FL: Psychological Assessment Resources.

Hollich, G. J., Hirsh-Pasek, K., Golinkoff, R. M., Brand, R. J., Brown, E., Chung, H. L., … Rocroi, C. (2000). Breaking the language barrier: An emergentist coalition model for the origins of word learning. *Monographs of the Society for Research in Child Development, 65*(3, Serial No. 262), v-123.

Hollos, M., Larsen, U., Obono, O., & Whitehouse, B. (2009). The problem of infertility in high fertility populations: Meanings, consequences and coping mechanisms in two Nigerian communities. *Social Science & Medicine, 68,* 2061–2068.

Holm, S. M., Forbes, E. E., Ryan, N. D., Phillips, M. L., Tarr, J. A., & Dahl, R. E. (2009). Reward-related brain function and sleep in pre/early pubertal and mid/late pubertal adolescents. *The Journal of Adolescent Health, 45,* 326–334.

Holmboe, K., Nemoda, Z., Fearon, R. M. P., Sasvari-Szekely, M., & Johnson, M. H. (2011). Domanine D4 receptor and serotonin transporter gene effects on the longitudinal development of infant temperament. *Genes, Brain, and Behavior, 10,* 513–522. doi:10.1111/j.1601–183X.2010.00669.x

Holtzman, J. (2009). Simple, effective—and inexpensive—strategies to reduce tooth decay in children. *ICAN: Infant, Child, & Adolescent Nutrition, 1,* 225–231. doi:10.1177/1941406409338861

Hook, J. L. (2010). Gender inequality in the welfare state: Sex segregation in housework, 1965–2003. *American Journal of Sociology, 115,* 1480–1523. doi:10.1086/651384

Hook, J. L. (2012). Working on the weekend: Fathers' time with family in the United Kingdom. *Journal of Marriage and Family, 74,* 631–642. doi:10.1111/j.1741–3737.2012.00986.x

Hooper, L. M. (2007). The application of attachment theory and family systems theory to the phenomena of parentification. *The Family Journal: Counseling and Therapy for Couples and Families, 15,* 217–223. doi:10.1177/1066480707301290

Horn, J. L., & Cattell, R. B. (1967). Age differences in fluid and crystallized intelligence. *Acta Psychologica, 26,* 107–129.

Houdmont, J., Zhou, J., & Hassard, J. (2011). Overtime and psychological well-being among Chinese office workers. *Occupational Medicine, 61,* 270–273.

Hougaard, K. S., & Hansen, Å. M. (2007). Enhancement of developmental toxicity effects of chemicals by gestational stress. A review. *Neurotoxicology and Teratology, 29,* 425–445.

Howard, K. S. (2010). Paternal attachment, parenting beliefs and children's attachment. *Early Child Development and Care, 180,* 157–171.

Howlin, P., Magiati, I., Charman, T., & MacLean, W. E., Jr. (2009). Systematic review of early intensive behavioral interventions for children with autism. *American Journal on Intellectual and Developmental Disabilities, 114,* 23–41. doi:10.1352/2009.114:23–41

Howson, C. P., Kinney, M. V., & Lawn, J. E. (Eds.). (2012). *Born too soon: The global action report on preterm birth.* Retrieved from http://www.who.int/pmnch/media/news/2012/201204_borntoosoon-report.pdf

Hrabosky, J. I., & Thomas, J. J. (2008). Elucidating the relationship between obesity and depression: Recommendations for future research. *Clinical Psychology: Science and Practice, 15,* 28–34.

Hrdy, S. B. (2009). *Mothers and others: The evolutionary origins of mutual understanding.* Cambridge, MA: Harvard University Press.

Hsia, Y., & Maclennan, K. (2009). Rise in psychotropic drug prescribing in children and adolescents during 1992–2001: A population-based study in the UK. *European Journal of Epidemiology, 24,* 211–216. doi:10.1007/s10654–009–9321–3

Hu, F. B. (2011). Globalization of diabetes: The role of diet, lifestyle, and genes. *Diabetes Care, 34,* 1249–1257. doi:10.2337/dc11–0442

Huang, C. (2010). Mean-level change in self-esteem from childhood through adulthood: Meta-analysis of longitudinal studies. *Review of General Psychology, 14,* 251–260. doi:10.1037/a0020543

Huang, C.-C. (2009). Mothers' reports of nonresident fathers' involvement with their children: Revisiting the relationship between child support payment and visitation. *Family Relations, 58,* 54–64. doi:10.1111/j.1741–3729.2008.00534.x

Huang, D., Kapur, A. K., Ling, P., Purssell, R., Henneberry, R. J., Champagne, C. R., ..., Francescutti, L. H. (2010). CAEP position statement on cellphone use while driving. *Canadian Journal of Emergency Medicine, 12,* 365–370. Retrieved from http://caep.ca/sites/default/files/caep/files/cell_phone_use_while_driving_2010.pdf

Huang, Y. (2012, May 30). SUSTC enrolls 180 scholarship students. *China Daily.* Retrieved from http://www.chinadaily.com.cn/china/2012-05/30/content_15427093.htm

Hubbard, R., & Lindsay, R. M. (2008). Why *p* values are not a useful measure of evidence in statistical significance testing. *Theory and Psychology, 18,* 69–88.

Huberty, T. J. (2012). *Anxiety and depression in children and adolescents: Assessment, intervention, and prevention.* New York, NY: Springer.

Huesmann, L. R., Dubow, E. F., & Boxer, P. (2009). Continuity of aggression from childhood to early adulthood as a predictor of life outcomes: Implications for the adolescent-limited and life-course-persistent models. *Aggressive Behavior, 35,* 136–149. doi:10.1002/ab.20300

Hugdahl, K., & Westerhausen, R. (2010). *The two halves of the brain: Information processing in the cerebral hemispheres.* Cambridge, MA: MIT Press.

Hughes, K. A. (2010). Mutation and the evolution of ageing: From biometrics to system genetics. *Philosophical Transactions of the Royal Society B: Biological Sciences, 365,* 1273–1279. doi:10.1098/rstb.2009.0265

Hughes, S. M., & Gore, A. C. (2007). How the brain controls puberty, and implications for sex and ethnic differences. *Family & Community Health, 30*(Suppl. 1), S112-S114.

Huh, S. Y., Rifas-Shiman, S. L., Taveras, E. M., Oken, E., & Gillman, M. W. (2011). Timing of solid food introduction and risk of obesity in preschool-aged children. *Pediatrics, 127,* e544-e551. http://pediatrics.aappublications.org/content/127/3/e544.abstract doi:10.1542/peds.2010-0740

Huijbregts, S. K., Tavecchio, L., Leseman, P., & Hoffenaar, P. (2009). Child rearing in a group setting: Beliefs of Dutch, Caribbean Dutch, and Mediterranean Dutch caregivers in center-based child care. *Journal of Cross-Cultural Psychology, 40,* 797–815. doi:10.1177/0022022109338623

Human Resources and Skills Development Canada. (2012, December 14). Government of Canada highlights prohibition of mandatory retirement [Press release]. Retrieved from http://news.gc.ca/web/article-eng.do?nid=712429

Human Resources Development Canada, Applied Research Branch, Strategic Policy. (2000, October). *Dropping out of high school: Definitions and costs* (Catalogue No. MP32–29/01-1E). Retrieved from http://s3.amazonaws.com/zanran_storage/www.hrsdc.gc.ca/ContentPages/2411732.pdf

Hummert, M. L. (2011). Age stereotypes and aging. In K. W. Shaie & S. L. Willis (Eds.), *Handbook of the psychology of aging* (7th ed., pp. 249–262). Boston, MA: Elsevier/Academic Press.

Hurd, M. (1993). Minority language children and French immersion: Additive multilingualism or subtractive semi-lingualism? *Canadian Modern Language Review, 49,* 514–525.

Husain, N., Chaudhry, N., Tomenson, B., Jackson, J., Gater, R., & Creed, F. (2011). Depressive disorder and social stress in Pakistan compared to people of Pakistani origin in the UK. *Social Psychiatry and Psychiatric Epidemiology, 46,* 1153–1159. doi:10.1007/s00127–010–0279-y

Huston, A. C., & Aronson, S. R. (2005). Mothers' time with infant and time in employment as predictors of mother-child relationships and children's early development. *Child Development, 76,* 467–482.

Huston, A. C., & Ripke, M. N. (2006). Middle childhood: Contexts of development. In A. C. Huston & M. N. Ripke (Eds.), *Developmental contexts in middle childhood: Bridges to adolescence and adulthood* (pp. 1–22). New York: Cambridge University Press.

Huver, R. M. E., Otten, R., de Vries, H., & Engels, R. C. M. E. (2010). Personality and parenting style in parents of adolescents. *Journal of Adolescence, 33,* 395–402.

Hvistendahl, M. (2011, May 6). China's population growing slowly, changing fast. *Science, 332,* 650–651.

Hyde, J. S., Lindberg, S. M., Linn, M. C., Ellis, A. B., & Williams, C. C. (2008, July 25). Gender similarities characterize math performance. *Science, 321,* 494–495.

Hyson, M., Copple, C., & Jones, J. (2006). Early childhood development and education. In K. A. Renninger & I. E. Sigel (Eds.), *Handbook of child psychology: Vol. 4. Child psychology in practice* (6th ed., pp. 3–47). Hoboken, NJ: Wiley.

I

Iacovidou, N., Varsami, M., & Syggellou, A. (2010). Neonatal outcome of preterm delivery. In G. Creatsas & G. Mastorakos (Eds.), *Annals of the New York Academy of Sciences: Vol. 1205. Women's health and disease* (pp. 130–134). Malden, MA: Blackwell.

Idler, E. (2006). Religion and aging. In R. H. Binstock & L. K. George (Eds.), *Handbook of aging and the social sciences* (6th ed., pp. 277–300). Amsterdam, The Netherlands: Elsevier.

Imai, M., Kita, S., Nagumo, M., & Okada, H. (2008). Sound symbolism facilitates early verb learning. *Cognition, 109,* 54–65.

Imamoglu, Ç. (2007). Assisted living as a new place schema: A comparison with homes and nursing homes. *Environment and Behavior, 39,* 246–268.

Inbar, Y., Botti, S., & Hanko, K. (2011). Decision speed and choice regret: When haste feels like waste. *Journal of Experimental Social Psychology, 47,* 533–540.

Inglehart, R. (1990). *Culture shift in advanced industrial society.* Princeton, NJ: Princeton University Press.

Inhelder, B., & Piaget, J. (1958). *The growth of logical thinking from childhood to adolescence: An essay on the construction of formal operational structures.* New York, NY: Basic Books.

Inhelder, B., & Piaget, J. (1964). *The early growth of logic in the child.* New York, NY: Harper & Row.

Insel, B. J., & Gould, M. S. (2008). Impact of modeling on adolescent suicidal behavior. *Psychiatric Clinics of North America, 31,* 293–316.

Institute of Medicine, Committee on Food Marketing and the Diets of Children and Youth. (2006). *Food marketing to children and youth: Threat or opportunity?* Washington, DC: National Academies Press.

Inzlicht, M., & Schmader, T. (2012). *Stereotype threat: Theory, process, and application.* New York, NY: Oxford University Press.

Ipsos News Center. (1999, January 10). Three quarters (73%) of Canadians believe Robert Latimer ended his daughter's life out of compassion [Press release]. Available from http://www.ipsos-na.com/news-polls/pressrelease.aspx?id=760

Irwin, S., Galvez, R., Weiler, I. J., Beckel-Mitchener, A., & Greenough, W. (2002). Brain structure and the functions of FMR1 protein. In R. Jensen Hagerman & P. J. Hagerman (Eds.), *Fragile X syndrome: Diagnosis, treatment, and research* (3rd ed., pp. 191–205). Baltimore, MD: Johns Hopkins University Press.

Ispa, J. M., Fine, M. A., Halgunseth, L. C., Harper, S., Robinson, J., Boyce, L., ... Brady-Smith, C. (2004). Maternal intrusiveness, maternal warmth, and mother-toddler relationship outcomes: Variations across low-income ethnic and acculturation groups. *Child Development, 75,* 1613–1631. doi:10.1111/j.1467–8624.2004.00806.x

Issa, J.-P. (2011). Epigenetic variation and cellular Darwinism. *Nature Genetics, 43,* 724–726.

IVF.ca (2007). Human assisted reproduction live birth rates for Canada [Press release]. Retrieved from http://www.ivf.ca/results.htm

Iyengar, S. S., & Lepper, M. R. (2000). When choice is demotivating: Can one desire too much of a good thing? *Journal of Personality and Social Psychology, 79,* 995–1006.

Izard, C. E. (1978). Emotions and emotion-cognition relationships. In M. Lewis & L. A. Rosenblum (Eds.), *The development of affect* (pp. 389–413). New York, NY: Plenum.

Izard, C. E. (2009). Emotion theory and research: Highlights, unanswered questions, and emerging issues. *Annual Review of Psychology, 60,* 1–25. doi:10.1146/annurev.psych.60.110707.163539

Izard, C. E., Fine, S., Mostow, A., Trentacosta, C., & Campbell, J. (2002). Emotion processes in normal and abnormal development and preventive intervention. *Development & Psychopathology, 14,* 761–787.

J

Jack, C. R. J., Lowe, V. J., Weigand, S. D., Wiste, H. J., Senjem, M. L., Knopman, D. S., ... Petersen, R. C. (2009). Serial PIB and MRI in normal, mild cognitive impairment and Alzheimer's disease: Implications for sequence of pathological events in Alzheimer's disease. *Brain, 132*(Pt. 5), 1355–1365. doi:10.1093/brain/awp062

Jackson, A. (2001). Poverty and racism. *Perception, 24,* 4.

Jackson, J. S. (2012, May 24). *The masquerade of racial group differences in psychological sciences.* Paper presented at the 24th Annual Convention of the Association for Psychological Science, Chicago, IL.

Jackson, S. L., & Hafemeister, T. L. (2011). Risk factors associated with elder abuse: The importance of differentiating by type of elder maltreatment. *Violence and Victims, 26,* 738–757.

Jacob, J. I. (2009). The socio-emotional effects of non-maternal childcare on children in the USA: A critical review of recent studies. *Early Child Development and Care, 179,* 559–570.

Jacoby, L. L., & Rhodes, M. G. (2006). False remembering in the aged. *Current Directions in Psychological Science, 15,* 49–53.

Jaffee, S. R., Caspi, A., Moffitt, T. E., Polo-Tomás, M., & Taylor, A. (2007). Individual, family, and neighborhood factors distinguish resilient from non-resilient maltreated children: A cumulative stressors model. *Child Abuse & Neglect, 31,* 231–253.

James, R. (2007). Sexually transmitted infections. In M. S. Tepper & A. Fuglsang Owens (Eds.), *Sexual health: Vol. 4. State-of-the-art treatments and research* (pp. 235–267). Westport, CT: Praeger/Greenwood.

James, S., Simmons, C. P., & James, A. A. (2011, November 11). Mosquito trials. *Science, 334,* 771–772.

Janssen, I., Katzmarzyk, P. T., Boyce, W. F., Vereecken, C., Mulvihill, C., Roberts, C., ... Pickett, W. (2005). Comparison of overweight and obesity prevalence in school-aged youth from 34 countries and their relationships with physical activity and dietary patterns. *Obesity Reviews, 6,* 123–132. doi:10.1111/j.1467–789X.2005.00176.x

Jasny, B. R., Chin, G., Chong, L., & Vignieri, S. (2011, December 2). Again, and again, and again ... *Science, 334,* 1225.

Jastrzembski, T. S., Charness, N., & Vasyukova, C. (2006). Expertise and age effects on knowledge activation in chess. *Psychology and Aging, 21,* 401–405.

Jenson, J. M., & Fraser, M. W. (2006). *Social policy for children & families: A risk and resilience perspective.* Thousand Oaks, CA: Sage.

Jessop, D. C., & Wade, J. (2008). Fear appeals and binge drinking: A terror management theory perspective. *British Journal of Health Psychology, 13,* 773–788.

Jetté, M., & Des Groseilliers, L. (2000). Survey description and methodology. In *Longitudinal study of child development in Québec (ELEDQ 1998–2002)* (Vol 1, No. 1). Quebec, QC: Institut de la Statistique du Québec.

Jia, J., Wang, F., Wei, C., Zou, A., Jia, X., Li, F., ... Dong, X. (2014). The prevalence of dementia in urban and rural areas of China. *Alzheimer's & Dementia, 10,* 1–9. doi: 10.1016/j.jalz.2013.01.012

Johnson, C. A., & Wilkinson, M. E. (2010). Vision and driving: The United States. *Journal of Neuro-Ophthalmology, 30,* 170–176.

Johnson, E. K., & Tyler, M. D. (2010). Testing the limits of statistical learning for word segmentation. *Developmental Science, 13,* 339–345. doi:10.1111/j.1467–7687.2009.00886.x

Johnson, M. (2007). Our guest editors talk about couples in later life. *Generations, 31*(3), 4–5.

Johnson, M. H., & Fearon, R. M. P. (2011). Commentary: Disengaging the infant mind: Genetic dissociation of attention and cognitive skills in infants – Reflections on Leppänen et al. (2011). *Journal of Child Psychology and Psychiatry, 52,* 1153–1154. doi:10.1111/j.1469–7610.2011.02433.x

Johnson, M. H., Grossmann, T., & Kadosh, K. C. (2009). Mapping functional brain development: Building a social brain through interactive specialization. *Developmental Psychology, 45,* 151–159.

Johnson, S. C., Dweck, C. S., Chen, F. S., Stern, H. L., Ok, S.-J., & Barth, M. (2010). At the intersection of social and cognitive development: Internal working models of attachment in infancy. *Cognitive Science, 34,* 807–825. doi:10.1111/j.1551–6709.2010.01112.x

Johnson, W. (2010). Understanding the genetics of intelligence: Can height help? Can corn oil? *Current Directions in Psychological Science, 19,* 177–182. doi:10.1177/0963721410370136

Johnston, L. D., O'Malley, P. M., Bachman, J. G., & Schulenberg, J. E. (2009). *Monitoring the Future national survey results on drug use, 1975–2008: Vol. II. College students and adults ages 19–50* (NIH Publication No. 08–6418). Bethesda, MD: National Institute on Drug Abuse.

Johnston, L. D., O'Malley, P. M., Bachman, J. G., & Schulenberg, J. E. (2010). *Monitoring the Future national results on adolescent drug use: Overview of key findings, 2009* (NIH Publication No. 09–7403). Bethesda, MD: National Institute on Drug Abuse.

Jokela, M. (2012). Birth-cohort effects in the association between personality and fertility. *Psychological Science, 12,* 835–841.

Jokela, M., Elovainio, M., Kivimäki, M., & Keltikangas-Järvinen, L. (2008). Temperament and migration patterns in Finland. *Psychological Science, 19,* 831–837.

Jones, D., & Crawford, J. (2005). Adolescent boys and body image: Weight and muscularity concerns as dual pathways to body dissatisfaction. *Journal of Youth and Adolescence, 34,* 629–636.

Jones, K. L. (1997). *Smith's recognizable patterns of human malformations.* Philadelphia, PA: Saunders.

Jones, L. A., Sinnott, L. T., Mutti, D. O., Mitchell, G. L., Moeschberger, M. L., & Zadnik, K. (2007). Parental history of myopia, sports and outdoor activities, and future myopia. *Investigative Ophthalmology & Visual Science, 48,* 3524–3532.

Jones, M. C. (1965). Psychological correlates of somatic development. *Child Development, 36,* 899–911.

Jones, R. M. (2011). Psychosocial development and first substance use in third and fourth grade students: A short-term longitudinal study. *Child Development Research, 2011.* doi:10.1155/2011/916020

Jong, J.-T., Kao, T., Lee, L.-Y., Huang, H.-H., Lo, P.-T., & Wang, H.-C. (2010). Can temperament be understood at birth? The relationship between neonatal pain cry and their temperament: A preliminary study. *Infant Behavior and Development, 33,* 266–272.

Jopp, D., & Rott, C. (2006). Adaptation in very old age: Exploring the role of resources, beliefs, and attitudes for centenarians' happiness. *Psychology and Aging, 21,* 266–280.

Jordan, A. H., & Monin, B. (2008). From sucker to saint: Moralization in response to self-threat. *Psychological Science, 19,* 809–815.

Juan, S. (2010, January 14). C-section epidemic hits China. *China Daily.* Retrieved from http://www.chinadaily.com.cn/index.html

Jurkovic, G. J., & Casey, S. (2000). Parentification in immigrant Latino adolescents. In G. P. Kuperminc (Chair), *Proyecto Juventud: A multidisciplinary study of immigrant Latino adolescents.* Symposium conducted at the meeting of the Society for Applied Anthropology, San Francisco, CA.

Jurkovic, G. J., Morrell, R., & Casey, S. (2001). Parentification in the lives of high-profile individuals and their families: A hidden source of strength and distress. In B. E. Robinson & N. Chase (Eds.), *High-performing families: Causes, consequences, and clinical solutions* (pp. 92–113). Washington, DC: American Counseling Association.

Jyrkkä, J., Mursu, J., Enlund, H., & Lönnroos, E. (2012). Polypharmacy and nutritional status in elderly people. *Current Opinion in Clinical Nutrition & Metabolic Care, 15,* 1–6. doi: 10.1097/MCO.0b013e32834d155a

K

Kachel, A. F., Premo, L. S., & Hublin, J.-J. (2011). Modeling the effects of weaning age on length of female reproductive period: Implications for the evolution of human life history. *American Journal of Human Biology, 23,* 479–487. doi:10.1002/ajhb.21157

Kagan, J. (2008). In defense of qualitative changes in development. *Child Development, 79,* 1606–1624.

Kagan, J., & Herschkowitz, N. (2005). *A young mind in a growing brain.* Mahwah, NJ: Erlbaum.

Kagicibasi, C. (1996). *Family and human development across cultures: A view from the other side.* Mahwah, NJ: Erlbaum.

Kahneman, D. (2011). *Thinking, fast and slow.* New York, NY: Farrar, Straus and Giroux.

Kalambouka, A., Farrell, P., Dyson, A., & Kaplan, I. (2007). The impact of placing pupils with special educational needs in mainstream schools on the achievement of their peers. *Educational Research, 49,* 365–382.

Kalaria, R. N., Maestre, G. E., Arizaga, R., Friedland, R. P., Galasko, D., Hall, K., … Antuono, P. (2008). Alzheimer's disease and vascular dementia in developing countries: Prevalence, management, and risk factors. *The Lancet Neurology, 7,* 812–826.

Kalliala, M. (2006). *Play culture in a changing world.* Maidenhead, England: Open University Press.

Kalmijn, M. (2010). Country differences in the effects of divorce on well-being: The role of norms, support, and selectivity. *European Sociological Review, 26,* 475–490. doi:10.1093/esr/jcp035

Kalra, S. K., & Barnhart, K. T. (2011). In vitro fertilization and adverse childhood outcomes: What we know, where we are going, and how we will get there. A glimpse into what lies behind and beckons ahead. *Fertility and Sterility, 95,* 1887–1889.

Kanner, A. M. (2012). *Depression in neurologic disorders: Diagnosis and management.* Chichester, West Sussex: John Wiley & Sons.

Kapornai, K., & Vetró, Á. (2008). Depression in children. *Current Opinion in Psychiatry, 21,* 1–7.

Kärnä, A., Voeten, M., Little, T. D., Poskiparta, E., Kaljonen, A., & Salmivalli, C. (2011). A large-scale evaluation of the KiVa antibullying program: Grades 4–6. *Child Development, 82,* 311–330. doi:10.1111/j.1467–8624.2010.01557.x

Karney, B. R., & Bradbury, T. N. (2005). Contextual influences on marriage: Implications for policy and intervention. *Current Directions in Psychological Science, 14,* 171–174.

Kärtner, J., Borke, J., Maasmeier, K., Keller, H., & Kleis, A. (2011). Sociocultural influences on the development of self-recognition and self-regulation in Costa Rican and Mexican toddlers. *Journal of Cognitive Education and Psychology, 10,* 96–112.

Kärtner, J., Keller, H., & Yovsi, R. D. (2010). Mother–infant interaction during the first 3 months: The emergence of culture-specific contingency patterns. *Child Development, 81,* 540–554. doi:10.1111/j.1467–8624.2009.01414.x

Kastenbaum, R. (2006). *Death, society, and human experience* (9th ed.). Boston, MA: Allyn and Bacon.

Kastenbaum, R. (2012). *Death, society, and human experience* (11th ed.). Boston, MA: Pearson.

Katz, K. S., Jarrett, M. H., El-Mohandes, A. A. E., Schneider, S., McNeely-Johnson, D., & Kiely, M. (2011). Effectiveness of a combined home visiting and group intervention for low income African American Mothers: The Pride in Parenting program. *Maternal and Child Health Journal, 15,* 75–84. doi:10.1007/s10995–011–0858-x

Kaufman, K. R., & Kaufman, N. D. (2006). And then the dog died. *Death Studies, 30,* 61–76.

Kaushik, M., Sontineni, S. P., & Hunter, C. (2010). Cardiovascular disease and androgens: A review. *International Journal of Cardiology, 142,* 8–14. doi:10.1016/j.ijcard.2009.10.033

Kavanaugh, R. D. (2011). Origins and consequences of social pretend play. In P. Nathan & A. D. Pellegrini (Eds.), *The Oxford handbook of the development of play* (pp. 296–307). New York, NY: Oxford University Press.

Keating, D. P. (2004). Cognitive and brain development. In R. M. Lerner & L. D. Steinberg (Eds.), *Handbook of adolescent psychology* (2nd ed., pp. 45–84). Hoboken, NJ: Wiley.

Kegel, C. A. T., Bus, A. G., & van IJzendoorn, M. H. (2011). Differential susceptibility in early literacy instruction through computer games: The role of the dopamine D4 receptor gene (DRD4). *Mind, Brain, and Education, 5,* 71–78. doi:10.1111/j.1751–228X.2011.01112.x

Keil, F. C. (2011, February 25). Science starts early. *Science, 331,* 1022–1023.

Kelemen, D., Callanan, M. A., Casler, K., & Perez-Granados, D. R. (2005). Why things happen: Teleological explanation in parent-child conversation. *Developmental Psychology, 41,* 251–264.

Kellehear, A. (2008). Dying as a social relationship: A sociological review of debates on the determination of death. *Social Science & Medicine, 66,* 1533–1544. doi:10.1016/j.socscimed.2007.12.023

Kellehear, A., & Ritchie, D. (2003). *Seven dying Australians.* Bendigo, Victoria, Australia: St. Luke's Innovative Resources.

Keller, H., Borke, J., Chaudhary, N., Lamm, B., & Kleis, A. (2010). Continuity in parenting strategies: A cross-cultural comparison. *Journal of Cross-Cultural Psychology, 41,* 391–409. doi:10.1177/0022022109359690

Keller, H., Yovsi, R., Borke, J., Kärtner, J., Jensen, H., & Papaligoura, Z. (2004). Developmental consequences of early parenting experiences: Self-recognition and self-regulation in three cultural communities. *Child Development, 75*, 1745–1760.

Kelley, S. J., & Whitley, D. M. (2003). Psychological distress and physical health problems in grandparents raising grandchildren: Development of an empirically-based intervention model. In B. Hayslip & J. H. Patrick (Eds.), *Working with custodial grandparents* (pp. 127–144). New York, NY: Springer.

Kellman, P. J., & Arterberry, M. E. (2006). Infant visual perception. In D. Kuhn & R. S. Siegler (Eds.), *Handbook of child psychology: Vol. 2. Cognition, perception, and language* (6th ed., pp. 109–160). Hoboken, NJ: Wiley.

Kelly, D., Faucher, L., & Machery, E. (2010). Getting rid of racism: Assessing three proposals in light of psychological evidence. *Journal of Social Philosophy, 41*, 293–322. doi:10.1111/j.1467–9833.2010.01495.x

Kelly, J. R. (1993). *Activity and aging: Staying involved in later life.* Newbury Park, CA: Sage.

Kemp, C. L. (2005). Dimensions of grandparent-adult grandchild relationships: From family ties to intergenerational friendships. *Canadian Journal on Aging, 24*, 161–177.

Kempe, R. S., & Kempe, C. H. (1978). *Child abuse.* Cambridge, MA: Harvard University Press.

Kempner, J., Perlis, C. S., & Merz, J. F. (2005, February 11). Forbidden knowledge. *Science, 307*, 854.

Kendler, K. S., Eaves, L. J., Loken, E. K., Pedersen, N. L., Middeldorp, C. M., Reynolds, C., ... Gardner, C. O. (2011). The impact of environmental experiences on symptoms of anxiety and depression across the life span. *Psychological Science, 22*, 1343–1352. doi:10.1177/0956797611417255

Kennedy, Q., Taylor, J. L., Reade, G., & Yesavage, J. A. (2010). Age and expertise effects in aviation decision making and flight control in a flight simulator. *Aviation, Space, and Environmental Medicine, 81*, 489–497.

Kennedy, S., & Bumpass, L. (2008). Cohabitation and children's living arrangements: New estimates from the United States. *Demographic Research, 19*, 1663–1692.

Kéri, S. (2009). Genes for psychosis and creativity. *Psychological Science, 20*, 1070–1073. doi:10.1111/j.1467–9280.2009.02398.x

Kerns, K. A., Brumariu, L. E., & Seibert, A. (2011). Multi-method assessment of mother-child attachment: Links to parenting and child depressive symptoms in middle childhood. *Attachment & Human Development, 13*, 315–333. doi:10.1080/14616734.2011.584398

Kerr, M., Stattin, H., & Burk, W. J. (2010). A reinterpretation of parental monitoring in longitudinal perspective. *Journal of Research on Adolescence, 20*, 39–64. doi:10.1111/j.1532–7795.2009.00623.x

Kesselring, T., & Müller, U. (2011). The concept of egocentrism in the context of Piaget's theory. *New Ideas in Psychology, 29*, 327–345.

Kessler, R. C., Amminger, G. P., Aguilar-Gaxiola, S., Alonso, J., Lee, S., & Üstün, T. B. (2007). Age of onset of mental disorders: A review of recent literature. *Current Opinion in Psychiatry, 20*, 359–364.

Kestenbaum, R., Farber, E. A., & Sroufe, A. (1989). Preschoolers: Relation to attachment history. In N. Eisenberg (Ed.), *Empathy and related emotional responses: New directions for child development* (pp. 51–XX). San Francisco, CA: Jossey-Bass.

Keyes, C. L. M. (2007). Promoting and protecting mental health as flourishing: A complementary strategy for improving national mental health. *American Psychologist, 62*, 95–108.

Keysers, C., & Gazzola, V. (2010). Social neuroscience: Mirror neurons recorded in humans. *Current Biology, 20*, R353-R354.

Khaleque, A., & Rohner, R. P. (2002). Perceived parental acceptance-rejection and psychological adjustment: A meta-analysis of cross-cultural and intracultural studies. *Journal of Marriage & the Family, 64*, 54–64.

Khan, L. K., Sobush, K., Keener, D., Goodman, K., Lowry, A., Kakietek, J., & Zaro, S. (2009, July 24). Recommended community strategies and measurements to prevent obesity in the United States. *Morbidity and Mortality Weekly Report Recommendations and Reports, 58*(RR07), 1–26.

Khoury-Kassabri, M. (2009). The relationship between staff maltreatment of students and bully-victim group membership. *Child Abuse & Neglect: The International Journal, 33*, 914–923.

Kiang, L., & Harter, S. (2008). Do pieces of the self-puzzle fit? Integrated/fragmented selves in biculturally-identified Chinese Americans. *Journal of Research in Personality, 42*, 1657–1662.

Kiang, L., Witkow, M., Baldelomar, O., & Fuligni, A. (2010). Change in ethnic identity across the high school years among adolescents with Latin American, Asian, and European backgrounds. *Journal of Youth and Adolescence, 39*, 683–693. doi:10.1007/s10964–009–9429–5

Kiernan, S. P. (2010). The transformation of death in America. In N. Bauer-Maglin & D. Perry (Eds.), *Final acts: Death, dying, and the choices we make* (pp. 163–182). New Brunswick, NJ: Rutgers University Press.

Killen, M. (2007). Children's social and moral reasoning about exclusion. *Current Directions in Psychological Science, 16*, 32–36.

Killen, M., Margie, N. G., & Sinno, S. (2006). Morality in the context of intergroup relationships. In M. Killen & J. G. Smetana (Eds.), *Handbook of moral development* (pp. 155–183). Mahwah, NJ: Erlbaum.

Killen, M., & Smetana, J. (2007). The biology of morality: Human development and moral neuroscience. *Human Development, 50*, 241–243.

Kim, D.-S., & Kim, H.-S. (2009). Body-image dissatisfaction as a predictor of suicidal ideation among Korean boys and girls in different stages of adolescence: A two-year longitudinal study. *The Journal of Adolescent Health, 45*, 47–54.

Kim, E. C. (2009). "Mama's family": Fictive kinship and undocumented immigrant restaurant workers. *Ethnography, 10*, 497–513. doi:10.1177/1466138109347000

Kim, H. K., Laurent, H. K., Capaldi, D. M., & Feingold, A. (2008). Men's aggression toward women: A 10-year panel study. *Journal of Marriage and Family, 70*, 1169–1187.

Kim, H. S. (2011). Consequences of parental divorce for child development. *American Sociological Review, 76*, 487–511.

Kim, H. S., & Chu, T. Q. (2011). Cultural variation in the motivation of self-expression. In D. Dunning (Ed.), *Social motivation* (pp. 57–78). New York, NY: Psychology Press.

Kim, H. S., Sherman, D. K., & Taylor, S. E. (2008). Culture and social support. *American Psychologist, 63*, 518–526.

Kim, J. S. (2011). Excessive crying: Behavioral and emotional regulation disorder in infancy. *Korean Journal of Pediatrics, 54*, 229–233. doi:10.3345/kjp.2011.54.6.229

Kim-Cohen, J., Moffitt, T. E., Caspi, A., & Taylor, A. (2004). Genetic and environmental processes in young children's resilience and vulnerability to socioeconomic deprivation. *Child Development, 75*, 651–668.

King, P. E., & Furrow, J. L. (2004). Religion as a resource for positive youth development: Religion, social capital, and moral outcomes. *Developmental Psychology, 40*, 703–713. doi:10.1037/0012-1649.40.5.703

King, P. E., & Roeser, R. W. (2009). Religion and spirituality in adolescent development. In R. M. Lerner & L. Steinberg (Eds.), *Handbook of adolescent psychology: Vol. 1. Individual bases of adolescent development* (3rd ed., pp. 435–478). Hoboken, NJ: Wiley.

King, S., Waschbusch, D. A., Pelham, W. E., Frankland, B. W., Corkum, P. V., & Jacques, S. (2009). Subtypes of aggression in children with attention deficit hyperactivity disorder: Medication effects and comparison with typical children. *Journal of Clinical Child and Adolescent Psychology, 38*, 619–629.

King, W. J., MacKay, M., Sirnick, A., & The Canadian Shaken Baby Study Group. (2003). *Canadian Medical Association Journal, 168*, 155–159. Retrieved from http://www.cmaj.ca/content/168/2/155.full

Kinnunen, M.-L., Kaprio, J., & Pulkkinen, L. (2005). Allostatic load of men and women in early middle age. *Journal of Individual Differences, 26*, 20–28. doi:10.1027/1614-0001.26.1.20

Kirby, D., & Laris, B. A. (2009). Effective curriculum-based sex and STD/HIV education programs for adolescents. *Child Development Perspectives, 3*, 21–29. doi:10.1111/j.1750–8606.2008.00071.x

Kirby, M., Maggi, S., & D'Angiulli, A. (2011). School start times and the sleep–wake cycle of adolescents. *Educational Researcher, 40*, 56–61. doi:10.3102/0013189x11402323

Kirkorian, H. L., Pempek, T. A., Murphy, L. A., Schmidt, M. E., & Anderson, D. R. (2009). The impact of background television on parent–child interaction. *Child Development, 80*, 1350–1359. doi:10.1111/j.1467–8624.2009.01337.x

Kisilevsky, B. S., Hains, S. M. J., Brown, C. A., Lee, C. T., Cowperthwaite, B., Stutzman, S. S., ... Wang, Z. (2009). Fetal sensitivity to properties of maternal speech and language. *Infant Behavior and Development, 32*, 59–71. doi: 10.1016/j.infbeh.2008.10.002

Kisilevsky, B. S., Hains, S. M., Lee, K., Xie, X., Huang, H., Ye, H. H., ... Wang, Z. (2003). Effects of experience on fetal voice recognition. *Pyschological Science, 14*, 220–224.

Kiuru, N., Burk, W. J., Laursen, B., Salmela-Aro, K., & Nurmi, J.-E. (2010). Pressure to drink but not to smoke: Disentangling selection and socialization in adolescent peer networks and peer groups. *Journal of Adolescence, 33*, 801–812.

Klaczynski, P., Daniel, D. B., & Keller, P. S. (2009). Appearance idealization, body esteem, causal attributions, and ethnic variations in the development of obesity stereotypes. *Journal of Applied Developmental Psychology, 30*, 537–551.

Klaczynski, P. A. (2001). Analytic and heuristic processing influences on adolescent reasoning and decision-making. *Child Development, 72*, 844–861.

Klaczynski, P. A. (2011). Age differences in understanding precedent-setting decisions and authorities' responses to violations of deontic rules. *Journal of Experimental Child Psychology, 109*, 1–24.

Klatsky, A. L. (2009). Alcohol and cardiovascular diseases. *Expert Review of Cardiovascular Therapy, 7*, 499–506. doi:10.1586/erc.09.22

Klaus, P. (2005). Crimes against persons age 65 or older, 1993–2002. Washington, DC: Bureau of Justice Statistics.

Klaus, S. F., Ekerdt, D. J., & Gajewski, B. (2012). Job satisfaction in birth cohorts of nurses. *Journal of Nursing Management, 20*, 461–471. doi:10.1111/j.1365–2834.2011.01283.x

Klimstra, T. A., Luyckx, K., Germeijs, V., Meeus, W. H. J., & Goossens, L. (2012). Personality traits and educational identity formation in late adolescents: Longitudinal associations and academic progress. *Journal of Youth and Adolescence, 41*, 346–361. doi: 10.1007/s10964–011–9734–7

Kline, K. K. (2008). *Authoritative communities: The scientific case for nurturing the whole child*. New York, NY: Springer.

Kochanska, G. (1991). Socialization and temperament in the development of guilt and conscience. *Child Development, 62*, 1379–1392.

Kochanska, G., Aksan, N., Prisco, T. R., & Adams, E. E. (2008). Mother-child and father-child mutually responsive orientation in the first 2 years and children's outcomes at preschool age: Mechanisms of influence. *Child Development, 79*, 30–44.

Kochanska, G., Barry, R. A., Jimenez, N. B., Hollatz, A. L., & Woodard, J. (2009). Guilt and effortful control: Two mechanisms that prevent disruptive developmental trajectories. *Journal of Personality and Social Psychology, 97*, 322–333. doi:10.1037/a0015471

Kohen, D., Uppal, S., Khan, S., & Visentin, L. (2006). *Access and barriers to educational services for Canadian children with disabilities*. Retrieved from http://www.ccl-cca.ca/pdfs/OtherReports/201009KohenUppalKhanVisentinFullReport.pdf

Kohlberg, L. (1963). The development of children's orientations toward a moral order: I. Sequence in the development of moral thought. *Vita Humana, 6*, 11–33.

Kohlberg, L., Levine, C., & Hewer, A. (1983). *Moral stages: A current formulation and a response to critics*. New York, NY: Karger.

Kohyama, J., Mindell, J. A., & Sadeh, A. (2011). Sleep characteristics of young children in Japan: Internet study and comparison with other Asian countries. *Pediatrics International, 53*, 649–655. doi:10.1111/j.1442–200X.2010.03318.x

Kolb, B., & Whishaw, I. Q. (2008). *Fundamentals of human neuropsychology* (6th ed.). New York, NY: Worth.

Kolpin, R. (1999). *Global links: Connecting Canada*. Toronto: Oxford University Press.

Koltko-Rivera, M. E. (2006). Rediscovering the later version of Maslow's hierarchy of needs: Self-transcendence and opportunities for theory, research, and unification. *Review of General Psychology, 10*, 302–317.

Konner, M. (2007). Evolutionary foundations of cultural psychology. In S. Kitayama & D. Cohen (Eds.), *Handbook of cultural psychology* (pp. 77–105). New York, NY: Guilford Press.

Konner, M. (2010). *The evolution of childhood: Relationships, emotion, mind*. Cambridge, MA: Harvard University Press.

Kooij, D. T. A. M., Annet, H. D. E., Lange, P. G. W., Jansen, R. K., & Dikkers, J. S. E. (2011). Age and work-related motives: Results of a meta-analysis. *Journal of Organizational Behavior, 225*, 197–225.

Kopp, C. B. (2011). Development in the early years: Socialization, motor development, and consciousness. *Annual Review of Psychology, 62*, 165–187. doi:10.1146/annurev.psych.121208.131625

Koppen, J. (2009). *Effect of the economy on housing choices*. Washington, DC: AARP.

Korenblum, M. (2004). Antidepressant use in adolescence: We're asking the wrong questions. *Paediatrics and Child Health, 9*, 539–540.

Kossowsky, J., Wilhelm, F. H., Roth, W. T., & Schneider, S. (2012). Separation anxiety disorder in children: Disorder-specific responses to experimental separation from the mother. *Journal of Child Psychology and Psychiatry, 53*, 178–187. doi:10.1111/j.1469–7610.2011.02465.x

Kovacs, M., Joormann, J., & Gotlib, I. H. (2008). Emotion (dys)regulation and links to depressive disorders. *Child Development Perspectives, 2*, 149–155. doi:10.1111/j.1750–8606.2008.00057.x

Kovas, Y., Hayiou-Thomas, M. E., Oliver, B., Dale, P. S., Bishop, D. V. M., & Plomin, R. (2005). Genetic influences in different aspects of language development: The etiology of language skills in 4.5-year-old twins. *Child Development, 76*, 632–651.

Kramer, A. F., Fabiani, M., & Colcombe, S. J. (2006). Contributions of cognitive neuroscience to the understanding of behavior and aging. In J. E. Birren & K. W. Schaie (Eds.), *Handbook of the psychology of aging* (6th ed., pp. 57–83). Amsterdam, The Netherlands: Elsevier.

Krampe, R. T., Schaefer, S., Lindenberger, U., & Baltes, P. B. (2011). Lifespan changes in multi-tasking: Concurrent walking and memory search in children, young, and older adults. *Gait & Posture, 33*, 401–405. doi:10.1016/j.gaitpost.2010.12.012

Krause, N. (2006). Social relationships in late life. In R. H. Binstock & L. K. George (Eds.), *Handbook of aging and the social sciences* (6th ed., pp. 181–200). Amsterdam, The Netherlands: Elsevier.

Krebs, D. L. (2008). Morality: An evolutionary account. *Perspectives on Psychological Science, 3*, 149–172.

Krebs, J. R. (2009). The gourmet ape: Evolution and human food preferences. *American Journal of Clinical Nutrition, 90*, 707S–711S. doi:10.3945/ajcn.2009.27462B

Krenk, L., Rasmussen, L. S., Siersma, V. D., & Kehlet, H. (2012). Short-term practice effects and variability in cognitive testing in a healthy elderly population. *Experimental Gerontology, 47*, 432–436. doi:10.1016/j.exger.2012.03.011

Krieger, N. (2002). Is breast cancer a disease of affluence, poverty, or both? The case of African American women. *American Journal of Public Health, 92*, 611–613.

Krieger, N. (2003). Does racism harm health? Did child abuse exist before 1962? On explicit questions, critical science, and current controversies: An ecosocial perspective. *American Journal of Public Health, 93*, 194–199.

Kriger, M., & Seng, Y. (2005). Leadership with inner meaning: A contingency theory of leadership based on the worldviews of five religions. *The Leadership Quarterly, 16*, 771–806.

Kröger, E., Andel, R., Lindsay, J., Benounissa, Z., Verreault, R., & Laurin, D. (2008). Is complexity of work associated with risk of dementia? The Canadian Study of Health and Aging. *American Journal of Epidemiology, 167*, 820–830. doi:10.1093/aje/kwm382

Kroger, J. (2007). *Identity development: Adolescence through adulthood* (2nd ed.). Thousand Oaks, CA: Sage.

Kroger, J., Martinussen, M., & Marcia, J. E. (2010). Identity status change during adolescence and young adulthood: A meta-analysis. *Journal of Adolescence, 33*, 683–698.

Kronenberg, M. E., Hansel, T. C., Brennan, A. M., Osofsky, H. J., Osofsky, J. D., & Lawrason, B. (2010). Children of Katrina: Lessons learned about postdisaster symptoms and recovery patterns. *Child Development, 81*, 1241–1259. doi:10.1111/j.1467–8624.2010.01465.x

Kryzer, E. M., Kovan, N., Phillips, D. A., Domagall, L. A., & Gunnar, M. R. (2007). Toddlers' and preschoolers' experience in family day care: Age differences and behavioral correlates. *Early Childhood Research Quarterly, 22*, 451–466.

Kübler-Ross, E. (1969). *On death and dying*. New York, NY: Macmillan.

Kübler-Ross, E. (1975). *Death: The final stage of growth*. Englewood Cliffs, NJ: Prentice-Hall.

Kuehn, B. M. (2011). Scientists find promising therapies for fragile x and Down syndromes. *The Journal of the American Medical Association, 305*, 344–346. doi:10.1001/jama.2010.1960

Kuh, G. D., Gonyea, R. M., & Williams, J. M. (2005). What students expect from college and what they get. In T. Miller, B. E. Bender, & J. H. Schuh (Eds.), *Promoting reasonable expectations: Aligning student and institutional views of the college experience* (pp. 34–64). San Francisco, CA: Jossey-Bass.

Kuhlmann, I., Minihane, A., Huebbe, P., Nebel, A., & Rimbach, G. (2010). Apolipoprotein E genotype and hepatitis C, HIV and herpes simplex disease risk: A literature review. *Lipids in Health and Disease, 9*, 8.

Kuhn, D., & Franklin, S. (2006). The second decade: What develops (and how). In D. Kuhn & R. Siegler (Eds.), *Handbook of child psychology: Vol. 2. Cognition, perception, and language* (6th ed., pp. 953–993). Hoboken, NJ: Wiley.

Kuhn, L., Sinkala, M., Thea, D., Kankasa, C., & Aldrovandi, G. (2009). HIV prevention is not enough: Child survival in the context of prevention of mother to child HIV transmission. *Journal of the International AIDS Society, 12*, 36.

Kumar, S., Calvo, R., Avendano, M., Sivaramakrishnan, K., & Berkman, L. F. (2012). Social support, volunteering and health around the world: Cross-national evidence from 139 countries. *Social Science & Medicine, 74*, 696–706. doi:10.1016/j.socscimed.2011.11.017

Kun, J. F. J., May, J., & Noedl, H. (2010). Surveillance of malaria drug resistance: Improvement needed? *Future Medicine, 7*, 3–6. doi:10.2217/thy.09.82

Kuo, H.-K., Leveille, S. G., Yu, Y.-H., & Milber, W. P. (2007). Cognitive function, habitual gait speed, and late-life disability in the National Health and Nutrition Examination Survey (NHANES) 1999–2002. *Gerontology, 53*, 102–110.

Kuperberg, A. (2012). Reassessing differences in work and income in cohabitation and marriage. *Journal of Marriage and Family, 74*, 688–707. doi:10.1111/j.1741–3737.2012.00993.x

Kuppens, S., Grietens, H., Onghena, P., & Michiels, D. (2009). Associations between parental control and children's overt and relational aggression. *British Journal of Developmental Psychology, 27*, 607–623.

Kutob, R. M., Senf, J. H., Crago, M., & Shisslak, C. M. (2010). Concurrent and longitudinal predictors of self-esteem in elementary and middle school girls. *Journal of School Health, 80*, 240–248. doi:10.1111/j.1746–1561.2010.00496.x

L

LaBar, K. S. (2007). Beyond fear: Emotional memory mechanisms in the human brain. *Current Directions in Psychological Science, 16*, 173–177. doi:10.1111/j.1467–8721.2007.00498.x

Labouvie-Vief, G. (1990). Wisdom as integrated thought: Historical and developmental perspectives. In R. J. Sternberg (Ed.), *Wisdom: Its nature, origins, and development* (pp. 52–83). Cambridge, England: Cambridge University Press.

Labouvie-Vief, G., Grühn, D., & Mouras, H. (2009). Dynamic emotion-cognition interactions in adult development: Arousal, stress, and the processing of affect. In H. B. Bosworth & C. Hertzog (Eds.), *Aging and cognition: Research methodologies and empirical advances* (pp. 181–196). Washington, DC: American Psychological Association.

Lachman, M. E., & Bertrand, R. M. (2001). Personality and the self in midlife. In M. E. Lachman (Ed.), *Handbook of midlife development* (pp. 279–309). New York, NY: Wiley.

Lachman, M. E., Neupert, S. D., & Agrigoroaei, S. (2011). The relevance of control beliefs for health and aging. In K. W. Schaie & S. L. Willis (Eds.), *Handbook of the psychology of aging* (7th ed., pp. 175–190). Boston, MA: Elsevier/Academic Press.

Lachman, M. E., Rosnick, C. B., & Röcke, C. (2009). The rise and fall of control beliefs and life satisfaction in adulthood: Trajectories of stability and change over ten years. In H. B. Bosworth & C. Hertzog (Eds.), *Aging and cognition: Research methodologies and empirical advances* (pp. 143–160). Washington, DC: American Psychological Association.

LaFontana, K. M., & Cillessen, A. H. N. (2010). Developmental changes in the priority of perceived status in childhood and adolescence. *Social Development, 19*, 130–147. doi:10.1111/j.1467–9507.2008.00522.x

Laible, D., Panfile, T., & Makariev, D. (2008). The quality and frequency of mother-toddler conflict: Links with attachment and temperament. *Child Development, 79*, 426–443.

Lalande, K. M., & Bonanno, G. A. (2006). Culture and continuing bonds: A prospective comparison of bereavement in the United States and the People's Republic of China. *Death Studies, 30*, 303–324.

Lam, R. W. (2012). *Depression* (2nd ed.). Oxford, UK: Oxford University Press.

Lamb, M. E. (1976). Twelve-month olds and their parents: Interaction in a laboratory playroom. *Developmental Psychology, 12*, 237–244. doi:10.1037–0012–1649.12.3.237

Lamb, M. E. (Ed.). (2010). *The role of the father in child development* (5th ed.). Hoboken, NJ: Wiley.

Lambert, N. M., Fincham, F. D., Stillman, T. F., Graham, S. M., & Beach, S. R. H. (2010). Motivating change in relationships. *Psychological Science, 21*, 126–132. doi:10.1177/0956797609355634

Lambourne, K., & Donnelly, J. E. (2011). The role of physical activity in pediatric obesity. *Pediatric Clinics of North America, 58*, 1481–1491. doi:10.1016/j.pcl.2011.09.004

Landis, S., & Insel, T. R. (2008, November 7). The "neuro" in neurogenetics. *Science, 322*, 821.

Landy, F. J., & Conte, J. M. (2007). *Work in the 21st century: An introduction to industrial and organizational psychology* (2nd ed.). Malden, MA: Blackwell.

Lane, R. F., Shineman, D. W., & Fillit, H. M. (2011). Beyond amyloid: A diverse portfolio of novel drug discovery programs for Alzheimer's disease and related dementias. *Alzheimer's Research & Therapy, 3*, 36. doi:10.1186/alzrt99

Lane, S. D., Cherek, D. R., Pietras, C. J., & Steinberg, J. L. (2005). Performance of heavy marijuana-smoking adolescents on a laboratory measure of motivation. *Addictive Behaviors, 30*, 815–828.

Lang, F. R., Wagner, J., & Neyer, F. J. (2009). Interpersonal functioning across the lifespan: Two principles of relationship regulation. *Advances in Life Course Research, 14*, 40–51.

Lange, M. A. (2011). The Arab youth and the dawn of democracy. *KAS International Reports, 5*, 20–29. Retrieved from http://www.kas.de/wf/doc/kas_22803-544-2-30.pdf?110516131303

Langenkamp, A. G. (2010). Academic vulnerability and resilience during the transition to high school. *Sociology of Education, 83*, 1–19. doi:10.1177/0038040709356563

Langlois, K. A., Samokhavalov, A. V., Rehm, J., Spence, S. T., & Connor Gorber, S. (2012). *Health state descriptions for Canadians: Mental illnesses* (Catalogue No. 82–619–M—No. 004). Retrieved from http://www.statcan.gc.ca/pub/82-619-m/82-619-m2012004-eng.pdf

Langlois, S., & Turner, A. (2012). *Aboriginal languages in Canada: Language, 2011 Census of Population* (Catalogue No. 98–314–X2011003). Retrieved from http://www12.statcan.gc.ca/census-recensement/2011/as-sa/98-314-x/98-314-x2011003_3-eng.pdf

Långström, N., Rahman, Q., Carlström, E., & Lichtenstein, P. (2010). Genetic and environmental effects on same-sex sexual behavior: A population study of twins in Sweden. *Archives of Sexual Behavior, 39*, 75–80. doi:10.1007/s10508–008–9386–1

Laperrière, J. P. (2009). *Analyse comparative de la forme des messages publicitaires pouvant s'adresser aux enfants.* Retrieved from http://www.archipel.uqam.ca/2034/1/M10834.pdf

Lara-Cinisomo, S., Fuligni, A. S., & Karoly, L. A. (2011). Preparing preschoolers for kindergarten. In D. M. Laverick & M. Renck Jalongo (Eds.), *Transitions to early care and education* (Vol. 4, pp. 93–105). New York, NY: Springer.

Laraway, K. A., Birch, L. L., Shaffer, M. L., & Paul, I. M. (2010). Parent perception of healthy infant and toddler growth. *Clinical Pediatrics, 49*, 343–349. doi:10.1177/0009922809343717

LaRochelle-Côté, S. (2013). *Employment instability among younger workers.* Retrieved from http://www.statcan.gc.ca/pub/75-004-m/75-004-m2013001-eng.htm

LaRochelle-Côté, S., & Gilmore, J. (2009). *Canada's employment downturn* (Catalogue No. 75–001-X). Retrieved from http://www.statcan.gc.ca/pub/75-001-x/2009112/pdf/11048-eng.pdf

Larzelere, R., Cox, R., & Smith, G. (2010). Do nonphysical punishments reduce antisocial behavior more than spanking? A comparison using the strongest previous causal evidence against spanking. *BMC Pediatrics, 10*, 10.

Laumann, E. O., & Michael, R. T. (2000). *Sex, love, and health in America: Private choices and public policies.* Chicago, IL: University of Chicago Press.

Laurino, M. Y., Bennett, R. L., Saraiya, D. S., Baumeister, L., Doyle, D. L., Leppig, K., ... Raskind, W. H. (2005). Genetic evaluation and counseling of couples with recurrent miscarriage: Recommendations of the National Society of Genetic Counselors. *Journal of Genetic Counseling, 14*, 165–181. doi:10.1007/s10897–005–3241–5

Laursen, B., Bukowski, W. M., Nurmi, J.-E., Marion, D., Salmela-Aro, K., & Kiuru, N. (2010). Opposites detract: Middle school peer group antipathies. *Journal of Experimental Child Psychology, 106*, 240–256.

Laursen, B., & Collins, W. A. (2009). Parent-child relationships during adolescence. In R. M. Lerner & L. D. Steinberg (Eds.), *Handbook of adolescent psychology: Vol. 2. Contextual influences on adolescent development* (3rd ed., pp. 3–42). Hoboken, NJ: Wiley.

Laursen, B., & Mooney, K. S. (2007). Individual differences in adolescent dating and adjustment. In R. C. M. E. Engels, M. Kerr, & H. Stattin (Eds.), *Friends, lovers, and groups: Key relationships in adolescence* (pp. 81–92). Hoboken, NJ: Wiley.

Lavallee, T. (2005). Honouring Jordan: Putting First Nations children first and funding fights second. *Paediatric Child Health, 10*, 527–529.

Lavelli, M., & Fogel, A. (2005). Developmental changes in the relationship between the infant's attention and emotion during early face-to-face communication: The 2-month transition. *Developmental Psychology, 41*, 265–280.

Lawrence, J., Alcock, D., McGrath, P., Kay, J., MacMurray, S. B., & Dulberg, C. (1993). The development of a tool to assess neonatal pain. *Neonatal Network, 12*, 59–66.

Layden, T. (2004, November 15). Get out and play! *Sports Illustrated, 101*, 80–93.

Leach, P. (1997). *Your baby & child: From birth to age five* (3rd ed.). New York, NY: Knopf.

Leach, P. (2009). *Child care today: Getting it right for everyone.* New York, NY: Knopf.

Leadbeater, B. J., & Hoglund, W. L. G. (2009). The effects of peer victimization and physical aggression on changes in internalizing from first to third grade. *Child Development, 80*, 843–859.

Leaper, C. (1994). Exploring the consequences of gender segregation on social relationships. In C. Leaper (Ed.), *Childhood gender segregation: Causes and consequences* (pp. 67–86). San Francisco, CA: Jossey-Bass.

Leatherdale, S. T., & Ahmed, R. (2011). Screen-based sedentary behaviours among a nationally representative sample of youth: Are Canadian kids couch potatoes? *Chronic Diseases and Injuries in Canada, 31*, 141–146.

LeBlanc, M. M., & Barling, J. (2004). Workplace aggression. *Current Directions in Psychological Science, 13*, 9–12.

Lee, E., Spitze, G., & Logan, J. R. (2003). Social support to parents-in-law: The interplay of gender and kin hierarchies. *Journal of Marriage and Family, 65*, 396–403.

Lee, H. Y., Gibson, P., & Chaisson, R. (2011). Elderly Korean immigrants' socially and culturally constructed definitions of elder neglect. *Journal of Aging Studies, 25*, 126–134. doi:10.1016/j.jaging.2010.08.015

Lee, I.-M., Ewing, R., & Sesso, H. D. (2009). The built environment and physical activity levels: The Harvard Alumni Health Study. *American Journal of Preventive Medicine, 37*, 293–298.

Lee, J., & Bean, F. D. (2007). Reinventing the color line: Immigration and America's new racial/ethnic divide. *Social Forces, 86*, 561–586.

Lee, J. M., Kaciroti, N., Appugliese, D., Corwyn, R. F., Bradley, R. H., & Lumeng, J. C. (2010). Body mass index and timing of pubertal initiation in boys. *Archives of Pediatric and Adolescent Medicine, 164*, 139–144. doi:10.1001/archpediatrics.2009.258

Lee, K. S., & Ono, H. (2012). Marriage, cohabitation, and happiness: A cross-national analysis of 27 countries. *Journal of Marriage and Family, 74*, 953–972. doi:10.1111/j.1741–3737.2012.01001.x

Lee, S., & Shouse, R. C. (2011). The impact of prestige orientation on shadow education in South Korea. *Sociology of Education, 84*, 212–224. doi:10.1177/0038040711411278

Leman, P. J., & Björnberg, M. (2010). Conversation, development, and gender: A study of changes in children's concepts of punishment. *Child Development, 81*, 958–971. doi:10.1111/j.1467-8624.2010.01445.x

Lepper, M. R., Greene, D., & Nisbett, R. E. (1973). Undermining children's intrinsic interest with extrinsic reward: A test of the "overjustification" hypothesis. *Journal of Personality & Social Psychology, 28*, 129–137.

Lerner, C., & Dombro, A. L. (2004). Finding your fit: Some temperament tips for parents. *Zero to Three, 24,* 42–45.

Lerner, R. M. (2010). *The handbook of life-span development.* Hoboken, NJ: Wiley.

Leslie, M. (2012, March 23). Gut microbes keep rare immune cells in line. *Science, 335,* 1428.

Levin, H. M. (2005, October). The social costs of inadequate education. In H. H. Levin (Chair), *Teachers College Symposium on Educational Equity.* Symposium conducted at the meeting of The Campaign for Educational Equity, Columbia University, New York, NY.

Levinson, D. J. (1978). *The seasons of a man's life.* New York, NY: Knopf.

Levy, B. (2009). Stereotype embodiment: A psychosocial approach to aging. *Current Directions in Psychological Science, 18,* 332–336.

Levy, B., & Langer, E. (1994). Aging free from negative stereotypes: Successful memory in China among the American deaf. *Journal of Personality & Social Psychology, 66,* 989–997.

Levy, B. R. (2000). Handwriting as a reflection of aging self-stereotypes. *Journal of Geriatric Psychiatry, 33,* 81–94.

Levy, B. R., & Myers, L. M. (2004). Preventive health behaviors influenced by self-perceptions of aging. *Preventive Medicine, 39,* 625–629.

Lewin-Benham, A. (2008). *Powerful children: Understanding how to teach and learn using the Reggio approach.* New York, NY: Teachers College Press.

Lewis, M. (1992). *Shame: The exposed self.* New York, NY: The Free Press.

Lewis, M. (2007). Early emotional development. In A. Slater & M. Lewis (Eds.), *Introduction to infant development* (pp. 216–232). New York, NY: Oxford University Press.

Lewis, M. (2010). The emergence of consciousness and its role in human development. In W. F. Overton & R. M. Lerner (Eds.), *The handbook of life-span development, Vol 1: Cognition, biology, and methods* (pp. 628–670). Hoboken, NJ: Wiley.

Lewis, M. (2011). Inside and outside: The relation between emotional states and expressions. *Emotion Review, 3,* 189–196. doi:10.1177/1754073910387947

Lewis, M., & Brooks, J. (1978). Self-knowledge and emotional development. In M. Lewis & L. A. Rosenblum (Eds.), *Genesis of behavior: Vol. 1. The development of affect* (pp. 205–226). New York, NY: Plenum Press.

Lewis, M., & Kestler, L. (2012). *Gender differences in prenatal substance exposure.* Washington, DC: American Psychological Association.

Lewis, M., & Ramsay, D. (2005). Infant emotional and cortisol responses to goal blockage. *Child Development, 76,* 518–530.

Lewis, S., & Ariyachandra, T. (2011). Seniors and social networking. *Journal of Information Systems Applied Research, 4,* 4–18.

Lewkowicz, D. J. (2010). Infant perception of audio-visual speech synchrony. *Developmental Psychology, 46,* 66–77. doi:10.1037/a0015579

Li, Y., & Lerner, R. M. (2011). Trajectories of school engagement during adolescence: Implications for grades, depression, delinquency, and substance use. *Developmental Psychology, 47,* 233–247. doi:10.1037/a0021307

Libertus, K., & Needham, A. (2010). Teach to reach: The effects of active vs. passive reaching experiences on action and perception. *Vision Research, 50,* 2750–2757. doi:10.1016/j.visres.2010.09.001

Libertus, M. E., & Brannon, E. M. (2009). Behavioral and neural basis of number sense in infancy. *Current Directions in Psychological Science, 18,* 346–351. doi:10.1111/j.1467-8721.2009.01665.x

Lichter, D. T., Qian, Z., & Mellott, L. M. (2006). Marriage or dissolution? Union transitions among poor cohabiting women. *Demography, 43,* 223–240.

Lillard, A., & Else-Quest, N. (2006, September 29). Evaluating Montessori education. *Science, 313,* 1893–1894.

Lillard, A. S. (2005). *Montessori: The science behind the genius.* New York, NY: Oxford University Press.

Lim, B. Y. (2004). The magic of the brush and the power of color: Integrating theory into practice of painting in early childhood settings. *Early Childhood Education Journal, 32,* 113–119.

Limber, S. P. (2011). Development, evaluation, and future directions of the Olweus Bullying Prevention Program. *Journal of School Violence, 10,* 71–87. doi:10.1080/15388220.2010.519375

Lin, I.-F. (2008a). Consequences of parental divorce for adult children's support of their frail parents. *Journal of Marriage and Family, 70,* 113–128.

Lin, I.-F. (2008b). Mother and daughter reports about upward transfers. *Journal of Marriage and Family, 70,* 815–827.

Lincove, J. A., & Painter, G. (2006). Does the age that children start kindergarten matter? Evidence of long-term educational and social outcomes. *Educational Evaluation and Policy Analysis, 28,* 153–179

Lindau, S. T., & Gavrilova, N. (2010). Sex, health, and years of sexually active life gained due to good health: Evidence from two US population based cross sectional surveys of ageing. *British Medical Journal, 340,* c810. doi:10.1136/bmj.c810

Lindfors, K., Elovainio, M., Wickman, S., Vuorinen, R., Sinkkonen, J., Dunkel, L., & Raappana, A. (2007). Brief report: The role of ego development in psychosocial adjustment among boys with delayed puberty. *Journal of Research on Adolescence, 17,* 601–612.

Linn, S., & Novosat, C. L. (2008). Calories for sale: Food marketing to children in the twenty-first century. In A. B. Jordan (Ed.), *Annals of the American Academy of Political and Social Science: Vol. 615. Overweight and obesity in America's children: Causes, consequences, solutions* (pp. 133–155). Thousand Oaks, CA: Sage.

Lipton, J. S., & Spelke, E. S. (2003). Origins of number sense: Large-number discrimination in human infants. *Psychological Science, 14,* 396–401. doi:10.1111/1467-9280.01453

Liston, B. (2011, March 22). Peanut allergy stirs controversy at Florida school. *Reuters.* Retrieved from http://www.reuters.com/article/2011/03/22/us-peanut-allergy-idUSTRE72L7AQ20110322

Liszkowski, U., Schäfer, M., Carpenter, M., & Tomasello, M. (2009). Prelinguistic infants, but not chimpanzees, communicate about absent entities. *Psychological Science, 20,* 654–660. doi:10.1111/j.1467–9280.2009.02346.x

Liu, C., Spector, P. E., & Shi, L. (2007). Cross-national job stress: A quantitative and qualitative study. *Journal of Organizational Behavior, 28,* 209–239.

Liu, D., Wellman, H. M., Tardif, T., & Sabbagh, M. A. (2008). Theory of mind development in Chinese children: A meta-analysis of false-belief understanding across cultures and languages. *Developmental Psychology, 44,* 523–531.

Liu, H., Wang, Q., Keesler, V., & Schneider, B. (2011). Non-standard work schedules, work-family conflict and parental well-being: A comparison of married and cohabiting unions. *Social Science Research, 40,* 473–484. doi:10.1016/j.ssresearch.2010.10.008

Livas-Dlott, A., Fuller, B., Stein, G. L., Bridges, M., Mangual Figueroa, A., & Mireles, L. (2010). Commands, competence, and *cariño*: Maternal socialization practices in Mexican American families. *Developmental Psychology, 46,* 566–578. doi:10.1037/a0018016

Livingston, G. (2011, October 12). *In a down economy, fewer births.* Washington, DC: Pew Social & Demographic Trends.

Lleras-Muney, A. (2005). The relationship between education and adult mortality in the United States. *Review of Economic Studies, 72,* 189–221.

Lloyd-Fox, S., Blasi, A., Volein, A., Everdell, N., Elwell, C. E., & Johnson, M. H. (2009). Social perception in infancy: A near infrared spectroscopy study. *Child Development, 80,* 986–999. doi:10.1111/j.1467–8624.2009.01312.x

Lobstein, T., & Dibb, S. (2005). Evidence of a possible link between obesogenic food advertising and child overweight. *Obesity Reviews, 6,* 203–208. doi:10.1111/j.1467–789X.2005.00191.x

LoBue, V., & DeLoache, J. S. (2011). Pretty in pink: The early development of gender-stereotyped colour preferences. *British Journal of Developmental Psychology, 29,* 656–667. doi:10.1111/j.2044–835X.2011.02027.x

Löckenhoff, C. E., De Fruyt, F., Terracciano, A., McCrae, R. R., De Bolle, M., Costa Jr, P. T., ... Yik, M. (2009). Perceptions of aging across 26 cultures and their culture-level associates. *Psychology and Aging, 24,* 941–954. doi:10.1037/a0016901

Loe, I. M., & Feldman, H. M. (2007). Academic and educational outcomes of children with ADHD. *Journal of Pediatric Psychology, 32,* 643–654. doi:10.1093/jpepsy/jsl054

Loeber, R., & Burke, J. D. (2011). Developmental pathways in juvenile externalizing and internalizing problems. *Journal of Research on Adolescence, 21,* 34–46. doi:10.1111/j.1532–7795.2010.00713.x

Loes, C., Pascarella, E., & Umbach, P. (2012). Effects of diversity experiences on critical thinking skills: Who benefits? *Journal of Higher Education, 83,* 1–25.

Löfmark, R., Nilstun, T., Cartwright, C., Fischer, S., van der Heide, A., Mortier, F., ... Consortium, t. E. (2008, February 12). Physicians' experiences with end-of-life decision-making: Survey in 6 European countries and Australia. *BMC Medicine.* Retrieved from http://www.biomedcentral.com/1741-7015/6/4

Longmore, M., Eng, A., Giordano, P., & Manning, W. (2009). Parenting and adolescents' sexual initiation. *Journal of Marriage and Family, 71,* 969–982.

Lopez, O. L., Kuller, L. H., Becker, J. T., Dulberg, C., Sweet, R. A., Gach, H. M., & Dekosky, S. T. (2007). Incidence of dementia in mild cognitive impairment in the cardiovascular health study cognition study. *Archives of Neurology, 64,* 416–420. doi:10.1001/archneur.64.3.416

Lövdén, M., Xu, W., & Wang, H.-X. (2013). Lifestyle change and the prevention of cognitive decline and dementia: What is the evidence? *Current Opinion in Psychiatry, 26,* 239–243. doi: 10.1097/YCO.0b013e32835f4135

Lovecky, D. V. (2009). Moral sensitivity in young gifted children. In D. Ambrose & T. Cross (Eds.), *Morality, ethics, and gifted minds* (pp. 161–176). New York, NY: Springer.

Lovell, B., & Wetherell, M. A. (2011). The cost of caregiving: Endocrine and immune implications in elderly and non elderly caregivers. *Neuroscience & Biobehavioral Reviews, 35,* 1342–1352. doi:10.1016/j.neubiorev.2011.02.007

Low, D. (2013, September 24). *In memory of Dr. Donald Low* [Video file]. Retrieved from http://www.youtube.com/watch?v=q3jgSkxV1rw

Lowell, D. I., Carter, A. S., Godoy, L., Paulicin, B., & Briggs-Gowan, M. J. (2011). A randomized controlled trial of Child FIRST: A comprehensive home-based intervention translating research into early childhood practice. *Child Development, 82,* 193–208. doi:10.1111/j.1467–8624.2010.01550.x

Lucas, R. E., Clark, A. E., Georgellis, Y., & Diener, E. (2003). Reexamining adaptation and the set point model of happiness: Reactions to changes in marital status. *Journal of Personality and Social Psychology, 84,* 527–539. doi:10.1037/0022-3514.84.3.527

Ludington-Hoe, S. (2011). Thirty years of kangaroo care science and practice. *Neonatal Network: The Journal of Neonatal Nursing, 30,* 357–362. doi:10.1891/0730-0832.30.5.357

Luengo-Prado, M. J., & Sevilla, A. (2013). Time to cook: Expenditure at retirement in Spain. *The Economic Journal, 123,* 764–789. doi:10.1111/j.1468–0297.2012.02546.x

Luking, K. R., Repovs, G., Belden, A. C., Gaffrey, M. S., Botteron, K. N., Luby, J. L., & Barch, D. M. (2011). Functional connectivity of the amygdala in early-childhood-onset depression. *Journal of the American Academy of Child & Adolescent Psychiatry, 50,* 1027–1041.e1023.

Luna, B., Padmanabhan, A., & O'Hearn, K. (2010). What has fMRI told us about the development of cognitive control through adolescence? *Brain and Cognition, 72,* 101–113.

Lundquist, G., Rasmussen, B. H., & Axelsson, B. (2011). Information of imminent death or not: Does it make a difference? *Journal of Clinical Oncology, 29,* 3927–3931. doi:10.1200/JCO.2011.34.6247

Lustig, C., Shah, P., Seidler, R., & Reuter-Lorenz, P. A. (2009). Aging, training, and the brain: A review and future directions. *Neuropsychology Review, 19,* 504–522. doi:10.1007/s11065–009–9119–9

Luthar, S. S., Cicchetti, D., & Becker, B. (2000). The construct of resilience: A critical evaluation and guidelines for future work. *Child Development, 71,* 543–562.

Luthar, S. S., D'Avanzo, K., & Hites, S. (2003). Maternal drug abuse versus other psychological disturbances: Risks and resilience among children. In S. S. Luthar (Ed.), *Resilience and vulnerability: Adaptation in the context of childhood adversities* (pp. 104–129). New York, NY: Cambridge University Press.

Lutz, W., & Samir, K. C. (2011, July 29). Global human capital: Integrating education and population. *Science, 333,* 587–592.

Luxmoore, N. (2012). *Young people, death, and the unfairness of everything.* London, England: Jessica Kingsley.

Lynch, S. M., & Brown, J. S. (2011). Stratification and inequality over the life course. In R. H. Binstock & L. K. George (Eds.), *Handbook of aging and the social sciences* (7th ed., pp. 105–117). San Diego, CA: Academic Press.

Lynn, R., & Mikk, J. (2007). National differences in intelligence and educational attainment. *Intelligence, 35,* 115–121.

Lynne, S. D., Graber, J. A., Nichols, T. R., Brooks-Gunn, J., & Botvin, G. J. (2007). Links between pubertal timing, peer influences, and externalizing behaviors among urban students followed through middle school. *Journal of Adolescent Health, 40,* 181. e187–181.e113.

Lyons-Ruth, K., Bronfman, E., & Parsons, E. (1999). Maternal frightened, frightening, or atypical behavior and disorganized infant attachment patterns. *Monographs of the Society for Research in Child Development, 64*(3, Serial No. 258), 67–96.

M

Ma, L., Phelps, E., Lerner, J. V., & Lerner, R. M. (2009). Academic competence for adolescents who bully and who are bullied: Findings from the 4-H Study of Positive Youth Development. *The Journal of Early Adolescence, 29,* 862–897. doi:10.1177/0272431609332667

Maccoby, E. E. (1990). Gender and relationships: A developmental account. *American Psychologist, 45,* 513–520.

Maccoby, E. E. (1998). *The two sexes: Growing up apart, coming together.* Cambridge, MA: Belknap Press.

Macdonald, D., & Wilson, D.. (2013). *Poverty or prosperity: Indigenous children in Canada.* Retrieved from https://www.policyalternatives.ca/sites/default/files/uploads/publications/National%20Office%2C%20Manitoba%20Office/2013/06/WorkLife_Poverty%20or%20Prosperity.pdf

Macgregor, S., Lind, P. A., Bucholz, K. K., Hansell, N. K., Madden, P. A. F., Richter, M. M., ... Whitfield, J. B. (2009). Associations of ADH and ALDH2 gene variation with self report alcohol reactions, consumption and dependence: An integrated analysis. *Human Molecular Genetics, 18,* 580–593. doi:10.1093/hmg/ddn372

Macmillan, R., & Copher, R. (2005). Families in the life course: Interdependency of roles, role configurations, and pathways. *Journal of Marriage and Family, 67,* 858–879.

MacPhee, D. (1981). *Knowledge of Infant Development Inventory (KIDI).* Unpublished manuscript, Educational Testing Service, Ewing, New Jersey.

Magnuson, K., & Berger, L. M. (2009). Family structure states and transitions: Associations with children's well-being during middle childhood. *Journal of Marriage and Family, 71,* 575–591. doi:10.1111/j.1741–3737.2009.00620.x

Mahler, M. S., Pine, F., & Bergman, A. (1975). *The psychological birth of the human infant: Symbiosis and individuation.* New York, NY: Basic Books.

Maisto, A. S., Galizio, M., & Connors, G. J. (2011). *Drug use and abuse* (6th ed.). Belmont, CA: Wadsworth/Cengage Learning.

Majercsik, E. (2005). Hierachy of needs of geriatric patients. *Gerontology, 51,* 170–173.

Makimoto, K. (1998). Drinking patterns and drinking problems among Asian-Americans and Pacific Islanders. *Alcohol Health and Research World, 22,* 270–275.

Malina, R. M., Bouchard, C., & Bar-Or, O. (2004). *Growth, maturation, and physical activity* (2nd ed.). Champaign, IL: Human Kinetics.

Malloy, M. H. (2009). Impact of cesarean section on intermediate and late preterm births: United States, 2000–2003. *Birth: Issues in Perinatal Care, 36,* 26–33.

Man, G. (1994). The astronaut family phenomenon: Examining consequences of the diaspora of the Hong Kong children. In J. DeBernardi, F. Forth, & S. Niessen (Eds.), *Proceedings of the 21st meetings of the Canadian Council for Southeast Asian Studies* (pp. 269–281). Edmonton, AB: University of Alberta.

Man, G. (2013). Families in the Chinese disapora: Transnational Hong Kong and mainland Chinese families in Canada. In C. Kwok-Bun (Ed.), *The handbook on families in Chinese societies* (pp. 157–168). New York, NY: Routledge.

Manago, A. M., Taylor, T., & Greenfield, P. M. (2012). Me and my 400 friends: The anatomy of college students' Facebook networks, their communication patterns, and well-being. *Developmental Psychology, 48,* 369–380. doi:10.1037/a0026338

Mancini, A. D., & Bonanno, G. A. (2006). Marital closeness, functional disability, and adjustment in late life. *Psychology and Aging, 21,* 600–610.

Mandemakers, J. J., & Dykstra, P. A. (2008). Discrepancies in parent's and adult child's reports of support and contact. *Journal of Marriage and Family, 70,* 495–506.

Mangels, J. A., Good, C., Whiteman, R. C., Maniscalco, B., & Dweck, C. S. (2012). Emotion blocks the path to learning under stereotype threat. *Social Cognitive and Affective Neuroscience, 7,* 230–241. doi:10.1093/scan/nsq100

Mann, J. R., McDermott, S., Bao, H., & Bersabe, A. (2009). Maternal genitourinary infection and risk of cerebral palsy. *Developmental Medicine & Child Neurology, 51,* 282–288.

Mann, R. D., & Andrews, E. B. (Eds.). (2007). *Pharmacovigilance* (2nd ed.). Hoboken, NJ: Wiley.

Mann, T., & Ward, A. (2007). Attention, self-control, and health behaviors. *Current Directions in Psychological Science, 16*, 280–283. doi:10.1111/j.1467–8721.2007.00520.x

Manzi, C., Vignoles, V. L., Regalia, C., & Scabini, E. (2006). Cohesion and enmeshment revisited: Differentiation, identity, and well-being in two European cultures. *Journal of Marriage and Family, 68*, 673–689.

Manzoli, L., Villari, P., Pironec, G. M., & Boccia, A. (2007). Marital status and mortality in the elderly: A systematic review and meta-analysis. *Social Science & Medicine, 64*, 77–94.

Mar, R. A. (2011). The neural bases of social cognition and story comprehension. *Annual Review of Psychology, 62*, 103–134. doi:10.1146/annurev-psych-120709-145406

Mar, R. A., Tackett, J. L., & Moore, C. (2010). Exposure to media and theory-of-mind development in preschoolers. *Cognitive Development, 25*, 69–78.

Marazita, J. M., & Merriman, W. E. (2011). Verifying one's knowledge of a name without retrieving it: A u-shaped relation to vocabulary size in early childhood. *Language Learning and Development, 7*, 40–54. doi:10.1080/15475441.2010.496099

Marchand, A., Drapeau, A., & Beaulieu-Prévost, D. (2011). Psychological distress in Canada: The role of employment and reasons for non-employment. *International Journal of Social Psychiatry, 58*, 596–604.

Marcia, J. E. (1966). Development and validation of ego-identity status. *Journal of Personality & Social Psychology, 3*, 551–558.

Marcia, J. E., Waterman, A. S., Matteson, D. R., Archer, S. L., & Orlofsky, J. L. (1993). *Ego identity: A handbook for psychosocial research.* New York, NY: Springer-Verlag.

Marcovitch, S., Boseovski, J. J., Knapp, R. J., & Kane, M. J. (2010). Goal neglect and working memory capacity in 4- to 6-year-old children. *Child Development, 81*, 1687–1695. doi:10.1111/j.1467–8624.2010.01503.x

Marcus, G. F., & Rabagliati, H. (2009). Language acquisition, domain specificity, and descent with modification. In J. Colombo, P. McCardle, & L. Freund (Eds.), *Infant pathways to language: Methods, models, and research disorders* (pp. 267–285). New York, NY: Psychology Press.

Margolis, R., & Myrskylä, M. (2011). A global perspective on happiness and fertility. *Population and Development Review, 37*, 29–56. doi:10.1111/j.1728–4457.2011.00389.x

Margrett, J. A., Daugherty, K., Martin, P., MacDonald, M., Davey, A., Woodard, J. L., … Poon, L. W. (2011). Affect and loneliness among centenarians and the oldest old: The role of individual and social resources. *Aging & Mental Health, 15*, 385–396. doi:10.1080/13607863.2010.519327

Marlow-Ferguson, R. (Ed.). (2002). *World education encyclopedia: A survey of educational systems worldwide* (2nd ed.). Detroit, MI: Gale Group.

Marschark, M., & Spencer, P. E. (2003). *Oxford handbook of deaf studies, language, and education.* New York, NY: Oxford University Press.

Marsh, L., McGee, R., Nada-Raja, S., & Williams, S. (2010). Text bullying and traditional bullying among New Zealand secondary school students. *Journal of Adolescence, 33*, 237–240.

Marshall, K. (2008). Fathers' use of paid parental leave. *Perspectives on Labour and Income.* Retrieved from http://www.statcan.gc.ca/pub/75-001-x/2008106/pdf/10639-eng.pdf

Marsiske, M., & Margrett, J. A. (2006). Everyday problem solving and decision making. In J. E. Birren & K. W. Schaie (Eds.), *Handbook of the psychology of aging* (6th ed., pp. 315–342). Burlington, MA: Elsevier Academic Press.

Martel, L., Malenfant, E. C., Morency, J-D., Lebel, A., Bélanger, A., & Bastien, N. (2012). *Projected trends to 2031 for the Canadian labour force.* Retrieved from http://www.statcan.gc.ca/pub/11-010-x/2011008/part-partie3-eng.htm

Martin, A. J. (2009). Motivation and engagement across the academic life span: A developmental construct validity study of elementary school, high school, and university/college students. *Educational and Psychological Measurement, 69*, 794–824. doi:10.1177/0013164409332214

Martin, C., Fabes, R., Hanish, L., Leonard, S., & Dinella, L. (2011). Experienced and expected similarity to same-gender peers: Moving toward a comprehensive model of gender segregation. *Sex Roles, 65*, 421–434. doi:10.1007/s11199–011–0029-y

Martin, C. L., Korneinko, O., Schaefer, D. R., Hanish, L. D., Fabes, R. A., & Goble, P. (2013). The role of sex of peers and gender-typed activities in young children's peer affiliative networks: A longitudinal analysis of selection and influence. *Child Development, 84*, 921–937. doi: 10.1111/cdev.12032

Martin, C. L., & Ruble, D. N. (2010). Patterns of gender development. *Annual Review of Psychology, 61*, 353–381. doi:10.1146/annurev.psych.093008.100511

Martin, I. M., & Kamins, M. A. (2010). An application of terror management theory in the design of social and health-related anti-smoking appeals. *Journal of Consumer Behaviour, 9*, 172–190. doi:10.1002/cb.293

Masche, J. G. (2010). Explanation of normative declines in parents' knowledge about their adolescent children. *Journal of Adolescence, 33*, 271–284.

Mascolo, M. F., Fischer, K. W., & Li, J. (2003). Dynamic development of component systems of emotions: Pride, shame, and guilt in China and the United States. In R. J. Davidson, K. R. Sherer, & H. Hill Goldsmith (Eds.), *Handbook of affective sciences* (pp. 375–408). Oxford, England: Oxford University Press.

Mashburn, A. J., Justice, L. M., Downer, J. T., & Pianta, R. C. (2009). Peer effects on children's language achievement during pre-kindergarten. *Child Development, 80*, 686–702. doi:10.1111/j.1467–8624.2009.01291.x

Maslow, A. H. (1954). *Motivation and personality.* New York, NY: Harper.

Maslow, A. H. (1970). *Motivation and personality* (2nd ed.). New York, NY: Harper & Row.

Masoro, E. J. (2006). Are age-associated diseases an integral part of aging? In E. J. Masoro & S. N. Austad (Eds.), *Handbook of the biology of aging* (6th ed., pp. 43–62). Amsterdam, The Netherlands: Elsevier Academic Press.

Masoro, E. J., & Austad, S. N. (2011). Forward. In E. J. Masoro & S. N. Austad (Eds.), *Handbook of the biology of aging* (7th ed., pp. xi–xii). San Diego, CA: Academic Press.

Masten, A. S. (2004). Regulatory processes, risk, and resilience in adolescent development. In R. E. Dahl & L. P. Spear (Eds.), *Annals of the New York Academy of Sciences: Vol. 1021. Adolescent brain development: Vulnerabilities and opportunities* (pp. 310–319). New York, NY: New York Academy of Sciences.

Masten, C. L., Guyer, A. E., Hodgdon, H. B., McClure, E. B., Charney, D. S., Ernst, M., ... Monk, C. S. (2008). Recognition of facial emotions among maltreated children with high rates of post-traumatic stress disorder. *Child Abuse & Neglect, 32,* 139–153.

Mathison, D. J., & Agrawal, D. (2010). An update on the epidemiology of pediatric fractures. *Pediatric Emergency Care, 26,* 594–603.

Matsumoto, D. (2004). Reflections on culture and competence. In R. J. Sternberg & E. L. Grigorenko (Eds.), *Culture and competence: Contexts of life success* (pp. 273–282). Washington, DC: American Psychological Association.

Matthews, F. E., Arthur, A., Barnes, L. E., Bond, J., Jagger, C., Robinson, L., & Brayne, C. (2013). A two-decade comparison of prevalence of dementia in individuals aged 65 years and older from three geographical areas of England: Results of the Cognitive Function and Ageing Study I and II. *The Lancet, 382,* 1405–1412. doi:10.1016/S0140–6736(13)61570–6

Mattis, J. S., & Mattis, J. H. (2011). Religiosity and spirituality in the lives of African American children. In N. E. Hill, T. Mann, & H. E. Fitzgerald (Eds.), *African American children and mental health* (pp. 125–149). Santa Barbara, CA: Praeger.

Mattison, J. A., Roth, G. S., Beasley, T. M., Tilmont, E. M., Handy, A. M., Herbert, R. L., ... de Cabo, R. (2012). Impact of caloric restriction on health and survival in rhesus monkeys from the NIA study. *Nature, 489,* 318–321.

Maxfield, M., Pyszczynski, T., Kluck, B., Cox, C. R., Greenberg, J., Solomon, S., & Weise, D. (2007). Age-related differences in responses to thoughts of one's own death: Mortality salience and judgments of moral transgressions. *Psychology and Aging, 22,* 341–353. doi:10.1037/0882-7974.22.2.341

May, V., Mason, J., & Clarke, L. (2012). Being there, yet not interfering: The paradoxes of grandparenting. In S. Arber & V. Timonen (Eds.), *Contemporary grandparenting: Changing family relationships in global contexts* (pp. 139–158). Bristol, UK: Policy Press.

Mazzocco, M. M. M., & Ross, J. L. (2007). *Neurogenetic developmental disorders: Variation of manifestation in childhood.* Cambridge, MA: MIT Press.

McAdams, D. P. (2006). The redemptive self: Generativity and the stories Americans live by. *Research in Human Development, 3,* 81–100.

McAdams, D. P., Bauer, J. J., Sakaeda, A. R., Anyidoho, N. A., Machado, M. A., Magrino-Failla, K., ... Pals, J. L. (2006). Continuity and change in the life story: A longitudinal study of autobiographical memories in emerging adulthood. *Journal of Personality, 74,* 1371–1400. doi:10.1111/j.1467–6494.2006.00412.x

McAdams, D. P., & Olson, B. D. (2010). Personality development: Continuity and change over the life course. *Annual Review of Psychology, 61,* 517–542. doi:10.1146/annurev.psych.093008.100507

McCall, R. B., Groark, C. J., & Fish, L. (2010). A caregiver–child socioemotional and relationship rating scale. *Infant Mental Health Journal, 31,* 201–219. doi:10.1002/imhj.20252

McCartney, K., Burchinal, M., Clarke-Stewart, A., Bub, K. L., Owen, M. T., Belsky, J., & The NICHD Early Child Care Research Network. (2010). Testing a series of causal propositions relating time in child care to children's externalizing behavior. *Developmental Psychology, 46,* 1–17, 17a.

McClain, L. R. (2011). Better parents, more stable partners: Union transitions among cohabiting parents. *Journal of Marriage and Family, 73,* 889–901.

McClain, P. D., Johnson Carew, J. D., Walton, E., Jr., & Watts, C. S. (2009). Group membership, group identity, and group consciousness: Measures of racial identity in American politics? *Annual Review of Political Science, 12,* 471–485. doi:10.1146/annurev.polisci.10.072805.102452

McCormick, C. M., Mathews, I. Z., Thomas, C., & Waters, P. (2010). Investigations of HPA function and the enduring consequences of stressors in adolescence in animal models. *Brain and Cognition, 72,* 73–85.

McCrae, R. R., & Terracciano, A. (2006). National character and personality. *Current Directions in Psychological Science, 15,* 156–161. doi:10.1111/j.1467–8721.2006.00427.x

McCue, H. (2012). *Education of Aboriginal people.* Retrieved from http://www.thecanadianencyclopedia.com/en/article/aboriginal-people-education/

McDaniel, M. A., & Bugg, J. M. (2012). Memory training interventions: What has been forgotten? *Journal of Applied Research in Memory and Cognition, 1,* 45–50. doi:10.1016/j.jarmac.2011.11.002

McDonald, S. D., Han, Z., Mulla, S., Murphy, K. E., Beyene, J., & Ohlsson, A. (2009). Preterm birth and low birth weight among *in vitro* fertilization singletons: A systematic review and meta-analyses. *European Journal of Obstetrics & Gynecology and Reproductive Biology, 146,* 138–148.

McFadden, S. H., & Basting, A. D. (2010). Healthy aging persons and their brains: Promoting resilience through creative engagement. *Clinics in Geriatric Medicine, 26,* 149–161.

McGrath, S. K., & Kennell, J. H. (2008). A randomized controlled trial of continuous labor support for middle-class couples: Effect on cesarean delivery rates. *Birth, 35,* 92–97.

McGreary, K. (2007). Preconception health framework. Retrieved from http://www.aphp.ca/pdf/Preconception%20Report%20proof%2004.26.07.pdf

McIntyre, D. A. (2002). *Colour blindness: Causes and effects.* Chester, UK: Dalton.

McIntyre, R. S., Konarski, J. Z., Soczynska, J. K., Wilkins, K., Panjwani, G., Bouffard, B., ... Kennedy, S. H. (2006). Medical comorbidity in bipolar disorder: Implications for functional outcomes and health service utilization. *Psychiatric Services, 57,* 1140–1144.

McKay, A. (2013). Trends in Canadian national and provincial territorial teen pregnancy rates: 2001–2010. *The Canadian Journal of Human Sexuality, 21,* 161–175. Retrieved from http://www.sieccan.org/pdf/TeenPregancy.pdf

McKown, C., & Strambler, M. J. (2009). Developmental antecedents and social and academic consequences of stereotype-consciousness in middle childhood. *Child Development, 80,* 1643–1659. doi:10.1111/j.1467–8624.2009.01359.x

McLanahan, S. (2009). Fragile families and the reproduction of poverty. *The ANNALS of the American Academy of Political and Social Science, 621,* 111–131. doi:10.1177/0002716208324862

McLendon, A., & Shelton, P. (2011–2012, Winter). New symptoms in older adults: Disease or drug? *Generations, 35*(4), 25–30.

McLeod, B. D., Wood, J. J., & Weisz, J. R. (2007). Examining the association between parenting and childhood anxiety: A meta-analysis. *Clinical Psychology Review, 27,* 155–172.

McLeod, J. D., Pescosolido, B. A., Takeuchi, D. T., & Falkenberg White, T. (2004). Public attitudes toward the use of psychiatric medications for children. *Journal of Health and Social Behavior, 45,* 53–67.

McLeod, P., Sommerville, P., & Reed, N. (2005). Are automated actions beyond conscious access? In J. Duncan, L. Phillips, & P. McLeod (Eds.), *Measuring the mind: Speed, control, and age* (pp. 359–372). New York: Oxford University Press.

McLoyd, V. C., Aikens, N. L., & Burton, L. M. (2006). Childhood poverty, policy, and practice. In K. A. Renninger & I. E. Sigel (Eds.), *Handbook of child psychology: Vol. 4. Child psychology in practice* (6th ed., pp. 700–775). Hoboken, NJ: Wiley.

McLoyd, V. C., Kaplan, R., Hardaway, C. R., & Wood, D. (2007). Does endorsement of physical discipline matter? Assessing moderating influences on the maternal and child psychological correlates of physical discipline in African American families. *Journal of Family Psychology, 21,* 165–175.

McManus, I. C., Moore, J., Freegard, M., & Rawles, R. (2010). Science in the making: Right Hand, Left Hand. III: Estimating historical rates of left-handedness. *Laterality: Asymmetries of Body, Brain and Cognition, 15,* 186–208. doi:10.1080/13576500802565313

McMullen, K. (2004). *Children of immigrants: How well do they do in school? Education matters* (Catalogue No. 81–004–XIE). Retrieved from http://www.statcan.gc.ca/pub/81-004-x/200410/7422-eng.htm

McNamee, C., & Raley, K. (2011). A note on race, ethnicity and nativity differentials in remarriage in the United States. *Demographic Research, 24,* 293–231.

McNulty, J. K., & Fincham, F. D. (2012). Beyond positive psychology? Toward a contextual view of psychological processes and well-being. *American Psychologist, 67,* 101–110. doi:10.1037/a0024572

Meadows, S. (2006). *The child as thinker: The development and acquisition of cognition in childhood* (2nd ed.). New York, NY: Routledge.

Meaney, M. J. (2010). Epigenetics and the biological definition of gene × environment interactions. *Child Development, 81,* 41–79.

Meece, J. L., & Eccles, J. S. (2010). *Handbook of research on schools, schooling, and human development.* New York, NY: Routledge.

Meeus, W. (2011). The study of adolescent identity formation 2000–2010: A review of longitudinal research. *Journal of Research on Adolescence, 21,* 75–94. doi:10.1111/j.1532–7795.2010.00716.x

Mehta, C. M., & Strough, J. (2009). Sex segregation in friendships and normative contexts across the life span. *Developmental Review, 29,* 201–220.

Meier, A., Hull, K. E., & Ortyl, T. A. (2009). Young adult relationship values at the intersection of gender and sexuality. *Journal of Marriage and Family, 71,* 510–525. doi:10.1111/j.1741–3737.2009.00616.x

Meisami, E., Brown, C. M., & Emerle, H. F. (2007). Sensory systems: Normal aging, disorders, and treatments of vision and hearing in humans. In P. S. Timiras (Ed.), *Physiological basis of aging and geriatrics* (4th ed., pp. 109–136). New York, NY: Informa Healthcare.

Melhem, N. M., Porta, G., Shamseddeen, W., Payne, M. W., & Brent, D. A. (2011). Grief in children and adolescents bereaved by sudden parental death. *Archives of General Psychiatry, 68,* 911–919.

Mellor, M. J., & Brownell, P. J. (Eds.). (2006). *Elder abuse and mistreatment: Policy, practice, and research.* New York, NY: Haworth Press.

Menacker, F., & Hamilton, B. E. (2010, March). Recent trends in cesarean delivery in the United States. Hyattsville, MD: National Center for Health Statistics.

Mendle, J., Harden, K. P., Brooks-Gunn, J., & Graber, J. A. (2010). Development's tortoise and hare: Pubertal timing, pubertal tempo, and depressive symptoms in boys and girls. *Developmental Psychology, 46,* 1341–1353. doi:10.1037/a0020205

Mendle, J., Leve, L. D., Van Ryzin, M., Natsuaki, M. N., & Ge, X. (2011). Associations between early life stress, child maltreatment, and pubertal development among girls in foster care. *Journal of Research on Adolescence, 21,* 871–880. doi:10.1111/j.1532–7795.2011.00746.x

Mendleson, R. (2009, February 23). No room for gifted kids. *Maclean's.* Retrieved from http://www2.macleans.ca/2009/02/23/no-room-for-gifted-kids

Mennella, J. A., Jagnow, C. P., & Beauchamp, G. K. (2001). Prenatal and postnatal flavor learning by human infants. *Pediatrics, 107,* e88.

Menon, M., Tobin, D. D., Corby, B. C., Menon, M., Hodges, E. V. E., & Perry, D. G. (2007). The developmental costs of high self-esteem for antisocial children. *Child Development, 78,* 1627–1639. doi:10.1111/j.1467–8624.2007.01089.x

Menon, U. (2001). Middle adulthood in cultural perspectives: The imagined and the experienced in three cultures. In M. E. Lachman (Ed.), *Handbook of midlife development* (pp. 40–74). New York, NY: Wiley.

Meririnne, E., Kiviruusu, O., Karlsson, L., Pelkonen, M., Ruuttu, T., Tuisku, V., & Marttunen, M. (2010). Brief report: Excessive alcohol use negatively affects the course of adolescent depression--One year naturalistic follow-up study. *Journal of Adolescence, 33,* 221–226.

Merriam, S. B. (2009). *Qualitative research: A guide to design and implementation.* San Francisco: Jossey-Bass.

Merriman, W. E. (1999). Competition, attention, and young children's lexical processing. In B. MacWhinney (Ed.), *The emergence of language* (pp. 331–358). Mahwah, NJ: Erlbaum.

Merz, E. C., & McCall, R. B. (2011). Parent ratings of executive functioning in children adopted from psychosocially depriving institutions. *Journal of Child Psychology and Psychiatry, 52*(5), 537–546. doi:10.1111/j.1469–7610.2010.02335.x

Merzenich, H., Zeeb, H., & Blettner, M. (2010). Decreasing sperm quality: A global problem? *BMC Public Health, 10,* 24. doi:10.1186/1471-2458–10–24

Mesquita, B., & Leu, J. (2007). The cultural psychology of emotion. In S. Kitayama & D. Cohen (Eds.), *Handbook of cultural psychology* (pp. 734–759). New York, NY: Guilford Press.

Messer, K., Trinidad, D. R., Al-Delaimy, W. K., & Pierce, J. P. (2008). Smoking cessation rates in the United States: A comparison of young adult and older smokers. *American Journal of Public Health, 98,* 317–322. doi:10.2105/ajph.2007.112060

Messinger, D. M., Ruvolo, P., Ekas, N. V., & Fogel, A. (2010). Applying machine learning to infant interaction: The development is in the details. *Neural Networks, 23,* 1004–1016. doi:10.1016/j.neunet.2010.08.008

Meteyer, K., & Perry-Jenkins, M. (2010). Father involvement among working-class, dual-earner couples. *Fathering, 8,* 379–403.

Meyer, D. R., Skinner, C., & Davidson, J. (2011). Complex families and equality in child support obligations: A comparative policy analysis. *Children and Youth Services Review, 33,* 1804–1812. doi:10.1016/j.childyouth.2011.05.011

Meyer, M. H. (2012). Grandmothers juggling work and grandchildren in the United States. In S. Arber & V. Timonen (Eds.), *Contemporary grandparenting: Changing family relationships in global contexts* (pp. 71–90). Bristol, UK: Policy Press.

Midgett, J., Ryan, B. A., Adams, G. R., & Corville-Smith, J. (2002). Complicating achievement and self-esteem: Considering the joint effects of child characteristics and parent-child interactions. *Contemporary Educational Psychology, 77,* 132–143. doi:10.1006.ceps.2001.1083

Miklowitz, D. J., & Cicchetti, D. (Eds.). (2010). *Understanding bipolar disorder: A developmental psychopathology perspective.* New York, NY: Guilford.

Milan, A. (2013). *Fertility: Overview, 2009 to 2011* (Catalogue No. 91–209-X). Retrieved from http://www.statcan.gc.ca/pub/91-209-x/2013001/article/11784-eng.pdf

Milan, A., & Bohnert, N. (2012). *Fifty years of families in Canada: 1961 to 2011: Families, households and marital status, 2011 Census of Population* (Catalogue No. 98–312-X2011003). Retrieved from http://www12.statcan.gc.ca/census-recensement/2011/as-sa/98-312-x/98-312-x2011003_1-eng.pdf

Milan, A., Hou, F., & Wong, I. (2006). Learning disabilities and child altruism, anxiety, and aggression. *Canadian Social Trends* (Catalogue No. 11–008). Retrieved from http://www.statcan.gc.ca/pub/11-008-x/2006001/pdf/9197-eng.pdf

Milan, A., Maheux, H., & Chui, T. (2010). *A portrait of couples in mixed unions* (Catalogue No. 11–008-X). Retrieved from http://www.statcan.gc.ca/pub/11-008-x/2010001/article/11143-eng.htm#tphp

Milan, A., Vézina, M., & Wells, C. (2007) *Family portrait: Continuity and change in Canadian families and households in 2006: Provinces and territories: Quebec.* Retrieved from http://www12.statcan.gc.ca/census-recensement/2006/as-sa/97-553/p24-eng.cfm

Milkman, K. L., Chugh, D., & Bazerman, M. H. (2009). How can decision making be improved? *Perspectives on Psychological Science, 4,* 379–383.

Miller, G. (2010, November 26). New clues about what makes the human brain special. *Science, 330,* 1167.

Miller, G. E., Lachman, M. E., Chen, E., Gruenewald, T. L., Karlamangla, A. S., & Seeman, T. E. (2011). Pathways to resilience: Maternal nurturance as a buffer against the effects of childhood poverty on metabolic syndrome at midlife. *Psychological Science, 22,* 1591–1599. doi:10.1177/0956797611419170

Miller, J. G. (2004). The cultural deep structure of psychological theories of social development. In R. J. Sternberg & E. L. Grigorenko (Eds.), *Culture and competence: Contexts of life success* (pp. 111–138). Washington, DC: American Psychological Association.

Miller, P., & Plant, M. (2010). Parental guidance about drinking: Relationship with teenage psychoactive substance use. *Journal of Adolescence, 33,* 55–68.

Miller, P. H. (2011). *Theories of developmental psychology* (5th ed.). New York, NY: Worth.

Miller, S. W. (2011–2012). Medications and elders: Quality of care or quality of life? *Generations, 35*(4), 19–24.

Mills-Koonce, W. R., Garrett-Peters, P., Barnett, M., Granger, D. A., Blair, C., & Cox, M. J. (2011). Father contributions to cortisol responses in infancy and toddlerhood. *Developmental Psychology, 47,* 388–395. doi:10.1037/a0021066

Minagawa-Kawai, Y., van der Lely, H., Ramus, F., Sato, Y., Mazuka, R., & Dupoux, E. (2011). Optical brain imaging reveals general auditory and language-specific processing in early infant development. *Cerebral Cortex, 21,* 254–261. doi:10.1093/cercor/bhq082

Mindell, J. A., Sadeh, A., Wiegand, B., How, T. H., & Goh, D. Y. T. (2010). Cross-cultural differences in infant and toddler sleep. *Sleep Medicine, 11,* 274–280.

Minister of Justice. (1988). *Canadian multiculturalism act.* Ottawa, ON: Author.

Mintz, T. H. (2005). Linguistic and conceptual influences on adjective acquisition in 24- and 36-month-olds. *Developmental Psychology, 41,* 17–29.

Minuchin, S. (1974). *Families and family therapy.* Cambridge, MA: Harvard University Press.

Minuchin, S., Montalvo, B., Guerney, B., Rosman, B., & Schumer, F. (1967). *Families of the slums.* New York, NY: Basic Books.

Mishra, R. C., Singh, S., & Dasen, P. R. (2009). Geocentric dead reckoning in Sanskrit- and Hindi-medium school children. *Culture & Psychology, 15,* 386–408. doi:10.1177/1354067x09343330

Misra, D. P., Caldwell, C., Young, A. A., & Abelson, S. (2010). Do fathers matter? Paternal contributions to birth outcomes and racial disparities. *American Journal of Obstetrics and Gynecology, 202,* 99–100.

Mitchell, B., Carleton, B., Smith, A., Prosser, R., Bromwell, M., & Kozyrskyj, A. (2008). Trends in psychostimulant and antidepressant use by children in 2 Canadian provinces. *Canadian Journal of Psychiatry, 53,* 152–159.

Mitchell, B. A. (2010). Happiness in midlife parental roles: A contextual mixed methods analysis. *Family Relations, 59,* 326–339. doi:10.1111/j.1741–3729.2010.00605.x

Mitchell, T. L., & Maracle, D. T. (2005). Healing the generations: Post-traumatic stress and the health status of Aboriginal populations in Canada. *Journal of Aboriginal Health, 2,* 14–23. Retrieved from http://www.naho.ca/jah/english/jah02_01/JournalVol2No1ENG4headinggenerations.pdf

Moen, P., & Spencer, D. (2006). Converging divergences in age, gender, health, and well-being: Strategic selection in the third age. In R. H. Binstock & L. K. George (Eds.), *Handbook of aging and the social sciences* (6th ed., pp. 127–144). Amsterdam: Elsevier.

Moen, P., Sweet, S., & Swisher, R. (2005). Embedded career clocks: The case of retirement planning. In R. Macmillan (Ed.), *The structure of the life course: Standardized? Individualized? Differentiated?* (pp. 237–265). Greenwich, CT: Elsevier/JAI Press.

Moffat, S. D. (2005). Effects of testosterone on cognitive and brain aging in elderly men. In R. G. Cutler, S. M. Harman, C. Heward, & M. Gibbons (Eds.), *Longevity health sciences: The Phoenix conference* (Vol. 1055, pp. 80–92). New York, NY: New York Academy of Sciences.

Moffitt, T. E. (2003). Life-course-persistent and adolescence-limited antisocial behavior: A 10-year research review and a research agenda. In B. B. Lahey, T. E. Moffitt, & A. Caspi (Eds.), *Causes of conduct disorder and juvenile delinquency* (pp. 49–75). New York, NY: Guilford Press.

Moffitt, T. E., Caspi, A., & Rutter, M. (2006). Measured gene-environment interactions in psychopathology: Concepts, research strategies, and implications for research, intervention, and public understanding of genetics. *Perspectives on Psychological Science, 1,* 5–27.

Moffitt, T. E., Caspi, A., Rutter, M., & Silva, P. A. (2001). *Sex differences in antisocial behaviour: Conduct disorder, delinquency, and violence in the Dunedin Longitudinal Study.* New York, NY: Cambridge University Press.

Molina, B. S. G., Hinshaw, S. P., Swanson, J. W., Arnold, L. E., Vitiello, B., Jensen, P. S., ... Houck, P. R. (2009). The MTA at 8 years: Prospective follow-up of children treated for combined-type ADHD in a multisite study. *Journal of the American Academy of Child & Adolescent Psychiatry, 48,* 484.

Molitor, A., & Hsu, H.-C. (2011). Child development across cultures. In K. D. Keith (Ed.), *Cross-cultural psychology: Contemporary themes and perspectives* (pp. 75–109). Malden, MA: Wiley-Blackwell.

Moloney, M., MacKenzie, K., Hunt, G., & Joe-Laidler, K. (2009). The path and promise of fatherhood for gang members. *British Journal of Criminology, 49,* 305–325. doi:10.1093/bjc/azp003

Monahan, K. C., Steinberg, L., & Cauffman, E. (2009). Affiliation with antisocial peers, susceptibility to peer influence, and antisocial behavior during the transition to adulthood. *Developmental Psychology, 45,* 1520–1530.

Monastersky, R. (2007, January 12). Who's minding the teenage brain? *Chronicle of Higher Education, 53,* A14–A18.

Monks, C. P., & Coyne, I. (2011). *Bullying in different contexts.* New York, NY: Cambridge University Press.

Monserud, M. A., & Elder, G. H. (2011). Household structure and children's educational attainment: A perspective on coresidence with grandparents. *Journal of Marriage and Family, 73,* 981–1000. doi:10.1111/j.1741–3737.2011.00858.x

Monteiro, C. A., Conde, W. L., & Popkin, B. M. (2004). The burden of disease from undernutrition and overnutrition in countries undergoing rapid nutrition transition: A view from Brazil. *American Journal of Public Health, 94,* 433–434.

Monteiro, C. A., Conde, W. L., & Popkin, B. M. (2007). Income-specific trends in obesity in Brazil: 1975–2003. *American Journal of Public Health, 97,* 1808–1812. doi:10.2105/ajph.2006.099630

Montgomery, L., & Williams, S. (2010). *Countries with the highest college graduation rates.* Retrieved from http://www.csmonitor.com/USA/Education/2010/0809/Countries-with-the-highest-college-graduation-rates/Ireland-43.9-percent

Moody, R. A. (1975). *Life after life: The investigation of a phenomenon—Survival of bodily death.* Atlanta, GA: Mockingbird Books.

Moon, M. (2011). The effects of divorce on children: Married and divorced parents' perspectives. *Journal of Divorce & Remarriage, 52,* 344–349. doi:10.1080/10502556.2011.585093

Moore, G. A., & Calkins, S. D. (2004). Infants' vagal regulation in the still-face paradigm is related to dyadic coordination of mother-infant interaction. *Developmental Psychology, 40,* 1068–1080.

Moore, K. L., Boscardin, W. J., Steinman, M. A., & Schwartz, J. B. (2012). Age and sex variation in prevalence of chronic medical conditions in older residents of U.S. nursing homes. *Journal of the American Geriatrics Society, 60,* 756–764. doi:10.1111/j.1532–5415.2012.03909.x

Moore, K. L., & Persaud, T. V. N. (2003). *The developing human: Clinically oriented embryology* (7th ed.). Philadelphia, PA: Saunders.

Moore, K. L., & Persaud, T. V. N. (2007). *The developing human: Clinically oriented embryology* (8th ed.). Philadelphia, PA: Saunders/Elsevier.

Moore, S., & Rosenthal, D. (2006). *Sexuality in adolescence: Current trends* (2nd ed.). New York, NY: Routledge.

Morasch, K. C., & Bell, M. A. (2009). Patterns of brain-electrical activity during declarative memory performance in 10-month-old infants. *Brain and Cognition, 71,* 215–222.

Morbidity and Mortality Weekly Report (MMWR). (2008, July 11). Disparities in secondhand smoke exposure—United States, 1988–1994 and 1999–2004. *Morbidity and Mortality Weekly Report, 57,* 744–747.

Morbidity and Mortality Weekly Report (MMWR). (2010, June 4). Youth Risk Behavior Surveillance—United States, 2009. *MMWR Surveillance Summaries, 59*(SS5), 1–142.

Morbidity and Mortality Weekly Report (MMWR). (2011, June 10). Sexual identity, sex of sexual contacts, and health-risk behaviors among students in grades 9–12—Youth risk behavior surveillance, selected sites, United States, 2001–2009. *Morbidity and Mortality Weekly Report Surveillance Summaries, 60*(SS07), 1–133.

Morbidity and Mortality Weekly Report (MMWR). (2012, June 8). Youth risk behavior surveillance—United States, 2011. *Morbidity and Mortality Weekly Report, 61*, 4–162.

Morelli, G. A., & Rothbaum, F. (2007). Situating the child in context: Attachment relationships and self-regulation in different cultures. In S. Kitayama & D. Cohen (Eds.), *Handbook of cultural psychology* (pp. 500–527). New York, NY: Guilford Press.

Moreno, C., Laje, G., Blanco, C., Jiang, H., Schmidt, A. B., & Olfson, M. (2007). National trends in the outpatient diagnosis and treatment of bipolar disorder in youth. *Archives of General Psychiatry, 64*, 1032–1039. doi:10.1001/archpsyc.64.9.1032

Moreno, R. P. (1991). Maternal teaching of preschool children in minority and low-status families: A critical review. *Early Childhood Quarterly, 6*, 395–410.

Morgan, I. G. (2003). The biological basis of myopic refractive error. *Clinical and Experimental Optometry, 86*, 276–288.

Morning, A. (2008). Ethnic classification in global perspective: A cross-national survey of the 2000 census round. *Population Research and Policy Review, 27*, 239–272.

Morris, A. S., Silk, J. S., Steinberg, L., Myers, S. S., & Robinson, L. R. (2007). The role of the family context in the development of emotion regulation. *Social Development, 16*, 361–388.

Morris, D. H., Jones, M. E., Schoemaker, M. J., Ashworth, A., & Swerdlow, A. J. (2011). Familial concordance for age at natural menopause: Results from the Breakthrough Generations Study. *Menopause, 18*, 956–961.

Morris, J. A., Jordan, C. L., & Breedlove, S. M. (2004). Sexual differentiation of the vertebrate nervous system. *Nature Neuroscience, 7*, 1034–1039.

Morrison, F. J., Ponitz, C. C., & McClelland, M. M. (2010). Self-regulation and academic achievement in the transition to school. In S. D. Calkins & M. A. Bell (Eds.), *Child development at the intersection of emotion and cognition* (pp. 203–224). Washington, DC: American Psychological Association.

Morrison, M., Tay, L., & Diener, E. (2011). Subjective well-being and national satisfaction. *Psychological Science, 22*, 166–171. doi:10.1177/0956797610396224

Morrissey, T. (2009). Multiple child-care arrangements and young children's behavioral outcomes. *Child Development, 80*, 59–76. doi:10.1111/j.1467–8624.2008.01246.x

Morrow, D. G., Ridolfo, H. E., Menard, W. E., Sanborn, A., Stine-Morrow, E. A. L., Magnor, C., … Bryant, D. (2003). Environmental support promotes expertise-based mitigation of age differences on pilot communication tasks. *Psychology & Aging, 18*, 268–284.

Morrow-Howell, N., & Freedman, M. (2006–2007). Bringing civic engagement into sharper focus. *Generations, 30*(4), 6–9.

Mosher, C. E., & Danoff-Burg, S. (2007). Death anxiety and cancer-related stigma: A terror management analysis. *Death Studies, 31*, 885–907. doi:10.1080/07481180701603360

Mõttus, R., Johnson, W., & Deary, I. J. (2012). Personality traits in old age: Measurement and rank-order stability and some mean-level change. *Psychology and Aging, 27*, 243–249. doi:10.1037/a0023690

Moulson, M. C., Westerlund, A., Fox, N. A., Zeanah, C. H., & Nelson, C. A. (2009). The effects of early experience on face recognition: An event-related potential study of institutionalized children in Romania. *Child Development, 80*, 1039–1056.

Mroczek, D. K., Spiro, A., III, & Griffin, P. W. (2006). Personality and aging. In J. E. Birren & K. W. Schaie (Eds.), *Handbook of the psychology of aging* (6th ed., pp. 363–377). Amsterdam, NL: Elsevier.

Mrozek-Budzyn, D., Kieltyka, A., & Majewska, R. (2010). Lack of association between measles-mumps-rubella vaccination and autism in children: A case-control study. *The Pediatric Infectious Disease Journal, 29*, 397–400.

Mueller, C. E., Bridges, S. K., & Goddard, M. S. (2011). Sleep and parent-family connectedness: Links, relationships and implications for adolescent depression. *Journal of Family Studies, 17*, 9–23.

Mulder, P. J., & Johnson, T. S. (2010). The Beginning Breastfeeding Survey: Measuring mothers' perceptions of breastfeeding effectiveness during the postpartum hospitalization. *Research in Nursing & Health, 33*, 329–344. doi:10.1002/nur.20384

Mulholland, A. (2013, October 18). *Rasouli life-support case: SCC rules consent needed before ending treatment.* Retrieved from http://www.ctvnews.ca/canada/rasouli-life-support-case-scc-rules-consent-needed-before-ending-treatment-1.1502434

Müller, U., Dick, A. S., Gela, K., Overton, W. F., & Zelazo, P. D. (2006). The role of negative priming in preschoolers' flexible rule use on the dimensional change card sort task. *Child Development, 77*, 395–412.

Mullis, I. V. S., Martin, M. O., Foy, P. & Arora, A. (2012a). *TIMSS 2011 international results in mathematics.* Retrieved from http://timss.bc.edu/timss2011/downloads/T11_IR_Mathematics_FullBook.pdf

Mullis, I. V. S., Martin, M. O., Foy, P., & Drucker, K. T. (2012b). *PIRLS 2011 international results in reading.* Chestnut Hill, MA: TIMSS & PIRLS International Study Center, Boston College.

Munck, H. (2009). Early intervention and fatherhood: Denmark. In J. K. Nugent, B. Petrauskas, & T. B. Brazelton (Eds.), *The newborn as a person: Enabling healthy infant development worldwide* (pp. 101–111). Hoboken, NJ: Wiley.

Muñoz, C., & Singleton, D. (2011). A critical review of age-related research on L2 ultimate attainment. *Language Teaching, 44*, 1–35. doi:10.1017/S0261444810000327

Munroe, R. H., Shimmin, H. S., & Munroe, R. L. (1984). Gender understanding and sex role preference in four cultures. *Developmental Psychology, 20*, 673–682.

Munroe, R. L., & Romney, A. K. (2006). Gender and age differences in same-sex aggregation and social behavior: A four-culture study. *Journal of Cross-Cultural Psychology, 37*, 3–19.

Muraco, A. (2006). Intentional families: Fictive kin ties between cross-gender, different sexual orientation friends. *Journal of Marriage and Family, 68,* 1313–1325.

Murphy, B., Zhang, X., & Dionne, C. (2012). Chapter 3: Low income across groups of people. In *Low income in Canada: A multi-line and multi-index perspective* (Catalogue No. 75F0002MW). Retrieved from http://www.statcan.gc.ca/pub/75f0002m/2012001/chap3-eng.htm

Murphy, M. (2011). Long-term effects of the demographic transition on family and kinship networks in Britain. *Population and Development Review, 37*(Suppl. 1), 55–80. doi:10.1111/j.1728–4457.2011.00378.x

Murphy, S. L., Xu, J., & Kochanek, K. D. (2012). Deaths: Preliminary data for 2010. *National Vital Statistics Reports, 60*(4).

Murray, C. J. L., Kulkarni, S. C., Michaud, C., Tomijima, N., Bulzacchelli, M. T., Iandiorio, T. J., & Ezzati, M. (2006). Eight Americas: Investigating mortality disparities across races, counties, and race-counties in the United States. *PLoS Medicine, 3,* e260.

Musick, K., & Bumpass, L. (2012). Reexamining the case for marriage: Union formation and changes in well-being. *Journal of Marriage and Family, 74,* 1–18. doi:10.1111/j.1741–3737.2011.00873.x

Mustard, C. A., Bielecky, A., Etches, J., Wilkins, R., Tjepkema, M., Amick, B. C., … Aronson, K. J. (2013). Mortality following unemployment in Canada, 1991–2001. *BMC Public Health, 13,* 441. doi:10.1186/1471-2458-13-441

Mustard, J. F. (2006). Experience-based brain development: Scientific underpinnings of the importance of early child development in the global world. *Paediatrics & Child Health, 11,* 571–572.

Mustonen, U., Huurre, T., Kiviruusu, O., Haukkala, A., & Aro, H. (2011). Long-term impact of parental divorce on intimate relationship quality in adulthood and the mediating role of psychosocial resources. *Journal of Family Psychology, 25,* 615–619. doi:10.1037/a0023996

Mutti, D. O., & Zadnik, K. (2009). Has near work's star fallen? *Optometry & Vision Science, 86,* 76–78. doi:10.1097/OPX.0b013e31819974ae

N

Nadeau, J. H., & Dudley, A. M. (2011, February 25). Systems genetics. *Science, 331,* 1015–1016.

Nagata, C., Nakamura, K., Wada, K., Oba, S., Hayashi, M., Takeda, N., & Yasuda, K. (2010). Association of dietary fat, vegetables and antioxidant micronutrients with skin ageing in Japanese women. *British Journal of Nutrition, 103,* 1493–1498. doi:10.1017/S0007114509993461

Naicker, K., Wickham, M., & Colman, I. (2012). Timing of first exposure to maternal depression and adolescent emotional disorder in a national Canadian cohort. *PLoS ONE, 7*(3). doi:10.1371/journal.pone.0033422

Naninck, E. F. G., Lucassen, P. J., & Bakker, J. (2011). Sex differences in adolescent depression: Do sex hormones determine vulnerability? *Journal of Neuroendocrinology, 23,* 383–392. doi:10.1111/j.1365–2826.2011.02125.x

Naqvi, R., Liberman, D., Rosenberg, J., Alston, J., & Strauss, S. (2013). Preventing cognitive decline in healthy older adults. *Canadian Medical Association Journal, 185,* 881–885. doi:10.1503/cmaj.121488

Narayan, C. R., Werker, J. F., & Beddor, P. S. (2010). The interaction between acoustic salience and language experience in developmental speech perception: Evidence from nasal place discrimination. *Developmental Science, 13,* 407–420. doi:10.1111/j.1467–7687.2009.00898.x

Narvaez, D., & Lapsley, D. K. (2009). Moral identity, moral functioning, and the development of moral character. In D. Bartels, C. Bauman, L. Skitka & D. Medin (Eds.), *Psychology of learning and motivation* (Vol. 50, pp. 237–274). San Diego, CA: Academic Press.

National Advisory Council on Aging. (2005). *Seniors on the margins: Seniors from ethnocultural minorities* (Catalogue No. H88–5/1-2005E). Retrieved from http://seniorspolicylens.ca/Root/Materials/Seniors%20From%20Ethnocultural%20Minorities%20NACA%202005.pdf

National Association for the Education of Young Children (NAEYC). (2012). All criteria document. Retrieved from http://www.naeyc.org/files/academy/file/AllCriteriaDocument.pdf

National Center for Health Statistics. (2010). *Health, United States, 2009: With special feature on medical technology.* Author: Government Printing Office.

National Center for Health Statistics. (2011). *Health, United States, 2010: With special feature on death and dying.* Hyattsville, MD: Author.

National Crime Prevention Centre. (2013). *Bullying prevention in schools: Executive summary.* Retrieved from http://www.publicsafety.gc.ca/cnt/rsrcs/pblctns/bllng-prvntn-smr/index-eng.aspx

National Defence and the Canadian Armed Forces. (2013). *Welcome to the CF family resources site.* Retrieved from http://www.forces.gc.ca/en/caf-community-health-services-r2mr-deployment/deployment-resources-family-members.page

National Epidemiologic Database for the Study of Autism in Canada (NEDSAC). (2012). *Findings from the National Epidemiologic Database for the Study of Autism in Caada (NEDSAC): Changes in the prevalence of autism spectrum disorders in Newfoundland and Labrador, Prince Edward Island, and Southeastern Ontario.* Retrieved from http://www.nedsac.ca/Publications/FamilyUpdates/NEDSAC_Report_March2012_Key_Findings.pdf

National Institute of Child Health and Human Development (NICHD) Early Child Care Research Network (Ed.). (2005). *Child care and child development: Results from the NICHD Study of Early Child Care and Youth Development.* New York, NY: Guilford Press.

National Institute of Child Health and Human Development (NICHD) Early Child Care Research Network. (2007). Age of entry to kindergarten and children's academic achievement and socioemotional development. *Early Education and Development, 18,* 337–368.

National Seniors Council. (2010). *Report of the National Seniors Council on volunteering among seniors and positive and active aging.* Retrieved from http://www.seniorscouncil.gc.ca/eng/research_publications/volunteering/page07.shtml

Native Women's Association of Canada. (2012). *Healthy babies & children.* Retrieved from http://www.nwac.ca/programs/healthy-babies-children

Neave, N. (2008). *Hormones and behaviour: A psychological approach.* New York, NY: Cambridge University Press.

Needleman, H. L., & Gatsonis, C. A. (1990). Low-level lead exposure and the IQ of children: A meta-analysis of modern studies. *Journal of the American Medical Association, 263,* 673–678.

Needleman, H. L., Schell, A., Bellinger, D., Leviton, A., & Allred, E. N. (1990). The long-term effects of exposure to low doses of lead in childhood. *New England Journal of Medicine, 322,* 83–88. doi:10.1056/NEJM199001113220203

Neimeyer, R. A., & Currier, J. M. (2009). Grief therapy: Evidence of efficacy and emerging directions. *Current Directions in Psychological Science, 18,* 352–356. doi:10.1111/j.1467–8721.2009.01666.x

Nelson, C. A., III, Zeanah, C. H., Fox, N. A., Marshall, P. J., Smyke, A. T., & Guthrie, D. (2007, December 21). Cognitive recovery in socially deprived young children: The Bucharest Early Intervention Project. *Science, 318,* 1937–1940.

Nelson, L. J., Hart, C. H., & Evans, C. A. (2008). Solitary-functional play and solitary-pretend play: Another look at the construct of solitary-active behavior using playground observations. *Social Development, 17,* 812–831. doi:10.1111/j.1467–9507.2008.00470.x

Nelson, R. M., & DeBacker, T. K. (2008). Achievement motivation in adolescents: The role of peer climate and best friends. *Journal of Experimental Education, 76,* 170–189.

Nelson, T. D. (2011). Ageism: The strange case of prejudice against the older you. In R. L. Weiner & S. L. Willborn (Eds.), *Disability and aging discrimination: Perspectives in law and psychology* (pp. 37–47). New York, NY: Springer.

Neugarten, B. L., & Neugarten, D. A. (1986). Changing meanings of age in the aging society. In A. J. Pifer & L. Bronte (Eds.), *Our aging society: Paradox and promise* (pp. 33–52). New York, NY: Norton.

Neumann, A., van Lier, P., Frijns, T., Meeus, W., & Koot, H. (2011). Emotional dynamics in the development of early adolescent psychopathology: A one-year longitudinal study. *Journal of Abnormal Child Psychology, 39,* 657–669. doi:10.1007/s10802–011–9509–3

Nevin, R. (2007). Understanding international crime trends: The legacy of preschool lead exposure. *Environmental Research, 104,* 315–336. doi:10.1016/j.envres.2007.02.008

Nevin, R., Jacobs, D. E., Berg, M., & Cohen, J. (2008). Monetary benefits of preventing childhood lead poisoning with lead-safe window replacement. *Environmental Research, 106,* 410–419.

Newell, K. M., Vaillancourt, D. E., & Sosnoff, J. J. (2006). Aging, complexity, and motor performance. In J. E. Birren & K. W. Schaie (Eds.), *Handbook of the psychology of aging* (6th ed., pp. 163–182). Amsterdam, The Netherlands: Elsevier.

Newnham, C. A., Milgrom, J., & Skouteris, H. (2009). Effectiveness of a modified mother-infant transaction program on outcomes for preterm infants from 3 to 24 months of age. *Infant Behavior and Development, 32,* 17–26.

Ng, E. (2010). *Demographic and socio-economic profile of immigrant seniors in Canada.* Retrieved from http://canada.metropolis.net/events/metropolis_presents/priority_seminar/presentations/ng_panel4_e.pdf

Ng, N., Weinehall, L., & Öhman, A. (2007). 'If I don't smoke, I'm not a real man'—Indonesian teenage boys' views about smoking. *Health Education Research, 22,* 794–804. doi:10.1093/her/cyl104

Nic Gabhainn, S., Baban, A., Boyce, W., Godeau, E., & The HBSC Sexual Health Focus Group. (2009). How well protected are sexually active 15-year olds? Cross-national patterns in condom and contraceptive pill use 2002–2006. *International Journal of Public Health, 54,* 209–215. doi:10.1007/s00038–009–5412–x

Niccols, A. (2007). Fetal alcohol syndrome and the developing socio-emotional brain. *Brain and Cognition, 65,* 135–142.

Nicholson, B., & Parker, L. (2009). *Attached at the heart: 8 proven parenting principles for raising connected and compassionate children.* Bloomington, IN: iUniverse.com.

Nicoladis, E., & Genesee, F. (1996). A longitudinal study of pragmatic differentiation in young bilingual children. *Language Learning, 46,* 439–464. doi:10.1111/j.1467–1770.1996.tb01243.x

Nielsen, M. (2006). Copying actions and copying outcomes: Social learning through the second year. *Developmental Psychology, 42,* 555–565.

Nielsen, M., & Tomaselli, K. (2010). Overimitation in Kalahari Bushman children and the origins of human cultural cognition. *Psychological Science, 21,* 729–736. doi:10.1177/0956797610368808

Nimrod, G. (2007). Expanding, reducing, concentrating and diffusing: Post retirement leisure behavior and life satisfaction. *Leisure Sciences, 29,* 91–111.

Nishida, T. K., & Lillard, A. S. (2007). The informative value of emotional expressions: 'Social referencing' in mother-child pretense. *Developmental Science, 10,* 205–212.

Nishina, A., & Juvonen, J. (2005). Daily reports of witnessing and experiencing peer harassment in middle school. *Child Development, 76,* 435–450.

Nordgren, L. F., van Harreveld, F., & van der Pligt, J. (2009). The restraint bias: How the illusion of self-restraint promotes impulsive behavior. *Psychological Science, 20,* 1523–1528. doi:10.1111/j.1467–9280.2009.02468.x

Norris, D. J. (2010). Raising the educational requirements for teachers in infant toddler classrooms: Implications for institutions of higher education. *Journal of Early Childhood Teacher Education, 31,* 146–158. doi:10.1080/10901021003781221

Northcott, H. C., & Petruik, C. R. (2011). The geographic mobility of elderly Canadians. *Canadian Journal on Aging, 30,* 311–322. doi:10.1353/cja.2011.0045

Nsamenang, A. B. (2004). *Cultures of human development and education: Challenge to growing up African.* New York, NY: Nova Science.

Nucci, L., & Smetana, J. G. (1996). Mothers' concepts of young children's arenas of personal freedom. *Child Development, 67,* 1870–1886. doi:10.1111/j.1467–8624.1996.tb01833.x

Nucci, L., & Turiel, E. (2009). Capturing the complexity of moral development and education. *Mind, Brain, and Education, 3,* 151–159. doi:10.1111/j.1751–228X.2009.01065.x

Nugent, J. K., Petrauskas, B. J., & Brazelton, T. B. (2009). *The newborn as a person: Enabling healthy infant development worldwide.* Hoboken, NJ: Wiley.

Nunavut Department of Education. (2008). *Nunavut education Act 2008.* Retrieved from http://www.edu.gov.nu.ca/apps/UPLOADS/fck/file/EdAct/EA004c-CSFNGuide.pdf

Nyberg, L., & Bäckman, L. (2011). Memory changes and the aging brain: A multimodal imaging approach. In K. W. Schaie & S. L Willis (Eds.), *Handbook of the psychology of aging* (7th ed., pp. 121–131). San Diego, CA: Academic Press.

O

O'Caoimh, R., Gao, Y., Gallagher, P. F., Eustace, J., McGlade, C., & Molloy, D. W. (2013). Which part of the Quick mild cognitive impairment screen (Qmci) discriminates between normal cognition, mild cognitive impairment and dementia? *Age and Ageing, 42,* 324–330. doi: 10.1093/ageing/aft044

O'Donnell, L., Stueve, A., Duran, R., Myint-U, A., Agronick, G., Doval, A. S., & Wilson-Simmons, R. (2008). Parenting practices, parents' underestimation of daughters' risks, and alcohol and sexual behaviors of urban girls. *Journal of Adolescent Health, 42,* 496–502.

O'Donnell, V., & Tait, H. (2003). *Aboriginal peoples survey 2001— Initial findings: Well-being of the non-reserve Aboriginal population* (Catalogue No. 89–589-XIE). Retrieved from http://www.statcan.gc.ca/pub/89-589-x/pdf/4228565-eng.pdf

O'Leary, C. M., Nassar, N., Zubrick, S. R., Kurinczuk, J. J., Stanley, F., & Bower, C. (2010). Evidence of a complex association between dose, pattern and timing of prenatal alcohol exposure and child behaviour problems. *Addiction, 105,* 74–86. doi:10.1111/j.1360–0443.2009.02756.x

O'Malley, A. J., & Christakis, N. A. (2011). Longitudinal analysis of large social networks: Estimating the effect of health traits on changes in friendship ties. *Statistics in Medicine, 30,* 950–964.

O'Neil, K. A., Conner, B. T., & Kendall, P. C. (2011). Internalizing disorders and substance use disorders in youth: Comorbidity, risk, temporal order, and implications for intervention. *Clinical Psychology Review, 31,* 104–112.

O'Rahilly, R. R., & Müller, F. (2001). *Human embryology & teratology* (3rd ed.). New York: Wiley-Liss.

O'Rourke, N., Cappeliez, P., & Claxton, A. (2010a). Functions of reminiscence and the psychological well-being of young-old and older adults over time. *Aging & Mental Health, 15,* 272–281. doi:10.1080/13607861003713281

O'Rourke, N., Neufeld, E., Claxton, A., & Smith, J. Z. (2010b). Knowing me-knowing you: Reported personality and trait discrepancies as predictors of marital idealization between long-wed spouses. *Psychology and Aging, 25,* 412–421. doi:10.1037/a0017873

Oakes, L. M. (2011). *Infant perception and cognition: Recent advances, emerging theories, and future directions.* New York, NY: Oxford University Press.

Oberlander, T. F., & Miller, A. R. (2011). Antidepressant use in children and adolescents: Practice touch points to guide paediatricians. *Paediatrics and Child Health, 16,* 549–553.

Ochsner, K. N., Hughes, B., Robertson, E. R., Cooper, J. C., & Gabrieli, J. D. E. (2009). Neural systems supporting the control of affective and cognitive conflicts. *Journal of Cognitive Neuroscience, 21,* 1842–1855. doi:10.1162/jocn.2009.21129

Offit, P. A. (2008). *Autism's false prophets: Bad science, risky medicine, and the search for a cure.* New York, NY: Columbia University Press.

Ogden, C. L., Gorber, S. C., Dommarco, J. A. R., Carroll, M., Shields, M., & Flegal, K. (2011). The epidemiology of childhood obesity in Canada, Mexico and the United States. In L. A. Moreno, I. Pigeot, & W. Ahrens (Eds.), *Epidemiology of obesity in children and adolescents* (Vol. 2, pp. 69–93). New York, NY: Springer.

Ogrodnik, L. (2010). *Child and youth victims of police-reported violent crime, 2008* (Catalogue No. 85F0033M). Retrieved from http://www.statcan.gc.ca/pub/85f0033m/85f0033m2010023-eng.pdf

Okazaki, S., Okazaki, M., & Sue, S. (2009). Clinical personality assessment with Asian Americans. In J. N. Butcher (Ed.), *Oxford handbook of personality assessment* (pp. 377–395). New York, NY: Oxford University Press.

Oldershaw, L. (2002). *A national survey of parents of young children.* Toronto, ON, Canada: Invest in Kids.

Olshansky, S. J., Antonucci, T., Berkman, L., Binstock, R. H., Boersch-Supan, A., Cacioppo, J. T., … Rowe, J. (2012). Differences in life expectancy due to race and educational differences are widening, and many may not catch up. *Health Affairs, 31,* 1803–1813. doi:10.1377/hlthaff.2011.0746

Olson, K. R., & Dweck, C. S. (2008). A blueprint for social cognitive development. *Perspectives on Psychological Science, 3,* 193–202.

Olson, K. R., & Dweck, C. S. (2009). Social cognitive development: A new look. *Child Development Perspectives, 3,* 60–65. doi:10.1111/j.1750–8606.2008.00078.x

Olson, S. L., Lopez-Duran, N., Lunkenheimer, E. S., Chang, H., & Sameroff, A. J. (2011). Individual differences in the development of early peer aggression: Integrating contributions of self-regulation, theory of mind, and parenting. *Development and Psychopathology, 23,* 253–266. doi:10.1017/S0954579410000775

Olweus, D., Limber, S., & Mahalic, S. F. (1999). *Bullying prevention program.* Boulder, CO: Center for the Study and Prevention of Violence, Institute of Behavioral Science, University of Colorado at Boulder.

Ontai, L. L., & Thompson, R. A. (2008). Attachment, parent-child discourse and theory-of-mind development. *Social Development, 17,* 47–60.

Ontario Dental Association (2008). *Oral health issues for Ontarians: Tooth decay in Ontario's children: An ounce of prevention—A pound of cure.* Retrieved from http://www.oda.on.ca/images/pdfs/ODA_SpecialReport_WEB_booklet.pdf

Ontario Ministry of Education. (2000). *Individual education plans: Standards for development, program planning, and implementation.* Retrieved from http://www.edu.gov.on.ca/eng/general/elemsec/speced/iep/iep.pdf

Ontario Ministry of Education. (2010). *The full-day early learning—kindergarten program.* Retrieved from http://www.edu.gov.on.ca/eng/curriculum/elementary/kindergarten_english_june3.pdf

Ontario Ministry of Education. (2012). *Student success/Learning to 18.* Available from http://www.edu.gov.on.ca/eng/teachers/studentsuccess/index.html

Onunaku, N. (2005). *Improving maternal and infant mental health: Focus on maternal depression.* Retrieved from http://main.zerotothree.org/site/DocServer/maternaldep.pdf

Oregon Public Health Division. (2014). *Oregon's Death with Dignity Act—2013.* Retrieved from http://public.health.oregon.gov/ProviderPartnerResources/EvaluationResearch/DeathwithDignityAct/Documents/year16.pdf

Organisation for Economic Co-operation and Development (OECD). (2006). *Education at a glance: OECD indicators—2006 edition.* Retrieved from http://www.oecd.org/edu/skills-beyond-school/37393408.pdf

Organisation for Economic Co-operation and Development (OECD). (2009). Infant mortality. In *OECD factbook 2009: Economic, environmental and social statistics.* doi:10.1787/factbook-2009-en

Organisation for Economic Co-operation and Development (OECD). (2010a). *PISA 2009 results: Learning to learn: Vol. 3. Student engagement, strategies and practices.* Retrieved from http://www.oecd-ilibrary.org/education/pisa-2009-results-learning-to-learn_9789264083943-en

Organisation for Economic Co-operation and Development (OECD). (2010b). *PISA 2009 survey results.* Retrieved from http://ourtimes.wordpress.com/2008/04/10/oecd-education-rankings/

Organisation for Economic Co-operation and Development (OECD). (2011). *Education at a glance 2011: OECD indicators.* Paris, France: OECD.

Organisation for Economic Co-operation and Development (OECD). (2013). *Pensions at a glance 2013: OECD and G20 indicators.* Retrieved from http://www.oecd.org/pensions/public-pensions/OECDPensionsAtAGlance2013.pdf

Ormerod, T. C. (2005). Planning and ill-defined problems. In R. Morris & G. Ward (Eds.), *The cognitive psychology of planning* (pp. 53–70). New York, NY: Psychology Press.

Osberg, L. (2001). Poverty among senior citizens. In P. Grady & A. Sharpe (Eds.), *The state of economics in Canada: Festschrift in honour of David Slater.* Ottawa, ON: Centre for the Study of Living Standards.

Osorio, S. N. (2011). Reconsidering Kwashiorkor. *Topics in Clinical Nutrition, 26,* 10–13.

Ostfeld, B. M., Esposito, L., Perl, H., & Hegyi, T. (2010). Concurrent risks in sudden infant death syndrome. *Pediatrics, 125,* 447–453. doi:10.1542/peds.2009–0038

Ostrovsky, Y. (2004). Life cycle theory and the residential mobility of older Canadians. *Canadian Journal on Aging, 23* (Suppl.), S23–S37.

Over, H., & Gattis, M. (2010). Verbal imitation is based on intention understanding. *Cognitive Development, 25,* 46–55.

Overbeek, G., Stattin, H., Vermulst, A., Ha, T., & Engels, R. C. M. E. (2007). Parent-child relationships, partner relationships, and emotional adjustment: A birth-to-maturity prospective study. *Developmental Psychology, 43,* 429–437.

Oyekale, A. S., & Oyekale, T. O. (2009). Do mothers' educational levels matter in child malnutrition and health outcomes in Gambia and Niger? *The Social Sciences, 4,* 118–127.

P

Pace, C. S., Zavattini, G. C., & D'Alessio, M. (2011). Continuity and discontinuity of attachment patterns: A short-term longitudinal pilot study using a sample of late-adopted children and their adoptive mothers. *Attachment & Human Development, 14,* 45–61. doi:10.1080/14616734.2012.636658

Padilla-Walker, L. M., Barry, C. M., Carroll, J. S., Madsen, S. D., & Nelson, L. J. (2008). Looking on the bright side: The role of identity status and gender on positive orientations during emerging adulthood. *Journal of Adolescence, 31,* 451–467.

Pagani, L. S., Fitzpatrick, C., Barnett, T. A., & Dubow, E. (2010). Prospective associations between early childhood television exposure and academic, psychosocial, and physical well-being by middle childhood. *Archives of Pediatrics & Adolescent Medicine, 164,* 425–431. doi: 10.1001/archpediatrics.2010.50

Paganini-Hill, A., Kawas, C. H., & Corrada, M. M. (2011). Activities and mortality in the elderly: The leisure world cohort study. *The Journals of Gerontology Series A: Biological Sciences and Medical Sciences, 66A,* 559–567. doi:10.1093/gerona/glq237

Pahwa, R., & Lyons, K. (2013). *Handbook of Parkinson's disease* (5th ed.). Boca Raton, FL: CRC Press.

Paik, A. (2011). Adolescent sexuality and the risk of marital dissolution. *Journal of Marriage and Family, 73,* 472–485. doi:10.1111/j.1741–3737.2010.00819.x

Painter, J. N., Willemsen, G., Nyholt, D., Hoekstra, C., Duffy, D. L., Henders, A. K., … Montgomery, G. W. (2010). A genome wide linkage scan for dizygotic twinning in 525 families of mothers of dizygotic twins. *Human Reproduction, 25,* 1569–1580. doi:10.1093/humrep/deq084

Palagi, E. (2011). Playing at every age: Modalities and potential functions in non-human primates. In P. Nathan & A. D. Pellegrini (Eds.), *The Oxford handbook of the development of play* (pp. 70–82). New York, NY: Oxford University Press.

Palmore, E. (2005). Three decades of research on ageism. *Generations, 29*(1), 87–90.

Pape, B., & Galipeault, J. P. (2002). *Mental health promotion for people with mental illness: A discussion paper.* Ottawa, ON: Public Health Agency of Canada.

Paradis, J., & Genesee, F. (1996). Syntactic acquisition in bilingual children: Autonomous or interdependent? *Studies in Second Language Acquisition, 18,* 1–25. doi: http://dx.doi.org/10.1017/S0272263100014662

Pardini, M., & Nichelli, P. F. (2009). Age-related decline in mentalizing skills across adult life span. *Experimental Aging Research, 35,* 98–106. doi:10.1080/03610730802545259

Park, D. C., & Reuter-Lorenz, P. (2009). The adaptive brain: Aging and neurocognitive scaffolding. *Annual Review of Psychology, 60,* 173–196. doi:10.1146/annurev.psych.59.103006.093656

Park, D. J. J., & Congdon, N. G. (2004). Evidence for an "epidemic" of myopia. *Annals, Academy of Medicine, Singapore, 33,* 21–26.

Park, H., Bothe, D., Holsinger, E., Kirchner, H. L., Olness, K., & Mandalakas, A. (2011). The impact of nutritional status and longitudinal recovery of motor and cognitive milestones in internationally adopted children. *International Journal of Environmental Research and Public Health, 8,* 105–116.

Park, J. (2011). *Retirement, health, and employment among those 55 plus* (Catalogue no. 75–001-X). Retrieved from http://www.statcan.gc.ca/pub/75-001-x/2011001/pdf/11402-eng.pdf

Park, J.-T., Jang, Y., Park, M. S., Pae, C., Park, J., Hu, K.-S., ... Kim, H.-J. (2011). The trend of body donation for education based on Korean social and religious culture. *Anatomical Sciences Education, 4,* 33–38. doi:10.1002/ase.198

Parke, R. D., & Buriel, R. (2006). Socialization in the family: Ethnic and ecological perspectives. In N. Eisenberg (Ed.), *Handbook of child psychology: Vol. 3. Social, emotional, and personality development* (6th ed., pp. 429–504). Hoboken, NJ: Wiley.

Parke, R. D., Coltrane, S., Duffy, S., Buriel, R., Dennis, J., Powers, J., ... Widaman, K. F. (2004). Economic stress, parenting, and child adjustment in Mexican American and European American families. *Child Development, 75,* 1632–1656.

Parladé, M. V., & Iverson, J. M. (2011). The interplay between language, gesture, and affect during communicative transition: A dynamic systems approach. *Developmental Psychology, 47,* 820–833. doi:10.1037/a0021811

Parten, M. B. (1932). Social participation among pre-school children. *The Journal of Abnormal and Social Psychology, 27,* 243–269. doi: 10.1037/h0074524

Parveen, S., & Morrison, V. (2009). Predictors of familism in the caregiver role: A pilot study. *Journal of Health Psychology, 14,* 1135–1143. doi:10.1177/1359105309343020

Parylak, S. L., Koob, G. F., & Zorrilla, E. P. (2011). The dark side of food addiction. *Physiology & Behavior, 104,* 149–156.

Pascarella, E. T. (2005). Cognitive impacts of the first year of college. In R. S. Feldman (Ed.), *Improving the first year of college: Research and practice* (pp. 111–140). Mahwah, NJ: Erlbaum.

Pascarella, E. T., & Terenzini, P. T. (1991). *How college affects students: Findings and insights from twenty years of research.* San Francisco, CA: Jossey-Bass.

Pasch, L. A., & Bradbury, T. N. (1998). Social support, conflict, and the development of marital dysfunction. *Journal of Consulting and Clinical Psychology, 66,* 219–230.

Pashler, H., McDaniel, M., Rohrer, D., & Bjork, R. (2008). Learning styles: Concepts and evidence. *Psychological Science in the Public Interest, 9,* 105–119. doi:10.1111/j.1539–6053.2009.01038.x

Passel, J. S., Wang, W., & Taylor, P. (2010). *Marrying out: One-in-seven new U.S. marriages is interracial or interethnic.* Retrieved from http://www.pewsocialtrends.org/files/2010/10/755-marrying-out.pdf

Patel, V. L., Arocha, J. F., & Kaufman, D. R. (1999). Expertise and tacit knowledge in medicine. In R. J. Sternberg & J. A. Horvath (Eds.), *Tacit knowledge in professional practice: Researcher and practitioner perspectives* (pp. 75–99). Mahwah, NJ: Erlbaum.

Patrick, H., Kaplan, A., & Ryan, A. M. (2011). Positive classroom motivational environments: Convergence between mastery goal structure and classroom social climate. *Journal of Educational Psychology, 103,* 367–382.

Patrick, M. E., & Schulenberg, J. E. (2011). How trajectories of reasons for alcohol use relate to trajectories of binge drinking: National panel data spanning late adolescence to early adulthood. *Developmental Psychology, 47,* 311–317. doi:10.1037/a0021939

Patterson, D. (2007, July 10). Re: *Creative correction* [Online customer book review]. Retrieved from http://www.amazon.com/Creative-Correction-Lisa-Whelchel/product-reviews/1589971280?pageNumber=3

Pausch, J. (2012). *Dream new dreams: Reimagining my life after loss.* New York, NY: Crown Archetype.

Pausch, R. (Producer). (2007). *Randy Pausch last lecture: Achieving your childhood dreams.* [Video] Retrieved from http://www.youtube.com/watch?v=ji5_MqicxSo

Pearce, T. (2012, August 23). 'Gifted'—what is it good for? *The Globe and Mail.* Retrieved from http://www.theglobeandmail.com/news/national/education/gifted---what-is-it-good-for/article570688/?page=all

Pearson, B. Z. (2008). *Raising a bilingual child: A step-by-step guide for parents.* New York, NY: Living Language.

Pearson, B. Z., & Fernandez, S. C. (1994). Patterns of interaction in the lexical development in two languages of bilingual infants. *Language Learning, 44,* 617–653.

Pearson, B. Z., Fernandez, S. C., & Oller, D. K. (1993). Lexical development in bilingual infants and toddlers: Comparison to monolingual norms. *Language Learning, 43,* 93–120. doi: 10.1111/j.1467–1770.1993.tb00174.x

Pedersen, N. L., Spotts, E., & Kato, K. (2005). Genetic influences on midlife functioning. In S. L. Willis & M. Martin (Eds.), *Middle adulthood: A lifespan perspective* (pp. 65–98). Thousand Oaks, CA: Sage.

Pellegrini, A. D. (2009). Research and policy on children's play. *Child Development Perspectives, 3,* 131–136. doi:10.1111/j.1750–8606.2009.00092.x

Pellegrini, A. D. (2011). Introduction. In P. Nathan & A. D. Pellegrini (Eds.), *The Oxford handbook of the development of play* (pp. 3–6). New York, NY: Oxford University Press.

Pellegrini, A. D., Dupuis, D., & Smith, P. K. (2007). Play in evolution and development. *Developmental Review, 27,* 261–276.

Pellegrini, A. D., & Smith, P. K. (Eds.). (2005). *The nature of play: Great apes and humans.* New York, NY: Guilford Press.

Pelletier, J. (2012). *Key findings from year 1 of full-day early learning kindergarten in Peel.* Retrieved from http://www.oise.utoronto.ca/atkinson/UserFiles/File/Publications/Peel_Year_1_FDELK_Summary_Report.pdf

Pellis, S. M., & Pellis, V. C. (2011). Rough-and-tumble play: Training and using the social brain. In P. Nathan & A. D. Pellegrini (Eds.), *The Oxford handbook of the development of play* (pp. 245–259). New York, NY: Oxford University Press.

Peng, D., & Robins, P. K. (2010). Who should care for our kids? The effects of infant child care on early child development. *Journal of Children and Poverty, 16*, 1–45.

Pennisi, E. (2007, May 25). Working the (gene count) numbers: Finally, a firm answer? *Science,* 1113.

Perez, L., Helm, L., Sherzai, A., Jaceldo-Siegl, K., & Sherzai, A. (2012). Nutrition and vascular dementia. *The Journal of Nutrition, Health & Aging, 16*, 319–324.

Perfetti, J., Clark, R., & Fillmore, C.-M. (2004). Postpartum depression: Identification, screening, and treatment. *Wisconsin Medical Journal, 103*, 56–63.

Perls, T. T. (2008). Centenarians and genetics. In C. Y. Read, R. C. Green, & M. A. Smyer (Eds.), *Aging, biotechnology, and the future* (pp. 89–99). Baltimore, MD: Johns Hopkins University Press.

Perner, J. (2000). About + belief + counterfactual. In P. Mitchell & K. Riggs (Eds.), *Children's reasoning and the mind* (pp. 367–401). Hove, England: Psychology Press.

Perner, J., & Lang, B. (2002). What causes 3-year-olds' difficulty on the dimensional change card sorting task? *Infant and Child Development, 11*, 93–105. doii:10.1002/icd.299

Peron, E. P., & Ruby, C. M. (2011–2012, Winter). A primer on medication use in older adults for the non-clinician. *Generations, 35*(4), 12–18.

Perron, A., Brendgen, M., Boivin, M., Vitaro, F., & Tremblay, R. E. (2011). *Playing sports improves academic performances for victimized children.* Paper presented at the SRCD 2011 Biennial Meeting, Montreal, Quebec, Canada.

Perry, D. G., & Pauletti, R. E. (2011). Gender and adolescent development. *Journal of Research on Adolescence, 21*, 61–74. doi:10.1111/j.1532-7795.2010.00715.x

Perry, W. G., Jr. (1981). Cognitive and ethical growth: The making of meaning. In A. W. Chickering (Ed.), *The modern American college: Responding to the new realities of diverse students and a changing society* (pp. 76–116). San Francisco, CA: Jossey-Bass.

Perry, W. G., Jr. (1999). *Forms of intellectual and ethical development in the college years: A scheme.* San Francisco, CA: Jossey-Bass.

Peters, E., Dieckmann, N. F., & Weller, J. (2011). Age differences in complex decision making. In K. W. Schaie & S. L. Willis (Eds.), *Handbook of the psychology of aging* (7th ed., pp. 133–151). San Diego, CA: Academic Press.

Petersen, I., Martinussen, T., McGue, M., Bingley, P., & Christensen, K. (2011). Lower marriage and divorce rates among twins than among singletons in Danish birth cohorts 1940–1964. *Twin Research and Human Genetics, 14*, 150–157.

Peterson, J. B., & Flanders, J. L. (2005). Play and the regulation of aggression. In R. E. Tremblay, W. W. Hartup, & J. Archer (Eds.), *Developmental origins of aggression* (pp. 133–157). New York, NY: Guilford Press.

Peterson, J. W., & Sterling, Y. M. (2009). Children's perceptions of asthma: African American children use metaphors to make sense of asthma. *Journal of Pediatric Health Care, 23*, 93–100.

Pettit, G. S., Erath, S. A., Lansford, J. E., Dodge, K. A., & Bates, J. E. (2011). Dimensions of social capital and life adjustment in the transition to early adulthood. *International Journal of Behavioral Development, 35*, 482–489. doi:10.1177/0165025411422995

Pew Commission on Children in Foster Care. (2004). *Fostering the future: Safety, permanence and well-being for children in foster care.* Retrieved from http://pewfostercare.org/research/docs/FinalReport.pdf

Pew Forum on Religion & Public Life. (2012, July 31). *Two-thirds of democrats now support gay marriage.* Retrieved from http://www.pewforum.org/Politics-and-Elections/2012-opinions-on-for-gay-marriage-unchanged-after-obamas-announcement.aspx

Pew Research Center. (2009, June 29). *Growing old in America: Expectations vs. reality.* Retrieved from http://www.pewsocialtrends.org/2009/06/29/growing-old-in-america-expectations-vs-reality/

Pfeffer, J. (2007). Human resources from an organizational behavior perspective: Some paradoxes explained. *Journal of Economic Perspectives, 21*, 115–134. doi:10.1257/jep.21.4.115

Pfeifer, J. H., Dapretto, M., & Lieberman, M. D. (2010). The neural foundations of evaluative self-knowledge in middle childhood, early adolescence, and adulthood. In P. D. Zelazo, M. Chandler, & E. Crone (Eds.), *Developmental social cognitive neuroscience* (pp. 141–164). New York, NY: Psychology Press.

Pfeiffer, R. E. (2012). *Parkinson's disease and nonmotor dysfunction.* New York, NY: Springer.

Phillips, D. A., Fox, N. A., & Gunnar, M. R. (2011). Same place, different experiences: Bringing individual differences to research in child care. *Child Development Perspectives, 5*, 44–49. doi:10.1111/j.1750-8606.2010.00155.x

Phillips, M. L. (2010). Coming of age? Neuroimaging biomarkers in youth. *American Journal of Psychiatry, 167*, 4–7. doi:10.1176/appi.ajp.2009.09101546

Phillips, T. M., & Pittman, J. F. (2007). Adolescent psychological well-being by identity style. *Journal of Adolescence, 30*, 1021–1034.

Phinney, J. S. (2006). Ethnic identity exploration in emerging adulthood. In J. J. Arnett & J. L. Tanner (Eds.), *Emerging adults in America: Coming of age in the 21st century* (pp. 117–134). Washington, DC: American Psychological Association.

Piaget, J. (1932). *The moral judgment of the child* (M. Gabain, Trans.). London: K. Paul, Trench, Trubner & Co.

Piaget, J. (1932/1997). *The moral judgment of the child* (M. Gabain, Trans.). New York, NY: Simon and Schuster.

Piaget, J. (1945/1962). *Play, dreams and imitation in childhood* (C. Gattegno & F. M. Hodgson, Trans.). New York, NY: Norton.

Piaget, J. (1954). *The construction of reality in the child* (M. Cook, Trans.). New York, NY: Basic Books.

Piaget, J. (1972). *The psychology of intelligence.* Totowa, NJ: Littlefield.

Piaget, J., & Inhelder, B. (1969). *The psychology of the child.* New York, NY: Basic Books.

Piaget, J., Voelin-Liambey, D., & Berthoud-Papandropoulou, I. (2001). *Problems of class inclusion and logical implication* (R. L. Campbell, Ed. and Trans.). Hove, East Sussex, England: Psychology Press.

Pianta, R. C., Barnett, W. S., Burchinal, M., & Thornburg, K. R. (2009). The effects of preschool education. *Psychological Science in the Public Interest, 10,* 49–88. doi:10.1177/1529100610381908

Pietrefesa, A. S., & Evans, D. W. (2007). Affective and neuropsychological correlates of children's rituals and compulsive-like behaviors: Continuities and discontinuities with obsessive-compulsive disorder. *Brain and Cognition, 65,* 36–46.

Pignotti, M. S. (2010). The definition of human viability: A historical perspective. *Acta Pædiatrica, 99,* 33–36. doi:10.1111/j.1651–2227.2009.01524.x

Pilkington, P. D., Windsor, T. D., & Crisp, D. A. (2012). Volunteering and subjective well-being in midlife and older adults: The role of supportive social networks. *The Journals of Gerontology Series B: Psychological Sciences and Social Sciences, 67B,* 249–260. doi:10.1093/geronb/gbr154

Pin, T., Eldridge, B., & Galea, M. P. (2007). A review of the effects of sleep position, play position, and equipment use on motor development in infants. *Developmental Medicine & Child Neurology, 49,* 858–867.

Pinker, S. (2007). *The stuff of thought: Language as a window into human nature.* New York, NY: Viking.

Pinker, S. (2011). *The better angels of our nature: Why violence has declined.* New York, NY: Viking.

Pinquart, M., & Silbereisen, R. K. (2006). Socioemotional selectivity in cancer patients. *Psychology and Aging, 21,* 419–423.

Pinquart, M., & Sörensen, S. (2011). Spouses, adult children, and children-in-law as caregivers of older adults: A meta-analytic comparison. *Psychology and Aging, 26,* 1–14. doi:10.1037/a0021863

Pitskhelauri, G. Z. (1982). *The longliving of Soviet Georgia* (G. Lesnoff-Caravaglia, Trans.). New York, NY: Human Sciences Press.

Planalp, S., & Trost, M. R. (2008). Communication issues at the end of life: Reports from hospice volunteers. *Health Communication, 23,* 222–233.

Pluess, M., & Belsky, J. (2009). Differential susceptibility to rearing experience: The case of childcare. *Journal of Child Psychology and Psychiatry and Allied Disciplines, 50,* 396–404.

Pluess, M., & Belsky, J. (2010). Differential susceptibility to parenting and quality child care. *Developmental Psychology, 46,* 379–390.

Pogrebin, A. (2009). *One and the same: My life as an identical twin and what I've learned about everyone's struggle to be singular.* New York, NY: Doubleday.

Poldrack, R. A., Wagner, A. D., Gotlib, I. H., & Hamilton, J. P. (2008). Neuroimaging and depression: Current status and unresolved issues. *Current Directions in Psychological Science, 17,* 159–163. doi:10.1111/j.1467–8721.2008.00567.x

Pollet, S. L. (2010). Still a patchwork quilt: A nationwide survey of state laws regarding stepparent rights and obligations. *Family Court Review, 48,* 528–540. doi:10.1111/j.1744–1617.2010.01327.x

Poon, L. W. (2008). What can we learn from centenarians? In C. Y. Read, R. C. Green & M. A. Smyer (Eds.), *Aging, biotechnology and the future* (pp. 100–110). Baltimore, MD: Johns Hopkins University.

Popham, L. E., Kennison, S. M., & Bradley, K. I. (2011a). Ageism and risk-taking in young adults: Evidence for a link between death anxiety and ageism. *Death Studies, 35,* 751–763.

Porter, R. H., & Reiser, J. J. (2005). Retention of olfactory memories by newborns. In R. T. Mason, P. M. LeMaster, & D. Müller-Schwarze (Eds.), *Chemical signals in vertebrates* (pp. 300–307). New York, NY: Springer.

Posner, M. I., Rothbart, M. K., Sheese, B. E., & Tang, Y. (2007). The anterior cingulate gyrus and the mechanism of self-regulation. *Cognitive, Affective & Behavioral Neuroscience, 7,* 391–395.

Potter, D. (2010). Psychosocial well-being and the relationship between divorce and children's academic achievement. *Journal of Marriage and Family, 72,* 933–946. doi:10.1111/j.1741–3737.2010.00740.x

Poulin-Dubois, D., & Chow, V. (2009). The effect of a looker's past reliability on infants' reasoning about beliefs. *Developmental Psychology, 45,* 1576–1582.

Poulsen, P., Esteller, M., Vaag, A., & Fraga, M. F. (2007). The epigenetic basis of twin discordance in age-related diseases. *Pediatric Research, 61*(5, Pt. 2), 38R–42R.

Powell, K. (2006). Neurodevelopment: How does the teenage brain work? *Nature, 442,* 865–867.

Powledge, T. M. (2007, October). Easing hormone anxiety. *Scientific American, 297,* 32, 34.

Prado, C. G. (2008). *Choosing to die: Elective death and multiculturalism.* New York, NY: Cambridge University Press.

Pratt, M. W., Norris, J. E., Cressman, K., Lawford, H., & Hebblethwaite, S. (2008). Parents' stories of grandparenting concerns in the three-generational family: Generativity, optimism, and forgiveness. *Journal of Personality, 76,* 581–604.

Presser, H. B., Gornick, J. C., & Parashar, S. (2008). Gender and nonstandard work hours in 12 European countries. *Monthly Labor Review, 131,* 83–103.

Preston, T., & Kelly, M. (2006). A medical ethics assessment of the case of Terri Schiavo. *Death Studies, 30,* 121–133.

PREVNet.ca. (n.d.). *Facts & solutions.* Retrieved from http://www.prevnet.ca/bullying/bullying-facts

Priest, L. (2010). Canada's reputation for low infant mortality takes stunning decline. *The Globe and Mail.* Retrieved from http://www.theglobeandmail.com/news/politics/canadas-reputation-for-low-infant-mortality-takes-stunning-decline/article1211391/

Programme for International Student Assessment (PISA). (2009). *Learning mathematics for life: A perspective from PISA.* Paris, France: OECD.

Proulx, C. M., Helms, H. M., & Buehler, C. (2007). Marital quality and personal well-being: A meta-analysis. *Journal of Marriage and Family, 69,* 576–593.

Provasnik, S., Kastberg, D., Ferraro, D., Lemanski, N., Roey, S., & Jenkins, F. (2012). *Highlights from TIMSS 2011: Mathematics and science achievement of U.S. fourth- and eighth-grade students in an international context.* Washington, DC: National Center for Education Statistics, Institute of Education Sciences, U.S. Department of Education.

Pryor, J. H., DeAngelo, L., Blake, L. P., Hurtado, S., & Tran, S. (2011). *The American freshman: National norms fall 2011.* Los Angeles, CA: Higher Education Research Institute, UCLA.

Public Health Agency of Canada (PHAC). (2008). *Canadian guidelines for sexual health education.* Ottawa, ON: Author.

Public Health Agency of Canada (PHAC). (2009). *Child and youth injury in review, 2009 edition—Spotlight on consumer product safety.* Retrieved from http://www.phac-aspc.gc.ca/publicat/cyi-bej/2009/index-eng.php

Public Health Agency of Canada (PHAC). (2010). *Canadian incidence study of reported child abuse and neglect–2008: Major findings.* Available from http://www.phac-aspc.gc.ca/cm-vee/csca-ecve/2008/index-eng.php

Public Health Agency of Canada (PHAC). (2011a). *Joint statement on safe sleep: Preventing sudden infant deaths in Canada.* Retrieved from http://www.phac-aspc.gc.ca/hp-ps/dca-dea/stages-etapes/childhood-enfance_0-2/sids/pdf/jsss-ecss2011-eng.pdf

Public Health Agency of Canada (PHAC). (2011b). *Vaccines present diseases.* Retrieved from http://www.phac-aspc.gc.ca/im/iyc-vve/prevention-eng.php#diseases

Public Health Agency of Canada (PHAC). (2012a). *Summary: Estimates of HIV prevalence and incidence in Canada, 2011.* Retrieved from http://www.phac-aspc.gc.ca/aids-sida/publication/survreport/estimat2011-eng.php

Public Health Agency of Canada (PHAC). (2012b). *Joint statement on shaken baby syndrome.* Retrieved from http://www.phac-aspc.gc.ca/hp-ps/dca-dea/publications/js-dc-sbs/js-dc-sbs-eng.php

Public Health Agency of Canada (PHAC). (2012c). *Varicella (chicken pox).* Retrieved from http://www.phac-aspc.gc.ca/im/vpd-mev/varicella-eng.php

Public Health Agency of Canada (PHAC), & Canadian Institute for Health Information (CIHI). (2011). *Obesity in Canada: A joint report from the Public Health Agency of Canada and the Canadian Institute for Health Information* (Catalogue No. HP5–107/2011E-PDF). Retrieved from http://www.phac-aspc.gc.ca/hp-ps/hl-mvs/oic-oac/index-eng.php

Puhl, R. M., & Heuer, C. A. (2010). Obesity stigma: Important considerations for public health. *American Journal of Public Health, 100,* 1019–1028. doi:10.2105/AJPH.2009.159491

Pullmann, H., & Allik, J. (2008). Relations of academic and general self-esteem to school achievement. *Personality and Individual Differences, 45,* 559–564.

Pulvermüller, F., & Fadiga, L. (2010). Active perception: Sensorimotor circuits as a cortical basis for language. *Nature Reviews Neuroscience, 11,* 351–360.

Puri, S., & Nachtigall, R. D. (2010). The ethics of sex selection: A comparison of the attitudes and experiences of primary care physicians and physician providers of clinical sex selection services. *Fertility and Sterility, 93,* 2107–2114.

Q

Qiu, C., von Strauss, E., Bäckman, L., Winblad, B., & Fratiglioni, L. (2013). Twenty-year changes in dementia occurrence suggest decreasing incidence in central Stockholm, Sweden. *Neurology, 80,* 1888–1894. doi: 10.1212/WNL.0b013e318292a2f9

Qualls, S. H., & Kasl-Godley, J. E. (2010). *End-of-life issues, grief, and bereavement: What clinicians need to know.* Hoboken, NJ: Wiley.

Quindlen, A. (2012). *Lots of candles, plenty of cake.* New York, NY: Random House.

R

Rabkin, N., & Hedberg, E. C. (2011). *Arts education in America: What the declines mean for arts participation.* Washington, DC: National Endowment for the Arts.

Race, Ethnicity, and Genetics Working Group of the National Human Genome Research Institute. (2005). The use of racial, ethnic, and ancestral categories in human genetics research. *American Journal of Human Genetics, 77,* 519–532.

Rajaratnam, J. K., Marcus, J. R., Flaxman, A. D., Wang, H., Levin-Rector, A., Dwyer, L., ... Murray, C. J. L. (2010). Neonatal, postneonatal, childhood, and under-5 mortality for 187 countries, 1970–2010: A systematic analysis of progress towards Millennium Development Goal 4. *Lancet, 375,* 1988–2008. doi:10.1016/S0140–6736(10)60703–9

Ramakrishnan, U., Goldenberg, T., & Allen, L. H. (2011). Do multiple micronutrient interventions improve child health, growth, and development? *Journal of Nutrition, 141,* 2066–2075. doi:10.3945/jn.111.146845

Ramani, G. B., Brownell, C. A., & Campbell, S. B. (2010). Positive and negative peer interaction in 3- and 4-year-olds in relation to regulation and dysregulation. *Journal of Genetic Psychology, 171,* 218–250.

Ramscar, M., & Dye, M. (2011). Learning language from the input: Why innate constraints can't explain noun compounding. *Cognitive Psychology, 62,* 1–40.

Raphael, D. (2010). The health of Canada's children. Part 1: Canadian children's health in comparative perspective. *Pediatrics & Child Health, 15,* 23–29.

Ray, J. G., Sgro, M., Mamdani, M. M., Glazier, R. H., Bocking, A., Hilliard, R., & Urquia, M. L. (2012). Birth weight curves tailored to maternal world region. *Journal of Obstetrics Gynaecology Canada, 34,* 159–171.

Raymond, N., Beer, C., Glazebrook, C., & Sayal, K. (2009). Pregnant women's attitudes towards alcohol consumption. *BMC Public Health, 9,* 175–183.

Reche, M., Valbuena, T., Fiandor, A., Padial, A., Quirce, S., & Pascual, C. (2011). Induction of tolerance in children with food allergy. *Current Nutrition & Food Science, 7,* 33–39.

Reece, E. A., & Hobbins, J. C. (Eds.). (2007). *Handbook of clinical obstetrics: The fetus & mother handbook* (2nd ed.). Malden, MA: Blackwell.

Reed, K., Beeds, N., Elijah, M. J., Lickers, K., & McLeod, N. (2011). *Aboriginal peoples in Canada.* Toronto, ON: Pearson.

Reese, E., Bird, A., & Tripp, G. (2007). Children's self-esteem and moral self: Links to parent-child conversations regarding emotion. *Social Development, 16*, 460–478.

Reeskens, T., & Wright, M. (2011). Subjective well-being and national satisfaction: Taking seriously the "Proud of what?" question. *Psychological Science, 22*, 1460–1462. doi:10.1177/0956797611419673

Reid, M., & Reczek, C. (2011). Stress and support in family relationships after hurricane Katrina. *Journal of Family Issues, 32*, 1397–1418. doi:10.1177/0192513x11412497

Reijntjes, A., Thomaes, S., Boelen, P., van der Schoot, M., de Castro, B. O., & Telch, M. J. (2011). Delighted when approved by others, to pieces when rejected: Children's social anxiety magnifies the linkage between self- and other-evaluations. *The Journal of Child Psychology and Psychiatry, 52*, 774–781. doi:10.1111/j.1469–7610.2010.02325.x

Reis, H. T., & Collins, W. A. (2004). Relationships, human behavior, and psychological science. *Current Directions in Psychological Science, 13*, 233–237.

Renk, K., Donnelly, R., McKinney, C., & Agliata, A. K. (2006). The development of gender identity: Timetables and influences. In K.-S. Yip (Ed.), *Psychology of gender identity: An international perspective* (pp. 49–68). Hauppauge, NY: Nova Science.

Renkema, L. J., Stapel, D. A., Maringer, M., & van Yperen, N. W. (2008). Terror management and stereotyping: Why do people stereotype when mortality is salient? *Personality and Social Psychology Bulletin, 34*, 553–564. doi:10.1177/0146167207312465

Rentfrow, P. J. (2010). Statewide differences in personality: Toward a psychological geography of the United States. *American Psychologist, 65*, 548–558.

Rentfrow, P. J., Gosling, S. D., & Potter, J. (2008). A theory of the emergence, persistence, and expression of geographic variation in psychological characteristics. *Perspectives on Psychological Science, 3*, 339–369. doi:10.1111/j.1745–6924.2008.00084.x

Rettig, M. (2005). Using the multiple intelligences to enhance instruction for young children and young children with disabilities. *Early Childhood Education Journal, 32*, 255–259.

Reuter-Lorenz, P. A., & Sylvester, C.-Y. C. (2005). The cognitive neuroscience of working memory and aging. In R. Cabeza, L. Nyberg, & D. Park (Eds.), *Cognitive neuroscience of aging: Linking cognitive and cerebral aging* (pp. 186–217). New York, NY: Oxford University Press.

Reutskaja, E., & Hogarth, R. M. (2009). Satisfaction in choice as a function of the number of alternatives: When "goods satiate". *Psychology and Marketing, 26*, 197–203. doi:10.1002/mar.20268

Reynolds, A. J. (2000). *Success in early intervention: The Chicago child-parent centers.* Lincoln, NE: University of Nebraska Press.

Reynolds, A. J., & Ou, S.-R. (2011). Paths of effects from preschool to adult well-being: A confirmatory analysis of the child-parent center program. *Child Development, 82*, 555–582. doi:10.1111/j.1467–8624.2010.01562.x

Reynolds, A. J., Temple, J. A., White, B. A. B., Ou, S.-R., & Robertson, D. L. (2011). Age 26 cost–benefit analysis of the child-parent center early education program. *Child Development, 82*, 379–404. doi:10.1111/j.1467–8624.2010.01563.x

Rhee, K. (2008). Childhood overweight and the relationship between parent behaviors, parenting style, and family functioning. In A. B. Jordan (ed.), *Annals of the American Academy of Political and Social Science: Vol. 615. Overweight and obesity in America's children: Causes, consequences, solutions* (pp. 12–37). San Diego, CA: Sage.

Riccio, C. A., & Rodriguez, O. L. (2007). Integration of psychological assessment approaches in school psychology. *Psychology in the Schools, 44*, 243–255. doi:10.1002/pits.20220

Riccio, C. A., Sullivan, J. R., & Cohen, M. J. (2010). *Neuropsychological assessment and intervention for childhood and adolescent disorders.* Hoboken, NJ: Wiley.

Ridenour, T. A., Meyer-Chilenski, S., & Reid, E. E. (2012). Developmental momentum toward substance dependence: Natural histories and pliability of risk factors in youth experiencing chronic stress. *Drug and Alcohol Dependence, 123*(Suppl. 1), S87–S98.

Rieger, G., & Savin-Williams, R. C. (2012). Gender nonconformity, sexual orientation, and psychological well-being. *Archives of Sexual Behavior, 41*, 611–621.

Riggs, S. A., & Riggs, D. S. (2011). Risk and resilience in military families experiencing deployment: The role of the family attachment network. *Journal of Family Psychology, 25*, 675–687. doi:10.1037/a0025286

Riordan, J. (Ed.). (2005). *Breastfeeding and human lactation* (3rd ed.). Sudbury, MA: Jones and Bartlett.

Riordan, J., & Wambach, K. (Eds.). (2009). *Breastfeeding and human lactation* (4th ed.). Sudbury, MA: Jones and Bartlett.

Ripke, M. N., Huston, A. C., & Casey, D. M. (2006). Low-income children's activity participation as a predictor of psychosocial and academic outcomes in middle childhood and adolescence. In A. C. Huston & M. N. Ripke (Eds.), *Developmental contexts in middle childhood: Bridges to adolescence and adulthood* (pp. 260–282). New York, NY: Cambridge University Press.

Rivas-Drake, D., & Mooney, M. (2009). Neither colorblind nor oppositional: Perceived minority status and trajectories of academic adjustment among Latinos in elite higher education. *Developmental Psychology, 45*, 642–651.

Rivers, I., Poteat, V. P., Noret, N., & Ashurst, N. (2009). Observing bullying at school: The mental health implications of witness status. *School Psychology Quarterly, 24*, 211–223.

Rix, S. E. (2011). Employment and aging. In R. H. Binstock & L. K. George (Eds.), *Handbook of aging and the social sciences* (7th ed., pp. 193–206). San Diego, CA: Academic Press.

Robb, K., Simon, A., & Wardle, J. (2009). Socioeconomic disparities in optimism and pessimism. *International Journal of Behavioral Medicine, 16*, 331–338. doi:10.1007/s12529–008–9018–0

Robelen, E. W. (2011, April 5). Study finds more students learning Mandarin Chinese. *Education Week*, p. 5. Retrieved from http://www.edweek.org/ew/contributors/erik.robelen.html

Roberts, B. W., Walton, K. E., & Viechtbauer, W. (2006). Patterns of mean-level change in personality traits across the life course: A meta-analysis of longitudinal studies. *Psychological Bulletin, 132*, 1–25.

Roberts, K. C., Shields, M., de Groh, M., Aziz, A., & Gilbert, J-A. (2012). *Overweight and obesity in children and adolescents: Results from the 2009 to 2011 Canadian health measures survey by Statistics Canada* (Catalogue No. 82–003-x). Retrieved from http://www.statcan.gc.ca/pub/82-003-x/2012003/article/11706-eng.htm

Roberts, L. (2007, October 26). Battling over bed nets. *Science, 318,* 556–559.

Roberts, R. D., & Lipnevich, A. A. (2012). From general intelligence to multiple intelligences: Meanings, models, and measures. In K. R. Harris, S. Graham, T. Urdan, S. Graham, J. M. Royer & M. Zeidner (Eds.), *APA educational psychology handbook: Vol. 2. Individual differences and cultural and contextual factors* (pp. 33–57). Washington, DC: American Psychological Association.

Roberts, S. (2010, January 1). *Travis Pastrana breaks world record for longest rally car jump on New Year's Eve.* Retrieved from http://www.nydailynews.com

Roberts, W., & Strayer, J. (2008). Empathy, emotional expressiveness, and prosocial behavior. *Child Development, 76,* 449–470. doi:10.1111/j.1467–8624.1996.tb01745.x

Robinson, O. C., Demetre, J. D., & Corney, R. (2010). Personality and retirement: Exploring the links between the Big Five personality traits, reasons for retirement and the experience of being retired. *Personality and Individual Differences, 48,* 792–797.

Robson, R. (2010). Notes on my dying. In N. Bauer-Maglin & D. Perry (Eds.), *Final acts: Death, dying, and the choices we make* (pp. 19–28). New Brunswick, NJ: Rutgers University Press.

Roche, A. F., & Sun, S. S. (2003). *Human growth: Assessment and interpretation.* Cambridge, UK: Cambridge University Press.

Rodkin, P. C., & Roisman, G. I. (2010). Antecedents and correlates of the popular-aggressive phenomenon in elementary school. *Child Development, 81,* 837–850. doi:10.1111/j.1467–8624.2010.01437.x

Rodrigue, K. M., & Kennedy, K. M. (2011). The cognitive consequences of structural changes to the aging brain. In K. W. Schaie & S. L. Willis (Eds.), *Handbook of the psychology of aging* (7th ed., pp. 73–91). San Diego, CA: Academic Press.

Roebers, C. M., Schmid, C., & Roderer, T. (2009). Metacognitive monitoring and control processes involved in primary school children's test performance. *British Journal of Educational Psychology, 79,* 749–767.

Roelfs, D. J., Shor, E., Davidson, K. W., & Schwartz, J. E. (2011). Losing life and livelihood: A systematic review and meta-analysis of unemployment and all-cause mortality. *Social Science Medicine, 72,* 840–854.

Roenneberg, T., Allebrandt, K., Merrow, M., & Vetter, C. (2012). Social jetlag and obesity. *Current Biology, 22,* 939–943.

Rogoff, B. (2003). *The cultural nature of human development.* New York, NY: Oxford University Press.

Roiphe, A. (2009). Grandmothers should be seen and not heard. In B. Graham (Ed.), *Eye of my heart: 27 writers reveal the hidden pleasures and perils of being a grandmother* (pp. 241–250). New York, NY: HarperCollins.

Romano, E., Babchishin, L., Pagani, L. S., & Kohen, D. (2010). School readiness and later achievement: Replication and extension using a nationwide Canadian survey. *Developmental Psychology, 46,* 995–1007. doi: 10.1037/a0018880

Ron, P. (2009). Daughters as caregivers of aging parents: The shattering myth. *Journal of Gerontological Social Work, 52,* 135–153.

Ronay, R., & von Hippel, W. (2010). The presence of an attractive woman elevates testosterone and physical risk taking in young men. *Social Psychological and Personality Science, 1,* 57–64. doi: 10.1177/1948550609352807

Rondal, J. A. (2010). Language in Down syndrome: A life-span perspective. In M. A. Barnes (Ed.), *Genes, brain, and development: The neurocognition of genetic disorders* (pp. 122–142). New York, NY: Cambridge University Press.

Roopnarine, J. L. (2011). Cultural variations in beliefs about play, parent-child play, and children's play: Meaning for childhood development. In P. Nathan & A. D. Pellegrini (Eds.), *The Oxford handbook of the development of play* (pp. 19–39). New York, NY: Oxford University Press.

Rose, A. J., & Asher, S. R. (2004). Children's strategies and goals in response to help-giving and help-seeking tasks within a friendship. *Child Development, 75,* 749–763.

Rose, S. (2008, January 31). Drugging unruly children is a method of social control [Correspondence]. *Nature, 451,* 521.

Roseberry, S., Hirsh-Pasek, K., Parish-Morris, J., & Golinkoff, R. M. (2009). Live action: Can young children learn verbs from video? *Child Development, 80,* 1360–1375.

Rosenberg, R., Mandell, D., Farmer, J., Law, J., Marvin, A., & Law, P. (2010). Psychotropic medication use among children with autism spectrum disorders enrolled in a national registry, 2007–2008. *Journal of Autism and Developmental Disorders, 40,* 342–351. doi:10.1007/s10803–009–0878–1

Rosenfield, R. L., Lipton, R. B., & Drum, M. L. (2009). Thelarche, pubarche, and menarche attainment in children with normal and elevated body mass index. *Pediatrics, 123,* 84–88. doi:10.1542/peds.2008–0146

Rosow, I. (1985). Status and role change through the life cycle. In R. H. Binstock & E. Shanas (Eds.), *Handbook of aging and the social sciences* (2nd ed., pp. 62–93). New York, NY: Van Nostrand Reinhold.

Rosowsky, E. (2007). Loss of the 'supplementary spouse' in marriages in later life. *Generations, 31*(3), 38–40.

Rossi, E., Schippers, M., & Keysers, C. (2011). Broca's area: Linking perception and production in language and actions. In S. Han & E. Pöppel (Eds.), *Culture and neural frames of cognition and communication* (pp. 169–184). New York, NY: Springer Berlin Heidelberg.

Rossignol, D., Rossignol, L., Smith, S., Schneider, C., Logerquist, S., Usman, A., … Mumper, E. (2009). Hyperbaric treatment for children with autism: A multicenter, randomized, double-blind, controlled trial. *BMC Pediatrics, 9,* 21.

Rössler, W., Hengartner, M. P., Ajdacic-Gross, V., Haker, H., Gamma, A., & Angst, J. (2011). Sub-clinical psychosis symptoms in young adults are risk factors for subsequent common mental disorders. *Schizophrenia Research, 131,* 18–23.

Rotermann, M. (2008). *Trends in teen sexual behaviour and condom use.* Statistics Canada Health Reports (Catalogue No. 82–003-X). Retrieved from http://www.statcan.gc.ca/pub/82-003-x/2008003/article/10664-eng.pdf

Rotermann, M. (2012). *Sexual behaviour and condom use of 15- to 24-year-olds in 2003 and 2009/2010* (Catalogue No. 82–003-x). Retrieved from http://www.statcan.gc.ca/pub/82-003-x/2012001/article/11632-eng.htm

Roth, D. L., Ackerman, M. L., Okonkwo, O. C., & Burgio, L. D. (2008). The four-factor model of depressive symptoms in dementia caregivers: A structural equation model of ethnic differences. *Psychology and Aging, 23,* 567–576. doi:10.1037/a0013287

Roth, D. L., Mittelman, M. S., Clay, O. J., Madan, A., & Haley, W. E. (2005). Changes in social support as mediators of the impact of a psychosocial intervention for spouse caregivers of persons with Alzheimer's disease. *Psychology and Aging, 20,* 634–644.

Rothbart, M. K., & Bates, J. E. (2006). Temperament. In N. Eisenberg (Ed.), *Handbook of child psychology: Vol. 3. Social, emotional, and personality development* (6th ed., pp. 99–166). Hoboken, NJ: Wiley.

Rothbaum, F., Morelli, G., & Rusk, N. (2011). Attachment, learning and coping: The interplay of cultural similarities and differences. In M. J. Gelfand, C. Chiu, & Y. Hong (Eds.), *Advances in culture and psychology* (Vol. 1, pp. 153–216). New York, NY: Oxford University Press.

Rothermund, K. (2005). Effects of age stereotypes on self-views and adaptation. In W. Greve, K. Rothermund, & D. Wentura (Eds.), *The adaptive self* (pp. 223–242). Cambrige, MA: Hogrefe & Huber.

Rothrauff, T. C., Cooney, T. M., & An, J. S. (2009). Remembered parenting styles and adjustment in middle and late adulthood. *The Journals of Gerontology Series B: Psychological Sciences and Social Sciences, 64B,* 137–146. doi:10.1093/geronb/gbn008

Rovee-Collier, C. (1987). Learning and memory in infancy. In J. Doniger Osofsky (Ed.), *Handbook of infant development* (2nd ed., pp. 98–148). New York, NY: Wiley.

Rovee-Collier, C. (1990). The "memory system" of prelinguistic infants. In A. Diamond (Ed.), *The development and neural bases of higher cognitive functions* (Vol. 608, pp. 517–542). New York, NY: New York Academy of Sciences.

Rovee-Collier, C., & Cuevas, K. (2009). The development of infant memory. In M. L. Courage & N. Cowan (Eds.), *The development of memory in infancy and childhood* (2nd ed., pp. 11–41). New York, NY: Psychology Press.

Rovi, S., Chen, P.-H., & Johnson, M. S. (2004). The economic burden of hospitalizations associated with child abuse and neglect. *American Journal of Public Health, 94,* 586–590.

Rubin, K. H. (2004). *Three things to know about friendships.* Retrieved from http://www.rubin-lab.umd.edu/pubs/Downloadable%20pdfs/kenneth_rubin/Friendship/Three%20Things%20to%20Know%20about%20Friendship.pdf

Rubin, K. H., Bukowski, W., & Parker, J. (1998). Peer interactions, relationships, and groups. In N. Eisenberg (Ed.), *Handbook of child psychology: Social, emotional, and personality development* (5th ed.). (pp. 619–700). New York, NY: Wiley.

Rubin, K. H., Coplan, R. J., & Bowker, J. C. (2009). Social withdrawal in childhood. *Annual Review of Psychology, 60,* 141–171. doi:10.1146/annurev.psych.60.110707.163642

Ruble, D. N., Martin, C. L., & Berenbaum, S. (2006). Gender development. In N. Eisenberg (Ed.), *Handbook of child psychology: Vol. 3. Social, emotional, and personality development* (6th ed., pp. 858–932). Hoboken, NJ: Wiley.

Ruder, D. B. (2008, September-October). The teen brain. *Harvard Magazine, 111,* 8–10.

Rueda, M. R., Rothbart, M. K., Saccomanno, L., & Posner, M. I. (2007). Modifying brain networks underlying self regulation. In D. Romer & E. F. Walker (Eds.), *Adolescent psychopathology and the developing brain: Integrating brain and prevention science* (pp. 401–419). Oxford, UK: Oxford University Press.

Rulfs, M. (2011). Marking death: Grief, protest and politics after a fatal traffic accident *Grassroots memorials: The politics of memorializing traumatic death* (pp. 145–168). New York, NY: Berghahn Books.

Ruthig, J. C., Trisko, J., & Stewart, T. L. (2012). The impact of spouse's health and well-being on own well-being: A dyadic study of older married couples. *Journal of Social and Clinical Psychology, 31,* 508–529. doi:10.1521/jscp.2012.31.5.508

Rutter, M. (2006). The psychological effects of early institutional rearing. In P. J. Marshall & N. A. Fox (Eds.), *The development of social engagement: Nerurobiolgoical perspectives* (pp. 355–391). New York, NY: Oxford University Press.

Rutter, M., Colvert, E., Kreppner, J., Beckett, C., Castle, J., Groothues, C., ... Sonuga-Barke, E. J. S. (2007). Early adolescent outcomes for institutionally-deprived and non-deprived adoptees: I. Disinhibited attachment. *Journal of Child Psychology and Psychiatry, 48,* 17–30.

Rutter, M., Sonuga-Barke, E. J., Beckett, C., Castle, J., Kreppner, J., Kumsta, R., ... Gunnar, M. R. (2010). Deprivation-specific psychological patterns: Effects of institutional deprivation. *Monographs of the Society for Research in Child Development, 75*(1, Serial No. 295), 1–252.

Rutters, F., Nieuwenhuizen, A. G., Vogels, N., Bouwman, F., Mariman, E., & Westerterp-Plantenga, M. S. (2008). Leptin-adiposity relationship changes, plus behavioral and parental factors, are involved in the development of body weight in a Dutch children cohort. *Physiology & Behavior, 93,* 967–974.

Ruys, J. H., de Jonge, G. A., Brand, R., Engelberts, A., C., & Semmekrot, B. A. (2007). Bed-sharing in the first four months of life: A risk factor for sudden infant death. *Acta Pædiatrica, 96,* 1399–1403.

Ryan, R. M., & Deci, E. L. (2000). Self-determination theory and the facilitation of intrinsic motivation, social development, and well-being. *American Psychologist, 55,* 68–78.

Ryan, S., Franzetta, K., Manlove, J., & Holcombe, E. (2007). Adolescents' discussions about contraception or STDs with partners before first sex. *Perspectives on Sexual and Reproductive Health, 39,* 149–157.

Ryan, S., Franzetta, K., Manlove, J. S., & Schelar, E. (2008). Older sexual partners during adolescence: Links to reproductive health outcomes in young adulthood. *Perspectives on Sexual and Reproductive Health, 40,* 17–26.

Rydell, R. J., & Boucher, K. L. (2010). Capitalizing on multiple social identities to prevent stereotype threat: The moderating role of self-esteem. *Personality and Social Psychology Bulletin, 36,* 239–250. doi:10.1177/0146167209355062

S

Saarni, C., Campos, J. J., Camras, L. A., & Witherington, D. (2006). Emotional development: Action, communication, and understanding. In N. Eisenberg (Ed.), *Handbook of child psychology: Vol. 3. Social, emotional, and personality development* (6th ed., pp. 226–299). Hoboken, NJ: Wiley.

Sabatino, C. P. (2010). The evolution of health care advance planning law and policy. *Milbank Quarterly, 88,* 211–239. doi:10.1111/j.1468–0009.2010.00596.x

Sacks, O. W. (1995). *An anthropologist on Mars: Seven paradoxical tales.* New York, NY: Knopf.

Sadeh, A., Mindell, J. A., Luedtke, K., & Wiegand, B. (2009). Sleep and sleep ecology in the first 3 years: A web-based study. *Journal of Sleep Research, 18,* 60–73.

Sadeh, A., Tikotzky, L., & Scher, A. (2010). Parenting and infant sleep. *Sleep Medicine Reviews, 14,* 89–96.

Sadler, T. W. (2012). *Langman's medical embryology* (12th ed.). Baltimore, MD: Lippincott Williams & Wilkins.

Saewyc, E. M. (2011). Research on adolescent sexual orientation: Development, health disparities, stigma, and resilience. *Journal of Research on Adolescence, 21,* 256–272. doi:10.1111/j.1532–7795.2010.00727.x

Saewyc, E. M., Taylor, D., Homma, Y., & Ogilvie, G. (2008). Trends in sexual health and risk behaviours among adolescent students in British Columbia. *The Canadian Journal of Human Sexuality, 17,* 1–14.

Saffran, J. R., Werker, J. F., & Werner, L. A. (2006). The infant's auditory world: Hearing, speech, and the beginnings of language. In D. Kuhn & R. S. Siegler (Eds.), *Handbook of child psychology: Vol. 2. Cognition, perception, and language* (pp. 58–108). Hoboken, NJ: Wiley.

Sahlberg, P. (2011). *Finnish lessons: What can the world learn from educational change in Finland?* New York, NY: Teachers College Press.

Sakai, C., Lin, H., & Flores, G. (2011). Health outcomes and family services in kinship care: Analysis of a national sample of children in the child welfare system. *Archives of Pediatrics & Adolescent Medicine, 165,* 159–165.

Salkind, N. J. (2004). *An introduction to theories of human development.* Thousand Oaks, CA: Sage.

Salmivalli, C. (2010). Bullying and the peer group: A review. *Aggression and Violent Behavior, 15,* 112–120.

Salthouse, T. A. (2006). Mental exercise and mental aging: Evaluating the validity of the "use it or lose it" hypothesis. *Perspectives on Psychological Science, 1,* 68–87.

Salthouse, T. A. (2010). *Major issues in cognitive aging.* New York, NY: Oxford University Press.

Salvatore, J., & Shelton, J. N. (2007). Cognitive costs of exposure to racial prejudice. *Psychological Science, 18,* 810–815.

Sam, D. L., & Virta, E. (2001). Social group identity and its effect on the self-esteem of adolescents with immigrant background in Norway and Sweden. In R. G. Craven & H. W. Mars (Eds.), *Self-concept theory, research and practices: Advances for the new millennium* (pp. 366–378). Sydney, AU: Self Research Center, University of Western Sydney.

Samarin, B., & Chuang, S. S. (2012, March). *Mothers, fathers, sons, and daughters: An exploration in parent-youth relationships in Croatian families.* Poster presented at the biennial meetings of the Society for Research on Adolescence, Vancouver, BC.

Samji H., & Wardman A. E. D. (2009). First Nations communities and tobacco taxation: A commentary. *American Indian and Alaska Native Mental Health Research, 6,* 1–10.

Sander, T. H., & Putnam, R. D. (2010). Still bowling alone? The post-9/11 split. *Journal of Democracy, 21*(1), 9–16.

Sanders, G. (2010). The dismal trade as culture industry. *Poetics, 38,* 47–68. doi:10.1016/j.poetic.2009.08.001

Sandstrom, M. J., & Zakriski, A. L. (2004). Understanding the experience of peer rejection. In J. B. Kupersmidt & K. A. Dodge (Eds.), *Children's peer relations: From development to intervention* (pp. 101–118). Washington, DC: American Psychological Association.

Sanson, A., Smart, D., & Misson, S. (2011). Children's socio-emotional, physical, and cognitive outcomes: Do they share the same drivers? *Australian Journal of Psychology, 63,* 56–74. doi:10.1111/j.1742–9536.2011.00007.x

Santelli, J. S., & Melnikas, A. J. (2010). Teen fertility in transition: Recent and historic trends in the United States. *Annual Review of Public Health, 31,* 371–383. doi:10.1146/annurev.publhealth.29.020907.090830

Santosh, P. J., & Canagaratnam, M. (2008). Paediatric bipolar disorder—An update. *Psychiatry, 7,* 349–352.

Saraceno, C. (2010). Social inequalities in facing old-age dependency: A bi-generational perspective. *Journal of European Social Policy, 20,* 32–44. doi:10.1177/0958928709352540

Saskatchewan Education. (2000). *Directions for diversity: Enhancing supports to children and youth with diverse needs.* Retrieved from http://www.education.gov.sk.ca/Directions-for-Diversity

Sassler, S., Addo, F. R., & Lichter, D. T. (2012). The tempo of sexual activity and later relationship quality. *Journal of Marriage and Family, 74,* 708–725. doi:10.1111/j.1741–3737.2012.00996.x

Satariano, W. (2006). *Epidemiology of aging: An ecological approach.* Sudbury, MA: Jones and Bartlett.

Saul, S. (2008, July 26). Weight drives the young to adult pills, data says. *New York Times.* Retrieved from http://www.nytimes.com/2008/07/26/business/26kidmed.html?pagewanted=all

Saunders, C. M. (1978). *The management of terminal disease.* London, England: Arnold.

Savic, I. (Ed.). (2010). *Progress in Brain Research: Vol. 186. Sex differences in the human brain, their underpinnings and implications.* Amsterdam, The Netherlands: Elsevier.

Saw, S.-M., Cheng, A., Fong, A., Gazzard, G., Tan, D. T. H., & Morgan, I. (2007). School grades and myopia. *Ophthalmic and Physiological Optics, 27,* 126–129.

Saxton, M. (2010). *Child language: Acquisition and development.* Thousand Oaks, CA: SAGE.

Saylor, M. M., & Sabbagh, M. A. (2004). Different kinds of information affect word learning in the preschool years: The case of part-term learning. *Child Development, 75,* 395–408.

Scannapieco, M., & Connell-Carrick, K. (2005). *Understanding child maltreatment: An ecological and developmental perspective.* New York, NY: Oxford University Press.

Scarf, M. (2008). *September songs: The good news about marriage in the later years.* New York, NY: Riverhead Books.

Scarr, S. (1985). Constructing psychology: Making facts and fables for our times. *American Psychologist, 40,* 499–512. doi:10.1037/0003-066x.40.5.499

Schaal, B., Marlier, L., & Soussignan, R. (2000). Human fetuses learn odours from their pregnant mother's diet. *Chemical Senses, 25,* 729–737. doi:10.1093/chemse/25.6.729

Schachter, S. R. (2003). 9/11: A grief therapist's journal. In M. Lattanzi-Licht, K. Doka, & J. D. Gordon (Eds.), *Living with grief: Coping with public tragedy* (pp. 15–25). New York, NY: Brunner-Routledge.

Schafer, G. (2005). Infants can learn decontextualized words before their first birthday. *Child Development, 76,* 87–96.

Schaie, K. W. (2005). *Developmental influences on adult intelligence: The Seattle longitudinal study* (Rev. ed.). New York, NY: Oxford University Press.

Schanler, R. J. (2011). Outcomes of human milk-fed premature infants. *Seminars in Perinatology, 35,* 29–33. doi:10.1053/j.semperi.2010.10.005

Scharlach, A., Graham, C., & Lehning, A. (2012). The "Village" model: A consumer-driven approach for aging in place. *The Gerontologist, 52,* 418–427. doi:10.1093/geront/gnr083

Schauer, D. P., Arterburn, D. E., Livingston, E. H., Fischer, D., & Eckman, M. H. (2010). Decision modeling to estimate the impact of gastric bypass surgery on life expectancy for the treatment of morbid obesity. *Archives of Surgery, 145,* 57–62. doi:10.1001/archsurg.2009.240

Scheffler, R. M., Brown, T. T., Fulton, B. D., Hinshaw, S. P., Levine, P., & Stone, S. (2009). Positive association between attention-deficit/hyperactivity disorder medication use and academic achievement during elementary school. *Pediatrics, 123,* 1273–1279. doi:10.1542/peds.2008–1597

Scheibehenne, B., Greifeneder, R., & Todd, P. M. (2010). Can there ever be too many options? A meta-analytic review of choice overload. *Journal of Consumer Research, 37,* 409–425. doi:10.1086/651235

Schermerhorn, A. C., D'Onofrio, B. M., Turkheimer, E., Ganiban, J. M., Spotts, E. L., Lichtenstein, P., ... Neiderhiser, J. M. (2011). A genetically informed study of associations between family functioning and child psychosocial adjustment. *Developmental Psychology, 47,* 707–725. doi:10.1037/a0021362

Schmader, T. (2010). Stereotype threat deconstructed. *Current Directions in Psychological Science, 19,* 14–18. doi:10.1177/0963721409359292

Schmader, T., Johns, M., & Forbes, C. (2008). An integrated process model of stereotype threat effects on performance. *Psychological Review, 115,* 336–356. doi:10.1037/0033-295x.115.2.336

Schneider, S. K., O'Donnell, L., Stueve, A., & Coulter, R. W. S. (2011). Cyberbullying, school bullying, and psychological distress: A regional census of high school students. *American Journal of Public Health, 102,* 171–177. doi:10.2105/ajph.2011.300308

Schneider, W., & Lockl, K. (2008). Procedural metacognition in children: Evidence for developmental trends. In J. Dunlosky & R. A. Bjork (Eds.), *Handbook of metamemory and memory* (pp. 391–409). New York, NY: Psychology Press.

Schofield, T. J., Martin, M. J., Conger, K. J., Neppl, T. M., Donnellan, M. B., & Conger, R. D. (2011). Intergenerational transmission of adaptive functioning: A test of the interactionist model of SES and human development. *Child Development, 82,* 33–47. doi:10.1111/j.1467–8624.2010.01539.x

Schön, D., Boyer, M., Moreno, S., Besson, M., Peretz, I., & Kolinsky, R. (2008). Songs as an aid for language acquisition. *Cognition, 106,* 975–983.

Schore, A., & McIntosh, J. (2011). Family law and the neuroscience of attachment, part I. *Family Court Review, 49,* 501–512. doi:10.1111/j.1744–1617.2011.01387.x

Schreck, C. J., Burek, M. W., Stewart, E. A., & Miller, J. M. (2007). Distress and violent victimization among young adolescents: Early puberty and the social interactionist explanation. *Journal of Research in Crime and Delinquency, 44,* 381–405.

Schulenberg, J., O'Malley, P. M., Bachman, J. G., & Johnston, L. D. (2005). Early adult transitions and their relation to well-being and substance use. In R. A. Settersten, Jr., F. F. Furstenberg, & R. G. Rumbaut (Eds.), *On the frontier of adulthood: Theory, research, and public policy* (pp. 417–453). Chicago, IL: University of Chicago Press.

Schupp, J., & Sharp, J. (2012). Exploring the social bases of home gardening. *Agriculture and Human Values, 29,* 93–105. doi:10.1007/s10460–011–9321–2

Schwartz, A. E., Stiefel, L., Rubenstein, R., & Zabel, J. (2011). The path not taken: How does school organization affect eighth-grade achievement? *Educational Evaluation and Policy Analysis, 33,* 293–317. doi:10.3102/0162373711407062

Schwartz, P. D., Maynard, A. M., & Uzelac, S. M. (2008). Adolescent egocentrism: A contemporary view. *Adolescence, 43,* 441–448.

Schweinhart, L. J., Montie, J., Xiang, Z., Barnett, W. S., Belfield, C. R., & Nores, M. (2005). *Lifetime effects: The High/Scope Perry Preschool Study through age 40.* Ypsilanti, MI: High/Scope Press.

Schweinhart, L. J., & Weikart, D. P. (1997). *Lasting differences: The High/Scope Preschool Curriculum Comparison Study through age 23.* Ypsilanti, MI: High/Scope Educational Research Foundation.

Schytt, E., & Waldenström, U. (2010). Epidural analgesia for labor pain: Whose choice? *Acta Obstetricia et Gynecologica Scandinavica, 89,* 238–242. doi:10.3109/00016340903280974

Scott, L. S., & Monesson, A. (2010). Experience-dependent neural specialization during infancy. *Neuropsychologia, 48,* 1857–1861.

Scott, L. S., Pascalis, O., & Nelson, C. A. (2007). A domain-general theory of the development of perceptual discrimination. *Current Directions in Psychological Science, 16,* 197–201.

Sebastian, C., Burnett, S., & Blakemore, S.-J. (2008). Development of the self-concept during adolescence. *Trends in Cognitive Sciences, 12,* 441–446.

Sebastián-Gallés, N. (2007). Biased to learn language. *Developmental Science, 10,* 713–718. doi:10.1111/j.1467-7687.2007.00649.x

Sedivy, J. M., Munoz-Najar, U. M., Jeyapalan, J. C., & Campisi, J. (2008). Cellular senescence: A link between tumor suppression and organismal aging? In L. P. Guarente, L. Partridge, & D. C. Wallace (Eds.), *Molecular biology of aging* (pp. 185–214). Cold Spring Harbor, NY: Cold Spring Harbor Laboratory Press.

Seelaar, H., Rohrer, J. D., Pijnenburg, Y. A. L., Fox, N. C., & van Swieten, J. C. (2011). Clinical, genetic and pathological heterogeneity of frontotemporal dementia: A review. *Journal of Neurology, Neurosurgery & Psychiatry, 82,* 476–486. doi:10.1136/jnnp.2010.212225

Seery, M. D. (2011). Resilience: A silver lining to experiencing adverse life events? *Current Directions in Psychological Science, 20,* 390–394. doi:10.1177/0963721411424740

Seifer, R., LaGasse, L. L., Lester, B., Bauer, C. R., Shankaran, S., Bada, H. S., … Liu, J. (2004). Attachment status in children prenatally exposed to cocaine and other substances. *Child Development, 75,* 850–868.

Seki, F. (2001). The role of the government and the family in taking care of the frail elderly: A comparison of the United States and Japan. In D. N. Weisstub, D. C. Thomasma, S. Gauthier, & G. F. Tomossy (Eds.), *Aging: Caring for our elders* (pp. 83–105). Dordrecht, The Netherlands: Kluwer.

Seligman, H. K., & Schillinger, D. (2010). Hunger and socioeconomic disparities in chronic disease. *New England Journal of Medicine, 363,* 6–9. doi:10.1056/NEJMp1000072

Senioropolis.com. (n.d.). *Nursing home rates across Canada.* Retrieved from http://www.senioropolis.com/article-general.asp?ID=41

Senju, A., Southgate, V., Miura, Y., Matsui, T., Hasegawa, T., Tojo, Y., … Csibra, G. (2010). Absence of spontaneous action anticipation by false belief attribution in children with autism spectrum disorder. *Development and Psychopathology, 22,* 353–360. doi:10.1017/S0954579410000106

Setlik, J., Bond, G. R., & Ho, M. (2009). Adolescent prescription ADHD medication abuse is rising along with prescriptions for these medications. *Pediatrics, 124,* 875–880. doi:10.1542/peds.2008-0931

Settersten, R. A. (2002). Social sources of meaning in later life. In R. S. Weiss & S. A. Bass (Eds.), *Challenges of the third age: Meaning and purpose in later life* (pp. 55–79). London, England: Oxford University Press.

Shai, I., & Stampfer, M. J. (2008). Weight-loss diets—Can you keep it off? *American Journal of Clinical Nutrition, 88,* 1185–1186. doi:10.3945/ajcn.2008.26876

Shakya, H. B., Usita, P. M., Eisenberg, C., Weston, J., & Liles, S. (2012). Family well-being concerns of grandparents in skipped generation families. *Journal of Gerontological Social Work, 55,* 39–54. doi:10.1080/01634372.2011.620072

Shanahan, M. J., & Hofer, S. M. (2011). Molecular genetics, aging, and well-being: Sensitive period, accumulation, and pathway models. In R. H. Binstock & L. K. George (Eds.), *Handbook of aging and the social sciences* (7th ed., pp. 135–147). San Diego, CA: Academic Press.

Shanahan, T., & Lonigan, C. J. (2010). The National Early Literacy Panel: A summary of the process and the report. *Educational Researcher, 39,* 279–285. doi:10.3102/0013189x10369172

Shannon, J. B. (Ed.). (2007). *Eating disorders sourcebook: Basic consumer health information about anorexia nervosa, bulimia nervosa, binge eating, compulsive exercise, female athlete triad, and other eating disorders* (2nd ed.). Detroit, MI: Omnigraphics.

Shapiro, E. S., Zigmond, N., Wallace, T., & Marston, D. (Eds.). (2011). *Models for implementing response to intervention: Tools, outcomes, and implications.* New York, NY: Guilford Press.

Shapiro, J. A. (2009). Revisiting the central dogma in the 21st century. In G. Witzany (Ed.), *Annals of the New York Academy of Sciences: Vol. 1178. Natural genetic engineering and natural genome editing* (pp. 6–28). Malden, MA: Wiley.

Shapiro, M. F. (2011). *Mothers' feelings about physical and emotional intimacy twelve to fifteen months after the birth of a first child.* (M.S.W. Thesis), Smith College, Northampton, MA. Retrieved from https://dspace.smith.edu/handle/11020/23004

Sharif, K. W., & Coomarasamy, A. (Eds.). (2012). *Assisted reproduction techniques: Challenges and management options.* Chichester, West Sussex, UK: Wiley-Blackwell.

Sharkey, S. S., Hudak, S., Horn, S. D., James, B., & Howes, J. (2011). Frontline caregiver daily practices: A comparison study of traditional nursing homes and the green house project sites. *Journal of the American Geriatrics Society, 59,* 126–131. doi:10.1111/j.1532-5415.2010.03209.x

Sharpe, A. & Arsenault, J-F. (2010). *Investing in Aboriginal education in Canada: An economic perspective.* Retrieved from http://www.csls.ca/reports/csls2010-03.pdf

Sharples, T. (2009, January 4). Have Americans gone nuts over food allergies? *Time.* Retrieved from http://content.time.com/time/health/article/0,8599,1869095,00.html

Shattuck, P. T. (2006). The contribution of diagnostic substitution to the growing administrative prevalence of autism in US special education. *Pediatrics, 117,* 1028–1037. doi:10.1542/peds.2005-1516

Sheehy, G. (1976). *Passages: Predictable crises of adult life.* New York, NY: Dutton.

Sheldon, P. (2012). Profiling the non-users: Examination of life-position indicators, sensation seeking, shyness, and loneliness among users and non-users of social network sites. *Computers in Human Behavior, 28,* 1960–1965. doi:10.1016/j.chb.2012.05.016

Shepard, T. H., & Lemire, R. J. (2004). *Catalog of teratogenic agents* (11th ed.). Baltimore, MD: Johns Hopkins University Press.

Sherblom, S. (2008). The legacy of the "Care challenge": Re-envisioning the outcome of the justice-care debate. *Journal of Moral Education, 37*, 81–98.

Shields, M., Carroll, M. D., & Ogden, C. L. (2011). *Adult obesity prevalence in Canada and the United States.* Retrieved from http://www.cdc.gov/nchs/data/databriefs/db56.htm

Shih, M., Pittinsky, T. L., & Ambady, N. (1999). Stereotype susceptibility: Identity salience and shifts in quantitative performance. *Psychological Science, 10*, 80–83. doi: 10.1111/1467-9280.00111

Shirom, A., Toker, S., Berliner, S., Shapira, I., & Melamed, S. (2008). The effects of physical fitness and feeling vigorous on self-rated health. *Health Psychology, 27*, 567–575. doi:10.1037/0278-6133.27.5.567

Shirtcliff, E. A., Dahl, R. E., & Pollak, S. D. (2009). Pubertal development: Correspondence between hormonal and physical development. *Child Development, 80*, 327–337. doi:10.1111/j.1467-8624.2009.01263.x

Shumaker, S. A., Ockene, J. K., & Riekert, K. A. (Eds.). (2009). *The handbook of health behavior change* (3rd ed.). New York, NY: Springer.

Siegel, L. A., & Siegel, R. M. (2007). Sexual changes in the aging male. In M. S. Tepper & A. Fuglsang Owens (Eds.), *Sexual health: Vol. 2. Physical foundations* (pp. 223–255). Westport, CT: Praeger/Greenwood.

Siegler, R. S. (2009). Improving the numerical understanding of children from low-income families. *Child Development Perspectives, 3*, 118–124. doi:10.1111/j.1750-8606.2009.00090.x

Siegler, R. S., & Chen, Z. (2008). Differentiation and integration: Guiding principles for analyzing cognitive change. *Developmental Science, 11*, 433–448. doi:10.1111/j.1467-7687.2008.00689.x

Sierra, F., Hadley, E., Suzman, R., & Hodes, R. (2009). Prospects for life span extension. *Annual Review of Medicine, 60*, 457–469. doi:10.1146/annurev.med.60.061607.220533

Silk, T. J., & Wood, A. G. (2011). Lessons about neurodevelopment from anatomical magnetic resonance imaging. *Journal of Developmental & Behavioral Pediatrics, 32*, 158–168.

Sillars, A., Smith, T., & Koerner, A. (2010). Misattributions contributing to empathic (in)accuracy during parent-adolescent conflict discussions. *Journal of Social and Personal Relationships, 27*, 727–747. doi:10.1177/0265407510373261

Silton, N. R., Flannelly, L. T., Flannelly, K. J., & Galek, K. (2011). Toward a theory of holistic needs and the brain. *Holistic Nursing Practice, 25*, 258–265. doi:10.1097/HNP.0b013e31822a0301

Silva, K. G., Correa-Chávez, M., & Rogoff, B. (2010). Mexican-heritage children's attention and learning from interactions directed to others. *Child Development, 81*, 898–912. doi:10.1111/j.1467-8624.2010.01441.x

Silventoinen, K., Hammar, N., Hedlund, E., Koskenvuo, M., Ronnemaa, T., & Kaprio, J. (2008). Selective international migration by social position, health behaviour and personality. *European Journal of Public Health, 18*, 150–155. doi:10.1093/eurpub/ckm052

Silver, W. (2007). *Crime statistics in Canada, 2006* (Catalogue No. 85–002-XIE). Ottawa, ON: Statistics Canada. Retrieved from http://www.statcan.gc.ca/pub/85-002-x/85-002-x2007005-eng.pdf

Silverstein, M. (2006). Intergenerational family transfers in social context. In R. H. Binstock & L. K. George (Eds.), *Handbook of aging and the social sciences* (6th ed., pp. 165–180). Amsterdam: Elsevier.

Silverstein, M., Gans, D., Lowenstein, A., Giarrusso, R., & Bengtson, V. L. (2010). Older parent–child relationships in six developed nations: Comparisons at the intersection of affection and conflict. *Journal of Marriage and Family, 72*, 1006–1021. doi:10.1111/j.1741–3737.2010.00745.x

Silvia, P. J., & Sanders, C. E. (2010). Why are smart people curious? Fluid intelligence, openness to experience, and interest. *Learning and Individual Differences, 20*, 242–245.

Simmons, J. P., Nelson, L. D., & Simonsohn, U. (2011). False-positive psychology: Undisclosed flexibility in data collection and analysis allows presenting anything as significant. *Psychological Science, 22*, 1359–1366. doi:10.1177/0956797611417632

Simpkins, S. D., Fredricks, J. A., Davis-Kean, P. E., & Eccles, J. S. (2006). Healthy mind, healthy habits: The influence of activity involvement in middle childhood. In A. C. Huston & M. N. Ripke (Eds.), *Developmental contexts in middle childhood: Bridges to adolescence and adulthood* (pp. 283–302). New York, NY: Cambridge University Press.

Simpson, J. A., & Rholes, W. S. (2010). Attachment and relationships: Milestones and future directions. *Journal of Social and Personal Relationships, 27*, 173–180. doi:10.1177/0265407509360909

Sinardet, D., & Mortelmans, D. (2009). The feminine side to Santa Claus. Women's work of kinship in contemporary gift-giving relations. *The Social Science Journal, 46*, 124–142.

Singleton, D., & Muñoz, C. (2011). Around and beyond the critical period hypothesis. In E. Hinkel (Ed.), *Handbook of research in second language teaching and learning* (Vol. 2, pp. 407–425). Mahwah, NJ: Erlbaum.

Sinnott, J. D. (1998). *The development of logic in adulthood: Postformal thought and its applications.* New York, NY: Plenum Press.

Sinnott, J. D. (2008). Cognitive and representational development in adults. In K. B. Cartwright (Ed.), *Literacy processes: Cognitive flexibility in learning and teaching* (pp. 42–68). New York, NY: Guilford.

Siu, A. F. Y. (2007). Using friends to combat internalizing problems among primary school children in Hong Kong. *Journal of Cognitive and Behavioral Psychotherapies, 7*, 11–26.

Skinner, B. F. (1957). *Verbal behavior.* New York, NY: Appleton-Century-Crofts.

Skipper, M. (2011). Epigenomics: Epigenetic variation across the generations. *Nature Reviews Genetics, 12*, 740.

Slaby, R. G., & Frey, K. S. (1975). Development of gender constancy and selective attention to same-sex models. *Child Development, 46*, 849–856.

Slack, J. M. W. (2012). *Stem cells: A very short introduction.* New York, NY: Oxford University Press.

Slaughter, V., & Griffiths, M. (2007). Death understanding and fear of death in young children. *Clinical Child Psychology and Psychiatry, 12*, 525–535. doi:10.1177/1359104507080980

Slessor, G., Phillips, L. H., & Bull, R. (2008). Age-related declines in basic social perception: Evidence from tasks assessing eye-gaze processing. *Psychology and Aging, 23,* 812–822. doi:10.1037/a0014348

Slining, M., Adair, L. S., Goldman, B. D., Borja, J. B., & Bentley, M. (2010). Infant overweight is associated with delayed motor development. *The Journal of Pediatrics, 157,* 20–25.e21.

Sloan, J. (2011–2012, Winter). Medicating elders in the evidence-free zone. *Generations, 35*(4), 56–61.

Sloan, K. (2009). The role of personality in a manager's learning effectiveness. *European Journal of Social Sciences, 12,* 31–42.

Sloane, S., Baillargeon, R., & Premack, D. (2012). Do infants have a sense of fairness? *Psychological Science, 23,* 196–204. doi:10.1177/0956797611422072

Slobin, D. I. (2001). Form-function relations: How do children find out what they are? In M. Bowerman & S. Levinson (Eds.), *Language acquisition and conceptual development* (pp. 406–449). Cambridge, UK: Cambridge University Press.

Slutske, W. S., Moffitt, T. E., Poulton, R., & Caspi, A. (2012). Undercontrolled temperament at age 3 predicts disordered gambling at age 32: A longitudinal study of a complete birth cohort. *Psychological Science, 23,* 510–516. doi:10.1177/0956797611429708

Small, M. F. (1998). *Our babies, ourselves: How biology and culture shape the way we parent.* New York, NY: Anchor Books.

Smetana, J. G. (1981). Preschool children's conceptions of moral and social rules. *Child Development, 52,* 1333–1336.

Smetana, J. G. (2002). Culture, autonomy, and personal jurisdiction in adolescent-parent relationships. In R. V. Kail & H. W. Reese (Eds.), *Advances in child development and behavior* (Vol. 29, pp. 51–87). New York, NY: Academic Press.

Smetana, J. G., Daddis, C., & Chuang, S. S. (2003). "Clean your room!": A longitudinal investigation of adolescent-parent conflict and conflict resolution in middle-class African American families. *Journal of Adolescent Research, 18,* 631–650. doi:10.1177/0743558403254781

Smetana, J. G., Metzger, A., & Campione-Barr, N. (2004). African American late adolescents' relationships with parents: Developmental transitions and longitudinal patterns. *Child Development, 75,* 932–947.

Smetanin, P., Kobak, P., Briante, C., Stiff, D., Sherman, G., & Ahmad, S. (2009). *Rising tide: The impact of dementia in Canada 2008 to 2038.* Retrieved from http://www.alzheimer.ca/~/media/Files/national/Advocacy/ASC_Rising_Tide_Full_Report_e.ashx

Smith, A. (2010, August 11). *Home broadband 2010.* Retrieved from http://pewinternet.org/Reports/2010/Home-Broadband-2010.aspx

Smith, C. W. D., & Lundquist, M. (2005). *Soul searching: The religious and spiritual lives of American teenagers.* Oxford, UK: Oxford University Press.

Smith, G. (2011). FAAMA: Inside the U.S. school allergy law. *Allergic Living.* Retrieved from http://allergicliving.com/index.php/2011/01/12/qa-faama-school-allergy-law/

Smith, G. R., Williamson, G. M., Miller, L. S., & Schulz, R. (2011). Depression and quality of informal care: A longitudinal investigation of caregiving stressors. *Psychology and Aging, 26,* 584–591. doi:10.1037/a0022263

Smith, P. K. (2010). *Children and play: Understanding children's worlds.* Chichester, West Sussex, UK: Wiley-Blackwell.

Smith, P. K., Mahdavi, J., Carvalho, M., Fisher, S., Russell, S., & Tippett, N. (2008). Cyberbullying: Its nature and impact in secondary school pupils. *Journal of Child Psychology and Psychiatry, 49,* 376–385.

Smith, P. K., Pepler, D. J., & Rigby, K. (2004). *Bullying in schools: How successful can interventions be?* New York, NY: Cambridge University Press.

Smylie, J., Fell, D., Ohlsson, A., & The Joint Working Group on First Nations, Indian, Inuit, and Métis Infant Mortality of the Canadian Perinatal Surveillance System. (2010). A review of Aboriginal infant mortality rates in Canada: Striking and persistent Aboriginal/non-Aboriginal inequities. *Canadian Journal of Public Health, 101,* 143–148.

Smyth, J. M. (2007). Beyond self-selection in video game play: An experimental examination of the consequences of massively multi-player online role-playing game play. *CyberPsychology & Behavior, 10,* 717–727.

Sneed, J. R., Schwartz, S. J., & Cross, W. E., Jr. (2006). A multicultural critique of identity status theory and research: A call for integration. *Identity: An International Journal of Theory and Research, 6,* 61–84. doi:10.1207/s1532706xid0601_5

Sneed, J. R., & Whitbourne, S. K. (2005). Models of the aging self. *Journal of Social Issues, 61,* 375–388.

Sniderman, A. S. (2012, August 8). Aboriginal students: An education underclass. *Maclean's.* Retrieved from http://www2.macleans.ca/2012/08/08/an-education-underclass/

Snow, D. (2006). Regression and reorganization of intonation between 6 and 23 months. *Child Development, 77,* 281–296.

Snow, C. E., & Kang, J. Y. (2006). Becoming bilingual, biliterate, and bicultural. In K. A. Renninger & I. E. Sigel (Eds.), *Handbook of child psychology: Vol. 4. Child psychology in practice* (6th ed., pp. 75–102). Hoboken, NJ: Wiley.

Snow, C. E., Porche, M. V., Tabors, P. O., & Harris, S. R. (2007). *Is literacy enough? Pathways to academic success for adolescents.* Baltimore, MD: Brookes.

Snyder, J., Schrepferman, L., Oeser, J., Patterson, G., Stoolmiller, M., Johnson, K., & Snyder, A. (2005). Deviancy training and association with deviant peers in young children: Occurrence and contribution to early-onset conduct problems. *Development & Psychopathology, 17,* 397–413.

Snyder, T. D., & Dillow, S. A. (2010). *Digest of education statistics, 2009* (Vol. 2010). Washington, DC: National Center for Education Statistics.

Sobal, J., & Hanson, K. L. (2011). Marital status, marital history, body weight, and obesity. *Marriage & Family Review, 47,* 474–504. doi:10.1080/01494929.2011.620934

Sobotka, T., & Testa, M. R. (2008). Attitudes and intentions toward childlessness in Europe. In C. Höhn, D. Avramov, & I. E. Kotowska (Eds.), *European Studies of Population: Vol. 16. People, population change and policies* (Vol. 1, pp. 177–211). The Hague, Netherlands: Springer.

Soenens, B., & Vansteenkiste, M. (2010). A theoretical upgrade of the concept of parental psychological control: Proposing new insights on the basis of self-determination theory. *Developmental Review, 30,* 74–99.

Sokol, R. Z. (2009). Is androgen therapy indicated for aging men? *Sexuality, Reproduction & Menopause, 7,* 27–30.

Soley, G., & Hannon, E. E. (2010). Infants prefer the musical meter of their own culture: A cross-cultural comparison. *Developmental Psychology, 46,* 286–292.

Solomon, A., Sippola, R., Soininen, H., Wolozin, B., Tuomilehto, J., Laatikainen, T., & Kivipelto, M. (2010). Lipid-lowering treatment is related to decreased risk of dementia: A population-based study (FINRISK). *Neuro-Degenerative Diseases, 7,* 180–182. doi:10.1159/000295659

Sonnenschein, S., Stapleton, L. M., & Benson, A. (2010). The relation between the type and amount of instruction and growth in children's reading competencies. *American Educational Research Journal, 47,* 358–389. doi:10.3102/0002831209349215

Sorkin, D. H., & Rook, K. S. (2006). Dealing with negative social exchanges in later life: Coping responses, goals, and effectiveness. *Psychology and Aging, 21,* 715–725.

Soska, K. C., Adolph, K. E., & Johnson, S. P. (2010). Systems in development: Motor skill acquisition facilitates three-dimensional object completion. *Developmental Psychology, 46,* 129–138.

Sowell, E. R., Thompson, P. M., & Toga, A. W. (2007). Mapping adolescent brain maturation using structural magnetic resonance imaging. In D. Romer & E. F. Walker (Eds.), *Adolescent psychopathology and the developing brain: Integrating brain and prevention science* (pp. 55–84). Oxford, UK: Oxford University Press.

Spear, L. P. (2011). Adolescent neurobehavioral characteristics, alcohol sensitivities, and intake: Setting the stage for alcohol use disorders? *Child Development Perspectives, 5,* 231–238. doi:10.1111/j.1750–8606.2011.00182.x

Spearman, C. E. (1927). *The abilities of man, their nature and measurement.* New York, NY: Macmillan.

Specht, J., Egloff, B., & Schmukle, S. C. (2011). Stability and change of personality across the life course: The impact of age and major life events on mean-level and rank-order stability of the Big Five. *Journal of Personality and Social Psychology, 101,* 862–882. doi:10.1037/a0024950

Spencer, J. P., Blumberg, M. S., McMurray, B., Robinson, S. R., Samuelson, L. K., & Tomblin, J. B. (2009). Short arms and talking eggs: Why we should no longer abide the nativist–empiricist debate. *Child Development Perspectives, 3,* 79–87.

Spencer, J. P., Clearfield, M., Corbetta, D., Ulrich, B., Buchanan, P., & Schöner, G. (2006). Moving toward a grand theory of development: In memory of Esther Thelen. *Child Development, 77,* 1521–1538.

Spinillo, A., Montanari, L., Gardella, B., Roccio, M., Stronati, M., & Fazzi, E. (2009). Infant sex, obstetric risk factors, and 2-year neurodevelopmental outcome among preterm infants. *Developmental Medicine & Child Neurology, 51,* 518–525.

Spittle, A. J., Treyvaud, K., Doyle, L. W., Roberts, G., Lee, K. J., Inder, T. E., ... Anderson, P. J. (2009). Early emergence of behavior and social-emotional problems in very preterm infants. *Journal of the American Academy of Child and Adolescent Psychiatry, 48,* 909–918.

Spitz, R. A. (1946). Hospitalism: A follow-up report on investigation described in Volume I, 1945. *The Psychoanalytic Study of the Child, 2,* 113–117.

Sroufe, L. A. (2012, January 28). Ritalin gone wrong. *New York Times,* p. SR1. Retrieved from http://www.nytimes.com/2012/01/29/opinion/sunday/childrens-add-drugs-dont-work-long-term.html?pagewanted=all

Sroufe, L. A., Egeland, B., Carlson, E. A., & Collins, W. A. (2005). *The development of the person: The Minnesota study of risk and adaptation from birth to adulthood.* New York, NY: Guilford Press.

St. Petersburg-USA Orphanage Research Team. (2008). The effects of early social-emotional and relationship experience on the development of young orphanage children. *Monographs of the Society for Research in Child Development, 73*(3, Serial No. 291), 1–262.

Staff, J., & Schulenberg, J. (2010). Millennials and the world of work: Experiences in paid work during adolescence. *Journal of Business and Psychology, 25,* 247–255. doi:10.1007/s10869–010–9167–4

Statistics Canada. (2002). *Self-rated health, by age group and sex, household population aged 12 and over, Canada, 2000/01.* Retrieved from http://www.statcan.gc.ca/pub/82-221-x/00502/t/pdf/4195348-eng.pdf

Statistics Canada. (2003). *Canadian Community Health Survey—Mental Health and Well-being.* Available from http://www.statcan.gc.ca/pub/82-617-x/index-eng.htm

Statistics Canada. (2004, February 17). *Spotlight: Grandparents.* Retrieved from http://www.statcan.gc.ca/pub/11-002-x/2004/02/04804/4072395-eng.htm

Statistics Canada. (2006, May 16). *2006 census of population.* Available from http://www12.statcan.gc.ca/census-recensement/2006/index-eng.cfm

Statistics Canada. (2008a, April 2). *2006 census: Ethnic origin, visible minorities, place or work and mode of transportation.* Retrieved from http://www.statcan.gc.ca/daily-quotidien/080402/dq080402a-eng.htm

Statistics Canada. (2008b). *Participation, graduation and dropout rates.* Retrieved from http://www.statcan.gc.ca/pub/81-595-m/2008070/6000003-eng.htm

Statistics Canada. (2008c, October 21). *Study: Caring for seniors.* Retrieved from http://www.statcan.gc.ca/daily-quotidien/081021/dq081021a-eng.htm

Statistics Canada. (2009). *Live births, by geography: Age of mother.* Retrieved from http://www.statcan.gc.ca/pub/84f0210x/2009000/t003-eng.pdf

Statistics Canada. (2010a). *Economic fact sheet* (Catalogue No. 11-008-X). Retrieved from http://www.statcan.gc.ca/pub/11-008-x/2010001/article/11133-eng.pdf

Statistics Canada. (2010b). *Ethnic diversity and immigration.* Retrieved from http://www.statcan.gc.ca/pub/11-402-x/2010000/chap/imm/imm-eng.htm

Statistics Canada. (2010c). *General social survey: Time use.* Retrieved from http://www.statcan.gc.ca/daily-quotidien/110712/dq110712b-eng.htm

Statistics Canada. (2010d). *Population projections: Canada, the provinces and territories.* Retrieved from http://www.statcan.gc.ca/daily-quotidien/100526/dq100526b-eng.htm

Statistics Canada. (2011a). *Births 2008* (Catalogue No. 84F0210X). Retrieved from http://www.statcan.gc.ca/pub/84f0210x/84f0210x2008000-eng.pdf

Statistics Canada. (2011b). *Breastfeeding, 2009.* Retrieved from http://www.statcan.gc.ca/pub/82-625-x/2010002/article/11269-eng.htm

Statistics Canada. (2011c). *Canadian health measures survey: Lead, bisphenol A and mercury.* Retrieved from http://www.statcan.gc.ca/daily-quotidien/100816/dq100816a-eng.htm

Statistics Canada. (2011d). *Elections…by the numbers.* Retrieved from http://www42.statcan.gc.ca/smr08/2011/smr08_152_2011-eng.htm

Statistics Canada. (2011e). *Physical activity during leisure time, 2010.* Retrieved from http://www.statcan.gc.ca/pub/82-625-x/2011001/article/11467-eng.htm

Statistics Canada. (2011f). *Women in Canada: A gender-based statistical report.* Retrieved from http://www.statcan.gc.ca/pub/89-503-x/89-503-x2010001-eng.pdf

Statistics Canada. (2012a). *2011 Census of population: Linguistic characteristics of Canada.* Retrieved from http://www.statcan.gc.ca/daily-quotidien/121024/dq121024a-eng.htm

Statistics Canada. (2012b). *Labour force characteristics by age and sex.* Retrieved from http://www.statcan.gc.ca/tables-tableaux/sum-som/l01/cst01/labor20a-eng.htm

Statistics Canada. (2012c). *Life expectancy at birth, by sex, by province.* Retrieved from http://www.statcan.gc.ca/tables-tableaux/sum-som/l01/cst01/health26-eng.htm

Statistics Canada. (2012d). *Motor vehicle accidents causing death, by sex and by age group.* Retrieved from http://www.statcan.gc.ca/tables-tableaux/sum-som/l01/cst01/health112a-eng.htm

Statistics Canada. (2012e). *Portrait of families and living arrangements in Canada* (Catalogue No. 98–312–2011001). Retrieved from http://www12.statcan.gc.ca/census-recensement/2011/as-sa/98-312-x/98-312-x2011001-eng.pdf

Statistics Canada. (2012f). *Study: Suicide rates, an overview, 1950 to 2009.* Retrieved from http://www.statcan.gc.ca/daily-quotidien/120725/dq120725a-eng.htm

Statistics Canada. (2012g). *Suicides and suicide rate, by sex and by age group (females no.).* Retrieved from http://www.statcan.gc.ca/tables-tableaux/sum-som/l01/cst01/hlth66c-eng.htm

Statistics Canada. (2012h). *Suicides and suicide rate, by sex and by age group (males rate).* Retrieved from http://www.statcan.gc.ca/tables-tableaux/sum-som/l01/cst01/hlth66e-eng.htm

Statistics Canada. (2012i). *Table 102–0509: Deaths in hospital and elsewhere, Canada, provinces and territories* [Data set]. Available from http://www5.statcan.gc.ca/cansim/pick-choisir?lang=eng&p2=33&id=1020509

Statistics Canada. (2012j). *Table 102–0561: Leading causes of death, total population, by age group and sex, Canada* [Data set]. Available from http://www5.statcan.gc.ca/cansim/pick-choisir?lang=eng&p2=33&id=1020561

Statistics Canada. (2012k). *Table 251–0013: Youth custody and community services (YCCS), admissions to correctional services, by most serious offence* [Data set]. Available from http://www5.statcan.gc.ca/cansim/pick-choisir?lang=eng&p2=33&id=2510013

Statistics Canada. (2012l). *Table 477–0019: Postsecondary enrolments, by registration status, pan-Canadian standard classification of education (PCSCE), classification of instructional programs, primary grouping (CIP_PG), sex and immigration status* [Data set]. Available from http://www5.statcan.gc.ca/cansim/a05?searchTypeByValue=1&lang=eng&id=4770019&pattern=4770019

Statistics Canada. (2012m). *Table 477–0020: Postsecondary graduates, by pan-Canadian standard classification of education (PCSCE), classification of instructional programs, primary grouping (CIP_PG), sex and immigration status* [Data set]. Available from http://www5.statcan.gc.ca/cansim/a05?lang=eng&id=4770020

Statistics Canada. (2012n). *Youth crime, 2011.* Retrieved from http://www.statcan.gc.ca/pub/85-005-x/2012001/article/11749-eng.htm

Statistics Canada. (2013a). *Aboriginal peoples: First Nations people, Métis, and Inuit* (Catalogue No. 99–011–X2011001). Retrieved from http://www12.statcan.gc.ca/nhs-enm/2011/as-sa/99-011-x/99-011-x2011001-eng.pdf

Statistics Canada. (2013b). *Blood lead concentrations in Canadians, 2009 to 2011.* Retrieved from http://www.statcan.gc.ca/pub/82-625-x/2013001/article/11779-eng.htm

Statistics Canada. (2013c). *Canadian Health Measures Survey: Directly measured physical activity of Canadian, 2007 to 2011.* Retrieved from http://www.statcan.gc.ca/daily-quotidien/130530/dq130530d-eng.htm

Statistics Canada. (2013d). *Health profile, December 2013* [Data set]. Available from https://www12.statcan.gc.ca/health-sante/82-228/details/page.cfm?Lang=E&Tab=1&Geo1=PR&Code1=13&Geo2=PR&Code2=01&Data=Rate&SearchText=New%20Brunswick&SearchType=Contains&SearchPR=01&B1=All&Custom=&GeoLevel=PR&GeoCode=13

Statistics Canada. (2013e). *Living arrangements of young adults aged 20 to 29* (Catalogue No. 98–312–X2011003). Retrieved from http://www12.statcan.gc.ca/census-recensement/2011/as-sa/98-312-x/98-312-x2011003_3-eng.pdf

Statistics Canada. (2013f). *Overweight and obese adults (self-reported), 2012.* Retrieved from http://www.statcan.gc.ca/pub/82-625-x/2013001/article/11840-eng.htm

Statistics Canada. (2013g). *Study: Economic downturn and educational attainment, 2008 to 2011.* Retrieved from http://www.statcan.gc.ca/daily-quotidien/120621/dq120621c-eng.htm

Statistics Canada. (2013h). *Table 051–0001: Estimates of population by age group and sex for July 1, Canada, provinces and territories* [Data set]. Available from http://www5.statcan.gc.ca/cansim/a26?lang=eng&retrLang=eng&id=0510001&paSer=&pattern=&stByVal=1&p1=1&p2=31&tabMode=dataTable&csid=

Statistics Canada. (2013i). *Table 102–0504: Death and mortality rates, by age group and sex, Canada, provinces and territories.* Available from http://www5.statcan.gc.ca/cansim/a26?lang=eng&retrLang=eng&id=1020504&pattern=102-0501..102-0510&tabMode=dataTable&srchLan=-1&p1=-1&p2=31

Statistics Canada. (2013j). *Table 102–4516: Live births and fetal deaths (stillbirths), by place of birth (hospital and non-hospital), Canada, provinces and territories* [Data set]. Available from http://www5.statcan.gc.ca/cansim/pick-choisir?lang=eng&p2=33&id=1024516

Statistics Canada. (2013k). *Table 105–0501: Health indicator profile, annual estimates, by age group and sex, Canada, provinces, territories, health regions (2012 boundaries) and peer groups* [Data set]. Available from http://www5.statcan.gc.ca/cansim/a26?lang=eng&retrLang=eng&id=1050501&pattern=&csid=

Statistics Canada. (2013l). *Table 358–0152: Canadian internet use survey, internet use, by age group and household income for Canada, provinces and census metropolitan areas (CMAs)* [Data set]. Available from http://www5.statcan.gc.ca/cansim/pick-choisir?lang=eng&p2=33&id=3580152

Statistics Canada. (2013m). *Table 358–0153: Canadian internet use survey, internet use, by age group, internet activity, sex, level of education and household income* [Data set]. Available from http://www5.statcan.gc.ca/cansim/pick-choisir?lang=eng&p2=33&id=3580153

Statistics Canada. (2013n). *Victims and persons accused of homicide, by age and sex.* Retrieved from http://www.statcan.gc.ca/tables-tableaux/sum-som/l01/cst01/legal10a-eng.htm

Statistics Canada. (2014a). *Detailed mother tongue (158), generation status (4), knowledge of official languages (5), number of non-official languages spoken (5), age groups (10) and sex (3) for the population in private households of Canada, provinces and territories, 2011 National Household Survey* [Data file]. Retrieved from http://www12.statcan.gc.ca/nhs-enm/2011/dp-pd/dt-td/rp-eng.cfm?lang=e&apath=3&detail=0&dim=0&fl=a&free=0&gc=0&gid=0&gk=0&grp=0&pid=105400&prid=0&ptype=105277&s=0&showall=0&sub=0&temporal=2013&theme=95&vid=0&vnamee=&vnamef=

Statistics Canada. (2014b). *Table 102–0551: Death and mortality rate, by selected grouped causes, age group and sex, Canada* [Data set]. Available from http://www5.statcan.gc.ca/cansim/a26?lang=eng&retrLang=eng&id=1020551&paSer=&pattern=&stByVal=1&p1=1&p2=37&tabMode=dataTable&csid=

Statistics Canada. (2014c). *Table 282–0004: Labour force survey estimates (LFS), by educational attainment, sex and age group* [Data set]. Available from http://www5.statcan.gc.ca/cansim/a26?lang=eng&retrLang=eng&id=2820004&paSer=&pattern=&stByVal=1&p1=1&p2=-1&tabMode=dataTable&csid=

Statistics Canada. (2014d). *Visible minority (15), immigrant status and period of immigration (11), age groups (10) and sex (3) for the population in private households of Canada, provinces, territories, census metropolitan areas and census agglomerations, 2011 National Household Survey* [Data set]. Available from https://www12.statcan.gc.ca/nhs-enm/2011/dp-pd/dt-td/rp-eng.cfm?lang=e&apath=3&detail=0&dim=0&fl=a&free=0&gc=0&gid=0&gk=0&grp=1&pid=105392&prid=0&ptype=105277&s=0&showall=0&sub=0&temporal=2013&theme=95&vid=0&vnamee=&vnamef=

Staudinger, U. M., & Lindenberger, U. (2003). Why read another book on human development? Understanding human development takes a metatheory and multiple disciplines. In U. M. Staudinger & U. E. R. Lindenberger (Eds.), *Understanding human development: Dialogues with lifespan psychology* (pp. 1–13). Boston, MA: Kluwer.

Stavrova, O., Fetchenhauer, D., & Schlösser, T. (2012). Cohabitation, gender, and happiness: A cross-cultural study in thirty countries. *Journal of Cross-Cultural Psychology, 43,* 1063–1081. doi:10.1177/0022022111419030

Stawski, R. S., Almeida, D. M., Lachman, M. E., Tun, P. A., & Rosnick, C. B. (2010). Fluid cognitive ability is associated with greater exposure and smaller reactions to daily stressors. *Psychology and Aging, 25,* 330–342.

Steele, C. M. (1997). A threat in the air: How stereotypes shape intellectual identity and performance. *American Psychologist, 52,* 613–629.

Steemers, J. (2010). *Creating preschool television: A story of commerce, creativity and curriculum.* New York, NY: Palgrave Macmillan.

Stein, A. (2006). *Shameless: Sexual dissidence in American culture.* New York, NY: New York University Press.

Steinberg, L. (2004). Risk taking in adolescence: What changes, and why? In R. E. Dahl & L. P. Spear (Eds.), *Adolescent brain development: Vulnerabilities and opportunities* (Vol. 1021, pp. 51–58). New York, NY: New York Academy of Sciences

Steinberg, L. (2008). A social neuroscience perspective on adolescent risk-taking. *Developmental Review, 28,* 78–106.

Steinberg, L., & Monahan, K. C. (2011). Adolescents' exposure to sexy media does not hasten the initiation of sexual intercourse. *Developmental Psychology, 47,* 562–576. doi:10.1037/a0020613

Steiner, M., & Young, E. A. (2008). Hormones and mood. In J. B. Becker, K. J. Berkley, N. Geary, E. Hampson, J. P. Herman, & E. Young (Eds.), *Sex differences in the brain: From genes to behavior* (pp. 405–426). New York, NY: Oxford University Press.

Steingraber, S. (2007). *The falling age of puberty in U.S. girls: What we know, what we need to know.* Retrieved from http://www.breastcancerfund.org/assets/pdfs/publications/falling-age-of-puberty.pdf

Stel, V. S., Smit, J. H., Pluijm, S. M. F., & Lips, P. (2004). Consequences of falling in older men and women and risk factors for health service use and functional decline. *Age and Ageing, 33,* 58–65.

Sterck, E. H. M., & Begeer, S. (2010). Theory of Mind: Specialized capacity or emergent property? *European Journal of Developmental Psychology, 7,* 1–16.

Sterling, P. (2012). Allostasis: A model of predictive regulation. *Physiology & Behavior, 106,* 5–15.

Stern, M. J., & Adams, A. E. (2010). Do rural residents really use the internet to build social capital? An empirical investigation. *American Behavioral Scientist, 53,* 1389–1422. doi:10.1177/0002764210361692

Stern, Y. (2013). Cognitive reserve: Implications for assessment and intervention. *Folia Phoniatrica et Logopaedica, 65,* 49–54. doi:10.1159/000353443

Sternberg, R. J. (1988). Triangulating love. In R. Sternberg & M. L. Barnes (Eds.), *The psychology of love* (pp. 119–138). New Haven, CT: Yale University Press.

Sternberg, R. J. (1996). *Successful intelligence: How practical and creative intelligence determine success in life.* New York, NY: Simon & Schuster.

Sternberg, R. J. (2003). *Wisdom, intelligence, and creativity synthesized.* New York, NY: Cambridge University Press.

Sternberg, R. J. (2006a). A duplex theory of love. In R. J. Sternberg & K. Weis (Eds.), *The new psychology of love* (pp. 184–199). New Haven, CT: Yale University Press.

Sternberg, R. J. (2006b). Introduction. In J. C. Kaufman & R. J. Sternberg (Eds.), *The international handbook of creativity* (pp. 1–9). New York, NY: Cambridge University Press.

Sternberg, R. J. (2012). Why I became an administrator … and why you might become one too. *Observer, 25*(2), 21–22.

Sternberg, R. J., & Weis, K. (2006). *The new psychology of love.* New Haven, CT: Yale University Press.

Sterns, H. L., & Huyck, M. H. (2001). The role of work in midlife. In M. E. Lachman (Ed.), *Handbook of midlife development* (pp. 447–486). New York, NY: Wiley.

Stevenson, J. C., Hodis, H. N., Pickar, J. H., & Lobo, R. A. (2011). HRT and breast cancer risk: A realistic perspective. *Climacteric, 14*, 633–636. doi:10.3109/13697137.2011.590618

Stevenson, O. (2007). *Neglected children and their families* (2nd ed.). Malden, MA: Blackwell.

Stevenson, R. J., Oaten, M. J., Case, T. I., Repacholi, B. M., & Wagland, P. (2010). Children's response to adult disgust elicitors: Development and acquisition. *Developmental Psychology, 46*, 165–177.

Stigler, J. W., & Hiebert, J. (2009). *The teaching gap: Best ideas from the world's teachers for improving education in the classroom* (1st Free Press trade paperback ed.). New York, NY: Free Press.

Stiles, J., & Jernigan, T. (2010). The basics of brain development. *Neuropsychology Review, 20*, 327–348. doi:10.1007/s11065-010-9148-4

Stine-Morrow, E. A. L., & Basak, C. (2011). Cognitive interventions. In K. W. Schaie & S. L. Willis (Eds.), *Handbook of the psychology of aging* (7th ed., pp. 153–171). San Diego, CA: Academic Press.

Stine-Morrow, E. A. L., Noh, S. R., & Shake, M. C. (2010). Age differences in the effects of conceptual integration training on resource allocation in sentence processing. *Quarterly Journal of Experimental Psychology, 63*, 1430–1455. doi:10.1080/17470210903330983

Stipek, D., Recchia, S., & McClintic, S. (1992). Self-evaluation in young children. *Monographs of the Society for Research in Child Development, 57*, 1–98.

Stoltenborgh, M., van IJzendoorn, M. H., Euser, E. M., & Bakermans-Kranenburg, M. J. (2011). A global perspective on child sexual abuse: Meta-analysis of prevalence around the world. *Child Maltreatment, 16*, 79–101. doi:10.1177/1077559511403920

Stone, R. (2011, April 8). Daring experiment in higher education opens its doors. *Science, 332*, 161.

Stone, R. I. (2006). Emerging issues in long-term care. In R. H. Binstock & L. K. George (Eds.), *Handbook of aging and the social sciences* (6th ed., pp. 397–418). Amsterdam, The Netherlands: Elsevier.

Strasburger, V. C., Wilson, B. J., & Jordan, A. B. (2009). *Children, adolescents, and the media* (2nd ed.). Los Angeles, CA: Sage.

Straus, M. A., & Paschall, M. J. (2009). Corporal punishment by mothers and development of children's cognitive ability: A longitudinal study of two nationally representative age cohorts. *Journal of Aggression, Maltreatment & Trauma, 18*, 459–483.

Strauss, J. (2012). Psychotropic medications in the elderly. In S. Ryan Barnett (Ed.), *Manual of geriatric anesthesia* (pp. 399–418). New York, NY: Springer.

Strayer, J., & Roberts, W. (2004). Children's anger, emotional expressiveness, and empathy: Relations with parents' empathy, emotional expressiveness, and parenting practices. *Social Development, 13*, 229–254. doi:10.1111/j.1467–9507.2004.000265.x

Streissguth, A. P., & Connor, P. D. (2001). Fetal alcohol syndrome and other effects of prenatal alcohol: Developmental cognitive neuroscience implications. In C. A. Nelson & M. Luciana (Eds.), *Handbook of developmental cognitive neuroscience* (pp. 505–518). Cambridge, MA: MIT Press.

Stroebe, M., Schut, H., & Boerner, K. (2010). Continuing bonds in adaptation to bereavement: Toward theoretical integration. *Clinical Psychology Review, 30*, 259–268.

Strohm, C., Seltzer, J., Cochran, S., & Mays, V. (2009). "Living Apart Together" relationships in the United States. *Demographic Research, 21*, 177–214.

Strouse, D. L. (1999). Adolescent crowd orientations: A social and temporal analysis. In J. A. McLellan & M. J. V. Pugh (Eds.), *The role of peer groups in adolescent social identity: Exploring the importance of stability and change* (pp. 37–54). San Francisco, CA: Jossey-Bass.

Stuart, J., & Ward, C. (2011). Predictors of ethno-cultural identity conflict among South Asian immigrant youth in New Zealand. *Applied Developmental Science, 15*, 117–128. doi:10.1080/10888691.2011.587717

Stubben, J. D. (2001). Working with and conducting research among American Indian families. *American Behavioral Scientist, 44*, 1466–1481.

Sturdee, D. W., & Pines, A. (2011). Updated IMS recommendations on postmenopausal hormone therapy and preventive strategies for midlife health. *Climacteric, 14*, 302–320. doi:10.3109/13697137.2011.570590

Subcommittee on Attention-Deficit/Hyperactivity Disorder, Steering Committee on Quality Improvement Management. (2011). ADHD: Clinical practice guideline for the diagnosis, evaluation, and treatment of attention-deficit/hyperactivity disorder in children and adolescents. *Pediatrics, 128*, 1007–1022. doi:10.1542/peds.2011-2654

Substance Abuse and Mental Health Services Administration (SAMHSA). (2009). *Results from the 2008 National Survey on Drug Use and Health: National findings.* Rockville, MD: U.S. Department of Health and Human Services.

Sue, D. W. (2010). *Microaggressions and marginality: Manifestation, dynamics, and impact.* Hoboken, NJ: Wiley.

Suh, E. M., Diener, E., & Updegraff, J. A. (2008). From culture to priming conditions: Self-construal influences on life satisfaction judgments. *Journal of Cross-Cultural Psychology, 39,* 3–15. doi:10.1177/0022022107311769

Sun, R., & Liu, Y. (2008). The more engagement, the better? A study of mortality of the oldest old in China. In Y. Zeng, D. L. Poston, Jr., D. Ashbaugh Vlosky, & D. Gu (Eds.), *Healthy longevity in China* (pp. 177–192). Dordrecht, The Netherlands: Springer.

Suris, J.-C., Michaud, P.-A., Akre, C., & Sawyer, S. M. (2008). Health risk behaviors in adolescents with chronic conditions. *Pediatrics, 122,* e1113–1118. http://pediatrics.aappublications.org/cgi/content/abstract/122/5/e1113 doi:10.1542/peds.2008-1479

Susman, E. J., Houts, R. M., Steinberg, L., Belsky, J., Cauffman, E., DeHart, G., ... for the Eunice Kennedy Shriver NICHD Early Child Care Research Network. (2010). Longitudinal development of secondary sexual characteristics in girls and boys between ages 9–1/2 and 15–1/2 years. *Archives of Pediatrics & Adolescent Medicine, 164,* 166–173. doi:10.1001/archpediatrics.2009.261

Sutin, A. R., & Costa, P. T., Jr. (2010). Reciprocal influences of personality and job characteristics across middle adulthood. *Journal of Personality, 78,* 257–288. doi:10.1111/j.1467–6494.2009.00615.x

Sutphin, G. L., & Kaeberlein, M. (2011). Comparative genetics of aging. In E. J. Masoro & S. N. Austad (Eds.), *Handbook of the biology of aging* (7th ed., pp. 215–242). San Diego, CA: Academic Press.

Sutton-Smith, B. (2011). The antipathies of play. In P. Nathan & A. D. Pellegrini (Eds.), *The Oxford handbook of the development of play* (pp. 110–115). New York, NY: Oxford University Press.

Swain, M., Lapkin, S., Rowen, N., & Hart, D. (1990). The role of mother tongue literacy in third language learning. *Language, Culture and Curriculum, 3,* 65–81. doi:10.1080/07908319009525073

Sweeney, M. M. (2010). Remarriage and stepfamilies: Strategic sites for family scholarship in the 21st century. *Journal of Marriage and Family, 72,* 667–684. doi:10.1111/j.1741–3737.2010.00724.x

Syed, M., & Azmitia, M. (2010). Narrative and ethnic identity exploration: A longitudinal account of emerging adults' ethnicity-related experiences. *Developmental Psychology, 46,* 208–219.

Szaflarski, M., Cubbins, L. A., & Ying, J. (2011). Epidemiology of alcohol abuse among US immigrant populations. *Journal of Immigrant and Minority Health, 13,* 647–658. doi:10.1007/s10903–010–9394–9

T

Tacken, M., & van Lamoen, E. (2005). Transport behaviour and realised journeys and trips. In H. Mollenkopf, F. Marcellini, I. Ruoppila, Z. Széman, & M. Tacken (Eds.), *Enhancing mobility in later life: Personal coping, environmental resources and technical support. The out-of-home mobility of older adults in urban and rural regions of five European countries* (pp. 105–139). Amsterdam, The Netherlands: IOS Press.

Taga, K. A., Markey, C. N., & Friedman, H. S. (2006). A longitudinal investigation of associations between boys' pubertal timing and adult behavioral health and well-being. *Journal of Youth and Adolescence, 35,* 401–411.

Tajfel, H., & Turner, J. C. (1986). The social identity theory of intergroup behaviour. In S. Worchel & W. G. Austin (Eds.), *Psychology of intergroup relations* (pp. 7–24). Chicago, IL: Nelson-Hall.

Talwar, V., Harris, P. L., & Schleifer, M. (2011). *Children's understanding of death: From biological to religious conceptions.* New York, NY: Cambridge University Press.

Tamay, Z., Akcay, A., Ones, U., Guler, N., Kilic, G., & Zencir, M. (2007). Prevalence and risk factors for allergic rhinitis in primary school children. *International Journal of Pediatric Otorhinolaryngology, 71,* 463–471.

Tamis-LeMonda, C. S., Bornstein, M. H., & Baumwell, L. (2001). Maternal responsiveness and children's achievement of language milestones. *Child Development, 72,* 748–767.

Tamis-LeMonda, C. S., Way, N., Hughes, D., Yoshikawa, H., Kalman, R. K., & Niwa, E. Y. (2008). Parents' goals for children: The dynamic coexistence of individualism and collectivism in cultures and individuals. *Social Development, 17,* 183–209. doi:10.1111/j.1467–9507.2007.00419.x

Tanaka, H., Black, J. M., Hulme, C., Stanley, L. M., Kesler, S. R., Whitfield-Gabrieli, S., ... Hoeft, F. (2011). The brain basis of the phonological deficit in dyslexia is independent of IQ. *Psychological Science, 22,* 1442–1451. doi:10.1177/0956797611419521

Tanaka, Y., & Nakazawa, J. (2005). Job-related temporary father absence (Tanshinfunin) and child development. In D. W. Shwalb, J. Nakazawa, & B. J. Shwalb (Eds.), *Applied developmental psychology: Theory, practice, and research from Japan* (pp. 241–260). Greenwich, CT: Information Age.

Tanner, J. L., Arnett, J. J., & Leis, J. A. (2009). Emerging adulthood: Learning and development during the first stage of adulthood. In M. C. Smith & N. DeFrates-Densch (Eds.), *Handbook of research on adult learning and development* (pp. 34–67). New York, NY: Routledge/Taylor & Francis Group.

Tarullo, A. R., Garvin, M. C., & Gunnar, M. R. (2011). Atypical EEG power correlates with indiscriminately friendly behavior in internationally adopted children. *Developmental Psychology, 47,* 417–431.

Tarullo, A. R., & Gunnar, M. R. (2006). Child maltreatment and the developing HPA axis. *Hormones and Behavior, 50,* 632–639. doi:10.1016/j.yhbeh.2006.06.010

Taubes, G. (2009, July 17). Prosperity's plague. *Science, 325,* 256–260.

Tay, M. T.-H., Au Eong, K. G., Ng, C. Y., & Lim, M. K. (1992). Myopia and educational attainment in 421,116 young Singaporean males. *Annals, Academy of Medicine, Singapore, 21,* 785–791.

Taylor, A. C., Robila, M., & Lee, H. S. (2005). Distance, contact, and intergenerational relationships: Grandparents and adult grandchildren from an international perspective. *Journal of Adult Development, 12,* 33–41.

Taylor, J. H. (Ed.). (2010). *Journey through the afterlife: Ancient Egyptian book of the dead.* London, England: British Museum Press.

Taylor, R. D., Seaton, E., & Dominguez, A. (2008). Kinship support, family relations, and psychological adjustment among low-income African American mothers and adolescents. *Journal of Research on Adolescence, 18,* 1–22.

Taylor, S. E. (2006). Tend and befriend: Biobehavioral bases of affiliation under stress. *Current Directions in Psychological Science, 15,* 273–277.

Taylor, S. E., Klein, L. C., Lewis, B. P., Gruenewald, T. L., Gurung, R. A. R., & Updegraff, J. A. (2000). Biobehavioral responses to stress in females: Tend-and-befriend, not fight-or-flight. *Psychological Review, 107,* 411–429.

Taylor-Butts, A., & Bressan, A. (2008). *Youth crime in Canada, 2006* (Catalogue No. 85–002-XIE). Retrieved from http://www.statcan.gc.ca/pub/85-002-x/85-002-x2008003-eng.pdf

Teachman, J. (2008). Complex life course patterns and the risk of divorce in second marriages. *Journal of Marriage and Family, 70,* 294–305.

Teachman, J. (2010). Work-related health limitations, education, and the risk of marital disruption. *Journal of Marriage and Family, 72,* 919–932. doi:10.1111/j.1741–3737.2010.00739.x

Teitel, E. (2013, June 15). Why we need to get in bed with modern sex ed. *Maclean's.* Retrieved from http://www2.macleans.ca/2013/06/15/we-need-to-get-into-bed-with-modern-sex-ed/

ter Bogt, T., Schmid, H., Nic Gabhainn, S., Fotiou, A., & Vollebergh, W. (2006). Economic and cultural correlates of cannabis use among mid-adolescents in 31 countries. *Addiction, 101,* 241–251.

Thelen, E., Fisher, D. M., Ridley-Johnson, R., & Griffin, N. (1982). The effects of body build and arousal on newborn infant stepping. *Developmental Psychobiology, 15,* 447–453. doi:10.1002/dev.420150506

Thelen, E., & Smith, L. B. (2006). Dynamic systems theories. In R. M. Lerner (Ed.), *Handbook of child psychology: Vol. 1. Theoretical models of human development* (6th ed., pp. 258–312). Hoboken, NJ: Wiley.

Thiele, D. M., & Whelan, T. A. (2008). The relationship between grandparent satisfaction, meaning, and generativity. *International Journal of Aging and Human Development, 66,* 21–48.

Thomaes, S., Reijntjes, A., Orobio de Castro, B., Bushman, B. J., Poorthuis, A., & Telch, M. J. (2010). I like me if you like me: On the interpersonal modulation and regulation of preadolescents' state self-esteem. *Child Development, 81,* 811–825. doi:10.1111/j.1467–8624.2010.01435.x

Thomas, A., & Chess, S. (1977). *Temperament and development.* Oxford, England: Brunner/Mazel.

Thomas, A. K., & Bulevich, J. B. (2006). Effective cue utilization reduces memory errors in older adults. *Psychology and Aging, 21,* 379–389.

Thomas, D. (1957). *The collected poems of Dylan Thomas* (6th ed.). New York, NY: New Directions.

Thomas, E. M. (2010). *Recent trends in upper respiratory infections and asthma among young Canadian children* (Catalogue No. 82–003-XPE). Retrieved from http://www.statcan.gc.ca/pub/82-003-x/2010004/article/11364-eng.pdf

Thomas, M. S. C., & Johnson, M. H. (2008). New advances in understanding sensitive periods in brain development. *Current Directions in Psychological Science, 17,* 1–5.

Thomas, R., DiLillo, D., Walsh, K., & Polusny, M. A. (2011). Pathways from child sexual abuse to adult depression: The role of parental socialization of emotions and alexithymia. *Psychology of Violence, 1,* 121–135. doi:10.1037/a0022469

Thomas, W. H. (2007). *What are old people for? How elders will save the world* (Paperback ed.). Acton, MA: VanderWyk & Burnham.

Thompson, C. A., & Siegler, R. S. (2010). Linear numerical-magnitude representations aid children's memory for numbers. *Psychological Science, 21,* 1274–1281. doi:10.1177/0956797610378309

Thompson, E. M., & Morgan, E. M. (2008). "Mostly straight" young women: Variations in sexual behavior and identity development. *Developmental Psychology, 44,* 15–21.

Thompson, R. A. (2006). The development of the person: Social understanding, relationships, conscience, self. In N. Eisenberg (Ed.), *Handbook of child psychology: Vol. 3. Social, emotional, and personality development* (6th ed., pp. 24–98). Hoboken, NJ: Wiley.

Thompson, R. A., & Raikes, H. A. (2003). Toward the next quarter-century: Conceptual and methodological challenges for attachment theory. *Development & Psychopathology, 15,* 691–718.

Thornton, A., Axinn, W. G., & Xie, Y. (2007). *Marriage and cohabitation.* Chicago, IL: University of Chicago Press.

Thorson, J. A. (1995). *Aging in a changing society.* Belmont, CA: Wadsworth.

Thurber, J. (1999). The secret life of James Thurber. In J. Thurber (Ed.), *The Thurber carnival* (pp. 35–41). New York, NY: Harper Perennial.

Tidwell, L. C., & Walther, J. B. (2002). Computer-mediated communication effects on disclosure, impressions, and interpersonal evaluations: Getting to know one another a bit at a time. *Human Communication Research, 28,* 317–348. doi:10.1111/j.1468–2958.2002.tb00811.x

Tikotzky, L., Sharabany, R., Hirsch, I., & Sadeh, A. (2010). "Ghosts in the Nursery:" Infant sleep and sleep-related cognitions of parents raised under communal sleeping arrangements. *Infant Mental Health Journal, 31,* 312–334. doi:10.1002/imhj.20258

Tilling, K., Lawlor, D. A., Davey Smith, G., Chambless, L., & Szklo, M. (2006). The relation between components of adult height and intimal-medial thickness in middle age: The Atherosclerosis Risk in Communities Study. *American Journal of Epidemiology, 164,* 136–142. doi:10.1093/aje/kwj184

Tilton-Weaver, L., Kerr, M., Pakalniskeine, V., Tokic, A., Salihovic, S., & Stattin, H. (2010). Open up or close down: How do parental reactions affect youth information management? *Journal of Adolescence, 33,* 333–346.

Timiras, M. L. (2007). The skin. In P. S. Timiras (Ed.), *Physiological basis of aging and geriatrics* (4th ed., pp. 345–352). New York, NY: Informa Healthcare.

Timiras, P. S., & De Martinis, M. (2007). The pulmonary respiration, hematopoiesis, and erythrocytes. In P. S. Timiras (Ed.), *Physiological basis of aging and geriatrics* (4th ed., pp. 277–296). New York, NY: Informa Healthcare.

Tishkoff, S. A., Reed, F. A., Friedlaender, F. R., Ehret, C., Ranciaro, A., Froment, A., ... Williams, S. M. (2009, May 22). The genetic structure and history of Africans and African Americans. *Science, 324,* 1035–1044.

Titus, D. N. (2007). Strategies and resources for enhancing the achievement of mobile students. *NASSP Bulletin, 91,* 81–97. doi:10.1177/0192636506298362

Tokunaga, R. S. (2010). Following you home from school: A critical review and synthesis of research on cyberbullying victimization. *Computers in Human Behavior, 26,* 277–287.

Tomalski, P., & Johnson, M. H. (2010). The effects of early adversity on the adult and developing brain. *Current Opinion in Psychiatry, 23,* 233–238. doi:10.1097/YCO.0b013e3283387a8c

Tomasello, M. (2006). Acquiring linguistic constructions. In D. Kuhn & R. S. Siegler (Eds.), *Handbook of child psychology: Vol. 2. Cognition, perception, and language* (6th ed., pp. 255–298). Hoboken, NJ: Wiley.

Tomasello, M. (2011). Language develpment. In U. Goswami (Ed.), *The Wiley-Blackwell handbook of childhood cognitive development* (2nd ed., pp. 239–257). West Sussex, UK: Blackwell.

Tomasello, M., & Herrmann, E. (2010). Ape and human cognition. *Current Directions in Psychological Science, 19,* 3–8. doi:10.1177/0963721409359300

Tornstam, L. (2005). *Gerotranscendence: A developmental theory of positive aging.* New York, NY: Springer.

Toutain, S. (2010). What women in France say about alcohol abstinence during pregnancy. *Drug and Alcohol Review, 29,* 184–188.

Townsend, J., Godfrey, M., & Denby, T. (2006). Heroines, villains and victims: Older people's perceptions of others. *Ageing & Society, 26,* 883–900.

Tracy, E. E. (2009, August). Does home birth empower women, or imperil them and their babies? *OBG Management, 21,* 45–52.

Trautmann-Villalba, P., Gschwendt, M., Schmidt, M. H., & Laucht, M. (2006). Father-infant interaction patterns as precursors of children's later externalizing behavior problems: A longitudinal study over 11 years. *European Archives of Psychiatry and Clinical Neuroscience, 256,* 344–349.

Treas, J., & Gubernskaya, Z. (2012). Farewell to moms? Maternal contact for seven countries in 1986 and 2001. *Journal of Marriage and Family, 74,* 297–311.

Tremblay, A., & Chaput, J.-P. (2012). Obesity: The allostatic load of weight loss dieting. *Physiology & Behavior, 106,* 16–21.

Tremblay, M. S., Warburton, D. E., Janssen, I., Paterson, D. H., Latimer, A. E., Rhodes R. E., ... Duggan, M. (2011). New Canadian physical activity guidelines. *Applied Physiology Nutrition and Metabolism, 36,* 36–58. doi:10.1139/H11–009

Tremblay, R. E., Nagin, D. S., Séguin, J. R., Zoccolillo, M., Zelazo, P. D., Boivin, M., ... Japel, C. (2004). Physical aggression during early childhood: Trajectories and predictors. *Pediatrics, 114,* 43–50. doi: 10.1542/peds.1141.e43

Trickett, P. K., Negriff, S., Ji, J., & Peckins, M. (2011). Child maltreatment and adolescent development. *Journal of Research on Adolescence, 21,* 3–20. doi:10.1111/j.1532-7795.2010.00711.x

Troll, L. E., & Skaff, M. M. (1997). Perceived continuity of self in very old age. *Psychology & Aging, 12,* 162–169.

Trommsdorff, G., & Cole, P. M. (2011). Emotion, self-regulation, and social behavior in cultural contexts. In X. Chen & K. H. Rubin (Eds.), *Socioemotional development in cultural context* (pp. 131–163). New York, NY: Guilford Press.

Tronick, E. (2007). *The neurobehavioral and social-emotional development of infants and children.* New York, NY: Norton.

Tronick, E., & Beeghly, M. (2011). Infants' meaning-making and the development of mental health problems. *American Psychologist, 66,* 107–119. doi:10.1037/a0021631

Tronick, E. Z. (1989). Emotions and emotional communication in infants. *American Psychologist, 44,* 112–119.

Tronick, E. Z., & Weinberg, M. K. (1997). Depressed mothers and infants: Failure to form dyadic states of consciousness. In L. Murray & P. J. Cooper (Eds.), *Postpartum depression and child development* (pp. 54–81). New York, NY: Guilford Press.

Trudeau, L., Spoth, R., Randall, G., Mason, W., & Shin, C. (2012). Internalizing symptoms: Effects of a preventive intervention on developmental pathways from early adolescence to young adulthood. *Journal of Youth and Adolescence, 41,* 788–801. doi:10.1007/s10964–011–9735–6

Truman, J. L., & Planty, M. (2012). *Criminal victimization, 2011.* Washington, DC: U.S. Department of Justice.

Truog, R. D. (2007). Brain death—Too flawed to endure, too ingrained to abandon. *The Journal of Law, Medicine & Ethics, 35,* 273–281.

Trzesniewski, K. H., Donnellan, M. B., Moffitt, T. E., Robins, R. W., Poulton, R., & Caspi, A. (2006). Low self-esteem during adolescence predicts poor health, criminal behavior, and limited economic prospects during adulthood. *Developmental Psychology, 42,* 381–390.

Tsao, F.-M., Liu, H.-M., & Kuhl, P. K. (2004). Speech perception in infancy predicts language development in the second year of life: A longitudinal study. *Child Development, 75,* 1067–1084.

Tudge, J. (2008). *The everyday lives of young children: Culture, class, and child rearing in diverse societies.* New York, NY: Cambridge University Press.

Turcotte, M., & Schellenberg, G. (2006). *A portrait of seniors in Canada.* Retrieved from http://www.statcan.gc.ca/pub/89-519-x/89-519-x2006001-eng.pdf

Turcotte, M., & Zhao, J. (2004). *A portrait of Aboriginal children living in non-reserve areas: Results from the 2001 Aboriginal Peoples Survey* (Catalogue No. 89–597-XWE). Retrieved from http://data.library.utoronto.ca/datapub/codebooks/cstdli/aps/aps01ch/aps2001portrait-children.pdf

Turiel, E. (1979). Distinct conceptual and developmental domains: Social convention and morality. In H. E. Howe & G. B. Keasey (Eds.), *Nebraska symposium on motivation, 1977: Vol. 25. Social cognitive development* (pp. 77–116). Lincoln, NE: University of Nebraska.

Turiel, E. (1983). *The development of social knowledge: Morality and convention.* Cambridge, UK: Cambridge University.

Turiel, E. (2006). The development of morality. In N. Eisenberg (Ed.), *Handbook of child psychology: Vol. 3. Social, emotional, and personality development* (6th ed., pp. 789–857). Hoboken, NJ: Wiley.

Turiel, E. (2008a). The development of children's orientations toward moral social, and personal orders: More than a sequence in development. *Human Development, 51,* 21–39. doi: 10.1159/000113154

Turiel, E. (2008b). Thought about actions in social domains: Morality, social conventions, and social interactions. *Cognitive Development, 23,* 136–154.

Turley, R. N. L., & Desmond, M. (2011). Contributions to college costs by married, divorced, and remarried parents. *Journal of Family Issues.* doi:10.1177/0192513x10388013

Turner, V. D., & Berkowitz, M. W. (2005). Scaffolding morality: Positioning a socio-cultural construct. *New Ideas in Psychology, 23,* 174–184. doi:10.1016/j.newideapsych.2006.04.002

Twenge, J. M., Gentile, B., DeWall, C. N., Ma, D., Lacefield, K., & Schurtz, D. R. (2010). Birth cohort increases in psychopathology among young Americans, 1938–2007: A cross-temporal meta-analysis of the MMPI. *Clinical Psychology Review, 30,* 145–154.

Twenge, J. M., Konrath, S., Foster, J. D., Campbell, W. K., & Bushma, B. J. (2008). Egos inflating over time: A cross-temporal meta-analysis of the narcissistic personality inventory. *Journal of Personality, 76,* 875–902.

Tye-Murray, N., Spehar, B., Myerson, J., Sommers, M. S., & Hale, S. (2011). Cross-modal enhancement of speech detection in young and older adults: Does signal content matter? *Ear and Hearing, 32,* 650–655.

U

U.S. Bureau of the Census. (2011). *Statistical abstract of the United States: 2012* (131st ed.). Washington, DC: U.S. Government Printing Office.

U.S. Department of Health and Human Services. (2011). *The Surgeon General's call to action to support breastfeeding.* Washington, DC: U.S. Department of Health and Human Services, Office of the Surgeon General.

U.S. Department of Health and Human Services, Administration for Children and Families. (2010). *Head Start impact study: Final report.* Washington, DC: Author.

U.S. Preventive Services Task Force. (2002). Postmenopausal hormone replacement therapy for primary prevention of chronic conditions: Recommendations and rationale. *Annals of Internal Medicine, 137,* 834–839.

Uchida, S., Hara, K., Kobayashi, A., Otsuki, K., Yamagata, H., Hobara, T., … Watanabe, Y. (2011). Epigenetic status of Gdnf in the ventral striatum determines susceptibility and adaptation to daily stressful events. *Neuron, 69,* 359–372.

Uddin, M., Koenen, K. C., de los Santos, R., Bakshis, E., Aiello, A. E., & Galea, S. (2010). Gender differences in the genetic and environmental determinants of adolescent depression. *Depression and Anxiety, 27,* 658–666. doi:10.1002/da.20692

Umberson, D., Pudrovska, T., & Reczek, C. (2010). Parenthood, childlessness, and well-being: A life course perspective. *Journal of Marriage and Family, 72,* 612–629. doi:10.1111/j.1741-3737.2010.00721.x

UNESCO. (2008). *Global education digest: Comparing education statistics across the world.* Montreal, Quebec, Canada: UNESCO Institute for Statistics.

UNESCO. (2009). *Global education digest 2009: Comparing education statistics across the world.* Montreal, Quebec, Canada: UNESCO Institute for Statistics.

Ungar, M. (2008). Resilience across cultures. *British Journal of Social Work, 38,* 218–235. doi:10.1093/bjsw/bcl343

UNICEF (Children's Fund). (2008). *The state of the world's children 2009: Maternal and newborn health.* New York, NY: Author.

UNICEF (United Nations Children's Fund). (2012). *The state of the world's children 2012: Children in an urban world.* New York, NY: United Nations.

United Nations. (2011). *The millennium development goals report 2011.* New York, NY: Author.

United Nations. (2012). *World population prospects: The 2010 revision.* New York, NY: Population Division of the United Nations Department of Economic and Social Affairs of the United Nations Secretariat.

United Nations Human Rights, Office of the High Commissioner for Human Rights. (1990). *Convention on the rights of the child.* Retrieved from http://www.ohchr.org/en/professionalinterest/pages/crc.aspx

Unnever, J. D. (2005). Bullies, aggressive victims, and victims: Are they distinct groups? *Aggressive Behavior, 31,* 153–171.

Utendale, W. T., & Hastings, P. D. (2011). Developmental changes in the relations between inhibitory control and externalizing problems during early childhood. *Infant and Child Development, 20,* 181–193. doi:10.1002/icd.691

Uttal, W. R. (2000). *The war between mentalism and behaviorism: On the accessibility of mental processes.* Mahwah, NJ: Erlbaum.

V

Vaillant, G. E. (2002). *Aging well: Surprising guideposts to a happier life from the landmark Harvard Study of Adult Development.* Boston, MA: Little Brown.

Vaillant, G. E. (2008). *Spiritual evolution: A scientific defense of faith.* New York, NY: Broadway Books.

van den Akker, A., Deković, M., Prinzie, P., & Asscher, J. (2010). Toddlers' temperament profiles: Stability and relations to negative and positive parenting. *Journal of Abnormal Child Psychology, 38,* 485–495. doi:10.1007/s10802–009–9379–0

van den Ban, E., Souverein, P., Swaab, H., van Engeland, H., Heerdink, R., & Egberts, T. (2010). Trends in incidence and characteristics of children, adolescents, and adults initiating immediate- or extended-release methylphenidate or atomoxetine in the Netherlands during 2001–2006. *Journal of Child and Adolescent Psychopharmacology, 20,* 55–61. doi:10.1089/cap.2008.0153

van den Berg, P. A., Mond, J., Eisenberg, M., Ackard, D., & Neumark-Sztainer, D. (2010). The link between body dissatisfaction and self-esteem in adolescents: Similarities across gender, age, weight status, race/ethnicity, and socioeconomic status. *The Journal of Adolescent Health, 47,* 290–296.

van den Berg, S. M., & Boomsma, D. I. (2007). The familial clustering of age at menarche in extended twin families. *Behavior Genetics, 37,* 661–667.

van den Hoonaard, D. K. (2002). Attitudes of older widows and widowers in New Brunswick, Canada towards new partnerships. *Ageing International, 27,* 79–92. doi: 10.1007/s12126–002–1016-y

van der Houwen, K., Stroebe, M., Schut, H., Stroebe, W., & Bout, J. v. d. (2010). Mediating processes in bereavement: The role of rumination, threatening grief interpretations, and deliberate grief avoidance. *Social Science & Medicine, 71,* 1669–1676. doi:10.1016/j.socscimed.2010.06.047

van IJzendoorn, M. H., & Bakermans-Kranenburg, M. J. (2010). Invariance of adult attachment across gender, age, culture, and socioeconomic status? *Journal of Social and Personal Relationships, 27,* 200–208. doi:10.1177/0265407509360908

van IJzendoorn, M. H., Bakermans-Kranenburg, M. J., Pannebakker, F., & Out, D. (2010). In defence of situational morality: Genetic, dispositional and situational determinants of children's donating to charity. *Journal of Moral Education, 39,* 1–20.

van Ijzendoorn, M. H., Belsky, J., & Bakermans-Kranenburg, M. J. (2012). Serotonin transporter genotype 5HTTLPR as a marker of differential susceptibility? A meta-analysis of child and adolescent gene-by-environment studies. *Translational Psychiatry, 2,* e147.

van Leijenhorst, L., Zanolie, K., Van Meel, C. S., Westenberg, P. M., Rombouts, S. A. R. B., & Crone, E. A. (2010). What motivates the adolescent? Brain regions mediating reward sensitivity across adolescence. *Cerebral Cortex, 20,* 61–69. doi:10.1093/cercor/bhp078

van Praag, H. M., de Kloet, E. R., & van Os, J. (2004). *Stress, the brain and depression.* New York, NY: Cambridge University Press.

Van Puyvelde, M., Vanfleteren, P., Loots, G., Deschuyffeleer, S., Vinck, B., Jacquet, W., & Verhelst, W. (2010). Tonal synchrony in mother-infant interaction based on harmonic and pentatonic series. *Infant Behavior and Development, 33,* 387–400.

van Soelen, I. L. C., Brouwer, R. M., Peper, J. S., van Beijsterveldt, T. C. E. M., van Leeuwen, M., de Vries, L. S., … Boomsma, D. I. (2010). Effects of gestational age and birth weight on brain volumes in healthy 9 year-old children. *The Journal of Pediatrics, 156,* 896–901.

Van Zundert, R. M. P., Van Der Vorst, H., Vermulst, A. A., & Engels, R. C. M. E. (2006). Pathways to alcohol use among Dutch students in regular education and education for adolescents with behavioral problems: The role of parental alcohol use, general parenting practices, and alcohol-specific parenting practices. *Journal of Family Psychology, 20,* 456–467. doi:10.1037/0893-3200.20.3.456

Vaughan, A. M., & Kappe, S. H. I. (2012). Malaria vaccine development: Persistent challenges. *Current Opinion in Immunology, 24,* 324–331.

Veenstra, R., Lindenberg, S., Munniksma, A., & Dijkstra, J. K. (2010). The complex relation between bullying, victimization, acceptance, and rejection: Giving special attention to status, affection, and sex differences. *Child Development, 81,* 480–486. doi:10.1111/j.1467-8624.2009.01411.x

Vega, W.A., Aguilar-Gaxiola, S., Andrade, L., Bijl, R., Borges, G., Caraveo-Anduaga, J. J., … Wittchen, H.-U. (2002). Prevalence and age of onset for drug use in seven international sites: Results from the international consortium of psychiatric epidemiology. *Drug and Alcohol Dependence, 68,* 285–297.

Vélez, C. E., Wolchik, S. A., Tein, J.-Y., & Sandler, I. (2011). Protecting children from the consequences of divorce: A longitudinal study of the effects of parenting on children's coping processes. *Child Development, 82,* 244–257. doi:10.1111/j.1467–8624.2010.01553.x

Verbakel, E., & Jaspers, E. (2010). A comparative study on permissiveness toward euthanasia: Religiosity, slippery slope, autonomy, and death with dignity. *Public Opinion Quarterly, 74,* 109–139. doi:10.1093/poq/nfp074

Verbruggen, F., & Logan, G. D. (2008). Automatic and controlled response inhibition: Associative learning in the go/no-go and stop-signal paradigms. *Journal of Experimental Psychology: General, 137,* 649–672. doi: 10.1037/a0013170

Vered, K. O. (2008). *Children and media outside the home: Playing and learning in after-school care.* Houndmills, Basingstoke, Hampshire, England: Palgrave Macmillan.

Verona, S. (2003). Romanian policy regarding adoptions. In V. Little (Ed.), *Adoption update* (pp. 5–10). New York, NY: Nova Science.

Véronneau, M.-H., & Dishion, T. (2010). Predicting change in early adolescent problem behavior in the middle school years: A mesosystemic perspective on parenting and peer experiences. *Journal of Abnormal Child Psychology, 38,* 1125–1137. doi:10.1007/s10802–010–9431–0

Véronneau, M.-H., Vitaro, F., Brendgen, M., Dishion, T. J., & Tremblay, R. E. (2010). Transactional analysis of the reciprocal links between peer experiences and academic achievement from middle childhood to early adolescence. *Developmental Psychology, 46,* 773–790. doi:10.1037/a0019816

Vézina, M. & Crompton, S. (2012). *Volunteering in Canada* (Catalogue No. 11–008-X). Retrieved from http://www.statcan.gc.ca/pub/11-008-x/2012001/article/11638-eng.pdf

Viadero, D. (2007, April 5). Long after Katrina, children show symptoms of psychological distress. *Education Week, 26*(32), 7.

Victora, C. G., Adair, L., Fall, C., Hallal, P. C., Martorell, R., Richter, L., & Sachdev, H. S. (2008). Maternal and child undernutrition: Consequences for adult health and human capital. *Lancet, 371,* 340–357.

Vieno, A., Nation, M., Pastore, M., & Santinello, M. (2009). Parenting and antisocial behavior: A model of the relationship between adolescent self-disclosure, parental closeness, parental control, and adolescent antisocial behavior. *Developmental Psychology, 45,* 1509–1519.

Vihman, M. (1998). A developmental perspective on codeswitching: Conversations between a pair of bilingual siblings. *International Journal of Bilingualism, 2,* 45–84. doi:10.1177/136700699800200103

Virji-Babul, N., Rose, A., Moiseeva, N., & Makan, N. (2012). Neural correlates of action understanding in infants: Influence of motor experience. *Brain and Behavior, 2,* 237–242. doi:10.1002/brb3.50

Vital Signs Canada (VSC). (2009). *Health: Incidence of low birth weight.* Retrieved from http://www.vitalsignscanada.ca/en/findings-53-health-incidence-of-low-birth-weight-2009

Vitale, S., Sperduto, R. D., & Ferris, F. L., III. (2009). Increased prevalence of myopia in the United States between 1971–1972 and 1999–2004. *Archives of Ophthalmology, 127,* 1632–1639. doi:10.1001/archophthalmol.2009.303

Vitaro, F., Barker, E. D., Boivin, M., Brendgen, M., & Tremblay, R. E. (2006). Do early difficult temperament and harsh parenting diffentially predict reactive and proactive aggression? *Journal of Abnormal Psychology, 34,* 681–691.

Vittrup, B., & Holden, G. W. (2010). Children's assessments of corporal punishment and other disciplinary practices: The role of age, race, SES, and exposure to spanking. *Journal of Applied Developmental Psychology, 31,* 211–220.

Vogel, I., Verschuure, H., van der Ploeg, C. P. B., Brug, J., & Raat, H. (2010). Estimating adolescent risk for hearing loss based on data from a large school-based survey. *American Journal of Public Health, 100,* 1095–1100. doi:10.2105/ajph.2009.168690

Vogel, L. (2011). Dying a "good death". *Canadian Medical Association Journal, 183,* 2089–2090.

Vohs, K. D., & Baumeister, R. F. (2013). *Handbook of self-regulation research, theory, and applications* (2nd ed.). New York, NY: Guilford Press.

von dem Knesebeck, O., Pattyn, E., & Bracke, P. (2011). Education and depressive symptoms in 22 European countries. *International Journal of Public Health, 56,* 107–110. doi:10.1007/s00038–010–0202-z

von Mutius, E., & Vercelli, D. (2010). Farm living: Effects on childhood asthma and allergy. *Nature Reviews Immunology, 10,* 861–868.

Vonderheid, S. C., Kishi, R., Norr, K. F., & Klima, C. (2011). Group prenatal care and doula care for pregnant women. In A. Handler, J. Kennelly, & N. Peacock (Eds.), *Reducing racial/ethnic disparities in reproductive and perinatal outcomes: The evidence from population-based interventions* (pp. 369–400). New York, NY: Springer.

Voorpostel, M., & Blieszner, R. (2008). Intergenerational solidarity and support between adult siblings. *Journal of Marriage and Family, 70,* 157–167.

Voorpostel, M., & Schans, D. (2011). Sibling relationships in Dutch and immigrant families. *Ethnic and Racial Studies, 34,* 2027–2047.

Voorpostel, M., & van der Lippe, T. (2007). Support between siblings and between friends: Two worlds apart? *Journal of Marriage and Family, 69,* 1271–1282.

Voosen, P. (2013, July 15). A brain gone bad. *The Chronicle Review.* Retrieved from http://chronicle.com/article/A-Brain-Gone-Bad/140167/

Vouloumanos, A., & Werker, J. F. (2007). Listening to language at birth: Evidence for a bias for speech in neonates. *Developmental Science, 10,* 159–164.

Voydanoff, P. (2007). *Work, family, and community: Exploring interconnections.* Mahwah, NJ: Erlbaum.

Vukic, A., Gregory, D., Martin-Misener, R., & Etowa, J. (2011). Aboriginal and western conceptions of mental health and illness. *Pimatisiwin: A Journal of Aboriginal and Indigenous Community Health, 9,* 65–86. Retrieved from http://www.pimatisiwin.com/online/wp-content/uploads/2011/08/04VukicGregory.pdf

Vygotsky, L. S. (1934/1987). *Thinking and speech* (N. Minick, Trans. R. W. Rieber & A. S. Carton Eds. Vol. 1). New York, NY: Plenum Press.

Vygotsky, L. S. (1934/1994). The development of academic concepts in school aged children (T. Prout, Trans.). In R. van der Veer & J. Valsiner (Eds.), *The Vygotsky reader* (pp. 355–370). Cambridge, MA: Blackwell.

W

Wagner, L., & Lakusta, L. (2009). Using language to navigate the infant mind. *Perspectives on Psychological Science, 4,* 177–184. doi:10.1111/j.1745–6924.2009.01117.x

Wagner, P. A. (2011). Socio-sexual education: A practical study in formal thinking and teachable moments. *Sex Education: Sexuality, Society and Learning, 11,* 193–211.

Wahlstrom, D., Collins, P., White, T., & Luciana, M. (2010). Developmental changes in dopamine neurotransmission in adolescence: Behavioral implications and issues in assessment. *Brain and Cognition, 72,* 146–159.

Waldinger, R. J., & Schulz, M. S. (2010). What's love got to do with it? Social functioning, perceived health, and daily happiness in married octogenarians. *Psychology and Aging, 25,* 422–431. doi:10.1037/a0019087

Walsh, B. A., & Petty, K. (2007). Frequency of six early childhood education approaches: A 10-year content analysis of early childhood education journal. *Early Childhood Education Journal, 34,* 301–305.

Walsh, M., Hickey, C., & Duffy, J. (1999). Influence of item content and stereotype situation on gender differences in mathematical problem solving. *Sex Roles, 41,* 219–240. doi:10.1023/A:1018854212358

Walsh, R. (2011). Lifestyle and mental health. *American Psychologist, 66,* 579–592. doi:10.1037/a0021769

Wan, X., Nakatani, H., Ueno, K., Asamizuya, T., Cheng, K., & Tanaka, K. (2011, January 21). The neural basis of intuitive best next-move generation in board game experts. *Science, 331,* 341–346.

Wanberg, C. R. (2012). The individual experience of unemployment. *Annual Review of Psychology, 63,* 369–396.

Wang, H., & Wellman, B. (2010). Social connectivity in America: Changes in adult friendship network size from 2002 to 2007. *American Behavioral Scientist, 53,* 1148–1169. doi:10.1177/0002764209356247

Wang, J., & Candy, T. R. (2010). The sensitivity of the 2- to 4-month-old human infant accommodation system. *Investigative Ophthalmology and Visual Science, 51,* 3309–3317. doi:10.1167/iovs.09–4667

Wang, W., & Taylor, P. (2011, March 9). *For millennials, parenthood trumps marriage.* Washington, DC: Pew Social and Demographic Trends.

Ward, L. M., Epstein, M., Caruthers, A., & Merriwether, A. (2011). Men's media use, sexual cognitions, and sexual risk behavior: Testing a mediational model. *Developmental Psychology, 47,* 592–602. doi:10.1037/a0022669

Ward, R. A., & Spitze, G. D. (2007). Nestleaving and coresidence by young adult children: The role of family relations. *Research on Aging, 29,* 257–277.

Wardman, A. E. D., & Khan, N. A. (2005). Registered Indians and tobacco taxation: A culturally-appropriate strategy? *Canadian Journal on Public Health, 96,* 451–453. Retrieved from http://journal.cpha.ca/index.php/cjph/article/viewFile/653/653

Warick, J. (2010, January 21). Canada's infant mortality rate highest in Saskatchewan. *Canwest News Service.* Retrieved from http://www.vancouversun.com/story_print.html?id=2469882&sponsor=

Warneken, F., & Tomasello, M. (2009). The roots of human altruism. *British Journal of Psychology, 100,* 455–471.

Warren, C. W., Jones, N. R., Eriksen, M. P., & Asma, S. (2006). Patterns of global tobacco use in young people and implications for future chronic disease burden in adults. *Lancet, 367,* 749–753.

Washington, H. A. (2006). *Medical apartheid: The dark history of medical experimentation on Black Americans from colonial times to the present.* New York, NY: Doubleday.

Wastesson, J. W., Parker, M. G., Fastbom, J., Thorslund, M., & Johnell, K. (2012). Drug use in centenarians compared with nonagenarians and octogenarians in Sweden: A nationwide register-based study. *Age and Ageing, 41,* 218–224. doi:10.1093/ageing/afr144

Watson, J. B. (1924/1998). *Behaviorism.* New Brunswick, NJ: Transaction.

Watson, J. B. (1928). *Psychological care of infant and child.* New York, NY: Norton.

Waxman, S. R., & Lidz, J. L. (2006). Early word learning. In D. Kuhn & R. S. Siegler (Vol. Eds.), *Handbook of child psychology: Vol. 2. Cognition, perception, and language* (6th ed., pp. 299–335). Hoboken, NJ: Wiley.

Weaver, I. C. G., Cervoni, N., Champagne, F. A., D'Alessio, A. C., Sharma, S., Seckl, J. R., ... Meaney, M. J. (2004). Epigenetic programming by maternal behavior. *Nature Neuroscience, 7,* 847–854. doi:10.1038/nn1276

Weikum, W. M., Vouloumanos, A., Navarra, J., Soto-Faraco, S., Sebastian-Galles, N., & Werker, J. F. (2007, May 25). Visual language discrimination in infancy. *Science, 316,* 1159.

Weiler, R., Stamatakis, E., & Blair, S. (2010). Should health policy focus on physical activity rather than obesity? Yes. *British Medical Journal, 340,* c2603.

Weisgram, E. S., Bigler, R. S., & Liben, L. S. (2010). Gender, values, and occupational interests among children, adolescents, and adults. *Child Development, 81,* 778–796. doi:10.1111/j.1467-8624.2010.01433.x

Weiss, C. C., Carolan, B. V., & Baker-Smith, E. C. (2010). Big school, small school: (Re)testing assumptions about high school size, school engagement and mathematics achievement. *Journal of Youth and Adolescence, 39,* 163–176. doi:10.1007/s10964–009–9402–3

Wellman, H. M., Cross, D., & Watson, J. (2001). Meta-analysis of theory-of-mind development: The truth about false belief. *Child Development, 72,* 655–684.

Wendelken, C., Baym, C. L., Gazzaley, A., & Bunge, S. A. (2011). Neural indices of improved attentional modulation over middle childhood. *Developmental Cognitive Neuroscience, 1,* 175–186. doi:10.1016/j.dcn.2010.11.001

Wenner, M. (2009, February). The serious need for play. *Scientific American Mind, 20,* 23–29.

Wente, M. (2010, June 17). The immigration debate we don't want to have: Aqsa's murder raises some extremely troubling questions about integration. *The Globe and Mail.* Retrieved from http://www.theglobeandmail.com/commentary/the-immigration-debate-we-dont-want-to-have/article4322200/

Werheid, K., Gruno, M., Kathmann, N., Fischer, H., Almkvist, O., & Winblad, B. (2010). Biased recognition of positive faces in aging and amnestic mild cognitive impairment. *Psychology and Aging, 25,* 1–15. doi:10.1037/a0018358

Werner, E. E. (1979). *Cross-cultural child development: A view from the planet Earth.* Monterey, CA: Brooks/Cole.

Werner, E. E., & Smith, R. S. (1992). *Overcoming the odds: High risk children from birth to adulthood.* Ithaca, NY: Cornell University Press.

Werner, E. E., & Smith, R. S. (2001). *Journeys from childhood to midlife: Risk, resilience, and recovery.* Ithaca, NY: Cornell University Press.

Werner, N. E., & Hill, L. G. (2010). Individual and peer group normative beliefs about relational aggression. *Child Development, 81,* 826–836. doi:10.1111/j.1467–8624.2010.01436.x

Wertsch, J. V., & Tulviste, P. (2005). *L. S. Vygotsky and contemporary developmental psychology.* New York, NY: Routledge.

Whalley, L. J., Duthie, S. J., Collins, A., R., Starr, J. M., Deary, I. J., Lemmon, H.,... Staff, R. T. (2013). Homocysteine, antioxidant micronutrients and late onset dementia. *European Journal of Nutrition, 53,* 277–285. doi:10.1007/s00394–013–0526–6

Whelchel, L. (2005). *Creative correction: Extraordinary ideas for everyday discipline.* Wheaton, IL: Tyndale House.

Whitbourne, S. K. (2008). *Adult development & aging: Biopsychosocial perspectives* (3rd ed.). Hoboken, NJ: John Wiley & Sons.

Whitbourne, S. K., Sneed, J. R., & Sayer, A. (2009). Psychosocial development from college through midlife: A 34-year sequential study. *Developmental Psychology, 45,* 1328–1340.

Whitfield, K. E., & McClearn, G. (2005). Genes, environment, and race: Quantitative genetic approaches. *American Psychologist, 60,* 104–114.

Whitmore, H. (2001). Value that marketing cannot manufacture: Cherished possessions as links to identity and wisdom. *Generations, 25*(3), 57–63.

Whittle, S., Yap, M. B. H., Sheeber, L., Dudgeon, P., Yücel, M., Pantelis, C., ... Allen, N. B. (2011). Hippocampal volume and sensitivity to maternal aggressive behavior: A prospective study of adolescent depressive symptoms. *Development and Psychopathology, 23,* 115–129. doi:10.1017/S0954579410000684

Wicherts, J. M., Dolan, C. V., & van der Maas, H. L. J. (2010). The dangers of unsystematic selection methods and the representativeness of 46 samples of African test-takers. *Intelligence, 38,* 30–37.

Widhalm, K., Fritsch, M., Widhalm, H., Silberhumer, G., Dietrich, S., Helk, O., & Prager, G. (2011). Bariatric surgery in morbidly obese adolescents: Long-term follow-up. *International Journal of Pediatric Obesity, 6*(Suppl. 1), 65–69. doi:10.3109/17477166.2011.606817

Wijdicks, E. F. M., Varelas, P. N., Gronseth, G. S., & Greer, D. M. (2010). Evidence-based guideline update: Determining brain death in adults: Report of the Quality Standards Subcommittee of the American Academy of Neurology. *Neurology, 74*, 1911–1918. doi:10.1212/WNL.0b013e3181e242a8

Wilkens, R., Tjepkema, M., Mustard, C., & Choinière, R. (2008). *The Canadian census mortality follow-up study, 1991 through 2001* (Component of Statistics Canada Cataolgue No. 82–003-X). Retrieved from http://www.statcan.gc.ca/pub/82-003-x/2008003/article/10681-eng.pdf

Willett, W. C., & Trichopoulos, D. (1996). Nutrition and cancer: A summary of the evidence. *Cancer Causes Control, 7*, 178–180.

Williams, A. L., Khattak, A. Z., Garza, C. N., & Lasky, R. E. (2009). The behavioral pain response to heelstick in preterm neonates studied longitudinally: Description, development, determinants, and components. *Early Human Development, 85*, 369–374. doi:10.1016/j.earlhumdev.2009.01.001

Williams, C., Sutcliffe, A., & Sebire, N. J. (2010). Congenital malformations after assisted reproduction: Risks and implications for prenatal diagnosis and fetal medicine. *Ultrasound in Obstetrics and Gynecology, 35*, 255–259. doi:10.1002/uog.7589

Williams, K. N., Herman, R., Gajewski, B., & Wilson, K. (2009). Elderspeak communication: Impact on dementia care. *American Journal of Alzheimer's Disease and Other Dementias, 24*, 11–20. doi:10.1177/1533317508318472

Williams, L. (n.d.). *Aboriginal Head Start Program.* Retrieved from http://www.niichro.com/Child/child4.html

Williamson, R. A., Meltzoff, A. N., & Markman, E. M. (2008). Prior experiences and perceived efficacy influence 3-year-olds' imitation. *Developmental Psychology,*

Wilson, S. M., & Ngige, L. W. (2006). Families in sub-Saharan Africa. In B. B. Ingoldsby & S. D. Smith (Eds.), *Families in global and multicultural perspective* (2nd ed., pp. 247–273). Thousand Oaks, CA: Sage.

Winner, B., Peipert, J. F., Zhao, Q., Buckel, C., Madden, T., Allsworth, J. E., & Secura, G. M. (2012). Effectiveness of long-acting reversible contraception. *New England Journal of Medicine, 366*, 1998–2007. doi:10.1056/NEJMoa1110855

Witherington, D. C., Campos, J. J., & Hertenstein, M. J. (2004). Principles of emotion and its development in infancy. In G. Bremner & A. Fogel (Eds.), *Blackwell handbook of infant development* (Paperback ed., pp. 427–464). Malden, MA: Blackwell. (Reprinted from: Paperback).

Wittassek, M., Koch, H. M., Angerer, J., & Brüning, T. (2011). Assessing exposure to phthalates – The human biomonitoring approach. *Molecular Nutrition & Food Research, 55*, 7–31. doi:10.1002/mnfr.201000121

Wittrock, M. C. (2010). Learning as a generative process. *Educational Psychologist, 45*, 40–45.

Wolchik, S. A., Ma, Y., Tein, J.-Y., Sandler, I. N., & Ayers, T. S. (2008). Parentally bereaved children's grief: Self-system beliefs as mediators of the relations between grief and stressors and caregiver-child relationship quality. *Death Studies, 32*, 597–620.

Wolf, N. S. (Ed.). (2010). *Comparative biology of aging.* New York, NY: Springer.

Wong, P. T. P., & Tomer, A. (2011). Beyond terror and denial: The positive psychology of death acceptance. *Death Studies, 35*, 99–106. doi:10.1080/07481187.2011.535377

Wood, J. M. (2002). Aging, driving and vision. *Clinical and Experimental Optometry, 85*, 214–220. doi:10.1111/j.1444-0938.2002.tb03040.x

Woods, D. W., Piacentini, J., & Walkup, J. T. (2007). *Treating Tourette syndrome and tic disorders: A guide for practitioners.* New York, NY: Guilford Press.

Woodward, A. L., & Markman, E. M. (1998). Early word learning. In D. Kuhn & R. S. Siegler (Eds.), *Handbook of child psychology: Vol. 2. Cognition, perception and language* (5th ed., pp. 371–420). New York: Wiley.

Woollett, K., Spiers, H. J., & Maguire, E. A. (2009). Talent in the taxi: A model system for exploring expertise. *Philosophical Transactions of the Royal Society of London, 364*, 1407–1416. doi:10.1098/rstb.2008.0288

World Bank. (2010). *What can we learn from nutrition impact evaluations?* Washington, DC: The International Bank for Reconstruction and Development.

World Bank. (2014). *Fertility rates, total (birth per woman* [Data set]. Retrieved from http://data.un.org/data.aspx?d=wdi&f=indicator_code%3asp.dyn.tfrt.in#wdi

World Health Organization (WHO). (2002). *Ageing and life course: Elder abuse.* Retrieved from http://www.who.int/ageing/projects/elder_abuse/en/

World Health Organization (WHO). (2005). *Sexually transmitted infections among adolescents: Issues in adolescent health and development.* Geneva, Switzerland: Author.

World Health Organization (WHO). (2010, October 5). *WHO global infobase: NCD indicators.* Retrieved from https://apps.who.int/infobase/Indicators.aspx

World Health Organization (WHO). (2012, February). *Poliomyelitis.* Retrieved from http://www.who.int/mediacentre/factsheets/fs114/en/

World Health Organization (WHO). (2013a, July). *Poliomyelitis* [Fact sheet]. Retrieved from http://www.who.int/mediacentre/factsheets/fs114/en/

World Health Organization (WHO). (2013b). *Sexual and reproductive health: Defining sexual health.* Retrieved from http://www.who.int/reproductivehealth/topics/sexual_health/sh_definitions/en/

World Health Organization (WHO). (2013c, July). *The top 10 causes of death* [Fact sheet]. Retrieved from http://who.int/mediacentre/factsheets/fs310/en/

World Health Organization UNAIDS. (2011). *Progress in scale-up of male circumcision for HIV prevention in Eastern and Southern Africa: Focus on service delivery.* Retrieved from http://whqlibdoc.who.int/publications/2011/9789241502511_eng.pdf

Worrell, F. C. (2008). Nigrescence attitudes in adolescence, emerging adulthood, and adulthood. *Journal of Black Psychology, 34,* 156–178. doi:10.1177/0095798408315118

Worthy, D. A., Gorlick, M. A., Pacheco, J. L., Schnyer, D. M., & Maddox, W. T. (2011). With age comes wisdom: Decision making in younger and older adults. *Psychological Science, 22,* 1375–1380. doi:10.1177/0956797611420301

Wosje, K. S., Khoury, P. R., Claytor, R. P., Copeland, K. A., Hornung, R. W., Daniels, S. R., & Kalkwarf, H. J. (2010). Dietary patterns associated with fat and bone mass in young children. *American Journal of Clinical Nutrition, 92,* 294–303. doi:10.3945/ajcn.2009.28925

Wright, M. W., & Bruford, E. A. (2011). Naming 'junk': Human non-protein coding RNA (ncRNA) gene nomenclature. *Human Genomics, 5,* 90–98.

Wu, P.-L., & Chiou, W.-B. (2008). Postformal thinking and creativity among late adolescents: A post-Piagetian approach. *Adolescence, 43,* 237–251.

Wurm, S., Tomasik, M., & Tesch-Römer, C. (2008). Serious health events and their impact on changes in subjective health and life satisfaction: The role of age and a positive view on ageing. *European Journal of Ageing, 5,* 117–127.

Wurtele, S. K. (2009). "Activities of older adults" survey: Tapping into student views of the elderly. *Educational Gerontology, 35,* 1026–1031. doi:10.1080/03601270902973557

X

Xu, Y. (2010). Children's social play sequence: Parten's classic theory revisited. *Early Child Development and Care, 180,* 489–498. doi:10.1080/03004430802090430

Y

Yamaguchi, S., Greenwald, A. G., Banaji, M. R., Murakami, F., Chen, D., Shiomura, K., … Krendl, A. (2007). Apparent universality of positive implicit self-esteem. *Psychological Science, 18,* 498–500.

Yan, B., & Arlin, P. (1995). Nonabsolute/relativistic thinking: A common factor underlying models of postformal reasoning? *Journal of Adult Development, 2,* 223–240. doi:10.1007/bf02251038

Yang, D., Sidman, J., & Bushnell, E. W. (2010). Beyond the information given: Infants' transfer of actions learned through imitation. *Journal of Experimental Child Psychology, 106,* 62–81.

Yerys, B. E., & Munakata, Y. (2006). When labels hurt but novelty helps: Children's perseveration and flexibility in a card-sorting task. *Child Development, 77,* 1589–1607.

Yeung, W. J., & Conley, D. (2008). Black-White achievement gap and family wealth. *Child Development, 79,* 303–324.

Youn, G., Knight, B. G., Jeong, H.-S., & Benton, D. (1999). Differences in familism values and caregiving outcomes among Korean, Korean American, and White American dementia caregivers. *Psychology & Aging, 14,* 355–364.

Young, E. A., Korszun, A., Figueiredo, H. F., Banks-Solomon, M., & Herman, J. P. (2008). Sex differences in HPA axis regulation. In J. B. Becker, K. J. Berkley, N. Geary, E. Hampson, J. P. Herman, & E. Young (Eds.), *Sex differences in the brain: From genes to behavior* (pp. 95–105). New York, NY: Oxford University Press.

Young, J. K. (2010). Anorexia nervosa and estrogen: Current status of the hypothesis. *Neuroscience & Biobehavioral Reviews, 34,* 1195–1200.

Young-Wolff, K. C., Enoch, M.-A., & Prescott, C. A. (2011). The influence of gene-environment interactions on alcohol consumption and alcohol use disorders: A comprehensive review. *Clinical Psychology Review, 31,* 800–816.

Yuen, J. (2010). *Job-education match and mismatch: Wage differentials.* Retrieved from http://www.statcan.gc.ca/pub/75-001-x/2010104/pdf/11149-eng.pdf

Z

Zacher, H., & Frese, M. (2011). Maintaining a focus on opportunities at work: The interplay between age, job complexity, and the use of selection, optimization, and compensation strategies. *Journal of Organizational Behavior, 32,* 291–318. doi:10.1002/job.683

Zachry, A. H., & Kitzmann, K. M. (2011). Caregiver awareness of prone play recommendations. *The American Journal of Occupational Therapy, 65,* 101–105.

Zahn-Waxler, C., Park, J.-H., Usher, B., Belouad, F., Cole, P., & Gruber, R. (2008). Young children's representations of conflict and distress: A longitudinal study of boys and girls with disruptive behavior problems. *Development and Psychopathology, 20,* 99–119.

Zalenski, R. J., & Raspa, R. (2006). Maslow's hierarchy of needs: A framework for achieving human potential in hospice. *Journal of Palliative Medicine, 9,* 1120–1127. doi:10.1089/jpm.2006.9.1120

Zani, B., & Cicognani, E. (2006). Sexuality and intimate relationships in adolescence. In S. Jackson & L. Goossens (Eds.), *Handbook of adolescent development* (pp. 200–222). Hove, East Sussex, UK: Psychology Press.

Zapf, J. A., & Smith, L. B. (2007). When do children generalize the plural to novel nouns? *First Language, 27,* 53–73. doi:10.1177/0142723707070286

Zentall, S. R., & Morris, B. J. (2010). "Good job, you're so smart": The effects of inconsistency of praise type on young children's motivation. *Journal of Experimental Child Psychology, 107,* 155–163.

Zentner, M., & Bates, J. E. (2008). Child temperament: An integrative review of concepts, research programs, and measures. *European Journal of Developmental Science, 2,* 7–37.

Zernike, K. (2012, August 14). Youth driving laws limit even the double date. *New York Times,* pp. A-1, A-3.

Zero to Three. (2013). *FAQ's on the brain.* Retrieved from http://www.zerotothree.org/child-development/brain-development/faqs-on-the-brain.html#fullydeveloped

Zettel, L. A., & Rook, K. S. (2004). Substitution and compensation in the social networks of older widowed women. *Psychology and Aging, 19,* 433–443. doi:10.1037/0882-7974.19.3.433

Zettel-Watson, L., Ditto, P. H., Danks, J. H., & Smucker, W. D. (2008). Actual and perceived gender differences in the accuracy of surrogate decisions about life-sustaining medical treatment among older spouses. *Death Studies, 32,* 273–290.

Zhang, B., Wright, A. A., Huskamp, H. A., Nilsson, M. E., Maciejewski, M. L., Earle, C. C., ... Prigerson, H. G. (2009). Health care costs in the last week of life: Associations with end-of-life conversations. *Archives of Internal Medicine, 169,* 480–488.

Zhang, D. (2010). Language maintenance and language shift among Chinese immigrant parents and their second-generation children in the U.S. *Bilingual Research Journal, 33,* 42–60.

Zhang, S., & Kline, S. L. (2009). Can I make my own decision? A cross-cultural study of perceived social network influence in mate selection. *Journal of Cross-Cultural Psychology, 40,* 3–23. doi:10.1177/0022022108326192

Zhang, X., Yeung, D. Y., Fung, H. H., & Lang, F. R. (2011). Changes in peripheral social partners and loneliness over time: The moderating role of interdependence. *Psychology and Aging, 26,* 823–829.

Zhu, Q., Song, Y., Hu, S., Li, X., Tian, M., Zhen, Z., ... Liu, J. (2010). Heritability of the specific cognitive ability of face perception. *Current Biology, 20,* 137–142.

Zhu, W. X., & Hesketh, T. (2009). China's excess males, sex selective abortion and one child policy: Analysis of data from 2005 national intercensus survey. *British Medical Journal, 338,* b121. doi:10.1136/bmj.b1211

Zhu, Y., Zhang, L., Fan, J., & Han, S. (2007). Neural basis of cultural influence on self-representation. *NeuroImage, 34,* 1310–1316.

Zimmermann, C. (2012). Acceptance of dying: A discourse analysis of palliative care literature. *Social Science & Medicine, 75,* 217–224. doi:10.1016/j.socscimed.2012.02.047

Zimprich, D., & Martin, M. (2009). A multilevel factor analysis perspective on intellectual development in old age. In H. B. Bosworth & C. Hertzog (Eds.), *Aging and cognition: Research methodologies and empirical advances* (pp. 53–76). Washington, DC: American Psychological Association.

Zine, J. (2008). Honour and identity: An ethnographic account of Muslim girls in a Canadian Islamic school. *Topia, 19,* 35–61.

Zolotor, A. J., Burchinal, M., Skinner, D., Rosenthal, M., & Investigators, & The Key Family Life Project Investigators. (2008). Maternal psychological adjustment and knowledge of infant development as predictors of home safety practices in rural low-income communities. *Pediatrics, 121,* e1668–e1675. doi:10.1542/peds.2007–1255

Zolotor, A. J., & Puzia, M. E. (2010). Bans against corporal punishment: A systematic review of the laws, changes in attitudes and behaviours. *Child Abuse Review, 19,* 229–247. doi:10.1002/car.1131

Zosuls, K. M., Martin, C. L., Ruble, D. N., Miller, C. F., Gaertner, B. M., England, D. E., & Hill, A. P. (2011). "It's not that we hate you": Understanding children's gender attitudes and expectancies about peer relationships. *British Journal of Developmental Psychology, 29,* 288–304. doi:10.1111/j.2044–835X.2010.02023.x

NAME INDEX

Note: The Name Index comprises individuals who are named in the text as well as parenthetically cited authors and organizations. Organizations may also appear in the Subject Index. Statutes are listed in the Subject Index. Page numbers followed by *f* indicate numbered figures, photos or photo captions; those followed by *t* indicate tables; those followed by *n* indicate source notes.

SUBJECT INDEX

Note: Individuals who are discussed in the text or named in parenthetical citations appear in the Name Index. Organizations are listed in the Subject Index when discussed in the text, but in the Name Index when listed in a citation. Statutes are listed in the Subject Index. Page numbers followed by *f* indicate numbered figures, photos, or captions accompanying photos or figures; those followed by *t* indicate tables.